THE WORLD'S GREATEST
WINE ESTATES

A MODERN PERSPECTIVE

ROBERT M. PARKER, JR.

SIMON & SCHUSTER
New York   London   Toronto   Sydney

Simon & Schuster
Rockefeller Center
1230 Avenue of the Americas
New York, NY 10020

Simon & Schuster and colophon are registered trademarks of Simon & Schuster, Inc.

For information regarding special discounts for bulk purchases, please contact
Simon & Schuster Special Sales at 1-800-456-6798 or business@simonandschuster.com

Designed by Joel Avirom, Jason Snyder, and Meghan Day Healey
Map illustrations by Jason Snyder

Manufactured in the United States of America

1 3 5 7 9 10 8 6 4 2

Library of Congress Cataloging-in-Publication Data
Parker, Robert M., date.
The world's greatest wine estates: a modern perspective / Robert M. Parker, Jr.; [map illustrations by Jason Snyder].
p. cm.
1. Wine and winemaking. 2. Vintners. I. Title.
TP548.P288 2005
641.2'2—dc22   2005050885

ISBN-13: 978-0-7432-3771-0
ISBN-10: 0-7432-3771-4

For Pat and Maia

Here, back, down a long
and straight track
I have chose the long road—
That leads me to god knows
So I can't stop right now
—FROM "FITZCARRALDO"
BY THE FRAMES

CONTENTS

TRYING TO DEFINE GREATNESS

More than anything, this is a book about artists, craftspeople, revolutionaries, and traditionalists who have one overwhelming trait in common—they are irrefutably dedicated to the pursuit of excellence, and their hearts, souls, and enormous talents are reflected in wines of singular personality and achievement. The people behind the wines in this book range from isolated hermits to savvy and sophisticated world travelers. Their wines emerge from cellar conditions that in some cases could be described as medieval at best to those that resemble the command center at NASA, with the finest technology money can buy. As diverse as they and their wines are, they share an inexhaustible commitment to their vineyards, a passion to produce as fine a wine as is humanly possible, and a vision that the joys of wine are infinite and represent the pinnacle of a civilized society. In short, they have taken a commonplace beverage and transformed it into art.

That said, there is something surreal, bordering on demented, about trying to define the concept of greatness, especially in an agricultural product, but let me offer my point of view.

A WORKABLE DEFINITION OF GREATNESS

THE ELEMENTS OF A GREAT WINE

What is a great wine? This is one of the most controversial subjects of the vinous world. Isn't greatness in wine, much like a profound expression of art or music, something very personal and subjective? As much as I agree that the appreciation and enjoyment of art, music, or wine is indeed personal, high quality in wine, as in art and music, does tend to be subject to widespread agreement (except for the occasional contrarian). Few art aficionados would disagree with the fact that Picasso, Rembrandt, Bacon, Matisse, Van Gogh, or Michelangelo were extraordinary artists. And though certainly some dissenters can be found regarding the merits of composers such as Chopin, Mozart, Beethoven, or Brahms, or in the more modern era, such musicians/songwriters as Bob Dylan, the Beatles, or the Rolling Stones, the majority opinion is that these people have produced exceptional music.

It is no different with wine. Most wine drinkers agree that the legendary wines of the 20th century—1945 Mouton Rothschild, 1945 Haut-Brion, 1947 Cheval Blanc, 1947 Pétrus, 1961 Latour, 1982 Mouton Rothschild, 1982 Le Pin, 1982 Léoville-Las-Cases, 1989 Haut-Brion, 1990 Margaux, and 1990 Pétrus, to name some of the most renowned red Bordeaux—are profoundly riveting. Tasting is indeed subjective, and no one should feel forced to feign fondness for a work by Picasso or Beethoven, much less a bottle of 1961 Latour, but as with most of the finest things in life, there is considerable agreement as to what represents high quality.

Two things that all can agree on are the origin and production of the world's finest wines. Great wines emanate from well-placed vineyards with microclimates favorable to specific types of grapes. Profound wines, whether they are from France, Italy, Spain, California, or Australia, are also the product of conservative viticultural practices that emphasize low yields, and physi-

1

ologically rather than analytically ripe fruit. After 27 years spent tasting over 300,000 wines, I have never tasted a superb wine that was made from underripe fruit. Does anyone enjoy the flavors of an underripe orange, peach, apricot, or cherry? Low yields and ripe fruit are essential for the production of extraordinary wines, yet it is amazing how many wineries never seem to understand this fundamental principle.

In addition to the commonsense approach of harvesting mature fruit, and pruning to discourage the vine from overproducing, the winery's individual winemaking philosophy is of paramount importance. Exceptional wines (whether they be red, white, or sparkling) emerge from a similar philosophy, which includes the following: 1) permit the vineyard's *terroir* (soil, microclimate, distinctiveness) to express itself; 2) allow the purity and characteristics of the grape varietal, or blend of varietals, to be faithfully represented in the wine; 3) produce a wine without distorting the personality and character of a particular vintage by excessive manipulation; 4) follow an uncompromising, noninterventionist winemaking philosophy that eschews the food-processing, industrial mindset of high-tech winemaking—in short, give the wine a chance to make itself naturally without the human element attempting to sculpt or alter the wine's intrinsic character; 5) follow a policy of minimal handling, clarification, and treatment of the wine so that what is placed in the bottle represents as natural an ex-

pression of the vineyard, varietal, and vintage as is possible. In keeping with this overall philosophy, winemakers who attempt to reduce such traumatic clarification procedures as fining and filtration, while also lowering sulphur levels (which can dry out a wine's fruit, bleach color from a wine, and exacerbate the tannin's sharpness), produce wines with far more aromatics and flavors, as well as more enthralling textures. These are wines that offer consumers their most compelling and rewarding drinking experiences. Assuming there is a relatively broad consensus as to how the world's finest wines originate, what follows is my working definition of an exceptional wine. In short, what are the characteristics of a great wine?

1. The ability to please both the palate and the intellect. Great wines have the ability to both satisfy the senses and challenge the intellect. The world offers many delicious wines that have pure hedonistic value, but are not complex. Whether a wine satisfies the intellect is a more subjective issue. Wines that experts call "complex" are those that offer multidimensional aromatic and flavor profiles, and have more going for them than simply ripe fruit and a satisfying, pleasurable, yet one-dimensional quality.

2. The ability to hold the taster's interest. I have often remarked that the greatest wines I have ever tasted could be easily recognized by bouquet alone. They are wines that could never be called monochromatic, simple, or "grape juice magnets" as a friend called them. Profound wines hold the taster's interest, not only providing an initial tantalizing tease, but possessing a compelling aromatic intensity and nuance-filled layers of flavors.

3. The ability to offer intense aromas and flavors without heaviness. I could make an analogy here to eating in the finest restaurants. Extraordinary cooking is characterized by its purity, intensity, balance, texture, and compelling aromas and flavors. What separates exceptional cuisine from merely good cooking, as well as great wines from good wines, is their ability to offer extraordinary intensity of flavor without heaviness. Wineries in the New World (especially in Australia and California) can easily produce wines that are oversize, bold, big, rich, but heavy. Europe's finest wineries, with many centuries' more experience, have mastered the ability to obtain intense flavors without heaviness. However, New World viticultural areas (particularly in California) are quickly catching up, as evidenced by the succession of remarkable wines produced in Napa, Sonoma, and elsewhere in the Golden State during the 1990s. Many of California's greatest wines of the 1990s have sacrificed none of their power and richness, but no longer possess the rustic tannin and oafish feel on the palate that characterized so many of their predecessors of ten and twenty years ago.

4. The ability to taste better with each sip. Most of the finest wines I have ever drunk were better with the last sip than the first, revealing more nuances and more complex aromas and flavors as the wine unfolded in the glass. Do readers ever wonder why the most interesting and satisfying glass of wine is often the one that finishes the bottle?

5. The ability to improve with age. This is, for better or worse, an indisputable characteristic of great wines. One of the enduring misconceptions disseminated by the European wine writers is the idea that in order for a wine to be exceptional when mature, it had to be nasty when young. My experience has revealed just the opposite—wines that are acidic, astringent, and generally fruitless and charmless when young become even nastier and less drinkable when old. With that being said, new vintages of top wines are often unformed and in need of 10 or 12 years of cellaring (in the case of top California Cabernets, Bordeaux, and Rhône wines), but those wines should always possess a certain accessibility so that even inexperienced wine tasters can tell the wine is—at the minimum—made from very ripe fruit. If a wine does not exhibit ripeness and richness of fruit when young, it will not develop nuances with aging. Great wines unquestionably improve with age. I define "improvement" as the ability of a wine to become significantly more enjoyable and interesting in the bottle, offering more pleasure old than when it was young. Many wineries (especially in the New World) produce wines they claim "will age," but this is nothing more than a public relations ploy. What they should really say is that they "will survive." They can endure 10–20 years of bottle age, but they were more enjoyable in their exuberant youthfulness.

6. The ability to display a singular personality. When one considers the greatest wines produced, it is their singular personalities that set them apart. The same can be said of the greatest vintages. The abused description "classic vintage" has become nothing more than a reference to what a viticultural region does in a typical (normal) year. Exceptional wines from exceptional vintages stand far above the norm, and they can always be defined by their singular qualities—their aromas and their flavors and textures. The opulent, sumptuous qualities of the 1982 and 1990 red Bordeaux, the rugged tannin and immense ageability of the 1986 red Bordeaux, the seamless, perfectly balanced 1994 Napa and Sonoma Cabernet Sauvignons and proprietary blends, and the plush, sweet fruit, high alcohol, and glycerin of the 1990 Barolos and Barbarescos, are all examples of vintage individuality.

7. The ability to reflect the place of origin. An Asian proverb seems particularly applicable when discussing the ballyhooed French concept of *terroir*: "Knowing in part may make a fine tale, but wisdom comes from seeing the whole." And so it is with this concept of *terroir*, that hazy, intellectually appealing notion that a plot of soil plays the determining factor in a wine's character. The French are more obsessed with the issue of *terroir* than anyone else in the world. And why not? Many of that country's most renowned vineyards are part of an elaborate hierarchy of quality based on their soil and exposition. And the French would have everyone believe that no one on planet Earth can equal the quality of their Pinot Noir, Chardonnay, Cabernet, Syrah, etc. because their privileged *terroir* is unequaled. One of France's most celebrated wine regions, Burgundy, is often cited as the best place to search for the fullest expression of *terroir*. Advocates of *terroir* (the terroirists) argue that a particular piece of ground contributes a character that is distinctive and apart from that same product grown on different soils and slopes. Burgundy, with its classifications of grand cru and premier cru vineyards, village vineyards, and generic viticultural areas, is the terroirists' "raison d'être." Of course, they claim they can taste a wine's *terroir* only if they have not seen the label.

Lamentably, *terroir* has become such a politically correct buzzword that in some circles it is an egregious error not to utter some profound comments about finding "a sense of somewhereness" when tasting a Vosne–Romanée–Les Malconsorts or a Latricières-Chambertin. Leading terroirists make a persuasive and often eloquent case about the necessity of finding, as one observer puts it, "the true voice of the land" in order for a wine to be legitimized.

Yet like so many things about wine, especially tasting it, there is no scientific basis for anything the terroirists propose. What they argue is what most Burgundians and owners of France's finest vineyards give lip service to—that for a wine to be authentic and noble it must speak of its *terroir*.

On the other side of this issue are the "realists," or should I call them modernists. They suggest that *terroir* is merely one of many factors that influence a wine's style, quality, and character. Soil, exposition, and microclimate (*terroir*) most certainly impart an influence, but so do the following:

Rootstock—Is it designed to produce prolific or small crop levels?

Yeasts—Does the winemaker use the vineyard's wild yeasts or are commercial yeasts employed? Every yeast, wild or commercial, will give a wine a different set of aromatics, flavor, and texture.

Yields and Vine Age—High yields result in diluted wine. Low yields, usually less than two tons per acre or 35–40 hectoliters per hectare, result in wines with much more concentration and personality. Additionally, young vines have a tendency to overproduce, whereas old vines produce small berries and less wine. Crop thinning is often employed with younger vineyards to increase the level of concentration.

Harvest Philosophy—Is the fruit picked underripe (with greener, cooler red fruit flavors) to preserve more acidity, or fully ripe (with darker fruit flavors and lower acids) to emphasize the lushness and opulence of a given varietal?

Vinification Techniques and Equipment—There are an amazing number of techniques that can change the wine's aromas and flavors. Moreover, equipment choice (different presses, destemmers, etc.) can have a profound influence on the final wine.

Elevage (or the wine's upbringing)—Is the wine brought up in oak barrels, concrete vats, stainless-steel vats, or large oak vats (which the French call *foudres*)? What is the percentage of new oak? Of these elements, only oak exerts an influence on the wine's character. Additionally, transferring wine (racking) from one container to another has an immense impact on a wine's bouquet and flavor. Is the wine allowed to remain in long contact with its lees (believed to give the wine more aromatic complexity and fullness)? Or is it racked frequently for fear of picking up an undesirable lees smell?

Fining and Filtration—Even the most concentrated and profound wines that terroirists consider quintessential examples of the soil can be eviscerated and stripped of their personality and richness by excessive fining and filtering. Does the winemaker treat the wine with kid gloves, or is the winemaker a manufacturer/processor bent on sculpturing the wine?

Bottling Date—Does the winemaker bottle early to preserve as much fruit as possible, or does he bottle later to give the wine a more mellow, aged character? Undoubtedly, the philosophy of when to bottle can radically alter the character of a wine.

Cellar Temperature and Sanitary Conditions—Some wine cellars are cold and others are warm. Different wines emerge from cold cellars (development is slower and the wines are less prone to oxidation) than from warm cellars (the maturation of aromas and flavors is more rapid and the wines are quicker to oxidize). Additionally, are the wine cellars clean or dirty?

These are just a handful of factors that can have extraordinary impact on the style, quality, and personality of a wine. As the modernists claim, the choices that man himself makes, even when they are unquestionably in pursuit of the highest quality, can contribute far more to a wine's character than the vineyard's *terroir*.

If you are wondering where I stand on *terroir*, I do believe it is an important component in the production

of fine wine. However, I would argue that the most persuasive examples of *terroir* do not arise from Burgundy, but rather, from white wine varietals planted in Alsace and Germany. If one is going to argue *terroir*, the wine has to be made from exceptionally low yields; fermented with only the wild yeasts that inhabit the vineyard; brought up in a neutral medium, such as old barrels, cement tanks, or stainless steel; given minimal cellar treatment; and bottled with little or no fining or filtration.

Terroir, as used by many of its proponents, is often a convenient excuse for upholding the status quo. If one accepts the fact that *terroir* is everything and is essential to legitimize a wine, how should consumers evaluate the wines from Burgundy's most famous grand cru vineyard, Chambertin? This 32-acre vineyard boasts 23 different proprietors. But only a handful of them appear

committed to producing an extraordinary wine. Everyone agrees this is a hallowed piece of ground, but I can think of only a few producers—Domaine Leroy, Domaine Ponsot, Domaine Rousseau, Domaine des Chézeaux (Ponsot made the wine for Chézeaux)—that produce wines that merit the stratospheric reputation of this vineyard. Yet the Chambertins of three of these producers, Leroy, Ponsot, and Rousseau, are completely different in style. The Ponsot wine was the most elegant, supple, and round; Leroy's is the most tannic, backward, concentrated, and meaty; and Rousseau's is the darkest-colored, most dominated by new oak, and most modern in style, taste, and texture. As for the other 18 or 20 producers (and I am not even thinking about the various *négociant* offerings), what Burgundy wine enthusiasts are likely to encounter on retailers' shelves ranges from mediocre to appallingly thin and insipid. What wine, may I ask, speaks for the soil of Chambertin? Is it the wine of Leroy, the wine of Ponsot, the wine of Rousseau?

Arguments such as this can be made with virtually any significant Burgundy vineyard. Consider Corton-Charlemagne and four of its most celebrated producers. The firm of Faiveley owns the most prized parcel atop this famous hill, and they make a compellingly elegant Corton-Charlemagne. Stylistically, it is the antithesis of the super-concentrated, lavishly oaky, broadly flavored, alcoholic Corton-Charlemagne made by Louis Latour. Again, Domaine Leroy makes a backward, hard, tough Corton-Charlemagne that resembles a tannic red more than a white wine. Domaine Coche-Dury makes a wine with extraordinary mineral components, as well as remarkable richness, unctuosity, and opulence where the oak takes a back seat to the wine's fruit and texture. Which of these Corton-Charlemagnes has that notion of "somewhereness" that is raised by the terroirists to validate the quality of a vineyard?

Are terroirists kindergarten intellectuals who should be doing more tasting and less talking? Of course not. But they can be accused of naïvely swallowing the tallest tale in winedom. On the other hand, the realists should recognize that no matter how intense and concentrated a wine can be from a modest vineyard in Givry, it will never have the sheer complexity and class of a Vosne-Romanée grand cru from a conscientious producer.

In conclusion, it is fundamental that no great wine can be made from mediocre *terroir,* and any top wine must, to some degree, reflect its place of origin. Yet wine enthusiasts need to think of *terroir* as you do salt, pepper, and garlic. In many dishes they can represent an invaluable component, imparting wonderful aromas and flavors. But if consumed alone, they are usually difficult to swallow. Moreover, all the hyperventilation over *terroir* obscures the most important issue of all—identifying and discovering those producers who make wines worth drinking and savoring!

8. The passion and commitment of the producers. Think it over—the artist who produces a wine has one chance every 12 months. First is the 11 months of work leading up to the vintage. And then there is the most important decision made in the course of the year—the date to harvest, which, once made, cannot be undone. The fruit can be too ripe or not ripe enough, so getting it perfect is their goal, but perfection is no easy accomplishment, particularly given the vagaries of Mother Nature. These producers work virtually every day of the year, either in the vineyard or in the winery. They are the custodians for the new wine in the cellar. They are groundskeepers responsible for manicuring, pruning, and taking care of the vineyard's health, its crop size, and its overall balance. These producers have to be quick learners. A chef can have a bad day in the kitchen and 24 hours later be back on his or her brilliant and creative game. A wine producer puts in 11 months of labor, but over the course of a 10–20 day harvest, only gets that one chance to prove his or her worth.

These producers, to a man and woman, all have an enviable passion, intensity, and commitment to hard work. They refuse to compromise, and they recognize their responsibilities as the custodians of special pieces of property. Their sole purpose is to deliver to the consumer the most natural, uncompromised, unmanipulated expression of their vineyard, vintage, and varietal that is humanly possible. For the most part, the vast majority of the men and women behind great wines are humble servants of Mother Nature.

Most of the producers in this book are, I am sure, capable of pursuing more lucrative careers in other fields of work, but they are wedded to the concept that wine is not a business but a culture that ties together man, nature, and land. It embodies civilization at its finest, and is capable of bringing together diverse people to share the joy of a beverage that has been an important component of every major civilization in the Western world.

THE IMPORTANCE OF HISTORY

What makes this a modern view of the great wines of the world is that, while I consider the producer's history important, it is not the only factor. Many of the wines in this book originate from relative newcomers, some merely a decade old, but I am so convinced by the commitment of their makers and of the potential of their vineyard sites that I have taken the risk of including them. I did arbitrarily decide that any winery that hadn't produced at least ten vintages—a nanosecond in the time line of wine—couldn't be included. That said, the majority of these wineries do have considerable histories and pedigree. But to me the pedigree, hype, price, etc. are less important than the ability of a vineyard and/or winery to produce high-quality wine in virtually every vintage. Track record is one of the paramount considerations on my list, and the producers who are included have an extraordinary record of achievement even in vintages when Mother Nature was unkind.

THE IMPORTANCE OF THE FUTURE

Great wines attract a crowd, and this is ever so evident over the last quarter of a century. The recognition of greatness encourages other serious producers to ratchet up their level of performance. In the future, the producers who have been recognized for producing the greatest wines of the world in my opinion will be a beacon to hundreds of other producers, who will emulate their passion and commitment to quality.

GLOBALISM: THE WINE WORLD'S BIGGEST MYTH

One of the overwhelmingly specious arguments in the wine world today is that as the market becomes ever more global, the international companies are producing only monochromatic wines from a limited number of varieties in order to appeal to the largest customer base. This line of thinking ignores the true realities of a wine world that has become enormously more compli-

cated, diverse, and broad. The principal assertion of these critics is that globalization has resulted in bland, standard wine quality. As a result, individuality and artisanal winemaking are being replaced by oceans of vapid wines with the same taste. The appalling weakness of this argument is that there is never any specific evidence provided by the accusers to back up these broad and generally baseless allegations.

If the truth be known, wine quality is significantly superior today to what it was a mere 10 or 25 years ago. Moreover, there is substantial evidence that diversity of wine styles is manifoldly far greater today than it was 10 or 20 years ago. How many world-class wines were made from Italy's indigenous varietals, Aglianico, Nero d'Avola, or Piedirosso, a decade ago? None. However, today in southern Italy these grapes are enjoying a renaissance.

How many interesting wines emerged from outside Spain's Rioja region 10 or 20 years ago? A decade ago,

did anyone get turned on by the glorious old vine *cuvées* of Mourvèdre, Tempranillo, Grenache/Carignan, or Mencía? Numerous world-class wines are being produced not only from these varietals, but from exciting new regions such as Priorato, Toro, Jumilla, and Bierzo. How does that fit into the globalists' argument that the world of wine has narrowed and become less diverse?

This broadening of the wine world is not limited to only one or two countries. Serious table wines from indigenous varietals in Portugal are emerging in ever increasing quantities, and many of them are very interesting as well as distinctive. The rediscovery of old vineyards of Grenache and Carignan in Algeria, Lebanon, and Morocco is just one more persuasive example that the wine world has expanded in a positive and diverse fashion.

A decade ago, nobody was talking about the vinous bounty and artisanal producers of Australia, from Barossa and McLaren Vale in the south to the Margaret River in the west. The only conversation about Australia 10 or 20 years ago was about the giant corporations that had a stranglehold on the U.S. market. Hundreds of small quality-oriented wineries are now routinely represented in top wine shops throughout the United States. And let's not forget the increasingly interesting wines emerging from Tasmania and New Zealand that did not exist a mere decade ago. There is no standardized globalist taste to these wines any more than there is in any other viticultural region.

America's homegrown wines have also expanded significantly, not just in quality, but in diversity. Consider such newly emerging viticultural wine regions as the Sonoma Coast, Anderson Valley, the limestone ridges west of Paso Robles, and the Santa Rita Hills. Distinctive, exceptionally high-quality wines routinely emerge from these regions, yet all of them were unknown *terroirs* 15–20 years ago.

Moreover, how many different styles of wine exist in Oregon and Washington today? Even a narrow-minded conservative interested in preserving the status quo at all costs would agree that the number of quality wineries has more than quadrupled in the last decade, and whether it is Pinot Noir, Cabernet Sauvignon, or Pinot Gris, they taste different.

The growing internationalism of the wine industry has in fact created more competition. We now have significantly more young men and women trying to create distinctive and original wines from viticultural areas that are either being rediscovered or newly created. Many of the members of this younger winemaking generation are succeeding.

The overwhelming evidence is that globalization (i.e., standardization) is largely a fabricated problem with no credible supporting evidence. Everywhere I go, I see more "hands-off" rather than hands-on winemaking, more organic and biodynamic farming, and more producers cognizant of their responsibilities as custodians of a privileged piece of property.

Let's go one step further and look at the great bastion of traditional winemaking—France. It is irrefutable that 20 years ago it was the huge *négociant* firms of Alsace, Burgundy, and the Rhône Valley that controlled the image of those regions' wines. They were the ones who upheld the monopoly certain estates had on the market, and thus controlled the region's international reputation. Today, the emergence of artisanal and high-quality small and moderate-size estates from Alsace, Burgundy, and the Rhône Valley has completely revolutionized the world's image of these regions. A quest for high quality and individualistic, distinctive wines has also taken place in the Languedoc-Roussillon and the Loire Valley. Just how many newly energized estates making high-quality wines (and very different styles) have emerged from these viticultural regions? Is it 50 or 100? It is more. More than 200 estates did not make wine or did not make wine fit to drink 10 or 15 years ago, but now play proudly on the world stage of quality.

Lastly, consider France's most conservative viticultural region of all—Bordeaux. In Bordeaux, not only are the famed classified-growths making far better wines than they did two decades ago, but there has been an emergence of dedicated, conscientious men and women, especially in St.-Emilion, Pomerol, and the satellite appellations east of these two hallowed viticultural areas, pushing the quality higher and higher.

The globalization argument is an appealing one to reactionary romantics and their offspring, the pleasure police, in that they appear to fear any change as well as wines from both new regions and new producers that actually taste good. Like disingenuous politicians, they tend to believe that by repeating such gibberish over and over, it will somehow become an accepted truism.

TRYING TO DEFINE GREATNESS

To put this in a slightly different context, if I were writing this book 25 years ago, approximately 70% of these estates would not have been included. They were either producing mediocre wine or they did not even exist. The number of truly great wines in the world would probably have been less than five dozen, and all would have been from France, particularly Bordeaux, Burgundy, and Champagne.

There are convincing reasons why there are so many great wines today, and what changes have brought us so many of these finest wines.

The best example is Bordeaux, the region of the wine world that dominates this book and is clearly the most influential viticultural area in the world. It is there that the strongest arguments about dramatically improved quality can be made, but most of these arguments apply equally to every top viticultural region in the world for the very same reasons. Change the geography, the names of the grapes, the names of the producers, and the names of the estates, and you see that while Bordeaux may still be the epicenter for the world's greatest wines, what it does and how it does it is widely emulated elsewhere, but with different *terroirs*, different grapes, and totally different styles of wine.

So why is modern-day wine so much better than it was a mere 20, 30, 40, or 50 years ago? I list the reasons in three categories: 1) significant changes in the vineyard; 2) progressive changes in the wine cellar and fermentation techniques; and 3) changes in the wine's *élevage* (upbringing) and bottling.

Significant changes in the vineyard

Bordeaux has always led the world in vineyard care and management. In the 1960s and 1970s, octogenarian professor Dr. Emile Peynaud and famed professor of oenology Dr. Pascal Ribeau-Gayon, head of the department of oenology at the University of Bordeaux between 1977 and 1995, began advocating significant changes in viticultural management. They recommended later harvest dates in order to achieve riper fruit with lower acid levels as well as sweeter tannin and greater fruit characteristics. Later harvesting automatically produces wines lower in acidity and slightly higher in alcohol, and, if the harvest has not been undone by rain, exceptional fruit and ripeness can be achieved. This advice is 30–40 years old.

Along with these changes, modern-day sprays and treatments aimed at preventing rot in the vineyard were begun in the 1970s and increased in the 1980s. Recent good vintages such as 2002, 1999, 1994, 1983, 1979, and 1978 would undoubtedly have been destroyed by mildew in the 1950s and 1960s. At the same time, there was greater acceptance of the philosophy of going back to the vineyard (where most serious wine producers believe 90% of the quality emerges) to promote more organic techniques to encourage the health of the vines. There was also a movement toward developing a better understanding of viticulture. New techniques (called "extreme" or "radical" viticulture) became standard practice in the late 1980s and 1990s. This included the curtailing of yields by aggressive pruning in the winter and spring, and crop thinning (cutting off bunches of grapes) in summer to encourage lower yields. With extremely healthy vines, yields would be expected to rise, but thanks to pruning and crop thinning, yields have dropped significantly for the top estates, from highs of 60–100 hectoliters per hectare in the mid-1980s to 25–50 hectoliters per hectare in recent vintages. Other more radical viticulture techniques include leaf pulling (to encourage air flow as well as more contact with the sun), shoot positioning (to enhance sun exposure), and the ongoing research with clones and rootstocks designed to eliminate those that produce overly prolific crops of large-size berries. Harvesting grapes is also done with much more care, and in smaller containers designed to prevent bruising and skin breakage.

In 2005, the Bordeaux vineyards are healthier, have lower vigor, and are producing smaller and smaller berries and crops of higher and higher quality fruit. All of this is designed to produce the essence of the *terroir*, enhance the character of the vintage, and reveal the personality of the varietal or blend.

Progressive changes in the wine cellar and fermentation techniques

The famed first-growths Haut-Brion and Latour were two of the earliest estates to invest in temperature-controlled stainless-steel fermenters, Haut-Brion in the early 1960s, and Latour in 1964. The advantage of temperature-controlled fermenters, which are now being replaced by some avant garde producers with open-top temperature-controlled wood fermenters (an

adaptation of the old wooden vats used prior to the advent of temperature-controlled steel), is that they allow a producer to harvest as late as possible, picking grapes at full phenolic maturity with high sugars. Assuming weather permits, producers can harvest at their leisure, and bring in fully mature grapes knowing that at the push of a button they can control the temperature of each of their fermentation vats. In the old days, picking fully mature grapes often happened by accident, and in fact was often discouraged as fully ripe grapes were tricky to vinify. Many of the Médoc 1947s, not to mention some of the 1929s, were ruined by excessive volatile acidity, since producers did not have the ability to control fermentation temperatures. If temperatures soar to dangerously high levels, the yeasts that convert the sugar into alcohol are killed, setting off a chain reaction that results in spoiled wines. This was frequently a problem when harvests occurred during hot weather. The stories of producers throwing in blocks of ice to cool down

their fermentations are not just vineyard legend; it actually happened in 1947, 1949, and 1959. Certainly the advent of temperature-controlled fermenters, whether steel or wood, has been a remarkable technological advancement in wine quality, and has resulted in significantly better wines with fewer defects and sweeter fruit, as well as riper tannin and lower acidity.

Moreover, all of the top properties are now doing an extraordinary selection (or culling out damaged or vegetal material) on what they call the *table de tri* (sorting table). A labor force inspects the grapes as they come into the cellars, and discards any that appear rotten, unripe, unhealthy, or blemished. The degree of inspection varies from property to property, but it is safe to assume that those properties producing the finest wines practice the most severe selection. Some perfectionist estates have a second *table de tri* after the grapes are destemmed. (This means another sorting team searches through the destemmed grape bunches

to further pull out any vegetal material, stems, leaves, or questionable-looking berries.)

Cold soaks, or prefermentation macerations, have become increasingly à la mode. They have been used in the past in some of the colder northern viticulture areas (Burgundy and the northern Rhône) simply because the cellars were so cold, and fermentations often did not kick off for four or five days. Cold soaks have been gathering support among avant garde producers, who believe four- to eight-day cold soaks will extract more phenolic material, greater aromatics, and darker colors. Some of the more radical producers actually add dry-ice pellets to the soaking/macerating grape must to promote bouquet and color development.

Fermentations, which used to be 10–15 days, are now often extended, the theory being that the molecular chain that forms the tannin structure will become sweeter and riper with prolonged fermentations of 21–30 or more days.

The bottom line is that every top property has invested in state-of-the-art temperature-controlled fermenters, whether they be stainless steel or the smaller open-top wood type (which have become the rage in St.-Emilion over the last decade). All the top properties do a severe triage before and sometimes after destemming. More and more properties use cold soaks, and some use extended macerations. Overall, the vinification of modern-day wine is done under strictly supervised, temperature-controlled conditions in a far more sanitary, healthy environment than 30 or 50 years ago. It is a far cry from the seat-of-your-pants fermentations of the past that could become stuck or troubled, thus causing the development of unwanted organisms and/or volatile acidity.

Lastly, the most controversial technique in the wine cellar today is the use of reverse osmosis (a technique that involves pushing the grape must through an apparatus to remove water) and entrophy (the removal of

TRYING TO DEFINE GREATNESS

water under a vacuum system to concentrate the grape must). In the past, the technique generally employed was called *saignée,* which consisted of siphoning off a portion of the juice in the fermentation tank to increase the percentage of skins to grape must. That worked reasonably well, but in the early 1980s some top châteaux (Léoville-Las-Cases was among the first) discreetly began using reverse osmosis. These concentration techniques have now been in use for 20 years, and while I was initially skeptical, the fact is that Léoville-Las-Cases has been producing wines of first-growth quality. In years when there is good ripeness but dilution from harvest rains, these machines, when used with discretion, can increase the quality of the wine with apparently no damage. At many top châteaux, reverse osmosis is now standard operating procedure, but only in years where there is some dilution from harvest rain. It is not without risks. The danger is that you not only concentrate the wine, you concentrate the defects as well. That is why such practices must still be approached with caution. However, in the hands of talented, capable operators who use them prudently as well as selectively, it is hard to argue that they are actually changing the character of the wine. After being skeptical, even critical of these machines, I have come to believe they work well when used properly. Yet, many producers foolishly do not do the work necessary to curtail yields, and use these concentrators recklessly as a safety gap, with traumatic results. They will never produce profound wines.

Changes in the wines' élevage *(upbringing) and bottling*
Perhaps the primary reason for improved quality as well as uniformity of Bordeaux wines has been the movement, encouraged by Dr. Emile Peynaud and Dr. Pascal Ribeau-Gayon (and their protégés), to bottle wines over a much shorter period of time (one to two weeks) as opposed to bottling on demand, or over a six to nine–month period (often the case 30–50 years ago). Prior to 1970, many châteaux sold barrels of their wines to brokers, even shipping them to merchants in England or Belgium who then bottled the wines at their leisure. Thankfully, that practice came to a halt nearly 30 years ago. Today, the shorter time in barrel has resulted in wines that are more primary and richer in fruit, and have far greater potential to develop in the

bottle. This trend has occurred throughout the finest vineyards.

In addition, sanitation in the cellars has changed dramatically in the past 25 years. Many critics claim the percentage of new oak has jumped significantly, and there is no doubting that far more new oak is seen in Bordeaux than there was 20 or 30 years ago. A great advantage in working with new oak is that it is sanitary. Part of the problem when working with old oak is that it is a fertile home for unwanted bacteria, resulting in off flavors and potential spoilage problems. However, if the wine does not have sufficient concentration and depth to stand up to new oak, the producer would be wiser to use a neutral vessel for aging. One Burgundian (actually a Belgian, Jean-Marie Guffens) put the issue of new oak in perspective, saying, "never has a wine been over-oaked . . . it's been under-wined." While new oak is an ingredient that works well with Cabernet Sauvignon, Merlot, Cabernet Franc, Syrah, and Petit Verdot, excessive use will destroy the flavors and obliterate varietal character, vintage personality, and *terroir* characteristics.

A controversial (actually it's not, but is perceived as such by uninformed observers) practice initiated by some smaller estates is malolactic fermentation in barrel. Virtually all serious red wines go through malolactic fermentation, which, in short, is the conversion of sharp, tart malic acids in the grape must into softer, creamier, lower lactic acids. For the most part, the largest estates continue to do malolactic in tank, and then move the wine into barrels for 16–20 months aging. Small estates prefer to do malolactic in barrel because they believe it integrates the wood better and gives the wine a more forward sweetness early in life, making the young, grapy wine more appealing to wine journalists/critics who descend on Bordeaux every spring to taste the newest vintage. Malolactic in barrel is not new. It has been practiced in Burgundy for decades, and was often utilized a century ago. It fell out of favor when large fermentation vats were developed. Malolactic in barrel gives a wine a certain seductiveness/sexiness early in its life, but at the end of a 12-month period, there is virtually no difference between a wine given malolactic in barrel and one where malolactic occurs in tank and is subsequently moved to barrel. The latter wines often start life more slowly, but at the end of a year they have absorbed their wood just as well as those that have had malolactic in barrel.

Significant changes in the selection process have also resulted in tremendous improvements in many wines. It is not unusual for an estate included in this book to declassify 35% or more of their production in order to put only the finest essence of their vineyard into the top wine. Much of the declassified juice goes into the second wine. The development of second wines is not new. Léoville-Las-Cases instituted a second wine more than 100 years ago, and Château Margaux has been producing one nearly as long. However, in the 1980s and 1990s, the selection process for top Bordeaux estates became increasingly draconian. Now most serious properties also produce a third wine, or sell it in bulk.

Other changes in the *élevage* of long-lived red wines include less racking and brutal movement of the wines. Today, many wines are moved under gas, and the racking process (often done 3–4 times during the first year) has been modified, as many progressive winemakers believe it bruises the wine and causes accelerated development as well as fruit desiccation. A small group of producers has begun aging their wines on the lees, another technique borrowed from the Burgundians. Lees are sedimentary materials consisting of yeasts and solid particles that often separate after fermentation and after the wine has been pressed into tank and barrel. These progressives feel that aging on the lees, assuming they are healthy lees, adds more texture, richness, vineyard character, and varietal personality. I tend to agree with them. However, there is no doubting that many a great Bordeaux has been produced that was never aged on any significant lees. Lees aging remains controversial in Bordeaux, where it is regarded as an avant garde technique.

Another new development has been microbullage, which originated in France's appellation of Madiran to sweeten and soften the notoriously hard tannin of those wines, and quickly caught on in Cahors, and to a certain extent St.-Emilion. This technique involves the diffusion of tiny amounts of oxygen through a tube into fermentation vats postfermentation, or into the actual barrels during the wines' upbringing. In Bordeaux (primarily St.-Emilion), the talented Stéphane Derenoncourt has had success with this technique for wines he oversees. The philosophy behind microbullage (or micro-oxygenation) is sound. The idea is to avoid labor-intensive and sometimes brutal/traumatic racking, and feed the wine oxygen in a reductive state while it is aging in the barrel. It is believed that this measured, oxidative process preserves more of the *terroir* and fruit character than a harsher racking process. A variation of this technique is called *clicage*. It is essentially the same thing, but the term is applied only to those who use micro-oxygenation in barrel, not tank. Early results from those producers who practice this technique have been positive. The wines have not fallen apart (as their critics warned), and in truth, there is no reason they should, since the technique itself, if not abused, is far more gentle than traditional racking.

The addition of tannic, highly pigmented press wine to the higher-quality "free-run juice" was often applied in ancient times without any regard for balance/harmony. Today, it is done judiciously or not at all, depending on whether or not the wine needs it. Small, measured dosages are frequently added incrementally to ensure that the wine does not end up with an excess of tannin.

Lastly, perhaps the single most important factor after the selection process is the decision whether to fine and/or filter, and the degree to which this is done. Both procedures can eviscerate a wine, destroying texture as well as removing aromatics, fruit, and mid-palate flesh. In the old days, a wine was rarely filtered, but egg-white fining was often done in order to soften the harsh tannin. Moreover, years ago, grapes were often unripe and not destemmed, so the tannin was extremely aggressive, even vegetal. Fining helped soften this astringency. Today, with later harvests and for the other reasons already expressed, the tannin is sweeter, and unless the wine has a bacterial problem (suspended proteins or other matter that makes the wine unattractive aesthetically), there is no need to perform the heavy finings and filtrations of the past.

In summary, less fining and filtering are practiced today, resulting in wines with more intense flavors, texture, aromatics, and *terroir* character. Most of the finest estates take an intelligent approach and do not employ fining and filtering unilaterally, but on a vintage by vintage basis. The good news, and one of the reasons Bordeaux is so much better today, is that wineries actually make a decision about whether fining or filtering is necessary, as opposed to doing it automatically (which was the situation during the 1960s, 1970s, and early 1980s).

The finest wines of today are far superior to the wines of 20–50 years ago for all of the above reasons. Today, one sees more of the *terroir* essence and vintage character in a bottle than was the case 20, 30, 40, or 50 years ago. Not only are the wines more accessible young, but the aging curve of top wines has been both broadened and expanded. Contrary to the doom and gloom predictions from uninformed critics, most vintages of today will live longer and drink better during the entire course of their lives than their predecessors.

However, there are some negatives to consider. For example, some of the prodigious 1947 Bordeaux (such as Pétrus, Latour à Pomerol, l'Evangile, Lafleur, and most notably Cheval Blanc) had residual sugar, elevated volatile acidity, and extremely high alcohol, as well as pH levels that would cause most modern-day oenologists to faint. Sadly, despite all the improvements that have been made, few modern-day oenologists would permit a wine

such as the 1947 Cheval Blanc ever to get into the bottle under the name Cheval Blanc. Anyone who has tasted a pristine bottle of this wine recognizes why most competent observers feel this is one of the most legendary wines ever produced in Bordeaux. All of its defects are outweighed by its extraordinary positive attributes. It is also these defects that often give the wine its individuality and character. So, a word of warning: Despite all the techniques designed to make higher quality, there is still a place for wines with a handful of defects that give them undeniable character as well as greatness. Somehow, all these new techniques need to make an allowance for wines such as these 1947s.

That being said, there is no question that: 1) the increased knowledge of viticulture, vinification, and weather that exists today has resulted in greater wines; 2) the improved health of the vineyards has resulted in higher-quality grapes; 3) the movement toward more natural winemaking has led to less traumatic bruising of the fruit and wine; 4) the preservation of the fruit, vintage, and *terroir* characteristics has reached a pinna-

cle because of these soft handling techniques; and 5) the bottling process today is aimed at putting the essence of the vineyard into the bottle in a less oxidized and evolved condition. Logically, it makes sense that these wines will have the ability to age better and longer than their predecessors.

It cannot be underscored strongly enough: The ignorant belief that the wines of today are more forward, and therefore shorter lived, is a myth. Additional myths include the previously mentioned fallacious assertion that wines taste too much alike, and that there are fewer artisans/artists crafting diverse wines than in the past. As already stated, this is the most foolish accusation of the romantic reactionaries who have yet to offer any specific evidence to support their statements. In truth, their nonsensical observations are betrayed by the realities of today's wine world.

Wines today are produced from healthier, riper fruit, and thus they possess lower acidity as well as sweeter tannin. Analytically, modern-day great vintages have indices of tannin and dry extract as high as or higher than the legendary vintages of the past. However, because their tannin is sweeter and the acidity lower, they can be enjoyed at an earlier age. This does not compromise their aging potential. Two examples would be 1959 Bordeaux, which was considered entirely too low in acidity to age (most of the great 1959s are still in pristine condition), and 1982 Bordeaux, which many uninformed observers claimed would have to be drunk by 1990 for fear the wine would turn into vinegar. The finest 1959s are still evolving, with the best wines possessing another 20–30 years of life. The top 1982 Bordeaux have—at the minimum—30 to 50 years of longevity.

Think it over. Does anyone want to return to the wine world of 30 or 40 years ago when (1) fewer than one-fourth of the most renowned estates made wines worthy of their official pedigree; (2) dirty, unclean aromas were rationalized as part of the *terroir* character; (3) disappointingly emaciated, austere, excessively tannic wines from famous *terroirs* were labeled "classic" by a subservient wine press that existed on the largesse of the wine industry; (4) wines were made from underripe grapes and were too high in acidity and tannin to ever fully become harmonious; (5) there was no young generation of creative artists fashioning compelling wines from unknown *terroirs* and unfashionable grapes; and (6) there was no worldwide revolution in quality.

Nevertheless, the arguments will continue to be made that modern-day wines won't age as well as earlier efforts from the same estates, or even worse, that high technology and globalization have completely destroyed individuality in wines. Of course, one of the historical fallacies about Bordeaux, Burgundy, Italy, or California is that older vintages aged well. In truth, there are only a dozen or so wines from great vintages of these regions that ever aged well. Most of the wines of these vintages were defective or fell apart before they ever became drinkable.

In short, let no one state that there are not great wines made traditionally as well as compelling wines made in a modern style. The reactionaries of the wine world who continue to decry modern-styled wines are most likely threatened by newcomers and by a young generation of men and women taking less renowned pieces of property, and less prestigious varietals, and exploiting them to their fullest potential.

As a general rule, great wines are made in relatively limited quantities. It tends to be a fundamental condition of winedom that the world's finest wines simply do not exist in industrial-size quantities. The closest consumers will get to significant quantities are at the large Bordeaux estates that can produce 20,000–30,000 cases of compelling wine. However, these are the exceptions to the rule. Most of the wines in this book are only available in 400–500 to 2,000–3,000 case lots, which is a microscopic quantity given the world's insatiable demand.

While many of these wines will not be found at your neighborhood mom-and-pop liquor store, top wine shops in every major metropolitan area receive limited allocations from even the smallest estates. The one place where all these wines can be found, even older, historic vintages, is the wine auction place.

Wine auctions have become the wine consumer's preferred source for that limited-production wine, rarified wine, or a great wine from an ancient vintage. The most famous auction venues are the houses of Christie's and Sotheby's, but they have plenty of noteworthy competition. Some notable auction wine houses include Zachys in New York; the Chicago Wine Company in Chicago; Morrell Wine Auctions, a New York–based retail auction house; and winebid.com, winecommune.com, and eBay.com (all Internet sites). Readers who are interested in trying to latch on to a bottle or case of these limited-production gems should get on the mailing lists of these wine auction houses, or sign up on the Internet for the online services.

Buying wine at auction has several downsides. There are commissions to pay, the provenance of the bottle must be authenticated, and the condition of the cellar from which it was procured by the auction house should be verified. A recent supreme court decision seemingly in favor of more flexibility regarding the direct purchase and shipment of wines to wine consumers may not lead to full and unrestricted access to wine, as legal authorities were in disagreement about its true significance at the time of publication.

WINESPEAK

Not surprisingly, wine-tasting jargon constitutes an entire language system that frequently sounds pretentious and silly to the non–wine geek. However, it is no different from any specialized language for a limited-interest subject. At the end of this book there is a glossary of wine terms that includes most of the operative wine vocabulary used in this book.

ARGENTINA

Ironically, for over 200 years, members of virtually every family in Argentina worked in viticulture or winemaking, yet only in the last 10 to 15 years has a new generation of Argentinian vignerons begun to realize this country's, and particularly the province of Mendoza's, extraordinary potential. In the past the industry was plagued by the general philosophy that quantity was preferable to quality. Now their finest wines can compete on the world stage. Argentina's greatest visionary is Nicolás Catena, and his crusade for high-altitude vineyards and conservative viticultural practices has resulted in one after another breakthrough wines that have pushed Argentina to the forefront of the modern winemaking revolution. The other irony is that Malbec, a grape long considered challenging and often disappointing in France, produces prodigious wines of great perfume, quality, and longevity in Argentina. Malbec is the red wine hope of Argentina, but the upstart wine industry has also been successful with Cabernet Sauvignon, Merlot, and another famed French variety, Chardonnay.

WINES:

Catena Zapata (Cabernet Sauvignon and Malbec)

Cabernet Sauvignon Nicolás Catena Zapata Vineyard

Cabernet Sauvignon Agrelo Vineyard

Chardonnay Adrianna Vineyard Catena Alta

Malbec Angélica Vineyard Catena Alta

CLASSIFICATION: Mendoza, Argentina

OWNER: Nicolás Catena

ADDRESS: Calle Cobos, (5519) Agrelo, Luján de Cuyo, Mendoza, Argentina

TELEPHONE: 54 261 490 0214 / 0215 / 0216

TELEFAX: 54 261 490 0217

E-MAIL: export@catenazapata.com

WEBSITE: www.catenawines.com

CONTACT: Jeff Mausbach (jeffm@catenazapata.com)

VISITING POLICY: Guided tours in English, Spanish, French, or German, Monday through Friday, 9 A.M.–6 P.M. All visits are by appointment only with 24 hours' advance notice.

VINEYARDS

SURFACE AREA: 1,032 acres in six vineyard sites

GRAPE VARIETALS: Malbec, Chardonnay, Cabernet Sauvignon, Merlot, Pinot Noir, Sauvignon Blanc, Cabernet Franc, Semillon, Syrah, Petit Verdot, Sangiovese, Tanat

AVERAGE AGE OF THE VINES: 23 years (oldest planted 1930; youngest planted 1997)

DENSITY OF PLANTATION: The more than 70-year-old Angélica Vineyard is planted at 5,500 plants per hectare. All of the newer vineyards are planted at 4,000 plants per hectare.

AVERAGE YIELDS: 8 metric tons per hectare (4 tons per acre)

WINEMAKING AND UPBRINGING

All the grapes are harvested by parcels and vinified in separate lots so that their progression can be followed. State-of-the-art temperature-controlled fermentations and aging in French oak are parts of a winemaking and upbringing philosophy that is very much in the Bordeaux tradition. New oak is important as a seasoning, kept well in the background so that the *terroir* character and fruit of the wines can come forward.

ANNUAL PRODUCTION

Catena Alta Chardonnay: 24,900 bottles

Catena Alta Cabernet Sauvignon: 66,000 bottles

Catena Alta Malbec: 66,000 bottles

Nicolás Catena Zapata: 42,000 bottles

AVERAGE PRICE (VARIABLE DEPENDING ON VINTAGE): $15–80

GREATEST RECENT VINTAGES

2003, 2002, 2001 (Chardonnay only), 1997 (Cabernet Sauvignon only), 1996 (Malbec only)

The Catena family's roots lie deep in the Italian wine–growing province of Marche. In fact, Nicola Catena was the son of a vineyard worker. He emigrated to Argentina in the 19th century and settled his family in Mendoza, which was just beginning to develop a reputation as a grape-growing region. In 1902, Nicola Catena planted his first vineyard. In 1963, his grandson Nicolás Catena, after receiving a Ph.D. in economics, took over the business.

Nicolás Catena credits California with completely changing the way he looked at viticulture and winemaking. In 1982 he was invited to be a visiting professor at the Department of Agricultural Economics of the University of California at Berkeley, and he used his weekends to visit Napa Valley. Completely flabbergasted by the amount of investment and research done by Robert Mondavi and his family, he became convinced that similar efforts in Argentina could yield splendid results. As he says candidly, after spending time at Robert Mondavi and seeing the results of their research in both the vineyards and winemaking, he thought, "My God, why not try this in Mendoza?" Catena returned home in the early 1980s and began a research project designed to find Mendoza's finest growing regions and microclimates for growing Chardonnay, Cabernet Sauvignon, and Malbec. He also designed his research to ascertain which selection of clonal material from both Europe and California would be best suited for the grape-growing condition and soils in Mendoza. All of this went against the local philosophy of grape growers, who believed that larger and larger crops would mean better wine, as opposed to lower yields and proper rootstocks and clonal material.

His wines were first released in the United States in 1991, and they were immediate successes, both the Chardonnay and the Cabernet Sauvignon. He followed those up with a more serious line of wines under the Catena Alta label, which was even more positively received. These were the best lots of Cabernet Sauvignon, Malbec, and Chardonnay from the Catena Zapata vineyards. His flagship wine, the Nicolás Catena Zapata, a Cabernet Sauvignon and Malbec blend, debuted in 1997. The wine had already competed in Argentina in a number of blind tastings against the famous French wines of Latour, Haut-Brion, and some of the best of Napa Valley, and consistently came out first or second. The results encouraged Catena and suggested that there was unrealized upside for his vineyards.

While these tasting notes are largely for single-vineyard wines, Nicolás Catena is moving more and more to microclimate blending, recognizing that a more complex wine can evolve from blending different varietals from different altitudes. As a result, most of the upcoming releases that will hit the market after 2005 will be microclimate blends carrying the Mendoza

Nicolás Catena and his daughter Laura

appellation instead of specific vineyard designations. The exception is the Catena Alta Chardonnay, which will continue to be sourced entirely from the Adrianna Vineyard. Though none has been released at the time of this writing, the Bodega Catena Zapata will start bottling single-vineyard Malbecs starting with the 2002s.

Among the principal vineyards used for the Bodega Catena Zapata wines is the Angélica Vineyard, 195 acres of alluvial soils of clay, rock, and sand planted entirely with Malbec and Cabernet Sauvignon except for a small parcel of Chardonnay. This vineyard was named after Catena's mother. The Uxmal Vineyard, planted on limestone, sand, and clay soils, has many different varietals planted in it, but primarily Cabernet Sauvignon, Chardonnay, Malbec, and then smaller quantities of Merlot, Sauvignon Blanc, Semillon, Syrah, Sangiovese, Cabernet Franc, and Petit Verdot. The Adrianna Vineyard (267 acres) is dominated by Malbec, followed by Merlot, Chardonnay, Cabernet Sauvignon, Pinot Noir, Viognier, and Sauvignon Blanc. The Domingo Vineyard, named after Nicolás Catena's fa-

ther, is an 87-acre vineyard planted primarily with Chardonnay but with some Pinot Noir and Cabernet Sauvignon. The Virginia Vineyard, named after another member of the Catena family, is a 147-acre vineyard planted mostly with Chardonnay, but also with some Merlot and Malbec. Lastly, the Nicasia Vineyard, named after Nicolás Catena's maternal grandmother, is again primarily a Malbec vineyard, but also with some plantings of Chardonnay, Cabernet Franc, Tannat, Tokai, and Merlot. All these vineyards are planted at relatively lofty elevations from 2,850 feet (Angélica Vineyard) to an amazing 4,830 feet (the Adrianna Vineyard).

Nicolás Catena, backed up admirably by his daughter Laura, is one of South America's greatest visionaries, and the wines reflect his uncompromising crusade to produce the finest wines Argentina can achieve.

CABERNET SAUVIGNON NICOLAS CATENA ZAPATA

1999 Cabernet Sauvignon Nicolás Catena Zapata

RATING: 94 points

Nicolás Catena's flagship wine does justice to his name. A blend of 82% Cabernet Sauvignon and 18% Malbec, the 1999 Nicolás Catena Zapata bursts from the glass with spice-laden blackberries. While it does not have the 1997's blockbuster fruit, its graceful, seamless personality reveals huge depth. Medium-bodied and satin textured, this elegant, flavorful wine displays clove-tinged black cherries, jammy blackberries, and hints of licorice whose flavors linger throughout its supple, exceedingly long finish. Anticipated maturity: now–2015+.

1997 Cabernet Sauvignon Nicolás Catena Zapata

RATING: 95 points

The 1997 Cabernet Sauvignon Nicolás Catena Zapata is a selection of the finest barrels in the Catena Alta cellars. About 5% Malbec was blended into the 1,000-case lot. This wine may also be marketed in some countries under the name Cuvée Unico. It reveals a dense black/purple color as well as a sensational nose of crème de cassis intermixed with toasty oak. Unevolved and supple, with enormous concentration and richness in addition to a funky, grilled meat flavor, this huge, full-bodied wine is surprisingly well balanced and symmetrical for its size. It should drink well for another 10–15 years.

CATENA ALTA CABERNET SAUVIGNON ZAPATA VINEYARD

1999 Catena Alta Cabernet Sauvignon Zapata Vineyard

RATING: 91 points

The dark ruby–colored 1999 Catena Alta Cabernet Sauvignon Zapata Vineyard has chocolate, raspberry, and blackberry aromas. Unlike the 1997, which was 100% Cab, this wine contains 10% Malbec. It is highly concentrated, extracted, and backward. Layers of cassis, blackberries, spices, and dark cherries can be found in its tightly wound and tannic (yet ripe) character as well as in its admirably long finish. Bravo to Nicolás Catena and Pepe Galante for putting together such a marvelous lineup of wines. Anticipated maturity: now–2010.

1997 Catena Alta Cabernet Sauvignon Zapata Vineyard

RATING: 92 points

The dark ruby–colored 1997 Catena Alta Cabernet Sauvignon Zapata Vineyard has awesome richness to its aromatic profile, revealing candied black fruits, spices, and cassis. This magnificent, hugely rich wine is fat, medium to full–bodied, plump, and, simply put, gorgeous. It is powerful yet elegant, crammed with a myriad of sweet blackberries and assorted currants. Its finish reveals copious quantities of ripened tannin. It is a superb wine that merits comparison with the world's finest Cabernets. Anticipated maturity: now–2012+.

CATENA ALTA CHARDONNAY ADRIANNA VINEYARD

2001 Catena Alta Chardonnay Adrianna Vineyard

RATING: 93 points

Boasting impressive aromatic depth, the spicy pear-scented 2001 Catena Alta Chardonnay Adrianna Vineyard is medium to full–bodied, oily-textured, broad, and expansive. Its luscious mouth-feel, while rich and supple, retains admirable freshness and purity. Candied white fruits, anise, and hints of butterscotch (not from oxidation) can be found in this sumptuous offering. Drink it over the next four years.

CATENA CABERNET SAUVIGNON AGRELO VINEYARD

1999 Catena Cabernet Sauvignon Agrelo Vineyard

RATING: 90 points

The medium to dark ruby–colored 1999 Catena Cabernet Sauvignon Agrelo Vineyard is a highly aromatic, blackberry-dominated wine. It is hugely concentrated and viscous, coating the taster's palate with wave after wave of blackberry liqueur. Its flavors last throughout the extraordinarily long finish. This is an exceptionally well-made wine that puts to shame many California Cabernets at two to three times the price. Anticipated maturity: now–2010+.

CATENA ZAPATA

1999 Catena Zapata

94+ points

Bursting from the glass with spice-laden blackberries, this wine may not have the 1997's blockbuster fruit, but it still reveals huge depth to its graceful, seamless personality. It is a medium-bodied, satin-textured, elegantly flavored wine that displays clove-tinged black cherries, jammy blackberries, and hints of licorice. Its flavors linger throughout its supple, exceedingly long finish. Anticipated maturity: now–2012.

1997 Catena Zapata

95 points

A spectacular effort and a breakthrough wine for Nicolás Catena, this inky, dense black/purple–colored wine shows a sensational core of crème de cassis intertwined with toasty oak. Unevolved and supple, with enormous concentration, this huge, full-bodied wine is surprisingly well balanced and symmetrical for its size. Anticipated maturity: now–2015.

AUSTRALIA

It is nearly impossible to believe that 25 years ago there were only a handful of Australian wines available in the United States. Even the wine considered by many observers to be one of the greatest produced in the Southern Hemisphere, the renowned Penfolds Grange, was not exported to America until 1977. However, Australian wines have proliferated over the last 2–3 decades, and now the shelves of virtually every retailer are filled with hundreds of Australian selections.

The real glories are the classic old-vine, South Australian *cuvées* made of Shiraz, Grenache, and, occasionally, blends of those two varietals with Cabernet Sauvignon. South Australia is a large area that encompasses many diverse appellations, the most well known being Barossa Valley, McLaren Vale, Clare Valley, Eden Valley, Adelaide Hills, and Coonawarra. It also includes such far-flung viticultural regions as Wrattonbully, the Fleurieu Peninsula, Riverland, Padthaway, Mount Benson, Langhorne Creek, and Kangaroo Island. There is no other place in the world that can match the kind of wines being produced from old Shiraz and Grenache vines in the McLaren Vale and Barossa vineyards. Yet, these offerings are often criticized by Eurocentric oenophiles who mock them as too rich, thick, alcoholic, woody, and flamboyant. While some wines are guilty as charged, the finest of these efforts, even though they are incredibly rich, powerful, and intense early in life, are capable of maturing into far more graceful and civilized wines after 10–15 years in the bottle. In short, while I do not believe that anyone in Australia can successfully duplicate the classics of Europe, neither can anyone else in the world produce such distinctive and original wine as many South Australian wineries can. The irony is that 30 years ago, the Australian government encouraged farmers to tear up their ancient vines of Shiraz and Grenache and replace them with popular international varieties such as Merlot and Cabernet Sauvignon, which the bureaucrats believed represented the future of viticulture in Australia. Thankfully many farmers refused, and today it is irrefutable that Australia's finest dry wines emerge from these once endangered old-vine vineyards.

Another irony about Australian wines is that the homegrown critics seem to share the Eurocentrics' bias against the power and potency of many of the old-vine *cuvées* of Grenache and Shiraz. There seems to be considerable agreement among the Aussie wine press that the Barossa, Eden Valley, and McLaren Vale wineries should put on the brakes and produce wines that do little more than imitate French, Spanish, or Italian efforts. This would be a disaster, since no country has demonstrated the ability to compete with the great classics of France, Spain, or Italy, and by the same token, no European country can duplicate Australia's finest efforts. Without the fundamental climatic conditions that are conducive to making elegant, finesse-styled wines, those Australian wineries that believe they can outperform Europe frequently turn out innocuous, manipulated wines with little soul or character.

Elegant wines do emerge from Australia, particularly in the areas of Victoria and Western Australia, primarily the Margaret River. Victoria is an interesting area, producing Syrah, Cabernet Sauvignon, and occasionally, Merlot and Grenache that combine richness with finesse. Readers should look for some of the finest offerings from such sub-viticultural regions as Bendigo, Geelong, Grampians, and Pyrenees, and the Yarra Valley should always be considered. Victoria is also the home of one of Australia's (and the wine world's) greatest treasures, the stupendous fortified wines of Rutherglen, which are as good as any fortifieds produced in Europe. Moreover, except for the rare, limited-edition, ancient Solera *cuvées*, they can still be purchased for a song.

WINE: Draycott Shiraz

OWNERS: Rick and Bronwyn Burge

ADDRESS: P.O. Box 330, Barossa Valley Highway, Lyndoch, SA, 5351, Australia

TELEPHONE: 61 8 8524 4644

TELEFAX: 61 8 8524 4444

E-MAIL: draycott@burgefamily.com.au

WEBSITE: www.burgefamily.com.au

CONTACT: Rick Burge

VISITING POLICY: Open Thursday to Monday, 10 A.M.–5 P.M., closed Tuesday and Wednesday

VINEYARDS

SURFACE AREA: 25 acres (10 hectares)

GRAPE VARIETALS: Shiraz, Grenache, Cabernet Sauvignon, Mourvèdre, Merlot, Zinfandel, Nebbiolo, Touriga, Souzao, Semillon, Muscat Blanc

AVERAGE AGE OF THE VINES: Draycott Shiraz comes from low-yielding Shiraz vines planted in the 1960s together with grapes from more recent plantings (12–15 years old)

DENSITY OF PLANTATION: Approximately 660 vines per acre

AVERAGE YIELDS: Shiraz vineyards average 1.5–2.5 tons per acre

WINEMAKING AND UPBRINGING

Rick Burge has a policy of nonintervention. Most of the Shiraz is dry-grown in the Barossa, with minimal fungicide spraying and an absence of any fertilizers. Some irrigation is permitted in extraordinary drought conditions, only to maintain the health of the vine and bud fruitfulness for the following season. Believing it's the vineyard, not the man, that makes the wine, Rick Burge sees his job as simply to translate what fruit has been given to him into a complete product in the winery. He strongly believes that harvest cannot occur until the flavors are ripe and the tannins are mature. By pruning for lower yields and practicing well-ventilated canopy management, he works to achieve the right formula for full tannin maturity and flavor ripeness while maintaining reasonable pH and acid levels. He uses oak like a chef, for seasoning rather than dominating the flavor or texture. For the Draycott Shiraz, French oak is used, with a few larger American oak puncheons. The percentage of new oak used in any vintage is between 25 and 35%, and the time a wine spends in wood 11–13 months.

When asked to sum up his personal philosophy, Rick Burge says, "Aiming to make great wine requires a degree of humility. With success comes the realization of relatively how little you really know about this wonderful beverage, life's lubricant. Keep the bullshit and hype to a minimum, and allow consumers to catch on to your product of their own accord."

ANNUAL PRODUCTION

Draycott Shiraz: production is variable

AVERAGE PRICE (DEPENDING ON VINTAGE): $27–60

GREAT RECENT VINTAGES

2003, 2002, 2001, 1998, 1996, 1991, 1990, 1986

This brilliant winemaker in the Barossa Valley (Australia's epicenter for old-vine Grenache and Shiraz) comes from an English immigrant family from Wiltshire that settled in South Australia in 1855. In the late 1920s, faced with plummeting grape prices, the Burge family had to decide to either leave the grapes on the vine to rot, since there were no purchasers, or learn how to make wine. Rick Burge's grandfather Percival decided that it was time to make wine. This 25-acre, single-estate vineyard, which is composed of the Draycott, Olive Hill, and Garnacha blocks, yields approximately 75 tons of fruit, and in its short history has produced some marvelous vintages, such as 1986, 1990, 1991, 1996, 1998, 2001, 2002, and 2003. They were known from the 1930s through the early 1980s primarily for their dessert wines, but Rick Burge steered the company toward premium table wines.

Rick Burge

DRAYCOTT SHIRAZ

2001 Premium Draycott Shiraz

RATING: 95 points

Burge's flagship wine is the limited-production (480 cases) 2001 Premium Draycott Shiraz (a blend of 90% Shiraz, 6% Mourvèdre, and 4% Grenache from vines averaging 40 years in age). Half was aged in French oak and half in American. The 2001 continues the beautiful succession of Draycott *cuvées* made since 1986. Its saturated purple color is accompanied by aromas of crème de cassis, melted licorice, camphor, and a hint of vanilla. Full-bodied and dense, with stunning purity, a multilayered texture, and a voluptuous finish, this is classic Barossa Shiraz, powerful yet well balanced. It will drink well for 15+ years. In short, it's a stunner!

2000 Premium Draycott Shiraz

RATING: 92 points

Burge's top Shiraz is no longer designated "Reserve," but is blended into the "Premium" Draycott *cuvée*. The rich, full-bodied, dense purple–colored 2000 Premium Draycott Shiraz emerges from a vintage that is not as highly regarded as the 2001 and 2002. The 2000 is a lavishly concentrated effort offering aromas of sweet blackberry jam intermixed with acacia flowers, pepper, and spicy new oak. Aged in equal parts French and American oak, it is opulent, full-bodied, and pure, with an impressively layered texture. Already gorgeous to drink, it should evolve for 7–8 years, possibly longer.

1998 Draycott Shiraz

RATING: 90 points

The 1998 Draycott Shiraz shows fatness, a broad, expansive texture, low acidity, and a sweet, jammy, blackberry, smoky cassis character. The wine is long, pure, and full-bodied (the alcohol is 14.9%). Drink it over the next 7–8 years for its exuberant, powerful, in-your-face style.

1998 Draycott Reserve Shiraz

RATING: 99 points

It would be difficult to find a better Shiraz than the 1998 Draycott Reserve Shiraz. Sadly, only 195 cases were produced of this wine, which was made from a 40-year-old vineyard. The color is a saturated blue/purple that looks more like vintage port than dry table wine. A spectacular bouquet of melted chocolate, licorice, blackberry jam, blueberries, and cassis is accompanied by an awesomely concentrated, massively proportioned wine that somehow has just enough acid-

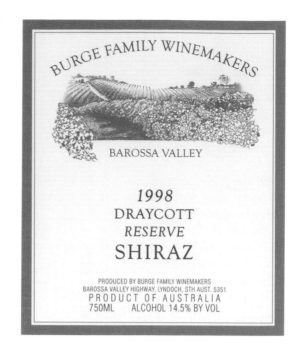

ity and tannin to both pull it together and provide some delineation. The wine is gorgeously pure, with massive power and weight, and a finish that lasts for nearly a minute. Low acidity, high glycerin, 14.5% alcohol, and thrilling levels of extract/concentration make for a nearly perfect drinking experience. Anticipated maturity: now–2025+.

1996 Draycott Shiraz

RATING: 92 points

The 1996 Draycott Shiraz exhibits a saturated purple color, and a terrific nose of raspberry jam intermixed with crushed pepper, tar, and earth. Sweet and unctuously textured, with full body, outstanding purity, and impressive levels of glycerin and extract, this large-scaled Shiraz can be drunk now or cellared for 11+ years.

1996 Draycott Reserve Shiraz

RATING: 95 points

The 1996 Draycott Reserve Shiraz offers an opaque purple color, followed by aromas of toasty new oak intermixed with blackberry jam, prune liqueur, and pepper. Deep, with monstrous levels of extract and viscousness, this superb, multilayered, fabulously concentrated Shiraz has managed to retain its harmony and balance. It is velvety-textured enough to be drunk now, but should evolve and develop more complexity with another 2–3 years of cellaring. It will keep for two decades or more.

WINES:

Grand Muscadelle (Tokay)

Grand Muscat

Rare Muscadelle (Tokay)

Rare Muscat

OWNER: William (Bill) Chambers

ADDRESS: Barkly Street, Rutherglen, Victoria, 3685, Australia

TELEPHONE: 61 2 6032 8641

TELEFAX: 61 2 6032 8101

E-MAIL: wchambers@netc.net.au

CONTACT: William Chambers

VISITING POLICY: Monday to Saturday, 9 A.M.–5 P.M.; Sunday 11 A.M.–5 P.M.; closed Good Friday, Christmas Day, and Anzac Day morning; buses by appointment

VINEYARDS

SURFACE AREA: Approximately 120 acres

GRAPE VARIETALS: Muscat, Muscadelle, Shiraz, Cabernet Sauvignon, Riesling, Cinsault, Touriga, Gouais, Palomino

AVERAGE AGE OF THE VINES: 25 years

DENSITY OF PLANTATION: 600 vines per acre

AVERAGE YIELDS: 1–2 tons per acre

WINEMAKING AND UPBRINGING

For Muscats and Tokays, all from wine from their own vineyards, *terroir* is important. These wines are placed in old wood, preferably barrels that have held Muscat or Tokay before. These aged wines are topped up once or twice in a decade.

ANNUAL PRODUCTION

Figures are confidential.

Grand Muscadelle (Tokay)

Grand Muscat

Rare Muscadelle (Tokay)

Rare Muscat

AVERAGE PRICE (VARIABLE DEPENDING ON VINTAGE): $70–280 (375 ml)

GREAT RECENT VINTAGES

The fortified wines are blended with various vintages.

Stephen and Bill Chambers

The first William Chambers was born in 1807 at Weston Longville in Norfolk, England. He brought his family to Australia in 1856 after training as a gardener and working in France, where he and his sons gained some experience in vineyard culture for hothouses.

By the late 1850s, the Chambers family had established itself in the Rutherglen area. They planted vines on a site opposite the vineyards of a German settler and winemaker, Anton Ruche, who, the family believes, was the man who introduced and instructed William in the art of fine winemaking.

Upon William's death in 1876, Philip, his only surviving son, kept the business going and purchased more prime land for vine cultivation. He named the property "Rosewood," after the rose hedges that were planted in the channels separating the fields from the house. After Philip's death, William —known as Will—took over the family and business responsibilities.

In 1895 there were 14,000 acres of vines in the Rutherglen district, but by the end of the century, phylloxera had devastated the vineyards, many of which were never replanted. It took a great deal of hard work and heartache to recover from this setback, and replanting at Rosewood was not completed until 1917.

Will overcame adversities, and went on to win championship prizes and medals for his fortified wines at wine shows in Victoria, Sydney, and Brisbane. During his many years of exhibiting in Melbourne, he won the

championship on 27 occasions and remained actively involved in all facets of the business until his death in 1956.

Upon the death of his grandfather, William "Bill" Chambers, a gold medal graduate from Roseworthy with first-class honors in oenology, and the fourth generation of the family to make wine at Rosewood, returned after eight years with the Stanley Wine Company to run the family operation.

Chambers is a respected wine judge with an excellent palate and has judged at all capital city shows and many regional shows throughout Australia.

Under Bill Chambers's careful guidance, the vineyards have been extended and improved, and the cellars, a happy collection of tin sheds, have seen new casks and equipment, insulation, refrigeration, and a large dam and irrigation system to help them through the dry seasons.

In 2001, Bill's son Stephen undertook his first vintage, becoming the fifth generation of his family to make wine at Rosewood and carry on the tradition.

The vines, many of which are over 80 years old, are set in acidic red-brown soil and grow in vineyards with names like Neilson's, The Convent, and the Horse Paddock. Old vines such as these are highly valued, as they bring distinct characteristics not evident in fruit from younger vines. Unlike newer plantings, these vines were planted with a number of varieties in the same vineyard.

Summers at Rosewood are hot but usually not humid, with long hours of sunshine and temperatures ranging from 15°–40°C. Winter is cold, with frosts sometimes affecting bud burst.

The following tasting notes are just for the four *cuvées,* which are actually all different ages of the Solera system. Because of that, the tasting notes don't vary that much from bottling to bottling. There is also a less expensive wine (simply called Muscat or Muscadelle [Tokay]) that wouldn't qualify for entry in this book, but is certainly a great introduction to the William Chambers style.

N.V. Grand Muscadelle (Tokay)

RATING: 97 points

The Grand Muscadelle (Tokay) possesses a deep amber color as well as extraordinary concentration, and additional caramel, toffee, fig, prune, and raisin aromas and flavors. This incredibly rich, unctuous, full-throttle offering is never cloying because of its good acidity.

N.V. Grand Muscat

RATING: 99 points

The Grand Muscat's deep amber color is accompanied by aromas and flavors of coffee liqueur, brown sugar, molasses, prunes, figs, and a bevy of spices. It is just extraordinary stuff!

N.V. Rare Muscadelle (Tokay)

RATING: 99 points

At the top level, the Rare Muscadelle (Tokay) boasts a deep amber color along with a rich, sumptuous nose of molasses, brown sugar, and a smorgasbord of spices and flavors. It has a whopping, unctuous texture, amazing concentration, and a powerful, heady finish.

N.V. Rare Muscat

RATING: 100 points

Even more prodigious than the Rare Muscadelle (Tokay), the Rare Muscat reveals a dark amber color, a fabulous bouquet, great concentration, as well as remarkable sweetness and length, but manages to avoid being cloying or over-the-top. I have cellared half-bottles of these fortifieds for over 15 years, and there has been no degradation of quality during that time. However, once opened, they should be consumed within 3–4 days.

WINES: All of the single-vineyard Grenaches and Syrahs

OWNER: Roman Bratasiuk

ADDRESS: 363 The Parade, Kensington Park, SA, 5068, Australia

TELEPHONE: 61 8 8364 1484

TELEFAX: 61 8 8364 1484

E-MAIL: clarendonhills@bigpond.com

WEBSITE: www.clarendonhills.com.au

CONTACT: Roman Bratasiuk

VISITING POLICY: By appointment only

VINEYARDS

SURFACE AREA: 200 acres

GRAPE VARIETALS: Grenache, Merlot, Syrah, Cabernet Sauvignon

AVERAGE AGE OF THE VINES: Grenache—75 years; Merlot—25 years; Syrah—75 years; Cabernet Sauvignon—60 years

DENSITY OF PLANTATION: 3 feet in rows; 6 feet between rows

AVERAGE YIELDS: 1.5–2 tons per acre

WINEMAKING AND UPBRINGING

There are no secrets or razzle-dazzle tricks at Clarendon Hills. Old vines (dry-grown, hand-pruned, and hand-picked) produce tiny quantities of fruit that is fermented with natural yeasts in open stainless-steel tanks for 14–21 days. All French oak is used and the wine matures for 18 months (mainly on gross lees). No fining or filtration is tolerated, as Clarendon Hills aims to produce pure expressions of the variety and vineyard that age well and complement the dining experience.

Roman Bratasiuk

ANNUAL PRODUCTION

Clarendon Vineyard Grenache: 9,000 bottles

Kangarilla Vineyard Grenache: 11,000 bottles

Blewitt Springs Vineyard Grenache: 9,000 bottles

Hickinbotham Vineyard Grenache: 8,000 bottles

Romas Vineyard Grenache: 8,000 bottles

Liandra Vineyard Syrah: 14,000 bottles

Moritz Vineyard Syrah: 12,000 bottles

Brookman Vineyard Syrah: 8,000 bottles

Hickinbotham Vineyard Syrah: 8,000 bottles

Piggott Range Vineyard Syrah: 7,000 bottles

Astralis Vineyard Syrah: 8,000 bottles

AVERAGE PRICE (VARIABLE DEPENDING ON VINTAGE): $40–90

GREAT RECENT VINTAGES

2003, 2002, 2001 (all three exceptional); also 1998, 1996, 1992

Roman Bratasiuk is a larger-than-life producer in McLaren Vale who has dedicated himself to naturally made wines from old-vine vineyards. While he makes some very serious Merlots and Cabernet Sauvignons, his single-vineyard Grenaches and Syrahs are world-class wines. Like most of the producers in this book, his policy of low yields, and minimal intervention, and his respect for individual sites and the character of the varietal, vineyard, and vintage are paramount. He refers to himself as following the "Jurassic Park" school of viticulture when compared to many of the high-tech, modern wineries that are sprinkled across McLaren Vale. A lover of France's finest wines, he spends enormous amounts of time in that country, tasting at the best addresses for Syrah and Grenache as well as Cabernet Sauvignon and Merlot. France is clearly his reference point and one of the reasons he chooses to age his wines in French rather than American oak, though the latter is very popular in South Australia. The percentage of new oak varies from around 30% for the Grenaches to higher levels for the Syrahs to 100% for his flagship Astralis Vineyard Syrah. His wines have elegance combined with the homegrown power of Australia, and aging potential that is unusual for such ripe and concentrated wines.

Bratasiuk has rarely gotten accolades from the Australian press, largely because of his stubbornness and overall contempt for a wine press that seems largely bought and paid for by the large Australian wine companies. Aside from that, there is no question that one taste of a Clarendon Hills wine will prove that both power and elegance can be achieved by conscientious winemakers who are passionate about their work as well as their legacy.

GRENACHE

2003 Blewitt Springs Vineyard Old Vines Grenache

RATING: 94 points

According to Roman Bratasiuk, the "Dolly Parton" of Grenache is the 2003 Blewitt Springs Vineyard Old Vines Grenache, from a vineyard whose soils include quartz, sand, and loam. This opulent, voluptuous, deep ruby/purple–colored effort offers a heady mixture of red and black fruits, incense, licorice, and full-bodied, viscous, exuberant flavors. Drink this delicious offering over the next decade. Anticipated maturity: now–2012.

2003 Clarendon Vineyard Old Vines Grenache

RATING: 93 points

The brilliant, evolved 2003 Clarendon Vineyard Old Vines Grenache (head-pruned vines planted in 1920) reveals notes of sweet cherry jam intermixed with licorice and sandy/loamy soil undertones. Full-bodied, opulent, and lush, it should be consumed over the next 7–10 years.

2003 Hickinbotham Vineyard Old Vines Grenache

RATING: 93 points

The elegant, deep ruby/purple–hued 2003 Hickinbotham Vineyard Old Vines Grenache exhibits notes of raspberries, strawberries, and cherries along with hints of fig and charcoal. It possesses more density than the Clarendon Vineyard cuvée. Anticipated maturity: now–2012.

2003 Kangarilla Vineyard Old Vines Grenache

RATING: 94 points

The 2003 Kangarilla Vineyard Old Vines Grenache (planted in sandy soils overlaying heavy clay) is the richest of the 2003 Grenaches except for the top-of-the-line Romas. Provocative aromas of black cherries, raspberries, earth, sandstone, and balsam are followed by a wine with huge body, fabulous concentration, and wonderful minerality/delineation. Noticeable tannin suggests 1–2 years of cellaring is required; it should drink well for 10–15.

2003 Romas Vineyard Old Vines Grenache

RATING: 96 points

Clarendon Hills' flagship Grenache, the 2003 Romas Vineyard Old Vines Grenache is the densest, most exotic of these wines. Produced from a parcel of vines in the highest section of the Blewitt Springs Vineyard, it boasts a dense ruby/plum color, a raspberry and blackberry–scented perfume with hints of underbrush, incense, and camphor, an unctuously textured mouth-feel, marvelous elegance, and an incredibly intoxicating personality. Rich and dense, it will benefit from 1–3 years of bottle age, and should last for 12–15 years.

2002 Blewitt Springs Vineyard Old Vines Grenache

RATING: 93 points

The 2002 Blewitt Springs Vineyard Old Vines Grenache exhibits candied cherry, kirsch, pepper, and licorice scents along with a Château Rayas–like raspberry component. Opulent and rich, with seamless integration of acidity, wood, and tannin, this medium to full–bodied, gorgeously elegant, intensely flavored 2002 is strikingly complex as well as showy. It will provide immense pleasure over the next decade.

2002 Clarendon Vineyard Old Vines Grenache

RATING: 95 points

A sexy concoction of kirsch, melted licorice, and flowers emerges from the 2002 Clarendon Vineyard Old Vines Grenache. With a sumptuous texture, full body, a splendidly concentrated mid-palate, and an expansive, blockbuster finish offering a bit of tannin, but primarily abundant fruit and glycerin, this impeccably well-balanced whopper should drink well for 10–14 years.

2002 Hickinbotham Vineyard Old Vines Grenache

RATING: 92 points

The Pinot Noir–like 2002 Hickinbotham Vineyard Old Vines Grenache is less sexy than the 2003, revealing more mineral and herbs as well as a more structured, harder character. Notes of smoke and earth emerge from this big, tightly knit Grenache. Give it 2–3 more years of bottle age, and drink it over the following 12–15 years. I do not think it will ever attain the hedonistic heights of the 2003 Hickinbotham.

2002 Kangarilla Vineyard Old Vines Grenache

RATING: 94 points

The expansive, full-bodied 2002 Kangarilla Vineyard Old Vines Grenache offers aromas and flavors of pure kirsch. With in-your-face levels of fruit and glycerin, an unctuous texture, and a huge finish, it should drink well for 10–15 years.

2002 Romas Vineyard Old Vines Grenache

RATING: 96 points

The 2002 Romas Vineyard Old Vines Grenache's saturated ruby/purple color is followed by a superb bouquet of black fruits, truffles, Asian spices, figs, and licorice. Powerful, rich, and up-front, this layered, intensely concentrated Grenache can be drunk now or cellared for 10–12 years. Production of these Grenache *cuvées* ranges from 800–1,000 cases each. Interestingly, while discussing the 2002 vintage versus the 2001, Roman Bratasiuk said he thought the 2001 Grenache *cuvées* were better than his 2002s, but that the latter vintage produced the finest Syrahs he has yet made.

2001 Blewitt Springs Vineyard Old Vines Grenache

RATING: 95 points

The dense plum/purple–colored 2001 Blewitt Springs Vineyard Old Vines Grenache offers a heady concoction of red as well as black fruits, flowers, incense, balsam wood, and spice. On the palate, it is prodigiously thick, rich, viscous, and packed and stacked. Difficult to resist, this exuberant, full-throttle wine should be at its peak between now and 2012.

2001 Clarendon Vineyard Old Vines Grenache

RATING: 95 points

The 2001 Clarendon Vineyard Old Vines Grenache's soaring aromatics envelop the olfactory senses, offering up notes of freshly ground pepper, spice box, plums, figs, black cherries, and balsam wood. Full-bodied, thick, and unctuously textured, with great finishing acidity that gives delineation and uplift to the wine's enormous concentration and overall purity, it is a stunning example of old-vine Grenache that should drink well for a decade.

2001 Hickinbotham Vineyard Old Vines Grenache

RATING: 92 points

The 2001 Hickinbotham Vineyard Old Vines Grenache is a winner. This full-bodied, earthy, peppery wine is loaded with licorice-imbued black and red fruits. Expressive, elegant, and lush, it should be drunk over the next decade.

2001 Kangarilla Vineyard Old Vines Grenache

RATING: 95–97 points

The fabulous, dense purple–colored 2001 Kangarilla Vineyard Old Vines Grenache (produced from 80-year-old vines) reveals a sensational perfume of violets as well as blackberries, raspberries, and sweet cherries. Full-bodied, packed and stacked, with great intensity, seamlessness, and voluptuousness that lingers on the palate for nearly 45 seconds, this profound Grenache should drink well for 15 years.

2001 Romas Vineyard Old Vines Grenache

RATING: 98 points

It is too soon to say if the 2001 Romas Vineyard Old Vines Grenache is the finest Roman Bratasiuk has made to date, but it is hard to believe anything will ever top this. The nearly perfect 2001 Romas reveals a broodingly deep plum/purple color. At first reticent aromatically, it explodes with aeration to reveal a pure, peppery, raspberry and blackberry–scented bouquet with hints of spice, underbrush, and incense in the background. Enormously concentrated yet not over-the-top or too extracted, this beautifully pure, full-bodied Grenache saturates/stains the palate with fruit, glycerin, and flavor. In short, it's a tour de force! Anticipated maturity: now–2016.

1999 Blewitt Springs Vineyard Old Vines Grenache

RATING: 92 points

Lovers of flamboyant Grenache will get a blast from the exotic, over-the-top 1999 Blewitt Springs Vineyard Old Vines Grenache (14.5% alcohol). This wine has jammy, raspberry notes intermixed with notes of peach/apricot, suggesting ripe fruit. The wine is full-bodied, powerful, super-concentrated, and coats the mouth with enviable levels of glycerin and sweet fruit. The wine is long, luscious, and a total hedonistic turn-on. Drink it over the next 6–7 years.

1999 Kangarilla Vineyard Old Vines Grenache

RATING: 91 points

Châteauneuf du Pape–like is the 1999 Kangarilla Vineyard Old Vines Grenache (14.5% alcohol). This wine ratchets up the level of volume, depth, and length, offering kirsch, black raspberry, and cherry notes intermixed with roasted herbs and balsam wood notes. The wine is textured, full-bodied, and offers a plum/ruby color. I would opt for drinking this over the next 3–5 years.

1999 Romas Vineyard Old Vines Grenache

RATING: 92 points

The 1999 Romas Vineyard Old Vines Grenache suggests new oak, and exhibits some toasty smells. In addition to that, there are dense, concentrated kirsch and raspberry notes intermixed with chewy, ripe, full-bodied, heavy, high-alcohol (14.5%) flavors. Full-bodied, with admirable structure, weight, and volume, it will last for another 7–9 years.

1998 Blewitt Springs Vineyard Old Vines Grenache

RATING: 92 points

The dark ruby–colored 1998 Blewitt Springs Vineyard Old Vines Grenache offers copious quantities of raspberry and cherry jam intermixed with spicy wood, earth, herb, and pepper scents. Heady, high alcohol gives the wine additional levels of glycerin, which coat the palate and teeth. Dense, chewy, and ripe, this large-scaled Grenache can be drunk now or cellared for another 5–7 years.

1998 Clarendon Vineyard Old Vines Grenache

RATING: 93 points

This fabulous wine is still young and vigorous, with a dark plum/ruby color and a very sweet nose of kirsch intermixed with almost overripe peach and cherry notes. Very full-bodied, fleshy, with succulent texture yet superb underlying structure and decent acidity, this is a blockbuster old-vine Grenache to drink over the next 10–13+ years.

1998 Kangarilla Vineyard Old Vines Grenache

RATING: 90 points

The 1998 Kangarilla Vineyard Old Vines Grenache exhibits a medium ruby color, a peppery, Provençal herb–scented nose, soft, earthy, medium to full–bodied flavors, moderate tannin, and a rich, well-concentrated finish. Drink it over the next 5–7 years.

SYRAH

2003 Astralis Vineyard Syrah

RATING: 99+ points

There are generally 600–800 cases of what is becoming Australia's greatest Syrah, Clarendon Hills' Astralis. I have previously made the argument that, compared to its closest competition, the famed Penfolds Grange, Astralis is (1) a more natural wine, without added tannin, (2) made from a single vineyard, (3) not the product of a corporate committee, (4) aged in French versus American oak, and (5) clearly an expression of a specific *terroir*. However, that said, this wine is meant to be drunk from about age 10 onward, not in its youth. The 2003 Astralis Vineyard Syrah stood out as a spectacular offering, possibly as good as the virtually perfect 2002. Its inky/black/purple color is accompanied by superb aromas of white flowers, chocolate, black fruits, and espresso roast. Full-bodied, unctuously textured, and gorgeously pure, it should be cellared for 5–8 years. Anticipated maturity: 2012–2025+.

2003 Brookman Vineyard Syrah

RATING: 95 points

Truly great stuff, the 2003 Brookman Vineyard Syrah boasts a dense purple color in addition to a rich, pure nose of blueberries, blackberries, camphor, spice, and truffles. With superb fruit, great texture, well-integrated tannin, and a long finish, it will drink well for 10–15 years.

2003 Hickinbotham Vineyard Syrah

RATING: 95+ points

The 2003 Hickinbotham Vineyard Syrah is a prodigious effort. With fabulous notes of melted licorice, smoke, asphalt, crème de cassis, and roasted *jus de viande,* this full-bodied, dense yet remarkably elegant, well-balanced Syrah should hit its peak in 2–3 years, and last for 15+.

2003 Liandra Vineyard Syrah

RATING: 93 points

The 2003 Liandra Vineyard Syrah offers a tremendous perfume of black fruits, incense, pepper, vanilla, and licorice. Full-bodied, with beautiful integration of its structural elements as well as tremendous purity (a characteristic of all the

Clarendon Hills wines), it should hit its stride in 2–3 years, and last for 12–15.

2003 Moritz Vineyard Syrah

RATING: 93 points

The 2003 Moritz Vineyard Syrah is characterized by its extraordinary balance and purity. This saturated ruby/purple-colored, elegant Syrah offers up sweet aromas of black fruits, flowers, espresso, and white chocolate. Rich, long, velvety-textured, and well balanced, it should drink well young, hit its peak in 5–7 years, and last for 15–16.

2003 Piggott Range Vineyard Syrah

RATING: 93+ points

From rocky shale/slate soils, the 2003 Piggott Range Vineyard Syrah should only be purchased by patient consumers. Possessing enormous structure, but also magnificent extract and richness, it offers up aromas of crushed minerals, flowers, blackberry and blueberry liqueur, and pepper. Medium to full–bodied, dense flavors reveal striking elegance as well as balance. There is plenty of tannin lurking under the surface, so I suspect it will need 4–5 years of cellaring. It should keep for 20–25 years. The 2003 is very French in style.

2002 Astralis Vineyard Syrah

RATING: 99 points

The 2002 Astralis Vineyard Syrah rivals the greatest wines Roman Bratasiuk has made in his 15-year career. This compelling, black/blue-hued offering from 75-year-old Syrah vines tastes like blood of the vine. An extraordinary perfume of flowers, crème de cassis, blackberries, roasted meat, new saddle leather, and earth is followed by a wine with sweet tannin, sensational concentration, full body, an unctuous texture, and a full-throttle, tannic finish. Yet it reveals unbelievable elegance and finesse. Too many Eurocentric elitists argue that Australian wines are too rich and over-the-top, but all of these offerings have been made by someone with great talent and vision who takes the extraordinary ripeness and purity of fruit available from these old-vine vineyards and crafts them into wines that are quite European in style, just richer and denser. The 2002 Astralis is a tour de force. Anticipated maturity: 2012–2025+.

2002 Brookman Vineyard Syrah

RATING: 96 points

Remarkably, the 2002 Brookman Vineyard Syrah is even more compelling than the 2003. Still an infant, it exhibits a saturated blue/purple color as well as a marvelous perfume of blueberry and blackberry liqueur intermixed with scents of flowers, graphite, vanilla, coffee, and licorice. It possesses great intensity, a wealth of fruit and glycerin covering substantial tannin, and a spectacular finish that lasts over a minute. Give

it 3–5 more years of bottle age, and enjoy it over the following two decades.

2002 Hickinbotham Vineyard Syrah

RATING: 97 points

The stupendous 2002 Hickinbotham Vineyard Syrah exhibits a saturated purple color as well as an extraordinary bouquet of ink, blackberry liqueur, crème de cassis, smoke, licorice, and espresso. Massively endowed, with great concentration yet tremendous structure and definition, it is an example of what Roman Bratasiuk does so well: marry old-vine power and concentration with extraordinary definition and elegance. It may be the finest example I have yet tasted from this vineyard. While approachable, it should last for 20+ years.

2002 Liandra Vineyard Syrah

RATING: 93 points

The beautiful 2002 Liandra Vineyard Syrah exhibits aromas of pepper, black fruits, acacia flowers, and subtle new oak. Full-bodied, with an expansive mid-palate in addition to a gorgeously long finish, it is an elegant yet well-endowed Syrah to drink over the next 10–15 years.

2002 Moritz Vineyard Syrah

RATING: 95 points

The meaty, earthy-styled 2002 Moritz Vineyard Syrah boasts fabulous concentration, wonderful density, a saturated purple color, and notes of creosote, acacia flowers, blackberries, and cassis. It comes across as an Australian version of a hypothetical blend of 50% Cornas and 50% Hermitage. Give it 2–3 years of bottle age, and enjoy it over the following 15+ years.

2002 Piggott Range Vineyard Syrah

RATING: 97 points

Absolutely fabulous, but extremely backward, the saturated black/purple–colored 2002 Piggott Range Vineyard Syrah reveals that minerality/crushed-rock characteristic in the nose along with notes of roasted meats, blackberry and blueberry liqueur, truffles, spice, and espresso. This dense, fabulously endowed Syrah inundates the palate with layers of crème de cassis, loads of glycerin, and unbelievable definition as well as focus. Four to five years of cellaring is recommended, as this is a wine for patient connoisseurs. It should easily age for two decades. The distinctive roasted character of the Piggott Range Syrahs is noteworthy since this vineyard is a natural amphitheater planted with 35- to 40-year-old Syrah vines.

2001 Astralis Vineyard Syrah

RATING: 99 points

The 2001 Astralis Vineyard Syrah may be just as compelling as the 2002. Tighter because of being in the bottle, it is an extraordinary effort that offers the essence of graphite, blackberry liqueur, espresso, and acacia flowers, all combining into a smorgasbord for the senses. Sensationally concentrated, with sweet tannin, but neither as weighty nor as over-the-top as might be expected for a wine of such extreme richness, it is an extraordinarily well-delineated Syrah that should hit its prime in 10–12 years, and last for 30–40. Hail Caesar . . . I mean Roman!

2001 Brookman Vineyard Syrah

RATING: 94 points

The impressive 2001 Brookman Vineyard Syrah reveals a saturated blue/purple color as well as gorgeous aromas of smoke, licorice, acacia flowers, and black fruits. Full-bodied and dense, this killer Syrah should age effortlessly for 20 years.

2001 Hickinbotham Vineyard Syrah

RATING: 95 points

This Hickinbotham Syrah blew me away. The 2001 Hickinbotham Vineyard Syrah boasts glorious amounts of blackberry liqueur intermixed with melted licorice, vanilla, smoke, and earth in a full-bodied, unctuously textured, viscous style with great purity as well as palate persistence. The finish lasts nearly 60 seconds. Anticipated maturity: 2007–2020.

2001 Liandra Vineyard Syrah

RATING: 93 points

The 2001 Liandra Vineyard Syrah offers up fragrant aromas of acacia flowers intermixed with blackberries, currants, licorice, and vanilla. Powerful and intense yet surprisingly restrained and measured, it builds incrementally in the mouth. Anticipated maturity: now–2018.

2001 Moritz Vineyard Syrah

RATING: 93 points

The 2001 Moritz Vineyard Syrah comes across as a more elegant version of the 2002. It is profoundly concentrated, with floral notes intermixed with blackberries, creosote, earth, and background oak. Although fabulously rich and long, the large-framed 2001 will hit its peak by 2007, and last until 2020.

2001 Piggott Range Vineyard Syrah

RATING: 96 points

The 2001 Piggott Range Vineyard Syrah may be one of several Clarendon Hills' Syrah *cuvées* that stand toe-to-toe with its 2002 sibling. A giant Syrah, it boasts an enormously rich nose of black fruits, subtle vanilla, smoke, and a hint of graphite. Extremely full-bodied, thick, and prodigious, it will be at its finest between 2008 and 2025.

1999 Astralis Vineyard Syrah

RATING: 92 points

Showing better than when I originally tasted it, the wine seems to open a bit, but is still backward. A saturated purple color offers up concentrated blackberry fruit intermixed with licorice and barbecue spice. The wine is large-scaled, very intense, with a multidimensional, layered personality. This wine should be at its best in about 6–7 years. Anticipated maturity: 2008–2025.

1998 Astralis Vineyard Syrah

RATING: 98 points

Just beginning to emerge from a relatively dormant state, this wine was showing the best it has yet performed, suggesting again that Clarendon Hills wines behave more like European wines in terms of needing time in the bottle. The saturated blue/purple color offers up notes of ripe black fruits intermixed with graphite, vanilla, mineral, and spice. Extremely thick, with a viscous texture, good underlying tannin and acidity, and fabulous length (nearly 50 seconds), this is certainly a prodigious effort that is now living up to the fame and extraordinary quality of this vintage. Nevertheless, I thought the wine needed about five years of cellaring three years ago, but now I tend to think it needs at least another 4–6 years of cellaring before it will begin to become an adolescent. It is a majestic, multidimensional, individualistic wine that certainly is world-class and undoubtedly profound. Anticipated maturity: 2007–2030.

1998 Brookman Vineyard Syrah

RATING: 94 points

The 1998 Brookman Vineyard Syrah (900 cases) is a Hermitage-like wine. With a larger-than-life personality, high extraction, opaque purple color, dense, concentrated, peppery, cassis, mineral, and licorice–scented nose, full body, an unctuous texture, and a spectacular finish, this superb effort can be drunk now as well as over the next 10–15 years.

1998 Hickinbotham Vineyard Syrah

RATING: 92 points

The black/purple-colored 1998 Hickinbotham Vineyard Syrah (600 cases) reveals extraordinary intensity. This wine exhibits smoky cassis, blackberry, melted asphalt, and toasty oak aromas, purity of fruit, an earthy, peppery character, and massive extract and richness. Drink this blockbuster Syrah over the next 7–10 years.

1998 Piggott Range Vineyard Syrah

RATING: 92 points

Closed but exceptionally impressive is the 1998 Piggott Range Vineyard Syrah (900 cases). Exhibiting slightly revealing aromas, with coaxing, some mint-tinged blackberry fruit emerges.

Extremely powerful, with remarkable purity, intensity, and extraction, this Syrah should keep for another 10–15 years.

1997 Astralis Vineyard Syrah

RATING: 98 points

The essence of vineyard and the varietal, the 1997 Astralis has a saturated purple color and is just beginning to show more nuances, such as the telltale Syrah characteristics of pepper, melted asphalt, as well as a wealth of blackberry and crème de cassis. The new oak seems to have been sucked up completely, and the wine shows softness and evolution. Nevertheless, it is still a very youthful, backward, spectacular wine that has surreal levels of richness and potential complexity. Anticipated maturity: 2006–2024.

1996 Astralis Vineyard Syrah

RATING: 97 points

This wine remains a baby and in need of another 10 more years of cellaring. A mammoth, blockbuster wine with awesome layers of flavor extract, huge, high tannin, and magnificent, concentrated cassis fruit, this full-bodied wine shows beautifully integrated tannin, acidity, and alcohol, but still has a personality more like a barrel sample than a wine that is already seven years old. Anticipated maturity: 2009–2040.

1995 Astralis Vineyard Syrah

RATING: 96 points

Fabulous nose of blackberry liqueur intermixed with blackberry, smoke, a touch of bacon, and some floral notes, this wine reveals aromatic nuances. The wine is phenomenally thick, rich, and as good as Syrah can be in either the New or the Old World. There is no doubt there is a luxurious wealth of fruit, glycerin, and mass to a wine that is also remarkably well balanced. Anticipated maturity: 2006–2027.

1994 Astralis Vineyard Syrah

RATING: 95 points

The debut vintage (only 150 cases were produced) of this wine first came to my attention at a blind tasting. The wine still has a dense purple color and a sweet nose of black fruits intermixed with espresso, licorice, truffle, and smoke. Very full-bodied, opulently textured, with sweet tannin and a finish that goes on for a good 40–45 seconds, this wine is evolved, but could still benefit from another 3–4 years of cellaring. It will keep for at least two decades.

WINES: The single-vineyard Shiraz *cuvées* and Roennfeldt
wines

OWNERS: Michael and Annabelle Waugh

ADDRESS: Radford Road, Seppeltsfield, SA, 5360, Australia

TELEPHONE: 61 8 85628 103

TELEFAX: 61 8 85628 259

E-MAIL: greenockcreek@ozemail.com.au

CONTACT: Michael or Annabelle Waugh

VISITING POLICY: Open every day except Tuesdays, Good
Friday, and Christmas Day, 11 A.M–5 P.M.

VINEYARDS

SURFACE AREA: 45 acres

GRAPE VARIETALS: Shiraz, Cabernet Sauvignon, Grenache

AVERAGE AGE OF THE VINES: 35 years

DENSITY OF PLANTATION: Rows average 12 feet apart, with
vines at 7–8 feet spacings. Approximately 480 per acre.

AVERAGE YIELDS: 1–1.75 tons per acre

WINEMAKING AND UPBRINGING

The aim at Greenock Creek is to produce big, soft reds with
good alcohol, fruit, and acid balance that will cellar for a considerable length of time. The fruit is fermented in four to
eight–ton open masonry fermenters and then transferred to
hogsheads and left for malolactic fermentation to occur. The
two Roennfeldt Road wines are left in new oak (the Shiraz in
American and the Cabernet Sauvignon in French) for 36
months, bottled, and cellared for two years before release. The
other Shiraz and Cabernet Sauvignon are put into American
and French hogsheads, respectively, for 28 months, and the
Grenache in French oak for 16 months. Aged hogsheads
(puncheons) predominate, with a ratio of new to old of about
12 to 1. The wines are bottled unfiltered in July and released
in mid-September each year.

ANNUAL PRODUCTION

Cornerstone Grenache: 2,250 bottles

Cabernet Sauvignon: 3,500 bottles

Seven Acre Shiraz: 5,000 bottles

Creek Block Shiraz: 2,750 bottles

Alice's Shiraz: 15,000 bottles

Apricot Block Shiraz: 9,000 bottles

Roennfeldt Road Shiraz: 2,500 bottles

Roennfeldt Road Cabernet Sauvignon: 600 bottles

AVERAGE PRICE (VARIABLE DEPENDING ON VINTAGE):

Roennfeldt Road *cuvées*: $220–300

Shiraz single-vineyard *cuvées*: $45–85

GREAT RECENT VINTAGES

The first Greenock Creek vintage was only in 1984, so there isn't a lot to choose from. Suffice it to say they haven't had a poor vintage yet, but consider the 1992 and 1994 vintages among the best.

This is a very traditional producer who has accumulated some very old, dry-farmed, low-yielding Barossa vineyard sites, and is producing large-scaled, big reds with good acid balance and tremendous aging potential. The proprietors, Michael and Annabelle Waugh, are disciples of Rockford's Rocky O'Callaghan (one of the Barossa's pioneers of old-vine Shiraz). They make some very fine traditional Grenache and Cabernet Sauvignon, but their greatest wines are the single-vineyard *cuvées* of Shiraz and their two Roennfeldt *cuvées* of Shiraz and Cabernet Sauvignon. All this comes from sites that were planted at the end of the 1800s, in soils that range from deep alluvian-like clay to red loam over limestone and bluestone with harsh granite interspersed amongst sandy loam. The Waughs purchase no fruit; thus the quantities produced are at the mercy of Mother Nature from vintage to vintage. Their top vineyards are as follows:

Roennfeldt Road Shiraz (Marananga Vineyard): This is three acres of 70-year-old vines, grown on heavy red loam, that averages one ton of fruit per acre.

Roennfeldt Road Cabernet Sauvignon (Marananga Vineyard): Only a one-acre vineyard of 70-year-old vines, grown on heavy clay loam, it also averages one ton of fruit per acre.

Creek Block Shiraz (Seppeltsfield Vineyard): Fifty-year-old vines, producing 2–2.5 tons per acre, this vineyard is planted in rich alluvial soil.

Seven Acre Shiraz (Seppeltsfield Vineyard): This is a 7-acre parcel of Shiraz grown in red sandy loam over limestone and bluestone, cropped at a very low 1–1.5 tons per acre.

Apricot Block Shiraz (Marananga Vineyard): The newest wine from the Waughs, it is planted on a steeply sloped 9-acre parcel that consists of considerable granite and sandy loam soils. These are young vines, planted in 1995.

Alice's Shiraz (Seppeltsfield Vineyard): This is a 14-acre block of heavy and light sandy loam soils on a gentle western-facing slope that produces 1–1.5 tons per acre. This is the Waughs' youngest vineyard, planted in 1997.

For a producer whose first vintage was only in 1984, despite the history of this old Barossa vineyard they emanate from, they have been exceptionally consistent, not only in the great years in the Barossa, but also in the more challenging years. I have been consistently astounded by the quality of wines, which is no doubt due to the commitment of the owners, but also to winemaker Chris Ringland, who is one of Australia's genius wine producers.

ROENNFELDT ROAD CABERNET SAUVIGNON

1998 Roennfeldt Road Cabernet Sauvignon
RATING: 100 points
This 1998 possesses the concentration of the greatest classics ever produced in such Bordeaux vintages as 1945, 1947, 1959, 1961, and 1982. It is an amazing aromatic expression of crème de cassis, a massive, full-bodied red with a finish that lasts well over 60 seconds. For its size and concentration, it is, surprisingly, not heavy, just super-endowed. This Cabernet Sauvignon needs 2–3 more years of cellaring, and should drink well for two decades. Unfortunately, quantities are extremely limited for this spectacular, world-class Australian red.

1997 Roennfeldt Road Cabernet Sauvignon
RATING: 93+ points
The 1997 Roennfeldt Road Cabernet Sauvignon is a full-bodied, inky ruby/purple–colored effort revealing extraordinarily intense notes of crème de cassis fruit intermixed with underbrush, vanilla, and cedar/tobacco. Already complex as well as formidably endowed, with exceptional intensity, purity, power, and a 60+-second finish, this Barossa Valley legend should age for two decades. Anticipated maturity: now–2025.

1996 Roennfeldt Road Cabernet Sauvignon
RATING: 94 points
Made by winemakers Michael Waugh and Chris Ringland at the Rockford winery in Barossa, the 1996 Roennfeldt Road Cabernet Sauvignon (120 cases from 50-year-old vines) was aged for three years in new French oak. Its 13.4% alcohol is modest by Barossa standards. An opaque purple color is followed by gorgeous aromas of blueberry and blackberry liqueur intermixed with flower, camphor, and vanilla scents. Marvelously rich and full-bodied, with a viscous texture, superb purity, and a multilayered, skyscraper personality, this is profound stuff! Anticipated maturity: now–2020.

1995 Roennfeldt Road Cabernet Sauvignon

RATING: 99 points

The 1995 Roennfeldt Road Cabernet Sauvignon is 100% Cabernet Sauvignon from 50-year-old vines. The wine was aged for three years in new French oak. It has soaked up the wood beautifully. This is an unctuous, blockbuster, opaque, purple-colored wine with a classic nose of charcoal, black currants, cedar, minerals, and licorice. The wine has phenomenal intensity, great purity, a huge, ripe, yet balanced attack, a multilayered mid-palate, and an awesome finish. The mid-palate seems to have layers of fruit that just cascade over the palate with no hard edges. This is a terrific classic that can be approached now but ideally needs 1–2 more years of cellaring. Anticipated maturity: now–2025.

ROENNFELDT ROAD SHIRAZ

1998 Roennfeldt Road Shiraz

RATING: 98+ points

Like the Roennfeldt Road Cabernet Sauvignon, the 1998 Roennfeldt Road Shiraz (235 cases), made from yields of .75–1 ton of fruit per acre, possesses extraordinary concentration. A massive, full-bodied red, it is an amazing aromatic expression of blackberry, melted road tar, and truffles with a finish that lasts well over 60 seconds. For its size and concentration, it is, surprisingly, not heavy, just super-endowed. The Shiraz is a bit more accessible than the Cabernet Sauvignon, but still primary. Unfortunately, quantities are extremely limited for this spectacular, world-class Australian red. Anticipated maturity: 2007–2025+.

1997 Roennfeldt Road Shiraz

RATING: 98+ points

The nearly perfect 1997 Roennfeldt Road Shiraz boasts a dense opaque purple color in addition to celestial aromas of blackberry liqueur, melted road tar, truffles, and earth. It is full-bodied, with massive layers of fruit and glycerin that cascade over the palate in a seamless, beautifully balanced fashion, and a 55-second finish. This enormous wine is fabulously young with its entire future ahead of it. It should hit its peak in 3–4 years, and last for two decades.

1996 Roennfeldt Road Shiraz

RATING: 100 points

This amazing achievement boasts an inky/black/purple color as well as a striking perfume of smoke, charcoal, blackberry liqueur, and a hint of toast. In the mouth, it is fabulously concentrated and tremendously pure, with layer upon layer of flavors that unfold incrementally. Mouth-staining, but not over-the-top, it would be hard to find a more concentrated wine anywhere in the world. Although the tannin is high, it is obscured by the wealth of fruit and glycerin. A tour de force in winemaking, it is probably worth the high cost of admission. Anticipated maturity: now–2018.

1995 Roennfeldt Road Shiraz

RATING: 100 points

This is a syrup of Shiraz, with compelling blackberry liqueur intermixed with minerals, smoke, and truffles. Huge in the mouth but not overbearing, this wine has a finish that goes on for nearly a minute. With great purity, massive extraction, and a blockbuster, multidimensional personality, this is one of the greatest Shirazes I have ever tasted. Anticipated maturity: now–2030.

SHIRAZ SINGLE-VINEYARD *CUVÉES*

2001 Apricot Block Shiraz

RATING: 99+ points

The 2001 Apricot Block Shiraz represents a spectacular example of Barossa Shiraz. Dense ruby/purple, with a fragrant bouquet of black raspberry, acacia flowers, tar, and spice, it is a dense, full-bodied Shiraz possessing fabulous intensity, great purity, and a multitiered, skyscraper-like mid-palate. It can be drunk young or cellared through 2018–2020.

2001 Creek Block Shiraz

RATING: 100 points

A perfect wine, the magnificent inky purple 2001 Creek Block Shiraz exhibits notes of burning embers, melted road tar, truffles, blackberries, and crème de cassis. With huge glycerin and a full-bodied, sensational finish, it represents the essence of wine. Anticipated maturity: 2008–2020.

2001 Seven Acre Shiraz

RATING: 98 points

The dense purple 2001 Seven Acre Shiraz is an opulent hussy boasting magnificent fruit concentration, enormous body as well as length, and surprising elegance and purity. As always, the fruit and vineyard character dominate because no new oak is utilized in these offerings. Anticipated maturity: 2008–2022.

2000 Apricot Block Shiraz

RATING: 96 points

A candidate for wine of the vintage in the Barossa, it possesses an opaque ruby/purple color as well as tremendous fruit intensity, enormous body, great purity, and a skyscraper-like mid-palate and texture. This dense, chewy Barossa classic has a finish that lasts over 60 seconds. Although still somewhat primary, it reveals tremendous potential, even from this challenging vintage. Anticipated maturity: now–2018.

2000 Seven Acre Shiraz

RATING: 94+ points

The 2000 Seven Acre Shiraz appears more earth-driven than the Apricot Block, revealing notes of tar, creosote, crème de cassis, licorice, and a hint of truffles. While firmer and more tannic, savage, and animal-like than its sibling, it possesses extraordinary density, power, and richness. Anticipated maturity: now–2014.

1999 Apricot Block Shiraz

RATING: 93 points

Its opaque purple color is accompanied by aromatic fireworks (white flowers, pepper, sweet blackberry liqueur, and cassis). This beautifully pure, full-bodied, multidimensional, layered Shiraz exhibits low acidity as well as ripe tannin. Enjoy this stunning, flamboyant effort over the next 12–14 years.

1999 Creek Block Shiraz

RATING: 96 points

The aromas of crème de cassis, new saddle leather, vanilla, spice box, and cedar are reminiscent of a first-growth Bordeaux. As the wine sits in the glass, more Shiraz characteristics (asphalt and blackberries) emerge. Sensationally concentrated and extremely full-bodied, with monster extract, yet not over-the-top, it possesses beautifully integrated tannin as well as acidity. This profound Shiraz should age effortlessly for two decades. Anticipated maturity: 2006–2020.

1999 Seven Acre Shiraz

RATING: 94 points

The powerhouse 1999 Seven Acre Shiraz boasts an opaque purple color along with a sweet nose of melted licorice intermixed with blackberry jam, white flowers, pepper, and a hint of toast. It offers layers of gorgeous fruit, voluptuousness, density, great purity, and a finish that lasts nearly 40 seconds. This stunning Shiraz (750 cases) typifies what can be produced at the pinnacle of winemaking in the Barossa Valley. Anticipated maturity: now–2019.

1998 Apricot Block Shiraz

RATING: 94 points

This 100% Shiraz shows an opaque garnet/purple color and a sweet nose of melted asphalt, smoke, blackberry, and cassis. Extremely full-bodied with great intensity, tremendous purity, and impeccable overall harmony among its rather large-scale elements, this dense, super-extracted wine should be at its best between now and 2020.

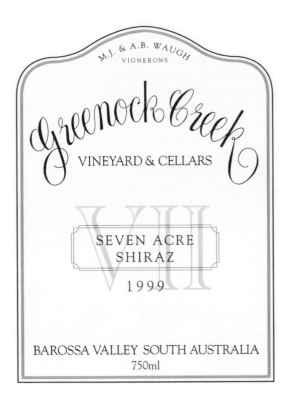

1998 Creek Block Shiraz

RATING: 98 points

The wine shows terrific notes of beef blood, new saddle leather, blackberry liqueur, smoke, and earth. Extremely full-bodied yet seamless, with dazzling levels of extract and ripeness, this is a tour de force in winemaking, but sadly, there is too little of it. It looks to have the potential to go 20–30 years.

1998 Seven Acre Shiraz

RATING: 92 points

An elegant wine for the normally powerful Greenock Creek style, this wine exhibits dark ruby/purple color, and a bouquet of black raspberries intermixed with blackberry, currant, pepper, and spicy wood. The wine is deep, full-bodied, and beautifully knit. Some tannin still needs to be resolved in the finish, but this wine should age beautifully for 10–13 more years.

1997 Creek Block Shiraz

RATING: 95 points

Revealing an opaque purple color, the 1997 Creek Block Shiraz exhibits sweet aromatics as well as a firm mouth-feel. This intense offering could be called Syrup of Shiraz. Full-bodied, massively concentrated and extracted, this gigantic wine is long and rich. Look for this wine to be drinkable young, yet keep for two decades.

1997 Seven Acre Shiraz

RATING: 94 points

The opaque purple-colored 1997 Seven Acre Shiraz offers a knockout nose of cassis intertwined with cherries and licorice, great intensity and purity, huge body, and layers of glycerin that coat the palate. The wine's low acidity and gorgeous fruit make it irresistible now, but it will develop more complexity over the next 4–5 years and drink well for two decades.

1996 Creek Block Shiraz

RATING: 96 points

The 1996 Creek Block Shiraz exhibits a dense purple color, and a spectacular nose of roasted coffee intermixed with cassis, blackberries, licorice, and spice. The wine displays amazing ripeness, an unctuous texture, full-bodied palate, and a finish that lasts for 45+ seconds. Its high alcohol and tannin are nearly concealed by the wine's amazing concentration. Anticipated maturity: now–2020.

1996 Seven Acre Shiraz

RATING: 97 points

The 1996 Seven Acre Shiraz possesses complexity in the nose (violets?), as well as a delineated palate. It is an enormous, massive, fabulously concentrated yet symmetrical wine. Anticipated maturity: now–2025.

1995 Creek Block Shiraz

RATING: 95 points

This wine possesses a modest 14.1% alcohol. It is more akin to blackberry jam or dry port than wine, but it does not taste as heavy as one might initially suspect given the thickness and richness of fruit. It possesses a mineral character underlying the full-bodied, massive concentration. It is also slightly tannic and closed, although still accessible as well as capable of turning heads at any wine tasting. Look for this monster Shiraz to become even more civilized over the following 10–15 years. This is a massive, opulently textured, extraordinary wine.

1995 Seven Acre Shiraz

RATING: 98 points

This wine boasts an opaque purple color, and a splendidly sweet, rich nose of blackberry liqueur, cherries, cassis, tar, and pepper. Only 25% new oak was utilized in the aging process, but that is not even discernible given the wine's extraordinary richness and purity of fruit. Layers of viscously textured fruit cascade over the palate with precision and purity. This is a fabulous, nearly perfect Shiraz that should age effortlessly for two decades or more. An amazing wine!

WINES:
Eclipse (70% Grenache, 30% Shiraz)
Reserve Shiraz
Reserve Cabernet Sauvignon
OWNERS: Noon Winery Pty. Ltd., Drew and Raegan Noon
ADDRESS: Rifle Range Road, P.O. Box 88, McLaren Vale, SA, 5171, Australia
TELEPHONE: 61 8 8323 8290
TELEFAX: 61 8 8323 8290
CONTACT: Drew or Rae
VISITING POLICY: Cellar Door is open for only a brief period each year for sales (approximately four weekends from November); phoning in advance to check stock availability and opening times is recommended prior to visiting.

VINEYARDS

SURFACE AREA: Grenache—9.88 acres; Shiraz—3.95 acres; Cabernet—2.96 acres
GRAPE VARIETALS: Grenache, Shiraz, Cabernet
AVERAGE AGE OF THE VINES: Grenache planted 1934–1943; Shiraz planted early 1960s; Cabernet planted early 1970s
DENSITY OF PLANTATION: Approximately 1,800 vines per hectare
AVERAGE YIELDS: 2–4 tons per acre (30–60 hectoliters per hectare)

WINEMAKING AND UPBRINGING

The wines are made in small quantities, by hand, using traditional open fermenters and basket presses. They are matured in a combination of small (300-liter) and large (2,500–4,500-liter) oak for a period of 18 months before bottling (in September of the year following the harvest) without fining or filtration.

They are made and matured with the minimum of additives or manipulation, as naturally as possible.

ANNUAL PRODUCTION

Eclipse: 12,000 bottles (their signature red—Grenache 70%, Shiraz 30%)
Reserve Shiraz: 4,500 bottles
Reserve Cabernet: 6,000 bottles
AVERAGE PRICE (VARIABLE DEPENDING ON VINTAGE): $45–60

GREAT RECENT VINTAGES

The Noons would rank the seasons (since they took over prior to the 1997 vintage) as follows:
Excellent: 1998, 2002
Good: 1997, 2001
Average: 1999, 2000

Noon was started by Drew's father, David, a former French teacher, who in 1976 took the plunge and left his teaching job to produce red wines for a living. The production is based on estate-grown old Grenache bush vines. Historically, David Noon purchased a little Shiraz to blend with the Grenache to produce the signature wine—a full-bodied red he initially marketed as "Burgundy," but which is now called Eclipse. Noon also used to purchase some Cabernet because at the time it was considered by most red drinkers in Australia to be the premium red wine.

Very little about the production methods or the quantities produced has changed over the past 27 years.

The source of the purchased grapes varied until 1987, when the Noons began buying fruit only from the

Drew Noon

Borrett family at Langhorne Creek. The quality of the grapes was outstanding. Over the years the Noons became good friends with the Borrett family, and they have provided a consistent, single-vineyard source for the Noon Reserve Shiraz and Cabernet.

There are no future plans to expand production for fear of losing some control, possibly even quality and consistency.

It is a true micro-winery with superb products that are undeniably of world-class quality. Drew Noon and his wife, Rae, have taken an estate originally planted by his father, on over 10 acres of chocolaty sandy loams and red clay soils between 1934 and 1945, and pushed the quality since the late 1990s to exhilarating levels. Interestingly enough, Drew Noon was a trained oenologist before becoming a winemaker and is one of the few masters of wine in Australia. The Noons are part of the young, open-minded generation that is guided by one goal: to produce the most uncompromising product possible.

With their incredible perfume and extraordinary purity and layers of fruit, these are attention-getting wines, but there is a restraint, balance, and complexity that is remarkable. Noon's wines taste like the essence of their respective varietals, pushing concentration and extract to the limit, although I have never sensed that they were over-the-top. These are wines of extraordinary depth and richness, with amazing upside potential in the bottle. Life is too short not to be drinking the wines of Drew and Rae Noon.

CABERNET SAUVIGNON RESERVE

2002 Cabernet Sauvignon Reserve

RATING: 96 points

This wine exhibits a striking bouquet of graphite, crème de cassis, new saddle leather, Chinese black tea, and vanilla. The complex aromatics are followed by a full-bodied wine of compelling purity and nobleness with layers of concentration as well as intensity. One of the most prodigious Australian Cabernet Sauvignons ever made, it should hit its prime in 3–5 years, and last for two decades or more.

2001 Cabernet Sauvignon Reserve

RATING: 93–96 points

Noon's brilliant 2001 Cabernet Sauvignon Reserve offers layered, pure crème de cassis flavors nicely touched by wood,

acidity, alcohol, and tannin. Incredibly pure and intense, with a long, heady finish, this seamless classic should age effortlessly for 12–15 years. Yeah!

2000 Cabernet Sauvignon Reserve

RATING: 95 points

The opaque blue/black/purple–colored 2000 Cabernet Sauvignon Reserve is even more impressive from bottle than it was from barrel. This is a great effort displaying first-growth quality. It boasts a stunningly pure nose of crème de cassis, cedar, licorice, smoke, and vanilla. As it sits in the glass, notions of chocolate also emerge. This full-bodied Cabernet builds incrementally in the mouth. The finish lasts for 45 seconds. A magnificent wine with seamlessness and profound concentration. It should still be drinking well at age 25.

1999 Cabernet Sauvignon Reserve

RATING: 94 points

The 1999 Cabernet Sauvignon Reserve could easily be called a Pauillac from Australia. Dense ruby/purple, a classic Cabernet nose of cedarwood, smoke, cassis, mineral, lead pencil, and new oak soars from the glass. In the mouth, it is full-bodied, with fabulous concentration and multilayered texture, high levels of glycerin, and a seamless, concentrated, long finish with well-integrated tannin, acidity, and alcohol. This is no wimpish wine at 14.6% alcohol, but sadly, there are only 290 cases of this 100% Cabernet Sauvignon made from 25–30-year-old vines. Anticipated maturity: now–2020.

1998 Cabernet Sauvignon Reserve

RATING: 98 points

Nearly perfect, this black/purple-colored 1998 Cabernet offers extraordinary sweet black cherry/black currant aromas as well as huge, gorgeously proportioned, voluptuously textured flavors that last for over 50 seconds. The wine reveals no hotness from the high alcohol, unbelievable purity, symmetry, and the potential to improve for 10–15 years. It should keep for two decades or more. This is a tour de force in winemaking, and it performed better when the bottle was opened 48 hours prior to the tasting. This is an exceptional wine from an Australian genius!

1997 Cabernet Sauvignon Reserve

RATING: 95 points

Although it displays a port-like viscosity, it is dry, with none of the late-harvest, pruny, Amarone characteristics often found in wines of such massive ripeness. Extremely full-bodied, pure, and well balanced, this Cabernet is still unevolved and youthful, but it appears to possess all the potential required to develop into something profound. Anticipated maturity: now–2025.

ECLIPSE

2002 Eclipse

RATING: 97 points

The 2002 Eclipse (70% Grenache and 30% Shiraz) is a brilliant exercise in vineyard sourcing and management. The result is a prodigious dense ruby/purple–colored red boasting a glorious perfume of black fruits, licorice, vanilla, graphite, and Asian spices as well as a touch of incense. Full-bodied, gorgeously pure, elegant, and seamless, it's hard to know how this beauty will age, but I suspect it should be consumed during its first 10–12 years of life.

2001 Eclipse

RATING: 94 points

The 2001 Eclipse (65% Grenache and 35% Shiraz) is still closed aromatically, but with coaxing reveals potentially fabulous quality. An opaque purple color is followed by aromas of charcoal, smoke, blackberries, and sweet cherries. This full-bodied, rich, beautifully delineated effort is extraordinarily pure as well as incredibly persistent on the palate (close to one minute). Aged in a combination of new and old large American oak hogsheads for 18 months and bottled unfiltered, it appears to have tremendous upside potential, although I suspect many readers will not be able to defer their gratification . . . and why should they? Drink it over the next decade.

1999 Eclipse

RATING: 94 points

The 1999 Eclipse (a blend of 66% Grenache and 34% Shiraz) tips the scales at a hefty 14.9% alcohol. The wine has an opaque purple color as well as a fabulously sweet nose of blackberry and cassis interspersed with licorice, truffle, and vanilla. Full-bodied, heady, layered, ripe, pure, and sumptuous, it is a dazzling 1999 to drink over the next 15–16 years.

1998 Eclipse

RATING: 96 points

The 1998 Eclipse possesses a whopping 15.7% alcohol, which is totally concealed by the dense, blackberry liqueur–scented and flavored fruit. Notes of cassis, toast, pepper, and licorice can also be found in this thick, full-bodied effort. It is a phenomenally rich, super-extracted wine of astonishing intensity. The tannin is sweet, the acidity low, and the wine unreal. Drink it over the next 10–15+ years. This is another tour de force winemaking effort that performed better from the bottle when it was opened 48 hours prior to the tasting.

1997 Eclipse

RATING: 94 points

The opaque purple-colored 1997 Eclipse (65% Grenache, 35% Shiraz blend) somehow manages to hide its 16.3% alcohol. The wine offers up cherry/blackberry liqueur–like aromas and flavors, an unctuous texture, and despite its ripeness, size, and richness, does not taste like a heavyweight, late-harvest, pruny wine. It seems to me that vineyards in this viticultural area (Langhorne Creek) can achieve an extraordinarily high degree of alcohol without the pruny flavors often associated with less alcoholic wines. This unfiltered beauty is extremely intense, yet should evolve into a civilized, spectacular Shiraz/Grenache blend that will age well for 10–15+ years.

SHIRAZ RESERVE

2002 Shiraz Reserve

RATING: 99 points

Flirting with perfection, the blue/purple-colored 2002 Shiraz Reserve has the texture reminiscent of motor oil. This full-bodied, remarkably intense Shiraz possesses great purity and richness as well as a broad palate. As concentrated as Shiraz can get, it is also impeccably well balanced, elegant, and bursting with personality/soul. It is the kind of wine that is hard to duplicate anywhere else in the world. It's gratifying to see that certain winemakers refuse to put the brakes on when producing something of this ilk. Anticipated maturity: 2006–2016+.

2001 Shiraz Reserve

RATING: 99 points

The 2001 Shiraz Reserve possesses amazing aromatics, purity, texture, and richness. This 2001, which tips the scales at a lofty 15.8% alcohol, is intense and full-bodied as well as remarkably elegant for a wine of such mass and intensity. Its impenetrable inky/black/purple color is accompanied by explosive aromatics, and is bursting with deep, rich, well-balanced flavors revealing seamlessly integrated wood, alcohol, acidity, and tannin. Profoundly deep, rich, and intense, it will hit its peak in 3–4 years, and should last for 15+. This is truly compelling old-vine Shiraz!

1999 Shiraz Reserve

RATING: 96 points

The hugely extracted, massive 1999 Shiraz Reserve tips the scales at 15.2% alcohol. From Shiraz vines that average 35–40 years of age, it was aged in a combination of small and large oak barrels as well as puncheons. An opaque blue/purple color and a knockout nose of blackberry liqueur intermixed with spice box, pepper, asphalt, and licorice soar from the glass. Opulent and viscous, with tremendous palate presence, beautifully integrated acidity, tannin, and alcohol, this superb, larger-than-life wine is a tour de force for a lighter-weight vintage such as 1999. Anticipated maturity: now–2020.

1998 Shiraz Reserve

RATING: 98 points

The opaque black/blue–colored 1998 Shiraz displays a fascinating bouquet of violets, black raspberry and blackberry liqueur, cedar, fruitcake, and pepper. Surreal levels of glycerin and richness are present in this full-bodied, surprisingly supple-textured wine. The finish lasts for several minutes. This is another brilliant winemaking effort. Anticipated maturity: now–2020.

1997 Shiraz Reserve

RATING: 98 points

The 1997 Shiraz Reserve comes close to resembling a dry vintage port. It boasts an opaque black/purple color, followed by a sumptuous nose of licorice, Asian spices, tar, and concentrated blackberry fruit. Thick in the mouth, with remarkably full body and surprising balance, the alcohol (15.8%), tannin, and acidity are lost in the cascades of fruit. Anticipated maturity: now–2025.

WINES:

Grange

Bin 707 Cabernet Sauvignon

OWNER: Southcorp Wines

ADDRESSES:

Penfolds Magill Estate Winery, 78 Penfold Road, Magill, SA, 5072, Australia

Penfolds Nuriootpa Winery, Tanunda Road, SA, 5355, Australia

TELEPHONE: Magill Estate—61 412 208 634; Nuriootpa—61 8 8568 9389

TELEFAX: Magill Estate—61 8 882391182; Nuriootpa—61 8 8568 9493

E-MAIL: Magill Estate—penfolds.magill@cellar-door.com.au; Nuriootpa—penfolds.bv@cellar-door.com.au

WEBSITE: www.penfolds.com

CONTACT: Magill—David Matters; Nuriootpa—Lea Tatt

VISITING POLICY:

Magill Estate Winery Cellar Door: Open 7 days from 10:30 A.M.–4:30 P.M., except closed Christmas Day, New Year's Day, and Good Friday

Nuriootpa Winery Cellar Door: Open Monday to Friday, 10 A.M.–5 P.M.; Saturday, Sunday, and public holidays, except closed Christmas Day, New Year's Day, and Good Friday

VINEYARDS

SURFACE AREA:

Kalimna Vineyard—378 acres planted; 700 acres total

Koonunga Hill Vineyard—146.5 acres planted; 160 acres total

Penfolds Magill Estate Vineyard—12.9 acres

Penfolds McLaren Vale Vineyards—122.9 acres

GRAPE VARIETALS: Cabernet Sauvignon, Shiraz, Grenache, Semillon, Chardonnay, Mataro, Merlot, Sangiovese, Riesling, Sauvignon Blanc, Traminer, others

AVERAGE AGE OF THE VINES:

Kalimna Vineyard—Block 42 (for Bin 707) 120 years; remaining vines 50 years

Koonunga Hill Vineyard—half 30 years; remaining 7 years

Penfolds Magill Estate Vineyard—most 50 years; small parcel 15 years

Penfolds McLaren Vale Vineyards—half 38 years; remaining 14 years

DENSITY OF PLANTATION: All the vineyards range from 1,200–2,000 vines per hectare

AVERAGE YIELDS: Yields average 1–9 tons of fruit per hectare depending on the vineyard and varietal. For Grange and Bin 707, the yields are very low, usually 1–3 tons per hectare.

WINEMAKING AND UPBRINGING

The winemaking approach at Penfolds is the "stamp" that distinguishes its wines. After a rigorous selection of physiologically ripe fruit, with particular attention paid to tannin ripeness, the wine is then framed by the judicious use of oak aligned to specific wine style. The overarching objective is to achieve a rich mid-palate, excellent color, and longevity once bottled.

ANNUAL PRODUCTION

Grange: 8,000–10,000 cases

Bin 707 Cabernet Sauvignon: 10,000–14,000 cases

AVERAGE PRICE (VARIABLE DEPENDING ON VINTAGE): $45–185

GREAT RECENT VINTAGES

2001, 1998, 1996, 1991, 1990, 1986, 1982, 1978, 1976, 1971

Max Schubert (1915–1994), the former Penfolds chief winemaker, said, "True excellence is a constant and endless journey, it is not a destination."

The Penfolds firm, one of the most successful in Australian wine history, has a 150-year legacy of excellence, but it is best known for a wine that many observers have called the greatest wine of the Southern Hemisphere, the Penfolds Grange.

The name Penfolds comes from a young English doctor who migrated from England. Born in 1811, he was the youngest of 11 children and studied medicine at St. Batholomew's Hospital, London, graduating in 1838. Like many doctors, he had a firm belief in the medicinal value of wine, so he planted vine cuttings from the south of France next to his cottage in Magill, on the outskirts of Adelaide, in 1845. He and his wife, Mary, called this house "The Grange," after his wife's home in England.

Dr. Penfold died in 1870, but his wife continued to own the vineyards and winery, which was mostly dedicated to producing fortified wines (port and sherry). The scale of this operation was remarkable. Historical records show that in 1881 there were close to 500,000 liters of wine stored at the Magill estate, which according to the folks at Penfolds was nearly one-third of all the wine produced in South Australia at that time.

The production of fortified wines and some brandy, with only a small amount of dry table wine, continued through the Second World War, when consumer tastes began to change. By 1950, Max Schubert (who began in the early 1930s as a teenage messenger boy for the company) had taken more control of winemaking and instituted a profound change in the direction of the winemaking at Penfolds.

In 1951, following a visit to Europe, Schubert produced the first experimental vintage of Grange Hermitage, a Shiraz-based wine inspired by the long-lived wines of France's Rhône Valley. Little did Schubert know that six decades later this would be considered one of the flagship wines of the wine world and the reference point for most Australian winemakers who wanted to produce a world-class red wine.

Penfolds produces a huge bevy of other wines, the best of which, in my opinion, has been the Bin 707 Cabernet Sauvignon. The Penfolds family gave up partial control of the estate in 1962, when the company went public, and finally relinquished their controlling interest in 1976.

BIN 707 CABERNET SAUVIGNON

1998 Bin 707 Cabernet Sauvignon

RATING: 90 points

The outstanding 1998 Bin 707 Cabernet Sauvignon is a thick, rich, full-bodied Cabernet emphasizing copious quantities of cassis fruit. Pure, with nicely integrated oak, acidity, and tannin, it cuts a broad swath across the palate. While still young and grapy, this 1998 is loaded with potential. Anticipated maturity: now–2015.

1994 Bin 707 Cabernet Sauvignon

RATING: 90 points

Penfolds' most impressive 1994 Cabernet Sauvignon is the Bin 707. This murky plum–colored, blockbuster, backward, exceptionally tannic Cabernet displays abundant quantities of blackberry and cassis fruit, a heavy overlay of toasty vanilla from new oak casks, and mouth-searing levels of tannin. Although the wine is closed, it is firmly structured and enormously endowed in the mouth. Consume this offering over the next 15+ years.

1993 Bin 707 Cabernet Sauvignon

RATING: 94 points

The three luxury-priced 1993 offerings from Penfolds include a spectacular Bin 707 Cabernet Sauvignon. This opaque purple–colored wine exhibits a huge, jammy, black currant, vanilla, licorice, and earthy-scented nose, as well as massive concentration of fruit, glycerin, and body. Readers will find plenty of sweet tannin in the awesomely endowed finish. This blockbuster, monster-sized Cabernet Sauvignon is accessible because of its low acidity and ripe tannin. The formidable extract suggests it will drink well for another 5–10+ years.

GRANGE

1999 Grange

RATING: 92 points

The 1999 Grange does not come close to such great Granges as the 1998, 1996, 1991, and 1990. Dense ruby/purple to the edge, with a bouquet of blackberries, mulberries, and floral-like aromas, and medium to full body, the 1999 has an acid punch, but also tremendous layers of fruit and extract. Not massive, but elegant and nicely layered, it requires another 2–3 years of cellaring, and should last for 12–15 years.

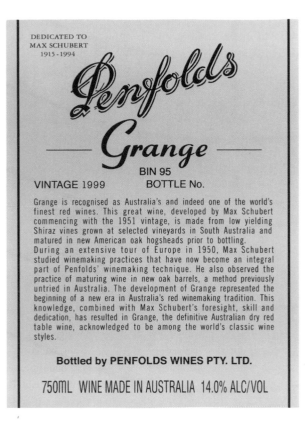

1998 Grange

RATING: 99 points

The 1998 Grange will be legendary. A blend of 97% Shiraz and 3% Cabernet Sauvignon, it tips the scales at a whopping 14.5% alcohol. The inky/purple color is followed by an extraordinarily intense nose of crème de cassis intermixed with blueberry and floral notes. As the wine sits in the glass, aromas of meat, plums, and cola also emerge. It is a seamless effort with sweet tannin, well-integrated acidity, sensational extract, and layer upon layer of blackberry and cassis fruit that stain the palate and fill the mouth. Its harmony, freshness, and remarkable length (the finish lasts nearly a minute) suggest an all-time classic. Anticipated maturity: 2006–2030.

1997 Grange

RATING: 94 points

The 1997 Grange (a blend of 96% Shiraz and 4% Cabernet Sauvignon) looks to be a classic Grange, although slightly softer and more forward than the backward 1996. The saturated purple–colored 1997 offers a gorgeously sweet nose of blackberry liqueur, cherries, camphor, chocolate, plums, and mocha. The wine is opulently textured, extremely soft, layered, and seductive, with Grange's telltale personality well displayed, but in a seamless, seductive style. This is a superb Grange that can hold its own against the more heralded 1996. Anticipated maturity: now–2022.

1996 Grange

RATING: 93 points

This dark purple–colored wine exhibits notes of sweet plum, blackberry, and cassis intermixed with some licorice, chocolate, and espresso. It is a blend of 94% Shiraz and 6% Cabernet Sauvignon that tips the scales at 14+% alcohol. The wine is layered, unctuously textured, and full bodied, with tremendous intensity, moderately high tannin, and a 40-second finish. The wine needs a good 4–5 years of cellaring. Anticipated maturity: 2006–2025. This Grange should ultimately merit a higher score when it is closer to its plateau of drinkability.

1995 Grange

RATING: 92 points

An impressive Grange that may ultimately prove to be underrated, like many wines from this vintage. The 1995, a blend of 94% Shiraz and 6% Cabernet Sauvignon, exhibits a saturated plum/purple color and a sweet blackberry liqueur nose intermixed with cassis, licorice, and new oak. The wine is textured, jammy, full-bodied, with impressive levels of extract, glycerin, and black fruit flavors. It is long, ripe, with unobtrusive acidity and tannin. Anticipated maturity: now–2018.

1994 Grange

RATING: 91 points

This is the first vintage where Grange went to a bottle with laser-etched identification numbers to preclude the possibility of fraudulent bottles. The wine, a blend of 89% Shiraz and 11% Cabernet Sauvignon, shows some toasty oak mixed with notes of root vegetables, damp earth, blackberry liqueur, prune, and licorice. The wine is dense, full-bodied, not terribly complex in the mouth, but layered and rich. I would not be surprised to see the rating on this wine improve as this youthful Grange continues to evolve. Anticipated maturity: now–2020.

1993 Grange

RATING: 91 points

1993 was a very light harvest because of excessive rainfall and mild growing conditions. This wine performed well, although it would not appear to have the nuances of the finest vintages of Grange. The wine, a blend of 86% Shiraz and 14% Cabernet Sauvignon, has an opaque purple color, a sweet nose of black currants intermixed with cedar, and earthy, almost truffle-like notes intermixed with some camphor. The wine is full-bodied, dense, somewhat monolithic, but very concentrated, powerful, and long. Anticipated maturity: now–2018.

1992 Grange

RATING: 92 points

This is a very aromatic Grange that seems to be the product of a vintage where the wines are showing extremely well young. It is dense purple, with a sweet blackberry/cherry nose and some subtle cedar and licorice in the background, unctuously textured, thick, full, without as many nuances as some of the greatest vintages of Grange, but very concentrated and dense. Anticipated maturity: now–2017.

1991 Grange

RATING: 93 points

This wine is generous, open, and sweet in its personality. Dense purple, this blend of 95% Shiraz and 5% Cabernet Sauvignon shows great fruit, a very lush, open-knit style with full body, high glycerin, low acidity, and superb purity. It is a very jammy, voluptuous wine, dominated by its crème de cassis fruit intermixed with tar and licorice. Anticipated maturity: now–2017.

1990 Grange Hermitage

RATING: 94 points

The 1990 is the greatest, most complete, and richest Grange since the monumental 1986. It rivals the 1986, 1982, 1981, and 1980 as the finest "young" Grange. The wine's opaque purple color is followed by a sweet nose of jammy black raspberry and cassis fruit intermingled with scents of minerals, licorice, and toasty oak. Extremely full-bodied, with that layered, multidimensional feel that sets a truly profound Grange apart from just an outstanding one, the wine is fabulously concentrated, unctuous, and with a finish that lasts over 50 seconds. It is in need of another 1–2 years of cellaring. It should last through the first two decades of the 21st century.

1990 Grange

RATING: 92 points

Three bottles opened seemed uncharacteristically compressed, and the wine very dumb and closed. This is certainly a very complete, rich Grange that has been universally praised in all wine circles. Nevertheless, it is not showing well at present, although it is weighty and dense. What left me looking for an answer were the somewhat cool climate characteristics of the wine, with an almost menthol note to the red and black currant fruit. The wine showed some tart acidity as well. I suspect this wine is just closed down, needing a good 4–5 years to reemerge. It seemed uncharacteristic of Grange, but the three bottles opened all were identical in their development. The color is certainly a healthy saturated purple, and the wine is large-scaled and balanced on the palate. That any Grange could behave in such an unforthcoming way is puzzling, but I am still an optimist about this vintage's ultimate potential. Anticipated maturity: 2007–2025.

1989 Grange Hermitage

RATING: 93 points

A very hedonistic, almost decadent style of Grange, this blend of 91% Shiraz and 9% Cabernet Sauvignon from three grape sources—Kalimna in the Barossa, Penfolds' other sources in the Barossa, and McLaren Vale—is a gorgeously opulent, almost Pomerol-like Grange with an overripe characteristic to the fruit. Cherry liqueur intermixed with cranberry and cassis presented in a seductive, full-bodied, very soft, forward style is truly not the classic Grange in the sense of having huge structure and massive concentration, but this wine is loaded, very corpulent, and fleshy. The wine is going to last for up to two decades, but it will be uncommonly succulent and delicious to drink young, as it was last year. Among the young vintages of Grange, this is perhaps the most flattering wine that they have produced over the last 20 years, at least for such a relatively young wine. Anticipated maturity: now–2018.

1988 Grange Hermitage

RATING: 91 points

A blend of 94% Shiraz and 6% Cabernet Sauvignon, this is an uncharacteristically soft, fruity Grange. This wine shows a syrupy crème de cassis, earthy note, some pepper, and caramel. It is somewhat soft and accessible for such a relatively young Grange, but there is plenty of structure and tannin in the finish. It is certainly perfumed and more evolved than some of its siblings that are actually older, chronologically speaking. This wine has sweet, full-bodied, plum, cherry, and cassis flavors, with some distinct truffle and asphalt notes. Anticipated maturity: now–2016.

1987 Grange Hermitage

RATING: 90 points

A light, elegant style of Grange made with a blend of 90% Shiraz and 10% Cabernet Sauvignon, this wine has a deep ruby/purple color and a spicy, peppery nose with some new oak, black cherry, and blackberry flavors. The wine shows some dry tannin in the finish that may ultimately prove worrisome given the less-than-massive style of this vintage. Nevertheless, there is still a lot to like in this wine, which is very pure, ripe, and medium to full–bodied. Anticipated maturity: now–2016.

1986 Grange Hermitage

RATING: 99 points

A current as well as future legend, this has long been considered by Penfolds' winemaking team as the greatest Grange of the 1980s. And why not? A blend of 87% Shiraz and 13% Cabernet Sauvignon, it tips the scales at nearly 14% alcohol. I have been fortunate to have this wine nearly a dozen times, and I have consistently rated it 96–100. It was virtually perfect in June 2002, exhibiting an opaque purple color and a provocative nose of crème de cassis intermixed with smoke, chocolate, licorice, new saddle leather, and pepper. The wine is fleshy, massively concentrated, and multidimensional, with the extraordinary power, beautifully integrated acidity, tannin, and alcohol that seem to only occur in the greatest vintages. Moreover, the wine is still a baby and ideally in need of another 2–4 years of cellaring. This is a Grange to kill for. Anticipated maturity: now–2030.

1985 Grange Hermitage
RATING: 90? points

Considered a more "restrained" Grange, this wine has balance but a somewhat foursquare/monolithic character with dry, astringent tannin in the finish, hence the question mark. The color is still a healthy dense purple, and the wine shows the telltale peppery, asphalt, earthy, crème de cassis characteristics, but the tannin seems to be increasingly problematic. As always, it is still a young wine, so the question that begs to be answered with time is, "Is it just unevolved and backward, or is it too tannic?" Anticipated maturity: now–2015.

1984 Grange Hermitage
RATING: 94 points

The best showing ever for this wine from my perspective, this blend of 95% Shiraz and 5% Cabernet Sauvignon is considered a relatively forward, accessible style of Grange. The color is still a dark plum/purple, and the wine shows plenty of sweet cassis, with notes of chocolate and toasty oak. The wine is opulent and luscious, with great intensity, full body, and fabulous extract. The acidity seems relatively low and integrated, and the tannins quite ripe. Drink it over the next 12–18 years.

1983 Grange Hermitage
RATING: 92 points

The earliest harvest on record at Penfolds, the 1983 vintage was characterized by devastating bush fires, followed by enormous flooding in March. A blend of 94% Shiraz and 6% Cabernet, the wine still shows considerable tannin in its flavors, but enormously powerful, rich, high-acid characteristics. It is somewhat of a paradox to taste. The wine seems very youthful, very backward, and still in need of at least another 3–4 years of cellaring. Whether it will all come together in a seamless classic remains open to conjecture. Anticipated maturity: 2006–2020.

1982 Grange Hermitage
RATING: 95 points

One of my favorite vintages of Grange to actually drink at present is the 1982, a vintage that Max Schubert called, in his low-key manner, "very good." A blend of 94% Shiraz and 6% Cabernet Sauvignon, this is a wine with an open-knit, seductive style. Dense ruby/purple with sweet black raspberry, jammy plum, and currant flavors, the wine tastes like dry vintage port, but also seems to be approaching full maturity. The wine seems low in acidity and sweet in tannin, with firmness, ripeness, richness, and powers of seduction. The wine is gorgeously opulent and impossible to resist. Anticipated maturity: now–2016.

1981 Grange Hermitage
RATING: 94 points

Winemaker John Duval called the 1981 a "big, tannic Grange." It is just that, a very powerful, inky, purple-colored wine that is still almost primary and unevolved in its surprising youthfulness. This formidably endowed, broodingly backward, thick, full-bodied, muscular wine has a boatload of chocolate-infused plum, caramel, and cassis flavors. With high tannin, huge grip, and some propensity toward austerity, this is a monster Grange that may not totally assimilate the high levels of tannin, but there are plenty of reasons to be optimistic about its future. Anticipated maturity: now–2025.

1980 Grange Hermitage
RATING: 94 points

A fabulous Grange, this was a light harvest, and the blend ended up being 96% Shiraz and 4% Cabernet Sauvignon. The wine still seems very youthful, made in a very voluptuous, blockbuster Grange style. The wine has a dense ruby/purple color with no amber. A nose of melted asphalt, pepper, crème de cassis, and blackberries changes little in the glass, but with airing, some sweeter plum, prune, and chocolate emerge in a very full-bodied, powerful, seamlessly constructed wine with perfect levels of glycerin and extract. It is just now reaching its plateau of drinkability. Anticipated maturity: now–2016.

1979 Grange Hermitage
RATING: 92 points

Max Schubert commented in 1993 that this vintage, a blend of 87% Shiraz and 13% Cabernet Sauvignon, was "not quite up to the mark." For technicians, this was the last vintage to use white capsules on the bottle, with Penfolds moving to the crimson red foils in 1980. The wine is deep ruby garnet with an unusual nose of root vegetables mixed with cola, caramel, black currant, and tar. Relatively attenuated in the finish but sweet on the attack, this wine seems to be narrowing out, with the tannins becoming increasingly dominant. If this is typical of the direction the evolution of this wine is taking, it is not reassuring. The wine is certainly still full, but may ultimately tend to dry out rather than blossom and prove expansive. This is a vintage to monitor closely. Anticipated maturity: now–2016.

1978 Grange Hermitage

RATING: 95 points

A wine that seems to get better every time I have it, the 1978 Grange, a blend of 90% Shiraz and 10% Cabernet Sauvignon, has turned out to be a blockbuster wine with extraordinary intensity, a voluptuous palate, notes of camphor, coffee, jammy black fruits, leather, and crème de cassis. As the wine sits in the glass, pepper and melted asphalt make an appearance. Very unctuously textured, thick, and chewy, this wine is soft, with a very succulent style. Its color is showing just a touch of amber as this wine approaches its plateau of maturity. Drink it now and over the next 20 years.

1977 Grange Hermitage

RATING: 93 points

This is considered a good rather than outstanding Grange, but I have consistently found this wine to be superb. A blend of 91% Shiraz and 9% Cabernet Sauvignon from a relatively cool growing year, this wine has full body and a gorgeously complex nose of coffee, crème de cassis, caramel, leather, and a subtle hint of pepper and eucalyptus. The wine is very rich and still somewhat unevolved, with more new oak showing through than most vintages of Grange. The wine still has a dense ruby/purple color and seems to need at least another 2–3 years to reach full maturity, with a very sweet, chewy style but exceptional balance. Anticipated maturity: now–2018.

1976 Grange Hermitage

RATING: 100 points

Consistently one of the most awesome wines ever made at Grange, this blend of 89% Shiraz and 11% Cabernet Sauvignon (13.9% alcohol) was the first Australian wine to cost $20 upon release. I have had this wine six separate times, every time rating it between 96 and 100. It had a phenomenal showing at Penfolds' Magill estate. The color is an opaque purple, the wine massive, full-bodied, and to me, the quintessential Grange. Notes of blackberry liqueur intermixed with cassis, charcoal, new saddle leather, and underbrush resonate from the glass. Huge, thick, unctuously textured, with extraordinary concentration but perfect harmony among all of its elements, this is a prodigious Grange that is still not fully mature. Anticipated maturity: now–2020. A legend for sure!

1975 Grange Hermitage

RATING: 92 points

A blend of 90% Shiraz and 10% Cabernet Sauvignon, this vintage was considered a "good yet tannic Grange." Certainly the tannins have become beautifully integrated in this sweet, expansive, full-bodied wine, with notes of subtle leather, melted asphalt, blackberry, and coffee. It is a very powerful, rich, deep, muscular wine with enormous concentration, plenty of glycerin and sweetness, and remarkable freshness and vigor. Drink it over the next 12–15 years.

1973 Grange Hermitage

RATING: 90 points

A blend of 95% Shiraz and 5% Cabernet Sauvignon, this was considered "a good wine from an undistinguished vintage." It certainly was outstanding in June 2002 in Adelaide, showing a terrific nose of blackberry jam intermixed with sweet earth, plum, brown sugar, and tobacco. Full-bodied, deep, rich, and fully mature, this layered, concentrated, very fresh wine even exhibited some espresso-infused chocolate in the finish. It should drink well for another 4–6 years.

1971 Grange Hermitage

RATING: 96 points

I have had this wine on five separate occasions and on each occasion it has been a prodigious example of Grange Hermitage. The wine has consistently revealed the fruit levels, intensity, and complexity that are the hallmarks of a classic Grange. In fact, it is the first great Grange Hermitage since the debut vintage of 1955. The color is a mature garnet with considerable amber/orange at the edge. The magnificent aromatic profile includes scents of cedar, caramel, coffee, toffee, chocolate, and gobs of jammy black cherry and currant fruit. It could easily be mistaken for an old, magnificent Pomerol given its voluptuous texture, glorious richness, unctuosness, and phenomenal concentration, fat, and length. The wine has been fully mature since I first tasted it in 1990, yet it is capable of lasting for another 2–3 years. This is the real thing!

WINES:

The Factor

Descendant

RunRig

Les Amis

OWNER: David Powell

ADDRESS: Roennfeldt Road, Marananga, SA, 5356, Australia

TELEPHONE: 61 8 8562 4155

TELEFAX: 61 8 8562 4195

E-MAIL: dave@torbreck.com

WEBSITE: www.torbreck.com

CONTACT: Liz Ellis, Cellar Door Manager,
    cellardoor@torbreck.com

VISITING POLICY: Open 7 days, 10 A.M.–6 P.M.; closed Good
    Friday and Christmas Day

VINEYARDS

SURFACE AREA: 250 acres

GRAPE VARIETALS: Shiraz, Grenache, Mataro, Viognier,
    Marsanne, Roussanne, Semillon, Frontignac

AVERAGE AGE OF THE VINES: 60 years

DENSITY OF PLANTATION: 1,500 vines per hectare

AVERAGE YIELDS: 23 hectoliters per hectare

WINEMAKING AND UPBRINGING

At Torbreck the philosophy is that great wines are made in the vineyard and then nurtured through to the bottle. The fruit is sourced from predominantly old vines from various sub-regions across the Barossa Valley. Fruit is harvested according to flavor ripeness, as opposed to sugar levels, hence they obtain optimal tannin and physiological ripeness on the vine. Winemaking techniques are very traditional, starting with gentle destemming of the grapes, which are then slowly pumped into open fermentation vessels and pumped over twice a day. A complete *délestage* is mandatory once a day. There is no extended maceration, and when fermentation is finished, all skins are pressed with a basket press. Secondary malolactic fermentation is carried out naturally in barrel utilizing the indigenous cultures of each of the single vineyard components.

The full range of Torbreck wines is an expression of the Barossa's finest and oldest vines as well as the Rhône-oriented philosophy that has so captivated Dave Powell. They mainly use seasoned oak, and in some instances, such as with the Cuvée Juveniles, they use no oak at all. The wines that do mature in oak can spend up to 30 months, as is the case with RunRig, and these icon wines also incorporate a small percentage of new French oak. Torbreck does not filter or fine any of the wines, preferring the flavors, textures, and style that are enhanced by their noninterventionist approach to winemaking. Torbreck's goal is to keep the wines focused and balanced between rich, ripe fruit and a subtle, harmonious use of oak.

ANNUAL PRODUCTION

Woodcutters Semillon: 60,000 bottles

Woodcutters Shiraz: 120,000 bottles

Cuvée Juveniles: 60,000 bottles

The Steading: 60,000 bottles

The Struie: 48,000 bottles

The Factor: 18,000 bottles

Descendant: 12,000 bottles

RunRig: 18,000 bottles

Les Amis: 1,800 bottles

The Bothie: 12,000 bottles

AVERAGE PRICE (DEPENDING ON VINTAGE): $25–150

GREAT RECENT VINTAGES

2002, 2001, 1998

Although Torbreck is only 10 years old, they have access to some of the oldest vineyards in Australia's most hallowed wine region, the Barossa Valley.

David Powell was born and raised in Adelaide, South Australia. His father was an accountant, and Dave soon

found himself on a similar career path, studying economics at Adelaide University. While a student, he was introduced to wine by an uncle, and soon he found himself spending more and more time in the Barossa Valley.

After leaving the university, Dave spent the next 25 years learning the art of winemaking in famous vineyards and winemaking regions in Europe, the United States, and, of course, the Barossa Valley. The experience showed him the value of the Barossa's unique attributes and convinced him of the importance of the valley's vineyard heritage when others felt that it was well past its use-by date.

In the early 1990s, David Powell set about approaching local landowners concerning their neglected vineyards, most of which were lifeless and overgrown. Over time Powell nurtured them back to health, and was rewarded with a few small parcels of dry grown fruit that he made into wine. Following this, contracts were negotiated for the use of these vineyards and the old practice of share farming was resurrected in the Barossa Valley. The name Torbreck came from a forest in Scotland where Powell had worked while under contract with the Scottish forestry commission. The contracts that he negotiated secured a regular supply of the best Barossa Shiraz, Grenache, and Mataro as well as ensuring that he obtained fruit from some of the oldest vines in the world.

Realizing the potential that the Barossa had for Rhône varietals, both red and white, Powell bought a 30-acre property in Marananga and planted Viognier, Marsanne, and Roussanne vines. Part of the property in Marananga, known as the Descendant vineyard, is planted with Shiraz vines that are grown exclusively for the Descendant. Powell also took cuttings from each of the RunRig vineyards, planting them in 1995–1996. In 1999 Powell purchased another two old vineyards and six more came under the Torbreck share-farming scheme. His contracts with local growers multiplied, and by the end of 2003 he had secured long-term contracts with 35 local growers for old-vine parcels.

Dave Powell has quickly established himself as one of the geniuses of Rhône Valley–influenced blockbuster red wines from Australia. I have extolled his previous vintages, and the quality (and prices) continues to soar, as these are some of the most exciting wines produced not only in Australia but in the world. These are wines of enormous strength but also riveting individuality

and extraordinary purity and symmetry. The reds are all spectacular, even some of the less expensive *cuvées*. Of course, the RunRig has become one of the most fashionable wines in the world, and it deserves billing as the Guigal Côte-Rôtie La Mouline of Australia.

These wines not only make for compelling drinking, but also a huge amount of fun, and isn't that what it's all about?

DESCENDANT

2002 Descendant
RATING: 96 points
A magnificent effort, the dense ruby/purple–colored 2002 Descendant offers gorgeous aromas of crushed blackberries, raspberries, licorice, acacia flowers, and the added notes of honeysuckle and apricots from the touch of Viognier in this Shiraz-dominated wine. Full-bodied and opulently textured, with good tannin, structure, purity, and a broad, expansive finish that lasts nearly a minute, it needs 1–2 years of cellaring, and should keep for 12–15+.

2001 Descendant
RATING: 98 points
The 2001 Descendant is a blend of 92% Shiraz and 8% Viognier cropped at approximately 1.5 tons of fruit per acre. This spectacular Australian red offers an aromatic smorgasbord of honeysuckle intermixed with blackberry and crème de cassis, licorice, coffee, and spice. There is fabulous fruit purity, tremendous intensity, and great balance with flavor, power, and elegance all combined into a riveting example of Barossa Valley wine. It should drink well for another 8–10 years.

2000 Descendant
RATING: 94 points
The 2000 Descendant is a single-vineyard Shiraz that includes 8% Viognier. This exotic offering boasts an inky purple color along with a gorgeously sweet nose of blackberry liqueur intermixed with licorice and Viognier's honeysuckle character. It has great texture, fabulous length (the finish lasts for 50 seconds), and incredible fruit purity. I would not be surprised to see it firm up in the bottle. This pedal-to-the-metal, full-throttle Shiraz is a singular expression of Barossa Valley fruit. Anticipated maturity: now–2015.

1999 Descendant
RATING: 93 points
The 1999 Descendant is a blend of 92% Shiraz and 8% Viognier. Its dense purple color is followed by blackberry, crème de cassis, and floral aromas, huge body, terrific fat and glyc-

erin, and a seamless, decadently rich finish. For drinking in its first 7–8 years of life, it is a tour de force in pleasure.

1997 Descendant

RATING: 96 points

The 1997 Descendant (100% Shiraz fermented on Viognier pomace) is Australia's quintessential example of power and elegance. While not massive, its level of concentration is extraordinary. This black/purple-colored wine offers a feminine, silky voluptuousness allied to fascinating levels of richness, unbelievably sweet tannin, and layers of flavor. In the glass, the wine develops magnificently. A bottle kept open for 48 hours displayed additional nuances and complexity. Full-bodied but not heavy, this is a tour de force in winemaking, as well as a thrilling Shiraz to drink. No other wine from Australia remotely resembles it. In truth, the closest wine to which it could be compared is Marcel Guigal's single-vineyard Côte-Rôtie La Turque. Anticipated maturity: now–2011.

THE FACTOR

2002 The Factor

RATING: 99 points

Remarkably, the 2002 The Factor (100% Shiraz) may be even more awesome than the 2001. It boasts a blackberry liqueur–like intensity with chocolaty richness intermixed with blackberries, raspberries, and cherries. The unctuous texture, refreshing acidity, and sweet tannin frame up this magnificent wine. It should drink well for 15+ years. Interestingly, the 2002 The Factor did not have the Côte-Rôtie–like roasted element found in the 2001, no doubt because 2002 was much cooler than the record heat experienced in 2001.

2001 The Factor

RATING: 98 points

A 100% Shiraz offering, the exquisite 2001 possesses a more roasted, Côte-Rôtie character than its Shiraz siblings. Blackberry, blueberry, espresso roast, smoke, and a roasted component are found in this intense, rich effort along with considerable structure, fabulous density, and a broad, deep, profound palate. Anticipated maturity: now–2014.

2000 The Factor

RATING: 95 points

The 2000 The Factor has benefitted from the fact that Powell decided not to produce a RunRig in 2000. It is a compelling wine of great richness, multiple dimensions, and glorious levels of blackberry liqueur–like fruit intermixed with crème de cassis, melted licorice, espresso, and leather. Sweet, expansive, and opulent, it is a lusty, hedonistic, mouth-staining Shiraz that should drink well for another 8–13 years.

1999 The Factor

RATING: 97 points

The spectacular 1999 offers an opaque inky/blue/purple color, accompanied by scents of new saddle leather, pepper, creosote, smoke, and blackberry liqueur. This full-bodied, marvelously concentrated, stunningly pure Shiraz is the qualitative equivalent of this estate's flagship offering, the RunRig. Anticipated maturity: now–2016.

1998 The Factor

RATING: 93 points

A stunning effort is the 1998 The Factor. Supple, with a telltale, ostentatious bouquet of black fruits intermixed with smoke, licorice, and melted asphalt, this super-extracted, velvety-textured, sumptuous, pure, rich, impeccably well-balanced Shiraz is best consumed during its first decade of life. Anticipated maturity: now.

LES AMIS

2002 Les Amis

RATING: 99 points

One of the most remarkable wines in Torbreck's portfolio is the 100% Grenache *cuvée*, the 2002 Les Amis. It is made from an old, dry-farmed Grenache vineyard planted in 1901 that escaped the pull-up of old vines that afflicted Barossa and McLaren Vale 30 years ago when the government's intelligentsia was encouraging vineyard development in cool climate areas, and had concluded that warmer South Australia areas, such as Barossa and McLaren Vale, were irrelevant. Obviously, this was a blunder of extraordinary proportions. Luckily, some old vineyards were saved. Les Amis is David Powell's homage to the most underrated great red wine of the world, France's Châteauneuf-du-Pape. What is amazing about this wine is that Grenache tends to do poorly in a lot of new oak, but this *cuvée* spends 18 months in new French oak, which is completely absorbed by the extraordinary Greenock Creek fruit. A marvelous effort, it boasts an inky/ruby/purple color as well as an extraordinarily provocative perfume of crushed raspberries and black cherry liqueur. This full-bodied, multidimensional red inundates the palate with fruit, glycerin, and intensity. It has the highest alcohol content of all the Torbreck wines (16.5%), which tend to average 14.5%. Nevertheless, it is refreshing, vigorous, and incredibly well delineated. No doubt the old vines are the key to such a magnificent achievement. It should drink well for 10–12 years, possibly longer.

2001 Les Amis

RATING: 96 points

The debut vintage of Les Amis, the 2001, is 100% Grenache fashioned from ancient pruned vines. It tips the scales at 15% alcohol, but somehow manages to conceal its oak. A majestic red of great ripeness, richness, and copious quantities of kirsch, pepper, and spice, there is not a hard edge to be found in this dense, full-bodied offering. Sadly, there are only 100 cases of this compelling wine. It should be consumed over the next 4–6 years.

RUNRIG

2001 RunRig

RATING: 99+ points

Constantly flirting with perfection, the 2001 RunRig is a worthy successor to the blockbuster, surreal 1998. A blend of 97% Shiraz and 3% Viognier, this is Torbreck's flagship offering. Sourced from old vines, some close to 140 years of age, it is fashioned from four sectors of Barossa—Marananga, Koonunga Hill, Moppa, and Greenock. The powerful, full-bodied 2001 exhibits aromas of crème de cassis, blackberry liqueur, ink, espresso, graphite, and apricot marmalade. The impression on the palate is one of marvelous richness and expansive texture, a multilayered skyscraper soaring across the palate with no heaviness. It is a tour de force in winemaking, but give it 2–3 years of bottle age, and drink it over the following 15–20+ years.

1999 RunRig

RATING: 97 points

The 1999 RunRig is an unfined/unfiltered beauty of remarkable concentration and intensity. The RunRig is a structured, muscular effort with phenomenal density, dry vintage port-like concentration, and magnificent notes of smoke, blackberries, cassis, leather, and coffee. A hint of Viognier's sweet marmalade character comes through as the wine sits in the glass. This majestic Shiraz, one of the greatest wines made in the New World, should be cellared for another 3–4 years, and drunk over the following 2–3 decades.

1998 RunRig

RATING: 99 points

A blend of 97% Shiraz and 3% Viognier, aged completely in French oak for approximately 18 months prior to bottling, the 1998 may well be the most concentrated RunRig to date. The color is an opaque purple, and the bouquet offers an exotic concoction of tropical fruit, blackberry liqueur, crème de cassis, smoke, and honeysuckle notes. Once past the exhilarating fragrance, the wine is sumptuous and full-bodied, with a skyscraper-like profile of fabulous concentration and length that builds in the mouth. The black-fruits-galore scenario unfolds to reveal beautifully integrated wood, acidity, tannin, and alcohol (14.5%). The balance is virtually perfect, and the finish lasts for nearly a minute. This luxurious, compelling gem displays a level of complexity and delineation that is rare in a wine of such size. Anticipated maturity: now–2016.

1997 RunRig

RATING: 98 points

Torbreck's 1997 RunRig is spectacular. This huge, exotic wine, which offers up blueberry liqueur, cassis, flowers, a touch of overripe peaches, and sweet vanilla, is a rich, full-bodied, supple-textured wine. It represents Australia's answer to Marcel Guigal's Côte-Rôtie La Mouline. The oak is beautifully integrated. The wine is low in acidity, and the impact on the palate is one of awesome levels of fruit, richness, and complexity. This amazing wine may even merit a perfect rating. It should drink well for another 6–8 years.

1996 RunRig

RATING: 96 points

Sensational aromatics leap from the glass, offering up cherry liqueur, smoke, toast, roasted herbs, and blackberry fruit. It is full-bodied, with exquisite concentration, an unctuous texture, low acidity, and beautifully integrated tannin and alcohol (14.5%). This staggering wine can be drunk now or cellared for another 5–7 years.

1995 RunRig

RATING: 95 points

This is a lavishly rich, compelling effort with spectacular aromatics as well as flavors. From the toasty vanilla, bacon fat, black raspberry, blackberry, and cassis aromas to its stunningly proportioned, thick, medium to full–bodied flavors, this seamless, silky-textured, juicy, succulent wine is a total turn-on. With airing, some tannin emerges, and the wine still tastes youthful. The RunRig can be drunk now, but it promises to evolve effortlessly for another 6–12 years.

WINES:

Hanisch Shiraz

Heysen Shiraz

OWNER: The Binder family (Principal: Rolf G. Binder)

ADDRESS: Winery—Seppeltsfield Road, Dorrein via Tanunda;
Postal—P.O. Box 126, Tanunda, SA, 5352, Australia

TELEPHONE: 61 8 8562 3300

TELEFAX: 61 8 8562 1177

E-MAIL: cellar@veritaswinery.com

WEBSITE: www.veritaswinery.com

CONTACT: Rolf Binder

VISITING POLICY: Cellar Door—Monday to Friday, 10 A.M.–
4:30 P.M.; weekends/holidays, 11 A.M.–4 P.M.; groups
and tours—by invitation only

VINEYARDS

SURFACE AREA: Total area of vineyard is 98.8 acres split over
two vineyards—Chri Ro Estate and Western Ridge

GRAPE VARIETALS: 34.6 acres of Shiraz

AVERAGE AGE OF THE VINES: Shiraz planted in 1972 and 1985

DENSITY OF PLANTATION: Plantings pre-1990: 3.5 meters by
3.0 meters; post-1990: 3.0 meters by 2.0 meters

AVERAGE YIELDS: Reds, 3–8 tons per hectare

WINEMAKING AND UPBRINGING

The philosophy of Veritas Winery is to let the vineyard tell its
own story. The crushing is designed to leave as many berries
whole as possible in the fermentation, which is done in 8-ton
open fermenters. They use heading-down boards on some
fermentations, which give a rich, full-palate wine, and the majority are managed through pump-overs, which tend to give
more weight and back palate structure.

Veritas's old screw press has been in use since the company was established in 1955. The initial pressing extracts and
macerates the skins, but the final pressure on the cake is soft,
giving an almost gentle "basket press" effect. They want to
avoid pressing too hard, as they prefer to leave a few liters in
the cake than have hardness in the wine.

Rolf Binder, the winemaker, has an expression that "the
wine is the hand and the fruit is the glove," and they must fit
well together. The correct use of oak is vital, and new oak is
used sparingly. The tendency is to use older reshaven oak,
which imports less oak aggression and more fine oak flavor to
the wine. As Binder says, "Barossa fruit has such an intense
full fruit, why hammer it with lots of oak?"

The premium wines such as Hanisch and Heysen spend
22 months in oak. The final blending and finishing of the

wines is very important. After barrel selection and blending,
the wines will generally receive a very light fining of egg white
and a very gentle filtration pre-bottling.

Veritas has shied away from modern technology because
it believes that the process of making wine is a very simple
one, and sees no reason to fix what isn't broken.

ANNUAL PRODUCTION

Hanisch Shiraz: 3,600 bottles

Heysen Shiraz: 7,000 bottles

AVERAGE PRICE (VARIABLE DEPENDING ON VINTAGE): $30–80

GREAT RECENT VINTAGES

2002, 2001, 1998, 1996, 1994, 1991

Veritas was established as a winery in 1955 by Rolf
Binder's parents, Rolf and Fransiska Binder, post-
war immigrants to Australia from Europe.

Rolf Sr. came to Australia with literally nothing, but
was fortunate to have enough knowledge of languages
that he could work as a court interpreter. It was at court
that he met two gentlemen, Chris Vohrer and Wilhelm
Abel, who had established the original winery in the
Barossa Valley. Rolf Sr. had studied chemistry before the

Rolf Binder

war and felt winemaking was a logical extension. Vohrer and Abel offered him an apprenticeship, and after a decade of learning the trade, Rolf Sr. was given the opportunity to purchase the winery. In 1955 he bought the property and renamed it "Veritas Winery."

The initial production was of fortified wines, with a few dry reds on the side. The business was established by doing "house deliveries" to many areas of the state, which helped spread the word about the company's wines.

In the mid-1960s, Rolf Sr. purchased some land that was partially planted with old Shiraz and Mataro vines. In 1972, much of the uncultivated land was planted to vines, and christened the Heysen and Hanisch vineyards.

In the early 1980s, daughter Christa and then Rolf Jr. graduated from Roseworthy Agricultural College and joined the winemaking business. Rolf began working at Veritas in 1982, while Christa went offsite for experience and returned to Veritas ten years later, bringing vast skills in white wine–making.

Rolf Jr. worked hard to shift away from fortified wines and develop the company's red wine style. During the 1980s, the company continued to develop its vineyards, planting more Shiraz, Mataro, Semillon, Riesling, and Cabernet Sauvignon.

There is no question that the two Shiraz *cuvées* from the Hanisch and Heysen vineyards are world-class wines of extraordinary aromatic and flavor dimension. Both wines give indications of evolving for 15–20 years, and seem very capable of competing with the famous wine of South Australia, the Penfolds Grange.

HANISCH SHIRAZ

2002 Hanisch Shiraz
RATING: 98 points

The blockbuster 2002 Hanisch Shiraz possesses a dense purple color, extraordinary richness, an incredible perfume of creosote, blueberries, blackberries, and cassis, and velvety tannin that suggests great ripeness as well as wonderful integration of all its structural components. With full body, stunning depth, a multilayered mouth-feel, tremendous purity, and a 60+-second finish, this unevolved yet accessible Shiraz should hit its prime in 2–3 years, and last for 12–15 or longer. This is a brilliant Barossa Valley Shiraz!

2001 Hanisch Shiraz
RATING: 92+ points

The 2001 Hanisch Shiraz perfume is reminiscent of some of the great Diamond Creek Cabernets of the mid- and late 1970s. Scorched earth, crème de cassis, blackberry, licorice, and smoky aromas emerge from this dense purple-colored Shiraz. Opulent, rich, and full-bodied, with more forward fruit than the Heysen *cuvée*, and a 45-second finish, this stunning effort should be at its finest between now and 2016.

1999 Hanisch Shiraz
RATING: 92 points

The 1999 Hanisch Shiraz boasts an inky purple color as well as a terrific nose of jammy black fruits intermixed with licorice, new saddle leather, and pepper. Full-bodied and seamless, with exceptional concentration and purity, this large-scaled yet well-balanced wine should drink well for 9–10 years. It is far more evolved and accessible than the 1998 or 1996 were at similar ages. Anticipated maturity: now–2012.

1998 Hanisch Shiraz

RATING: 99 points

The virtually perfect 1998 Hanisch Shiraz offers up notes of beef blood, blackberries, and jammy cassis liqueur. This viscous but not heavy, massive, full-bodied, fabulously concentrated 1998 has a finish that lasts for just under a minute. It represents the essence of Shiraz. Three hundred cases were produced. It can be drunk now because it is so luxuriously rich, but don't expect secondary nuances to develop for at least another 3–6 years. It should keep for 20–25, at the minimum.

1997 Hanisch Shiraz

RATING: 97 points

The 1997 Hanisch Shiraz tastes like a dry vintage port. Opaque purple–colored, with a knockout bouquet of blackberries, leather, and forest scents intermixed with licorice and pepper, this intense, super-concentrated, phenomenally extracted Shiraz is beyond massive. Amazingly well balanced and delineated for its gargantuan size, it is accessible and soft enough to be drunk now, but it is just beginning its long life, which should take it past two decades of evolution. Anticipated maturity: now–2020+.

1996 Hanisch Shiraz

RATING: 97 points

I was blown away by the 1996 Hanisch Shiraz (15.1% alcohol). It boasts copious quantities of jammy blueberry and blackberry fruit intermixed with truffle, tar, licorice, and chocolaty aromas. This is a spectacularly intense, massive, old-vine Shiraz that comes across more as a dry port than a dry table wine. With an unctuous texture as well as a finish that lasts for 40+ seconds, this terrific wine should last for another 20–25+ years. Wow!

HEYSEN SHIRAZ

2002 Heysen Shiraz

RATING: 93+ points

The 2002 Heysen Shiraz is a deep ruby/purple-hued, tightly knit effort that reveals an intriguing, distinctive nose of spice box and flowers. It possesses admirably intense flavors of flowers and blackberries, multiple layers, full body, and firm tannin. Give it 2–3 years of cellaring, and enjoy it over the following 12–15.

2001 Heysen Shiraz

RATING: 90+ points

The saturated purple-colored 2001 Heysen Shiraz was closed (at least on the day I tasted it), but offers a tight but promising nose of damp forest floor scents interwoven with blackberry liqueur and a hint of tar. Full-bodied, chewy, and unctuous, with high tannin (largely concealed by the wealth of fruit), this primary effort has a promising upside. Anticipated maturity: now–2020.

1998 Heysen Shiraz

RATING: 96 points

An opaque black/purple is accompanied by an ostentatious bouquet of raspberries, blackberries, currants, and cherries. With airing, the bouquet also offers up smoke, pepper, licorice, and earth. In the mouth, the wine is unctuously textured and extremely full-bodied, with great purity as well as layers of flavor. It is a dazzling example of what Australia can do so well. Four hundred cases of this classic were produced. Anticipated maturity: now–2020.

1997 Heysen Shiraz

RATING: 96 points

This opaque black/purple–colored wine reveals aromas of flowers, licorice, blackberries, and new saddle leather. This full-bodied, fat, succulent, low-acid wine is one of the most concentrated and intense that Shiraz drinkers will ever taste. Long, powerful, and concentrated, it can be drunk now, but will age effortlessly for twenty years. Anticipated maturity: now–2020.

1996 Heysen Shiraz

RATING: 91 points

This killer Shiraz with an opaque purple color is peppery, tarry, sweet, and layered, with jammy blackberry fruit and hints of subtle new oak. This is a massive, powerful, full-bodied wine with a finish that goes on and on. Still youthful, it promises to age easily for another 7–10 years.

AUSTRIA

A strong argument can be made that the finest Austrian wines are the best-kept secret of the wine world. These exciting wines are loaded with flavor, and are remarkably complex, with a striking depth of minerality found in only a handful of wines in the world. Of course, Austria is a very small wine-producing country, and the best wines are hardly good values, but they are great wines.

The Austrian wine culture is among the oldest in Europe. The Celts produced wine until the Roman conquest displaced them with their own brand of viticulture. As in most areas of Europe, the majority of medieval viticulture was controlled by monasteries, and that remained largely unchanged until the famous phylloxera scourge of the 1880s destroyed virtually all of Austria's vineyards. Of course, the 20th century saw the demise of the Austro-Hungarian empire, two World Wars, and a complete devastation of the Austrian economy. By that time much of Austrian wine culture was a caricature of cheap wine and industrial farming at its worst. Most of the Austrian wine production following the Second World War was designed to foster the desire for inexpensive sweet swill that German supermarkets bought in industrial quantities. Perhaps it was inevitable, but all of this came to a catastrophic end in 1985 when some growers in Austria, as well as in Italy, were found to be adding diethylene glycol (a commonly used antifreeze agent) to sweeten their wines artificially. The adulteration scandal virtually destroyed what was left of Austria's reputation, but the silver lining is that the great producers only strengthened their resolve and tried harder to resurrect the image of Austrian wines.

Since then, Austrian wines have made considerable inroads into the elitist wine culture. Even the most jaded connoisseurs now recognize the brilliance and compelling quality of Austria's greatest Rieslings and Grüner Veltliners. The most hallowed Austrian wine region remains, irrefutably, the Wachau, where very powerful, dry wines of

BURGENLAND

Neusiedler See

• Podersdorf Am See
• Frauenkirchen

Sankt Andrä
am Zicksee

WEINGUT
ALOIS KRACHER
Illmitz

Apetlon
Wallern

Austria | Hungary

VIENNA ○

AUSTRIA

impressive aging potential are produced by the top growers. These are wines of undeniable character with aromas and flavors that resonate *terroir*. They are not shy wines, and the most powerful of them, called Smaragd, usually contains 13–14% alcohol despite being quite dry. In nearby Kremstal and Kamptal, wine styles change a bit as one runs into more Chardonnay, some good sparkling wines, and occasionally an innocuous Pinot Noir. In other regions of Austria, wine quality is decidedly mixed and often only an individual grower transcends the mediocrity of the region. However, there are good wines being made in increasing numbers, and even some rather attractive red wines emerging from Burgenland, the main viticultural region for reds. The great shining success story in the Burgenland (from one of the four sub-appellations, the Neusiedlersee) is the prodigious portfolio of Alois Kracher, whose wines are profiled in the pages that follow. Of course, there are other viticultural areas of Austria, particularly Styria and some of the sub-appellations of lower Austria such as Thermenregion and Weinviertel, but with one notable exception, it is the finest producers of Wachau that play on the world's stage of compelling wines.

WEINGUT FRANZ HIRTZBERGER

WINES:

Grüner Veltliner Smaragd Honivogel
Riesling Smaragd Singerriedel
OWNERS: Irmgard and Franz Hirtzberger
ADDRESS: Kremser Strasse 8, 3620 Spitz, Austria
TELEPHONE: 43 27 13 22 09
TELEFAX: 43 27 13 22 09020
E-MAIL: weingut@hirtzberger.com
WEBSITE: www.hirtzberger.com
CONTACT: Contact the winery at the above address
VISITING POLICY: By appointment only

VINEYARDS

SURFACE AREA: 30 acres
GRAPE VARIETALS: 45% Grüner Veltliner, 40% Riesling, the
     rest Pinot Gris, Pinot Blanc, and Chardonnay
AVERAGE AGE OF THE VINES: 25–30 years
DENSITY OF PLANTATION: 6,000–6,500 vines per hectare
AVERAGE YIELDS: 25–45 hectoliters per hectare

WINEMAKING AND UPBRINGING

All the wines are fermented in stainless steel and aged in the
rather traditional 30- to 50-hectoliter wooden barrels for
10–12 months prior to bottling.

ANNUAL PRODUCTION

Figures are confidential.

Grüner Veltliner Federspiel Rotes-Tor
Grüner Veltliner Smaragd Honivogel
Grüner Veltliner Smaragd Rotes-Tor
Riesling Smaragd Hochrain
AVERAGE PRICE (VARIABLE DEPENDING ON VINTAGE): $20–80

GREAT RECENT VINTAGES

2000, 1999, 1994

One of the great producers in Austria's Wachau Valley, Franz Hirtzberger, an undeniable perfectionist, took over the management of this estate from his father in 1983. His vineyards are all located at the western extremity of the Wachau, near the town of Spitz, an area considered to have some of the coldest *terroirs* of the Wachau. Hirtzberger has planted his vineyards with 45% Grüner Veltliner, 40% Riesling, and tiny smidgens of Pinot Gris, Pinot Blanc, and Chardonnay. One of his two greatest vineyards is Singerriedel, located just behind the family's 13th-century residence. Planted on steep south-southeast-facing slopes, Singerriedel produces one of the great Rieslings of Austria. His second great vineyard is Honivogel, which is planted primarily with Grüner Veltliner and grown on the lower slopes at the foot of the Singerriedel. Most wines at Hirtzberger require four to five years of bottle-age before their refinement, balance, depth, and exceptional complexity come forth.

Hirtzberger's perfectionist philosophy leads to wines that have almost a touch of magic in them, with very little residual sugar and incredibly delineated, clean, mineral-dominated styles. Along with F. X. Pichler, he is one of the two legendary producers in the Wachau.

Franz Hirtzberger

GRÜNER VELTLINER SMARAGD HONIVOGEL

2003 Grüner Veltliner Smaragd Honivogel

RATING: 94 points

Hirtzberger's 1990 Smaragd Honivogel is one of the finest Grüner Veltliners I've ever tasted. It has a nose that reveals expressive fennel-laden minerals. Its clay and mineral as well as pear flavors are ensconced in a rich, concentrated, deep, and bone-dry personality. This powerful behemoth possesses an exceptionally long and pure finish. Drink it between now and 2009–2010.

2000 Grüner Veltliner Smaragd Honivogel

RATING: 92 points

The medium-bodied and powerful 2000 Grüner Veltliner Smaragd Honivogel is a thick wine with roasted pear and spice aromas. This broad, intense offering is crammed with smoky white fruits whose flavors linger throughout its impressively long finish. Anticipated maturity: 2006–2014.

1999 Grüner Veltliner Smaragd Honivogel

RATING: 92 points

Honeysuckle, acacia blossoms, and stones can be discerned in the aromatics of the 1999 Grüner Veltliner Smaragd Honivogel. This tobacco, cedar, and mineral–flavored wine has gorgeous definition, precision, and focus. It is medium-bodied and silky-textured, and possesses a long, flavorful finish. Anticipated maturity: now–2008.

1997 Grüner Veltliner Smaragd Honivogel

RATING: 91 points

The 1997 Grüner Veltliner Smaragd Honivogel displays ripe white fruit aromas and a light to medium–bodied character that is intense, concentrated, and superbly balanced. The wine is armed with stunning grip, coating the palate with minerals, stones, and earth-like flavors. Drink this beauty between now and 2012.

1994 Grüner Veltliner Smaragd Honivogel

RATING: 90 points

The 1994 Grüner Veltliner Smaragd Honivogel was made from grapes harvested on November 15. The wine displays a terrific nose of ripe fruit and an exotic spice component. With ostentatious aromas and flavors, as well as a finish that lasts for 30+ seconds, this rich, deep, full-bodied, dry wine is a knockout example of Grüner Veltliner. It rivals those produced by F. X. Pichler and Ludwig Hiedler. Anticipated maturity: now–2011.

RIESLING SMARAGD SINGERRIEDEL

2000 Riesling Smaragd Singerriedel

RATING: 94 points

White flowers and minerals make up the nose of the wonderful 2000 Riesling Smaragd Singerriedel. This medium-bodied wine has a rich, thick, oily-textured character. Expansive waves of honeyed minerals and candied apples can be discerned in its dense core and extraordinarily long finish. Anticipated maturity: now–2016+.

1999 Riesling Smaragd Singerriedel

RATING: 94 points

This medium-bodied, silky-textured, and crystalline wine possesses depth, power, and richness. It is exceptionally well balanced, and is packed with mineral, pear, apple, and verbena flavors that linger in its long, precise finish. The Hirtzbergers began the tradition of passing through each vineyard multiple times during harvest, picking only the ripest grapes, in 1991. In 1999 it took five such passes (the last on December 1) to harvest the Riesling Smaragd Singerriedel. Anticipated maturity: now–2017. Bravo!

1994 Riesling Smaragd Singerriedel

RATING: 95 points

The powerful aromatics of the 1994 Riesling Smaragd Singerriedel exhibit honeyed mineral scents. On the palate, this medium-bodied wine has awesome depth, purity, and focus. Its never-ending character is slathered with almonds, chamomile, verbena, and pulpy pears. In most of the Wachau, 1994 was simply too warm a vintage. However, in the cooler climate around Spitz it was a special vintage. Drink it between now and 2013–2017.

WINES:

Welschriesling Trockenbeerenauslese (Nouvelle Vague)
Chardonnay Trockenbeerenauslese (Nouvelle Vague)
Scheurebe Trockenbeerenauslese (Zwischen den Seen)
Welschriesling Trockenbeerenauslese (Zwischen den Seen)
OWNER: Alois Kracher
ADDRESS: Apetlonerstrasse 37, A-7142 Illmitz, Austria
TELEPHONE: 43 2175 3377
TELEFAX: 43 2175 33774
E-MAIL: office@kracher.at
WEBSITE: www.kracher.com
CONTACT: Michaela Kracher
VISITING POLICY: By appointment only

VINEYARDS

SURFACE AREA: 50 acres
GRAPE VARIETALS: 30% Chardonnay, 40% Welschriesling, 10%
    Scheurebe, 10% Traminer, 10% Muskat-Ottonel
AVERAGE AGE OF THE VINES: 25 years
DENSITY OF PLANTATION: 6,500 vines per hectare
AVERAGE YIELDS: 15 hectoliters per hectare

Alois Kracher

WINEMAKING AND UPBRINGING

The Trockenbeerenausleses are classified in two categories: "Zwischen den Seen" covers the classic sweet wines of the region, which are fermented in stainless steel and aged in large casks. These are the fruit-driven varieties like Scheurebe, Welschriesling, and Muskat-Ottonel. The focus is on freshness and fruit. The "Nouvelle Vague" wines are internationally styled wines aged in small French oak barrels, like Traminer and Chardonnay. Both categories are mostly varietal wines. Long yeast contact is sought, which involves higher risks in vinification, yet these are minimized by modern equipment. Aging time in cask is about 20 months. Since 1991, the most characteristic wine of each vintage has been bottled as "Grande Cuvée." One third of the vines grow on sandy *terroir*, two thirds on gravelly soils.

ANNUAL PRODUCTION

The present range comprises a Beerenauslese and, if possible, an ice wine. Then there is the Collection series, which—depending on the vintage—includes a different number of Trockenbeerenausleses, all of which sport a distinctive golden label. Numbering of the Trockenbeerenausleses is done according to the concentration of the wines. The decisive factors in this respect include not only residual sugar, but also taste, acidity, alcohol, and extract.

Trockenbeerenauslese: 45,000 half bottles
Beerenauslese: 40,000 half bottles
Eiswein: 4,000 half bottles
Dry wines: 15,000 bottles
AVERAGE PRICE (VARIABLE DEPENDING ON VINTAGE): $50–100

GREAT RECENT VINTAGES

2000, 1998, 1995, 1981, 1979, 1976, 1973

In 1981, Alois "Luis" Kracher took over from his father, who was one of the first to recognize the potential of the Seewinkel district for the vinification of high-quality botrytised wines. Today, Alois Kracher, Sr. still takes care of the vineyards. His son, Alois Kracher, Jr., is the second generation involved in viticulture. He created a new dessert wine style, in which fruit, finesse, and balance are more important than sweetness, and he quickly became one of the most highly reputed sweet wine–makers of the world.

Alois Jr. is a wordly winemaker as capable of discussing the ingredients of intricate dishes with the world's greatest chefs as he is about viticulture in his vineyards, which are located just a short distance from Lake Neusidil. Ironically, he never wanted to take over his father's estate because he was trained as a chemical engineer, but when he did, like so many of the producers in this book, he did it without any compromises in his pursuit of perfection. This vineyard's soils are mostly black earth mixed with sand, and he vinifies everything with natural yeasts. Of course he produces the two distinctive styles of wine already mentioned, but just about everything Kracher does is of interest; he has even turned out some very limited production, very promising dry red wines to go along with his world-class sweet wines. He is also a partner with another wine producer in this book, Manfred Krankl of the California winery Sine Qua Non, and the two of them produce a dazzling array of sweet wines from South Central Coast grapes commercialized under the name "Mr. K."

CHARDONNAY TROCKENBEERENAUSLESE

2000 #3 Chardonnay Trockenbeerenauslese Nouvelle Vague

RATING: 94 points

Butterscotch, orange-flavored candies, and intense apricot aromas are found in the nose of the 2000 #3 Chardonnay Trockenbeerenauslese Nouvelle Vague. An oily-textured, medium to full–bodied effort, it has stupendous amplitude and excellent balance, and reveals loads of spicy, sweet yellow plum flavors. This bold, broad-shouldered, expressive wine (12.5% alcohol, 178.2 grams residual sugar/liter, and 6 grams/liter total acidity) should be consumed over the next 15 years.

2000 #7 Chardonnay Trockenbeerenauslese Nouvelle Vague

RATING: 94 points

Butterscotch, cream, and peaches are found in the nose of the syrupy 2000 #7 Chardonnay Trockenbeerenauslese Nouvelle Vague (7.5% alcohol, 295.9 grams residual sugar/liter, and 6.5 grams/liter total acidity). This creamy-textured wine's mouthfeel is as soft as a goosedown pillow. Its thick, full-bodied character has flavors reminiscent of butterscotch squares whipped into condensed milk. Drink it over the next 15 years.

1999 #7 Chardonnay Trockenbeerenauslese Nouvelle Vague

RATING: 96 points

The candied apple–scented 1999 #7 Chardonnay Trockenbeerenauslese Nouvelle Vague is an opulent, unctuous stunner. It is as thick as syrup yet focused and balanced, offering wave after wave of tangy pear and apple jams. Loads of spices, red currants, and apricots are also found throughout this wine's personality as well as in its seemingly unending finish. Drink it over the next 20–30+ years.

1998 #2 Chardonnay Trockenbeerenauslese Nouvelle Vague

RATING: 93 points

The pale yellow–colored 1998 #2 Chardonnay Trockenbeerenauslese Nouvelle Vague displays aromas of jammy peaches and apricots dusted with botrytis. Medium to full–bodied and thick, this is a sweet red raspberry, jellied apricot, candied peach, and spice–flavored wine. It is dense and oily textured, yet pure and fresh. Anticipated maturity: now–2020.

1998 #9 Chardonnay Trockenbeerenauslese Nouvelle Vague

RATING: 96 points

The oak, vanilla, toast, acacia blossom, and crème brûlée–scented 1998 #9 Chardonnay Trockenbeerenauslese Nouvelle Vague is an intensely sweet, fat, and candied wine. Full-bodied and powerful, this is a dense (yet harmonious) offering jam-packed with sugar-coated oranges, candied apples, and honey. Its seemingly unending finish reveals additional layers of luxurious jellied fruits. Drink this exceptional wine over the next 20–25 years.

1998 #13 Chardonnay Trockenbeerenauslese Nouvelle Vague

RATING: 98 points

The 1998 #13 Chardonnay Trockenbeerenauslese Nouvelle Vague is Kracher's most concentrated wine from this vintage. Cedar, spices, apricots, and overripe peaches are displayed by this full-bodied, muscular offering. It is hugely dense, almost syrupy, with loads of jammy and jellied fruits in its round, sexy personality. This Rubenesque wine has untold quantities of fruit (mostly apricots), spices, and botrytis in its expressive, seamless flavor profile. This harmonious, muscular, and graceful wine will retain its fruit for at least another 12 years, and will potentially age longer than anyone reading this book.

1996 #8 Chardonnay Trockenbeerenauslese Nouvelle Vague

RATING: 95 points

Kracher produced only 400 bottles of this wine, which contains 168 grams of residual sugar, 11.8% alcohol, and 9.6 grams of acidity. Coconut-laced overripe apricots and peaches are intermingled with botrytis scents in this fabulous TBA. It is Sauternes-like in its flavor profile yet fresher and livelier. This refined wine has superb delineation, breadth, and a creamy texture packed with toasty yellow fruits. Medium to full–bodied and impeccably focused, its finish reveals candied lemon flavors that seemingly last forever. Drink it between now and 2015.

1995 #13 Chardonnay Trockenbeerenauslese Nouvelle Vague

RATING: 96 points

This 800-bottle *cuvée* contains 250 grams of residual sugar, 8.5% alcohol, and 11 grams of acidity. Fermented and aged in new oak barrels, it was bottled after 16 months. It is the finest late harvest Chardonnay I have ever tasted. This masterpiece has pink grapefruit, white pepper, smoky scents, and a divine personality filled with baked papaya, mango, apricots, and peaches so thick it almost requires a knife and fork. Awesome balancing acidity and length! Drink it between now and 2030+.

SCHEUREBE TROCKENBEERENAUSLESE

2000 #5 Scheurebe Trockenbeerenauslese Zwischen den Seen

RATING: 96 points

The massive, full-bodied 2000 #5 Scheurebe Trockenbeerenauslese Zwischen den Seen (11.5% alcohol, 212.8 grams residual sugar/liter, and 6.5 grams/liter total acidity) bursts from the glass with peppery yellow fruit and spicy and botrytis aromas. Armed with the density and depth of 10W40 motor oil, it is a syrupy, jammy, viscous effort. Loads of jammy apricots, cherries, and peaches can be discerned in its spice-laden personality. Anticipated maturity: now–2030.

2000 #9 Scheurebe Trockenbeerenauslese Zwischen den Seen

RATING: 97 points

Sweet oak, botrytis, and jellied apricots emanate from the glass of the 2000 #9 Scheurebe Trockenbeerenauslese Zwischen den Seen. A diabetic's nightmare (6.5% alcohol, 347.8 grams residual sugar/liter, and 7.6 grams/liter total acidity), this full-bodied wine slathers itself onto the palate, revealing syrupy layers of jellied peaches and spiced dried apricots. It has unbelievable power, density, and length. Anticipated maturity: now–2045.

1999 #5 Scheurebe Trockenbeerenauslese Zwischen den Seen

RATING: 95 points

The spicy 1999 #5 Scheurebe Trockenbeerenauslese Zwischen den Seen offers aromatics reminiscent of juniper berries, cloves, and overripe peaches. This well-delineated yet jellied wine is rich, highly concentrated, dense, and prodigiously long in finish. Anticipated maturity: now–2030.

1999 #9 Scheurebe Trockenbeerenauslese Zwischen den Seen

RATING: 98 points

Flowers, spices, and apricots are found in the nose of the 1999 #9 Scheurebe Trockenbeerenauslese Zwischen den Seen. Lovers of apricot jam will adore this hyper-concentrated, jellied offering. Its immense size and depth is gorgeously buttressed by zesty acidity. This wine is as thick as the United States government's annual budget proposal. Drink it over the next 35+ years.

1998 #3 Scheurebe Trockenbeerenauslese Zwischen den Seen

RATING: 95 points

The orange/yellow-colored 1998 #3 Scheurebe Trockenbeerenauslese Zwischen den Seen explodes from the glass with spices, lychee nuts, roses, and candied white raisins. It is gorgeously focused, fresh, medium-bodied, and packed with smoky minerals as well as loads of jammy yellow fruits. This exceptionally long wine reveals a firm tannic backbone, a rarity for a white wine but typical of its varietal. It has an immensely impressive combination of power, concentration, balance, and elegance. Anticipated maturity: now–2020+.

1998 #12 Scheurebe Trockenbeerenauslese Zwischen den Seen

RATING: 93 points

The gold-colored 1998 #12 Scheurebe Trockenbeerenauslese Zwischen den Seen has a chemical-scented nose that also displays white pepper and graham cracker aromas. Medium to full–bodied and lush, this wine offers copious layers of jellied yellow fruits in its fat, yet wonderfully fresh personality. As its nose sheds its chemical notes with air, this wine offers a compote-like character that reveals caramel and butterscotch flavors. Readers who wish to drink this wine while it displays fruit should consume it over the next two to five years. Those who prefer aged, dark-colored, heavily botrytised wines dominated by burnt sugar flavors can drink it between 2007 and 2030+.

1996 #3 Scheurebe Trockenbeerenauslese Zwischen den Seen

RATING: 92 points

This 5,400-bottle *cuvée* contains 176 grams of residual sugar, 9.6% alcohol, and 11.6 grams of acidity. Smoky tropical fruits laced with botrytis are found in this TBA's aromatics. The wine has superb focus and an oily texture, as well as an expressive flavor profile crammed with intricate layers of sweet peaches, apricots, raspberries, and lemon. Drink it over the next 15 years.

1995 #3 Scheurebe Trockenbeerenauslese Zwischen den Seen

RATING: 94 points

There are 2,600 bottles of this 1995, which possesses 174 grams of residual sugar, 12% alcohol, and 9 grams of acidity. Fermented in used casks, it is then racked into stainless steel and bottled after 10 months. Mango, kiwi, and pink grapefruit aromas are followed by oily layers of lychee nut, minerals, steel, and crisp white grapes in a beguiling, superbly balanced, and elegant character. Anticipated maturity: now–2018+.

1995 #4 Scheurebe Trockenbeerenauslese Zwischen den Seen

RATING: 96 points

This 1,000-bottle offering includes 197 grams of residual sugar, 11.5% alcohol, and 10.5 grams of acidity. Fermented and aged in used casks, it is bottled after 10 months. Lychee, candied pink grapefruit, kiwi, and spicy smoke scents and a massive, powerful core of hugely rich floral, caramel-covered apricots, flowers, candied apples, and fresh herbs characterize this wine. Drink it between now and Armageddon (or when the cork disintegrates, whichever comes first).

1995 #6 Scheurebe Trockenbeerenauslese Zwischen den Seen

RATING: 94–96 points

There are 130 grams of residual sugar, 11% alcohol, and 9.5 grams of acidity (2,000 bottles produced) in the 1995, fermented and aged in used casks and bottled after 18 months. (This note is from a barrel sample, as the bottled sample I tasted was corked.) Candied pink grapefruit, white pepper, and spicy red berry (raspberries, cherries, and strawberries) scents are found in the oily, mango, papaya, banana, apricot, and sweet herbal tea–flavored wine. Drink it between now and 2020+.

1995 #14 Scheurebe Trockenbeerenauslese Zwischen den Seen

RATING: 96 points

With 310 grams of residual sugar, 7% alcohol, and 12 grams of acidity, this 2,300-bottle *cuvée* is fermented and aged in used casks and bottled after 18 months. Smoke, spice, thyme, rosemary, roasted herbs, candied apples, white pepper, and red currant aromas are followed by a massive silky core of sweet herbal teas, cherries, minerals, and spicy red fruits. (I find that highly concentrated white wines often exhibit red fruit aromas and flavors when they are young.) Unbelievably unctuous yet exquisitely refined due to its perfectly balanced acidity, this wine will still be drinking spectacularly when the theory behind *The Planet of the Apes* is unraveled.

WELSCHRIESLING TROCKENBEERENAUSLESE NOUVELLE VAGUE

1999 #10 Welschriesling Trockenbeerenauslese Nouvelle Vague

RATING: 98 points

The 1999 #10 Welschriesling Trockenbeerenauslese Nouvelle Vague, a wine Alois Kracher believes is his most concentrated of the 1999 vintage, offers white pepper–laced yellow fruits in its aromatics. Smoke, jellied peaches, jammy apricots, and loads of spices can be found in this viscous offering's character. It is immensely rich, almost painfully so, and is already revealing traces of caramel flavors that will, in time, significantly mark its character. It can be consumed over the next 35+ years. Bravo!

ZWISCHEN DEN SEEN

2000

WEINLAUBENHOF

KRACHER

BURGENLAND

WELSCHRIESLING
TROCKENBEEREN
AUSLESE

NUMMER 8

Süß · alc. 7,5% vol

e 375 ML

Abfüller
Prädikatswein "L"-E 7281/02
Kracher · A-7142 Illmitz

ÖSTERREICH · NEUSIEDLERSEE

WELSCHRIESLING TROCKENBEERENAUSLESE ZWISCHEN DEN SEEN

2000 #4 Welschriesling Trockenbeerenauslese Zwischen den Seen

RATING: 95 points

The 2000 #4 Welschriesling Trockenbeerenauslese Zwischen den Seen (11% alcohol, 212.4 grams residual sugar/liter, and 7.3 grams/liter total acidity) reveals smoky, botrytised peaches and spices in its aromatic profile. A syrupy, mango and passion fruit–flavored effort, it is an assertive, medium to full–bodied wine with a lively acid streak to give an appealingly zesty character. Anticipated maturity: now–2030.

2000 #8 Welschriesling Trockenbeerenauslese Zwischen den Seen

RATING: 98 points

The 2000 #8 Welschriesling Trockenbeerenauslese Zwischen den Seen (7.5% alcohol, 314.2 grams residual sugar/liter, and 7.2 grams/liter total acidity) displays scents of smoky apricots, mangoes, botrytis-laden papayas, and passion fruit. White pepper, jammy peaches, pears, assorted exotic fruits, and a myriad of spices are found in its viscous, syrup-like core. Immensely complex, dense, and outrageously concentrated, its interminable flavor profile refuses to relinquish its grasp on the palate. Drink it over the next 35–45+ years.

2000 #10 Welschriesling Trockenbeerenauslese Zwischen den Seen

RATING: 99 points

Given the gelatinous nature and increasing power of the previous wines, readers may understand the trepidation with which I approached the 2000 #10 Welschriesling Trockenbeerenauslese Zwischen den Seen (5.5% alcohol, 399.6 grams residual sugar/liter, and 7.8 grams/liter total acidity), after seeing it ooze its way from the bottle to my glass. Bronze-colored and molasses-scented, this is a wine of awesome depth, density, and richness. Akin to drinking honey, although no honey has ever been this complex, its super-thick, voluminous personality bastes the palate with oily apricot and canned-peach flavors. A piercing underlying acidity can be discerned through the viscous morass of fruit. Given the fact that acidity and sugar are preservatives, this wine will undoubtedly outlast its cork, and may outlive its bottle!

1998 #4 Welschriesling Trockenbeerenauslese Nouvelle Vague

RATING: 95 points

The 1998 #4 Welschriesling Trockenbeerenauslese Nouvelle Vague's color reveals hints of gold. This medium to full–bodied wine offers candied white raisin and caramel aromas. It is fat, thick, and dense on the palate. Loads of jellied fruits, spices, botrytis flavors, and overripe apricots conquer the taster's palate (my notes say "Wow! Rolling thunder!") and refuse to relinquish their grip for what seems like minutes. Remarkably, given this wine's intensity and thickness, it appears fresh, well balanced, and precise. Drink it over the next 20+ years.

1999 #8 Welschriesling Trockenbeerenauslese Zwischen den Seen

RATING: 96 points

The white pepper and apricot–scented 1999 #8 Welschriesling Trockenbeerenauslese Zwischen den Seen is a rich, concentrated behemoth. Pepper-laced white and yellow fruits can be found in this oily wine's character. It is powerful and deep, and possesses an exceedingly long finish. Anticipated maturity: now–2035+.

1998 #6 Welschriesling Trockenbeerenauslese Zwischen den Seen

RATING: 92 points

The 1998 #6 Welschriesling Trockenbeerenauslese Zwischen den Seen has a musty nose from its massive levels of botrytis (it wasn't corked) and also reveals loads of sweet white and yellow fruits. It is crammed with overripe fruit flavors, as well as the distinctive effects of spicy botrytis. This superbly focused wine has bountiful levels of acidity to cope with its lush, opulently thick character. Drink this refined, liquid botrytis over the next 15+ years.

1998 #11 Welschriesling Trockenbeerenauslese Zwischen den Seen

RATING: 96 points

The 1998 #11 Welschriesling Trockenbeerenauslese Zwischen den Seen has a yellow color with golden hues. It exhibits white peach, apricot, smoke, botrytis, and freshly cracked white-pepper aromas. Medium to full–bodied and elegant, this wine is stuffed with candied kumquats, jellied peaches, spices, and fresh apricots. It has an exceptional combination of refinement, power, and concentration. This decadently textured wine is intense, pure, and immensely long. Anticipated maturity: now–2030+.

1997 #7 Welschriesling Trockenbeerenauslese Zwischen den Seen

RATING: 94 points

The thick, almost impenetrable nose of the 1997 #7 Welschriesling Trockenbeerenauslese Zwischen den Seen offers spicy red and white fruit flavors. On the palate, this extraordinarily concentrated, thick, viscous, decadent, and backward wine is densely packed with untold quantities of red, yellow, and white fruits. It coats the palate with layers of honey-dripping fruit flavors that linger for two minutes or more. Drink this gorgeous, sweet wine over the next seven-plus years.

1996 #9 Welschriesling Trockenbeerenauslese Zwischen den Seen

RATING: 97 points

This 700-bottle *cuvée* possesses 231 grams of residual sugar, 9.8% alcohol, and 8.5 grams of acidity. The mind-boggling TBA #9 exhibits mouth-watering aromas of bergamots (a pear-shaped citrus fruit that is the primary flavoring in Earl Grey tea), raspberries, cherries, currants, and botrytis. Its satin-textured, medium to full–bodied character is super-concentrated, highly complex, and powerful. Layers of red fruits, mangoes, pineapples, papayas, and pink grapefruits can be found in its expressive personality and awesomely long finish. This magnificent wine can be drunk now or over the next 20 years.

1995 #1 Welschriesling Trockenbeerenauslese Zwischen den Seen

RATING: 93 points

There are 5,000 bottles of this wine, which possesses 195 grams of residual sugar per liter, 11% alcohol, and 8.5 grams acidity per liter. It is fermented in used casks and then racked into stainless steel to preserve the wine's freshness and bottled after 10 months. Flower and spice aromas are found in this sweet, earthy, apricot-jammed, and well-balanced nectar. It will be at its best between now and 2015+.

1995 #2 Welschriesling Trockenbeerenauslese Zwischen den Seen

RATING: 95 points

Fermented and aged in used casks and bottled after 10 months, this 1995 possesses 236 grams of residual sugar, 8.5% alcohol, and 10 grams of acidity. There are approximately 900 bottles. Aromatically revealing candied pineapples, this wine's super-thick core is packed with mineral, herbal, spicy, earthy, metallic, floral, apricot, peach, apple compote, and red berry flavors. Its striking, highly focused acidity perfectly balances the unctuous sweetness. A 40+-second finish! Drink it between now and 2020+.

WEINGUT JOSEF NIGL

WINES:

Riesling Privat

Riesling Senftenberger Hochäcker

OWNER: Martin Nigl

ADDRESS: Priel 8, A-3541 Senftenberg, Austria

TELEPHONE: 43 2719 2609

TELEFAX: 43 2719 2609 4

E-MAIL: info@weingutnigl.at

WEBSITE: www.weingutnigl.at

CONTACT: Martin Nigl

VISITING POLICY: Monday through Saturday, 8 A.M.–noon and 1–5 P.M.

VINEYARDS

SURFACE AREA: 63 acres

GRAPE VARIETALS: 40% Grüner Veltliner, 40% Riesling, the rest Sauvignon Blanc, Gelber Muskateller, Chardonnay, and Blauer Zweigelt

AVERAGE AGE OF THE VINES: 10–30 years

DENSITY OF PLANTATION: 6,000 vines per hectare

AVERAGE YIELDS: Grüner Veltliner: 40–50 hectoliters per hectare; Riesling: 30–40 hectoliters per hectare

WINEMAKING AND UPBRINGING

The Nigl family vinifies wine according to single vineyard and variety. Through appropriate yield reduction, neither chaptalization nor deacidification is necessary. The Nigl winery primarily uses steel tanks for vinification and maturing of its wines. Bottling time is spring (April and May).

ANNUAL PRODUCTION

Grüner Veltliner Kremser Freiheit: 15,000 bottles

Riesling Senftenberger Hochäcker: 6,000 bottles

Riesling Privat: 6,000 bottles

Grüner Veltliner Alte Reben: 3,200 bottles

Grüner Veltliner Privat: 4,800 bottles

AVERAGE PRICE (VARIABLE DEPENDING ON VINTAGE): $20–100

GREAT RECENT VINTAGES

2000, 1997

Joseph Nigl and his son Martin dared to devote their resources exclusively to winemaking less than two decades ago, making the speed of their ascent into the top class of Austrian winemakers even more astounding. Their vineyards are located both on the hillside terraces of the Kremstal and adjacent to a river valley, which experiences dramatic changes between day and night temperatures and encourages fog, all beneficial to ripening. These climatic factors also add spiciness, fruit, and elegance to the wines, according to Martin Nigl. Other estate vineyards are spread in several different locations, including parcels within the city of Krems. The drier climate, its predominantly loess soil, and other factors distinguish the wines of Krems from those of Senftenberg. Fermentation starts with natural yeast. From the substantial selection of Veltliner, the elegant "Piri" from Senftenberg and the noble, rich, highly extracted "Alte Reben" (old vines) are worth mentioning. The Riesling from the Hochäcker vineyard has been a favorite of most Austrian wine connoisseurs over the years. The more restrained "Piri" shows more fruit and elegance. Still others prefer the almost opulent Riesling of Kremsleiten. The best lots of these are labeled Privat and are outrageously delicious.

RIESLING KREMSER KREMSLEITEN

2000 Riesling Kremser Kremsleiten

RATING: 92 points

The outstanding 2000 Riesling Kremser Kremsleiten exhibits honeyed minerals in its nose. The wine is medium-bodied and bright. This focused, fruit-dominated offering displays well-extracted lemon, gravel, pear, and stone flavors. This fresh yet thick and rich wine should be drunk over the next seven years.

RIESLING KREMSLEITEN PIRI

2001 Riesling Kremsleiten Piri

RATING: 92 points

Smoky, honeyed minerals make up the aromatics of the 2001 Riesling Kremsleiten Piri. Its penetrating herbal tea, mineral, and apple flavors explode on the palate. The wine is light to medium–bodied and is particularly well balanced, extroverted, crammed with fruit, and powerful. Anticipated maturity: now–2012.

RIESLING PRIVAT

2001 Riesling Privat

RATING: 94 points

Rocks and citrus fruits burst from the glass of the 2001 Riesling Privat. This superb wine has a hugely concentrated, medium-bodied character jam-packed with crisp apples, candied lemons, and honeyed stones. This massively expressive offering is fresh and fruit dominated, and possesses an exceptionally long finish. Anticipated maturity: now–2016.

2000 Riesling Privat

RATING: 93 points

Aromatically, the 2000 Riesling Privat is dominated by sun-drenched minerals. On the palate, this superb offering exhibits the richness and depth common in wines from this warm, ripe year, yet it also displays a level of elegance and delineation that is stunning. The wine is highly detailed, with huge levels of dry extract and expressive pear, apple, mineral, and chalk flavors. Anticipated maturity: now–2015+.

1997 Riesling Privat

RATING: 94 points

The fennel-scented 1997 Riesling Privat has a powerful, layered personality filled with concentrated fruit. Apples, pears, and a brawny fennel/mint component can be found in its medium-bodied personality. This highly expressive, yet refined, intensely flavored wine has an admirably long, supple finish. Drink it over the next nine years.

RIESLING SENFTENBERGER HOCHÄCKER

2001 Riesling Senftenberger Hochäcker

RATING: 92 points

The 2001 Riesling Senftenberger Hochäcker sports a nose of minerals and stones. It is a wine of intense purity, power, and grace. The wine is medium-bodied, satin-textured, and expansive. Candied lemons, gravel, and smoky bacon can be found in its complex flavor profile as well as throughout its long, delineated finish. Anticipated maturity: now–2014.

2000 Riesling Senftenberger Hochäcker

RATING: 93 points

Sweet herbal teas can be discerned in the aromatics of the 2000 Riesling Senftenberger Hochäcker. Citrus fruits, stones, gravel, and powerfully concentrated underlying minerals make up this medium-bodied wine's personality. It is rich and satin-textured, and reveals an exceptionally long, pure finish. Anticipated maturity: now–2015.

WINES:

Riesling F. X. Unendlich

Grüner Veltliner Dürnsteiner Kellerberg

Riesling Smaragd Steinertal

Grüner Veltliner Smaragd M

OWNERS: Franz Xaver Pichler and Lucas Pichler

ADDRESS: Oberloiben 27, 3601 Dürnstein, Austria

TELEPHONE: 43 2732 85375

TELEFAX: 43 2732 85375 11

E-MAIL: winery@fx-pichler.at

WEBSITE: www.fx-pichler.at

CONTACT: Franz Xaver Pichler or Lucas Pichler

VISITING POLICY: By appointment

VINEYARDS

SURFACE AREA: 30 acres

GRAPE VARIETALS: 50% Grüner Veltliner, 47% Riesling, 3% Sauvignon Blanc

AVERAGE AGE OF THE VINES: 40 years

DENSITY OF PLANTATION: Flat—4,000 vines per hectare; terraces—6,000 vines per hectare

AVERAGE YIELDS: Flat—4,500 liters per hectare; terraces—4,000 liters per hectare

WINEMAKING AND UPBRINGING

This very individual winemaking is the product of a totally obsessed, erudite man. The wines are fermented with natural yeast from very low yields (there is vigorous crop-thinning throughout the year) and aged in old oak casks for four to six months (3,000 to 5,000 liters in size) after they have fermented for up to three weeks in temperature-controlled stainless-steel tanks. Pichler makes a point of saying there is no fining, no concentration of the must, and no chaptalization, as these wines are, in his words, "the essence of natural winemaking."

ANNUAL PRODUCTION

Grüner Veltliner "Frauenweingarten" Federspiel: 8,000 bottles

Grüner Veltliner "Klostersatz" Federspiel: 6,000 bottles

Grüner Veltliner "Von den Terrassen" Smaragd: 5,000 bottles

Grüner Veltliner "Loibnerberg" Smaragd: 6,000 bottles

Grüner Veltliner "Dürnsteiner Kellerberg" Smaragd: 6,000 bottles

Grüner Veltliner "M" (Monumental) Smaragd: 4,000 bottles

Riesling "Von den Terrassen" Smaragd: 6,000 bottles

Riesling "Steinertal" Smaragd: 7,000 bottles

Riesling "Loibnerberg" Smaragd: 8,000 bottles

F. X. Pichler and his son Lucas

Riesling "Dürnsteiner Kellerberg" Smaragd: 7,000 bottles
Riesling "M" (Monumental) Smaragd: 3,000 bottles
Riesling "Unendlich": 3,000 bottles
Sauvignon Blanc Smaragd: 3,000 bottles
AVERAGE PRICE (VARIABLE DEPENDING ON VINTAGE): $20–100

GREAT RECENT VINTAGES

2002, 2001, 1999, 1997, 1995, 1994, 1993, 1992, 1990, 1986, 1985, 1983, 1979, 1977, 1973

A lover of opera, part-time painter, and connoisseur of the world's finest art and sculpture, Franz Xaver Pichler, known to his collective peers as F. X., is as interesting as his wines. When F. X. and his talented, gregarious son Lucas are asked what they do differently from their neighbors, their answer is basically the same as every wine producer's in this book: "We work hard in the vineyards, wait longer than most for ripeness before harvesting, make many passes in the vineyards, and then we do *nothing*. We allow the wines to make themselves."

F. X. Pichler is the Romanée-Conti or Château Latour of Austria. There are many great producers in the Wachau, but F. X. Pichler is the name and reference point who everyone agrees simply does the best regardless of which of his wonderful vineyards the Riesling or Grüner Veltliner fruit emerges from—Loibnerberg, Kellerberg, or Steinertal. He is not bashful about the quality, affixing the letter "M" to some of his *cuvées,* for "monumental." While Pichler's wines are held in the highest esteem by the Austrian wine-drinking public, I have always had the impression that if they were made in France, his reputation would be as great as that of any estate in that hallowed country of winedom. Several 1990s drunk at the beginning of 2004 were still in extraordinary condition, and I have no doubt these wines can last for two decades or more in the top vintages.

F. X. Pichler is the fifth generation of this family-owned winery, and his wines are indeed the stuff of legend.

GRÜNER VELTLINER SMARAGD DÜRNSTEINER KELLERBERG

2000 Grüner Veltliner Smaragd Dürnsteiner Kellerberg

RATING: 92 points

The 2000 Grüner Veltliner Smaragd Dürnsteiner Kellerberg hails from a southeast-facing vineyard that typically enjoys cool evenings. Its mineral-dominated aromas lead to a lush, immensely rich character armed with a nugget of exotic fruits. This wine is so densely packed that it will require cellaring for its papaya, mango, and spiced pear flavors to blossom. Anticipated maturity: 2006–2014.

1999 Grüner Veltliner Smaragd Dürnsteiner Kellerberg

RATING: 91 points

The 1999 Grüner Veltliner Smaragd Dürnsteiner Kellerberg offers intense smoky mineral aromas as well as a light to medium–bodied character filled with gravel and apricots. While it lacks the tropical influence and hedonistic appeal of the 2000, this is an outstanding wine of depth, purity, and power. Anticipated maturity: now–2012.

1995 Grüner Veltliner Smaragd Dürnsteiner Kellerberg

RATING: 92 points

The yellow/gold-colored 1995 Grüner Veltliner Smaragd Dürnsteiner Kellerberg exhibits aromas of straw, stones, and peppery smoke. Tobacco, quinine, fennel, bright citrus fruits, ripe apricots, and a myriad of spices can be found in this boisterous wine's flavor profile as well as in its prodigious finish. Drink it between now and 2010–2011.

GRÜNER VELTLINER SMARAGD M

1999 Grüner Veltliner Smaragd M

RATING: 93 points

The gorgeous mineral and chamomile nose of the 1999 Grüner Veltliner Smaragd M is followed by a massive wine of intensity and delineation. Liquid minerals, crisp apples, and spices are found in this light to medium–bodied, rich, highly focused offering as well as throughout its immensely long finish. Drink it between now and 2012.

1997 Grüner Veltliner Smaragd M

RATING: 92 points

Fennel liqueur, pear, smoke, and minerals are found in the aromatics and flavors of the 1997 Grüner Veltliner Smaragd M. This light- to medium-bodied, silky-textured wine has great concentration and depth and enormous dry extract, as well as prodigious balance. Anticipated maturity: now–2009.

RIESLING F. X. UNENDLICH

2000 Riesling F. X. Unendlich

RATING: 97 points

The show-stopping 2000 Riesling F. X. Unendlich, produced from a blend of parcels (92% Loibenberg and 8% Kellerberg), displays perfumed, floral, honeysuckle-infused aromas. This medium to full–bodied wine possesses untold richness, concentration, power, and purity. Its liquid cloud-like texture carries forth waves of complex spiced pear, mineral, candied apple, and anise flavors that linger in its never-ending finish.

A note about the name: In 1991 F. X. Pichler dreamt of making a wine of such concentration and depth that its finish would be unending, and announced that if he were ever able to achieve this goal he'd name it Unendlich, which means "unending" in German. Seven years later he crafted his first Unendlich, the 1998. The 2000 is the second produced. Anticipated maturity: now–2020+.

1998 Riesling F. X. Unendlich

RATING: 94 points

The yellow-colored 1998 Riesling F. X. Unendlich offers smoky, botrytised aromas of stones and spices. This bone-dry wine has amazing balance and a humongous personality, as well as wave after wave of raspberry, white peach, pear, and papaya, whose botrytised flavors last throughout its interminable finish. Drink this concentrated behemoth now through 2011.

RIESLING SMARAGD DÜRNSTEINER KELLERBERG

2000 Riesling Smaragd Dürnsteiner Kellerberg

RATING: 92 points

Sweetened chamomile tea can be found in the aromas of the 2000 Riesling Smaragd Dürnsteiner Kellerberg. It is a dry, medium-bodied wine of outstanding richness that coats the taster's palate with lush waves of honeyed minerals, caramelized stones, and quince, whose flavors linger throughout its huge length. Anticipated maturity: now–2016.

1999 Riesling Smaragd Dürnsteiner Kellerberg

RATING: 92 points

The 1999 Riesling Smaragd Dürnsteiner Kellerberg displays spices, pears, and apples in its nose. This medium-bodied and lush wine is softly textured with an almost 2000-like richness, ripeness, and breadth. Layers of apples, white peaches, and minerals can be found in its long, supple finish. Drink it over the next nine years.

1998 Riesling Smaragd Dürnsteiner Kellerberg

RATING: 91 points

The spiced mineral–scented 1998 Riesling Smaragd Dürnsteiner Kellerberg reveals fewer effects of botrytis than other 1998s I've tasted. It is medium-bodied with a steely character and fresh mineral and spice flavors. Drink it over the next two to three years.

1997 Riesling Smaragd Dürnsteiner Kellerberg

RATING: 96 points

The demure, quartz-like aromas of the 1997 Riesling Smaragd Dürnsteiner Kellerberg lead to its magnificently complex and profound personality. Fennel, artichoke, raspberry, citrus, and currant flavors can be discerned in its fresh, medium-bodied character. This rich, satin-textured wine has admirable purity and an almost "unendlich" finish. Anticipated maturity: now–2018. Bravo!

1995 Riesling Smaragd Dürnsteiner Kellerberg

RATING: 94 points

The 1995 Riesling Smaragd Dürnsteiner Kellerberg offers a nose of citrus fruits, mint, and sweetened herbal teas. Bright limes, spicy fennel bulbs, and apricots can be found in its laser-like character. This light to medium–bodied effort is an almost linear, extremely long wine of huge concentration that requires cellaring. Anticipated maturity: now–2020.

1992 Riesling Smaragd Dürnsteiner Kellerberg

RATING: 93 points

F. X. Pichler's shockingly good 1992 Riesling Smaragd Dürnsteiner Kellerberg proves that great winemakers can overcome poor vintages. Its intense white flower and mineral aromas ("great nose!" indicate my notes) lead to a complex, powerful, opulent core of lush fruit. Honeysuckle-infused fennel is found throughout its creamy-textured character as well as in its long, pure finish. Drink this "off-vintage" beauty over the next four years.

WINES:

Riesling Smaragd Achleiten

Riesling Smaragd Klaus

Grüner Veltliner Smaragd Weissenkirchen Achleiten

Riesling Smaragd Wachstum Bodenstein

OWNERS: Ilse and Toni Bodenstein

ADDRESS: A-3610 Weissenkirchen 48, Austria

TELEPHONE: 43 2715 2248

TELEFAX: 43 2715 2532

E-MAIL: prager@weissenkirchen.at

WEBSITE: www.weingutprager.at

CONTACT: Ilse or Toni Bodenstein

VISITING POLICY: Open Monday through Saturday

VINEYARDS

SURFACE AREA: 35 acres

GRAPE VARIETALS: 75% Riesling and 25% Grüner Veltliner

AVERAGE AGE OF THE VINES:

Riesling—30 years (oldest: Klaus—47 years; Achleiten—
45 years)

Grüner Veltliner—35 years (oldest: Zwerithaler—55 years;
Achleiten—46 years)

DENSITY OF PLANTATION: 4,500–7,000 per hectare

AVERAGE YIELDS: Grüner Veltliner Smaragd—less than 6,000
kilograms per hectare; Riesling Smaragd—less than
5,000 kilograms per hectare

WINEMAKING AND UPBRINGING

The harvest usually occurs in mid-October and lasts through
the end of November. The grapes are always hand-harvested
with different passes, and only the ripest and healthiest make
it to the fermenting vats.

The grapes are destemmed and undergo fermentation
for no more than several hours to extract the aromatic sub-
stances from the skins. Chaptalization is never performed,
and after the grapes are pressed, the unfiltered must is fermented in steel tanks, primarily with indigenous yeasts. All
the Smaragd wines are totally dry. Fermentation usually occurs in three to four weeks, and there is no malolactic fermentation in order to preserve the transparency and minerality of
the wines. After two months of aging on the lees and fine
yeast, wines are racked, with the Grüner Veltliners stored in
large wooden *foudres* and the Rieslings in steel tanks. The
Grüner Veltliners spend approximately four months in the
foudres prior to bottling and the Rieslings five to six months.

ANNUAL PRODUCTION

Grüner Veltliner:

Federspiel, Hinter der Burg: 10,000 bottles

Smaragd, Weitenberg: 2,500 bottles

Smaragd, Zwerithaler: 2,500 bottles

Smaragd, Achleiten: 5,000 bottles

Riesling:

Federspiel, Steinriegl: 17,000 bottles

Federspiel, Ritzling: 3,000 bottles

Smaragd, Hollerin: 2,500 bottles

Smaragd, Kaiserberg: 3,000 bottles

Smaragd, Steinriegl: 6,000 bottles

Smaragd, Klaus: 6,500 bottles

Smaragd, Achleiten: 7,500 bottles

Smaragd, Wachstum Bodenstein: 3,500 bottles

AVERAGE PRICE (VARIABLE DEPENDING ON VINTAGE): $25–55

GREAT RECENT VINTAGES

2002, 2000, 1999, 1997, 1993, 1990

Best vintages from Franz Prager: 1979, 1969, 1959, 1953

While many generations of the Prager family have
worked in this historic winery, Ilse Prager Bodenstein and Toni Bodenstein are now responsible for
the estate's wines. Their central philosophy should
come as no surprise to anyone reading this book: "The
wines should reflect their vineyard sites."

The winery, first owned by a monastic order in
1302, was passed on to the Prager family in 1715. Interestingly, a letter that dates from 1715 in the archives of
the Prager family mentions three vineyards, Ritzling,
Hinter der Burg, and Steinriegl, all of which still remain
part of the estate. Franz Prager remains one of the region's viticultural pioneers and is still affectionately referred to as one of the "Wachau mafia" for putting this
region on the world map for high quality. His daughter
Ilse and son-in-law, Toni Bodenstein, who was originally trained as an environmental engineer, took over in
1988. Despite the fact that the estate encompasses 35
acres, the production is small, with just over 90,000
bottles produced in an abundant vintage. Virtually all
of the vineyards here are on extremely steep, terraced,
sloped hillsides and planted with 75% Riesling and
25% Grüner Veltliner.

GRÜNER VELTLINER SMARAGD WEISSENKIRCHEN ACHLEITEN

2000 Grüner Veltliner Smaragd Weissenkirchen Achleiten

RATING: 91 points

The 2000 Grüner Veltliner Smaragd Weissenkirchen Achleiten offers apricot, peach, and tea aromas in its highly expressive nose. This is a medium-bodied, layered, rich, intense, lush offering with powerful peppery apricot flavors. Anticipated maturity: now–2011.

RIESLING SMARAGD ACHLEITEN

2000 Riesling Smaragd Achleiten

RATING: 95 points

The flower and liquid-stone–scented 2000 Riesling Smaragd Achleiten is a feminine, focused, and refined wine. Its pure, laser-like personality is medium-bodied and displays complex waves of candied citrus zests, red currants, and minerals. This immensely long wine should be at its best between now and 2018+.

1999 Riesling Smaragd Weissenkirchen Achleiten

RATING: 92 points

The stone and mineral–scented 1999 Riesling Smaragd Weissenkirchen Achleiten is medium-bodied, powerful, and tightly wound. This citrus, mineral, and white fruit–dominated wine has outstanding intensity and complexity to its persistent personality. Drink it over the next three years.

RIESLING SMARAGD KLAUS

2000 Riesling Smaragd Klaus

RATING: 94 points

The 2000 Riesling Smaragd Klaus boasts complex white peach and apple aromas. This is a big and muscular, powerful, thick wine. Its profound core of apple-laced fruit is fresh, expressive, and velvety-textured. This exceptional, medium to full–bodied wine should be consumed between now and 2015+.

1999 Riesling Smaragd Weissenkirchen Klaus

RATING: 92 points

The 1999 Riesling Smaragd Weissenkirchen Klaus offers mineral, lemon, and pear aromas. Medium-bodied and silky-textured, it has outstanding depth, intensity, and focus. White flowers, gravel, minerals, and quinine (slightly reminiscent of a gin and tonic) can be found throughout its tangy flavor profile as well as in its impressively long finish. Drink it over the course of the next three to five years.

RIESLING SMARAGD WACHSTUM BODENSTEIN

2000 Riesling Smaragd Wachstum Bodenstein

RATING: 91 points

The 2000 Riesling Smaragd Wachstum Bodenstein reveals some yellow in its color (most Wachau wines are quite clear in their youth) as well as sweet herbal tea aromas interspersed with a powerful mineral component. Rich layers of honeyed minerals (this wine is virtually dry) are focused by its bright acidity. It is expressive, well balanced, flavorful, and powerful. Drink it between now and 2012.

1999 Riesling Smaragd Weissenkirchen Wachstum Bodenstein

RATING: 94 points

The superb 1999 Riesling Smaragd Weissenkirchen Wachstum Bodenstein has a nose of citrus fruits, flowers, white pepper, honeysuckle blossoms, and minerals. Medium-bodied and explosive, this powerful, gorgeously detailed, and intense wine coats the taster's palate with deep layers of liquid minerals and white fruits. It has exquisite balance, an expressive yet elegant personality, and a seemingly unending finish. Drink this wine over the course of the next five to seven years.

FRANCE

ALSACE This frontier zone, fought over by Germany and France for centuries, is perhaps the most underrated and underutilized source of great white wines in the world. Not only is it a fairy tale region graced with picturesque medieval villages, this is the site of some of the most extraordinary vineyards in France. Moreover, unlike most French wine regions, Alsace names most of its top wines after the varieties from which they are made. In the case of the greatest varietals, Riesling, Gewurztraminer, and Tokay Pinot Gris, the grape names are printed right on the labels, making them reasonably easy to understand. Some producers go further and vineyard-designate their wines as well, but few producers in Alsace blend across varietals.

Alsace was one of the last of the French wine regions to actually classify its best *terroirs*. Today there are 50 grand crus that can appear on the label in conjunction with the name of a varietal. What's confusing about Alsace wines is that it's virtually impossible to know whether they're dry, off-dry, slightly sweet, or very sweet. The wines

at the very top end of the dessert wine category, called Vendanges Tardives and Sélections de Grains Nobles, are indeed sweet wines, but everything below that, approximately 98% of the production, usually carries no indication, and consumers find out by pulling the cork and trying the wine. Also there are many growers who claim the grand cru system was poorly defined, and that there are many sites that deserve grand cru status but have not yet been recognized. Complicating matters further, there are many traditional producers in Alsace who largely ignore the vineyard-designated system and continue to name their wines with the variety and their personal hierarchy of quality—"Réserve" or "Special Cuvée."

The producers I have chosen to profile use minimal interventionist techniques to create wines of extraordinary ripeness, purity, and concentration that reflect intensely their *terroir*.

WINES:

Riesling Cuvée Sainte-Catherine

Riesling Grand Cru Schlossberg Cuvée Sainte-Catherine

Tokay Pinot Gris Cuvée Sainte-Catherine

Tokay Pinot Gris Cuvée Laurence

Tokay Pinot Gris Altenbourg Cuvée Laurence

Gewurztraminer Cuvée Théo

Gewurztraminer Altenbourg Cuvée Laurence

All the Sélection de Grains Nobles wines and Quintessence Sélection de Grains Nobles wines that are produced

CLASSIFICATION: Domaine Weinbach—Colette Faller et ses Filles

OWNERS: Colette, Catherine, and Laurence Faller

ADDRESS: Clos des Capucins, 25, Route du Vin, 68240 Kaysersberg, France

TELEPHONE: 33 03 89 47 13 21

TELEFAX: 33 03 89 47 38 18

E-MAIL: contact@domaineweinbach.com

WEBSITE: www.domaineweinbach.com

CONTACT: Catherine Faller or Laurence Faller

VISITING POLICY: Monday through Saturday, 9–11:30 A.M. and 2–5 P.M. by appointment; closed on Sundays and holidays

VINEYARDS

SURFACE AREA: 66 acres

GRAPE VARIETALS: 42% Riesling, 27% Gewurztraminer, 13% Tokay Pinot Gris, 6% Pinot Blanc and Auxerrois, 4.5% Sylvaner, 3.5% Muscat Ottonel and Muscat d'Alsace, .5% Chasselas, and 3.5% Pinot Noir

AVERAGE AGE OF THE VINES: 29 years

DENSITY OF PLANTATION: 5,800–6,500 vines per hectare

AVERAGE YIELDS: 40–45 hectoliters per hectare (2002: 40.5 hectoliters per hectare)

WINEMAKING AND UPBRINGING

The foremost concern at Weinbach is the quality of the grapes, and extraordinary attention is paid to their vineyards. All their vineyards have been cultivated organically and, since 1998, 23 acres have been farmed under strict biodynamic methods. The objectives are to keep the vines healthy, yields low, and allow each *terroir* to express itself in the most authentic possible way. In the winery, the philosophy of minimal interference is rigidly followed. Gentle, slow, whole-cluster pressing of the grapes is followed by fermentation in neutral oak *foudres* varying in capacity from 6 to 60 hectoliters, and ranging in age from 40 to over 100 years old. During fermentation, only indigenous yeasts are utilized, for the Fallers believe that these yeasts promote long, slow fermentations that enhance the depth and complexity in the wines as well as the nuances of the wines' places of origin. Their Rieslings are the slowest, often continuing to ferment until the summer following the harvest. Some of their very sweet Sélections de Grains Nobles or Quintessence de Grains Nobles fermentations can take as long as four to five years. The wines are bottled only in keeping with the biodynamic calendar.

ANNUAL PRODUCTION

Sylvaner Réserve: 7,000 bottles

Pinot Blanc Réserve: 11,000 bottles

Muscat Réserve: 5,000 bottles

Pinot Noir Réserve: 6,000 bottles

Riesling Réserve Personnelle: 7,000 bottles

Riesling Cuvée Théo: 8,000 bottles

Riesling Grand Cru Schlossberg: 14,000 bottles

Riesling Cuvée Sainte-Catherine: 12,000 bottles

Riesling Grand Cru Schlossberg Cuvée Sainte-Catherine: 6,000 bottles

Riesling Grand Cru Schlossberg Cuvée Sainte-Catherine "L'Inédit!": 2,000–4,000 bottles

Tokay Pinot Gris Cuvée Sainte-Catherine: 6,000 bottles

Tokay Pinot Gris Cuvée Laurence: 3,500 bottles

Tokay Pinot Gris Altenbourg Cuvée Laurence: 3,000 bottles

Gewurztraminer Réserve Personnelle: 5,500 bottles

Gewurztraminer Cuvée Théo: 6,000 bottles

Gewurztraminer Cuvée Laurence: 5,500 bottles

Gewurztraminer Altenbourg Cuvée Laurence: 5,500 bottles

Gewurztraminer Grand Cru Furstentum Cuvée Laurence: 4,000 bottles

Riesling GC Schlossberg Vendanges Tardives: 1,000 bottles

Riesling GC Schlossberg Sélection de Grains Nobles: 150–500 bottles

Riesling GC Schlossberg Quintessence de Grains Nobles: 150–250 bottles

Tokay Pinot Gris Altenbourg Vendanges Tardives: up to 2,000 bottles

Tokay Pinot Gris Altenbourg Sélection de Grains Nobles: 300–600 bottles

Tokay Pinot Gris Altenbourg Quintessence de Grains Nobles: 150–600 bottles (1995)

Gewurztraminer GC Mambourg Vendanges Tardives or SGN: 800 bottles

Gewurztraminer Altenbourg Vendanges Tardives: 2,000 bottles

Gewurztraminer GC Furstentum Vendanges Tardives: up to
2,500 bottles (1998)

Gewurztraminer Altenbourg Sélection de Grains Nobles:
200–800 bottles

Gewurztraminer GC Furstentum Sélection de Grains Nobles:
300–2,500 bottles (1998)

Gewurztraminer Altenbourg Quintessence de Grains Nobles:
150–250 bottles

(Vendanges Tardives, Sélections, and Quintessences de
Grains Nobles are not produced every year in every
grape variety and *terroir* depending on the potential of
the vintage and on the harvesting choices that are
made.)

AVERAGE PRICE (VARIABLE DEPENDING ON VINTAGE): $20–390

GREAT RECENT VINTAGES

2002, 2001, 2000, 1998, 1994, 1990, 1989, 1983

Domaine Weinbach is an ancient estate established
by the monks of the monastery of Capuchin in
1612. Written documents show that many of the Domaine Weinbach vineyards were originally planted as
early as 890. The Faller brothers acquired the property
in 1898, and it was their son and nephew, Théo, who became a prestigious and prominent figure in Alsace viticulture, and one of the area's strongest advocates of
limiting production, defining *terroirs,* and promoting
quality. After his death, his dynamic wife, Colette (also
one of the finest chefs of Alsace), took over, and when
her daughters, Catherine and Laurence, came of age,
they formed a triumvirate of women who are among
the most talented winemakers in the world. Today, Laurence Faller is the driving force, with her sister and
mother at her side. The jewel of the estate is the Clos des
Capucins, an actual, legitimate "clos" enclosed by four

Colette Faller (middle) with daughters Catherine and Laurence

walls that sits in front of the Fallers' romantically detailed house.

The Cuvée Théo wines, which are among their best, are named after the Faller patriarch, and of course there are now *cuvées* named after both daughters, Laurence and Catherine. Otherwise the nomenclature employed by the Fallers has always been somewhat confusing. The Clos des Capucins is 13+ acres in size, but that name appears on all the bottles. Their other holding is the grand cru vineyard Schlossberg, a steeply terraced south- and southeast-facing slope of primarily alluvial soils rich in clay, sand, and minerals sitting over a bedrock of granite. The vineyard is shared by the two villages of Kaysersberg, which is the home of Domaine Weinbach, and nearby Kientzheim. Laurence Faller has introduced subtle changes since taking control of the vinifications in the early 1990s: there has been a more draconian crop thinning in the vineyards, and a tendency to produce wines that are increasingly drier rather than sweeter. The Fallers also produce wines from two other grand cru vineyards, Furstentum (a south-southeast-facing, very steep slope of pebbly marl planted over limestone as well as sandstone) and Altenbourg (another steep southeast-facing slope with clay and limestone soils with a bit more gypsum intermixed with the primary soil types).

GEWURZTRAMINER ALTENBOURG CUVEE LAURENCE

2001 Gewurztraminer Altenbourg Cuvée Laurence
RATING: 92 points

The gloriously floral nose of the 2001 Gewurztraminer Altenbourg Cuvée Laurence leads to a lush, sensual, spicy personality. This hugely concentrated effort bastes the taster's palate with copious quantities of satin-textured waves of yellow plums, apricots, and spices whose effects linger in its extensive finish. It is an opulent, medium-bodied, flavor-packed Gewurz for drinking over the next six years.

2000 Gewurztraminer Altenbourg Cuvée Laurence
RATING: 95 points

According to Laurence Faller, this highly regarded estate's winemaker, "Unquestionably 2000 must be considered one of the finest vintages of the last decade. It reminds me of 1998 but with more botrytis, yet not too much."

The super-rich, opulent 2000 Gewurztraminer Altenbourg Cuvée Laurence is a more refined yet denser wine than the Cuvée Laurence. Described as "unctuous" by the ever gracious Madame Colette Faller, this domaine's matron, it is thickly textured, medium to full–bodied, balanced, and profound. Its potently spicy, flamboyant personality is crammed with fruit. Marilyn Monroe reincarnated as wine? Anticipated maturity: now–2014.

1999 Gewurztraminer Altenbourg Cuvée Laurence
RATING: 92 points

The white flower, peach, and smoke-scented 1999 Gewurztraminer Altenbourg Cuvée Laurence is a plump, well-focused, medium to full–bodied wine. Roses, spices, white peaches, and honeysuckle characterize its fat, deep personality. Additionally, this wine possesses an admirably long and pure finish. It is not an exotically styled or flavored Gewurztraminer, yet delivers loads of highly nuanced flavors in its rich yet delineated character. Anticipated maturity: now–2012.

1998 Gewurztraminer Altenbourg Cuvée Laurence
RATING: 93 points

A plethora of spices and plump yellow fruits can be discerned in the nose of the 1998 Gewurztraminer Altenbourg Cuvée Laurence. Medium-bodied, velvety-textured, and decadently styled, this thick, honeyed wine is packed with a compote of yellow fruits, cloves, and juniper berries. This extroverted, sexy wine should be consumed between now and 2010.

1994 Gewurztraminer Altenbourg Cuvée Laurence

RATING: 95 points

Domaine Weinbach's 1994 Gewurztraminers are all intense, spicy wines. Knowing that readers have either a love or hate relationship with this varietal, I recommend these Gewurztraminers only to those who are fond of ostentatious, in-your-face styles. The extraordinary 1994 Gewurztraminer Altenbourg Cuvée Laurence is a declassified Sélection de Grains Nobles. The finished alcohol is 16.4%, so this is not a wine to drink with delicately flavored cuisine. There is evidence of botrytis in its huge, honeyed, exotic nose. Massive, rich, and full-bodied, this is an off-dry, potent, blockbuster Gewurztraminer. Unfortunately, only 4,000 bottles were produced.

GEWURZTRAMINER ALTENBOURG QUINTESSENCE DE GRAINS NOBLES

2000 Gewurztraminer Altenbourg Quintessence de Grains Nobles

RATING: 97 points

A spectacular wine, the massive 2000 Gewurztraminer Altenbourg Quintessence de Grains Nobles (190 grams of residual sugar per liter) overflows with spiced pear, lily, rose, potpourri, and apricot aromas. On the palate, this full-bodied blockbuster is sweet, thick, oily-textured, and crammed with spicy candied apples as well as cherries, raspberries, and mangoes. Exceptionally well balanced, its flamboyant personality lasts for almost a minute. Bravo! Anticipated maturity: now–2030.

1999 Gewurztraminer Altenbourg Quintessence de Grains Nobles

RATING: 97 points

The 1999 Gewurztraminer Altenbourg Quintessence de Grains Nobles is a stunning spice and orange zest–scented wine. Medium to full–bodied and luxurious, it is satin-textured and feminine. This extraordinarily rich wine is reminiscent of syrup-drenched white peaches, lychee nuts, roses, and candy, yet it retains an admirably elegant touch. It is a magnificent wine with exceptional concentration and depth as well as a distinctive personality. Anticipated maturity: now–2025.

GEWURZTRAMINER ALTENBOURG VENDANGES TARDIVES

2001 Gewurztraminer Altenbourg Vendanges Tardives

RATING: 91 points

The wonderfully floral nose of the 2001 Gewurztraminer Altenbourg Vendanges Tardives precedes a sensual, seamless, plush personality. This rich yet well-focused, plump effort is loaded with spicy yellow fruits. Drink it between now and 2014.

1999 Gewurztraminer Altenbourg Vendanges Tardives

RATING: 94 points

The 1999 Gewurztraminer Altenbourg Vendanges Tardives explodes from the glass with roses, lychee nuts, and spices. Full-bodied, rich, and opulent, this is a compellingly huge yet elegant offering. Its exuberant personality possesses candied berries, rose water, violets, mangoes, poached pears, and clove notes. Anticipated maturity: now–2014.

GEWURZTRAMINER CUVEE D'OR QUINTESSENCE SELECTION DE GRAINS NOBLES

1994 Gewurztraminer Cuvée d'Or Quintessence Sélection de Grains Nobles

RATING: 98 points

Looking for a wine that is more concentrated than any Sauternes or sweet wine from France's Loire Valley? Check out the 1994 Gewurztraminer Cuvée d'Or Quintessence S.G.N. This wine offers mind-blowing extract, and an unctuous, super-concentrated, sweet style that is beautifully buttressed by zesty acidity. This remarkably pure, incredibly intense wine must be tasted to be believed. Wines such as this have seemingly infinite longevity (another 40+ years is possible). While the price may seem outrageously high, keep in mind that a half bottle will easily serve 12–16 people.

GEWURZTRAMINER CUVEE THEO

2000 Gewurztraminer Cuvée Théo

RATING: 90 points

The floral, spiced 2000 Gewurztraminer Cuvée Théo is light to medium–bodied, satin-textured, and feminine. Its rich, lively character offers loads of beautifully detailed flower-infused pears. Drink this delightful, smile-inducing wine through 2009.

1999 Gewurztraminer Cuvée Théo

RATING: 90 points

The lychee and rose–scented 1999 Gewurztraminer Cuvée Théo is a rich, expansive, medium-bodied offering. At this stage, this supple, lush, and fruit-packed (mostly white peaches and apricots) wine tastes more like a Pinot Gris than a Gewurztraminer. However, hints of mango and other exotic fruits come to the fore in its sumptuously textured finish. Drink it between now and 2007.

1994 Gewurztraminer Cuvée Théo

RATING: 94 points

I am a perennial buyer of a case of Domaine Weinbach's Gewurztraminer Cuvée Théo. (I still have two bottles of the glorious 1989, which remained a remarkably young, vibrant wine in 1996.) The 1994 (500 cases) displays a light gold color that appears more mature than the wine's age would suggest. An intense nose of white chocolate, pepper, lychee nuts, and rose petals is followed by a dense, smoky, oily wine with exceptional viscosity and flavor extraction. It is a full-throttle, decadent Gewurztraminer with a bold personality. It would be wonderful with a great Muenster cheese (one of my all-time favorite wine/cheese combinations), foie gras, or a hearty *choucroute garni* (an Alsatian sausage and sauerkraut, stick-to-your-ribs dish). Domaine Weinbach's 1994 Gewurztraminers are all intense, spicy wines. Anticipated maturity: now–2015.

GEWURZTRAMINER FURSTENTUM CUVEE LAURENCE

1999 Gewurztraminer Furstentum Cuvée Laurence

RATING: 92 points

Candied and jammy white peaches burst from the glass of the 1999 Gewurztraminer Furstentum Cuvée Laurence. This full-bodied, opulent, and lush wine is hugely rich and possesses impressive depth. Layers of sweet white fruits, spices, and mango are intermingled with hints of red berries throughout its sultry character and its exceptionally long, pure finish. This is a boisterous, full-flavored Gewurztraminer for drinking until 2011–2013.

GEWURZTRAMINER FURSTENTUM QUINTESSENCE DE GRAINS NOBLES

2001 Gewurztraminer Furstentum Quintessence de Grains Nobles

RATING: 100 points

A wine of extraordinary complexity, depth, and richness, the 2001 Gewurztraminer Furstentum Quintessence de Grains Nobles is liquid perfection. Its peppery, floral nose reveals lychee, rose, cherry, mango, and smoky botrytis scents. On the palate, poached/spiced pears, caramelized apples, candied citrus fruits, and a myriad of spices vie for the taster's attention. Medium to full–bodied, magnificently well focused, silky-textured, and sultry, this wine is sure to make your toes curl! Drink it between 2006 and 2020+. Wow!

RIESLING CUVEE SAINTE-CATHERINE

2001 Riesling Cuvée Ste.-Catherine

RATING: 93 points

From the estate's lowest-elevation parcel in the same vineyard, the spiced pear and lily–scented 2001 Riesling Cuvée Ste.-Catherine offers a powerful core of pears laced with pebbles and white pepper. Medium-bodied, rich, and concentrated, this wine boasts superb depth of fruit as well as magnificent purity of flavor. Anticipated maturity: 2006–2015.

2000 Riesling Cuvée Ste.-Catherine

RATING: 91 points

The pear-scented 2000 Riesling Cuvée Ste.-Catherine exhibits loads of depth in its linden and chamomile–flavored character. Light to medium–bodied, it is a concentrated, tightly wound, bone-dry, and complex wine. It has the capacity to become even better with cellaring. Drink it between now and 2015.

1999 Riesling Cuvée Ste.-Catherine

RATING: 90 points

Loads of minerals, stones, and herbal tea can be found in the delightful aromatics of the 1999 Riesling Cuvée Ste.-Catherine. A wine with lovely breadth to its rich, plump, and deep personality, it overflows with liquid mineral-like flavors. This lush, well-delineated wine is medium to full–bodied, and has an admirably persistent finish. Anticipated maturity: now–2010.

1997 Riesling Cuvée Ste.-Catherine

RATING: 92 points

Over 90% of the grapes used to craft the 1997 Riesling Cuvée Ste.-Catherine are from the 25–45-year-old vines in the lower portion of the Fallers' Schlossberg parcel. Displaying sweetened tea-laced minerals in its aromatics, this is a boldly expressive, medium to full–bodied, and refined wine. It boasts exquisite purity, power, breadth, and length in its chalky lemon juice flavors. Anticipated maturity: now–2010+.

1995 Riesling Cuvée Ste.-Catherine

RATING: 94 points

The 1995 Riesling Cuvée Ste.-Catherine offers an intriguing nose of quinine, red currants, and minerals. A darker straw/gold color is followed by a zesty, full-bodied, dry, floral-scented and -flavored wine that is exceptionally long and rich, with plenty of white peach–like flavors. This is an impressive, youthful yet compelling example of a large-scaled, elegant Riesling that admirably combines power and finesse. Anticipated maturity: now–2009.

RIESLING SCHLOSSBERG

2001 Riesling Schlossberg

RATING: 91 points

Produced from the estate's highest-elevation parcel in the Schlossberg grand cru, the 2001 Riesling Schlossberg reveals almond and white flower aromas. Medium-bodied and satin-textured, it exhibits flavors reminiscent of creamed minerals and pears. It has wonderful amplitude, richness (yet is de-tailed), concentration, and length. Anticipated maturity: now–2012.

2000 Riesling Schlossberg

RATING: 90 points

Produced from a parcel near the top of the vineyard, the 2000 Riesling Schlossberg has a floral nose and an intense, focused personality. A linear, bone-dry, light to medium–bodied effort, it is lace-like and reveals citrus-infused minerals. Antic-ipated maturity: now–2012.

1995 Riesling Schlossberg

RATING: 92 points

The medium-bodied 1995 Riesling Schlossberg reveals a fabulous nose of steel and minerals. Orange and passion fruit–like aromas make their appearance on the palate of this medium to full–bodied, highly extracted, dry yet backward Riesling. This superb, super-concentrated wine should keep until 2008–2013 and beyond.

RIESLING SCHLOSSBERG CUVEE STE.-CATHERINE

2001 Riesling Schlossberg Cuvée Ste.-Catherine

RATING: 95 points

French sugar-coated almond candies *(dragées)*, quartz, and stone-like aromas can be found in the nose of the 2001 Ries-ling Schlossberg Cuvée Ste.-Catherine. Armed with inspiring breadth, concentration, and richness, it reveals loads of stone, mineral, and pear flavors in its deep character. Rich yet highly focused and pure, this medium-bodied, satin-textured wine also sports an exceptionally long and detailed finish. Antici-pated maturity: 2006–2016.

2000 Riesling Schlossberg Cuvée Ste.-Catherine

RATING: 93 points

The gorgeous aromatics of the 2000 Riesling Schlossberg Cuvée Ste.-Catherine display honeysuckle blossoms, assorted white flowers, and minerals. Medium-bodied, this generous wine coats the taster's palate with powerful honeyed mineral ("out the wazoo!" read my notes) and pear flavors. This powerful, concentrated wine should be drunk over the next 9–11 years.

1999 Riesling Schlossberg Cuvée Ste.-Catherine

RATING: 91 points

The 1999 Riesling Schlossberg Cuvée Ste.-Catherine has vivid aromatic intensity in its mineral and quinine–scented nose. Loads of toasty minerals, sun-dried gravel, pears, and ber-

gamots can be found in its precise flavor profile. This wine has laser-like focus, yet has a silky-textured, fruit-forward character. Drink it between now and 2012.

1995 Riesling Schlossberg Cuvée Ste.-Catherine
RATING: 94 points

The light golden–colored 1995 Riesling Schlossberg Cuvée Ste.-Catherine offers a closed set of aromatics (with airing some apricot, peach, and mineral-like scents emerge), fabulous purity and ripeness, but extremely high acidity, and a backward, austere, medium to full–bodied style. This wine improves immensely in the glass, and is capable of lasting another 10 or more years.

1994 Riesling Schlossberg Cuvée Ste.-Catherine
RATING: 95 points

The 1994 Riesling Schlossberg Cuvée Ste.-Catherine is one of the most awesome dry Rieslings I have ever tasted. Extremely full-bodied and exceptionally concentrated, with spectacular aromatics (gravel, wet steel, oranges, and other citrus fruits), layers of concentration, and pinpoint precision, this admirably pure, exquisite Riesling may last for another decade or more. It is a tour de force in winemaking. Anticipated maturity: now–2020.

1993 Riesling Schlossberg Cuvée Ste.-Catherine
RATING: 94 points

The property's top Riesling Cuvée is the decadent, awesomely rich, full-bodied, dry 1993 Riesling Schlossberg Cuvée Ste.-Catherine. Fanatics of dry, full-throttle Riesling should make an effort to latch on to a bottle of this massively rich yet refreshingly light Riesling. The bouquet of tropical fruits, apples, and minerals is followed by layers of concentrated fruit. Despite all its intensity, power, and extract, the wine is not heavy or flabby. This wine is the essence of extremely ripe Riesling fruit grown in stony, mineral-filled soils. The finish lasts for nearly a minute.

RIESLING SCHLOSSBERG QUINTESSENCE DE GRAINS NOBLES

2001 Riesling Schlossberg Quintessence de Grains Nobles
RATING: 97 points

That botrytis was plentiful yet pure in 2001 is proven in this awe-inspiring Quintessence de Grains Nobles. Orange custard, candied blood oranges, and toasted almonds can be found in the profound aromas of the 2001 Riesling Schloss-

berg Quintessence de Grains Nobles. Broad, lush, and sensual, this wine is the essence of elegance. Its highly detailed, magnificently focused character reveals gorgeous candied orange, passion fruit, and floral flavors. Only 160 liters of this sublime nectar was produced. Anticipated maturity: 2009–2025+.

RIESLING SCHLOSSBERG SELECTION DE GRAINS NOBLES

2000 Riesling Schlossberg Sélection de Grains Nobles
RATING: 94 points

Hints of caramel are already visible on the edge of the glass of the 2000 Riesling Schlossberg Sélection de Grains Nobles (162 grams of residual sugar). Dominated by scents of botrytis, its nose leads to a thick, full-bodied, earthy personality. This jammy wine is dense and sweet and possesses an exceptionally long, fresh finish. Anticipated maturity: now–2014.

TOKAY PINOT GRIS ALTENBOURG QUINTESSENCE DE GRAINS NOBLES

2001 Tokay Pinot Gris Altenbourg Quintessence de Grains Nobles
RATING: 99 points

The 2001 Tokay Pinot Gris Altenbourg Quintessence de Grains Nobles bursts forth with aromas reminiscent of spice and botrytis-laden apricots, peach jam, cherries, and white pepper. This huge, massively rich wine contains 200 grams of residual sugar per liter yet is balanced and vinous (unlike some super-sweet, jelly-like dessert wines). Oodles of caramelized apricots, spices, and hints of tangy passion fruit can be found in its deep character as well as in its seemingly never-ending finish. Anticipated maturity: now–2030.

TOKAY PINOT GRIS ALTENBOURG SELECTION DE GRAINS NOBLES

2000 Tokay Pinot Gris Altenbourg Sélection de Grains Nobles

RATING: 96 points

Cotton candy and pipe smoke can be discerned in the aromatics of the 2000 Tokay Pinot Gris Altenbourg Sélection de Grains Nobles (160 grams of residual sugar per liter). A magnificent, medium to full–bodied beauty, it is thickly textured, dense, and concentrated. Its tangerine, apricot, and peach-filled character has superb delineation. Anticipated maturity: now–2025+.

1998 Tokay Pinot Gris Altenbourg Sélection de Grains Nobles

RATING: 99 points

The stunning 1998 Tokay Pinot Gris Altenbourg Sélection de Grains Nobles was produced from an entire parcel of vines, without sorting, so there is a reasonable quantity of this earth-shattering nectar (1,867 bottles). Its hyper-spicy nose displays loads of botrytis-infused smoky yellow fruits. On the palate, this full-bodied wine surges forth with a panoply of apricots, peaches, and sweetened herbal tea–like flavors. Intense and massively rich, it somehow maintains an unreal precision. This impeccably balanced offering is magnificently concentrated and extravagantly textured, yet impressively elegant and graceful. Anticipated maturity: 2006–2025+.

TOKAY PINOT GRIS CUVEE LAURENCE

2001 Tokay Pinot Gris Cuvée Laurence

RATING: 93 points

Smoked apricots are interspersed with earthy scents in the nose of the 2001 Tokay Pinot Gris Cuvée Laurence. A luxuriant wine, it is immensely ripe, sumptuous, and rich, yet well balanced. Intense layers of smoke-laden white peaches are found in this opulent, concentrated effort. Drink it between 2006 and 2015.

1997 Tokay Pinot Gris Cuvée Laurence

RATING: 92 points

The 1997 Tokay Pinot Gris Cuvée Laurence is a hedonistic, complex, focused, concentrated, and intense wine. Produced from vines located in the lower section of the Altenbourg vineyard, it displays honeysuckle and smoke-covered peach aromas. This superb wine has extraordinary balance, grip, and precision combined with lovely opulence. Anticipated maturity: now–2010.

1995 Tokay Pinot Gris Cuvée Laurence

RATING: 95 points

The two 1995 Tokay Pinot Gris offerings I tasted both possessed high extraction of flavor, stunning backbone and grip, and the vintage's telltale lofty acidity. The off-dry 1995 Tokay Pinot Gris Cuvée Laurence tastes like a Vendange Tardive. The wine has some residual sugar, but the acidity is so high that most readers would consider it to be dry. The intriguing nose of lemongrass, honeyed apricots, white peaches, and marmalade offers a dramatic introduction to this full-bodied, remarkably fresh wine that has massive doses of power and extract—all allied with unreal elegance and finesse. It is a winemaking tour de force. Drink this compelling wine between now and 2015.

TOKAY PINOT GRIS QUINTESSENCE DE GRAINS NOBLES

1997 Tokay Pinot Gris Quintessence de Grains Nobles

RATING: 96 points

As though its wines at the Sélection de Grains Nobles level were not concentrated and powerful enough to knock tasters off their feet, Domaine Weinbach crafts some of the most intense wines on earth under the Quintessence de Grains Nobles moniker. This jammy, syrupy nectar combines massive sugar levels with bracing acidity. Readers should be aware that this wine is meant for sipping in lieu of dessert. It is simply too intense and dominating to be matched with most foods. The sugar-coated peach and apricot-scented 1997 Tokay Pinot Gris Quintessence de Grains Nobles has superb elegance. It has the requisite acidity to balance its extraordinarily thick and juicy core of overripe yellow fruit, candied cherry, and raspberry jam–like flavors. Anticipated maturity: now–2030+.

WINES:

Riesling Clos Windsbuhl

Riesling Brand

Riesling Rangen de Thann Clos St.-Urbain

Pinot Gris Clos Windsbuhl

Pinot Gris Rangen de Thann Clos St.-Urbain

Gewurztraminer Clos Windsbuhl

Gewurztraminer Hengst

Gewurztraminer Rangen de Thann Clos St.-Urbain

Tokay Pinot Gris Clos Jebsal

Various Vendanges Tardives Sélection and Sélection de
Grains Nobles cuvées

CLASSIFICATION: Alsace

OWNERS: Olivier and Leonard Humbrecht

ADDRESS: 4, Route de Colmar, 68230 Turckheim, France

TELEPHONE: 33 03 89 27 02 05

TELEFAX: 33 03 89 27 22 58

E-MAIL: o.humbrecht@wanadoo.fr

CONTACT: Margaret or Olivier Humbrecht

VISITING POLICY: Visits by appointment only; sales—
8:30–11:30 A.M. and 1:30–5 P.M.

VINEYARDS

SURFACE AREA: 98.8 acres

GRAPE VARIETALS: 30% Riesling, 30% Gewurztraminer, 29%
Pinot Gris, 0.5% Pinot Noir, 1% Muscat, 9.5% vin de
table (Chardonnay, Auxerrois, Pinot Blanc)

AVERAGE AGE OF THE VINES: 30 years

DENSITY OF PLANTATION: 6,000–10,000 vines per hectare

AVERAGE YIELDS: 28-40 hectoliters per hectare

WINEMAKING AND UPBRINGING

Harvest usually takes place over the course of three months at
Zind-Humbrecht, as they will only pick a parcel when they
believe ripeness has been fully achieved. The grapes are
pressed whole-cluster, and they tend to include much of the
heavy lees so that the extraction of flavor and additional texture is optimized. Everything is moved by gravity and aged on
fine lees with very little use of sulfur. Fermentation is completely natural—indigenous yeast with no enzymes or added
agents such as oxygen, nitrogen, fining, or vitamins. The fermentations are slow at Zind-Humbrecht, ranging from 3 to
12 months, with even longer periods of time for the very
sweet wines. Bottling for the drier cuvées takes place between
12 and 18 months.

ANNUAL PRODUCTION

Bottle production varies significantly from vintage to vintage.

Zind

Muscat Herrenweg de Turckheim

Muscat Goldert

Riesling

Riesling Gueberschwihr

Riesling Turckheim

Riesling Thann

Riesling Herrenweg de Turckheim

Riesling Clos Häuserer

Riesling Heimbourg

Riesling Clos Windsbuhl

Riesling Brand

Riesling Rangen de Thann Clos St.-Urbain

Pinot Gris

Pinot Gris Herrenweg de Turckheim

Pinot Gris Rotenberg

Pinot Gris Heimbourg

Pinot Gris Clos Jebsal

Pinot Gris Clos Windsbuhl

Pinot Gris Rangen de Thann Clos St.-Urbain

Gewurztraminer Gueberschwihr

Gewurztraminer Turckheim

Gewurztraminer Wintzenheim

Gewurztraminer Herrenweg de Turckheim

Gewurztraminer Heimbourg

Gewurztraminer Clos Windsbuhl

Gewurztraminer Goldert

Gewurztraminer Hengst

Gewurztraminer Rangen de Thann Clos St.-Urbain

Gewurztraminer Clos Windsbuhl Vendange Tardive

Pinot Clos Jebsal Sélection de Grains Nobles

Pinot-Gris Rangen de Thann Clos St.-Urbain Sélection de
Grains Nobles

Pinot-Gris Windsbuhl Sélection de Grains Nobles

AVERAGE PRICE (VARIABLE DEPENDING ON VINTAGE): $35–475

GREAT RECENT VINTAGES

Olivier (1985 to today)—2002, 2001, 2000, 1998, 1995, 1994,
1990, 1989

Leonard (1951 to 1989)—1989, 1986, 1985, 1983, 1976, 1971,
1969, 1967, 1966, 1964, 1961

Larger than life not only in terms of their physiques but their well-earned reputations as well, the father-and-son team of Leonard and Olivier Humbrecht represent the pinnacle of winemaking in Alsace. This extraordinary estate, which includes some of the finest vineyards in France, has been at the head of a crusade for lower yields, more natural winemaking, and of course wines that are *terroir*-driven. Their estate holdings read like a "Who's Who" of Alsace, with significant parcels in the Brand, the Hengst, the Goldert, the Herrenweg, the Clos Häuserer, the Clos Windsbuhl, and of course their vineyard Clos St.-Urbain in the famed Rangen Vineyard. Every action taken has one objective—to produce the finest wine possible. Dense vineyard plantings, probably the lowest yields (by a long measure) in Alsace, and natural winemaking result in wines that are not only extraordinarily full flavored, but also age very impressively. Even some of the lower-level *cuvées* last 10 or even 20 years before tiring.

By French standards, Domaine Zind-Humbrecht is a relatively young winemaking estate, established by Leonard Humbrecht and Genevieve Zind in 1959. Their son Olivier, who has taken increasing control over the estate in the last decade, was France's first Master of wine. Though he downplays his achievement, his serious academic demeanor is never totally eclipsed by his otherwise down-to-earth, affable personality. While one could say his wines are the quintessence of traditional winemaking, Olivier Humbrecht is quick to apply modern solutions to age-old problems. In response to consumer confusion over which Alsace bottlings are dry or sweet, Humbrecht began printing a scale on the label of each of his bottles with numbers from 1 to 5 indicating the perceptible sweetness of the wines—"1" is totally dry; "2" not technically dry, but with the sweetness not apparent on the palate; "3" medium sweetness that gradually disappears with aging; "4" a sweet wine; "5" for extraordinary nectar-like elixirs produced under the Vendange Tardive and Sélection de Grains Nobles monikers. It is a simple system, designed to enlighten consumers about his wines.

Tasting through the cellars of Zind-Humbrecht is truly a lesson in how wine's aromas, flavors, texture, and overall personality are affected by the soil types and microclimates. There are the productive plains of Wintzenheim, the limestone-based soils of the Goldert and Hengst Vineyards, the gravel of Herrenweg, the marl of Clos Häuserer, the granite of Brand, the volcanic schist of Clos St.-Urbain, a parcel of the Rangen, or the varied marl, limestone, and sandstone soils of the Clos Windsbuhl. The last is their most famous vineyard. Though not yet a grand cru, Clos Windstahl is certainly proving it deserves to be one.

Few wines in the world reach the heights that Zind-Humbrecht's Rieslings, Gewurztraminers, and Pinot Tokay Gris attain. With a producer as accomplished as this, it is almost impossible to pick out the greatest wines, but the tasting notes provided may be enough to give the reader an accurate view of the wines.

GEWURZTRAMINER CLOS WINDSBUHL

2001 Gewurztraminer Clos Windsbuhl
RATING: 91 points
Honeyed spices make up the aromatic profile of the 2001 Gewurztraminer Clos Windsbuhl. Lush, satin-textured, and broad, it has superb mouth-feel as well as a long flavorful finish. Peppery pears and spices are found in its core. This is unquestionably an outstanding white wine, yet it is not a great Gewurztraminer as it lacks the varietal's archetypical flavors and expressiveness. Drink it now through 2011–2012.

2000 Gewurztraminer Clos Windsbuhl
RATING: 91 points
The 2000 Gewurztraminer Clos Windsbuhl is a dry, spice-scented wine. Rich layers of yellow fruits and flowers can be discerned in its detailed, medium-bodied character. Exhibiting outstanding depth of fruit and breadth, it is an elegant, finely etched Gewurztraminer. Anticipated maturity: now–2012.

1997 Gewurztraminer Clos Windsbuhl
RATING: 95 points
The pale green straw–colored 1997 Gewurztraminer Clos Windsbuhl soars from the glass with mouth-watering potpourri and spice aromas. This dry, medium to full–bodied, boisterous wine has extraordinary richness but is rendered light on its feet due to its high (but imperceptible) alcohol. Its gorgeously detailed character reveals pineapple-soaked minerals and flowers whose flavors last throughout its impressively long finish. Drink it now.

GEWURZTRAMINER CLOS WINDSBUHL VENDANGE TARDIVE

2001 Gewurztraminer Clos Windsbuhl Vendange Tardive

RATING: 95 points

This is the first time Olivier Humbrecht has fashioned a late-harvest Gewurztraminer from his parcel of Clos Windsbuhl. The jammy apricot-scented 2001 Gewurztraminer Clos Windsbuhl Vendange Tardive leads to a massively deep character packed with sweet white peaches and yellow plums. Medium to full–bodied and lush, this powerful, super-ripe, smoky wine is pure and exceptionally long in the finish. Anticipated maturity: now–2020.

GEWURZTRAMINER HENGST

2001 Gewurztraminer Hengst

RATING: 91 points

The sensual, lush 2001 Gewurztraminer Hengst is medium-bodied, silky-textured, and well balanced. Poached pears, spices, minerals, and apples are found in this effort's aromatic and flavor profiles. It should be consumed now through 2010.

2000 Gewurztraminer Hengst

RATING: 93 points

Medium to full–bodied and dense, the 2000 Gewurztraminer Hengst is a broad, ample wine with loads of richness. It possesses spiced pear, mineral, and candied apple aromas as well as flavors. Opulently textured, it should be consumed between now and 2013.

1999 Gewurztraminer Hengst

RATING: 92 points

The talcum powder, flower, and spice-scented 1999 Gewurztraminer Hengst has a delightful satin-textured character. Medium-bodied and fresh, this delineated and detailed wine regales the taster's palate with roses, violets, and hints of white fruits. Should be consumed between now and 2008–9.

1998 Gewurztraminer Hengst

RATING: 94 points

The magnificent, rose and lychee–scented 1998 Gewurztraminer Hengst is full-bodied and oily-textured. Thick, yet fresh, detailed, and polished, it is packed with lychee nut flavor as well. The wine's high level of alcohol (15.9%) slightly shows through the dense fruit, but its extroverted, focused, and fruit-dominated personality more than makes up for it. Anticipated maturity: now–2012.

1997 Gewurztraminer Hengst

RATING: 95 points

The extraordinarily floral and honeyed aromatics of the medium to full–bodied 1997 Gewurztraminer Hengst lead to an impeccably balanced character. Broad waves of minerals, pears, and candied apples drenched in lychee juice are found in its super-expressive core. This velvety-textured wine should be consumed now.

GEWURZTRAMINER HENGST VENDANGE TARDIVE

1994 Gewurztraminer Hengst Vendange Tardive

RATING: 99 points

The 1994 Gewurztraminer Hengst Vendange Tardive represents the essence of Gewurztraminer. It tastes dry despite nearly 5% residual sugar. The natural alcohol comes in at an amazing 17+%. Made from 30- and 65-year-old vines, this massive, remarkably intense, tannic, structured wine, is a smoky, mind-bogglingly rich wine that has to be tasted to be believed. It did not begin to hit its plateau of maturity until the turn of the century, and it will remain there for 20–25 years. It approaches perfection!

1990 Gewurztraminer Hengst Vendange Tardive

RATING: 96 points

The 1990 Gewurztraminer Hengst Vendange Tardive is great stuff, with a spectacular cherry, lychee nut, rose-scented nose; viscous, rich, chewy flavors that go on and on; and a huge, explosive finish. This giant of a wine is tied together with searingly high acidity. Anticipated maturity: now–2015.

GEWURZTRAMINER RANGEN DE THANN CLOS ST.-URBAIN

1999 Gewurztraminer Rangen de Thann Clos St.-Urbain

RATING: 91 points

The mineral-scented 1999 Gewurztraminer Rangen de Thann Clos St.-Urbain is more reminiscent of a Tokay Pinot Gris than a Gewurztraminer. Copious quantities of smoke and spice can be discerned in its lush yet detailed character. Minerals, metallic shavings, cinnamon, and cardamom can be found in its flavor profile. While it will not satisfy consumers yearning for an archetypal Gewurztraminer, those desiring a highly focused, spicy Tokay will be delighted with this offering. Drink it between now and 2008–9.

1998 Gewurztraminer Rangen de Thann Clos St.-Urbain

RATING: 97 points

The superlative 1998 Gewurztraminer Rangen de Thann Clos St.-Urbain Vendange Tardive has the amber/gold color of a Sélection de Grains Nobles. In the nose, candied oranges, botrytis, red berries, and earth compete for the taster's olfactory attention. A hedonist's delight, this full-bodied, decadently viscous offering is also refreshing to taste. The mouth-feel is tantamount to millions of tiny puffy pillows filled with caramel, cocoa, minerals, candied citrus fruit zests, and lemony stones. Seductive, intricate, and profound, it does not reflect any of its varietal's trademark lychee, rosewater, floral scents and flavors. It represents, according to Olivier Humbrecht, "the pure essence of the Rangen *terroir*." Anticipated maturity: now–2018+.

1997 Gewurztraminer Rangen de Thann Clos St.-Urbain

RATING: 98 points

Regrettably, only 500 bottles of the stunning, gold-colored 1997 Gewurztraminer Rangen de Thann Clos St.-Urbain exist. The result of microscopic yields (12–15 hectoliters per hectare), this nectar's aromas and flavors are presently dominated by fresh mangoes. When all is said and done, this full-bodied, detailed, magnificently refined, and hugely flavorful wine may merit a perfect score. The manner in which Humbrecht combines astronomical richness and power with impeccable precision and purity is pure genius. Stones, chalk, minerals, Asian teas, flint, roses, and innumerable tropical fruits are found in this blockbuster. Minutes after having been emptied, my glass continued to present awesome mineral and honeyed fruit scents. Readers fortunate enough to acquire this benchmark setter should consume it between now and 2010.

1996 Gewurztraminer Rangen de Thann Clos St.-Urbain

RATING: 95 points

The 1996 Gewurztraminer Rangen de Thann Clos St.-Urbain possesses nearly 17% alcohol and 2% residual sugar. The grapes were harvested during the first week of November. Its fermentation lasted 12 months! How do I describe such an intriguing, provocative, and multidimensional wine? Its medium gold color is followed by aromas of honeyed grapefruit, roasted coffee, white truffles, lychee nuts, and musty smells. Oily and viscous, with a honeyed tea–like character, this powerful, rich, exceptionally pure wine will continue to develop at a glacial pace over the next 10–20 years. This is a wine to consume by the spoonful, with only the richest of dishes—an indulgent but sumptuous combination.

1995 Gewurztraminer Rangen de Thann Clos St.-Urbain

RATING: 96 points

Four of the finest Gewurztraminers of the vintage are the 1995 Hengst, 1995 Clos Windsbuhl, 1995 Heimbourg, and 1995 Rangen de Thann Clos St.-Urbain. I suspect Clos St.-Urbain will be controversial. Unfortunately, few readers will ever get a chance to taste the 1995 Gewurztraminer Rangen, as only 450 bottles were produced. The wine exhibits an advanced deep golden color, an explosive, sweet, honeyed nose, monstrous extract, and a remarkably dry, full-bodied, super-intense finish that is nearly fatiguing to taste and analyze. Harvested at Sélection de Grains Nobles sugar levels, and made from a microscopic 9.5 hectoliters per hectare, this Gewurztraminer took nearly a year to complete fermentation. It is a dry, staggeringly concentrated wine. I suspect it could actually be classified as food—it's that rich! It will keep for another 12+ years.

GEWURZTRAMINER RANGEN CLOS ST.-URBAIN SELECTION DE GRAINS NOBLES

1993 Gewurztraminer Rangen Clos St.-Urbain Selection de Grains Nobles

RATING: 99 points

The 1993 Gewurztraminer Rangen Clos St.-Urbain Sélection de Grains Nobles is one of the most extraordinary sweet wines I have ever tasted. Only a minuscule 25 cases were produced, of which five made the trans-Atlantic trip to the United States. The wine displays a dense orange/caramel color; an awesome nose of orange marmalade; botrytised, exotic fruits; an unctuous, viscous, oily texture; spectacular acidity; and a finish that lasts for more than 60 seconds. It is almost too rich and intense to be classified as a beverage, so call it a food product. It is a glorious freak of nature that should drink well for another 40+ years.

GEWURZTRAMINER RANGEN DE THANN CLOS ST.-URBAIN VENDANGE TARDIVE

2000 Gewurztraminer Rangen de Thann Clos St.-Urbain Vendange Tardive

RATING: 98 points

The mind-boggling 2000 Gewurztraminer Rangen de Thann Clos St.-Urbain Vendange Tardive has the potential to merit a perfect score when its youthfully unevolved personality blossoms. This concentrated monster displays an unreal depth of fruit, huge levels of extract, and prodigious balance. Cherries, raspberries, currants, papayas, mangoes, and jammy apricots are interspersed with spices in this massively complex wine's flavor profile. Full-bodied, oily-textured, and potent, it is Gewurztraminer essence. Otherworldly! Anticipated maturity: 2008–2030.

PINOT GRIS CLOS WINDSBUHL

2001 Pinot Gris Clos Windsbuhl

RATING: 96 points

The 2001 Pinot Gris Clos Windsbuhl is a wine of huge ripeness. It has Vendange Tardive levels of sweetness (for Humbrecht it lacked enough botrytis to earn that moniker) yet retains a refined, balanced character. Minerals, smoky apricots, and white peaches are found in its aromatics. Silky-textured, medium to full–bodied, and powerful, it is a broad, intensely flavorful, decadent wine, crammed with smoke-laced poached pears and peaches, with a shockingly long, fruit-filled finish. Anticipated maturity: 2008–2025+.

1998 Pinot Gris Clos Windsbuhl

RATING: 93 points

The 1998 Pinot Gris Clos Windsbuhl does not reveal any influence of botrytis in its smoky, apricot-scented aromatics. Minerals, cherries, raspberries, and other assorted red fruits dominate its personality. This medium to full–bodied wine is pure, intricate, and wonderfully rich. Its extravagant character is satin-textured, luxurious, and elegant. Anticipated maturity: now–2012+.

1997 Pinot Gris Clos Windsbuhl

RATING: 93 points

The healthy, light straw–colored 1997 Pinot Gris Clos Windsbuhl has an intensely smoky, mineral, pear, and herb-scented nose. Medium-bodied and silky-textured, this wine is rich and ample. Layers of poached pears, minerals, and stones are found in its youthful, undeveloped personality. Anticipated maturity: now–2012.

1996 Pinot Gris Clos Windsbuhl

RATING: 95 points

Artichoke liqueur and hints of tangy citrus fruits are found in the aromatics of the pale straw–colored 1996 Pinot Gris Clos Windsbuhl. Broad, opulent, and medium to full–bodied, this wine's well-defined flavor profile is crammed with honeyed yellow fruits and candied lemons. Anticipated maturity: now–2012.

PINOT GRIS CLOS WINDSBUHL VENDANGE TARDIVE

1994 Pinot Gris Clos Windsbuhl Vendange Tardive

RATING: 98 points

The stunning, golden 1994 Pinot Gris Clos Windsbuhl Vendange Tardive displays a hugely botrytised smoke, honey, spice, and exotic fruit–scented nose. This decadently textured full-bodied wine coats the taster's palate with spice-laden mangoes, super-ripe apricots, and sweet peaches. It is a domineering wine, massive in its intensity of flavors and structure, yet remarkably maintains elegance and balance. Anticipated maturity: now–2020+.

1990 Pinot Gris Clos Windsbuhl Vendange Tardive

RATING: 100 points

Tasting this monumental Pinot Gris Clos Windsbuhl Vendange Tardive is a mind-boggling experience. It is stunning in its completeness. It has exemplary breadth, texture, refinement, balance, and length. While at first it is forward and appears to be giving all it's got, with time it begins to suggest an underlying power and concentration that will be displayed, with cellaring. The pale gold–colored 1990 boasts an immensely spicy nose of botrytis-laden candied apples. Full-bodied, velvety-textured, and opulent, it is an exquisite wine packed with quinces, poached pears, juniper berries, caramel-covered minerals, and hints of pineapple. Its pure, focused finish is unending, seemingly coating the palate for minutes. Extraordinarily, the density of fruit and balanced structure of this jewel completely covers the sugar. It is liquid heaven. Drink it between now and 2020.

RIESLING BRAND

2001 Riesling Brand

RATING: 98 points

Described by Olivier Humbrecht as "similar to the 1990 but with better balance," the 2001 Riesling Brand is one of the greatest dry Rieslings I have ever tasted. Its intensely ripe nose reveals complex liquid stone and smoky pear aromas. Medium to full–bodied, hugely concentrated and magnificently deep, this intricate wine inundates the palate with bitter almonds, liquid minerals, pears, flowers, and spices. This dry offering's finish is sumptuous, flavor packed, seamless, and unbelievably long. Typically, Rieslings from Brand age remarkably well, gaining complexity and power with time, so I would not be surprised to see this wine earn a perfect score in a few years. Wow! Anticipated maturity: 2008–2022.

2000 Riesling Brand

RATING: 97 points

"If a vineyard can ever have a perfect vintage, 2000 was for Brand," said Olivier Humbrecht. He added that the 2000 Riesling Brand "is like the 1989 or 1998 yet not as sweet and with additional richness, acidity, and botrytis." Its exuberant nose displays poached pears, white peaches, liquid minerals, and apricots. On the palate, this medium to full–bodied wine is immensely rich, ample, and plump. Layers of tea-laced minerals vie with copious white fruits for the taster's attention. Intricately laced, its powerful character lasts throughout its exceedingly long finish. This prodigious wine will be at its best between 2007 and 2020.

1999 Riesling Brand

RATING: 92 points

The liquid mineral–scented 1999 Riesling Brand, harvested at 25 hectoliters per hectare, is a velvety-textured, medium-bodied wine. The richest of Humbrecht's 1999 Rieslings, it has a sexy, lush, feminine character filled with ripe pears, fruit pulp, herbal tea, and spices. It has outstanding depth and a long finish that reveals berry-like fruits. Drink it between now and 2013.

1997 Riesling Brand

RATING: 96 points

The 1997 Brand joins the long list of stunning Rieslings crafted by Humbrecht from this southerly exposed hillside vineyard. An embracing, super-rich nose of spices, poached pears, and cherries gives way to a thickly textured, highly expressive, full-bodied core. This velvety bombshell is crammed with bergamots, acacia blossoms, honeyed white peaches, and clay, whose flavors last throughout its mind-boggling finish. Anticipated maturity: now–2012.

RIESLING BRAND VENDANGE TARDIVE

2000 Riesling Brand Vendange Tardive

RATING: 98 points

This full-bodied wine explodes from the glass with scents of lilies, peaches, apricots, and a myriad of spices. Unbelievably sexy, it is thick, dense, and botrytis laced. Its exotic, apricot puree–flavored character has extraordinary balance and an interminable finish. Wow! Anticipated maturity: 2007–2025.

RIESLING CLOS HAUSERER

2001 Riesling Clos Häuserer

RATING: 93 points

The aromatic profile of the 2001 Riesling Clos Häuserer features sweet pears and spices. An expansive, sultry offering, it slathers the palate with layers of gravel, quinine, spices, and mineral flavors. All of these elements linger in its exceptionally long finish. Medium-bodied and silky-textured, it displays huge richness and exquisite balance. Anticipated maturity: 2006–2014.

2000 Riesling Clos Häuserer

RATING: 92 points

Botrytis-dusted hazelnuts make up the aromatic profile of the 2000 Riesling Clos Häuserer. Citrus fruits are interspersed with minerals in its expansive, medium-bodied character. Exhibiting a lively, highly focused personality, it is also concentrated, deep, and well extracted. Anticipated maturity: 2006–2014.

1999 Riesling Clos Häuserer

RATING: 90 points

The talcum powder and mineral–scented 1999 Riesling Clos Häuserer is light-bodied, detailed, and delineated. This beautifully ripe, mineral and citrus fruit–flavored wine is bright, has outstanding grip, and possesses a long, herbal tea–laden finish. This beautifully nuanced wine may very well improve with age. Anticipated maturity: now–2012.

RIESLING CLOS WINDSBUHL

2001 Riesling Clos Windsbuhl

RATING: 94 points

The nose of the 2001 Riesling Clos Windsbuhl exhibits intensely spicy minerals and white flowers. From the coolest of Zind-Humbrecht's numerous vineyard holdings, the grapes that fashioned this broad, mouth-coating wine were harvested in November. Immensely pure and persistent, it boasts a stone, crisp pear, and mineral–packed medium-bodied character. Anticipated maturity: 2007–2015.

RIESLING CLOS WINDSBUHL VENDANGE TARDIVE

2000 Riesling Clos Windsbuhl Vendange Tardive

RATING: 97 points

Minerals, clove-spiked pears, and peaches make up the aromatic profile of the 2000 Riesling Clos Windsbuhl Vendange Tardive. This spectacular wine combines exceptional power and richness with magnificent detail and balance. Medium to full–bodied, plump, exuberant, and intense, its feminine flavor profile is dominated by spiced red berries. Drink it between 2007 and 2020+.

RIESLING RANGEN DE THANN CLOS ST.-URBAIN

2001 Riesling Rangen de Thann Clos St.-Urbain

RATING: 96 points

The powerful, virile 2001 Riesling Rangen de Thann Clos St.-Urbain explodes from the glass with smoky mineral scents. A wide, dense, concentrated, brooding wine, it is crammed with pears and minerals. Medium-bodied, satin-textured, and intense, this exceptional effort is a candidate for drinking between now and 2020.

2000 Riesling Rangen de Thann Clos St.-Urbain

RATING: 96 points

The botrytis, apricot, mineral, and quince–scented nose of the 2000 Riesling Rangen de Thann Clos St.-Urbain reveals awesome aromatic depth. This medium to full–bodied wine is hugely concentrated, densely packed with smoke-infused white fruits, and has exceptional balance. A profound, complex effort, it displays an awe-inspiring finish. Anticipated maturity: 2006–2018.

1998 Riesling Rangen de Thann Clos St.-Urbain

RATING: 94 points

The botrytis-laden 1998 Riesling Rangen de Thann Clos St.-Urbain fermented for over a year. Hints of gold appear in its color and its smoky, apricot, peach, and tropical fruit–filled nose is reminiscent of a Pinot Gris. On the palate, this opulent, medium to full–bodied wine is crammed with spiced apples, super-ripe yellow fruits, and layers of minerals, earth, and stones. Broad and intense, it is both sublimely rich and fresh. This impeccably balanced wine has the potential to become even grander with cellaring. Anticipated maturity: now–2014+.

1997 Riesling Rangen de Thann Clos St.-Urbain

RATING: 96 points

Analytically, the 1997 Riesling Rangen de Thann Clos St.-Urbain is identical to the stunning 1994. Produced from the steep southern-exposure slopes of the vineyard that is Alsace's Montrachet, it offers mind-blowing aromatic complexity, with well-defined flowers, stones, earth, and minerals competing with bergamots, pears, and white peaches for the taster's attention. On the palate it displays magnificent purity, delineation, elegance, power, richness, and focus. This medium to full–bodied, silky-textured wine is massively dense, concentrated, and intense without being heavy. Anticipated maturity: now–2015.

TOKAY PINOT GRIS CLOS JEBSAL

2001 Tokay Pinot Gris Clos Jebsal

RATING: 94 points

Notes of smoky botrytis can be discerned among the plum marmalade aromas of the 2001 Pinot Gris Clos Jebsal. Less sweet than the Rotenberg, it is a wide, medium-bodied, satin-textured wine crammed with white and yellow fruits. This deep, spicy effort is complex and well-structured, and reveals a long, quince-laced finish. Anticipated maturity: 2006–2020.

1997 Tokay Pinot Gris Clos Jebsal

RATING: 95 points

The 1997 Tokay Pinot Gris Clos Jebsal attained 15.3% alcohol while retaining 25 grams of residual sugar. This wine reveals a fresh bergamot and rose–scented nose. Thick, velvety-textured, full-bodied, and explosive, it possesses world-class power. Extremely floral, it has hints of stones in the background. Anticipated maturity: now–2020.

TOKAY PINOT GRIS CLOS JEBSAL SELECTION DE GRAINS NOBLES

2000 Tokay Pinot Gris Clos Jebsal Sélection de Grains Nobles

RATING: 98 points

Produced from 14 hectoliter per hectare yields, the 2000 Pinot Gris Clos Jebsal Sélection de Grains Nobles sports 147 grams of residual sugar per liter. Candied orange zest, yellow plums, apricots, and peaches are interspersed with smoke in the nose of this jammy, syrupy wine. A massive, hugely concentrated effort is crammed with spices, pepper, and a myriad of super-ripe yellow fruits. Anticipated maturity: 2007–2040.

1997 Tokay Pinot Gris Clos Jebsal Sélection de Grains Nobles

RATING: 97 points

The 1997 Tokay Pinot Gris Clos Jebsal Sélection de Grains Nobles is slightly gold colored and offers jammy apricot, cherry, and strawberry scents, as well as a hyper-dense, super-sweet character. It is full-bodied, intense, and packed with jellied yellow fruits and minerals. Anticipated maturity: now–2040.

TOKAY PINOT GRIS CLOS WINDSBUHL

2000 Tokay Pinot Gris Clos Windsbuhl

RATING: 95 points

The flamboyant 2000 Tokay Pinot Gris Clos Windsbuhl explodes with the scents of juicy peaches, spices, and apricots. Possessing awesome depth, this medium to full–bodied effort is crammed with minerals and poached pears. Most of the botrytis-affected bunches were sorted out so there is only a trace of noble rot in this exceptional, virtually dry wine's pure character. Anticipated maturity: 2006–2020.

1999 Tokay Pinot Gris Clos Windsbuhl

RATING: 93 points

The 1999 Tokay Pinot Gris Clos Windsbuhl has smoky mineral aromas. Medium-bodied, this silky-textured wine offers layers of apples, peaches, and white berries in its rich, lush, yet highly detailed, lace-like character. It has outstanding fat and depth, yet its fruit is, at present, youthfully restrained. This wine has immense complexity and an intense, powerful character. Drink it between now and 2015.

1997 Tokay Pinot Gris Clos Windsbuhl

RATING: 94 points

Candied apricots and exotic fruits emanate from a glass of the 1997 Tokay Pinot Gris Clos Windsbuhl. This hugely powerful, intense wine is full-bodied, dense, explosive, and fresh. While it lacks the delicate nuances of the previous offering, it regales the palate with untold quantities of yellow fruits and minerals. It is velvety-textured and complex, and its extensive finish offers loads of apricot and chalk flavors. Drink it between now and 2015+.

TOKAY PINOT GRIS RANGEN DE THANN CLOS ST.-URBAIN

2001 Tokay Pinot Gris Rangen de Thann Clos St.-Urbain

RATING: 94 points

With his parcel of Pinot Gris in the Rangen, Humbrecht again harvested twice. Those vines closest to the river Thur (indeed only a few yards away) were picked for a Sélection de Grains Nobles and those higher on the steep slope were vinified and bottled as the 2001 Pinot Gris Rangen de Thann Clos St.-Urbain (indice 3). Less opulent than the Clos Windsbuhl, this effort reveals gun flint, smoked minerals, and ripe-pear aromas. Highly elegant, it is a broad yet austere offering loaded with stones, smoke, pears, spices, and apples. This medium-bodied wine has superb balance and length. Anticipated maturity: now–2020.

2000 Tokay Pinot Gris Rangen de Thann Clos St.-Urbain

RATING: 97 points

A blockbuster of epic proportions, the compelling 2000 Tokay Pinot Gris Rangen de Thann Clos St.-Urbain has the breadth, body, and depth of a great red wine. This opulently structured offering is full-bodied, velvety-textured, and jam-packed with layers of minerals, smoke, and spice whose flavors seem to gain momentum in its interminable finish. Anticipated maturity: 2007–2025.

1997 Tokay Pinot Gris Rangen de Thann Clos St.-Urbain

RATING: 95 points

According to Olivier Humbrecht, the 1997 Tokay Pinot Gris Rangen de Thann Clos St.-Urbain fermented violently for three months. Toasted almonds and minerals are discernible in this full-bodied offering's aromatics. It has stellar focus, precision, complexity, power, and purity in its hyper-concentrated character. This bone-dry, fresh, hugely flavorful (yet lace-like), unbelievably long wine exhibits finely detailed mineral flavors reminiscent of a show-stopping Chablis. Anticipated maturity: now–2020.

1996 Tokay Pinot Gris Rangen de Thann Clos St.-Urbain

RATING: 95 points

The deep gold–colored 1996 Tokay Pinot Gris Rangen de Thann Clos St.-Urbain brought back memories of my childhood, when my mother would bake mincemeat pies. The wine's bouquet, an exotic concoction of spices, pie dough, *jus de viande,* and honey, soared from the glass of this awesomely endowed Pinot Gris. In the mouth, it tasted of white truffle oil, something I have only rarely experienced (on occasion, I have had white Hermitage as well as Hermitage Vin de Paille exhibit similar characteristics). Extremely full-bodied and thick, moderately sweet, and mammothly endowed, this is a winemaking monument. This wine will evolve gracefully through 2015–2017.

TOKAY PINOT GRIS RANGEN DE THANN CLOS ST.-URBAIN SELECTION DE GRAINS NOBLES

1998 Tokay Pinot Gris Rangen de Thann Clos St.-Urbain Sélection de Grains Nobles

RATING: 98 points

The 1998 Tokay Pinot Gris Rangen de Thann Clos St.-Urbain Sélection de Grains Nobles has 13.5% alcohol and 160 grams of residual sugar. Even though no new oak was employed, its aromatics reveal vanilla, powerful smoke, and spice scents. This is a raspberry, apricot, peach, spice, and toast-flavored wine with magnificent breadth and an unbelievably long finish. Even though its flavor profile is unctuous, almost jellied in character, it possesses brilliant focus. This is an extraordinary wine with an enormous upside. Drink it over the course of the next 20–25+ years.

WINES:

Riesling Clos Ste.-Hune

Riesling Clos Ste.-Hune Vendange Tardive or Hors Choix

CLASSIFICATION: Alsace

OWNER: Maison Trimbach

ADDRESS: 15, Route de Burgheim, 68150 Ribeauville, France

TELEPHONE: 33 03 89 73 60 30

TELEFAX: 33 03 89 73 89 04

E-MAIL: contact@maison-trimbach.fr

WEBSITE: www.maison-trimbach.fr

CONTACT: Bernard or Hubert Trimbach

VISITING POLICY: Monday through Friday, 8 A.M.–12 P.M., and 1:30–5:30 P.M.

VINEYARDS

SURFACE AREA: 63 acres of vines are owned by the estate, and contracts cover another 140 acres of vines

GRAPE VARIETALS: 41% Riesling, 33% Gewurztraminer, 15% Pinot Gris, 10% Pinot Blanc, and 1% Muscat

AVERAGE AGE OF THE VINES: 25–50+ years

DENSITY OF PLANTATION: 5,800–6,500 vines per hectare

AVERAGE YIELDS: 50 hectoliters per hectare

WINEMAKING AND UPBRINGING

None of the Trimbach wines are put through malolactic fermentation. They are all vinified and aged in stainless steel or neutral or old wood, and are bottled within 12 months of the vintage, except for some of the sweet rarities.

ANNUAL PRODUCTION

Gewurztraminer Cuvée des Seigneurs de Ribeaupierre: 3,000 cases

Riesling Clos Ste.-Hune: 7,000 bottles

Riesling Cuvée Frédéric-Emile: 3,000 cases

AVERAGE PRICE FOR THE RIESLING CLOS STE.-HUNE: $125–150

GREAT RECENT VINTAGES

1999, 1995, 1990, 1989, 1983, 1981, 1976, 1971, 1967

The Trimbach firm, one of the oldest in France, was founded by Jean Trimbach in 1626. Since the late 1800s, the estate has received great international recognition for its wines. Their finest wine emerges from the Clos Ste.-Hune, a 3.2-acre, totally enclosed site that represents a sub-parcel of the grand cru Rosacker Vineyard. (Under Alsace wine laws, any solely owned clos vineyard cannot claim grand cru status.) The Trimbach family has owned this site for over 200 years, with the first vintage produced in 1919. The Clos Ste.-Hune vines, planted in clay and limestone soils, are just under thirty years of age, and yields average around 50 hectoliters per hectare. Because this wine is so slow to develop and it ages well, the Trimbachs generally do not release any vintages until they have had at least four years of bottle age.

Clos Ste.-Hune is the quintessential Riesling. It is unquestionably the finest produced in France, and can rival any Riesling produced in the world. The Clos Ste.-Hune combines an extraordinary minerality with striking concentration and intensity, which are often hidden beneath exceptional levels of acidity. This can be a powerful, concentrated wine, but it always comes across as delicate, nuanced, and fresh.

RIESLING CLOS STE.-HUNE

2000 Riesling Clos Ste.-Hune

RATING: 93 points

A classy bouquet of white fruits, citrus, and honeyed grapefruit emerges from this medium-bodied, concentrated, focused white. Exhibiting stone, gravel, and citrus elements, it is quite concentrated under the veneer of crisp acidity. Consume it over the next 10–15 years.

1999 Riesling Clos Ste.-Hune

RATING: 94 points

Delicate lemon/lime notes with grassy, stony overtones are followed by a wine with superb depth and richness as well as a medium-bodied, intense finish. Still primary, it should be at its finest between 2007–2015.

1998 Riesling Clos Ste.-Hune

RATING: 92 points

Initially tightly knit, the 1998 evolves quickly to reveal ethereal lemon/lime characteristics intermixed with a hint of apricots, a steely minerality that comes across like digesting smoky stones, and a crisp, medium-bodied finish. I originally thought this vintage would be long lived, but I suspect it will evolve at a fast pace and thus should be consumed over the next 8–10 years.

1997 Riesling Clos Ste.-Hune

RATING: 91 points

The 1997 Riesling Clos Ste.-Hune displays strong floral aromas interlaced with ripe apricots. Reminiscent of a restrained Viognier, it reveals flavors of peaches, perfume, chalk, and honeysuckle blossoms in its opulently textured personality. This medium to full–bodied, extraordinarily rich wine possesses a superbly focused, mineral-dominated finish. As it sorts itself out in Trimbach's cold cellars it should come together to become one of the finest Clos Ste.-Hunes of the decade. Anticipated maturity: now–2012+.

1996 Riesling Clos Ste.-Hune

RATING: 93 points

Crisp, youthful aromas of lemons are found in the medium-bodied, dense, and highly focused 1996. It offers extraordinarily powerful layers of lime-drenched minerals, a vibrant satiny texture, and huge richness. This unbelievably long wine is massively structured, concentrated, and backward. Drink this gem between now and 2015.

1995 Riesling Clos Ste.-Hune

RATING: 94 points

The 1995 Riesling Clos Ste.-Hune is certainly one of the greatest wines to have been crafted from this tiny monopole (solely owned vineyard). A profound nose of creamed herbs, minerals, candied limes, and poached pears leads to a super-rich, dry, viscous core of fruit. Layer upon layer of stones, gravel, spiced apples, and liquid minerals captivate the palate for well over a minute. This is a riveting wine, with untold complexity, power, and precision. Anticipated maturity: now–2015+.

1983 Riesling Clos Ste.-Hune

RATING: 96 points

One of the greatest vintages for Trimbach's Clos Ste.-Hune, the 1983 is an extremely powerful, rich, amazingly well-delineated wine with a nose of honeyed green apples, liquid slate, and that petroleum note that is so much a part of the finest Rieslings from Alsace. This is about as big, rich, and dry as Riesling can get. Anticipated maturity: now–2016.

RIESLING CLOS STE.-HUNE VENDANGE TARDIVE

1989 Riesling Clos Ste.-Hune Vendange Tardive or Hors Choix

RATING: 99 points

While this is a Vendange Tardive, it is not a particularly sweet wine. It exhibits notes of honeysuckle and apricot jam along with fabulous minerality and fragrance. A full-bodied, intensely elegant effort with extraordinary nuance and delicacy, this magnificent wine is one of Trimbach's legendary offerings. Fully mature, it should remain at this plateau through 2012+.

BORDEAUX

It is irrefutable that Bordeaux dominates this book, and even though I was very draconian in my selection process, there are probably another two or three dozen estates that could easily have been added. There are many reasons for this, including an extraordinary talent pool of oenologists and wine producers, but also an exceptional commitment by the top château owners to stay ahead of the world marketplace, and the only way to do that is to achieve and maintain high quality.

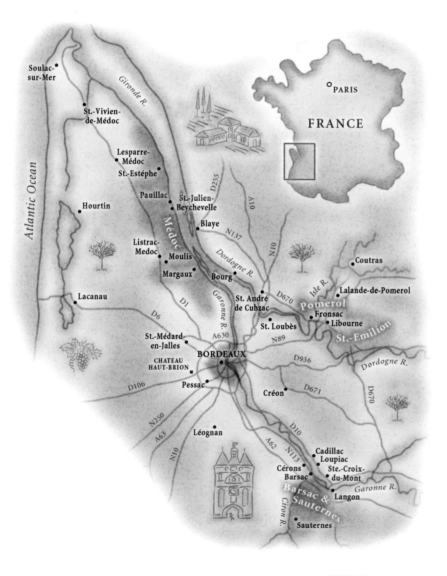

France is the epicenter of the world when it comes to the classification of vineyards and perceived wine quality. Nowhere is that more prevalent than in Bordeaux. It was there that in 1855 a group of wine brokers sat down and attempted to classify the region's finest estates. This historic categorization, known as the *1855 Classification of the Wines of Gironde,* was employed to both promote Bordeaux wines and establish some well-delineated quality benchmarks. The classification was based largely on the reputation of the vineyard as well as the price at which the wine sold. However, owners and winemakers changed, and because of negligence, ignorance, incompetence, or greed, many of these estates have gone through periods of producing

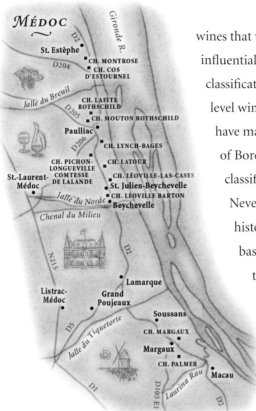

wines that were often unpalatable. However, the *1855 Classification* remains an influential document, and has been emulated in other parts of Bordeaux with classifications of the wines of Barsac and Sauternes, St.-Emilion, and even the lower-level wines often pejoratively referred to as Cru Bourgeois. All of these classifications have major imperfections, and exclude many notable properties. For example, one of Bordeaux's most renowned wine regions, Pomerol, has never had a classification, and not one Pomerol is included in any of the aforementioned lists. Nevertheless, the *1855 Classification of the Wines of Gironde* is still an important historical document. In my book *Bordeaux,* I offer my personal classification based on the quality of the wines over the last forty years. Personally, I believe this list is far more accurate than the one established in 1855. In the end, today's marketplace as well as the prices fetched by all Bordeaux determine the true de facto classification of Bordeaux wine quality. Despite the *1855 Classification,* the best wines are chosen by wine consumers, not wine brokers with vested interests. Moreover, they realize that Bordeaux is the reference point for the great wines of the world, and whether in Argentina, California, Australia, Italy, or Spain, every serious producer always wants to compare their finest effort with that which Bordeaux achieves.

Modern-day Bordeaux is so much better than what it was a mere 20, 30, 40, or even 50 years ago, and the number of top estates making fine wine today is at an all-time high. The estates deserve enormous credit. Their acceptance of essential progressive changes in the vineyard; their experimentation with techniques and adaptation of modern methods in the wine cellars; their belief in preserving the essence of the wine via more natural winemaking and upbringing, as well as less manipulative bottling; and of course, their keen awareness of the world competition— all of this has kept Bordeaux at the top of the pyramid of great wine quality.

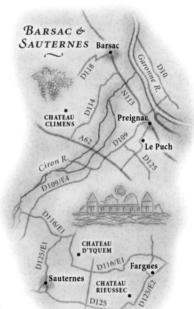

CLASSIFICATION: Premier Grand Cru Classé, Appellation
St.-Emilion Grand Cru

OWNER: De Boüard de Laforest family

ADDRESS: Château Angélus, 33330 St.-Emilion, France

TELEPHONE: 33 05 57 24 71 39

TELEFAX: 33 05 57 24 68 56

E-MAIL: chateau-angelus@chateau-angelus.com

WEBSITE: www.chateau-angelus.com

CONTACT: Hubert de Boüard de Laforest or Emmanuelle
d'Aligny

VISITING POLICY: By appointment only

VINEYARDS

SURFACE AREA: 57.8 acres

GRAPE VARIETALS: 50% Merlot , 47% Cabernet Franc, 3%
Cabernet Sauvignon

AVERAGE AGE OF THE VINES: 35 years

DENSITY OF PLANTATION: 7,000–8,000 vines per hectare

AVERAGE YIELDS: 25–30 hectoliters per hectare

WINEMAKING AND UPBRINGING

At least as many people work at the sorting tables as those
who work as pickers. No pump, no pipe to fill vats, but conveyor belts to carry whole berries into the vats (steel, wood,
concrete vats). Vats are wider than they are tall for the greatest
possible surface contact, and both punching down and
pumping over are employed with long macerations. Wines go
into barrel early, with malolactic fermentation in the barrel
(since 1983). The wines rest on their lees for 6–8 months
(since 1988). No fining, no filtration (since 1988). Aging in
barrel varies from 20 to 28 months. Bottling takes place in the
fall of the second year.

ANNUAL PRODUCTION

Château Angélus: 75,000 bottles

Carillon de l'Angélus: 10,000 bottles

AVERAGE PRICE (VARIABLE DEPENDING ON VINTAGE): $75–100

GREAT RECENT VINTAGES

2003, 2002, 2001, 2000, 1998, 1996, 1995, 1990, 1989

Near the famous St.-Emilion bell tower on the
renowned *pied de côte*, Château Angélus is the result of the passionate commitment of seven generations
of the Boüard de Laforest family. The property's name is
derived from one plot of vines where the Angélus bell
can be heard ringing from all three local churches simul-
taneously—the Chapel of Mazerat, the Church of St.-
Martin of Mazerat, and the Church of St.-Emilion.

Angélus is a St.-Emilion with great popular appeal.
With a large production (much of it exported), a lovely
label, and a charming, supple style of wine, Angélus has
been able to build a strong following among enthusiasts
of the wines of St.-Emilion. Angélus is located in the
Mazerat Valley, with vineyards planted on calcareous
clay loam and clay/sandy soil on the lower slopes. The
entire vineyard enjoys a perfect southern exposure.

In the 1960s and 1970s, Angélus produced a wine
that started life with a charming fruity intensity, then
proceeded to disintegrate in a matter of a few short
years. This all changed in the 1980s. The well-known
Bordeaux oenologist Michel Rolland was brought in to
consult, and he insisted that the property age the wine
in 100% oak casks. Previously, the wine had been aged
in vats and saw no oak aging at all. Fermenting the wine
in small oak casks (much like the Pomerol Le Pin)
tends to add an extraordinary amount of complexity
and intensity to the wine. However, only small estates
or those committed to spending huge sums of money
on labor can age their wine this way, because it is a
time-consuming, backbreaking process.

The results have been stunning. No doubt the young
proprietor, Hubert de Boüard de Laforest, is also making
a much stricter selection of only the best lots for the
final wine. Angélus was denied elevation to premier
grand cru status in the 1985 classification of the wines of
St.-Emilion, but it did receive that promotion in 1996.

The "new" Angélus style still emphasizes early accessibility, with intense, rich, supple, fat fruitiness. However, the wine is now much deeper colored and more
concentrated, and it has more supportive tannins to
help it age better. This was and still is accomplished by
applying commonsense viticultural techniques, lower

yields, a riper harvest, and then ostensibly not interfering in the winemaking. Angélus simply employed time-honored Burgundy winemaking techniques such as cold pre-fermentation macerations, malolactic in barrel, and an upbringing of the wine on its lees.

CHATEAU ANGELUS

2003 Château Angélus

RATING: 94–96 points

Once again, Angélus is one of Bordeaux's great successes thanks to the extraordinary hard work and skills of one of its owners, Hubert de Boüard de Laforest. The 2003 is a blend of 55% Cabernet Franc and 45% Merlot. Some *cuvées* of Cabernet Franc achieved nearly 16% natural alcohol. Inky/purple to the rim, with a stunning perfume of flowers, red and black fruits, lead pencil shavings, smoke, and roasted coffee, it is an opulent, heady effort possessing loads of glycerin, extremely low acidity, and a 60+-second finish. This hedonistic, intellec-

tually pleasing, full-bodied wine is a packed and stacked beauty. Thick, juicy flavors cascade over the palate, so I suspect this 2003 will drink well young, yet age for 15–20 years. It may be a modern-day version of its 1947 counterpart.

2002 Château Angélus

RATING: 92 points

A somewhat atypical Angélus given the high percentage of Cabernet Franc (47%, along with 50% Merlot and 3% Cabernet Sauvignon), this 2002 displays great class as well as potential complexity. Its blue/purple color is accompanied by a big, elegant, sweet wine that combines finesse with power and authority. Because of the high amount of Cabernet Franc, it may turn out to be one of the most aromatically compelling Angélus offerings to date. There is also robust tannin apparent in the long, medium to full–bodied finish. It is unquestionably one of St.-Emilion's most complete, concentrated, and provocative wines of 2002. Anticipated maturity: 2008–2020.

2001 Château Angélus

RATING: 93 points

Another brilliant performance by Hubert de Boüard, the 2001 Angélus (6,250 cases) is a more restrained and delineated version of the 2000. It has shed much of its tannin, and seems far more evolved and open-knit than I thought prior to bottling. Its deep purple color is followed by a rich nose of creosote, charcoal, blackberries, plums, cassis, and espresso roast. Elegant, medium-bodied, and rich, with a measured ripeness and moderate structure in the pure, nicely proportioned finish, it is less massive than either the 2000 or 2003, yet is also beautifully put together. Anticipated maturity: 2007–2017.

2000 Château Angélus

RATING: 96 points

An outrageously ripe, concentrated, dense effort, the 2000 offers up aromas of blackberry liqueur and vintage port. As the wine sits in the glass, graphite, wet stones, smoke, barbecue spices, and olives also make an appearance. It unfolds on the palate in layers, is full-bodied, big and rich yet incredibly poised, well balanced, and pure. Quite backward, this is one of the greatest Angélus made to date. Bravo! Anticipated maturity: 2009–2030.

1998 Château Angélus

RATING: 95+ points

A dazzling effort, the 1998 boasts an opaque purple color in addition to an exceptional bouquet of smoke, licorice, plums, black raspberries, and blackberries. As the wine sits in the glass, coffee and chocolate also emerge. Full-bodied, flamboyant, well delineated, and beautifully balanced as well as layered, with well-integrated tannin in the powerful, rich finish, this 1998 requires cellaring. Anticipated maturity: 2008–2025.

1996 Château Angélus

RATING: 91+ points

A massive, powerful Angélus, this wine exhibits a saturated black/ruby/purple color as well as an impressively endowed nose of dried herbs, roasted meats, new saddle leather, plum liqueur, and cassis. In the mouth, olive notes make an impression. This sweet, full-bodied, exceptionally concentrated wine is atypically backward and ferociously tannic. It was revealing more sweetness and forwardness immediately prior to bottling, but I would recommend three to four years of cellaring. Anticipated maturity: 2007–2025.

1995 Château Angélus

RATING: 95 points

A superb effort in this vintage, Angélus's opaque purple–colored 1995 is a massive, powerful, rich offering with plenty of ripe, sweet tannin. The wine's aromatics include scents of Provençal olives, jammy black cherries, blackberries, truffles, and toast. A very full-bodied wine, it is layered, thick, and pure. This is the most concentrated of the 1995 St.-Emilion premier grand crus. Anticipated maturity: now–2025.

1994 Château Angélus

RATING: 92 points

Another inky, purple/black-colored wine, the 1994 offers up heavenly scents of smoked meats, barbecue spices, hickory wood, and plenty of cassis and kirsch. The fruit's phenomenal purity and denseness, as well as its overall balance, is admirable in view of the massive, muscular personality of this huge, full-bodied wine oozing with extract. It is a tour de force in winemaking. Anticipated maturity: now–2020.

1990 Château Angélus

RATING: 96 points

This is a softer, fleshier, even more flamboyant version of the 1989. The acid seemed lower, the alcohol and glycerin levels slightly higher, but this dense, ruby/purple-colored wine, which shows a bit of pink at the edge, is developing beautifully, and is an example of a wine that is incredibly satisfying both hedonistically and intellectually. Very full-bodied, splendidly rich, pure, with intense notes of creosote, smoke, blackberry, and cassis, this provocative wine should drink well for at least another 10–15 years. Anticipated maturity: now–2015. How fascinating it always is to do a blind tasting between this vintage and the 1989.

1989 Château Angélus

RATING: 96 points

A great Angélus and one of the two or three best vintages made under the talented young Hubert de Boüard, this wine still has a youthful, saturated ruby/purple color and a sweet nose of melted licorice intermixed with crème de cassis, tapenade, cedar, spice box, and vanilla. Opulent and rich, it is one of the 1989s that justifies the lofty reputation of this vintage. Extremely full-bodied, this wine can be drunk now or cellared for at least another 10–15 years. Anticipated maturity: now–2015.

CLASSIFICATION: Premier Grand Cru Classé A St.-Emilion

OWNERS: Micheline, Catherine, and Alain Vauthier

ADDRESS: Château Ausone, 33330 St.-Emilion, France

TELEPHONE: 33 05 57 24 68 88

TELEFAX: 33 05 57 74 47 39

E-MAIL: château.ausone@wanadoo.fr

WEBSITE: www.château-ausone.com

VISITING POLICY: Wine professionals only

VINEYARDS

SURFACE AREA: 17.3 acres

GRAPE VARIETALS: 50% Merlot, 50% Cabernet Franc

AVERAGE AGE OF THE VINES: 50–55 years

DENSITY OF PLANTATION: 6,000–7,800 vines per hectare

AVERAGE YIELDS: 35 hectoliters per hectare

WINEMAKING AND UPBRINGING

Twenty-one to twenty-eight day fermentation and maceration in temperature-controlled wooden vats. Malolactics and 19–23 months aging in new oak barrels with rackings every 3 months. There is a light fining, but nary any filtration.

ANNUAL PRODUCTION

Château Ausone: 20,000–23,000 bottles

Chapelle d'Ausone: 7,000 bottles

AVERAGE PRICE (VARIABLE DEPENDING ON VINTAGE): $150–500

GREAT RECENT VINTAGES

2003, 2002, 2001, 2000, 1999, 1998, 1996, 1995, 1983, 1982, 1976

If the first-time visitor to Bordeaux has just one château and vineyard to visit, it should be the tiny Ausone property (visits are restricted to the wine trade). Perched on one of the hillsides outside the medieval walls of St.-Emilion, Ausone has a spectacular location, made all the more startling because of its tiny vineyard of very old vines and the extensive limestone caves that house the property's wine cellar. Ausone is named after the Roman poet Ausonius, who lived between A.D. 320 and 395. He was also known to have had a vineyard in the area (closer apparently to Bordeaux than to St.-Emilion), and while there are Roman ruins at Ausone, it is highly doubtful that Ausonius himself had anything to do with this estate.

Despite the great historical significance of Ausone and the fact that it has one of the most esteemed locations for making wine in all of Bordeaux (a steep southwestern slope), the record of wine quality was mediocre—even poor—during the 1960s and 1970s.

Ausone's minuscule production makes it almost impossible to find commercially. Even more rare than the famous Pomerol estate of Pétrus, yet considerably less expensive, Ausone has a style that is totally different from St.-Emilion's other famous estate, Cheval Blanc.

In spite of what appeared to be a cordial relationship between the two families that owned Ausone, there was internal bickering and constant friction over the philosophy of winemaking, and finally the Vauthier family bought out Madame Dubois-Challon in the mid-1990s. Winemaker Pascal Delbeck was replaced by Alain Vauthier, who receives oenological consultation from Libourne's Michel Rolland. While partisans complain that Ausone is now being made in a more forward, commercial style, this is nothing more than the whining of those who have an axe to grind. The most significant changes made under Vauthier/Rolland have been slightly later harvests if weather conditions permit, malolactic fermentation in barrel rather than tank, a stricter selection, and the introduction of a second wine. The initial efforts under the new regime have resulted in spectacular wines that display all of Ausone's elegance, finesse, and extraordinary mineral-based personality, as well as greater concentration and intensity. In fact, the development of these Ausones during their *élevage* in barrel and bottle has been brilliant, and the wines have lost none of their "typicity," as the Dubois-Challon/Delbeck supporters have opined. I expect Ausone to be more consistent and to reach even higher peaks of quality under the inspired leadership of Alain Vauthier.

CHATEAU AUSONE

2003 Château Ausone

RATING: 98–100 points

No one who knows Alain Vauthier will be surprised to learn that he has produced a 2003 Ausone that equals or surpasses his perfect 2000. A perfectionist in all senses, he oversees every detail and constantly keeps his mind open to new winemaking techniques that might enhance Ausone's extraordinary *terroir*. Made from 23 hectoliters per hectare, there are only 1,500 cases of the prodigious 2003 grand vin. A blend of 55% Cabernet Franc and 45% Merlot, it is one of the greatest wines I have ever tasted from cask. An inky/purple color is followed by an extraordinary crystalline, statuesque bouquet of flowers, raspberries, blackberries, liqueur of minerals, and a hint of quince. Extremely rich yet light and seamless with a nearly endless finish (it lasts for more than 70 seconds), this is an ethereal, monumental effort. In contrast to the 2000 at a similar age, it comes across as more flattering because of low acidity and higher alcohol. I suspect it will close down and reemerge in 10–20 years. This extraordinary *terroir* has produced an amazing 2003. Anticipated maturity: 2015–2050+.

2002 Château Ausone

RATING: 94 points

Alain Vauthier seemingly can do no wrong. A candidate for wine of the vintage, and clearly the finest 2002 from Bordeaux's right bank (a vintage that favors the Cabernet Sauvignon–based wines of the Médoc), the 2002 Ausone boasts an opaque blue/purple color as well as aromas reminiscent of liqueur of crushed rocks interwoven with raspberries, black currants, and licorice. It is extraordinarily pure, precise, and medium to full–bodied; it possesses huge levels of tannin, but they are balanced by equally prodigious levels of concentrated fruit. Although aged in 100% new oak, the wood is not detectable given the amazing concentration and texture of this profound 2002. It is another tour de force in winemaking from one of the most meticulous and conscientious wine producers in Bordeaux. Anticipated maturity: 2013–2060.

2001 Château Ausone

RATING: 98 points

Let's all stand and applaud Alain Vauthier. For the fourth straight vintage, he has produced one of the most compelling wines of the year. The 2001 Ausone has put on even more weight than I anticipated. The wine of the vintage, this inky/purple-colored 2001 boasts a provocative, floral perfume of crushed stones, raspberries, blackberries, crème de cassis, licorice, and smoke. What makes it so sensational are the layers of flavor and nuances that unfold as the wine sits in the glass as well as on the palate. An extraordinarily intense effort, but remarkably elegant and well balanced, it ideally needs another decade of cellaring; it should last for four to five decades! Alain Vauthier is a perfectionist, which is evidenced by what he has produced over the last half-dozen vintages at Ausone. Kudos to readers lucky enough to find a bottle or two . . . and to live long enough to enjoy them in their prime. Anticipated maturity: 2012–2050+.

2000 Château Ausone

RATING: 100 points

Alain Vauthier has produced a prodigious wine that masterfully captures the essence of Ausone's *terroir*. A saturated black/purple color is followed by sensational aromas of ink, cherries, blackberries, blueberries, and that wet stones/liquid minerality characteristic. The wine has phenomenal presence on the palate

as well as astonishing richness and purity. Despite its extract, power, and richness, it is remarkably light, with a surreal delicacy. It is a tour de force in winemaking and a compelling expression of this magical *terroir*. It should prove to be legendary, but sadly, anyone over the age of 50 will probably not live to see it come close to maturity. Anticipated maturity: 2020–2075.

1999 Château Ausone

RATING: 95 points

Is the 1999 Ausone the wine of the vintage? Dense purple color, a compelling bouquet of licorice, minerals, black and blueberry liqueur, extraordinary delineation, high tannin, superb extract, and phenomenal richness all are the stuff of a legend. This wine seems impossible to have emerged from a vintage like 1999. Alain Vauthier produced only 20,000 bottles because he eliminated one-fourth of the tiny crop. The result is out-and-out fabulous, but the wine needs 10–12 years of cellaring. Anticipated maturity: 2015–2050.

1998 Château Ausone

RATING: 94+ points

A dense opaque purple color offers up restrained but pure aromas of liquid minerals, blackberries, black raspberries, and flowers. Medium to full–bodied, with high tannin but a long, super-pure, symmetrical mouth-feel, this dazzling, extremely complex Ausone requires six to seven years of cellaring. Anticipated maturity: 2010–2050.

1997 Château Ausone

RATING: 91 points

One of the finest wines of the vintage, this dark purple–colored effort reveals black raspberry, blackberry, mineral, and floral aromas in its complex, multidimensional bouquet. In the mouth, it is medium-bodied, with sweet, ripe fruit, firm tannin, good acidity for the vintage, and a long, impressively endowed, moderately tannic finish. Moreover, it will be one of the vintage's longest-lived wines. Anticipated maturity: 2007–2020.

1996 Château Ausone

RATING: 93+ points

The color of the 1996 is a dense ruby/black/purple. Reluctant aromas of blueberries, blackberries, minerals, flowers, truffles, and subtle new oak eventually emerge. Elegant on the attack, with sweet ripeness and a delicate, concentrated richness, the hallmark of this wine is subtlety rather than flamboyance. A sweet mid-palate sets it apart from many of the uninspiring Ausones of the 1980s and 1970s. The wine is stylish, and presently understated, with tremendous aging potential. Anticipated maturity: 2008–2040.

1995 Château Ausone

RATING: 93 points

Ausone's extraordinary minerality is present in the 1995, yet there are more aromatics, a richer, more multidimensional palate impression, and a fuller texture—all with the *terroir* brilliantly expressed. The wine boasts a dense ruby/purple color and an emerging but tightly knit nose of spring flowers, minerals, earth, and black fruits. Rich, with an opulent texture and surprising sexiness for a young vintage of Ausone, the medium-bodied 1995 displays exquisite balance between its acid, tannin, alcohol, and fruit. Although it is not yet seamless, all the elements are present for an extraordinary evolution in the bottle. This wine will age at a glacial pace for 30–40 years. Anticipated maturity: 2010–2045.

1990 Château Ausone

RATING: 92+ points

The 1990 is not a charming, precocious wine. It is closed, but the color is a dense, dark ruby with no amber or orange at the edge. The fruit is sweeter, and the wine is more muscular, richer, and broader in the mouth, without losing Ausone's telltale minerality, spice, and curranty fruit. There is a good inner core of sweet fruit in this medium to full–bodied wine that needs another 15–20 years of cellaring. Can the 1990 possibly rival the 1983 or 1982? Perhaps . . . but don't bet on it. Anticipated maturity: 2008–2030.

1983 Château Ausone

RATING: 91 points

A very successful vintage for Ausone, this wine seems to be close to full maturity, but knowing the history of this château, it could very well last another 50 or more years. The wine shows a dark garnet color with considerable amber at the edge. Sweet notes of fruitcake, spice box, underbrush, licorice, and jammy red and black fruits tumble from the glass. The wine is medium-bodied, round, nearly opulent by the standards of this château, with a spicy, somewhat pinched finish. Anticipated maturity: now–2025+.

1982 Château Ausone

RATING: 91 points

Amber at the edge is evident in this dark garnet–colored wine. Sweet notes of weedy tobacco intermixed with red currant jam, spice box, and cedar jump from the glass of this relatively perfumed vintage for Ausone. The attack is sweet, with surprising glycerin and ripeness, but then the finish narrows out with plenty of tannin, hardness, and structure. The wine seems to have come out of its dormant stage, but where it's going is anyone's guess. Anticipated maturity: 2008–2030.

CHATEAU CHEVAL BLANC

CLASSIFICATION: Premier Grand Cru Classé A

OWNERS: Bernard Arnault and Albert Frère

ADDRESS: Château Cheval Blanc, 33330 St.-Emilion, France

TELEPHONE: 33 05 57 55 55 55

TELEFAX: 33 05 57 55 55 50

E-MAIL: contact@chateau-chevalblanc.com

WEBSITE: www.chateau-chevalblanc.com

CONTACT: Cécile Supéry

VISITING POLICY: By appointment only

VINEYARDS

SURFACE AREA: 91.4 acres

GRAPE VARIETALS: 58% Cabernet Franc, 42% Merlot

AVERAGE AGE OF THE VINES: 45 years

DENSITY OF PLANTATION: 8,000 vines per hectare

AVERAGE YIELDS: 35 hectoliters per hectare

WINEMAKING AND UPBRINGING

Twenty-one- to twenty-eight-day fermentation and maceration in temperature-controlled stainless-steel and concrete vats. After malolactics, 18 months of aging in new oak barrels with rackings every 3 months. Fining with egg whites, no filtration.

ANNUAL PRODUCTION

Château Cheval Blanc: 100,000 bottles

Le Petit Cheval: 40,000 bottles

AVERAGE PRICE (VARIABLE DEPENDING ON VINTAGE): $125–500

GREAT RECENT VINTAGES

2001, 2000, 1999, 1998, 1995, 1990, 1985, 1983, 1982

Cheval Blanc is undoubtedly one of Bordeaux's most profound wines. For most of the last 50 years or so, it has sat alone at the top of St.-Emilion's hierarchy, representing the finest wine this appellation can produce. However, since the renaissance began at Ausone, in addition to the revolution in quality led by St.-Emilion's *avant-garde garagistes* (unheralded producers pushing quality to the maximum), Cheval Blanc has

had to share some of the limelight. Cheval Blanc is a remarkably distinctive wine. Sitting right on the Pomerol border, in the St.-Emilion *graves* sector, with only a ditch and road separating its vineyards from those of l'Evangile and La Conseillante, it has for years been accused of making a wine that is as much a Pomerol as it is a St.-Emilion.

Among the "Big Eight" of Bordeaux, Cheval Blanc probably has the broadest window of drinkability. It is usually delicious when first bottled, yet it has the ability in the top years to gain weight and last. None of the Médoc first growths, or Pétrus in Pomerol, can claim to have such flexibility. Only Haut-Brion comes closest to matching Cheval Blanc's early drinkability and precociousness, as well as the stuffing and overall balance and intensity to age for 20–30 years. In the big, rich vintages, Cheval Blanc evolves exceptionally well, although one suspects that far too much of this wine is consumed long before its real majesty begins to emerge.

For me, Cheval Blanc is Cheval Blanc—it is like no other St.-Emilion or Pomerol I have ever tasted. The choice of grape varieties, equal parts Cabernet Franc and Merlot, is highly unusual. No other major château uses this much Cabernet Franc. Yet this grape reaches its zenith in Cheval Blanc's gravelly, sandy, and clay soil that is underpinned by a bed of iron rock, producing an extremely rich, ripe, intense, viscous wine.

The style of wine produced at Cheval Blanc has no doubt contributed to its immense popularity. Dark ruby in color, in the very good vintages it is an opulently rich and fruity wine, full bodied, voluptuous, and lush, and deceptively easy to drink when young. The bouquet is especially distinctive. At its best, Cheval Blanc is an even more fragrant wine than Médoc first growths such as Château Margaux. Scents of minerals, menthol, exotic spices, tobacco, and intense, superripe, black fruits can be overwhelming.

As the tasting notes demonstrate, Cheval Blanc can produce a decadently exotic wine of unbelievable depth and richness. However, in some vintages, it has been one of the most disappointing wines of the "Big Eight" châteaux of Bordeaux. Cheval Blanc was not a strong performer during the decades of the 1960s and 1970s. However, with the increasing attention to quality and detail provided by administrator Jacques Hébrard, the quality of this wine during the 1980s became more consistent. Hébrard's successor, Pierre Lurton, has pushed the quality and consistency of Cheval Blanc to even greater heights. The consecutive vintages of 2000, 1999, and 1998 were the finest Cheval Blanc since the splendid trilogy of 1949, 1948, and 1947.

Cheval Blanc, along with Haut-Brion, remains one of the two least expensive members of Bordeaux's "Big Eight."

CHATEAU CHEVAL BLANC

2003 Château Cheval Blanc

RATING: 89–92 points

It was not easy, as Pierre Lurton acknowledged, having a vineyard on gravelly soils in the stifling, unprecedented heat of the summer of 2003. Only 50% of the crop made it into Cheval Blanc, a blend of 60% Cabernet Franc and 40% Merlot (the highest percentage of Cabernet Franc in many years). A more delicate, elegant style of Cheval that's more into fruit than size, structure, and intensity, this soft, finesse-styled, medium-bodied effort reveals notes of cranberries, mangoes, cherries, and crushed stones in its moderately intense perfume. In the mouth, it is stylish, soft, pure, and builds incrementally. About 4% press wine was added to the final blend. The harvest, which produced only 30 hectoliters per hectare, was Cheval Blanc's earliest ever, with the Merlot picked between September 1 and 5, and the Cabernet Franc between September 10 and 15. Anticipated maturity: 2008–2018.

2002 Château Cheval Blanc

RATING: 89 points

I expected this wine to display more intensity, weight, and aromatic complexity. A blend of equal parts Cabernet Franc and Merlot, the dark ruby–colored 2002 Cheval Blanc exhibits muted aromas of cocoa, mint, cranberries, black cherries, and flowers. Medium-bodied with considerable vigor, freshness, and a cool climate personality, it does not possess the richness, body, or palate persistence found in the titanic 2000 and 1998 or the underrated 1999 and 2001. This is often an enigmatic wine to taste young, and it has a tendency to put on weight and reveal more character with cask as well as bottle age. We'll see. Anticipated maturity: 2007–2017.

2001 Château Cheval Blanc

RATING: 93 points

I was surprised by how soft, opulent, even voluptuous the 2001 Cheval Blanc performed out of bottle as this estate's wines tend to shut down when young. Its deep ruby/purple color was accompanied by sweet aromas of cranberries, black currants, menthol, Asian spices, and underbrush. This seductive blend of 60% Merlot and 40% Cabernet Franc reveals a lush sweetness, medium body, and ripe, well-integrated tannin. A racy effort filled with personality, it should be at its finest between 2007 and 2018.

2000 Château Cheval Blanc

RATING: 100 points

This blend of 53% Merlot and 47% Cabernet Franc boasts a saturated purple color along with a reticent but striking bouquet of blackberries, blueberries, truffles, and mocha. In spite of its tightness, aeration reveals scents of licorice, menthol, and saddle leather. Opulent and full-bodied, with low acidity, sweet tannin, and a 60-second finish, it is unquestionably as profound as the 1990 and 1982. I still believe the 2000 has the potential to be the most compelling Cheval Blanc since the mythical 1947 and 1949, but patience is required. Anticipated maturity: 2010–2030+.

1999 Château Cheval Blanc

RATING: 93 points

A blend of 59% Merlot and 41% Cabernet Franc, the complex, explosively fragrant 1999 Cheval Blanc is already showing well, which is a good sign for a wine that traditionally is reserved early in life but puts on weight and richness in the bottle. Stylistically, this wine is probably made from the same mold as vintages such as 1985, 1966, and 1962. The color is a dense ruby with purple nuances. Once past the blockbuster bouquet of menthol, leather, black fruits, licorice, and mocha, the wine reveals medium body, extraordinary elegance, purity, and sweet, harmonious flavors with no hard edges. A seamless beauty of finesse, charm, and concentration, 1999 has produced an exciting Cheval Blanc to drink relatively young. Anticipated maturity: 2006–2022.

1998 Château Cheval Blanc

RATING: 98+ points

I seriously underestimated this wine, as I tend to do with Cheval Blanc. A potentially immortal example that has gained significant weight since it was bottled, this blend of 55% Cabernet Franc and 45% Merlot has a saturated purple color and a glorious nose of menthol, plums, mulberries, new saddle leather, cocoa, and vanilla. Remarkably fuller bodied than I ever remembered it young, with an amazingly seamless texture and tremendous concentration and extract, this full-bodied yet gorgeously pure and elegant wine is impeccably balanced and certainly one of the all-time great Cheval Blancs. If it continues to improve as much as it has over the last three years since bottling, this wine will certainly rival the 2000, 1990, and 1982. Anticipated maturity: 2009–2030.

1996 Château Cheval Blanc

RATING: 90 points

The elegant, moderately weighted 1996 Cheval Blanc reveals a deep garnet/plum, evolved color. Quintessentially elegant, with a complex nose of black fruits, coconut, smoke, and toast, this medium-bodied wine exhibits sweet fruit on the attack, substantial complexity, and a lush, velvety-textured finish. It is very soft and evolved for a 1996. Anticipated maturity: now–2015.

1995 Château Cheval Blanc

RATING: 92 points

A pretty, attractive Cheval Blanc, the 1995 contains 50% Merlot and 50% Cabernet Franc. This wine has not developed as much fat or weight as its younger sibling, the 1996, but it appears to be an outstanding Cheval Blanc with an enthralling smoky, black currant, coffee, and exotic bouquet. Complex, rich, medium to full–bodied flavors are well endowed and pure, with surprisingly firm tannin in the finish. Unlike the sweeter, riper 1996, the 1995 may be more structured and potentially longer lived. Anticipated maturity: now–2020.

1990 Château Cheval Blanc

RATING: 100 points

This wine has overtaken its closest rival, the 1982. Dense ruby purple with only a bit of lightening at the edge, the explosive nose of black fruits and cassis intermixed with coffee, menthol, and leather is followed by an opulent, splendidly concentrated wine that is sheer nectar. With no hard edges, gorgeously integrated glycerin, tannin, acidity, and alcohol are all present in this seamless classic. The wine has been gorgeous since youth, but is now revealing more aromatic and flavor nuances into the game. This is spectacular stuff! Anticipated maturity: now–2015.

1985 Château Cheval Blanc

RATING: 93 points

A rather seductive style of Cheval Blanc that has been delicious from its youth, this wine continues to develop beautifully. Although it seems to have attained full maturity, the wine shows plenty of sweet plum, mocha, coffee, and black currant fruit intermixed with some menthol, chocolate, and cola. The wine is lush, medium to full–bodied, very soft, and ideal for drinking now and over the next 5–7 years.

1983 Château Cheval Blanc

RATING: 94 points

A glorious wine, and one of the candidates for the wine of the vintage, Cheval Blanc's 1983 shows far more evolved color than its older sibling, the 1982. With explosive aromatic notes of sweet jammy plum, black currant, smoke, coffee, and Asian spice, opulent, medium to full–bodied and lush, this is a gorgeous, very sexy, seductive style of Cheval Blanc that has been consistently delicious from the time it was bottled. It shows no signs of decline despite some increasing amber in the color. The tannins are still sweet, the fruit very present, and the wine totally intact. Anticipated maturity: now–2010.

1982 Château Cheval Blanc

RATING: 96 points

This was consistently a perfect wine early in its life, but it seems to be going through a stage where the tannins are more present, and the extraordinarily exotic opulence that the wine had when young, while still present, is not now as dominant a characteristic. Nevertheless, there is plenty to admire in this full-bodied, very lush Cheval Blanc that has reached full maturity. Sweet notes of red and black fruits intermixed with licorice, spice box, and incense jump from the glass. On the palate, the wine is layered and very rich. It seems to develop interesting nuances the more it sits in the glass, and then suddenly takes a dive. A fascinating Cheval Blanc, and certainly the greatest Cheval Blanc after the 1964 and before the 1990. Anticipated maturity: now–2016.

1964 Château Cheval Blanc

RATING: 96 points

A blockbuster Cheval Blanc and probably the greatest Cheval Blanc made during the 1960s and 1970s, this wine still has a dense, murky garnet color and knockout aromatics of coffee, black fruit, and spice box. The wine is opulent and fleshy with enormous glycerin and power. It is still very muscular, also with slightly robust tannins to shed, but this wine seems almost immortal in terms of longevity. My best guess is that, from pristinely stored bottles, this wine is still in late adolescence and not yet at its peak of maturity. Anticipated maturity: now–2025.

CLASSIFICATION: Second Growth in 1855

OWNER: Mr. Michel Reybier has been the new owner of the Château since 2000.

ADDRESS: Cos d'Estournel, 33180 St.-Estèphe, France

TELEPHONE: 33 05 56 73 15 50

TELEFAX: 33 05 56 59 72 59

E-MAIL: estournel@estournel.com

WEBSITE: www.estournel.com

CONTACT: Jean-Guillaume Prats

VISITING POLICY: Private tours and tastings, by reservation only. Open from Monday to Friday. Tours in French or English.

VINEYARDS

SURFACE AREA: 160.1 acres

GRAPE VARIETALS: 60% Cabernet Sauvignon, 30% Merlot, 2% Cabernet Franc

AVERAGE AGE OF THE VINES: 35 years

DENSITY OF PLANTATION: 8,000–10,000 vines per hectare

AVERAGE YIELDS: 40 hectoliters per hectare

WINEMAKING AND UPBRINGING

Severe pruning is done in the vineyard in order to maintain the yields *lutte raisonnée* (reasonably low). Cos d'Estournel is vinified in concrete vats and Les Pagodes de Cos in steel.

Cold pre-macerations last for 10–15 days and are adapted to the extraction according to the vintage and phenolic ripeness. The wine is aged in oak barrels for 18–22 months.

While Cos maintains a healthy respect for tradition, it is not averse to innovation and conducts new experiments every year.

ANNUAL PRODUCTION

Cos d'Estournel: 200,000 bottles

Les Pagodes de Cos: 130,000 bottles

AVERAGE PRICE (VARIABLE DEPENDING ON VINTAGE): $35–125

GREAT RECENT VINTAGES

2003, 2002, 2001, 2000, 1996, 1995, 1989, 1986, 1985, 1982

Louis Gaspard d'Estournel was born in 1762, during the reign of Louis XV, and died in 1853 under Napoleon III at the remarkable age of 91. During his life, he had one sole passion: Cos. In the early and mid-19th century, Cos d'Estournel's wine fetched prices higher than many of the most prestigious Bordeaux and was exported as far away as India. In fact, Louis Gaspard d'Estournel became known as "the Maharajah of St.-Estèphe."

In 1852, overwhelmed with debts he had accumulated in order to extend and beautify his estate, Louis Gaspard d'Estournel sold the estate to Martyns, a London banker. He was permitted by Martyns to stay and live on the land, and he died there in 1853, two years before the supreme consecration of his work—the classification of 1855 placed Cos d'Estournel at the head of the St.-Estèphes.

In 1869, Martyns sold Cos d'Estournel to the Errazu, an aristocratic Basque family who resold it to the Hostein brothers in 1889. In 1917, Cos d'Estournel was

purchased by Fernand Ginestet, one of the leading Bordeaux wine merchants. His grandsons, Jean-Marie, Yves, and Bruno Prats, inherited the château.

In 1998, the Prats brothers sold Cos d'Estournel to the Merlaut family, the owners of the Taillan group, and to Argentinian investors represented by Mr. Moyano.

Sold again in 2000, Cos d'Estournel now belongs to the Société des Domaines Reybier, directed by Jean-Guillaume Prats, great-grandson of Fernand Ginestet and son of Bruno Prats, who was also the manager of Cos d'Estournel from 1970 to 1998.

This château, which resembles an Asian pagoda, sits on a ridge immediately north of the Pauillac border, looking down on its famous neighbor, Lafite Rothschild. Between 1982 and 1996, the wines had gone from one strength to another, and in most vintages Cos d'Estournel could be expected to produce one of the Médoc's finest wines. After a brief lackluster intermission (1997–1999), the château quickly rebounded.

Atypically for a Médoc, Cos is distinguished by the high percentage of Merlot used in the blend, 40%, and the above-average use of new oak casks, 60–100%. This proportion of Merlot is among the highest used in the Haut-Médoc and accounts for the fleshy, richly textured character so noticeable in recent vintages of Cos d'Estournel.

This is one of the few major Bordeaux estates that was adamantly in favor of filtration of wine, before both cask aging and bottling. However, former manager and owner Bruno Prats belonged to the avant garde of new wine technology and in 1989 decided to eliminate the second filtration prior to the bottling. In 2002, his son, the estate manager Jean-Guillaume Prats, decided to eschew any filtration at all. The results speak for themselves—Cos d'Estournel, after having to play runner-up to Montrose in the 1950s and 1960s, emerged in the 1980s as one of the most popular wines in Bordeaux. Readers should also note that Cos d'Estournel has been particularly successful in difficult vintages, specifically 1993, 1992, and 1991. In spite of the recent changes in ownership, this estate remains impeccably managed and put together a brilliant trilogy of wines between 2001 and 2003.

COS D'ESTOURNEL

2003 Cos d'Estournel

RATING: 96–98 points

Under the inspired ownership of Michel Reybier and his talented winemaking team, led by Jean-Guillaume Prats, Cos d'Estournel's quality has been on the rise since the 2000 vintage. The 2003 is one of the greatest offerings this hallowed estate has ever produced. This 15,000-case *cuvée* is a blend of 70% Cabernet Sauvignon (atypically high), 27% Merlot, 2% Petit Verdot, and 1% Cabernet Franc. With a pH of 3.72, and 13.5% alcohol, it is a substantial yet extraordinarily elegant claret. There are no hints of overripeness (prunes, saddle leather, etc.) or exoticism, just classic black currant, melted licorice, blackberry, smoke, and spice notes. Seventy percent of the crop made it in to this *cuvée,* which was fashioned from low yields of 30 hectoliters per hectare. Cos d'Estournel appears to have done everything right, waiting to harvest fully ripe fruit (the Merlot between September 12 and 14, and the Cabernet Franc and Cabernet Sauvignon between September 18 and 25). The wine possesses a thickness and unctuousness typical of the top 2003 northern Médocs, as well as remarkable definition and elegance. It is the most impressive young Cos I have ever tasted. However, the tannin is high, so it will require patience. Anticipated maturity: 2012–2030. Bravo!

2002 Cos d'Estournel

RATING: 94 points

A brilliant effort for the vintage, the 2002 Cos d'Estournel is a blend of 58% Cabernet Sauvignon, 38% Merlot, 3% Cabernet Franc, and 1% Petit Verdot made from low yields of 32 hectoliters per hectare. It is an outstanding expression of Bordeaux elegance married to surprising power, yet it never goes over the top. Complex aromatics include scents of smoke, licorice, red as well as black currants, vanilla, spice box, and Asian spices. The wine is medium-bodied, with great purity and elegance, a superb mouth-feel and texture, and a long, rich finish. It is not a huge blockbuster, but clearly Jean-Guillaume Prats fully exploited his vineyard's potential and did not try to overdo it, as some of his colleagues did. Anticipated maturity: 2008–2022.

2001 Cos d'Estournel

RATING: 93 points

A beautiful effort, the 2001 Cos d'Estournel (65% Cabernet Sauvignon and 35% Merlot) exhibits a poised, noble bouquet of black currants, cedar, spice box, and licorice. A hint of truffles emerges as it sits in the glass. Medium-bodied with sweet fruit (mostly black) and nicely integrated wood, it builds incrementally in the mouth, ending with a 50-second finish. Drink this stylish, restrained yet substantial claret over the next 15+ years.

2000 Cos d'Estournel

RATING: 92+ points

This wine puts on weight and grows in stature every time I go back to it. In fact, from the bottle it was better than ever. A blend of 60% Cabernet Sauvignon, 38% Merlot, and 2% Cabernet Franc, the 2000 Cos d'Estournel suffers only in comparison with its successor, the 2001. Deep bluish purple in color with a reticent but emerging bouquet of cedar, licorice, blueberry, cassis, vanilla, and lead pencil shavings, this medium-bodied, slightly sinewy Cos d'Estournel has relatively high tannin, an excellent mid-palate, and a persistent finish. Purity and classicism are hallmarks of this top-flight wine. Anticipated maturity: 2010–2022.

1996 Cos d'Estournel

RATING: 93+ points

Made from 65% Cabernet Sauvignon and 35% Merlot, this is a huge, backward wine reminiscent of the 1986 Cos d'Estournel. The 1996 possesses an opaque purple color as well as pure aromatics consisting of cassis, grilled herbs, coffee, and toasty new oak. Massive in the mouth and one of the most structured and concentrated young Cos d'Estournels I have ever tasted, this thick, structured, tannic wine has closed down significantly since bottling. It requires 2–3 years of cellaring, and it should last for 30–35 years. It is a fabulous Cos, but patience is required. Anticipated maturity: 2006–2030.

1995 Cos d'Estournel

RATING: 95 points

A wine of extraordinary intensity and accessibility, the 1995 Cos d'Estournel is a sexier, more hedonistic offering than the muscular, backward 1996. Opulent, with forward aromatics (gobs of black fruits intermixed with toasty scents and a boat-load of spice), this terrific Cos possesses remarkable intensity, full body, and layers of jammy fruit nicely framed by the wine's new oak. Because of its low acidity and sweet tannin, the 1995 will be difficult to resist young, although it will age for two to three decades. Anticipated maturity: now–2025.

1990 Cos d'Estournel

RATING: 95 points

The 1990 has consistently charmed tasters with its flashy display of opulent Merlot (about 40% of the blend) mixed with jammy Cabernet Sauvignon. This super-concentrated wine possesses a roasted herb, sweet, jammy black fruit–scented nose, infused with opulent and succulent licorice, spice box, and cedar. Pure and full-bodied, this concentrated wine has entered its plateau of maturity. The wine is open, flattering, and impossible to resist. Anticipated maturity: now–2015.

1986 Cos d'Estournel

RATING: 93+ points

The 1986 is a highly extracted wine, with a black/ruby color (some pink is showing at the rim) and plenty of toasty, smoky notes in its bouquet that suggest ripe plums, licorice, and black currants. Evolving at a glacial pace, it exhibits massive, huge, ripe, extremely concentrated flavors with impressive depth and richness. It possesses power, weight, and tannin, and it is a wine for long-term aging. Anticipated maturity: now–2020.

1985 Cos d'Estournel

RATING: 92 points

Forward, with a fabulously scented toasty bouquet and concentrated red and black fruits (especially black cherries), the 1985 is rich, lush, long, and medium to full–bodied. Very fragrant, with gobs of sweet black fruits, minerals, and spice in both its flavors and aromatics, this wine is fully mature and not likely to improve. Anticipated maturity: now–2010.

1982 Cos d'Estournel

RATING: 96 points

Like many 1982s, Cos d'Estournel was flattering, opulent, and easy to drink in its youth. The 1982 is atypically thick, super-concentrated, rich, and powerful. The wine reveals no signs of age in its opaque dark ruby/purple color. The tannin is present, yet the wine reveals that fabulous inner core of sweet, jammy, black currant and black cherry fruit. There is considerable glycerin and body in this youthful but immensely promising example of Cos d'Estournel that has entered its plateau of maturity. It has at least 15 years of life remaining. Anticipated maturity: now–2018.

CLASSIFICATION: There is no official classification of the wines in Pomerol.

OWNER: Famille Durantou/GFA du Château L'Eglise-Clinet

ADDRESS: L'Eglise-Clinet, 33500, Pomerol, France

TELEPHONE: 33 05 57 259 659

TELEFAX: 33 05 57 252 196

E-MAIL: eglise@denis-durantou.com

WEBSITE: www.eglise-clinet.com

CONTACT: Denis Durantou

VISITING POLICY: By appointment only

VINEYARDS

SURFACE AREA: 11.12 acres

GRAPE VARIETALS: 85% Merlot, 15% Cabernet Franc

AVERAGE AGE OF THE VINES: 40 years

DENSITY OF PLANTATION: 6,500–7,000 vines per hectare

AVERAGE YIELDS: 35–38 hectoliters per hectare

WINEMAKING AND UPBRINGING

Fifteen- to twenty-one-day fermentation and maceration in small temperature-controlled stainless-steel tanks of 30- to 50-hectoliter capacity. Fifteen to eighteen months aging with 40–70% new oak. Fining, no filtration.

ANNUAL PRODUCTION

Château L'Eglise-Clinet: 12,000–15,000 bottles

La Petite Eglise: 15,000–20,000 bottles

AVERAGE PRICE (VARIABLE DEPENDING ON VINTAGE): $90–150

GREAT RECENT VINTAGES

2001, 2000, 1998, 1995, 1990, 1989, 1988, 1986, 1985

From a family estate dating from the 18th century, L'Eglise-Clinet is one of the least-known Pomerol estates. A typically fat, succulent, juicy, richly fruity style of Pomerol, this wine is admirably and traditionally made, but because of the tiny production, it is rarely tasted. The vineyard is well situated on the plateau of Pomerol behind the church, where deep gravel beds intermingle with sand, clay, and iron.

L'Eglise-Clinet is one of the few Pomerol vineyards that was not replanted after the 1956 killing freeze (nor was there any vine damage in the frosts of 1985 and 1987), and consequently it has very old vines, a few of which exceed 100 years in age.

Until 1983, Pierre Lasserre, the owner of the bigger and better-known Pomerol property of Clos René, farmed this vineyard under the *métayage* system (a type of vineyard rental agreement) and turned out a wine that was rich, well balanced, supple, firm, and always well vinified. Since then, the winery has been run by the young, extremely dedicated Denis Durantou, who is trying to take this tiny vineyard to the very top of the unofficial Pomerol hierarchy. His secrets to success include a remarkable commitment to quality, the age of the vines (they average 40–45 years), plus the fact that in abundant and/or difficult vintages one-fourth of the crop is relegated to the second wine, called La Petite L'Eglise. One cannot applaud the efforts of Denis Durantou enough.

The price for a bottle of L'Eglise-Clinet is high, as connoisseurs recognize that this is one of the top dozen wines of the appellation.

2002 Château L'Eglise-Clinet

RATING: 90 points

An exceptionally strong effort from vigneron Denis Durantou, who works his vineyard brilliantly and makes truly fine wines, this dense ruby/purple-colored Pomerol offers up aromas of pure raspberries and cherries, subtle wood, and a hint of earth. It is moderately tannic, medium to full-bodied, intense, and pure. A noteworthy success for the vintage, it will be at its finest between 2008 and 2018.

2001 Château L'Eglise-Clinet

RATING: 94 points

Denis Durantou has turned in one of the vintage's most substantial wines, a tour de force in 2001. Sadly, there are only 1,500 cases of this 85% Merlot /15% Cabernet Franc blend. A beauty, this brilliant effort boasts a dense ruby/purple color as well as a glorious nose of red and black fruits, flowers, sweet oak, and hints of licorice as well as truffles. Opulent, medium to full–bodied, concentrated, tannic, and persistent on the palate (the finish lasts 40 seconds), give it 2–4 years of cellaring, and drink it between 2007 and 2020.

2000 Château L'Eglise-Clinet

RATING: 96 points

Truly spectacular, this could be another of the great classics that Durantou has produced over recent years. For now, it is hard to believe it could rival or eclipse the fabulous 1998 or, for that matter, the 1995, but the 2000 has gone from strength to strength in its evolution. From bottle, it is dazzling. The saturated ruby/purple color offers up pure fruit notes of mulberries, figs, and cassis intermixed with hints of licorice and toasty oak. Revealing great palate presence, tremendous texture, sweet tannin, relatively low acidity, and a finish that exceeds 60 seconds, this wine, I assume, will close down, not to reopen for nearly a decade. This is a profound example from a proprietor who has never subscribed to the new, progressive/razzle-dazzle techniques being employed by some of the cutting-edge producers. Here it is low-yield, ripe-fruit, and non-interventionist winemaking at its purest. Anticipated maturity: 2010–2035+.

1999 Château L'Eglise-Clinet

RATING: 92 points

The 1999 L'Eglise-Clinet has evolved beautifully. One of the stars of the vintage, it is an extraordinary expression of elegance married to power. An opaque purple color is followed by aromas of black raspberries, currants, licorice, graphite, truffles, and earth. Sweet and expansive, it is a model of pu-

rity, symmetry, and balance. Moderate tannin suggests some more cellaring is required. Anticipated maturity: now–2025.

1998 Château L'Eglise-Clinet

RATING: 94+ points

This effort should turn out to be one of the longest-lived Pomerols of the vintage. It is backward and has closed down since bottling, but make no mistake about it . . . this is a dazzling, serious *vin de garde*. An opaque purple color is followed by a restrained but promising bouquet of sweet black raspberries intermixed with vanilla, caramel, and minerals. The wine is full-bodied, powerfully tannic, beautifully textured, and crammed with extract (an assortment of black fruits). Although it is bursting at the seams, purchasers will need to wait a minimum of three to four years. Anticipated maturity: 2008–2035.

1997 Château L'Eglise-Clinet

RATING: 91 points

One of the vintage's most concentrated, seductive, and age-worthy offerings, this dark ruby/purple–colored 1997 possesses gorgeous symmetry, abundant quantities of seductive black raspberry and cherry fruit, full body, a fat, chewy mid-palate, and roasted blackberries, coffee, and toasty oak in the finish. A superb effort for the vintage, it can be drunk now (because of its low acidity and sweet tannin), or cellared for 12+ years. Bravo!

1996 Château L'Eglise-Clinet

RATING: 93 points

One of the few profound Pomerols in 1996, L'Eglise-Clinet turned out an uncommonly rich, concentrated wine that is performing well from bottle, even though it is displaying a tightly knit structure. The dark ruby/purple color is followed by notes of charcoal, jammy cassis, raspberries, and a touch of *sur-maturité*. Spicy oak emerges as the wine sits in the glass. It is fat, concentrated, and medium to full–bodied, with a layered, multidimensional, highly nuanced personality. This muscular Pomerol will be at its apogee until 2020.

1995 Château L'Eglise-Clinet

RATING: 96 points

One of the vintage's most awesome wines, L'Eglise-Clinet's 1995 has been fabulous from both cask and bottle. The color is opaque purple. The wine is closed aromatically, but it does offer a concoction of black raspberries, kirsch, smoke, cherries, and truffles. Full-bodied and rich, with high tannin but profound levels of fruit and richness, this dense, exceptionally well-delineated, layered, multidimensional L'Eglise-Clinet only hints at its ultimate potential. This looks to be a legend in the making. I could not get over the extraordinary texture of this wine in the mouth. Intensity and richness without heaviness—a tour de force in winemaking! Anticipated maturity: 2010–2030.

1990 Château L'Eglise-Clinet

RATING: 92 points

Seemingly close to its plateau of maturity, yet at the same time still relatively youthful and fresh, the dark plum/purple–colored 1990 is beginning to have a hint of amber at the edge. A sweet nose of cola, black cherry jam, smoke, malt chocolate, and earth is followed by a full-bodied, opulently textured wine with very little acidity, still noticeable tannin, a very chewy mid-section, and a sweet, layered finish. A very impressive wine that continues to go from strength to strength. Anticipated maturity: now–2023.

1985 Château L'Eglise-Clinet

RATING: 95 points

The last time I tasted this superstar of the vintage was next to a very herbal, green, emaciated Pétrus (one of the great disappointments of the vintage). This wine still has a very saturated opaque ruby/purple color that is far less evolved than almost any other 1985. The wine has sweet cranberry, black cherry, and blackberry fruit notes intermixed with mineral, cold steel, and a hint of cedar. Rich, full-bodied, with fabulous purity, a very well-delineated feel in the mouth, enormous richness, and a long finish that goes on for nearly 45 seconds, the wine seems to grow incrementally in the glass with increasing amounts of air, and is certainly a 1985 that has evolved at a snail's pace compared to most wines of this vintage. Anticipated maturity: now–2023.

CLASSIFICATION: There is no official classification of the wines in Pomerol.

OWNER: Domaines Barons de Rothschild (Lafite)

ADDRESS: Château L'Evangile, 33500 Pomerol, France

TELEPHONE: 33 05 57 55 45 55

TELEFAX: 33 05 57 55 45 56

E-MAIL: evangile@wanadoo.fr

WEBSITE: www.lafite.com

CONTACT: Jean Pascal Vazart

VISITING POLICY: By appointment only, Monday–Friday

VINEYARDS

SURFACE AREA: 34.6 acres

GRAPE VARIETALS: 78% Merlot, 22% Cabernet Franc

AVERAGE AGE OF THE VINES: 35 years

DENSITY OF PLANTATION: 6,000–7,500 vines per hectare

AVERAGE YIELDS: 38 hectoliters per hectare

WINEMAKING AND UPBRINGING

L'Evangile is the product of a traditional culture with a manual harvest as well as strict selections in the vineyard. Vinification takes place in small to moderately sized cement and stainless-steel vats. In most vintages, the wines spends 18–20 months primarily in new oak barrels, a change under the Rothschild administration as new oak was rare under the Ducasse ownership.

ANNUAL PRODUCTION

Château L'Evangile: 2,000–3,000 cases per year

Blason de L'Evangile: 2,000–3,000 cases per year

AVERAGE PRICE (VARIABLE DEPENDING ON VINTAGE): $50–175

GREAT RECENT VINTAGES

2001, 2000, 1998, 1995, 1990, 1985, 1982, 1975

L'Evangile appeared in the 1741 land registry under the name of Fazilleau. At the turn of the 19th century, the estate was already in much of its current configuration, stretching over some 32 acres, when it was sold to a lawyer named Isambert, who renamed the estate "L'Evangile."

In 1862, L'Evangile was purchased by Paul Chaperon, whose descendants, the Ducasse family, would remain the property's owners until 1990. Paul Chaperon was the man who made the estate famous. By 1868, L'Evangile was considered and registered as an "Upper-Pomerol 1st growth wine." After Chaperon's death around 1900, his descendants managed the estate until Louis Ducasse took over the property in the early 1960s. At that point the estate was in decline, having been damaged by the frosts of 1956. Ducasse made considerable efforts to renew the vineyard and restore the L'Evangile name. After his death in 1982, his widow, Simone Ducasse, continued the family's role in running the estate.

In 1990, Domaines Barons de Rothschild (Lafite) acquired L'Evangile from the Ducasse family. The Rothschilds' first moves were to make a more discriminating selection of the finest lots, and to create a second wine, Blason de L'Evangile. They also endeavored to enhance the vines' health with an incremental restoration and renewal plan that was finally completed in 1998.

A total renovation of the tank room and the *chais* in 2003/2004 completed the property's reconfiguration.

Anyone who has tasted the 2001, 2000, 1998, 1995, 1990, 1989, 1985, 1982, 1975, 1961, 1950, and 1947 L'Evangiles knows full well that this property can make wines of majestic richness and compelling character. Bordered on the north by the Who's Who of vineyards, La Conseillante, Vieux Château Certan, and Pétrus, and on the south by the great St.-Emilion Cheval Blanc, the 34.6-acre vineyard is brilliantly situated on deep, gravelly soil mixed with both clay and sand. With these advantages, I believe that L'Evangile (though never a model of consistency) can produce wines that rival Pétrus, Lafleur, and Cheval Blanc, which is now the case.

The Rothschild family (of Lafite Rothschild) purchased a controlling interest in 1990, but in 2000 they and Albert Frère (a wealthy Belgian who also has an interest in Cheval Blanc) became 100% owners. They are fully aware of the unlimited potential of this estate, and L'Evangile may soon be challenging Pétrus and Lafleur in both quality and, lamentably, price.

The late Louis Ducasse fervently believed in the distinctiveness of his vineyard, and often browbeat visiting wine critics with his observation that L'Evangile was as good as, and even more complex than, the neighboring Pétrus. The remarkable Madame Ducasse died in her

mid-nineties, several years ago, when she was still running day-to-day operations at L'Evangile. I remember having lunch with this amazing woman in the early 1990s, when she poured the 1964, 1961, and 1947 from her personal cellar. At the end of a sumptuous lunch of gigantic portions of truffles, *ris de veau,* and *filet de boeuf,* I remarked that the only person who had eaten everything, and who had finished each glass of glorious wine even more quickly than the guests, was Madame Ducasse!

Now that L'Evangile is completely under Rothschild ownership, I fully anticipate this property will challenge Pétrus as well as Cheval Blanc year in and year out. It is a magical vineyard, as evidenced by the great wines produced in years when there was nothing declassified for a second wine and a somewhat seat-of-the-pants vinification and upbringing of the wine. That will all change under the perfectionist regime of the Rothschilds. This is a Pomerol with a great track record already that looks poised to attain even greater heights . . . and prices.

CHATEAU L'EVANGILE

2002 Château L'Evangile

RATING: 90 points

One of the most impressive Pomerols of the vintage, the deep ruby/purple–colored 2002 L'Evangile (75% Merlot and 25% Cabernet Franc) exhibits big, sweet aromas of blackberries, raspberries, and hints of earth as well as truffles. It possesses admirable depth and palate persistence, medium body, outstanding freshness, rich, ripe fruit, good underlying acidity, and a nicely layered finish. I would have expected its nearby neighbor, Cheval Blanc, to perform this well. Kudos to L'Evangile's manager, Jean-Pascal Vazart, for a commendable job with his first vintage. Anticipated maturity: 2007–2018.

2001 Château L'Evangile

RATING: 91 points

While not up to the quality level of the stratospheric 2000, the deep ruby/purple-colored 2001 L'Evangile is a beauty. Revealing notes of beef blood, black fruits, and white flowers, it is medium-bodied and lush, with sweet tannin, a pliant, opulent texture, and a long, rich finish revealing hints of forest floor, truffles, and licorice. Anticipated maturity: 2006–2017.

2000 Château L'Evangile

RATING: 96+ points

I kept a bottle of this wine open for 11 days in early 2003, recorking each evening after pouring an ounce or two for evaluation. The wine simply refused to oxidize, hitting its stride on day 3, and then beginning to drop some fruit by day 8. A fabulous L'Evangile, it rivals such recent great vintages as 1998, 1995, 1990, and of course, 1982. With aeration, the thick, unctuous, saturated purple color is followed by scents of blueberries, blackberries, truffles, acacia flowers, tar, and graphite. Full-bodied, with tremendous opulence, intensity, and purity as well as silky tannin and a long, powerful, concentrated finish, with a hint of cocoa/chocolate, this was a modern-day clone of the 1975, I initially thought, but now I am not so sure. The 2000 is a prodigious, intense, powerful offering, but the tannins are clearly sweeter than those of the controversial 1975. Anticipated maturity: 2008–2030+.

1998 Château L'Evangile

RATING: 95+ points

A blend of 80% Merlot and 20% Cabernet Franc aged in 45% new oak, this terrific, dense ruby/purple–colored L'Evangile is stuffed with concentrated blackberry and raspberry fruit. There is also an acacia-like floral character that gives the wine even more complexity. Notes of toffee, licorice, and truffles add to the aromatic fireworks. The wine is full-bodied, with superb purity as well as moderate tannin in the finish. A worthy rival of the 2000, the 1998 should be the finest L'Evangile since the superb 1995 and 1990. Anticipated maturity: 2009–2035.

1995 Château L'Evangile

RATING: 92 points

This wine is closed, backward, and marginally less impressive from the bottle than from cask. Still an outstanding L'Evangile, is may prove longer lived than the sumptuous 1990, though perhaps not as opulently styled. It remains one of the year's top efforts. The dense ruby/purple color is accompanied by aromas of minerals, black raspberries, earth, and spice. The bottled wine seems toned down (too much fining and filtration?) compared with the pre-bottling samples, which had multiple layers of flesh and flavor dimension. High tannin in the finish and plenty of sweet fruit on the palate suggest this wine will turn out to be extra special. Could it have been even better if the filters had been junked in favor of a natural bottling? I think so, yet that being said, the wine's ferocious tannin level cannot conceal its outstanding ripeness, purity, and depth. Anticipated maturity: 2007–2020.

1994 Château L'Evangile

RATING: 90 points

One of the vintage's most notable successes, L'Evangile's 1994 has a dense plum/ruby color, a sweet nose of licorice, black raspberry, and currant with a hint of roasted herbs and damp soil. Medium to full-bodied, very opulent, it has considerable richness in the front end and mid-section. Like most of the best 1994s, the one defect is the lack of sweetness and the relatively dry, tannic finish. Nevertheless, this is top-notch stuff from a vintage that provides many good surprises, although the style of the wines tend to be relatively firm, muscular, and structured. Anticipated maturity: now 2020.

1990 Château L'Evangile

RATING: 96 points

A fabulous example of L'Evangile at its best. Dense ruby/purple with some amber at the edge, this wine has a gorgeous nose of black truffles intermixed with caramel, malt chocolate, sweet black raspberries, and blackberries. The wine is full-bodied with loads of glycerin giving it a very opulent, almost viscous feel on the palate. It still tastes youthful, but has always been accessible throughout its entire life. The wine does have plenty of tannin, but most of it is concealed by the wealth of fruit extract and the wine's viscosity. It is a sensational L'Evangile that is just beginning to develop the secondary nuances of adolescence. Anticipated maturity: now–2024.

1985 Château L'Evangile

RATING: 95 points

A beautiful L'Evangile and one of the vintage's top successes, the color is still a very dense ruby/purple with only a bit of lightening at the edge. A classic nose of liquid intermixed with black raspberries, blackberries, licorice, and a hint of truffle jumps from the glass of this medium to full–bodied, very concentrated, well-balanced, sweet, authoritatively powerful yet at the same time elegant wine. It has reached full maturity, where it should rest for some time to come. Anticipated maturity: now–2017.

1982 Château L'Evangile

RATING: 98 points

A spectacular wine that seems to put on weight every time I go back to it, this old-style wine (meaning reminiscent of some of the late 1940s vintages) has an opaque, murky plum/purple color with only a bit of lightening at the edge. The nose offers up notes of new saddle leather intermixed with very jammy notes of blackberry liqueur, licorice, smoke, beef blood, and truffles; it is a total turn-on. Very opulent, viscous, and intense, with full body, great richness, and loads of glycerin, this wine seems set for at least another 15–20 years of evolution. A remarkable effort and, to my taste, the greatest L'Evangile made after 1975 and 1961. Anticipated maturity: now–2025.

CLASSIFICATION: First Growth in 1855

OWNER: Domaine Clarence Dillon SA

ADDRESS: Château Haut-Brion, 135, avenue Jean Jaurès, 33600 Pessac, France

MAILING ADDRESS: c/o Domaine Clarence Dillon, 33608 Pessac Cedex, France

TELEPHONE: 33 05 56 00 29 30

TELEFAX: 33 05 56 98 75 14

E-MAIL: info@haut-brion.com or visites@haut-brion.com

WEBSITE: www.haut-brion.com

CONTACT: Turid Hoel-Alcaras or Carla Kuhn

VISITING POLICY: By appointment only, Monday–Thursday, 8:30–11:30 A.M. and 2–4:30 P.M.; Friday, 8:30–11:30 A.M.

VINEYARDS

SURFACE AREA: 106.7 acres

GRAPE VARIETALS: 45% Cabernet Sauvignon, 37% Merlot, 18% Cabernet Franc

AVERAGE AGE OF THE VINES: 36 years

DENSITY OF PLANTATION: 8,000 vines per hectare

AVERAGE YIELDS: 35–45 hectoliters per hectare

WINEMAKING AND UPBRINGING

In the temperature-controlled battery of stainless-steel tanks (Haut-Brion was the first major château to utilize them, in 1961), the young wine ferments and macerates for 15–20 days. The wine is gently moved to 100% new oak (a tradition at Haut-Brion since the 18th century) and is aged for 22–26 months, depending on the strength and power of the vintage. The wine is egg-white fined but only filtered if essential.

RED WINE PRODUCTION

Château Haut-Brion: 132,000 bottles

Château Bahans Haut-Brion: 88,000 bottles

AVERAGE PRICE (VARIABLE DEPENDING ON VINTAGE): $50–300

WHITE WINE PRODUCTION

Château Haut-Brion: 7,800 bottles

Les Plantiers du Haut-Brion: 5,000 bottles

AVERAGE PRICE (VARIABLE DEPENDING ON VINTAGE): $75–100

GREAT RECENT VINTAGES

2003, 2000, 1998, 1995, 1990, 1989, 1985, 1982, 1975

Spanning five centuries, the history of Haut-Brion is one of the oldest and most illustrious of any vineyard.

In 1488, four years before Columbus discovered America, Jean de Pontac, the true founder of the domaine, was born. On April 23, 1525, Monsieur de Pontac, then 37 years old and a civil and criminal registrar with the Parliament of Bordeaux, married Jeanne de Bellon. As part of her dowry, Mlle. de Bellon, daughter of the mayor of Libourne, brought the lands known as "Haut-Brion" in the village of Pessac.

Jean de Pontac carefully planned and built the château. One of the most powerful men of Bordeaux, Pontac married three times, fathered 15 children, and lived to the age of 101. His fourth son, Arnaud II de Pontac, Bishop of Bazas, inherited most of his Haut-Brion property, but not the château.

One of Pontac's heirs, Arnaud de Pontac, had considerable interest in the vineyard surrounding the château. An expert wine-grower, he adopted techniques such as topping up and racking casks and conducted tastings to see how his wines aged. Arnaud de Pontac's Haut-Brion was something new and became known in England as "New French Claret." For the first time it was sold as "Haut-Brion" instead of "Graves," the generic term used until then.

At the end of the 17th century, the fame of Haut-Brion wine spread throughout Europe. Diarist Samuel Pepys tasted the wine on April 10, 1663, at the Royal Oak Tavern in London, and later famously remarked, "There I drank a sort of French wine called Ho-Bryan which hath a good and most particular taste which I never before encountered."

By the middle of the 18th century, it had become the practice to bottle the wine at the château. In January 1769, M. Viallon, the cellarmaster of Haut-Brion, noted in his account books the bottling of 13 *barriques* of the 1764 vintage. Nine years later, he noted a new bottling of the same vintage. It was likely that wines were bottled only after receiving orders. The beneficial tannin in the wood allowed Viallon to keep the wines in barrels for eight years or more. Bottling, despite its high cost, rapidly became profitable. Haut-Brion sold its

1784 vintage for 325 pounds per barrel. In 1787, this same vintage was worth 600 pounds per barrel and, by 1789, it was worth 700.

Thomas Jefferson, then an envoy from the United States to Paris, came to Haut-Brion on May 25, 1787. The day after his visit to the vineyard, Jefferson wrote to his friend in Virginia, Francis Eppes: "I cannot deny myself the pleasure of asking you to participate in a parcel of wine. It is of the vineyard Obrion, one of the four established as the very best, and it is of the vintage 1784. Six dozen bottles will be packed and separately sent to you."

In a letter to John Bondfield, honorary American consul in Bordeaux, Jefferson wrote: "Haut-Brion is a wine of the first rank and seems to please the American palate more than all the others that I have been able to taste in France." His correspondence shows that, thanks to his gifts and counsel, the wines of Haut-Brion were served at the White House not only by Jefferson when he was president, but by Presidents Washington, Madison, and Monroe as well.

In 1855, the Bordeaux Chamber of Commerce, acting on behalf of the Committee of the Paris Universal Exposition, undertook the classification of the great growths of the Gironde. Sixty-two vineyards were judged worthy to be ranked, and only four were given the honor of "First Growth." Haut-Brion was among these, alongside Lafite, Margaux, and Latour.

In 1870, a bottle of Haut-Brion sold for 5 pounds sterling (almost 25 dollars at that time), which, in constant values, is about five times today's price.

In 1875, the firm of Eschenauer, which had a monopoly on the sale of the estate's wines, boasted of a record price for a single bottle—100 pounds! The wines of Haut-Brion then brought the highest prices in Bordeaux.

Meanwhile disaster dogged the vineyard: in 1852, an attack of oïdium; in 1881, rampant mildew; in 1885, the phylloxera scourge struck. Of these three diseases, the most devastating were oïdium and mildew. The harvests from 1851 to 1854 and from 1881 to 1884 were scarcely a fifth of normal. Paradoxically, phylloxera was not immediately damaging to the production, but its eradication was infinitely more costly and ruinous for the vintners. It required the grafting and replanting of all the vines of Bordeaux with resistant American rootstock. At Haut-Brion, replanting was completed in 1900.

In 1933, Clarence Dillon, an American banker and financier, was looking for an estate in France. Accompanied by his nephew, Dillon visited several regions, including Bordeaux where, guided by the famed courtier Daniel Lawton, he visited Cheval Blanc, Margaux, and finally Haut-Brion—all of which were presumably for sale. But Dillon procrastinated.

In 1934, the proprietor offered Haut-Brion to the city of Bordeaux on the condition that it maintain the vineyard "in perpetuity." His offer was refused. One of Dillon's associates, having heard of this move, cabled him, "Haut-Brion can be bought if you act fast." Dillon finally responded, "Act fast."

At the outbreak of war in 1939, Dillon returned to the United States, having left the château—at that point set up as a field hospital—at the disposal of the French government. His nephew, Seymour Weller, who had become a French citizen and president of the Haut-Brion, directed the property during the German occupation. The château was taken over by the occupying forces and became a rest home for Luftwaffe pilots.

The style of wine at Haut-Brion has changed over the years. The magnificently rich, earthy, almost sweet wines of the 1950s and early 1960s gave way in the period 1966–1974 to a lighter, leaner, easygoing, somewhat simplistic style of claret that lacked the richness and depth one expects from a first growth. Whether this was intentional or just a period in which Haut-Brion was in a bit of a slump remains a question in search of an answer. The staff at Haut-Brion is quick-tempered and sensitive about such a charge. Starting with the 1975 vintage, the wines have again taken on more of the customary earthy richness and concentration that existed before the 1966–1974 era. The quality of Haut-Brion began to rebound in 1975. Haut-Brion today is undoubtedly making wine that merits its first-growth status. In fact, the wines from 1979 onward have consistently proven to be among the finest produced in the region, as well as a personal favorite.

Jean Delmas, who administered Haut-Brion between 1961 and 2003, is widely regarded as one of the most talented and knowledgeable winemakers/administrators in France, if not the world. His extraordinary state-of-the-art research with clonal selections is unsurpassed in France. With the advent of the super-abundant crops during the 1980s, Delmas began, much like his counterpart in Pomerol, Christian Moueix of Château Pétrus, to crop-thin by cutting off grape bunches. This has no doubt accounted for the even greater concentration and extraordinary quality of the 1989, which may be the most compelling Haut-Brion made since the 1959 and 1961, and a modern-day legend.

It is interesting to note that in blind tastings Haut-Brion often comes across as the most aromatic as well as the most forward and lightest of all the first growths. In truth, the wine is deceptive. It's not all that light, just different, particularly when tasted alongside the more oaky, fleshy, and tannic wines of the Médoc and the softer, Merlot-dominated wines from the right bank. Despite the precociousness, it has the ability to gain weight as well as texture, and to age for 30 or more years in top vintages, giving it a broader window of drinkability than any other first growth. Aromatically, a great vintage of Haut-Brion has no peers.

Coinciding with improvements in the quality of Haut-Brion since 1975 has been the increased quality of the second label, Bahans Haut-Brion. Bahans is now one of the best second wines of Bordeaux, surpassed in certain vintages only by the renowned second wine of Château Latour, Les Forts de Latour.

The white wine made at Haut-Brion continues to be rated the finest of the Graves region. However, at the request of the proprietors it has never been classified, because the production is so tiny. Nevertheless, under Jean Delmas, who has sought to make a white Graves with the opulent texture of a prodigious Montrachet, the white wine has gone from strength to strength. Recent vintages such as 2003, 2001, 1998, 1994, 1989, and 1985 have been astonishing wines of majestic richness and complexity.

On a personal note, I should also add that after more than 30 years of intensely tasting as many Bordeaux wines as I can, the only general change I have noticed in my taste has been a greater and greater affection for Haut-Brion. The smoky, mineral, cigar box, sweet black currant character of this wine has increasingly appealed to me as I have gotten older and, as Jean Delmas would undoubtedly state, wiser as well. Jean Delmas retired in 2003, proudly allowing his son, Jean-Philippe, to take over the management of this great estate.

CHATEAU HAUT-BRION

2003 Château Haut-Brion

RATING: 95–98 points

This was the last vintage overseen by the venerable Jean Delmas. He retired this year and made way for his son, Jean-Philippe, to continue the nearly nine-decades-old family tradition of managing Haut-Brion's cellars.

In a year that Mother Nature challenged the Graves vignerons to overcome the freakish weather conditions, the perfectionist Delmas did everything right. Towering over the competition in his sector, this profound wine (a blend of 58% Merlot, 31% Cabernet Sauvignon, and 11% Cabernet Franc) represents 60% of the crop, and possesses a high natural alcohol level of just over 13% as well as an extremely high pH of 3.8. In that sense, it ranks alongside such great vintages as 1990, 1989, 1961, and 1959. However, unlike any of those years, in 2003, the Merlot harvest began on an unprecedented early date (August 25), and by September 15, the entire crop had been brought in. Even more unusual, the grapes for the extraordinarily profound 2003 Haut-Brion-Blanc were picked between August 13 and 15!

The 2003 Haut-Brion reveals the vintage's opulence and low acidity, but it possesses an even higher tannin level than the 2000. A deep ruby/purple color accompanies classic aromas of cranberries, scorched earth, minerals, and blue as well as black fruit notes. It hits the palate with considerable richness and intensity, but is neither overripe nor heavy. Cropped at low yields of 36 hectoliters per hectare, it has a good inner core of depth as well as sweetness. I do not think it will hit the heights of the perfect 1989, but it is a beautifully made, broad, medium to full–bodied claret with vigor, freshness, great texture, and not one trace of overripeness. Anticipated maturity: 2009–2025.

2002 Château Haut-Brion

RATING: 92 points

Perhaps because in relatively cool years the first-growth *terroirs* tend to be brilliant, Haut-Brion has turned out a beautifully classic, precise, and focused 2002 boasting a deep ruby/purple color as well as strikingly elegant aromatics (crushed stones, plums, black cherries, currants, figs, and earth). The wine possesses impressively measured power and elegance offered in a medium-bodied, nicely structured, exceptionally pure format. It is unusual for Haut-Brion to dominate La Mission Haut-Brion at such a young age, but it certainly does in the 2002 vintage. Anticipated maturity: 2010–2024.

2001 Château Haut-Brion

RATING: 94 points

Haut-Brion's 2001, which was bottled late (the end of September 2003), possesses an unmistakable nobility as well as a burgeoning complexity. Plum/purple to the rim, this blend of 52% Merlot, 36% Cabernet Sauvignon, and 12% Cabernet Franc is playing it close to the vest, having closed down considerably after bottling. Nevertheless, it reveals pure notes of sweet and sour cherries, black currants, licorice, smoke, and crushed stones. Medium-bodied with excellent purity, firm tannin, and an angular, structured finish, it requires five to seven years of cellaring. Anticipated maturity: 2009–2020+.

2000 Château Haut-Brion

RATING: 98+ points

It will always be tempting to compare the 2000 Haut-Brion with the perfect 2000 La Mission Haut-Brion. However, this wine is not as fat, unctuous, flamboyant, or voluminous as La Mission. Like a great diplomat, it is a wine of intensity, authority, and measured restraint. A supremely elegant offering, its dense ruby/purple color and burgeoning perfume of scorched earth, liquid minerals, plums, black currants, cherries, lead pencil, and subtle spicy oak are followed by a delicate yet powerfully flavorful, multilayered, highly nuanced, and extraordinarily pure and seamless wine. There have been so many recent classics from Haut-Brion, it is premature to suggest the 2000 is better than the 1998, 1995, 1990, or 1989, but it is certainly a prodigious wine of great persistence, length, and complexity. A blend of 51% Merlot, 42% Cabernet Sauvignon, and 7% Cabernet Franc, it should prove to be uncommonly long-lived, even by the standards of Haut-Brion. Anticipated maturity: 2012–2040.

1999 Château Haut-Brion

RATING: 93 points

Deep plum, currant, and mineral notes emerge from the concentrated, beautifully balanced, pure 1999 Haut-Brion. It seems to be cut from the same cloth as years such as 1985 and 1979. A hint of graphite as well as minerals is obvious in the abundant fruit. Medium to full–bodied, nuanced, subtle, deep, and provocatively elegant, it is made in a style that only Haut-Brion appears capable of achieving. The finish is extremely long, the tannins sweet, and the overall impression one of delicacy interwoven with power and ripeness. Anticipated maturity: 2007–2025.

1998 Château Haut-Brion

RATING: 96+ points

This is a prodigious Haut-Brion. It exhibits a dense ruby/purple color in addition to a tight but incredibly promising nose of smoke, earth, minerals, lead pencil, black currants, cher-

ries, and spice. This full-bodied wine unfolds slowly but convincingly on the palate, revealing a rich, multitiered, stunningly pure, symmetrical style with wonderful sweetness, ripe tannin, and a finish that lasts for nearly 45 seconds. It tastes like liquid nobility. There is really no other way of describing it. The 1998 is unquestionably the finest Haut-Brion since the fabulous 1989 and 1990, and the titanic 2000. However, patience is warranted, as it is not as flashy and forward as those three vintages. Anticipated maturity: 2008–2035.

1996 Château Haut-Brion

RATING: 95 points

Only 60% of the total production made it into the final blend, which consists of 50% Merlot, 39% Cabernet Sauvignon, and 11% Cabernet Franc. This wine has completely shut down since it was first bottled. Nevertheless, there is immense potential. This is a relatively structured, backward style of Haut-Brion, without the up-front succulence that some of the sweeter vintages such as 1989 and 1990 provide. The wine has a deep ruby color to the rim and a subtle but emerging nose of scorched earth, dried herbs, black currants, smoke, and a hint of fig. The wine is very concentrated, powerfully tannic,

with medium body and outstanding equilibrium, but currently the wine seems to have settled into a very dormant state. Anticipated maturity: 2008–2035.

1995 Château Haut-Brion

RATING: 96 points

It is fun to go back and forth between the 1995 and 1996, two superb vintages for Haut-Brion. The 1995 seems to have sweeter tannin and a bit more fat and seamlessness when compared to the more structured and muscular 1996. Certainly 1995 was a vintage that the brilliant administrator Jean Delmas handled flawlessly. The result is a deep ruby/purple–colored wine with a tight but promising nose of burning wood embers intermixed with vanilla, spice box, earth, mineral, sweet cherry, black currant, plum-like fruit, medium to full body, a high level of ripe but sweet tannin, and a finish that goes on for a good 40–45 seconds. This wine is just beginning to emerge from a very closed state in which it was unyielding and backward. Anticipated maturity: 2006–2035.

1994 Château Haut-Brion

RATING: 92 points

This is one of the surprise sleeper wines of the vintage that has more successes than many people suspect in spite of all the rain. The tremendous drainage enjoyed by the Haut-Brion vineyard worked in its favor during this wet September harvest. The color is deep plum/ruby with a bit of lightening at the edge. Notes of compost, truffle, earth, spice box, dried herbs, and licorice compete with sweet black cherry and currant fruit. The wine is medium-bodied, with a relatively plump, chewy feel to it. It is certainly one of the top half-dozen or so wines of the vintage. The tannins are still there, but the wine seems far more accessible than the two bigger wines that Haut-Brion produced in 1995 and 1996. Anticipated maturity: now–2024.

1990 Château Haut-Brion

RATING: 98 points

A profound Haut-Brion and one of the great Haut-Brions of the last 25 years, this wine got somewhat lost in the enormous shadow cast by the immortal 1989. It continues to go from strength to strength and is actually more evolved than the 1989, but is showing the classic Haut-Brion scorched earth, fragrant smoked herbs, tobacco, sweet currant, fig, and black currant nose. A very opulent/voluptuously textured wine with full body, great concentration, superb purity, low acidity, and very sweet, seamlessly integrated tannin, the wine is already showing great complexity and accessibility, and is extremely difficult to resist. Anticipated maturity: now–2020.

1989 Château Haut-Brion

RATING: 100 points

This continues to be one of the immortal wines and one of the greatest young Bordeaux wines of the last half-century. Consistently prodigious and almost a sure bet to top the scoring card of any blind tasting of this vintage as well as other years, the 1989 Haut-Brion is a seamless, majestic classic and a tribute to this phenomenal *terroir* and its singular characteristics. The wine still has a very thick, viscous-looking ruby/purple color, a spectacular, young but awesome smorgasbord of aromas ranging from scorched earth, liquid minerals, graphite, blackberry and black currant jam to toast, licorice, and spice box. The levels of fruit, extract, and glycerin in this viscous, full-bodied, low-acid wine are awe inspiring. The brilliant symmetry of the wine, extraordinary purity, and seamlessness are the hallmarks of a modern-day legend. It is still in its pre-adolescent stage of development, and I would not expect it to hit its full plateau of maturity for another two or three years, but this should be an Haut-Brion that rivals the greatest ever made at this estate. Life is too short not to drink this wine as many times as possible! A modern-day clone of the 1959? Anticipated maturity: now–2030.

1988 Château Haut-Brion

RATING: 92 points

A more firmly structured Haut-Brion, built somewhat along the lines of the 1996, this dark, garnet-colored wine is showing notes of licorice, underbrush, compost, truffles, dried herbs, creosote, and sweet black cherries and currants. Medium-bodied, rich, but still structured, this wine unfolds incrementally on the palate, showing superb density and a lot of complex Graves elements. It is just beginning to hit its plateau of full maturity. Anticipated maturity: now–2025.

1986 Château Haut-Brion

RATING: 94 points

This wine continues to be backward, but the bouquet is beginning to develop secondary nuances from roasted herbs and sweet cigar tobacco to compost, leathery notes, and plenty of sweet cherry and black currant fruit. I had somewhat higher hopes for it a decade ago. The wine is still youthful, quite pure, medium to full–bodied, but somewhat elevated, austere tannins in the finish at age 18 are starting to make me think they will never become fully integrated. As always, making a judgment call on a wine destined to have a half-century of life is sometimes difficult, given the varying stages it goes through, but I wonder if this wine will turn out to be as profound as I once predicted. Anticipated maturity: 2008–2030.

1985 Château Haut-Brion

RATING: 95 points

A gloriously seductive, classic Haut-Brion showing the most savory side of this elegant, finesse-styled wine, the 1985 Haut-Brion has reached its plateau of full maturity. The color is a deep ruby/garnet with some lightening at the edge. A very complex nose of cedar, dried herbs, smoke, creosote, and black cherries, plums, and currants jumps from the glass. In the mouth, it is round, concentrated, medium to full–bodied, with a velvety texture and beautifully integrated alcohol, acidity, and tannin. A beauty! Anticipated maturity: now–2012.

1982 Château Haut-Brion

RATING: 96 points

As far as first-growth 1982s go, this wine is certainly not one of the profound examples of the vintage. Jean Delmas has always compared it to the 1959, and perhaps it will magically put on weight and length and ultimately be comparable to that perfect wine. However, this wine seems a far cry from the immortal 1989, and even such recent Haut-Brion greats as the 2000, 1998, 1996, 1995, and 1990. Nevertheless, it is still a relatively youthful wine, with a deep ruby color that is just revealing a bit of pink at the edge. The wine shows sweet red currant, plum, and sweet mineral notes, followed by a medium-bodied, very elegant style, with ripe tannin, beautiful fruit, and a 45-second length. Its youthfulness is not surprising, but the wine does not seem to have the weight, opulence, and viscosity of the top 1982s. Anticipated maturity: now–2022.

CLASSIFICATION: Premier Cru Classé 1855

OWNER: Domaines Barons de Rothschild (Lafite)

ADDRESS: Château Lafite Rothschild, 33250 Pauillac, France

TELEPHONE: 33 05 56 73 18 18

TELEFAX: 33 05 56 59 26 83

E-MAIL: clesure@lafite.com

WEBSITE: www.lafite.com

CONTACT: Charles Chevallier (or Cécilia Lesure for appointments)

VISITING POLICY: By appointment only, Monday–Friday

VINEYARDS

SURFACE AREA: 247.1 acres

GRAPE VARIETALS: 70% Cabernet Sauvignon, 25% Merlot, 3% Cabernet Franc, and 2% Petit Verdot

AVERAGE AGE OF THE VINES: 30 years

DENSITY OF PLANTATION: 8,500 vines per hectare

AVERAGE YIELDS: 50 hectoliters per hectare

WINEMAKING AND UPBRINGING

After a manual harvest, the grapes are sorted in the vineyard. A classical vinification in oak and stainless-steel vats ensues, with three weeks of maceration depending on the chosen varietals, maturity, and extractability of the tannins. Eighteen to twenty months in new oak barrels (made at Lafite's own cooperage) complete the young wine's maturation. Lafite is very lightly fined and filtered prior to bottling.

ANNUAL PRODUCTION

Château Lafite Rothschild: 18,000–25,000 cases

Carruades de Lafite: 20,000–25,000 cases

AVERAGE PRICE (VARIABLE DEPENDING ON VINTAGE): $150–750

GREAT RECENT VINTAGES

2003, 2002, 2001, 2000, 1999, 1998, 1996, 1995, 1990, 1988, 1986, 1983, 1982

The name Lafite comes from the Gascon language term *"la hite,"* which means "hillock." The first known reference to Lafite dates back to the 13th century, but it wasn't until the 17th century that the property began to earn its reputation as a winemaking estate. Jacques de Ségur is credited with the planting of the Lafite vineyard in the 1670s and in the early 1680s.

By the early 18th century, Lafite had found its market in London. Between 1732 and 1733, Robert Walpole, the prime minister, purchased a barrel of Lafite every three months.

Marquis Nicolas Alexandre de Ségur improved the winemaking techniques, and above all enhanced the prestige of the wines in foreign markets and the Versailles court. He became known as "The Wine Prince," and Lafite's wine became "The King's Wine," with the support of an able ambassador, the Maréchal de Richelieu. In 1755, Richelieu was appointed governor of Guyenne, and upon his return to Paris, Louis XV remarked, "Maréchal, you look twenty-five years younger than you did when you left for Guyenne." Richelieu responded, "Does his Majesty not yet know that I've at long last found the Fountain of Youth? I have found that Château Lafite wines make invigorating cordials—they are as delicious as the ambrosia of the Gods of Olympus."

The Count de Ségur, in considerable debt, was forced to sell Château Lafite in 1784. Nicolas Pierre de Pichard, the first president of the Bordeaux Parliament, and a relative of the count, used the "kinship rights" legislation to purchase the estate.

By the late 1780s, Lafite had an international following that included such dignitaries as Thomas Jefferson, future president of the United States. While serving as ambassador to the Versailles Court, Jefferson acquired a passion for winemaking and considered developing it in his own country. During his stay in Bordeaux in May 1787, he detailed the hierarchy of the growths and designated Château Lafite as one of the four leading wines.

The Ségur family's stewardship of Lafite ended brutally with the execution of Nicolas Pierre de Pichard during the French Revolution. In the lobby of Château Lafite is an ancient poster announcing the public sale of the property on September 12, 1797. The estate was then described as "the leading Médoc wine, producing the finest wines in all of Bordeaux."

In 1815, the famous Bordeaux firm of wine experts, Lawton, published an initial classification of

Médoc wines in their brokerage house log and proclaimed Lafite wines "the most superb in all of Médoc." The vintage rankings of the Universal Paris Exposition in 1855 officially classified Lafite as a first growth, ranking it a "leader among fine wines."

In August 1868, Baron James de Rothschild purchased Château Lafite, which had once again been placed up for public sale. Baron James, who was head of the French branch of the Rothschild family, passed away just three months after purchasing Lafite. The estate then became the joint property of his three sons: Alphonse, Gustave, and Edmond. At that time the estate boasted 183 acres of vineyards. Coincidentally, the 1868 Lafite became the highest-priced wine of the vintage, setting a record that would remain for the entire century.

The end of the 19th century and the first half of the 20th century were devastating. The phylloxera crisis, followed by World War I and the Great Depression, led to a precipitous dive in prices. The Depression caused an unprecedented financial crisis that forced the Rothschilds to sell part of the estate's vineyard area. Despite these trials, several great vintages were produced—1899, 1900, 1906, 1926, and 1929.

World War II deepened the gloom, and with the June 1940 defeat of France, the Germans occupied the Médoc. The Rothschild family properties were confiscated and placed under public administration to serve as agricultural vocational schools. A German garrison was entrenched for the entire length of the occupation at Château Lafite Rothschild and Château Mouton Rothschild, and the château suffered from requisitions and ransacking of ancient vintages. The Barons de Rothschild recovered possession of Château Lafite Rothschild at the end of 1945.

Baron Elie led a program to restore the vineyards and the buildings, and to fully restructure the property's administration. The brilliant 1953 and very good 1955 were evidence of the estate's renewal, but the Bordeaux vineyard suffered terrible frosts in February of 1956 before producing a new cycle of exceptional vintages in 1959 and 1961. The 1960s rounded out the renaissance with the addition of new markets, particularly the United States.

After the 1973–1976 international oil crisis hit Bordeaux, the château rebounded once again with the 1975

and 1976 vintages under the management of Baron Eric de Rothschild. In the vineyard, the replanting and restoration work continued, fertilizing was reevaluated, and herbicide treatment limited. In the cellars, a stainless-steel tank complex was installed alongside oak tanks, and a new circular aging *chai*.

Lafite remains Bordeaux's most famous property and wine, and—with its elegant, undersized, and understated label—has become a name synonymous with wealth, prestige, history, respect, and wines of remarkable longevity.

While the vintages since 1975 have witnessed a succession of superlative Lafites, wines produced between 1961 and 1974 were of surprising mediocrity for a first growth. It has always remained a mystery to me why more wine critics did not cry foul after tasting some of the Lafite wines made during this period. The official château's position has always been that the wines were made in a light, elegant style and were simply overmatched in blind tastings by bigger, more robust wines. Certainly such things do happen, but the mediocrity of Lafite was particularly obvious in very fine vintages—1971, 1970, 1966, 1961, 1949, 1945—in which the wines were surprisingly deficient in color, excessively dry, overly oaked, and abnormally high in acidity. Several vintages—1974, 1971, 1969—were complete failures yet released for high prices under the Lafite name.

The reasons for such missteps are not likely to ever be revealed by the Rothschild family, but the problems in the 1960s and early 1970s seem to correlate with the following: First, the absentee owners lived in Paris and only casually supervised the goings-on at Lafite. Certainly Lafite has been diligently managed by the concerned and committed Eric de Rothschild since 1975. Second, the wine at Lafite was often aged a minimum of 32 to 36 months in oak barrels, whereas now 20 to 30 months is maximum, which no doubt causes Lafite to taste fruitier and fresher. Third, the current winemaking staff at Lafite picks the grapes later, to obtain greater ripeness and lower acidity in their wines, and the selection process is undoubtedly more severe. Since 1990, it has not been unusual for Lafite to eliminate a whopping 60% of the harvest, either selling it off in bulk or relegating it to the second wine. Finally, Lafite Rothschild is being bottled over a shorter period of time. There were unsubstantiated reports that Lafite often dragged out the bottling operation over as many as 8 to 12 months, allowing unacceptable levels of bottle variation. Today the entire crop is bottled within 2 or 3 weeks.

Regardless of the past, Lafite Rothschild is now producing compelling wines, and the turnabout in quality that clearly began in 1975 accelerated in the mid-1990s when Charles Chevallier was asked to manage the estate. One could successfully argue that since 1981, Lafite Rothschild has produced some of the Médoc's best wines in years such as 2003, 2002, 2001, 2000, 1999, 1998, 1996, 1995, 1990, 1988, 1987, 1986, 1983, 1982, and 1981.

CHATEAU LAFITE ROTHSCHILD

2003 Château Lafite Rothschild

RATING: 98–100 points

This is one of the most profound wines I have ever tasted. Some say that 2003 is an atypical vintage for Lafite, but it reminded me of the 1982 at a similar stage. Extrapolating backward, could the 2003 also resemble what the 1959 might have tasted like in March 1960? Revealing enormous richness, flesh, and succulence, the 2003 Lafite Rothschild is one of the candidates for wine of the vintage. A blend of 86% Cabernet Sauvignon, 9% Merlot, 3% Cabernet Franc, and 2% Petit Verdot (the Merlot was harvested between September 8 and 12, and the Cabernet Sauvignon between September 15 and 24), it possesses ethereal richness as well as perfume. Yields were a low 34 hectoliters per hectare, there is just under 13% natural alcohol, and the pH level is frightfully high at 3.9 with a total acidity of only 2.9. These figures are nearly identical to such ripe, concentrated vintages as 1982 and 1959. Inky/ruby/purple-colored with a spectacular, ripe perfume of black fruits, cedar, Asian soy, and balsamic vinegar, it exhibits massive richness yet is remarkably fresh and lively on the palate for such an unctuous effort (amazing levels of glycerin). In that sense, it is atypical, but like the 1982, I suspect the 2003 will become more delineated as the tannin emerges over the next one to two years. An amazing textural impression left me scratching my head, as I have never tasted a Lafite Rothschild quite like this. This is one first growth worth mortgaging the house for! Anticipated maturity: 2010–2035.

2002 Château Lafite Rothschild

RATING: 94 points

As I have indicated in the past, under the administration of Charles Chevallier, Lafite Rothschild has produced a tremendous succession of monumental, possibly historic wines since 1994. The 2002 will only add to Chevallier's illustrious résumé. Forty-seven percent of the crop made it into the grand vin, a blend of 87% Cabernet Sauvignon, 9.5% Merlot, and 3.5% Cabernet Franc. It smells and tastes like liqueur of lead pencil intermixed with cassis and cherry jam. Opaque purple to the rim, relatively light on its feet, but super-concentrated and intense, it is reminiscent of a lighter-weight 1996, a wine that merited a perfect score. More forward than the 1996, the 2002 is extraordinarily concentrated, riveting juice that has impeccable harmony. Anticipated maturity: 2011–2038.

2001 Château Lafite Rothschild

RATING: 94 points

The 2001 Lafite Rothschild's deep, saturated plum/purple color is accompanied by lead pencil liqueur–like notes intermixed with sweet red and black currants, plums, and cedar.

This blend of 86.5% Cabernet Sauvignon and 13.5% Merlot is a classic example of Lafite. Extremely elegant, medium-bodied, with intense concentration, richness, and sweet tannin, it appears to be on a rapid evolutionary track, at least in comparison to recent Lafite vintages that have been far more backward and powerful. The classy 2001 should be at its finest between 2007 and 2018.

2000 Château Lafite Rothschild

RATING: 100 points

Well, well, well—Lafite Rothschild does it again. Ever since manager Charles Chevallier was transferred from his beloved Sauternes property of Rieussec (also owned by the Rothschilds) to Lafite in 1994, there has been a succession of profound wines to emerge from this noble estate. The 2000 Lafite Rothschild, a blend of 93.3% Cabernet Sauvignon and 6.7% Merlot (only 36% of the crop made the grade) has an opaque ruby/purple color, followed by an extraordinary aromatic expression of liquid minerals/stones interwoven with the telltale graphite notes, mulberry, black currants, caramel, and tobacco. In the mouth, it is remarkably light on its feet, but somehow seems to pack intense flavors into layer upon layer of fruit and richness that cascade over the palate. A compelling wine, with extraordinary precision, great intensity, and a seamlessness in spite of what are obviously elevated levels of tannin, this wine was provocatively open and beautiful when tasted in January and February 2003, but I am sure it will soon close down. The finish lasted a whopping 72 seconds! This is utterly fascinating stuff. Anticipated maturity: 2011–2050.

1999 Château Lafite Rothschild

RATING: 95 points

This Lafite Rothschild sports an engraved "1999" on the bottle along with an eclipse to mark that significant historical event of August 1999. A quintessential offering from Lafite Rothschild, this prodigious wine is both elegant and intensely flavored and almost diaphanous in its layers that unfold with no heaviness. An opaque ruby/purple color is accompanied by a complex bouquet of lead pencil, graphite, cedar, crème de cassis, toast, and vanilla. Medium-bodied with extravagant layers of richness yet little weight and a finish that is all sweetness, ripeness, and harmony, this extraordinary Lafite increasingly appears to be a modern-day clone of the majestic 1953. A mere one-third of the crop made it into the grand vin! Anticipated maturity: 2007–2030.

1998 Château Lafite Rothschild

RATING: 98 points

A blend of 81% Cabernet Sauvignon and 19% Merlot, this wine represents only 34% of Lafite's total harvest. In a less-than-perfect Médoc vintage, it has been spectacular since birth, putting on more weight and flesh during its élevage. This opaque purple-colored 1998 is close to perfection. The spectacular nose of lead pencil, smoky, mineral, and black currant fruit soars majestically from the glass. The wine is elegant yet profoundly rich, revealing the essence of Lafite's character. The tannin is sweet, and the wine is spectacularly layered yet never heavy. The finish is sweet, superrich, yet impeccably balanced and long (50+ seconds). Anticipated maturity: 2007–2035.

1997 Château Lafite Rothschild

RATING: 92 points

Only 26% of the crop made it into the final blend, resulting in only 15,000 cases of the 1997 Lafite Rothschild. Readers should not ignore this wine because of the negative press surrounding the 1997 vintage. It boasts an opaque dense purple color in addition to a gorgeously sweet, expansive perfume of cedarwood, black currants, lead pencil, and minerals, a fat mid-palate, medium body, explosive fruit and richness, soft tannin, and a velvety texture. It is a beautiful, compelling Lafite Rothschild that can be drunk young, yet promises to evolve for 15+ years. Although one of the most forward Lafites ever tasted, it is all the more captivating because of this characteristic. Don't miss it! Anticipated maturity: now–2017.

1996 Château Lafite Rothschild

RATING: 100 points

Tasted six times since bottling, the 1996 Lafite Rothschild is unquestionably this renowned estate's greatest wine since the 1986 and 1982. Will the 2000 be this profound? Only 38% of the crop was deemed grand enough to be put into the final blend, which is atypically high in Cabernet Sauvignon (83% Cabernet Sauvignon, 7% Cabernet Franc, 7% Merlot, and 3% Petit Verdot). This massive wine may be the biggest, largest-scaled Lafite I have ever tasted. It will require many years to come around, so I suspect all of us past the age of 50 might want to give serious consideration to whether we should be laying away multiple cases of this wine. It is also the first Lafite Rothschild to be put into a new engraved bottle, designed to prevent fraudulent imitations. The wine exhibits a thick-looking, ruby/purple color and a knockout nose of lead pencil, minerals, flowers, and black currant scents. Extremely powerful and full-bodied, with remarkable complexity for such a young wine, this huge Lafite is oozing with extract and richness, yet has managed to preserve its quintessentially elegant personality. This wine is even richer than it was prior to bottling. It should unquestionably last for 40–50 years. Anticipated maturity: 2012–2050.

1995 Château Lafite Rothschild

RATING: 95 points

The 1995 Lafite Rothschild (only one-third of the harvest made it into the final blend) is 75% Cabernet Sauvignon, 17% Merlot, and 8% Cabernet Franc. It exhibits a dark ruby purple color and a sweet, powdered mineral, smoky, weedy, cassis-scented nose. Beautiful sweetness of fruit is present in this medium-bodied, tightly knit, but gloriously pure, well-delineated Lafite. The 1995 is not as powerful or as massive as the 1996, but it is beautifully made with outstanding credentials, in addition to remarkable promise. Anticipated maturity: 2008–2028.

1994 Château Lafite Rothschild

RATING: 90+ points

Made from nearly 100% Cabernet Sauvignon, this dark ruby/purple–colored wine is stubbornly backward, unappealing, and severe and astringent on the palate. There is plenty of weight, and the wine possesses admirable purity, with no suggestion of herbaceousness or underripe fruit, but the wine's personality refuses to be coaxed from the glass. The 1994 Lafite may turn out to be austere and disappointing flavorwise, but possesses a fabulous set of aromatics (does that sound reminiscent of the 1961, another Lafite that was primarily Cabernet Sauvignon?). I am not giving up on this wine, but purchasers should be willing to wait another 5 years before pulling a cork. Anticipated maturity: 2010–2030.

1990 Château Lafite Rothschild

RATING: 92 points

The 1990 is a ripe, rich, well-textured, yet elegant, mouth-filling style of Lafite. The wine possesses excellent richness, a hint of the unmistakable Lafite perfume of minerals, cedar, graphite, and red fruits, medium to full body, moderate weight, admirable richness, and overall balance. Tannin is very noticeable in the finish. It should be a 40- to 50-year Lafite. As outstanding as I believe it will ultimately turn out to be, I do not think the 1990 Lafite matches the sheer class, quality, and complexity of the 2000, 1998, 1996, 1988, 1986, and 1982. Anticipated maturity: 2008–2040.

1989 Château Lafite Rothschild

RATING: 90 points

A classic Lafite, the 1989 is just coming out of a period of dormancy. This dark ruby-colored, medium-bodied wine reveals new oak in the nose and a spicy finish. It is a quintessentially elegant, restrained, understated style of Lafite. In the final analysis, this wine lacks the profound depth and mid-section of the estate's greatest efforts. Anticipated maturity: 2006–2025.

1988 Château Lafite Rothschild

RATING: 94 points

The 1988 is a classic expression of Lafite. This deeply colored wine (deep plum/ruby) exhibits the telltale Lafite bouquet of cedar, subtle herbs, dried pit fruits, minerals, asphalt, lead pencil, and cassis. Extremely concentrated, with brilliantly focused flavors and huge tannins, this backward yet impressively endowed Lafite Rothschild looks increasingly like the wine of the vintage! Anticipated maturity: now–2035.

1986 Château Lafite Rothschild

RATING: 100 points

At 15 years of age, the 1986 Lafite was accessible yet still had the personality of a young, adolescent wine. The prodigious 1986 possesses outstanding richness, a deep color, medium body, a graceful, harmonious texture, and superb length. The penetrating fragrance of cedar, chestnuts, minerals, and rich fruit is a hallmark of this wine. Powerful, dense, rich, and tannic, as well as medium to full–bodied, with awesome extraction of fruit, this Lafite has immense potential. Patience is still required. Anticipated maturity: now–2040.

1983 Château Lafite Rothschild

RATING: 92 points

The wine exhibits a deep ruby/garnet color with only a slight amber at the edge. The perfumed nose of lead pencil, toast, red and black fruits, minerals, and roasted herbs is provocative. In the mouth, this wine displays considerable body for a Lafite, plenty of power, and a fleshy, rich, sweet mid-palate. Long, elegant, plump, and surprisingly fleshy, this outstanding example of Lafite seems largely forgotten given the number of high-quality vintages during the golden decade of the 1980s. Anticipated maturity: now–2019.

1982 Château Lafite Rothschild

RATING: 100 points

Still extraordinarily youthful, this large-scaled (massive by Lafite's standards) wine should prove to be the greatest Lafite made after the 1959. It continues to offer an exceptionally intense, compelling bouquet of herbs, black currants, vanilla, lead pencil, and cedar. The wine reveals considerable tannin as well as amazing, atypical power and concentration for Lafite. The hallmark elegance of this wine has not been compromised because of the vintage's tendency to produce powerful and unctuously textured, thick, juicy wines. Rich, full, and still youthful, this has turned out to be a fabulous Lafite Rothschild, and a modern-day clone of the 1959. Anticipated maturity: now–2040.

CLASSIFICATION: There is no official classification of the wines in Pomerol.

OWNERS: Jacques Guinaudeau and family

ADDRESS: Château Lafleur, 33500 Pomerol, France

MAILING ADDRESS: Château Grand Village, 33240 Mouillac, France

TELEPHONE: 33 05 57 84 44 03

TELEFAX: 33 05 57 84 83 31

CONTACT: Sylvie or Jacques Guinaudeau

VISITING POLICY: By appointment only

VINEYARDS

SURFACE AREA: 11.1 acres

GRAPE VARIETALS: 50% Cabernet Franc, 50% Merlot

AVERAGE AGE OF THE VINES: More than 30 years

DENSITY OF PLANTATION: 5,900 vines per hectare

AVERAGE YIELDS: 38 hectoliters per hectare

WINEMAKING AND UPBRINGING

Fermentations and macerations last 15–21 days depending upon the vintage. Wines are transferred directly into oak barrels for malolactics, where they remain for 18–20 months in cask (one-third to one-half new oak). Wines are fined with fresh egg whites but not systematically filtered.

ANNUAL PRODUCTION

Château Lafleur: 12,000 bottles

Les Pensées de Lafleur: 3,000 bottles

AVERAGE PRICE (VARIABLE DEPENDING ON VINTAGE): $200–500+

GREAT RECENT VINTAGES

2003, 2001, 2000, 1999, 1995, 1990, 1989, 1985, 1982

I have always had a personal attachment to this tiny Pomerol vineyard. In the mid-1970s, when I first started tasting the wines of Lafleur, I could find nothing written about them. Yet in my small tasting group we frequently found the wine to be every bit as compelling as Pétrus. I made my first visit to Lafleur in 1978, speaking very little French, and found the two elderly proprietors (now deceased), sisters Thérèse and Marie Robin, decrepit, but even then both were utterly charming. Despite the advanced age of these two spinsters,

they would ride their bikes out to Le Gay, the official reception center for both Lafleur and Le Gay, on my visits in the late 1970s. They were no doubt amused by my size, referring to me as Monsieur Le Taureau (Bull). I probably did look a bit oversized walking in the tiny *chai*, where the barrels, as well as a bevy of ducks, chickens, and rabbits, were housed. The Lafleur château was, and remains today, more of a barn than a winery. It always amazed me how wines of such great extraction and utterly mind-blowing character could be produced in such filthy conditions at the time.

Today Lafleur is both owned and managed by the niece and nephew, Sylvie and Jacques Guinaudeau. They took responsibility starting with the 1985 vintage and purchased it in 2002. One of their first decisions was to refuse to bottle any 1987 Lafleur. Instead they introduced a second wine, Les Pensées de Lafleur. This is rather remarkable given the tiny production of this micro-estate. The cellars remain the same, though devoid of ducks, chickens, and rabbits, as well as the dung they left behind. Additionally, Lafleur now benefits from 50% new oak casks for most vintages.

Is the wine any better? Certainly Lafleur remains one of the few wines of Pomerol that is consistently capable of challenging, and in some cases surpassing, Pétrus. Even the late Jean-Pierre Moueix once admitted this to me, and I have been fortunate to have had Lafleur and Pétrus side by side enough times to know the former is a wine every bit as extraordinary as Pétrus. In many vintages, from an aromatic point of view, it is more complex than Pétrus, no doubt because of the old-vine Cabernet Franc the vineyard possesses.

Much of the greatness of Lafleur lies in the soil, which is a deep, gravelly bed enriched with iron and some sand but also characterized by extremely important deposits of phosphorus and potassium. Over the years the yields have been tiny, reflecting the motto of the Robin sisters' father: "Quality surpasses quantity."

Old vintages of Lafleur are legendary, but the history of the property has not been without mixed results. The 1971 and 1970 should have been better, and more recently, the 1981 is flawed by the presence of fecal aromas. However, the wine is being overseen by an oenologist, and even though the old vines (there was no replanting at Lafleur after the freeze of 1956) are having to be grubbed up, the average age is still impressive.

Since 1982 (the 1982 and 1983 were made by Christian Moueix and his ultra-conservative oenologist Jean-Claude Berrouet), Lafleur has become less exotic and perhaps more influenced by the modern-day oenologists' obsession with technical parameters. Nevertheless, Lafleur, measured by the highest standards of Bordeaux, still remains one of the most distinctive, exotic, and greatest wines—not only from Pomerol, but in the world.

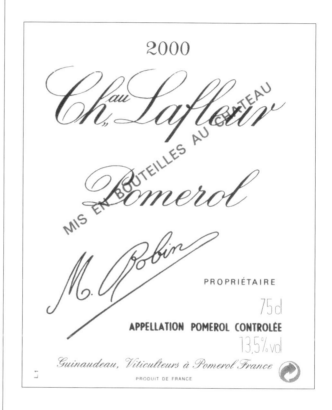

CHATEAU LAFLEUR

2003 Château Lafleur

RATING: 93–96 points

At Lafleur, the Merlot was harvested on September 1 and 2, and the Cabernet Franc on September 12 and 13. Surprisingly high alcohol as well as low acidity are found in this terrific Lafleur. It has had its press wine added, and the result is a dense ruby/purple–colored effort revealing aromas of flowers, blueberries, raspberries, mulberries, and cherries. Extraordinary elegance as well as intensity, and a low-acid, high-pH style with considerable power suggest it will be drinkable at an earlier age than most of its predecessors. I suspect the alcohol level is between 13 and 13.5%, and the pH is somewhere in the 3.8–4.0 range. Anticipated maturity: 2008–2020+.

2002 Château Lafleur

RATING: 91 points

Somewhat of a revelation in a vintage that was obviously difficult in this appellation, Lafleur's 2002 represents the essence of old vines with structured, deep, concentrated flavors. This medium-bodied, dense ruby/purple–colored effort exhibits impressive purity as well as a persistent, long palate offering a kiss of sweet kirsch and licorice. Some jagged tannin needs to be resolved if this wine is to merit a score in the low nineties. However, it will be very long-lived, especially for a Pomerol. Anticipated maturity: 2011–2025.

2001 Château Lafleur

RATING: 92+ points

Performing slightly less impressively from bottle than it did from cask, this wine's Cabernet Franc element has come forward, revealing a distinctive herbal, bell pepper, vegetal character that kept my score from going higher. Nevertheless, there is plenty to like about this 2001 Pomerol. It possesses a saturated ruby/purple color, powerful aromas (kirsch, raspberries, and blackberries), an earthy, muscular, chunky character, and the most tannic personality of any Pomerol I tasted. While not the huge blockbuster Lafleur can often produce, it is well built. Anticipated maturity: 2009–2019.

2000 Château Lafleur

RATING: 100 points

I am not surprised the 2000 Lafleur has garnered the magical three-digit score. From bottle, the wine boasts a dense plum/purple color in addition to a gorgeous nose of kirsch intermixed with hints of black truffles, raspberries, and minerals. The tannin is present but seems to creep up only upon intense inspection. Lafleur is enormously endowed, rich, and full-bodied, with a tremendous chewiness and, at the same time, sensuality. Pure, massive, and rich, with exceptional levels of glycerin and fruit nearly concealing high levels of tannin, and a 60+-second finish, this is a remarkable achievement, and . . . just maybe the finest Lafleur since the 1982. Anticipated maturity: 2012–2040+.

1999 Château Lafleur

RATING: 93 points

A brilliant success, the 1999 is one of the stars of the vintage. Lafleur's 1999 is atypically powerful and concentrated, with an inky, saturated purple color followed by a sensational nose of black cherry jam intermixed with liquid minerals, raspberries, and licorice. Super-concentrated, extraordinarily pure, with moderately high tannin, this dense, powerful, impressively endowed wine should turn out to be a classic for Lafleur. Anticipated maturity: 2010–2025.

1998 Château Lafleur

RATING: 94 points

This wine was incredibly tannic and backward from cask, but out of bottle it has shrugged off the excess tannin and seems to be developing far better than I thought it would. The color is dense ruby/purple, and the wine shows notes of sweet kirsch and blackberry liqueur, with a liquid minerality and a hint of violets. The wine is full-bodied, quite tannic, very dense and backward, but gorgeously concentrated, pure, and intense. This looks to be a classic Lafleur meant for significant long-term aging. Anticipated maturity: 2015–2040+.

1996 Château Lafleur

RATING: 92+ points

Another Lafleur that has come on in bottle, in contrast to the pre-bottling tastings where the wine was painfully backward and austere; I still tend to think it represents a modern-day clone of the gorgeous 1966. It is not the most intense and expansive Lafleur, but it has a saturated ruby/purple color, a sweet nose of minerals, black raspberries, blackberries, and almost steely mineral liquidity to it. A powerful wine with Médoc-like tannin and structure, the wine is still very closed but much more promising and less of a gamble than I thought early on. Nevertheless, this is a wine for patient connoisseurs. Anticipated maturity: 2012–2030+.

1995 Château Lafleur

RATING: 93+ points

Another amazingly backward, tannic Lafleur that has an opaque ruby/purple color and a tight but promising nose of blackberry liqueur intermixed with blueberries, raspberries, and minerals, this wine is full-bodied, has searingly dry, astringent tannins, but a layered, very large-scaled, weighty feel in the mouth. The wine is very young, formidable, but oh so prodigious. I cannot see this wine being ready to drink for at least two decades, and it may actually need more time than the 1998. Anticipated maturity: 2020–2050.

1994 Château Lafleur

RATING: 91 points

Still backward, but one of the great successes of the vintage, the 1994 still has a deep ruby/purple color, notes of plums, a hint of prunes, earth, truffle, and mineral. As the wine sits in the glass, some of the steely mineral Lafleur character emerges. This remains an excruciatingly tannic, backward, medium to full–bodied wine that needs plenty of cellaring. I am not so sure the tannins will always mesh, given the fact that this wine does not quite have the concentration that some of the other top vintages of Lafleur possess. Anticipated maturity: 2010–2025.

1990 Château Lafleur

RATING: 96 points

Still developing but becoming more formed, this wine shows fabulous extract, a dense purple color, and a sweet nose of kirsch that is almost similar to the famed Château Rayas of Châteauneuf du Pape. This wine is full-bodied, somewhat exotic, but still very youthful and not yet in its adolescence. The viscous texture, profound richness in the mouth, and extraordinary purity all suggest a potential legend in the making. The wine still needs considerable cellaring. Anticipated maturity: 2008–2040.

1989 Château Lafleur

RATING: 96 points

The 1989 Lafleur, tasted side by side with the 1990 on two occasions in 2002, plays it closer to the vest. The wine needs far more coaxing to produce the licorice, black cherry liqueur, earth, and truffle notes from the nose. In the mouth, the wine is full-bodied, tannic, backward, and very tightly knit, with mouth-searing levels of tannin and extremely high extract. The tannins are firmer, the fruit seemingly less sweet, but still extremely ripe, and the evolutionary process is far slower in the 1989 than the 1990. Anticipated maturity: 2012–2045.

1988 Château Lafleur

RATING: 93 points

Consistently one of the strongest candidates for the wine of the vintage, Lafleur's 1988 has a dark plum/ruby color and a gorgeous nose of white flowers intermixed with kirsch and raspberries. The wine is sweet, round, and beautifully pure, with moderate tannin, medium to full body, and great elegance and complexity. This wine has come around faster than I would have thought. Anticipated maturity: now–2025.

1986 Château Lafleur

RATING: 93 points

Dark, dense ruby/purple, with very little evolution to the color, Lafleur's 1986 seems frozen in time, a structured, tannic, backward monster that still needs considerable cellaring. No matter how much airing I have given this wine, it does not ever seem to emerge from its cloak of tannin and structure. The fruit seems sweet, and the wine has Lafleur's telltale notes of kirsch intermixed with raspberries, minerals, flowers, and truffles. The wine is medium-bodied, weighty in the mouth, but so, so tannic and backward. Will it ever blossom? Anticipated maturity: 2008–2035.

1985 Château Lafleur

RATING: 94 points

This is one of the greatest wines of the vintage, possibly the slowest to mature and potentially its longest lived. Tasted next to Pétrus twice in 2002, the 1985 Lafleur seemed like it came from a different vintage. It was not herbal like the Pétrus; it was far denser, the color more saturated, and it had more body, volume, and intensity. In fact, the Pétrus looked like an emaciated, herbaceous, thin cousin to Lafleur. This wine is very special, with notes of figs, plums, minerals, violets, black raspberries, and licorice. Still a dense, saturated ruby/purple with full body, great purity, and fabulous fruit, this is an immense vintage for Lafleur, and it certainly ranks as one of the greatest wines this small micro-estate has ever produced. Anticipated maturity: 2008–2030.

1983 Château Lafleur

RATING: 92 points

Fully mature, yet still in far better condition than most 1983 Pomerols, Lafleur's 1983 has a medium ruby color with considerable pink at the edge. A very exotic, almost kinky nose of Asian spice, licorice, truffle, and jammy kirsch is followed by a medium to full–bodied, plum, fleshy wine with sweet tannin and low acidity in a very evolved style. Certainly among the very good vintages of Lafleur over the last 20 years, this is the most evolved and drinkable. Anticipated maturity: now–2015.

1982 Château Lafleur

RATING: 100 points

Tasted five times in 2002, once in 2003, this wine, on each occasion, stood out as a colossal effort even in this great vintage. The wine still has a very dense, murky ruby/purple color, a nearly overripe nose of black cherry liqueur intermixed with raspberries, minerals, smoke, and some cold steel as well as white flowers that soars from the glass with tremendous force and staying power. Very thick, with a viscous texture reminiscent of some of the late 1940s vintages of Pomerol, high extract, and huge, opulent flavors—this wine hits the palate with a cascade of glycerin, fruit, and extract. Almost over the top, but surprisingly well delineated for its massive size, this is an extraordinary, concentrated, fabulously compelling wine that should prove to be immortal. The wine has never tasted better in its entire life than in recent tastings, yet it still seems relatively young. Anticipated maturity: now–2025.

CLASSIFICATION: Premier Grand Cru Classé—Pauillac—First
Growth

OWNER: Mr. François Pinault

ADDRESS: Château Latour, Saint-Lambert, 33250 Pauillac,
France

TELEPHONE: 33 05 56 73 19 80

TELEFAX: 33 05 56 73 19 81

E-MAIL: info@chateau-latour.com

WEBSITE: www.chateau-latour.com

CONTACT: Sonia Favreau (Guest Relation Manager)

VISITING POLICY: Open Monday–Friday, except on French
public holidays, 8:30 A.M.–12:30 P.M. and 2–5 P.M.
Individual and free tours, by
appointment only. Groups
are limited to 15 people.

VINEYARDS

SURFACE AREA: 163 acres

GRAPE VARIETALS: 75% Cabernet
Sauvignon, 4% Cabernet Franc, 20%
Merlot, 1% Petit Verdot

AVERAGE AGE OF THE VINES: 50 years old
(Château Latour); 35 years old (Les
Forts de Latour); 10 years old
(Pauillac)

DENSITY OF PLANTATION: 10,000 vines per
hectare

AVERAGE YIELDS: 51 hectoliters per hectare

WINEMAKING AND UPBRINGING

During fermentation, two daily pumpings-over are carried
out at a temperature of 29–30°C. Depending on the vintage
and structure of the wine, one to three racking operations are
performed during the alcoholic fermentation. Vatting lasts
between 15 and 25 days, depending on the grape variety and
age of the plot. The press wines undergo malolactic fermentation in barrels before blending with the free-run wine, always
accomplished before the end of February. The grand vin is
aged in new oak barrels for 16 to 18 months. Bottling takes
place each year between June and July.

ANNUAL PRODUCTION

Château Latour: 180,000 bottles

Les Forts de Latour: 150,000 bottles

Pauillac: 40,000 bottles

AVERAGE PRICE (VARIABLE DEPENDING ON VINTAGE): $125–500

GREAT RECENT VINTAGES

2003, 2002, 2001. 2000, 1996, 1995, 1990, 1982

Château Latour's viticultural estate began history in
1378, at the height of the Hundred Years' War. Acquired in 1670 by the de Ségur family, Château Latour
remained in the hands of its heirs for nearly 200 years,
until 1963.

The reputation of Château Latour for making
wines of great color, complexity, and purity of fruit, as
well as powerful and long-lasting
character, was established in the
19th century. In 1855, at the time of
the classification of the greatest
wines of the Médoc and Graves for
the International Exhibition in Paris,
Château Latour was classified as a
first growth.

Between 1963 and 1993,
Château Latour came under British
stewardship, at which time investments were made in the vineyard,
vat-house, and cellar. Two world-
renowned British writers, Hugh
Johnson and the late Harry Waugh,
served as advisors to Château Latour
during this era. The château returned
to French hands in 1993, when it was
purchased by Mr. François Pinault, a wine lover and connoisseur of Château Latour, who essentially purchased
the estate that made his favorite wine. He is also a perfectionist, and vintages under his ownership have gone from
strength to strength.

Impressively situated on the Pauillac/St.-Julien
border, immediately north of the walled vineyard of
Léoville-Las-Cases, Latour's vineyard can be spotted
easily from the road because of the creamy-colored,
fortress-like tower. Notably depicted on the wine's label,
this formidable tower overlooking the vineyards and
the Gironde River remains from the 17th century, when
it was built on the site of a 15th-century fortress used
by the English to fend off attacks by pirates.

The wine produced here has been an impeccable model of consistent excellence, in great, mediocre, and poor vintages. For that reason, many have long considered Latour to be the Médoc's finest wine. Latour's reputation for making Bordeaux's best wine in mediocre or poor vintages—such as 1974, 1972, and 1960—has been totally justified, although in some poor Bordeaux vintages—1984, 1980, and 1977—Latour's wines were surprisingly light and eclipsed in quality by a number of other châteaux. The wine of Latour also has a remarkable record of being stubbornly slow-developing, requiring a good 20–25 years of bottle age to shed its considerable tannic clout and reveal its stunning power, depth, and richness. This style, often referred to by commentators as virile, masculine, and tough, may have undergone a subtle yet very perceptible softening up between 1983 and 1989. This was adamantly denied by the staff at Latour, but my tastings suggest a more gentle and accessible style. Fortunately, this ignoble trend was quickly abandoned, as Latour has once again been producing blockbuster wines since 1990.

While the 1982 and to a lesser extent the 1986 are undeniably great Latours, on the whole the estate did not have a distinguished decade. It was no secret that the *cuverie* was too small to handle the gigantic crop sizes of 1986, 1985, and 1983. As a consequence, the fermentation tanks had to be emptied too soon in order to make room for the arriving grapes. The underground cellars and *cuverie* were subsequently enlarged—just in time to handle 1989, the largest vintage ever harvested in Bordeaux. In 2000, a massive renovation project costing millions has given Latour a state-of-the-art winemaking and storage facility. However, an objective tasting analysis of the 1989, 1988, 1985, and 1983 Latours leaves one with the impression that in these years, Latour is a significantly lighter, less powerful and concentrated wine than it was in any decade earlier in the last century. However, the decade of the 1990s witnessed a return to form, and under the impeccable administration of François Pinault and his man on the spot, Frédéric Engerer, nothing less than perfection has been tolerated.

Latour remains one of the most concentrated, rich, tannic, and full-bodied wines in the world. When mature, it has a compelling bouquet of fresh walnuts and leather, black currants and gravelly mineral scents. On the palate, it can be a wine of extraordinary richness, yet it is never heavy.

CHATEAU LATOUR

2003 Château Latour

RATING: 98–100 points

One of the three greatest young Bordeaux I have ever tasted, Château Latour's 2003 is one of the candidates for wine of the vintage (Latour's 2002 is *the* wine of the vintage in my opinion). This great estate has produced a freakishly rich, concentrated Pauillac revealing no evidence of overripeness or too much weight. A blend of 81% Cabernet Sauvignon, 18% Merlot, and 1% Petit Verdot, only 53% of the production made it into the 2003 Latour, which tips the scales at 13% alcohol. Manager Frédéric Engerer told me that 6% press wine was added to the final blend. The Merlot harvest occurred between September 8 and 13, and the Cabernet Sauvignon between September 22 and 30. A remarkable effort, it boasts a black/purple color in addition to an extraordinary bouquet of crème de cassis, blackberries, and subtle sweet oak in the background. A massive, multilayered texture inundates the palate with a seamless wealth of glycerin, extract, and richness. Tasters must search especially hard to find the structure and tannin. In that sense, the 2003 is reminiscent of how the 1982 performed at the same age. Tasted next to the undeniably great 2000 Latour, the 2003 came across as almost twice as concentrated, with a fruit presence that had to be tasted to be believed. In fact, I do not believe I have ever tasted a Latour like this. I wonder how the 1961 would have tasted at a similar period? Extraordinarily pure, with a finish that lasted more than 70 seconds, this is a tour de force as well as a modern-day legend in the making. Sadly, Latour's small production means that only 10,000 cases will be produced. Anticipated maturity: 2010–2040?

2002 Château Latour

RATING: 96 points

No guts, no glory? If I had to choose today, this would be my pick for the wine of the vintage. It is a colossal, remarkably concentrated, highly extracted, formidably endowed Latour as well as a potential legend in the making. It will be interesting to see how such recent great Latours as the 2000 and 1996 stand up against the 2002, which will probably never have the acclaim of those two vintages. The meticulous Frédéric Engerer told me that yields were a measly 23–24 hectoliters per hectare, and the final blend was 74% Cabernet Sauvignon, 25% Merlot, and dollops of Cabernet Franc and Petit Verdot. The pH is remarkably high (3.87) and the natural alcohol (no chaptalization) is over 13%, so this is a surprisingly powerful offering. It demonstrates that those who picked late benefitted from the Indian summer. About 51% of the production made it into the grand vin. So what's it taste like? This is a behemoth that is also extraordinarily pure and elegant. Opaque purple to the rim, it boasts a strikingly intense liquid minerality, crème de cassis, and licorice-scented nose. The wine's incredible purity, fascinating texture, full-bodied power, and massive display of fruit, extract, and harmony suggest a monumental Latour that will require a considerable amount of time to become drinkable. I do not believe it is as backward as the 2002 Mouton, but certainly it is far less accessible than the 2002 Lafite. The brilliant 2002 Latour is a tour de force from a great estate that has hit, all cylinders, producing a surprisingly profound wine in an irregular vintage. Anticipated maturity: 2015–2050+.

2001 Château Latour

RATING: 95 points

This effort from the newly renovated Château Latour is performing even better from bottle than it did from cask. In the Médoc, Latour looks to be the wine of the vintage, and is probably surpassed by only a handful of right-bankers such as Ausone and Pavie. A brilliant offering, which should be drinkable much earlier than the blockbuster 2000, the 2001 Latour boasts an inky/ruby/purple color to the rim as well as a glorious bouquet of black currants, crushed stones, vanilla, and hints of truffles and oak. A blend of 80% Cabernet Sauvignon and the balance primarily Merlot with a touch of Cabernet Franc and Petit Verdot, it reveals a sweetness on the palate that is atypical for such a young Latour. The beautiful integration of tannin, acidity, and wood is stunning. The wine flows across the palate with fabulous texture, purity, and presence. This luscious, full-bodied Latour was surprisingly open-knit on the three occasions I tasted it from bottle. However, do not mistake its aging ability, as this 2001, despite its precociousness, will last 20–25 years. Anticipated maturity: 2007–2025.

2000 Château Latour

RATING: 98+ points

There are only 14,000 cases (only 48% of the crop made it into the grand vin) of the 2000, which flirts with perfection. Truly great stuff, it reveals perfect equilibrium, great finesse, yet colossal size, with a thickness and density that rival the brilliant 1996. This saturated black ruby/purple–colored wine seems almost discreet on first inspection, but with aeration, notes of vanilla, exceptionally pure mineral-infused crème de cassis, and earth emerge. Full-bodied and tannic, it should come close to exemplifying perfection. Latour's 2000 is hard to compare with previous vintages. It obviously does not have the opulence of the 1990 and 1982, yet there is an extraordinary purity, delineation, seamlessness, and freshness to this wine that sets it apart from previous vintages. In any event, it is prodigious, with at least five decades of evolution ahead of it. Anticipated maturity: now–2050.

1999 Château Latour

RATING: 93 points

Readers looking for a modern-day version of Latour's magnificent 1971 or 1962 should check out the sensational 1999 Latour. A big, concentrated offering, it exhibits a dense ruby/purple color and a classic nose of minerals, black currants, leather, and vanilla. Long, ripe, and medium-bodied, with high levels of sweet tannin, this surprisingly full, concentrated 1999 should be drinkable in five years; it will last for three decades.

1998 Château Latour

RATING: 90 points

Not a blockbuster, super-concentrated classic such as the 1996, 1995, 1990, or 1982, the 1998 possesses a dark garnet/purple color in addition to a complex bouquet of underbrush, cedar, walnuts, and licorice-tinged black currants. Although medium to full–bodied and moderately tannic, it lacks the expansiveness in the mid-palate necessary to be truly great. Moreover, the tannin is slightly aggressive, although that is hardly unusual in such a young Latour. Anticipated maturity: 2009–2030.

1996 Château Latour

RATING: 99 points

A spectacular Latour, the 1996 may be the modern-day clone of the 1966, only riper. This vintage, which is so variable in Pomerol, St.-Emilion, and Graves, was fabulous for the late-harvested Cabernet Sauvignon of the northern Médoc because of splendid weather in late September and early October. An opaque purple color is followed by phenomenally sweet, pure aromas of cassis infused with subtle minerals. This massive offering possesses unreal levels of extract, full body, intensely ripe but abundant tannin, and a finish that lasts for nearly a minute. More classic and denser than the 1995, it displays the potential for 50–75 years of longevity. Although it is still an infant, it would be educational to taste a bottle. Anticipated maturity: 2015–2050.

1995 Château Latour

RATING: 96+ points

A beauty, the opaque, dense purple–colored 1995 exhibits jammy cassis, vanilla, and minerals in its fragrant but still youthful aromatics. Medium to full–bodied, with exceptional purity, superb concentration, and a long, intense, ripe, 40-second finish, this is a magnificent example of Latour. As the wine sat in the glass, scents of roasted espresso and toasty new oak emerged. This classic will require considerable cellaring. Anticipated maturity: 2012–2050.

1990 Château Latour

RATING: 96 points

This is not the awesome blockbuster I thought it would be. Though a dark ruby/purple color, it does not possess the saturation found in vintages such as 2000, 1996, and 1995. There is a roasted, earthy, hot-year character with extremely low acidity, fleshy, seductive, opulently textured flavors, and a full-bodied finish with considerable amounts of glycerin and tannin. The wine was sweet, accessible, and seductive on the attack, but it closed down in the mouth; it needs at least 5 years of further cellaring. It will last 25–30 years, but is it the immortal classic many observers, including myself, thought it was? Anticipated maturity: 2010–2036.

1988 Château Latour

RATING: 91 points

The best showing yet for a wine from this underrated vintage, the dark garnet–colored 1988 Latour reveals slight amber at the edge. A bouquet of melted tar, plums, black currants, cedar, and underbrush is followed by a sweet entry with medium to full body, excellent ripeness, and mature tannin. It is a classic, elegant Latour with more meaty, vegetable-like flavors than are found in a riper year, such as 1990 and 1989. The 1988 has just begun to enter its plateau of maturity, where it should remain for 25 years. Anticipated maturity: now–2025.

1986 Château Latour

RATING: 90+ points

The 1986 has consistently been outstanding, falling just short of sublime. The spicy, peppery bouquet reveals aromas of dried herbs and red currant fruit. Medium-bodied, austere, but youthful, vigorous, and concentrated, this wine still requires 4–5 years of cellaring. It is surpassed in this vintage (which favored the northern Médoc and Cabernet Sauvignon) by its rivals, Lafite Rothschild and Mouton Rothschild. Anticipated maturity: now–2020.

CLASSIFICATION: Second Growth in 1855

OWNERS: The Barton family

ADDRESS: Château Léoville Barton, 33250 St.-Julien-Beychevelle, France

TELEPHONE: 33 05 56 59 06 05

TELEFAX: 33 05 56 59 14 29

E-MAIL: chateau@leoville-barton.com

WEBSITE: www.leoville-barton.com

CONTACT: Anthony Barton

VISITING POLICY: By appointment only; weekdays, 9–11 A.M., 2–4 P.M.

VINEYARDS

SURFACE AREA: 123.6 acres

GRAPE VARIETALS: 72% Cabernet Sauvignon, 20% Merlot, 8% Cabernet Franc

AVERAGE AGE OF THE VINES: 30 years

DENSITY OF PLANTATION: 9,000 vines per hectare

AVERAGE YIELDS: 50 hectoliters per hectare

WINEMAKING AND UPBRINGING

This Bordeaux is a poster child for traditional methods of winemaking, aside from the use of modern equipment such as a destemmer, a press, and temperature control. Fermentation takes place in oak vats of 200 hectoliters at 30–32°C. After fermentation, the grapes are left in the vats for about two weeks, after which the juice is drawn off into another vat for the malolactic fermentation. After this the wine is transferred into oak barrels (50% new). The wine is racked every three months and fined with egg white in the water. Bottling takes place in July of the second year.

ANNUAL PRODUCTION

Château Léoville Barton: 264,000 bottles

Réserve de Léoville Barton: 55,000 bottles

AVERAGE PRICE (VARIABLE DEPENDING ON VINTAGE): $30–100

GREAT RECENT VINTAGES

2003, 2000, 1996, 1995, 1990, 1986, 1985, 1982

The three Léovilles (Las Cases, Poyferré, and Barton) were originally all part of one large Léoville estate. Hugh Barton bought about a quarter of the vineyard in 1826 and this became Léoville Barton. The property has remained in the hands of the family up to the present time, a record broken by only one other property, Château Langoa Barton, bought by the same Hugh Barton in 1821. According to his great-great-grandson Anthony Barton, there is an enduring misconception that the reason for this long ownership is because the Bartons were Irish, therefore not subject to French law, which required all assets to be divided equally among the children. This is not the case, as the Bartons are fully under French jurisdiction.

Léoville Barton is generally acknowledged to have a huge qualitative edge on its sibling, Langoa Barton. Both properties are owned by Anthony Barton. Unlike other proprietors, Barton uses only a small amount of the supple, fleshy Merlot in the blend (although it was increased to 20% with plantings in the mid-1980s), whereas the proportion of Cabernet Sauvignon is high not only for the commune of St.-Julien, but for the Médoc in general.

Léoville Barton is made at Langoa Barton because there is no château at Léoville. The main vineyard for Léoville Barton sits immediately behind the town of St.-Julien Beychevelle, and runs in a westerly direction, where it intersects with the large vineyard of Château Talbot.

The inconsistencies of the 1970s have been replaced by a consecutive string of brilliantly successful wines in the 1980s, 1990s, and the early 21st century. Since 1985 Anthony Barton has refined rather than changed the traditional style of this wine. Among all the top wines of St.-Julien, it represents the finest value.

CHATEAU LEOVILLE BARTON

2003 Château Léoville Barton

RATING: 93–95+ points

One of the superstars of the vintage, Léoville Barton's 2003 (tasted four times with identical notes) is a powerfully rich, muscular offering possessing a saturated plum/purple color as well as high levels of tannin, low acidity, and inky flavors that have profound depth as well as penetration on the palate. It recalls the 2000 in color saturation and power, but has lower acidity, and a fleshier, fatter mouth-feel. I would assume the alcohol is also slightly high. This formidably endowed St.-Julien should prove to be one of the longest-lived wines of the vintage. It will require 4–8 years of cellaring, and will keep for 25–30 years. It is another brilliant offering from Anthony Barton, who has demonstrated a Midas touch over the last 15 or so years.

2002 Château Léoville Barton

RATING: 92 points

A deep ruby/purple color is accompanied by reticent aromas that require coaxing from the glass. There is a surprising amount of new oak, an unusual component given this estate's wood regime. This is an excruciatingly tannic, backward offering with medium to full body, big, tough tannin (making palate penetration difficult), abundant depth, glorious extract buried underneath the structure, and a pure, rich finish. This appears to be another classic Léoville Barton that should be purchased only by patient connoisseurs. Anticipated maturity: 2011–2025.

2001 Château Léoville Barton

RATING: 92+ points

Consistent from bottle (I tasted it three times), this is an outstanding offering, although not quite at the prodigious level of the 2000. Civilized and approachable for a young Léoville-Barton, it exhibits a saturated plum/purple color along with classic Bordelais aromas of damp earth, crème de cassis, smoke, vanilla, and tobacco. Medium to full–bodied and rich, with high but well-integrated tannin, and a long, 40+- second finish, it should turn out to be a brilliant effort, and one of the stars of the Médoc. However, patience is essential. Anticipated maturity: 2008–2020.

2000 Château Léoville Barton

RATING: 96 points

Absolutely spectacular from bottle, but frightfully closed and backward, with massive power and structure, the saturated purple-colored 2000 Léoville Barton is one of the greatest wines ever made at this estate. The wine has smoky, earthy notes intermixed with graphite, camphor, damp earth, jammy cassis, cedar, and a hint of mushroom. Enormous, even monstrous in the mouth, with tremendous extraction, broodingly backward dense flavors, and copious tannins, this should prove to be one of the longest-lived wines of the vintage and one of the most compelling Léoville Bartons ever made. However, anyone unable to defer gratification for at least a decade should steer clear of this behemoth. Anticipated maturity: 2015–2040.

1998 Château Léoville Barton

RATING: 91 points

This opaque purple-colored, muscular, full-bodied, classically made St.-Julien displays impressive concentration, chewy, highly extracted flavors of black fruits, iron, earth, and spicy wood, a powerful mouth-feel, and three decades of longevity. A pure, uncompromising, traditionally styled wine, it is to be admired for its authenticity, class, and quality. Anticipated maturity: 2007–2035.

1996 Château Léoville Barton

RATING: 92+ points

The impressive 1996 is a classic. Although backward, it exhibits a dense ruby/purple color in addition to abundant black currant fruit intertwined with spicy oak and truffle-like scents. The wine is brilliantly made, full-bodied, and tightly structured, with plenty of muscle and outstanding concentration and purity. It should turn out to be a long-lived Léoville Barton (almost all this estate's recent top vintages have shared that characteristic) and somewhat of a sleeper of the vintage. However, patience is required. Anticipated maturity: 2007–2030.

1995 Château Léoville Barton

RATING: 91 points

Somewhat closed and reticent after bottling but still impressive, this 1995 possesses a dark ruby/purple color, as well as an oaky nose with classic scents of cassis, vanilla, cedar, and spice. Dense and medium to full–bodied, with softer tannin and more accessibility than the 1996, but not quite the packed and stacked effect on the palate, the 1995 is an outstanding textbook St.-Julien. Anticipated maturity: now–2025.

1990 Château Léoville Barton

RATING: 94 points

Still backward, tannic, and formidably endowed, but beginning to budge from its infancy, this opaque garnet/purple-colored wine offers up notes of licorice, damp earth, sweet black currants, wood, and some underbrush. Very full-bodied, with huge amounts of glycerin and concentration backed up by some impressive levels of tannin, this wine is one of the more backward 1990s but is just beginning to move out of infancy into adolescence. It is an exceptional wine that seems to have gotten even better than I predicted it would be from the cask and from its life early in the bottle. Anticipated maturity: now–2030.

1986 Château Léoville Barton

RATING: 91+ points

Still backward (frustratingly so), this wine shows a very dark ruby color with a hint of pink at the rim. The aromatics are beginning to emerge from just pure fruit-driven notes to secondary characteristics. Sweet earth, truffle, black currant, underbrush, and licorice emerge with coaxing. In the mouth, the wine is powerful and dense, with high tannin, impressive concentration, and a formidable, sort of old-style personality. The best 1986 Médocs are terrific wines, but have never been wines that show a lot of charm. Like so many of its siblings from the Médoc, the wines are admired more than they are actually enjoyed. I still have high hopes that everything will come together. Anticipated maturity: 2006–2030.

1985 Château Léoville Barton

RATING: 92 points

The 1985 is a gorgeous example that may well represent a more modern-day clone of the splendid 1953. Dark ruby/garnet with an open-knit, complex, ripe nose of sweet red as well as black currants, vanilla, fruitcake, tobacco, cedar, and earth, the wine is medium-bodied with exceptional sweetness, soft tannin, and a supple, very nicely layered finish. A classic mid-weight Bordeaux, it will drink now and over the next decade. Anticipated maturity: now–2010.

1982 Château Léoville Barton

RATING: 94 points

Still one of the most backward wines of the vintage, Léoville Barton's 1982 is a wine of huge extract, high tannin, and a somewhat ancient style that recalls some of the Bordeaux of the late 1940s. The color is still a dense, even murky, opaque ruby/garnet. The wine offers up notes of licorice, cedar, black truffles, and sweet currant fruit. I had the wine twice in 2002, and my tasting notes were almost identical to the last time I had it, in 1997, showing just how slowly this wine is evolving. The wine is enormous in the mouth but still has some rather gritty, high tannins. It is a classic St.-Julien, with meat and black currants, great structure, and an amazingly youthful, vigorous feel. I would not touch a bottle for another five or six years. Anthony Barton thinks it is more "rustic" than younger vintages. No new oak was used in 1982. Anticipated maturity: 2009–2035.

CLASSIFICATION: Second Growth in 1855

OWNER: SC du Château Léoville-Las-Cases (the Delon family)

ADDRESS: Château Léoville-Las-Cases, 33250 St.-Julien-Beychevelle, France

TELEPHONE: 33 05 56 73 25 26

TELEFAX: 33 05 56 59 18 33

E-MAIL: leoville-las-cases@wanadoo.fr

CONTACT: Jacqueline Marange

VISITING POLICY: By appointment only

VINEYARDS

SURFACE AREA: 240 acres

GRAPE VARIETALS: 65% Cabernet Sauvignon, 19% Merlot, 13% Cabernet Franc, 3% Petit Verdot

AVERAGE AGE OF THE VINES: 30 years

DENSITY OF PLANTATION: 8,000 vines per hectare

AVERAGE YIELDS: 42–50 hectoliters per hectare

WINEMAKING AND UPBRINGING

Twelve- to twenty-day fermentation and maceration in temperature-controlled wooden, concrete, and stainless-steel vats. Twelve to twenty-four months' aging in barrels with 50–100% new oak depending upon the vintage. Fining, no filtration.

ANNUAL PRODUCTION

Château Léoville-Las-Cases: 216,000 bottles

Clos du Marquis: 240,000 bottles

AVERAGE PRICE (VARIABLE DEPENDING ON VINTAGE): $50–150

GREAT RECENT VINTAGES

2003, 2002, 2000, 1998, 1996, 1995, 1990, 1986, 1982

Léoville-Las-Cases is unquestionably one of the great names and wines of Bordeaux. Situated next to Latour, Léoville-Las-Cases' picturesque main vineyard of more than 100 acres is the enclosed vineyard depicted on the wine's label. The estate is one of Bordeaux's largest, and while the meticulous and passionate commitment to quality may be equaled by several others, it is surpassed by no one. The man responsible was the late Michel Delon, and more recently, his son Jean-Hubert. Michel Delon was a proud man who was as admired as he was scorned. His critics, and there were many, claimed he played games when selling his wines, doling out tiny quantities in great vintages to artificially drive up the price. Yet no one can argue about the splendid quality of his wines, the product of an almost maniacal obsession to be the finest, not just in St.-Julien, but in the entire Médoc! Who else would declassify more than 50% of their crop in an abundant vintage such as 1986 or an astonishing 67% in 1990? Who else would introduce not only a second wine, but a third wine (Bignarnon) as well? Who else would lavishly install marble floors in the air-conditioned *chais*? Like him or not, Michel Delon, ably assisted by Michel Rolland (not the Libourne oenologist) and Jacques Depoizier, consistently made one of the greatest wines in the Médoc during the 1980s and 1990s. His son seems more than capable of continuing in the path of his father.

The wines of Léoville-Las-Cases were erratic in the post–World War II era, yet the period from 1975 onward has witnessed the production of a string of successes. Vintages such as 2000, 1996, 1995, 1994, 1990, 1986, 1985, 1982, 1978, and 1975 have come close to perfection. In fact, these wines are as profound as most of the Médoc's first growths in those vintages.

In comparison to Ducru-Beaucaillou, its chief rival in St.-Julien, the wines of Léoville-Las-Cases tend to be a shade darker in color, more tannic, larger scaled, more concentrated, and, of course, built for extended cellaring. They are traditional wines, designed for connoisseurs who must have the patience to wait the 10–15 years necessary for them to mature properly. Should a reclassification of Bordeaux's 1855 classification take place, Léoville-Las-Cases, like Ducru-Beaucaillou and possibly Léoville Barton and Gruard Larose, would merit and receive serious support for first-growth status.

CHATEAU LEOVILLE-LAS-CASES

2003 Château Léoville-Las-Cases

RATING: 94–96+ points

Extremely small yields of only 21.2 hectoliters per hectare, from a harvest that began on September 11 and ended September 26, the 2003 Léoville-Las-Cases is a blend of 70.2% Cabernet Sauvignon, 17.2% Merlot, and 12.6% Cabernet Franc. The 13.27% alcohol is slightly less than the record alcohol level attained here in 2002, and the pH is 3.82. Only 54% of the harvest made it into the grand vin. Still a large-scaled, monolithic wine, it will no doubt move up the scale as it sorts itself out and becomes more delineated. Inky ruby/purple-colored, it possesses the classic Las-Cases purity and balance along with layer upon layer of ripe, pure black cherry and black currant fruit wrapped around a solid core of minerals and subtle oak. Medium to full-bodied, with sweet tannin, but not as opulent as many of its peers, this classically proportioned, well-delineated 2003 is another brilliant achievement from Jean-Hubert Delon and his staff. Anticipated maturity: 2010–2030.

2002 Château Léoville-Las-Cases

RATING: 95 points

A sensational effort from Jean-Hubert Delon, the 2002 Léoville-Las-Cases (a blend of 66.7% Cabernet Sauvignon, 14.5% Merlot, 13.9% Cabernet Franc, and the rest Petit Verdot) possesses the highest natural alcohol of any vintage produced at Las-Cases (a whopping 13.5%, compared to 2000's 12.9%, 1982's 12.8%, and 1990's 13.2%). Yields were a low 27 hectoliters per hectare. Approximately 43% of the production made it into the 2002. The wine has tremendously high measurements of extract and phenolics. The color is nearly black/purple, and the wine looks like syrup of Léoville-Las-Cases. Dense, concentrated, broodingly backward as well as tannic, but oh, so promising and intense, the 2002 reveals tremendous purity, great intensity, and a finish that lasts for 45 seconds. Clearly Léoville-Las-Cases has produced a wine of first-growth quality (what's new?) that competes for the wine of the vintage moniker. Anticipated maturity: 2015–2030+.

2001 Château Léoville-Las-Cases

RATING: 93+ points

Jean-Hubert Delon thinks the 2001 Léoville-Las-Cases could turn out to be as good as his 2000. I'm not sure I agree, but it may come close. A blend of 69% Cabernet Sauvignon, 19.5% Merlot, and the rest Cabernet Franc, the 2001 (which represents only 40% of the production) reveals notes of sweet vanilla intermixed with pure cassis, black cherries, and lead pencil shavings. Elegant and medium-bodied, it possesses a saturated purple color, high tannin, and a structured, backward feel in the mouth. This quintessentially elegant Las-Cases needs another five to seven years to hit its plateau of maturity. It will be one of the Médoc's longest-lived wines of the vintage. Anticipated maturity: 2011–2030.

2000 Château Léoville-Las-Cases

RATING: 99 points

This wine has put on weight and, as impressive as it was from cask, it is even more brilliant from bottle. Only 35% of the crop made it into the 2000 Léoville-Las-Cases, a blend of 76.8% Cabernet Sauvignon, 14.4% Merlot, and 8.8% Cabernet Franc. The wine is truly profound, with an opaque purple color and a tight but promising nose of vanilla, sweet cherry liqueur, black currants, and licorice in a dense, full-bodied, almost painfully rich, intense style with no hard edges. This seamless classic builds in the mouth, with a finish that lasts more than 60 seconds. Still primary, yet extraordinarily pure, this compelling wine, which continues to build flavor intensity and exhibit additional layers of texture, is a tour de force in winemaking and certainly one of the great Léoville-Las-Cases. In that sense, it pays homage to perfectionist former proprietor Michel Delon, who passed away in 2000. Anticipated maturity: 2012–2040.

1999 Château Léoville-Las-Cases

RATING: 91 points

The 1999 Léoville-Las-Cases possesses a dense purple color as well as classic aromas of vanilla, black cherries, and currants mixed with subtle toasty oak. While medium-bodied with sweet tannin, it remains young, backward, and unevolved (unusual for a 1999). Its extraordinary purity and overall harmony give it a character all its own. This excellent Las-Cases will be at its finest between 2006 and 2022. This is one of the wines of the vintage!

1998 Château Léoville-Las-Cases

RATING: 93 points

The 1998 has turned out to be one of the vintage's superb Médocs. It boasts an opaque black/purple color as well as a classic Léoville-Las-Cases display of gorgeously pure black raspberries and cherries, smoke, and graphite. A classic entry on the palate reveals firm tannin, medium to full body, superb concentration and purity, as well as a totally symmetrical mouth-feel. This wine is a worthy successor to such classic Las-Cases vintages as 1996, 1995, and 1988. Anticipated maturity: 2006–2025.

1996 Château Léoville-Las-Cases

RATING: 98+ points

A profound Léoville-Las-Cases, this is one of the great modern-day wines of Bordeaux, rivaling what the estate has done in vintages such as 2000, 1990, 1986, and 1982. The 1996's hallmark remains a *sur-maturité* (overripeness) of the Cabernet Sauvignon grape. Yet the wine has retained its intrinsic classicism, symmetry, and profound potential for complexity and elegance. The black/purple color is followed by a spectacular nose of cassis, cherry liqueur, toast, and minerals. It is powerful and rich on the attack, with beautifully integrated tannin, massive concentration, yet no hint of heaviness or disjointedness. As this wine sits in the glass, it grows in stature and richness. It is a remarkable, seamless, palate-staining, and extraordinarily elegant wine—the quintessential St.-Julien made in the shadow of its next-door neighbor, Latour. Despite the sweetness of the tannin, I would recommend cellaring this wine for another four or five years. Anticipated maturity: 2010–2040.

1995 Château Léoville-Las-Cases

RATING: 95 points

If it were not for the prodigious 1996, everyone would be concentrating on getting their hands on a few bottles of the fabulous 1995 Léoville-Las-Cases, which is one of the vintage's great success stories. The wine boasts an opaque ruby/purple color and exceptionally pure, beautifully knit aromas of black fruits, minerals, vanilla, and spice. On the attack, it is staggeringly rich yet displays more noticeable tannin than its younger sibling. Exceptionally ripe cassis fruit, the judicious use of toasty new oak, and a thrilling mineral character intertwined with the high quality of fruit routinely obtained by Las-Cases make this a compelling effort. There is probably nearly as much tannin as in the 1996, but it is not as perfectly sweet as in the 1996. The finish is incredibly long in this classic. Only 35% of the harvest was of sufficient quality for the 1995 Léoville-Las-Cases. Anticipated maturity: 2008–2025.

1994 Château Léoville-Las-Cases

RATING: 91 points

One of the more massive Médocs of the vintage, this opaque purple-colored wine exhibits fabulous richness and volume in the mouth. Layers of pure black cherry and cassis fruit are intermixed with stony, mineral-like scents, earth, as well as high-quality toasty oak. Medium to full–bodied, with a sweet, rich entry, this wine possesses plenty of tannin yet impressive extract and length. Léoville-Las-Cases is one of the half-dozen great wines of the Médoc in 1994. Anticipated maturity: now–2025.

1990 Château Léoville-Las-Cases

RATING: 97 points

I underestimated this wine young, as it continues to put on weight and character. In fact, of the great vintages of Léoville-Las-Cases, this is one of the more forward wines, largely because of the seamlessness of the 1990 and its exceptionally sweet tannin, combined with relatively low acidity. The color remains a healthy opaque dark plum/purple. The classic Las-Cases nose of sweet black currants, cherries, minerals, lead pencil, and vanilla soars from the glass. Very full-bodied, expansive, and super-concentrated, yet so symmetrical and perfectly balanced (always a hallmark of Léoville-Las-Cases), this wine seems youthful yet very approachable. Anticipated maturity: now–2035.

1989 Château Léoville-Las-Cases

RATING: 90 points

Dark ruby (a far less saturated color than the 1990, for example), this wine offers up a somewhat internationally styled nose of new oak and ripe black currant fruit, with a hint of mineral and graphite. It is a medium-weight, relatively elegant style of wine without nearly the power, density, and layers of concentration that the 1990 possesses. As with so many 1989s, there is a feeling that the selection was not as strict as it could have been, or that the harvest occurred perhaps a few days earlier than it should have in order to achieve full phenolic ripeness. This wine will continue to improve for at least another 15 or more years, and while it is an outstanding wine, it is hardly a profound example of Léoville-Las-Cases. Anticipated maturity: now–2016.

1988 Château Léoville-Las-Cases

RATING: 92 points

This wine continues to show brilliantly and is certainly a more successful effort than the more renowned and expensive 1989. The color is a dark, murky garnet/purple. The wine shows notes of underbrush, fruitcake, cedar, black cherries, and currants. The wine still shows some moderate tannins in the mouth, but the fruit is sweet, the wine is expansive, and the overall impression is a very symmetrical, medium to full–bodied, rather classic Médoc. Anticipated maturity: now–2020.

1986 Château Léoville-Las-Cases
RATING: 100 points
The late Michel Delon always thought that this was the greatest vintage he had produced. We often tasted it side by side with the 1982, because I always preferred the latter vintage. Of course, the two vintages are quite different in style. The 1986 is a monument to classicism, with great tannin, extraordinary delineation, and a huge, full-bodied nose of sweet, ripe cassis fruit intermixed with vanilla, melon, fruitcake, and a multitude of spices. The wine has always been phenomenally concentrated yet wonderfully fresh and vigorous. It still seems young, yet it is hard to believe it is not close to full maturity. It is a great example of Léoville-Las-Cases and another compelling reason to take a serious look at the top Cabernet Sauvignon–based Médocs of 1986. Anticipated maturity: now–2035.

1985 Château Léoville-Las-Cases
RATING: 94 points
The 1985 is a gorgeously open-knit Las-Cases with a sweet nose of lead pencil, sweet black cherries and currants, and a hint of underbrush and new oak. Medium to full–bodied with expansiveness, supple tannins, and outstanding concentration, this is a beautifully made wine that still tastes like it is an adolescent and may have an even greater upside as it continues to age. The low acidity and sweet tannin, however, suggest it has entered its plateau of maturity. Anticipated maturity: now–2018.

1982 Château Léoville-Las-Cases
RATING: 100 points
Still stubbornly backward, yet beginning to budge from its preadolescent stage, this dense, murky ruby/purple-colored wine offers up notes of graphite, sweet caramel, black cherry jam, cassis, and minerals. The nose takes some coaxing; decanting two to four hours prior to service is highly recommended. For such a low-acid wine, it is huge, well delineated, extremely concentrated, and surprisingly fresh. Perhaps because I lean more toward the hedonistic view of wine than the late Michel Delon, I have always preferred this to the 1986, but the truth is that any lover of classic Médoc should have both vintages in his cellar, as they represent perfection in the glass. This wine has monstrous levels of glycerin, extract, and density, but still seems very youthful and tastes more like a seven-to eight-year-old Bordeaux than one that is past its 20th birthday. A monumental effort. Anticipated maturity: now–2035.

CLASSIFICATION: Second Growth in 1855

OWNER: GFA Domaine St.-Julien

ADDRESS: Léoville Poyferré, 33250 St.-Julien-Beychevelle, France

TELEPHONE: 33 05 56 59 08 30

TELEFAX: 33 05 56 59 60 09

E-MAIL: lp@leoville-poyferre.fr

WEBSITE: www.leoville-poyferre.fr

CONTACT: Didier Cuvelier

VISITING POLICY: By appointment, Monday–Friday, 9 A.M.–noon and 2–5:30 P.M.

VINEYARDS

SURFACE AREA: 197.6 acres

GRAPE VARIETALS: 65% Cabernet Sauvignon, 25% Merlot, 8% Petit Verdot, 2% Cabernet Franc

AVERAGE AGE OF THE VINES: 25 years

DENSITY OF PLANTATION: 8,000 vines per hectare

AVERAGE YIELDS: 45–50 hectoliters per hectare

WINEMAKING AND UPBRINGING

Seven-day fermentation and fifteen- to thirty-day maceration in temperature-controlled tanks. Twenty-two months' aging in barrels with 75% new oak. Fining with egg whites, no filtration.

ANNUAL PRODUCTION

Château Léoville Poyferré: 250,000 bottles

Moulin-Riche: 130,000 bottles

AVERAGE PRICE (VARIABLE DEPENDING ON VINTAGE): $25–55

GREAT RECENT VINTAGES

2003, 2000, 1996, 1990, 1983, 1982

Like the two other Léoville siblings, Poyferré was once part of the great Médoc estate owned by the Marquis de Léoville. After it was confiscated during the French Revolution, Monsieur Poyferré was one of three buyers who acquired the estate at public auction.

Talk to just about any knowledgeable Bordelais about the potential of the vineyard of Léoville Poyferré, and they will unanimously agree that Poyferré has the capacity to produce one of the Médoc's most profound red wines. In fact, some will argue that Léoville Poyferré has better soil than any of the other second-growth St.-Juliens. However, the story of Léoville Poyferré since

1961 is largely one of disappointments, though it has the makings of a happy ending. Modernizations to the cellars, the introduction of a second wine, the elevated use of new oak, the increasingly watchful eyes of Didier Cuvelier, and the genius of the Libourne oenologist Michel Rolland have finally pushed Léoville Poyferré into the elite of St.-Julien. The two finest vintages of the 1980s remain the gloriously fruity 1983 and the prodigious 1982. Both years exhibit the depth and richness that this property is capable of attaining. In the 1990s, a top 1990 followed by strong efforts in 1995, 1996, and 2000 suggest this estate has begun to finally exploit its considerable potential. Both the 2002 and 2003 have continued the optimism of the last 10–15 years.

CHATEAU LEOVILLE POYFERRE

2003 Château Léoville Poyferré

RATING: 94–96 points

A huge success for Poyferré, this 2003, tasted three separate times with similar notes, reveals a saturated ruby/purple color, explosive aromatics, and ripe yet remarkably fresh, vibrant flavors that cascade over the palate with enormous concentration, depth, and precision. The wood, acidity, tannin, and alcohol are all beautifully integrated in this fabulous effort. It is reminiscent of the compelling 1990. Anticipated maturity: 2009–2025.

2002 Château Léoville Poyferré
RATING: 92–94 points
One of the stars of the vintage, this 2002 reveals a saturated-to-the-rim purple color as well as a big, sweet, provocative nose of earth, licorice, crème de cassis, and toasty new oak. It possesses medium to full body, great purity, tangy underlying acidity, and an impressively long, 40-second finish. This top-flight St.-Julien should hit its prime in five to eight years, and last for more than two decades. Bravo!

2001 Château Léoville Poyferré
RATING: 90 points
Sweet notions of plums, black currants, caramel, and spicy oak are provocative and alluring. Subtle but substantial, layered, and textured, with medium body as well as sexy, upfront flavors, low acidity, and ripe tannin, this beauty is among the most evolved and flamboyant of the appellation. Nevertheless, it should age well. Anticipated maturity: now.

2000 Château Léoville Poyferré
RATING: 95 points
Wow, this wine has really come on strong. A brilliant effort, it boasts an opaque purple color in addition to a gorgeously sweet nose (make that explosive nose) of blackberries and crème de cassis intermixed with minerals, smoke, and earth. The 2000 is opulent, full-bodied, and much more accessible than either of its two Léoville siblings, Léoville-Las-Cases or Léoville Barton, with low acidity, sweet tannin, and a layered, sumptuous finish. It continues to improve dramatically and looks to be a great success, rivaling the brilliant 1996 and 1990. Anticipated maturity: 2009–2030.

1996 Château Léoville Poyferré
RATING: 93 points
This fabulous 1996 was tasted three times from bottle, and it is unquestionably, along with the 2000, the finest wine produced by this estate since their blockbuster 1990. Medium to full–bodied with a saturated black/purple color, the nose offers notes of cedar, jammy black fruits, smoke, truffles, and subtle new oak. In the mouth, there is impressive fruit extraction, a tannic, full-bodied structure, and a classic display of power and finesse. The longer it sat in the glass, the more impressive the wine became. Backward and massive in terms of its extract and richness, this should prove to be a sensational

Léoville Poyferré for drinking over the next three decades. Anticipated maturity: 2007–2028.

1995 Château Léoville Poyferré
RATING: 90+ points
While not as backward as the 1996, the opaque purple-colored 1995 is a tannic, unevolved, dense, concentrated wine that will require another two or three years of cellaring. The 1995 exhibits toast, black currant, mineral, and subtle tobacco in its complex yet youthful aromatics. Powerful, dense, concentrated cassis and blueberry flavors might be marginally softer than in the 1996, but there is still plenty of grip and structure to this big wine. Anticipated maturity: now–2030.

1990 Château Léoville Poyferré
RATING: 96 points
One of the profound Léoville Poyferrés of the last 25 years, this wine, so open in its youth, seems to be shutting down ever so slightly, based on three tastings in 2002. The color still remains a saturated, dense, opaque ruby/purple. The nose has great purity of jammy, sweet cassis fruit intermixed with hints of espresso, vanilla, white flowers, and minerals. Very full-bodied with low acidity, extremely high tannin, yet fabulous extract and a layered personality, this is a prodigious Léoville Poyferré. Anticipated maturity: 2008–2030.

1983 Château Léoville Poyferré
RATING: 91 points
One of the superstar 1983s that is not beginning to crack up and decline, Léoville Poyferré's effort exhibits a dark garnet color, a sweet nose of plum liqueur intermixed with licorice, black currants, weedy tobacco, and *herbes de Provence.* The wine is round and seductive with a certain degree of opulence, low acidity, gorgeous fruit, and a nicely layered palate impression. Drink it by 2010.

1982 Château Léoville Poyferré
RATING: 94 points
A great Léoville Poyferré, not nearly as majestic as the 1990, but chunkier, more muscular, with high levels of tannins equaled by prodigious levels of extract and density, this wine still exhibits a youthful deep purple color. The tannins seem less polished than in more recent vintages, but the wine is so concentrated and massive that clearly it looks set to overcome the brutality of its tannin structure. The wine is very full-bodied, very concentrated, and somewhat of a sleeper in this vintage. It still needs time in the cellar. Anticipated maturity: 2006–2025.

CLASSIFICATION: Fifth Growth of the 1855 classification

OWNERS: The Cazes family

ADDRESS: Château Lynch-Bages, 33250 Pauillac, France

TELEPHONE: 33 05 56 73 24 00

TELEFAX: 33 05 56 59 26 42

E-MAIL: infochateau@lynchbages.com

WEBSITE: www.lynchbages.com

CONTACT: Jean-Michel Cazes

VISITING POLICY: By appointment (mail or telephone). Open every day, including weekends. Closed on Christmas Day and January 1.

VINEYARDS

SURFACE AREA: 235 acres

GRAPE VARIETALS:

Red—73% Cabernet Sauvignon, 10% Cabernet Franc, 15% Merlot, 2% Petit Verdot

White—40% Semillon, 40% Sauvignon, 20% Muscadelle

AVERAGE AGE OF THE VINES:

Red—35 years

White—15 years

DENSITY OF PLANTATION:

Red—8,700 vines per hectare

White—8,700 vines per hectare

AVERAGE YIELDS: 50 hectoliters per hectare

WINEMAKING AND UPBRINGING

Fermentation takes place in 35 stainless-steel temperature-controlled vats, a system that has been adapted regularly and modernized over the years. Nearly 20 years ago Lynch-Bages introduced an extraction method that involves frequent *délestage* (rack and return) during fermentation in order to extract powerful, rich tannin. This has now become a standard winemaking procedure in Bordeaux. At Lynch-Bages, 20 small underground vats make *délestage* an easy task thanks to the simple flow of gravity. The wine is completely run off the vat, causing the cap to break up, as well as facilitating homogenous extraction, then sent back in the vat at a later time.

At *écoulage* (racking of the vats) time, the wine is sent directly in the barrels. Malolactic fermentation is conducted in vats and barrels (50%). Only a very light filtering takes place for polish. The wine is aged the traditional way for 12–15 months in oak barrels (60% of which are new every year) and racked regularly in the traditional way (from barrel to barrel).

ANNUAL PRODUCTION

Château Lynch-Bages: 38,000 cases

Haut-Bages Averous: 8,000 cases

AVERAGE PRICE (VARIABLE DEPENDING ON VINTAGE): $35–85

GREAT RECENT VINTAGES

2000, 1996, 1990, 1989, 1986, 1982

This château is located just west of Bordeaux's Route du Vin (D2) as one approaches the dull, commercial town of Pauillac from the south. It is situated on a small ridge called, not surprisingly, the Bages plateau, which rises above the town and the adjacent Gironde River. The luxury hotel/restaurant Château Cordeillan-Bages sits directly in front of Lynch-Bages. Until recently the kindest thing that could be said about the winery buildings was that they were utilitarian. However, Lynch-Bages has benefitted enormously from a major face-lift and renovation. The château now sports a fresh façade, new cellars with large stainless-steel tanks, and a state-of-the-art tasting room. Except for these recent changes, this large estate has remained essentially intact since the 16th century.

The winery takes its name from Thomas Lynch, the son of an Irish immigrant whose family ran the property during the 17th and 18th centuries, and the Bages plateau. After Thomas Lynch sold Lynch-Bages, it passed through the hands of several wine merchants before being purchased in 1937 by Jean-Charles Cazes, the grandfather of the current proprietor, Jean-Michel Cazes. Jean-Charles Cazes was already a renowned proprietor and winemaker, having directed the fortunes of one of the leading Cru Bourgeois of St.-Estèphe, Château Les Ormes de Pez. He continued to handle both châteaux until 1966, when his son André, a prominent politician who had been the mayor of Pauillac for nearly two decades, took control. André's reign lasted until 1973, when Jean-Michel Cazes assumed control of both Lynch-Bages and Les Ormes de Pez. Jean-Michel made perhaps the smartest decision of his business career in 1976 when he hired the brilliant Daniel

Llose as director of Château Lynch-Bages and Les Ormes de Pez.

After the great success Lynch-Bages enjoyed under Jean-Michel's father, André, in the 1950s (1959, 1957, 1955, 1953, and 1952 were all among the top wines of that decade) and in the 1960s (1966, 1962, and 1961), Jean-Michel's inheritance consisted of a disappointing 1972 still in cask. Even his first vintage, 1973, was largely a washout. This was followed by another disappointing year in 1974 and, for Lynch-Bages, less than exhilarating wine from the sometimes troublesome vintage of 1975. Jean-Michel Cazes recognized that the old wooden vats created sanitation problems and also made it difficult to control the proper fermentation temperature in both cold and hot years. At the same time (the late 1970s), Cazes flirted with a newer style, producing several vintages of Lynch-Bages that were lighter and more elegant. Longtime fans and supporters of Lynch-Bages were dismayed. Fortunately, after Jean-Michel Cazes installed 25 large stainless-steel vats in 1980, the slump in quality between 1971 and 1979 came to an abrupt end. Lynch-Bages produced a competent 1981 and continued to build on that success with highly successful wines in nearly every vintage since.

The vineyard itself is located midway between Mouton Rothschild and Lafite Rothschild to the north,

and Latour, Pichon Longueville Comtesse de Lalande, and Pichon-Longueville Baron to the south. Despite the enormous amount of modernization and rebuilding that has taken place at Lynch-Bages, the general philosophy of making wine remains traditional yet enlightened. Since 1980, as I have mentioned, the vinification has taken place in new steel tanks. After that, the wine is put directly into small French oak casks.

In the famous *1855 Classification of the Wines of Gironde,* Lynch-Bages was positioned in the last tier as a fifth growth. I know of no professional in the field today who would not argue that its present-day quality is more akin to a second growth. Englishman Oz Clarke lightheartedly argues that those responsible for the 1855 classification must have been essentially Puritans because they "couldn't bear to admit that a wine as openheartedly lovely as Lynch-Bages could really be as important as other less-generous growths."

Just as it is difficult not to enjoy a bottle of Lynch-Bages, so is it difficult not to appreciate the affable, seemingly always open and gregarious Jean-Michel Cazes, the man who engineered Lynch-Bages's stratospheric rise to international prominence. The confident Cazes attended school in America and speaks English like a native. He has a global vision, and anyone who talks with him knows he wants his wines to be lusty, open, and direct yet also reflect the class and character of a top Pauillac. For that reason he always prefers vintages such as 1985 and 1982 to more tannic and severe years such as 1988 and 1986. He is also an untiring ambassador for not only his own wines but also for the wines of the entire Bordeaux region. There rarely seems to be a conference, symposium, or international tasting of Bordeaux where one does not encounter Monsieur Cazes. There is no other producer in Pauillac (with the possible exception of Madame Lencquesaing of Pichon-Lalande) who travels so extensively and who speaks so eloquently of both his beloved Lynch-Bages and of all the wines of Bordeaux. President Chirac finally recognized this man's enormous contributions to French prestige and culture in 2001, bestowing on him that country's highest decoration, knighthood in the Legion of Honor.

CHATEAU LYNCH-BAGES

2002 Château Lynch-Bages

RATING: 90 points

A classic offering possessing the weight of the 1999, but without that vintage's charm, this structured, tannic 2002 offers a dense ruby/purple color, medium to full body, and the telltale Lynch-Bages black currant and earthy nose. There is good power on the attack, mid-palate, and finish. It will need two or three years of cellaring, and should age nicely for twelve to fifteen years. If more texture and length develop with bottle age (and they should), this wine will merit an outstanding score. Anticipated maturity: 2009–2020.

2000 Château Lynch-Bages

RATING: 95+ points

An utterly profound Lynch-Bages, this wine continues to remind me of a hypothetical blend of the 1990 and 1989. Interestingly, when I asked Jean-Michel Cazes to rank his top four vintages of Lynch-Bages, he ranked the 1989 first, followed by three vintages that he said were essentially equivalent in quality—1990, 1996, and 2000. The 2000 Lynch-Bages exhibits a dense purple color, loads of glycerin and extract, big, muscular, sweet crème de cassis notes, with hints of new saddle leather, earth, and tobacco leaf. The 2000 is forceful yet plush, with a thick, juicy, succulent mid-palate, ripe tannin, and a long, layered finish. I know it will be tempting to pull corks

on this wine in its youth, but it really will not hit its stride for a few more years and will last for at least twenty-five. Anticipated maturity: 2008–2025.

1999 Château Lynch-Bages

RATING: 90 points

A modern-day clone of this estate's wonderful 1962, the dense ruby/purple–colored 1999 reveals forward, open-knit notes of crème de cassis and earth. Fleshy, medium to full–bodied, and succulent, with supple tannin, excellent balance, and a long, pure, ripe finish, this seductive effort will drink well for 12–15 years, possibly longer.

1996 Château Lynch-Bages

RATING: 91+ points

Lynch-Bages has turned out an outstanding 1996 that is less forward than the 1995 or 1990 and built along the lines of the tannic, blockbuster 1989. It offers an opaque purple color and outstanding aromatics consisting of dried herbs, tobacco, cassis, and smoky oak. Full-bodied and classic in its proportions, this dense, chewy, pure Lynch-Bages will have considerable longevity. Anticipated maturity: now–2025.

1995 Château Lynch-Bages

RATING: 90 points

While most 1995 Médocs remain stubbornly closed, Lynch-Bages is attractive and soft, yet reveals obvious tannin in the background. The 1995 is not made in the blockbuster style of the 1996, 1990, 1989, or 1986. Deep ruby colored, with an evolved nose of sweet, smoky, earthy, black currant fruit, this fleshy, round, seductive, fat, and fruity Lynch-Bages should drink well young, yet age for 10+ years. Anticipated maturity: now–2015.

1990 Château Lynch-Bages

RATING: 95 points

A sumptuous, even flamboyant wine, the 1990 is a forward, flattering, and delicious-to-drink wine, in contrast to the more massive, backward, tannic 1989. Lynch-Bages' 1990 offers sweet, beefy, leathery, black currant aromas intermingled with smoky, toasty oak and roasted herbs. The wine offers a hedonistic turn-on of fruit, extract, and high levels of glycerin, all crammed into a full-bodied, supple-textured, rich, powerful, low-acid Lynch-Bages with no hard edges. Anticipated maturity: now–2020.

1989 Château Lynch-Bages

RATING: 95 points

The opaque, purple-colored 1989 is less evolved and showy than the 1990. However, it looks to be a phenomenal example of Lynch-Bages, perhaps the finest vintage in the last 30 years. Oozing with extract, this backward, muscular, dense wine possesses great purity, huge body, and a bulldozer-like power that charges across the palate. It is an enormous wine with unbridled quantities of power and richness. Anticipated maturity: now–2020.

1988 Château Lynch-Bages

RATING: 90 points

Undoubtedly, the 1988 Lynch-Bages is among the biggest wines produced in the northern Médoc in this vintage. The saturated ruby/purple color suggests excellent ripeness and plenty of concentration. The oaky bouquet exhibits roasted black raspberries, currants, and licorice, as well as an earthy, robust character. The wine is full-bodied, rich, with an attractive cedary, herbaceous, black-fruit character. This fleshy, broad-shouldered wine characterizes the style of the château. Anticipated maturity: now–2010.

1986 Château Lynch-Bages

RATING: 90 points

The 1986 is dark purple in color and extremely rich and tannic. But are the tannins too prominent and astringent? I doubt that anyone will be capable of answering that question for at least a decade. As for now, this wine is more admirable for its remarkable size and weight than for charm and enjoyability. Impressively built and approaching maturity, this is still a very youthful wine. Anticipated maturity: now–2020.

1985 Château Lynch-Bages

RATING: 90 points

This has been a deliciously charming, seductive wine since its birth. Fully mature, this plum/garnet-colored wine offers a fragrant bouquet of sweet black currant fruit intermixed with smoky toasty oak and roasted herbs. Medium-bodied (with far less girth, weight, and richness than the 1990, 1989, 1986, and 1982), the 1985 Lynch-Bages is a gorgeously fleshy, well-proportioned wine that should continue to drink well for another four or five years. Its low acidity, corpulent fleshiness, sweet tannin, and amber edge suggest full maturity. Anticipated maturity: now–2006.

1982 Château Lynch-Bages

RATING: 94 points

The 1982 Lynch-Bages continues to develop well. Delicious since age five to six, it remains a husky, forceful, grapy, exuberant wine with gobs of cassis fruit presented in an unctuously textured, thick, succulent style. The wine has not developed much complexity aromatically, but it is a weighty, textbook example of a wine from this popular estate. Full-bodied, soft, and supple, it will continue to drink well for 10–12 more years.

CLASSIFICATION: First Growth in 1855

OWNERS: The Mentzelopoulos family

ADDRESS: Château Margaux, 33460 Margaux, France

MAILING ADDRESS: BP31, 33460 Margaux, France

TELEPHONE: 33 05 57 88 83 83

TELEFAX: 33 05 57 88 31 32

E-MAIL: chateau-margaux@chateau-margaux.com

WEBSITE: www.chateau-margaux.com

CONTACT: Tina Bizard (Telephone: 33 05 57 88 83 93)

VISITING POLICY: By appointment, Monday–Friday, 10 A.M.–
noon and 2–4 P.M.

VINEYARDS

SURFACE AREA: 192.7 acres (under vine)

GRAPE VARIETALS: 75% Cabernet Sauvignon, 20% Merlot, 5%
Cabernet Franc and Petit Verdot

AVERAGE AGE OF THE VINES: 35 years

DENSITY OF PLANTATION: 10,000 vines per hectare

AVERAGE YIELDS: 45 hectoliters per hectare

WINEMAKING AND UPBRINGING

Three week fermentation and maceration in temperature-controlled wooden vats. Eighteen to twenty-four months' aging in new oak barrels. Fining, no filtration.

ANNUAL PRODUCTION

Château Margaux: 200,000 bottles

Pavillon Rouge du Château Margaux: 200,000 bottles

AVERAGE PRICE (VARIABLE DEPENDING ON VINTAGE): $75–350

GREAT RECENT VINTAGES

2003, 2000, 1996, 1995, 1990, 1986, 1985, 1983, 1982

The approach to the great aristocrat of the Southern Médoc, Château Margaux, is a splendid sight. First-time visitors are surprised and delighted to come upon this noble château, tucked discreetly in a small park just north of Château Palmer.

The estate's history can be traced to the 12th century, when it was known as "La Mothe de Margaux." Its wine history begins somewhat later. Between 1522 and 1582, Pierre de Lestonnac began a systematic replacement of fields, then used primarily to produce cereal crops, with vineyards. By 1705, the *London Gazette* was offering the first sale of Château Margoose, and the wine first appeared in Christie's catalogue with the 1771 vintage.

England's prime minister, Sir Robert Walpole, purchased four casks (about 100 cases) every three months and, according to the château's archives, "did not always pay." Thomas Jefferson, while the American ambassador to France, also had a fondness for Château Margaux, and both drank and paid for the 1784, a wine about which he remarked, "There cannot be a better bottle of Bordeaux."

In the 20th century, Château Margaux began compulsory château bottling with the 1924 vintage, but hard times followed. The disastrous decade of the 1930s, followed by war, led to the sale of the estate, which was acquired by the Ginestets in 1950. Wine quality was variable except for a monumental 1953, and after a distressing period of mediocrity in the 1960s and 1970s—when far too many wines lacking richness, concentration, and character were produced under the inadequately financed administration of Pierre and Bernard Ginestet (the international oil crisis and wine market crash of 1973 and 1974 proved their undoing)—Margaux was sold in 1977

to André and Laura Mentzelopoulos. Lavish amounts of money were immediately spent on the vineyards and the winemaking facilities. Emile Peynaud was retained as a consultant to oversee the vinification of the wine. Apprehensive observers expected the passing of many harvests before the wines of Margaux would reflect the new financial and spiritual commitments to excellence, but it took just one vintage, 1978, for the world to see just how great Margaux could be.

Unfortunately, André Mentzelopoulos died before he could see the full transformation of a struggling first-growth into a brilliantly consistent wine of stunning grace, richness, and complexity. His elegant wife, Laura, and more recently his savvy, street-smart daughter Corinne, run the show. They are surrounded by considerable talent—most notably, manager Paul Pontallier. The immediately acclaimed 1978 Margaux was followed by a succession of brilliantly executed wines that are so

stunning, rich, and balanced that it is not unfair to suggest that during the 1980s there was no better wine made in all of Bordeaux than that of Margaux.

The style of the rejuvenated wine at Margaux is one of opulent richness, a deep, multidimensional bouquet with a fragrance of ripe black currants, spicy vanilla oakiness, and violets. The wine is now considerably fuller in color, richness, body, and tannin than the wines made under the pre-1977 Ginestet regime.

Margaux also makes a dry white wine. Pavillon Blanc du Château Margaux is produced entirely from a 29.6-acre vineyard planted exclusively with Sauvignon Blanc. It is fermented in oak barrels and bottled after 10 months' aging in cask. Trivia buffs will want to know that it is made at the small building, called Château Abel-Laurent, several hundred yards up the road from the magnificent château of Margaux. It is the Médoc's finest white wine, crisp, fruity, subtly herbaceous, and oaky.

1986 Château Margaux

RATING: 98 points

A magnificent example of Château Margaux and one of the most tannic, backward Margaux of the last 50 years, the 1986 continues to evolve at a glacial pace. The color is still a dense ruby/purple with just a hint of lightening at the rim. With several hours of aeration, the aromatics become striking, with notes of smoke, toast, crème de cassis, mineral, and white flowers. Very full-bodied, with high but sweet tannin, great purity, and a very masculine style, this wine should prove nearly immortal in terms of its aging potential. It is beginning to budge from its infantile stage and approach adolescence. Anticipated maturity: 2008–2050.

1985 Château Margaux

RATING: 95 points

Approaching full maturity, this beautifully sweet Château Margaux has a dense plum/purple color and a huge, sweet nose of black currants intermixed with licorice, toast, underbrush, and flowers. Medium to full-bodied with supple tannin and a fleshy, juicy, very succulent and multilayered mid-palate, this expansive, velvety wine has entered its plateau of maturity, where it should remain (assuming good storage) for at least another 10–15 years. A very delicious, seductive, and opulent Château Margaux to drink over the next two decades. Anticipated maturity: now–2015.

1983 Château Margaux

RATING: 96 points

As I have noted consistently, this can be a breathtaking wine, but having tasted it close to a dozen times since 1998, I found that over half the bottles were marred by tainted corks. In fact, one would almost wonder if there was a TCA problem in part of the wine storage area. The percentage of corked half-bottles is even higher than in the regular format. However, when clean, this 1983, which has seemingly reached full maturity far faster than I would have guessed a mere four years ago, has a dense, murky plum/purple color and a gorgeous nose of smoked herbs, damp earth, mushrooms, and sweet crème de cassis intermixed with vanilla and violets. The wine is medium to full-bodied, deep, rich, and powerful, with sweet tannins and loads of fruit concentration. Anticipated maturity: now–2020.

1982 Château Margaux

RATING: 98+ points

At one time I thought the 1983 was the more classic and better effort from Château Margaux, but I am human: The 1982 has overtaken the 1983 and is obviously the superior effort. It started off life as a somewhat ruggedly constructed, powerful, masculine, even coarse style of Château Margaux with high levels of tannin, huge extract, and richness. Increasingly civilized, with the tannin becoming seamlessly integrated, this opaque purple/garnet-colored wine offers up hints of incense, sweet truffles, smoke, black currants, flowers, and damp earth. Very full-bodied, with remarkable levels of glycerin, extract, and tannin, this is probably the largest-scaled, most concentrated Château Margaux under the Mentzelopoulos administration. It is doubtful it will ever rival the 2000, 1996, or 1990 for pure finesse or elegance. In spite of its high levels of tannin, it does not seem to have the classicism of these vintages, but this wine goes from strength to strength and is quickly becoming one of the all-time compelling efforts of Château Margaux. Anticipated maturity: now–2035.

CLASSIFICATION: Classified growth (red wines)

OWNER: Domaine Clarence Dillon SA

ADDRESS: Château La Mission Haut-Brion, 67, rue Peybouquey, 33400 Talence, France

MAILING ADDRESS: c/o Domaine Clarence Dillon, Château Haut-Brion, 33608 Pessac Cedex, France

TELEPHONE: 33 05 56 00 29 30

TELEFAX: 33 05 56 98 75 14

E-MAIL: info@haut-brion.com or visites@haut-brion.com

WEBSITE: www.mission-haut-brion.com

CONTACT: Carla Kuhn

VISITING POLICY: By appointment only, Monday–Thursday, 9–11:30 A.M. and 2–4:30 P.M.; Friday, 9–11:30 A.M.

VINEYARDS

SURFACE AREA: 51.6 acres

GRAPE VARIETALS: 45% Merlot, 48% Cabernet Sauvignon, 7% Cabernet Franc

AVERAGE AGE OF THE VINES: 21 years old

DENSITY OF PLANTATION: 10,000 vines per hectare

AVERAGE YIELDS: 45 hectoliters per hectare

WINEMAKING AND UPBRINGING

At La Mission there is a manual harvest, with first sorting done on tables set up on trucks out among the vines. Vats are stainless steel, 4,755 gallons. A computer program manages the fermentation and the pumping-over in the vat controlling the homogenization and temperature after measuring the heat of the must and the marc. Average temperature of fermentation is 30°C. The wines are aged in 100% new barrels for 22 months. They are fined with fresh egg whites and generally bottled without filtration.

ANNUAL PRODUCTION

Château La Mission Haut-Brion: 72,000 bottles

La Chapelle de la Mission Haut-Brion: 36,000 bottles

AVERAGE PRICE (VARIABLE DEPENDING ON VINTAGE): $125–500

GREAT RECENT VINTAGES

2000, 1998, 1995, 1990, 1989, 1985, 1982

Once part of the Haut-Brion estate, La Mission Haut-Brion in Talence produces one of the greatest wines in the entire Bordeaux region. This estate sits across the road (RN 250), confronting its longtime

rival, Haut-Brion, and has maintained a record of virtually unmatched brilliance that covers much of the 20th century.

In 1682 the proprietor bequeathed the domaine of La Mission Haut-Brion to a religious order founded by St. Vincent de Paul that went by the name "Preachers of the Mission." A chapel was built, which is still on the premises. La Mission's religious affiliate guaranteed a certain popularity. It graced the tables of such notable people as the Archbishop of Bordeaux, the Maréchal de Richelieu, and the Governor of Guyenne. After the French Revolution, the property was divested from the monks and sold, but its reputation continued to spread.

The wine of La Mission began to appear on celebrated tables all over the globe. La Mission archives show that in 1922 the 1918 vintage Lafite was selling at 8F a bottle, Margaux and Latour for 9F, and La Mission for 10F! Only Haut-Brion went for more at 14F a bottle. Following the First World War (in 1919), Frédéric Woltner and his family became owners of La Mission. The Woltners were impassioned vintners imbued with a desire to continually improve their product. They remained owners for most of the 20th century and are largely responsible for La Mission's current reputation as a world-class wine.

In 1983, the Dillon family, owners of Château Haut-Brion, bought Château La Mission Haut-Brion from the descendants of the Woltner family. Domaine Clarence Dillon SA under the presidency of the Duchesse de Mouchy (daughter of the late Douglas Dillon, former ambassador to France and secretary of the treasury under President Kennedy) and the management of Jean-Bernard Delmas took control. Their active pursuit of quality included the study and use of home-grown clonal selections for replanting, the modernization of the old *chais* in 1987, and the building of a state-of-the-art new *cuvier*. The combination of new oenological science with the old magic of La Mission tradition has earned this ancient estate the reputation of being one of the most modern, and most outstanding, wineries in the world.

Under the nearly 65-year reign of the Woltners, La Mission Haut-Brion built an enormous reputation. Woltner's genius was widely recognized in Bordeaux. He was known as a gifted taster and oenologist and pioneered the installation of easy-to-clean, metal, glass-lined fermentation tanks in 1926. Many observers attributed the dense, rich, powerful, fruity character of La Mission to these short, squat vats that, because of their shape, tended to increase the grape-skin-to-juice contact during the fermentation. These vats were replaced under the new administration with the computer-controlled, state-of-the-art fermenters in 1987.

La Mission Haut-Brion's style of wine has always been one of intense richness, full body, great color and extract, and plenty of tannin. I have had the pleasure of

tasting all of the best vintages of La Mission back to 1921, and it is a wine that can easily last 30–50 years in the bottle. It has always been a much richer and more powerful wine than that of its archrival Haut-Brion. For this reason, as well as remarkable consistency in poor and mediocre vintages (along with Latour in Pauillac, it has had the finest record in Bordeaux for good wines in poor vintages), La Mission had become one of the most popular wines of Bordeaux.

Since 1983 Jean Delmas has moved quickly to put his winemaking stamp on the wines of this estate. After the property was sold in 1983, the winemaking staff was promptly dismissed and Delmas increased the percentage of Merlot to 45%, lowering the percentages of Cabernet Sauvignon and Cabernet Franc. He also began to replace the old oak casks, which the Woltner regime had not been able to do due to financial difficulties. Now La Mission, like Haut-Brion, is aged in 100% new oak.

The first vintages under Delmas were very good but lacked the power and extraordinary richness seen in La Mission in previous top years. They were technically correct wines that lacked a bit of soul and personality. However, with the installation of a state-of-the-art winemaking facility in time for the 1987 vintage, the quality of the wine quickly returned to that of its glory years. The wine is cleaner, and flaws (such as elevated

levels of volatile acidity and rustic tannin that appeared in certain older vintages of La Mission) have not reared their unpleasant heads under the meticulous management of Jean Delmas. After a transitional period between 1983 and 1986, La Mission Haut-Brion produced one of the very best wines of the vintage in 1987, a beauty in 1988, and a sumptuous, perfect 1989, the latter wine undoubtedly the finest La Mission of the decade. Vintages of the 1990s, while more vexing because of rainy Septembers, have all produced wines that are among the finest in Bordeaux. Of course, the 2000 is immortal, the 1998 nearly so.

It is unlikely that the newer style of La Mission will age as long as older vintages, but neither will it be as unapproachable, tannic, and occasionally rustic. In the final analysis, La Mission Haut-Brion remains a wine of first-growth quality.

CHATEAU LA MISSION HAUT-BRION

2003 Château La Mission Haut-Brion

RATING: 90–92 points

Like its renowned sibling, Haut-Brion, the 2003 La Mission Haut-Brion tips the scales at 13.25% alcohol, and 60% of the crop was used in the final blend. Although firm, powerful, and closed, with a dense purple color, high tannin, and a tight personality with some austerity to shed, there is plenty of size and depth to this 52% Cabernet Sauvignon, 40% Merlot, and 8% Cabernet Franc blend. There is nothing about this 2003 that reminds me of either the 1989 or 1990. In fact, it comes across like a more obviously tannic vintage such as 1995, and seems completely dominated at this stage of its evolution by its first-growth brethren, Haut-Brion. Anticipated maturity: 2010–2025.

2002 Château La Mission Haut-Brion

RATING: 90 points

Extensive amounts of dry tannin in the finish may prove to be a liability after bottling. Nevertheless, this 2002 possesses plenty of power, a dense ruby/purple color, and a sweet nose of hot rocks intermixed with black currants, plums, cherries, and spice box. Medium-bodied and tannic, it cuts a large swath across the palate. The tannin will need to be monitored. If it becomes better integrated, this wine will be outstanding as well as long lived. At this stage, it is similar in structure to the 1996 and 1988. Anticipated maturity: 2008–2020.

2001 Château La Mission Haut-Brion

RATING: 91+ points

Like its more famous neighbor, Haut-Brion, the 2001 La Mission Haut-Brion has closed down considerably since bottling. A blend of 62% Cabernet Sauvignon, 35% Merlot, and 3% Cabernet Franc, it possesses an inky/purple color (deeper than Haut-Brion's) in addition to a tight but promising bouquet of scorched earth, wood, tar, black currants, and a hint of hickory wood. Medium-bodied, firm, muscular, and virile, it is a candidate for long-term cellaring. Anticipated maturity: 2010–2020+.

2000 Château La Mission Haut-Brion

RATING: 100 points

A superstar of this great vintage, the 2000 La Mission Haut-Brion is as profound as the 1989, 1982, and 1975. It is more structured and tannic than the 1989, more civilized and refined, but not as thick as the 1982, and sweeter as well as purer than the 1975. The 2000 is neither flamboyant nor accessible, but what upside potential it possesses! In time, one might have to return to the prodigious duo of 1959 and 1961 to find a La Mission with this much potential. While still tight from bottling, its inky purple color is accompanied by extravagantly sweet aromas of blackberries, blueberries, toast, scorched earth, coffee, asphalt, graphite, and smoke. Super-intense and unctuously textured, with a sumptuous mid-palate and finish, this is an explosively rich, layered effort that possesses everything I could ever want from a *terroir* that has given me as much hedonistic and intellectual pleasure as any other wine in the world. It is an amazing achievement for Jean-Bernard Delmas, his son, Jean-Phillipe, and the entire winemaking team. The phenomenal aftertaste goes on for more than a minute. Anticipated maturity: 2011–2045.

1999 Château La Mission Haut-Brion

RATING: 91 points

Beautifully complex, with notes of cherry liqueur, plums, cigar smoke, fresh tobacco, and scorched earth, the deep, elegant, yet precise, medium to full–bodied 1999 La Mission Haut-Brion is cut from the same mold as the 1985, 1983, 1971, and 1962. Not a heavyweight, it is gorgeously complex, supple, and both hedonistic and intellectual. Anticipated maturity: now–2018.

1998 Château La Mission Haut-Brion

RATING: 94 points

Complex aromas of scorched earth, minerals, black fruits, lead pencil, and subtle wood accompany this classic, full-bodied La Mission. It boasts superb purity, an expansive, concentrated mid-palate, and sweet tannin in the long, muscular yet refined finish. This superb wine, which requires three to four years of cellaring, gets my nod as the finest La Mission since the super duo produced in 1990 and 1989. Anticipated maturity: 2007–2030.

1996 Château La Mission Haut-Brion
RATING: 90 points
A backward, somewhat austere, muscular style of La Mission Haut-Brion, the color is still a dense, opaque ruby/purple and the aromatics are shut down but promising, offering up black fruit, a hint of chocolate, and some sweet oak. The wine is a brawny, full-bodied La Mission that is going to take some time to reach its apogee. It may remain a somewhat austere wine compared to the top vintages for La Mission. Anticipated maturity: 2008–2025.

1995 Château La Mission Haut-Brion
RATING: 94 points
Emerging from a very backward state, the 1995 La Mission has a dense ruby/purple color to the rim. Its nose of smoke, sweet charred earth intermixed with black currant and blueberry as well as mineral is beginning to gain intensity. In the mouth this structured, muscular, medium to full–bodied wine has impressive levels of concentration, extract, and tannin. The wine is still very youthful, and not even an adolescent in terms of its development, but quite long in the mouth and extremely promising. Anticipated maturity: 2010–2030.

1994 Château La Mission Haut-Brion
RATING: 91 points
A superb La Mission from a difficult vintage, this wine shows classic scorched-earth notes intermixed with a hint of dried herbs, pepper, sweet tobacco, and smoky black currant and cherry fruit. It is medium to full–bodied, with loads of glycerin, surprising depth, and no evidence of dilution or vegetal tannins. Anticipated maturity: now–2015.

1990 Château La Mission Haut-Brion
RATING: 96 points
Like its more elegant and feminine sibling, Haut-Brion, the 1990 La Mission has continued to build weight and richness and is now certainly one of the great La Missions of the last 25 years. The wine has a deep ruby/purple/plum color and a sweet nose of Provençal herbs intermixed with cedar, scorched earth, creosote, and black currant as well as blackberry. Very full-bodied, even viscous, with low acidity and layers of concentration, this is a spectacular La Mission Haut-Brion that is already showing considerable complexity. Anticipated maturity: now–2025.

1989 Château La Mission Haut-Brion
RATING: 100 points
This is a profound bottle of La Mission Haut-Brion with a deep ruby/purple color and a gorgeous nose of espresso, tar, tobacco, mineral, and blackberry, blueberry, and black currant fruit. The extraordinary smorgasbord of aromatics is matched by a full-bodied, viscous, opulent style of wine with sweet, jammy fruit yet enough tannin and acidity to provide uplift and definition. Still somewhat of an adolescent in terms of its development, and far less evolved than its gorgeous sibling, the 1990, this is a prodigious, multidimensional wine and a modern-day legend. Anticipated maturity: now–2025.

1988 Château La Mission Haut-Brion
RATING: 90 points
A very concentrated, sweet, yet at the same time well-delineated 1988 that has a dark plum/garnet color with some lightening at the edge, this rather muscular, earthy wine shows notes of creosote, scorched earth, deep, sweet black cherries, coffee, and a hint of chocolate. It is a chewy, dense wine that will never be the most harmonious La Mission, but it is mouth-filling and substantial. Anticipated maturity: now–2014.

1982 Château La Mission Haut-Brion
RATING: 100 points
The most powerful, concentrated, and enormously endowed La Mission Haut-Brion of any vintage between 1975 and 2000, this wine still seems very backward and yet oh so promising. I have gone back and forth over its life, wondering whether it is a modern-day clone of the 1961 or the 1959, but more and more I am leaning toward the 1959. The wine has a murky, opaque plum/garnet color with no lightening at the edge. With hours of aeration, the wine begins to reveal a prodigious perfume of black fruits, scorched earth, licorice, truffles, and some graphite as well as damp earth. Enormously concentrated, with extraordinary power and depth, this wine continues to remind me of a modern-day equivalent of the 1959. The 1989 is an interesting comparison, as is the 2000. The 1989 has sweeter tannin, more finesse and elegance, but perhaps not the sheer power, muscle, and palate impact of the extraordinary 1982. Both of them are pure perfection for my palate, but completely different in style. The 2000 has as much extract and power but tastes slightly more refined. The 1982 still reveals plenty of tannin, which should guarantee it at least another three decades of longevity. This is clearly a 50-year wine. Anticipated maturity: 2007–2040.

CHATEAU LA MONDOTTE

CLASSIFICATION: AOC St.-Emilion

OWNERS: Counts von Neipperg

ADDRESS: Château La Mondotte, BP34, 33330 St.-Emilion, France

TELEPHONE: 33 05 57 24 71 33

TELEFAX: 33 05 57 24 67 95

E-MAIL: info@neipperg.com

WEBSITE: www.neipperg.com

CONTACT: Count Stephan von Neipperg

VISITING POLICY: No visits

VINEYARDS

SURFACE AREA: 11.1 acres

GRAPE VARIETALS: 75% Merlot, 25% Cabernet Franc

AVERAGE AGE OF THE VINES: 45 years old

DENSITY OF PLANTATION: 5,500 vines per hectare

AVERAGE YIELDS: 25 hectoliters per hectare

WINEMAKING AND UPBRINGING

This small treasure of a vineyard is located east of the St.-Emilion limestone plateau. The clay soil, excellent ripeness, and low yields help produce wines that are opulent, very deep in color, and extremely well structured. Incredibly ripe fruit and finesse come through on the palate.

At harvest, grapes are hand-picked and double sorted before and after destemming. Fermentation takes place in thermo-controlled oak vats for 25 days. Extraction is achieved by punching down the cap of skin. The wine is aged on its lees in barrels (90–100% new every year) over about 18 months, with no fining or filtering.

ANNUAL PRODUCTION

La Mondotte: 9,500 bottles

AVERAGE PRICE (VARIABLE DEPENDING ON VINTAGE): $150–250

GREAT RECENT VINTAGES

2003, 2001, 2000, 1998, 1996

The ancient von Neipperg family, members of the aristocracy, can trace their origins back to the early 12th century. In subsequent centuries, the family produced many famous soldiers and statesmen, but never lost touch with its winemaking roots or its attachment to viticulture.

In 1971 Count Joseph-Hubert von Neipperg bought four St.-Emilion châteaux—Canon La Gaffe-

lière, La Mondotte, Clos de l'Oratoire, and Peyreau. Although the family acquired all four at the same time, they initially invested the most effort and money into Canon La Gaffelière. In 1983, Count von Neipperg offered his son Stephan the opportunity to take charge of the St.-Emilion châteaux. Stephan accepted and appointed Stéphane Derenoncourt cellarmaster.

The extraordinary success achieved by Château La Mondotte in an incredibly short period of time deserves special mention. Although it was purchased at the same time as the other von Neipperg estates in St.-Emilion, up until recently La Mondotte was very much overshadowed by Château Canon La Gaffelière and Clos de l'Oratoire. However, the 1996 La Mondotte won an extraordinary reception and brought Stephan von Neipperg and his littlest estate into the limelight.

When asked why he did not realize La Mondotte's potential sooner, Stephan von Neipperg explains, "People often ask me this question. . . . The answer is mostly to do with economics. The investments we have made at Canon La Gaffelière since 1984 and at Clos de l'Oratoire since 1991 consumed most of our energy. When these two estates were in fine form, we were able to concentrate on the small La Mondotte estate, which we knew from the beginning was outstanding.

"Our success was a by-product of our efforts. We wanted to apply our wine-growing philosophy to a jewel of an estate. Its small size was an ideal opportunity to try out some of our ideas. The ability to work with very small volumes also meant that we could make technical tests quickly and relatively inexpensively.

"The most important factor is the personality of each *terroir*. There is no way mediocre soil can produce a great wine. When we make wine at La Mondotte, we do not adapt our winemaking style to fit any preconceived taste criteria. For instance, it would be absurd to say that La Mondotte is the Pétrus of St.-Emilion. The *terroir* imposes its own style."

La Mondotte is one of the most concentrated young Bordeaux I have tasted. Whether it is trying to be the Pétrus or Le Pin of St.-Emilion is irrelevant, for this wine is made superbly. It is a showcase offering that is already turning heads and causing some unwanted jealousy.

LA MONDOTTE

2003 La Mondotte
RATING: 93–96 points
This vineyard, which sits on classic clay/limestone hillsides, enjoyed great success in 2003. A blend of 80% Merlot and 20% Cabernet Franc, this wine exhibits an inky/purple color along with a gorgeously deep, ethereal bouquet of espresso roast, blackberries, crème de cassis, minerals, and flowers. It is rich and full-bodied, with low acidity, obvious power, and tremendous elegance as well as definition. Not a blockbuster, it is a beautifully layered, textured St.-Emilion that builds incrementally, revealing tremendous purity and sense of place. Anticipated maturity: 2007–2018.

2002 La Mondotte
RATING: 90 points
Tasted three separate times, this appears to be the least inspiring La Mondotte produced since the debut vintage of 1996. A blend of 80% Merlot and 20% Cabernet Franc, it exhibits a dense purple color, sweet cranberry and blackberry fruit, and a good texture, but astringent tannin, a dry, overly extracted, narrow, and disjointed finish. Perhaps more barrel aging will bring out additional character as well as texture. While the 2002 is excellent, possibly outstanding, it is not up to the quality of previous vintages produced under the guidance of Stephan von Neipperg and his talented consultant, Stéphane Derenoncourt. Anticipated maturity: 2008–2016.

2001 La Mondotte
RATING: 94 points
Made in an elegant, surprisingly low-key style for La Mondotte, the concentrated, delicious, opaque purple–colored 2001 builds incrementally on the palate. An impressive bouquet of black cherries, crème de cassis, toast, and minerals is followed by a medium to full–bodied effort with nicely integrated wood, acidity, and tannin as well as a long finish. Anticipated maturity: now–2017.

2000 La Mondotte

RATING: 98+ points

From an 11.3-acre vineyard cropped at 25 hectoliters per hectare, this blend of 80% Merlot and 20% Cabernet Franc is a candidate for perfection. The 2000 La Mondotte has a saturated, inky purple color to the rim and a tight but enormously promising nose of blackberry and cassis intermixed with cherry, vanilla, espresso, mocha, and a hint of acacia flower. This unfined and unfiltered wine is enormously rich, with great intensity, fabulous purity, a layered texture, and a viscous, full-bodied finish that goes on for nearly one minute. In spite of its size, the wine has remarkable finesse and delineation. This is another tour de force in winemaking from Stephan von Neipperg and Stéphane Derenoncourt. Anticipated maturity: 2007–2030.

1999 La Mondotte

RATING: 94 points

Along with the 1997, the 1999 is the most forward and accessible La Mondotte yet produced. Its opaque purple color is followed by a glorious nose of candied black fruits, graphite, licorice, and underbrush. Full-bodied and sumptuous, La Mondotte possesses amazing extract and richness for the vintage. Its high tannin is hidden by a wealth of glycerin, fruit, and extract. Moreover, the finish lasts for 35–45 seconds. This is an amazing achievement in 1999. Anticipated maturity: now–2020.

1998 La Mondotte

RATING: 96+ points

An amazing tour de force in winemaking, this massive, opaque black/purple-colored offering boasts an extraordinarily pure nose of black fruits intermixed with cedar, vanilla, fudge, and espresso. It is unctuously textured, with exhilarating levels of blackberry/cassis fruit and extract, as well as multiple dimensions that unfold on the palate. The 50-second finish reveals moderately high tannin. Despite its similarity to dry vintage Port, it is not a wine to drink early. It is a colossal wine! Anticipated maturity: 2008–2030.

1997 La Mondotte

RATING: 94 points

An amazing effort and unquestionably one of the wines of the vintage, La Mondotte's 1997 boasts a saturated purple color as well as an explosive nose of blackberries, violets, minerals, and sweet toasty oak. Huge and massive, yet gorgeously proportioned, it possesses an unctuous texture with no hard edges. More seductive and easier to drink than the behemoth 1996, it should be consumed between now and 2015.

1996 La Mondotte

RATING: 97 points

The 1996 La Mondotte is amazing for both its appellation and the vintage, revealing a remarkable level of richness, profound concentration, and integrated tannin. The thick purple color suggests a wine of extraordinary extract and richness. This super-concentrated wine offers a spectacular nose of roasted coffee, licorice, blueberries, and black currants intermixed with smoky new oak. It possesses full body, a multidimensional, layered personality with extraordinary depth of fruit, a seamless texture, amazing viscosity, and a long, 45-second finish. The tannin is sweet and well integrated. A dry, vintage Port! This blockbuster St.-Emilion should be at its best between 2006 and 2025.

CLASSIFICATION: Second Growth in 1855

OWNER: Jean-Louis Charmolüe

ADDRESS: Château Montrose, 33180 St.-Estèphe, France

TELEPHONE: 33 05 56 59 30 12

TELEFAX: 33 05 56 59 38 48

WEBSITE: www.chateaumontrose-charmolue.com

CONTACT: Philippe de Laguarigue

VISITING POLICY: by appointment only; Monday–Friday,
8:30 A.M.–12:00 P.M., 2–5:30 P.M.

VINEYARDS

SURFACE AREA: 169.2 acres

GRAPE VARIETALS: 64% Cabernet Sauvignon, 31% Merlot, 4%
Cabernet Franc, 1% Petit Verdot

AVERAGE AGE OF THE VINES: 39 years

DENSITY OF PLANTATION: 9,000 vines per hectare

AVERAGE YIELDS: 42 hectoliters per hectare (in the past 13 years,
from 52 to 32 hectoliters per hectare)

WINEMAKING AND UPBRINGING

Alcoholic fermentations are traditionally driven in thermo-
regulated stainless-steel tanks. During these fermentations,
daily pumpings-over and massive pumpings-over (by bleed-

Jean-Louis Charmolüe and his wife

ing half of the tank in an underground tank before pumping
it back) are done. The total vatting lasts about 21 days, with
the exact length decided according to the character of the vintage. The malolactic fermentations are in stainless-steel tanks.

Château Montrose spends 18–19 months in barrels with
50–70% new wood. The wine is racked every 3–4 months
and fined in barrels with fresh egg whites. The wines are not
filtered.

ANNUAL PRODUCTION

Château Montrose: 150,00–200,000 bottles
La Dame de Montrose: 85,000–160,000 bottles

AVERAGE PRICE (VARIABLE DEPENDING ON VINTAGE): $50–150

GREAT RECENT VINTAGES

2003, 2002, 2001, 2000, 1996, 1995, 1990, 1989, 1986, 1982

In 1778, Etienne-Théodore Dumoulin acquired a ridge
of 80 hectares (200 acres) that was covered with
heather. The flowers inspired him to name his new property "Mont-Rose." The château was built in 1815. By
1825 there were 12–15 acres of vines, and by 1832 the
estate had been increased to 85 acres.

In 1855 Château Montrose was classified among
the second growths of the Médoc. At that time, the annual production varied from 100 to 150 tonneaux—the
equivalent of 10,000 to 15,000 cases. The property remained in the hands of the Dumoulin family until 1866,
when it was sold to Mathieu Dollfus. When Mathieu
Dollfus died, Château Montrose was sold by his successors to Jean Hostein, who was the owner of Châteaux
Cos d'Estournel and Pomys, two nearby vineyards.

In 1896, Mr. Hostein resold the property to his son-
in-law Louis Charmolüe. Since that time it has remained
in the Charmolüe family, whose coat of arms appears on
the label. Until 1925 it was under the direction of Louis
Charmolüe, then Albe Charmolüe until 1944, and then
Mrs. Yvonne Charmolüe until 1960, at which point she
ceded control to her son, Jean-Louis Charmolüe.

Since then the technical buildings have been improved, especially with the construction of a new cellar
in 1983 and a new winery in 2000.

One of the Médoc's best-situated vineyards and one of the commune's most impeccably clean and well-kept cellars, Montrose was for years associated with huge, dense, powerful wines that needed several decades of cellaring to be soothing enough to drink. For example, Jean Paul Jauffret, the former head of Bordeaux's CIVB, served me the 1908 Montrose in 1982, blind, to see if I could guess its age. The wine had plenty left in it and tasted like it was at least 30 years younger.

The affable owner Jean-Louis Charmolüe has obviously lightened the style of Montrose in response to declining consumer demand for dense, excruciatingly tannic wines. The change in style is particularly noticeable with the vintages of the late 1970s and early 1980s, as more Merlot has been introduced into the blend at the expense of Cabernet Sauvignon and Petit Verdot. Montrose fans were not amused by the "nouveau" style. Since 1986 Montrose returned to a more forceful, muscular style, reminiscent of pre-1975 vintages. Certainly the 2003, 2000, 1996, 1990, and 1989 vintages for Montrose produced the kind of true blockbuster wines not seen from this property since 1961. Moreover, in these vintages, the wines are of first-growth quality. Anyone who has had the pleasure of drinking some of Montrose's greatest vintages—1970, 1964, 1961, 1959, 1955, and 1953—can no doubt attest to the fact that Montrose produced a bevy of massive wines that deserve to be called the Latour of St.-Estèphe. The wines of Montrose were especially strong in the period from 1953 to 1971 and from 1989 to the present, when they were usually among the finest wines produced in the northern Médoc.

Visitors to St.-Estèphe will find the modest château of Montrose situated on the high ground with a magnificent view of the Gironde River. The property, owned by the Charmolüe family, does make a worthy visit, given the splendid *cuverie* with its old, huge, open oak vats and striking new barrel and fermentation cellar.

CHATEAU MONTROSE

2003 Château Montrose

RATING: 96–100 points

A whopping 78% of the production made it into the prodigious 2003 Montrose. Harvested between September 11 and 26, this 62% Cabernet Sauvignon, 34% Merlot, 3% Cabernet Franc, and 1% Petit Verdot blend was fashioned from low yields of 35 hectoliters per hectare. The pH is high (3.9), and the alcohol is 13.2%. Imagine it as a blend of the compelling 1989 and 1990. This inky/purple-colored 2003 boasts a spectacular, flamboyant perfume of crème de cassis, new wood, smoke, crushed rocks, and white flowers. Magnificently rich, unctuously textured, and full-bodied, with huge presence on the palate, and a finish that exceeds 60 seconds, this is a legendary effort from Montrose. It is capable of rivaling the wines produced in 2000, 1990, and 1989. Given its low acidity and incredible performance already, it should drink well in 5–6 years, and last for 25–30.

2002 Château Montrose

RATING: 91 points

Only 56% of the production made it into Montrose, a blend of 62% Cabernet Sauvignon, 32% Merlot, 4% Cabernet Franc, and 2% Petit Verdot. The color is a saturated ruby/purple, but the wine was revealing a monolithic personality, with a slightly pinched, hard, tannic finish. There are complex aromas as well as a sweet attack, but the sinewy aftertaste and abrupt, tannic finish may keep this 2002 from meriting an outstanding score. Anticipated maturity: 2010–2020.

2001 Château Montrose

RATING: 91 points

Sweet notes of earth, compost, and thick, juicy black currant as well as cherry characteristics jump from the glass of this dense purple–colored 2001. Medium bodied and rich, with moderately high tannin as well as surprising power and density, it is the most backward St.-Estèphe of the vintage. A blend of 62% Cabernet Sauvignon, 34% Merlot, and the rest Petit Verdot and Cabernet Franc, it requires 5–6 years of cellaring, and should drink well for 15–16.

2000 Château Montrose

RATING: 96 points

This estate has frequently hit the bull's-eye with recent vintages, and the 2000 Montrose is the finest effort produced since the compelling 1990 and 1989. This gigantic tannic, backward effort boasts a saturated inky purple color followed by a huge nose of acacia flavors, crushed blackberries, crème de cassis, vanilla, hickory smoke, and minerals. Extremely full-bodied, powerful, dense, and multilayered, this unreal

Montrose should last for 30+ years. A blend of 63% Cabernet Sauvignon, 31% Merlot, 4% Cabernet Franc, and 2% Petit Verdot, this is a special wine that has exceptional purity and length. Anticipated maturity: 2010–2040.

1999 Château Montrose

RATING: 90 points

The black/purple-colored 1999 Montrose offers up notes of pure black fruits intermixed with minerals, smoke, and earth. Extremely concentrated, surprisingly powerful and dense, with moderate tannin, its size, strength, and medium to full–bodied power are atypical for the vintage. Anticipated maturity: 2006–2025.

1998 Château Montrose

RATING: 90+ points

A classic effort, the 1998 Montrose exhibits a dense purple color in addition to a sweet nose of jammy cassis, licorice, earth, and smoke. It is a powerful and full-bodied wine with well-integrated tannin. Given Montrose's tendency to shut down, it is performing better out of bottle than I expected. Anticipated maturity: now–2030.

1996 Château Montrose

RATING: 91+ points

The 1996 Montrose reveals outstanding potential. It boasts a saturated dark ruby/purple color and aromas of new oak, jammy black currants, smoke, minerals, and new saddle leather. This multilayered wine is rich and medium to full–bodied, with sweet tannin, a nicely textured, concentrated mid-palate, and an impressively long finish. Anticipated maturity: 2009–2025.

1995 Château Montrose

RATING: 93 points

An explosively rich, exotic, fruity Montrose, the 1995 displays even more fat and extract than the 1996. There is less Cabernet Sauvignon in the 1995 blend, resulting in a fuller-bodied, more accessible, and friendlier style. The wine exhibits an opaque black/ruby/purple color, as well as a ripe nose of black fruits, vanilla, and licorice. Powerful yet surprisingly accessible (the tannin is velvety and the acidity low), this terrific example of Montrose should be at its peak until 2028.

1994 Château Montrose

RATING: 90 points

An opaque purple color suggests a wine of considerable intensity. One of the most successful 1994s of the northern Médoc, the wine presents closed aromatics of jammy black fruits, plums, spice, and earth. On the palate, there is impressive extract, purity, and copious amounts of sweet black currant fruit nicely balanced by moderate yet ripe tannin. Medium bodied, with excellent to outstanding concentration, this impressive Montrose is approachable now and will hold until 2020.

1990 Château Montrose

RATING: 100 points

This majestic wine is remarkably rich, with a distinctive nose of sweet, jammy fruit, liquefied minerals, new saddle leather, and grilled steak. In the mouth, the enormous concentration, extract, high glycerin, and sweet tannin slide across the palate with considerable ease. It is a huge, corpulent, awesomely endowed wine that is relatively approachable, as it has not yet begun to shut down and lose its baby fat. Because of its enormous sweetness, dense concentration, high extract, and very low acidity, the 1990 Montrose can be appreciated today, yet this is a legend for the future. Anticipated maturity: now–2030.

1989 Château Montrose

RATING: 97 points

An outstanding Montrose, the 1989 is one of the vintage's superstars. It possesses an opaque dark ruby/purple color, a sweet nose of minerals, black fruits, acacia flower, cedar, and wood. A full-bodied, highly extracted wine with low acidity and moderate tannin in the long finish, it has developed even more richness and layers of flavors than I originally thought. It has layers of sweet fruit as well as an elevated level of glycerin. A brilliant effort, the 1989 Montrose is very close in quality to the perfect 1990. Anticipated maturity: now–2025.

1986 Château Montrose

RATING: 91 points

Made during a period when Montrose was flirting with a lighter style, the 1986 is one of the beefier efforts from that short-lived detour. The wine reveals a dense ruby/purple color with only a hint of lightening at the edge. Fleshy, muscular, and powerful, with aromas of red and black fruits, mineral, and spice, this medium to full–bodied, tannic, brawny Montrose is still youthful yet accessible. It possesses a layered, chewy character, along with plenty of sweet tannin in the finish. Anticipated maturity: now–2025.

1982 Château Montrose

RATING: 91 points

The 1982 Montrose has developed rapidly, yet it remains a candidate for another 10 years of delicious drinking. The wine reveals a healthy dark ruby/garnet color, followed by a fragrant, sweet nose of black fruits intermingled with new oak, licorice, and floral scents. Full-bodied and opulent, with dusty tannin in the finish, this gorgeously proportioned, rich, concentrated wine can be drunk now. A very impressive example of Montrose that has consistently been atypically evolved and forward. Anticipated maturity: now–2015.

CHATEAU MOUTON ROTHSCHILD

CLASSIFICATION: First Growth in 1973

OWNER: Baroness Philippine de Rothschild GFA

ADDRESS: Château Mouton Rothschild, 33250 Pauillac, France

TELEPHONE: 33 05 56 59 22 22

TELEFAX: 33 05 56 73 20 44

E-MAIL: webmaster@bpdr.com

WEBSITE: www.bdpr.com

CONTACT: Patrick Léon, technical manager; Hervé Berland, commercial director

VISITING POLICY: Tours by appointment only (telephone 33 05 56 73 21 29 or telefax 33 05 56 73 21 28); Monday–Thursday, 9:30–11 A.M. and 2–4 P.M.; Friday, 9:30–11 A.M. and 2–3 P.M.; from April to October: open every weekend and holiday (four visits only—9:30 A.M., 11 A.M., 2 P.M., and 3:30 P.M.)

VINEYARDS

SURFACE AREA: 205 acres

GRAPE VARIETALS: 77% Cabernet Sauvignon, 12% Merlot, 9% Cabernet Franc, 2% Petit Verdot

AVERAGE AGE OF THE VINES: 46 years

DENSITY OF PLANTATION: 8,540 vines per acre

AVERAGE YIELDS: 40–50 hectoliters per hectare

WINEMAKING AND UPBRINGING

The harvest is done manually and put into small baskets. When it reaches the vat room, the entire crop is worked over on sorting tables prior to destemming in order to take away all the vegetal parts and keep only perfect berries. Afterward, berries are pulled down into vats by gravity.

The vats of Château Mouton Rothschild are all made of wood, and each block of the estate is vinified in accordance with the genuine art of winemaking. Alcoholic fermentation takes about one week.

After the fermenting/maceration period, which takes 4–5 weeks, the wines are poured directly into new oak barrels. Following the malolactic fermentation, the lots of wines are blended. Afterward the wine is aged in barrels for 18–22 months. The wines are regularly racked in a traditional manner every 4 months. The goal is to produce strong wines with good aging potential.

ANNUAL PRODUCTION

Château Mouton Rothschild: 300,000 bottles

Le Petit Mouton de Mouton Rothschild: 43,000 bottles

Aile d'Argent (white Bordeaux): 13,000 bottles

AVERAGE PRICE (VARIABLE DEPENDING ON VINTAGE): $125–300

GREAT RECENT VINTAGES

2003, 2002, 2000, 1998, 1996, 1995, 1989, 1986, 1982

In 1853, Baron Nathaniel de Rothschild, a member of the English branch of the family, bought Château Brane-Mouton and renamed it Château Mouton Rothschild. In 1922, his great-grandson Baron Philippe de Rothschild (1902–1988) purchased the property.

In 1924, Baron Philippe was the first to introduce château bottling. In 1926, he built the famous *grand chai*, the 100-meter first-year cellar, which has become a major attraction for visitors to Mouton. In 1933, he enlarged the family estate by purchasing the neighboring Château Mouton d'Armailhacq, classified in 1855, and renamed Château d'Armailhac.

Mouton-Rothschild, the place and wine, are the singular creations of the late Baron Philippe de Rothschild. No doubt when he took over the estate at the age of 21, his aspirations for Mouton were high. But he raised the estate's profile higher than anyone could have imagined. He has been the only person able to effectuate a change in the 1855 classification of the wines of the Médoc.

After many years of lobbying, in 1973, Mouton-Rothschild was officially classified a first growth. The flamboyant baron changed his defiant wine labels from *"Premier ne puis, second ne daigne, Mouton suis"* ("First I cannot be, second I will not call myself, Mouton I am") to *"Premier je suis, second je fus, Mouton ne change"* ("First I am, second I was, Mouton does not change").

The Baron died in January 1988, and his daughter, the equally charismatic Philippine, is now the spiritual head of this winemaking empire. She continues to receive extraordinary assistance from the talented Mouton team led by Hervé Berland.

There is no question that some of the greatest bottles of Bordeaux I have ever drunk have been Moutons. The 2003, 2000, 1996, 1995, 1986, 1982, 1959, 1955, 1953, 1947, 1945, and 1929 are stunning examples of Mouton at its best. However, I have also experienced too many mediocre vintages of Mouton, which are embarrassing for a first growth and obviously irritating for a paying consumer. The 1990, 1980, 1979, 1978, 1977, 1976, 1974, 1973, 1967, and 1964 fell well below first-growth standards. Even the 1990 and 1989, two renowned vintages, produced wines that were surprisingly austere and lacking the concentration expected from a first growth in a superb vintage.

Nevertheless, the reasons for the commercial success of this wine are numerous. To begin with, the labels of Mouton are collector's items. Since 1945, Baron Philippe de Rothschild has commissioned an artist to do an annual painting, which is depicted on the top of the label. There has been no shortage of masters to appear on the Mouton Rothschild labels, from such Europeans as Miró, Picasso, Chagall, and Cocteau, to the Americans Warhol, Motherwell, and, in 1982, John Huston. Second, the opulence of Mouton in the great vintages differs significantly in style from the austere elegance of Lafite Rothschild and the powerful, tannic, dense, and muscular Latour. Third, the impeccably kept château itself, with its superb wine museum, is the Médoc's (and possibly the entire Bordeaux region's) top tourist attraction.

CHATEAU MOUTON ROTHSCHILD

2003 Château Mouton Rothschild

RATING: 95–98 points

Made from low yields of 28 hectoliters per hectare, this profound blend of 76% Cabernet Sauvignon, 14% Merlot, 8% Cabernet Franc, and 2% Petit Verdot possesses a finished pH of 3.8, alcohol of 12.9% (nearly identical to Lafite Rothschild in that sense), and 3.5 total acidity (much higher than the other first growths). The 2003 is similar in style to Mouton's 1982, but softer and more pliable than that wine was at the same age. The Cabernet Sauvignon harvest began on the same day it did in both 1982 and 1947, an interesting coincidence. Black/purple colored to the rim, with a gorgeous nose of espresso roast intermixed with classic Mouton crème de cassis–like notes, its powerful, unctuous flavors cascade over the palate, revealing tremendous intensity as well as strong tannin. This enormously endowed 2003 is still sorting itself out, but it is unquestionably one of the greatest efforts of the vintage. If my instincts are correct, it is the ripest, most flamboyant Mouton Rothschild since the 1982. Anticipated maturity: 2012–2035.

Baroness Philippine and Baron Philippe de Rothschild

2002 Château Mouton Rothschild

RATING: 94+ points

Another candidate for wine of the vintage, there are only 20,000 cases of the 2002 Mouton Rothschild (there are 25,000 cases of the 2000). Made from low yields of 31 hectoliters per hectare, it is a blend of 78% Cabernet Sauvignon, 12% Merlot, 9% Cabernet Franc, and 1% Petit Verdot. The color may be the most saturated and opaque of any Médoc Cabernet-based 2002. It is a broad-flavored offering displaying telltale crème de cassis intermixed with smoke, cocoa, leather, and licorice. Still excruciatingly tannic, but incredibly dense, powerful, and rich, the phenolic measurements were nearly off the charts for this full-bodied, monster-sized Mouton. Given most Moutons' track records, I suspect the 2002 will shut down after bottling, and perhaps need a minimum of 10–15 years to reemerge. This is unquestionably a *vin de garde* for long-term cellaring. Anticipated maturity: 2015–2040.

2001 Château Mouton Rothschild

RATING: 90 points

A blend of 86% Cabernet Sauvignon, 12% Merlot, and 2% Cabernet Franc, the opaque purple–colored, chunky 2001 Mouton Rothschild does not possess the finesse and stature

tannic, and backward. Twenty-four to forty-eight hours of aeration only hints at its ultimate potential. This blockbuster will be exceptionally long-lived. It is not as expressive as the other first-growth Médocs, but give it time. Anticipated maturity: 2015–2050+.

1999 Château Mouton Rothschild

RATING: 93 points

Mouton's 1999 (78% Cabernet Sauvignon, 18% Merlot, and 4% Cabernet Franc) represents 60% of the total production. The beautiful 1999 Mouton Rothschild may be a modern-day clone of their 1985 or 1962. Its saturated ruby/purple color is followed by sumptuous aromas of cedarwood, crème de cassis, wood smoke, coffee, and dried herbs. Forward, lush, and full-bodied, it is already complex as well as succulent, fleshy, and long. Tannin in the finish suggests more nuances will emerge in one or two years. It is a complex, classic Mouton. Anticipated maturity: now–2030.

1998 Château Mouton Rothschild

RATING: 96 points

The 1998 Mouton has emerged as the greatest wine produced at this estate since the perfect 1986, of which the 1998 is somewhat reminiscent. Like many of its 1998 peers, it has filled out spectacularly. Now in the bottle, this opaque black/purple–colored offering has increased in stature, richness, and size. A blend of 86% Cabernet Sauvignon, 12% Merlot, and 2% Cabernet Franc (57% of the production was utilized), it is an extremely powerful, super-concentrated wine offering notes of roasted espresso, crème de cassis, smoke, new saddle leather, graphite, and licorice. It is massive in the mouth, with awesome concentration, mouth-searing tannin levels, and a saturated flavor profile that grips the mouth with considerable intensity. This is another 50-year Mouton, but patience will be required as it will not be close to drinkability for about a decade. However, this wine rivals the 1995, 1990, and 1986! Anticipated maturity: 2012–2050.

1997 Château Mouton Rothschild

RATING: 90 points

Only 55% of the harvest was utilized for the 1997 Mouton Rothschild. One of the most forward and developed Moutons over recent years, it possesses all the charm and fleshiness this vintage can provide. A blend of 82% Cabernet Sauvignon, 13% Merlot, 3% Cabernet Franc, and 2% Petit Verdot, the wine exhibits a dense ruby/purple color and an open-knit nose of cedarwood, blackberry liqueur, cassis, and coffee. Fleshy, ripe, and mouth-filling, with low acidity, soft tannin, and admirable concentration and length, this delicious Pauillac should age for 15+ years. It is an impressive effort for this vintage.

often achieved by this first growth. It offers a telltale cassis-scented nose, and a monolithic, medium to full–bodied style with relatively high, austere tannin in the finish (a characteristic I also noticed in cask). A dry, angular, backward effort for the vintage, it should be forgotten for at least a decade. Let's hope the fruit continues to expand and sweeten, but that's no sure thing. Anticipated maturity: 2013–2025+.

2000 Château Mouton Rothschild

RATING: 97+ points

As I predicted in my first report on the millennium vintage in April 2001, Philippine de Rothschild could be expected to do something special with her presentation of 2000 and she has exceeded everyone's expectations. Those who have seen the extraordinary packaging of the 2000 Mouton Rothschild must certainly realize this is a brilliant achievement. The bottle is extraordinary, and likely to have nearly as much value empty as full! Her genius is obvious, but it's what's inside that counts! The 2000 Mouton Rothschild is at its best with about 24–48 hours of decanting. A blend of 86% Cabernet Sauvignon and 14% Merlot, the wine offers a saturated ruby/purple color in addition to reticent but promising aromas of toast, coffee, licorice, crème de cassis, and roasted nuts. Dense, chewy, and backward, with tremendous purity and density in addition to obvious toasty oak, it is full-bodied, powerful,

1996 Château Mouton Rothschild

RATING: 94+ points

This estate's staff believes that the 1996 Mouton Rothschild is far more complex than the 1995, but less massive. I agree that among the first growths, this wine is showing surprising forwardness and complexity in its aromatics. It possesses an exuberant, flamboyant bouquet of roasted coffee, cassis, smoky oak, and soy sauce. The impressive 1996 Mouton Rothschild offers impressive aromas of black currants, framboise, coffee, and new saddle leather. This full-bodied, ripe, rich, concentrated, superbly balanced wine is paradoxical in the sense that the aromatics suggest a far more evolved wine than the flavors reveal. Anticipated maturity: 2007–2030.

1995 Château Mouton Rothschild

RATING: 95+ points

This profound Mouton is more accessible than the more muscular 1996. A blend of 72% Cabernet Sauvignon, 19% Merlot, and 9% Cabernet Franc, it reveals an opaque purple color and reluctant aromas of cassis, truffles, coffee, licorice, and spice. In the mouth, the wine is "great stuff," with superb density, a full-bodied personality, rich mid-palate, and a layered, profound finish that lasts for 40+ seconds. There is outstanding purity and high tannin, but my instincts suggest this wine is lower in acidity and slightly fleshier than the brawnier, bigger 1996. Anticipated maturity: 2010–2030.

1994 Château Mouton Rothschild

RATING: 90 points

The 1994 Mouton exhibits a dense, saturated purple color, followed by a classic Mouton nose of sweet black fruits intermingled with smoke, toast, spice, and cedar. Medium to full–bodied, with outstanding concentration, a layered feel, plenty of tannin, and rich, concentrated fruit, this wine is similar to the fine 1988. Anticipated maturity: now–2025.

1989 Château Mouton Rothschild

RATING: 90 points

The 1989 Mouton Rothschild is the superior wine, but in no sense is this a compelling wine if compared with the Moutons produced in 2000, 1998, 1996, 1995, 1986, and 1982. The 1989 displays a dark ruby color that is already beginning to reveal pink and amber at the rim. The bouquet is surprisingly evolved, offering up scents of cedar, sweet black fruits, lead pencil, and high levels of toasty oak. An elegant, medium-bodied, restrained wine, it is beautifully made, stylish, and not dissimilar to the 1985, but ultimately lacking the profound depth one anticipates in the greatest vintages. It is an excellent to outstanding Mouton that is close to full maturity. It will drink well for 15–20 years. Anticipated maturity: now–2020.

1988 Château Mouton Rothschild

RATING: 92 points

One of the biggest Médocs of the vintage, the dense garnet/plum–colored 1988 Mouton has an attractive aroma of Asian spices, dried herbs, minerals, coffee, black currants, and sweet oak. Much like the 1989, the bouquet is alluring. The flavors continue to add bulk and the wine is better than I initially thought. In the mouth, it is a much firmer, tougher, more obviously tannic wine than the 1989, with full body and admirable ripeness. This is a muscular, large-scaled 1988 that will last another 15–20 years. I clearly underestimated this wine in its infancy. If the truth be known, it is superior to the more renowned vintages of 1990 and 1989! Anticipated maturity: 2008–2030.

1986 Château Mouton Rothschild

RATING: 100 points

An enormously concentrated, massive Mouton Rothschild, comparable in quality, but not style, to the 1982, 1959, and 1945, this impeccably made wine is still in its infancy. Interestingly, in 1998 I had this wine served to me blind from a magnum that had been opened and decanted 48 hours previously. Even then, it still tasted like a barrel sample! I suspect the 1986 Mouton Rothschild requires a minimum of 15–20

more years of cellaring; it has the potential to last for 50–100 years! Given the outrageously high prices being fetched by recent vintages, it appears this wine might still be one of the "relative bargains" in the fine-wine marketplace. I wonder how many readers will be in shape to drink it when it does finally reach full maturity. The telltale characteristics of this wine are pure Moutonian—crème de cassis in abundance, exhilarating purity, and awesome layers of finish. It still tastes like a wine of five or six years old! A tour de force! Anticipated maturity: 2008–2060.

1985 Château Mouton Rothschild

RATING: 90+ points

While the estate compares their 1985 to their 1959, it is more akin to their 1989, 1962, or 1953. The rich, complex, well-developed bouquet of Asian spices, toasty oak, herbs, and ripe fruit is wonderful. On the palate, the wine is also rich, forward, long, and sexy. It ranks behind both Haut-Brion and Château Margaux in 1985. Readers looking for a savory, boldly scented Mouton should search out other vintages, as this is a tame, forward, medium-weight, elegant wine that is fully mature. It is capable of lasting another 15+ years. Anticipated maturity: now–2015.

1982 Château Mouton Rothschild

RATING: 100 points

The saturated purple–colored Mouton-Rothschild remains the most backward and unevolved wine of 1982. It flaunted a knockout, fabulously rich, and ostentatious personality during its first 5–6 years after bottling. Since the late 1980s it has gradually closed down, and it is hard to estimate when this wine might reemerge. I routinely decant this wine 12–24 hours prior to service. The thick, unctuously textured, jammy fruit and enormous flavor concentration remain the hallmarks of the vintage, but the wine is extremely unevolved and behaves like a wine that is less than a decade old. This massive, powerful example of Mouton exhibits huge tannin and immense body. Significantly richer than the 1970 or 1961, it is not farfetched to suggest that it is comparable to either the 1959 or 1945! Owners who do not want to commit infanticide should cellar it for another 5–10 years. Like Latour, the 1982 Mouton Rothschild is a potential 50–60-year wine, but far less accessible than the 1982 Latour. To those masochists who lack discipline, be sure to decant this wine at least 8–12 hours in advance. The wine will reveal its extraordinary potential with approximately 30 hours of breathing in a closed decanter. A legend! Anticipated maturity: 2007–2065.

CLASSIFICATION: Third Growth in 1855

OWNER: SC Château Palmer

ADDRESS: Château Palmer, Cantenac, 33460 Margaux, France

TELEPHONE: 33 05 57 88 72 72

TELEFAX: 33 05 57 88 37 16

E-MAIL: chateau-palmer@chateau-palmer.com

WEBSITE: www.chateau-palmer.com

CONTACT: Bernard de Laage de Meux, development manager

VISITING POLICY: By appointment; every day from April until October; Monday through Friday from November to March

VINEYARDS

SURFACE AREA: 128.4 acres

GRAPE VARIETALS: 47% Merlot, 47% Cabernet Sauvignon, 6% Petit Verdot

AVERAGE AGE OF THE VINES: 38 years old

DENSITY OF PLANTATION: 10,000 vines per hectare

AVERAGE YIELDS: 45 hectoliters per hectare

WINEMAKING AND UPBRINGING

The hand-harvested grapes are carefully identified according to variety and vineyard plot as soon as they arrive in the vat room. They are analyzed, then destemmed and crushed. Grapes from each plot are separately fermented in one of the château's 42 vats, which enables the estate to have a better idea of each plot's qualities and potential with every passing year.

The grapes ferment in the vat for 8–10 days. The wine is pumped over several times a day to facilitate fermentation and enhance the extraction of phenolic compounds. The wine is kept on the skins for about 20 days. Temperatures are carefully controlled during this maceration phase, and the

wine is frequently tasted to decide the right moment to run it off from the vat. The free-run wine is separated from the lees, which are put through a wine press to produce the press wine. The free-run and press wine both go through malolactic fermentation to stabilize the wine and lower its acidity.

As soon as malolactic fermentation is over, the wine is racked and put into oak barrels, where it will age for 18–21 months, and then bottled unfiltered.

ANNUAL PRODUCTION

Château Palmer: 120,000–140,000 bottles

Alter Ego de Palmer: 80,000–100,000 bottles

AVERAGE PRICE (VARIABLE DEPENDING ON VINTAGE): $75–125

GREAT RECENT VINTAGES

2002, 2001, 2000, 1999, 1995, 1989, 1983

Charles Palmer, a major-general in the British army under Wellington, acquired this property in 1814, as the Napoleonic era came to an end. Over the next four decades, the general invested his fortune in the estate, extending the property by buying plots of neighboring vineyards.

The property was sold to a group of bankers named Péreire in 1853. The new owners were leading 19th-century entrepreneurs and were responsible for the reconstruction of Paris under the direction of Georges-Eugène Haussmann and Napoleon III. They commissioned the architect Burguet in 1856 to build the elegant château with its unmistakable towers.

The depression of the 1930s forced them to sell Palmer, which had by then fallen into a state of neglect. The estate was bought by families of Bordeaux négociants, Sichel from Britain, Mähler-Besse from Holland, and Ginestet-Miahle from Bordeaux. Thanks to their efforts, Palmer's reputation and prosperity were restored by the 1970s.

Palmer's impressive turreted château is majestically situated adjacent to Bordeaux's Route du Vin (D2), in the middle of the tiny village of Issan. Tourists consider it a worthy spot to stop for a photograph. More important to wine enthusiasts is the fact that the château also produces one of Bordeaux's greatest wines.

Palmer can be as profound as any of the first growths. In vintages such as 2002, 2001, 2000, 1999, 1998, 1996, 1995, 1989, 1983, 1975, 1970, 1967, 1966, and 1961, it can be better than many of them. While Palmer is officially a third growth, the wine sells at a price level between the first and second growths, no doubt reflecting the high respect Bordeaux merchants, foreign importers, and consumers throughout the world have for this wine.

Palmer is still a traditionally made wine, and the enviable track record of success is no doubt attributable to a number of factors. The *assemblage* (blend of grapes) at Palmer is unique in that a very high percentage of Merlot (47%) is used to make the wine. This high proportion of Merlot no doubt accounts for Palmer's Pomerol-like richness, suppleness, and generous, fleshy character. However, its compelling fragrance is quintessentially Margaux. Palmer also has one of the longest maceration periods (20–28 days), wherein the grape skins stay in contact with the grape juice. This explains the richness of color, excellent extract, and abundant

tannins that are found in most vintages of Palmer. Finally, this is an estate whose proprietors remain adamantly against the filtration of their wine.

Palmer consistently made the best wine of the Margaux appellation between 1961 and 1977, but the resurgence of Château Margaux in 1978, which has now taken the place at the top of the Margaux hierarchy, has—for the moment—left Palmer in the runner-up spot, although Palmer's most recent performances suggest first-growth aspirations. The significant cellar renovations of the late 1990s and the introduction of a second wine have all resulted in even greater wines at Palmer.

The style of Palmer's wine is one characterized by a sensational fragrance and bouquet. I have always felt that Palmer's great vintages can often be identified in blind tastings by smell alone. The bouquet has the forward fruity richness of a great Pomerol but the complexity and character of a Margaux. The wine's texture is rich, often supple and lush, but always deeply fruity and concentrated.

2003 Château Palmer

RATING: 88–91 points

The 2003 Palmer exhibits an evolved style along with a deep ruby/purple–tinged color, sexy, complex aromatics, and medium body. While it lacks the great depth this estate achieved in the last three vintages, it should be delicious upon release, and age for 15+ years. A blend of 68% Cabernet Sauvignon, 20% Merlot, and 12% Petit Verdot and made from extremely low yields of 25 hectoliters per hectare, it is a wine of undeniable finesse, fruit, and elegance. Although it does not possess the weight and power of Palmer's finest vintages, if its mid-palate fills out a bit, it will be an outstanding effort. Anticipated maturity: 2006–2018.

2002 Château Palmer

RATING: 93 points

A tour de force in winemaking, the 2002 Palmer (52% Cabernet Sauvignon, 40% Merlot, and 8% Petit Verdot) exhibits great intensity along with tremendously complex and compelling aromatics of acacia flowers, crème de cassis, a hint of espresso, and vague notions of underbrush. Although extremely concentrated, full-bodied, and dense, with blistering levels of tannin in the finish, there is enough extract and glycerin to provide balance. Nevertheless, this will be a Palmer to forget for 7–10 years. There are 8,500 cases of this brilliant effort that is in the same qualitative league as the 2000. Anticipated maturity: 2012–2025+.

2001 Château Palmer

RATING: 90+ points

A virile, muscular effort for this estate, the 2001 Palmer (a blend of 51% Cabernet Sauvignon, 44% Merlot, and 5% Petit Verdot) exhibits a saturated purple color to the rim. Although closed and backward, it is surprisingly powerful, layered, and formidably endowed, revealing hints of charcoal, black fruits, earth, and underbrush. There is a lot going on in this offering, but it needs five to seven years of cellaring to resolve its high tannin. Anticipated maturity: 2010–2022.

2000 Château Palmer

RATING: 96 points

The 2000 Palmer may ultimately be as good as the 1999, but it is altogether a different animal. If the 1999 is pure Palmer elegance and femininity, the 2000 is more masculine, powerful, muscular, and tannic. Only 50% of the production made it into the grand vin, a blend of 53% Cabernet Sauvignon and 47% Merlot. While it is still revealing plenty of tannin, the tannin has sweetened. A dense inky/purple color is accompanied by a wine with abundant extract as well as a brawny, expansive

mouth-feel. It will require more patience than the seductive 1999. Anticipated maturity: 2010–2035.

1999 Château Palmer

RATING: 95 points

One of the superstars of the vintage, 1999 is the greatest Palmer made since 1961 and 1966. A blend of 48% Cabernet Sauvignon, 46% Merlot, and 6% Petit Verdot, it boasts a staggering bouquet of violets and other spring flowers intermixed with licorice, black currants, and subtle wood. Only 50% of the production made it into the grand vin. A multidimensional, compelling effort with both power and elegance, it offers sweet tannin along with flavors that caress the palate and a 45-second finish. This is terrific stuff! Anticipated maturity: now–2025.

1998 Château Palmer

RATING: 91 points

A classic Margaux, the 1998 Palmer has put on weight and fleshed out during its *élevage* in barrel. It displays a dense purple color as well as a sumptuous bouquet of black fruits, licorice, melted asphalt, toast, and a touch of acacia flowers. Full-bodied with brilliant definition, this blend of equal parts Merlot and Cabernet Sauvignon, with a dollop of Petit Verdot, will age well for 20–25 years. It is one of the Médoc's, as well as the Margaux appellation's, finest wines of the vintage. Anticipated maturity: now–2028.

1996 Château Palmer

RATING: 91+ points

This wine, a blend of 55% Cabernet Sauvignon, 40% Merlot, and 5% Petit Verdot, is performing well in bottle. It boasts an impressively saturated purple color, in addition to a backward yet intense nose of black plums, currants, licorice, and smoke. Following terrific fruit on the attack, the wine's structure and tannin take over. This impressively endowed, surprisingly backward Palmer may develop into a modern-day version of the 1966. There is plenty of sweet fruit. The tannin is well integrated, but the wine requires two to three years of cellaring. Anticipated maturity: 2007–2028.

1995 Château Palmer

RATING: 90 points

This wine includes an extremely high percentage of Merlot (about 43%). It is a gloriously opulent, low-acid, fleshy Palmer that will be attractive early and keep well. Dark ruby/purple–colored, with smoky, toasty new oak intertwined with gobs of jammy cherry fruit and floral and chocolate nuances, this medium to full–bodied, plump yet elegant wine is impressive. Anticipated maturity: now–2020.

1990 Château Palmer

RATING: 90 points

This wine has become more delineated after a period of seeming diffuse and disjointed. Dark plum/garnet in color, the 1990 has a sweet nose of baked fruit, spice box, incense, and sweet licorice intermixed with some chocolate, plum, and black cherries. This lush, low-acid, velvety-textured wine has reached full maturity yet promises to last at this level for at least 5–10 years when properly stored. The wine shows real up-front, luscious depth in a very sexy, open-knit style. Anticipated maturity: now–2012.

1989 Château Palmer

RATING: 95 points

One of the superstars of the vintage, Palmer's 1989 retains a dark plum/purple color with some pink and a hint of amber creeping in at the rim. A big nose of charcoal, white flowers (acacia?), licorice, plums, and black currants comes from the glass of this elegant, medium to full–bodied, very concentrated, seamlessly made wine. Gorgeous, seemingly fully mature, yet brilliantly balanced, this wine may well turn out to be a modern-day clone of the glorious 1953. Anticipated maturity: now–2020.

1983 Château Palmer

RATING: 98 points

This wine goes from strength to strength and is certainly a candidate for wine of the vintage. It has surpassed even Château Margaux in recent tastings. The color is an opaque plum/purple. The wine has a fabulously complex nose of smoked duck, white flowers, cedar, Asian spice, crème de cassis, melted licorice, and espresso. Super-concentrated, very powerful, full-bodied, and huge, this is undeniably one of the biggest, most concentrated, and powerful Palmers made in the last 40 years. The wine has thrown off the rugged tannins that were so prominent during its first 10–15 years of life and has become increasingly seamless and compelling. Potentially this wine remains the most extraordinary Palmer after the 1961. Anticipated maturity: now–2020.

CLASSIFICATION: Premier Grand Cru Classé B

OWNERS: Gérard and Chantal Perse

ADDRESS: Château Pavie, 33330 St.-Emilion, France

TELEPHONE: 33 05 57 55 43 43

TELEFAX: 33 05 57 24 63 99

E-MAIL: vignobles.perse@wanadoo.fr

WEBSITE: www.vignoblesperse.com

CONTACT: Delphine Rigau or Christine Fritegotto (by fax or e-mail only)

VISITING POLICY: By appointment only

VINEYARDS

SURFACE AREA: 103.7 acres

GRAPE VARIETALS: 70% Merlot, 20% Cabernet Franc, 10% Cabernet Sauvignon

AVERAGE AGE OF THE VINES: 43 years

DENSITY OF PLANTATION: 5,500 vines per hectare

AVERAGE YIELDS: 28–30 hectoliters per hectare

WINEMAKING AND UPBRINGING

The estate has three distinct *terroirs,* each of which has its own microclimate—the limestone plateau; the Côte (or "slope,") with dense, deep clay soil; and the Pied de Côte (or "foot of the slope"), which is mostly sandy clay with some gravel. The Pavie *terroir* offers a variety of favorable wine-growing features—meager soil, excellent south-facing sun exposure, good natural drainage thanks to the slope, and a topography that is shielded from the north wind and thus naturally frost-resistant. Nevertheless, Pavie's slope vineyards do not ripen particularly early,

which entails greater climatic risks. This is why Gérard Perse aims to keep the yields particularly low.

When Gérard Perse acquired the vineyard in 1998, basic vineyard practices at Pavie were radically redefined. He set in motion a major replanting program, done by scientifically matching grape varieties and soil types. Cabernet Franc was planted in 30% of the vineyard (in the most prestigious parts of the *terroir*) and the rest 60% Merlot and 10% Cabernet Sauvignon.

Perse has completely restructured the cellar facilities as well. A new vat room was built to replace the previous one, which contained large vats incompatible with the new plot-by-plot vineyard management. Twenty temperature-controlled wooden vats were bought, corresponding to each of the twenty vineyard plots.

Perse also installed a new and highly innovative grape reception system, which uses a conveyor belt to transport grapes from the sorting table to the top of the vats, where they are crushed and destemmed before going into the vat.

The former aging cellar, buried halfway up the slope, was too cold and wet, and so that was replaced as well. The new aging cellar, which adjoins the fermentation cellar, was painstakingly planned to take both aesthetics and technical considerations into account. Pavie's cellar is truly revolutionary. It is one of the most beautiful and efficient in the Bordeaux region.

The Pavie *terroir* produces wine that is characterized by its remarkable power. Fermentation temperatures are kept moderate and the wine does not stay too long on the skins in order to preserve finesse. The wine's natural richness and strength makes malolactic fermentation and aging possible in 100% new oak barrels.

ANNUAL PRODUCTION

Château Pavie: 100,000 bottles

AVERAGE PRICE (VARIABLE DEPENDING ON VINTAGE): $125–275

GREAT RECENT VINTAGES

2003, 2002, 2001, 2000, 1999, 1998

Historical documents confirm that the first vines in St.-Emilion were planted at Pavie and Ausone in the 4th century. However, it was not until the 19th century, when the property was owned by the Talleman and Pigasse families, that wine-growing at Pavie became reasonably well known.

In 1855, the Bordeaux *négociant* Ferdinand Bouffard bought all of the Fayard-Talleman family's share. He then went on to acquire several neighboring vineyards, forming one 50-hectare (123.5-acre) vineyard in a single block. Bouffard named most of his newly constituted estate "Pavie." It included another, separately managed vineyard, which later became known as Pavie-Decesse.

A few years later, at the end of the First World War, Ferdinand Bouffard sold the estate to Albert Porte. He, in turn, sold it to the Valette family in 1943, who owned it until its sale to Gérard Perse in 1998.

Pavie has the largest vineyard of all the St.-Emilion premier grand cru classes, with a production seven times the size of one of its neighbors, Ausone, and twice that of the adjacent vineyard, La Gaffelière. The vineyard is superbly situated with a full southerly exposure just to the southeast of St.-Emilion (a five-minute drive) on the eastern section of the hillsides of the town.

Prior to the Perse acquisition, Pavie, despite the large production and popularity, had not been a top performer among the St.-Emilion first growths. In many vintages the wine was too light and feebly colored, with a tendency to brown and mature at an accelerated pace. Fortunately, this period of inconsistency is past history. However, this is not a St.-Emilion to drink young; most vintages have been stubbornly backward at their outset, and a minimum of 7–10 years of bottle age is required for mellowing. The wine was particularly disappointing during the 1990s, and this undoubtedly played a role in Mr. Valette's decision to sell the estate. The quality skyrocketed with Perse's first vintage, in 1998. What he has achieved in a mere seven years since is one of the most compelling stories of modern-day Bordeaux. Today, Pavie is one of the world's greatest wines and, in St.-Emilion, exceeded only in price, not quality, by Cheval Blanc.

CHATEAU PAVIE

2003 Château Pavie

RATING: 96–100 points

Another off-the-chart effort from perfectionist proprietors Chantal and Gérard Perse, the 2003 Pavie was cropped at 30 hectoliters per hectare. A blend of 70% Merlot, 20% Cabernet Franc, and 10% Cabernet Sauvignon, it is a wine of sublime richness, minerality, delineation, and nobleness. Representing the essence of one of St.-Emilion's greatest *terroirs*, the limestone and clay soils were perfect for handling the torrid heat of 2003. Inky/purple to the rim, it offers up provocative aromas of minerals, black and red fruits, balsamic vinegar, licorice, and smoke. It traverses the palate with extraordinary richness as well as remarkable freshness and definition. The finish is tannic, but the wine's low acidity and higher-than-normal alcohol (13.5%) suggests it will be approachable in four or five years. Anticipated maturity: 2011–2040. A brilliant effort, it, along with Ausone and Pétrus, is one of the three greatest offerings of the right bank in 2003.

2002 Château Pavie

RATING: 95 points

This wine includes the small production previously bottled as La Clusière as the Pavie vineyard now encompasses just under 92 acres. A blend of 70% Merlot, 20% Cabernet Franc, and 10% Cabernet Sauvignon, Pavie is once again a candidate for wine of the vintage, a tribute to Chantal and Gérard Perse, who are unwavering in their commitment to produce one of Bordeaux's most long-lived and complex wines. There are approximately 8,000 cases of the 2002, which was macerated for four to five weeks with malolactic fermentation and aging in 100% new oak. Like every Pavie produced under Perse, it will be bottled unfined and unfiltered. The color is a saturated dense purple. The wine possesses that liquid minerality that denotes a great *terroir*, along with a tremendously sweet liqueur of black currants and cherries intermixed with melted licorice and spice box. Dense and full-bodied yet remarkably elegant and delineated, this is a stunning achievement for the 2002 vintage. It is capable of three decades of ageability. Anticipated maturity: 2008–2025.

2001 Château Pavie

RATING: 96 points

One of the candidates for wine of the vintage . . . again, the 2001 Pavie. From a magnificent south-facing vineyard planted primarily on limestone soil, it is a blend of 70% Merlot, 20% Cabernet Franc, and 10% Cabernet Sauvignon. After a six-week maceration, it spent nearly twenty-four months in new oak prior to being bottled unfined and unfiltered. Some Bordeaux brokers think it might be even better than the 2000 Pavie, but I do not agree. The inky ruby/purple–colored 2001 exhibits a tight but promising nose of crushed stones, a liqueur of blackberries, cherries, and black currants, and subtle smoke and licorice in the background. It is powerful, with impressive elegance, fine harmony among its elements, a multi-layered texture, and a finish that lasts for 50+ seconds. There is considerable tannin, but it is well integrated. Give it three or four years, and drink it over the next two decades. A profound effort for the vintage, it is an example of perfectionist proprietors pushing the envelope of quality.

2000 Château Pavie

RATING: 100 points

Give Gérard Perse credit. People thought his numerous assurances that 2000 was the greatest Pavie ever produced were premature as well as arrogant. However, after tasting this extraordinary blend of 60% Merlot, 30% Cabernet Franc, and 10% Cabernet Sauvignon (made from low yields of 28–30 hectoliters per hectare) six separate times in 2003, I found that it is unquestionably one of the most monumental wines Bordeaux has ever produced. Bottled in March 2003, about nine months later than other 2000s, the color is an opaque purple, and the bouquet offers up notes of liquid minerals, blackberries, cherries, and cassis intermixed with spice box, cedar, and white flowers. On the palate, it exhibits a massive display of richness and extract, yet with pinpoint delineation and vibrancy as well as a 60+-second finish, this is the kind of phenomenal wine that Perse's critics were afraid he might produce—a no-compromise, immortal wonder that represents the essence of one of Bordeaux's greatest *terroirs*. Life is too short not to own and consume the 2000 Pavie. Anticipated maturity: 2012–2050.

1999 Château Pavie

RATING: 95 points

A candidate for wine of the vintage, the 1999 Pavie boasts an opaque ruby/purple color in addition to gorgeous aromas of crushed minerals, smoke, licorice, cherry liqueur, and black currants. It is exceptionally pure and multilayered, with stunning texture and overall balance. The tannin level suggests one to two years of cellaring is warranted; it should age gracefully for 25+ years. Anticipated maturity: now–2030.

1998 Château Pavie

RATING: 95+ points

A 50-year wine, this opaque, purple-colored offering exhibits a strong, precise nose of black fruits, liquid minerals, smoke, and graphite. Extremely full-bodied yet brilliantly delineated, powerful, and awesomely concentrated, it boasts a fabulous mid-palate as well as a finish that lasts for nearly a minute. This *vin de garde* requires two to three years of cellaring. A tour de force in winemaking! Anticipated maturity: 2006–2045.

1990 Château Pavie

RATING: 90 points

This is the most impressive Pavie between 1982 and 1998, and certainly the last very noteworthy effort from the late proprietor Jean-Paul Valette. Dark ruby with some amber at the edge, the spicy, herb-tinged nose offers up notes of earth, black cherries, minerals, and spice box. Medium to full–bodied, meaty, and fleshy, with low acidity and moderate tannin, this wine seems to have approached its plateau of maturity. Anticipated maturity: now–2015.

CLASSIFICATION: There is no official classification of the wines in Pomerol.

OWNER: SC Château Pétrus

ADDRESS: Pétrus, 33500 Pomerol, France

MAILING ADDRESS: c/o SA Ets Jean-Pierre Moueix, BP 129, 54, quai du Priourat, 33502 Libourne, France

TELEPHONE: 33 05 57 51 78 96

TELEFAX: 33 05 57 51 79 79

CONTACT: Frédéric Lospied

VISITING POLICY: By appointment and exclusively for professionals of the wine trade dealing with the firm

VINEYARDS

SURFACE AREA: 28.4 acres

GRAPE VARIETALS: 95% Merlot, 5% Cabernet Franc

AVERAGE AGE OF THE VINES: 35 years

DENSITY OF PLANTATION: 6,500 vines per hectare

AVERAGE YIELDS: 36 hectoliters per hectare

WINEMAKING AND UPBRINGING

Twenty- to twenty-four-day fermentation and maceration in temperature-controlled concrete tanks. Twenty months' aging in 100% new oak barrels. Fining, no filtration.

ANNUAL PRODUCTION

Pétrus: 25,000–30,000 bottles

AVERAGE PRICE (VARIABLE DEPENDING ON VINTAGE): $250–500+

GREAT RECENT VINTAGES

2003, 2001, 2000, 1998, 1990, 1989, 1982

For one of the most cherished and expensive wines of the world, Pétrus has little significant history. The owner of Libourne, Hotel Loubat, was the majority owner of Pétrus until the late Jean-Pierre Moueix secured partial ownership in 1961 and 100% of the estate in 2002. The original vineyard of 16 acres was enlarged, and significantly so, by the acquisition of 12-plus acres in 1969 (a part of the Gazin estate). The wine was little known until the late 1940s, when vintages such as 1945, 1947, and 1950 created considerable excitement.

Now the most celebrated wine of Pomerol, Pétrus has, during the last four decades, become one of Bordeaux's most renowned as well as expensive red wines.

A humble building, renovated in 2004, boasts a vineyard situated on a buttonhole of clay in the middle of Pomerol's plateau. The tiny 28.4-acre vineyard renders wines that are treated as well and as carefully as any wines produced on earth. The legendary Jean-Pierre Moueix (1913–2003), a noble and erudite man, single-handedly established the reputation of not only Pétrus but also of all the wines of Pomerol. He founded his firm in Libourne in 1937, and developed a marketplace in Belgium and northern Europe for many of the area's greatest wines. His success allowed him to purchase many of the better vineyards, the most renowned of which were Trotanoy (1953), La Fleur–Pétrus (1953), Magdelaine (1954), and Pétrus, which he partially owned until its outright acquisition in 2002.

While the property is owned by Jean-Francois Moueix, a very private person, it is his younger brother (by one year), Christian Moueix, who is responsible for the viticultural management and winemakery. This is the same Christian Moueix who owns the flagship/reference estate Dominus in Napa Valley. Christian Moueix couldn't be more different from his reclusive brother. Tall, handsome, charismatic, outgoing, and married to an American, he looks like a *Vanity Fair* cover story, but looks and personality aside, he is a brilliant winemaker. After the two brothers make their selection, most vintages of Pétrus turn out to be 100% pure Merlot.

There have been a tremendous number of legendary Pétrus vintages, which no doubt has propelled prices into the stratosphere. Yet as Pétrus has become deified by much of the world's wine press, one must ask, particularly in view of this property's track record from 1976 on, "Is Pétrus as great today as it once was?" There is no doubt that Pétrus slumped in vintages such as 1988, 1986, 1983, 1981, 1979, 1978, and 1976, but since 1989 Pétrus has been in top form, producing a succession of brilliant wines. The 2003, 2000, 1998, 1990, 1989, 1975, 1971, 1970, 1964, 1961, 1950, 1948, 1947, 1945, 1929, and 1921 are among the most monumental wines I have ever tasted.

2003 Pétrus

RATING: 96–98+ points

The only Pomerol vineyard to be planted in a deep bed of blue clay, Pétrus, which harvested its Merlot in a mere three days during the first week of September (2, 3, and 4), did not suffer as much from the record-breaking heat as many of its neighbors, whose vineyards are planted in more gravelly soils. Hence it has produced one of the finest 2003s of Bordeaux's right bank. However, the production is small, with only 1,650 cases made. The alcohol of 13–13.5% was not as high as Christian Moueix suspected, but the acidity levels were low, and the pH running at 3.9 plus, which gives the wine a fat, multilayered, fleshy, textural mouth-feel. The deep ruby/purple color is accompanied by an exceptional nose of jammy red and black fruits intermixed with notions of licorice, vanilla, and underbrush. Full-bodied and opulent, with great intensity as well as noteworthy freshness, and no evidence of overripeness (prunes, raisins, etc.), this blockbuster is a remarkable achievement, especially given the style of other Pomerols produced adjacent to this hallowed vineyard. Anticipated maturity: 2010–2030.

2002 Pétrus

RATING: 92 points

Considering the fact that Christian Moueix was contemplating not making a 2002 Pétrus, I was surprised by how strongly this wine performed. However, production was cut in half, with only 1,800 cases produced. The resulting offering has the potential to be the top wine of the appellation. A deep plum/purple color is followed by sweet aromas of mulberries, black cherries, vanilla, and hints of truffles as well as licorice. It is impressively pure and medium to full–bodied, with moderately high tannin in the finish. This is not a blockbuster, brawny, super-concentrated Pétrus, but it is one of the biggest 2002s made in Pomerol. Moreover, it will possess as much longevity as L'Evangile, Lafleur, or Le Gay, three other noteworthy Pomerols. Anticipated maturity: 2011–2025.

2001 Pétrus

RATING: 95+ points

The brilliant Le Pin aside, this is a candidate for one of the wines of the vintage. The 2001 Pétrus (2,160 cases produced) exhibits more depth and richness than any other Pomerol I tasted. Its deep, saturated ruby/plum/purple color is accompanied by a tight but promising bouquet of vanilla, cherry liqueur, melted licorice, black currants, and notions of truffles and earth. Rich, full-bodied, and surprisingly thick as well as intense, there is plenty of structure underlying the wealth of fruit and extract. Give it three to six years of cellaring and drink it over the following two decades, as it promises to be one of the longest-lived wines of the vintage, not to mention one of the most concentrated.

I told Christian Moueix (although I'm not sure he agreed with me) that his best wines of 2001 reminded me of the 1971s in style, but with slightly less tannin and more fat.

2000 Pétrus

RATING: 100 points

Another magical effort from Pétrus, the 2000 has continued to gain weight and stature. From the bottle, it is another perfect wine, much like the 1998. The color is inky plum/purple to the rim and the nose, which starts slowly, begins to roar after several minutes, offering up scents of smoke, blackberries, cherries, licorice, and an unmistakable truffle/underbrush element. On the palate, this enormous effort is reminiscent of dry vintage port, with fabulous ripeness, a huge, unctuous texture, enormous body, and a colossal 65-second finish. I did not have the benefit of tasting it side by side with the equally perfect 1998, but it appears the 2000 is a more massive, macho/masculine wine, with more obvious tannin and structure than the seamless 1998. It is another wine to add to the legacy of the great vintages of Pétrus. Anticipated maturity: 2015–2050.

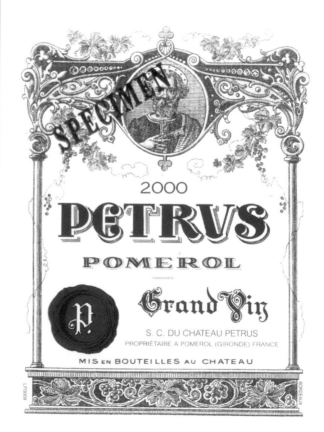

1999 Pétrus

RATING: 94 points

This wine is turning out much in the style of such wonderful Pétrus vintages as 1967 and 1971. Although not as compelling as either the 1998 or 2000, it displays beautiful intensity and finesse in a more evolved style than one normally expects from this estate. The wine has a dense, nearly opaque ruby/purple color, sweet black cherry, mulberry, and truffle–infused fruit, full body, low acidity, admirable purity, and sweet tannin. Only 2,400 cases were produced. It should be ready to drink in 3–4 years, and it will last for two decades. Anticipated maturity: 2007–2030.

1998 Pétrus

RATING: 100 points

Christian Moueix feels the 1998 is even better than his 1989 or 1990, and ultimately he may be proven right. However, it will be five or six years or more before it can be known which of these profound efforts might turn out to be the most compelling. The 1998 Pétrus is unquestionably a fabulous effort boasting a dense plum/purple color as well as an extraordinary nose of black fruits intermixed with caramel, mocha, and vanilla. Exceptionally pure, super-concentrated, and extremely full-bodied, with admirable underlying acidity as well as sweet tannin, it reveals a superb mid-palate in addition to the luxurious richness for which this great property is known. The finish lasts for 40–45 seconds. Patience will definitely be required. Production was 2,400 cases, about 1,600 cases fewer than normal. Anticipated maturity: 2010–2040.

1997 Pétrus

RATING: 91 points

The backward 1997 (2,300 cases produced) needs another two or three years of cellaring. The dense plum/ruby/purple color is accompanied by a closed bouquet of mocha, dried tomato skin, and black fruits. In the mouth, it is one of the most muscular 1997s, exhibiting outstanding concentration, length, intensity, and depth, copious tannin, and a fine mouth-feel. Consider the 1997 Pétrus a modern-day version of their superb 1967. Anticipated maturity: 2006–2025.

1996 Pétrus

RATING: 92 points

The 1996 Pétrus is a big, monolithic, foursquare wine with an impressively opaque purple color and sweet berry fruit intermixed with earth, toast, and coffee scents. Full-bodied and muscular, with high levels of tannin and a backward style, this wine (less than 50% of the production was bottled as Pétrus) will require patience. It is a mammoth example, but without the sweetness of the 1997 or the pure, exceptional richness and layers of the multidimensional 1995. Anticipated maturity: 2010–2035.

1995 Pétrus

RATING: 95+ points

Unquestionably one of the vintage's superstars, the 1995 Pétrus is taking on a personality similar to the extraordinarily backward, muscular 1975. This is not a Pétrus that could be approached in its youth (i.e., the perfect duo of 1989 and 1990). The wine exhibits an opaque ruby/purple color, followed by a knockout nose of toast, jammy black fruits, and roasted coffee. On the palate, it possesses teeth-staining extract levels, massive body, and rich, sweet black fruits buttressed by powerful, noticeable tannin. A formidably endowed wine with layers of extract, this is a huge, tannic, monstrous Pétrus that will last for 50+ years. Anticipated maturity: 2012–2050.

1994 Pétrus

RATING: 92 points

Opaque purple/black in color, with a sweet vanilla, toast, jammy cherry, and cassis nose, this full-bodied, densely packed wine reveals layers of flavor and an inner core of sweetness with huge quantities of glycerin and depth. A tannic, classic style of Pétrus, with immense body, great purity, and a backward finish, this wine will be at its apogee between 2006 and 2035.

1993 Pétrus

RATING: 90 points

A candidate for the most concentrated wine of the vintage, this 1993 exhibits a saturated purple/plum color and a sweet nose of black fruits, Asian spices, and vanilla. Huge and formidably rich, this powerful, dense, super-pure wine is a tour de force in winemaking. For a vintage not known for wines of this immense richness and length, this brawny, splendidly endowed Pétrus possesses low acidity and high tannin, suggesting that 8–10 years of cellaring are required. This should be a 30-year wine, as well as the vintage's longest-lived effort. Anticipated maturity: now–2016.

1990 Pétrus

RATING: 100 points

This is a spectacular Pétrus, made much in the style of the 1970 or a more modern-day version of the 1947. This wine still has a very dense, ruby/purple color with no lightening at the rim. With considerable aeration the wine offers up spectacular aromas of caramel, sweet vanilla, and black cherry and blackberry liqueur, with a hint of tobacco and cedar. The wine is massively big, viscous, and full-bodied, with low acidity but magnificent richness and an almost seamless personality. The wine remains youthful and not even in its adolescence, but it has a certain accessibility, even though so much is yet to come. This is a compellingly great Pétrus, slightly sweeter and more opulent than the 1998, and perhaps on a quicker evolutionary track than the 1998 or 1989. Anticipated maturity: 2007–2040.

1989 Pétrus

RATING: 100 points

This wine is more tightly knit and more tannic, but every bit the blockbuster, concentrated effort that its younger sibling, the 1990, is. It seems to need more coaxing from the glass, but the color is virtually identical—a dense ruby/purple with no lightening at the edge. In the mouth the wine cuts a broad swath, with spectacular intensity, richness, massive concentration, and high levels of tannin, yet the wine is fabulously well delineated and, like its sibling, has a finish that goes on for nearly a minute. It does not seem to be quite as evolved as the 1990, and my instincts suggest there is a bit more tannin, but both are as prodigious as Pétrus can be. Anticipated maturity: 2010–2040.

1988 Pétrus

RATING: 91 points

This wine has become increasingly herbaceous, and with the tannins pushing through the fruit, it is also becoming more aggressive. The wine started off life with an impressively deep ruby/purple color, but is now showing some amber at the edge. A medium-bodied, rather elegant style of Pétrus, it has a distinctive cedary, almost celery component intermixed with a hint of caramel, sweet mulberry, and black cherry fruit. It has aged far less evenly than I would have thought and is probably best drunk over the next 8–10 years.

1982 Pétrus

RATING: 90–98 points

I have gone through a complete case of this wine, stored perfectly, and this has been a perplexingly irregular wine to taste. Some bottles are spectacular—sweet, rich, full-bodied, opulent—but even those have a distinctive herbaceousness to the nose, which offers up notes of chocolate, cedar, black cherry jam, and currants. It is full-bodied, tannic, and, from the best bottles, very concentrated and rich. Other bottles seem somewhat vegetal and roasted, with sweetness but not the prodigious qualities of other bottles. It is hard to know what is really going on. The wine seems to be close to full maturity, but should hold where well stored for at least another two decades. As a postscript, from cask, this wine is still to this day one of the most memorable wines I have ever tasted and certainly a perfect wine. From my perspective, though, it has never lived up to that after bottling, which I suspect involved entirely too much fining and filtration, something that has not been done at Pétrus since the late 1980s. Anticipated maturity: now–2023.

CHATEAU PICHON-LONGUEVILLE BARON

CLASSIFICATION: Second Growth in 1855

OWNER: AXA Millésimes

ADDRESS: Château Pichon-Longueville Baron, 33250 Pauillac, France

TELEPHONE: 33 05 56 73 17 17

TELEFAX: 33 05 56 73 17 28

E-MAIL: infochato@pichonlongueville.com

WEBSITE: www.chateaupichonlongueville.com

CONTACT: Christian Seely, managing director; Jean-René Matignon, technical director

VISITING POLICY: Every weekday, 9 A.M.–12:30 P.M. and 2–6:30 P.M.; Saturday and Sunday, by appointment; visit and tasting free for groups under 15 persons; 3 euros per person for groups of 15 or more.

VINEYARDS

SURFACE AREA: 173 acres

GRAPE VARIETALS: 60% Cabernet Sauvignon, 35% Merlot, 4% Cabernet Franc, 1% Petit Verdot

AVERAGE AGE OF THE VINES: 27 years

DENSITY OF PLANTATION: 9,000 vines per hectare

AVERAGE YIELDS: 45 hectoliters per hectare

WINEMAKING AND UPBRINGING

The oldest part of the château's *terroir,* mainly planted with Cabernet Sauvignon, is selected for the first wine. The younger plots, composed of some 49 acres, mainly Merlot, are used for the production of the property's second wine, Les Tourelles de Longueville. The plots are kept separate in order to maintain a regular style and quality from one vintage to the other.

Particular attention is brought to the Cabernet Sauvignon grapes to make sure that they are not harvested too early. In 1991, Pichon-Baron installed a maturity index that monitors the evolution of the phenolic components of the grapes, in order to understand the maturation in relation to the type of *terroir*. The main objective at Pichon-Baron is to preserve the quality of the fruit and its primary aromas.

Alcoholic and partly malolactic fermentation are carried out in stainless-steel vats of 50 to 220 hectoliters. The smaller vats are used for the smaller plots and are vinified apart. The yeasts for the alcoholic fermentation are chosen specifically as well. The fermentation takes place between 26 and 31°C with frequent pumping over of the juice. The maceration of the skins lasts from 5 to 15 days, during which regular tasting vat by vat is carried out.

The best lots (for the grand vin) are barrel-aged after the vinification. The assemblage takes place after several barrel tastings in the course of the first phase of the aging process. The final blend is made in late February or the beginning of March. The aging in barrels lasts for approximately 16 months in 60–80% new oak.

ANNUAL PRODUCTION

Château Pichon-Longueville Baron: 240,000 bottles

Les Tourelles de Longueville: 150,000 bottles

AVERAGE PRICE (VARIABLE DEPENDING ON VINTAGE): $40–100

GREAT RECENT VINTAGES

2003, 2002, 2001, 2000, 1998, 1996, 1995, 1990, 1989, 1988, 1986, 1982

The existing château was built in 1851 by Raoul de Pichon Longueville and was owned by the Bouteiller family between 1933 and 1988. It was purchased by AXA Millésimes, and totally restored under the management of Jean-Michel Cazes.

In 1989, an architectural competition for the construction of modern viticultural buildings was organized in collaboration with the Georges Pompidou Centre in Paris. The owners chose the design of the French-American team of Jean de Gastines and Patrick Dillon, an ambitious architectural project that successfully marries tradition and modernity.

In 2001, Jean-Michel Cazes retired from AXA Millésimes, and Englishman Christian Seely took over the management of all the properties in Bordeaux and abroad—Châteaux Pichon-Longueville, Pibran, Cantenac Brown, Suduiraut, Petit-Village, Quinta do Noval (Port), Disznökó (Tokaj), and Château Belles Eaux, since December 2002 in the Coteaux du Languedoc.

As a consequence, Pichon-Longueville Baron, frequently called Pichon-Baron, now merits its prestigious second-growth status.

The vineyard is superbly situated on gravelly soil with a full southerly exposure. Much of the vineyard is adjacent to that of Château Latour. It has been speculated that the lack of brilliance in many of Pichon-Baron's wines in the 1960s and 1970s was a result of both casual viticultural practices and poor cellar management. I remember passing by the cellars on a tor-

Christian Seely

ridly hot afternoon in July, only to see the newly bottled vintage stacked up outside the cellars, roasting in the relentless sunshine. Such recklessness has no doubt stopped.

Rhetoric and public relations efforts aside, the best evidence that Pauillac once again has two great Pichons are the wines that have been produced at Pichon-Baron since 1986. This château has proven to be one of the great superstars of the 1990s. This is routinely one of the Médoc's most majestic wines.

CHATEAU PICHON-LONGUEVILLE BARON

2003 Château Pichon-Longueville Baron

RATING: 92–94+ points

Reminiscent of Pichon-Baron's triumphant 1990, the 2003 is powerful and alcoholic (13.46%) for a cru classé Bordeaux, with a high pH of 3.85, and low acidity (3.1). Made from 31 hectoliters per hectare, this blend of 65% Cabernet Sauvignon and 35% Merlot exhibits an inky/purple color along with a big, thick, juicy nose of soy sauce, blackberries, crème de cassis, minerals, and flowers. Full-bodied and powerful, with terrific fruit purity as well as depth, this beauty should become increasingly delineated as it evolves in barrel. The finish lasts for 45+ seconds. Anticipated maturity: 2009–2025.

2002 Château Pichon-Longueville Baron

RATING: 91 points

This is not one of this estate's most inspiring efforts. Nevertheless, it is a potentially outstanding wine . . . if everything comes together. Surprisingly aromatic and evolved, it offers notes of black fruits, underbrush, toasty oak, and a hint of mocha. Soft and fleshy, with medium body as well as outstanding purity, but not the power, density, or concentration expected, it is a very fine effort that falls behind such recent vintages as 2001 and 2000. Anticipated maturity: now–2014.

2001 Château Pichon-Longueville Baron

RATING: 92 points

A successful effort for this vintage in the Médoc, this deep ruby/purple–colored Pauillac exhibits class, nobility, and breeding, along with black currant liqueur, licorice, and incense notes. Sweet, expansive, fleshy, and medium to full–bodied, with good structure, ripe tannin, and a long, 30–35 second finish, it can be drunk now, but it will last for 12–15 years. I had this wine three separate times out of bottle, and it is performing significantly better than it did from cask.

2000 Château Pichon-Longueville Baron

RATING: 96 points

A spectacular effort, this is a profound Pichon-Baron and clearly my favorite vintage of this wine since the 1989 and 1990. An inky purple color offers up notes of barbecue spices intermixed with new saddle leather, crème de cassis, melted licorice, creosote, and a hint of vanilla. The wine is full–bodied, tremendously concentrated, with sweet tannin and a seamless finish that goes on for close to one minute. This wine has great purity, tremendous texture, and fabulous upside potential. This is a prodigious 2000! Anticipated maturity: 2008–2028.

1998 Château Pichon-Longueville Baron

RATING: 90 points

A definitive Pauillac, the dense purple–colored 1998 Pichon-Baron offers up a sweet bouquet of licorice, smoke, asphalt, blackberries, and crème de cassis. In the mouth, the wine is elegant rather than full blown, with medium body, sweet fruit, nice texture on the attack and mid-palate, and moderate tannin in the long finish. No, this is not as profound as the 1996, 1990, or 1989, but it is an outstanding effort. Anticipated maturity: 2006–2020.

1996 Château Pichon-Longueville Baron

RATING: 91 points

Pichon-Longueville Baron's 1996's high percentage of Cabernet Sauvignon (about 80%) has resulted in a wine that has put on weight. An opaque purple color is accompanied by

beautiful aromas of tobacco, new saddle leather, roasted coffee, and cassis. It is dense, medium to full–bodied, and backward, with moderately high tannin, but plenty of sweet fruit, glycerin, and extract to balance out the wine's structure. This well-endowed, classic Pauillac should be at its finest from 2007 to 2028.

1995 Château Pichon-Longueville Baron
RATING: 90 points
A stylish, elegant, more restrained style of Pichon-Baron with less obvious new oak than usual, this deep ruby/purple–colored wine offers a pure black currant–scented nose with

subtle aromas of coffee and smoky toasty oak. In the mouth, the wine displays less weight and muscle than the 1996, but it offers suave, elegant, rich fruit presented in a medium to full–bodied, surprisingly lush style. Anticipated maturity: now–2016.

1990 Château Pichon-Longueville Baron
RATING: 96 points
A fabulous effort, the dense, purple-colored 1990 Pichon-Longueville exhibits the roasted overripeness of this vintage, but it manages to keep everything in perspective. The wine is opulent and flamboyant, with lower acidity and noticeably

less tannin than the 1989. It is equally concentrated, with a more evolved nose of cedar, black fruits, earth, minerals, and spices. On the palate, the wine offers sensational quantities of jammy fruit, glycerin, wood, and sweet tannin. It is far more fun to taste and drink (more hedonistic) than the more structured, backward, yet exceptional 1989. Ideally, readers should have both vintages in their cellars. The 1990 can be drunk now as well as over the next 25+ years.

1989 Château Pichon-Longueville Baron

RATING: 95+ points

Evolving at a glacial pace, the 1989 Pichon-Longueville exhibits an opaque, dense purple color that suggests a massive wine of considerable extraction and richness. The dense, full-bodied 1989 is brilliantly made, with huge, smoky, chocolaty, cassis aromas intermingled with scents of toasty oak. Well layered with a sweet inner core of fruit, this awesomely endowed, backward, tannic, prodigious 1989 needs additional cellaring; it should last for three decades or more. It is unquestionably a great Pichon-Longueville Baron. Anticipated maturity: 2006–2030.

1988 Château Pichon-Longueville Baron

RATING: 90 points

The 1988 Pichon-Longueville Baron promises to be one of the most successful wines of this vintage. Surprisingly large-scaled for a 1988, with a bouquet of oak, cassis, and licorice, it is deep in color (some pink and amber are emerging), rich, softly tannic, as well as medium to full–bodied. It has thrown off its cloak of tannin and inched into full maturity. Anticipated maturity: now–2010.

1982 Château Pichon-Longueville Baron

RATING: 92 points

I certainly bungled the early reviews of this wine! In barrel and early in bottle, it was a big, ripe, fruit bowl of a wine with virtually no acidity or structure in evidence. However, it is safe to say the one component Bordeaux never lacks, even in the ripest, fattest vintages, is tannin. As this wine has evolved it has become much more delineated as well as classically proportioned. In fact, it is an exceptional example of Pichon-Longueville Baron produced during a period when this estate was best known for the mediocrity of its wines. Fully mature, the 1982 reveals a dense, opaque ruby/purple/garnet color, and a huge nose of cedar, sweet cassis, and spice. The wine's full body, marvelous concentration, a 1982-like opulence and unctuousness, and a thick, jammy, moderately sweet finish all combine to offer a splendid drinking experience. Given its ripe, creamy personality, this wine should be drunk over the next 10–15 years.

CLASSIFICATION: Second Growth in 1855

OWNER: May-Eliane de Lencquesaing

ADDRESS: Pichon-Longueville Comtesse de Lalande, 33250 Pauillac, France

TELEPHONE: 33 05 56 59 19 40

TELEFAX: 33 05 56 59 26 56

E-MAIL: pichon@pichon-lalande.com

WEBSITE: www.pichon-lalande.com

CONTACT: accueil@pichon-lalande.com and above telephone and fax numbers

VISITING POLICY: By appointment only

VINEYARDS

SURFACE AREA: 185.3 acres

GRAPE VARIETALS: 45% Cabernet Sauvignon, 35% Merlot, 12% Cabernet Franc, 8% Petit Verdot

AVERAGE AGE OF THE VINES: 30 years

DENSITY OF PLANTATION: 9,000 vines per hectare

AVERAGE YIELDS: 45 hectoliters per hectare

WINEMAKING AND UPBRINGING

Eighteen- to twenty-four-day fermentation and maceration in temperature-controlled stainless-steel tanks. Eighteen to twenty months' aging in barrels that are renewed by half every year. Racking every three months. Fining. No filtration.

ANNUAL PRODUCTION

Château Pichon-Longueville Comtesse de Lalande: 180,000 bottles

Réserve de la Comtesse: 160,000 bottles

AVERAGE PRICE (VARIABLE DEPENDING ON VINTAGE): $50–125

GREAT RECENT VINTAGES

2003, 2002, 2001, 2000, 1996, 1995, 1986, 1982

Mentioned by Louis XIV while visiting the Médoc in the late 18th century, this estate was once part of the large viticultural empire of Pierre Mazure de Rauzan. It was the prize in a dowry given to his daughter Thérèse, who married Jacques de Pichon-Longueville in 1700. It stayed in the family until 1850, when three-fifths was inherited by the three sisters of Baron Pichon. In 1926 the vineyards of the three sisters were formally joined together, and it is this property union that now constitutes Pichon-Lalande.

At present, Pichon-Longueville Comtesse de Lalande (Pichon-Lalande) is unquestionably the most popular and, since 1978, one of Pauillac's most consistently brilliant wines. It can rival the three famous first growths of this commune. The wines of Pichon-Lalande have been very successful since 1961, but there is no question that in the late 1970s and early 1980s, under the energetic helm of Madame de Lencquesaing (who is affectionately called La Générale by her peers), the quality rose dramatically.

The wine is made in an intelligent manner and is darkly colored, supple, fruity, and smooth enough to be drunk young. It has the distinction, along with Château Palmer in Margaux, of being one of the most famous Médoc estates to use a significant quantity of Merlot in the blend. Yet Pichon-Lalande has the requisite tannin, depth, and richness to age gracefully for 10–20 years. The high proportion of Merlot (35%) no doubt accounts for part of the wine's soft, fleshy characteristic.

Significant investments in the winemaking facilities were made during the 1980s. A new *cuvier* was built in 1980 and a new barrel-aging cellar and tasting room (with a spectacular vista of neighboring Château Latour), in 1988. A fine museum now sits atop the barrel room, and renovations of the château were completed in 1990. Madame Lencquesaing resides at the château, which sits across the road from Pichon-Longueville Baron. The estate's vineyards lay both in Pauillac and St.-Julien, the latter region often credited as the reason for Pichon-Lalande's supple style.

PICHON-LONGUEVILLE COMTESSE DE LALANDE

2003 Pichon-Lalande

RATING: 93–95 points

Fashioned from low yields of 39 hectoliters per hectare, Pichon-Lalande's harvest began on September 17, and lasted until the end of the month. A powerful effort for this estate (13% alcohol), with a pH of 3.8, and total acidity of 3.15, this blend of 65% Cabernet Sauvignon, 31% Merlot, and 4% Petit Verdot possesses an opaque purple color to the rim as well as lovely aromas of spring flowers, crème de cassis, blackberries,

and a hint of roasted espresso. Dense, opulent, and medium to full–bodied, with outstanding purity, and no trace of over-ripeness, it should drink well young, and last for 15–20 years. Although it reveals a more classic style than the 1982 did at a similar stage, its similarities with that vintage are unmistakable. Anticipated maturity: 2008–2020.

2002 Pichon-Lalande
RATING: 94 points
A tannic, super-concentrated effort from Pichon-Lalande, this is a blend of 51% Cabernet Sauvignon, 34% Merlot, 9% Cabernet Franc, and 6% Petit Verdot, from yields of only 33 hectoliters per hectare (45 hectoliters in 2000). It possesses a saturated purple color in addition to a firm but promising bouquet of figs, black currant liqueur, licorice, lavender, and background smoky oak. Tannic, classically structured, exceptionally pure and layered as well as tremendously persistent

and long in the mouth, this will not be a wine to drink in its youth. Medium-bodied, it will require 7–8 years of cellaring. It is a very impressive but structured effort from this famous estate. Anticipated maturity: 2012–2025.

2001 Pichon-Lalande
RATING: 93 points
A distinctive bouquet of violets, soy, pepper, blackberries, cassis, and tree bark gives this 2001 a singular style. This dense ruby/purple–colored blend of 50% Cabernet Sauvignon, 36% Merlot, and a whopping 14% Petit Verdot exhibits plenty of structure, wonderful sweetness, a closed style, but a rich, textured, persistent character. The unusually large percentage of Petit Verdot gives the wine more structure and less initial charm. This beauty needs some time in the cellar. Anticipated maturity: 2007–2018.

2000 Pichon-Lalande

RATING: 97 points

The 2000 Pichon-Longueville Comtesse de Lalande is spectacular, and certainly a noteworthy rival to the 1996, 1995, and even the extraordinary 1982. A blend of 50% Cabernet Sauvignon, 34% Merlot, 10% Petit Verdot, and the rest Cabernet Franc, this effort has a dense saturated purple color, a singular/distinctive yet possibly controversial aromatic smorgasbord existing of crème de cassis, vanilla, and violets, but also tapenade and tree bark. No doubt the Petit Verdot has imparted a certain almost olive-like component to the wine's aromatic profile. In the mouth, it is a wine of extraordinary density, opulence, great presence, and richness. As the 2000 sits in the glass, notes of lavender and melted licorice emerge along with the distinctive tapenade aromas interwoven with crème de cassis, espresso roast, and cedar. The wine is full-bodied, with extraordinary purity and a tremendous texture. I suspect this wine will be relatively approachable young but evolve effortlessly. This is a dramatic, almost flamboyant style that is not classic Pauillac in one sense, but a classic wine. Anticipated maturity: 2007–2025.

1996 Pichon-Lalande

RATING: 96 points

The 1996 Pichon-Lalande is awesome. For Pichon-Lalande, the percentage of Cabernet Sauvignon utilized in the final blend is atypically high. This wine normally contains 35–50% Merlot in the blend, but the 1996 is a blend of 75% Cabernet Sauvignon, 15% Merlot, 5% Cabernet Franc, and 5% Petit Verdot. Only 50% of the estate's production made it into the grand vin. The color is a saturated ruby/purple. The nose suggests sweet, nearly overripe Cabernet Sauvignon, with its blueberry/blackberry/cassis scents intermixed with high-quality, subtle, toasty new oak. Deep and full-bodied, with fabulous concentration and a sweet, opulent texture, this wine was singing in full harmony when I tasted it in January 2002. Given the wine's abnormally high percentage of Cabernet Sauvignon, I would suspect it will close down. It possesses plenty of tannin, but the wine's overwhelming fruit richness dominates its personality. Could the 1996 turn out to be as extraordinary as the 1982? Anticipated maturity: 2007–2025.

1995 Pichon-Lalande

RATING: 95 points

The 1995 is an exquisite example of Pichon-Lalande with the Merlot component giving the wine a coffee/chocolaty/cherry attribute to go along with the two Cabernets' complex blackberry/cassis fruit. The wine possesses an opaque black/ruby/purple color, and sexy, flamboyant aromatics of toast, black fruits, and cedar. Exquisite on the palate, this full-bodied, layered, multidimensional wine should prove to be one of the vintage's most extraordinary success stories. Anticipated maturity: now–2020.

1994 Pichon-Lalande

RATING: 91 points

One of the stars of the vintage, this opaque, purple-colored wine possesses a gorgeously perfumed, exotic, smoky, black currant, Asian spice, and sweet vanilla bouquet. It is followed by thick, rich, moderately tannic flavors that exhibit medium to full body, good structure, outstanding purity, and a classically layered, long, pure finish. This terrific Pichon-Lalande should evolve effortlessly for 15–18 years. Anticipated maturity: now–2020.

1989 Pichon-Lalande

RATING: 93 points

Approaching full maturity, Pichon-Lalande's 1989 has a deep ruby/plum color with some lightening at the edge. The nose offers sweet plums and crème de cassis intermixed with vanilla and graphite. The wine is lush, medium to full-bodied, and layered with texture, low acidity, sweet tannin, and the hallmark purity and elegance this estate routinely produces. Some tannins remain, but this wine has reached its plateau of maturity, where it should remain for another 10–15 years. Anticipated maturity: now–2017.

1988 Pichon-Lalande

RATING: 90 points

Somewhat austere but very successful for the vintage, Pichon-Lalande's 1988 has a dark garnet color and an intriguing nose of compost, earth, black currants, licorice, and weedy tobacco. The wine is medium-bodied with a sweet, relatively expansive mid-palate and slightly rugged tannins in the increasingly attenuated finish. This wine has reached full maturity and should be drunk over the next 5–10 years. Anticipated maturity: now–2015.

1986 Pichon-Lalande

RATING: 94 points

Just now emerging from a very clumsy dormant period, Pichon-Lalande's dense ruby/purple–colored 1986 still has the color of a 4–5-year-old wine. This is the most tannic and backward Pichon-Lalande after 1975 and before 1996. The wine was completely closed down until just recently. The wine shows notes of cedar, black currants, earth, spice box, and licorice, followed by a medium to full–bodied, very concentrated, intense palate with a still-noticeable tannic structure, a relatively big, muscular style for Pichon-Lalande. Anticipated maturity: now–2015.

1985 Pichon-Lalande

RATING: 90 points

Fully mature, this wine shows some pink at the edge, a sweet nose of herb-tinged cherries and black currants intermixed with dusty notes and new oak. The wine is medium-bodied, elegant, very flattering, and perfumed. It does not have the weight, depth, or dimensions of the top vintages, but is quite seductive. Anticipated maturity: now.

1983 Pichon-Lalande

RATING: 90 points

This wine seems to be just beginning to turn the corner and was excellent in its most recent tasting. For much of its life it has been a stunning wine, not far off the mark from the prodigious 1982. The color is still a healthy dark garnet with some amber creeping in at the edge. The wine shows a very distinctive nose of asphalt, tobacco, and cigar box, intermixed with some sweet cherries and black currants. In the mouth it is medium to full–bodied, but the fruit seems to be fading ever so slightly. In the finish, the tannins and acidity are beginning to poke through. Nevertheless, this is still underrated and always a sleeper vintage for Pichon-Lalande, but it requires consumption. Anticipated maturity: now.

1982 Pichon-Lalande

RATING: 100 points

I tasted this wine at least half a dozen times in 2002, and keep waiting for it to fall off. It was prodigious in its early days, and in bottle continues to be one of the most satisfying wines of this great vintage, both intellectually and hedonistically. The color is still a dense, dark garnet/plum/purple. The nose offers spectacularly sweet crème de cassis intermixed with plums and cherries, vanilla, and smoke. The wine is full-bodied, opulently textured, very plush, with a viscous texture and extravagant quantities of fruit, glycerin, and alcohol. It has always been incredibly low in acidity, very decadent, and about as hedonistic as a Pichon-Lalande—or any Bordeaux, for that matter—can be. It has surprised me with its longevity and should still continue to show no amber at its rim nor any evidence of breaking up. However, I wouldn't push my luck, as this wine is already over 20 years old. Anticipated maturity: now–2012.

CLASSIFICATION: There is no official classification of the wines in Pomerol.

OWNER: SC Château Trotanoy

ADDRESS: Trotanoy, 33500 Pomerol, France

MAILING ADDRESS: c/o SA Ets Jean-Pierre Moueix, BP 129, 54, quai du Priourat, 33502 Libourne

TELEPHONE: 33 05 57 51 78 96

TELEFAX: 33 05 57 51 79 79

CONTACT: Frédéric Lospied

VISITING POLICY: By appointment and exclusively for professionals of the wine trade dealing with the firm

VINEYARDS

SURFACE AREA: 17.8 acres

GRAPE VARIETALS: 90% Merlot, 10% Cabernet Franc

AVERAGE AGE OF THE VINES: 35 years

DENSITY OF PLANTATION: 6,200 vines per hectare

AVERAGE YIELDS: 39 hectoliters per hectare

WINEMAKING AND UPBRINGING

Twenty-day fermentation and maceration in temperature-controlled concrete tanks. Twenty months' aging in barrels with 40% new oak. Fining, no filtration.

ANNUAL PRODUCTION

Château Trotanoy: 30,000 bottles
No second wine is produced.

AVERAGE PRICE (VARIABLE DEPENDING ON VINTAGE): $75–225

GREAT RECENT VINTAGES

2003, 2001, 2000, 1998, 1982

Trotanoy has historically been one of the great wines of both Pomerol and all of Bordeaux. Since 1976, Trotanoy has equalled the quality of a second growth. In vintages prior to 1976, Trotanoy was often as profound as a first growth.

Since 1953, Trotanoy has been owned by the firm of Jean-Pierre Moueix. The château is unmarked. The vineyards of this modest estate, which lie a kilometer to the west of Pétrus between the church of Pomerol and the village of Catusseau, are situated on soil of clay and gravel. The wine is vinified and handled in exactly the same way as Pétrus (which is owned and managed by the same family), except only 40% new oak barrels are used each year.

Until the late 1970s, Trotanoy was an opulently rich, intense, full-bodied wine that usually needed a full decade of cellaring to reach its zenith. In some vintages the power, intensity, and concentration came remarkably close to matching that of Pétrus. It had an enviable track record of producing good, sometimes brilliant, wines in poor Bordeaux vintages. The 1967, 1972, and 1974 are examples of three vintages in which Trotanoy was among the best two or three wines of the entire Bordeaux region.

In the late 1970s the style became lighter, although Trotanoy appeared to return to full form with the extraordinarily opulent, rich, decadent 1982. Until 1995 there was a succession of good, rather than thrilling, wines. There is no question that there has been some major replanting of the microscopic vineyard of Trotanoy, and that the quality shifted at the same time that production from these younger vines was blended in. Whatever the case might be, Trotanoy no longer seems to be one of the top three or four wines of Pomerol, and it was surpassed in the 1980s (with the exception of the 1982 vintage) by such châteaux as Clinet, L'Eglise Clinet, Vieux Château Certan, Le Pin, Lafleur, La Fleur de Gay, L'Evangile, La Conseillante, and even Le Bon Pasteur in certain vintages. However, thanks to the competitiveness and talent of Christian Moueix and his staff, this situation appears to be changing. Recent vintages have all been strong, including a beautiful 1995 and sensational 1998, as well as 2000, 2001, and 2003.

Trotanoy is an expensive wine because it is highly regarded by connoisseurs the world over. Yet it rarely sells for more than half the price of Pétrus—a fact worth remembering since it does (in certain vintages) have more than just a casual resemblance to the great Pétrus itself.

CHATEAU TROTANOY

2003 Château Trotanoy

RATING: 90–92+ points

One of the most muscular, formidably tannic offerings of Pomerol (somewhat atypical for the vintage), the heady, full-bodied, powerful Trotanoy will need four to six years of cellaring. The tannin borders on being rustic, but there is a lot going on in this deep ruby/purple–colored 2003. Hints of scorched earth, multivitamins, black cherries, new saddle leather, and earth emerge from this impressive claret. The harvest was freakishly early, with the Merlot picked on September 2, 3, and 4, and the Cabernet Franc on September 9. Anticipated maturity: 2008–2020.

2001 Château Trotanoy

RATING: 90+ points

This virile offering's dense plum/garnet color is followed by aromas of saddle leather, undergrowth, and black fruits. Made in a brooding, medium-bodied, backward style for the vintage, it possesses good weight and richness, firm tannin, and a hint of truffles. Less charming and developed than La Fleur–Pétrus, this powerful, structured 2001 requires 2–3 years of cellaring, and should keep for 12–15.

2000 Château Trotanoy

RATING: 92+ points

I don't think this wine will ever live up to the extraordinary 1998, but it is not far off the mark. Dense plum/garnet–colored, it is closed aromatically, but aeration brings out hints of figs, black cherries, earth, and cedar. Sweet on the attack, dense, powerful, medium to full–bodied, and tannic, with a broodingly backward finish, patience will be required. Anticipated maturity: 2009–2030.

1998 Château Trotanoy

RATING: 96+ points

The finest Trotanoy since the 1961, this structured, formidably endowed, deep ruby/purple–colored, full-bodied, superrich wine exhibits notes of toffee, truffles, and abundant blackberry, cherry, and currant fruit. It cuts a large swath across the palate and possesses copious but sweet tannin as well as a chewy, muscular mid-palate and finish. This is a compelling effort from one of the great vineyards of Pomerol. Anticipated maturity: 2006–2035.

1995 Château Trotanoy

RATING: 93 points

Certainly the best Trotanoy between 1998 and 1982, the 1995 has a deep saturated ruby color that is dark to the rim. Relatively shut down when tasted in 2002 on several occasions, the wine, with coaxing, does offer some notes of earth, raspberry, black cherries, and a hint of licorice. Medium to full–bodied, powerful, and backward, it is an impressively constituted Trotanoy that is relatively large scaled, but the huge level of tannin also means it might be a modern-day version of the 1970. Time will tell. Anticipated maturity: 2010–2025.

1990 Château Trotanoy

RATING: 90 points

Very evolved and far more mature than its bigger sibling (the 1990 Pétrus), this dark, plum-colored wine is already showing some amber at the edge. It is forward and sweet, with sweet-and-sour cherry fruit intermixed with a hint of herbs, licorice, fig, and earth. The wine is medium-bodied with sweet fruit, low acidity, and a very nicely layered finish. All things considered, it is a very elegant, understated Trotanoy that is outstanding, but well behind the best Pomerols of the vintage. Anticipated maturity: now–2012.

1982 Château Trotanoy

RATING: 92 points

Fully mature, gorgeously fragrant, with a knockout nose of sweet herbs intermixed with toast, jammy strawberry, and black cherry fruit, as well as mocha and cedar, this dense, garnet-colored wine is medium to full–bodied, expansive, lush, with low acidity and a long, concentrated finish with considerable glycerin. It is not going to improve, but certainly this wine will hold for at least another 10–15 years.

CLASSIFICATION: Grand Cru

OWNER: Jean-Luc Thunevin and Murielle Andraud

ADDRESS: Château de Valandraud, 6, rue Guadet, F-33330 St.-Emilion, France

TELEPHONE: 33 05 57 55 09 13

TELEFAX: 33 05 57 55 09 12

E-MAIL: thunevin@thunevin.com

WEBSITE: www.thunevin.com

CONTACT: Jean-Luc Thunevin

VISITING POLICY: No visits

VINEYARDS

SURFACE AREA: 19.8 acres

GRAPE VARIETALS: 70% Merlot, 25% Cabernet Franc, 2.5% Malbec, 2.5% Cabernet Sauvignon

AVERAGE AGE OF THE VINES: 30 years

DENSITY OF PLANTATION: 6,500 vines

AVERAGE YIELDS: 30–40 hectoliters per hectare

WINEMAKING AND UPBRINGING

All grapes are hand-harvested from organically farmed vineyards. After a cold maceration, the vinification is very Burgundian (cold maceration, malolaction in barrel, aging on the lees), with not only pumping-over but *pigéage*. Malolactics take place in barrel, and the wine rests on its lees until the first racking. After 18 months in 100% new oak, the wine is bottled unfined and unfiltered.

ANNUAL PRODUCTION

Château de Valandraud: 11,000 bottles

Virginie de Valandraud: 10,000 bottles

AVERAGE PRICE (VARIABLE DEPENDING ON VINTAGE): $175–250

GREAT RECENT VINTAGES

2003, 2002, 2001, 1998, 1995, 1994, 1993

In 1989, Jean-Luc Thunevin and his wife, Murielle Andraud, purchased a small plot of 0.6 hectares in the valley of St.-Emilion between Pavie-Macquin and La Clotte. They undertook their first vintage in 1991, which they bottled themselves.

Since then, they have bought other plots and properties in St.-Sulpice de Faleyrens, in St.-Emilion, and in St.-Etienne de Lisse. Château de Valandraud is not officially classified but it is considered by many wine pro-fessionals as one of the best châteaux in all of the Bordeaux area. The obsessive-compulsive, highly talented proprietor Thunevin has the Cheshire cat's grin these days given the publicity and prices his unfined, unfiltered, superrich Valandraud is fetching. With Murielle Andraud, Thunevin established a microscopic estate from selected parcels in St.-Emilion. Having had experience with running wine shops and restaurants in St.-Emilion, and also being involved in the wine trade, Thunevin knows what it means to produce great wine.

Obviously the jury is still out as to how well Valandraud ages, but the wine is enormously rich, concentrated, and beautifully delineated. It has been extraordinary even in such difficult vintages as 1994, 1993, and 1992. More than any other St.-Emilion property, Valandraud has become the micro-treasure sought by billionaire wine collectors throughout the world. While Thunevin has no shortage of critics (largely the jealous aristocracy of Bordeaux), his influence continues to expand. He is one of the most sought-after consultants, and his dedication and commitment to excellence, as well as his tremendous palate (infinitely helped by his equally talented partner), has turned many obscure wines in St.-Emilion and its satellites into prime-time players for quality-minded consumers.

Along with Michel Rolland, Thunevin has inspired an entire new generation of young vignerons to produce wine of higher and higher quality. For this, all of Bordeaux has benefitted enormously.

CHATEAU DE VALANDRAUD

2003 Château de Valandraud

RATING: 93–96 points

The well-known Jean-Luc Thunevin, who has done so much to inspire a young generation of St.-Emilion wine producers, may have produced the finest wine in this estate's short history. Cropped at 28 hectoliters per hectare, there are just over 1,000 cases of this blend of 50% Merlot, 40% Cabernet Franc, and small portions of Malbec and Cabernet Sauvignon. An inky/blue/purple color accompanies a powerful perfume of black fruits, underbrush, licorice, crushed stones, cocoa, espresso, and spice box. It hits the palate with a thunderous display of power and fruit. With beautifully integrated tannin, a ripe personality, and a 50-second finish, this serious effort may be the biggest and longest-lived Valandraud has yet produced. Anticipated maturity: 2008–2020+.

2002 Château de Valandraud

RATING: 93 points

Another strong effort from Murielle Andraud and Jean-Luc Thunevin, the 2002 Valandraud possesses a saturated ruby/purple color in addition to scents of chocolate, espresso, black currants, and cherries. Dense, medium to full–bodied, concentrated, and muscular, the 2002 is less silky and opulent than the 2001, but still impressively endowed and well balanced. It should shed much of its tannin in 2–5 years, and drink well for 12–15+. Anticipated maturity: 2007–2018.

2001 Château de Valandraud

RATING: 94 points

As hard as it may be to believe, Valandraud's 2001 is better than their 2000. One of the great efforts from Murielle Andraud and Jean-Luc Thunevin, the 2001 Valandraud boasts a saturated plum/purple color as well as a sumptuously sweet nose of Valrhona chocolate intertwined with espresso roast, blackberries, cherry jam, and currants. Full-bodied, opulent, voluptuously textured, pure, rich, and seriously endowed, this is a brilliant effort from Bordeaux's leading revolutionary. Anticipated maturity: 2007–2020.

2000 Château de Valandraud

RATING: 93 points

Jean-Luc Thunevin tends to be humble when he talks about his 2000, as if there were something wrong with it. Well, it is a spectacular wine, and having tasted it three times from bottle, I am in love with it. Dense purple, with a glorious nose of espresso, cocoa, chocolate, plum, black currant, and cherry, offering a true smorgasbord of heavenly delights, this medium to full–bodied wine still shows some relatively firm tannin, but the low acidity, layered, multitextured mouth-feel, and tremendous purity are hallmarks of the Thunevin wine-making style. However, this might be one Valandraud that actually needs three to five years of cellaring prior to drinking. Anticipated maturity: 2008–2019.

1999 Château de Valandraud

RATING: 90 points

Sweet coffee, mocha, leather, black cherry, and currant flavors dominate the pure, well-delineated, opulently textured, hedonistic 1999 Valandraud. It possesses definition, length, and a singular personality. Anticipated maturity: now–2015.

1998 Château de Valandraud

RATING: 93 points

A classic St.-Emilion, the 1998 exhibits a dark plum/purple color as well as an elegant nose of mocha, coffee, cherries, blackberries, and chocolate. It has turned out to have more finesse and be less exotic than past vintages. This medium to full–bodied, beautifully concentrated wine reveals chocolate overtones in the aromas and flavors. With exceptional purity, balance, and length, it should turn out to be one of the most elegant Valandrauds yet produced. Anticipated maturity: now–2020.

1996 Château de Valandraud

RATING: 91 points

This 1996 has firmed up significantly since bottling. This viscous wine displays the telltale thickness of color (saturated, dark ruby/plum/purple). The exotic bouquet is just beginning to form, offering up notes of iodine, roasted coffee, jammy black fruits, and toast. In the mouth, it is medium to full–bodied, with sweet tannin, terrific texture, and outstanding purity and length. Anticipated maturity: now–2018.

1995 Château de Valandraud

RATING: 95 points

This splendid Valandraud ranks with the finest wines Jean-Luc Thunevin has produced. The wine exhibits an opaque purple color and a sensational nose of roasted herbs, black fruits (cherries, currants, and blackberries), and high-class toasty oak (the latter component is more of a nuance than a

Jean-Luc Thunevin

dominant characteristic). Very concentrated, with layers of fruit, glycerin, and extract, yet seamlessly constructed, this wine contains the stuff of greatness and appears to be the finest Valandraud yet produced. The finish lasts for more than 30 seconds. The wine's high tannin is barely noticeable because of the ripeness and richness of fruit. Anticipated maturity: now–2020.

1994 Château de Valandraud

RATING: 92+ points

An opaque purple color and a closed set of aromatics (sweet black currant and woodsy, smoky aromas emerge with airing) are revealed in this blockbuster 1994. The wine possesses fabulous purity, great flavor intensity, a sweet inner core of fruit on the mid-palate, and a full-bodied, layered, viscous finish. It is unquestionably one of the finest wines of the vintage. Anticipated maturity: now–2020.

1993 Château de Valandraud

RATING: 93 points

This is undoubtedly one of the most concentrated wines of the vintage. The color is an opaque purple, and the wine exhibits fabulously sweet, ripe, black cherry, and cassis fruit nicely infused with subtle oak and a touch of minerals and truffles. Full-bodied, with exceptional density and no hard edges, the unbelievably concentrated 1993 Valandraud is a tour de force, in a vintage that does not seem capable of producing wines such as this. Drink it over the next 15–20 years.

CHATEAU CLIMENS

CLASSIFICATION: First Growth in 1855

OWNER: Bérénice Lurton

ADDRESS: Château Climens, 33720 Barsac, France

TELEPHONE: 33 05 56 27 15 33

TELEFAX: 33 05 56 27 21 04

E-MAIL: contact@chateau-climens.fr

WEBSITE: www.chateau-climens.fr

CONTACT: Bérénice Lurton

VISITING POLICY: By appointment only, Monday–Friday, 8:30 A.M.–noon, 2–6 P.M.; closed in August and during the harvest

VINEYARDS

SURFACE AREA: 74 acres

GRAPE VARIETALS: 100% Semillon

AVERAGE AGE OF THE VINES: 35 years

DENSITY OF PLANTATION: 6,600 vines per hectare

AVERAGE YIELDS: 13 hectoliters per hectare for the estate, 7 hectoliters per hectare for the first wine (on average over 20 years)

WINEMAKING AND UPBRINGING

The Climens *terroir* is incomparable. Situated on the highest point of the Barsac appellation, it stretches out around the château in a single continuous vineyard. The red soil, dotted with stones, is made up of a thin layer of clayey, ferruginous sand on a substratum of fissured starfish limestone.

The combination of these soils and the slope create excellent natural drainage. Aided by specific weather conditions of alternating mist and sun, the grapes are subject to an early development of noble rot, or *Botrytis cinerea*. This microscopic mushroom develops on ripe grapes, inducing the concentration and structure modification necessary for the elaboration of great sweet wines.

Each grape is carefully checked on a sorting tray in the vineyard before being pressed in the cellars. Then the grapes must undergo fermentation in barrels, without the addition of cultured yeasts.

The beginning of the maturation takes place on the fine lees, to aid the development of delicate fresh fruit and floral aromas. Barrel fermentation also allows vinification in small separate volumes.

The wines are tasted repeatedly over several months until the final blend truly represents the best of the vintage. Integrity at Climens is paramount, and lesser vintages are declassified, such as the 1984, 1987, 1992, and 1993. Climens stays in barrel approximately 20 months, after which it is bottled.

ANNUAL PRODUCTION

Château Climens: 25,000 bottles

Cyprès de Climens: 10,500 bottles

AVERAGE PRICE (VARIABLE DEPENDING ON VINTAGE): $45–125

GREAT RECENT VINTAGES

2003, 2002, 2001, 2000, 1999, 1997, 1991, 1990, 1989, 1988, 1986, 1983

The most famous estate of the Barsac/Sauternes region is, without question, Château d'Yquem, which makes the most concentrated and expensive sweet white wine in France. But the wine I find most companionable with food, and most complex and compelling to drink, is that of Château Climens in Barsac. Climens has been owned since 1971 by the Lurton family, which presides over a considerable empire of Bordeaux estates, including the famous Margaux properties of Châteaux Brane Cantenac, Durfort-Vivens, and Desmirail. All of these properties produce good wine, but none of them has quite the standing in its respective commune that Château Climens has in Barsac.

For much of the last two centuries, Climens has been considered one of the two leading estates in the commune of Barsac (the other is Coutet). The 72-acre vineyard and modest one-story château (the only distinguishing physical characteristics are two slate-roofed

towers at each end) is located just north of the tiny village of La Pinesse, sitting on the highest plateau of the Barsac region, a full 70 feet above sea level. Most observers claim that this elevation contributes to the vineyard's excellent drainage, which gives Climens a distinct advantage over lower-lying properties in wet years.

While the names of most châteaux here can be traced back to former owners, no one is quite sure how Climens acquired its name. For most of the 19th century the château was owned by the Lacoste family, who produced a wine they called Château Climenz-Lacoste. At that time the vineyard's 70 acres achieved an annual production of 6,000 cases, but the devastating effects of

phylloxera in the late 19th century destroyed most of the vineyards in Bordeaux, including those of Climens. In 1871, Climens was sold to Alfred Ribet, the owner of another estate called Château Pexoto, which was subsequently absorbed into what is today known as Château Sigalas Rabaud.

In 1885, Ribet sold the property to Henri Gounouilhou, whose family managed Climens until the dynamic Lucien Lurton purchased it in 1971. It was Gounouilhou, director of Bordeaux's most famous daily newspaper, *Sud-Ouest,* and his successors who raised not only the level of quality at Climens but also the public's awareness of this great estate. The legendary vintages of 1947, 1937, and 1929 enabled Climens to surpass the reputation of its larger neighbor, Château Coutet, and rival even that of the great Château d'Yquem.

The Lurtons, Brigitte and Bérénice, have merely enhanced the extraordinary reputation of this outstanding property. Their only change has been the removal of the small quantities of Muscadelle planted in the gravel, red sand, and clay-like soil of the vineyard. The current plantings, which they believe produce the best wine from the *terroir* of Château Climens, are 100% Semillon. The Lurtons eschew Sauvignon in the blend because it has a tendency to lose its aroma after several years. The average age of the vines is maintained at an impressive 35 years, as the Lurtons believe in replanting only 3–4% of the vineyard per year. In addition, their yield of 16 hectoliters per hectare remains one of the smallest of all the estates in the Sauternes/Barsac region. (Today, when most major wine-producing estates are doubling the yields from their vineyards, Climens commendably maintains an average annual production of only 3,333 cases, from a vineyard area 1.6 acres larger than it was in the mid-19th century.) No doubt this statistic alone accounts for the exceptional concentration and quality of the wine produced.

The wine is fermented in cask and aged for 12–18 months in 55-gallon barrels before being bottled. In most vintages, 33% new oak is used; this is believed to develop the proper marriage of honeyed pineapple-and-apricot-flavored fruit with the vanilla toastiness of new oak barrels.

What makes Climens so precious is that it produces the region's most compellingly elegant wine. There is no doubt that for sheer power, viscosity, and opulence, Climens will never rival Château d'Yquem, nor even Château Rieussec, Château Suduiraut, and the luxurious, rare Cuvée Madame of Château Coutet. However, if one measures the greatness of a wine by its extraordinary balance and finesse, Climens not only has no peers, it deserves the reputation as the most quintessentially graceful wine of the region. Many Sauternes can border on the cloying, but in the top vintages Climens seems to combine a rich, luscious, exotic character of honeyed pineapple fruit with a remarkable inner core of lemony acidity—giving the wine zestiness, precision to its flavors, and a profound, hauntingly pleasurable bouquet.

Consistently one of the most profound wines of Barsac/Sauternes, this wine, made from 100% Semillon, is one of the most ravishing examples of just how much elegance can be built into a powerful racehorse style of wine.

CHATEAU CLIMENS

2003 Château Climens

RATING: 94–97 points

Atypically powerful, unctuous, and rich, the 2003 Climens, even at this early date, is vaguely reminiscent of the 1990. Light goldish–colored with a green hue, the wine shows oodles of honeysuckle, very sweet, powerful flavors, an unctuous texture, and already burgeoning complexity. The wine seems on a relatively faster evolutionary track than the monumental 2001, and perhaps is also slightly sweeter and fuller, but whether it ever achieves that wine's surreal elegance remains to be seen. Nevertheless, this is a brilliant effort. Anticipated maturity: 2010–2035.

2002 Château Climens

RATING: 94 points

I suspect most readers will find it hard to get excited about the 2002 vintage for the sweet wines of Barsac and Sauternes after what appears to be a prodigious 2001. However, 2002 is a very fine wine, superior to such vintages as 2000. This wine possesses plenty of botrytis, but has neither the impressive definition nor supreme elegance of the 2001. This is a sweet, full-bodied, fat, concentrated, intense effort that is showing well, but somewhat in the style of the 1989. Anticipated maturity: 2010–2035.

2001 Château Climens

RATING: 100 points

A prodigious offering, the 2001 Climens' light medium gold color with a greenish hue is followed by ethereal aromas of tropical fruits (primarily pineapple), honeysuckle, and flowers. It is a medium-bodied wine of monumental richness, extraordinary precision/delineation, great purity, and moderate sweetness. The finish seemingly lasts forever. This monumental effort is the stuff of legends. Anticipated maturity: 2010–2040+.

2000 Château Climens

RATING: 89+ points

The proprietors are extremely happy with what they were able to produce in 2000. Even though the vintage has a bad reputation, those producers who included only the early-picked grapes in their final blend have often turned out wines that are close to being exceptional. The yields for this were microscopic (four hectoliters per hectare) and the wine, although somewhat monolithic (I tasted it right after bottling), shows honeyed citrus, pineapple, a hint of pear, and a bit of butter and honeysuckle. The wine is medium-bodied and elegant, with superb purity, always a hallmark of this great estate. Anticipated maturity: 2007–2020.

1999 Château Climens
RATING: 90 points
Medium-deep gold, this wine shows relatively high acidity, a somewhat monolithic character, but great purity, with the telltale honeysuckle, pineapple, and some tropical fruits, along with mineral and a very subtle dose of oak. Only 63% of the crop made it into this Climens, and the wine was produced from nine hectoliters per hectare in the vintage that took place between September 19 and October 18. This wine should be very long lived, but obviously will never hit the highlights of the great vintages such as 2001, 1997, 1996, 1990, 1989, and 1988. Anticipated maturity: 2008–2025.

1998 Château Climens
RATING: 92 points
This is a very precocious and evolved style of Climens that should be immensely pleasing to all those looking for a moderately sweet Barsac to drink over the next 15–20 years. Made from 13 hectoliters per hectare (64% of the crop made it into this Climens), this 100% Semillon Barsac shows a medium-gold color with some green undertones. The wine has superb ripeness and unctuousness on the palate, with terrific intensity; decent acidity; and evolved honeysuckle, buttery, tropical fruit, and botrytised flavors. Anticipated maturity: now–2020.

1997 Château Climens
RATING: 93 points
A great classic from Climens, with the telltale nose of white flowers intermixed with buttered pineapple, citrus, honeysuckle, and vanilla, this medium to full–bodied wine has great precision, purity, and stature. Anticipated maturity: now–2022.

1996 Château Climens
RATING: 90 points
A very delicate, finesse-styled Climens (made from 100% Semillon), this wine has pretty, almost steely citrus notes, with a hint of honeysuckle and buttery grapefruit. The wine shows good acidity and builds incrementally in the mouth. It is not a heavyweight, monster-size wine by any means, but it is pure elegance and pedigree. Anticipated maturity: now–2015.

1990 Château Climens
RATING: 96 points
This vintage for Climens goes from strength to strength. The yields, which were a microscopic 10 hectoliters per hectare, have produced nearly 3,000 cases of a spectacular wine that has a medium-deep-gold color and a gorgeous nose of honeysuckle, vanilla, pineapple, acacia, crème brûlée, and roasted nuttiness. In the mouth, it is full-bodied, atypically powerful for a Climens (the residual sugar of 130 grams per liter is very high for this estate), and the massive finish goes on for well over a minute. In spite of such exceptional richness, there is good acidity, giving the wine uplift and definition. Anticipated maturity: now–2035.

1989 Château Climens
RATING: 94 points
This wine has continued to evolve, and although I still prefer its two closest siblings, the elegance of the 1988 and the power and mass of the 1990, this is a profound example of Climens. Produced from 11 hectoliters per hectare, this wine achieved 14.5% alcohol and has 123 grams per liter of residual sugar. The wine shows deep medium-gold color, a glorious nose of

crème brûlée intermixed with lanolin, candle wax, honeyed citrus, vanilla, and something that seems vaguely similar to passion fruit. Very full-bodied, quite sweet, with exceptional concentration, this looks to be a glorious Climens and has proved far better out of bottle than I thought from cask. Anticipated maturity: now–2025.

1988 Château Climens
RATING: 96 points
One of my all-time favorite Climens, but far less evolved than the 1990 or 1989, this is the quintessential elegant style of Barsac. Made from 12 hectoliters per hectare, with 14.4% sugar and 106 grams of residual sugar per liter, this wine has a very classy, delicate nose of tangerine skin, melted butter, overripe pineapples, and subtle toasty oak. The wine is medium to full–bodied, does not quite have the mass and sweetness of either the 1990 or the 1989, but there seem to be more nuances, and its lightness on its feet is impressive for a wine of such power and richness. This is a glorious Climens that still needs time in the bottle. Anticipated maturity: 2006–2025.

1986 Château Climens
RATING: 96 points
Another extraordinary Climens from a tiny crop (less than 1,000 cases) that achieved 14.5% alcohol and residual sugar of 101 grams per liter, the 1986 Climens shows a deep-gold color and a crème brûlée nose with orange marmalade, pineapple liqueur, and tropical fruits, along with some coconut and vanilla in the nose. The wine is medium to full–bodied, with great concentration, very impressive levels of botrytis, and a long finish with hints of caramel and marmalade in an unctuous yet well-delineated style. Anticipated maturity: now–2020.

1983 Château Climens
RATING: 93 points
A beautiful wine that continues to go from strength to strength, the honey, popcorn, pineapple, and grapefruit notes are present, along with hints of candle wax and lanolin. The wine is very rich, with good acidity, considerable botrytis, and a full-bodied, expansive, intense mouth-feel. Another brilliant wine that seems to be closer to its plateau of maturity. Anticipated maturity: now–2016.

CLASSIFICATION: First Growth in 1855

OWNER: Domaines Barons de Rothschild (Lafite)

ADDRESS: Château Rieussec, 33210 Fargues, France

TELEPHONE: 33 05 57 98 14 14

TELEFAX: 33 05 57 98 14 10

WEBSITE: www.lafite.com

CONTACT: Eric Kohler

VISITING POLICY: By appointment only (Monday–Friday)

VINEYARDS

SURFACE AREA: 186 acres

GRAPE VARIETALS: 90% Sémillon, 6% Sauvignon,
    4% Muscadelle

AVERAGE AGE OF THE VINES: 25 years

DENSITY OF PLANTATION: 7,300 vines per hectare

AVERAGE YIELDS: 15 hectoliters per hectare

WINEMAKING AND UPBRINGING

Rieussec's philosophy is based on very strict selection during the successive sortings and also when assembling the Château Rieussec. Fermentation takes place in oak barrels that come from the Château Lafite cooperage. Each year 60% new oak barrels are used for the *élevage* of the Château Rieussec; it takes around 30 months for the Grand Vin.

ANNUAL PRODUCTION

Château Rieussec: Production varies depending on the vintage, but average is 6,000 cases per year (but no production in 1993 and low production in 2000 with just 3,000 cases).

Château de Cosse (or Clos Labère), second wine of Château Rieussec, Sauternes: 2,000 to 6,000 cases per year

"R" de Rieussec, white dry, Graves: Average 2,000 cases per year

AVERAGE PRICE (VARIABLE DEPENDING ON VINTAGE): $45–100

GREAT RECENT VINTAGES

2003, 2002, 2001, 2000, 1990, 1989, 1988

In the 18th century, the Rieussec estate belonged to the Carmes de Langon monks. The estate was confiscated during the French Revolution and sold at a public sale as an "object of national heritage" to Mr. Marheilhac, the owner of Château La Louvière in Léognan.

Rieussec's history reflects many owners: Charles Crepin (1870), Paul Defolie (1892), Mr. Bannil (1907), then the Gasqueton family (owner of Château Calon-Ségur of Saint-Estèphe), P. F. Berry during the war (an American citizen and brother of the Vicomte de Bouzet),

Mr. Balaresque (1957), and Albert Vuillier (1971), who was passionate about Sauternes "sweet wines."

Approaching the Sauternes appellation, visitors can spot Château Rieussec and its prominent lookout tower on one of the highest hillsides. The Rieussec vineyard, spread across the hillsides of Fargues and Sauternes overlooking the left bank of the Garonne, has the highest altitude after Yquem. Quite surprising for a Bordeaux property, the entire vineyard is one single unit, much of it bordering the hallowed Yquem.

Rieussec has always had an outstanding reputation, but after its acquisition by Albert Vuillier in 1971, the quality improved even more, largely because of the increase in new oak and more frequent passes through the vineyard to harvest only heavily botrytised grapes. In fact, some critics of Rieussec claim that the color of Vuillier's wines become too deep as they age (like the 1976, for example). Vuillier sold Rieussec to the Domaines Barons de Rothschild, which has spared no expense and permitted no compromise in the making of Rieussec. The results have been truly profound offerings that are now routinely among the top three or four wines of the appellation. Wealthy collectors will no doubt argue for decades whether 2003, 2002, 2001, 1990, 1989, or 1988 produced the most profound Rieussec.

CHÂTEAU RIEUSSEC

2003 Château Rieussec

RATING: 93–96 points
Light to medium gold in color with a crème brûlée nose intermixed with hints of toffee, caramelized oranges, and melted butter, this full-bodied, rather lavish, extravagantly rich wine is quite intense, chewy, and sweet, yet has good acidity and nicely integrated wood and alcohol. This is a big Rieussec that comes close to rivaling the extraordinary 2001. Anticipated maturity: 2011–2028.

2002 Château Rieussec

RATING: 94 points
Medium gold with a roasted tropical fruit nose, hints of orange marmalade, and crème brûlée, this is a medium to full–bodied, very rich, dense wine that exhibits enormous potential. It is somewhat fruitier than the prodigious 2001. Anticipated maturity: 2009–2035.

2001 Château Rieussec

RATING: 99 points
A monumental effort, the 2001 Rieussec boasts a light to medium–gold color in addition to a fabulous perfume of honeysuckle, smoky oak, caramelized tropical fruits, crème brûlée, and Grand Marnier. The wine is massive and full-bodied yet neither over the top nor heavy because of good acidity. With intense botrytis as well as a 70–75-second finish, this amazing Sauternes will be at its apogee between 2010 and 2035.

2000 Château Rieussec

RATING: 91 points
The very deep golden, almost amber color reminds me of the 1983 in its youth. Orange marmalade, crème brûlée, brown butter, and smoke all emerge from the relatively complex, very attractive, and full-bodied 2000. The wine has tremendous density, good acidity, and loads of fruit and botrytis. This is undoubtedly a candidate for the wine of the vintage in Sauternes. Anticipated maturity: now–2018.

1999 Château Rieussec

RATING: 91 points
Very good acidity characterizes this backward, somewhat tightly knit but honeyed wine, with notes of white flowers, peach, caramel, and relatively good botrytis. The wine is medium to full–bodied, not the most extravagant or flamboyant of Rieussecs because of its rather tightly knit personality, but long, layered, and impressive. However, patience is required. Anticipated maturity: 2006–2020.

1998 Château Rieussec

RATING: 92 points
A very strong effort from Rieussec, this wine shows medium deep-gold color and a sweet nose of smoky, toasty oak, vanilla, coconut, honeysuckle, peach, and even some pineapple. It is very rich, very sweet, and in contrast to its younger sibling, the 1999, very forward and evolved. Drink it over the next 12–15 years. It is a candidate for the wine of the vintage.

1997 Château Rieussec

RATING: 93 points
A terrific example of Rieussec, this full-bodied, very sweet wine shows tremendous botrytis and loads of honeysuckle, caramel, peach, and crème brûlée in a full-bodied, very flamboyant, opulent style. There is enough acidity to provide uplift and to balance out the relatively high level of sugar (120 grams per liter). Like most vintages, this is a blend of 90% Semillon, 7% Sauvignon, and 3% Muscadelle. Anticipated maturity: now–2025.

1996 Château Rieussec

RATING: 92+ points

Deep gold with notes of new oak, smoke, caramel, crème brûlée, and honeysuckle, this relatively sweet yet structured wine seems to have closed down since I first tasted it after bottling. The wine is layered, very full, with a tremendous upside. However, patience will be required, as this looks to be a potentially very long-lived Rieussec. Anticipated maturity: 2008–2040.

1990 Château Rieussec

RATING: 94 points

A spectacular wine with a relatively evolved gold color, the tremendous nose of spice box intermixed with caramelized peaches, apricots, and honeysuckle soars from the glass. The wine is very full-bodied, thick, and juicy, with just enough acidity to balance out the wine's power and intense sweetness. This is layered, very viscous stuff that seems to be drinkable already but no doubt will last for another 20–25 years. Anticipated maturity: now–2025.

1989 Château Rieussec

RATING: 93 points

What fun can be had, as I had in 2003, tasting the great trilogy of Rieussecs—1990, 1989, and 1988—together. The 1989 seems to be a synthesis in style between the more delicate, elegant, nuanced, almost restrained 1988 and the muscular, blockbuster 1990. This is no wimpish wine, however. The medium deep-gold color is not quite as intense as the 1990, but certainly darker than the 1988. The big, smoky, earthy nose offers up notes of crème brûlée, honeysuckle, ripe pineapples, and other tropical fruits. The wine is quite full-bodied, with low acidity, very sweet, and luxuriously rich, with a viscous texture and a huge, concentrated finish. This wine seems to continue to put on weight and become even more impressive, much like the 1990. Anticipated maturity: now–2025.

1988 Château Rieussec

RATING: 94 points

Perhaps it is the sheer delicacy of this wine that has always impressed me. It seems to take a backseat to the more flamboyant and powerful 1990 and 1989, but the nuances, the very polite yet authoritatively intense notes of coconut, orange marmalade, crème brûlée, honeysuckle, and some oak all seem to be beautifully integrated in both the aromas and flavors. The wine is full-bodied, not as sweet as either the 1990 or 1989, but extremely stylish, with good acidity and tremendous delineation and uplift. It is a brilliant Rieussec that should prove almost immortal. Anticipated maturity: now–2035.

1986 Château Rieussec

RATING: 90 points

This wine seems to have become less impressive as it has aged. Perhaps it has just shut down, but I always seemed to score it one to three points higher than I did recently. The wine has a deep medium-gold color, a sweet nose of honeysuckle, white corn, peach, and some toasty oak. The wine is medium to full-bodied, with a hint of marmalade, apricot, and roasted nuts. Good acidity gives the wine elegance and definition. However, the finish seems to be drying out and is noticeably shorter than it once was. Perhaps this wine is just going through an awkward stage. Anticipated maturity: now–2015.

1983 Château Rieussec

RATING: 92 points

Light golden with just the slightest tint of green, the 1983 Rieussec, from an excellent year for Sauternes, is certainly one of this property's greatest wines. Well structured, with excellent acidity and a deep, long, rich, full-bodied, viscous texture, this wine, despite the richness and power, is neither heavy nor cloying. It has gorgeous balance and a very long, lingering, spectacular finish. One of the great successes of the vintage. Anticipated maturity: now.

CLASSIFICATION: First Growth in 1855

OWNER: LVMH

ADDRESS: Château d'Yquem, 33210 Sauternes, France

TELEPHONE: 33 05 57 98 07 07

TELEFAX: 33 05 57 98 07 08

E-MAIL: info@yquem.fr

WEBSITE: www.yquem.fr

CONTACT: Valérie Lailheugue

VISITING POLICY: Appointments arranged for professionals and wine lovers upon written request. Visits are organized Monday–Friday only in the afternoon, at 2 or 3:30 P.M.

VINEYARDS

SURFACE AREA: 308.8 acres, of which 254.2 are in production

GRAPE VARIETALS: 80% Semillon, 20% Sauvignon

AVERAGE AGE OF THE VINES: 30 years (3 hectares pulled out and 3 hectares replanted each year)

DENSITY OF PLANTATION: 6,500 vines per hectare

AVERAGE YIELDS: 8 hectoliters per hectare

WINEMAKING AND UPBRINGING

Several successive pickings of individual grapes, exclusively those affected by *Botrytis cinerea* ("noble rot"); 20 degrees potential alcohol of minimal level (1145 density). There are on average six selective pickings that can be spread over six weeks.

Fermentation and maturing occurs in 100% new stave-wood barrels. The wine is matured for three and a half years before bottling. There is never any chaptalization.

ANNUAL PRODUCTION

Château d'Yquem: 110,000 bottles on average

"Y": dry white Bordeaux produced only in certain years, provided some very restrictive conditions are met. The first vintage was 1959. The existing vintages are 2000, 1996, 1994, 1988, 1986, 1985, 1980, 1979, 1978, 1977, 1973, 1972, 1971, 1969, 1968, 1966, 1965, 1964, 1962, 1960, 1959.

AVERAGE PRICE (VARIABLE DEPENDING ON VINTAGE): $200–500

GREAT RECENT VINTAGES

2001, 1999, 1997, 1995, 1990, 1989, 1988, 1986, 1983

Historians can verify that the land surrounding the estate was known as Yquem as far back as 1593, when the name was mentioned in a land conveyance. The château, or parts of it, was constructed in the 12th century. By the time the Lur Saluces family became owners in 1785, the wine had already developed an international reputation. Thomas Jefferson had ordered 250 bottles of the 1784, and later acquired 360 bottles of 1787 on behalf of President George Washington, and another 120 bottles for himself. Yquem became even more popular in Russia, where the tsars were great admirers and purchasers of this elixir. Certainly Yquem's fame has never wavered since.

Yquem, located in the heart of the Sauternes region, sits magnificently atop a small hill overlooking the surrounding vineyards of many of the premiers crus classés. Between 1785 and 1997 this vast estate was in the hands of just one family. Comte Alexandre de Lur Saluces is the most recent member of this family to manage it, having taken over for his uncle in 1968. In 1997, the extended family sold the estate to the giant Moët-Hennessy conglomerate. The sale was unsuccessfully contested by Comte de Lur Saluces, who was retained as administrator until 2004, when he was replaced with Pierre Lurton, who also manages Cheval Blanc.

Yquem's greatness and uniqueness are certainly a result of a number of factors. First, it has a perfect location that is said to have its own microclimate. Second, the Lur Saluces family installed an elaborate drainage system with more than 60 miles of pipes. The third, which is the biggest reason why Yquem is so superior to its neighbors, is a fanatical obsession with producing only the finest wines regardless of financial loss or trouble.

At Yquem they proudly boast that only one glass of wine per vine is produced. The grapes are picked one by one at perfect maturity by a group of 150 pickers, who frequently spend six to eight weeks at Yquem and go through the vineyard a minimum of four times. In 1964 they canvassed the vineyard thirteen separate times, and harvested grapes that were ultimately deemed unsuitable, leaving Yquem with no production

whatsoever in that vintage. Few winemaking estates are willing or financially able to declassify the entire crop.

Yquem has unbelievable aging potential. Because it is so rich, opulent, and sweet, the majority is consumed before it ever reaches its tenth birthday. However, Yquem almost always needs 15–20 years to show best, and the great vintages will be fresh and decadently rich for as long as 50–75 or more years. The greatest Yquem I ever drank was the 1921. It was remarkably fresh and alive, with a luxuriousness and richness I shall never forget.

This passionate commitment to quality does not stop in the vineyard. The wine is aged for more than three years in new oak casks, and 20% of the total crop volume is lost due to evaporation. When the chateau's management deems the wine ready for bottling, a severe selection of only the best casks is made. In excellent years, such as 1980, 1976, and 1975, 20% of the barrels

were eliminated. In difficult years, such as 1979, 60% of the wine was declassified, and in the troublesome vintage of 1978, 85% of the wine was declared unworthy of being sold as Yquem. To my knowledge, no other property has such a ruthless selection process. Yquem is never filtered for fear of removing some of the richness.

Yquem also produces a dry wine called "Y." It is a distinctive wine, with a bouquet not unlike that of Yquem, but oaky and dry to the taste and usually very full-bodied and noticeably alcoholic. It is a powerful wine and, to my palate, best served with a rich food such as foie gras. Yquem, unlike other famous Bordeaux wines, is not sold *en primeur* or as a wine future. The wine is usually released four years after the vintage at a very high price, but given the labor involved, the risk, and the brutal selection process, it is one of the few luxury-priced wines that merits a stratospheric price tag.

CHATEAU D'YQUEM

2001 Château d'Yquem

RATING: 100 points

An example of perfection, the 2001 Yquem reveals a hint of green in its light gold color. While somewhat reticent aromatically, with airing it offers up honeyed tropical fruit, orange marmalade, pineapple, sweet crème brûlée, and buttered nut–like scents. In the mouth, it is full-bodied with gorgeously refreshing acidity as well as massive concentration and unctuousness. Everything is uplifted and given laser-like focus by refreshing acidity. This large-scale, youthful Yquem should take its place among the most legendary vintages of the past, and will age effortlessly for 75+ years. Anticipated maturity: 2010–2075.

1998 Château d'Yquem

RATING: 95 points

The 1998 Yquem is a great success. Made in an elegant style, it is not a blockbuster such as 1990, 1989, and 1988. It is well delineated, with wonderfully sweet aromas of crème brûlée, pineapples, apricots, and white flowers. Medium to full–bodied, it is not as sweet as the biggest/richest Yquem vintages, but it is gorgeously pure, precise, and strikingly complex. Already approachable, it should evolve for 30–50 years . . . without a doubt.

1997 Château d'Yquem

RATING: 96 points

A sensational Yquem, and probably the best Yquem since the 1990, although I would not discount the 1996 finally turning out to be nearly this good. Yquem's 1997 shows a light-gold color and a gorgeous nose of caramel, honeysuckle, peach, apricot, and smoky wood. The wine is very full-bodied, unctuously textured, with good underlying acidity and loads of sweetness and glycerin. It looks to be a very great vintage for Yquem. Anticipated maturity: now–2055.

1996 Château d'Yquem

RATING: 95+ points

Compared with the rather flamboyant aromatics of the 1997, Yquem's 1996 plays it closer to the vest, although there is a lot below the surface; it just needs more coaxing. Light gold with a tight but promising nose of roasted hazelnuts intermixed with crème brûlée, vanilla beans, honey, orange marmalade, and peach, this medium to full–bodied Yquem has loads of power but a sense of restraint and a more measured style. The acidity also seems to be holding the wine close to the vest. The weight is there, the texture impressive, and the purity, as always, impeccable. Patience will probably be a virtue with this vintage. Anticipated maturity: 2012–2060.

1995 Château d'Yquem

RATING: 93 points

Hints of honeysuckle, orange marmalade, vanilla beans, and toasty oak are present in the moderately intense aromatics. In the mouth the wine is medium to full–bodied, with good acidity, a somewhat monolithic character at present, but a long, concentrated, relatively sweet finish, with good acidity. Anticipated maturity: 2007–2035.

1994 Château d'Yquem

RATING: 90 points

Disjointed early in its life, this wine seems to be taking on more weight and focus. Medium gold, with a honeyed nose intermixed with toast, coconut, and a hint of pineapple as well as peaches, this medium-bodied Yquem is not one of the more ostentatious vintages, but exceptionally well made and certainly capable of lasting 30+ years. Anticipated maturity: 2008–2030.

1990 Château d'Yquem

RATING: 98+ points

A colossal Yquem from a blockbuster, very powerful, and very sweet vintage in the Barsac/Sauternes region, this medium gold–colored wine is evolving at a glacial pace, as is so common with this singular sweet wine. The nose has not moved much over the last five or six years, but plenty of coconut, tropical fruit, honeysuckle, and crème caramel notes emerge. Very full-bodied, extremely viscous, yet with enough acidity to provide uplift and focus, this is an enormously constituted Yquem that should be one of the great vintages for this château, and one to last nearly 100 years. Like most vintages, it can be drunk in its infancy (that's where it is, even though it is 14 years old), but it will continue to develop even greater nuances. Anticipated maturity: now–2075.

1989 Château d'Yquem

RATING: 98 points

What a remarkable trilogy of vintages for Château d'Yquem (I am speaking of the 1990, 1989, and 1988). This vintage leans more toward the 1990 than 1988 in style. It is a very unctuously textured, medium gold–colored Yquem that is oozing with honey-soaked oranges, pineapples, apricots, and peaches. This is a very powerful, rich, thick wine, with loads of glycerin, fabulous aromatics, and seemingly low acidity, but mind-boggling levels of depth and concentration, and a finish that goes on for well over a minute. Like the 1990, it is a bit more flamboyant than its more restrained sibling, the 1988, and tends to be more impressive in terms of power and richness than the more nuanced 1988. A great, great Yquem! Anticipated maturity: now–2065.

1988 Château d'Yquem

RATING: 99 points

This remarkable wine is much more backward, less flamboyant, and more gentlemanly than the 1990 or 1989. Its light-golden color is more youthful than its younger siblings, the bouquet powerful but restrained, with subtle yet intense notes of coconut, orange marmalade, crème brûlée, peach, and white corn emerging very gently but authoritatively. In the mouth it builds incrementally, as this is a wine of enormous richness and power but far higher acidity than the 1990 or 1989. The wine is relatively light on its feet for such a powerful, highly extracted, and sensational effort. This is certainly one of the great Yquems, and probably more along the style of the 1975 than more recent vintages. Anticipated maturity: 2010–2070.

1987 Château d'Yquem

RATING: 90 points

A sleeper vintage for Yquem, hardly one of the great Yquems, but well made, more medium-bodied than full, with a relatively precocious/evolved personality, the 1987 Yquem shows notes of buttered hazelnuts, crème brûlée, smoke, and peach jam. It is moderately sweet but showing evidence of approaching full maturity. Anticipated maturity: now–2020.

1986 Château d'Yquem

RATING: 97 points

Starting to show some secondary nuances after nearly 18 years (this is just additional evidence of how slow this wine ages), the 1986 has a medium-gold color and a gorgeous nose of vanilla beans intermixed with sweet, honey-drenched apricots, peaches, and hazelnuts. The wine is very opulent and full-bodied, with good underlying acidity and loads of botrytis. There is considerable sweetness and, again, a finish that goes on well past 60 seconds. This is a brilliant Yquem, somewhat less obviously complex and delineated when compared to the 1988, and less flamboyant than either the 1990 or 1989. Nevertheless, there is authority, power, richness, and immense upside potential. It is still a very young wine, just approaching its adolescence. Anticipated maturity: now–2050.

1985 Château d'Yquem

RATING: 90 points

A somewhat monolithic Yquem that has never developed, this wine has straightforward notes of tropical fruit and seems to lack the botrytis and honeysuckle that most of the great vintages possess. It is medium to full–bodied, with plenty of weight and sweetness, but a certain monochromatic style. Am I being too severe? Anticipated maturity: now–2020.

1983 Château d'Yquem

RATING: 98 points

A wine that is just hitting its adolescence, this spectacular Yquem is the great vintage of the early 1980s and the best Yquem since 1976 and before the trilogy of 1990, 1989, and 1988. The wine has a medium-gold color and an extraordinary nose of honey-dripped coconuts, pineapple, caramel, crème brûlée, orange marmalade, and no doubt a few other items. Unctuously textured and full-bodied, with massive richness and great sweetness, this is a seamless classic that will probably be immortal. My point score continues to go up, but the wine still is young. Anticipated maturity: now–2075.

BURGUNDY

In the school of wine, Burgundy is as simple as first grade and as hard to understand as postgraduate school. A glass of Burgundy can seem incredibly easy, seductive, charming, and appealing. These wines are perfumed, silky, expansive, and complex. However, buying Burgundy can be dangerous; such famous names as Chambertin and Clos de Vougeot are available in 30 or more distinctive styles and quality levels, even though they are all officially called grand crus.

As a wine, Burgundy is a temperamental as well as schizophrenic mistress. When it is great, no other Pinot Noir or Chardonnay–based wine can rival or eclipse it. Unfortunately, more frequently than not, Burgundy is disappointing, and her past is littered with admirers who quickly became disenchanted and took their discretionary income to other wine regions of the world, never to return—and that is a shame.

Perhaps it is the fickleness of the Pinot Noir grape, which is difficult to grow, vinify, and bottle, or the fact that Burgundy makes so little wine, at least at the top level, and there are far too many suitors, many of whom have more money than either wine smarts or discriminating taste. Thus, a producer who wants to do the best job possible in the vineyard and cellar is often a casualty of greed and indifference instead. The producers profiled in the following chapter are Burgundy's finest, and they have proven this time and time again, even in difficult vintages. They continually transcend what Mother Nature throws their way, making compelling wines in both great and mediocre vintages.

Burgundy, arguably the most legendary wine-producing region in France, encompasses five regions. The northernmost area, Chablis, makes only white wines from Chardonnay. The tenderloin section, the Côte d'Or (meaning the "hill of gold"), includes two famous hillside slopes, the Côte de Beaune and Côte de Nuits. This is the area that attracts worldwide interest as well as the highest prices. South of the Côte d'Or remain the largely unexplored, backwater viticultural regions of the Côte Chalonnais and the vast, up-and-coming Mâconnais. Further south is Beaujolais. While technically located in the Rhône, Beaujolais has historically been considered part of Burgundy.

Burgundy's continental climate differs significantly from the maritime climate of Bordeaux as well as the inland climates of eastern France, notably Alsace. While it does not get as hot in Burgundy as it does in Bordeaux, Burgundy receives as much sunlight as Bordeaux. Anyone who has spent a summer evening in Burgundy will no doubt remember the 10:30 P.M. sunsets.

All of the Burgundy producers included in this book are from the Côte d'Or. The "hill of gold" refers to the deep golden brown color the vineyards take on in autumn. This is surely the most scrutinized and inspected stretch of real estate in the world. Historically, the monks of the Abbey of Citeaux exploited these hills, but during the last two centuries, the French government has examined every field, valley, crevice, and outcropping and determined that more than 30 vineyards in a 31-mile stretch of limestone are capable of producing grand cru red and white Burgundies. Approximately 300 of these fields were deemed suitable to produce premier cru red and white Burgundies. The overly bureaucratic French government, which can be criticized for many things, appears to have gotten it right, as the finest Burgundies truly are the premier and grand crus.

The excruciating complexity of Burgundy is best illustrated by Clos de Vougeot, one of its most famous grand cru vineyards. This 124-acre vineyard had more than 75 different proprietors the last time the land records were checked. Some of these proprietors sell their wines to large brokers who then blend it together, and others estate-bottle their wines. So the consumer is comforted in any given vintage with four to five dozen Clos de Vougeots. Moreover, all are entitled to grand cru status and all are frighteningly expensive. Yet only a small percentage are interesting to drink. Contrast that with a property of approximately the same size as Clos de Vougeot, Bordeaux's 120-acre Château Latour, where there is only one proprietor, one winemaker, and one wine.

Burgundy was best summarized by the late A. J. Liebling in his classic book *Between Meals,* where he wrote, "Burgundy has the advantage—to which a young palate is particularly sensitive—of a clear, direct appeal, immediately pleasing and easy to comprehend on a primary level. Burgundy is a lovely thing when you can get anybody to buy it for you."

WINES:

Volnay Champans

Volnay Clos des Ducs

Volnay Taillepieds

OWNER: Jacques d'Angerville

ADDRESS: Clos des Ducs, 21190 Volnay, France

TELEPHONE: 33 03 80 21 61 75

TELEFAX: 33 03 80 21 65 07

E-MAIL: domaine.angerville@wanadoo.fr

CONTACT: Renaud de Villette

VISITING POLICY: By appointment only

VINEYARDS

SURFACE AREA: 37 acres

GRAPE VARIETALS: Pinot Noir, Chardonnay

AVERAGE AGE OF THE VINES: 25 years

DENSITY OF PLANTATION: 10,000 vines per hectare

AVERAGE YIELDS: 37 hectoliters per hectare

WINEMAKING AND UPBRINGING

Not much has changed at d'Angerville over the years. There has always been a manual harvest, a 3–4 day pre-fermentation cold maceration, and an 8–10 day maceration period with pump-overs, after which the wine is moved directly to French oak casks, of which about 15% are new. Prior to bottling, the wine is racked and given a light egg-white fining as well as a light filtration. Most vintages spend 18–20 months in barrel.

ANNUAL PRODUCTION

Volnay Champans: 20,000 bottles

Volnay Clos des Ducs: 11,000 bottles

Volnay Taillepieds: 5,000 bottles

AVERAGE PRICE (VARIABLE DEPENDING ON VINTAGE): $35–55

GREAT RECENT VINTAGES

2002, 1999, 1996, 1993, 1990, 1985, 1978, 1976

This beautiful estate on the hillside in the village of Volnay has great historical significance. In 1804, Baron du Mesnil assembled in "Vollenay" (around the Clos des Ducs) parcels of vines that in the 12th century had been part of the famous vineyard belonging to the Dukes of Burgundy. After the phylloxera crisis, the Marquis d'Angerville, the great-grandson of Baron du Mesnil, devoted himself to the replanting of his domaine, in Volnay, with selected Pinot Noir vines. He was an ardent promoter of domaine-bottling and direct sales, and his influence on quality and estate-bottling in Burgundy is significant.

The late Jacques, Marquis d'Angerville, was without a doubt one of the finest producers in Burgundy. Charming, sensitive, and intelligent, he was one of the region's great gentlemen. D'Angerville saw his father ostracized by other winemakers because of his attempts to combat dishonest practices in the 1930s and 1940s in Burgundy. This commitment to the appellation laws, and the practice of planting only the finest clones of Pinot Noir, has continued to the present day.

All of the vineyards face southeast and lie upon deposits of marly limestone. The rocky soil retains the sun's heat, reflecting it back toward the grapes, hastening their maturation. The slope is often quite steep, ensuring proper drainage.

The estate now includes 37 acres of vineyards, with the top parcel being the *monopole* vineyard, Volnay Clos des Ducs. I have also had good luck with the Volnay Taillepieds and Volnay Champans. The wines are generally made in a light, delicate style that in certain vintages has left me desiring a bit more richness and flesh. In the late 1970s and early 1980s, there was a bit too much fining and filtration. However, vintages since the late 1980s have been consistently superb, achieving more texture and intensity without losing any of their lacy delicacy and finesse. In most vintages, the d'Angerville wines need 5–6 years of bottle age. Great vintages require several additional years. These wines generally hit their peak at 10–12 years of age and can last for two decades or more.

VOLNAY CHAMPANS

1999 Volnay Champans

RATING: 90 points

The medium to dark ruby–colored 1999 Volnay Champans, from a four-hectare parcel where 50% of the vines are 40 years of age and the balance over 10 years, displays a sweet blackberry nose. Medium-bodied, this wine has an excellent depth of fruit, a supple, velvety texture, and a fresh personality. Loads of intense blackberry, cassis, plum, and spice flavors can be found in its juicy and expressive character. Drink it now–2011.

1996 Volnay Champans

RATING: 91 points

The medium ruby–colored 1996 Volnay Champans has a creamy, cherry-scented nose and an outstanding, sweet, medium-bodied, and supple character packed with ripe black cherries and minerals. This lovely and well-focused wine should be at its peak now–2016.

1995 Volnay Champans

RATING: 91 points

The medium to dark ruby–colored 1995 Volnay Champans displays highly expressive cherry and mineral aromas as well as superb flavors reminiscent of unctuous blueberries, strawberries, and Asian spices. Concentrated and well balanced, this full-bodied and refined wine can be drunk through 2006.

VOLNAY CLOS DES DUCS

1999 Volnay Clos des Ducs

RATING: 94 points

Produced from the Marquis d'Angerville's two-hectare parcel, the 1999 Volnay Clos des Ducs has a marvelous nose of bing cherries, kirsch, *griottes* (morello cherries), and violets. This wine is medium to full–bodied and gorgeously balanced, and it possesses the outstanding depth of velvety-textured fruit. It coats the taster's palate with cherries and blackberries, blueberries, flowers, and spices whose flavors last throughout its extraordinarily long, pure, and silky finish. This harmonious, refined beauty has copious amounts of superripe tannin that can be discerned under its waves of fruit. It has the density, balance, and structure for mid- to long-term cellaring. Anticipated maturity: now–2012+.

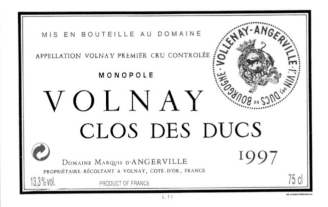

1997 Volnay Clos des Ducs

RATING: 92 points

The dark ruby–colored 1997 Volnay Clos des Ducs displays super aromas of soy sauce, hoisin, and spices. This powerful yet elegant wine is jam-packed with sweet black fruits, flowers, stones, and herbs. A powerful, complex, and complete wine, it should be drunk by 2008.

1996 Volnay Clos des Ducs

RATING: 92 points

Sporting a medium to dark ruby–color, the 1996 Volnay Clos des Ducs offers mouth-watering aromas of cream-covered black cherries and the inviting scents of a deep-dish cherry pie. Powerful and explosive layers of sweet red and black fruits greet the palate in this profound, broad, concentrated, and complex wine. It is slightly more structured, intense, and extracted than Volnay Taillepieds. Projected maturity: now–2008.

1995 Volnay Clos des Ducs

RATING: 91 points

Offering a gorgeous, saturated black/purple color, the 1995 Volnay Clos des Ducs has a sublime nose of violets, roses, and superripe plums, cherries, and blueberries. Full-bodied, oily-textured, and impressively concentrated, this wine has a mouthwatering core of Asian spices, fresh herbs, and deeply sweet red and black fruits. Its purity, precision, and elegance are simply mind-boggling. Anticipated maturity: now–2010.

1993 Volnay Clos des Ducs

RATING: 90 points

The dark ruby/purple–colored 1993 Volnay Clos des Ducs offers a sweet attack, layers of black cherry flavors, medium body, and considerable finesse, class, and character. The long finish reveals beautifully integrated tannin and oak. Drink it between now and 2015.

VOLNAY TAILLEPIEDS

2002 Volnay Taillepieds

RATING: 91 points

As is typical for this wine, the 2002 Volnay Taillepieds displays a boisterous nose of plump, sweet black fruits. On the attack and mid-palate, this effort is extremely broad, lush, and intense. Its red and black cherry fruit is intermingled with herbs, spices, and minerals. Medium to full–bodied, it has outstanding depth, loads in reserve, and the structure for aging. Anticipated maturity: 2008–2017.

2000 Volnay Taillepieds

RATING: 91 points

Aromatically demure, the black cherry–scented 2000 Volnay Taillepieds has a magnificent personality. Broad, sexy, expressive, and deep, it coats the taster's palate with loads of plump, sensual red cherries and blackberries. It has a satin-textured, gorgeous mouth-feel, a flamboyant personality, and lovely breadth as well as length. It lacks the complexity of the Marquis d'Angerville's finest wines, yet delivers tons of supple fruit. Drink it by 2007.

1999 Volnay Taillepieds

RATING: 93 points

The outstanding 1999 Volnay Taillepieds has zesty, dark fruit aromas. It is medium to full–bodied, ample, broad, and packed with copious amounts of jammy and juicy plums, black currants, Asian spices, and black cherries. This is a powerful yet refined, seamless wine with prodigiously ripened tannin. Its finish is long, silky, and pure. Drink it between now and 2008.

1997 Volnay Taillepieds

RATING: 90 points

Aromatically, the medium to dark ruby–colored 1997 Volnay Taillepieds offers dark plums, violets, and candied black cherries. It is an expansive, medium to full–bodied wine with great concentration, breadth, and richness. This is a thick, satin-textured, muscular, and well-structured wine. Stones, black fruits, and fresh herbs can be found in its fresh, yet plump, flavor profile. Anticipated maturity: now.

1996 Volnay Taillepieds

RATING: 91+ points

Produced from yields below 40 hectoliters per hectare (admirable for 1996), the Volnay Taillepieds exhibits beguiling aromas of black cherries, blackberries, and spices. On the palate, this complex, concentrated, and extracted wine is beautifully refined—sumptuous, yet structured. It is expansive, broad, medium- to full-bodied, and packed with juicy cassis and blueberries. This well-balanced and fruit-driven wine has an admirably persistent finish that displays loads of ripe tannins. Anticipated maturity: now–2010.

1995 Volnay Taillepieds

RATING: 93 points

The dark ruby/purple–colored 1995 Volnay Taillepieds possesses beguiling aromas of deeply spicy blackberries and cherries, and a massively thick, highly structured, hugely extracted and sweet flavor profile oozing with tangy and lively dark cherries, cassis, and wild blueberries. Notes of vanilla and Asian spices can be detected in this wine's exemplary finish. Anticipated maturity: now–2009.

WINES:

Bonnes Mares

Chevalier-Montrachet

Criots-Bâtard-Montrachet

Mazis-Chambertin

Meursault Les Narvaux

Puligny-Montrachet Les Folatières

OWNER: Lalou Bize-Leroy

ADDRESS: St.-Romain, 21190 Meursault, France

TELEPHONE: 33 03 80 21 23 27

TELEFAX: 33 03 80 21 23 27

CONTACT: Madame Lalou Bize-Leroy or Madame Bettina
    Roemer

VISITING POLICY: Visits must be arranged through distributors
    and agents of the Domaine d'Auvenay wines.

VINEYARDS

SURFACE AREA: 12 acres

GRAPE VARIETALS: Pinot Noir, Chardonnay, Aligoté

AVERAGE AGE OF THE VINES: 65 years

DENSITY OF PLANTATION: 10,000 vines per hectare

AVERAGE YIELDS: 22.5 hectoliters per hectare

WINEMAKING AND UPBRINGING

D'Auvenay's winemaking is identical to Domaine Leroy's except for *cuvées* of already made wine that Lalou Bize-Leroy purchases.

ANNUAL PRODUCTION

Bonnes Mares: 870–1,160 bottles

Chevalier-Montrachet: 560–814 bottles

Criots-Bâtard-Montrachet: 140–290 bottles

Mazis-Chambertin: 580–1,010 bottles

Meursault Les Narvaux: 1,160–3,500 bottles

Puligny-Montrachet Les Folatières: 800–2,800 bottles

AVERAGE PRICE (VARIABLE DEPENDING ON VINTAGE): $150–600

GREAT RECENT VINTAGES

2003, 2002, 2001, 2000, 1999, 1997, 1996, 1994, 1993, 1991, 1990

Domaine d'Auvenay has taken a backseat since Lalou Bize-Leroy's acquisition in 1988 of the Domaine Charles Noellat in Vosne-Romanée. This is the *négociant* arm of the Leroy firm, and even though they possess some beautiful parcels of vines, the wines are

made very much in the Lalou Bize-Leroy style, meaning full-bodied, very concentrated, long-lived, and the bottled essence of a *terroir*. However, the ownership remains in the name of Madame Bize-Leroy. The most important thing for readers to know is that the quality is every bit as exceptional at Domaine d'Auvenay as it is at the more famous Domaine Leroy in Vosne-Romanée.

BONNES MARES

2002 Bonnes Mares

RATING: 93 points

The 2002 Bonnes Mares displays aromas of coffee beans, earth, rocks, violets, and sweet, superripe berries. This masculine, medium to full–bodied effort is medium to dark ruby–colored and reveals espresso beans and black fruits in its deep, muscular personality. Its tannin is slightly firm, and it exhibits a hint of alcoholic warmth. That being said, it is a wine of exceptional concentration and balance. Anticipated maturity: 2007–2016.

1999 Bonnes Mares

RATING: 93 points

The medium to dark ruby–colored 1999 Bonnes Mares reveals toasted almond, blackberry, and floral aromas. This plum, licorice, and cherry-flavored wine is medium to full–bodied, highly structured, fresh, and precise. It coats the palate with compelling layers of sweet, dark flavors, as well as loads of ripe yet firm tannins. It also possesses an extraordinarily long finish. Anticipated maturity: now–2015+.

1997 Bonnes Mares

RATING: 94 points

The dark ruby/purple–colored 1997 Bonnes Mares exhibits deep aromas of baked plums, blackberries, and sealing wax. It is a thick, full-bodied, jammy wine with plump layers of roasted dark fruits and hints of leather and stones. While opulent, intense, and powerful, this wine is also tightly wound and well structured. Its almost overripe character expresses itself in a thick, verging on waxy, texture. Anticipated maturity: now–2010.

1996 Bonnes Mares

RATING: 95 points

This dark-colored wine has a violet and cookie dough–laced nose that gives way to a velvety-textured, massively concentrated, masculine, broad-shouldered, and powerful character. Full-bodied, thick, highly structured, intense, and extraordinarily proportioned, this wine is crammed with candied blackberries, cassis, beef blood, and loads of supple tannins. Its immensely long finish tails off after 40 seconds on notes of sweet blueberries and vanilla-imbued oak. Anticipated maturity: now–2015+.

1995 Bonnes Mares

RATING: 93 points

Made from yields averaging 15 hectoliters per hectare, Domaine d'Auvenay's superb 1995 Bonnes Mares displays a fabulously perfumed, elegant nose of roses in addition to red and dark fruits. In the mouth, this explosive, intensely powerful, and structured wine offers deeply roasted, lush, dark fruits. Full-bodied, it has a brilliant combination of elegance and power (a hallmark of great wines). Anticipated maturity: now–2008.

1993 Bonnes Mares

RATING: 92 points

Not surprisingly, the 1993 Bonnes Mares is a massive, muscular, lumbering giant of a wine with a strong mineral component woven into the wine's immense concentration of red and black fruits. Full-bodied, spicy, this should turn out to be a monumental wine that will last 20–25 more years.

CHEVALIER-MONTRACHET

2002 Chevalier-Montrachet

RATING: 99 points

The 2002 Chevalier-Montrachet boasts aromas of liquid minerals and fresh flowers. This silky, graceful, powerful wine offers mouth-coating waves of honeyed minerals, sappy resin, and spices in its exceptionally classy, detailed, and awesomely balanced personality. In addition, this noble, majestic effort possesses a finish that lasts for almost a minute. In short, it is a stunning, awe-inspiring example of its world-renowned vineyard. Anticipated maturity: 2008–2020.

2001 Chevalier-Montrachet

RATING: 93 points

White peaches and pears can be discerned in the nose of the 2001 Chevalier-Montrachet. This highly concentrated wine displays layers of minerals, gravel, and white fruits. It has outstanding depth, balance, grip, and length. Anticipated maturity: now–2014.

2000 Chevalier-Montrachet

RATING: 92 points

Creamy minerals and vanilla yogurt can be found in the aromatics of the 2000 Chevalier-Montrachet. Medium-bodied, it has a sultry, silky texture, a mineral-laden personality, and a broad yet vivacious character. The wine also has a long, pure finish. Anticipated maturity: now–2014.

1999 Chevalier-Montrachet

RATING: 93 points

The highly expressive nose of the 1999 Chevalier-Montrachet displays limestone and mineral aromas. Medium-bodied and satin-textured, it is crammed with flavors of stones, gravel, metal, pear, and candied citrus. This intense, concentrated wine possesses superb purity, delineation, and richness. Anticipated maturity: now–2014.

1997 Chevalier-Montrachet

RATING: 96 points

The 1997 Chevalier-Montrachet is certainly one of the stars of the vintage. Aromatically, it reveals rocks, stones, and salty seashells. This magnificent masterpiece has a personality of unheard-of intensity, ripeness, and focus. Its overpowering minerality is gorgeously precise, revealing traces of anise, pears, and oak spices that last throughout the stupendous finish. Drink it between now and 2012.

1996 Chevalier-Montrachet

RATING: 98 points

The 1996 Chevalier-Montrachet from Domaine d'Auvenay is mind-boggling. Fresh, lively, and perfumed aromas of minerals and spicy oak, and touches of candied orange rinds, give way to a velvety, full-bodied, massively ripe, and hugely concentrated personality. This wine's purity, precision, delineation, and focus render its citrus fruit and minerality compelling. At present a touch austere, it possesses unbridled power, intensity, and concentration of fruit. It should hit its stride around 2010, and last until well past 2020.

CRIOTS-BATARD-MONTRACHET

2002 Criots-Bâtard-Montrachet

RATING: 95 points

The fresh, mineral-dominated nose of the 2002 Criots-Bâtard-Montrachet leads to a hugely concentrated, deep, oily-textured personality packed with flavors of syrupy stones, spices, pears, sappy minerals, and copious spices. Medium-bodied and powerful, it also has an extraordinarily long, flavor-packed finish. Anticipated maturity: 2006–2018.

2001 Criots-Bâtard-Montrachet

RATING: 96 points

One of the "wines of the vintage," the 2001 Criots-Bâtard-Montrachet explodes from the glass with powerful aromas of minerals and smoke. A magnificent elixir, it paints a broad swath across the palate, revealing stunning quantities of liquid minerals and syrupy stones. Massively concentrated, deep, and complete, it has a finish that simply refuses to relinquish its hold on the taster's palate. Wow! Anticipated maturity: now–2014.

2000 Criots-Bâtard-Montrachet

RATING: 93 points

The 2000 Criots-Bâtard-Montrachet bursts from the glass with intense toast, mineral, and smoke aromas. This plush, medium-bodied wine offers layers of spicy minerals, buttered toast, and creamy pears in its deep, satin-textured, and persistent flavor profile. Anticipated maturity: now–2014.

1999 Criots-Bâtard-Montrachet

RATING: 93 points

The 1999 Criots-Bâtard-Montrachet has powerful mineral aromas. This oily-textured wine is thick, fat, and dense, yet remains elegant and focused. It is harmonious and muscular, and the flavors of its intense mineral-laden core last throughout the extraordinarily long finish. Anticipated maturity: now–2014.

1996 Criots-Bâtard-Montrachet

RATING: 96 points

An amazingly complex and profound minerality is evident on the nose of the Criots-Bâtard-Montrachet. Its character is tightly wound, defined, medium to full–bodied, and racy. Stones, gravel, metals, and white flowers are found in this vibrant yet dense and oily-textured wine. The awesomely long finish holds the palate captive for at least 45 seconds, with its

precise mineral and chalk flavors. It will be at its peak between 2007 and 2018.

MAZIS-CHAMBERTIN

2002 Mazis-Chambertin

RATING: 99 points

The dark ruby–colored 2002 Mazis-Chambertin is the darkest, broadest, biggest, and most concentrated of all of Lalou Bize-Leroy's 2002s. Madame Bize-Leroy says that it reminds her of the stupendous 1985 Mazis-Chambertin she produced from the Hospices de Beaune. Its superripe blackberry, spice, herb, and clove aromas lead to a full-bodied personality reminiscent of liquid wax. Hugely deep, perfectly balanced, this chewy, classy wine slathers the taster's palate with untold quantities of black fruits and Asian spices. It is a stunning example of its vineyard and vintage. Anticipated maturity: 2009–2020.

1999 Mazis-Chambertin

RATING: 95 points

The dark ruby–colored 1999 Mazis-Chambertin has an awesome nose that reveals violets, intense blackberries, and sweet cherries. This profound wine has admirable focus, great purity, harmony, and a mind-bogglingly long finish. Loads of tangy *griottes* (morello cherries) can be found throughout this exceptional wine's character. It is powerful, elegant, and extroverted. Anticipated maturity: 2006–2018+.

1997 Mazis-Chambertin

RATING: 95 points

Surprisingly, Domaine d'Auvenay's 1997 Mazis-Chambertin is forward, opulent, and luxuriant. This dark, almost black-colored effort displays jammy and waxy cherry fruit scents. Its concentrated, rich, deep, and intensely sweet character is crammed with red fruits galore. This velvety-textured wine's amazingly long finish reveals superbly ripe, supple tannins. An extraordinary effort in any vintage, in this irregular one, it stands as a testimony to Bize-Leroy's immense talents and dedication. Anticipated maturity: now–2014+.

1996 Mazis-Chambertin

RATING: 97 points

Revealing a black color with bright purple tints, this wine has a brooding nose of jammy blackberries and stones. This thick (almost syrupy), massively powerful, muscular, and backward wine is even bigger, denser, and more concentrated than the Bonnes Mares. Layers of black cherries, cassis, minerals, iron shavings, and plums can be found in this blockbuster's superbly focused and extraordinarily delicious personality. Its prodigiously long and persistent finish makes that of the previous wine almost seem short! Anticipated maturity: 2006–2020.

1995 Mazis-Chambertin

RATING: 95 points

The 1995 Mazis-Chambertin was made from amazingly low yields (nine hectoliters per hectare). Possessing a very dark, almost black color, and an engulfing, deeply intense, brooding nose, this wine's oily texture, wild berries, and spices intertwined with minerals and rocks must be tasted to be believed. Highly structured, full-bodied, and powerful, this super-concentrated offering will be drinkable between now and 2010.

MEURSAULT LES NARVAUX

2002 Meursault Les Narvaux

RATING: 93 points

The medium-bodied 2002 Meursault Les Narvaux has aromatic and flavor profiles packed with smoky minerals, stones, spices, and pears. This detailed, pure, concentrated wine lingers on the palate for up to 40 seconds. Anticipated maturity: now–2014.

2001 Meursault Les Narvaux

RATING: 93 points

Spiced liquid minerals can be found in the nose of the 2001 Meursault Les Narvaux. Deep, intense, massively concentrated, and displaying sublime purity of fruit, this medium-bodied wine offers a silky-textured, hugely spicy personality.

Its overpowering spice flavors explode on the taster's palate and linger throughout its exceptional finish. Anticipated maturity: now–2012.

2000 Meursault Les Narvaux

RATING: 92 points

Intense spice and mineral aromas can be found in the aromatics of the 2000 Meursault Les Narvaux. Medium-bodied and intense, this is a zesty yet lush wine, crammed with fresh pear, lemon, and spice flavors. It has outstanding depth and a bright acid streak that runs uninhibited from the attack through this wine's persistent finish. Anticipated maturity: now–2012.

1999 Meursault Les Narvaux

RATING: 90 points

The mineral- and stone-scented 1999 Meursault Les Narvaux is light to medium–bodied, concentrated, and refined. It has outstanding depth to its stone, pear, and mineral-flavored personality, as well as an extremely long, pure finish. Anticipated maturity: now–2008.

1997 Meursault Les Narvaux

RATING: 92 points

The 1997 Meursault Les Narvaux displays an oak-imbued and rich, white fruit–laden nose. This massive, thick, chewy, and medium to full–bodied offering is crammed with expansive metal, mineral, and hazelnut flavors. Madame Bize-Leroy attributed this level of unbelievable ripeness and superb bal-

Meursault Les Narvaux 2002
Appellation Meursault Contrôlée

Mis en Bouteille au Domaine par Lalou Bize-Leroy, S.C. du Domaine d'Auvenay, Meursault, France

ance to "low yields and respect for the vine as well as nature." This beauty should be at its peak between now and 2008.

1996 Meursault Les Narvaux

RATING: 96 points

Domaine d'Auvenay's 1996 Meursault Narvaux is a masterpiece. Extraordinarily complex aromas of freshly cut flowers, hazelnuts, and minerals are followed by a thick, full-bodied, profound, hyper-concentrated personality. Layer upon layer of highly extracted white peaches, poached and spiced pears, anise, and liquid minerals coat the palate in this magnificently balanced and focused wine. This offering's mind-blowing finish is at least a minute long. Its massive ripeness and powerful, expressive flavors, married with bright and lively acidity, render this a wine that will easily age for decades given proper storage. Anticipated maturity: 2006–2020+.

1995 Meursault Les Narvaux

RATING: 94 points

The attention-getting 1995 Meursault Les Narvaux has an awesome sweet and spicy component on the nose and an incredibly viscous and oily-textured mouth-feel. Powerful flavors of flowers and nuts float through the taster's mouth in a finish that easily lasts 30 seconds. Drink between now and 2010.

PULIGNY-MONTRACHET LES FOLATIERES

2002 Puligny-Montrachet Les Folatières

RATING: 91 points

The smoky, mineral-laden nose of the 2002 Puligny-Montrachet Les Folatières leads to a light to medium–bodied, slate-dominated personality. Tight yet exhibiting gorgeous depth, it coats the palate with resiny, smoky minerals. It should be drunk between now and 2014.

2001 Puligny-Montrachet Les Folatières

RATING: 92 points

White flowers and intensely ripe pears are found in the profound aromatics of the 2001 Puligny-Montrachet Les Folatières. Armed with gorgeous concentration, depth, and focus, this smoky mineral-flavored wine also reveals a finish of impressive length and elegance. Anticipated maturity: now–2010.

1999 Puligny-Montrachet Les Folatières

RATING: 90 points

The 1999 Puligny-Montrachet Les Folatières is aromatically demure yet rich and deep on the palate. Medium-bodied and plump, it coats the palate with minerals, flowers, and spices that lead seamlessly to its admirably long finish. Anticipated maturity: now–2009.

1996 Puligny-Montrachet Les Folatières

RATING: 95 points

The Puligny-Montrachet Les Folatières possesses a floral and mineral-laden nose as well as a highly refined, feminine, superbly focused, oily-textured, medium to full body. This pure, muscular, and expansive wine is packed with flavors reminiscent of fresh hazelnut butter, white flowers, anise, and candied pears. It is a concentrated, elegant, and extremely persistent wine that expresses both power and lace-like delicacy. It should be at its best between now and 2015+.

1995 Puligny-Montrachet Les Folatières

RATING: 94 points

With an intense nose of bakery spices and floral notes reminiscent of a spring meadow, the 1995 Puligny-Montrachet Les Folatières has the same oily texture as the equally great 1995 Meursault Les Narvaux. This wine has a very floral, medium to full–bodied mouth, and great length; it should be at its peak between now and 2012.

1989 Puligny-Montrachet Les Folatières

RATING: 98 points

One hundred and seventy-five cases of this wine, which could easily pass for a Montrachet, were produced from yields that averaged 24 hectoliters per hectare. That is about one-third of what other top producers get from their Chardonnay vineyards. Not surprisingly, the 1989 possesses an awesome bouquet of minerals, butter, and tropical fruits. In the mouth, there is extraordinary richness, amazing viscosity (oil of Chardonnay), and an intensity level that is rarely encountered. This monumental white Burgundy should last through 2010.

WINES:

Corton-Charlemagne

Meursault-Perrières

OWNER: Jean-François Coche-Dury

ADDRESS: 9 rue Charles Giraud, 21190 Meursault, France

TELEPHONE: 33 03 80 21 24 12

TELEFAX: 33 03 80 21 67 65

VISITING POLICY: Clients only

VINEYARDS

SURFACE AREA: 26.4 acres

GRAPE VARIETALS: Chardonnay, Aligoté, Gamay, Pinot Noir

AVERAGE AGE OF THE VINES: 25–35 years

DENSITY OF PLANTATION: 10,000–12,000 vines per hectare

AVERAGE YIELDS: 35–45 hectoliters per hectare

WINEMAKING AND UPBRINGING

Coche-Dury employs straightforward winemaking practices, including gentle pressings (he uses an old Vaslin), aging of the wine in a maximum of 50% new Allier oak (only the top *cuvées*) for 18–20 months, two rackings, and no filtration at bottling. Coche-Dury believes that more than 90% of a wine's quality comes from the vineyard. Among Burgundian producers, he is one of the most flexible about harvesting. Sometimes he is among the first, other years among the last.

ANNUAL PRODUCTION

Corton-Charlemagne: 1,500–2,000 bottles

Meursault-Perrières: 3,000 bottles

AVERAGE PRICE (VARIABLE DEPENDING ON VINTAGE):

Corton-Charlemagne: $230

Meursault-Perrières: $150

GREAT RECENT VINTAGES

2002, 2001, 2000, 1996, 1995, 1992, 1990, 1989, 1986

Fifty-year-old Jean-François Coche-Dury (Dury is his wife's family name) is one of Burgundy's legendary winemakers. Tall, thin, and bespectacled, he produces some of the region's longest-lived, most aromatically complex, and compellingly textured white wines. His two greatest whites are Meursault-Perrières and Corton-Charlemagne, both among the half-dozen finest white Burgundies produced in nearly every vintage. He also fashions terrific Meursault Les Rougeots, Meursault Les Narvaux, and several other village Meursaults. More recently, he has produced a top-notch Puligny-Montrachet Enseignères. A small amount of red wine is also made. Coche's whites age magnificently, and wines from the early eighties, even in vintages not considered great (1981 and 1982), were still young, beautifully made efforts when tasted in the early part of the 21st century. Coche is well known for his extraordinary flexibility and work in the vineyards. Low yields and impeccable viticulture are the keys to producing his finest wines, which are never over-oaked and often need 4–5 years of bottle age before they strut their pedigree. He is one of the few producers in Meursault, Puligny-Montrachet, and Chassagne-Montrachet to have half of his Chardonnay vineyards planted with the *cordon de royat* system, which results in dramatically lower yields. I visited Jean-François Coche-Dury nearly every year for more than 15 years, and the only time I ever saw him smile was when the tasting was over and he was telling me good-bye. This is a very serious as well as great winemaker.

CORTON-CHARLEMAGNE

2002 Corton-Charlemagne

RATING: 96 points

Caramel-coated apples, melons, and white flowers are exhibited in the nose of the intense 2002 Corton-Charlemagne. Medium-bodied, plush, and pure, its flavor profile is reminiscent of golden raisins, quartz, minerals, and spices. This is a complex, exceptionally ripe wine with superb balance, depth, and length. Anticipated maturity: 2007–2016.

2001 Corton-Charlemagne

RATING: 98 points

A myriad of spices and anise-spiked pears are found in the highly expressive nose of the 2001 Corton-Charlemagne. Medium to full–bodied, with levels of dry extract that would tip the scales, and a supple, fleshy character of intense width and power, this wine is amazing. Magnificently supple yet focused, boisterous yet refined, thick yet balanced, it possesses a finish that easily lasts for more than a minute. It has all the earmarks of perfection. This velvety-textured wine is jam-packed with minerals immersed in pear syrup and copious spices (including clove, ginger, and juniper berries), as well as a distinctive note of applesauce. It is layered, opulent, and sexy, while remaining nuanced and seamless. Anticipated maturity: now–2015.

2000 Corton-Charlemagne

RATING: 95 points

The toasted oak–scented 2000 Corton-Charlemagne has the austerity found in many of this vineyard's wines in the 2000 vintage. However, it is vinous, rich, and broad. Pure flavors of minerals, toast, and spices can be found in its highly delineated, profound offering. Anticipated maturity: now–2015.

1996 Corton-Charlemagne

RATING: 96+ points

This full-bodied Corton-Charlemagne, displaying unbelievable depth to its spicy pear, white peach, and floral aromas, is an awesomely rich, as well as perfectly delineated and balanced, wine. This oily-textured tour de force has an embracing, almost enveloping flavor profile crammed with intense stones, minerals, superripe pears, waves of nuts and minerals, and touches of grilled toast. The taster's palate is held prisoner by the interminable layers and layers of concentrated, highly extracted, and powerful fruit that roll across it, each sublimely defined and focused by this wine's racy acidity. Anticipated maturity: now–2010.

1992 Corton-Charlemagne

RATING: 96 points

The 1992 Corton-Charlemagne reveals a huge, spicy, vanilla, buttery, coconut, and tropical fruit–scented nose; astonishingly rich, unctuously textured flavors that linger on the palate; and enough glycerin, extract, and alcohol to satisfy the most demanding hedonist. It is softer than the exceptional Corton-Charlemagnes made in 1990 and 1989.

1990 Corton-Charlemagne

RATING: 98 points

Light-medium straw in color, with a honeyed bouquet of brioche, pear, peach, and hazelnut, this exquisite wine is full-bodied, intensely flavorful, and still youthful. Drink it during the next 10–12 years.

1989 Corton-Charlemagne

RATING: 98 points

It is hard to believe, but Coche-Dury's 1989 Corton-Charlemagne is even better than his spectacular 1986. Unbelievably concentrated, it exhibits superb depth, good acidity, and a penetrating earthy, mineral quality. The finish lasts more than a minute. It may have more structure and aging potential than the 1986. Given the worldwide interest in the micro-quantities produced of this wine, it will be nearly impossible to find. Anticipated maturity: now–2016.

1986 Corton-Charlemagne

RATING: 99 points

When first released, this was one of the most flamboyant Corton-Charlemagnes of the vintage. It has now taken on more definition and structure, and may disprove my theory about the limited aging potential of Coche-Dury's wines. The wine still boasts a spectacular, stony, mineral-scented nose intermingled with aromas of overripe oranges and apples. Full-bodied, with admirable concentration, crisp acidity, and far more definition and focus than it initially exhibited, this large-scale yet perfectly balanced wine should continue to drink well for another decade.

MEURSAULT-PERRIERES

2002 Meursault-Perrières

RATING: 96 points

Described by Coche-Dury as "hyper-ripe," the 2002 Meursault-Perrières sports a nose of sweet candied apples. It is broad, rich, hugely concentrated, deep, and amazingly long in the finish. Fat layers of pure, detailed minerals and gravel can be found in its complex personality. Anticipated maturity: 2007–2016.

2001 Meursault-Perrières

RATING: 98+ points

The towering aromatics of the 2001 Meursault-Perrières reveal oodles of candied apples, flowers, minerals, pears, and gravel. A wine of unbelievable purity and breadth, it conquers the palate with flavors of bacon-laced minerals, spiced stones, smoky pears, and buttered toast. Satin-textured, lush, and medium-bodied, this awe-inspiring wine is complete. Described by the exceedingly modest Coche-Dury as "un vin de grande classe" (a

wine of great class), it has perfect balance, harmony, and un-heard-of depth. Anticipated maturity: now–2017.

2000 Meursault-Perrières

RATING: 96 points

The 2000 Meursault-Perrières reveals spices, cinnamon, and vanilla in its deep, concentrated character. Medium to full–bodied, it explodes on the palate with pears, apples, butter, gravel, stones, and minerals. It is velvety-textured and lush and it exhibits massive depth and an intensely pure, powerful, and deep character. This is a Perrières that will give Coche-Dury's 1996 a run for its money. Anticipated maturity: now–2015.

1999 Meursault-Perrières

RATING: 91 points

The 1999 Meursault-Perrières has a shy yet deep smoke, mineral, and spice-laden nose. This highly refined, gorgeously detailed wine is packed with minerals, toast, spices, and crisp pears. Medium-bodied, concentrated, and harmonious, this beautiful offering also possesses an extremely long and pure finish. Anticipated maturity: 2010–2020.

1997 Meursault-Perrières

RATING: 93 points

The 1997 Meursault-Perrières displays lovely aromas of can-died limes, lemons, minerals, rocks, and smoke. This is a hugely rich, medium to full–bodied, viscously textured wine. It has great class, and its peach, stone, earth, clay, and red berry–filled flavor profile has enormous elegance. Were it not for an austere and lightly dusty finish, I would have been even more enamored of this offering's rich panoply of flavors and exquisite texture. Anticipated maturity: now–2007+.

1996 Meursault-Perrières

RATING: 99 points

Tasting the 1996 Meursault-Perrières is an out-of-this-world experience! This masterpiece has perfect balance, focus, and delineation. It is vibrant and spiritual, and as complex a wine as I can imagine. It attacks the palate with waves of candied lemons, marzipan, creamed hazelnuts, pears, grilled oak, curry, red berries, and loads of minerals. It is truly mind-blowing! Anticipated maturity: now–2010.

1995 Meursault-Perrières

RATING: 98 points

Jean-François Coche-Dury produced a total of 900 bottles (at 18 hectoliters per hectare) of his otherworldly 1995 Meursault-Perrières. This quintessentially elegant wine re-veals liquid minerals intertwined with flowers, spices, and stones. The French would say it is "aérien," or spiritual. On the palate, this highly defined and hyper-concentrated, thick, full-bodied yet perfectly delineated Meursault-Perrières exhibits waves of toasted almonds, hazelnuts, and wet stones and has an unbelievably long finish. Literally minutes after having tasted it, my palate remained permeated with its sumptuous flavors. Those few people lucky enough to secure a few bottles of this gem should consume it between now and 2014.

1992 Meursault-Perrières

RATING: 93 points

The 1992 Meursault-Perrières (350 cases produced) offered a compelling bouquet of steel, minerals, ripe honeyed apple, fruit, and floral aromas. The long, full-bodied, rich, multidimen-sional, chewy flavors were decadent. Anticipated maturity: now.

1989 Meursault-Perrières

RATING: 97 points

Jean-François Coche-Dury's 1989 Meursault-Perrières smells and tastes as if it were a Montrachet. If there is one premier cru vineyard in Burgundy that merits elevation to grand cru status, it must be Les Perrières in Meursault. Its huge nose of minerals, lemons, apple blossoms, and buttered toast was fol-lowed by a wine with immense richness, massive structure, and layer upon layer of Chardonnay fruit. Crammed with glycerin, extract, alcohol, and intensity, it represents a wine-making tour de force! Anticipated maturity: now.

1986 Meursault-Perrières

RATING: 96 points

With only a handful of exceptions, my experience with Coche-Dury's wines has taught me that they are about as profound as any white Burgundy one is likely to find. The 1986 Meursault-Perrières revealed huge aromas of sweet, buttery apple, grilled nuts, and smoke. The fabulous texture and richness that Coche-Dury routinely achieves was evident, as were a fascinat-ing, unctuous richness, enough acidity to provide focus, and a spectacularly long finish. Anticipated maturity: now.

WINES:

Charmes-Chambertin
Griotte-Chambertin
OWNER: Famille Claude Dugat
ADDRESS: 1 place Cure, 21220 Gevrey-Chambertin, France
TELEPHONE: 33 03 80 34 36 18
TELEFAX: 33 03 80 58 50 64
VISITING POLICY: No visits

VINEYARDS

SURFACE AREA: 12.35 acres
GRAPE VARIETAL: Pinot Noir
AVERAGE AGE OF THE VINES: 35–45 years
DENSITY OF PLANTATION: 10,000–12,000 vines per hectare
AVERAGE YIELDS: 30–35 hectoliters per hectare

WINEMAKING AND UPBRINGING

This estate takes a relatively modern approach to winemaking using a 3–5 day cold pre-fermentation maceration, 100% destemming, fermentation temperatures that rise to 34°C, and a three-plus-week *cuvaison.* The wines are then moved into oak casks for malolactic fermentation. After 16–18 months of aging, they are bottled unfiltered. Approximately 50% new oak is utilized, although the grand crus can see up to 100%. These are supple-textured, exceptionally fragrant wines possessing loads of sweetness as well as complexity. According to Dugat, the wines age well for 15 or more years.

ANNUAL PRODUCTION

Charmes-Chambertin: 1,500–2,500 bottles
Griotte-Chambertin: 1,500–2,500 bottles
AVERAGE PRICE (VARIABLE DEPENDING ON VINTAGE):
Charmes-Chambertin: $110
Griotte-Chambertin: $160

GREAT RECENT VINTAGES

2003, 2002, 1999, 1997, 1996, 1990

A relatively recent estate bottler, for many years Claude Dugat sold his wine to some of Burgundy's finest *négociants,* who then bottled under someone else's name. One if his most well-known purchasers was Lalou Bize-Leroy at Maison Leroy, which is where I first learned of Dugat's old vines and high-quality winemaking. Dugat, a self-effacing, modest man, is extremely meticulous in both the vineyard and the cellars, a characteristic reflected in his wines. These are known as modern-styled Burgundies because they can be drunk young, but they age well.

CHARMES-CHAMBERTIN

2002 Charmes-Chambertin

RATING: 97 points
The magnificently expressive 2002 Charmes-Chambertin boasts a floral, spicy nose packed with fresh red fruits. Spicy, concentrated, powerful, yet elegant, this cherry-dominated, medium-bodied wine exhibits spice box and coffee notes in its extensive finish. Harmonious, refined, and extroverted, it is a candidate for drinking between 2006 and 2015.

2001 Charmes-Chambertin

RATING: 92 points
From one of Gevrey's warmest *terroirs,* the 2001 Charmes-Chambertin offers aromas of black cherries and blackberries. Light to medium–bodied, it slathers the palate with copious red and black cherries whose effects linger in its long, yet firm finish. Anticipated maturity: now–2012.

2000 Charmes-Chambertin

RATING: 94 points
Displaying the darker aromas and flavors typical for a Claude Dugat Charmes-Chambertin, the 2000 offers plummy black-

berry scents as well as a grapy, black cherry–dominated personality. An intensely flavored, powerful wine, it has superb concentration, grip, and density of fruit as well as an exceptionally long, ripe finish. Anticipated maturity: now–2011.

1999 Charmes-Chambertin
RATING: 96 points

The medium to dark ruby–colored 1999 Charmes-Chambertin has a mouthwatering nose of Asian spices, blackberries, and black cherries. This luscious, opulent, medium to full–bodied wine is creamy-textured and refined. Loads of red cherries, spices, and candied raspberries, and touches of sweet oak, can be found in this luxurious offering. It has an awesome depth of fruit as well as loads of exquisitely ripened, supple tannins. Additionally, this wine has an exceptionally long, pure finish. Drink it between now and 2012.

1998 Charmes-Chambertin
RATING: 93 points

Produced from 22-hectoliter-per-hectare yields, the medium to dark ruby–colored 1998 Charmes-Chambertin displays massive amounts of red and black fruit aromas. Medium to full–bodied and chewy-textured, it coats the palate with blackberries, black cherries, and cassis. This intense, concentrated, and velvety-textured wine has firm tannins that are immersed in sweet, well-ripened fruit. Drink it between now and 2008.

1997 Charmes-Chambertin
RATING: 95 points

Crafted from yields below 30 hectoliters per hectare, the medium to dark ruby–colored 1997 Charmes-Chambertin displays candied red cherry and spicy aromas. On the palate, it is opulent, sexy, refined, and gorgeously velvety. Flavors reminiscent of cinnamon-laced, red cherry jam coat the palate, and linger for up to 30 seconds or more. This hedonistic wine will offer superb drinking until 2009.

1996 Charmes-Chambertin
RATING: 98 points

I have no argument with anyone who states that this wine merits a perfect score. It is a dark ruby/purple–colored wine that regales the olfactory senses with sweet and perfumed red and black cherry scents that are lively, profound, and verging on jammy—reminiscent of the filling of a deep dish cherry pie. On the palate, this wondrous wine's combination of superripe candied red fruits and violets with virtually perfect precision and purity of flavors is mind-boggling. This complex, velvety-textured, chewy, and delineated wine is utterly extraordinary and otherworldly. Anticipated maturity: 2006–2012.

1995 Charmes-Chambertin
RATING: 92 points

While many offerings from Charmes-Chambertin are disappointingly weak, Claude Dugat's consistently outstanding offerings reinforce the point that the vineyard deserves its grand cru status. In 1995 Dugat produced another spectacular Charmes. Medium to dark ruby–colored with touches of purple, this elegant gem's thick texture and cascade of fat, chewy black fruits are divine. Spiced with toasty oak, long and refined, this wine should drink well through 2007.

1993 Charmes-Chambertin
RATING: 96 points

The 1993 Charmes-Chambertin (165 cases produced for the world) boasts layers of flavor, a saturated, deep ruby/purple color, a huge attack, and considerable tannin and muscle, as well as an inner sweetness and that profound mid-palate not found in many 1993s. This wine has it all—ripeness, richness, structure, purity, and complexity. Anticipated maturity: now–2014.

1992 Charmes-Chambertin
RATING: 94 points

The 1992 Charmes-Chambertin is a candidate for the wine of the vintage. A superb expression of red Burgundy, it possesses a huge, forceful, sweet, jammy nose of black and red fruits, smoke, and oak. Full-bodied, with layers of ripe fruit that cascade across the palate, this sensational, marvelously rich, well-delineated red Burgundy is a marvel to smell and taste. Anticipated maturity: now.

1991 Charmes-Chambertin
RATING: 92 points

The Dugats make spectacular Griottes and Charmes-Chambertins, and their 1991s will make believers of anyone who doubted what heights this vintage was capable of achieving. Combine the character of the Griottes with aromas of black truffles and smoked meats and nuts, add some additional length and richness, and you have Dugat's 1991 Charmes-Chambertin. Anticipated maturity: now.

1990 Charmes-Chambertin
RATING: 96 points

The 1990 Charmes-Chambertin was so concentrated, voluptuous, and chewy that the overall impression was one of layer upon layer of sweet, jammy Pinot fruit crammed into a wine that coats the mouth with such purity and intensity it had to be tasted to be believed. An oenologist might quibble over the low acid, as well as the element of *sur-maturité* in the wine, but, wow, what extraordinary flavor dimension and richness this wine possesses. Anticipated maturity: now.

2002 Griotte-Chambertin

Dugat's 2002 Griotte-Chambertin is denser, broader, and more layered than his Charmes. Aromatically, it explodes from the glass with a myriad of spices. On the palate, flavors of espresso beans intermingle with those of red cherries, blackberries, and mocha. Broad, ample, and seductive, it is a sensual, hugely concentrated wine with an admirably long, fruit-packed finish. Anticipated maturity: 2006–2016.

2001 Griotte-Chambertin

RATING: 91 points

Bing cherries and spices make up the aromatic profile of the 2001 Griotte-Chambertin. As is typical for Dugat's wines, it explodes on the palate revealing loads of candied fruits. Red cherries, jammy strawberries, and currants are found throughout its attack and mid-palate, giving way in the finish to a firmly tannic backbone. Anticipated maturity: now–2012.

2000 Griotte-Chambertin

RATING: 94 points

Chocolate-covered blackberries are found in the aromas of the 2000 Griotte-Chambertin. A big, juicy, medium to full-bodied, backward wine, it has massive depth, concentration, and density. Its velvety-textured core of fruit reveals mocha-laced black cherries and blackberries, as well as hints of toasted oak. In addition, its amazingly long finish displays a firm (yet ripe) tannic backbone and roasted dark fruits. If this wine blossoms (as I expect it will) with cellaring, it will ultimately be one of the wines of the vintage. Anticipated maturity: 2006–2014.

1999 Griotte-Chambertin

RATING: 96 points

The tangy cherry, Asian spice, and hoisin sauce–scented 1999 Griotte-Chambertin is medium to dark ruby–colored. This silky-textured beauty is loaded with creamed cherries, blackberry syrup, spices, and vanilla. It is fresh, focused, sexy, yet well-structured. Its immensely appealing fruit flavors last throughout its exceptional finish. Drink it between now and 2012.

1998 Griotte-Chambertin

RATING: 93 points

The 1998 Griotte-Chambertin was produced from even lower yields than the Charmes-Chambertin. Medium to dark ruby–colored, and boasting black cherry aromas, this velvety-textured wine is intense and persistent. Copious quantities of candied raspberries and cherries are found in its elegant, layered character. Drink it between now and 2008.

1997 Griotte-Chambertin

RATING: 94 points

Fashioned from a yield of 22 hectoliters per hectare, the 1997 Griotte-Chambertin verges on being dark ruby–colored. At first glance, this wine appeared to be reticent, yet with aeration, it revealed sweet black fruits, fresh herbs, perfume, and spices. On the palate, pruney fruits, nutmeg, cinnamon, brown sugar, licorice, and superripe blackberries are found in this broad, plump wine. In the Dugat style, it is quite expansive, medium to full–bodied, and eminently drinkable. Its complex flavors seemingly last forever. It has power, grace, magnificent depth, and a beguiling satin texture. Anticipated maturity: now–2010.

1996 Griotte-Chambertin

RATING: 98+ points

It would take a writer of Shakespeare's eloquence to do justice to this wine. It has a deep ruby/purple color and spiritual aromas of raspberry and cherry jam, violets, perfume, and Asian spices. Its aromatic purity, definition, and depth were so captivating that I feared the palate could not match up. Wrong! An explosion of satin-laced fruit greeted my tongue. Layer upon layer of perfectly ripened, sweet and jammy cherries, candied violets, roses, and blueberries provided a levitating experience. For minutes I could neither see nor feel my surroundings—nor did I care to—as this wine took my senses hostage. It is velvety, supple, powerful, stylish, refined, and

Griotte-Chambertin
Grand Cru
APPELLATION CONTRÔLÉE
MIS EN BOUTEILLE À LA PROPRIÉTÉ
VIN NON FILTRÉ
13.6% vol.   75 cl
L GRIO   Cellier des Dîmes XIII°
CLAUDE DUGAT
PROPRIÉTAIRE-VITICULTEUR A GEVREY-CHAMBERTIN (CÔTE-D'OR) FRANCE

concentrated, and it possesses the backbone (as silky as can be imagined!) to allow this heavenly offering to evolve magnificently. Its awesomely long finish has loads of fruit-drowned, soft, and round tannins. Anticipated maturity: 2006–2016.

1995 Griotte-Chambertin
RATING: 99 points
This is a mesmerizing wine. It is dark ruby–colored, almost inky black, with bright streaks of purple on the edges. Aromatically, it reveals an unreal depth of intense black fruits that give way to an explosion of black cherries, plums, blackberries, blueberries, violets, mocha, café au lait, sweet oak, and Asian spices. Wave upon wave of luscious fruit unfold on the palate in this opulent and hedonistic offering's velvety-textured core. Perfectly balanced and harmonious, intense yet soft, structured yet supple, it is a tour de force. Anticipated maturity: now–2010.

1993 Griotte-Chambertin
RATING: 100 points
A vintage that has been recklessly promoted as a "great" year (when, in fact, there are too many astringent, austere, angular, thin-tasting wines for "greatness") has also produced some astonishing Burgundies that are as compelling as any I have ever tasted. Dugat's 1993 Griotte-Chambertin is a religious experience, and not because it was made in a historic abbey/wine cellar. The color is an intense, saturated ruby/purple. The nose is classic, offering a penetrating fragrance combining profound quantities of red and black fruits, with toast, earth, and spice. Medium to full–bodied, with the essence of Pinot Noir distilled to its naked purity, this phenomenally intense, velvety-textured wine possesses exceptional fruit extraction that has been but-

tressed by sweet, ripe tannin. It is absurdly rich and seductive, yet also powerful and structured—a tour de force in winemaking! The 1993 is an even greater wine than Dugat's 1990. Anticipated maturity: now–2015.

1992 Griotte-Chambertin
RATING: 93 points
The 1992 Griotte-Chambertin displays a deep, saturated ruby/purple color and a huge, stunning bouquet of black fruits and spicy, toasty new oak. With rich, full-bodied, wonderfully expansive, pure flavors, superb harmony, and well-integrated acidity and tannin, this spectacularly endowed, rich, lusty red Burgundy should drink well through 2008.

1991 Griotte-Chambertin
RATING: 91 points
The opaque, dark ruby color of the 1991 Griotte-Chambertin was followed by a dazzling bouquet of roasted herbs, smoky oak, and black cherries. Sumptuous, sweet, expansive, and loaded with flavor and extraction, this decadent, superrich red burgundy required consumption by the end of 2003.

1990 Griotte-Chambertin
RATING: 99 points
While similar to the 1990 Charmes-Chambertin, the Griotte-Chambertin is even richer and longer, with a fragrance that could fill a room. Again, the characteristic style of Claude Dugat is for phenomenally sweet, opulent extraction of fruit complemented by toasty new oak. This massive yet exceptionally concentrated, supple wine exhibits a finish that lasts nearly 90 seconds. It is a monumental example of red Burgundy that should drink well through 2010.

WINES:

Chambertin

Charmes-Chambertin

Mazis-Chambertin

OWNER: Bernard Dugat-Py

ADDRESS: B. P. 31, Cour de l'Aumônerie, 21220 Gevrey-
Chambertin, France

TELEPHONE: 33 03 80 51 82 46

TELEFAX: 33 03 80 51 86 41

E-MAIL: dugat-py@wanadoo.fr

WEBSITE: www.dugat-py.com

CONTACT: Jocelyne or Bernard Dugat-Py

VISITING POLICY: No visits

VINEYARDS

SURFACE AREA: 21 acres

GRAPE VARIETALS: 97% Pinot Noir, 3% Chardonnay

AVERAGE AGE OF THE VINES: 50 years

DENSITY OF PLANTATION: 11,000 vines per hectare

AVERAGE YIELDS: 30 hectoliters per hectare

WINEMAKING AND UPBRINGING

Dugat's winemaking philosophy is to employ "the least inter-
ventionalistic procedures possible," always trying to preserve the
quality of the fruit so the appellation's full expression comes
through in the bottle. One hundred percent destemming is usually done, but there are exceptions (2002), and the fermentation,
which takes place in cement as well as wood fermenters, can last
for four weeks. New oak is employed according to the vintage's
concentration and can be as low as 20%, or significantly higher.
The wines generally spend 14–20 months in barrel and are bottled without fining or filtration. Dugat's magnificent cellars are
essentially the underground crypt of the local church.

ANNUAL PRODUCTION

Chambertin: 270 bottles

Charmes-Chambertin: 2,000 bottles

Mazis-Chambertin: 900 bottles

AVERAGE PRICE (VARIABLE DEPENDING ON VINTAGE): $125–450

GREAT RECENT VINTAGES

2003, 2002, 2001, 1999, 1996

Two rising superstars, Bernard and Jocelyne Dugat-Py,
are relative latecomers in the somewhat sated world
of Burgundy. They purchased their first vineyard parcel

in 1973, and their first vinification was in 1975. Bernard
and his father, Pierre, quickly established reputations as
conservative vignerons. Some of their top wines were
purchased by well-known *négociant* firms for commin-
gling with other *cuvées*. I first heard Dugat's name while
talking to several *négociants* about some of the finest
growers in the Gevrey-Chambertin. Today, Jocelyne and
Bernard work side by side along with their son, Loic.
They continue to build their estate: In 1998, they purchased a tiny parcel in the premier cru Petite Chapelle
(100 cases produced), and in 2003 they added a tiny parcel of old-vine Pommard as well as old-vine Meursault.

For the past decade, this 21-acre domaine has consistently produced exceptional wines, a testimony to the
relentless pursuit of quality exhibited by Dugat, Jocelyne, and their son Loic. "Yes, it's true that we live in the
vineyards, working from morning to night, but the primary reasons we don't have the same problems as many
others in Burgundy is that we concentrate on having
low yields and are fortunate enough to have old vines,"
says Bernard Dugat.

Readers should note these Burgundies are not
meant for near-term consumption, as they are intense,
concentrated efforts that represent the essence of
Dugat's vineyard sites. Even in lighter vintages they require 4–6 years of cellaring. In great years, they beg for
10–12 years of bottle age.

CHAMBERTIN

2002 Chambertin

RATING: 98 points

Produced from 80-year-old vines planted at a 14,000-vines-per-hectare density, the 2002 Chambertin was whole-cluster fermented in this particular vintage because of the tiny amount produced, and crushed by foot by Bernard's son, Loic. Its waxy, black cherry aromas are intermingled with notes of tar, licorice, mint, and spices. Viscous, hugely powerful, and dense, it saturates the palate with rocks, herbs, coffee, and black fruit pastes. Immensely concentrated and profound, it must be tasted to be believed, yet since only 198 liters (about 260 bottles) of this amazing elixir were produced in 2002, only the wealthiest and luckiest wine enthusiasts will ever experience it. Anticipated maturity: 2012–2030+.

2001 Chambertin

RATING: 98 points

A prodigious wine, Dugat's black-colored 2001 Chambertin boasts a blackberry, chocolate, tar, and dark cherry–filled nose. Medium to full–bodied, supple, sweet, and thick, its voluminous, harmonious character conquers the palate with unbelievably dense layers of lush black fruits. A viscous yet perfectly balanced effort, it sports an imposing, seemingly unending finish. This stately Burgundy transcends its vintage. Wow! Anticipated maturity: now–2020+.

1999 Chambertin

RATING: 98 points

The 1999 Chambertin is a magnificent, show-stopping wine. It is black-colored and bursts from the glass with licorice, cookie dough, blackberry, and cassis aromas. This is a massive, full-bodied wine with loads of sweet candied black fruits, licorice, freshly laid asphalt, spice, fresh herbs, and toasty oak flavors. It is mind-numbingly powerful, conquering the taster with wave upon wave of supple, syrup-like fruit whose flavors last throughout its seemingly unending finish. This blockbuster Burgundy should be cellared for a minimum of 10 years and may last up to 20 or more years after that. It is one of the rare wines from this region that I would have no qualms about cellaring for 30 years.

1997 Chambertin

RATING: 96 points

A hedonistic fruit bomb, the 1997 Chambertin reveals creamy, wild red berries, cherry pie filling, fruitcake, blueberry jam, milk chocolate, and hints of white pepper. This is a chewy, almost syrupy-textured monster with candied and jellied red fruit flavors that saturate the palate and seemingly linger forever. Drink this extraordinary offering over the next 10–12 years.

CHARMES-CHAMBERTIN

2002 Charmes-Chambertin

RATING: 97 points

Reminiscent of liquid satin, the candied black fruit, rose, and spice–scented 2002 Charmes-Chambertin seduces with its mouth-coating, harmonious personality. Loads of dark cherries, blackberries, spices, and raspberries are found in this generous, awesomely ripe wine. "Sweet, sweet, sweet" read my notes. Decadently powerful yet supple, and armed with great purity, it will be at its finest between 2007 and 2017.

2001 Charmes-Chambertin

RATING: 95 points

Chocolate-covered black cherries can be discerned in the viscous aromas of the 2001 Charmes-Chambertin. This huge, medium to full–bodied wine has exceptional depth of fruit. Its personality displays a flavor profile reminiscent of cherry syrup laced with vanilla beans. Ample, lush, and rich, its stupendous finish reveals waves of fruit and copious, exquisitely ripened tannin. Anticipated maturity: now–2015.

2000 Charmes-Chambertin

RATING: 96 points

The 2000 Charmes-Chambertin boasts a violet-spice and black cherry–scented nose. This dense, syrupy wine is medium to full–bodied and layered with powerful chocolate-covered black cherries. Its magnificent personality is luxuriant, well-structured, and exceedingly long. Anticipated maturity: 2007–2018.

1999 Charmes-Chambertin

RATING: 94 points

The 1999 Charmes-Chambertin is medium to dark ruby–colored and offers a knockout nose of sweet cherries, smoked bacon, and mint. This is a huge, medium to full–bodied wine that is highly concentrated and expansive. Untold quantities of blackberries, cherries, and spices, and hints of new toasty oak, can be discerned in its layered character. This powerful yet feminine wine is loaded with ripe tannin. Anticipated maturity: now–2012+.

1998 Charmes-Chambertin

RATING: 93 points

Bernard Dugat's 1998 Charmes-Chambertin (one-third Mazoyères and two-thirds from the Charmes sector) is dark ruby–colored and offers a hugely spicy, candied cherry–scented nose. Loads of black fruits and sweet cherries, as well as asphalt and oak, can be found in this broad, medium to full–bodied wine. Sweet, almost jammy fruit coats the taster's palate throughout this offering's well-ripened personality and long, focused finish. Anticipated maturity: now–2010.

1997 Charmes-Chambertin

RATING: 94 points

One hundred cases of the dark ruby–colored 1997 Charmes-Chambertin were produced. Its magnificently sweet nose is crammed with cherries and creamy vanilla aromas. It is charming and sexy. Medium to full–bodied, it offers loads of syrupy blackberries and cherries in addition to possessing the required structure for cellaring. Anticipated maturity: now–2009.

MAZIS-CHAMBERTIN

2002 Mazis-Chambertin

RATING: 96+ points

The masculine, firm, and deep 2002 Mazis-Chambertin explodes from the glass with profound aromas of chocolate, blackberry jam, cassis, and black cherry paste. This monstrously powerful wine assaults the palate with waves of velvety black fruits, tar, licorice, and Asian spices. Hyper-ripe yet structured and balanced, it displays copious quantities of tannin in its exceptionally long, intense finish. Anticipated maturity: 2009–2025.

2001 Mazis-Chambertin

RATING: 95 points

The masculine, foursquare 2001 Mazis-Chambertin is a brooding monster. Chewy-textured, it saturates the palate with highly extracted black fruits. This massively concentrated, backward wine is dense and loaded with ripe yet firm tannin. Anticipated maturity: 2007–2017.

2000 Mazis-Chambertin

RATING: 97 points

Candied blackberries and cherries are found in the nose of the awesome 2000 Mazis-Chambertin. A thick, yet juicy wine, it coats the taster's palate with jammy black cherries. Medium to full–bodied, it is bold, dense, deep, expansive, and hugely concentrated. Its considerable tannin, discernible in its prodigious finish, is perfectly ripe, almost sweet. Drink this awesome effort between 2007 and 2020.

1999 Mazis-Chambertin

RATING: 95 points

Produced from 55- to 60-year-old vines, the dark-colored 1999 Mazis-Chambertin is profound. Its licorice, black cherry syrup, and chocolate chip cookie dough–scented nose leads to a hugely powerful, medium to full–bodied character. This road tar, blackberry, cassis, and spice-flavored wine has the density, structure, and balance for moderate to long-term aging. Anticipated maturity: 2006–2015+.

1998 Mazis-Chambertin

RATING: 93 points

Produced from 60-year-old vines, the 1998 Mazis-Chambertin Vieilles Vignes has a tar and blackberry–scented nose. This muscular, masculine, and highly expressive wine is full-bodied, inky, and firmly structured. Massively concentrated and intense, this may be one of the rare tannic Pinot Noirs whose fruit can sustain cellaring. Anticipated maturity: now–2008+.

1997 Mazis-Chambertin

RATING: 95 points

Crafted from 53- and 56-year-old vines, the dark ruby–colored 1997 Mazis-Chambertin exhibits sweet black fruits, Asian spices, and hints of saddle leather in its austere and brooding aromatics. This full-bodied, broad-shouldered, muscular wine has flavors reminiscent of soy sauce, hoisin, earth, leather, and cassis. Anticipated maturity: now–2012.

WINES:

Bonnes Mares

Chambertin-Clos de Bèze

Chevalier-Montrachet Les Demoiselles

Corton-Charlemagne

Le Montrachet

Musigny

OWNER: The Kopf family

ADDRESS: 21 rue Eugene Spuller, B.P. 117, 21200 Beaune, France

TELEPHONE: 33 03 80 22 10 57

TELEFAX: 33 03 80 22 56 03

E-MAIL: contact@louisjadot.com

WEBSITE: www.louisjadot.com

CONTACT: Pierre-Henry Gagey

VISITING POLICY: By appointment only

VINEYARDS

SURFACE AREA: 336 acres

GRAPE VARIETALS: Chardonnay, Pinot Noir, Gamay

AVERAGE AGE OF THE VINES: 20–80 years

DENSITY OF PLANTATION:

Côte d'Or: 10,000–12,000 per hectare

Beaujolais: 8,000–10,000 per hectare

AVERAGE YIELDS:

Grands crus: 35 hectoliters per hectare

Premiers crus: 40 hectoliters per hectare

Villages wines: 45 hectoliters per hectare

Regional appellations: 55 hectoliters per hectare

WINEMAKING AND UPBRINGING

PINOT NOIR: Everything is destemmed. Then there follows a long maceration in open wooden vats and stainless-steel tanks for a month. The alcoholic fermentation is done only with indigenous yeasts. During maceration, the wine is punched down twice a day, with relatively high fermentation temperatures to encourage maximum extraction. The wine is then moved into barrels. An average of 30% new oak is used for the red wines, with a slightly higher percentage utilized for the premier and grand crus. Malolactic fermentation takes place in barrel, and the wine is aged 10–20 months, depending on the vintage. No fining is done at bottling, but a light polishing filtration is employed.

CHARDONNAY: The grapes are fermented in stainless-steel tanks, and once alcoholic fermentation begins, they are quickly moved to French barrels to complete the alcoholic and partial malolactic fermentation. Louis Jadot is one of the few estates that systematically blocks part of the malolactic process in order to preserve more acidity. In such fragile low-acid vintages as those of 1982, 1983, 1989, and 2003, this has added longevity and character to the wines. The white wines spend 10–20 months in barrels, of which approximately 30% are new.

ANNUAL PRODUCTION

Bonnes Mares: 750 cases

Chambertin-Clos de Bèze: 450–500 cases

Chevalier-Montrachet Les Demoiselles: 275–300 cases

Corton-Charlemagne: 700–750 cases

Le Montrachet: 25–50 cases

Musigny: 25 cases

AVERAGE PRICE (VARIABLE DEPENDING ON VINTAGE): $50–200

GREAT RECENT VINTAGES

Red Burgundy: 2002, 1999, 1997, 1996, 1993, 1990, 1989, 1985

White Burgundy: 2002, 1999, 1996, 1992, 1990, 1986, 1985

In terms of quality, the firm of Louis Jadot is among the finest *négociants* in Burgundy. The firm also has extensive vineyard holdings. This operation was run with meticulous attention to detail by the late André Gagey, and more recently by his dynamic son, Pierre-Henry Gagey. True gentlemen, both Gageys are among Burgundy's most conscientious protectors of quality.

This firm was established in 1859 by the Jadot family with their purchase of the renowned Beaune premier cru vineyard, Clos des Ursules. In 1985, it was purchased by an American family, the Kopfs of New York, and the owners have continued to purchase top-quality vineyards when they become available. In 1986, they acquired the famous estate of Clair-Dau (42 acres), and in December 1989 they bought the cellars and vineyards of Maison Champet (15.6 acres). That was followed by the brilliant acquisitions of the famed Moulin à Vent estate in Beaujolais, Château des Jacques in 1996, and Château de Bellevue in Beaujolais in 2001.

A cooperage (for fabricating their own barrels) called Cadus was created in 1996, and in 1997 they completed the construction of a state-of-the-art winery, La Sablier, as Pierre-Henry Gagey states, "to maximize the expression of *terroir* in our wines."

They have consistently vinified all grapes from their own vineyards as well as those purchased under contract with growers, something that is rarely practiced by other *négociants*.

BONNES MARES

2002 Bonnes Mares

RATING: 97 points

Armed with huge quantities of fruit and perfectly ripened tannin, the medium to full–bodied 2002 Bonnes Mares explodes from the glass with stunning aromas of candied blueberries, rocks, and red cherries. This massive, broad, enormously rich wine could ultimately, like the Chapelle and Clos de Bèze, earn a perfect score. Its velvety waves of sensual red and black fruits are interspersed with nuanced notes of spices, mocha, flowers, and minerals. While enormously powerful and ripe, it magically retains its freshness and sports an ethereal quality that is difficult to put into words. It is a tour de force in winemaking! Anticipated maturity: 2009–2020+.

2001 Bonnes Mares

RATING: 90 points

Gorgeous aromas of spiced red cherries can be found in the nose of the 2001 Bonnes Mares. Medium-bodied, pure, and well-balanced, this silky-textured wine boasts a dark cherry and black raspberry–filled flavor profile. It is well-concentrated, ripe, and expressive. Anticipated maturity: now–2012.

1997 Bonnes Mares

RATING: 93 points

The stunning, dark purple–colored 1997 Bonnes Mares enthralls the nose with its extraordinary baked-blackberry aromas. This is a wine of unbelievable power and concentration and exceptional extraction. Deep layers of cocoa powder–dusted figs and prunes vie for the taster's attention with a compote of red cherries, stones, and creamed mocha flavors. This full-bodied, velvety-textured, *sur-maturité* wine lingers on the palate for at least 40 seconds. It is a prodigiously breathtaking Burgundy. Anticipated maturity: now–2012+.

1996 Bonnes Mares

RATING: 94+ points

This dark ruby–colored wine is unbelievable and has the potential to be Jadot's finest 1996. An awesome nose of deep black cherries intermingled with sautéed mushrooms, underbrush, stones, and minerals is followed by an amazingly powerful yet tense personality. Complex layers of intense, precise, pure, and earthy fruit cascade over the palate in this full-bodied, thickly textured, muscular, masculine, and well-delineated wine. The harmonious juxtaposition of this offering's outstanding depth and richness and its elegant focus is mind-blowing. A tour de force! Anticipated maturity: now–2010+.

1995 Bonnes Mares

RATING: 91+ points

The spectacular 1995 Bonnes Mares jumps from the glass with aromas of blackberries, cherries, flowers, and minerals. It is a massively concentrated, powerful, full-bodied wine packed with stones, wild cherries, red currants, and touches of iron, tar, and chocolate for additional complexity. Highly structured and with an exceptionally long finish, it should hold through 2012.

1993 Bonnes Mares

RATING: 90 points

The outstanding 1993 Bonnes Mares is more tannic than the Clos St.-Denis, but not as concentrated or supple as the Chambolle-Musigny Les Amoureuses. This well-made wine offers good sweetness and medium body, but it is not as impressive as some of the previous vintages, particularly the 1990. Anticipated maturity: now–2016.

1990 Bonnes Mares

RATING: 96 points

The sweet, open-knit 1990 Bonnes Mares reveals layer upon layer of fruit and huge body, yet there is a sense of elegance and precision to its lavish richness and huge, perfumed personality. This extraordinary red Burgundy is soft and more developed than either the Chambertin-Clos de Bèze or Chambertin. Anticipated maturity: 2006–2018.

1987 Bonnes Mares

RATING: 90 points

The 1987 Bonnes Mares is truly great, and one of the very top wines of the vintage. It has a gorgeous, complete bouquet of herbs, rich berry fruits, spicy new oak, and exotic spices. Rich, with a chewy, fleshy texture, and fresh acidity, it has one of the longest finishes of any wine I have tasted from this vintage. It should be drunk up now.

CHAMBERTIN-CLOS DE BEZE

2002 Chambertin-Clos de Bèze

RATING: 96

Black fruits are interspersed with licorice and earth in the nose of the medium to full–bodied 2002 Chambertin-Clos de Bèze. This concentrated, deep, noble wine is crammed with perfectly ripe fruit and tannin. Loads of blackberries, licorice, plums, black cherries, stones, and flowers can be discerned in its complex flavor profile. Its finish, described in my notes as "completely unreal," is exceedingly long, fruit-filled, and suave. If stored in a cold cellar, this wine would be an ideal selection for serving to a 2002 baby on his or her 21st birthday. Anticipated maturity: 2010–2024.

1997 Chambertin-Clos de Bèze

RATING: 94 points

The 1997 Chambertin-Clos de Bèze was harvested at an unheard of (for Burgundy) 14.2 natural potential alcohol. This black/purple–colored benchmark setter offers saliva-inducing aromas of cookie dough and cherry syrup. Immensely ripe and concentrated, yet pure, fresh, and noble, it conquers the taster with unending layers of jammy compote-like fruit flavors. Awesomely dense, deep, fresh, and refined, it seamlessly combines the New World's overripeness and fruit-forward characteristics with Burgundy's trademark balance, elegance, and structure. It should be at its peak of maturity between now and 2015.

1996 Chambertin-Clos de Bèze

RATING: 92+ points

This magnificent offering has a saturated black/ruby color and an enthralling nose of candied cherries, roses, blackberries, stones, earth, and toasty oak. It is full-bodied, velvety-textured, and unbelievably dense, yet superbly focused. Fresh and lively layers of red cherries, clay, currants, and Asian spices can be found in this powerful, intense, classy, and persistent wine. It should hit its peak around 2006 and can be cellared through 2014.

1995 Chambertin-Clos de Bèze

RATING: 91 points

Jadot's opaque, black-colored Chambertin-Clos de Bèze reveals superripe cherries and prunes intertwined with roasted notes of coffee, herbs, and stones. This wine's immense, full-bodied personality is packed with massive, thick, viscous, highly extracted and concentrated black fruits. Unapproachable, this behemoth will be at its peak between now and 2015.

1990 Chambertin-Clos de Bèze

RATING: 96 points

The outstanding 1990's saturated, dark ruby/purple color is followed by sweet, jammy aromas framed by noticeable smoky new oak. The magnificent richness and highly structured and delineated style, as well as the explosively rich finish, all make for a show-stopping impression. Anticipated maturity: now–2017.

1988 Chambertin-Clos de Bèze

RATING: 92 points

Not surprisingly, the Chambertin-Clos de Bèze, always a winner from this house, received 26 days of maceration in 1988. The result is a beautifully scented wine smelling of exotic spices, soy sauce, ground beef, and lots of ripe berry fruit. It is full-bodied and very rich but is not comparable to the celestial 1985. Nevertheless, it is an outstanding red Burgundy from this vintage. Anticipated maturity: now–2010.

CHEVALIER-MONTRACHET LES DEMOISELLES

1999 Chevalier-Montrachet Les Demoiselles

RATING: 92 points

The 1999 Chevalier-Montrachet Les Demoiselles has gorgeous, mouthwatering aromas of almonds and flowers. Medium to full–bodied, sexy, broad, and opulent, this wine is also well-delineated and refined. Flowers, crisp pears, and candied apples are found throughout its pure, fresh, and impressively long finish. Anticipated maturity: now–2015.

1998 Chevalier-Montrachet Les Demoiselles

RATING: 92 points

Typically one of Jadot's longest-lived whites, the 1998 Chevalier-Montrachet Les Demoiselles will live up to its reputation. Flowers, stones, and minerals are found in its aromatics. This medium-bodied wine has admirable breadth, delineation, richness, and freshness in its character. Minerals and candied lemons can be found throughout its flavor profile and persistent finish. Anticipated maturity: now–2010.

1997 Chevalier-Montrachet Les Demoiselles

RATING: 93 points

Jadot's 1997 Chevalier-Montrachet Les Demoiselles is a fabulous wine. Its nose reveals nuts, minerals, and stones. An offering of outstanding richness and density, its flavor profile is crammed with candied hazelnuts and almonds, as well as spicy minerals. It also has an ethereal quality found in the best Chevaliers. This is one of the rare 1997s from the Côte de Beaune that will age for at least a decade. Drink it between now and 2012.

1996 Chevalier-Montrachet Les Demoiselles

RATING: 97 points

Jadot's 1996 Chevalier-Montrachet Les Demoiselles, one of Burgundy's perennial stars, is a stunner. Its aromatic purity and precision is something to behold, displaying extraordinary depth and ripeness as well as loads of liquid minerals. On the palate, it has unbridled power, a full body, an oily texture, and exquisite anise, spice, pear, and floral flavors. This highly delineated and wonderfully structured wine will require patience. Consume it before 2015.

1995 Chevalier-Montrachet Les Demoiselles

RATING: 96 points

The 1995's nose displays butter, minerals, stones, and spice. The flavors present fabulous harnessed fruit with well-integrated acidity. This high-class wine possesses formidable structure and impressive persistence. Regrettably, there were only 100 cases produced of this sublime Chevalier. Anticipated maturity: now–2017.

1989 Chevalier-Montrachet Les Demoiselles

RATING: 96 points

Less than 100 cases were made of the 1989 Chevalier-Montrachet Les Demoiselles, which was the tightest, most backward wine I tasted from Jadot. Even more unevolved than the Montrachet, it needs 5–10 years of cellaring and should last for 20–30 years. It is absolutely magnificent with its subtle yet authoritative bouquet of minerals and superripe fruit. In the mouth, there is high acidity, formidable depth, and a texture that is oh, so chewy. It is the essence of Chardonnay. Anticipated maturity: now–2022.

CORTON-CHARLEMAGNE

2002 Corton-Charlemagne

RATING: 96 points

Aromatically, the powerful, dense, explosive 2002 Corton-Charlemagne offers spices, minerals, gravel, and pears. Its awesome aromatics are followed by a muscular, intense personality of exceptional purity. Spices, earth, poached pears, apples, white peaches, and ginger can be found throughout this blockbuster's flavor profile, as well as in its super-impressive finish. Drink this elegant, muscle-bound gem between 2009 and 2019.

2000 Corton-Charlemagne

RATING: 91 points

The 2000 Corton-Charlemagne has a creamy, talcum powder and mocha–scented nose. Medium to full–bodied, supple, and velvety-textured, it is an intensely flavored offering. It bastes the palate with creamed fruit and mineral flavors. Drink this harmonious, lush wine between now and 2012.

1996 Corton-Charlemagne

RATING: 92 points

The 1996 Corton-Charlemagne has a deep, rich, and ripe bouquet packed with white fruits. On the palate, it is an oily-textured, medium to full–bodied, and dense wine with metal, mineral, sweet candied nut, buttered popcorn, and poached pear flavors. Anticipated maturity: now–2008.

1995 Corton-Charlemagne

RATING: 92 points

Jadot's 1995 Corton-Charlemagne is one of those rare Cortons with class and finesse, in contrast to the majority of Cortons, which are big, powerful, and brawny wines that rely on their strength to awe the drinker. With reticent, nearly concealed ripe fruit aromas, this tightly knit wine offers great richness (green apple essence) and a long, persistent flavor. Thick-textured and medium to full–bodied, it should last until 2012.

1989 Corton-Charlemagne

RATING: 95 points

Normally one of the slowest grand crus to evolve, the 1989 should mature at a glacial pace. Spectacularly concentrated, it possesses a reticent nose that needs coaxing from the glass. After 10–15 minutes, aromas of minerals, oranges, ripe pineapples, and buttery baked apples soar from the glass. Extremely long and full-bodied, with blockbuster length and intensity, this is spectacular Corton-Charlemagne in a vintage that produced many dazzling wines from that appellation. Anticipated maturity: now–2022.

1986 Corton-Charlemagne

RATING: 94 points

The immensely promising 1986 still tastes young and backward. While full-bodied and expansive on the palate, the acidity is higher than normal. Anticipated maturity: now–2012.

1983 Corton-Charlemagne

RATING: 95 points

The spectacular 1983 offers superripe aromas of oranges, baked apples, and honeysuckle. This flamboyant wine possesses exceptional glycerin and extraction of fruit in addition to mind-numbing levels of alcohol. Anticipated maturity: now.

LE MONTRACHET

2002 Le Montrachet

RATING: 95 points

The 2002 Le Montrachet reveals a highly expressive nose of sap-laden rocks, spices, and ginger. On the palate, this medium to full–bodied, velvety-textured effort is seamless, rich, broad, and ample. Loads of spices, hazelnuts, cloves, pears, and honeyed minerals can be discerned in its complex, harmonious character. Its pure, lush personality and impressively bold flavors linger throughout its long, suave finish. Anticipated maturity: 2008–2020.

2000 Le Montrachet

RATING: 91+ points

The mineral and spice–scented 2000 Le Montrachet is light to medium–bodied, yet rich and satin-textured. Highly focused, this wine exhibits outstanding depth and concentration. Waves of minerals intermingled with citrus fruits and pears can be discerned throughout its expressive character as well as in its lengthy finish. Anticipated maturity: now–2012.

1999 Le Montrachet

RATING: 94 points

Harvested at 13.6% natural potential alcohol, the 1999 Le Montrachet has a magnificent spice cake, almond paste, and hazelnut–laden nose. Medium to full–bodied and suggestive of drinking liquid velvet, this is a big, deep, broad, and well-focused wine. Pears, apples, stones, and a myriad of spices can be found throughout its highly expressive and flavorful character. It is a huge success for the vintage, and an exceptional wine in its own right. It should stand the test of time. Anticipated maturity: now–2014.

1998 Le Montrachet

RATING: 92 points

In 1998, Maison Louis Jadot purchased its Le Montrachet from two growers, producing a total of eight barrels (200 cases). The wine's acacia, spice, stone, and mineral nose gives way to a lively, broad-shouldered, medium to full–bodied personality. This magnificent wine offers layers and layers of ripe white fruits, hints of toasted nuts, gravel, and poached pears. It wonderfully unites muscle with grace, and explosive, expressive fruit with refinement. Anticipated maturity: now–2012+.

1996 Le Montrachet

RATING: 96 points

The 1996 Le Montrachet exhibits earth, wild mushroom, smoke, and mineral aromas as well as a hugely concentrated, extracted, and intensely complex personality. Copious quantities of Brazil nuts, gravel, spiced pears, buttered toast, and flowers saturate the palate in this velvety-textured, magnificently balanced, and full-bodied blockbuster. Its admirably long finish appears to last close to 40 seconds. Anticipated maturity: 2006–2015.

1995 Le Montrachet

RATING: 95 points

Possessing a harnessed, super-tightly wound nose of sweet fruit and steely components, the 1995 Le Montrachet is a compelling wine. Jam-packed with dense underlying fruit and minerals, its powerful racy mouth is just waiting to explode to the surface. The brilliant use of oak is impeccable and provides a gorgeous spiciness to the wine. Full-bodied, complex, intense and long, it will age effortlessly for 20+ years. Anticipated maturity: now–2017.

1992 Le Montrachet

RATING: 93 points

The 1992 Le Montrachet exhibits a huge nose of minerals, cherries, oranges, and honeysuckle. Full-bodied, ripe, and long, with fine underlying acidity, and plenty of weight and richness in the finish, it should drink well until 2008.

1989 Le Montrachet

RATING: 98 points

The super-opulent, highly extracted 1989 Le Montrachet conjures up everything that this 19.76-acre grand cru vineyard should, but so rarely does, produce. There is density, balance, a haunting combination of minerals and ripe fruit, and a finish that exceeds 60 seconds. This big, splendidly concentrated wine should be at its finest between now and 2017.

MUSIGNY

2002 Musigny

RATING: 96 points

Sadly, Jadot only produces tiny amounts of Musigny, but those lucky enough to secure some of the 2002 will be enthralled. Its boisterous aromas greet the nose with flowers, spices, raspberries, and cherries. On the palate, this medium to full–bodied effort is coiled, waiting to strike. Cloves, sweet red fruits, candied blackberries, violets, and roses can be discerned in its tightly wound personality. A wine of power and harmony, it is chewy-textured and dense and has a firm structure that demands cellaring. Anticipated maturity: 2010–2024.

2001 Musigny

RATING: 91 points

Medium to dark ruby–colored and exhibiting a nose of candied orange rinds as well as sweet blackberries, the 2001 Musigny is a long, lush wine. This medium-bodied offering broadens on the palate to reveal an enticing panoply of spiced red fruits. Anticipated maturity: now–2012.

1999 Musigny

RATING: 90 points

The oak-scented, medium to dark ruby–colored 1999 Musigny offers a medium-bodied, tangy character. This floral, feminine, well-made, elegant wine displays sweet red cherry and raspberry flavors in its long, satin-textured character. It lacks the depth and power of Jadot's finest Musignys, yet is an outstanding, highly detailed, and delicious wine. Drink it between now and 2012.

1997 Musigny

RATING: 94 points

Awesome, but very structured and masculine, the dark ruby–colored 1997 Musigny regales the nose with its blueberry and spiced-toast aromas. This firm, muscular, and verging-on-foursquare wine displays black cherry, blackberry, rock, and mineral flavors. This powerhouse is immensely complex and persistent. Anticipated maturity: now–2012+.

1996 Musigny

RATING: 93+ points

The dark ruby–colored 1996 Musigny offers sublime aromas of violets, roses, and blackberries dusted with baby powder and has a full-bodied, thickly textured, powerful, yet controlled personality. Its flavor profile is tense and tightly wound, but extraordinary layers of chocolate-covered cherries, sweetly charred oak, and coffee are discernable. It has the elegant femininity of a ballerina and the muscle of a body builder. Its seemingly unending finish is buttressed by loads of ripe tannins. Drink it between now and 2010.

1995 Musigny

RATING: 90 points

Jadot's dark-colored 1995 Musigny reveals touches of cinnamon and blackberries in its intensely floral nose. On the palate, this full-bodied, velvety-textured, powerful wine explodes with copious quantities of roasted herbs, coffee, blackberries, and violets and has an admirable finish. Anticipated maturity: now–2012.

1993 Musigny

RATING: 92 points

Jadot's great 1993 Musigny boasts spectacular concentration, a super, penetrating fragrance of red and black fruits intermingled with the judicious use of toasty oak, medium to full body, admirable structure, and noticeable, ripe tannin that contributes to an overall sense of equilibrium. Anticipated maturity: now–2015.

1990 Musigny

RATING: 93 points

The 1990 Musigny (75 cases produced) is a textbook example of this vineyard. The color is deep ruby. The nose consists primarily of sweet black cherries and new oak. In the mouth, there is a soft, velvety texture, as well as medium to full body, low acidity, and gentle tannins in the long finish. Anticipated maturity: now.

WINES:

Meursault Les Charmes

Meursault Les Genevrières

Meursault Les Perrières

Le Montrachet

Volnay Santenots-du-Milieu

OWNERS: Lafon family

ADDRESS: Clos de la Barre, 21190 Meursault, France

TELEPHONE: 33 03 80 21 22 17

TELEFAX: 33 03 80 21 61 64

E-MAIL: comtes.lafon@wanadoo.fr

VISITING POLICY: No visits

VINEYARDS

SURFACE AREA: 34 acres, 19.8 acres in Meursault

GRAPE VARIETALS: Chardonnay, Pinot Noir

AVERAGE AGE OF THE VINES: 25–50 years

DENSITY OF PLANTATION: 10,000–12,000 vines per hectare

AVERAGE YIELDS: 25–45 hectoliters per hectare

WINEMAKING AND UPBRINGING

Low yields, ripe fruit, and a non-interventionist winemaking process are the norm at Lafon. The deep, cold cellars allow for a slow *élevage* (upbringing). Both the Chardonnays and the Pinot Noirs are aged on their lees for long periods. Lafon is flexible with respect to bottling, allowing the most concentrated vintages to rest 24 months prior to being bottled, whereas the lighter vintages are bottled earlier. There is rarely any type of clarification as the wines have a tendency to settle naturally in this cold environment. The Pinot Noir is largely

Dominique Lafon and his father

destemmed and given more new oak (up to 50% new) than the Chardonnay (20–35% new). Like the whites, the red wines are also bottled without filtration.

ANNUAL PRODUCTION

Meursault Les Charmes: 1,000 cases

Meursault Les Genevrières: 1,150 cases

Meursault Les Perrières: 450–500 cases

Le Montrachet: 125–150 cases

Volnay Santenots-du-Milieu: 300–500 cases

AVERAGE PRICE (VARIABLE DEPENDING ON VINTAGE): $100–500

GREAT RECENT VINTAGES

2002, 2000, 1999, 1996, 1995, 1990, 1989, 1985

One of the reference points for white Burgundy, Domaine des Comtes Lafon is run by Dominique Lafon and his brother, Bruno. Dominique is both a sophisticated, globe-trotting ambassador for Burgundy and a brilliant vineyard specialist and winemaker. Some of the finest, most elegant and ageworthy white Burgundies emerge from this 34-acre estate, graced with a handsome château-like building. Comtes Lafon's cellars are among the deepest and coldest in Burgundy, and for that reason, the upbringing of the wines has always been prolonged. The wines typically age on their lees undisturbed for nearly two years so that they can be bottled without filtration. However, some older vintages were oxidized at bottling and only got worse, so there appears to be a trend toward bottling earlier. The classics include Le Montrachet and Meursault Les Perrières (the most mineral-dominated), but both Meursault Les Genevrières and Meursault Les Charmes (the fatter and more obvious wine) are close behind.

Dominique Lafon, who took over from his father in 1987, practices traditional winemaking, but he keeps an open mind about ways he can continue to improve some of the world's most extraordinary wines. However, he believes the most important part of the winemaking philosophy he has inherited from generations of Lafons is "the courage to do nothing."

MEURSAULT LES CHARMES

2002 Meursault Les Charmes

RATING: 95 points

Lafon's 2002 Meursault Les Charmes is exceptional. Its awesome aromatics display spiced oak, peach, apricot, and yellow plum scents. Medium to full–bodied, decadent, and expansive, this intense wine bursts on the palate with silky, powerful waves of spices and yellow fruits. Even though it has massive richness and a broad-shouldered, muscular character, this beauty also displays graceful elegance. Anticipated maturity: now–2013.

2001 Meursault Les Charmes

RATING: 94 points

The spectacular 2001 Meursault Les Charmes reveals a boisterous nose of cloves, pears, spices, and white peaches. Hugely expansive, powerful, chewy-textured, and supple, this velvety wine slathers the palate with white pepper–laced apple compote whose flavors linger in its 45-second finish. Drink this beauty before 2012.

2000 Meursault Les Charmes

RATING: 92 points

The mineral, apple, and pear–scented 2000 Meursault Les Charmes is a wine that combines both power and finesse. It explodes on the palate with candied pear, butter, anise, and spiced apple flavors that, while highly expressive, seem delicate and lace-like. It is medium-bodied, precise, and exceptionally long in the finish. Anticipated maturity: now–2011.

1999 Meursault Les Charmes

RATING: 90 points

Talcum powder, perfume, and flowers can be discerned in the aromatics of the 1999 Meursault Les Charmes. Medium-bodied and silky, it offers toast, mineral, white currant, and crisp pear flavors. It is tangy, flavorful, extremely well balanced, and graceful. This wine also boasts an admirably long, smooth finish. Anticipated maturity: now–2010.

1997 Meursault Les Charmes

RATING: 92 points

The 1997 Meursault Les Charmes offers an extraordinarily elegant nose of earth, minerals, nuts, and flowers. This vivacious, medium to full–bodied, and harmonious wine has sweet mineral, chalk, citrus, and floral flavors. It is rich, gorgeously refined, and velvety-textured. Drink it between now and 2008.

1996 Meursault Les Charmes

RATING: 94 points

Lafon segregates the grapes from the youngest of his Meursault Les Charmes vines, blending them with his village Meursault *cuvée*. The most intense and concentrated berries are earmarked for his premier cru bottling. His dedication to quality is evidenced by the 1996's tantalizing floral, white peach, and toast aromas. Medium to full–bodied, thick, and yet feminine and gracious, this superb offering combines power with lace-like definition. Ripe white peaches, flower blossoms, and traces of anise are found in this precise, pure, and ageworthy beauty. Anticipated maturity: now–2010.

1995 Meursault Les Charmes

RATING: 93 points

The 1995 Meursault Les Charmes exhibits piercing and refined floral aromas, as well as a great saturation of powerful mineral and flint flavors. Anticipated maturity: now–2009.

1989 Meursault Les Charmes

RATING: 98 points

The blockbuster 1989 Meursault Les Charmes is one of the richest, most intense wines I have ever tasted from Lafon. This wine exhibits amazing amounts of glycerin, and an extraction level that is usually found only in the finest white Burgundy grand crus. The huge nose of superripe apples, buttered toast, and nuts is followed by a wine of decadent richness and phenomenal length and poise. All of this is held together by crisp acidity, another indication that this 1989 vintage, for all its precociousness and unctuous fruit, is going to evolve well. Anticipated maturity: now–2010

MEURSAULT LES GENEVRIERES

2002 Meursault Les Genevrières

RATING: 93 points

Mouthwatering aromas of yellow plums, white peaches, apricots, and a myriad of spices can be discerned in the nose of the 2002 Meursault Genevrières. This fresh, satiny-textured, medium-bodied wine has a fabulous satiny mouth-feel. Honeyed minerals are intermingled with spicy plums in its deep, long character. Anticipated maturity: now–2012.

2001 Meursault Les Genevrières

RATING: 91 points

The almond paste–scented 2001 Meursault Les Genevrières is oily-textured, lush, and medium-bodied. Sporting a fabulous mouth-feel, this wine conquers the palate with satiny layers of ripe white peaches and pears. Fresh, pure, and long in the finish, it should be consumed between now and 2009.

2000 Meursault Les Genevrières

RATING: 93 points

The gorgeous 2000 Meursault Les Genevrières reveals juniper berries, spices, and anise in its aromatics. Rich, fat, and vinous, this is a spice fruit bomb with a sexy, fruit-forward character and a long, persistent finish. It is concentrated, deep, and dense. Enjoy this highly expressive wine until 2012.

1997 Meursault Les Genevrières

RATING: 93 points

The 1997 Meursault Les Genevrières is spectacular! As he poured it, Lafon enthusiastically said, "It is the best wine of my life. I'm very proud of it." Sweet almond cookies intermingled with juicy citrus fruits can be found in this beauty's aromas. It explodes on the palate with richly textured and expansive flavors reminiscent of spiced apples, earth, minerals, and mangoes. This is a medium to full–bodied, intensely flavored, and opulent wine that is amazingly refined. Its exceptionally long finish lasted for at least 40 seconds. Impressive! Anticipated maturity: now–2008+.

1996 Meursault Les Genevrières

RATING: 95 points

Surprisingly, the 1996 Meursault Les Genevrières finished its malolactic fermentation prior to completing its alcoholic fermentation, a rarity in this vintage. Golden aromas of ripe pears, dried flowers, and white peaches complement the wine's immense concentration, intensity of flavor, and superb definition on the palate. This wine's massive yet elegant, full-bodied, opulent, and oily character is jam-packed with spicy poached pears, cloves, juniper berries, fresh herbs, and cardamom. Anticipated maturity: now–2009.

1995 Meursault Les Genevrières

RATING: 92 points

The 1995 Meursault Les Genevrières offers beautiful roasted fruit aromas; a fat, oily texture; sweet, salty nut flavors; and excellent balance. This full-bodied wine should be drunk between now and 2007.

1989 Meursault Les Genevrières

RATING: 94 points

Lafon's 1989 Meursault Les Genevrières was the most subtle and restrained of his 1989s. Completely closed when tasted in November, all of its potential and quality is evident at the back of the mouth, where there is an explosively long, rich, super-concentrated finish. Anticipated maturity: now–2007.

MEURSAULT LES PERRIERES

2002 Meursault Les Perrières
RATING: 96 points

Revealing aromas reminiscent of exotic spices awash in stone liqueur, the 2002 Meursault Les Perrières is a wine of huge depth, concentration, and complexity. Medium-bodied, pure, and layered, it offers gravel, earth, pear, and nutmeg throughout its character as well as in its lengthy oak-tinged finish. Anticipated maturity: 2006–2014.

2001 Meursault Les Perrières
RATING: 91 points

Spices, gravel, and smoke can be detected in the nose of the 2001 Meursault Les Perrières. It does not have the flesh, opulence, and depth of Lafon's finest 2001s, but it delivers loads of purity and elegance. Spiced minerals and candied lemons make up the character of this delineated, refined wine. Anticipated maturity: now–2010.

2000 Meursault Les Perrières
RATING: 94 points

The 2000 Meursault Les Perrières exhibits intense smoke and mineral scents, and possesses great aromatic depth. Medium to full-bodied and vinous, this seamless stone and mineral-laden wine is rich, well balanced, and exceptionally long in the finish. Anticipated maturity: now–2012.

1997 Meursault Les Perrières
RATING: 93 points

The magnificent 1997 Meursault Les Perrières displays profound aromas of stones, limes, flowers, and crisp pears. This thick, dense, and satin-textured wine offers loads of caramel-covered apples, fresh butter, minerals, and oak spices in its explosive yet elegant personality. It is full-bodied, fat, and impeccably balanced, and it possesses a stupendously long finish. Anticipated maturity: now–2009+.

1996 Meursault Les Perrières
RATING: 98 points

The breathtaking 1996 Meursault Les Perrières has an extraordinarily well-defined and elegant nose of stones, earth, and minerals. As Lafon tasted it, he smiled and said, "Yes, it is classic, like the Charmes." Classic to me means representative of the norm, and this wine is more than that; it is an exquisite example of the heights this vineyard can attain. Harmonious, lively, gorgeously delineated, silky-textured, rich, medium to full-bodied, and profoundly deep, this wine's stone and mineral flavors seems to linger on the palate indefinitely. This magnificent wine should be consumed between now and 2012.

1995 Meursault Les Perrières
RATING: 93 points

The 1995 Meursault Les Perrières has deep mineral and earth tones in the nose, and toasty, nutty, iron flavors in the mouth. Powerful and full-bodied, it possesses great length and balance. Drink it between now and 2010.

1989 Meursault Les Perrières
RATING: 97 points

The 1989 Meursault Les Perrières exhibits exceptional flavor: the telltale mineral, cold steel, gunflint sort of nose of a textbook Perrières; sensational fruit extraction; and a whoppingly long, crisp finish. Despite its enormous size, the wine is remarkably well balanced. Anticipated maturity: now–2017.

LE MONTRACHET

2002 Le Montrachet
RATING: 98+ points

The medium-bodied 2002 Le Montrachet has an awesome aromatic profile of resin, minerals, spices, poached pears, red currants, and oak. On the palate, this wine seemingly gains in strength, coming at the taster with increasingly bold waves of white pepper–laced, sappy minerals, white fruits, and oak. Its more-than-45-second finish regales the mouth with additional layers of candied apple, ginger, and buttered toast. Anticipated maturity: 2007–2017.

2001 Le Montrachet

RATING: 96 points

While not a blockbuster, Domaine Lafon's medium-bodied 2001 Le Montrachet is a stunning, awe-inspiring wine. Spiced pears and vanilla can be found in its complex aromatics. On the palate, this oily-textured wine reveals sublime power, depth, concentration, purity, expanse, and class. Loads of spice-laden pears, candied apples, buttered toast, acacia blossoms, and well-defined minerals are detected in its flavor profile. Its sultry finish, which still bathes the palate in spices after a minute, is mind-numbing. Anticipated maturity: 2010–2025.

2000 Le Montrachet

RATING: 94 points

The spice and anise–scented 2000 Le Montrachet is a lush, medium-bodied wine. Soft layers of creamed minerals and spices can be found in its broad, soft character. It is expansive and reveals loads of underlying minerals in its persistent finish. Anticipated maturity: 2006–2018.

1999 Le Montrachet

RATING: 94 points

Lafon's 1999 Le Montrachet is one of the vintage's few blockbusters. Boisterous flowers, minerals, and pears can be discerned in its explosive aromatics. Medium-bodied and impeccably delineated as well as nuanced, this rich, broad, and opulent wine is exceptionally refined. Satin-textured and loaded with stones, pears, apples, toast, hints of crème brûlée and vanilla bean, this wine is powerful, harmonious, elegant, and complete. Its majestic finish displays buttered toast as well as a myriad of spices. Anticipated maturity: now–2016.

1998 Le Montrachet

RATING: 92 points

Dominique Lafon's parcel of Le Montrachet produced his highest yields (30 hectoliters per hectare) in 1998. Four and a half barrels of this magnificent nectar were made. Harvested at 14% natural potential alcohol, it reveals pears, peaches, apricots, and flowers in its intense aromatic profile. Medium to full–bodied, expansive, and palate-coating, this elegant, classy, and rich wine is crammed with spices, white fruits, and minerals. It has outstanding presence, detail, and focus. It is not a muscular wine, yet possesses considerable underlying power in its precise character. This tour de force has an extraordinarily long, delineated, and mineral-laden finish. Anticipated maturity: now–2012+.

1997 Le Montrachet

RATING: 96 points

The 1997 Le Montrachet exhibits deep aromas of stones, minerals, honeysuckle blossoms, candied hazelnuts, and sweet oak spices. It is extraordinarily expansive and pure, richly textured, and superbly delineated. Akin to liquid silk, it has enormously ripe yet fresh flavors of red currants, raspberries, minerals, peaches, apricots, and poached pears that persist in the finish. Anticipated maturity: now–2020.

1996 Le Montrachet

RATING: 99 points

Harvested at a whopping 14% potential natural alcohol, Lafon's mind-blowing 1996 Le Montrachet is brilliant. Sublime mineral, stone, smoke, and toasted-nut aromatics are followed by a wondrous, concentrated, extracted, and sublimely classy personality. Oily layers of liquid minerals, red berries, anise, hazelnuts, and white flowers can be found in this massive, full-bodied, mouth-coating, and palate-saturating wine. Incredibly, just when the taster believes the palate has realized the brunt of this explosive gem's assault on the senses, it expands to even greater heights. The wine has a compellingly long finish. This is a tour de force! Anticipated maturity: 2010–2025.

1995 Le Montrachet

RATING: 94 points

Possessing a super-tight and unyielding nose, this full-bodied 1995 Le Montrachet displays intense, minerally fruit and striking elegance. While not as forward or sultry as expected, it has a superb structure. Anticipated maturity: now–2024.

1991 Le Montrachet

RATING: 92 points

The 1991 Le Montrachet is not an easy wine to evaluate. The color is significantly deeper than that of the Meursaults. There are scents of overripe apricots and oranges, in addition to minerals and honey. Full-bodied, high in acidity, with massive weight, but a disjointed personality, this wine looks to be magnificent, but idiosyncratic. An immensely impressive wine, it has been controversial. Anticipated maturity: now–2018.

1989 Le Montrachet

RATING: 96 points

The 1989 Le Montrachet, of which there are about 60 cases, offers steely, mineral aromas reminiscent of the Meursault Les Perrières. In the mouth, there is awesome concentration, surprisingly high acidity for the vintage, and exhilarating definition and length. I am not sure it will ever offer the drama and opulence of the 1989 Meursault Les Charmes, or the intensity of the 1989 Meursault Les Perrières, but it is an extraordinary effort from the Comtes Lafon. Anticipated maturity: now–2020.

VOLNAY SANTENOTS-DU-MILIEU

2002 Volnay Santenots-du-Milieu

RATING: 94 points

An exceptional effort, the 2002 Volnay Santenots-du-Milieu explodes from the glass with awesome scents of flowers and dark cherries. Superbly balanced, its concentrated, medium to full–bodied core of fruit displays sappy, expansive waves of dense black cherries. Exquisitely ripe, yet fresh, it reveals a prolonged finish studded with additional layers of dark fruits. Anticipated maturity: 2007–2019.

1999 Volnay Santenots-du-Milieu

RATING: 92 points

The outstanding dark ruby–colored 1999 Volnay Santenots-du-Milieu has subtle cherry, currant, and jammy black raspberry aromas. Medium-bodied and packed with loads of red and black fruits, it is a zesty, concentrated, tangy, blackberry, cherry, raspberry, and red currant–flavored wine. It is lively, and fresh in the finish. Anticipated maturity: now–2009.

1997 Volnay Santenots-du-Milieu

RATING: 92 points

The bright, dark ruby–colored 1997 Volnay Santenots-du-Milieu yielded only 25 hectoliters per hectare and was harvested at a whopping 13.5% natural potential alcohol. Of course, it was not chaptalized. It offers intense aromas of plummy cherries. Its awesome aromatics reveal the *sur-maturité* (overripeness) levels of Lafon's harvest. This is a mouth-coating, medium to full–bodied, broad, velvety wine that abounds with layers and layers of sweet black fruits. Its candied, almost confectionary, finish is extremely long and reveals supple, ripe tannins. Anticipated maturity: now–2007.

1996 Volnay Santenots-du-Milieu

RATING: 93 points

Consistently Lafon's finest red wine, the dark ruby–colored Volnay Santenots-du-Milieu is magnificent. Intense and profound blackberry aromas are followed by a massive explosion of red and black cherries. It possesses amazing richness, freshness, juiciness, and depth, as well as admirable concentration, complexity, harmony, and balance. Its persistent finish reveals fresh herbs, candied raspberries, cherries, and supple tannins. Drink this gem between now and 2007.

CHEVALIER-MONTRACHET

2002 Chevalier-Montrachet

RATING: 95+ points

Gorgeous aromas of minerals, gravel, and spices are found in the big, rich, opulent 2002 Chevalier-Montrachet. Medium-bodied and velvety-textured, this lush, spicy wine coats the palate with layers of toasted minerals, honey, and pears. Anticipated maturity: 2006–2015.

2000 Chevalier-Montrachet

RATING: 92 points

The aromatically intense 2000 Chevalier-Montrachet boasts toasted mineral scents. This medium-bodied wine is vinous, deep, and packed with floral, mineral flavors. Anticipated maturity: now–2013.

1999 Chevalier-Montrachet

RATING: 91 points

Pure and nuanced mineral aromas make up the nose of the 1999 Chevalier-Montrachet. Expansive, broad, and deep, this spicy mineral and pear–flavored wine is harmonious and well-balanced. It has a long, crisp, crystalline, and softly textured finish. Drink it between now and 2011.

1996 Chevalier-Montrachet

RATING: 96 points

The elegant, refined, 1996 Chevalier-Montrachet displays rock, mineral, and flower aromas. This medium to full–bodied and perfectly balanced wine's precision is mind-blowing. Chalk, rock dust, stones, and crisp pears are found in its superbly focused flavor profile. Drink it between now and 2010.

1995 Chevalier-Montrachet

RATING: 95 points

The 1995 Chevalier-Montrachet is spectacular. Racy, floral, fresh, and engaging on the nose, the wine's awesome entry is filled with intense flavors of minerals and toasted apricots. Silky-textured, full-bodied, classy, and refined, it can be enjoyed now and through 2018.

1992 Chevalier-Montrachet

RATING: 97 points

This is a well-knit, expansively flavored, full-bodied, super-concentrated white Burgundy displaying a honeyed orange, roasted nut, overripe apple–scented nose; a buttery, creamy texture; super-extraction of flavor; and a long finish. It explodes on the back of the palate and looks to have great longevity. Anticipated maturity: now–2012.

1989 Chevalier-Montrachet

RATING: 95 points

The 1989 Chevalier-Montrachet was the firmest and least forthcoming of Leflaive's 1989s from an aromatic perspective. It also exhibited the longest finish. This honeyed, creamy-textured wine possesses superb acidity for a 1989. Anticipated maturity: now–2007.

1983 Chevalier-Montrachet

RATING: 94 points

This is one of those rare examples of a 1983 that is formidably powerful as well as young and backward. I do not know how Leflaive was able to achieve a monstrous-sized wine that has remained so fresh and unevolved for nearly a decade. A huge wine by Leflaive's standards, and more massive and alcoholic than the domaine would prefer, it has turned out to be one of the great 1983s. Anticipated maturity: now–2010.

PULIGNY-MONTRACHET LES COMBETTES

2000 Puligny-Montrachet Les Combettes

RATING: 91 points

The 2000 Puligny-Montrachet Les Combettes's nose is composed of candied pears and apples. Medium-bodied and vinous, this is a well-balanced, harmonious, and broad wine. It is feminine, crammed with minerals, flowers, and pears, as well as butter, and has an extensive finish. Anticipated maturity: now–2014.

1995 Puligny-Montrachet Les Combettes

RATING: 93 points

Displaying a sublime explosion of intense, candied white flower aromas, the Puligny-Montrachet Les Combettes (1995 produced 175 cases, and 1996 a whopping 400 cases!) has a silky texture and a huge burst of sweet floral fruits complemented by a judicious use of oak. This superb and refined, medium to full–bodied wine should drink well until 2007.

1992 Puligny-Montrachet Les Combettes

RATING: 94 points

The 1992's formidable nose of grilled hazelnuts, butter, steel, and flowers is mind-blowing. With its huge, unctuous, thick, chewy flavors, the wine has magnificent extraction of flavor and enough acidity to provide definition to its sizeable components. The finish is rich, long, and mouth-filling. It should be drunk up now.

2000 Puligny-Montrachet Les Pucelles

RATING: 92 points

Toasted minerals are found in the nose of the 2000 Puligny-Montrachet Les Pucelles. Light to medium–bodied and highly defined, this wine has outstanding depth to its silky, lush personality. Minerals and pears are found in this concentrated wine's character as well as in its supple, fresh, and exceptionally long finish. Anticipated maturity: now–2014.

1995 Puligny-Montrachet Les Pucelles

RATING: 93 points

A stunning wine, the 1995 Puligny-Montrachet Les Pucelles displays an intensely spicy and floral nose, followed by a complex flavor profile of deeply roasted peaches, apricots, and minerals. This medium to full–bodied wine has a driving raciness reminiscent of Jadot's 1995 Montrachet. Anticipated maturity: now–2012.

1992 Puligny-Montrachet Les Pucelles

RATING: 96 points

Marrying power with finesse, the 1992 Puligny-Montrachet Les Pucelles is a classic. Richer and more unctuous than usual, it possesses fabulous clarity and definition and a great bouquet of oranges/tangerines combined with toasty vanilla, buttered popcorn, and apple scents. Sensationally concentrated, with layers of flavor beautifully buttressed by vibrant acidity, this is a magnificent wine. Anticipated maturity: now–2010.

1989 Puligny-Montrachet Les Combettes

RATING: 92 points

The 1989 Puligny-Montrachet Les Combettes possessed a buttery, hazelnut sort of fragrance; wonderfully lush, rich, concentrated flavors; plenty of glycerin and body; and a long, lusty finish. It should have been consumed by the end of 2002.

1985 Puligny-Montrachet Les Combettes

RATING: 92 points

This exceptionally elegant, vividly fresh wine offered attractive aromas of lemon rind, herbs, and grilled nuts reminiscent of a top Meursault. The characteristic Leflaive elegance, medium-bodied weight, and excellent richness and purity were all apparent. It should have been drunk before the turn of the century.

DOMAINE LEROY

WINES:

Chambertin

Clos de la Roche

Corton-Renardes

Latricières-Chambertin

Musigny

Richebourg

Romanée-St.-Vivant

Vosne-Romanée Les Beaux Monts

Vosne-Romanée Aux Brûlées

OWNER: Leroy SA

ADDRESS: 15 Rue de la Fontaine, 21700 Vosne-Romanée, France

TELEPHONE: 33 03 80 21 21 10

TELEFAX: 33 03 80 21 63 81

E-MAIL: domaine.leroy@wanadoo.fr

WEBSITE: www.domaine-leroy.com

CONTACT: Madame Lalou Bize-Leroy or Monsieur Frédéric Roemer

VISITING POLICY: By appointment only

VINEYARDS

SURFACE AREA: 56 acres

GRAPE VARIETALS: Pinot Noir, Chardonnay, and Aligoté

AVERAGE AGE OF THE VINES: 60 years

DENSITY OF PLANTATION: 10,000 vines per hectare

AVERAGE YIELDS:

1993—15.38 hectoliters per hectare

1994—17.18 hectoliters per hectare

1995—15.31 hectoliters per hectare

1996—24.86 hectoliters per hectare

1997—15.38 hectoliters per hectare

1998—16.64 hectoliters per hectare

1999—24.50 hectoliters per hectare

2000—22.31 hectoliters per hectare

2001—17.23 hectoliters per hectare

2002—15.22 hectoliters per hectare

WINEMAKING AND UPBRINGING

The wines of Domaine Leroy are produced biodynamically, which prohibits the use of all chemicals, including weed killers, pesticides, and synthetic fertilizers, and emphasizes the importance of the Earth's cycles and essential rhythms throughout the year.

In the vineyard, each rootstock must express in its way the particular character and typicity of the site. Leroy is adamant about removal of suckers and excess green grapes. There is a draconian sorting at the *cuverie,* no destemming, and a prolonged *cuvaison*/vatting in traditional wooden vats.

ANNUAL PRODUCTION

Chambertin: 900–1,750 bottles

Clos de la Roche: 800–1,750 bottles

Corton-Renardes: 1,200–2,000 bottles

Latricières-Chambertin: 600–1,650 bottles

Musigny: 600–875 bottles

Richebourg: 1,150–2,700 bottles

Romanée-St.-Vivant: 900–3,000 bottles

Vosne-Romanée Les Beaux Monts: 4,000–6,900 bottles

Vosne-Romanée Aux Brûlées: 290–580 bottles

AVERAGE PRICE (VARIABLE DEPENDING ON VINTAGE): $250–600+

GREAT RECENT VINTAGES

2003, 2002, 1999, 1996, 1995, 1993, 1990

Today, this is the greatest estate in Burgundy, producing uncompromising wines of irrefutable longevity and intensity. Ironically, the estate is often criticized for reasons totally unrelated to quality.

More than a century ago, in 1868, François Leroy founded Maison Leroy in the one-horse village of Auxey-Duresses, near Meursault, and Leroy has remained a traditional family business ever since. At the end of the 19th century, François's son, Joseph, and Joseph's wife, Louise Curteley, enlarged their small wine brokerage business, selecting the finest wines and the top sites to grow the best grapes in Burgundy.

Their son, Henri Leroy, joined the family business in 1919. He expanded further by creating a subsidiary branch near Cognac, that produced *eaux de vie de vin*. He also established a distillery at Segonzac, in the heart of the Grande Champagne area. In 1942, he purchased half of the Domaine de la Romanée-Conti from Jacques Chambon, and devoted himself to this domaine for the following 40 years, developing it into what is referred to by the international cognoscenti as the *fleuron de la Bourgogne*, or "the gem of Burgundy."

Henri's daughter, Lalou, an intense, wiry, diminutive fireball, joined the family business in 1955. A devout "terroirist," Lalou learned through constant tastings the essential characteristics of each *terroir* from each vineyard. While I do not always agree with her on what *terroir* encompasses, I admire her strong convictions.

Lalou was content to run the family's *négociant* business, Domaine d'Auvenay, until 1988, when she decided to expand Leroy's own vineyards, purchasing the 35-acre estate of Charles Noellat in Vosne-Romanée and Philippe-Rémy's 8.5-acre Gevrey-Chambertin vineyard. Leroy's estate vineyards now include Bourgogne rouge, Bourgogne blanc, and Bourgogne Aligoté (approximately 16 acres of generic appellation); Auxey-Duresses (approximately 12 acres of village appellation); Volnay-Santenots Premier Cru "Les Santenots-du-Milieu" (approximately 16 acres of premier cru); Pommard Les Vignots and Les Trois Follots; Savigny-les-Beaune Premier Cru Les Narbantons; Nuits-St.-Georges Aux Allots, Aux Lavières, and Au Bas de Combe; Vosne-Romanée Les Geneivrières; Vosne-Romanée Premier Cru Aux Brûlées and Les Beaux Monts; Chambolle-Musigny Les Fremières; Chambolle-Musigny Premier Cru Les Charmes; Gevrey-Chambertin; and Gevrey-Chambertin Premier Cru Les Combettes.

Leroy owns nine vineyards in the grand crus areas (approximately 17 acres), including Corton-Charlemagne (white wine), Corton-Renardes, Richebourg, Romanée-St.-Vivant, Clos de Vougeot, Musigny, Clos de la Roche, Latricières-Chambertin, and Chambertin.

Until January 1, 1992, Leroy was the distributor of Domaine de le Romanée-Conti wines, and the Leroy family still owns 50% of the DRC's shares.

In Burgundy, Lalou Bize-Leroy may have as many critics as I once did. Some producers accuse her of illegally doctoring her wines because she obtains such a deep color. Others claim she is hiding hundreds of cases of grand crus in other cellars since her yields "cannot possibly be so low." Of course, all of this is nonsense, not to mention appallingly jealous behavior from producers who are scared to death that other growers might decide to follow in Lalou's footsteps. For nearly 15 years, Bize-Leroy has stood at the top of the Burgundy pyramid, alone both literally and figuratively in her pursuit of the finest wine Burgundy can produce. It is almost criminal to try to describe wines that may be the greatest red Burgundies I will ever taste in my life. As even the immodest Lalou Bize-Leroy says, these wines are "an accident of nature." Tasting them, with their extraordinary ripeness, unctuousness, and opulence, with no hard tannin to be found, makes one think that, yes, low yields do translate into physiologically ripe fruit, concentrated wines, and exquisite quality. It goes without saying that everything in this cellar is aged in 100% new French oak (you cannot detect any oak in the wines because of their concentration) and bottled without fining or filtration.

Much has been written about the dynamic Madame Lalou Bize-Leroy. Some of it has been malicious and motivated strictly by insidious jealousy. Certainly, it is easy to complain about her pricing structure (these are the most expensive wines of Burgundy), yet there should never be any criticism of her philosophy of what Burgundy should be. Her wines are among the noblest and purest expressions of Pinot Noir and Chardonnay in Burgundy. They are treated with the care of a pampered child, are never filtered, and are bottled barrel by barrel. Given the size of her wines and their power and structure, in a cool, damp cellar they will last 20–25 years.

I am not alone in believing her wines are the reference point for Burgundy. Jacques Pusais, a renowned oenologist, remarked, "Here we are at the Louvre; these are cultural moments about wine and its language." Jean Lenoir, a very popular writer, compared Leroy's cellars "to the Bibliothèque Nationale, a place of reference for great works of art."

On a personal note, I have known Lalou Bize-Leroy for over 25 years. Although a delicately framed woman, she has a bigger-than-life personality. In spite of her extraordinary personality and no doubt ruthless business style, she comes across as a fragile person pushing herself to the very edge of winedom, trying to do the finest job possible. There are two sides to every argument, but I have never met anyone more committed to guarding the great traditions of Burgundy than Lalou Bize-Leroy. The loss of her beloved husband, Marcel, in 2004, was an enormous blow. A quiet, dignified man, he was the strong and silent influence behind the exuberant Lalou. I hope she will respond to his absence as she has to every other challenge in her life—by going back to the vineyard and beating the competition on the playing field . . . something she has always done very well.

CHAMBERTIN

2002 Chambertin
RATING: 98 points
Madame Leroy's stunning 2002 Chambertin bursts from the glass with profound aromas of blackberries, tar, and licorice. This expansive, hugely concentrated, deep wine is medium- to full-bodied, powerful, and seamless. With flavors of mocha, black fruit, and florals, this effort is noble, well balanced, and perfectly harmonious, and it possesses an extraordinarily long finish. Anticipated maturity: 2012–2035

2001 Chambertin
RATING: 91 points
The 2001 Chambertin displays smoked bacon, spice, and black fruit aromas. Medium-bodied, with a supple, broad personality, its fruit-forward character offers black raspberry, cherry, and cassis flavors whose effects linger in its long, silky finish. It doesn't have the depth, power, and presence of Leroy's finest Chambertins, yet is seamless, friendly, and generous. Anticipated maturity: now–2025.

2000 Chambertin
RATING: 95 points
Medium to dark ruby–colored, the 2000 Chambertin exhibits tar-laced, spicy, black fruit aromas. This magnificent wine combines the generosity of fruit found in the finest offerings of the vintage with a power, depth, structure, and concentration that is typically lacking in the 2000s. Its intense, muscular flavor profile coats the taster's palate with waves of superripe plums and blackberries whose effects linger throughout its regal, sweet finish. Certainly one of the finest reds produced in 2000, it will be at its peak of maturity between now and 2014.

1999 Chambertin
RATING: 95 points
The medium to dark ruby–colored 1999 Chambertin reveals a nose of fresh herbs, spices, blackberries, and violets. Medium to full–bodied, intense, and powerful, this wine is loaded with dark fruits and toast flavors. It is a structured, stony wine that has an outstanding, muscular, masculine personality. Anticipated maturity: 2006–2025.

1998 Chambertin
RATING: 94 points
The medium to dark ruby–colored 1998 Chambertin exhibits a nose of dark fruits and fresh herbs that gives way to a broad, medium to full–bodied character. This wine has massive layers of tarry black fruit, yet also possesses the woody, scraping tannins that may spell future doom for many wines from this vintage. Either drink it in the very near term with a dish containing lots of tannin-hiding fat, or wait 7+ years and pray.

1997 Chambertin
RATING: 97 points
Sweet plums and jammy cherries can be found in the aromatics of the dark ruby/purple–colored 1997 Chambertin. Medium to full–bodied and ample, it is velvety-textured, plump, and packed with plummy baked cherries. This wine's personality envelopes the palate with lush fruit and spices. It is well structured, concentrated, and immensely long in the finish. Anticipated maturity: 2006–2015.

1996 Chambertin
RATING: 96 points
The dark ruby/purple–colored 1996 Chambertin exhibits lively berry and rose aromas. It has huge depth to its tightly wound, closed personality. This medium to full–bodied, foursquare, dark, fruit-flavored wine will require patience. Anticipated maturity: 2006–2012+.

1995 Chambertin

RATING: 93 points

The 1995 Chambertin is medium to dark ruby–colored and reveals hints of amber along the edge of the glass. Aromatically, it displays plums, cherries, and hints of mint. It is a full-bodied, foursquare, long-term wine with unbelievable concentration of fruit. Tarry blackberries and black cherries are intermingled with herbs in this backward behemoth. Anticipated maturity: 2007–2014.

1993 Chambertin

RATING: 91 points

The astringency of the tannins in this wine raised concerns. It shows amber in its medium to dark ruby color and has admirable concentration of dark berry fruit, yet it is rugged and dry. The 1993 has evolved smoke, tobacco, cedar, and herbal aromas and flavors. Anticipated maturity: now–2016.

1991 Chambertin

RATING: 92 points

The ruby–colored 1991 Chambertin reveals herbal red fruit aromas. It has superb depth, definition, and concentration, as well as boatloads of dark fruit, yet it also possesses a monstrous level of tannin. It could be magnificent in a decade or more, or may dry out. Anticipated maturity: 2010+?

1990 Chambertin

RATING: 94 points

The medium to dark ruby–colored 1990 Chambertin has a sweet black currant and blackberry–scented nose. Medium to full–bodied, it has a soft entry that expands and coats the palate with intense red and black fruits. This concentrated, focused, and immensely persistent wine will be at its finest between now and 2010.

1985 Chambertin

RATING: 96 points

One of the great successes of the vintage, the dark ruby/purple–colored 1985 possessed aromas of jammy black fruit intertwined with notes of prunes, damp earth, spices, and meat. In the mouth, there was superb concentration, medium body, integrated soft tannins, and a whoppingly long finish. Anticipated maturity: now–2010.

CLOS DE LA ROCHE

2002 Clos de la Roche

RATING: 96 points

The ruby-colored 2002 Clos de la Roche sports an earthy, herbal, black fruit and spice–packed nose. Medium-bodied, deep, and fresh, this structured, somewhat tannic wine offers flavors reminiscent of red cherries, raspberries, and spices. It has lovely purity, concentration, and length. Anticipated maturity: 2015–2030.

2001 Clos de la Roche

RATING: 93 points

As is often the case, Leroy's Clos de la Roche was a standout in the 2001 vintage. Its beguiling aromatics burst forth, displaying spicy, jammy cherries and raspberries. Deep plummy red fruits, black raspberries, juniper berries, cinnamon, and a myriad of other spices can be discerned in its gorgeously deep, muscular personality. Lush, expansive, and concentrated, it is a medium-bodied wine with a long, tannin-filled finish. Anticipated maturity: 2006–2013.

2000 Clos de la Roche

RATING: 93 points

Subtle notes of cheese rinds are interspersed with sweet black cherries in the complex aromatics of the 2000 Clos de la Roche. An extracted, medium to full–bodied wine of exceptional concentration, it boasts a flavor profile with copious quantities of stony black fruits, and a powerful, muscular character. Its firm yet astonishingly long finish reveals some stemmy, woody tannin, a characteristic that kept its score from being higher. Anticipated maturity: now–2012.

1999 Clos de la Roche

RATING: 96 points

The medium to dark ruby–colored 1999 Clos de la Roche has sweet black cherry, earth, and plum-like aromas. This powerful, intense, meaty wine is filled with plums, blackberries, gelatinous veal stock, and Asian spices. It is pure, muscular, dense, and profound. Anticipated maturity: 2006–2018.

1998 Clos de la Roche

RATING: 96 points

The medium to dark ruby–colored 1998 Clos de la Roche has huge quantities of sweet cherry, blackberry, and violet-infused blueberries; a huge velvety-textured character; and a full body. However, it is astonishingly tannic and firm. While this wine may have the requisite power and depth to sustain significant cellaring, will it outlast its rugged tannins? Anticipated maturity: 2007–2016.

1997 Clos de la Roche

RATING: 98 points

The medium to dark ruby–colored 1997 Clos de la Roche displays complex blackberry, fresh herb, spice, stone, and jammy strawberry scents. It is magnificently defined yet decadently fashioned, with luxurious layers of cassis, leather, asphalt, blackberries, and violets that coat the palate. Broad, focused, and delineated, it is also highly concentrated and muscular. Anticipated maturity: 2007–2014.

1996 Clos de la Roche

RATING: 99 points

The dark ruby/purple–colored 1996 Clos de la Roche reveals beguiling aromas of perfume, violets, blackberries, and juniper-smoked bacon. It is medium to full–bodied and offers a chewy-textured flavor profile filled with fresh cherries, licorice, raspberries, road tar, and blueberries. It is massively concentrated, intense, and powerful, and possesses an amazingly long, pure finish. This complete wine's harmony and extravagant personality is something to savor. Anticipated maturity: 2009–2015+.

1995 Clos de la Roche

RATING: 94 points

The black currant, blackberry, balsam, and spice–scented 1995 Clos de la Roche has loads of cassis, blueberry, and black cherry fruit in its medium to full–bodied, super-concentrated character. At present it is painfully tannic and backward, yet its admirable fruit (so incredibly evident in its infancy) may well blossom in time to regain command of this offering. Anticipated maturity: 2007–2015.

1993 Clos de la Roche

RATING: 98 points

The dark ruby with amber–colored 1993 Clos de la Roche is a showstopper. It has penetrating aromas of cassis, blackberry, stones, and wild herbs. On the palate, leather, boysenberries, assorted dark fruits, and a myriad of spices can be discerned in its complex and decadently fashioned personality. This 1993 unquestionably has the requisite power, richness, concentration, and density of fruit to stand up to its solid backbone. Anticipated maturity: now–2015.

1991 Clos de la Roche

RATING: 92 points

The medium to dark ruby–colored 1991 Clos de la Roche has exotic wood (cedar and balsam), cassis, stone, and black fruit aromas. It is at its peak of maturity, showing evidence of evolved fruit flavors, caramelized leaves, and sweet cedar. A chewy-textured and firm wine, its fruit appears to be evolving faster than its firm structure. Anticipated maturity: now–2009.

1990 Clos de la Roche

RATING: 98 points

The stellar 1990 Clos de la Roche has a medium to dark ruby color and dense, dark, berry aromas. It possesses a youthful, almost impenetrable core of thick, lush blackberries, juniper berries, plums, cloves, and blueberries that coat the palate.

This medium to full–bodied wine has exquisite equilibrium and focus, as well as a seemingly unending, luxurious finish. Anticipated maturity: now–2010.

1989 Clos de la Roche

RATING: 94 points

The 1989 Clos de la Roche is ruby/amber-colored and offers dense currant aromas. This medium to full–bodied, ample mouthful of a wine is crammed with layers of cedary cherries, stones, and touches of mint. It has a sexy satin texture, lovely definition, gorgeous harmony, and a long supple finish. Anticipated maturity: now–2008.

CORTON-RENARDES

2002 Corton-Renardes

RATING: 95 points

Flowers, candied blackberries, and stones can be found in the nose of the ruby-colored 2002 Corton-Renardes. This ample, broad, medium-bodied wine is sweet, plush, and fruit-forward. Black fruits and spices are found throughout its personality as well as in its long, ripe, pure finish. Drink it between 2007 and 2015.

1999 Corton-Renardes

RATING: 97 points

The dark ruby–colored 1999 Corton-Renardes was harvested at 14.9% natural potential alcohol. ("I almost made port," said Madame Bize-Leroy.) A prodigious effort, it exhibits a nose of candied cherries, jammy strawberries, and blueberry jelly. On the palate, this magnificent wine is indescribably intense and powerful, yet is majestically harmonious and elegant. Loads of cherries and other assorted red fruits are intermingled with spices, fresh herbs, and hints of new oak in its velvety-textured, full-bodied character. This gem also possesses a stupendously long, pure, and supple finish. Anticipated maturity: 2006–2018.

1998 Corton-Renardes

RATING: 95 points

The medium to dark ruby–colored 1998 Corton-Renardes is awesome. Its profound dark cherry aromas lead to a medium to full–bodied, broad, and complex core of red cherries, spices, plums, and vanilla-infused oak. This expansive wine is deep, well balanced, and velvety-textured, and has a long, flavor-packed finish. Anticipated maturity: now–2012.

1997 Corton-Renardes

RATING: 96 points

The almost black-colored 1997 Corton-Renardes boasts a nose filled with sweet black plums and cherries. On the palate, it is ample and full-bodied, and it coats the mouth with layers of superripe dark fruits, stones, and supple tannins. Anticipated maturity: now–2012.

1996 Corton-Renardes

RATING: 94 points

The dark-colored 1996 Corton-Renardes displays fresh blackberry aromas. This satin-textured wine is lively, densely packed with red/black fruits and stones, as well as herbs, and has a firm, tannic finish. Still youthfully backward, it will require a half-dozen years or more of cellaring. Drink it between 2007 and 2012.

1995 Corton-Renardes

RATING: 93 points

The 1995 Corton-Renardes has an impressively dark color and sweet and spicy dark fruit aromas, as well as a hugely concentrated, backward personality. Highly structured and dense, this wine has a powerful nugget of black stony fruit that will require cellaring to be exposed. Anticipated maturity: now–2010+.

1993 Corton-Renardes

RATING: 94 points

The 1993 Corton-Renardes has a slightly amber robe and complex, lightly evolved aromas of herbs and black pit fruits. Medium to full–bodied and hugely concentrated, it opens with spectacular, lushly textured, intense fruit, and then slams shut on hard tannins. Its color, aromatics, and fruit seem to be evolving without much softening of the tannins, yet it has loads of fruit to spare. Anticipated maturity: now.

1990 Corton-Renardes

RATING: 92 points

The 1990 Corton-Renardes has a demure, stone- and boysenberry-scented nose. This medium to full–bodied, silky-textured wine has great depth of dark cherry fruit in its flavor profile. It remains youthfully healthy, with primary fruit flavors intermingled with hints of secondary perfumes and a structured, solid finish. Anticipated maturity: now–2010.

LATRICIERES CHAMBERTIN

2002 Latricières-Chambertin

RATING: 96 points

Flowers, spices, rocks, clove, and licorice explode from the glass of the 2002 Latricières-Chambertin. Medium to full–bodied, masculine, and muscular, this wine coats the taster's palate with cassis, blackberries, and perfume. It is intensely concentrated and powerful, yet remains lively and detailed. Anticipated maturity: 2008–2019.

1999 Latricières-Chambertin

RATING: 94 points

The demure, blackberry aromas of the medium to dark ruby–colored 1999 Latricières-Chambertin lead to a masculine, highly structured, and firm personality. This wine is intense, loaded with stony blackberry fruits and roasted black currants. This dense, powerful, chewy wine should be at its peak of maturity between 2006 and 2018.

1998 Latricières-Chambertin

RATING: 95 points

The medium to dark ruby–colored 1998 Latricières-Chambertin displays a mouthwatering nose of spicy blackberries, cinnamon, and blueberries. Medium to full–bodied and ample, it is velvety-textured and muscular, and has an impressively long finish. This powerful wine is firmly structured, yet appears to have the requisite density of fruit to sustain its tannin over the short to medium term. Anticipated maturity: now–2008.

1997 Latricières-Chambertin

RATING: 93 points

The dark ruby/purple–colored 1997 Latricières-Chambertin displays floral, lively, sweet blackberry, cherry, and plum aromas. On the palate, baked plums, tobacco, spices, and cedar can be found in this concentrated, backward wine. It has superb depth, power, and complexity, yet is presently tightly wound and firm. Anticipated maturity: now–2012+.

1996 Latricières-Chambertin

RATING: 97 points

The dark ruby/purple-colored 1996 Latricières-Chambertin offers fresh, pure blueberry aromas. This massive, full-bodied wine has stupendous depth, breadth, and length to its blackberry, cherry, and floral character. It is immensely powerful as well as concentrated and has its vintage's trademark freshness and grip. Anticipated maturity: 2006–2012+.

1995 Latricières-Chambertin

RATING: 95 points

The medium to dark ruby–colored 1995 Latricières-Chambertin is already showing hints of amber along the edge of the glass. Cedar, tangy strawberries, and herbs can be discerned in its somewhat evolved bouquet. Its personality is rustic, hard, and tannic, yet continues to show glimpses of the extraordinary concentration of fruit that marked this vintage in its infancy. Blackberries, cassis, and thick cherries can be discerned in its deep core. If its fruit expands with time, this wine will be a showstopper. If not, the anticipated maturity is 2006–2010+.

long haul, it may well have the capacity to be a 40-year wine. Anticipated maturity: 2010–2020+.

1990 Richebourg

RATING: 96 points

The magnificent, healthy medium to dark ruby–colored 1990 Richebourg has stupendous depth and complexity to its dark fruit-dominated aromas. Soy and hoisin sauces, cherries, and raspberries can be discerned in its deep, medium to full–bodied character. This satin-textured wine remains youthfully vibrant and should benefit from additional cellaring. Anticipated maturity: now–2010+.

1989 Richebourg

RATING: 93 points

The lovely 1989 Richebourg appears to be one of the rare wines from its vintage to still have the capacity to age and ameliorate. It possesses a medium to dark ruby and amber color, as well as dense, dark berry and caramelized aromas. On the palate, it is medium to full–bodied and offers loads of sweet red cherry, plum, black pepper, juniper berry, and spice. Broad, well structured, and velvety-textured, it also has an exceptionally long and flavorful finish. Drink it now–2011 or 2012.

ROMANEE-ST.-VIVANT

2001 Romanée-St.-Vivant

RATING: 91 points

The medium ruby–colored 2001 Romanée-St.-Vivant has a highly expressive nose of superripe grapes, blackberries, and violets. Medium-bodied, it slathers the palate with layers of floral blackberry and cassis flavors. This fruit-forward wine displays outstanding depth, a plump, flavorful personality, and some hints of stemminess in the finish. It should be drunk now–2011 or 2012.

2000 Romanée-St.-Vivant

RATING: 92 points

The boldly spicy, plummy, black fruit–filled nose of the 2000 Romanée-St.-Vivant leads to a highly extracted, intense personality. Medium-bodied as well as uncharacteristically inky, this blackberry- and cassis-laden wine suffers somewhat from a rough, woody finish. It is unquestionably outstanding, with loads of roasted black fruits, yet one has to wonder what would have been achieved with a softer hand in vinification. Drink it between now and 2010.

1999 Romanée-St.-Vivant

RATING: 91 points

The medium ruby–colored 1999 Romanée-St.-Vivant has delicate floral, spice, and berry aromas. This medium-bodied, concentrated wine is complex and refined, yet backward, closed, and tannic. Time will tell whether this lace-like Burgundy will survive its firm structure. Anticipated maturity: 2006–2012.

1998 Romanée-St.-Vivant

RATING: 93 points

Red berries, raspberries, and cherries are found in the nose of the ruby–colored 1998 Romanée-St.-Vivant. Medium to full–bodied and elegantly styled, this strawberry jam and fresh raspberry-filled wine is intricate, well defined, and concentrated. Drink this feminine offering now–2010, 2011.

1997 Romanée-St.-Vivant

RATING: 95 points

Leroy's 1997 Romanée-St.-Vivant seems to have taken on weight, substance, and structure since I tasted it a year ago. Dark plums, spices, mocha, and dried prunes burst from the glass. This medium to full–bodied liquid velvet is packed with chewy red and black fruits. Anticipated maturity: now–2010+.

1996 Romanée-St.-Vivant

RATING: 97 points

The healthy, dark ruby/purple–colored 1996 Romanée-St.-Vivant reveals gorgeous dark currant, black cherry, and spice aromas. Its massively powerful, refined character has huge depth and concentration. Raspberries, both red and black, plums, and spices, as well as herbs make up its complex flavor profile. It remains youthfully firm and will require patience. Drink it between now and 2010+.

1995 Romanée-St.-Vivant

RATING: 95 points

The 1995 Romanée-St.-Vivant is dark ruby–colored with a very slight hint of amber. Dark berries and fresh herbs are found in its tightly wound aromatics. It is medium to full–bodied and massively concentrated, and has exemplary depth of dark, roasted black fruits. It is also fiercely tannic. Anticipated maturity: 2006–2020.

1993 Romanée-St.-Vivant

RATING: 99 points

The showstopping 1993 Romanée-St.-Vivant is beginning to show its age, with its dark mahogany robe revealing hints of amber. Aromatically, it exhibits a marvelous panoply of spices, flowers, herbs, and dark raspberry scents. Its flavor profile remains youthful, with profound layers of fresh red and black berries, rosemary, violets, and stones vying for the taster's attention. Firmly structured, powerful, and stupendously long in the finish, this is a wine for the ages. Anticipated maturity: now–2015.

1991 Romanée-St.-Vivant

RATING: 95 points

The ruby-colored 1991 Romanée-St.-Vivant boasts a terrific nose reminiscent of dark fruits blended with fresh herbs and traces of cocoa powder. This wine's deep and detailed character is loaded with mocha-infused red and black fruits. It is highly concentrated and elegant, and possesses an extremely long, supple finish. Anticipated maturity: now–2008+.

VOSNE-ROMANEE LES BEAUX MONTS

2002 Vosne-Romanée Les Beaux Monts

RATING: 96 points

The profound, medium ruby–colored 2002 Vosne-Romanée Les Beaux Monts has an intensely spicy, waxy, black fruit–dominated nose. On the palate, this wine expands magnificently, unleashing soft, velvety waves of fresh, pulp-laden red fruits. Concentrated, powerful, graceful, and well structured, it is a superb example of its vineyard's potential. Anticipated maturity: 2006–2015.

1999 Vosne-Romanée Les Beaux Monts

RATING: 93 points

The medium to dark ruby–colored 1999 Vosne-Romanée Les Beaux Monts reveals a complex nose of violets, roses, and bing cherries with copious quantities of ripe, supple tannin. This medium to full–bodied wine has remarkable depth of dark cherries, blackberries, and cassis-like fruit that lasts throughout the long, harmonious finish. It is a velvety-textured, extroverted, elegant, and boisterous wine for drinking between now and 2015.

1997 Vosne-Romanée Les Beaux Monts

RATING: 93 points

The 1997 Vosne-Romanée Les Beaux Monts exhibits red fruits, roses, and candied orange in its profound aromas. This tannic, backward, and hyper-concentrated wine is powerful and intense, yet elegant and precise. If this wine can cope with its very noticeable tannins, it will prove to be stunning. Anticipated maturity: now–2010+.

1996 Vosne-Romanée Les Beaux Monts

RATING: 96 points

This dark-colored wine is a cut above. Profound aromas of intensely sweet cherries, raspberries, stones, and earth give way to a full-bodied, extremely feminine, and massively ripe and vibrant core of roses, cherries, and candied blueberries. This silky-textured, hedonistic (yet wonderfully structured), and focused wine ends on an incredibly long and detailed finish. Anticipated maturity: now–2010+.

1995 Vosne-Romanée Les Beaux Monts

RATING: 94 points

Madame Leroy's top Vosne premier cru offering, the dark-colored Vosne-Romanée Les Beaux Monts (350 cases) exhibits invitingly spicy, deep red and black fruit aromas. The flavors are packed with fat, ripe cherries and touches of earth and cinnamon. Full-bodied, velvety-textured, incredibly long, and stunningly elegant, this gem will hold for 12–15 more years.

1993 Vosne-Romanée Les Beaux Monts

RATING: 96 points

The 1993 Vosne-Romanée Les Beaux Monts is less exotic and more classically structured than the Vosne-Romanée Aux Brûlées, with a more backward, tannic personality. Splendidly concentrated, powerful, and pure, it is a compelling wine. Anticipated maturity: now–2012.

1991 Vosne-Romanée Les Beaux Monts

RATING: 93 points

The gorgeous, saturated, deeply colored 1991 Vosne-Romanée Les Beaux Monts offers a sweet fragrance of chocolate, black fruits, herbs, and toasty vanilla, followed by a long, unctuously textured, layered wine with magnificent concentration, soft acid, and moderately ripe tannin in the finish. Drink it between now and 2010.

1990 Vosne-Romanée Les Beaux Monts

RATING: 98 points

Lalou Bize-Leroy's 1990 Vosne-Romanée Les Beaux Monts is a classic example of a top premier cru Vosne-Romanée. It does not soar from the glass with the exotic, smoky, roasted character of the Aux Brûlées, but it does offer subtly authoritative and persistent aromas of black fruits, herbs, underbrush, and sweet oak. While it displays exceptional concentration of flavor in the mouth, it is supported by higher levels of tannin and is a more structured, denser, richer wine than the Aux Brûlées. Since the tannins are more noticeable, it should last for 18 years or more.

VOSNE-ROMANEE AUX BRULEES

2002 Vosne-Romanée Aux Brûlées

RATING: 94 points

The highly perfumed nose of the 2002 Vosne-Romanée Aux Brûlées leads to a medium to full–bodied, candied character. This silky, plush wine is crammed with spices, juicy blueberries, and ripe blackberries, and displays superb balance and, though quite forward, an outstanding structure. Anticipated maturity: 2006–2015.

1997 Vosne-Romanée Aux Brûlées

RATING: 93 points

The ruby/purple-colored 1997 Vosne-Romanée Aux Brûlées reveals a richly spicy nose, filled with red and black cherries. This plump, glycerine-imbued, oily-textured, and broad wine displays superripe, spiced red fruit characteristics. Thick, harmonious, elegant, and extremely persistent, this complete wine should be at its best between now and 2010.

1996 Vosne-Romanée Aux Brûlées

RATING: 93 points

This dark-colored wine offers fresh and sweet berries, dried fruits, and intense grilled oak aromas. This highly concentrated, extracted, fresh, juicy, medium to full–bodied, and extremely elegant wine offers ripe cherries that seemingly burst on the palate. It is extremely complex, harmonious, and persistent. This gorgeously supple, silky, and sexy wine should be at its best between now and 2010.

1995 Vosne-Romanée Aux Brûlées

RATING: 92+ points

From a vineyard I adore for its forward, sultry style, the Vosne-Romanée Aux Brûlées (25 cases) reveals an enticing and exotic nose of spices and berries and a beautifully silky-textured palate crammed with lush red fruits and Asian spices. Attractive, opulent, and sensual, this medium to full–bodied wine should be at its peak between now and 2010.

1993 Vosne-Romanée Aux Brûlées

RATING: 99 points

Lalou Bize-Leroy's 1993 Vosne-Romanée Aux Brûlées is sweet, seductive, opulent, unctuous, thick, and rich, yet never heavy or overbearing. The taster truly senses the presence of something unreal. One of the more forward of the Leroy 1993s, this wine can be drunk now or cellared until 2014.

1990 Vosne-Romanée Aux Brûlées

RATING: 96 points

The sensational 1990 Vosne-Romanée Aux Brûlées dramatically lives up to its name. The roasted nose of meat and smoky black fruit is flashy and extroverted. In the mouth, this wine exhibits a broad-shouldered, expansive, succulent texture, with oodles of flavor and glycerin, as well as heady alcohol to go along with the spectacularly rich, unctuous finish. Even though the tannins are noticeable, it is a thrilling wine to drink at present. It should last through 2010.

WINE: Clos de la Roche
OWNER: Hubert Lignier
ADDRESS: 45 Grande Rue, 21220 Morey-St.-Denis, France
TELEPHONE: 33 03 80 51 87 40
TELEFAX: 33 03 80 51 80 97
E-MAIL: domaine.hubert-lignier@wanadoo.fr
CONTACT: Hubert Lignier
VISITING POLICY: By appointment only

VINEYARDS

SURFACE AREA: 21 acres
GRAPE VARIETALS: Pinot Noir—90%, Aligoté—5%,
    Gamay—5%
AVERAGE AGE OF THE VINES: 45 years
DENSITY OF PLANTATION: 10,500 vines per hectare
AVERAGE YIELDS: 35 hectoliters per hectare

WINEMAKING AND UPBRINGING

After 100% destemming, a 15–20 month vinification takes place in open tanks. There is usually a five-day pre-fermentation maceration, and only indigenous yeasts are used. After vinification, the wine is moved into wood (60% new and the rest one and two years old) for malolactic fermentation. It rests in wood for 12–16 months and is bottled with neither fining nor filtration.

ANNUAL PRODUCTION

Clos de la Roche: 4,000 bottles
AVERAGE PRICE (VARIABLE DEPENDING ON VINTAGE): $175–250

GREAT RECENT VINTAGES

2002, 1999, 1997, 1996, 1993, 1990, 1988

While this estate dates back five generations, only over the last several decades has the wine been estate-bottled and sold directly to a growing list of international clients. Prior to that, the entire production was sold to various *négociants.*

Hubert Lignier was preparing for retirement in 2003 when he suffered an enormous tragedy. His son, the talented winemaker Romain Lignier, fell ill following the 2003 harvest and was diagnosed with a brain tumor. He died in July 2004, at age 34. Romain already had been recognized by many as one of Burgundy's great up-and-coming young winemakers as well as a humanitarian (he was an avid cyclist and often guided blind bicyclists around the region). Hubert has resumed management of the estate along with other family members, including his wife, Françoise, and Romain's wife, Kellen.

The late Romain Lignier

CLOS DE LA ROCHE

2002 Clos de la Roche

RATING: 95 points
This estate's 2002 Clos de la Roche reveals a nose of candied red fruits, spices, earth, smoke, and blackberries. Satin-textured and fleshy in the attack, it offers powerful waves of fleshy red fruits. The extensive finish displays copious tannin, providing a firm backbone to the wine's sappy fruit. This concentrated, complex effort should be drunk between 2007 and 2016.

1999 Clos de la Roche

RATING: 94+ points
The 1999 Clos de la Roche is the darkest of Lignier's offerings, verging on dark ruby–colored. The black cherry, blackberry, licorice, and violet–scented nose leads to an explosive, immensely flavorful character. Medium to full–bodied and pure, this fresh, sweet wine is packed to the gills with cherries, raspberries, blueberries, and blackberries. Ample yet highly delineated, it has a magnificently long, fruit-filled finish. Anticipated maturity: 2006–2016.

1997 Clos de la Roche

RATING: 94 points

The saturated, medium to dark ruby–colored 1997 Clos de la Roche has intensely spicy, candle wax, and blackberry aromas. This full-bodied, broad wine is opulently textured and filled with sweet, plummy, red fruits and jammy candied cherries, as well as hints of hoisin sauce. Its extensive finish reveals loads of well-ripened, supple tannins. Anticipated maturity: now–2010.

1996 Clos de la Roche

RATING: 95 points

This wine is dark ruby–colored and offers a nose of extraordinary purity, depth, and richness. Scents of gravel, earth, violets, perfume, jammy blueberries, cassis, and black cherries and hints of road tar are followed by a velvety-textured, full-bodied, and magnificently concentrated wine. Candied cherries, stones, rosemary, spicy oak, Asian spices, and hints of chocolate can be found in this blockbuster's powerful yet graceful flavor profile and substantial finish. Armed with virtually perfect balance and harmony, an amazing depth of fruit, and copious quantities of seamless, satin-textured tannins, this marvel should prove to be one of the vintage's most ageworthy wines. Anticipated maturity: now–2018.

1995 Clos de la Roche

RATING: 97 points

This dark ruby–colored wine displays enthralling scents of candied hazelnuts, stones, fresh herbs, blackberries, blueberries, plums, and wet gravel basking in the sun. It is just as extraordinary and complex on the palate as its aromatics suggest, offering an awesomely intense, broad, and expansive character. This full-bodied, mouth-coating, oily-textured, and juicy yet immensely rich wine is redolent with blackberry, cassis, cedar, stone, and briery flavors. Its stunningly long finish offers copious quantities of fruit complemented by supple tannins. Drink it between 2006 and 2020+.

1993 Clos de la Roche

RATING: 93 points

The 1993 Clos de la Roche is medium to dark ruby–colored with hints of amber on the edge of the glass. Its initially kinky, slightly barnyard-like aromas blew off quickly to reveal loads of spicy cedar scents. Medium to full–bodied, this earth, stone, black fruit–laden wine is well concentrated and dense. It possesses its vintage's firm, dry, tannic backbone, but the depth of fruit has the potential to overcome this trait with age. Anticipated maturity: now–2010+.

1991 Clos de la Roche

RATING: 94 points

The dark-colored 1991 Clos de la Roche offers complex aromas of kirsch, stones, black cherries, and cedar. Medium bodied and well focused, it is in the transitional stage between youth and maturity. Sweet red cherries can still be discerned in its otherwise exotic wood and cigar box–flavored personality. This is a well-concentrated, elegant wine. Its long finish displays loads of gorgeously ripened tannins for additional structure. Anticipated maturity: now–2010.

1990 Clos de la Roche

RATING: 95 points

The ruby-colored robe of the 1990 Clos de la Roche is beginning to show touches of amber on the edge. The wine offers a rich, spicy nose of cedar and blackberries. On the palate, this full-bodied, broad, fat, and velvety-textured wine is packed with tobacco, cedar, spice, and superripe dark fruit flavors. Its plump, supple tannins and palate-coating, dense character are a hedonist's dream, while its complexity and refinement are made to order for those searching out intellectual delights. Anticipated maturity: now–2007.

DOMAINE MICHEL NIELLON

WINES:

Bâtard-Montrachet

Chevalier-Montrachet

OWNER: SCE Michel Niellon

ADDRESS: 1 rue Nord, 21190 Chassagne-Montrachet, France

TELEPHONE: 33 03 80 21 30 95

TELEFAX: 33 03 80 21 91 93

CONTACT: Michel Niellon

VISITING POLICY: Only for the estate's clients

VINEYARDS

SURFACE AREA: 17.3 acres

GRAPE VARIETALS: Chardonnay—66%, Pinot Noir—34%

AVERAGE AGE OF THE VINES: 7–77 years, with the oldest being
Chevalier-Montrachet (planted in 1962) and Bâtard-
Montrachet (planted in 1927)

DENSITY OF PLANTATION: 10,000 vines per hectare

AVERAGE YIELDS: 48–54 hectoliters per hectare

WINEMAKING AND UPBRINGING

Reasonable yields are followed by fermentation in stainless
steel tanks and then aging in oak casks. Niellon never uses
more than 20–25% new oak. Bottling, with both a fining and
light filtration, takes place 12–14 months later.

ANNUAL PRODUCTION

Bâtard-Montrachet: 700 bottles

Chevalier-Montrachet: 1,400 bottles

AVERAGE PRICE (VARIABLE DEPENDING ON VINTAGE): $50–200

GREAT RECENT VINTAGES

2002, 2001, 2000, 1999, 1995, 1992, 1990, 1982

This small estate was built slowly, starting with 7.5
acres that Michel Niellon inherited from his parents. He began working in the vineyards in 1948 (at age
14), an extremely difficult time, he tells me, given the
depressing post–World War II conditions. After completing his military service in 1957, Niellon began to
estate-bottle some of his wines, selling them to a few
friends and clients. His initial goal was to make a wine
that pleased him, above all.

One of the most extraordinary things about this
estate is that the wines never disappoint. I have been
buying them for more than 25 years, and Niellon is one
of those producers that transcends the vintage quality,
whether it is mediocre, good, or great. Moreover, as vintages from the early 1980s prove, Niellon's wines possess extraordinary aging potential.

Michel Niellon (left)

2002 Bâtard-Montrachet

RATING: 94 points

There are loads of rich mineral aromas in the nose of the 2002 Bâtard-Montrachet. Fat, rich, and plush, it coats the palate with resin-laced minerals. Armed with gorgeous depth, concentration, purity, and focus, this boldly flavored wine is a candidate for drinking between 2006 and 2012.

2001 Bâtard-Montrachet

RATING: 94 points

Niellon's 2001 Bâtard-Montrachet boasts an expressive nose of flowers, pears, and hints of vanilla. Medium-bodied, it broadens on the palate, revealing a thick, silky-textured core of spicy minerals and poached pears that lingers in its exceptional finish. This expansive, powerful wine retains a classy, refined personality even as it wows the taster with its depth and richness. Anticipated maturity: now–2013.

2000 Bâtard-Montrachet

RATING: 94 points

The 2000 Bâtard-Montrachet explodes from the glass with spiced pear aromas. This superb wine bastes the palate with tropical fruits, spices, candied apples, buttered toast, and hints of raspberries. Powerful and medium to full–bodied, it boasts an exceptionally long finish. Anticipated maturity: now–2012.

1999 Bâtard-Montrachet

RATING: 91 points

With coaxing, the aromatically muted, tightly wound 1999 Bâtard-Montrachet reveals a broad, concentrated, and deep personality. It is fresh, zesty, and tangy. Flavors of crisp pears and apples come to the fore with considerable air. Anticipated maturity: now–2011+.

1997 Bâtard-Montrachet

RATING: 93 points

The 1997 offers hyper-ripe pear and apple aromas, as well as a highly concentrated and extracted core of fruit. This is an extremely profound wine, with intense honeyed fruitcake flavors, as well as an opulent, viscous, and almost flabby texture. If it had better balance, there is no telling how high my score could have gone. Anticipated maturity: now–2012.

1996 Bâtard-Montrachet

RATING: 99 points

This grand cru is unbelievable, possessing everything I could hope for in a white wine. Is the Bâtard-Montrachet a candidate for a perfect score? Produced from 49-year-old vines, this benchmark-setting wine has such deep richness on the nose

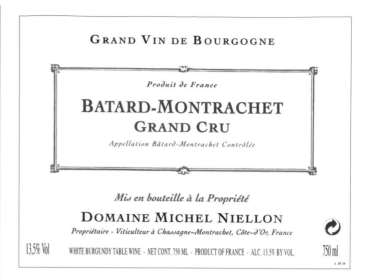

that it almost instills awe in the taster's heart and palate. Superripe fruits, white flowers, mulling spices, and sweet toast soar from the glass. This massive wine is a powerful, broad-shouldered, expansive, and mouth-coating monster that managed to retain extraordinary elegance and delineation—a rare achievement. This full-bodied wine offers layers of hazelnuts, roasted peaches, liquid minerals, and candied pears as well as a seemingly unending finish. It is a grand-slam home run! Anticipated maturity: now–2012.

1995 Bâtard-Montrachet

RATING: 93 points

The 1995 Bâtard-Montrachet sports a superb warm, enveloping spiciness on the nose with faint touches of citrus fruit. Superdeep rolls of roasted fruits bathed in mulling spices can be found in this velvety-textured, full-bodied wine. The only thing that prevents this Bâtard from receiving even higher praise is a lack of balancing acidity. Anticipated maturity: now–2015.

1992 Bâtard-Montrachet

RATING: 93 points

The 1992 Bâtard-Montrachet offers a huge nose and a mouth-feel of massively extracted Chardonnay fruit. Its mélange of aromas and flavors ranges from oranges, apples, and coconuts to vanilla butter cookies and honey. Huge and superrich, it is absolutely magnificent! Anticipated maturity: now–2008.

1991 Bâtard-Montrachet

RATING: 93 points

Niellon's yields in 1991 were a minuscule 20–25 hectoliters per hectare. The Bâtard-Montrachet (only 3 barrels, or 75 cases, were produced) was fat and rich with a long finish. Large-scaled, alcoholic, and sensationally perfumed, it was loaded with extraction. Anticipated maturity: now–2007.

1989 Bâtard-Montrachet

RATING: 96 points

The 1989 Bâtard-Montrachet exhibits a buttery, coconut-scented nose; huge, opulent, glycerin-laden flavors; spectacular depth; and a mind-blowing finish. How I wish all Montrachets would taste this good! Anticipated maturity: now–2012.

CHEVALIER-MONTRACHET

2002 Chevalier-Montrachet

RATING: 96 points

Loads of minerals, gravel, and crisp pears can be found in the aromatic profile of the 2002 Chevalier-Montrachet. This fleshy, light to medium–bodied wine is soft, satiny-textured, and deep. Its tangy, mineral-laced personality lingers in its long, pure finish. Anticipated maturity: now–2012.

2001 Chevalier-Montrachet

RATING: 95 points

The 2001 Chevalier-Montrachet bursts from the glass with spice, anise, and linden aromas. Surprisingly big and brawny for a Chevalier, it is lush, forward, chewy textured, and intense. This concentrated wine has superb depth and loads of gravel, stone, and mineral flavors intermingled with pears. In addition, it possesses a stunningly long, flavorful, elegant finish. Anticipated maturity: now–2013.

2000 Chevalier-Montrachet

RATING: 92 points

The 2000 Chevalier-Montrachet has a toasty, spicy nose. Well delineated, this medium-bodied wine has loads of gravel, mineral, stone, and apple flavors. It is tighter than the Bâtard, yet is intense and concentrated, and has a long, admirably pure finish. Anticipated maturity: now–2013.

1999 Chevalier-Montrachet

RATING: 92 points

Niellon's 1999 Chevalier-Montrachet reveals gorgeously pure mineral aromas. Medium-bodied, with a refined, highly delineated, and deep personality, this satin-textured wine offers stone, crisp pear, and apple flavors and a long finish. Anticipated maturity: now–2012.

1997 Chevalier-Montrachet

RATING: 92 points

The 1997 Chevalier-Montrachet reveals superb ripeness in its expressive mineral and chalk-packed nose. This fabulous offering is medium-bodied, rich, concentrated, and beautifully focused, and it has mouthwatering mineral flavors that last throughout its extended and bone-dry finish. Anticipated maturity: now–2009.

1996 Chevalier-Montrachet

RATING: 99 points

This grand cru is unbelievable, possessing everything I could hope for in a white wine. Is this a candidate for a perfect score? The profound 1996 Chevalier-Montrachet, produced from vines planted in 1968 and 1972, offers a mind-blowingly intricate, precise, and refined nose of minerals, chalk, rock dust, and flowers. On the palate, this breathtaking wine enthralls with its superbly defined and harmonious medium-to-full body. Each time I raised the glass to my lips, I found new flavors. Minerals, stones, gooseberry, plums, seashells, toast, raspberries, peaches, pears, honeysuckle blossoms, "champagne" currants, and flint can all be discerned in this silky, lovely, refined, and ethereal wine. Words simply cannot do it justice. Anticipated maturity: now–2012.

1995 Chevalier-Montrachet

RATING: 96 points

Niellon's profound 1995 Chevalier-Montrachet reveals an enticing, floral, super-spicy nose with touches of stones and minerals. Full-bodied, packed, and stacked, this wine has enormous potential. Anticipated maturity: 2007–2020.

1992 Chevalier-Montrachet

RATING: 90 points

The 1992 Chevalier-Montrachet has attributes similar to the Chassagne–Montrachet–Les Vergers. Although it is the most expensive wine from the Niellon portfolio, it is not as intense as several of his premier crus, and never as rich as the Bâtard-Montrachet. It is an outstanding, elegantly styled 1992. Anticipated maturity: now–2010.

DOMAINE DE LA ROMANEE-CONTI

WINES:

Grands Echézeaux
Le Montrachet
Richebourg
Romanée-Conti
La Tâche

OWNER: Société Civile du Domaine de la Romanée-Conti

ADDRESS: 1 rue Derrière le Four, 21700 Vosne-Romanée, France

TELEPHONE: 33 03 80 62 48 80

TELEFAX: 33 03 80 61 05 72

CONTACT: Aubert de Villaine

VISITING POLICY: Restricted to professionals referred by their
   distributors

VINEYARDS

SURFACE AREA: 62.5 acres

GRAPE VARIETALS: Pinot Noir, Chardonnay

AVERAGE AGE OF THE VINES: 45+ years

DENSITY OF PLANTATION: 11,000 vines per hectare

AVERAGE YIELDS: 25–30 hectoliters per hectare

WINEMAKING AND UPBRINGING

Aubert de Villaine makes it clear that each vintage presents its
own set of circumstances, and one always has to be flexible in
order to accommodate the nuances of nature. For many years,
this domaine has been cultivated biodynamically, although the
owners do not advertise this as much as other estates do. They
continue to replant with material that is indigenous to the domaine's own vineyards; they have never added newer clones.
At present, the average age of the vines is at least 45 years.

With respect to vinification, the fruit is never destemmed,
and there is a 5–6 day cold pre-maceration before the fermentation is allowed to begin. There is pumping-over and a bit of
pigéages on a daily basis. The maceration periods are relatively
long, but they avoid an exaggerated extraction of tannin. The
wines are always aged for at least 18 months in 100% new oak,
which the owners feel is the most sanitary condition for producing wines that are bottled without filtration.

ANNUAL PRODUCTION

Grands Echézeaux: 10,000 bottles
Le Montrachet: 3,000 bottles
Richebourg: 12,000 bottles
Romanée-Conti: 5,500 bottles
La Tâche: 20,000 bottles

AVERAGE PRICE (VARIABLE DEPENDING ON VINTAGE): $250–1,200+

GREAT RECENT VINTAGES

2003, 1999, 1990, 1979, 1978, 1971, 1966

There is no question that Domaine de la Romanée-
Conti, owned by the de Villaine, Bize-Leroy, and
Roche families, is Burgundy's most famous estate. In
fact, it might be the most famous wine estate in the
world. The abbreviation "DRC" has as much significance for the wine world as "IBM" and "GE" do in the
business world. The history of this estate goes back to an
entry dated July 18, 1760, in the Abbé de St.-Vivant's
archives that refers to the "vines of Romane," the vineyard that later became known as Romanée-Conti.

This estate was purchased in 1867 by a Santenay
négociant named J. M. Duvault-Blochet, who assembled
the different parcels. In 1942, Aubert de Villaine's
father, a descendent of Duvaut-Blochet's, sold half of
his interest in the DRC to Henri Leroy, a *négociant* in
Auxey-Duresses. Henri Leroy had two daughters, Lalou
Bize-Leroy and Pauline, who currently own two of the
major shares of the DRC. The de Villaine family shares
are much more fragmented (at last count there were
around 10 owners).

So what makes the DRC wines so famous, expensive, and revered? Unquestionably, in the greatest vintages, they literally stand alone, somewhat like the
mythical city of Minas Tirith in the *Lord of the Rings* tril-

Aubert de Villaine

ogy, a bright, shining empire that cannot be matched for beauty or power. In vintages such as the 2003, 1999, and 1990, no Pinot Noir in the world comes remotely close to what the DRC achieves.

However, the estate has a far more irregular record than is generally believed. The inconsistencies of certain vintages are somewhat shocking. In vintages such as the 2000, 1998, and 1995, some wines did not measure up to the two or three dozen finest Burgundies. In addition, through the mid-1980s there is tremendous bottle variation because the wines were bottled barrel by barrel. Now a small *cuvée* of approximately six barrels is blended together and then bottled. There are still variations among lots, as six barrels only represent approximately 3,600 bottles. There could be as many as six separate bottlings of La Tâche in an abundant year, four to five different bottlings of Echézeaux, and nearly that many for Richebourg. It seems, at least among wine lovers, that when wines are this profound, occasional irregularity and disappointing quality can be forgiven.

I have always felt the Domaine de la Romanée-Conti's single most compelling wine is La Tâche rather than Romanée-Conti, but there is something ethereal about a top vintage of the latter wine, even if it never has quite the flesh or concentration of La Tâche. Romanée-Conti's extraordinary perfume, power, and penetration make it special, but with only around 5,500

bottles produced each year, there is not enough for even the billionaires who want it.

La Tâche screams *terroir,* with such a distinctive aromatic and flavor character that it is easily discerned in any tasting. Produced from an extraordinary vineyard, it always seems to possess a mind-boggling level of concentration and intensity. As with all of the DRC wines, there can be disappointing vintages of La Tâche, but when it is fabulous, as it was in 1980, 1990, 1999, and 2003, it is fit for the wine gods.

There are several great Richebourg producers with whom the DRC must compete (Méo-Camuzet, Domaine Leroy, and the various bottlings from the Gros family), but when the people at DRC get their Richebourg right, as they did in 2003, 1999, 1990, and 1978, it's by far the finest made in Burgundy.

If there is a value in the Domaine de la Romanée-Conti's portfolio, it is the Grands Echézeaux. From a large grand cru vineyard, it exhibits the DRC's signature and is far superior to the producer's Echézeaux.

I must also mention the DRC Montrachet, the most concentrated and honeyed example of this vineyard that exists. Always made from extremely ripe fruit, it has a tendency to oxidize quickly in some vintages, but when the DRC is at its best, France's most concentrated and stunning dry white wine emerges from the domaine's holdings.

GRANDS ECHEZEAUX

2001 Grands Echézeaux

RATING: 90 points

Mouthwatering aromas of blackberries and spices can be found in the nose of the ruby-colored 2001 Grands Echézeaux. A seductive, medium-bodied, satin-textured wine, it coats the taster's palate with loads of dark fruits. This is a well-endowed, pure effort with a long, flavorful finish. Drink it from now until 2013.

1999 Grands Echézeaux

RATING: 98 points

The dark ruby–colored 1999 Grands Echézeaux has gorgeous talcum powder, perfume, and candied cherry aromas. This sumptuously sweet yet elegant, medium-bodied wine is crammed with blackberries and sugar-coated cherries. Oak shows through in this wine's satiny finish. Drink it from now until 2013.

1997 Grands Echézeaux

RATING: 91 points

The ruby-colored 1997 Grands Echézeaux offers red and black raspberry liqueur aromas. It is a medium to full–bodied, oily-textured wine that possesses good power and density. Smoked bacon, sweet wax, and spices are found in the fat, plump, seductive offering. Drink it from now until 2007.

1996 Grands Echézeaux

RATING: 93 points

This dark-colored wine displays a magnificently elegant nose of cassis, black cherries, and roses. This is an austere yet expansive, complex, medium- to full-bodied, ripe, and masculine wine. It is dense and powerful yet maintains a refined combination of muscle and class. Its tightly wound core offers red and black currants, cherries, minerals, and toasted oak flavors, all of which linger in its admirably focused and firm finish. Anticipated maturity: now–2012.

1995 Grands Echézeaux

RATING: 92 points

The 1995 Grands-Echézeaux is austere, masculine, backward, and dense. It offers superb black fruit flavors and a firm tannic backbone. Drink it between now and 2012+.

1993 Grands Echézeaux

RATING: 90 points

The 1993 Grands Echézeaux reveals a healthy dark ruby color. An attractive nose of red and black fruits and toast is followed by a medium-bodied, concentrated style with a firm, well-delineated, focused personality, and moderate tannin in the finish. Drink it between now and 2010.

1991 Grands Echézeaux

RATING: 93 points

The 1991 Grands Echézeaux exhibits a deep ruby/purple color, gorgeous as well as copious quantities of sweet, jammy, cassis fruit, and smoky, toasty new oak. Powerful, rich, medium to full–bodied, with exceptional concentration, this complex wine should be at its best between now and 2012.

1990 Grands Echézeaux

RATING: 98 points

The 1990 Grands Echézeaux offers abundant black raspberry and black cherry elements in its smoky, exotic nose, as well as a long, opulent, fleshy finish. It should drink well between now and 2010.

LE MONTRACHET

2002 Le Montrachet

RATING: 94 points

The bright, light straw–colored 2002 Montrachet bursts from the glass with spices, white pepper, pears, and flowers. Rich, medium to full–bodied, and lush, this wine has an oily-textured character that offers broad, ample layers of tangy apples, pulp-laden pears, anise, toasted nuts, and ginger snaps. This wine has superb depth, complexity, and length. Anticipated maturity: 2009–2018.

2001 Le Montrachet

RATING: 92 points

The 2001 was picked at 14% natural potential alcohol and reveals some hints of botrytis. Buttered toast, hazelnuts, and smoky spices are found in its aromatic profile. This plush, intense wine admirably combines muscular power with elegance. Light to medium–bodied, it is a fresh, delineated, spice-laden effort that is packed with pears and minerals. Drink it between now and 2012.

2000 Le Montrachet

RATING: 95 points

The Domaine de la Romanée-Conti's policy of late harvests for Montrachet leads to forward, expressive wines with flavorful personalities. The spice box–scented 2000 Montrachet is a huge, luscious, medium-bodied wine. Buttered, superripe apples, poached pears, honeyed minerals, and countless spices can be discerned in its extravagant personality. Rich, deep, and dense, it is the sexiest, most seductive Montrachet I've encountered. Anticipated maturity: now–2010.

1999 Le Montrachet

RATING: 93 points

The 1999 Montrachet reveals golden hues to its color and a nose of massive ripeness. Powerful spice scents are intermingled with tropical yellow fruits and anise in its aromatics. Medium to full–bodied, it is fat, plump, oily-textured, and unbelievably rich. Its layers of spices and hyper-ripe fruits are sensually decadent and linger on the taster's palate for a long while. This is a broad, massively dense Montrachet for drinking through 2011.

1998 Le Montrachet

RATING: 92 points

Notes of *Botrytis cinerea* (also known as "noble rot") are evident in the hedonistically appealing, bright gold–colored 1998 Montrachet's nose. Its honeyed spice and vanilla aromas are followed by a decadently sexy personality. This round, hyper-rich wine is crammed with overripe fruits, touches of caramel, and French toast soaked in syrup. It is magnificently flavorful and pleasing yet does not have the capacity to gain in complexity with cellaring. Drink this spicy fruit bomb now through 2006.

1997 Le Montrachet

RATING: 94 points

DRC's 1997 Montrachet reveals a goldish straw color and loads of tropical fruit, mineral, anise, and buttered aromas. This massive, medium to full–bodied, and dense wine displays layers of spice; creamy, superripe pears; crème brûlée; and hints of butterscotch in its opulent flavor profile. Velvety-textured and broad, it is forward yet well balanced. Drink it between now and 2012.

1996 Le Montrachet

RATING: 96 points

The DRC's light-colored 1996 Montrachet is spectacular. Its profound, rich, and embracing nose reveals toasted minerals, white fruits, and hints of lemon. On the palate it displays enormous complexity; a broad, layered core of tropical fruits (mostly mangoes); liquid minerals; and stones. It is terribly refined, bracing, satin-textured, medium to full–bodied, and mind-blowingly long in the finish. Its tightly wound core of fruit will require extended cellaring to blossom and reveal all of what this glorious wine has to offer. Anticipated maturity: now–2016.

1995 Le Montrachet

RATING: 99 points

Simply put, the 1995 Montrachet is a mind-boggling, virtually perfect wine. It displays breathtaking aromas of liquid minerals, creamed hazelnuts, candied chestnuts (*marrons glacés*), white flowers, anise, and buttered toast that seem to gain in expressiveness and intensity with time. On its utterly extraordinary palate, layer upon layer of stones, straw, minerals, grilled bread, and sweet white flowers can be found. Oily, full-bodied, magnificently concentrated, and extracted, this is as complex a wine as I have ever had the honor to pour over my lips and palate. Perfectly balanced and structured for the long haul, this wine also possesses one of the longest and purest finishes I have ever encountered. A winemaking tour de force! Anticipated maturity: 2008–2025.

1994 Le Montrachet

RATING: 93 points

The 1994 Montrachet has a deep mineral spice on the nose with touches of star anise and orange blossoms. In the mouth, it displays an awesome silky texture and good length, with touches of nuts and spices. This full-bodied wine has the components to be a great Montrachet, but it lacks the necessary drive to carry the fruit through to its summit. My impression is that this wine will age gracefully through 2007.

1991 Le Montrachet

RATING: 90 points

The 1991 Le Montrachet is a fat, unctuously styled wine made from yields of only 32 hectoliters per hectare. Although rich, it does not have the depth and power of vintages such as the 1990, 1989, and 1986. Soft and precocious because of low acidity, it should be drunk up now.

1990 Le Montrachet

RATING: 92 points

The 1990 Le Montrachet exhibits considerable opulence, as well as a telltale nose of coconut, buttered apples, and smoky, toasty new oak. Magnificently deep, expansive, and rich, with moderate acidity, it should prove to be a sensational DRC Le Montrachet. Anticipated maturity: now–2013.

1989 Le Montrachet

RATING: 99 points

Not surprisingly, the 1989 Montrachet is another awesome example from the Domaine de la Romanée-Conti. If pure, honeyed thickness and glycerin are what you are looking for, there is not a more concentrated Chardonnay produced in the world. The only wines I have ever tasted from the Americas that have a nectar-like richness such as this were the 1978 and 1980 Chalone, but that winery has now resorted to making much lighter, more commercially oriented products. There is nothing commercial about this 1989 Montrachet. It offers an awesome nose of honeyed, buttery, apple, intertwined with aromas of smoked nuts and toasty new oak. In the mouth, its extraordinary viscosity, thickness, and richness make it seem almost greasy. The finish is explosive, and while the alcohol must be over 14.5%, it cannot be detected because of the wine's phenomenal concentration. Anticipated maturity: now–2015.

1986 Le Montrachet

RATING: 95? points

The 1986 Montrachet wine continues to rank as one of the most memorable white wines I have ever tasted. The only criticism may be its heavyweight style. The light golden color is followed by a nose that zooms from the glass, offering a phenomenal fragrance of honey, smoked nuts, lavishly rich, buttery fruit, and toasty oak. The wine's viscosity, unctuousness, and extract level are mind-boggling. It represents the essence of Chardonnay, extremely full-bodied and concentrated, yet remarkably well balanced in spite of its massive size. Drink it up.

1985 Le Montrachet

RATING: 94 points

The light to medium straw–colored 1985 Montrachet appears to require another decade of aging before a more realistic assessment can be made on where this wine is going. It is still young, but I am not fully convinced that age will bring out all the complexity one would expect. Anticipated maturity: now–2015.

1983 Le Montrachet

RATING: 98 points

While reminiscent of the 1986, the mammoth-sized 1983 Le Montrachet is more backward and tightly knit. It offers an immense, honeyed nose of buttery popcorn, baked apples, coconuts, and ripe oranges. Unctuous, rich, and well structured, with an immense palate feel and lingering length, this huge, thick wine should last through 2010. It is an extraordinary success in a problematic vintage.

RICHEBOURG

2001 Richebourg

RATING: 92 points

The outstanding, medium to dark ruby–colored 2001 Richebourg reveals a nose of spiced cherries and creamy blackberries. It expands on the palate, displaying toasted oak–infused black cherry syrup. This hugely spicy, medium-bodied wine has wonderful depth and a friendly, juicy personality. Anticipated maturity: now–2012.

1999 Richebourg

RATING: 100 points

Magnificent, the 1999 Richebourg has a saturated, dark ruby color. It explodes from the glass with loads of superripe dark fruits, including blackberries, cassis, plums, and black cherries. This dense, plush, and broad wine has prodigious depth to its roasted red and black fruit–flavored personality. A myr-

iad of spices can be found in its chewy-textured, full-bodied, highly concentrated, powerful character. Its extraordinarily long finish is dominated by fruit, yet copious quantities of sweet and supple tannin can be discerned. Anticipated maturity: 2006–2018.

1997 Richebourg

RATING: 93 points

The ruby-colored 1997 Richebourg is big and flavorful. Its rose, violet, talcum powder, and crushed berry–scented nose leads to a boisterous, dense personality. Medium to full–bodied and loaded with spice—in particular freshly ground black pepper—and blackberries, this is a deeply ripe, expressive wine. Anticipated maturity: now–2009.

1996 Richebourg

RATING: 95 points

As is often the case with the youthful 1996 Richebourg, the nose was extremely reticent. After considerable coaxing, I had a peek at this offering's deeply ripe dark fruit aromatics. But what a flavor profile! A massive explosion of profound and intense cherries, raspberries, boysenberries, and strawberries coated my palate. It is a medium to full–bodied, densely fruited, and powerful wine that is perfectly balanced and delineated. Anticipated maturity: now–2018.

1995 Richebourg

RATING: 94 points

The 1995 Richebourg is spectacular. Powerful, dense, meaty, and thick, it is exceedingly long and possesses a firm tannic backbone that requires cellaring. Anticipated maturity: now–2018.

1993 Richebourg

RATING: 90 points

The 1993 Richebourg exhibits a dark ruby color, as well as flattering quantities of sweet, jammy, red and black fruits. With a husky framework and a sweet entry, this ripe, medium to full–bodied, moderately tannic, spicy, cleanly made wine exhibits the potential for 15–20 years of evolution. Drink it between now and 2015.

1990 Richebourg

RATING: 98 points

The DRC produced splendid wines in 1990, and the Richebourg is close to reaching its plateau of maturity. A dark ruby color reveals lightening at the edge. The stunning aromatics offer intense aromas of spring flowers, black fruits, licorice, and toasty new oak. Fleshy and medium to full–bodied, with a velvety-textured palate and sweet fruit, this smoky, rich, complex red Burgundy can be drunk now and over the next decade.

ROMANEE-CONTI

2001 Romanée-Conti

RATING: 93 points

The extroverted 2001 Romanée-Conti is medium to dark ruby–colored and displays intensely spicy black cherry aromas. Juicy and supple, as well as packed with spiced, candied black fruits, this medium-bodied wine is concentrated, lush, and velvety-textured. It reveals more tannin than its siblings, yet it is ripe and enveloped in fruit. Anticipated maturity: now–2014.

1999 Romanée-Conti

RATING: 98+ points

The medium to dark ruby–colored 1999 Romanée-Conti is mind-boggling. It has a hugely expressive nose of superripe black cherries, candied plums, and violets. Full-bodied and possessing a magnificent breadth of sweet, penetrating fruits, this is an unbelievably complex wine. It coats the palate with its velvety sweet cherries, jammy blackberries, and fruit-soaked tannin. Perfectly balanced and seamless, this gem has a remarkably long finish. This is a wine of exemplary precision, delineation, and power with indescribable class and refinement. Anticipated maturity: 2006–2020.

1997 Romanée-Conti

RATING: 95 points

The 1997 Romanée-Conti reveals a saturated, dark ruby color as well as a mouthwatering nose of leather, juniper berries, cherries, and spices. On the palate, it marvelously combines the powerful, ripe fruit characteristic of the vintage with magnificent delineation and elegance. Flavored with soy sauce, licorice, and flowers, as well as blackberries, this wine is dense and concentrated, yet lace-like and gloriously precise. It stands, as is expected given its rarity, price, and reputation, as one of the stars of the vintage. Anticipated maturity: now–2012+.

1996 Romanée-Conti

RATING: 97 points

The 1996 has a gorgeously bright, dark ruby/purple color and extremely complex aromatics of fresh herbs, Asian spices, creamy cherries, superripe blackberries, and vanilla-imbued oak. This superb wine offers a mouthful of silky-textured cherries, blueberries, plums, boysenberries, earth, minerals, and spiced oak. A masterpiece, this wine is full-bodied, dense (yet extremely elegant and defined), thickly textured, and immensely concentrated. Anticipated maturity: 2008–2025.

1995 Romanée-Conti

RATING: 95 points

This mind-boggling, complex 1995 Romanée-Conti boasts distinctive flavors of morel and porcini mushrooms intermingled with cassis and black cherries. It should be held at least another five years, and will easily last through 2020 given proper cellar conditions.

1993 Romanée-Conti

RATING: 91 points

The 1993 Romanée-Conti is extremely backward, tightly knit, and closed, with hard tannin, an excellent to outstanding mouth-feel, and a nearly impenetrable personality. Although this is usually a fragrant, intensely perfumed wine, the closed, tight 1993 exhibits few aromatics, medium body, and huge tannin. While the 1993 will last 20+ years, it is tough to judge just how good this wine will be. The score reflects the vineyard and historic reputation as much as what I was able to taste in the bottle. Anticipated maturity: now–2025.

1991 Romanée-Conti

RATING: 91 points

The 1991 Romanée-Conti reveals a deep color, but there is less color saturation than that possessed by La Tâche or Grands Echézeaux. Backward and medium to full–bodied, this is the most closed and impenetrable of all the 1991 DRC wines. No doubt its pedigree and breeding will emerge, but for now, I must rate Grands Echézeaux and La Tâche higher. Anticipated maturity: now–2015.

1990 Romanée-Conti

RATING: 99 points

The 1990 Romanée-Conti boasts a surprisingly saturated color that is the equal of La Tâche and Richebourg. The nose offers up sweet clove, cinnamon, and blackberry aromas intermingled with toasty, smoky new oak. Lavishly rich and full-bodied, with abundant tannins, this profound, surprisingly large-scaled, tannic wine boasts more muscle than usual. Anticipated maturity: now–2025.

LA TACHE

2002 La Tâche

RATING: 93 points

Soy sauce, candied blood oranges, and dark cherries make up the nose of the outstanding 2002 La Tâche. Extremely elegant and pure, this light to medium–bodied wine displays a superb satiny texture and a broad blackberry, black cherry, spice, and mineral–flavored character. It boasts a refined, noble personality with an exceedingly long, supple finish. The qualitative and ripeness differences between this wine and the Richebourg are striking as well as confounding. Anticipated maturity: 2009–2019.

2001 La Tâche

RATING: 92 points

Earthy blackberries can be discerned in the nose of the 2001 La Tâche. Suave, plush, and regal, it has a deep character that boasts loads of candied black fruits. This supple wine reveals superb clarity of fruit and an impressively long, fruit-filled finish. Anticipated maturity: now–2015.

1999 La Tâche

RATING: 100 points

The medium to dark ruby–colored 1999 La Tâche has sweet, tangy raspberry, black currant, candied cherry, leather, and spice aromas. This medium to full–bodied wine is harmonious, refined, and powerful. It is expansive, magnificently delineated, and feminine, particularly for La Tâche. Its flavor profile is crammed with an assortment of superripe red and black fruit laced with vanilla beans. It has loads of sweet tannin that can be detected in its admirable finish. Anticipated maturity: 2006–2025.

1997 La Tâche

RATING: 93 points

Dark-colored, the aromatically tight 1997 La Tâche reveals Asian spices, pepper, cherries, and black currants. This is a velvety-textured, expansive, and massively ripe wine boasting flavors reminiscent of licorice and blackberry jam. It has superb depth of fruit (particularly for this sometimes "simple" vintage), medium to full body, and admirable length to its supple finish. Anticipated maturity: now–2012.

1996 La Tâche

RATING: 96 points

The blockbuster 1996 La Tâche possesses a profound nose. It exhibits awesomely ripe red and black fruits, raw meat, and Asian spices, all of which are encased in sweet, toasty oak. This full-bodied, wide, thick, focused, harmonious, and intense wine releases amazingly powerful layers of candied black cherries and blackberries. It is structured, totally precise, and pure, and it possesses an exceptionally long finish loaded with abundant sweet tannins. Anticipated maturity: now–2020.

1995 La Tâche

RATING: 95 points

The 1995 La Tâche is intensely profound and superripe, yet harmonious. Its extraordinarily long finish (it tails off with a sweet kirsch kiss) flabbergasted me. I could not help but think of the finishes of two wines I love—Château Rayas and Château Lafleur. It appears to be holding an enormous amount in reserve and may ultimately merit higher ratings. It should be held at least until 2008, and will easily last through 2020 given proper cellar conditions.

1993 La Tâche

RATING: 90 points

The 1993 La Tâche reveals a tight but promising nose of smoky, game-like aromas intertwined with red and black fruits, minerals, and vanilla from new oak. Medium to full–bodied, with sweet, concentrated berry fruit, this tannic, spicy, backward wine appears to possess the requisite extraction to ensure a long, positive evolution. Drink it between now and 2020.

1991 La Tâche

RATING: 93 points

The 1991 La Tâche is a compelling wine. It possesses a deep color, as well as a telltale, decadent bouquet of smoked meats, jammy black fruits, and Asian spices. Expansive, full-bodied, and oozing with rich, sweet fruit, this example of La Tâche, despite its flamboyance, is structured, tannic, and in need of at least 3–4 more years of cellaring. It should last for 20 years. Anticipated maturity: now–2015.

1990 La Tâche

RATING: 100 points

The profound 1990 La Tâche is incredibly endowed, with an extraordinary perfume of Asian spices as well as jammy black raspberries, cherries, and blackberries infused with smoke, toast, and dried herbs. Full-bodied, but ethereal, with layers of flavor, as well as mind-boggling delicacy and complexity, it will be at its finest between now and 2015.

WINE: Musigny Vieilles Vignes

OWNER: Baronne de la Doucette

ADDRESS: Rue Ste.-Barbe, 21220 Chambolle-Musigny, France

TELEPHONE: 33 03 80 62 86 25

TELEFAX: 33 03 80 62 82 38

CONTACT: Baronne de la Doucette

VISITING POLICY: By appointment, Monday through Friday,
9 A.M.–12 P.M. and 2–6 P.M.

VINEYARDS

SURFACE AREA: 31 acres, of which there are 17.8 acres of
Musigny

GRAPE VARIETAL: Pinot Noir

AVERAGE AGE OF THE VINES: 40–50 years

DENSITY OF PLANTATION: 10,000–12,000 vines per hectare

AVERAGE YIELDS: 35–40 hectoliters per hectare

WINEMAKING AND UPBRINGING

The Comte de Vogüé wines are hand-harvested, largely
destemmed (although in 1990, 100% stems were retained),
fermented in vats, and kept in small oak barrels (40–45%
new) for 18 months. There is an egg-white fining and often a
light filtration. The wines are very dense as well as concentrated, no doubt because of low yields and the Musigny vineyard's limestone soils.

ANNUAL PRODUCTION

Musigny Vieilles Vignes: 900–1,000 cases

AVERAGE PRICE (VARIABLE DEPENDING ON VINTAGE): $200–300

GREAT RECENT VINTAGES

2003, 2002, 1995, 1990

This is the most significant estate in Chambolle-
Musigny because of its important vineyard holdings. It consists of 31 acres, with 17.8 acres in Le
Musigny (70% of that grand cru) and another 6.6 acres
in nearby Bonnes Mares. After producing extraordinary
wines in the late 1940s, this estate went into a slump,
not emerging until the late 1980s with the arrival of
winemaker François Millet in 1985. Vintages since 1990
have generally been spectacular. Not a wine to drink
young, this long-lived classic typically needs 10–15
years of cellaring in top vintages. The Vogüé wines are
not universally loved by Burgundy enthusiasts because
they are often accused of being too Bordelais-like in
their structure and density. However, my instincts suggest it is simply a matter of having more patience with
this firmly structured but immensely impressive wine.

François Millet

2002 Musigny Vieilles Vignes

RATING: 98 points

The extraordinary 2002 Musigny Vieilles Vignes will most likely not have as much cellaring potential as the great 1949, 1959, or 1990, yet in terms of quality it's in the same league as those jewels from the past. Sporting a profound nose of red cherries, spices, candied raspberries, and hints of oak, this noble, concentrated, refined wine reveals loads of flowers intermingled with red as well as black fruits in its complex personality. Unlike the bold, chewy, hyper-concentrated 1990, this is a feminine wine, a work of art with exquisite tannin. Anticipated maturity: 2007–2025.

1995 Musigny Vieilles Vignes

RATING: 93 points

One of the greatest wines of the vintage, Vogüé's 1995 Musigny Vieilles Vignes reminded me of Château Margaux at its best: an iron fist in a velvet glove. How can anything be this massive, powerful, and robust and yet also strikingly elegant and refined? Possessing a dark ruby color and an amazingly spicy, floral (roses), and black fruit–filled nose, this stupendous Burgundy has a thick, almost viscous, velvety texture, with copious quantities of fat, chewy red berries. Surprisingly, the fruit tastes almost stewed yet is perfectly and clearly delineated. Complex, intensely deep, and buttressed with huge but ripe tannins, this wine should be at its plateau of maturity between 2006 and 2016.

1993 Musigny Vieilles Vignes

RATING: 90 points

The 1993 Musigny Vieilles Vignes exhibits a Bordeaux-like structure and austerity. It is a deeply colored, rich, medium-bodied wine with plenty of tannin, admirable purity, and a measured feel on the palate. Assuming the fruit holds, it is capable of lasting through 2015.

1991 Musigny Vieilles Vignes

RATING: 93 points

Wealthy collectors should not miss the opportunity to see whether the 1991 equals or surpasses the 1990 Musigny Vieilles Vignes made at the Comte de Vogüé. The saturated, dense purple color is magnificent. The big, yet unformed, bouquet of framboise (raspberry), cassis, vanilla, and minerals suggests the wine is loaded. It is. Powerful, rich, concentrated, and marvelously clean and pure, this irrefutably impressively endowed, large-scaled red burgundy exhibits a Medoc-like austerity and structure, as well as a squeaky clean, international style. It should last an uncommonly long time for modern-day Burgundy. Very impressive!

1990 Musigny Vieilles Vignes

RATING: 96 points

A Bordeaux-like, saturated, dense ruby/purple color is followed by a tight-fisted nose and flavors of black fruits, underbrush, minerals, smoke, and new oak. Although extremely concentrated, the wine is broodingly backward, and not fun to drink . . . yet. This loaded effort should prove to be one of the longest-lived red Burgundies made in the last 20 years. Anticipated maturity: 2010–2025.

CHAMPAGNE

French Champagne is irrefutably the finest sparkling wine in the world. Despite the hoopla and vast sums of money invested in California, Italy, and elsewhere, in terms of quality, no other wine-producing region can compete. Yes, occasionally a small high-quality producer such as Italy's Bellavista can produce *cuvées* that challenge the best Champagne, but it is Champagne that stands alone at the top of the qualitative pyramid for sparkling wines.

A little over a quarter of a million bottles of Champagne are produced each year in this bucolic viticultural region, located 90 miles northeast of Paris. Champagne can be and sometimes is a blend of three grapes: Chardonnay, Pinot Noir, and Pinot Meunier. A Champagne called Blanc de Blancs must be 100% Chardonnay, while Blanc de Noirs is made from red wine grapes. The term "Crémant" signifies wine that is slightly less effervescent than typical Champagne. What I have always found surprising is that only 25% of the vineyards are planted with Chardonnay; Pinot Meunier dominates plantations with just over 40%; and Pinot Noir accounts for about 30%.

Champagne comes in many different styles, but the most desired tend to be the vintage *cuvées,* which (theoretically) are declared only in the finest years. They are typically richer in depth, deeper in flavor, and more expansive and perfumed than the nonvintage *cuvées* that every house produces. Nonvintage *cuvées* are often branded products designed for uniformity and consistency from year to year. Virtually every Champagne house also has a deluxe (prestige) *cuvée* that is generally vintage-dated and sold for a preposterous price. At their very essence, they can be extraordinary expressions of Champagne. And of course, there are the different styles of Champagne. "Brut," which is the most common, is a dry Champagne, but occasionally readers will see Champagnes called "brut zéro," which

are even drier. Those Champagnes called "sec" are off-dry, and "demi-sec" slightly sweet. And don't forget the glorious rosé Champagnes, which can be quite exquisite when made with the impeccable care that most Champagne houses tend to give them. They are more limited in production, but quite special.

Perhaps something more important than Champagne is what it symbolizes—life, joy, birth, marriage, anniversary, and . . . to celebrate one's good health.

WINES:
Vintage Grande Année
R.D.
Vieilles Vignes Françaises
CLASSIFICATION: Champagne
OWNER: Société Jacques Bollinger
ADDRESS: Champagne Bollinger, B.P. 4, 51160, Aÿ-Champagne, France
TELEPHONE: 33 03 26 53 33 66
TELEFAX: 33 03 26 59 85 59
E-MAIL: contact@champagne-bollinger.fr
WEBSITE: www.champagne-bollinger.fr
CONTACT: Ghislain de Montgolfier (president) or Hervé Augustin (general manager)
VISITING POLICY: Only professionals on request

VINEYARDS

SURFACE AREA: 387.8 acres
GRAPE VARIETALS: Pinot Noir, Pinot Meunier, Chardonnay
AVERAGE AGE OF THE VINES: 18 years
DENSITY OF PLANTATION: 8,300 vines per hectare
AVERAGE YIELDS: 10–12,000 kilograms per hectare as per the appellation

WINEMAKING AND UPBRINGING

Champagne Bollinger, one of the few remaining family-owned-and-managed Grandes Marques houses in Champagne, is known for the quality of its grand and premier crus vineyards. The house is also known for its continued use of traditional methods, including its almost exclusive use of Pinot Noir and Chardonnay, barrel fermentation, aging its reserve wines in magnums that are cork-sealed, and extra-aging on the lees of all its Champagnes. To ensure the continuity of its Champagnes' extraordinary character and quality, in 1992 Champagne Bollinger published its "Charter of Ethics and Quality" that outlines the requisite components of a great Champagne. At Bollinger, these are:

1. Over 70% of Bollinger's vineyards are located in grand and premier crus and have among the highest rating on Champagne's *echelle des crus* scale of any Champagne house, an average of 98%.

2. Two-thirds of Bollinger's production comes from the family's own vineyards, one of only two houses to own such a high percentage of its production.

3. Bollinger vintage Champagnes are made exclusively from Pinot Noir and Chardonnay. Bollinger uses over 60% Pinot Noir, the grape that gives Champagne its fullness and richness.

4. Barrel fermentation: Bollinger is one of very few houses that continue to ferment all their vintage-designated Champagnes and some nonvintage in small oak barrels and remains the only Champagne house that still employs a full-time cooper.

5. Individual crus: To preserve the character of each of its wines, Bollinger ferments each cru and each marc individually, and keeps each separate in traditional barrels until the assemblage, rather than fermenting in large stainless-steel vats where many marcs and even several crus could be required to fill a single vat with concomitant loss of individuality.

6. Bollinger Champagnes spend more time on the lees than those of most other houses, because the longer a Champagne from noble grapes rests on its lees, the more richness and complexity it acquires.

7. Reserve wines, exclusively of grand and premier crus, are individually aged, by variety, cru, and vintage, in cork-sealed magnums.

Ghislain de Montgolfier

ANNUAL PRODUCTION

Wines are sold under allocations.

Bollinger Grande Année: average 150,000 bottles sold
Bollinger Grande Année Rosé: average 10,000 bottles sold
Bollinger R.D.: average 30,000 bottles sold
Bollinger Vieilles Vignes Française: average 1,200 bottles sold
AVERAGE PRICE (VARIABLE DEPENDING ON VINTAGE): $65–125

GREAT RECENT VINTAGES

All the best become R.D.s—1990, 1988, 1985, 1982, 1981, 1979, 1976, 1975, 1973, 1970, 1969, 1966, 1964, 1961, 1959, 1955, 1953, 1952. The best might be 1990, 1985, 1981, 1975, 1969, 1961, 1953, and 1928.

A very old firm, founded in 1829, Bollinger exported its first Champagne to the United States in 1870. Following are the *cuvées* that represent some of the best wines in the world:

The recently disgorged R.D. Cuvée is essentially the same blend as the Grande Année, but it is kept longer on its yeast to give it more body, structure, and that undeniable toasty brioche character. It is usually released a good 10–12 years after the actual vintage.

The Grande Année comes completely from all the grand and premier cru vineyards. Approximately 16 crus are generally used in the assemblage of the Grande Année. Approximately 75% of the wine that you see comes from the grand crus and the rest from premier crus. While the blend changes each year, the most recent vintage, the 1996 Grande Année, was 70% Pinot Noir

and 30% Chardonnay. This wine is always fermented in small oak casks of 205, 225, and 410 liters, lot by lot, cru by cru, and grape variety by grape variety. This results in a very strict selection process. Bollinger uses only old casks (five years or older) to ensure that neither tannin nor oak flavors are imparted to the wines. The wines are bottled for a second fermentation with authentic cork stoppers, which ensure a better barrier against oxidation than the more commonly used crown caps. This also tends to guarantee a degree of freshness.

The Grande Année Rosé is usually a blend of nearly three-quarters Pinot Noir and the rest Chardonnay, made with only free-run juice and generally handled very much like the Grande Année Cuvée Brut.

The R.D., the most recent vintage being the exquisite 1990, was a blend of 69% Pinot Noir and 31% Chardonnay. After fermentation in small oak casks, the same as the Grande Année method, the wine is disgorged 10–12 years after the vintage then rested for three months prior to shipment to the export markets. It is a wine of extraordinary concentration and very full body.

The Vieilles Vignes Françaises *cuvée* always comes from just three parcels of grand cru vineyards in Aÿ and Bouzy, totaling a mere 1.5 acres. These are pre-phylloxera vines that are 100% Pinot Noir. Fermented in old oak barrels of 205 liters, the wine is disgorged by hand and, like the other great Champagnes of Bollinger, rested three months prior to being shipped to the export markets. In the most recent vintage, 1996, there were only 2,600 bottles produced.

As a hallmark of V.I.P. treatment, probably no Champagne is more famous in cinema or literature than Möet & Chandon's Dom Pérignon, but a strong argument can be made that Bollinger is a worthy second. The historical records reveal that Thomas Jefferson called Bollinger the best Champagne of the region when he visited Champagne in 1788. It wasn't Bollinger then, but the vineyard was ultimately acquired by Jacques Bollinger and is utilized in their Grande Année. Of course, Bollinger has most commonly appeared as the favorite Champagne of the fictional Secret Agent 007, James Bond. Bollinger Champagne has appeared in nine of the 20 James Bond films, most recently in *Die Another Day*.

WINES:

Grande Cuvée

Krug Vintage

Krug Rosé

Krug Clos du Mesnil

OWNER: Krug, Vins Fins de Champagne S.A.

ADDRESS: 5 rue Coquebert, 51100 Reims, France

TELEPHONE: 33 03 26 84 44 20

TELEFAX: 33 03 26 84 44 49

E-MAIL: krug@krug.fr

WEBSITE: www.krug.com

CONTACT: Rémi Krug

VISITING POLICY: Private visits only and by appointment only. Contact Mrs. Pascale Rousseau Monday to Friday.

VINEYARDS

SURFACE AREA: 49.4 acres

GRAPE VARIETALS: Pinot Noir, Chardonnay

AVERAGE AGE OF THE VINES: 15 years

DENSITY OF PLANTATION: 9,000 vines per hectare

AVERAGE YIELDS: Different every year

WINEMAKING AND UPBRINGING

These are probably some of the most traditionally made Champagnes available. Krug wines are best known for combining elegance with richness, power, intensity, and complexity. Krug ferments their Champagnes in small oak casks, which they believe allows the wine to breathe and express all of its potential aromas and tastes, but the wines are only in wood from the harvest until the end of December. The casks average 30–40 years of age, and new ones are purchased only when the oldest casks have actually become useless.

Five generations of Krugs have practiced making Champagne the same way. After the Krugs make their blends, the wines are aged for an extended period, 6 years for their Grand Cuvée and 10-plus years for their vintage years.

ANNUAL PRODUCTION

Approximately 100,000 bottles total are produced per year.

Krug Grande Cuvée "Multi-Vintage" Prestige Cuvée Krug

Krug Rosé ("multi-vintage")

Krug Clos du Mesnil

Krug Collection

AVERAGE PRICE (VARIABLE DEPENDING ON VINTAGE): $65–300

GREAT RECENT VINTAGES

1990, 1988, 1985, 1981, 1979, 1961, 1955, 1949, 1947, 1929, 1928

The Krug firm was founded in 1843 by Johann-Joseph Krug, who was born in Germany but became a naturalized French citizen. His son Paul eventually took over, and today five successive generations of Krugs have managed the firm. The two Krugs now at the helm, Henri, the president, and Rémi, the managing director, have done little to change the traditions of this great Champagne house. Their rigorous and very conservative policy of aging the wines for many years before releasing them seems almost at odds with the modern world, but thankfully this explains the rather mature, golden complexity of the Krug wines. Approximately 100,000 bottles of Krug are produced each year, but the demand far exceeds that.

The following is a description of the *cuvées,* as opposed to individual reviews:

Grand Cuvée: Representing well over three-fourths of the production of Krug, this wine, which comes from at least eight different vintages, is a blend of Pinot Noir, Pinot Meunier, and Chardonnay. There is no formula or

recipe, as the Grand Cuvée is created by blending and tasting. In most blends, Pinot Noir represents around 45–55%, Pinot Meunier 10–15%, and Chardonnay 35–45%, and the number of vintages can be as many as eight separate years blended together for complexity and richness. Rather interestingly, the Grand Cuvée was only launched in 1978.

Krug Vintage: One of the longest-lived Champagnes produced, the vintage years of Krug are famous for their richness, slightly oxidized style, but intense concentration and ability to hold up with aging potential. Perhaps one of the greatest Champagnes I ever tasted was the 1947 Krug Collection, which are so designated as their late-release vintages, often held back 30 or 40 years. The Krug Vintage, which varies but tends to be approximately anywhere from 30–50% Pinot Noir, 18–28% Pinot Meunier, and 30–40% Chardonnay, usually needs a good decade of bottle-aging, one of the reasons why Krug rarely releases it before it is 10 years of age. Some of the greatest vintages have been the 1982, 1979, 1975, 1964, 1962, 1959, and 1947.

Here is a breakdown of recent percentages for the Vintage Krug Champagne:

1989—47% Pinot Noir, 24% Pinot Meunier, 29% Chardonnay

1985—48% Pinot Noir, 22% Pinot Meunier, 30% Chardonnay

1982—54% Pinot Noir, 16% Pinot Meunier, 30% Chardonnay

1981—31% Pinot Noir, 19% Pinot Meunier, 50% Chardonnay

1979—36% Pinot Noir, 28% Pinot Meunier, 36% Chardonnay

1976—42% Pinot Noir, 26% Pinot Meunier, 32% Chardonnay

1975—50% Pinot Noir, 20% Pinot Meunier, 30% Chardonnay

1973—51% Pinot Noir, 16% Pinot Meunier, 33% Chardonnay

1971—47% Pinot Noir, 14% Pinot Meunier, 39% Chardonnay

1969—50% Pinot Noir, 13% Pinot Meunier, 37% Chardonnay

1966—48% Pinot Noir, 21% Pinot Meunier, 31% Chardonnay

1964—53% Pinot Noir, 20% Pinot Meunier, 27% Chardonnay

1962—36% Pinot Noir, 28% Pinot Meunier, 36% Chardonnay

1961—53% Pinot Noir, 12% Pinot Meunier, 35% Chardonnay

1959—50% Pinot Noir, 15% Pinot Meunier, 35% Chardonnay

Krug Rosé: A nonvintage blend usually of several years, and again made from Pinot Noir, Pinot Meunier, and Chardonnay. First produced in 1983, this rosé is one of the most copper-hued, palest of the rosé Champagnes in existence. It is also one of the richest, with biting austerity, very intense flavors, and a long finish. Along with the Louis Roederer Cristal Rosé and the Dom Pérignon Rosé, it is to me one of the three greatest rosé Champagnes in the world.

Clos du Mesnil: A 100% Chardonnay, produced from a 4.57-acre vineyard that has existed in the village of Le Mesnil since 1698, and which belonged to a Benedictine monastery until 1750. The vineyard was purchased by the Krugs in 1971. The first vintage was 1979, and it is 100% Chardonnay, all from the same vineyard. Production is rarely more than 15,000 bottles in an abundant year. The wine is extraordinarily elegant and intensely flavored, with a distinctive minerality/chalkiness.

WINE: Dom Pérignon

CLASSIFICATION: Champagne

OWNER: Moët-Hennessy

ADDRESS: 20 Avenue de Champagne, 51200 Epernay, France

TELEPHONE: 33 03 26 51 20 00

TELEFAX: 33 03 26 54 84 23

WEBSITE: www.moet.com

CONTACT: Frédéric Kumenal

VISITING POLICY: Monday through Friday, 9:30–11:30 A.M. and 2:30–4:30 P.M.

VINEYARDS

SURFACE AREA: Estate-owned vineyards as well as purchased grapes from long-term contract vineyards cover just under 1,900 acres

GRAPE VARIETALS: Chardonnay, Pinot Noir, Pinot Meunier

AVERAGE AGE OF THE VINES: 20–50+ years

DENSITY OF PLANTATION: Generally 5,000+ vines per hectare, but can vary

AVERAGE YIELDS: 46–65 hectoliters per hectare

WINEMAKING AND UPBRINGING

Moët & Chandon was one of the first Champagne houses to pioneer the use of stainless-steel tanks for fermentation. Their obsession with cleanliness has paid dividends in the great purity and quality of their Champagnes. They have a surprisingly "hands off" winemaking policy—unusual for a house this size—which results in Champagnes with considerable character. As for the renowned *cuvée* of Dom Pérignon, the best-known luxury Champagne in the world, the blend can vary from year to year, but the intention is to produce a Champagne of equal parts Chardonnay and Pinot Noir. Dom Pérignon can be disappointing in certain vintages (1992 and 1993), but its most recent great vintages (1990 and 1996) are flawless wines of extraordinary intensity and personality.

ANNUAL PRODUCTION

Production figures are confidential.

Brut Impériale
Brut Impériale Rosé
Dom Pérignon
Dom Pérignon Rosé
Nonvintage Brut

AVERAGE PRICE (VARIABLE DEPENDING ON VINTAGE): Dom Pérignon—$125; Dom Pérignon Rosé—$250

GREAT RECENT VINTAGES

1996, 1990, 1985, 1982, 1975

Moët & Chandon's winemaking team, led by the brilliant Richard Geoffroy, produces the world's most hyped luxury champagne in the world, the *cuvée* Dom Pérignon. The production figures for this wine have never been revealed, but the fact that it can be found in just about every luxury hotel and restaurant in the world suggests the numbers are staggering. We do know that the giant of champagne sells over 30 million bottles a year (about twice the amount sold by its nearest competitor, Veuve-Clicquot). The effort to produce such a consistently brilliant wine must be applauded. It is well known that Dom Pérignon comes primarily from grand cru vineyards in Aÿ, Bouzy, Cramant, and Verzenay as well as one premier cru vineyard in Haut Villers.

The history of Dom Pérignon is well known. It was named after Pierre Pérignon, a famous monk born in 1640, the son of a clerk to a local judge. At the age of 19 he entered the Benedictine order, and at age 28 he was appointed cellarmaster at the Abbey of Haut Villers. Though he was blind, he was reported to have extremely acute tasting abilities. A knowledgeable grape grower as well as winemaker, he was one of the first to teach blending skills in the Champagne region. While some chroniclers have said he actually invented Champagne, this has never been established historically. His greatest accomplishments were finding a way to keep the bubbles in the sparkling wine and reinforcing glass bottles by sealing them with corks.

Dom Pérignon was first put on the market in 1936, but it was not the first luxury *cuvée* of Champagne in the modern era (the Louis Roederer Cristal preceded it by many years). Recently declared vin-

tages include 1998, 1996, 1995, 1993, 1992, 1990, 1988, 1986, 1985, 1983, 1982, 1980, 1978, 1976, 1975, 1973, 1971, 1970, 1969, 1966, 1964, 1961, and 1959.

As for the Dom Pérignon Rosé, this incredibly rare, extravagantly priced rosé is everything its reputation suggests. Its first vintage was 1959, when it was created exclusively for the Shah of Iran. The first vintage released commercially in the United States was the 1962, but that wine was not officially marketed until 1970. The blend tends to include about two-thirds Pinot Noir vinified as a red wine from Bouzy, and approximately 35% Chardonnay. It can be exquisite. Most of the greatest rosé Champagnes I have ever tasted have been Dom Pérignon.

DOM PERIGNON

1996 Dom Pérignon

RATING: 98 points

I have had a lot of great vintages of Dom Pérignon, but I do not remember any as impressive as the 1996. Even richer than the brilliant 1990, the 1996 is still tightly wound, but reveals tremendous aromatic intensity, offering hints of bread dough, Wheat Thins, tropical fruit, and roasted hazelnuts. Medium-to full-bodied, with crisp acidity buttressing the wine's wealth of fruit and intensity, it comes across as extraordinarily zesty, well delineated, and incredibly long on the palate. Moet & Chandon deserves considerable accolades for this prodigious example of Dom Pérignon. Anticipated maturity: now–2020+

1995 Dom Pérignon

RATING: 95 points

A brilliant wine with a delicate straw color, creamy aromatics of brioche, orange rind, and hints of coffee and white currants, this exuberant, stylish, medium-bodied Champagne possesses intense flavors, a persistent effervescence (tiny bubbles that linger), and a dry, long finish. Anticipated maturity: now–2015.

1990 Dom Pérignon

RATING: 96 points

The profoundly rich 1990 Dom Pérignon is a creamy-textured, full-bodied offering that loses none of its elegance in spite of its flavor authority. It appears capable of surpassing the fabulous 1985 and 1982. The quality of the 1990 Champagne vintage is remarkable. Anticipated maturity: now–2012.

WINES:

Blanc de Chardonnay

Cuvée Winston Churchill

Vintage Brut

CLASSIFICATION: Champagne

OWNERS: Pol-Roger and de Billy families

ADDRESS: 1 rue Henri Lelarge, B.P. 199, 51200 Epernay, France

TELEPHONE: 33 03 26 59 58 00

TELEFAX: 33 03 26 55 25 70

E-MAIL: polroger@polroger.fr

WEBSITE: www.polroger.co.uk

CONTACT: Christian Pol-Roger

VISITING POLICY: No public tours. By appointment for professionals only.

VINEYARDS

SURFACE AREA: The company owns some 212 acres of vineyards on prime sites, drawing the remainder of its supplies from a further 212 acres contracted by individual growers.

GRAPE VARIETALS: Chardonnay, Pinot Noir, Pinot Meunier

AVERAGE AGE OF THE VINES: 15–20 years

DENSITY OF PLANTATION: 10,000 vines per hectare

AVERAGE YIELDS: 10 tons per hectare

WINEMAKING AND UPBRINGING

After clarification of the must (grape juice) at 8°C, the temperature of fermentation is closely controlled to ensure the optimum retention of fresh fruit character and aromas. The process is carried out in neutral vessels. Pol Roger believes that fermentation in oak barrels causes woody flavors to overtake the freshness of the grape, which all their vinification methods are designed to capture.

Their cellars, extending to some 7 km, are among the coolest (9.5°C) and the deepest in Epernay, which no doubt contributes to the famous Pol Roger mousse of minute bubbles and wines with characteristic elegance and structure. Over the years, the house has developed a reputation for Champagnes of great substance and aging potential. Since 1849 Pol Roger has never yielded to compromise—no overriding compulsion to expand or to impose its values on others, no concessions to passing fashions or the belief that larger is necessarily better.

ANNUAL PRODUCTION

Production figures are confidential.

Brut Reserve

Demi-Sec Rich

Brut Vintage

Blanc de Chardonnay Vintage

Rosé Vintage

Sir Winston Churchill Cuvée Vintage

AVERAGE PRICE (VARIABLE DEPENDING ON VINTAGE): $65–165

GREAT RECENT VINTAGES

1996, 1990, 1988, 1985, 1975, 1966, 1959, 1947, 1934, 1928, 1921, 1914, 1911, 1892

If there is one Vintage Brut Champagne that clearly qualifies for one of the world's greatest wines, it is that of Pol Roger. The blend changes and can be as high as 70% Pinot Noir (1952) but in general tends to be around 60–65% Pinot Noir with the balance Chardonnay. In fact, the 1952 may well be the only vintage that had under 40% Chardonnay. Made from 18 of the crus in the Epernay region, it is a full-bodied, deep, and concentrated wine but has the great vibrancy and delicacy of touch that makes top Champagne, and Pol Roger in particular, so special. The Brut Vintage can easily last for 30 or more years, and is clearly capable of outlasting many famous red wines of France. The other great *cuvée* Pol Roger pro-

ÉPERNAY. - Travail du Vin de Champagne - L'Emballage

duces is their Blanc de Chardonnay, one of the great Blanc de Blancs of Champagne, made only from Chardonnay grapes from the best cru vineyards of the Côtes des Blancs, Cramant, Le Mesnil, Oger, and Avize. This is perhaps the sexiest, most seductive of all the Pol Roger Champagnes, largely because often it can be drunk very young and does seem to have less aging potential than the Vintage Brut or the famed Cuvée Winston Churchill. The Cuvée Winston Churchill is by far the most robust, full-bodied, intense Champagne of the house, and is made only from the best vineyards in the best years. Pol Roger has always been very secretive about the blend, saying that it was a promise made to the Churchill family never to reveal the actual composition, but most observers have speculated that given its mas-

culinity and robustness, it is usually 65–70% Pinot Noir, and the rest Chardonnay. It was first launched in 1984 with the 1975 vintage, at that time produced only in magnums. That of course has changed. My favorites of this *cuvée*—and I have liked them all immensely—have been the 1990, 1985, 1982, and the 1979. I suspect when the 1996 is released, it will also become a legendary effort.

WINE:

Cristal Champagne

CLASSIFICATION: Champagne

OWNER: S.A. Champagne Louis Roederer, controlled by the Rouzaud family

ADDRESS: 21 boulevard Lundy, 51100 Reims, France

TELEPHONE: 33 03 26 40 42 11

TELEFAX: 33 03 26 61 40 45

E-MAIL: com@champagne-roederer.com

WEBSITE: www.champagne-roederer.com

CONTACT: Jean-Claude Rouzaud

VISITING POLICY: By recommendation and by appointment only

VINEYARDS

SURFACE AREA: 506 acres

GRAPE VARIETALS: Pinot Noir, Chardonnay

AVERAGE AGE OF THE VINES: 25 years

DENSITY OF PLANTATION: 8,300 vines per hectare

AVERAGE YIELDS: 10,000–12,000 kilograms per hectare

WINEMAKING AND UPBRINGING

The operative rules at Roederer include flexibility with respect to malolactic versus nonmalolactic fermentation, great selection, aging in large oak casks, and relatively early bottling.

ANNUAL PRODUCTION

Brut Premier Nonvintage: more than 2 million bottles

Grand Vin Sec Nonvintage: a few thousand

Carte Blanche Nonvintage: a few thousand

Blanc de Blancs Millésime: 13,000

Brut Millésime: 50,000

Brut Rosé Millésime: 40,000

Cristal Millésime: average 500,000

Cristal Rosé Millésime: 20,000

AVERAGE PRICE (VARIABLE DEPENDING ON VINTAGE): $150–175

GREAT RECENT VINTAGES

1996, 1995, 1990, 1985, 1982, 1979, 1974, 1970

This estate dates from 1776, when it was founded by a father and son by the name of Dubois. It didn't take the name of Roederer until 1833, when one of the partners in the firm, Louis Roederer, inherited the business from his uncle. It was under his leadership that the company began to exploit its name and produce Champagne. Remarkably, in 1868, Roederer Champagne sales exceeded 2.5 million bottles, most of it exported to Russia (although the United States was also a purchaser). Roederer Champagne became the darling of the Russian tsars, and in 1873 the archives of the Roederer firm record that 666,386 bottles of their Champagne (27% of the total production) were shipped to Russia. Three years later, in 1876, upon the request of tsar Alexander II, the *cuvée* Cristal was created for the exclusive use of the royal family. However, Roederer's market dominance came to a crashing halt in the aftermath of the Russian Revolution in 1917.

Today Louis Roederer is one of the rare family houses that is still totally independent. The company is managed by Jean-Claude Rouzaud, the grandson of Camille Olry-Roederer, who directed the company from 1932 until her death in 1975. She was renowned in France not only for her strong managerial personality, but because her racing stable produced one of the great champion trotters in horse racing history, Jamin. Today production and sales top 2.7 million bottles, and Roederer Champagnes, including their luxury *cuvée,* Cristal, are found in 80 countries.

Roederer takes an enlightened approach to winemaking, allowing far more flexibility than many other Champagne houses do. In some years malolactic fermentation is encouraged and completed, and in other years it is either done partially or not at all depending on their analysis of the grapes. The facilities themselves are air-conditioned and incredibly sanitary. All of their Reserve wines, which are the essence of Cristal, are kept in large wood *foudres,* which no doubt contributes to their full-bodied, rather heady style. The blend varies, but in general they try to produce a Cristal with 50–60% Pinot Noir and the rest Chardonnay. Rarely is there a Cristal vintage in which the percentage of Chardonnay drops below 40%. This is one interesting Champagne, because Roederer has managed to produce great vintages, particularly in 1974 and 1977, in what were by and large terrible vintages throughout France and even parts of Champagne. My favorite years have been the 1996, the 1990, and the 1982, but I have to say rarely have I ever been less than stunned by the quality of Louis Roederer's Cristal.

WINE: Champagne Salon

CLASSIFICATION: Champagne

OWNER: Laurent-Perrier Group

ADDRESS: Champagne Salon, 7 rue de la Brèche d'Oger, 51190 Le Mesnil-sur-Oger, France

TELEPHONE: 33 03 26 57 51 65

TELEFAX: 33 03 26 57 79 29

E-MAIL: champagne@salondelamotte.com

VISITING POLICY: By appointment only; closed on weekends

VINEYARDS

SURFACE AREA: Most fruit is secured from contracted grapes, primarily two sources

GRAPE VARIETALS: Chardonnay—100%

AVERAGE AGE OF THE VINES: 35–50 years old

DENSITY OF PLANTATION: 7,500–10,000 vines per hectare

AVERAGE YIELDS: 10,000 kilograms per hectare

WINEMAKING AND UPBRINGING

100% Le Mesnil/Oger cru. Fermentation takes place in stainless-steel tanks, and there is no malolactic fermentation. Aged an average of 10 years before disgorgement.

ANNUAL PRODUCTION

They produce one Champagne, and only in years they consider exceptional. Salon has released only 32 vintages since it was founded in 1921.

Champagne Salon: 50,000 bottles.

AVERAGE PRICE (VARIABLE DEPENDING ON VINTAGE): $65

GREAT RECENT VINTAGES

1999, 1997, 1996, 1995, 1990, 1988, 1985, 1982

One of the smallest of the great houses of Champagne, producing just over 4,000 cases a year, this small Champagne producer in Le Mesnil-Sur-Oger originated in 1867 with the birth of Eugene-Aime Salon. He began his career as a teacher and then became a successful fur trader, but eventually he secured enough money to buy one hectare of vineyard in Le Mesnil. In 1911 he made his first Champagne, and three years later formed the house that became known as Salon. Salon earned an early claim to fame when it became the house wine at the legendary restaurant Maxim's during the so-called "Roaring Twenties." Always 100% Chardonnay, Salon's quality is undeniable, and the fact that only one wine is made, and only in certain vintages, adds to its mystique. Also, the level of quality is impeccable, and because the wine is not put through malolactic fermentation, it retains very high natural acidity and seems to age for an amazingly long period of time. A 1964 tasted in 2002 was still spectacular.

Eugene-Aime Salon died in 1943, and in 1963 his family finally sold out to Besserat de Bellefon, who in turn sold Salon in 1989 to Laurent-Perrier. For years, the wine was matured in the large *demi-muid* wood casks, but the tradition was finally abandoned, although it is interesting that the nutty aromas and almost woodsy character of Salon are still present even though wood is no longer used. The average age of the vines still remains around 50+ years, and the two vineyards the wine comes from have a very specific warm microclimate in a relatively cool climate zone. One of my favorite vintages of Salon is 1990, but there have been so many great ones, it is almost unfair to compare them. The vintages of Salon that have been produced are 1999, 1997, 1996, 1995, 1990, 1988, 1985, 1983, 1982, 1979, 1976, 1973, 1971, 1969, 1966, 1964, 1961, 1959, 1955, 1953, 1952, 1951, 1949, 1948, 1947, 1946, 1943, 1937, 1934, 1928, 1925, and 1921.

WINE: La Grande Dame

CLASSIFICATION: Champagne

OWNER: Veuve Clicquot Ponsardin

ADDRESS: 12 rue du Temple, 51100 Reims, France

TELEPHONE: 33 03 26 89 54 40

TELEFAX: 33 03 26 40 60 17

WEBSITE: www.veuve-clicquot.com

VISITING POLICY: By appointment only; Monday through Saturday (from April 1 to October 30); Monday through Friday (from November 1 to March 31); possibility of booking via Website.

VINEYARDS

SURFACE AREA: 855 acres

GRAPE VARIETALS: Chardonnay, Pinot Noir, Pinot Meunier

AVERAGE AGE OF THE VINES: About 20 years

DENSITY OF PLANTATION: 8,500–9,500 plants per hectare

AVERAGE YIELDS: Very variable; from 5 tons (in 2003) to 12 tons per hectare

WINEMAKING AND UPBRINGING

All batches (grape varieties, crus, and even blocks) are kept separate and are fermented in temperature-controlled stainless steel with full malolactic fermentation.

Nonvintage: average 3 years of aging

Vintage: minimum 5–6 years of aging

La Grande Dame: minimum 6–7 years of aging

ANNUAL PRODUCTION

Production figures are confidential.

Nonvintage wines— Brut Yellow Label, Demi-Sec

Vintage wines—Vintage Reserve, Rosé Reserve, Rich Reserve

Vintage Prestige Cuvées—La Grande Dame, La Grande Dame Rosé

AVERAGE PRICE (VARIABLE DEPENDING ON VINTAGE): $50–135

GREAT RECENT VINTAGES

1996, 1990, 1955

Veuve Clicquot Ponsardin has been producing great champagnes since 1772. The story of this venerable house is intertwined with the work and personality of a remarkable woman, Madame Clicquot.

Philippe Clicquot, Madame Clicquot's father-in-law, set up the company to produce and sell Champagne. In 1775, Veuve Clicquot exported its Rosé Champagne for the first time, and today more than 85% of its production is sent abroad, both to countries with established consumer bases and those with developing markets. Veuve Clicquot Ponsardin is now positioned second to Moët & Chandon worldwide and is perceived by consumers as the most exclusive and prestigious of champagnes.

The 855 acres of vines currently owned by Veuve Clicquot were acquired over the years by Madame Clicquot and her successors. This vineyard has become one of the most important in the Champagne region both in terms of size and quality. The grapes used (Pinot Noir providing structure, Pinot Meunier roundedness, and Chardonnay freshness and elegance) are carefully selected each year from the best crus in the region.

The winemakers' knowledge of wines and winemaking has enabled Veuve Clicquot to make nonvintage champagnes such as their Brut Yellow Label or Demi-Sec of a consistent quality year after year, and to blend extraordinary vintage wines in years with a particularly good harvest.

La Grande Dame, Veuve Clicquot's most prestigious vintage, is made only during exceptional years with a blend of eight grand crus traditionally used by the house.

In 1987 Veuve Clicquot became part of LVMH, the leading group of luxury goods in the world. The source for this wine comes from the villages of Ambonnay, Bouzy, Avize, Cramant, Mesnil, Oger, and Verzenay. The wine has been vinified in stainless-steel tanks since 1962, and despite what is a relatively large production for a luxury *cuvée,* can age for 25–30 years in the best vin-

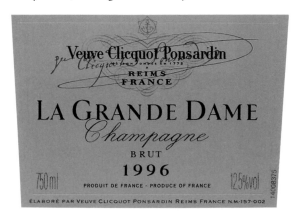

tages. The general blend can change, but in most vintages Veuve Clicquot aims for about 60% Pinot Noir and 38% Chardonnay from the original vineyards acquired by Madame Clicquot. This is always a Champagne with great vinosity, an almost black currant nose with the associated brioche notes. It is a quite ripe, very deep, and relatively full-bodied style of Champagne that handsomely repays aging. The great recent vintages for my palate have been 1996, 1990, and 1985. The vintages produced have included 1996, 1995, 1990, 1989, 1988, 1985, 1983, 1982, 1980, 1979, 1978, 1976, 1975, 1973, 1969, 1966, 1964, 1961, 1959, 1955, 1953, 1949, 1947, 1945, 1943, 1942, 1937, 1928, 1923, and 1919.

There are also very small quantities of La Grande Dame Rosé produced, but it is rarely seen in the marketplace.

THE LOIRE VALLEY

The Loire Valley is by far France's largest wine-producing region, stretching 635 miles from the warm foothills of the Massif Central (a short drive west from Lyon and the vineyards of the Rhône Valley) to the windswept shores of the Atlantic Ocean in Brittany. Most wine drinkers can name more historic Loire Valley châteaux than Loire Valley wines. That is a pity, because the Loire Valley wine-producing areas offer France's most remarkable array of wines from a wide range of varietals, the best known being Sauvignon Blanc and Chenin Blanc. But there are also Pinot Noir, Cabernet Franc, and a few other goodies planted in some of the world's oldest vineyards. Stylistically, white wines dominate the region, representing at least 95% of the production, and they range from bone-dry to amazingly sweet. The profiles that I chose came from a handful of the greatest producers in the world for both Sauvignon Blanc and Chenin Blanc (the latter wines in a range of both sweet and austere, dry styles).

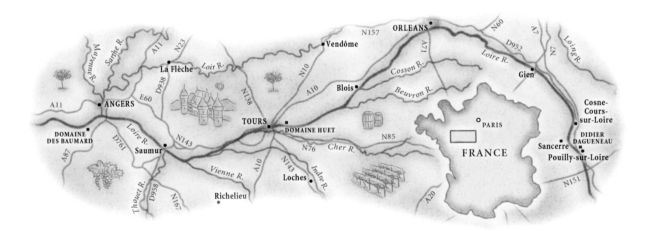

DOMAINE DES BAUMARD

WINES:

Quarts de Chaume

Coteaux du Layon Clos de Ste.-Catherine

Savennières Clos du Papillon

CLASSIFICATION: France, Val de Loire, Anjou

OWNER: s.c.e.a. Domaine des Baumard

ADDRESS: 8, rue de l'Abbaye, 49190 Rochefort sur Loire, France

TELEPHONE: 33 (0)2 41 78 70 03

TELEFAX: 33 (0)2 41 78 83 82

E-MAIL: contact@baumard.fr

WEBSITE: www.baumard.fr

CONTACT: Florent Baumard

VISITING POLICY: Open every day except Sundays and bank holidays, 10 A.M.–12 P.M. and 2–5:30 P.M.; call for appointment

VINEYARDS

SURFACE AREA: 101 acres (96.3 acres in production)

GRAPE VARIETALS: Chenin Blanc, Cabernet, Chardonnay, Verdelho de Madère, Groslot de Cinq Mars, Gamay

AVERAGE AGE OF THE VINES: 75% over 30 years; 20% 10–20 years; 5% less than 10 years

DENSITY OF PLANTATION: Depending on the parcel of vines, the vineyards are planted from 3,300 vines per hectare to as many as 5,000 vines per hectare

AVERAGE YIELDS: 30–40 hectoliters per hectare, with the sweet wines much smaller

WINEMAKING AND UPBRINGING

This is one of the most technically proficient estates in the wine world, with a rigorous policy of impeccable fermentations to protect against oxidation, very low temperatures to promote aromatic development and flavor delineation, and surprising flexibility about malolactic fermentation, which is encouraged in high-acid years and less so in the low-acid years. As Florent Baumard states so clearly, "The principles of vinification are, one, to preserve in the wine its qualities that make it digestible and appealing; secondly, to extract the very best qualities of the grape, recognizing that each vintage is completely different; thirdly, to produce a wine that guards its singular personality; and lastly, in all matters of vinification, never ignore progress and innovation."

Everything here is bottled relatively early, sometimes with a touch of CO_2 to preserve its freshness. The wines age magnificently, with even the drier Savennières having 20 or more years of aging potential and the sweeter wines from the Coteaux du Layon and Quarts de Chaume 25 to 50 years of aging potential.

ANNUAL PRODUCTION

Quarts de Chaume: 15,000 bottles

Coteaux du Layon Clos de Ste.-Catherine: 5,000 bottles

Savennières Clos du Papillon: 24,000 bottles

AVERAGE PRICE (VARIABLE DEPENDING ON VINTAGE): $20–80

GREAT RECENT VINTAGES

Wines produced by Jean Baumard—1976, 1969, 1961

Wines produced by Jean and Florent Baumard—1990, 1989

Wines produced by Florent Baumard—1997, 1996, 1995

The Baumard estate is one of the oldest in the Loire Valley, dating back to 1634, although the Baumards abandoned the nursery business for winemaking only three generations ago. Genius winemaker Jean Baumard, who retired in the mid-1990s, was a consummate professional and the leading technician of the Loire Valley, meticulously growing grapes and even more meticulously vinifying them. His son Florent took over the responsibilities of this highly regarded estate in 1995 and has added even more nuances to the wines, a seemingly impossible feat given the fact that Baumard wines have been the benchmarks for Savennières, Coteaux du Layon, and Quarts de Chaume for many decades. The château has its critics, who argue the wines are too pristine, too perfect, too technically soulless, but the complaints are usually from jealous winemakers who simply don't make wines as fresh, delineated, and crystalline, with such laser-like precision. The wines seem to have everything in place, no matter what vintage, and as many

Florent Baumard

commentators have already said, they are so flawless and polished that they almost seem to be the product of a scientist. Florent, who bears a striking resemblance to Hugh Grant, has added a bit of soul to his father's style, and this domaine continues to be one of the great shining success stories of France's past, present, and future.

COTEAUX DU LAYON CLOS DE STE.-CATHERINE

2002 Coteaux du Layon Clos de Ste.-Catherine
RATING: 94 points
Wonderfully sweet peach notes as well as hints of almond paste, brioche, and orange marmalade jump from the glass of this remarkably full-bodied, fresh, powerful wine. The smell of a spring flower garden lurks behind all of the fruit and concentration. The wine is very intense, with beautiful minerality and a touch of fig and white currant running through the finish. A magnificent wine with moderate sweetness, it should drink well for at least 20–25 years.

2001 Coteaux du Layon Clos de Ste.-Catherine
RATING: 92 points
Notes of white peach, honeysuckle, orange blossoms, green apple skins, and almost a hint of peppermint jump from the glass of this powerful yet very structured wine with loads of minerality and a long finish with good, crisp, almost raspy acidity. The wine is still a bit austere despite its sweetness, yet should age magnificently for 20–25 years.

1997 Coteaux du Layon Clos de Ste.-Catherine
RATING: 93 points
Displaying a super-expressive nose of quince, bergamots, and flowers, the medium to full–bodied 1997 Coteaux du Layon Clos de Ste.-Catherine is a powerful, hugely ripe wine. Broad, opulent, and oily-textured, this well-balanced offering is crammed with blood oranges, red berries, and assorted sugar candies. This is a wine that bursts with freshness and possesses a seemingly endless finish. Anticipated maturity: now–2020.

1996 Coteaux du Layon Clos de Ste.-Catherine
RATING: 94 points
Revealing aromas of sweet white flowers, quince, and minerals, this Coteaux du Layon Clos de Ste.-Catherine is a thick, unctuous, amazingly sweet and creamy, full-bodied wine. Layers of almond extract, fresh red currants, and sweetened herbal tea can be found in its lively and tightly wound personality. Superbly balanced and admirably long, this harmonious wine has the ability to age for over 20 years in an adequate cellar. Drink it between now and 2025.

QUARTS DE CHAUME

2002 Quarts de Chaume
RATING: 95 points
An extraordinary wine with notes of quince, honeysuckle, and white flowers, this very full-bodied wine has an amazing texture, great acidity, tremendous power and potency, but brilliant delineation and laser-like clarity. It offers an almost surreal combination of power, elegance, richness, and finesse. It should drink well for at least 30+ years.

1997 Quarts de Chaume
RATING: 94 points
Baumard's 1997 Quarts de Chaume was tasted five times over a six-month period and it is a remarkably consistent wine. With extended aeration it appears to gain in focus and freshness, a trait that is surprising in the generally heavy and super-ripe 1997 vintage. This dense, oily, jammy wine exudes caramelized minerals and honeyed aromas. On the palate, marzipan, candied grapefruit, and tropical fruits can be detected within its viscous, yet fresh, core. This massive offering will require some cellaring before reaching its peak. Drink it between now and 2020.

1996 Quarts de Chaume
RATING: 96 points
The Quarts de Chaume displays honeysuckle, liquid minerals, and touches of almond paste aromatically as well as a stunning, driven character with virtually perfect harmony and balance between its sweet superripe fruit and acidity. This floral and quince-laden, well-delineated wine has a seemingly unending finish. Anticipated maturity: now–2030+.

2000 Savennières Clos du Papillon

RATING: 90 points

This *cuvée* from Baumard exhibits an atypically open-knit style and a rather precocious personality. Notes of pear, almond, and flowers, in addition to some citrus and papaya, are present, and though this elegant, medium-bodied, very crisp wine lacks the depth of the greatest vintages of Clos du Papillon, it shows wonderful balance and an easygoing personality. This one begs for consumption between now and 2008.

1997 Savennières Clos du Papillon

RATING: 92 points

Mouthwatering scents of fruitcake, spices, and poached pears are found in the 1997 Savennières Clos du Papillon's nose. The wine offers loads of pears, apples, mangoes, and powerful spices in its thickly textured, medium to full body. Full-flavored, yet highly detailed, balanced, and precise, it can be enjoyed in the near term for its luscious fruit. With cellaring, this appellation's trademark minerality will blossom. Anticipated maturity: now–2010+.

1996 Savennières Clos du Papillon

RATING: 94 points

White flowers intermingled with verbena can be found in the 1996 Savennières Clos du Papillon's nose. This vibrant offering is rich, extremely delineated, medium-bodied, and super-focused, offering highly detailed flavors of herbal teas, minerals, flint, and lemon. This crystalline wine is as pure and sublimely balanced as a wine can be. Anticipated maturity: now–2020.

SAVENNIERES CLOS DU PAPILLON

2002 Savennières Clos du Papillon

RATING: 94 points

The 2002 Savennières Clos du Papillon explodes from the glass with intense mineral notes. Complex, medium-bodied, and profound, its concentrated core displays a panoply of flavors. Honeysuckle blossoms, sun-dried spices, almonds, chalk, and white flowers are detectable throughout its nuanced personality as well as in its prolonged finish. Drink it over the next 10–15 years.

2001 Savennières Clos du Papillon

RATING: 90 points

Hints of wet rocks, cold steel, flowers, lemon zest, and citrus oil are followed by a medium-bodied, austere wine with impressive minerality, a very dry, crisp, inner-concentrated mid-palate, and a long finish with zesty acidity. This very tightly knit wine should be at its best between 2007 and 2015.

WINES:

Pouilly-Fumé Pur Sang

Pouilly-Fumé Cuvée Silex

OWNER: Didier Dagueneau

ADDRESS: Rue Ernesto Che Guevara No. 1:3:5 and 7, 58150
St.-Andelain, France

TELEPHONE: 03 86 39 15 62

TELEFAX: 03 86 39 07 61

E-MAIL: silex@wanadoo.fr

CONTACT: Didier Dagueneau or Nathalie Julien

VISITING POLICY: By appointment only

VINEYARDS

SURFACE AREA: 29.6 acres

GRAPE VARIETALS: Blanc Fumé de Pouilly

AVERAGE AGE OF THE VINES: 7–77 years

DENSITY OF PLANTATION: 6,500 vines per hectare for the old
vines; 7,000 vines per hectare for the new plantings
(less than 10 years old)

AVERAGE YIELDS: 30–50 hectoliters per hectare

WINEMAKING AND UPBRINGING

One of the great winemakers and viticulturalists in the world,
Didier Dagueneau is a perfectionist, severely pruning, debud-
ding, deleafing, and cluster thinning his vines to keep his yields
among the lowest of the region. He will actually do successive
passes through the vineyard, much like a sweet wine producer,
simply to capture his grapes at their optimum peak of maturity. His cathedral-like winery, built in 1989, operates completely on gravity and is, as one might expect, impeccably clean.
There is no vinification formula; the grapes sometimes undergo a touch of skin contact, but in most vintages very little.
The grapes are very ripe and there is no destemming. While he
does utilize several varieties of commercial yeast, fermentation
always takes place in temperature-controlled stainless-steel
tanks or in less controlled oak barrels designed to his rigid requirements. He is a great believer in aging the wines on their
fine lees up until bottling and is opposed to malolactic fermentation regardless of how acidic any vintage might turn out to
be. He bottles at least four versions of Pouilly-Fumé, but his
two greatest are the Pur Sang and the Cuvée Silex.

ANNUAL PRODUCTION

Pouilly-Fumé Pur Sang: 24,000 bottles

Pouilly-Fumé Silex: 20,400 bottles

AVERAGE PRICE (VARIABLE DEPENDING ON VINTAGE): $60–75

GREAT RECENT VINTAGES

2002, 2000, 1999, 1998, 1990, 1986

Didier Dagueneau is the great master of Sauvignon
Blanc and one of the Loire Valley's most fascinating winemakers. Resembling a prophet with his long,
unruly hair and a full beard, Dagueneau immediately
strikes one as someone who is on a quest to do something very special in life. He has been a controversial
figure in France, condemning his neighbors, going on
French TV to point out their high yields and carelessly
managed vineyards, but he's trying to make a point.
Great wines can be produced, but such high quality is
costly and time-consuming, and requires hard work.
Despite his often inflammatory rhetoric and in-your-
face personality, this is a great winemaker who is trying
to produce Pouilly-Fumés that have grand cru–like
complexity, richness, and aging potential. He makes no
compromises—in the vineyards, in his modern cellars,
or in the wine. He both talks the talk and walks the
walk. Dagueneau has become an inspiration to the
younger generation in the Loire Valley and his wines are
a beacon of integrity and greatness.

POUILLY-FUME PUR SANG

2002 Pouilly-Fumé Pur Sang

RATING: 93 points

The 2002 Pouilly-Fumé Pur Sang is a wine of enormous power, concentration, and depth. A barrel-fermented, non-malolactic Sauvignon Blanc with extraordinary minerality, the 2002 has notes of orange peel, citrus oil, smoke, and wet rocks all presented in a very full-bodied, powerful, yet edgy style with great underlying acidity. Extraordinary elegance and the absence of anything intrusive make for a tour de force Sauvignon Blanc that should age beautifully for 10–15 years.

POUILLY-FUME CUVEE SILEX

2002 Pouilly-Fumé Cuvée Silex

RATING: 96 points

One of the greatest Pouilly-Fumés I have ever tasted, this wine satisfies both the intellect and the hedonistic senses. Barrel-fermented and always made from some of the oldest vines in the estate's and Silex's rich soils, this wine has a wonderful nose of flowers intermixed with a hint of white truffle, citrus oil, herb liqueur, melon, quince, and papaya. Extraordinary precision, huge, full-bodied flavors, yet fabulous, penetrating acidity make for one of the finest Sauvignon Blancs a person can taste. Anticipated maturity: now–2014.

WINES:

Vouvray Moëlleux Le Clos du Bourg

Vouvray Moëlleux Le Haut Lieu

Le Haut-Lieu Sec

Le Mont Sec

Vouvray Moëlleux Cuvée Constance

Vouvray Moëlleux Le Mont

CLASSIFICATION: Loire Valley

OWNERS: A consortium of Hungarian and American businessmen as well as Noël Pinguet

ADDRESS: Clos du Bourg, 11 rue de la Croix Buisée, 37210 Vouvray, France

TELEPHONE: 33 02 47 52 78 87

TELEFAX: 33 02 47 52 66 74

E-MAIL: huet.echansonne@wanadoo.fr

CONTACT: Call or write winery at above address

VISITING POLICY: By appointment only, Monday through Saturday, 9 A.M.–noon and 2–6 P.M.

VINEYARDS

SURFACE AREA: 100 acres

GRAPE VARIETALS: Chenin Blanc—100%

AVERAGE AGE OF THE VINES: 30–45+ years

DENSITY OF PLANTATION: 5,000–6,000 vines per hectare

AVERAGE YIELDS: 20–30 hectoliters per hectare and even much less for the rare sweet wine *cuvées*

WINEMAKING AND UPBRINGING

At this biodynamically run estate, the late Gaston Huet's son-in-law and one of the current owners, Noël Pinguet, employs slow, cool fermentations, after hand-harvesting the grapes in multiple passes. Fermentations tend to take place in very cramped quarters in stainless-steel tanks. Nothing goes through malolactic fermentation, as the life-preserving acidity of these great white wines is considered essential. Bottling usually takes place 12–14 months after the harvest, if not sooner.

ANNUAL PRODUCTION

Total production of all *cuvées* is 12,500 cases.

Vouvray Moëlleux Le Clos du Bourg

Le Haut-Lieu Sec

Le Mont Sec

Vouvray Moëlleux Cuvée Constance

AVERAGE PRICE (VARIABLE DEPENDING ON VINTAGE): $30–90

GREAT RECENT VINTAGES

2002, 1997, 1995, 1989

Known both as Domaine Le Haut-Lieu and Domaine Huet, this estate has been the preeminent property in Vouvray for decades. The engaging, dynamic Gaston Huet, a World War II hero, ran the domaine from 1947 until his death in 2002 at the age of 92. (His son-in-law, Noël Pinguet, had been making the wines and tending the vineyards.) Most likely because of France's draconian inheritance laws, Pinguet sold his controlling interest in Domaine Huet shortly after Gaston Huet's passing to a consortium composed of Hungary's István Szepsy (of Tokaji fame) and American businessmen.

Noël Pinguet, who remains as director and is a significant shareholder, has worked at the domaine since 1971 and has been solely responsible for its wines since 1976. For the past 29 years, this has been Noël Pinguet's winery. A soft-spoken yet extremely self-confident man, Pinguet strongly believes in working with what nature provides. He began shifting the estate to biodynamic farming in 1987, and converted all of its vineyards to this system by 1990. The vines are pruned tight to assure moderate yields. In the abundant 1997 vintage, the estate's yields were 37 hectoliters per hectare, extremely low by Vouvray standards. Pinguet has never chaptalized nor acidified a wine. In vintages where the grapes do not attain high ripeness levels (1976 and 1985, for example), he does not produce sweet wines.

This great estate is somewhat rare in Vouvray because the wines are kept separate from their respective vineyards until just prior to bottling. All the vineyards, which have a perfect southern exposure allowing them to achieve maximum ripeness, produce the richest and longest-lived wines of the appellation. Like most producers in Vouvray, this domaine produces a dry *cuvée* called *sec,* an off-dry, slightly sweet *cuvée* called *demi-sec* with 30 grams of residual sugar, and a sweet *cuvée* called *Moëlleux,* with residual sugars that can range from the low 30s to in excess of 70 to 100. The great vintages from Huet—1947, 1959, 1989, 1990, and certainly 1997 and 2002—were all wines that will keep 50 or more years. A 1947 Moëlleux drunk on New Year's Eve 2003 was quite extraordinary. The dry *cuvée,* called

Le Haut-Lieu Sec, is gorgeous to drink young but actually ages quite handsomely for up to a decade.

While many lamented the passing of the great Gaston Huet, a true legend in his lifetime, the extraordinary work done over many decades by Noël Pinguet will continue, as the current consortium seems committed to carrying on the extraordinary legacy built by Huet and Pinguet.

VOUVRAY MOELLEUX LE CLOS DU BOURG

1997 Vouvray Moëlleux Le Clos du Bourg 1er Trie
RATING: 95 points
Produced from vines planted in calcareous and stony soils, the 1997 Vouvray Moëlleux Le Clos du Bourg 1er Trie exudes aromas reminiscent of smoke, clay, chalk, and candied lemons. This medium-bodied, penetrating, superrich wine is balanced,

concentrated, and intense. Layers of earth, apples, figs, white peaches, and minerals can be found in this magnificent sweet wine's flavor profile and stupendous length. Presently somewhat austere and reserved, it will benefit from a few years of cellaring. Projected maturity: now–2025+.

VOUVRAY MOELLEUX CUVEE CONSTANCE

1997 Vouvray Moëlleux Cuvée Constance
RATING: 99+ points
Pinguet, in the finest sweet wine vintages, crafts a luxury *cuvée* from grapes sorted out of the harvests of his three finest vineyards (Le Clos du Bourg, Le Mont, and Le Haut-Lieu). The stunning, virtually perfect, 1997 Vouvray Moëlleux Cuvée Constance (named after his daughter) sports 150 grams of residual sugar per liter, 7.5 grams of acidity, and 12.5% alcohol. Tasting this sublime dessert wine brought tears to my eyes. So captivatingly pure, focused, and intricate, it is all but im-

possible to adequately describe. Its green and straw color reveals hints of gold. Aromatically, it titillates with scents of apricot jam, candied grapefruits, quince, bergamots, and flowers. On the palate fresh peaches, citrus fruits, honey, acacia blossoms, quinine, chalk, and lemony mangoes can be found. A medium to full–bodied, penetrating, yet perfectly balanced wine, it has a finish that seemingly lingers forever, revealing even more waves of minerals and fruit. It will require patience yet should easily evolve for 50 years or more. Bravo!

VOUVRAY MOELLEUX LE HAUT-LIEU

1997 Vouvray Moëlleux Le Haut-Lieu

RATING: 94 points

The 1997 Vouvray Moëlleux Le Haut-Lieu is crafted from a vineyard composed of clay, as well as calcareous and silica-based soils. It offers floral and sweet mineral aromas that lead to its hugely broad, honeyed character. It is densely packed with tropical fruits (mangoes, papaya, and hints of banana) as well as quince, clay, and honey flavors. As with its two siblings, it is stupendously long, easily lasting 45+ seconds; moreover, it can be cellared for decades. Projected maturity: now–2020+.

VOUVRAY MOELLEUX LE MONT

1997 Vouvray Moëlleux Le Mont

RATING: 90 points

The 1997 Vouvray Moëlleux Le Mont has a touch of gold in its otherwise straw color. It offers a nose of deeply honeyed chalk with hints of botrytis as well as a complex, quince, candied almond, and acacia blossom–flavored personality. Medium-bodied and exceptionally pure, this wine is rich, flavorful, and simply gorgeous. Drink it through 2014.

1997 Vouvray Moëlleux Le Mont 1er Trie

RATING: 96 points

The 1997 Vouvray Moëlleux Le Mont 1er Trie, from vines located on silica-based soils, bursts with mouthwatering honeysuckle and freshly cut flower aromas. This majestic, powerful, complex offering is crammed with red fruits, minerals, and floral flavors. Exquisitely balanced, it is harmonious, mouthcoating, and elegant. Anticipated maturity: now–2025+.

VOUVRAY LE MONT SEC

2002 Vouvray Le Mont Sec

RATING: 93 points

The 2002 Vouvray Le Mont Sec's bold limestone, herbal tea, and lemongrass aromas lead to a silky-textured, medium-bodied character crammed with honeyed chalk, spices, and almonds. Exceptionally well balanced, boisterously flavored, deep, and awesomely concentrated, it is a powerful, full-throttle wine with an immensely long finish. This is the finest dry Vouvray I've tasted to date. Bravo! While it may last longer, I suggest drinking it between now and 2010–2015.

VOUVRAY LE HAUT-LIEU SEC

2002 Vouvray Le Haut-Lieu Sec

RATING: 91 points

Nectar of lemongrass, limestone, fresh almonds, and honeysuckle blossoms can be found in both the aromatics and flavors of the 2002 Vouvray Le Haut-Lieu Sec. Medium to full–bodied, satin-textured, and focused, this outstanding wine has admirable depth and purity, as well as superb elegance. Wonderfully combining power and grace, this first-rate dry Vouvray also possesses an extremely long, fruit-packed finish. Drink it between now and 2013–2015.

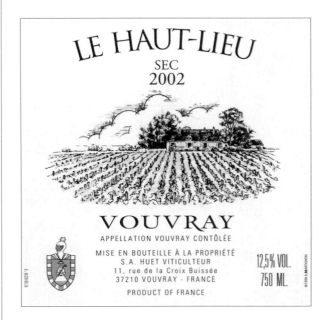

THE RHÔNE VALLEY

The Rhône Valley has always produced exhilarating as well as compelling wines, yet it seems perplexing that only a handful of them have the prestige and cachet of France's more hallowed regions such as Bordeaux, Burgundy, and Champagne. Certainly there have been fewer books and articles written about the Rhône, whose history dates back over 2,000 years and coincides with the Roman conquest of what was then known as Gaul. But many of its vineyards—after centuries of being ignored, misunderstood, underappreciated, and, one might also argue, undervalued—have finally arrived. They produce France's, and often the world's, most underrated great wines, and the celestially sublime wines of Côte Rôtie, Hermitage, Condrieu, and Châteauneuf-du-Pape have no rivals anywhere in the world.

The Rhône River actually starts in the icy depths of Switzerland, passing some of that country's wonderful hillside vineyards before it enters France just to the west of Geneva. It passes through the gorges of the Jura Mountains and then intersects and absorbs the waters of another famous French river, the Saône, at Lyon, one of France's greatest cities, long known for its gastronomic ambitions.

The northern viticultural region of the Rhône begins approximately twenty miles south of Lyon at Ampuis, where the terraced, steep hillsides of vineyards seem almost ready to tumble into the Rhône below them. About 60 miles later, the vineyards of the northern Rhône terminate at Valence, and one has to go another 60 or so miles before the great appellation of the southern Rhône, Châteauneuf-du-Pape, is visible with its ancient palace, partially destroyed by the Nazis, rising above the sleepy hillside village.

The most obvious geological characteristic of the northern Rhône vineyards, particularly Côte Rôtie, Condrieu, and Hermitage, is that most of the top vineyards are planted on very steep slopes made primarily of granite in Hermitage and limestone, schist, and some clays in Côte Rôtie and Condrieu. Châteauneuf-du-Pape, which is the largest *serious* appellation of the Rhône Valley, has more than 8,000 acres of vines and more than 300 proprietors and as many different expositions and soils. It is the home of some of the world's greatest wine producers, working with ancient vines and tiny yields to create wines that consistently produce a glorious perfume often reminiscent of an open-air Provençal marketplace. These wines have the added attraction of a full-throttle palate loaded with the red and black fruits that grow so easily in the region.

Thomas Jefferson, writing in 1787, said the white Hermitage was "the first wine in the world without single exception." The notorious Clement V—the French pope who established the papacy in Avignon instead of Rome—may or may not have planted some vines at a palace he built just to the north of Avignon in what is now the village of Châteauneuf-du-Pape.

The great grapes of the northern Rhône are limited to Syrah for the red wines and Marsanne, Roussanne, and Viognier for the whites. In the south, there is a smorgasbord of options, but the grape that dominates the region's most profound wines is Grenache, a grape more fickle than Pinot Noir but capable of extraordinary nobility in both its aromas and flavors. Grenache represents nearly 80% of the red vine plantings in Châteauneuf-du-Pape, with the balance about 5.6% Syrah, 4.7% Mourvèdre, and the rest a tiny bit of Cinsault, Vaccarèse, and Counoise.

CHATEAU DE BEAUCASTEL

WINES:

Châteauneuf-du-Pape

Châteauneuf-du-Pape Hommage à Jacques Perrin

Châteauneuf-du-Pape Roussanne Vieilles Vignes

OWNER: Perrin family

ADDRESS: Chemin de Beaucastel, 84350 Courthézon, France

TELEPHONE: 33 04 90 70 41 00

TELEFAX: 33 04 90 70 41 19

E-MAIL: contact@beaucastel.com

WEBSITE: www.beaucastel.com

CONTACT: François Perrin

VISITING POLICY: By appointment

VINEYARDS

SURFACE AREA: 320 acres

Whites: Cuvée Tradition—13.6 acres; Cuvée Vieilles Vignes—
5 acres

Reds: Regular *cuvée*—173 acres; Hommage à Jacques
Perrin—5 acres

GRAPE VARIETALS:

Whites: Blend: 80% Roussanne, 15% Grenache Blanc,
5% Clairette, Bourboulenc, Picardan; Cuvée Vieilles
Vignes: 100% Roussanne

Reds: Regular *cuvée*: 30% Grenache, 30% Mourvèdre,
10% Syrah, 10% Counoise, 5% Cinsault and other
varietals, mainly Vaccarèse and Muscardin; Hommage
à Jacques Perrin: 70% Mourvèdre, 15% Syrah,
10% Grenache, 5% Counoise

AVERAGE AGE OF THE VINES:

White: Cuvée Tradition—30 years; Cuvée Vieilles Vignes—
70 years

Red: Regular *cuvée*—50 years; Hommage à Jacques Perrin—
65–90+ years

DENSITY OF PLANTATION: 3,000–4,000 vines per hectare

AVERAGE YIELDS: 25–30 hectoliters per hectare

WINEMAKING AND UPBRINGING

Whites: Cuvée Vieilles Vignes—12 months total. Fermentation of 15–60 days, with 50% of the yield in stainless-steel tanks and 50% in one-year-old barrels.

Reds: Regular *cuvée*—24 months total. Fermentation of three weeks in cement tanks; the wine then goes into old oak casks for 8–18 months. Hommage à Jacques Perrin—Fermentation of three weeks in cement tanks; the wine then goes into old oak casks for 8–18 months. Bottling after 24 months, without filtration.

ANNUAL PRODUCTION

Cuvée Tradition: 1,625 cases

Cuvée Vieilles Vignes: 300–325 cases

Regular *cuvée*: 20,000–24,000 cases

Hommage à Jacques Perrin: 400–425 cases

AVERAGE PRICE (VARIABLE DEPENDING ON VINTAGE): $50–150

GREAT RECENT VINTAGES

2003, 2001, 2000, 1998, 1990, 1989, 1981

The fact that Beaucastel produces the longest-lived red wine of the southern Rhône is irrefutable. However, this estate also produces one of the Rhône Valley's greatest and most distinctive wines. The wine is made by totally organic methods. No chemicals are used in the vast 272-acre vineyard located in the northernmost sector of Châteauneuf-du-Pape near the town of Courthézon. More than 500 tons of manure are dumped on these vineyards whose vines, through a meticulously planned rotational replanting formula, maintain an average age of 50 years. The late Jacques Perrin, considered by many to be one of the Rhône Valley's most brilliant and philosophical winemakers, believed adamantly in three principles: (1) a wine must be made naturally, (2) the percentage of Mourvèdre in the blend must be significant, and (3) the wine's character and intrinsic qualities could not be compromised by

Jean-Pierre and François Perrin

concessions to modern technology. Jacques Perrin died in 1978, but his two sons, François and Jean-Pierre, were well indoctrinated with their father's beliefs, and have not only carried on his methodology but have further increased the quality of Beaucastel.

The vineyards of Beaucastel are one of the few major estates in Châteauneuf-du-Pape to have all 13 permitted varietals planted. For their red wines, Beaucastel is marked by the high percentage of Mourvèdre. The preferred blend here is 30% Grenache, 30% Mourvèdre, 10% Syrah, 1% Counoise, 5% Cinsault, and the rest Muscardin and Vaccarèse. They are augmenting the percentage of Mourvèdre and Counoise in their new plantings. For their white wine, they remain unique as well, using an unusually high percentage of 80% Roussanne, and the rest Bourboulenc, Clairette, and Grenache Blanc. The special *cuvée* is 100% Roussanne.

It is ironic that Beaucastel, while being America's best-known Châteauneuf-du-Pape, is undeniably the appellation's most atypical wine. The high percentage of Mourvèdre, combined with Counoise, Muscardin, and Vaccarèse, as well as the low percentage of Grenache, results in a wine that the Châteauneuf-du-Pape cognoscenti often call the antithesis of what is considered classic for the appellation. Yet the results are stunning, if unusual for a wine from this appellation. In top vintages, the red wine is usually a black/ruby or purple color, loaded with layers of fruit, tannin, and a multitude of fascinating scents and aromas. The Mourvèdre tends to give this Châteauneuf-du-Pape more structure and tannin, as well as an unmistakable perfume of animal and mushroom-like, tree-bark scents. Moreover, the finest vintages are often unflattering to drink young, but age, usually a minimum of 6–10 years, brings forth the distinctive aromatic profile and sweetness and richness of fruit.

As visitors to Beaucastel can attest, the rows of huge *foudres* in the air-conditioned underground cellars are visually impressive. After blending, the wine spends a year in these *foudres* until the bottling takes place. Because the traditional practice of bottling as the wine is sold results in bottle variation, Beaucastel constructed an underground storage facility beginning with the 1980 vintage. Since then, all 18,000–25,000 cases of Beaucastel are bottled at the same time, thus guaranteeing uniformity of quality from bottle to bottle. In keeping with the artisanal approach to viticulture and winemaking, Beaucastel is bottled after an egg-white fining; it is never filtered.

François Perrin is a youthful-looking, trim, articulate individual, and his handsome brother Jean-Pierre is the more outspoken and fiery of the two. The brothers have strong ideas about the issue of filtration. Both have experimented with filtration and have been shocked by the negative effect it has on a wine's bouquet, richness, body, and potential for development. It is not surprising that after three or four years of bottle age, most Beaucastels will shed considerable sediment, with the richer, more concentrated vintages caking the inside of the bottle.

The red *cuvée* of Beaucastel, which has had such an illustrious history, was joined by a special *cuvée*, called Hommage à Jacques Perrin, in the 2003, 2001, 2000, 1999, 1998, 1995, 1994, 1990, and 1989 vintages. The debut vintage, 1989, was inaugurated as a dedication to François and Jean-Pierre's father, Jacques, who had an enormous influence on them, and had steadfastly supported the use of Mourvèdre in the appellation. It is a super-concentrated blend of 60% Mourvèdre, 20% Grenache, 10% Syrah, and 10% Counoise that is aged in *foudre* and bottled later than Beaucastel's Châteauneuf-du-Pape. Given its thrilling level of quality, in addition to the tiny quantity produced, it became immortal the moment the first vintage was released.

The Perrins are contrarians. They support the Mourvèdre grape in Châteauneuf-du-Pape, and Beaucastel also prefers the fickle, often difficult-to-cultivate Roussanne to the more popular Grenache Blanc, Clairette, and Bourboulenc for their white wines. There are two *cuvées* of white Beaucastel, both of them the finest wines made in the appellation. Not only do they both have considerable longevity by the standards of white Châteauneuf-du-Pape, they are also the region's richest and most complex white wines. Both are Roussanne-based wines, with the regular *cuvée* made from 80% Roussanne, 15% Grenache Blanc, and the remaining 5% composed of Bourboulenc, Clairette, and Picpoul. This wine is augmented by a limited-production 100% old-vine Roussanne from a small parcel of 65-year-old vines. This wine, priced at a level that competes with grand cru white Burgundy, is vinified both in wood casks (some of which are new) and in stainless steel, and then blended together. It is put through full malolactic fermentation. It may be the world's greatest expression of Roussanne. The debut vintage was 1986. Every year has produced a compelling wine with at least 10–20 years of aging potential.

CHATEAUNEUF-DU-PAPE (RED)

2003 Châteauneuf-du-Pape

RATING: 90–93 points

Because of difficulties with some of the parcels of Mourvèdre due to the excessive drought and heat in August 2003, the classic blend of Beaucastel in 2003 has significantly more Grenache, about 50%, and only 20% Mourvèdre. In addition, there is a bit more Counoise and Syrah than normal, and in that sense it is more along the blending lines of the 1998. The wine shows very high levels of tannin, classic licorice notes intermixed with blackberry and pepper, a sweet, full-bodied palate impression, and some lofty tannins in the finish. My instincts suggest this wine is going to need a good 5–6 years of bottle age and then should drink well for 15–20 years.

2001 Châteauneuf-du-Pape

RATING: 96 points

Beaucastel has been on a terrific roll over the last four vintages. The 2001 Châteauneuf-du-Pape (which François Perrin feels is similar to the 1990, although I don't see that as of yet) is a 15,000-case blend of 30% Grenache, 30% Mourvèdre, 10% Syrah, 10% Counoise, and the balance split among the other permitted varietals of the appellation. This inky ruby/purple-colored *cuvée* offers a classic Beaucastel bouquet of new saddle leather, cigar smoke, roasted herbs, black truffles, underbrush, and blackberry as well as cherry fruit. It is a superb, earthy expression of this Mourvèdre-dominated *cuvée*. Full-bodied and powerful, it will undoubtedly close down over the next several years, not to reemerge for 7–8 years. Anticipated maturity: 2008–2025.

2000 Châteauneuf-du-Pape

RATING: 94 points

The opaque ruby/purple-colored 2000 Châteauneuf-du-Pape offers a profoundly sweet perfume of melted licorice, blackberries, and black cherries backed up by loads of glycerin, full body, and moderately high but sweet, well-integrated tannin. There is a seamlessness to the 2000 that will make it accessible early in life and thus atypical for Beaucastel. The 1985 behaved in this manner when young, but the 2000 possesses even more stuffing. Like its 2001 sibling, it is a classic blend of 30% Grenache, 30% Mourvèdre, 10% Syrah, 10% Counoise, and the balance other permitted varietals. Anticipated maturity: 2007–2025.

1999 Châteauneuf-du-Pape

RATING: 91 points

The prodigious 1999 Beaucastel boasts aromas of blackberry fruit intermixed with cassis, licorice, roasted meats, leather, and truffles. While it does not possess much fat or precociousness, it displays definition and elegance. This is a full-bodied, concentrated, classic Beaucastel. Anticipated maturity: 2007–2025.

1998 Châteauneuf-du-Pape

RATING: 96 points

The 1998 is unquestionably one of the great modern-day Beaucastels, but because of its high Grenache content, it is different from some of the other classics. Aromas and flavors of kirsch, licorice, earth, and new saddle leather dominate. Very full-bodied, intense, with surprisingly supple tannin, this is a more forward style, but with great longevity. Anticipated maturity: now–2031.

1995 Châteauneuf-du-Pape

RATING: 93 points

The 1995 exhibits a deep, dark ruby/purple color, and a provocative (probably controversial) aromatic profile of animal fur, tar, truffles, black cherries, cassis, licorice, and minerals. A medium to full–bodied wine, with a boatload of tannin, considerable grip and structure, and a weighty feel in the mouth, this appears to be a classic *vin de garde* made in the style of the 1978 Beaucastel (which is still not close to full maturity). Prospective purchasers over the age of 40 should be buying this wine for their children.

1990 Châteauneuf-du-Pape

RATING: 96 points

Two great back-to-back vintages are the 1990 and 1989. The more developed dark plum/garnet–colored 1990 boasts an incredible perfume of hickory wood, coffee, smoked meat, Asian spices, black cherries, and blackberries. Lush, opulent, and full-bodied, it is a fully mature, profound Beaucastel that will last another 15–20 years.

1989 Châteauneuf-du-Pape

RATING: 97 points

The 1989 is inkier/more purple in color than the 1990, with an extraordinarily sweet, rich personality offering up notes of smoke, melted licorice, black cherries, Asian spices, and cassis. Full-bodied and concentrated, it is one of the most powerful as well as highly extracted Beaucastels I have ever tasted. It requires another 3–4 years to reach its plateau of maturity, where it should remain for at least two decades.

1985 Châteauneuf-du-Pape

RATING: 91 points

One of the most charming Beaucastels since it was first bottled (and still holding on today), is the gorgeous 1985. Its
medium ruby color reveals considerable amber/pink at the
edge. This offering demonstrates that a wine does not need a
lot of tannin and power to age well; it's all about balance.
Velvety-textured, opulent, sweet, and appealing, this remains
a classic Beaucastel. Anticipated maturity: now–2008.

1981 Châteauneuf-du-Pape

RATING: 95 points

One of the all-time great classics, the 1981 is fully mature and
should be consumed. It's a big, sweet, candied fruit bomb offering notes of smoke, pepper, dried herbs, truffles, leather,
and cedar, as well as black and red currants. Full-bodied and
opulent, it is one of the most delicious, complex, and stunning
Beaucastels ever made. Anyone who has magnums of this wine
has the equivalent of liquid gold. Out of regular bottle, I would
recommend consumption over the next several years.

CHATEAUNEUF-DU-PAPE HOMMAGE A JACQUES PERRIN

2003 Châteauneuf-du-Pape Hommage à Jacques Perrin

RATING: 94–96 points

As with the classic *cuvée,* the Perrins deviated from the normal blend of this great wine and have added more Grenache
to it. Instead of 60% Mourvèdre, as in most vintages except
the 1998 and 2003, this is a blend of 40% Mourvèdre, 40%
Grenache, 10% Syrah, and 10% Counoise. Very closed, deep,
and formidably concentrated, with loads of muscle and tannin, this inky, purple-colored wine shows notes of blue and
black fruits intermixed with acacia flowers, licorice, and wild
mountain laurel notes. Quite intense, full-bodied, and very
tannic, this is a wine to forget for 7–10 years and drink over
the following 30–40 years.

2001 Châteauneuf-du-Pape Hommage à Jacques Perrin
RATING: 99 points

The 2001 Châteauneuf-du-Pape Hommage à Jacques Perrin is a blend of 60% Mourvèdre, 20% Grenache, 10% Counoise, and 10% Syrah. Full-bodied, excruciatingly backward, and nearly impenetrable, it boasts an inky/blue/purple color in addition to a promising nose of new saddle leather; melted asphalt; camphor; blackberries; smoky, roasted herbs; and Asian spices. A huge lashing of tannin as well as a formidable structure result in the antithesis of its more flattering, forward, and voluptuous sibling, the classic Beaucastel. Readers lucky enough to come across this *cuvée* should plan on waiting at least seven years before it begins to approach adolescence. Anticipated maturity: 2012–2040.

2000 Châteauneuf-du-Pape Hommage à Jacques Perrin
RATING: 97 points

The 2000 Châteauneuf-du-Pape Hommage à Jacques Perrin is a blend of 60% Mourvèdre, 20% Grenache, 10% Counoise, and 10% Syrah, the standard blend for this *cuvée* except for the 1998, which had 60% Grenache and only 20% Mourvèdre. The 2000 possesses an impenetrable black/purple color as well as a sumptuous bouquet of melted licorice, creosote, new saddle leather, blackberry and cherry fruit, and roasted meats. Sweet and full-bodied, with great intensity, huge power, and a finish that lasts for 67 seconds by my watch, this is an amazing tour de force in winemaking. Even in a flattering, forward-styled vintage such as 2000, it will need 6–7 more years of cellaring. Anticipated maturity: 2010–2040.

1999 Châteauneuf-du-Pape Hommage à Jacques Perrin
RATING: 96 points

The 1999 Châteauneuf-du-Pape Hommage à Jacques Perrin is closed and less expressive than the 2000, and perhaps more elegant and less weighty. Nevertheless, it is an enormously endowed effort revealing notes of licorice, blackberry and cherry fruit, melted asphalt, tapenade, truffles, and smoke. Chewy,

with more minerality than most vintages of this wine, it requires a minimum of 6–8 years of cellaring. It should last 35–40 years. Anticipated maturity: 2010–2035.

1998 Châteauneuf-du-Pape Hommage à Jacques Perrin
RATING: 100 points

The 1998 is an extraordinary effort, and from a purely hedonistic standpoint, probably my favorite Jacques Perrin, no doubt because of the high percentage of Grenache. It is an intense, full-bodied wine filled with notes of kirsch as well as an incredibly silky, expansive mouth-feel. It is one of the few vintages that was ready to drink within 3–4 years of the vintage, yet it is capable of lasting for three decades. It may not represent exactly what brothers François and Jean-Pierre Perrin are seeking (they mean this *cuvée* to emphasize the greatness of Mourvèdre), but it is an incredible wine. Anticipated maturity: now–2033.

1995 Châteauneuf-du-Pape Hommage à Jacques Perrin
RATING: 96 points

The 1995 remains tight, backward, and far less evolved than the 1998. The dense inky/purple color is accompanied by a floral, blueberry, mineral, and licorice-dominated bouquet. Huge and formidably endowed, but closed, tannic, and backward, it will be at its apogee between 2010 and 2030.

1994 Châteauneuf-du-Pape Hommage à Jacques Perrin
RATING: 93 points

The 1994 reveals an animal-styled personality with notes of beef blood, animal fur, wet dog, mushrooms, tree bark, licorice, spice, black currants, and cherries. Medium to full–bodied and rich, but slightly awkward compared to its siblings, it should be drinkable between 2006 and 2020. Hindsight suggests this might not have been a vintage in which to produce a Jacques Perrin.

1990 Châteauneuf-du-Pape Hommage à Jacques Perrin
RATING: 100 points

The perfection of the 1990 is based on a seamless, classic, harmonious concoction of flowers, melted licorice, blackberries, kirsch, blueberries, and Asian spices. An enormously full-bodied, sweet, expansive, amazing wine with a finish that lasts over a minute, it combines the extraordinary hedonism of the 1998 with an unbelievable intellectual appeal that makes it so hauntingly great. Even though it remains youthful, it can be drunk now or cellared for another 30 years.

1989 Châteauneuf-du-Pape Hommage à Jacques Perrin
RATING: 100 points

The less evolved 1989 boasts an even inkier purple color than the 1990. The most massive, biggest, most concentrated, and most structured of any of the Jacques Perrins, it is still 5–10 years away from full maturity. It has great intensity and is extraordinary to taste, but it is not a lot of fun to drink, if you know what I mean. In any event, this is a potentially perfect wine. The only question is, when will it hit its plateau of maturity? My guess is around 2010. Afterward, it should drink well for another 25 years.

CHATEAUNEUF-DU-PAPE ROUSSANNE VIEILLES VIGNES

2003 Châteauneuf-du-Pape Roussanne Vieilles Vignes
RATING: 94 points

Orange marmalade notes intermixed with other tropical fruits, lanolin, rosewater, and white currants jump from the glass of this very unctuously textured, full-bodied wine that has quite a bit of punch (14.5% alcohol), terrific texture, and a long, low-acid, honeyed finish. These are always best drunk very young and then forgotten during midlife, not to be retasted until they are 8–10 years of age.

2002 Châteauneuf-du-Pape Roussanne Vieilles Vignes
RATING: 90 points

The renowned 100% old-vine Roussanne, the 2002 Châteauneuf-du-Pape Roussanne Vieilles Vignes (from 86-year-old vines), does not possess the power typically found in this *cuvée*. Nevertheless, it is an outstanding effort with more elegance and lightness, which may appeal to those who generally find this offering too rich and liqueur-like. Allspice intermixed with acacia flowers, honey, and butter make an appearance in this medium-bodied 2002. With admirable depth and ripeness, it is a tribute to the draconian selection process practiced by Château de Beaucastel in this vintage. Drink it over the next 4–5 years.

2001 Châteauneuf-du-Pape Roussanne Vieilles Vignes
RATING: 97 points

The surreal 2001 Châteauneuf-du-Pape Roussanne Vieilles Vignes (100% Roussanne from 85-year-old vines) is pure liqueur of rose petals, marmalade, and honeysuckle. It is full-bodied, extraordinarily fresh and lively, and for me, one of the most singular expressions of white wine in the world. It is an amazing effort, but, sadly, there is little produced. My experience with most vintages of this *cuvée* suggests it should either be drunk during its first 2–3 years of life, or forgotten for a

decade. Increasingly, I tend to prefer it young. Anticipated maturity: now–2015.

2000 Châteauneuf-du-Pape Roussanne Vieilles Vignes
RATING: 99 points

The 2000 Châteauneuf-du-Pape Roussanne Vieilles Vignes is nearly perfect. It possesses great intensity and unctousness, yet extraordinary elegance with a viscous nose of honeyed caramel, pineapple, and apricots. Beautifully proportioned and full of mineral nuances, this is a tour de force in winemaking. Drink it over the next two years, and keep your fingers crossed that it will still deliver the same pleasure at age 10–15.

1999 Châteauneuf-du-Pape Roussanne Vieilles Vignes
RATING: 97 points

A singular effort of great concentration, the 1999 Châteauneuf-du-Pape Roussanne Vieilles Vignes exhibits honeysuckle, marmalade, rose petal, and acacia flower characteristics along with immense body, high glycerin, and good acidity. It can be drunk now but promises to last for another 10–12 years.

1998 Châteauneuf-du-Pape Roussanne Vieilles Vignes
RATING: 92 points

The 1998 Châteauneuf-du-Pape Roussanne Vieilles Vignes (produced from 50-year-old vines) may not be very ostentatious or concentrated, but it is an extremely impressive wine with aromas and flavors of grapefruit, orange marmalade, honey, and white flowers. Full-bodied, dense, and super-concentrated, this is a stunningly pure winemaking tour de force that admirably demonstrates what can be achieved in selected *terroirs* of the southern Rhône. It should age beautifully for another 15 years.

1997 Châteauneuf-du-Pape Roussanne Vieilles Vignes
RATING: 95 points

The 1997 Châteauneuf-du-Pape Roussanne Vieilles Vignes could easily be called the Montrachet or Chevalier-Montrachet of Châteauneuf-du-Pape. This *cuvée* has been remarkable in the past, and the 1997 is spectacular. It reveals lots of definition, as well as spectacular concentration, a viscous texture, honeyed floral and citrusy flavors, full body, and a finish that goes on for 40–50 seconds. A quintessential Roussanne, it is a great example of the heights this unheralded varietal can achieve. The 1997 should drink well for another 15 years or more.

WINE: Châteauneuf-du-Pape Réserve des Célestins

OWNER: Henri Bonneau

ADDRESS: 35, rue Joseph Ducos, 84230 Châteauneuf-du-Pape, France

TELEPHONE: Confidential

TELEFAX: Confidential

VISITING POLICY: A few select people have access to these cellars.

VINEYARDS

SURFACE AREA: 14.8 acres

GRAPE VARIETALS: 90% Grenache, 10% other varietals

AVERAGE AGE OF THE VINES: 30–45 years

DENSITY OF PLANTATION: 2,500–4,000 vines per hectare

AVERAGE YIELDS: 20–25 hectoliters per hectare

WINEMAKING AND UPBRINGING

An oenologist's nightmare (filthy cellars, ancient mold-covered barrels), this estate produces a profound wine that rests three to six years in small barrels and larger *demi-muids* and *foudres*. The wine is bottled without filtration when Henri Bonneau deems it ready.

ANNUAL PRODUCTION

Châteauneuf-du-Pape Réserve des Célestins: 1,500 cases

AVERAGE PRICE: $120–250

GREAT RECENT VINTAGES

2003, 2001, 2000, 1999, 1998, 1995, 1990, 1989, 1988, 1986, 1985, 1981

It is probably no coincidence that the idiosyncratic Henri Bonneau's hodgepodge of cellars is located at the *top* of the village of Châteauneuf-du-Pape. His wine, like that of Rayas, belongs in a class by itself. Although totally different from Rayas, both estates rely on shy-bearing old vines of Grenache for their power and richness. Bonneau's top *cuvée,* the Réserve des Célestins, is a formidable and massive wine—it is the biggest, most forceful and powerful wine of the southern Rhône Valley—but, wow, what a thrill it gives, provided you can get your hands on a bottle or two from the 1,500 cases Bonneau produces. A visit with the wry Henri Bonneau should be counted as one of life's more memorable

encounters. He is one of the most fascinating wine personalities I have ever met. His noted Provençal twang, vicious sense of humor ("I am not an oenologist; if I wanted prosperity and security, I would work for the government"), particularly when aimed at the French government, and encyclopedic knowledge of cuisine are added benefits when one considers just how extraordinary his wines are. In fact, if someone were to ask what is the quintessential traditionally styled Châteauneuf-du-Pape at the highest quality level, the answer can only be Henri Bonneau's Réserve des Célestins. The Bonneau family has been in Châteauneuf-du-Pape since the late 18th century.

Needless to say, tasting in this cellar is an unforgettable experience. Bonneau's cellar sets new standards for dinginess and crampedness. Excavation for Roman ruins below the cellar have left these caverns dotted with large black holes that can be crossed only by carefully walking across wood planks that keep visitors from falling 20–30 feet into a dark abyss. Like the late Jacques

Henri Bonneau

Reynaud, Bonneau is a legend in Châteauneuf-du-Pape, where he is widely admired as both a great winemaker and one of the village's most forceful personalities. Henri is now aided by his son, Marcel. His tiny domaine of nearly 15 acres includes most of his old vines (13 acres) in what many vignerons consider the finest *terroir* of Châteauneuf-du-Pape, La Crau. Bonneau's yields are reasonably low, but his description of how he makes the wines does not explain how he obtains the extraordinary complexity, richness, and intensity they possess. Bonneau's finest vintages have a distinct taste of concentrated beef blood, combined with a powerful, thick, and viscous texture. Given Henri's admiration of great food (he is a *copain* of one of France's great gourmands, Gérard Chave), it is no surprise that he often seems more comfortable discussing his favorite foods (e.g., goat testicles) than his wines.

Unlike many wines, particularly Burgundies, which are equally impressive in cask, a Châteauneuf-du-Pape from Bonneau always tastes even better out of bottle. Bonneau is willing to refuse to produce his Céléstins if conditions warrant. For example, the wine was not produced in 1987, 1991, 1993, or 2002. Bonneau is a late harvester, and he can be burned badly if he gets caught by October rains as he was in those years. Even when the weather cooperates, so little of his wine is made that it is almost impossible to find. When I first met him a decade ago he was unwilling to sell even one bottle in America. I consider it a personal triumph that now, after I've shared my enthusiasm in the *Wine Advocate*, several hundred cases of his liquid treasure make it to these shores. As one might expect, this has not endeared me to his clients in other countries.

Most of Bonneau's wines are enormous in concentration and character, much like the man himself. These wines are almost immortal in terms of ageability. As I have said before, the wines that emerge from Henri Bonneau's 15+ acres of old-vine Grenache planted on the famed sector called La Crau are majestic wines of extraordinary power, richness, and longevity. Everything done chez Bonneau makes no sense to modern-day oenologists. His cellars are deplorable, and the condition of his barrels (at least the outside of them) is frightful. However, it's what's inside that counts. The magic in those barrels represents the essence, the heart and soul, of Châteauneuf-du-Pape.

More than at any other wine cellar I have ever visited in the world, tasting chez Bonneau is like getting into a time machine and going back to Châteauneuf-du-Pape circa 1750–1800. If readers want to know what Châteauneuf-du-Pape tasted like 100 or 200 years ago, this is it. Long live Henri Bonneau!

CHATEAUNEUF-DU-PAPE RESERVE DES CELESTINS

2003 Châteauneuf-du-Pape Réserve des Célestins
RATING: 92–94+ points
This was still in tank and had not even been moved to *foudre* one year after the vintage, and was still trickling along in a slow fermentation, trying to digest the balance of its residual sugar. Behaving much like the 1998 or 1990, the wine has a dense ruby color to the rim, a very sweet, almost roasted nose reminiscent of a great Amarone, but with that tremendous kiss of kirsch and melted licorice as well as pepper. Quite full-bodied with natural alcohol well in excess of 16% (already), this looks to be another legendary wine in the making from Henri Bonneau, with the style not terribly dissimilar to the 1998 or 1990. It is very full-bodied, and the good news is that, by Bonneau's standards, it will be a bit more abundant in quantity since the vintage was so consistent for his parcels. He was comparing it to perhaps the 1947, which his father produced. Of course, this wine will probably get the standard Henri Bonneau *élevage*, meaning it will spend its life in smaller ancient oak barrels and larger *demi-muids* and small *foudres* until approximately 2009, and then be bottled at Henri Bonneau's discretion. It should have 30 years of aging potential at the minimum.

2001 Châteauneuf-du-Pape Réserve des Célestins
RATING: 92–95 points
Sweet and rich, with glycerin, alcohol, and muscle, is the dark plum/ruby–colored 2001 Châteauneuf-du-Pape Réserve des Célestins. Smelling like a concoction of kirsch, licorice, pepper, beef blood, smoke, and dried herbs, this full-throttle, dense, chewy offering has not begun to put on weight. However, it is a hefty specimen nevertheless. This full-throttle wine already possesses wonderful sweetness as well as huge amounts of lavender, and fig-like fruit, and a long, full-bodied, expansive finish. No doubt it will require 5–7 years of cellaring after release and should keep for 25+ years. It's a beauty.

2000 Châteauneuf-du-Pape Réserve des Célestins
RATING: 92–95 points
The 2000 Châteauneuf-du-Pape Réserve des Célestins did not taste terribly dissimilar from the 2000 Marie Beurrier, but it is a more beefy, brawny specimen, as if someone had dropped

some steroids into the Célestins. It is a huge, fat, fleshy effort, offering a wonderful concoction of fruitcake, charcuterie, prunes, raisins, kirsch, and blackberries in a full-bodied, velvety-textured, voluptuous style. If I were Bonneau, I'd bottle it, but then again, he always seems to make the correct decision about bottling dates, usually extending the *élevage* of his top *cuvées* for 4–5 years. This may seem mind-boggling, but the proof is in the bottle. The sexy, voluptuous 2000 will be the most forward Célestins Bonneau has released since I have been visiting him. Anticipated maturity: 2006–2020.

1999 Châteauneuf-du-Pape Réserve des Célestins

RATING: 94 points

Bonneau is high on this vintage in contrast to his dismissal of the 2000 vintage, which he says is "like a beautiful girl that's too sexually active at age 15, and too old at age 30." Last year he called the 2000 vintage "a nice whore." The 1999 is a more classic year, with firmer tannin, better acidity, and not the easy, "facile" style that Bonneau deplores. The 1999 Réserve des Célestins exhibits a dense plum/garnet color as well as a sumptuously sweet bouquet of roasted meats, liqueur of cherries, soy, Asian spices, licorice, and *garrigue.* It is a full-bodied wine with great freshness, concentrated fruit, and a long, 45-second finish. Like the 1988, initially it will be underappreciated, but it will blossom into something special. Anticipated maturity: 2008–2025.

1998 Châteauneuf-du-Pape Réserve des Célestins

RATING: 100 points

The entire production of Réserve des Célestins was bottled in late 2004. I thought it needed to be bottled in 2002! To quote Henri Bonneau, *"Ça c'est la confiture,"* meaning this is pure Châteauneuf-du-Pape jam, the essence of an appellation and his winemaking philosophy. Tipping the scales at 16% natural alcohol, it is a dead ringer for a modern-day version of the immortal 1990 Célestins. This is a wine of great intensity, and Bonneau's decision to hold it an extra year in barrel seems to have concentrated it even more than I thought possible. This profound beverage is worth doing just about anything legal, and possibly even illegal, to secure a bottle or two. It possesses a deep plum/ruby color as well as a gorgeously sweet nose of blackberry and black cherry liqueur; grilled aged beef; smoke; melted licorice; ground pepper; and sweet, nearly overripe figs. Massive in the mouth, with an unctuous texture that oozes glycerin and extract yet is also silky and surprisingly well balanced, this is a decadent, extravagantly rich, old-style Châteauneuf-du-Pape that is as good as it gets. Anticipated maturity: 2008–2030+.

1995 Châteauneuf-du-Pape Réserve des Célestins

RATING: 93 points

Although the 1995 remains tight and closed, it reveals classic Bonneau characteristics of roasted herbs, beef blood, cherries, cassis, licorice, and earth. These wines often taste as if someone took one of the old Grenache vines, threw it in a Cuisinart, liquefied it, added a bit of brandy, and then bottled it. This is classic Châteauneuf-du-Pape, the likes of which are increasingly difficult to find. Anticipated maturity: 2010–2025.

Châteauneuf-du-Pape

APPELLATION CHATEAUNEUF-DU-PAPE CONTROLÉE

Réserve des Célestins

Product of France
Alc. 14 % vol.

Red Rhone Wine
750 ml

HENRI BONNEAU, VIGNERON, CHATEAUNEUF-DU-PAPE (VAUCLUSE) FRANCE

1992 Châteauneuf-du-Pape Réserve des Célestins

RATING: 93 points

The 1992 is unquestionably the wine of the vintage. How Bonneau managed to produce such an amazing beverage continues to boggle my mind. It did not show that well when tasted from the various containers in the cramped cellars, but out of bottle it's the real deal! Aromas of grilled meats, barbecue spices, lavender, smoke, cedar, and kirsch soar from the glass of this dark plum/ruby–colored wine. Its power and richness in a vintage such as this are hard to believe. Long, chewy, and close to full maturity (unusual for a 10-year-old Réserve des Célestins), it can be drunk now and over the next 12 years.

1990 Châteauneuf-du-Pape Réserve des Célestins

RATING: 100 points

One of the greatest wines ever produced—anywhere—is the 1990. Having consistently merited 100 points (if my scoring system went higher, it would be there), it continues to perform like a young wine, yet is accessible enough to be appreciated for its extraordinary combination of power, complexity, and majestic layers of flavor. The color is a dark plum/ruby to the edge. The monumental bouquet offers up aromas of liquefied charcoaled beef intermixed with pepper, smoke, crème de cassis, kirsch, truffles, and new saddle leather. This full-bodied, viscous, prodigious Châteauneuf-du-Pape must be tasted to be believed. It is more like a food than a beverage. Anticipated maturity: now–2030.

1989 Châteauneuf-du-Pape Réserve des Célestins
RATING: 99 points

Inching closer and closer to the celestial 1990 is the 1989. This *cuvée* was fabulous when tasted in Bonneau's cellars, but it closed down after bottling. Possibly even more powerful and tannic than the 1990, as well as more backward, the 1989 looks to be a great classic. It is a Réserve des Célestins to forget for another 3–8 years. It possesses all the characteristics of the 1990, but everything is packed into a more linear personality. Amazing stuff! Anticipated maturity: 2009–2035.

1988 Châteauneuf-du-Pape Réserve des Célestins
RATING: 96 points

The 1988 is beginning to throw off its cloak of tannin and start its evolution. A dark plum/ruby color is accompanied by a sweet perfume of mushrooms, tree bark, black cherries macerated in brandy, and the telltale beef blood, lavender, cedar, and tobacco aromas. This full-bodied, powerful yet structured Réserve des Célestins does not reveal the pure breadth and depth of flavor found in the 1989 and 1990, but comes across as a mature example of the 1995. Anticipated maturity: now–2025.

1986 Châteauneuf-du-Pape Réserve des Célestins
RATING: 95 points

Few Châteauneuf-du-Papes from this vintage turned out well, and the few that did required consumption during their first decade of life. Bonneau's 1986 is just hitting full maturity. It offers a concoction of jammy, concentrated, licorice-infused black cherry fruit, with hints of tobacco, cedar, beef blood, smoked herbs, and Asian spices. As the wine sits in the glass, aromas of licorice, Peking duck, and other exotic scents emerge. An amazing effort, it may be the only Réserve des Célestins I own that can be classified as fully mature. Anticipated maturity: now–2020.

1981 Châteauneuf-du-Pape Réserve des Célestins
RATING: 93 points

Still youthful, this dark ruby/garnet–colored wine displays an immense nose of a smoky barbecue pit, black fruits, truffles, and aged beef. With a blast of glycerin, alcohol, and extract, this monster Châteauneuf-du-Pape has remarkable balance for its immense size. The color exhibits no signs of rust at the edge, only a slight lightening. Thick, juicy, and succulent, this is a lusty, hedonistic Châteauneuf-du-Pape that can be drunk now or cellared for another 20 years.

1978 Châteauneuf-du-Pape Réserve des Célestins
RATING: 99 points

When I drank this wine with Henri Bonneau at his home recently, it was so remarkably young it defied belief. This structured, tannic, profoundly concentrated wine represents the essence of Châteauneuf-du-Pape. The huge nose of smoked herbs, olives, beef blood, and black fruits is intense. The enormous concentration, freshness, and superb balance are hallmarks of this classically profound vintage for Châteauneuf-du-Pape. The wine reveals amazing extract and intensity, as well as a striking youthfulness. Still young, yet complete and complex, the 1978 should prove to be uncommonly long-lived, even by Henri Bonneau's standards. Anticipated maturity: now–2020.

WINES:

Châteauneuf-du-Pape Cuvée Centenaire

Châteauneuf-du-Pape Cuvée Tradition

OWNER: André Brunel

ADDRESS: 6, chemin du Bois de la Ville, 84230 Châteauneuf-du-Pape, France

TELEPHONE: 33 04 90 83 72 62

TELEFAX: 33 04 90 83 51 07

CONTACT: André Brunel

VISITING POLICY: By appointment only

VINEYARDS

SURFACE AREA: 53.4 acres

Whites: 4.9 acres; *Reds*: regular *cuvée*—42.9 acres; Cuvée Centenaire—5.6 acres

GRAPE VARIETALS: Grenache, Mourvèdre, Syrah, Grenache Blanc, Roussanne, Clairette, Bourboulenc, other varietals

AVERAGE AGE OF THE VINES:

Whites—30 years

Reds—regular *cuvée*—60 years; Cuvée Centenaire—100+ years (the Grenache vineyard was planted in 1889, and this represents at least 80% of the blend)

DENSITY OF PLANTATION: 2,500–4,000 vines per hectare

AVERAGE YIELDS: 20–30 hectoliters per hectare

WINEMAKING AND UPBRINGING

Whites: Fermentation of 15–21 days in stainless-steel vats, then 5 months in stainless-steel vats.

Reds: Regular *cuvée*—Fermentation of 3–4 weeks in enamel vats, then a percentage of yield goes into oak barrels, of which one-third are new and two-thirds 1–2 years old. The rest of the yield remains in enamel-lined cement vats for 18 months. Cuvée Centenaire: fermentation of 3–4 weeks in enamel vats, then 50% of the yield goes into new oak barrels for 18 months, and the rest stays in enamel vats. The wine is then blended and bottled unfiltered.

ANNUAL PRODUCTION

Regular cuvée: 6,900 cases

Cuvée Centenaire: 500 cases

AVERAGE PRICE (VARIABLE DEPENDING ON VINTAGE): $25–100; $175 for the Centenaire

GREAT RECENT VINTAGES

2003, 2001, 2000, 1998, 1995, 1990, 1989

André Brunel resembles the movie actor William Hurt. He must be in his mid-50s, but he looks 10 years younger, although a 12-foot fall off a large *foudre* in 2004 had him on his back recovering from surgery for nearly six months. He has always been one of the more serious producers in Châteauneuf-du-Pape. From this modestly sized estate, André Brunel produces powerful yet rich, elegant, concentrated wines that have gone from strength to strength since the late 1980s. His vineyards are morsellated, but a large segment is planted near Mont Redon, on the famed *galets roulés* (football-sized rocks). Brunel, who took over from his father in the early 1970s, comes from a family that has lived in Châteauneuf-du-Pape since the 18th century. His enthusiasm and leadership qualities have not gone unnoticed in the village, where he has a prominent position with one of the two syndicates that govern the appellation, as well as his own growers' group, Les Reflets.

Brunel has never been content to rest on his accomplishments, always challenging the old ways while examining and questioning newer methods. He has gradually increased the percentage of Roussanne in the very good white wine made at Les Cailloux, and in the red, Syrah and Mourvèdre have taken on increasing importance in the final blend. In 1989 Brunel launched a limited-production Cuvée Centenaire, made from a 5.6-acre parcel of vines that were planted in 1889. This wine is primarily Grenache.

The flexible approach to winemaking that exists at Les Cailloux extends to Brunel's position on destemming. Since Brunel recognized that the stems were often not physiologically mature and imparted too much acidity and bitterness, virtually all of the Mourvèdre and most of the Syrah and Grenache have been destemmed. Prior to 1988, Brunel kept an open mind with respect to fining and filtration. In vintages where the wine did not fall bright and clear, he did a minimal fining and filtering. In those years when there was no suspended protein or haziness, the wines were bottled unfiltered. However, since the 1988 vintage, Brunel decided to eliminate both fining and filtration for his red wines.

Brunel's wines were good though lacking consistency in the 1970s and early 1980s, but they have been in top form since the late 1980s. His Châteauneuf-du-Pape is usually drinkable when released, but it is capable of 10–15 years of aging. The Cuvée Centenaire, made in 1989, 1990, 1995, 1998, 2000, 2001, and 2003, is a wine of extraordinary opulence and richness, and, although very drinkable young, it is capable of lasting for two decades or more. André Brunel is one of the bright shining lights of Châteauneuf-du-Pape.

CHATEAUNEUF-DU-PAPE

2003 Châteauneuf-du-Pape

RATING: 91–93 points

A very 1990s-styled Châteauneuf-du-Pape, the 2003 Les Cailloux shows loads of glycerin and a big, spicy, peppery nose with dried Provençal herbs intermixed with cherry liqueur. A very broad, expansive wine, relatively high in alcohol (typical of this vintage) and with a long, silky finish that has tremendous persistence, this wine can be drunk now as well as over the next 12–14 years.

2001 Châteauneuf-du-Pape

RATING: 91 points

The 2001 Châteauneuf-du-Pape, an unfined/unfiltered blend of 65% Grenache, 20% Mourvèdre, and 15% Syrah, is more structured than the open-knit 2000 or the muscular 1998. The 2001 is a dense, archetypical effort offering a classic bouquet of Provençal herbs intermixed with loamy soil, Asian spice, kirsch, cedar, and tobacco aromas. Sweet, peppery, black cherry jam–like flavors emerge in the mouth. Dense, full-bodied, rich, and spicy. Anticipated maturity: now–2014.

2000 Châteauneuf-du-Pape

RATING: 91 points

The 2000 Châteauneuf-du-Pape is pure sex in a bottle. A fragrant bouquet offers up aromas of spice box, cedar, pepper, jammy cherries, and a hint of plums and prunes. Dense, full-bodied, and evolved, but gorgeously succulent, this is a seamless, voluptuous Châteauneuf-du-Pape. Its fragrance, tactile mouthfeel, and explosive finish make for a sumptuous Châteauneuf-du-Pape to drink now and over the next 10–12 years.

1999 Châteauneuf-du-Pape

RATING: 90 points

The famed Cuvée Centenaire (produced from 100+-year-old vines) was included in the Cuvée Classique in 1999. Made in an evolved style for proprietor André Brunel, the 1999 Châteauneuf-du-Pape exhibits a dark plum/ruby color as well

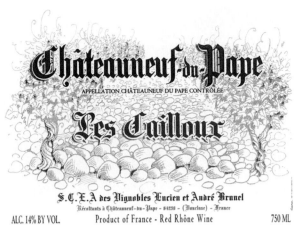

as a sweet, spicy nose of red and black fruits mixed with *garrigue,* pepper, spice box, and tobacco. Rich, full-bodied, layered, and undeniably captivating, this sumptuous, forward, flavorful, savory Châteauneuf can be drunk now and over the next 10–12 years.

1998 Châteauneuf-du-Pape

RATING: 91 points

Les Cailloux's regular *cuvée* has evolved into a blend of 65% Grenache, 20% Mourvèdre, 10% Syrah, and 5% miscellaneous varietals aged both in barrel and *foudre.* The classic 1998 represents a blend of traditional and progressive winemaking techniques. A southern Rhône nose of *garrigue* pepper, wood spice, and gorgeously sweet black cherry and plum-like flavors are intense as well as alluring. Once one is past the bouquet, this dark ruby/garnet–colored wine offers a full-bodied, powerful, layered impression, with impressive levels of glycerin, ripe fruit, and extract. Tannin is present, but it is sweet. This 1998 will easily drink well for 10–12 years.

1995 Châteauneuf-du-Pape

RATING: 92 points

I would not classify 1995 as a great year for Châteauneuf-du-Pape—although it is certainly excellent, and overall the finest vintage since 1990—but you would never know that by tasting André Brunel's sumptuous 1995s. The 1995 Châteauneuf-du-Pape is a precocious, medium to full–bodied, lush, layered, complex wine offering up abundant quantities of sweet black cherry and kirsch fruit in a spicy, compelling bouquet. This multidimensional, low-acid wine displays plenty of earth, smoke, and truffle notes to accompany the kirsch, plum, and prune-like fruit. Sweet and rich in the mouth, with an explosive finish, it should drink well for another 5–8 years.

1990 Châteauneuf-du-Pape

RATING: 95 points

The traditional *cuvée* of 1990 is stunning. Fully mature, it offers up a delicious perfume of Asian spices, cedar, leather, black cherries, plums, and prunes. Luscious and viscous, it is a terrific effort. Anticipated maturity: now–2010.

CHATEAUNEUF-DU-PAPE CUVEE CENTENAIRE

2003 Châteauneuf-du-Pape Cuvée Centenaire

RATING: 95–97+ points

André Brunel thinks this is the best Cuvée Centenaire produced since the 1998, and I'm not going to disagree. It is a bit more forward and plump than the more structured 2001, seems to have greater depth and intensity than the brilliant 2000, but aren't we just splitting hairs at this level of quality? It is deep ruby/purple–tinged to the rim with an extraordinarily explosive bouquet of dried Provençal herbs, ground pepper, kirsch, plum, raspberry, and black currant. Very powerful, concentrated flavors imbued with considerable levels of glycerin show remarkable freshness and precision for their extraordinary intensity and fleshiness. The wine is a great example of power married to elegance, with a finish well over one minute. According to Brunel, there is plenty of tannin, but it seems completely absorbed by the wine's flesh, glycerin, and relatively big alcohol (easily 15.5–16%, but extraordinarily well hidden). This wine should drink well for 20+ years and be a bit more approachable in its youth than the 2001.

2001 Châteauneuf-du-Pape Cuvée Centenaire

RATING: 96 points

The Cuvée Centenaire is produced from ancient-vine (planted in 1889) Grenache (80% of the blend, along with 8% Syrah and 12% Mourvèdre). The 2001 Châteauneuf-du-Pape Cuvée Centenaire is superior to the 2000, but slightly behind the 1998. This fabulous wine boasts a dense ruby/purple color as well as a provocative perfume of incense, black tea, plums, figs, and kirsch. As it sits in the glass, this full-bodied, dense 2001 offers up notes of pepper, smoke, and balsam wood. Rich and voluptuous with great length, massive body, and a structured, long, heady, tannic finish, its alcohol must be over 15%, but it is well concealed by the wine's great concentration. Anticipated maturity: 2007–2020.

2000 Châteauneuf-du-Pape Cuvée Centenaire

RATING: 96 points

The heady 2000 Châteauneuf-du-Pape Cuvée Centenaire is more evolved than either the 2001 or 1998. Extremely full-bodied, with low acidity and a knockout bouquet of black-berry and cherry jam intermixed with licorice, pepper, and dried Provençal herbs, this sexy, voluptuous, enormously concentrated 2000 possesses a huge, silky, seamless finish. Drink this irresistible effort now and over the next 12–15 years.

1998 Châteauneuf-du-Pape Cuvée Centenaire

RATING: 100 points

The 1998 Cuvée Centenaire is an awesome Châteauneuf-du-Pape. This is the essence of both Châteauneuf-du-Pape and the Grenache grape. The wine boasts a deep ruby/purple color as well as an extraordinary bouquet of melted, jammy black cherry, raspberry, and currant fruit mixed with pepper and spice box. In the mouth, it is rich, full-bodied, and unctuously textured, with extraordinary purity, and laser-like definition for a wine of such massive concentration and depth. The finish lasts for nearly a minute. This spectacular, youthful, amazingly accessible offering is a tour de force in winemaking, and a tribute to just how great Châteauneuf-du-Pape can be. Anticipated maturity: now–2025.

1995 Châteauneuf-du-Pape Cuvée Centenaire

RATING: 94 points

1995 was a powerful vintage for Brunel. The Cuvée Centenaire remains a young, promising wine offering notes of licorice, cedar, vanilla, and sweet black currant/cherry fruit presented in a full-bodied, virile style. Anticipated maturity: 2007–2018.

1990 Châteauneuf-du-Pape Cuvée Centenaire

RATING: 100 points

One of the greatest vintages for André Brunel, aside from his extraordinary succession of vintages from 1998–2001, is 1990. The perfect Cuvée Centenaire is still dense ruby/purple–colored with a sumptuous nose of white flowers, raspberry and cherry liqueur, smoke, and mineral scents. The gorgeous aromatics are followed by an unctuously textured, pure wine that combines the best of Châteauneuf-du-Pape with the floral, earthy complexity of a great grand cru red Burgundy. This is a riveting tour de force in winemaking. Don't miss it. Anticipated maturity: now–2020.

1989 Châteauneuf-du-Pape Cuvée Centenaire

RATING: 94 points

The 1989 remains a young, tight, difficult to penetrate wine that is loaded with potential. Licorice, black fruits, Asian spices, and vanilla emerge from the dense, saturated purple color. It remains somewhat closed and firm, yet powerful, with abundant tannin as well as extraction. Anticipated maturity: 2008–2018.

WINES:

Ermitage Pavillon (Red)

Ermitage L'Orée (White)

Ermitage Le Méal (Red)

Ermitage Le Méal (White)

Ermitage L'Ermite (Red)

Ermitage L'Ermite (White)

Châteauneuf-du-Pape Barbe Rac

Côte Rôtie La Mordorée

OWNER: SA M. Chapoutier (Président du Conseil d'Administration: Michel Chapoutier)

ADDRESS: 18, avenue Docteur Paul Durand, 26600 Tain l'Hermitage, France

TELEPHONE: Office—33 04 75 08 28 65; Cellar—33 04 75 08 92 61

TELEFAX: Office—33 04 75 08 81 70; Cellar—33 04 75 08 96 36

E-MAIL: michel.chapoutier@chapoutier.com

WEBSITE: www.chapoutier.com

CONTACT: Caveau de Tain l'Hermitage

VISITING POLICY: Visits and tastings by appointment only; contact the cellar.

VINEYARDS

SURFACE AREA: 151.95 acres

Côte Rôtie—13.6 acres

Hermitage—76.6 acres

Châteauneuf-du-Pape—61.75 acres

GRAPE VARIETALS:

Côte Rôtie—100% Syrah

Hermitage—Syrah (red); Marsanne (white)

Châteauneuf-du-Pape—Grenache, Syrah, Grenache Blanc, Clairette, Bourboulenc, Roussanne

AVERAGE AGE OF THE VINES:

Côte Rôtie—Mordorée: 50+ years

Hermitage—Sélections Parcellaires: 60–100 years

Châteauneuf-du-Pape: 50–80 years

DENSITY OF PLANTATION:

Côte Rôtie—10,000 vines per hectare

Hermitage—8,000–10,000 vines per hectare

Châteauneuf-du-Pape—5,100 vines per hectare

AVERAGE YIELDS:

Côte Rôtie—Mordorée: 15–18 hectoliters per hectare

Hermitage—Sélections Parcellaires: 15–18 hectoliters per hectare

Châteauneuf-du-Pape—15–25 hectoliters per hectare

WINEMAKING AND UPBRINGING

A true biodynamically run estate since 1989, the objective has been to produce the purest and most natural expressions of *terroir* possible. Every decision is based on enhancing the characteristics of a wine's *terroir*, varietal character, and vintage trademark. In short, it is the earth that inspires this firm.

ANNUAL PRODUCTION

Côte Rôtie—Mordorée: 6,500 bottles

Hermitage—L'Ermite (red): 6,000 bottles; Pavillon: 9,000 bottles; Méal (red): 6,000 bottles; De l'Orée: 8,000 bottles; Méal (white): 5,000 bottles; L'Ermite (white): 1,500 bottles; Vin de Paille: 3,000 bottles (37.5 cl); Sizeranne: 35,000 bottles; Chante Alouette: 22,000 bottles; Mure de Larnage (white): 2,600 bottles; Mure de Larnage (red): 5,000 bottles

Châteauneuf-du-Pape—Barbe Rac: 8,000 bottles

AVERAGE PRICE (VARIABLE DEPENDING ON VINTAGE): $50–250

GREAT RECENT VINTAGES

2003, 2001, 2000, 1999, 1998, 1997, 1996, 1995, 1991, 1990, 1989

This famous old firm, founded in 1808, is the proprietor of a significant 175 acres of vines in five Rhône Valley appellations. A venerable Rhône *négociant,* Chapoutier muddled along in recent decades, content to produce good, traditional Rhône wines, but rarely did they make superb wine. With the retirement of Max Chapoutier in 1989, his energetic, brilliant son Michel took over. In my career, I have never witnessed a more significant jump in quality and change in winemaking philosophy than what has since occurred in the Chapoutier cellars. What Michel Chapoutier has accomplished has caused ripples around the wine world. He has completely revamped the winemaking and *élevage* programs for the Chapoutier wines, and the results are wines that rival the Rhône Valley's greatest wine producer, Marcel Guigal.

With respect to the white wines, Michel Chapoutier was influenced primarily by André Ostertag and Marcel Deiss of Alsace. In essence, his basic goal was to "go back to the earth," reducing the signature of the winemaker and raising the level of the typicity and vineyard charac-

ter of the wine. As the young Chapoutier says, "Everything is in the soil and vines." It is his intention to "kill the character of the grape, but bring up the quality of the soil." To this end, Chapoutier decided to farm his vineyards biodynamically, and to use only wild yeast for the fermentation. In both 1988 and 1989 the vineyards were pruned back and grape bunches were cut off to reduce the yields to a conservative 30–35 hectoliters per hectare for both the red and white wines.

Michel Chapoutier gives full credit for the direction of his red wine–making style to his consultations with Gérard Chave and Marcel Guigal. The first thing he did was to throw out the old chestnut *foudres* (a hallmark of the old Chapoutier style) and replace them with small oak casks. There is total destemming except for the red wines from St.-Joseph and Côte Rôtie, as well as a *cuvaison* that lasts for three to three and one-half weeks. The two most significant changes included not only the raising of the wines in small oak barrels, but also Chapoutier's decision to neither fine nor filter his finest red or white wines prior to bottling.

In the 15 years (1989–2004) that Michel Chapoutier and the brilliant oenologist Alberic Mazoyer have had control of the winemaking, few wine firms in the world have produced more extraordinary wines. At the same time, few firms have engendered more controversy and animosity. Michel Chapoutier is an outspoken advocate of biodynamic farming as described by the guru of this approach to organic farming, German professor Rudolph Steiner, whose book *Agriculture* was the product of numerous lectures he presented in 1924 in Germany. While Chapoutier's critics tend to dismiss biodynamic farming as a cult or wizardry, more and more high-quality producers (e.g., Lalou Bize-Leroy, Nicolas Joly, and others) are moving in this direction, recognizing that decades of overdependence on chemicals, fertilizers, and sprays has wreaked enormous damage on the vineyards' health. Michel Chapoutier is the first to acknowledge the debt he owes such more traditional producers as Marcel Guigal, Gérard Chave, François and Jean-Pierre Perrin, and the late Jacques Reynaud. Yet in his pursuit of quality he has a tendency to provoke controversy wherever he goes. His brash statements can appear undiplomatic and, at times, scathingly critical of his colleagues. All of this is a shame, since producers, members of the wine industry, and consumers committed to quality should be Chapoutier supporters rather than detractors. While I am not sure he's capable of restraining his youthful exuberance and obsessive nature when he feels growers with top vineyards are not pursuing high quality, it is an undeniable fact that Michel Chapoutier has become one of this planet's bright, shining lights.

Nearly a decade after assuming command of this firm, Michel Chapoutier is still not satisfied, pushing himself to achieve higher and higher quality. As he says, "In 1989, I knew how to make noise . . . now I know how to make music." He obviously feels his early efforts were simply monster, massive, intensely extracted wines, but today, the extraction is there, plus more complexity and finesse. Chapoutier by contrast believes those producers who filter are stripping their wines of their typicity, terroir, and personality, not to mention flavor. Another of his favorite quotes is, "Filtering wine is like making love with a condom."

In the past few years Chapoutier has completely renovated the cellars, installing air-conditioning and new small casks, and displaying meticulous attention to all details. This is a firm that believes in the "monocépage" (100% produced from a single grape varietal). Chapoutier's Côte Rôties are made from 100% Syrah, his white Hermitages are 100% Marsanne, and his Châteauneuf-du-Pape is 100% Grenache. He is a purist who believes that blending only mutes the character of the terroir and grape.

At the top of the Chapoutier hierarchy are the luxury cuvées made from parcels of extremely old vines and microscopic yields, aged 100% in new oak, and usually bottled without any fining or filtration. Reference-point wines for their appellations, they are among the greatest red and white wines produced in the world. From the southern Rhône comes the Châteauneuf-du-Pape Barbe Rac. In the north is the St.-Joseph Les Granits, an 80-year-old vineyard planted in pure granite on a hillside behind the village of Mauves; the Crozes-Hermitage Les Varonniers; the white Ermitage L'Orée, from ancient vines in Le Méal (often with yields of one-half ton of fruit per acre); the red Ermitage Le Pavillon, from 70- to 80-year-old vines in Les Bessards; and the Côte Rôtie La Mordorée, a parcel of vines 75–80 years old, a stone's throw from Guigal's famed La Turque. The production of these wines is frightfully small, from 400–700 cases, but the quality is prodigious.

The Chapoutiers claim they are the largest landholders in Hermitage, owning approximately 76 out of the total 321 acres there. Their cuvée of Le Pavillon comes from the oldest vines in Les Bessards, a vineyard in which the Chapoutiers own a 34.3-acre parcel. Grapes intended for Chapoutier's Hermitage are always destemmed for fear of extracting too much of the stemmy, vegetal component. Now that Michel Chapoutier has taken over the winemaking, Chapoutier is usually the last Hermitage producer to harvest.

Chapoutier's estate in Châteauneuf-du-Pape is called La Bernardine. This 61.75-acre property is unusual in the sense that it is planted with 100% Grenache. Michel Chapoutier believes in what he calls "monocépage" wines. He believes that if yields are restricted, these wines become the finest expressions of the terroir. La Bernardine was purchased in 1938, and consists of several parcels, with the largest pieces in the northern part of the appellation, near La Gardine, and on the eastern side of the appellation, near Vieux-Télégraphe and the village of Bédarrides. The oldest parcel, with vines planted in 1901, is on the western side of the appellation. Since 1989 this parcel has been culled from the La Bernardine blend and made into the luxury cuvée Barbe Rac. This 100% old-vine Grenache is designed to be a massive, huge, quintessential expression of Grenache, much like that of Jacques Reynaud's Château Rayas. Production of Barbe Rac varies from 500–700 cases per year, whereas La Bernardine produces up to 7,500 cases in a generous vintage. There is also a tiny quantity of white La Bernardine.

Chapoutier produces a good Côte Rôtie from a blend of purchased grapes and their estate vineyards. The real breakthrough in quality has been the luxury cuvée of Côte Rôtie called La Mordorée. This wine, which made its debut in 1990, is Michel Chapoutier's homage to Marcel Guigal's Côte Rôtie La Turque, La Mouline, and La Landonne. This spectacular wine is made from a selection of parcels of very old vines (averaging 75–80 years) that are located on the Côte Brune, adjacent to Guigal's La Turque.

These uncompromising offerings from a young genius are not meant for consumers who want something to drink immediately. They are the essence of biodynamically farmed vineyard sites cropped incredibly low, given extended fermentations with indigenous yeasts, and rarely touched until they go into the bottle unfined and unfiltered. In most vintages, they are not even racked off their lees, which only adds to their natural style. They are truly remarkable wines, but for most readers, patience is the operative rule, as they need a good 8–10 years to strut their stuff. For example, the 1989 and 1990 Le Pavillon are just beginning to reveal hints of secondary nuances. Both have 30–40 more years of aging potential.

Once moribund, since the late 1980s this firm has become one of the reference points for nearly all the Rhône Valley appellations under the direction of the brash yet immensely talented Michel Chapoutier. The single-vineyard offerings are as good as Rhône Valley wines can be. Moreover, Chapoutier continues to upgrade the quality of those wines offered in more significant quantities than the 500 or so cases each of the single-vineyard offerings.

Red Wines

CHATEAUNEUF-DU-PAPE BARBE RAC

2003 Châteauneuf-du-Pape Barbe Rac
RATING: 95–97 points
Michel Chapoutier thinks this is the best *cuvée* of this wine he has yet produced. Tipping the scales at nearly 16.5% alcohol, all of it submerged beneath a wealth of black cherry, plum, fig, and currant fruit intermixed with notes of sandalwood, underbrush, Provençal herbs, and pepper, this enormously constituted wine is very full-bodied, lush, and just remarkably intense and rich. There is some tannin, actually quite a bit of it by analysis, but it is largely concealed by the wine's wealth of glycerin, fruit, and extract. This wine should drink well for 15–20 years, possibly longer.

2001 Châteauneuf-du-Pape Barbe Rac
RATING: 95 points
The profound 2001 Châteauneuf-du-Pape Barbe Rac boasts a deep ruby/purple color as well as a nose of *garrigue*, licorice, kirsch, cassis, and new saddle leather. This superbly concentrated, full-bodied, multidimensional wine coats the palate with glycerin and sweet fruit. There is not a hard edge to be found, but wow, what intensity and length (the finish lasts for close to one minute). The 2001 should turn out to be a legendary effort capable of lasting 15–20 years.

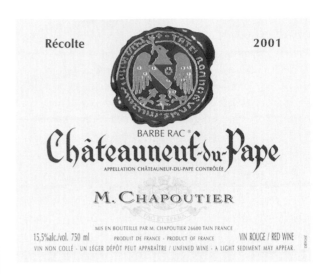

2000 Châteauneuf-du-Pape Barbe Rac
RATING: 95 points
The deep ruby/purple–colored 2000 Châteauneuf-du-Pape Barbe Rac boasts a fabulous perfume of kirsch, licorice, ground pepper, and a hint of Provençal herbs. Ripe, full-bodied, and concentrated, with huge quantities of glycerin as well as a finish that lasts for nearly 50 seconds, this spectacular Châteauneuf-du-Pape possesses a sweetness and endearing accessibility that make it hard to resist. It should be drinkable during its entire 20-year evolution. It's a wow, wow wine!

1999 Châteauneuf-du-Pape Barbe Rac
RATING: 92 points
The 1999 Châteauneuf-du-Pape Barbe Rac is a beautiful, medium dark ruby–colored effort with a gorgeously sweet nose of kirsch, Provençal herbs, licorice, earth, and spice. Cropped at an amazingly low 15 hectoliters per hectare, it possesses full body, super concentration, and a long finish. Anticipated maturity: now–2016.

1998 Châteauneuf-du-Pape Barbe Rac
RATING: 96 points
A dark plum/purple color is accompanied by a smoky kirsch, roasted meat, and saddle leather–scented bouquet. The wine took a full year to ferment dry. The result is a blockbuster, full-bodied, super-concentrated Châteauneuf-du-Pape with multiple nuances of spice and Christmas fruitcake, as well as a lusty, heady, alcoholic finish nicely balanced by abundant quantities of glycerin and dense, layered fruit. Don't hesitate to drink it now as well as over the next two decades.

1995 Châteauneuf-du-Pape Barbe Rac

RATING: 93 points

The 1995 Châteauneuf-du-Pape Barbe Rac is a fragrant wine with a dense purple color and a sensational Provençal nose of olives, jammy black cherries and raspberries, roasted herbs, and pepper. Extremely dense and huge in the mouth, with massive body, glycerin, and tannin, this powerful Châteauneuf-du-Pape requires cellaring. Anticipated maturity for this luxury *cuvée*: now–2020.

1994 Châteauneuf-du-Pape Barbe Rac

RATING: 93 points

The 1994 Barbe Rac possesses a textbook Provençal bouquet of lavender, *garrigue,* herbs, black olives, and jammy black-cherry scents. Powerful flavors bursting with extract and glycerin provide immense volume and force in the mouth, as well as a surprising sense of elegance and finesse. This full-bodied Châteauneuf-du-Pape will come around much sooner than the 1995, yet it will drink well for two decades.

1993 Châteauneuf-du-Pape Barbe Rac

RATING: 94 points

A sleeper vintage, the dense ruby/purple–colored, extremely concentrated 1993 offers a gloriously heady concoction of melted licorice, seaweed, black cherry liqueur, and smoke. It is a candidate for the wine of the vintage in Châteauneuf-du-Pape. Anticipated maturity: now–2012.

1990 Châteauneuf-du-Pape Barbe Rac

RATING: 96 points

The blockbuster 1990 is just now approaching full maturity. It possesses a dense ruby/purple color as well as a gorgeous bouquet of prunes, kirsch, balsam wood, incense, and fruitcake. Full-bodied, with a viscous texture and a long, concentrated finish exhibiting admirable purity and balance, it can be drunk now and over the next 10 -15 years.

1989 Châteauneuf-du-Pape Barbe Rac

RATING: 94 points

A classic for the vintage, the tight, muscular, tannic, saturated ruby/purple–colored 1989 requires another 3–5 years of cellaring. The bouquet offers up scents of Provençal herbs, pepper, *garrigue,* licorice, and gobs of kirsch. Full-bodied and powerful as well as extremely tannic, it will be drinkable between 2008 and 2020+.

COTE ROTIE LA MORDOREE

2003 Côte Rôtie La Mordorée

RATING: 96–100 points

Certainly the greatest Côte Rôtie Michel Chapoutier has made since the 1991, this inky/purple-colored wine has a glorious nose of graphite, flowers, blackberry, and cassis with a smoky tinge to these elements. Quite full-bodied and powerful (the yields were a minuscule 8–9 hectoliters per hectare), with awesome concentration, amazing power and muscle, and enough tannin to ensure this wine should be forgotten for 8–10 years, this is a modern-day legend in the making. Anticipated maturity: 2013–2035.

2001 Côte Rôtie La Mordorée

RATING: 90 points

The deep ruby/purple–colored 2001 Côte Rôtie La Mordorée is more dense, tannic, and earthy than its 2000 counterpart. Possessing additional structure as well as an undeniably backward character, this is a medium to full–bodied offering with the classic grilled meat, tapenade, herbal concoction found in many Côte Rôties. With a sweet attack but a narrow finish, it should turn out to be outstanding, but it will always be less charming and accessible than the 2000. Anticipated maturity: 2006–2014.

2000 Côte Rôtie La Mordorée

RATING: 90 points

Offering up scents of white flowers, black olives, cassis, and roasted notes, the 2000 is a seamless effort with well-integrated acidity and tannin as well as a big, plush, concentrated style that will provide delicious up-front drinking. Anticipated maturity: now–2012.

1999 Côte Rôtie La Mordorée

RATING: 95 points

The 1999 Côte Rôtie La Mordorée is the finest Chapoutier has produced since the 1991. Two bottles drunk over the last six months confirm this fabulous wine's potential, as it is just now beginning to emerge from a cloak of tannin. The 1999 has closed down since its pre-bottling tasting. The color is an inky purple, and the wine is dense and powerful, with notes of smoky blackberries, creosote, and espresso. Concentrated flavors reveal high levels of tannin and a rich, long, 45-second finish. This impressive 1999 will take longer to reach its plateau of drinkability than I previously thought. Anticipated maturity: 2009–2023.

1998 Côte Rôtie La Mordorée

RATING: 94 points

The 1998 exhibits an opaque ruby/purple color in addition to a spectacular nose of grilled toast, cured olives, cassis, fried bacon, and smoke. As it sits in the glass, additional nuances emerge. Deep, full-bodied, powerful, and concentrated, this 1998 is already approachable. The unctuous texture and long, 45-second finish suggest even greater promise for the future. Anticipated maturity: now–2020.

1997 Côte Rôtie La Mordorée

RATING: 93 points

The 1997 Côte Rôtie La Mordorée is an extremely expressive, open-knit, aromatic, and seductive example. Chapoutier believes it is the finest he has ever made. It is soft, accessible, and easy to understand. The saturated ruby/purple color is accompanied by telltale aromas of black raspberries, roasted herbs, smoke, and meat. The wine is medium to full–bodied and moderately tannic, with low acidity, superb concentration, and an intense black cherry, camphor-like, olive component. This wine should last for two decades.

1996 Côte Rôtie La Mordorée

RATING: 91 points

Made from microscopic yields of 15 hectoliters per hectare, it exhibits a saturated purple color and a reticent but promising nose of toasty new oak, cassis, black olives, and smoked game. In the mouth, the wine is medium to full–bodied and dense, but the high acidity and compressed, tightly knit style make it difficult to penetrate. The finish is long, but the wine is backward and unyielding. Anticipated maturity: 2006–2025.

1995 Côte Rôtie La Mordorée

RATING: 95 points

The 1995 is a superb wine. It possesses an intensely saturated black/purple color, and smoky, black raspberry, coffee, and chocolate-scented nose with black olives thrown in for complexity. Medium to full–bodied and rich, it is an extraordinary example of Côte Rôtie that possesses power as well as finesse. The 1995 should drink well from now to 2020.

1994 Côte Rôtie La Mordorée

RATING: 93 points

The classic 1994 is one of the stars of the vintage. It offers up a gorgeous black-raspberry, cassis, olive, and violet–scented nose. Amazingly complex (as are all great Côte Rôties), the wine hits the palate with copious amounts of fat, smoky, cassis-like fruit, medium body, sweet tannin, and a long, rich finish. While it is already stunningly aromatic, the flavors have yet to catch up with the wine's super bouquet. Anticipated maturity: now–2013.

1991 Côte Rôtie La Mordorée

RATING: 100 points

In the same class as the great single-vineyard Côte Rôties made by Marcel Guigal (i.e., La Mouline, La Turque, and La Landonne), La Mordorée is most akin to La Mouline in its seductive, otherworldly fragrance and layers of sweet, expansive, velvety-textured fruit. There were 400 cases made of this saturated purple–colored wine. Its huge bouquet and spectacularly rich, layered personality offer an astonishing example of what low yields from a naturally farmed vineyard and an unfined, unfiltered winemaking philosophy can achieve. Anticipated maturity: now–2020.

1990 Côte Rôtie La Mordorée

RATING: 94 points

The saturated dark ruby/purple color is followed by an awesome nose that offers copious quantities of sweet black fruits, flowers, toasty new oak, and smoky bacon fat. In the mouth there is superb concentration, a sweet, expansive texture, and a mind-boggling long finish. This lavishly rich, delicious Côte Rôtie is capable of lasting for another 5–7 years.

ERMITAGE L'ERMITE

2003 Ermitage L'Ermite

RATING: 98–100 points

One of the most compelling young wines I have ever tasted in my life, this wine tasted like liqueur of stones intermixed with a highly concentrated floral perfume as well as black currant liqueur. A wine of great precision, elegance, and amazing length and concentration, with a whopping 15.5% alcohol (blame the extraordinarily hot, dry summer of 2003 for that), this young, vibrant, huge but elegant wine is the kind of Hermitage that will surely be legendary. It could well be a 100-year wine, but I won't be around to know that for certain. Anticipated maturity: 2015–2060+.

2002 Ermitage L'Ermite

RATING: 94 points

Thanks to biodynamic farming and extraordinary attention to detail, Michel Chapoutier and his brilliant oenologist Alberic Mazoyer have produced the Hermitage of the vintage with this *cuvée* made from 15 hectoliters per hectare in a problematic vintage. Dense purple in color with a beautiful sweet nose of flowers, lead pencil shavings, crème de cassis, and some smoke, this full-bodied, rich, very concentrated wine has tremendous intensity and remarkable length. It tastes almost like liquid minerals intermixed with jammy black fruits. Anticipated maturity: 2012–2022.

2001 Ermitage L'Ermite

RATING: 98–100 points

The black-colored 2001 Ermitage L'Ermite may be equal to the perfect 1996. Awesome levels of kirsch, licorice, and white flowers are followed by a superbly concentrated, etched, long, deep wine with multiple layers, a fabulous texture, and virtually perfect balance as well as harmony. Possessing great stature and intensity, it is a monumental achievement. Anticipated maturity: 2012–2040.

2000 Ermitage L'Ermite

RATING: 99 points

I grossly underestimated the 2000 Ermitage L'Ermite from barrel. This wine, which emerges from largely pre-phylloxera vines planted on the dome of Hermitage, adjacent to the chapel that is perched there so photogenically, possesses extraordinary finesse and elegance. It reveals notes of liquid minerals intermixed with kirsch and blackberries. While it never possesses the power and breadth of flavor of Le Méal or Le Pavillon, L'Ermite appears to be a hypothetical blend of Bordeaux's Lafleur and Ausone, as it always displays a certain austerity early in life. The extraordinary 2000 flirts with perfection. A provocative wine with great minerality, finesse, and delineation, it blew me away when I tasted it from bottle. Anticipated maturity: 2009–2035.

1999 Ermitage L'Ermite

RATING: 96 points

The 1999 Ermitage L'Ermite is a wine that borders on perfection compared to its backward performance from barrel. There are usually 500–600 cases of the *cuvée,* but, sadly, in 1999 only 400 were produced. It comes from Chapoutier's oldest vines (most over 100 years of age), and represents the essence of both Hermitage and Syrah. From bottle, the 1999 L'Ermite reveals an old-style Lafleur character in its kirsch intermixed with raspberries, blackberries, and striking minerality. It has put on considerable weight since last year, but is essentially an elegant, ethereal effort with incredible intensity

as well as amazing lightness. It is a phenomenal expression of *terroir*. However, be forewarned: Anyone expecting to derive a lot of pleasure from this before another 10 years elapse will be disappointed. Anticipated maturity: 2015–2060.

1998 Ermitage L'Ermite

RATING: 98 points

Chapoutier's Ermitage L'Ermite possesses a transparent character that almost allows the taster to see through the wine's multiple levels. What stands out is the liqueur of granite liquid minerality. The elegant 1998 Ermitage L'Ermite rouge is light, but exquisitely balanced, with subtle notes of smoke and black currants. The flavors unfold gently and gracefully, with nothing overstated. The power is restrained, the tannin is well integrated, and the acidity is barely noticeable. However, the wine is fresh and beautifully delineated. Anticipated maturity: 2010–2040.

1997 Ermitage L'Ermite

RATING: 91–94 points

The fabulous 1997 Ermitage L'Ermite possesses the ripeness and exotic characteristics of a great Pomerol, but the structure, smoky minerality, and power of Hermitage. The color is a saturated black/ruby. The wine is rich, chewy, thick, and impeccably well balanced. This wine will be approachable in its youth, but is capable of lasting 30–40 years.

1996 Ermitage L'Ermite

RATING: 99 points

One of the candidates for France's wine of the vintage is unquestionably Chapoutier's 1996 Ermitage L'Ermite. In 1997 I reported that this was a virtually perfect wine made from a small parcel of vines, believed to be over 100 years old, located close to the tiny white chapel owned by the Jaboulets on the highest part of the Hermitage Hill. Yields were a minuscule 9 hectoliters per hectare. Now that this wine is in bottle, it is unbelievable! Unfortunately, only 30 cases were exported to the United States. The wine boasts a saturated black/purple color, as well as a phenomenal nose of rose petals, violets, blackberries, cassis, and toast. In the mouth, it is phenomenally rich, with a viscous texture, and a multidimensional, layered finish that lasts for over a minute. Its purity, perfect equilibrium, and unbelievable volume and richness are the stuff of legends. Anticipated maturity: 2010–2050.

ERMITAGE LE MEAL

2003 Ermitage Le Méal

RATING: 98–100 points

An absolutely magnificent wine with an inky, black/purple color, an explosive nose of violets interwoven with roasted meat, blackberry liqueur, smoke, and almost an indecipherable stony note, this wine has massive richness, a majestic palate, and great purity and length. It is a stunning wine that should prove a bit more forward and earlier maturing than Chapoutier's *cuvée* L'Ermite. It is a wine of great hedonism and intensity. Anticipated maturity: 2009–2040.

2002 Ermitage Le Méal

RATING: 91 points

A great testament to Michel Chapoutier is the 2002 Ermitage Le Méal. Notes of herbal tea intermixed with cassis, crushed stones, and wonderful meaty, blackberry notes, jump from the glass of this round, fleshy, opulently textured wine that is an extraordinary success for this problematic vintage. It is a very forward style, so drink it over the next 10–15 years.

2001 Ermitage Le Méal

RATING: 92–95 points

The dense purple–colored 2001 Ermitage Le Méal reveals aromas of blackberry liqueur, smoke, licorice, and toasty oak. While rich, it is neither as expansive nor as broad as the 2000. The 2001 possesses good acidity and delineation in addition to a tight, pinched but impressive finish that lasts for 40–45 seconds. It is certainly an outstanding, even profound effort, but not as compelling as previous vintages. Anticipated maturity: 2008–2030.

2000 Ermitage Le Méal

RATING: 95 points

The 2000 Ermitage Le Méal is better out of bottle than it was from cask. An opaque purple color is followed by a sumptuous nose of blackberry liqueur intermixed with ink, melted asphalt, camphor, and new saddle leather. Big, rich, broad, and expansive with a gorgeous texture as well as a 60-second finish, it is a full-bodied, opulent, surprisingly approachable offering. Anticipated maturity: 2007–2025.

1999 Ermitage Le Méal

RATING: 93 points

The 1999 Ermitage Le Méal will not be ready to drink for at least another dozen years. A dense ruby/purple color is accompanied by subtle notions of powdered stone, chalk, violets, cassis, graphite, and pepper. The wine is dense, tough-textured, tight, and tannic. It possesses considerable weight and depth, but it is not revealing the opulence it did in 2001. Anticipated maturity: 2015–2050.

1998 Ermitage Le Méal

RATING: 96 points

The 1998 Ermitage Le Méal rouge represents the essence of Hermitage: a wine of elegance, power, symmetry, and extraordinary purity. Aromas and flavors of black and red fruits as well as liquid granite emerge in this superb, multilayered wine of fabulous intensity and length. The finish lasts for nearly a minute. The tannin is high, and a decade of cellaring is warranted. This 1998 will last for half a century.

1997 Ermitage Le Méal

RATING: 91–94 points

The 1997 Ermitage Le Méal displays fat, plumpness, and richness, without losing the floral minerality. It is a finesse-styled Hermitage, with concentrated black fruits and a high-toned, structured, well-delineated personality. Because of low acidity and a plump, plush texture, this wine will be approachable at an early age. Anticipated maturity: now–2035.

1996 Ermitage Le Méal

RATING: 92 points

The 1996 Ermitage Le Méal (Chapoutier calls it the Lafite-Rothschild of Hermitage) is a mineral-dominated, high acid, medium to full–bodied, high-strung, extremely intellectual wine. It exhibits a saturated ruby/purple color, as well as mineral-dominated aromatics with notes of cassis, kirsch, and underbrush. It requires 7–12 years of cellaring. Although not the most charming, opulent, or viscous style of Hermitage, it does possess the strongest *terroir* character of any of Chapoutier's wines. I might call it the Ausone of Hermitage! Anticipated maturity: 2012–2040.

ERMITAGE LE PAVILLON

2003 Ermitage Le Pavillon

RATING: 99–100 points

What promises to be a perfect wine is the 2003 Ermitage Le Pavillon, made from yields of 12–15 hectoliters per hectare and tipping the scales at 15.5% alcohol. This is a 100-year wine, with a black/purple color and the viscosity of vintage port. The third word written in my tasting note was "Religious!" A gorgeous nose of acacia flowers, blackberry liqueur, blueberries, plums, and figs is followed by a wine with superb delineation, fabulous concentration, and an almost endless finish that I stopped timing at 92 seconds. There are huge tannins, but they are sweet and wrapped in the massive concentration this wine possesses. There have been so many great *cuvées* of Pavillon, but this might turn out to be the finest. Stylistically it, like its other siblings in 2003, has more of a similarity to the 1990 vintage, but there is such greater concentration because the yields were so tiny.

2002 Ermitage Le Pavillon

RATING: 91+ points

Made from 15 hectoliters per hectare, the brilliant 2002 Le Pavillon has fabulous aromatics, a relatively forward style for this wine, but tremendous muscle and intensity on the palate. Certainly Chapoutier made the three greatest *cuvées* of Hermitage in the troublesome vintage of 2002, and this broad, expansively flavored wine shows wonderfully sweet, meaty, blackberry fruit notes along with some floral hints. Very low in acidity, plump, and fleshy, it is one of the few Pavillons that can be drunk young but certainly will keep for 15 or more years.

2001 Ermitage Le Pavillon

RATING: 94 points

Year in and year out, one of the three greatest Hermitages made is Chapoutier's Le Pavillon. The 2001 Ermitage Le Pavillon exhibits a saturated ruby/purple color as well as a big, sweet nose of camphor, ink, crème de cassis, and hints of licorice as well as smoke. Although dense, rich, and full-bodied, the 2001 reveals more acidity in its delineated, nervous personality. Unquestionably great and intense, it will be less charming and precocious than its 2000 sibling. Anticipated maturity: 2010–2030.

2000 Ermitage Le Pavillon

RATING: 98 points

The black/blue-colored 2000 Ermitage Le Pavillon is brilliant out of bottle. Notes of graphite, ink, licorice, crème de cassis, and minerals jump from the glass of this syrup of Hermitage. Full-bodied, unctuously textured, gorgeously rich, spectacularly concentrated and long, it is a tour de force in winemaking. Anticipated maturity: 2007–2040.

1999 Ermitage Le Pavillon

RATING: 96 points

The prodigious 1999 Ermitage Le Pavillon boasts crème de cassis aromatics intermixed with unmistakable aromas of ink. It is full-bodied and fabulously concentrated as well as powerful, with a finish that lasts for 50 seconds. This saturated black/purple–colored 1999 exhibits remarkable symmetry, purity, and overall massive size all juxtaposed with a sense of elegance and restraint. It is a monumental achievement. Anticipated maturity: 2012–2040.

1998 Ermitage Le Pavillon

RATING: 98 points

The 1998 Ermitage Le Pavillon flirts with perfection . . . again. Revealing a striking bouquet of violets, blackberries, smoke, licorice, and minerals, it is luxuriously rich, full-bodied, and layered on the palate. It is a wine with a finish that lasts beyond a minute. Remarkably, yields were a mere 10 hectoliters per hectare. There is plenty of tannin in the finish, but it is ripe and well integrated. Anticipated maturity: 2010–2050.

1997 Ermitage Le Pavillon

RATING: 96 points

The 1997 Hermitage Le Pavillon displays a saturated purple color, and a fabulously intense nose of blackberry liqueur intermixed with floral scents, smoke, licorice, tar, and Chinese black tea aromas. There is wonderful concentration, massive body, and a monster finish in this decadently rich Hermitage. It possesses low acidity, but lots of concentration, extract, and length. Anticipated maturity: 2008–2035.

1996 Ermitage Le Pavillon

RATING: 96 points

The 1996 Ermitage Le Pavillon needs at least a decade of cellaring. The wine possesses a saturated black/purple color, in addition to fabulously sweet aromas of blackberries, framboise, blueberries, violets, roasted herbs, and meats. Massively concentrated and full-bodied, with staggering levels of extract, this wine is super pure, with high tannin, good but not intrusive acidity, and a 45-second finish. This is one of the superstars of the vintage in France! Anticipated maturity: 2010–2050.

1995 Ermitage Le Pavillon

RATING: 99 points

The 1995 Ermitage Le Pavillon offers a black/purple color and layers of cassis fruit, smoky, roasted meat, and mineral characteristics. It is huge but not heavy, gorgeously proportioned, and dazzlingly well defined. A monster Hermitage of immense proportions, it somehow manages to keep everything in balance. This backward Pavillon will require another 3–5 years of cellaring. It should age well through the first half of the 21st century.

1994 Ermitage Le Pavillon

RATING: 96 points

The 1994 Le Pavillon is a blockbuster, phenomenally concentrated wine. Le Pavillon is generally among the top three or four wines of France in every vintage! The 1994's opaque purple color and wonderfully sweet, pure nose of cassis and other black fruits intertwined with minerals, are followed by a wine of profound richness, great complexity, and full body. It is almost the essence of blackberries and cassis. There is huge tannin in this monster Hermitage, which somehow manages to keep its balance and elegance. The 1994 Ermitage Le Pavillon should be purchased only by those who are willing to invest 10–12 years of cellaring. It will not reach full maturity before 2010, after which it will last for 20 years.

1991 Ermitage Le Pavillon

RATING: 100 points

This is a Le Pavillon of mythical proportions. Produced from extremely old vines, some dating from the mid-19th century, with yields averaging under 15 hectoliters per hectare, this is the richest, most concentrated and profound wine made in Hermitage. The 1991 Ermitage Le Pavillon follows the pattern of the 1989 and 1990: It is another perfect wine. The saturated black/purple color is followed by a compelling bouquet of spices, roasted meats, and black and red fruits. Enormously concentrated yet with brilliant focus and delineation to its awesomely endowed personality, this extraordinary wine should age effortlessly for 3+ decades. Very powerful and full, yet displaying silky tannin, this is a seamless beauty! Anticipated maturity: now–2035.

1990 Ermitage Le Pavillon

RATING: 100 points

The 1990 Le Pavillon is as compelling as the 1989. It exhibits slightly less opulence but more power and weight. Black-colored, with an extraordinary perfume of licorice, sweet black currants, smoke, and minerals, it coats the palate with layer upon layer of decadently rich, super-concentrated, nearly viscous Syrah flavors. There is amazing glycerin, a chewy, unctuous texture, and phenomenal length. The tannins, which are considerable when analyzed, are virtually obscured by the massive quantities of fruit. My best guess for the aging potential of the Ermitage Le Pavillon is that it is more forward than both the Chave and Jaboulet Hermitages. It should last for 30–40 years.

1989 Ermitage Le Pavillon

RATING: 100 points

The 1989 Le Pavillon is a prodigious wine. Made from yields of 14 hectoliters per hectare, this parcel of old vines (averaging 70–80 years of age) has produced an opaque black/purple–colored wine, with a hauntingly stunning bouquet of violets, cassis, minerals, and new oak. In the mouth, the similarity in texture, richness, and perfect balance to the compelling 1986 Mouton Rothschild is striking, only this wine is richer and longer. This extraordinarily well-balanced wine will evolve for three decades or more. It is an enormous yet amazingly well-delineated wine. Anticipated maturity: 2007–2035.

White Wines

ERMITAGE L'ERMITE

2003 Ermitage L'Ermite

RATING: 99–100 points

Prodigious, but sadly only 75 cases for the world, this is another 100-year Hermitage that tastes like the essence of Marsanne. Mind-boggling intensity, with amazing persistence of over 90 seconds, superb richness, and an almost liquefied honeyed minerality, this wine is one for the history books. Anticipated maturity: 2012–2099.

2002 Ermitage L'Ermite

RATING: 95 points

Yields of only 8 hectoliters per hectare produced an amazing and concentrated, full-bodied wine that tastes like liqueur of minerals. It is an extraordinary wine and no doubt controversial, but there are only 177 cases. Amazingly concentrated and obviously thick, yet elegant, this probably will drink better early, in its first 10–15 years of life, than its more prodigious sibling, the 2003.

2001 Ermitage L'Ermite

RATING: 96 points

Like all of these wines, the 2001 Ermitage l'Ermite is aged in *demi-muids* on its lees with malolactic in the barrel, considerable lees stirring, and bottled unfined and unfiltered. Displaying a liqueur of nut-like character along with hints of lychees, orange blossoms, and citrus oils in its pure, intensely mineral-styled personality, it is another prodigious effort that will have to take a back seat to the singular/remarkable 2000 L'Ermite. The 2001 should be at its finest between 2008 and 2030.

2000 Ermitage L'Ermite

RATING: 100 points

The 2000 Ermitage L'Ermite has a liquid mineral, crystalline expression. It is the essence of its grape as well as *terroir*. It may be the greatest expression of *terroir* I have seen outside of a handful of Alsatian Rieslings. It has that transparent character that terroirists talk more about than actually recognize. Drinking it is like consuming a liquefied stony concoction mixed with white flowers, licorice, and honeyed fruits. Frightfully pure, dense, and well delineated, as I said in 2001, "There is no real fruit character, just glycerin, alcohol, and liquid stones." That's about it, but wow, what an expression! Anticipated maturity: 2012–2050.

ERMITAGE LE MEAL

2003 Ermitage Le Méal

RATING: 98–100 points

Superlatives are easy, I suppose, but in all sincerity, I thought this might have been the single greatest white wine I have ever tasted in my life. Of course, it is not in bottle, but Chapoutier's wines do perform as well if not better from bottle than from barrel. An extraordinary wine (16.1% natural alcohol made from yields of 10–12 hectoliters per hectare) with incredible concentrated essence of honeyed citrus, liquid stone–like intensity, magnificent perfume, and amazing body and unctousness, yet surprisingly great freshness, this is a white Hermitage that will probably require 7–10 years of bottle age and last a century. It is one of the most provocative wines, white or red, dry or sweet, I have ever tasted. There are approximately 350 cases, so hopefully it will get spread around so many people can taste what an extraordinary achievement Michel Chapoutier has accomplished with this particular *cuvée*.

2002 Ermitage Le Méal

RATING: 95 points

An extraordinary achievement in this vintage, the 2002 Le Méal has notes of quince, crushed rock, and white flowers in a full-bodied, unctuously textured style that has amazing concentration, persistence, and length. It is a great white Hermitage that should keep for up to 30 years and is an incredible achievement in this vintage.

2001 Ermitage Le Méal

RATING: 93 points

The 2001 Ermitage Le Méal is more delineated, smoky, and citrusy, with less fat and unctousness than the 2000. Nevertheless, it is a big, thickly textured effort with huge notes of ripe honeysuckle, pear, and peach. Anticipated maturity: 2007–2020.

2000 Ermitage Le Méal

RATING: 97 points

The stunning 2000 Ermitage Le Méal represents a singular expression of white Hermitage. Offering up honeysuckle characteristics, gobs of fruit and glycerin, and more fat than the L'Orée, it is huge in the mouth, very buttery, and is a total hedonistic turn-on. I suspect additional nuances will develop as it ages. It will provide an enormous mouthful of wine over the next 4–5 years, and should keep for 40–50 years.

1999 Ermitage Le Méal

RATING: 95 points

Chapoutier's brilliant 1999 Ermitage Le Méal is essentially a liqueur of white Hermitage. Notes of pear liqueur intertwined with fino sherry, peaches, minerals, nuts, and licorice are offered in an amazingly concentrated, super-extracted style that manages to be delicate as well as precise. This is a 40- to 50-year dry white that will undoubtedly close down in 1–2 years and reemerge a decade later.

1998 Ermitage Le Méal

RATING: 96 points

The 1998 Ermitage Le Méal blanc offers aromas and flavors of butterscotch and caramel in its full-bodied, thick, juicy personality. It possesses liquid minerality but also reveals oak. This is an amazingly layered wine! Anticipated maturity: 2007–2030.

1997 Ermitage Le Méal

RATING: 96–100 points

The 1997 displays, in addition to cherry notes, an orange Grand Marnier characteristic to its fruit. It is an immense, full-bodied, fabulously powerful and concentrated dry white with a steely finish. There are approximately 300 cases of this spectacular offering. Anticipated maturity: 2012–2030.

ERMITAGE L'OREE

2003 Ermitage L'Orée

RATING: 98–100 points

Made from 12–15 hectoliters per hectare and tipping the scales at a whopping 14.5% alcohol, this awesome, concentrated wine is almost akin to the bottled essence of a dry white wine. It is totally dry, yet it has an unctuous texture, amazing concentration, and is probably not the easiest wine to match with food given its extraordinary intensity, power, and richness, yet it is a tour de force in winemaking and probably destined to live 50–75 or more years.

2002 Ermitage L'Orée

RATING: 93+ points

A gorgeous nose of honeysuckle, citrus, and crushed rocks jumps from the glass of the 2002 L'Orée. Very rich, full-bodied, with terrific minerality, this is a spectacular wine and is certainly one of the three white Hermitage *cuvées* of the vintage. (Not surprisingly, Chapoutier produced the other two as well.) Drink it over the next 10–15 years.

2001 Ermitage L'Orée

RATING: 94 points

The great American patriot and wine connoisseur Thomas Jefferson called Hermitage "the single greatest white wine of France." Slightly lower-keyed, but still prodigious, the 2001 Ermitage L'Orée does not possess the muscle, volume, or weight of the 2000, but it is a beautifully etched, elegant, intensely mineral wine offering hints of white flowers, citrus oils, and earth in its dense, full-bodied, chewy personality. Like its older sibling, it will be delicious in its first 3–4 years of life, then close down, to reemerge 10–12 years later. It will last for three decades or more.

2000 Ermitage L'Orée

RATING: 100 points

These wines usually flirt with perfection, which is the case with the 2000 Ermitage L'Orée. It boasts an amazing nose of licorice, minerals, acacia flowers, honeysuckle, and a hint of butter. Unctuously textured and full-bodied, with great intensity and purity, yet remarkably light on its feet, it can be drunk over the next 3–4 years, then forgotten for a decade, after which it will last for 40–50 years.

1999 Ermitage L'Orée

RATING: 99 points

The awesome 1999 Ermitage L'Orée flirts with perfection. It is full-bodied, with an incredible bouquet of liquid minerals, licorice, honeysuckle, citrus, and a hint of tropical fruits. The wine's fruit and glycerin have completely absorbed the 100% new oak aging. This is a winemaking tour de force, made from exceedingly low yields of 12–15 hectoliters per hectare (less than one ton of fruit per acre). However, readers should understand that these are often unusual wines to drink because they tend to show exceptionally well for 4–5 years after bottling, then close up until about age 12. They can last for 4–5 decades. Anticipated maturity: now–2006; 2012–2050.

1998 Ermitage L'Orée

RATING: 99 points

The 1998 Ermitage L'Orée's explosive bouquet offers a liquid minerality, honeyed tropical fruits, peaches, and acacia flowers. Amazingly, the 100% new oak treatment has been totally absorbed. The wine is extremely full-bodied, fresh, and pure, with an immense palate presence as well as finish. Anticipated maturity: now–2030.

1997 Ermitage L'Orée

RATING: 98 points

It is no secret that I adore Chapoutier's luxury *cuvée* of white Hermitage called L'Orée. It is a compelling white Hermitage. Made from 100% Marsanne, it is as rich and multidimensional as the fullest, most massive Montrachet money can buy. It is unctuously textured, yet extraordinarily and beautifully balanced. I suspect it will drink well early in life, and then shut down for a few years. It should last for 4–5 decades. It is a huge, chewy, multidimensional wine with spectacular concentration and richness. Notes of white flowers, honey, minerals, and peaches are present in astronomical quantities. In short, this wine must be tasted to be believed.

1996 Ermitage L'Orée

RATING: 99 points

This wine flirts with perfection. It is a compelling white Hermitage. It is unctuously textured, yet extraordinarily and beautifully balanced. I suspect it will drink well early in life, and then shut down for a few years. It should last for 4–5 decades. The 1996 possesses some of the most amazing glycerin levels I have ever seen in a dry white wine. In short, this wine must be tasted to be believed. Anticipated maturity: 2010–2040.

1995 Ermitage L'Orée

RATING: 97 points

Made from microscopic yields of 12 hectoliters per hectare, this wine possesses extraordinary intensity, full body, the multilayered texture, an intense, honeyed, mineral-like fruit flavor that oozes over the palate with remarkable richness, yet no sense of heaviness. Anticipated maturity: 2007–2025.

1994 Ermitage L'Orée

RATING: 99 points

This wine boasts a huge, flowery, superrich nose that is almost the essence of minerals and ripe fruit. Extremely powerful, full-bodied, and unctuously textured, this staggeringly great white Hermitage should last for 30–50+ years.

WINE: Châteauneuf-du-Pape
OWNERS: Earl Charvin G. et Fils
ADDRESS: Chemin de Maucoil, 84100 Orange, France
TELEPHONE: 33 04 90 34 41 10
TELEFAX: 33 04 90 51 65 59
E-MAIL: domaine.charvin@free.fr
WEBSITE: www.domaine-charvin.com
CONTACT: Laurent Charvin
VISITING POLICY: By appointment only

VINEYARDS

SURFACE AREA: 56.8 acres (19.76 acres Châteauneuf-du-Pape)
GRAPE VARIETALS: Grenache, Syrah, Mourvèdre, Vaccarèse
AVERAGE AGE OF THE VINES: Châteauneuf-du-Pape—65 years
DENSITY OF PLANTATION: 2,500–4,000 vines per hectare
AVERAGE YIELDS: Châteauneuf-du-Pape: 20–30 hectoliters per hectare

WINEMAKING AND UPBRINGING

The wine is vinified as well as aged in cement tanks, where it is kept for 20 months with little racking and no filtration at bottling. The objective is to preserve the wine's fresh aromas and intense fruit.

ANNUAL PRODUCTION

Châteauneuf-du-Pape: 30,000 bottles
AVERAGE PRICE (VARIABLE DEPENDING ON VINTAGE): $20–55

GREAT RECENT VINTAGES

2003, 2001, 2000, 1998, 1995, 1990 (the first vintage to be estate-bottled)

Laurent Charvin is a member of the sixth generation of his family to farm this estate, located in the Grés sector of Châteauneuf-du-Pape, since 1851. It took the family a mere 139 years to estate-bottle, as the family sold their entire production to brokers before beginning to estate-bottle in 1990. Charvin has enjoyed considerable success with his sumptuously styled, authoritatively flavored wines. The first estate-bottled wine, the terrific 1990 (I bought a case), and his recent vintages are all top wines. Charvin, perhaps the only Châteauneuf-du-Pape producer to indicate boldly on the front label that his wine is *nonfiltré*, fashions Châteauneuf-du-Pape that comes closest in style to that of Rayas. There is a splendidly pure, black-raspberry fruitiness to his wines, a wonderfully sweet, deep, concentrated mid-palate, and layers of flavor that unfold on the palate. Great Burgundy should possess a similar texture and purity, but it rarely does. Charvin, who has not yet been discovered by the masses, may indeed produce the Richebourg of Châteauneuf-du-Pape—for a very reasonable price.

Charvin's vineyard parcels are exceptionally well located in the Maucoil, Mont Redon, and La Gardine sectors. The soil is mainly rocky stones covering a limestone/clay base. Charvin, who has traditionally sold much of his production to several well-known *négociants,* continues to estate-bottle more of his liquid treasure.

CHATEAUNEUF-DU-PAPE

2003 Châteauneuf-du-Pape

RATING: 93–96 points
Another great success for Laurent Charvin, the 2003 Châteauneuf-du-Pape, a blend of 82% Grenache, 8% Syrah, 5% Mourvèdre, and 5% Vaccarèse that tips the scales at 14.5+% alcohol, has a gorgeous perfume of plums, raspberries, cherries, and currants. Dark garnet/ruby to the rim, this medium to full–bodied wine has silky tannins and an expansive mid-palate and finish, and just layers of fruit. It is a very sensual, soulful, sexy Châteauneuf-du-Pape that can be drunk young or cellared for 12–15+ years.

2001 Châteauneuf-du-Pape

RATING: 95 points
One of the most Burgundian-style wines of the appellation is Charvin's Châteauneuf-du-Pape, made in a style not dissimilar from the classic vintages of its neighbor, Rayas. The deep ruby–colored 2001 Châteauneuf-du-Pape reveals a gorgeously scented nose of kirsch, plums, and figs. It boasts an expansive, full-bodied palate; great purity; a sensual, silky texture; and a long, flowing finish with raspberries, cherries, licorice, and a hint of roasted Provençal herbs. Always a model of symmetry, balance, and complexity, this Charvin is as complex and elegant as Châteauneuf-du-Pape gets. Anticipated maturity: now–2016.

2000 Châteauneuf-du-Pape

RATING: 95 points

The glories at this estate are unquestionably their Châteauneuf-du-Papes. Fashioned from a blend of 82% Grenache, and the rest Syrah, Mourvèdre, and a dollop of Vaccarèse, the 2000 Châteauneuf-du-Pape initially appears closed, but with 30 minutes of airing, it explodes from the glass. A deep ruby/purple color is accompanied by a sweet nose of crème de cassis, kirsch, licorice, pepper, and underbrush. Voluptuously textured and exceptionally long (the finish lasts 45+ seconds), with silky tannin, low acidity, and full body, it is less tannic and delineated than the 2001, but it offers a gorgeous, seductive mouthful of old-vine Châteauneuf-du-Pape. It will age effortlessly for 12–15 years. Readers who believe Châteauneuf-du-Pape cannot be a wine of finesse and elegance should taste Charvin!

1999 Châteauneuf-du-Pape

RATING: 92 points

A brilliant effort, the 1999 Châteauneuf-du-Pape (14% natural alcohol) exhibits a big, spicy nose of balsam; juicy, fat, black cherry and berry flavors; full body; a creamy texture; superb purity; and a long finish. It will provide abundant pleasure over the next 10–12 years.

1998 Châteauneuf-du-Pape

RATING: 96 points

There is no denying the 1998 is a sumptuous, extraordinarily compelling effort. Dark ruby–colored, with a gorgeous perfume of black raspberry liqueur intermixed with kirsch, pepper, spice box, and balsam, it displays superb depth, fabulous concentration, a boatload of glycerin, and a seamless finish. The enormous fruit admirably conceals the wine's high tannin. It can be drunk now, but promises to develop for two decades. Kudos to the young Laurent Charvin.

1995 Châteauneuf-du-Pape

RATING: 91 points

The 1995 Châteauneuf-du-Pape exhibits a dense purple color, as well as a sweet nose of black raspberries, cherries, and subtle *herbes de Provence*. It is an aromatic, full-bodied wine with

outstanding sweetness and layers of rich, spicy black fruits on the palate. Typical of the vintage, it reveals some tannin and relatively good acidity. I would suggest consuming it over the next 5–8 years.

1994 Châteauneuf-du-Pape

RATING: 91 points

The 1994 exhibits that telltale sweet, fragrant, black raspberry/kirsch-scented nose, sweet, expansive, chewy fruit, superb purity, an excellent marriage of power and elegance, and a soft, round, generous finish. This is a well-balanced, symmetrical Châteauneuf-du-Pape. Anticipated maturity: now–2008.

1990 Châteauneuf-du-Pape

RATING: 94 points

Charvin is a producer I am proud to have discovered while working in Châteauneuf-du-Pape. As was stated in both *The Wine Advocate* and my books, these wines have an affinity to the style of Rayas in their extraordinary purity, elegance, complexity, and black raspberry/kirsch-like fruit characteristics. The 1990 has reached full maturity, yet promises to hold for another 4–6 years. It offers sweet black raspberry and kirsch fruit notes, full body, admirable fat and succulence as well as amazing symmetry and freshness. This is great stuff!

WINES:

Hermitage

Hermitage (White)

Hermitage Cuvée Cathelin

OWNERS: Gérard and Jean-Louis Chave

ADDRESS: 36, avenue du St.-Joseph, 07300 Mauves, France

TELEPHONE: 33 04 75 08 24 63

TELEFAX: 33 04 75 07 14 21

CONTACT: Address letters to the family at the above address

VISITING POLICY: No visits

VINEYARDS

SURFACE AREA: 37.5 acres of Hermitage (24.7 acres in red; 12.35 acres in white)

GRAPE VARIETALS: *Red*—Syrah; *White*—20% Roussanne, 80% Marsanne

AVERAGE AGE OF THE VINES:

Red—45 years

White—60 years

DENSITY OF PLANTATION: 7,000–10,000 vines per hectare

AVERAGE YIELDS: 33 hectoliters per hectare

WINEMAKING AND UPBRINGING

At Chave, all the individual *terroirs* are vinified separately in both small, open wood and stainless-steel tanks. The white is vinified in barrel, a relatively new technique initiated by the son, Jean-Louis, in the mid-1990s. After 10–12 months, the father and son meticulously taste through the different *cuvées* and fashion the blend that becomes the legendary Chave Hermitage. The wines rest on their lees and the red wines spend 14 or more months in barrels and small *foudres* before being bottled with filtration. A luxury *cuvée*, somewhat of a radical

Gérard Chave

idea chez Chave, was inaugurated in 1990 for only the greatest of vintages. Thus, the famed Cuvée Cathelin has been made only in 1990, 1991, 1995, 1998, 2000, and 2003. It is significant to the Chaves that this *cuvée* be made only if there's no diminution of their classic *cuvée*.

ANNUAL PRODUCTION

Hermitage Blanc: 15,000 bottles

Hermitage Rouge: 30,000 bottles

Ermitage Cathelin: 2,500 bottles

AVERAGE PRICE (VARIABLE DEPENDING ON VINTAGE): $35–300

GREAT RECENT VINTAGES

2003, 2001, 1999, 1998, 1997, 1995, 1991, 1990, 1988

There can be no doubt that the son, Jean-Louis, and his papa, Gérard Chave—members of a family of growers that has been making Hermitage for six centuries—are among this planet's greatest winemakers. If I have trouble writing objectively about the Chaves, it is because of the fact that there is so much about them that I admire. Generous to a fault, uncommonly gracious, and bursting with a sincere joie de vivre, both Gérard and his son are great tasters, superb chefs, and brilliant raconteurs. Gérard possesses a depth of knowledge on an amazing array of subjects, ranging from the primary causes of gout (from which he suffers) to the viability of Zinfandel planted in Hermitage's granitic soils. Born in 1935, Gérard lives in the tiny, one-horse village of Mauves, across the river from Tain l'Hermitage and just south of Tournon. One blink of the eye when passing through Mauves and the passerby would no doubt miss the tiny, faded, rusting, brown and white metal sign hanging from the wall of a building inconspicuously announcing the cellars of "J. L. Chave—*Viticulteurs depuis 1481*." Gérard's big, sad, basset-hound eyes and long, pointed nose immediately suggest sympathy and warmth. For all his achievements, Chave is a remarkably modest man who remains unwaveringly committed to his passion for making wine in the same manner as his father before him, with no technological razzle-dazzle, and no compromises for consumers who want their wines to be already mature when released.

However, Chave is no provincial-thinking man blindly carrying on a tradition. Several trips to California and a keen sense of curiosity have informed him of the wonders, as well as dangers, of centrifuges and German micropore filtering machines that can clarify and stabilize a wine in a matter of minutes (as well as remove most of its flavor) so that no winemaker will ever have to worry about an unstable bottle. Yet he will have none of these methods, which he calls "the tragedy of modern winemaking." In his deep, damp, cobwebbed cellars, over 500 vintages of the Chave family's Hermitage have been allowed to clarify and stabilize naturally without the aid of chemicals or machines. No flavors have been sacrificed, and Chave sees no reason to change, because the old way, though much more troublesome and fraught with increased risk, produces wines of greater flavor, dimension, and depth.

Chave is not averse to experimentation if it can be proved that better wine will result. For instance, new oak barrels, pioneered by Marcel Guigal for his Côte Rôtie, and now à la mode in other houses in the Rhône Valley, have caused Chave to reflect. Despite the fact that Chave firmly believes that the intense richness of fruit produced at Hermitage does not require aging in new oak to give structure, he purchased *one* new barrel in 1985 to age one batch of his red Hermitage. Though a great admirer of Marcel Guigal, he believed that the toasty, vanilla character imparted by this new oak barrel to his Hermitage not only changed the character of the wine, but disguised its identity—to his Hermitage's detriment. But this 1985 experiment had an interesting conclusion. At the urging of his talented son, Jean-Louis, who spent time studying at the University of California at Davis, and who also received a master's degree in business in America, Chave

aged a small amount of his red Hermitage, largely from Les Bessards vineyard in 100% new oak casks. He agreed to do it in 1990 because the vintage was so extraordinary he knew the wine could absorb the new oak without losing its Hermitage typicity. When he blended together numerous lots of red Hermitage, this wine was kept separately and subsequently bottled in a heavy, old-fashioned bottle, with a red label. Called Cuvée Cathelin (after Chave's friend the painter Bernard Cathelin), it was also produced in 1991, 1995, 1998, 2000, and 2003. Interestingly, Gérard Chave continues to have mixed emotions about the importance of this deluxe *cuvée,* but the wine has received rave accolades from all who have been fortunate enough to taste it.

The Chave family now owns 37 acres on Hermitage Hill. Production ranges between 2,000 and 3,000 cases of Hermitage, and 500 cases of red St.-Joseph are produced from the 3.7 acres Chave owns in that appellation, although recent hillside plantings will increase the quantity of St.-Joseph.

There are no secrets as to why Chave's wines are great. It is because of low-yielding vines, a very late harvest producing physiologically ripe fruit, virtually no intervention in the winemaking or upbringing, and bottling with no filtration, and only insignificant fining. Tasting at Chave's cellars is always educational because it is the only place where the vineyards can be tasted separately before they are blended. I have done this numerous times and it is always a thrill to see his three white wine *cuvées,* one from his monopole vineyard, the 3.73 acres of 50- to 85-year-old vines of Péleat, the 9+ acres of 80-year-old vines of Les Rocoules, and his tiny parcel of 60-year-old vines of La Maison Blanche. Chave also owns a tiny parcel of very old-vine Roussanne on l'Hermite, which produces

an extraordinarily rich, complex, honeyed wine that manages to keep everything in balance while offering great finesse. Traditionally, this has always been blended with Chave's white Hermitage, but in 1994 it was kept separately. Chave's white Hermitage, a blend of 85% Marsanne and 15% Roussanne, aged after malolactic fermentation in both vats and barrels for 14–18 months, has benefitted from an increased percentage of new oak (largely Jean-Louis's influence). It is one of the finest white Hermitages of the appellation. Although Chapoutier's L'Orée, L'Ermite, and Méal offerings are richer and more powerful wines, they are made in such tiny quantities that they truly are impossible to find in the marketplace. Chave's white Hermitage drinks beautifully for 4–5 years after its release, and it then closes down, seemingly losing its fruit and becoming more monolithic and neutral, only to reemerge 10–15 years later with a roasted hazelnut, buttery, honeyed, slight fino sherry style that is exceptional. In the great vintages it can last for 20–30 years.

Chave's red wine vineyards include a parcel of very old vines in Les Rocoules, a 5-acre parcel of 80-year-old vines in Les Bessards, relatively young vines in l'Hermite, extremely old vines in Péleat, old vines in Les Beaumes, and 50-year-old vines in Le Méal. Each of these vineyards produces an Hermitage with slightly different aromatic, textural, and flavor profiles, but the sum of their parts always turns out to be far more interesting than any individual *cuvée.* The one exception may be the wine from Les Bessards, part of which, in the greatest years, becomes the Cuvée Cathelin.

Like so many top winemakers, Chave is never content to rest on his reputation. Concerned about having to do several bottlings because his cellars were not large enough to store the production from an entire vintage, he constructed a beautiful underground cellar in 1990 that allows one bottling and has sufficient room to store his entire production. In fact, there has been only one bottling of Chave Hermitage since 1983.

With respect to his red wine, perhaps Chave's most important decision is the date he chooses to harvest. Along with Chapoutier, he is the last to harvest. He has often said that he does not need an oenologist to know when to harvest. As Chave amusingly puts it, "I don't begin to think about picking until the chestnuts on my trees start falling." His goal is to achieve super ripeness and richness, which he claims are the primary ingredients of a great red wine. Delaying the harvest is always risky because torrential rains tend to plague France in early October. Chave keeps the wines from his vineyards separate for one year and then decides what will go into the final blend, going through an elaborate, laborious exercise of making various blends to see which turns out to be the finest. It is a long and tedious process, but as I have indicated, the final product is consistently better than the individual components, a testament to Chave's formidable tasting and blending abilities. In the finest years, Chave's red Hermitage is an immortal wine. Compared to the flashy, opulent style of Jaboulet's La Chapelle, and the extraordinarily concentrated masterpieces of Chapoutier's luxury *cuvées,* Chave's red Hermitage begins life slowly, but it never fails to impress after 7–10 years in bottle. Will it peak in 10, 15, or 20 years? His great vintages—1978, 1983, 1985, 1988, 1989, 1990, 1991, 1995, 1996, 1998, 1999, 2001, and 2003—are rivaled by few other producers in France.

Prior to 1978, Chave's wines were less consistent. Much of that is explained by the fact that when he took over for his father in 1970, he had to endure 1972, 1973, 1974, and 1975, all rain-plagued, extremely difficult years for Hermitage. While his 1976 did not turn out to be a successful wine, that year was also a tricky vintage given the extraordinary summer drought and heavy September rains.

Chave has also resurrected an old Hermitage practice of making a *vin de paille,* by taking whole bunches and leaving them on straw mats until they turn to raisins 60+ days after the harvest (usually in December), and then fermenting them, which not only produces microscopic quantities of juice, but unbelievably concentrated, intense, honeyed wines that are known to have aged for more than a century. When I tasted Chave's 1974 *vin de paille* I was struck by its extraordinary aromas of figs, apricots, roasted nuts, and honey. That wine was never commercialized, but in 1986 and 1989, Chave intentionally set out to produce tiny quantities of *vin de paille.* Both vintages are extraordinary.

This family-run estate continues to go from strength to strength, with the father-and-son team pushing all the right buttons to achieve success at all quality levels. Jean-Louis Chave is also responsible for several *négociant* wines.

HERMITAGE

2003 Hermitage

RATING: 98–100 points

While there will undoubtedly be a Cuvée Cathelin, this is the most provocative and extraordinary vintage I have tasted chez Chave in the 26 years I have been visiting this domaine. Every *cuvée* tasted before blending together had at least 16% and as much as 17% natural alcohol, yields were 10–15 hectoliters per hectare, and the potential unbelievable. The wine tastes more like dry vintage port than anything I have ever tasted at this estate, with amazing concentration yet remarkable freshness. Certainly Les Baumes (16.5% alcohol) tastes like crushed stones intermixed with crème de cassis. Even more stony in its unreal mineral richness and unctuousness was the *cuvée* l'Hermite. The two *cuvées* from Méal and Bessards were simply to die for, the most concentrated, intense Hermitages I have ever tasted, with extraordinary richness and power (16% alcohol). Of course, the yields were unprecedented, and the level of ripeness and richness unprecedented, so what we have is probably something for the archives of the Chave family, a wine of prodigious richness, longevity, and extraordinary intensity. It would be hard to believe that the Cuvée Cathelin, when they cull it out of this *cuvée,* can actually be any better, but it will obviously be a bit different as it tends to see a bit more small oak cask and/or new oak, and the bulk of it tends to come from their holdings in Les Bessards. Anticipated maturity: 2010–2045.

2002 Hermitage

RATING: 93 points

Along with some of the luxury *cuvées* from Chapoutier, this is by far one of the leading candidates for the wine of the vintage in the north. Over half the crop was eliminated, and the result is a wine with loads of licorice, cassis, and dense ruby/purple color, very forward by Chave standards, but ideal for drinking over the next 10 years. The wine has good earthy smokiness that permeates the concentrated black currant and heady flavors. Anticipated maturity: now–2016.

2001 Hermitage

RATING: 93+ points

Tasting through the component parts of the 2001 Hermitage reveals what should be an outstanding wine with a Burgundian-like finesse. The most elegant component emanates from Les Beaumes and Pelia, and the denser, thicker wines from Méal, l'Ermite, and Bessards. The wine will possess a dense ruby/purple color in addition to plenty of sweet cassis fruit, medium body, noticeably high tannin, and gorgeous purity as well as symmetry. It will be built along the lines of the 1996 rather than the 2000 or 1999. Anticipated maturity: 2008-2028.

2000 Hermitage

RATING: 96 points

Along with the single-vineyard offerings from Michel Chapoutier, Chave's 2000 Hermitage is a candidate for this appellation's wine of the vintage. A dense ruby/purple color is accompanied by sumptuous aromas of licorice, blackberries, currants, spice box, and earth. Deep, full-bodied, and rich, with moderately high tannin, it is atypical for the vintage given its structure and density (two characteristics most 2000 northern Rhônes lack). It is a brilliant achievement in a challenging year. Anticipated maturity: 2007–2035.

1999 Hermitage

RATING: 96 points

The dense, saturated purple–colored 1999 Hermitage had been bottled only 24 hours before my visit in 2002. It is a brilliant effort. The wine exhibits fabulous texture, purity, and sweetness, as well as a finish that lasts for nearly a minute. There is high tannin, remarkably rich, concentrated extract, and telltale Hermitage fruit characteristics (blackberries, cassis), minerals, and spice. This is the greatest vintage Chave has produced since 1990. Anticipated maturity: 2009–2027.

1998 Hermitage

RATING: 93 points

The 1998 Hermitage rouge is a tannic, backward, large-scaled, dense ruby/purple–colored wine with high tannin, sensational extract, and formidable power and length. Anticipated maturity: 2007–2030.

1997 Hermitage

RATING: 94 points

The 1997 Hermitage rouge is unusual in its fruit-forward, user-friendly style. The color is a dense ruby/purple. The gorgeous, evolved bouquet of cassis, minerals, herbs, underbrush, and licorice is intense. Creamy-textured, full-bodied, and opulent, this low-acid, gloriously ripe, layered 1997 can be drunk now, but promises to be even better with another 2–3 years of cellaring. It will last for 20–25 years.

1996 Hermitage

RATING: 91 points

The 1996 red Hermitage possesses the vintage's tangy acidity, as well as a saturated ruby/purple color, and copious quantities of smoke, cassis, fennel, and minerals in the moderately intense, still young aromatics. The wine displays beautiful balance, outstanding purity, and a medium-bodied, rich, elegant personality. Anticipated maturity: 2009–2030.

1995 Hermitage

RATING: 95 points

The magnificent 1995 Hermitage is one of the classic Rhônes of the vintage. The wine, which had just been bottled when I tasted it, was revealing no signs of fatigue. The color is opaque purple, and the wine is beautifully made, offering up scents of violets and black currants, along with the telltale aromas of tar, truffle, mineral, and earth. This wine could be called the Musigny of Hermitage. It is medium to full–bodied (less massive than the 1990 and 1989), with good underlying acidity, and powerful but sweet tannin in the finish. Do not expect the 1995 to possess the power of the 1989 or 1990, as it is made along the lines of the 1991, but even more fragrant. Anticipated maturity: 2006–2030.

1994 Hermitage

RATING: 93 points

The 1994 red Hermitage appears to be superb. Originally it tasted like a richer sibling of the 1985. Tasted a year later, it was significantly richer, but with the 1985's softness, elegance, and precocious appeal. The wine possesses a black/ruby/purple color; an intense, smoky, cassis, and mineral-scented nose; full body; superb density; a soft attack; good grip; and a long, impressively endowed finish. It is a wine of undeniable power, spice, tannin, fruit, silk, and fat—what else can you ask for? It should last for 25+ years.

1990 Hermitage

RATING: 99 points

1990 is the Hermitage appellation's greatest vintage since 1978, and maybe since 1961. I have been tasting Chave's Hermitage since the great 1978 vintage, and the black-colored 1990 is unquestionably the most massive and concentrated wine he has yet produced. Perhaps the real difference between it and the splendid 1989 is that the 1990 exhibits a more roasted character to its nose, as well as a bit more tannin and concentration in the mouth. Except for that, they are both mind-boggling, monumental bottles of red Hermitage. The 1990, which offers huge aromas of tar, roasted cassis fruit, and hickory, as well as astonishing concentration, will not be interesting to drink young. Anticipated maturity: now–2040.

1989 Hermitage

RATING: 95 points

The 1989 is finally beginning to reveal all its glory. This is a tannic, formidably endowed wine. Its black/ruby/purple color; the intensely fragrant nose of jammy cassis, minerals, and spices; and the full-bodied, rich, concentrated style are unmistakable. An enormously rich, backward Hermitage, it does not share the roasted character or sheer massiveness and tannic clout of the 1990, but it is a spectacularly concentrated Hermitage that will age effortlessly for 20–30 years. Anticipated maturity: now–2030.

1988 Hermitage

RATING: 93 points

This opaque, dark ruby/purple–colored wine reveals a tightly knit nose of cassis, minerals, and tar. Full-bodied, with superb concentration, the 1988 Chave Hermitage exhibits more astringent, tougher tannin than either the 1989 or 1990. While it appears more structured, it has nowhere near the weight and dazzling opulence of its two younger siblings. Nevertheless, this is a superb Hermitage. Anticipated maturity: now–2020.

1985 Hermitage

RATING: 91 points

Chave produced the best red Hermitage of this vintage. Yet for Chave, 1985 was not a year he cares to remember. Holding back the tears, he sadly states that his beloved mother, as well as his faithful sidekick, his dog, passed away that year. A sentimentalist, Chave is likely to put a little of this vintage into the huge reservoir of old vintages that his family has faithfully cellared throughout this century. His 1985 avoided the over-supple style of some of the other reds of this vintage. The wine's deep ruby color exhibits some lightening at the edge. The intense fragrance of smoked meat, cassis, and Provençal olives is followed by a rich, full-bodied, velvety-textured wine that is just beginning to reach its apogee. Anticipated maturity: now–2012.

1983 Hermitage

RATING: 93 points

Chave has always loved the 1983, a sentiment I share, but the tannin in the wine is worrisome. It seems to me that his 1983 has the potential to be super, but it still remains charmless and austere. Deep, dark ruby in color with some amber at the edge, it has a profound concentration of ripe, smoky, berry fruit and Asian spices, full body, exceptional depth and length, as well as a formidable tannin level. Anticipated maturity: now–2025.

1982 Hermitage

RATING: 93 points

Like many of Chave's wines, the 1982 has gotten deeper and richer in the bottle after starting life a little diffuse and awkward. Fully mature, it offers a rich, silky palate with gobs of fruit, and unmistakable aromas and flavors of jammy berries, smoked barbecue, tar, and saddle leather. This is one of the most delicious Chave Hermitages to drink. Anticipated maturity: now–2008.

1978 Hermitage

RATING: 96 points

This has always been one of Chave's single greatest vintages, possibly equaled in recent years by 1989, 1991, 1994, and 1995, and possibly surpassed by 1990. Memorizing its aromas, its flavors, its texture, and its length is a quick education in what great wine is all about. Still an infant, with a murky, dark ruby/garnet color, this wine offers a smoky, tar, cassis, herb, and grilled meat set of aromatics, huge body, and mouth-searing tannin. When last tasted in 1995 it was still a very youthful wine—after nearly two decades of cellaring! Anticipated maturity: now–2025.

HERMITAGE BLANC

2003 Hermitage Blanc

RATING: 94–98 points

This is unbelievably the greatest white Hermitage I have ever tasted at Chave, and even both Gérard and Jean-Louis Chave told me they were actually having to rethink everything that centuries of the Chave family have learned about winemaking. Tasting the three major components that will be blended together, Péleat, Rocoules, and L'Hermite, the wine, made from yields of 10–15 hectoliters per hectare and with a minimum of 16% natural alcohol, has extraordinary richness, with the wonderful gun flint, *goût du pétrol,* that sometimes appears in certain Alsace Rieslings, tremendous buttery, unctuous texture, yet remarkable freshness and vivaciousness. The Chaves were saying there is virtually no acidity in the finished wine analytically, yet the wine tastes as if it has good acidity. The only explanation would be *terroir* and extremely old vines and tiny yields, because this is a wine of extraordinary extraction. Who knows how it will age, but Chave tends to think this is probably like the great 1929 his ancestors produced, a wine of enormous richness, high alcohol, but virtually no acidity. It will be fascinating to follow. Anticipated maturity: now–2025.

2001 Hermitage Blanc

RATING: 93 points

I tasted component parts of the 2001 Hermitage Blanc. Aromas of acacia flowers, honeysuckle, and citrus were followed by a medium to full–bodied white with loads of glycerin as well as heady fruit and alcohol. Elegant and crisper, it is more obviously backward than the 2000. Anticipated maturity: now–2017.

2000 Hermitage Blanc

RATING: 95 points

A 1,000-case blend of 80% Marsanne and 20% Roussanne, the profound 2000 Hermitage Blanc boasts a terrific perfume of honeysuckle, white flowers, peaches, citrus, and minerals. Displaying an unctuous texture along with tremendous glycerin, richness, and depth, it will undoubtedly close down after a few years in the bottle, but for now, it is a spectacularly rich, multidimensional white Hermitage to drink young, then forget about for 5–10 years, after which it will last for 15–20 years.

1999 Hermitage Blanc

RATING: 94 points

The 1999 Hermitage Blanc is a glorious effort. It is a 1,000-case blend of 80% Marsanne and 20% Roussanne, all from Les Rocoules, Maison Blanche, L'Ermite, and Péleat. It is an oily, unctuously textured wine with low acidity and fabulous, concentrated honeysuckle, citrus, liquid mineral, and acacia flower–like flavors. The finish lasts for nearly 45 seconds. It will be gorgeous young but evolve for two decades or more.

1998 Hermitage Blanc

RATING: 92 points

A retasting of the 1998 Hermitage Blanc confirmed its brilliant quality. It is an elegant, floral-scented, structured white Hermitage. It boasts fabulous concentration, but is less flattering and precocious than either the 1999 or 2000. If the latter two wines lean toward a flamboyant style, the 1998 should prove to be one of the more muscular, long-lived, backward efforts requiring patience. Anticipated maturity: now–2015.

1997 Hermitage Blanc

RATING: 94 points

One of my favorite white Hermitages to drink now is the 1997, which has much in common with the 2000. It is an unctuously textured, full-bodied white with an evolved personality. However, there is no doubting its user-friendly, forward style or honeyed character.

1996 Hermitage Blanc

RATING: 93 points

The bottled 1996 Hermitage white is sensational. It is a powerful, heady, alcoholic, deep, chewy, superb white Hermitage offering notes of grilled nuts; sherry fino-like scents; thick, juicy, honeyed citrus; and a touch of peach and roses. Structured and powerful, it should have considerable longevity. Anticipated maturity: now–2025.

1995 Hermitage Blanc

RATING: 94 points

The 1995 white Hermitage had been assembled when I visited in 1997 and was awaiting bottling. The wine is low in acidity, but fabulously rich, with an extraordinary floral, honeysuckle, peach-like fruit character. With awesome intensity and an unctuous texture, this may be the finest white Hermitage Chave has ever produced. It is powerful and extremely showy

at present. Given its equilibrium and overall density, this wine should last 20+ years. Chave said the yields were a minuscule 20 hectoliters per hectare in 1995, versus 30 hectoliters per hectare in 1996 (about one-half the yield of most top white Burgundy producers' Chardonnay vineyards).

Chave's white wine always went through full malolactic fermentation, but now there is *bâtonnage* (stirring the lees), as well as more barrel fermentation and a greater percentage of new oak. I have always loved Chave's white Hermitage, and have been buying it consistently since the 1978 vintage. However, I must say that if the 1994 signaled a new level of quality, the 1995 and 1996 continue that, with both vintages producing blockbuster white Hermitages that possess the texture of a great white Burgundy, in addition to extraordinary intensity and richness. Americans have never taken a liking to white Hermitage, but it ages as well as the red, and if you do not drink it during the first 2–3 years after the vintage, it is best to wait for two decades to consume it, as it goes through a long, stubborn, dumb period.

1994 Hermitage Blanc

RATING: 94 points

The 1994 white Hermitage is one of the most seductive, perfumed, multilayered, and profoundly textured white Hermitages I have tasted from Chave. The unctuous texture and superb nose of honeyed white flowers and minerals are followed by a wine of exceptional depth, richness, and balance. Anticipated maturity: now–2015.

1991 Hermitage Blanc

RATING: 90 points

The fat, rich 1991 Hermitage Blanc offers a big, juicy nose of acacia flowers and honeyed fruit, medium to full body, and loads of flavor. While it is not as broadly flavored or as powerful as the 1990 and 1989, it is a delicious, well-made, excellent example of white Hermitage. Anticipated maturity: now.

1990 Hermitage Blanc

RATING: 92 points

This bold, rich, powerful wine exhibits a floral, honeyed, apricot, fig, and roasted nut–scented nose. It has considerable size, as well as copious fat and fruit. Still approachable, this full-bodied, rich wine is a candidate for several decades of cellaring. It had not begun to close up when last tasted. Anticipated maturity: now–2015.

1989 Hermitage Blanc

RATING: 92 points

The 1989 Hermitage Blanc is low in acidity, expansive, and weighty, and makes for a huge, chewy mouthful of white wine. The honeyed, somewhat unctuous personality of the wine is more dominant in the 1989 than in the 1988, but there remains the head-turning, beautiful, flowery aromas, sensational concentration, super ripeness, and low acidity. Chave believes the latter component is always a characteristic of the greatest Hermitage vintages. Anticipated maturity: now–2015.

HERMITAGE CUVEE CATHELIN

2000 Hermitage Cuvée Cathelin
RATING: 91+ points
The 2000 Hermitage Cuvée Cathelin is very limited and very closed. At present I actually prefer the classical *cuvée,* but this wine is every bit as concentrated—it just seems very high in tannin, backward, and in need of a good 7–10 years of cellaring. It should round into shape with considerable aeration, but the only day I was able to taste it from bottle, it was quite shut down and closed but very promising. Anticipated maturity: 2011–2030+.

1998 Hermitage Cuvée Cathelin
RATING: 98 points
The opaque black/purple–colored 1998 Hermitage Cuvée Cathelin (200 cases) offers a huge nose of smoked licorice, blackberry, cassis, new saddle leather, and vanilla. Tasting like liqueur of Syrah, it is extremely full-bodied and awesomely concentrated, with formidable tannin as well as mind-blowing levels of extract and density. The tannin is sweet, and the wine seamless for a young Chave Hermitage. Anticipated maturity: 2010–2040.

1995 Hermitage Cuvée Cathelin
RATING: 95+ points
A very firmly structured, totally closed style of wine, this deep ruby/purple wine has an enormously promising nose of cassis, licorice, and truffle. It is medium to full–bodied with a hint of new oak, high concentration, and equally high tannins. Patience is mandatory. Anticipated maturity: 2012–2025.

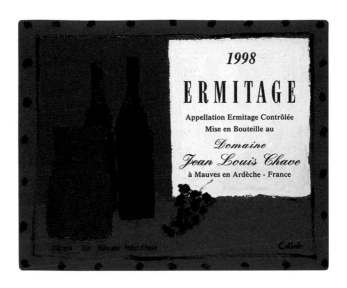

1991 Hermitage Cuvée Cathelin
RATING: 98 points
In 1991, Chave made 2,500 bottles of a Hermitage Cuvée Cathelin that is significantly richer and more profound than the classic *cuvée.* It offers an opaque dark purple color, and a huge nose of cassis, vanilla, smoke, and flowers. Full-bodied, dense, and powerful, this is a deeply concentrated, rich, compelling bottle of Hermitage. Anticipated maturity: now–2025.

1990 Hermitage Cuvée Cathelin
RATING: 100 points
The Cuvée Cathelin, more influenced by new oak than the classic *cuvée,* is a prodigious wine. Remarkably, the new oak takes a back seat to the wine's superb raw materials. The wine exhibits fabulous concentration, richness, intensity, and length, as well as a mind-boggling finish. It is not superior to the classic *cuvée,* just different. The Cuvée Cathelin possesses more of an international new oak signature, but awesome extract and potential. The 1990 Cuvée Cathelin should not be drunk for 10–15 years; it has the potential to last for 30–50 years!

WINES:

Châteauneuf-du-Pape

Châteauneuf-du-Pape La Cuvée du Papet

Classification: AOC Châteauneuf-du-Pape / AOC Côtes du
Rhône (SCEA Clos du Mont-Olivet)

OWNER: Sabon family

ADDRESS: 15, avenue St.-Joseph, 84230 Châteauneuf-du-Pape,
France

TELEPHONE: 33 04 90 83 72 46

TELEFAX: 33 04 90 83 51 75

E-MAIL: clos.montolivet@wanadoo.fr

VISITING POLICY: Cellar Door Sales: Chemin du Bois de la
Ville, 84230 Châteauneuf-du-Pape, from Monday to
Thursday, 8 A.M.–noon, Friday, 8 A.M.–noon, 2–5 P.M.
On Saturday or if you want to meet the owners, by
appointment.

VINEYARDS

SURFACE AREA: Châteauneuf-du-Pape—62 acres

GRAPE VARIETALS:

Châteauneuf-du-Pape: *Red*—Grenache, Syrah, Mourvèdre,
Cinsault, others; *White*—Clairette, Bourboulenc,
Roussanne, Grenache Blanc

AVERAGE AGE OF THE VINES: *Red*—60+ years; *White*—50 years;
Cuvée du Papet—60–80 years

DENSITY OF PLANTATION: 3,200–3,500 stocks per hectare

AVERAGE YIELDS: Châteauneuf-du-Pape—32 hectoliters per
hectare

WINEMAKING AND UPBRINGING

The red winemaking is very traditional. The Syrah, the
Mourvèdre, and some young Grenache are now destemmed.
During the fermentation, the temperature is controlled
around 30°C. There is significant pumping-over. After malolactic fermentation, the wine spends a few months in cement
vats, then is blended and spends at least 10 months in neutral
wood casks.

ANNUAL PRODUCTION

Clos du Mont-Olivet Red: 70,000 bottles

Cuvée du Papet: 10,000 bottles

AVERAGE PRICE (VARIABLE DEPENDING ON VINTAGE): $50–125

GREAT RECENT VINTAGES

2003, 2000, 1998, 1995, 1990, 1989, 1988, 1985

The pioneer of the estate is Seraphin Sabon, who
moved to Châteauneuf-du-Pape when he married a
girl from the village. He started working in his father-in-
law's vineyard and created the Clos du Mont-Olivet in
1932. His son Joseph took over and had three sons, Jean-
Claude, Pierre, and Bernard, all of whom are in charge
of the estate. (Joseph died on the 4th of July, 2002.)

The Clos du Mont-Olivet is one of the very best
Châteauneuf-du-Papes. They produce a splendidly rich,
old-style Châteauneuf-du-Pape from ancient vines (an
average age of 60 years) grown on 62 acres of vineyards.
Another 19 acres of Côtes du Rhône (near Bollène) is
also farmed by the Sabon brothers. As for the red, my
only criticism of the Sabons is their practice of "bottling upon ordering," meaning that the same vintages
may spend different amounts of time in the large oak
foudres, depending on the level of demand. The 1978
was bottled over a period of eight years! Lest anyone
think I do not understand the difficulty for small domaines that have neither the financial capacity nor the
space to buy all the corks, labels, and bottles to do one
bottling, it is incumbent upon the powers that be in
Châteauneuf-du-Pape to recognize that this issue needs
to be resolved. Given the potential for exquisite wines in
this appellation, it is a shame that the French government and producers have not allocated enough resources to provide a solution to this problem. Still, I
believe if consumers purchase the early bottlings, truly
remarkable wines can emerge in Sabon's great years,
such as 1957, 1967, 1970, 1971, 1976, 1978, 1979, 1985,
1988, 1989, 1990, 1995, 1998, 2000, and 2003. The
wines of this estate will keep a good 10–15+ years in the
top vintages, even longer in great years such as 1978,
1989, 1990, 1998, 2000, and 2003.

The Sabons can boast four generations of winemakers. The name Mont-Olivet comes from a notary
public who owned a vineyard of the same name in 1547.
The morsellated vineyard parcels are almost all on
clay/limestone-based soil with a rocky carpet. The top
parcels are in the north, the eastern sector, and in the
southern section near the *lieu-dit* Les Gallimardes. The
"clos" of Mont-Olivet is a specific vineyard of nearly 20

acres, all on the plateau just north of Domaine La Solitude. From this parcel of old vines, the Sabons produce their famed Cuvée du Papet (named after the grandfather Seraphin). The Cuvée du Papet was only produced in 1989, 1990, 1998, 2000, and 2003, and as the tasting notes that follow enthusiastically attest, it is an exquisite wine. Approximately 600 cases were made.

The Sabons—father and sons

CHATEAUNEUF-DU-PAPE

2003 Châteauneuf-du-Pape

RATING: 92–95 points

A very classic Provençal nose of resiny notes intermixed with ground pepper, *garrigue,* balsam wood, and sweet and sour cherries is backed up by a fleshy, sexy, full-bodied wine with very low acidity, high glycerin and alcohol, and a lush, forward personality. It should drink well for 12–15 years.

2000 Châteauneuf-du-Pape

RATING: 90 points

Surprisingly, the 2000 Châteauneuf-du-Pape is firmer-styled than the 2001, with a salty, sea breeze, iodine, *garrigue,* pepper, and kirsch–scented nose. This traditional Châteauneuf possesses medium to full body, outstanding density, admirable ripeness, and moderate tannin. Enjoy it between now and 2015.

1995 Châteauneuf-du-Pape

RATING: 90 points

The 1995 Châteauneuf-du-Pape reveals a deep ruby color with purple nuances. A sexy, ripe wine, it offers up aromas of kirsch, black raspberries, and pepper, along with fine glycerin and moderate tannin. It is not massive or huge, nor does it possess the rustic tannin that characterizes some years of Clos du Mont-Olivet. Rather, it is lush, full-bodied, forward, round, and concentrated. This delicious Châteauneuf will provide ideal drinking between now and 2016.

1994 Châteauneuf-du-Pape

RATING: 91 points

The 1994 Châteauneuf-du-Pape is one of the top wines of the vintage. Dark ruby/purple–colored, it exhibits a textbook Châteauneuf-du-Pape bouquet of black olives, salty sea breezes, *garrigue,* and masses of black cherry/plum-like fruit. Extremely full-bodied, with high extraction, admirable glycerin, a dense, supple attack, and a chewy mid-palate, this is a layered, concentrated, impressively long Châteauneuf-du-Pape. Anticipated maturity: now–2007.

1990 Châteauneuf-du-Pape

RATING: 90 points

The 1990 is a highly concentrated, backstrapping, muscular, big wine. The color is a dark ruby/purple. With swirling, a spicy, peppery nose of *herbes de Provence* and cassis fruit is apparent. Full-bodied and impressively endowed, this large-scaled wine is just beginning to shed its cloak of tannin. Anticipated maturity: now–2010.

1989 Châteauneuf-du-Pape

RATING: 90 points

Lovers of Châteauneuf-du-Pape will have immense pleasure comparing Clos du Mont-Olivet's 1989 and 1990. The 1989 has begun to close down, but it is a beautifully made, intense, full-bodied wine with some of the Provençal *garrigue* character, along with smoke, jammy black cherries, and dusty tannin. The wine is full-bodied and highly extracted, with plenty of purity, richness, and length. It reveals more delineation with perhaps less jamminess when compared to the 1990, but this is splitting hairs. Anticipated maturity: now–2012.

1988 Châteauneuf-du-Pape

RATING: 90 points

The 1988 has a super bouquet of Asian spices, black cherries, cedar, chocolate, and coffee. It is extremely full-bodied, and possibly as concentrated as the 1989 and 1990. With intense, rich, wonderfully pure fruit, this wine is well balanced and impressive. Anticipated maturity: now–2008.

CHATEAUNEUF-DU-PAPE LA CUVÉE DU PAPET

2003 Châteauneuf-du-Pape La Cuvée du Papet
RATING: 92–95 points

The best Cuvée du Papet since the 1998, this wine shows powerful kirsch notes that emerge from its dark ruby/plum color. Sweet, full-bodied, expansive flavors show great fruit; broad, heady levels of alcohol and glycerin; plenty of *garrigue;* spice box; pepper; and earth. This is quite a full-throttle wine that finished with some noticeably firm tannins. Anticipated maturity: 2007–2020.

2000 Châteauneuf-du-Pape La Cuvée du Papet
RATING: 92 points

The 2000 Châteauneuf-du-Pape La Cuvée du Papet boasts a dense plum/purple color as well as a sweet bouquet of balsam wood, dried herbs, black cherries, currants, plums, and figs. Full-bodied, powerful, and tannic, it is not a Châteauneuf-du-Pape for those wanting immediate gratification, as it requires 3–5 years of cellaring. I am not convinced it is as profound as the 1998 or 1990, but it is a top-flight effort that should age for two decades. Anticipated maturity: now–2020.

1998 Châteauneuf-du-Pape La Cuvée du Papet
RATING: 95 points

A wine I underestimated post-bottling, this wine has put on weight and developed an intoxicating perfume of balsam wood, pepper, kirsch, and tobacco. Thick, unctuously textured, full-bodied, and gorgeously pure, it is more evolved than expected, but there is no doubting this Châteauneuf will drink well for more than a decade. It is still slightly behind the otherworldly qualities of the 1990 Cuvée du Papet. Anticipated maturity: now–2018.

1990 Châteauneuf-du-Pape La Cuvée du Papet
RATING: 98 points

This wine's evolution has been surprising. Believe me, if I had known it was going to develop into a nearly perfect wine, I would have bought more. The dark ruby color reveals slight lightening at the edge. Stunning aromatics offer up classic Châteauneuf-du-Pape aromas of balsam wood, *garrigue,* kirsch, blackberries, and pepper. An extraordinarily voluptuously textured effort, with layers of concentration, no sense of heaviness, mouth-staining levels of richness, and more than 14.5% alcohol, this astonishing wine proves what old-vine Grenache can achieve. Given its vigor, exuberance, and extraordinary richness, this wine has remarkable freshness for such size and power. It will drink well for another 10–15+ years.

1989 Châteauneuf-du-Pape La Cuvée du Papet
RATING: 94 points

The 1989 Cuvée du Papet offers up huge aromas of Provençal herbs, roasted nuts, and sweet, jammy, exotic fruits. In the mouth its decadence and opulence must be tasted to be believed. This unctuous, wonderfully rich wine makes for splendid drinking at present, but it promises to be even better with bottle age. It is an astonishing, old-style, traditionally made Châteauneuf-du-Pape, the likes of which are rarely seen in today's high-tech world where wines are so often made within strictly formulated parameters. Anticipated maturity: now–2020.

WINE: Châteauneuf-du-Pape

OWNER: Paul Avril family

ADDRESS: 13, avenue Pierre de Luxembourg, 84230 Châteauneuf-du-Pape, France

TELEPHONE: 33 04 90 83 70 13

TELEFAX: 33 04 90 83 50 87

E-MAIL: clos-des-papes@clos-des-papes.com

WEBSITE: http://www.clos-des-papes.fr

CONTACT: Paul-Vincent Avril

VISITING POLICY: By appointment only

VINEYARDS

SURFACE AREA: 35 hectares of Châteauneuf-du-Pape (10% white); 5 hectares of *vin de table (petit vin d'avril)*

GRAPE VARIETALS:

Red—65% Grenache, 20% Mourvèdre, 10% Syrah, 5% other

White—Same percentage of all six *cépages blanc*

AVERAGE AGE OF THE VINES: 40 years

DENSITY OF PLANTATION: 3,300 vines per hectare

AVERAGE YIELDS: 28 hectoliters per hectare for the last 10 vintages

WINEMAKING AND UPBRINGING

The objective is the maximum expression of *terroir*. Fermentations and macerations, in large vats, usually take three weeks. The wines spend most of their early life in tank, and then in late spring after the vintage, they are moved to large wood *foudres*. After 14–15 months, the wines are assembled and bottled without filtration.

ANNUAL PRODUCTION

Clos des Papes (red): 100,000 bottles

AVERAGE PRICE (VARIABLE DEPENDING ON VINTAGE): $45–60

GREATEST RECENT VINTAGES

2003, 2001, 2000, 1999, 1998, 1995, 1993, 1990, 1989, 1988, 1985, 1981, 1979, 1978

The Avril family has been making wine in Châteauneuf-du-Pape since the beginning of the 18th century. The current master of ceremonies is Paul Avril, now aided by his talented son, Vincent. Clos des Papes has always been considered one of the appellation's reference-point wines. Sometimes such a reputation does not mesh with one's tasting experiences, but the Clos des Papes wines are brilliant. Moreover, Paul, Vincent, and Madame Avril are three of the most generous and gracious vignerons in the southern Rhône. This is an estate that visitors to the region should not hesitate to visit, not only for the quality wines, but for the warm welcome extended by the Avrils.

The estate's name derives from the vineyard's name, which was once part of the old papal vineyard located within the walls of what is now a ruined château. The other 17 parcels are spread out over the entire Châteauneuf-du-Pape appellation, from the sandy soils to the west and southeast, to the rocky plateau limestone/clay soils of the north and northeast. Paul Avril has gradually decreased the amount of Grenache in his blend, while increasing the Syrah and Mourvèdre. In principle, the wine is largely made of Grenache, Syrah, and Mourvèdre, but this is one estate that has other plantations, particularly Muscardin, Counoise, and Vaccarèse. A dollop of each of these varietals is usually included in the blend. Vinification is traditional, and, since the mid-1990s, the Avrils have destemmed all the red

Paul and Vincent Avril

grapes, although flexibility is the operative mode of action at this estate.

Only one red and one white wine are produced, as the Avrils do not believe in making a luxury *cuvée*, saying that anything of lesser quality is sold in bulk to *négociants*. The wines, which were always bottled without fining or filtration, did go through both of these processes in the early and mid-1980s. The Avrils were disappointed by the results and abandoned filtration starting with the 1988 vintage. Generally they do not even fine the wine if it does not taste too tannic, and the red wine has always been one of the finest of the appellation.

Clos des Papes is one of the few Châteauneuf-du-Papes that is rarely flattering to drink young, with most top vintages needing 5–8 years to blossom. Not surprisingly, Clos des Papes is one of the appellation's longest-lived wines—a wine for passionate amateurs of Châteauneuf-du-Pape.

CHATEAUNEUF-DU-PAPE

2003 Châteauneuf-du-Pape

RATING: 96–98 points

This will undeniably turn out to be one of the most profound wines made at this great estate. The early harvest, among the earliest ever recorded, produced a very powerful, concentrated wine (yields were 24 hectoliters per hectare and the average degree of alcohol 15%). This blend of 65% Grenache, 20% Mourvèdre, 10% Syrah, and the rest Counoise and Muscardin is quite stunning and spiritually made along the lines of the great 1990. Deep ruby/purple to the rim with a gorgeous nose of black fruits, flowers, a hint of raspberry, fig, plum, as well as licorice, in the mouth the wine is extremely full-bodied, very large-scaled, but has remarkable freshness

and definition with some firm but sweet tannin in the finish. Very long, concentrated, and massive, this wine will benefit from 2–3 years of cellaring and should drink well for up to two decades. This is a very great Clos des Papes.

2001 Châteauneuf-du-Pape

RATING: 95 points

Paul Avril feels that purchasers of the 2001 Châteauneuf-du-Pape should "wait ten years" before drinking it. A blend of 65% Grenache, 20% Mourvèdre, 10% Syrah, and 5% Counoise, all aged in large wood *foudres* prior to being bottled without filtration, was produced from low yields of 27 hectoliters per hectare. A deep ruby/purple color is accompanied by a sweet bouquet of figs, raspberries, new saddle leather, autumnal forest floor, and resiny notes. Full-bodied with beautiful purity as well as a strikingly rich mouth-feel, this seriously endowed Châteauneuf admirably conceals its 14.5% alcohol. A structured finish and impressive extract levels suggest considerable longevity. This firmly tannic, intensely concentrated 2001 boasts great aromatic and palate presence, but it remains young and unevolved. Anticipated maturity: 2009–2020+.

2000 Châteauneuf-du-Pape

RATING: 95 points

The 2000 Châteauneuf-du-Pape reveals 14.6% alcohol, and is stylistically similar to the great 1990. The 2000 is open-knit and fat, with higher levels of glycerin as well as a more corpulent style than the structured, backward 2001. A deep ruby/purple color is followed by sweet, black cherry/kirsch-like notes presented in a voluptuous, full-throttle, intense style. It is already revealing such secondary nuances as pepper, *garrigue*, and truffles. Chewy, full-bodied, and moderately tannic, this *cuvée* is accessible, but not ready to drink. Anticipated maturity: 2007–2025.

1999 Châteauneuf-du-Pape

RATING: 94 points

While the 1999 performed better than the 1998, it remains firm and closed, offering plenty of sweet kirsch and blackberry fruit, licorice, spice, and floral aromas. Structured, medium to full–bodied, and moderately tannic, it should be at its finest between 2006 and 2020.

1995 Châteauneuf-du-Pape

RATING: 92 points

1995 was a very good, but firmly structured, tannic vintage for nearly all Châteauneuf-du-Pape producers. The wines do not display the generosity of the 1998s or 2000s, but the finest examples are admirably concentrated. Clos des Papes' closed, spicy 1995 exhibits more animal-like notes than the sweeter, more fruit-dominated vintages of 1998, 1999, 2000, and 2001.

Nevertheless, it is big, full, and promising. Anticipated maturity: now–2020.

1990 Châteauneuf-du-Pape

RATING: 96 points

From a fabulous vintage, the 1990 is one of the greatest offerings from Clos des Papes. This was the last vintage vinified with 100% stems, and the result is a full-bodied, opulent, sweet, multidimensional, expansive Châteauneuf-du-Pape. It has hit its plateau of maturity, where it should rest for 10–15 years. Terrific!

1989 Châteauneuf-du-Pape

RATING: 92 points

Like many of the best wines from this vintage, the 1989 remains a big, muscular, virile, closed Châteauneuf boasting an impressive ruby/purple color displaying no signs of degradation. Still young and vibrant, with hints of saddle leather, roasted herbs, licorice, and black fruit, as well as excruciatingly high tannin, this vintage may behave like the 1978. The only concern is when will these wines reach maturity? Anticipated maturity: 2008–2025.

1981 Châteauneuf-du-Pape

RATING: 92 points

Drinking better than ever, the 1981 has blossomed gorgeously in the bottle. A huge nose of sweet red and black fruits, caramel, smoke, roasted herbs, and olives is followed by a full-bodied, flamboyant wine with gobs of fruit. The color remains a youthful deep ruby with no amber at the edge. Powerful, yet elegant and mouth-filling, this is a sumptuous example of Clos des Papes. Anticipated maturity: now.

1978 Châteauneuf-du-Pape

RATING: 99 points

The virtually perfect 1978 still possesses a dark, dense plum/garnet color to the rim. An extraordinary nose of black tea intermixed with licorice, figs, truffles, black currants, and cherries is to die for. The wine is full-bodied and dense, with melted licorice and truffle flavors dominating the palate. Powerful yet harmonious, this is one of the modern-day classics of Châteauneuf-du-Pape. Anticipated maturity: now–2012.

THE RHÔNE VALLEY

Hermitage Les Bessards

Hermitage Marquise de la Tourette

Côte Rôtie La Landonne

OWNER: Champagne Deutz

ADDRESS: Z.A. de l'Olivet, 07300 St.-Jean de Muzols, Tournon
sur Rhône, France

TELEPHONE: 33 04 75 08 60 30

TELEFAX: 33 04 75 08 53 67

E-MAIL: jacques.grange@delas.com

WEBSITE: www.delas.com *(under construction)*

CONTACT: Jacques Grange

VISITING POLICY: By appointment only

VINEYARDS

SURFACE AREA: 34.6 acres

GRAPE VARIETALS: Syrah (100% red); Marsanne (90% white);
Roussanne (10% white)

AVERAGE AGE OF THE VINES: 50–60 years

DENSITY OF PLANTATION: 7,000–8,000 vines per hectare

AVERAGE YIELDS: 30–35 hectoliters per hectare

WINEMAKING AND UPBRINGING

The harvest window is a minimum 12 degrees potential alcohol, 0.50 TA and 3.5 pH, but the significant parameter that determines harvesting time is the taste of the grapes. The entire harvest is hand-picked, so steep are the terraces.

No sulfur dioxide is added to the whole berries due to the pre-cold maceration that the fruit goes through before fermentation.

The Syrah grapes are totally destemmed, then poured by gravity into small concrete tanks of 90 hl capacity, covered by epoxy.

Before starting fermentation, the juices are pre-cold macerated (cold soak) around 15°C for three days. This particular technique dissolves anthocyanins and tannins slowly to stabilize color and to free intracellular components in order to obtain greater texture and flavor. Indigenous yeast is generally used depending on the fruit quality to obtain slower fermentation and get more complexity.

Once the pre-cold maceration is completed, the juices start fermenting at temperatures between 28° and 30°C. Two plungings and pump-overs are applied once a day in order to softly extract tannins and color.

After minimal racking and pressing, the wines usually complete their malolactic fermentation in oak. A few of the wines are matured in a combination of stainless-steel tanks and oak barrels.

The top *cuvées* are bottled without fining or filtering.

ANNUAL PRODUCTION

Hermitage Les Bessards (red): 6,000 bottles

Hermitage Marquise de la Tourette (red): 30,000 bottles

Côte Rôtie La Landonne: 2,500 bottles

AVERAGE PRICE (VARIABLE DEPENDING ON VINTAGE): $75–150

GREAT RECENT VINTAGES

2003, 1999, 1998, 1997

The winery was founded in 1835 when Charles Audibert and Philippe Delas bought "Maison Junique," a 40-year-old winery that they renamed Audibert and Delas. The house's reputation spread quickly worldwide after the winery brought home numerous awards from international competitions, notably a gold medal in Sydney in 1879.

Philippe Delas had two sons, Henri and Florentin. The latter married the daughter of Charles Audibert, further strengthening the bond between the families. In 1924, the brothers succeeded the founders and changed the name of the house to Delas Frères.

After World War II, under Florentin's son Jean, the family house experienced rapid growth. When his son Michel took control of Delas Frères in 1960, the winery had become one of the major houses in the northern Rhône, where it owned and controlled vineyards in Hermitage, Cornas, Côte Rôtie, and Condrieu. In 1977

Michel Delas decided to retire from the wine industry and sold the winery to the Lallier-Deutz family.

In 1981, under the new ownership of Champagne Deutz, the house moved to its current premises in St. Jean de Muzols, a small village located on the outskirts of Tournon, across the river from Tain l'Hermitage. The winery building, set amidst the vineyards of Ste.-Epine, in the heart of the St.-Joseph appellation, covers more than 3,000 square meters.

The Delas wines are crafted by a panel of experts headed by winemaker Jacques Grange, who joined Delas in 1997. Jacques Grange is a *bourguignon* who graduated from the University of Dijon, where he obtained his Diplôme National d'Oenologie in 1988. After four years working for the firm of Chapoutier, he joined Jean-Luc Colombo as a personal assistant. In 1999, Jacques took responsibility for Delas. As a simple but highly dedicated man, he says, "I am *bourguignon* working for a Champagne house in the Rhône Valley."

The winery was updated with enlarged capacity, modern equipment such as a new concrete tank farm, the riddance of old and inadequate oak *foudres,* and the implementation of new barrels and small wood *barriques.*

COTE ROTIE LA LANDONNE

2003 Côte Rôtie La Landonne
RATING: 96–100 points
A very small crop picked at the end of August (unprecedented) produced an inky/purple-colored wine with notes of roasted/scorched earth, graphite, black plums, cassis, and cherries. In the mouth, there is terrific elegance allied to considerable power and brawn. Although this wine was aged in 100% new oak, it has been absorbed completely by the influence of *barriques.* Anticipated maturity: 2008–2020+.

2001 Côte Rôtie La Landonne
RATING: 93 points
The plum/purple-colored 2001 Côte Rôtie La Landonne reveals this vineyard's roasted characteristics in its mineral, Asian spice, licorice, graphite, blackberry, and raspberry-scented and flavored personality. It has an atypical earthy character as well as fine sweetness, ripeness, and considerable aromatic complexity. A medium to full–bodied, long, rich, and impressive wine, it also possesses high tannin in addition to noticeable acidity, suggesting patience will be a virtue. Anticipated maturity: 2009–2020.

1999 Côte Rôtie La Landonne
RATING: 96 points
The limited *cuvée* from the Cote Brune, the 1999 Côte Rôtie La Landonne is prodigious. Readers lucky enough to track down a bottle or two will own a legend in the making. However, another 4–5 years of cellaring are required before this wine rounds into drinkable form. An opaque black/purple color is accompanied by sublime aromas of licorice, espresso, scorched earth, tapenade, bacon fat, and blackberry/cassis. This is a wine of great intensity, explosive richness, and brutally high tannin. This compelling, majestic Côte Rôtie should be at its finest between 2008 and 2025.

1998 Côte Rôtie La Landonne
RATING: 95 points
The opaque black/purple-colored 1998 Côte Rôtie La Landonne offers vanilla, espresso, licorice, blackberry, and cassis scents and flavors with scorched earth and olive notes in the background. Extremely full-bodied, tannic, and monstrous on the palate, it possesses huge ripeness and extraction, as well as mouth-searing levels of tannin. This wine will need another 5–7 years of bottle age; it should drink well for 3–4 decades.

1997 Côte Rôtie La Landonne
RATING: 94 points
Sadly, there are only 2,000 bottles and 150 magnums of the extraordinary 1997 Côte Rôtie La Landonne. Made from 100% Syrah, it boasts a black/purple color as well as a sumptuous nose of roasted meats, black fruits, minerals, scorched earth, and licorice. This superb, fabulously concentrated wine has plenty of sweet tannin in addition to gorgeous layers of fruit and extract. Anticipated maturity: now–2020.

HERMITAGE LES BESSARDS

2003 Hermitage Les Bessards

RATING: 94–96+ points

By the standards of the vintage, the 13.6% alcohol is relatively low for this year in the northern Rhône. This dense, purple-colored wine, made from yields of 20–25 hectoliters per hectare, has a smoky, earthy nose with hints of lard, very pure crème de cassis, and sweet cherries, marvelous integration of wood, low acidity, high tannin, and a very full-bodied, powerful, brawny style that will require 5–10 years of cellaring. Anticipated maturity: 2011–2030.

2001 Hermitage Les Bessards

RATING: 92+ points

Delas's luxury *cuvée* is top-flight, even in the challenging 2001 vintage. The inky-colored 2001 Hermitage Les Bessards boasts pure cassis notes intermixed with hints of licorice and tar. Sweet, ripe, concentrated, full-bodied, and impressively endowed, it is only for readers with cold cellars and considerable discipline, as 5–7 years of cellaring will be warranted. Anticipated maturity: 2010–2035.

2000 Hermitage Les Bessards

RATING: 90 points

The titan of Delas's portfolio is their luxury *cuvée*, Hermitage Les Bessards. The 2000 Hermitage Les Bessards should prove to be outstanding. The color is a deep blue/purple, and the nose offers classic aromas of crème de cassis, melted licorice, and creosote. It is sweet yet unevolved. This medium to full-bodied effort does not have the affliction of many 2000 northern Rhônes, that is a hole in the middle. It is ripe, fleshy, and rich, with moderately high tannin. It will last for about 20 years. Anticipated maturity: 2008–2025.

1999 Hermitage Les Bessards

RATING: 95 points

The compelling 1999 Hermitage Les Bessards exhibits an opaque purple color along with an extraordinary bouquet of blackberry fruit, crème de cassis, creosote, and minerals. The wine is full-bodied, with great purity as well as palate presence. This super-extracted, rich wine is only for those with considerable patience. It reveals considerable structure. Anticipated maturity: 2010–2035.

1998 Hermitage Les Bessards

RATING: 96 points

The 1998 Hermitage Les Bessards reveals licorice, coffee, cassis, minerals, smoke, and meat scents, full body, great depth, teeth-coating tannin, and a persistent, sweet, well-delineated, 45-second finish. It will be at its peak between 2007 and 2035.

1997 Hermitage Les Bessards

RATING: 94 points

The spectacular 1997 Hermitage Les Bessards is a very profound wine. Black/purple-colored, with a spectacular crème de cassis, mineral, spicy new wood, and floral-scented nose, this full-bodied, blockbuster Hermitage possesses a sweet attack (from concentration, glycerin, and extract, not sugar), prodigious concentration and length, and unbelievable potential. This teeth-staining, mouth-coating wine will not hit its prime for another 1–2 years; it will last for 25 years. It is an amazing accomplishment in a vintage such as 1997! Anticipated maturity: 2006–2025.

1991 Hermitage Les Bessards

RATING: 92 points

The 1991 Les Bessards (named after one of the tenderloin vineyards of the great dome of granite—the hill of Hermitage) is an impressive, outstanding wine with a deep purple color, plenty of peppery cassis fruit and minerals in the nose, tightly wound, full-bodied flavors that exhibit terrific extract, and a long, muscular, powerful finish. It should keep for 20–30 years.

1990 Hermitage Les Bessards

RATING: 93 points

The blockbuster, deep purple–colored 1990 Les Bessards is dense and rich, with more opulence and sweetness than the 1991, as well as more power and concentration. Massive and broad-shouldered, this exquisite wine is one of the finest Hermitages I have ever tasted from Delas. Patience is required. Anticipated maturity: now–2030.

HERMITAGE MARQUISE DE LA TOURETTE

2003 Hermitage Marquise de la Tourette

RATING: 92–94 points

A very tannic, powerful, concentrated wine with a black/purple color, a wonderful, sweet nose of smoky cassis and flowers, huge body, wonderful elegance and purity, and a long, concentrated, textured finish. Give this wine 4–5 years of cellaring and drink over the following two decades.

2001 Hermitage Marquise de la Tourette

RATING: 91 points

The 2001 Hermitage Marquise de la Tourette boasts a terrific honeysuckle-scented nose in addition to sweet, spicy, textured notes of rose petals and ripe, buttery fruit presented in a full-bodied, dense, chewy format. This *cuvée* includes both Marsanne and Roussanne in the blend. It will drink well during its first 4–5 years of life, then close down for 5 or so years before reemerging.

2000 Hermitage Marquise de la Tourette

RATING: 90 points

The deep ruby/purple–colored 2000 Hermitage Marquise de la Tourette (which includes the declassified Les Bessards) offers up aromas of crème de cassis, creosote, vanilla, and Asian spices. Dense, rich, and medium to full–bodied, this elegant, finesse-styled Hermitage has taken on more weight as the result of the addition of Les Bessards to the blend. Anticipated maturity: 2006–2017.

1998 Hermitage Marquise de la Tourette

RATING: 92 points

The 1998 Hermitage Marquise de la Tourette exhibits a remarkably huge, chewy mid-palate as well as formidable persistence, but it is very tannic and backward. Readers who are not willing to invest another 5–7 years of cellaring should forget about this wine. Some toasty new oak is present, but the primary characteristic is the layers of black fruits intertwined with minerals.

JEAN-MICHEL GERIN

WINES:

Côte Rôtie Les Grandes Places
Côte Rôtie La Landonne

OWNER: Jean-Michel Gerin

ADDRESS: 19, rue de Montmain-Verenay, 69420 Ampuis, France

TELEPHONE: 33 04 74 56 16 56

TELEFAX: 33 04 74 56 11 37

E-MAIL: gerin.jm@wanadoo.fr

VISITING POLICY: By appointment only

VINEYARDS

SURFACE AREA: Côte Rôtie—17.3 acres; Condrieu—5 acres

GRAPE VARIETALS: Côte Rôtie—90% Syrah, 10% Viognier

AVERAGE AGE OF THE VINES: Côte Rôtie—20–25 years

DENSITY OF PLANTATION: 10,000 vines per hectare

AVERAGE YIELDS:

Côte Rôtie: 37–38 hectoliters per hectare

Condrieu: 34–45 hectoliters per hectare

WINEMAKING AND UPBRINGING

Côte Rôtie—Champin Le Seigneur: 18–20 months in
25% new oak barrels and 75% 1, 2, and 3 years old;
Les Grandes Places: 20 months minimum in 100% new
oak barrels; La Landonne: same as Les Grandes Places

Condrieu—10 months, one-third of yield in new oak and
two-thirds in inox vats

ANNUAL PRODUCTION

Côte Rôtie—Champin Le Seigneur: 25,000 bottles; Les
Grandes Places: 6,000 bottles; La Landonne: 2,000
bottles

AVERAGE PRICE (VARIABLE DEPENDING ON VINTAGE): $50–150

GREAT RECENT VINTAGES

2003, 2001, 2000, 1999, 1998, 1995, 1991

A relatively new estate (created in 1983) with estate-bottling introduced only in 1987, this is one of the success stories of the 1990s. The brilliant Jean-Michel Gerin has propelled his estate into the top echelon of French wine producers. The Gerins have long been growers in Côte Rôtie, and Jean-Michel's father, Alfred, is a well-known political figure in the northern Rhône as a one-time mayor of Ampuis and a legislator in the French government.

Alfred's young, enthusiastic, exuberant son, Jean-Michel, began his own domaine in 1991. He had the intelligence to bring aboard the famed Cornas oenologist Jean-Luc Colombo, and he has been drawing rave reviews for his wines ever since, even after Colombo's departure. There are three *cuvées* of Côte Rôtie produced at this estate. The Champin Le Seigneur, which is made from a blend of parcels with both young and old vines, represents the bulk of Gerin's production. The two luxury *cuvées* are called Les Grandes Places, after the Côte Brune vineyard of the same name, and La Landonne, which made its debut in 1996. It is planted mostly in 80-year-old vines and a handful of younger vines. Unlike his father, Jean-Michel believes new oak casks make a major contribution to the quality of Côte Rôtie. Both top *cuvées* are aged for at least 20 months in 100% new-oak casks, and bottled, like the other *cuvées,* with no filtration.

COTE ROTIE LES GRANDES PLACES

2003 Côte Rôtie Les Grandes Places

RATING: 94–96 points

An astonishing 14% natural alcohol was achieved from this hillside vineyard. Very low acidity gives the wine a voluptuous, very opulent mouth-feel. Notes of raspberry jam intermixed with some flowers and black fruits jump from the glass of this full-bodied, very flamboyant Côte Rôtie. Quite broad, expansive, and very concentrated, with huge levels of extract and glycerin, this is a stunning Côte Rôtie that can be drunk young or cellared for 12–15 years.

2001 Côte Rôtie Les Grandes Places

RATING: 92 points

Fashioned from 100% Syrah, the 2001 Côte Rôtie Les Grandes Places is virile and masculine, offering a dense ruby/purple color as well as a bouquet of roasted earth, licorice, minerals, blackberries, and cassis. Tannic, medium-bodied, and chewy, it requires cellaring. Anticipated maturity: 2007–2016.

2000 Côte Rôtie Les Grandes Places

RATING: 90 points

The 2000 Côte Rôtie Les Grandes Places reveals more graphite, crème de cassis, blackberry, and earthy aromas. With airing, scents of Asian spices and new saddle leather also emerge.

Medium-bodied, structured, tannic, and closed but promising, this 2000 will be at its peak between 2007 and 2015.

1999 Côte Rôtie Les Grandes Places
RATING: 95 points

The sumptuous, profound 1999 Côte Rôtie Les Grandes Places (625 cases) is great stuff in an outrageously ripe, concentrated vintage. A Syrah masterpiece, this opaque purple-colored offering beautifully juxtaposes its muscle, power, and depth with considerable elegance and precision. The tannin is sweet, the acidity adequate, and the wine layered, majestically rich, full-bodied, and moderately tannic. It can be drunk now, but another 1–2 years of cellaring will be beneficial. Anticipated maturity: now–2020.

1998 Côte Rôtie Les Grandes Places
RATING: 91 points

Although tannic, the 1998 Côte Rôtie Les Grandes Places (500 cases produced) is loaded with flavor and potential. From a well-known vineyard on the Côte Brune, this wine was aged in 100% new oak, with malolactic fermentation taking place in barrel. Moreover, it was bottled unfined and unfiltered. A dense ruby/purple color is accompanied by aromas of blackberries, raspberries, cherries, licorice, and charcoal. Dense and full-bodied, with high tannin, it will benefit from a year or two of cellaring, and should keep for 15+ years.

1997 Côte Rôtie Les Grandes Places
RATING: 90–91 points

The splendid 1997 Côte Rôtie Les Grandes Places reveals an impressively saturated opaque purple color. The nose offers up gorgeous quantities of superripe black raspberries, blackberries, toasty oak, smoke, and toast. Expansive and full-bodied, with fabulous concentration, outstanding purity, and low acidity, this is a hedonistic, lush, heady, decadently styled Côte Rôtie to consume over the next 7–10+ years.

1996 Côte Rôtie Les Grandes Places
RATING: 90 points

The 1996 Côte Rôtie Les Grandes Places is concentrated and rich. The wine exhibits a dark ruby color with purple nuances and plenty of toast notes intermixed with blackberry and raspberry fruit. The wine is medium to full–bodied and fleshy, with good acidity, but it is tannin that gives a wine structure and grip as opposed to acidity. Anticipated maturity: now–2012.

1995 Côte Rôtie Les Grandes Places
RATING: 90 points

The superb 1995 Côte Rôtie Les Grandes Places boasts a dense black/ruby/purple color, and a gorgeously fragrant nose of jammy cassis intermixed with smoky, toasty oak, and layers of ripe, concentrated black fruit (primarily black raspberries and cassis). This medium-bodied, concentrated Côte Rôtie has not lost its sense of elegance and overall balance. Anticipated maturity: now–2015.

2003 Côte Rôtie La Landonne

RATING: 94–96 points

A fabulous nose of scorched earth, bacon fat, white flowers, and black fruits jumps from the glass of this brawny, dense, very full-bodied, super-concentrated wine that seems to represent almost the essence of the Syrah grape. Very rich, almost unctuously textured, this is a potential legend in the making. Anticipated maturity: 2008–2022+.

2001 Côte Rôtie La Landonne

RATING: 92 points

Made from 100% Syrah, the 2001 Côte Rôtie La Landonne exhibits a saturated blue/purple color in addition to pure notes of liquefied minerals intermixed with creosote, blackberries, and blueberries. Dense, ripe, peppery, and rich, this is an impressive effort for the vintage, but patience is warranted. Anticipated maturity: 2007–2018.

2000 Côte Rôtie La Landonne

RATING: 91 points

The deep plum/purple–colored 2000 Côte Rôtie La Landonne reveals a great aromatic complexity as well as a large volume and density. Deep, chewy, and medium-bodied, with tremendous purity and ripeness, it exhibits all the scorched earth/black fruit characteristics found in Côte Rôties from the northern sector of the appellation. It also possesses plenty of tannin (sweet), so cellaring is recommended. Anticipated maturity: now–2015.

1999 Côte Rôtie La Landonne

RATING: 94 points

This is a marvelous example of the vintage. It boasts a roasted, meaty, smoky-scented nose with notions of minerals, blackberries, and underbrush. It is full-bodied, thick, and muscular, with superb extraction. This inky/purple-colored wine needs another 2–4 years of cellaring. Anticipated maturity: now–2020.

1998 Côte Rôtie La Landonne

RATING: 91 points

The 1998 Côte Rôtie La Landonne displays an earthy, roasted meat, smoky component reminiscent of baked minerals. Thrilling levels of blackberry and prune-like fruit are found in the bouquet and flavors. Deep, full-bodied, and opulently textured, with the glycerin and concentration concealing lofty tannin, this wine should be at its best between now and 2018.

1997 Côte Rôtie La Landonne

RATING: 90–93 points

The 1997 Côte Rôtie La Landonne boasts a saturated black/purple color, as well as seductive, sweet oak in the aromas that, with airing, becomes increasingly intermixed with plums, blackberries, licorice, and bacon fat. Surprisingly silky and more seductive than I would have expected from this Côte Brune vineyard, this rich, low-acid, concentrated Côte Rôtie should prove to be a head-turner. Anticipated maturity: now–2012.

WINES:

Côte Rôtie Château d'Ampuis

Côte Rôtie La Mouline

Côte Rôtie La Landonne

Côte Rôtie La Turque

Condrieu La Doriane

Ermitage Ex Voto (Red)

Ermitage Ex Voto (White)

OWNER: Guigal family

ADDRESS: Château d'Ampuis, 69420 Ampuis, France

TELEPHONE: 33 04 74 56 10 22

TELEFAX: 33 04 74 56 18 76

E-MAIL: contact@guigal.com

WEBSITE: www.guigal.com

CONTACT: Guigal family

VISITING POLICY: Open from Monday to Friday, 8 A.M.–noon, 2–6 P.M.; tour and tasting by appointment only.

VINEYARDS

SURFACE AREA: 109 acres

Côte Rôtie—49.4 acres

Condrieu—5 acres

Hermitage—10 acres

GRAPE VARIETALS:

Côte Rôtie —Syrah and Viognier

Condrieu—Viognier

Hermitage white—Marsanne and Roussanne

Hermitage red—Syrah

AVERAGE AGE OF THE VINES: Between 25 and 110 years old; 40 years average

DENSITY OF PLANTATION: 10,000 vines per hectare

AVERAGE YIELDS: 33 hectoliters per hectare for vineyards in Côte Rôtie and Condrieu

WINEMAKING AND UPBRINGING

All vineyards are hand-harvested.

The Viogniers (Condrieus) go through a skin contact for about 8–10 hours. They are then pressed with a pneumatic press, and the decantation is done at a low temperature. Alcoholic fermentation takes place in new oak casks or stainless-steel vats. Both are temperature controlled around 16°C, with *bâtonnage* for the part in barrels and malolactic fermentation always occurring.

The Syrah wines are vinified in a traditional way, including *remontage* (pumping-over) and pigéage (punching down). The alcoholic fermentation is done at a high temperature and the vatting lasts between 3 and 4 weeks. The aging is unique, and actually unprecedented—more than 30 months for the Côte Rôtie and Hermitage, 38 months in new oak casks only for the Côte Rôtie Château d'Ampuis, and a whopping 42 months in new oak casks only for the Côte Rôtie La Mouline, La Turque, La Landonne, and the newest luxury wine, the Ermitage Ex Voto.

According to Marcel Guigal, "Only oak can, with constancy and perfection, ensure the subtle interchange which enables wine to develop and improve under the watchful eye of man. Oak alone is capable of enhancing the raw material created from fruit and soil, with delicate hints of wood, vanilla, or choice tannins. Oak reveals the authenticity of wine without ever dominating it, gives it expression while profoundly respecting its balance, origin, and vintage. Day after day the wine is refined, developing and blossoming in the barrels."

ANNUAL PRODUCTION

Côte Rôtie La Mouline: 5,000 bottles

Côte Rôtie La Turque: 4,800 bottles

Côte Rôtie La Landonne: 10,000 bottles

Côte Rôtie Château d'Ampuis: 28,000 bottles

Condrieu La Doriane: 10,000 bottles

Ermitage Ex Voto: 5,000 bottles

AVERAGE PRICE (VARIABLE DEPENDING ON VINTAGE): $25–250

GREAT RECENT VINTAGES

2003, 2001, 1999, 1998, 1995, 1991, 1985, 1983, 1978, 1976

Truly a family enterprise, the Guigal firm, started only in 1946 by Marcel Guigal's father, Etienne, is one of the world's success stories. From this firm's Côtes du Rhône to excellent Châteauneuf-du-Pape, exquisite Condrieu, and mind-boggling reference-point Côte Rôties, there is no winemaker on planet Earth who has produced so many compelling wines irrespective of the vintage conditions as Marcel Guigal. Since I began visiting Guigal annually in the late 1970s, his production must have increased more than fiftyfold, and there have been times when I feared such expansion could not occur without a decline in quality. Yet annual tasting in Guigal's cellars has proved time and time again that my fears have been unfounded. In fact, days of sniffing, swirling, and spitting in the Guigal cellars are among the most memorable and instructive days most wine enthusiasts could spend. The quality and distinctiveness of each of his wines is equaled in few other cellars in the world.

What is the key to Guigal's success? In Guigal's own vineyards, which are cultivated organically with no chemical fertilizers or treatments, there is a notoriously late harvest aimed at picking grapes that are nearly bursting because of their supermaturity. The late harvest, plus extremely low yields and minimal intervention in the wine cellar (minimal rackings and absolutely no filtration), all combine to form spectacularly fragrant, rich, profound wines. The same prerequisites are applicable to the juice that Guigal purchases to fashion his blends of Côtes du Rhône, Hermitage, Condrieu, and Châteauneuf-du-Pape. He buys only from producers who have old vines and low yields and who harvest late.

Marcel Guigal, more than any wine producer I have ever met, believes the genius of his wines is as much in their upbringing as it is in their *terroir*. His father was, as the French say, a gifted *éleveur,* and Marcel, and now his son, Philippe, have translated their understanding of a wine's life in barrel, *foudre,* tank, and vat into high art. The proof is always in the bottle, and at Guigal, the final bottled wine is always significantly better than when tasted from vat, *foudre,* or barrel. The Guigals have always practiced very long aging regimes for their top reds, often going against conventional oenological wisdom, but time and time again, they prove to be the masters.

Whatever Guigal produces, his name will be forever synonymous with the appellation's most riveting examples of Côte Rôtie. Wealthy Rhône wine enthusiasts have been known to do just about everything to try to locate a bottle or two of Guigal's super-rare and expensive single-vineyard Côte Rôtie La Landonne, La Mouline, and La Turque. La Mouline is almost always the first vineyard to be harvested. From a distance, the vines look as if they are sitting in a naturally occurring Roman arena, terraces of vines on concave slopes with a full southerly exposition. That perfect exposure to sunlight ensures that these grapes ripen several days before those of La Turque or La Landonne. Moreover, La Mouline can be harvested in a mere 3–4 hours. Once the grapes are harvested (La Mouline's vines average 60 years of age, and readers should keep in mind that there is about 11% Viognier planted on this small parcel),

La Mouline is given a slow, warm, very long fermentation, but with no punching down of the cap for fear of extracting too much tannin. It is Guigal's goal to make La Mouline the most silky, elegant, and complex of his Côte Rôties, and by regularly pumping the juice gently over the cap he obtains extraordinary concentration, but no rough edges. The first vintage of La Mouline was 1966, but it was not until 1969 and 1976 that this single-vineyard wine became a superstar.

Guigal's second single-vineyard wine is La Landonne, made from a collection of small plots of land on an extremely steep slope located in the northern part of the appellation on the Côte Brune. Guigal began buying small parcels of La Landonne in 1972 and planting them in 1974. La Landonne has a south-southeast orientation, and is usually harvested after La Mouline. In contrast to the vinification of La Mouline, La Landonne is fermented in a closed tank with a system of automatic *pigéage* to extract as much flavor and intensity as possible. There is no Viognier planted in the La Landonne vineyard, and the strong iron content of the soil results in a wine that is among the most concentrated, extracted, and powerful produced in the world.

The last vineyard to be harvested is La Turque, Guigal's youngest vineyard. Situated on a convex slope with a southern orientation, La Turque enjoys sunshine throughout the day. The slope is not nearly as steep as that of La Landonne, and yields tend to be slightly higher, about 35–40 hectoliters per hectare instead of the 25–36 hectoliters at La Mouline and La Landonne. Additionally, slightly higher acidity is noticeable in La Turque, and thus Guigal perennially harvests this vineyard very late in order to have extremely high sugar levels to achieve the right acid balance. La Turque is usually harvested in one day. La Turque receives essentially the same vinification as La Landonne in closed tanks with considerable *pigéage*. Like all Guigal's Côte Rôties, destemming is rarely practiced, although in 1995 Guigal was shocked that the grapes were so physiologically ripe yet the stems were still green and full of acidity. A partial destemming was done in 1995. All three of these *cuvées* are put in 100% new-oak casks and racked two to three times during their first year, and one to two times during the second year. During the third year of upbringing in 100% new-oak casks, there is rarely more than one racking. These wines are bottled after 42 months in new oak barrels, and are neither fined nor filtered. What is so remarkable is that after 3–4 years in bottle, it is almost impossible to tell they were ever aged in new oak, given their extraordinary richness and profound personalities.

What do great vintages of these wines taste like? Looking at my notes over the last 25 years, and extrapolating from the best vintages of these three extraordinary wines, this is what readers might expect:

La Mouline—This is the *cuvée* with the highest percentage of Viognier, which can vary from 8–12% depending on the vintage. It is one of the world's most intensely perfumed wines, offering in the great vintages nearly otherworldly aromas of bacon fat, toast, cassis, white flowers, black raspberries, and occasionally Provençal olives. Because of the Viognier and the vineyard's *terroir,* La Mouline is the most supple and seductive of Guigal's single-vineyard treasures. It is often delicious at birth and continues to offer voluptuously textured, hedonistic drinking for 15–20 years. Only the most tannic and concentrated vintages, such as 1976, 1978, 1983, 1985, 1988, and 1998, produced La Moulines that required cellaring. La Mouline is the Mozart of the Guigal portfolio.

La Landonne—More like Brahms, La Landonne, coming from very steep terraces on the Côte Brune, with its distinctively high iron content, produces a wine of enormous massiveness and concentration. Since there is no Viognier in the blend (this is 100% Syrah), La Landonne is usually the most opaque purple, sometimes almost black, with extraordinary density and power, as well as a brooding backwardness that is extremely impressive, almost intimidating. La Landonne is the most tannic wine made in Côte Rôtie, and as Guigal often claims, it is meant to survive 30–40 years of cellaring. This is clearly a wine for enthusiasts who have both patience and a good, cold cellar, as it usually requires a minimum of 8–10 years of cellaring, even in lighter-weight years. Aromatically and flavor-wise, La Landonne offers much more smoke, licorice, Asian spice, grilled meat, and cassis aromas and flavors.

La Turque—La Turque represents a synthesis in style between La Mouline and La Landonne. It comes from the Côte Brune, but the vineyard is far closer to the Côte Blonde than La Landonne. While it is not as tannic or muscular as La Landonne, it is as concentrated as the latter wine, with nearly the same compelling aromatics as La Mouline. In many respects, it tastes as if it wants to be the Rhône's answer to Burgundy's great duo of grand cru vineyards, Richebourg and Musigny. It usually possesses a saturated dark purple color (darker than La Mouline, but not as opaque as La Landonne), great flavor intensity and extraction, more structure than La Mouline, but not nearly the tannic force and power of La Landonne, with extraordinary density and richness of taste, without any heaviness. Very delicious when released, but less aromatically evolved than La Mouline, it is a wine that should, in top vintages, have 20–25 years of aging potential.

Château d'Ampuis is meant to be well above the quality of Guigal's Brune et Blonde, but without the elevated stature of his three single-vineyard wines. The first vintage was 1995 (coincidentally the first vintage that Marcel Guigal's son, Philippe, did the harvest and assisted his father in the vinification). In tasting through the six vineyards that make up this extraordinary wine, it is obvious that this is going to be one of the finest wines of the appellation. Aged both in barrel and in specially designed *foudres,* it has a character closer to La Turque than La Landonne or La Mouline.

Of the approximately 25,000 cases of wine produced in an average Condrieu harvest, Marcel Guigal accounts for 45% of the appellation's production. In 1986, Guigal was a minor player in Condrieu. But even then he had his eye on the appellation, recognizing the enormous potential and rarity of Condrieu. Since that time, he purchased from Patrice Porte a superb 4.5-acre hillside vineyard from which he produces his luxury *cuvée* La Doriane. Its debut vintage was 1994. Only 500–600 cases of this sumptuous wine from the Côtes Colombier emerge, and there is no likelihood of additional production since this is a single-vineyard *cuvée.* The rest of Guigal's production comes from grapes (not juice) Guigal purchases in his capacity as a *négociant.*

Guigal has pioneered *macération particulaire* (a low-temperature fermentation with the skins of the grapes for 4–8 hours) and full malolactic fermentation for his Condrieu. He also advocates destemming the Viognier to prevent the wine from tasting too acidic or green. The results have been irrefutable—superb wines. The newest superb edition to this portfolio made its

debut in 2003, the Ex Voto, a 4,500-bottle *cuvée* from Guigal's holdings in Hermitage.

As when any person has reached the top of their profession, critics consider it fashionable to be cynical and wait for the empire to tumble. However, I do not believe this will happen as long as Marcel Guigal has control of this firm. With the capable assistance of his wife, and with his son, Philippe—who is beginning to show the dedication, seriousness, and commitment that his father and grandfather have exhibited—the elements for Guigal's continued reign of success remain in place. And one final thought: It would be very easy for someone in Guigal's position to travel in luxury to any exotic location in the world, but this is not part of the man. He is more often at work, getting his hands dirty. I say that one will always eat well in a restaurant where the chef is pale, sweaty, overweight, and sporting a dirty apron. In contrast, there have been only a few times in my life where I have eaten well when the chef was tan and wearing a spotless apron! By analogy, Marcel Guigal is the chef who is always in the kitchen. Sporting his beret, which seems to have been planted on his head, Guigal knows the location of every barrel and *foudre* in his vast underground cellars, and when it was last tasted or racked. In the past 26 years I have spent visiting wineries and vignerons, I have never seen a producer as fanatical about quality as Marcel Guigal.

Marcel Guigal and Philippe

CONDRIEU LA DORIANE

2003 Condrieu La Doriane
RATING: 96 points

This is a tricky vintage to vinify, but Guigal, who harvested these grapes in August, did 100% barrel fermentation as well as lees aging and *bâtonnage*. He normally produces 10,000 bottles of this wine, but in 2003 the production was only 5,000, all from the famed Côte Chatillon. The wine shows tremendous exotic honeysuckle notes along with some lychee, ripe apricot, and pineapple, backed up with striking minerality. The wine is quite intense, very low in acidity, and seems destined to be a vintage to drink in its first several years of life.

2001 Condrieu La Doriane
RATING: 94 points

One of the appellation's most distinctive and complex offerings, it offers up a fragrant perfume of incense, smoke, honeysuckle, and jammy white fruits. Unctuously textured and full-bodied, with tremendous intensity, it should be drunk over the next 1–2 years, although past vintages have held up better in bottle than I predicted. Nevertheless, I prefer these whites in their youth.

1999 Condrieu La Doriane
RATING: 94 points

The 1999 Condrieu La Doriane emerges from Guigal's own vineyard, which he crop-thinned twice to lower yields. A stunning Condrieu, it offers intense aromas of peaches, apricots, and bananas, as well as a long, multilayered, rich, full-bodied palate with exquisite purity and intensity.

COTE ROTIE CHATEAU D'AMPUIS

2003 Côte Rôtie Château d'Ampuis
RATING: 95–97 points

The six components of this wine, all with at least 14% natural alcohol, all scored between 92 and 96 points, so I suspect this is going to be the greatest Château d'Ampuis that Guigal has produced, in keeping with his belief that never in his lifetime has he produced such profound wines as his 2003 Côte Rôties. Very rich, ravishing, concentrated wine with loads of structure but wonderful perfume, enormous concentration, and a somewhat freakishly dense, long finish, this is pretty spectacular stuff that should be relatively approachable when finally released and aged for 15 or more years.

2001 Côte Rôtie Château d'Ampuis
RATING: 94 points

Like many 2001 northern Rhônes in this vintage of tremendous aromatics—although perhaps not with the power and concentration of such great years as 1999 and 2003—beautiful bouquets are followed by wines with gorgeous richness, tremendous definition, and good, fresh, lively acidity. The 2001 Château d'Ampuis shows good weight, full-bodied, concentrated flavors, zesty acidity, and a tremendously evolved, perfumed style that is already showing well. A little bit of Viognier is incorporated into this *cuvée,* and the result in 2001 is a brilliant wine with great aromatics and the potential for up to 15 years of aging.

2000 Côte Rôtie Château d'Ampuis
RATING: 89 points

The light although richly fruity 2000 Côte Rôtie Château d'Ampuis exhibits a telltale toasty, roasted nose revealing aromas of sweet bacon fat, black cherries, and currants. It possesses medium body, soft tannin, and low acidity, but not the volume, depth, or length of its predecessor. Anticipated maturity: now–2010.

1999 Côte Rôtie Château d'Ampuis
RATING: 95 points

The 1999 Côte Rôtie Château d'Ampuis is the finest example yet of this blend fashioned from six hillside vineyards (La Garde, La Clos, La Grande Plantée, La Pommière, Pavillon Rouge, and Le Moulin). The fabulous 1999 boasts a dense ruby/purple color along with a sweet nose of roasted herbs, bacon, licorice, smoke, blackberries, cherry liqueur, and toast. Full-bodied and unctuously textured with hints of new saddle leather, tapenade, and crème de cassis, this large-scaled, well-delineated 1999 should hit its stride in another 3–4 years, and last for two decades.

1998 Côte Rôtie Château d'Ampuis
RATING: 93+ points

The extraordinary 1998 Côte Rôtie Château d'Ampuis is structured, powerful, and concentrated. It is deep ruby/purple with an earthy, smoky nose with bacon fat and black currants, and high tannin. This is unquestionably a vintage for patient connoisseurs, as it requires cellaring. It is dense, chewy, and muscular. This wine will be at its finest between 2007 and 2020.

1997 Côte Rôtie Château d'Ampuis
RATING: 91 points

The 1997 has a dense ruby color followed by gorgeous aromas of chocolate intermixed with road tar, cassis, smoke, and coffee. It is low in acidity, but ripe and concentrated with a voluptuous texture. This stunning Côte Rôtie is more developed and forward than the 1995, 1996, or 1998. Anticipated maturity: now–2018.

1996 Côte Rôtie Château d'Ampuis

RATING: 90 points

The dark ruby/purple color of the 1996 is followed by an intense nose of tapenade, dried herbs, licorice, leather, and black currants. The wine is nicely textured, soft, with less acidity than most 1996 Côte Rôties, and a layered, supple finish. Drink it over the next 7–10 years.

1995 Côte Rôtie Château d'Ampuis

RATING: 92 points

The 1995 Côte Rôtie Château d'Ampuis is a sensational offering. It boasts a dense, saturated deep ruby color, as well as a flamboyant, intense bouquet of crushed pepper, Provençal herbs, black raspberry jam, and smoky sweet oak. The wine is medium to full–bodied, with good underlying acidity, but much more voluptuous and unctuous than it appeared to be from cask. Long, concentrated, and explosively rich, this wine may merit an even higher score after it has had some time to mesh together in bottle. It is a terrific Côte Rôtie to drink over the next 5–10+ years.

COTE ROTIE LA LANDONNE

2003 Côte Rôtie La Landonne

RATING: 98–100 points

Black as midnight oil, this wine, which includes 100% stems, has a nose of roasted meats, blackberry and licorice liqueur, huge vanilla, and toasty, smoky notes. It also has a massive, unctuous texture, and a remarkable, full-bodied, concentrated finish with fabulous purity and length. It is quite an extraordinary wine and easily the biggest of these wines, but all of these 2003 single-vineyard Côte Rôties almost transcend their greatness with this very distinctive and individual vintage. Anticipated maturity: 2012–2040+.

2001 Côte Rôtie La Landonne

RATING: 95+ points

This is a very masculine, formidable wine with smoky dark fruits, a somewhat primordial personality, with good acidity, loads of tannin, huge body, and some hints of espresso, earth, herbs, and spice box. Of course, this is the only one of the single-vineyard Côte Rôties that is never destemmed, so that component gives the wine more tannin, acidity, and sometimes in cooler years such as 2001, a slight underlying note of underbrush. This is quite an intense, expressive wine but needs a good 5–10 years of cellaring. Anticipated maturity: 2011–2028.

2000 Côte Rôtie La Landonne

RATING: 91 points

The 2000 Côte Rôtie La Landonne is the finest of the three La-La's in this vintage. It displays the deepest ruby color as well as a big, earthy, leathery nose offering scents of blackberries, black currants, truffles, licorice, and graphite. Medium to full–bodied and moderately tannic, with more weight and length than its two peers, it will benefit from another 1–2 years of cellaring and drink well for 15 years.

1999 Côte Rôtie La Landonne

RATING: 100 points

I have given perfect scores to other vintages of La Landonne, but the black/purple-colored 1999 Côte Rôtie La Landonne may be the finest effort Guigal has ever coaxed out of this vineyard. It appears less animalistic than usual, offering gorgeously pure notes of incense, melted road tar, fried bacon, blackberries, blueberries, smoked meats, and vanilla. Completely out of this world in terms of flavor concentration and balance, the finish lasts well over 60 seconds. Anticipated maturity: 2007–2030.

1998 Côte Rôtie La Landonne

RATING: 100 points

The 1998 Côte Rôtie La Landonne is a perfect wine . . . at least for my palate. Its saturated black/purple color is accompanied by an extraordinary nose of smoke, incense, tapenade, creosote, blackberry, and currant aromas. It is densely packed with blackberry, truffle, chocolate, and leather-like flavors. The wine possesses high tannin, but perfect harmony, impeccable balance, and gorgeous integration of acidity, alcohol, and tannin. It is a tour de force in winemaking. Anticipated maturity: 2007–2025.

1997 Côte Rôtie La Landonne

RATING: 98 points

The nearly perfect 1997 Côte Rôtie La Landonne is an amazing achievement for the vintage. An astonishing saturated purple color is followed by scents of licorice, roasted meats, coffee, toasty oak, plums, and blackberries. The wine is extremely smoky, earthy, and *terroir*-driven. This 1997 offers exceptional expansiveness on the palate, sweet tannin, low acidity, and a ripe, robust finish. Another year of cellaring is warranted, but it is capable of lasting for two decades.

1996 Côte Rôtie La Landonne

RATING: 93 points

The 1996 Côte Rôtie La Landonne was herbaceous early in life, but is now revealing a black olive/tapenade, melted asphalt character in its smoky, earthy, animal, blackberry, leathery fruit. A masculine, full-bodied offering, it is drinkable now. Anticipated maturity: now–2018.

1995 Côte Rôtie La Landonne

RATING: 95 points

The brawny, black/purple-colored 1995 Côte Rôtie La Landonne reveals the animal, *sauvage* side of the Syrah grape. Licorice, prune, iron, and vitamin-like aromas compete with copious quantities of black fruits and smoke in this complex, structured, muscular, massive Côte Rôtie. It will require another year or two of cellaring, and should keep for 30+ years.

1994 Côte Rôtie La Landonne

RATING: 98 points

The 1994 Côte Rôtie La Landonne, which is more dominated by toasty new oak than the other two crus, is extremely muscular and powerful, with high tannin as well as fabulous extract. The wine reveals a dense black/purple color, and a tight nose with plenty of toast, olive, iron, and black fruit aromas. Anticipated maturity: now–2025.

1991 Côte Rôtie La Landonne

RATING: 99 points

The 1991 La Landonne will provide multimillionaires with plenty of pleasure over the next 20 years. They can also debate whether it or the perfect 1990 is the better wine. The 1991's bouquet offers huge, smoky, new saddle leather, licorice, Asian spice, meaty, and cassis scents. Black in color, with layers of richness, huge body, massive extraction, and a phenomenal finish, it is another legend from Marcel Guigal. It is the least precocious of the 1991s. Anticipated maturity: now–2018.

1990 Côte Rôtie La Landonne

RATING: 96 points

It possesses an opaque black color, and a huge truffle, licorice, cassis, and pepper–scented nose. While it is one of the most concentrated wines I have ever poured across my palate, it is perfectly balanced, with adequate underlying acidity, huge extraction of ripe fruit and tannin, and a phenomenal 70-second or longer finish. This is the essence of Syrah! Anticipated maturity: now–2020.

1989 Côte Rôtie La Landonne

RATING: 98 points

The 1989 single-vineyard Côte Rôties are magnificent. Reminiscent of Guigal's 1985s and 1982s, the black/purple-colored La Landonne possesses fabulous concentration and a sweet, expansive personality. It has plenty of tannin, but there is so much fruit that the tannin is largely concealed. This is another mammoth-sized wine with extraordinary extract. Anticipated a

1988 Côte Rôtie La Landonne

RATING: 100 points

An opaque purple color and a closed but exciting nose of truffles, minerals, Asian spices, and fruitcake characterizes the 1988 Côte Rôtie La Landonne. When the wine hits the mouth with its enormous weight and extraction of flavor, one can't help but be seduced by such enormous richness and purity. Nevertheless, there is still a remarkably high level of tannin (sweet rather than astringent), a youthful, unevolved fruit character, and flavors that stain the palate. After tasting this wine, one feels like brushing one's teeth . . . it is that rich. Anticipated maturity: now–2030.

1987 Côte Rôtie La Landonne

RATING: 96 points

Opaque purple, bordering on black in color, La Landonne's aromatics are the most subdued of the 1987s. Although still closed, this wine is very powerful, rich, thick, and represents the essence of the Syrah grape. That earthy, mineral, truffle, licorice component is just beginning to poke its head through this massively framed wine. It is remarkable that this vintage produced a wine of such extraordinary concentration and richness. Anticipated maturity: now–2020.

1986 Côte Rôtie La Landonne

RATING: 90 points

The 1986 La Landonne is an outstanding wine, though it lacks the magical perfume of La Mouline and the indescribable, riveting character of La Turque. It is more tannic and amply endowed, but among the splendid La Landonnes made during the 1980s, the 1986 does not possess the size or intensity of the greatest vintages. Anticipated maturity: now–2009.

1985 Côte Rôtie La Landonne

RATING: 100 points

Once again the darkest, thickest, most powerful, and formidably concentrated of Guigal's single-vineyard Côte Rôties, the 1985 La Landonne is also the least flattering and most intimidating. Like its two siblings, it is throwing a hefty sediment. The color is still a murky, inky purple. The nose offers up aromas of beef blood, vitamins (iron?), minerals, smoke, and truffles. Extremely thick, full-bodied, and massive, with noticeable tannin, this monster wine reveals no hard edges, but it does possess teeth-staining extract and power. It is a remarkable effort! Anticipated maturity: now–2025.

1983 Côte Rôtie La Landonne

RATING: 98+ points

This murky, purple/garnet-colored wine offers up an exotic nose of tea, smoked duck, licorice, truffles, and earth. Extraordinarily concentrated, and almost too rich to be called a beverage, this viscous, compellingly endowed, massive La Landonne possesses excruciatingly high tannin in the finish, but awesome levels of extract and glycerin. Anticipated maturity: now–2025.

1982 Côte Rôtie La Landonne

RATING: 95 points

For such a precocious vintage, the 1982 La Landonne remains a backward, beefy, smoky, chewy mouthful of tannic wine. It has thrown a huge amount of sediment, and the bottle is completely stained, as if it were a 15-year-old vintage port. The wine reveals an olive, earthy, licorice, mineral, smoked-meat nose, fabulous depth, and a huge, formidably endowed personality. It is monstrous and super-concentrated. Anticipated maturity: now–2025.

1980 Côte Rôtie La Landonne

RATING: 94 points

In contrast to the open-knit, fully mature 1980 La Mouline, the La Landonne is just beginning to open up and reach full maturity. It has thrown plenty of thick sediment, but it retains a dark, murky garnet color. The huge nose of roasted meats, Asian spices, truffles, minerals, and fruitcake is thrilling. Full-bodied, with huge quantities of fruit, and a gamy, rare steak–like taste, this is a thick, masculine, chewy wine that begs to be served with aged beef. Full-bodied and exceptionally concentrated, this is a tour de force for the vintage. Along with La Mouline, it is a candidate for the greatest wine made in France in 1980. Anticipated maturity: now–2010.

1979 Côte Rôtie La Landonne

RATING: 91 points

Surprisingly youthful, with a dark ruby/purple color revealing no signs of age, this wine seems more compact and tightly knit than many vintages of Guigal's Côte Rôties. Full-bodied and powerful, with good acidity and outstanding concentration and extract, this wine has aged at a glacial pace. Although not complex and somewhat monolithic, the 1979 La Landonne is loaded with fruit, glycerin, and body. The balance is there, so perhaps it is just a question of further patience. Anticipated maturity: now–2015.

1978 Côte Rôtie La Landonne

RATING: 96 points

The debut vintage for La Landonne, this formidably endowed, inky-colored monster is just beginning to open up and reveal its personality. As with La Mouline, there is an ounce of sediment in the bottom of the bottle. The color is a thick purple/black/garnet. The nose reveals a smoked meat, grilled steak, earthy, truffle, black-fruit character intermixed with mineral notes. Extremely powerful, rich, slightly tannic

flavors have enormous volume in the mouth. The wine still displays a rustic side to its tannin, but there is no doubting the excessively concentrated, prodigious amount of fruit, extract, glycerin, and character possessed by this wine. Anticipated maturity: now–2020.

COTE ROTIE LA MOULINE

2003 Côte Rôtie La Mouline

RATING: 98–100 points

Over 14% natural alcohol (the highest natural alcohol Guigal has ever produced), this wine is like pure vintage port of Côte Rôtie, somewhat 1999-ish in style but even more powerful and unctuously textured. The wine has a dense, ruby/purple color and an exotic nose of flowers intermixed with black fruits and honeysuckle. Very full-bodied, opulent, and just a complete hedonistic, intellectual turn-on, this looks to be one of the all-time great La Moulines, but unlike Guigal, I'm not ready to say it is better than the colossal 1999 or some of the other previous vintages that have been pure perfection. Given its power, extraordinary extract, and intensity, this wine should evolve for 20–25 years.

2001 Côte Rôtie La Mouline

RATING: 96 points

A beautiful nose of raspberries, sweet, jammy black cherries and currants, along with some exotic lychee and apricot marmalade jumps from the glass of this dense, opulent, full–bodied wine that shows a bit more tannin and structure than most vintages tend to do young. Quite aromatic, medium to full–bodied with good freshness and structure, this is a La Mouline to cellar for 4–5 years and drink over the following two decades.

2000 Côte Rôtie La Mouline

RATING: 90 points

The 2000 Côte Rôtie La Mouline, while lighter than the previous three vintages, possesses a deep ruby color in addition to a sweet perfume of white flowers, licorice, caramel, black raspberries, and currants. It is a medium-bodied, compactly built La Mouline with good fruit, low acidity, and an upfront, forward charm. It should drink well for 8–12 years.

1999 Côte Rôtie La Mouline

RATING: 100 points

The most developed, evolved, and forward of the three La-La's in this vintage is the dense purple–colored 1999 Côte Rôtie La Mouline. An extraordinary effort, it offers a smorgasbord of aromas and flavors. Scents of violets, raspberries, blackberries, roasted espresso, balsamic vinegar, and pepper tumble out of the glass. It is unctuously textured, full-bodied, and fabulously concentrated, with a tremendous purity and seamlessness that must be tasted to be believed. A wine of singular greatness, it can be drunk young, but should be at its finest between now and 2020.

1998 Côte Rôtie La Mouline

RATING: 97 points

The awesome 1998 Côte Rôtie La Mouline is a seamless, full-bodied classic with many characteristics of the 1997 La Landonne, but more structure, tannin, and muscle. It will last for 20 years. Stylistically, it is reminiscent of the 1988.

These tasting notes will not surprise any longtime readers. I have never made a secret of the fact that if I had only one wine left to drink, I would want it to be one of the great vintages of Guigal's Côte Rôtie La Mouline. This wine's aromatic fireworks, sumptuous texture, and seamless personality represent perfection. While the percentage of Viognier blended with Syrah can vary from 8–12%, this remains one of the world's most intensely perfumed and compelling wines, offering up bacon fat, toast, cassis, acacia flower, black raspberry, crème de cassis, and tapenade notes. A voluptuous texture, sweet tannin, and a satiny smooth demeanor are hallmarks of this La Mouline. Anticipated maturity: now–2025.

1997 Côte Rôtie La Mouline

RATING: 96 points

The spectacular, dense ruby/purple–colored 1997 Côte Rôtie La Mouline boasts a complex nose of violets, peaches, and cassis. Soft, voluptuous, medium to full–bodied, and incredibly seductive. Anticipated maturity: now–2015.

1996 Côte Rôtie La Mouline

RATING: 93 points

The 1996 Côte Rôtie La Mouline possesses the highest percentage of Viognier (17–18%) Guigal has ever included in this offering. The deep ruby/purple color is accompanied by a superb bouquet of spice box, cedar, leather, honeysuckle, and jammy black fruits. It is remarkably tender and soft for a vintage that produced high-acid wines. Medium-bodied, elegant, and complex, it is one of the more forward and evolved La Moulines, and thus should be drunk over the next 7–9 years.

1995 Côte Rôtie La Mouline

RATING: 95+ points

The 1995 Côte Rôtie La Mouline offers a compelling perfume as violets, black raspberries, coffee, pepper, and toast soar from the glass. Medium to full–bodied and lush, with a terrific multilayered texture and outstanding purity, this is a phenomenal example of La Mouline. It possesses enough structure and substance to last for two decades, although it will be delicious upon release. Anticipated maturity: now–2020.

1994 Côte Rôtie La Mouline

RATING: 96 points

The 1994 Côte Rôtie La Mouline possesses extraordinary intensity. A dark ruby/purple color is followed by a penetrating nose of sweet black raspberry fruit intertwined with aromas of coconut and apricots. Jammy black fruits continue on the palate of this full-bodied, silky-textured, sumptuously styled wine that is glorious to drink—even from barrel. It is an amazing La Mouline that offers all the elegance, suppleness, and sexiness this cru merits. Anticipated maturity: now–2018.

1991 Côte Rôtie La Mouline

RATING: 100 points

The black/purple-colored 1991 La Mouline appears to be a perfect wine in the making, with a staggering bouquet of violets, bacon fat, sweet cassis fruit, and toasty oak. The wine exhibits superb density. It is tasting even richer and more concentrated than it did during its first several years of life. With 8% Viognier in the blend and made from extremely low yields, it is a phenomenal wine. I find it very seductive. Anticipated maturity: now–2014.

1990 Côte Rôtie La Mouline

RATING: 99 points

The super-concentrated, opaque purple–colored 1990 La Mouline is similar in style to the otherworldly 1988. Extremely rich, with a huge, bacon fat, toasty, cassis, and floral-scented nose, as well as phenomenally rich flavors, it is a wine known for its voluptuousness and extraordinary intensity. Anticipated maturity: now–2018.

1989 Côte Rôtie La Mouline

RATING: 98 points

The saturated purple–colored 1989 La Mouline is an explosively rich wine, with its profound perfume of violets, black raspberries, and creamy, toasty new oak. Very full-bodied, with a dreamy opulence, gobs of fruit, an unctuous texture, and powerful finish, this wine manages to balance intensity with great elegance. Anticipated maturity: now–2016.

1988 Côte Rôtie La Mouline

RATING: 100 points

Among so many exceptional La Moulines, this is among the most profound. At the same time, it is atypically backward and has been slow to evolve. Still dark purple–colored, with only a hint of the flamboyant Mouline aromatics, this thick, super-concentrated, full-bodied, tannic La Mouline is massive and loaded with fruit, but still in need of time to fully shed its cloak of tannin. It is likely to be the longest-lived La Mouline since the 1978 and 1969. Anticipated maturity: now–2015.

1987 Côte Rôtie La Mouline

RATING: 95 points

Guigal's 1987 La Mouline is sensational. Considering the vintage, this must be the greatest wine produced in France in 1987. The color is a youthful purple, and the nose offers up sweet, pure aromas of jammy black raspberries, smoke, and honeysuckle, and vague whiffs of apricots. Thick, rich flavors coat the palate in a seamless, velvety-textured manner. This medium to full–bodied, marvelously concentrated wine has no hard edges, and is the epitome of voluptuousness and sumptuousness. This has been a glorious La Mouline to drink since its birth, and it shows no signs of age. Anticipated maturity: now–2007.

1986 Côte Rôtie La Mouline

RATING: 91 points

The 1986 La Mouline displays its characteristic exotic aroma of smoky oak, bacon fat, and spring flowers, which is followed by layer upon layer of opulent black fruits. The color is still very dark purple, with some lightening at the edge. There is more tannin and olive-flavored fruit than one normally finds in La Mouline. For a difficult vintage, this wine is remarkable. Anticipated maturity: now.

1985 Côte Rôtie La Mouline

RATING: 100 points

One of the all-time great La Moulines, this still youthful and unevolved wine does not have the tannic ferocity of the 1988, or the sheer force and intensity of the 1978, 1976, and 1969, but it represents the epitome of this single-vineyard wine. Everything fits perfectly in this full-bodied, black/purple-colored wine that reveals no garnet or amber at the edge of its color. The nose offers up a formidable array of overripe black raspberries and cherries intertwined with scents of cedar, chocolate, olives, and toast. Extremely full-bodied, with an unctuousness and opulence that must be tasted to be believed, this velvety-textured wine's finish lasts for over a minute. It is one of the most concentrated but profoundly endowed and well-balanced wines I have ever tasted. As with so many of the wines Guigal has produced from this vineyard, no matter how hard one tries to articulate its glories, words are simply inadequate. The 1985 has achieved full maturity. Anticipated maturity: now–2012.

1983 Côte Rôtie La Mouline

RATING: 100 points

Still backward, but beginning to throw considerable sediment and reveal some amber at the edge, this wine reveals a distinctive violet, cassis, bacon-fat aroma intermixed with smoked duck and Asian spice components. Extremely full-bodied and sturdy, with noticeable tannin, this husky, powerful, concentrated La Mouline is less seductive than many vintages. In fact, in 1983, it behaves more like La Landonne. Many 1983s have proven less exciting than initial predictions because of the refusal of the harsh tannins to melt away, but the tannin is clearly falling away in the 1983 La Mouline. There is still a wealth of fruit remaining. Anticipated maturity: now–2020.

1982 Côte Rôtie La Mouline

RATING: 99 points

A fully mature example of La Mouline, the huge, smoky, bacon fat, cassis-scented perfume jumps from the glass of this seductive, hedonistic wine. The 1982 has been delicious from birth due to its low acidity and fat, open-knit character. There is no amber or lightening at the edge of its dark ruby/purple color. The wine exhibits a thick, unctuous texture, gobs of fruit, and plenty of heady alcohol in the blockbuster finish. Anticipated maturity: now–2008.

1980 Côte Rôtie La Mouline

RATING: 94 points

It is hard to believe this wine was aged for three years in new oak casks, given the fact that it no longer exhibits any aromas of toast, vanilla, or smoky new oak. The super-concentration of fruit has simply absorbed the oak, and the result is one of the top wines of the year in France. Still dark ruby/purple/garnet, with a huge smoked-meat and black-raspberry nose, this rich, voluptuous, concentrated wine has reached full maturity, but it promises to last for several decades. A glorious tasting experience. Anticipated maturity: now.

1979 Côte Rôtie La Mouline

RATING: 93 points

This wine continues to turn out better than I imagined. By the standards of La Mouline, it has higher acidity than normal, but that component has served it well, preserving the freshness and guaranteeing a relatively slow evolution. The wine exhibits an intense, gamy, Syrah nose, superrich, ripe flavors, and a full-bodied, long finish. Anticipated maturity: now.

1978 Côte Rôtie La Mouline

RATING: 100 points

I have had this wine more than two dozen times (lucky me), and it is one of the most thrilling wines ever. I loved it when it was an infant, and now that it may, or may not be, fully mature, I still think it is the quintessential expression of Guigal's La Mouline. The color remains an inky garnet, with no perceptible lightening at the edges. The celestial aromas include copious quantities of black raspberries, coconut, smoked duck, Asian spices, and violets. It overloads the olfactory senses. On the palate, this wine reveals unreal concentration, layers of thick, juicy fruit, beautifully integrated acidity and tannin, and a sumptuous finish that lasts for more than a minute. This seamless beauty is one of the greatest wines made in the 20th century. If I were forced to drink just one wine . . . let it be this! Anticipated maturity: now–2015.

1976 Côte Rôtie La Mouline

RATING: 100 points

The 1976 is even thicker, richer, and more jammy than some of the other great vintages of La Mouline. In essence, it is something between a dry red table wine and a vintage port. Of course it is not sweet, but it is so concentrated; one simply does not see wines such as this except for 1947 Pétrus or 1947 Cheval Blanc. The wine has thrown a couple of ounces of sediment. It offers a heavenly bouquet of sweet, floral-infused black raspberry/cassis fruit. Extremely unctuous and viscous, with mind-boggling concentration, this wine has always been exceptional to drink, but it continues to defy the aging curve. I have drunk my last bottle, so I am dependent on friends for future tastings. This is one of the legendary wines of the century! Anticipated maturity: now–2007.

COTE ROTIE LA TURQUE

2003 Côte Rôtie La Turque

RATING: 98–100 points

Black/purple to the rim, with an extraordinary nose of Asian spice, espresso roast, loads of black fruits, lead pencil shavings, and licorice, this wine's awesome texture hides considerable tannin and some powerful alcohol. This is a legendary effort and possibly the greatest La Turque made to date. Its finish goes on, much like La Mouline's, for almost 90 seconds. An amazing wine that is much less evolved than La Mouline but incredibly intense. Anticipated maturity: 2009–2030.

2001 Côte Rôtie La Turque

RATING: 95 points

A very powerful yet at the same time somewhat feminine style of Côte Rôtie with notes of scorched earth, bacon fat, blackberries, and licorice all presented in a relatively muscular, dense, chewy style with considerable tannin, this is a vintage to forget in the cellar for 4–5 years. Anticipated maturity: 2008–2025.

2000 Côte Rôtie La Turque

RATING: 91–93 points

The 2000 Côte Rôtie La Turque exhibits a deeper ruby color than the La Mouline, in addition to more smoke, melted tar, creosote, meat, pepper, incense, and leathery characteristics, medium to full body, and a moderately long finish. Consumption during its first 10–15 years of life is recommended.

1999 Côte Rôtie La Turque

RATING: 100 points

The 1999 Côte Rôtie La Turque reveals notes of toasty vanilla and espresso in addition to Asian spices, mocha, pepper, blackberries, creosote, and roasted meats. The exotic perfume is followed by a wine with phenomenal intensity, sweet, well-integrated tannin, huge body, and loads of concentrated fruit. It is a tour de force in winemaking. Anticipated maturity: 2006–2025.

1998 Côte Rôtie La Turque

RATING: 98 points

The 1998 Côte Rôtie La Turque may end up being a perfect wine. Its smoky black fruits intermixed with licorice, roasted meats, cassis, and flowers create an explosive, exotic perfume. The wine reveals considerable tannin, immense structure, and potentially legendary depth as well as intensity. Anticipated maturity: now–2022.

1997 Côte Rôtie La Turque

RATING: 96 points

The dense purple–colored, profound 1997 Côte Rôtie La Turque (5–7% Viognier added to the blend) offers crème de cassis, licorice, and espresso aromas as well as notions of melted asphalt. Compared to La Mouline, it has additional layers as well as structure, sweet tannin, and exhilarating levels of opulence and ripe fruit. Anticipated maturity: now–2018.

1996 Côte Rôtie La Turque

RATING: 95 points

The 1996 Côte Rôtie La Turque possesses a dark, saturated ruby/purple color, aromas of caramel, vanilla, and smoked cherry jam, medium to full body, outstanding ripeness, a plush, surprisingly soft finish, and loads of glycerin. This effort should be drunk over the next 9–12 years.

1995 Côte Rôtie La Turque

RATING: 98 points

The 1995 Côte Rôtie La Turque (about 7% Viognier in the blend) possesses a dense ruby/purple color, and roasted herb, olive, and Asian spice characteristics. It exhibits exceptional concentration and is velvety and concentrated. The fabulous 1995 La Turque is a virtually perfect wine, with flamboyance, harmony, and remarkable opulence and length. Anticipated maturity: 2007–2022.

1994 Côte Rôtie La Turque

RATING: 95 points

The exotic 1994 Côte Rôtie La Turque exhibits a dense purple color, and a fabulously scented nose of licorice, Asian spices, truffles, minerals, and gobs of black fruits. Full-bodied, with great richness, a multilayered personality, and an exotic, over-ripe character, this is a sensational, chocolaty, rich wine with more tannin than La Mouline. Anticipated maturity: now–2020.

1991 Côte Rôtie La Turque

RATING: 99 points

The 1991 La Turque behaves as if it wants to be the northern Rhône's answer to Richebourg and Musigny. However, with the exception of Domaine Leroy, you cannot find a Richebourg or Musigny with the richness and complexity possessed by this awesome wine. The saturated dark purple color is followed by a wine that is surprisingly lighter in the mouth than its great flavor intensity and rich extraction would suggest. It is a winemaking tour de force in that Guigal has been able to cram phenomenal levels of fruit, complexity, and richness into this velvety-textured wine without causing it to taste heavy. Anticipated maturity: now–2015.

1990 Côte Rôtie La Turque

RATING: 98 points

The 1990 La Turque offers an opaque purple color and an overwhelming perfume of jammy black cherries, cassis, toast, and minerals. With its sweet, generous, incredibly harmonious personality, it is an unforgettable wine. With sweet tannin, low acidity, and one of the most velvety-textured, decadently rich palates I have encountered, this fabulous wine has a finish that lasts more than a minute. Anticipated maturity: now–2016.

1989 Côte Rôtie La Turque

RATING: 99 points

The precocious, sweet, jammy 1989 La Turque's smoky, licorice, and black-raspberry aromas, as well as its phenomenal richness, make for another extraordinary tasting experience. Full-bodied, dense, and thick, this wine possesses the essence of black cherries. Still youthful, it is already gorgeous to drink. Anticipated maturity: now–2012.

1988 Côte Rôtie La Turque

RATING: 100 points

Deep purple–colored, with grilled meat and smoky, barbecue-like aromas beginning to emerge, along with lavishly ripe scents of black plums and cassis, the 1988 La Turque is not quite as suppressed aromatically as La Mouline. This thick, unctuously textured, full-bodied, monster wine is close to reaching its plateau of drinkability. The wine exhibits awesome concentration, terrific purity, and, amazingly, no evidence of the 42 months it spent in 100% new oak casks. Very full and rich, and potentially the longest-lived La Turque yet made, this wine should be legendary. Anticipated maturity: now–2015.

1987 Côte Rôtie La Turque

RATING: 96 points

A blast of roasted herb, licorice, and black fruit scents jumps from the glass of this full-bodied, superconcentrated 1987. Very pure, with some toast notes from new oak still present, this thick, juicy wine is soft, but its color and bouquet are more typical of a 3- or 4-year-old wine than one that is approaching 18 years of age. The finish is long and rich, with more tannin than in La Mouline. Anticipated maturity: now–2009.

1986 Côte Rôtie La Turque

RATING: 92 points

The fully mature 1986 La Turque has a bouquet of smoke, new saddle leather, roasted herbs, meat, and sweet, jammy black fruit. Medium to full–bodied, ripe, and intense, without the colossal richness of the finest vintages, this still youthful wine should continue to age well. Anticipated maturity: now–2006.

1985 Côte Rôtie La Turque

RATING: 100 points

The debut vintage for this wine was especially impressive in view of the fact that the vineyard was so young. The 1985 La Turque's color remains a dark purple, with no signs of amber or lightening. The nose explodes from the glass, revealing scents of jammy black fruits, licorice, lead pencil, and smoke. Sweet, thick, highly concentrated flavors contain enough acidity and soft wood tannin to give the wine a well-focused feel. This prodigiously endowed, rich wine should continue to evolve and offer accessible drinking for another 15+ years. Anticipated maturity: now–2012.

EX VOTO ERMITAGE

2003 Ex Voto Ermitage

RATING: 95–98+ points

From five acres of vineyards, representing about 30% from Les Bessards, 30% from Les Greffieux, 20% from Hermite, and 20% from Les Meurets, comes this 4,000-bottle *cuvée* that is Guigal's greatest red Hermitage to date. Certainly the vintage had a lot to do with it. Hot, tiny yields of 15–20 hectoliters per hectare, a natural alcohol content of 15%, and an extraordinary amount of concentration have provided a black/purple-colored wine with gorgeous notes of crème de cassis, flowers, licorice, and a hint of road tar. This wine is voluptuously textured, has loads of tannin, but it is quite sweet and round, and the finish goes on for well over a minute. Anticipated maturity: 2010–2030.

EX VOTO ERMITAGE WHITE

2003 Ex Voto Ermitage White

RATING: 96–100 points

This special *cuvée*, which will be aged nearly 18 months in 100% new oak, emerges 90% from the Les Meurets vineyard and 10% from the Hermite vineyard. The 2003 Ex Voto Ermitage White is quite an extraordinary wine, right up there with the great classics from Chave and the special single-vineyard wines of Chapoutier. Notes of honeysuckle, crushed minerals, flowers, white currants, and peaches all make an appearance in this wine, with great structure, extraordinary concentration, and probably 20–30 or more years of aging potential.

WINE: Hermitage La Chapelle

OWNER: Paul Jaboulet Aîné, S.A. (100% Jaboulet family)

ADDRESS: "Les Jalets," Route Nationale 7, 26600 La Roche sur Glun, France

TELEPHONE: 33 04 75 84 68 93

TELEFAX: 33 04 75 84 56 14

E-MAIL: info@jaboulet.com

WEBSITE: www.jaboulet.com

CONTACTS:

Michel Jaboulet (President)

Jacques Jaboulet (Oenologist)

Philippe Jaboulet (Director of the Jaboulet Estates)

Frédéric Jaboulet (Export Sales Manager)

Nicolas Jaboulet (Export Sales Manager)

Laurent Jaboulet (Oenologist)

Odile Jaboulet (Head of Public Relations)

VISITING POLICY: For appointments, contact (for American customers) Frederick Wildman or Mrs. Odila Galer Noël (212-355-0700); for other countries—Mr. Jean-Luc Chapel (33 04 75 84 68 93 or 06 07 83 28 87)

VINEYARDS

SURFACE AREA:

Hermitage red "La Chapelle," "La Petite Chapelle," "Le Pied de la Côte"—53.3 acres

AVERAGE AGE OF THE VINES: 40–50 years

DENSITY OF PLANTATION: According to the plantation method; 6,000 or 9,000 grape plants by hectare

AVERAGE YIELDS:

Hermitage red "La Chapelle," "La Petite Chapelle," "Le Pied de la Côte"—35 hectoliters per hectare

WINEMAKING AND UPBRINGING

All the red wines are destemmed and crushed. A meticulous selection in the vineyards is followed by fermentation at a temperature between 25 and 30°C. The maceration is made in tanks during three or four weeks with twice pumping-over daily. When the maceration is finished, the wines are transferred to oak cases for 12–18 months with traditional racking every three months. Only one-year-old casks are utilized.

ANNUAL PRODUCTION

Hermitage La Chapelle: 80,000–85,000 bottles

AVERAGE PRICE (VARIABLE DEPENDING ON VINTAGE): $65–200

GREAT RECENT VINTAGES

2003, 2001, 1990, 1989, 1988, 1985, 1983, 1979, 1978, 1969, 1966, 1961, 1949

The Jaboulet family may be the oldest in the Rhône, but all of the documented family history was destroyed during the French Revolution.

The Jaboulet Company was founded by Antoine Jaboulet (1807–1864), and his twin sons, Paul and Henri (1846–1892), expanded the family business. The elder son (*aîné* in French), Paul, established the company in its present form and gave it his own name. Since then, the company has been run by successive generations of sons.

The Jaboulet family business has been at Tain l'Hermitage since 1834. One hundred seventy years later, the original cellars are still in use, for the vinification, maturation, and aging of wines in oak casks. Recently, a new winery has been constructed within the architecture of the original building.

The Paul Jaboulet Aîné Company has also constructed a new building, in the neighboring town of La Roche de Glun, that houses offices, bottling lines, and storage and shipping facilities. Underground cellars were also excavated to enable more than one million bottles to age and mature in perfect conditions.

More recently, the underground quarries of Châteauneuf sur Isère have become the Vineum of Paul Jaboulet Aîné. The Vineum offers perfect natural conditions for maturing wine—a constant temperature of

12°C and humidity of more than 80% all year round. Two years of building work were needed to transform these quarries into an impressive space where over a million bottles are stored.

I would surmise that the family-owned company of Paul Jaboulet Aîné is the world's best-known producer of high-quality Rhône wine. Their most celebrated wine is the Hermitage La Chapelle (unquestionably one of the world's greatest dry red wines), named not after a specific vineyard, but after the tiny, white, solitary chapel that sits atop the steepest part of the Hermitage hill. This famous wine comes primarily from the two vineyards known as Le Méal and Les Bessards.

This is a large family, and the Jaboulets suffered a colossal tragedy in the late 1990s, when the firm's spokesperson and spiritual leader, the enormously talented and affable Gérard Jaboulet, suddenly died at a very young age. For several years, the firm seemed rudderless and quality declined, but all seemed back in order in time to capture the quality of the 2003s.

The increasing fame of the firm's stupendous Hermitage La Chapelle is not difficult to understand. An enormously concentrated wine, it normally takes a decade to throw off its tannic cloak. Even then it only hints at the majestic perfume and richness that will arise. In terms of longevity it is an almost immortal wine, and its quality and complexity equaled only by several dozen or so Bordeaux cru classés, a half-dozen or so Burgundies, and an equal number of other red Rhônes. This wine is made to last.

The Hermitage La Chapelle is not clarified, but is given a light filtration after malolactic fermentation. In the early 1980s, the Jaboulets did a prebottling filtration as well, but this practice was halted when they deemed it had an adverse impact on the finished wine. Curiously, Jaboulet is among the first to bottle his Hermitage; it rarely spends more than 12–14 months in wood. Compare that with 36+ months for Guigal, and 18–24 months for Chave. Today, only Michel Chapoutier bottles his Hermitage this quickly after a vintage. The Jaboulets explain that this has always been their method, and one hardly need argue, for the results speak for themselves. After a slump in quality (1998–2000), this wine bounced back with an excellent 2001 and brilliant 2003, the finest since 1990.

Most wine enthusiasts think of Hermitage as a thick, chewy wine with a dizzying degree of alcohol. However, the Hermitage La Chapelle, when mature at 15 or 20 years, is virtually interchangeable with a great Pauillac. In addition, the alcohol content rarely exceeds 13%. Much of the enormous impact this wine makes on the palate comes simply from its fabulous layers of fruit, which come from old vines grown in the granite soil of Le Méal and Les Bessards.

HERMITAGE LA CHAPELLE

2003 Hermitage La Chapelle
RATING: 93–95 points
In this vintage, 30% new oak was used but the yields were so tiny (16 hectoliters per hectare), only 45,000 bottles have been produced. Stylistically it is similar to the 1990 and undeniably the finest La Chapelle since that prodigious wine. Not quite the bell-ringer I had hoped for, but this is a brilliant La Chapelle with a deep ruby/purple–tinged color and a big, sweet nose of cassis, new saddle leather, roasted meat, and dried herbs. The wine is full-bodied, very pure, rich, and quite long in the finish. The natural alcohol is 14.1%, which is one of the highest ever recorded for this wine. It looks to be set for at least 20–30 years of longevity. Anticipated maturity: 2010–2030.

2001 Hermitage La Chapelle
RATING: 90 points
The 2001 Hermitage La Chapelle looks to be an excellent effort, perhaps the finest since 1997. This is welcome news, as this can be one of the world's greatest wines. After an extremely severe selection (something that may have been lacking in previous vintages), the 2001 boasts a deep ruby/purple color as well as a sweet nose of crème de cassis intermixed with licorice and earth. Full-bodied, sweet, rich, and moderately tannic, it should merit a score in the low 90s, a good sign after a succession of uninspiring efforts. Anticipated maturity: 2010–2020.

1997 Hermitage La Chapelle
RATING: 93 points
The 1997 Hermitage La Chapelle has begun to completely close down, which is surprising in view of how sweet, seductive, and precocious this vintage can be. However, the color seems to get deeper with exposure to air (the wine was far more drinkable after 24 hours of aeration than it was upon opening). The moderately intense bouquet exhibits plenty of ripe blackberry and cherry fruit, in addition to spicy, mineral characteristics. There is considerable weight and volume, but the wine is tight,

and nearly impenetrable, leaving an impression of a large, deep, foursquare monolith. This is an outstanding Hermitage La Chapelle that will have at least three decades of positive evolution. For readers intent on committing infanticide, open and decant it 12–24 hours in advance. The improvement is dramatic. Anticipated maturity: 2007–2025.

1996 Hermitage La Chapelle
RATING: 92 points
The 1996 Hermitage La Chapelle is immensely impressive. The acidity is high. The color is black/purple, and the wine is extremely concentrated, but unevolved and impossible to penetrate. It could turn out like the 1983 and never develop as well as its early promise suggests. Nevertheless, it is a massive effort with extraordinary concentration, but the high acidity requires a minimum of 7 years of cellaring. Anticipated maturity: 2012–2025.

1995 Hermitage La Chapelle
RATING: 90 points
A saturated purple/plum color is accompanied by gamy, blackberry, and smoked meat aromas. While this wine is rich and full-bodied, it has gritty, astringent tannin and an austere personality. It is a large-scaled, boldly flavored, but ferociously tannic La Chapelle. Anticipated maturity: 2010–2035.

1991 Hermitage La Chapelle
RATING: 90 points
The saturated, dark ruby/purple–colored 1991 La Chapelle is just beginning to reveal secondary nuances. Aromas of Asian spices, soy, grilled steak, pepper, and blackberries are beginning to emerge. Ripe and dense, with tart acidity (a cool vintage characteristic), it is a medium to full–bodied, concentrated, impressively endowed La Chapelle with surprising length and intensity. It looks to be slightly better than I originally suggested. Anticipated maturity: now–2020.

1990 Hermitage La Chapelle
RATING: 100 points
The modern-day equivalent of the 1961, the sexy and opulent 1990 La Chapelle deserves all the attention it has garnered. I had the 1990 at a Jaboulet vertical tasting in the fall of 1999, and again out of a double magnum three months later. On both occasions it was spectacular, clearly meriting a three-digit score. The color remains an opaque purple, with only a slight pink at the edge. Spectacular aromatics offer up aromas of incense, smoke, blackberry fruit, cassis, barbecue spice, coffee, and a touch of chocolate. As it sits in the glass, additional nuances of pepper and grilled steak emerge. There is extraordinary freshness for such a mammoth wine, in addition to abundant tannin, an amazing 60-second finish, and a level of glycerin and thick, fleshy texture that has to be tasted to be believed. Despite its youthfulness, the 1990 La Chapelle is lovely to drink, although it will be even better with another 1–2 years of cellaring; it should age for 35–40+ years. Anticipated maturity: now–2050.

1989 Hermitage La Chapelle
RATING: 96 points
This fabulous, blockbuster wine has been totally unevolved since bottling, but at a Jaboulet vertical tasting in 1999, it was beginning to reveal some of its formidable potential. A saturated opaque purple color is followed by aromas of cassis, minerals, and hot bricks/wood fire. Superripe and full-bodied, with a massive mid-section, teeth-staining extract, and mouth-searing tannin, it is a monster-sized La Chapelle. Anticipated maturity: 2010–2050.

1988 Hermitage La Chapelle
RATING: 92 points
This was the first vintage in the vertical tasting of La Chapelle in the fall of 1999 that was beginning to reveal considerable secondary nuances and color development. Opaque purple/garnet with a touch of amber at the edge, this sexy, rich effort is more pleasurable aromatically than on the palate. However, it possesses multiple dimensions as well as abundant aromas of cedar, damp forest, spice box, and Asian spices. The soaring bouquet suggested the wine was more mature in flavor than it turned out to be. The wine is dense, with a firm, noticeably tannic edge, full body, and concentrated, powerful flavors. It is a classy, understated La Chapelle that requires another year or two of cellaring. Anticipated maturity: now–2025.

1985 Hermitage La Chapelle
RATING: 91 points
A saturated dark plum/garnet color with amber at the edge is followed by an attractive smoky, underbrush, and truffle-scented wine with coffee, smoke, cedar, and jammy cassis/plum-like fruit. As the wine sits in the glass, notes of Chinese black tea, pepper, and soy emerge. There is surprising tannin and austerity in the finish, but the aromatics and attack were convincingly rich and intense. From my cellar, the 1985 appears to be developing at an evolved, precocious pace, but at the Jaboulets' vertical tasting in the fall of 1999, the wine revealed far more force, vigor, structure, and weight. Anticipated maturity: now–2025.

1982 Hermitage La Chapelle

RATING: 92 points

The 1982 is a wonderful surprise. It has put on weight yet retains its exotic, over-the-top style. Fully mature, but capable of lasting another decade or more, the 1982 La Chapelle possesses a dark garnet color with an amber edge. The glorious nose of Asian spices, roasted espresso, creamy cassis fruit, and hints of Peking duck lathered with hoisin sauce gives this wine, with its notes of prunes, plums, and cassis, an exotic yet compelling allure. Among all the vintages of the 1980s and 1990s, the 1982 is my favorite for current drinking. Sumptuous and full-bodied, with a creamy texture and sweet tannin, it is a dazzling La Chapelle for consuming through 2010.

1979 Hermitage La Chapelle

RATING: 90 points

This brilliant, dark ruby/purple–colored 1979 still retains a youthful vigor. Spicy, with plenty of smoke, dried herbs, pepper, and cassis fruit, this outstanding, smoky, gamy (smoked meats galore), full-bodied La Chapelle reveals some angularity and rough tannin in the finish, but all other signs are positive. While it does not possess the weight of the biggest, most muscular vintages of La Chapelle, it is an exciting wine. Anticipated maturity: now–2016.

1978 Hermitage La Chapelle

RATING: 100 points

Opaque plum/garnet–colored, with a fabulously sweet, youthful bouquet of licorice, incense, smoked meats, pepper, and blackberry/cassis fruit, the full-bodied 1978 La Chapelle is extremely young with astonishing vigor, velvety tannin, and a full-bodied, multidimensional, layered personality. The finish lasts for over 60 seconds. Remarkably fresh and not yet fully mature, the super-concentrated 1978 should continue to age well for another 25 years. Anticipated maturity: now–2030.

1971 Hermitage La Chapelle

RATING: 93 points

I purchased the 1971 La Chapelle inexpensively, and consumed more than three cases over the last three decades. It was delicious upon release, yet remarkably, it remains a thrilling wine. Resembling a Hermitage made in the image of Pomerol, this succulent, low-acid, silky-textured La Chapelle continues to age effortlessly, with no loss of fat or fruit. The color is opaque garnet with considerable amber at the edge. The hedonistic bouquet offers up smoky, dried herb, coffee, roasted meat, and blackberry/cassis aromas. Fully mature since the mid-1970s, this wine demonstrates what perfect balance can mean in terms of the evolution of a great wine from a stunning *terroir*. The wine is full-bodied, hedonistic, opulently textured, exotic, and intensely fragrant and rich. How much longer it will age is the question, but it is revealing no signs of decline. Drink it up.

1970 Hermitage La Chapelle

RATING: 94 points

I was lucky to buy early and enjoy the 1970 multiple times. It has always been a fabulous La Chapelle. The showing at the Jaboulet vertical tasting in 1999 was totally in keeping with the way this wine has always performed. In a blind tasting it could easily be mistaken for a first-growth Pauillac.

The dark garnet color reveals light amber at the edge. The spectacular aromatics (always a characteristic of very ripe vintages of La Chapelle) exhibit telltale Asian spice, soy, smoked meats, chocolate, pepper, blackberry, and cassis fruit scents. Lush, ripe, full-bodied, and oozing with concentration and glycerin, this expansive, voluptuously textured La Chapelle is fully mature, sumptuous, and gorgeously pure and long. The perfectly integrated tannin and acidity are nearly obscured by the wine's flesh, succulence, and intensity. Anticipated maturity: now–2010.

1966 Hermitage La Chapelle

RATING: 94 points

The 1966 La Chapelle's bouquet possessed the most spectacular and persistent aromas of any wine in the Jaboulet vertical tasting in 1999. Dried herbs, new saddle leather, soy, roasted duck, grilled steak, and copious quantities of cassis, blackberry, and prune notes soared from the glass of this spectacularly fragrant effort. The promise exhibited by the bouquet did not come through on the palate. And while the smoky, peppery, exotic spice characteristics and multilayered richness are still present, the wine begins to disintegrate as it sits in the glass. Nevertheless, there is still plenty of life remaining in this glycerin-imbued, expansive, lush, low-acid, concentrated La Chapelle. From pristinely stored bottles as well as magnums, it may be one of the more thrilling La Chapelles. It should be drunk up.

1964 Hermitage La Chapelle

RATING: 93 points

This fully mature La Chapelle exhibits a dark garnet color with considerable amber at the edge. Aromas of wood fires, smoke, leather, Asian spices, roasted vegetables, and meats emerge from the wine's bouquet. Burly, brawny, fat, and full, with low acidity, high alcohol, and copious glycerin and fruit, this 1964 is initially sumptuous, creamy-textured, and spectacular to drink, but it quickly cracks up as it sits in the glass. I have not had much previous experience with this vintage, but I suspect it was close to perfect when drunk in its prime (the 1970s and early 1980s). However, it is clearly at the end of its useful life, and should be consumed quickly.

1962 Hermitage La Chapelle

RATING: 90 points

A La Chapelle on the verge of cracking up, this drinkable, earthy, spicy, garnet/amber-colored 1962 exhibits complex aromatics, a sweet, soft, round entry, medium body, a velvety texture, and opulent, fruity flavors. After 3–4 minutes in the glass, its acidity and tannin move to the forefront, and the fruit quickly fades. Interestingly, as it began to fade it took on the characteristics of an old Gruaud-Larose from the 1950s. Owners should consume it immediately.

1961 Hermitage La Chapelle

RATING: 100 points

This is unquestionably one of the greatest wines made in the 20th century. In the two dozen tastings where I have had the 1961 La Chapelle, I rated it 100 points twenty times. The opaque purple/garnet color is accompanied by spectacular aromatics representing the essence of old-vine Syrah (smoked meat, pepper, hoisin sauce, and soy). As the wine sits in the glass, notions of pepper, new saddle leather, grilled meat, and awesome levels of blackberry, plum, and black currant liqueur–like notes emerge. Extremely unctuous, with compelling concentration and purity, this full-bodied, seamless, mouth-filling 1961 is truly immortal. It still possesses a freshness and vigor that defy its 40+ years of age. It should continue to drink well for 15 years or more. Prodigious stuff! Anticipated maturity: now–2020.

1959 Hermitage La Chapelle

RATING: 90 points

I have had a half-dozen bottles of 1959 La Chapelle, and have always rated it in the upper 90s. At a Jaboulet vertical tasting in 1999, it appeared to be more evolved, with a saturated garnet color and a big, cedary, meaty, dried herb–scented bouquet with abundant smoke and spice. In the mouth, alcohol was burning its way through the flavors, and one could clearly see this wine was the product of an extremely hot, sunny year. Lusty, fully mature, but becoming disjointed, with the fruit fading and the alcohol and tannin taking over, this remains an outstanding wine, but I am convinced that pristine bottles are far better than this showing, and should be drunk over the next decade. In this condition, the wine requires immediate consumption.

1949 Hermitage La Chapelle

RATING: 94 points

A dazzling wine, the dark garnet/amber color of the 1949 La Chapelle is accompanied by aromas of molasses, exotic Asian spices, roasted duck, prune, and blackberry liqueur. In the mouth, this expansive, full-bodied, exotic wine exhibited terrific sweetness, awesome glycerin levels, sweet tannin, and, in addition to the aforementioned aromatic characteristics, coffee flavors. Full-bodied as well as extremely fresh, this offering not only drank fabulously well out of the bottle, but held up in the glass until I couldn't defer my gratification any longer. This tasting at the Jaboulets' in the fall of 1999 was the first time I had the 1949 La Chapelle, so I do not know what other bottles have revealed, but this was a profound example of a mature La Chapelle that has lived 50+ years with nary a blemish.

DOMAINE DE LA JANASSE

WINES:

Châteauneuf-du-Pape Cuvée Chaupin

Châteauneuf-du-Pape Vieilles Vignes

OWNERS: Aimé, Christophe, and Isabelle Sabon

ADDRESS: 27, chemin du Moulin, 84350 Courthézon, France

TELEPHONE: 33 04 90 70 86 29

TELEFAX: 33 04 90 70 75 93

E-MAIL: lajanasse@free.fr

WEBSITE: www.lajanasse.com

CONTACT: Christophe or Isabelle Sabon

VISITING POLICY: Tasting at the cellar from Monday through
Friday, 8 A.M.–noon and 2–6 P.M.; Saturday and Sunday
by appointment only.

VINEYARDS

SURFACE AREA: 136 acres total

GRAPE VARIETALS: Châteauneuf-du-Pape red—80% Grenache,
7% Syrah, 7% Mourvèdre, 6% other

AVERAGE AGE OF THE VINES: Châteauneuf-du-Pape red—50
years (ranging from 15 to 100 years). Chaupin emerges
from a parcel planted in 1912, and the Vieilles Vignes
from parcels between 60 and 100 years old.

DENSITY OF PLANTATION: Châteauneuf-du-Pape red—
Grenache: 3,500–4,500 vines per hectare; Syrah and
Mourvèdre—4,000–5,000 vines per hectare

AVERAGE YIELDS: Châteauneuf-du-Pape red: 20–30 hectoliters
per hectare

WINEMAKING AND UPBRINGING

The wine's early life consists of a severe triage (two sorting tables), 50% to 80% destemming, cold premaceration of 2–4
days, manual *pigéage,* and a 3–4 week maceration in tanks.
For the upbringing, the Grenache is always aged in large
foudres, the Syrah and Mourvèdre in smaller barrels. A very
tiny percentage of new oak is utilized, depending on the vintage. After 12–14 months, the wines are blended together. As a
general rule, about 30% of the Chaupin is aged in small barrels in contrast to the Vieilles Vignes, which sees about 35%
barrel treatment with a higher percentage of new oak. The
balance is aged in *foudre.* The wines are egg-white fined but
rarely filtered.

ANNUAL PRODUCTION

Châteauneuf-du-Pape Cuvée Chaupin: 12,000–16,000 bottles

Châteauneuf-du-Pape Vieilles Vignes: 10,000–15,000 bottles

AVERAGE PRICE (VARIABLE DEPENDING ON VINTAGE): $45–75

GREAT RECENT VINTAGES

2003, 2001, 2000, 1999, 1998, 1995, 1990

This estate has emerged in the last decade as one of
the bright shining stars of France. Aimé Sabon and
his yuppie, impeccably dressed son, Christophe, deserve
all the credit. Aimé had sold the entire production to
cooperatives until 1973, when he constructed a cellar
and began to estate-bottle. Christophe, who is in his
early 30s, took over the administration of the estate in
1991 after graduating in oenology from Beaune. He has
provided a degree of energy and enthusiasm that has
been translated into a bevy of superb wines. The
Châteauneuf-du-Papes from Domaine de la Janasse are
becoming so popular they are allocated, but readers
should also be aware that this family makes very fine
Côtes du Rhône as well as an impressive *vin de table*
from the southern Rhône.

The Domaine de la Janasse owns some superb
vineyard parcels. Like most Châteauneuf-du-Pape estates, they are morsellated, with 15 separate parcels.
This has led to three *cuvées* of wine, all of them dominated by Grenache. The regular *cuvée (cuvée classique)*
comes from relatively old-vine parcels, including a parcel of Le Crau, to the more sandy, claylike soil in the
northeastern section, not far from Courthézon. The
Cuvée Chaupin comes from a parcel of Grenache vines
planted in 1912. The Cuvée Vieilles Vignes comes from
multiple parcels with an average age of 80 years. Since
Christophe is continually experimenting with new
techniques, I would not be surprised to see more innovative additions to this portfolio of fine wine. He has
begun to do some destemming, although he remains
open-minded about how important destemming is in a
very ripe year, and he routinely employs crop thinning
in abundant years. Additionally, a tiny percentage of
new oak is used, primarily for the Cuvée Vieilles Vignes,
but small casks are widely employed for the non-
Grenache varietals. The results are some of the purest,
authoritatively flavored, yet undeniably elegant, suave,
and graceful wines being made in Châteauneuf-du-
Pape. They have the intensity of the old-style tradition-

alists, but the purity of a modernist. The Sabons have achieved a classic, rich, complex Châteauneuf-du-Pape without compromising its exuberance and intensity.

This is a brilliantly run Châteauneuf-du-Pape estate that in terms of quality has just reached the top level of the appellation's hierarchy. The wines are becoming international superstars. Domaine de la Janasse is also making some of the most delicious red and white Côtes du Rhône in the southern Rhône Valley.

CHATEAUNEUF-DU-PAPE CUVEE CHAUPIN

2003 Châteauneuf-du-Pape Cuvée Chaupin

RATING: 95–98 points

An extraordinary effort in this freakishly hot, dry year, this wine has an extraordinary nose of raspberry liqueur intermixed with a hint of orange rind, blackberry, licorice, and earth. Made from 100% Grenache, the wine has enormous body, relatively high alcohol (15%), and a tremendously long, concentrated finish. This is a beauty that should drink beautifully young because of its low acidity and huge levels of glycerin and suppleness but age nicely for up to 12–15 years.

2001 Châteauneuf-du-Pape Cuvée Chaupin

RATING: 95 points

The saturated purple/plum color is followed by a big, sweet bouquet of raspberries, black kirsch, and a hint of white flowers. Chewy and full-bodied, with slightly more structure and tannin than usual, this surprisingly elegant yet full-flavored 2001 will benefit from another 1–3 years of cellaring. The most backward and structured Chaupin made between 1998 and 2001, it could easily be mistaken for a top grand cru red Burgundy from a great vintage. Anticipated maturity: 2006–2015.

2000 Châteauneuf-du-Pape Cuvée Chaupin

RATING: 94 points

The 2000 Châteauneuf-du-Pape Cuvée Chaupin is the most voluptuous, sexy offering in the Janasse portfolio. It's the Brigitte Bardot of Châteauneuf-du-Papes—full-bodied, rich, and sexy. A sweet, expansive perfume of red and black fruits is followed by a wine of great purity and balance displaying a surprising combination of fat, power, and elegance. Already delicious because of its low acidity as well as its expansive, ripe fruit, it will drink well for 12–15 years. Don't miss this one, as it may be even more generous and sexy than the 1998.

1999 Châteauneuf-du-Pape Cuvée Chaupin

RATING: 91 points

The 1999 Châteauneuf-du-Pape Cuvée Chaupin's dense ruby/purple color is accompanied by a big, sweet bouquet of blackberries, cassis, and a hint of kirsch. This sexy, full-bodied, opulent 1999 combines fat and flesh with a sense of elegance, purity, and delineation. Already delicious, it will last for another 10–12 years.

1998 Châteauneuf-du-Pape Cuvée Chaupin

RATING: 93 points

The 1998 Châteauneuf-du-Pape Cuvée Chaupin (14.5% alcohol) is a voluptuous, opulently textured blockbuster with terrific fruit purity and gorgeous aromas of roasted herbs, kirsch, blackberries, and Asian spices. The palate impression is one of sweetness because of the wine's high glycerin and ripe, jammy fruit. The chewy, long finish lasts for 40+ seconds. It can be drunk now, but readers should save a bottle for drinking in about a decade. This is a brilliant effort from one of the Rhône's most accomplished young winemakers. Anticipated maturity: now–2018.

1995 Châteauneuf-du-Pape Cuvée Chaupin

RATING: 91 points

The 1995 Châteauneuf-du-Pape Cuvée Chaupin exhibits a denser ruby/purple color than the regular *cuvée*, a black raspberry–scented nose, more restraint, and a closed, tannic style. Full-bodied, with good flesh, this wine needs 1–2 years of cellaring. Long, textured, and well-defined, it will have a plateau of maturity between now and 2015. These are impeccably made offerings from one of the finest estates in Châteauneuf-du-Pape.

1994 Châteauneuf-du-Pape Cuvée Chaupin

RATING: 90 points

The 1994 Cuvée Chaupin reveals an intense, seductive nose of jammy cherries, kirsch, smoke, and *herbes de Provence*. Round, with good body, copious quantities of glycerin, and layers of fruit, this wine seems too delicious to last, but there is enough structure and acidity to provide another few years of hedonistic consumption. It also offers a whiff of that unmistakable Provençal *garrigue* smell. Anticipated maturity: now–2006.

1990 Châteauneuf-du-Pape Cuvée Chaupin

RATING: 90 points

The dark ruby/purple–colored 1990 Cuvée Chaupin displays a flamboyant nose of fiery black raspberries, roasted herbs, and chocolate. The wine has excellent concentration, gobs of glycerin and extraction, plenty of alcohol, and a long, moderately tannic finish. Anticipated maturity: now–2008.

CHATEAUNEUF-DU-PAPE VIEILLES VIGNES

2003 Châteauneuf-du-Pape Vieilles Vignes

RATING: 96–100 points

A wine of great intensity, with notes of melted licorice, crème de cassis, raspberry, and cherry jam, this wine is full-bodied, with superb purity and an unctuously textured, long finish of just over a minute. A brilliant, brilliant wine that should drink well for 12–15+ years.

2001 Châteauneuf-du-Pape Vieilles Vignes

RATING: 98 points

The spectacular 2001 Châteauneuf-du-Pape Vieilles Vignes is one of the monumental Châteauneuf-du-Papes of the vintage. A saturated plum/purple color reveals a thick, rich appearance. The wine combines freshness, power, elegance, and great intensity, all wrapped into a full-bodied, concentrated personality with phenomenal persistence on the palate. Remarkably pure, but neither overdone nor overripe, this spectacular, youthful Châteauneuf-du-Pape should hit its prime in 5–6 years and last for two decades. It is a brilliant tour de force!

2000 Châteauneuf-du-Pape Vieilles Vignes

RATING: 96+ points

The limited production Cuvée Vieilles Vignes (70% Grenache and 30% Syrah and Mourvèdre) was rocking when I tasted it. The 2000 Châteauneuf-du-Pape Vieilles Vignes represents the essence of kirsch intermixed with pepper. Sexy, full-bodied, layered, and multidimensional, it exhibits great intensity, even more length than the Chaupin, sweet fruit, adequate acidity, and ripe tannin. This is a flawless as well as seamless blockbuster to drink now and over the next 15–20 years.

1999 Châteauneuf-du-Pape Vieilles Vignes

RATING: 92 points

The floral (violets?)-scented, structured, backward, powerful 1999 Châteauneuf-du-Pape Vieilles Vignes boasts a dense purple color. Gorgeously rich flavors on the attack are followed by a heady, muscular, long wine that should age for two decades.

1998 Châteauneuf-du-Pape Vieilles Vignes

RATING: 96 points

I suppose one could say this wine was made in a quasi-modern style given its black/purple color and sweet nose of crème de cassis and raspberries. It is a great Châteauneuf-du-Pape, with power, elegance, immense purity, a majestic, multi-layered feel in the mouth, and a finish that lasts for 40+ seconds. Although it remains unevolved and somewhat grapy, everything is present for a fabulous evolution of two decades or more. Anticipated maturity: now–2021.

1995 Châteauneuf-du-Pape Vieilles Vignes

RATING: 93 points

The exceptional 1995 Châteauneuf-du-Pape Vieilles Vignes offers a saturated plum/purple color, as well as fabulous quantities of fruit. It is extremely rich and full-bodied, with a multifaceted nose of pepper, spice, black fruits (plums, cherries, and raspberries), and a touch of licorice and cedar. The wine is terrifically endowed, rich, and full-bodied, but not overbearing or excessively alcoholic. It will provide fabulous drinking between now and 2016.

1994 Châteauneuf-du-Pape Vieilles Vignes

RATING: 92 points

The 1994 Cuvée Vieilles Vignes is a full-bodied, deep wine with great stuffing, glycerin, smoke, kirsch, and cherry fruit, as well as more alcohol. It is a terrific young Châteauneuf-du-Pape that is already surprisingly developed and delicious. The wine hits the palate broadside with fruit, followed by plenty of ripeness, richness, and purity. There is some tannin, but the overall impression is one of gloriously ripe, rich fruit presented in a velvety-textured, beautifully well-focused format. Anticipated maturity: now–2010.

1990 Châteauneuf-du-Pape Vieilles Vignes

RATING: 92 points

The dark ruby–colored 1990 Cuvée Vieilles Vignes is a massive, highly extracted, densely colored wine with gobs of tannin and excellent aging potential. It boasts a whopping 15% natural alcohol. Still youthful, this is a noteworthy 1990. Anticipated maturity: now–2009.

WINES:

Châteauneuf-du-Pape

Châteauneuf-du-Pape Vieilles Vignes

OWNERS: Catherine and Sophie Armenier

ADDRESS: 7, rue A. Daudet, Chemin de la Gironde, 84100 Orange, France

TELEPHONE: 33 04 90 34 67 43

TELEFAX: 33 04 90 51 84 53

CONTACT: Write or call the Domaine

VISITING POLICY: No groups; visits or tastings by appointment only

VINEYARDS

SURFACE AREA: 40.5 acres of Châteauneuf rouge

GRAPE VARIETALS: Châteauneuf rouge—85% Grenache, 8% Mourvèdre, 5% Syrah, 2% Cinsault

AVERAGE AGE OF THE VINES:

10.1 acres of vines are 70–100 years old (24% of property)

13.1 acres of the vines are 40–53 years old (32%)

9.9 acres of the vines are 20–40 years old (24%)

7.5 acres of the vines are less than 20 years old (20%)

DENSITY OF PLANTATION: 3,300 vines per hectare

AVERAGE YIELDS: 25 hectoliters per hectare

WINEMAKING AND UPBRINGING

There is considerable flexibility at Marcoux, depending on the maturity of the fruit and the style of the vintage. Some vintages are totally destemmed, others are not. In general there is less destemming for the Cuvée Vieilles Vignes than their regular *cuvée*. The wines see little manipulation, very tiny amounts of SO_2, and are brought up in cement tanks as well as neutral wood. There is no fining or filtration at bottling.

ANNUAL PRODUCTION

Châteauneuf-du-Pape rouge: 27,000 bottles

Châteauneuf-du-Pape Vieilles Vignes: 4,000 bottles

AVERAGE PRICE (VARIABLE DEPENDING ON VINTAGE): $45–125

GREAT RECENT VINTAGES

2003, 2001, 2000, 1998, 1995, 1990, 1989

Catherine and Sophie Armenier

The two Armenier sisters, who took over from their brother Philippe in 1995, are an imposing duo. Sophie and Catherine are both intense, serious winemakers. Like their brother, they are disciples of biodynamic farming, inspired by the high-quality producers Lalou Bize-Leroy, Nicolas Joly, and Michel Chapoutier. The Armeniers cultivate their 53 acres of vineyards (40.5% Châteauneuf-du-Pape) following the astrological/homeopathic writings of the famed German professor Rudolf Steiner. As a result, yields are kept very low, and, not surprisingly, the quality is exceptionally high.

The Armenier family is impressively old—they can trace their origins in Châteauneuf-du-Pape to the 14th century (precisely 1344)—and so are their vines. The estate has an old-vine average of 40–50 years for the red wine grapes, and some are over 90 years old. There are at least 10 separate parcels, with the oldest vines located in Les Charbonnières, a vineyard in the eastern sector of the appellation, just west of the famed La Crau. Another parcel of extremely old vines is in Les Esquirons, a vineyard planted on sandy soil, just behind the château ruins. Fruit from these two parcels, plus another in the southern part of the appellation, covered with the famed *galets roulés* (football-sized rocks), make up the Vieilles Vignes *cuvée*. This can be one of the greatest red wines made in the world (the 1998 and 2000, for example), if not the single most phenomenal wine of Châteauneuf-du-Pape. It possesses a level of concentration and a vivid blackberry/blueberry fruitiness that are mind-boggling. Even lighter years, such as 1992 and 1993, are surprisingly powerful wines. This *cuvée,* which sees no new oak, but rather old barrels, *foudres,* and tanks, is always bottled without fining or filtration.

The regular *cuvée* of Marcoux is no wimpy wine either. In top vintages, it is a powerful Châteauneuf-du-Pape that is given the same *élevage* and, at least for the American importer, is bottled with no fining or filtering. Even the *cuvée* sold elsewhere in the world is given only a light filtration.

All of the cellar activity is guided by the stars (the ones in the sky), and there is virtually no manipulation of the wine. The grapes are not destemmed, and vinification, in spite of the lunar cycle, is traditional. With the extraordinary intensity it obtains, one would think that maceration must last a month or more, but that is rarely the case. In fact, in great years such as 1989 and 1990, the *cuvaison* was relatively short (two weeks), and in lighter years, such as 1993, it lasted for nearly a month. The red wines contain 80% Grenache, but the Armeniers have planted Vaccarèse, Counoise, Muscardin, and Terret Noir, in addition to the regular lineup of Cinsault, Syrah, and Mourvèdre.

While it is fashionable to rave about recent vintages of Philippe Armenier, his father, Elie, who died in 1980, also produced some classic Châteauneuf-du-Papes. Should you come across such older vintages as 1966, 1967, 1970, and 1978, do not hesitate to buy them, as they were classic, high-octane, superbly endowed Châteauneuf-du-Papes. This is an excellent reference-point estate for Châteauneuf-du-Pape.

The talented team of sisters Sophie and Catherine Armenier are gracefully carrying on the heritage of the Armenier family, which has been making Châteauneuf-du-Pape for only 700 years!

CHATEAUNEUF-DU-PAPE

2003 Châteauneuf-du-Pape
RATING: 91–93 points
Virtually 100% Grenache, this wine shows extraordinary concentration, with loads of raspberry and cassis fruit intermixed with some melted licorice. Its plush, full-bodied palate is characterized by a wine that must be at least 15% alcohol, huge body, seamlessness, and gorgeously long, concentrated finish. It is quite a complex, hedonistic wine to drink over the next 10–12 years.

2001 Châteauneuf-du-Pape
RATING: 90 points
The 2001 Châteauneuf-du-Pape (14.8% natural alcohol) is a sexy, surprisingly up-front Marcoux with a succulent personality, tremendous opulence, and loads of blackberry liqueur aromas intermixed with melted licorice, smoke, and Asian spices. Drink this low-acid, heady, plump, full-bodied, sexy Châteauneuf over the next 10–12 years.

2000 Châteauneuf-du-Pape
RATING: 92 points
The superb 2000 Châteauneuf-du-Pape exhibits a dark plum/purple color along with sumptuous notes of melted licorice, blackberries, cassis, cherries, prunes, and raisins. Layered with crème de cassis–like flavors and moderate tannin lurking beneath the surface, this is a sexy, lush, fragrant 2000. Low acidity and sweet tannin suggest it can be enjoyed now and over the next 12–15 years.

1999 Châteauneuf-du-Pape

RATING: 90 points

The dark ruby–colored 1999 Châteauneuf-du-Pape offers a gorgeous perfume of licorice, cherry jam, spring flowers, and blackberries. Relatively evolved (typical for Châteauneuf-du-Papes from this vintage), with sweet fruit, multiple layers of flavor, and a long, seamless finish, this captivating, opulent 1999 can be enjoyed now and over the next 8–10 years.

1998 Châteauneuf-du-Pape

RATING: 90 points

The 1998 Châteauneuf-du-Pape's peppery, plum, cherry liqueur, and cassis–scented nose is followed by opulent, long, open-knit flavors crammed with glycerin and alcohol. The high levels of richness and glycerin obscure much of the wine's structure and tannin. This sexy, voluptuously textured, creamy 1998 should drink gorgeously for 8–11+ years.

1990 Châteauneuf-du-Pape

RATING: 90 points

The 1990 reveals a dark ruby/purple color, and a huge nose of jammy, sweet black fruits and herbs. In the mouth, the sweetness, glycerin, high alcohol, and gorgeous extract levels make for a sumptuous drinking experience. The tannins are silky and the finish is formidable. Anticipated maturity: now–2006.

CHATEAUNEUF-DU-PAPE VIEILLES VIGNES

2003 Châteauneuf-du-Pape Vieilles Vignes

RATING: 99 points

A blend of 85% Grenache and 15% Syrah, this wine, which achieved 16.2% natural alcohol and comes from ancient vineyards, one part in La Crau and another sector in Les Gali-

mards, is quite extraordinary. The wine is deep blue/purple in color and has an extraordinary nose of melted licorice, crème de cassis, and scorched earth. It has tremendous body, magnificent concentration and intensity, loads of viscosity, and a full-throttle finish that goes on for well over a minute. It reminds me at this stage of the 2000 and 1998, but even more potent. It should last for 15–20+ years.

2001 Châteauneuf-du-Pape Vieilles Vignes

RATING: 96 points

The 2001 Châteauneuf-du-Pape Vieilles Vignes may not attain the perfection of the 1998 or the pure exuberance and voluptuousness of the 2000, but it is a brilliant effort. A wine of nobility as well as purity, this cuvée, made primarily from 50- to 100-year-old Grenache vines, exhibits a dark plum/purple color as well as a sumptuous bouquet of Provençal herbs, roasted meats, crème de cassis, blackberries, and violets. Floral and full-bodied, with a seamlessness that only old vines can provide, it possesses rich, concentrated, pure fruit, low acidity, and admirable delineation (because of its tannic structure). Give it 2–3 years of cellaring, and drink it over the following 15–18 years.

2000 Châteauneuf-du-Pape Vieilles Vignes

RATING: 98 points

The 2000 Châteauneuf-du-Pape Vieilles Vignes carries its 15% alcohol well. Though a compelling offering, and undoubtedly one of the wines of the vintage, it does not possess that magical extra dimension of greatness found in the 2003. Nevertheless, I would be thrilled to drink it anytime . . . anywhere! The floral component of white flowers intermixed with melted licorice, blackberry liqueur, plums, and prunes is followed by an expansive, sexy, silky-textured, full-bodied Châteauneuf with great depth, purity, and lusciousness. As with its younger sibling, the finish lasts for nearly a minute. Again, it is a singular expression of Châteauneuf-du-Pape that is totally different from its peers. Strikingly rich, dense, and opulent, with a breathtaking array of complexity and flavors, its low acidity, ripe tannin, and wealth of glycerin suggest drinking it now and over the next 15–16 years.

1999 Châteauneuf-du-Pape Vieilles Vignes

RATING: 91 points

Very good is the 1999 Châteauneuf-du-Pape Vieilles Vignes. Its dark ruby color with notions of pink at the rim is followed by a striking bouquet of violets intermixed with blackberry jam, licorice, and tapenade. This full-bodied, expansive, concentrated, spicy wine is dazzling stuff. Anticipated maturity: now–2016.

1998 Châteauneuf-du-Pape Vieilles Vignes
RATING: 100 points

Catherine and Sophie Armenier continue to fashion one of
France's greatest wines. There are 750 cases produced from 80%
Grenache, 10% Mourvèdre, and 10% miscellaneous varietals.

The profound, dense ruby/purple–colored 1998 reveals
telltale blackberry liqueur aromas and flavors, as well as a formidable level of glycerin, admirable richness, and a soaring
bouquet of black fruits, minerals, lavender, and exotic spices.
The finish lasts 50+ seconds, and the wine's purity and multiple
dimensions are staggering. This is a dazzling, full-throttle
Châteauneuf-du-Pape that is unbelievably concentrated, unctuous, well balanced, and silky-textured. There is not a rough
edge to be found. Anticipated maturity: now–2020.

1995 Châteauneuf-du-Pape Vieilles Vignes
RATING: 94 points

Unlike many wines from this vintage, the 1995 is approaching
full maturity. It exhibits a deep plum/purple color as well as a
sweet bouquet of figs, prunes, black raspberries, and blackberries (always a hallmark of this old-vine *cuvée*). Full-bodied
and unctuous, with high tannin, glycerin, and richness, it will
provide immense pleasure over the next 17–18 years.

1994 Châteauneuf-du-Pape Vieilles Vignes
RATING: 93 points

The 1994 Cuvée Vieilles Vignes appears to be an awesome
wine. The opaque dark ruby/purple color is accompanied by a
sensational nose of crushed black fruits, licorice, and truffles.
Full-bodied, with magnificent extraction of fruit and a layered, viscous texture, this unctuous, super-concentrated wine
has plenty of tannin lurking behind the ostentatious display
of richness. This is a dazzling Châteauneuf-du-Pape! Anticipated maturity: now–2012.

1990 Châteauneuf-du-Pape Vieilles Vignes
RATING: 96 points

The 1990 has been a consistently perfect wine for much of its
life. However, it appears to have turned the corner and lost
some of its most profound aspects. It is still an immortal
Châteauneuf-du-Pape, with a dense ruby/purple color in addition to a gorgeous nose of licorice, white flowers, blueberries, and blackberries. The wine is heady, with high alcohol,
an unctuous texture, and an extraordinarily ripe, concentrated finish. However, some bottles tasted seem far older
than others. I don't know whether it is a bottle variation
problem or a question of improper storage. Nevertheless,
pristine bottles remain candidates for perfection. Anticipated
maturity: now–2012.

1989 Châteauneuf-du-Pape Vieilles Vignes
RATING: 96 points

The 1989 is essentially equivalent to the 1990, with a more
muscular, backward personality as well as enormous concentration, density, and length. It offers up a telltale bouquet of
melted licorice, crème de cassis, blackberries, and blueberries.
Like the 1990s, the finish lasts for 60 seconds. Anticipated maturity: now–2020.

WINES:

Châteauneuf-du-Pape Cuvée de la Reine des Bois

Lirac Cuvée de la Reine des Bois

OWNER: Delorme family

ADDRESS: Chemin des Oliviers, F-30126 Tavel, France

TELEPHONE: 33 04 66 50 00 75

TELEFAX: 33 04 66 50 47 39

E-MAIL: info@domaine-mordoree.com

WEBSITE: www.domaine-mordoree.com *(under construction)*

CONTACT: Christophe Delorme

VISITING POLICY:

All year: Monday to Friday, 8 A.M.–noon, 1:30–6 P.M.;
   Saturday, 10 A.M.–noon, 3–6 P.M.

From beginning of May until the end of September: In addition
   to regular hours, the vineyard is open on Sundays and
   bank holidays from 10A.M.–noon, 3–6 P.M.

VINEYARDS

SURFACE AREA: Châteauneuf-du-Pape—12.47 acres; Lirac
   rouge—54.34 acres

GRAPE VARIETALS:

Châteauneuf-du-Pape—70% Grenache, 10% Mourvèdre,
   5% Syrah, 5% Vaccarèse, 5% Cinsault, 5% Counoise

Lirac rouge—40% Grenache, 35% Syrah, 20% Mourvèdre,
   5% Cinsault

AVERAGE AGE OF THE VINES: Châteauneuf-du-Pape—70 years;
   Lirac rouge—40 years

DENSITY OF PLANTATION: Châteauneuf-du-Pape—3,500 vines
   per hectare; Lirac rouge—4,000 vines per hectare

AVERAGE YIELDS: Châteauneuf-du-Pape—25 hectoliters per
   hectare; Lirac rouge—35 hectoliters per hectare

WINEMAKING AND UPBRINGING

Christophe Delorme's objective as a winemaker is to be unintrusive and maintain total respect for his *terroir* and the fruit it produces. His dream is to achieve a perfect balance between concentration, *terroir,* and flavors. For this reason the vinification is completely traditional and uses natural yeasts. The Delormes believe that 90% of the quality comes from the work in the vineyards. They have created an entirely natural ecosystem in their vineyards, avoiding all insecticides, fungicides, or herbicides, and have a sophisticated insect population to naturally fight vineyard diseases. As for the grapes, 100% are destemmed, there is a very long 30-day *cuvaison,* and for the Lirac, an *élevage* of 30% in oak barrels, 30% in neutral *foudres,* and 40% in stainless-steel tanks. For the Châteauneuf, one half is aged in small barrels and the other half in tanks.

ANNUAL PRODUCTION

Châteauneuf-du-Pape: 15,000–20,000 bottles

Lirac rouge: 40,000 bottles

AVERAGE PRICE (VARIABLE DEPENDING ON VINTAGE): $15–90

GREAT RECENT VINTAGES

2003, 2001, 2000, 1999, 1998, 1996

This exceptional 135-acre property located in Lirac is best known for its extraordinary Châteauneuf-du-Papes, which have been spectacular since the mid-1990s. Additionally, they produce the finest Liracs of the appellation. All the credit goes to the tall, handsome Christophe Delorme, who is as dedicated a terroirist and believer in organic viticulture as one can find in the southern Rhône. His vineyards are worked impeccably, and he is one of the finest white wine–makers in the area.

Mordorée's recent fame is based on its 12.47 acres in Châteauneuf-du-Pape, which consists of three parcels averaging 60 years in age, all planted in La Crau, Les Cabrières, and Bois la Ville. Delorme seems to be moving in the direction of biodynamic farming. He represents the best of an enlightened approach to winemaking that has one foot in the traditions of the past and one in the future.

Christophe Delorme and his daughter

CHATEAUNEUF-DU-PAPE CUVEE DE LA REINE DES BOIS

2003 Châteauneuf-du-Pape Cuvée de la Reine des Bois
RATING: 93–95+ points

A blend of 80% Grenache, 10% Mourvèdre, 3% Syrah, and the rest Vaccarèse and Cinsault, this wine has a huge, concentrated but very tannic personality, relatively high alcohol (a characteristic of the vintage) of 15.5%, and a deep purple color to the rim. Sweet and rich, with black currants, cherries, and plums in the aromatics and flavors; sensational concentration and body, but almost Bordeaux-like tannins in the finish, this wine will take some time to come around given the wine's structure. Anticipated maturity: 2008–2020+.

2001 Châteauneuf-du-Pape Cuvée de la Reine des Bois
RATING: 100 points

The 2001 Châteauneuf-du-Pape Cuvée de la Reine des Bois surpasses the extraordinary Reine des Bois produced in 2000, 1999, and 1998 . . . and that's saying something! An inky purple color is followed by a heady perfume of graphite, blackberries, kirsch, licorice, truffles, and charcoal. This full-bodied effort displays endless concentration in its pure, dense, generous flavors. It is broadly flavored, with beautifully integrated acidity, tannin, and alcohol. A blend of 78% Grenache, 10% Mourvèdre, and small quantities of Cinsault, Counoise, Syrah, and Vaccarèse, it is made from 60-year-old vines, and aged both in cask and neutral *foudres* from what are obviously very low yields. This classic Châteauneuf-du-Pape requires 3–5 years of cellaring; it will last for two decades. A modern-day legend, it is an example of what progressive winemaking can achieve without abandoning the traditions of the appellation.

2000 Châteauneuf-du-Pape Cuvée de la Reine des Bois
RATING: 97 points

The 2000 boasts an inky purple color in addition to a ravishing perfume of wood smoke, crème de cassis, blueberries, plums, figs, and a hint of graphite. Full-bodied, with sweet tannin, a layered richness, staggering ripeness, and a finish that lasts for nearly 50 seconds, this monumental Châteauneuf-du-Pape continues the unbelievable succession of superstar wines that began in 1998. Anticipated maturity: now–2020.

1999 Châteauneuf-du-Pape Cuvée de la Reine des Bois
RATING: 94 points

A candidate for wine of the vintage, the 1999 Châteauneuf-du-Pape Cuvée de la Reine des Bois boasts a saturated black/ruby color as well as amazing concentration of fruit extract (blackberries and cherries) intermixed with graphite and crème de cassis. Spectacularly concentrated, full-bodied, extremely pure, well-delineated, and opulent, this superb wine is forward and accessible. Anticipated maturity: now–2018.

1998 Châteauneuf-du-Pape Cuvée de la Reine des Bois
RATING: 99 points

This opaque purple-colored effort was among the most backward wines in the tasting. Although subdued aromatically, it is enormously endowed, concentrated, and fabulous in the mouth. With high tannin as well as extraordinary blackberry and cassis fruit mixed with minerals and subtle new oak, it cuts a huge swath across the palate but is not heavy. It is a quasi-modern-styled Châteauneuf-du-Pape but clearly has not lost its typicity. Anticipated maturity: now–2031.

1996 Châteauneuf-du-Pape Cuvée de la Reine des Bois
RATING: 94 points

The 1996 Châteauneuf-du-Pape Cuvée de la Reine des Bois is undoubtedly the wine of the vintage for Châteauneuf-du-Pape. From its youngest days, this offering possessed a level of concentration and intensity far beyond anything else produced in the village. Now that it is in bottle, it is a sensational wine, having more in common with a great vintage such as 1990 or 1989 than 1996. In that sense, it could be called atypical for the year. It boasts a saturated black/purple color, as well as a knockout nose of blackberry fruit intermixed with licorice, roasted herbs, and kirsch. Full-bodied, with a sweet, massive mid-palate, fabulous harmony, and outstanding concentration and length, this Châteauneuf, which achieved 14% alcohol naturally, is a gorgeously textured, superb wine that should continue to evolve for 10+ years. Bravo!

1994 Châteauneuf-du-Pape Cuvée de la Reine des Bois
RATING: 93 points

The dark ruby/purple–colored 1994 Cuvée de la Reine des Bois is special. The wine possesses immense body, superb extract, a sweet, flamboyant nose of black cherry jam, fruitcake, and smoke. Unctuous, thick, and full-bodied, with some tannin lurking in the background, this is a large-scaled yet drinkable Châteauneuf-du-Pape. Anticipated maturity: now–2010.

LIRAC CUVEE DE LA REINE DES BOIS

2003 Lirac Cuvée de la Reine des Bois
RATING: 91–93 points

As usual, equal parts Mourvèdre, Syrah, and Grenache, this wine shows a bit higher alcohol than usual, enormous concentration, and glycerin. Loads of black cherry and smoky berry fruit intermix with hints of new saddle leather, earth, and *barrique*. The wine is full-bodied, seamless, with beautiful integration of tannin, wood, and alcohol. It should drink well for 10–15 years.

2001 Lirac Cuvée de la Reine des Bois
RATING: 93 points

Spectacular, and certainly one of the great sleeper value picks of the southern Rhône in vintages such as 1998, 2000, and 2001, is the dense purple–colored, full-bodied 2001 Lirac Cuvée de la Reine des Bois. Made of equal parts Syrah, Grenache, and Mourvèdre from 40-year-old vines, it smells and tastes like Châteauneuf-du-Pape. Aromas and flavors of licorice, acacia flowers, blackberries, and cherry liqueur infused with espresso are found in this lush, hedonistic 2001. I have been working my way through a case of the 1998 Lirac Cuvée de la Reine des Bois, which is still a young wine. The 2001 is equally profound. Anticipated maturity: now–2012.

2000 Lirac Cuvée de la Reine des Bois
RATING: 90 points

Want a taste of what Mordorée does so well in Châteauneuf-du-Pape for less than one-third the price? This wine is a fine bargain. This deep purple–colored effort is crammed with cassis and cherry fruit nicely complemented by pepper, mineral, and licorice. The fat, jammy 2000 is a Lirac fruit/glycerin bomb. It should be drunk over the next 2–3 years.

1998 Lirac Cuvée de la Reine des Bois
RATING: 92 points

I previously reviewed the 1998 Lirac Cuvée de la Reine des Bois prior to bottling, and it is living up to my expectations. It exhibits a dark ruby/purple color as well as a moderately intense nose of black fruits, licorice, spice, pepper, and smoke. Displaying moderate tannin with exceptional concentration, it is one of those rare Liracs that will age for 10–15 years.

1996 Lirac Cuvée de la Reine des Bois
RATING: 90 points

This red wine possesses considerable richness and is a textbook example of the heights southern Rhône reds can attain. At $15 a bottle, it is a brilliant wine that is capable of lasting a decade. It boasts an opaque purple color, as well as a knockout nose of cassis, kirsch, black raspberries, truffles, pepper, and spice. Fat and superbly concentrated, yet with well-integrated acidity and tannin, this exquisite Lirac could easily pass for a top Châteauneuf-du-Pape in a blind tasting. Anticipated maturity: now–2008.

CHATEAU LA NERTHE

WINES:

Châteauneuf-du-Pape Cuvée des Cadettes

Châteauneuf-du-Pape Clos de Beauvenir

OWNER: Richard family (Alain Dugas, Manager)

ADDRESS: Route de Sorgues, 84230 Châteauneuf-du-Pape, France

TELEPHONE: 33 04 90 83 70 11

TELEFAX: 33 04 90 83 79 69

E-MAIL: la.nerthe@wanadoo.fr or
alain.dugas@chateau-la-nerthe.com

WEBSITE: www.chateau-la-nerthe.com

CONTACT: Alain Dugas

VISITING POLICY: By appointment only

VINEYARDS

SURFACE AREA: 225 acres (90 hectares)

GRAPE VARIETALS: Grenache, Syrah, Mourvèdre, Cinsault, Counoise, Muscardin, Terret Noir, Picpoul, Vaccarèse, Picardan, Roussanne, Clairette, Bourboulenc

AVERAGE AGE OF THE VINES: 40 years

DENSITY OF PLANTATION: 4,000 vines per hectare

AVERAGE YIELDS: 25 hectoliters per hectare

WINEMAKING AND UPBRINGING

Director Alain Dugas acquired his particular expertise in Châteauneuf-du-Pape by collaborating with Dr. Philippe Dufays, a specialist in local grape varieties and owner of the Domaine de Nalys. In 1985, Dugas was named director of Château La Nerthe.

One of La Nerthe's goals is to ensure the right balance of alcohol content and tannins. La Nerthe favors varieties with high aging potential, notably Syrah and Mourvèdre. The yields at La Nerthe are purposely kept low in order to produce highly concentrated grapes.

Another key policy is to blend the different varieties while they are still in the vats. Just as no chef would conceive of cooking vegetables separately for a casserole, so the winemakers at La Nerthe believe in bringing the grapes together early so their flavors can intermingle. This produces a clearly recognizable synergy of different grape varieties and a marriage of flavors that would be impossible to achieve by blending at a later stage.

Grape varieties with a high aging potential also require special conditions for maturing. While the "traditional" 800–1600 gallon cask is adequate for Grenache, it is not appropriate for the precious Mourvèdre and Syrah grapes, and La Nerthe employs small barrels. This is why their richest *cu-*

vées, Syrah and Mourvèdre are matured in barrels, to refine their tannins while respecting the nature of the grapes. La Nerthe's reintroduction of barrels to Châteauneuf renewed a 100-year-old tradition.

ANNUAL PRODUCTION

Châteauneuf-du-Pape Clos de Beauvenir (white): 400 cases

Châteauneuf-du-Pape Cuvée des Cadettes (red): 1,000 cases

AVERAGE PRICE (VARIABLE DEPENDING ON VINTAGE): $30–75

GREAT RECENT VINTAGES

2003, 2001, 2000, 1998, 1990, 1989

By the mid-18th century, wines from La Nerthe were already being sold in London, Moscow, and America. In 1782, Darluc wrote in his history of Provence: "The best wines are produced in the Clos de la Nerthe . . . they have a velvety texture and charm. The time to drink them is in their perfect maturity, when they are three to four years old." In 1784, La Nerthe wine was already being bottled on the estate.

The marquis of Tulle de Villefranche, owner of La Nerthe at the time, was one of the first to make Châteauneuf famous around the world, through an extended network of retailers. In the 19th century, Châteauneuf wine was already one-third more costly than the wine of neighboring villages, and when a local poet named Anselm Mathieu established a price list of all the different Châteauneuf wines in 1850, he found that La Nerthe was the most expensive. It was also considered the best. As early as 1822, Julian's Inventory of all the known vineyards ranked La Nerthe as a "first class wine," ahead of all the other Châteauneuf.

Around 1870, the vineyard was destroyed, along with almost all European vines, by the phylloxera disease. The Tulle de Villefranche family sold the property, which was one of the five major domaines of Châteauneuf, to Commander Joseph Ducos, an alumnus of France's prestigious engineering school. At La Nerthe, Joseph Ducos researched different types of grapes. Experimenting with 10 varieties, he determined the ideal quantity and specific flavor each one could bring to a blend. He noted, for example, that Grenache and Cinsault offered "alcohol,

warmth and mellowness" and should constitute up to 20% of the blend. More than a century ago, he already realized that a small portion of Grenache best expresses the *terroir* of La Nerthe. Mourvèdre, Syrah, Muscardin, and Camarèse (also called Vaccarèse) bring "strength, aging potential, freshness, and a thirst-quenching taste," and should constitute 40%. Counoise and Picpoul provide charm, freshness, and bouquet, and a special winey taste, termed vinosity, for another 30% of the blend. The white grapes, Clairette and Bourboulenc, in a proportion of 10%, bring finesse, warmth, and brilliance to red wine. All these grape varieties are approved under the strict regulations that govern which wines may carry the prestigious label A.O.C., Appellation d'Origine Contrôlée. Ducos himself is said to have introduced at least three of these varieties—Cinsault, Roussanne, and Camarèse— into the region.

The vineyards and château sit on the southeastern side of the village, well marked from the road but hidden by a large outcropping of trees. Records show that a merchant in Boston, Massachusetts, actually ordered barrels of La Nerthe in the late 18th century. The famous French poet Frédéric Mistral, who gave his name to the fierce, persistent winds of the region, called the

wine of La Nerthe *"un vin royal impérial et pontifical."* During World War II, the German air force used La Nerthe as its command control center and the property was badly damaged in the subsequent liberation of the area by the British and American forces. Until 1985, the estate was owned by the Dereumaux family and the wine was highly prized for its immense size and enormous palate-pleasing pleasure. In 1985 this famous property was purchased by the Richard family and a *négociant* firm, David and Foillard. Extensive renovations costing millions were made, and Alain Dugas was brought in to administer the resurrection of La Nerthe. Today, La Nerthe is the showpiece château of the southern Rhône Valley. In fact, it is the only château with the stature and grandeur of a top Médoc estate. The vineyards have been completely reconstituted, with the exception of the old-vine parcels that are still used to produce the famed Cuvée des Cadettes. The vineyard surface area includes 20 acres for the two white wine *cuvées* and 202 acres for the two red wines. In 1991 this acreage was increased dramatically by the acquisition of another Châteauneuf-du-Pape estate, La Terre Ferme.

La Nerthe was one of Châteauneuf-du-Pape's legendary wines during the 1960s and 1970s. I remember my first taste of the 1978 Cuvée des Cadettes, a wine that must have topped 16% alcohol. It was black in color, and to this day remains one of the most memorable Châteauneuf-du-Papes I have ever tasted. However, this style has been abandoned, first in favor of a more commercially oriented style. Gradually Alain Dugas began moving in a direction that suggests only the highest quality will be accepted, a refreshing perspective in view of the corporate mentality that often prizes quantity over quality. Dugas, an intense individual, seems to require perfection at all levels. The cellars are immaculate, and one can sense there is an element of precision about everything being done at La Nerthe, a complete contrast to the pre-1985 era.

The winemaking technique is relatively modern, with destemming, and vinification carried out in assorted tanks and vats. What is nontraditional is that the regular *cuvée* of Château La Nerthe then goes into both barrel and tank, with two-thirds being put in oak casks (one-half of which are new) and one-third in tanks. The wines are then blended prior to bottling. The regular *cuvée* has seen its percentage of Grenache decrease under the new ownership. Today it is a blend of 55% Grenache, with Syrah, Mourvèdre, Cinsault, Counoise, and a few dollops of other grapes. The Cuvée des Cadettes continues to be made from the original 12.4-acre parcel of vines 80–100 years old. It is a blend of primarily Grenache with Mourvèdre and Syrah, with Mourvèdre often dominating. It is aged in oak casks, of which a relatively high percentage are new. Since 1993, Alain Dugas has bottled the red wine *cuvées* without any filtration. There is no question that the fabulous raw potential of both the 1989 and 1990 Les Cadettes was compromised by both an overly zealous fining and filtration at bottling. That is not likely to happen again, and for that reason I believe this estate is ready to take its position with the very top properties in Châteauneuf-du-Pape.

CHATEAUNEUF-DU-PAPE CLOS DE BEAUVENIR

2001 Châteauneuf-du-Pape Blanc Clos de Beauvenir
RATING: 93 points

A luxury white *cuvée*, the 2001 Châteauneuf-du-Pape Clos de Beauvenir (62% Roussanne and 38% Clairette) ages as well as any other white Châteauneuf. The finest effort to date, the 2001 is a gloriously perfumed, honeyed wine possessing full body, terrific acidity, tremendous delineation, and a layered texture. A treat to drink (although nearly impossible to find), this loaded Châteauneuf-du-Pape will be drinkable between now and 2010.

1999 Châteauneuf-du-Pape Blanc Clos de Beauvenir
RATING: 91 points

The luxury *cuvée* of white Châteauneuf-du-Pape, the 1999 Clos de Beauvenir, is a blend of 62% Roussanne, 29% Clairette, 4% Bourboulenc, and 5% Grenache Blanc. Sadly, there are only 500 cases of this barrel-fermented offering. It possesses an exciting nose of honeyed citrus mixed with white flowers, honeysuckle, and a hint of wax. Dense, full-bodied, nicely textured, fresh, and lively, it is a substantial dry white that should age well for another 2–3 years. This white had its malolactic fermentation blocked, which, based on my experience tasting 15–20-year-old white Châteauneuf-du-Papes, means they tend to show extremely well young but fall into a dull, dumb, oxidized stage, only to reemerge after a decade.

1996 Châteauneuf-du-Pape Blanc Clos de Beauvenir
RATING: 90 points

The barrel-fermented 1996 Châteauneuf-du-Pape Clos de Beauvenir is a blend of 38% Roussanne and 47% Clairette, with the balance an assortment of other white wine varietals. The wine exhibits an excellent texture, beautiful honeyed pineapple/pear-like fruit, a chewy, full-bodied palate, and outstanding length. It appears to be one of the finest Beauvenirs La Nerthe has made. Dugas told me the yields were extremely low, averaging 15–20 hectoliters per hectare. Anticipated maturity: now–2009.

CHATEAUNEUF-DU-PAPE CUVEE DES CADETTES

2003 Châteauneuf-du-Pape Cuvée des Cadettes
RATING: 94–96 points

A brilliant success and possibly the best wine made at La Nerthe since the great 1998, there are 1,000 cases of this blend of 48% Grenache, 36% Syrah, and 16% Mourvèdre. Deep ruby purple to the rim, with a nose that hints of flowers, licorice, black fruits, and toasty oak, this wine exhibits enormous body, very pure, concentrated flavors, and moderate tannin in a finish that approaches one minute. This is a sensational wine, quite backward, but a bit more voluminous and endowed with fat, and a multitextured personality for this *cuvée*. Anticipated maturity: 2009–2025.

2001 Châteauneuf-du-Pape Cuvée des Cadettes
RATING: 95 points

The 2001 Châteauneuf-du-Pape Cuvée des Cadettes is the finest example of this *cuvée* since the 1998. This blend of 40% Grenache, 30% Mourvèdre, and 30% Syrah was aged in 100% new oak (to my knowledge the only wine of the appellation to receive such treatment, although the Cuvée des Generations of La Gardine sees a high percentage of small new oak casks). Remarkably, the oak is well integrated, which gives readers an idea of just how concentrated this 2001 is. A classic perfume of blackberry liqueur, smoky vanilla, new saddle leather, and graphite jumps from the glass of this dense purple–colored Châteauneuf. Full-bodied, with a terrific texture, a large, expansive mid-palate, and a blockbuster finish, this large-scaled, ageworthy wine should prove compelling. Anticipated maturity: 2007–2021.

2000 Châteauneuf-du-Pape Cuvée des Cadettes
RATING: 93 points

This *cuvée* represents the essence of the appellation, and has considerable potential for longevity. The 2000 Châteauneuf-du-Pape Cuvée des Cadettes is a blend of 38% Syrah, 35% Grenache, and 27% Mourvèdre. This blend includes the highest percentage of Syrah used in any Cuvée des Cadettes to date. It exhibits a dense ruby/purple color as well as a sweet, concentrated, opulent style with plenty of power, loads of sweet blackberry liqueur notes, and a touch of vanilla in the background. Sweet, chewy, plush, sexy, and voluptuous, it may not be the longest-lived example, but it is undeniably charming and disarming. Anticipated maturity: now–2016.

1999 Châteauneuf-du-Pape Cuvée des Cadettes
RATING: 91 points

The top *cuvée* of the most majestic estate in Châteauneuf-du-Pape, Château La Nerthe, the Cuvée des Cadettes is only made in the finest years. The blend changes from year to year, but it generally includes a high percentage of Mourvèdre. The 1999 (39% Grenache, 35% Syrah, and 26% Mourvèdre, all aged in barrel) does not reveal the fat of the 2000 or 1998, but it is an elegant, well-delineated effort with copious vibrancy, freshness, and cedar, black cherry and cassis fruit. Medium to full–bodied with a moderately muscular personality, it will benefit from 4–5 years of cellaring, and keep for 15–18.

1998 Châteauneuf-du-Pape Cuvée des Cadettes
RATING: 96 points

The 1998 Cuvée des Cadettes, which has put on considerable weight since I first tasted it, is a blend of 39% Grenache, 37% Mourvèdre, and 24% Syrah. It possesses a dense purple color as well as a glorious bouquet of blackberry liqueur intermixed with aromas of white flowers, licorice, and hints of minerals and *garrigue*. Full-bodied, chewy, and thick, its enormous wealth of fruit and glycerin conceals substantial tannin. To my taste, this classic is the greatest Des Cadettes made to date (but watch out for the 2001!). Anticipated maturity: 2006–2025.

1997 Châteauneuf-du-Pape Cuvée des Cadettes
RATING: 90 points

The outstanding 1997 Châteauneuf-du-Pape Cuvée des Cadettes (36% Grenache, 32% Mourvèdre, and 32% Syrah) is unquestionably one of the stars of this vintage. The color is a saturated ruby/purple. The nose offers up copious quantities of cassis, kirsch, new saddle leather, Asian spices, and earth. Rich and full-bodied, with a creamy texture, low acidity, and a luscious, massive finish for the vintage, this is a superb example from a light year. It should drink well for another 5–10 years.

1995 Châteauneuf-du-Pape Cuvée des Cadettes
RATING: 90 points

Fashioned from 44% Grenache and equal parts Mourvèdre and Syrah, the ruby/purple-colored 1995 Châteauneuf-du-Pape Cuvée des Cadettes offers tight but promising aromas of red and black fruits, scorched earth, wood smoke, and vanilla. Medium to full–bodied, tannic, and tightly knit, it requires another 4–5 years of cellaring (as do many 1995 Châteauneuf-du-Papes). Anticipated maturity: 2008–2016.

WINES:

Côte-Rôtie

Côte-Rôtie Cuvée Belle Hélène

OWNERS: Michel and Stéphane Ogier

ADDRESS: 3 Chemin du Bac, 69420 Ampuis, France

TELEPHONE: 33 04 74 56 10 75

TELEFAX: 33 04 74 56 01 75

E-MAIL: sogier@club-internet.fr

CONTACT: Stéphane Ogier

VISITING POLICY: By appointment only

VINEYARDS

SURFACE AREA: La Rosine—12.35 acres; Côte-Rôtie—6.4 acres

GRAPE VARIETALS: La Rosine—Syrah, Viognier, Roussanne;
    Côte-Rôtie—100% Syrah

AVERAGE AGE OF THE VINES:

La Rosine—60% of Syrah vines are 1–5 years old, 40%
    15 years old; the Viognier and Roussanne vines were
    planted in 2000

Côte-Rôtie—average 25 years old

DENSITY OF PLANTATION: La Rosine: 9,000 vines per hectare;
    Côte-Rôtie: 9,000–10,000 vines per hectare

AVERAGE YIELDS: La Rosine: 35–45 hectoliters per hectare;
    Côte-Rôtie: 30–40 hectoliters per hectare

WINEMAKING AND UPBRINGING

At this small estate, both father and son Ogier have taken a
very aggressive position of reducing the utilization of herbicides, with the parcel in the Côte-Rozier that produces the

Michel, Hélène, and Stéphane Ogier

Belle Hélène worked completely without herbicides. The intention is to do this throughout the estate. There is also serious crop-thinning in years of considerable abundance. At
present, 70–100% of the grapes are destemmed according to
the character of the vintage. They also believe in a five- to
seven-day cold maceration prior to kicking off the vinification. Macerations/*cuvaisons* tend to last a total of 20–30 days,
but again, this is dependent on the character of the vintage.
After fermentation, all the production is then moved into
225-liter barrels. The wines are not racked at all, as they are
allowed to rest on their lees until malolactic fermentation is
finished. The estate Côte-Rôtie generally spends 18 months in
oak, of which about 30–35% is new, and the Belle Hélène 30
months in oak barrels, of which 100% is new. The wines are
bottled with neither fining nor filtration.

ANNUAL PRODUCTION

Côte-Rôtie Domaine: 10,000 bottles

Côte-Rôtie Belle Hélène: 1,000–2,000 bottles

AVERAGE PRICE (VARIABLE DEPENDING ON VINTAGE): $45–150

GREAT RECENT VINTAGES

2003, 2001, 1999, 1998, 1991, 1985

Michel Ogier and his son own only 6.4 acres of
vines, mostly on the Côte Blonde, and have been
estate-bottling only since 1982. Previously the crop was
primarily sold to Marcel Guigal and Max Chapoutier.
The vineyard, which includes six different sites, 50% on
the Côte Blonde and 50% on the Côte Brune, includes
But de Mont, Lancement, Côte-Rozier, Champon, Bes-
set, and Serine. This is, in every sense, a family-run estate, and now that Stéphane has graduated from
oenology school in Beaune, the estate seems to have
taken an even greater interest in quality. The wines of
Ogier are possibly the most fragrant, sexy, supple, and
quintessentially elegant wines of the appellation, although certainly René Rostaing's Côte Blonde gives
them some competition in that area. Two additional
wines that merit serious attention were launched in
2001: the Embruns (100% Côte Brune from Vérenay)
and Lancement (100% Côte Blonde).

COTE ROTIE

2003 Côte Rôtie

RATING: 90–92 points

The harvest for the Ogier family was unprecedentedly early, starting August 26 and finishing September 2, a good 2–3 weeks before a normal harvest would have started. The results are wines that are quite concentrated, as the yields were very small but also higher in alcohol and surprisingly high in tannin. The 2003 Côte-Rôtie, which is a blend of approximately 60% from the Côte Blonde and 40% from the Côte Brune, shows a deep ruby/purple color, good acidity (some was added at the winery), and dense, concentrated raspberry and black currant fruit notes intermixed with some *barrique* smells, scorched earth, and tannin. The wine needs 4–5 years of cellaring because of its acid/tannin profile but should keep for 15 more years.

2001 Côte Rôtie

RATING: 91–94 points

The regular Côte Rôtie is a 10,000-bottle *cuvée* aged in *barrique* (of which 30% is new), with 15% stems utilized during the fermentation. It enjoys a cold maceration in barrel, a technique common in both Burgundy and Côte Rôtie, and recently implemented in Bordeaux. The 2001 Côte Rôtie is soft and sexy, but possesses more volume and intensity than the 2000. A roasted, herbaceous bouquet of crème de cassis, licorice, violets, spice box, and pepper emerges from this medium to full–bodied, broad, expansive 2001. The finish lasts 5–12 seconds longer than the 2000's. It appears to be Ogier's finest Côte Rôtie since the brilliant 1999 and should drink well for 10–15 years.

1999 Côte Rôtie

RATING: 95 points

The finest Côte Rôties Ogier has made (and he agrees) are the 1999s. The fabulous, opaque purple–colored 1999 Côte Rôtie, which spent two years in wood (30% new), reveals a glorious bouquet of bacon fat, crème de cassis, licorice, violets, and spice box. It is full-bodied, with sweet tannin, great presence in the mouth, and a knockout finish. Although it will be approachable in its youth, another year or two of cellaring will be beneficial. Anticipated maturity: now–2018. Michel Ogier and his son, Stéphane, are producing spectacular wines. The only problem is that production is small. Ogier's 1999s are magical.

1998 Côte Rôtie

RATING: 90 points

Ogier's regular *cuvée* of Côte Rôtie sees about 25–30% new oak. It spends 18 months in barrel, and over 70% of the grapes emerge from their holdings on the Côte Blonde. The 1998 Côte Rôtie exhibits scents and flavors of charred earth, smoke, minerals, and cassis. The wine is full-bodied, rich, and dense, with abundant tannin in the finish. The French might call it a true *vin de garde*. It needs another 1–2 years of cellaring, and will keep for 15–18+ years. This wine is bottled with no filtration.

1991 Côte Rôtie

RATING: 93 points

A sensational Côte Rôtie, this wine boasts exceptional elegance married to a velvety-textured, supple, rich fruitiness. Ogier's Côte Rôties are not as masculine or robust as others, relying more on complexity and finesse. The 1991 displays an ethereal bouquet of ripe cassis, bacon, vanilla, and violets. This deep, medium-weight wine with extraordinary finesse, fragrance, and length on the palate would embarrass many a Musigny from Burgundy. Drink it over the next 2–3 years.

1989 Côte Rôtie

RATING: 90 points

Ogier's 1989 Côte Rôtie exhibited an exceptional elegance and a perfume that could rival the greatest wines of Burgundy. With more tannin and structure than the 1990, as well as excellent color, it needed 2–3 years of cellaring when last tasted in 1994. There was no doubting its magnificent fragrance of spring flowers, black fruits, oak, and minerals. The flavors were tightly knit, and the precociousness suggested by the bouquet was not followed up on the palate. Anticipated maturity: now–2009.

COTE ROTIE CUVEE BELLE HELENE

2003 Côte Rôtie Cuvée Belle Hélène

RATING: 92–94+ points

Given the very tiny yields in 2003, there are only 100 cases of this wine, which comes completely from the Côte Brune vineyard of Côte-Rozier. Dense ruby/purple in color, with a scorched earth, bacon fat, blackberry, and raspberry–scented nose intermixed with licorice, roasted meat, and tar notes, this is a very brawny, powerful Belle Hélène with considerable tannin and good acidity. Anticipated maturity: 2010–2025.

2001 Côte Rôtie Cuvée Belle Hélène

RATING: 94+ points

The dense blue/purple–colored 2001 Côte Rôtie Cuvée Belle Hélène displays a sweet nose of black raspberry liqueur intertwined with crème de cassis, licorice, dried herbs, and toasty vanilla. Full-bodied and rich, with fabulous concentration as well as texture, it requires 4–5 years of cellaring, and should evolve for 15+ years.

2000 Côte Rôtie Cuvée Belle Hélène

RATING: 93 points

The 2000 Côte Rôtie Cuvée Belle Hélène is a fleshy, sexy, soft, opulently styled effort possessing more concentration than most of its 2000 peers. More flamboyant and showy than the monumental 1999, the rich, deep ruby/purple–colored, medium-bodied 2000 offers notes of cassis, licorice, pepper, and white flowers. This harmonious, seamless, extraordinary Côte Rôtie should provide immense pleasure over the next 10–12 years.

1999 Côte Rôtie Cuvée Belle Hélène

RATING: 100 points

The perfect 1999 Côte Rôtie Cuvée Belle Hélène is a seamless, majestic classic with the kind of concentration found only in Guigal's top *cuvées*. It boasts gorgeously sweet tannin, enormous levels of both extract and concentration, and is not only a tour de force in winemaking, but a huge Côte Rôtie Syrah fruit bomb with massive glycerin, layers of extract, and plenty of toasty new oak, which is marvelously integrated given the fact that it spent 30 months in 100% new-wood barrels prior to being bottled without filtration. This outstanding effort requires another 3–4 years of cellaring. Anticipated maturity: 2008–2030. Bravo!

1998 Côte Rôtie Cuvée Belle Hélène

RATING: 95 points

The wine is sumptuous, but it will obviously be almost impossible to find. This wine enjoys malolactic fermentation in *barrique*. The 1998 Côte Rôtie Cuvée Belle Hélène boasts an opaque black/purple color as well as a tight but promising nose of new saddle leather, roasted meats, dried herbs, black fruits, and minerals. It is extremely full-bodied, super-concentrated, ferociously backward and tannic, and possesses sufficient extract, fruit, and depth to balance out the wine's structure. This classic, gorgeously proportioned Côte Rôtie will last for a generation. Anticipated maturity: 2006–2025.

1997 Côte Rôtie Cuvée Belle Hélène

RATING: 92 points

The 1997 Côte Rôtie Cuvée Belle Hélène is backward rather than seductive and open-knit. It exhibits a deep ruby color with purple nuances, and sweet, toasty new oak aromas intertwined with jammy kirsch and crème de cassis. With airing, black olive scents also emerge in this complex, nicely nuanced, medium to full–bodied effort. The finish possesses sweet fruit. While the 1997 is low in acidity, it has a tannic grip. It requires a degree of patience, but it is a glorious Côte Rôtie. Anticipated maturity: now–2017.

DOMAINE DU PEGAU

WINES:

Châteauneuf-du-Pape Cuvée Réservée

Châteauneuf-du-Pape Cuvée da Capo

Châteauneuf-du-Pape Cuvée Laurence

OWNERS: Mr. and Mrs. Paul Féraud and Laurence Féraud

ADDRESS: 15, avenue Impériale, 84230 Châteauneuf-du-Pape, France

TELEPHONE: 33 04 90 83 72 70 or 33 04 90 83 56 61

TELEFAX: 33 04 90 83 53 02

E-MAIL: pegau@pegau.com

WEBSITE: www.pegau.com

CONTACT: Laurence Féraud

VISITING POLICY: Open Monday through Friday for visits and tastings, 8 A.M.–noon and 1:30–6 P.M.; weekends by appointment; group visits by appointment only.

VINEYARDS

SURFACE AREA: 56.8 acres total (42 acres in red AOC Châteauneuf-du-Pape, 2.47 acres in white AOC Châteauneuf-du-Pape, and about 12.35 acres in *vin de table*)

GRAPE VARIETALS: *Red*—75% Grenache, 15% Syrah, 10% Mourvèdre; *white*—60% Grenache, 20% Clairette, 10% Bourboulenc, 10% Roussanne

AVERAGE AGE OF THE VINES: 40–60 years (5 acres of 94 years— La Crau)

DENSITY OF PLANTATION: 3,300 vines per hectare

AVERAGE YIELDS: 30–33 hectoliters per hectare

WINEMAKING AND UPBRINGING

The vineyards of Domaine du Pégau are carefully cultivated by hand. The wine calendar begins in December with pruning, *la taille*, which is carried out at intervals until March. Later in the year the green vine branches are snapped by hand. Preselecting the buds with the best development and exposure is what predetermines both the quality and volume of the future crop.

Throughout the year the soils are aerated and every two years organic matter is worked into the ground. Weedkillers are not used. When necessary, the vines are treated with sulfur and copper sulfate for their preventative and curative traits.

When the grapes have reached optimal maturity they are hand-picked and carefully separated. The vinification processes are natural and traditional. For the red wine there is a brief *foulage* (a process which breaks the skin of the grape to free the juice) and then the whole bunches are put in the vats. This process of maceration may last 15 days and continues until all the sugars have been transformed into alcohol. When this alcoholic fermentation is completed, the juice is decanted to large oak *foudres* where it will mature for a minimum of 18 months before bottling.

ANNUAL PRODUCTION

Cuvée Laurence: 6,000 bottles (only in specific vintages)

Cuvée da Capo: 4,000–5,000 bottles (only in great vintages)

Total of Cuvée Réservée: 63,000–74,000 bottles

AVERAGE PRICE (VARIABLE DEPENDING ON VINTAGE): $40–200

GREAT RECENT VINTAGES

2003, 2001, 2000, 1998, 1995, 1990, 1989, 1981

The Féraud family have been winemakers in Châteauneuf-du-Pape for over 150 years. Although the vineyards have changed hands a number of times, tradition and the knowledge handed down over generations have ensured that the Féraud wine is always an authentic product of its *terroir*.

The family has been producing wine in the region of Châteauneuf since 1670. The holdings have grown slowly, and in 1987 the Domaine du Pégau was incorporated as a partnership between father and daughter, Paul and Laurence. The name "Pégau" is a Provençal dialect word for the clay pitcher traditionally used to serve wine at the table, dating back to the 14th century and the time of the Avignon popes.

Laurence and Paul Féraud

The vineyards of the domaine comprise eight parcels, totaling 18 hectares (42 acres) of Châteauneuf's best *terroirs,* with the favored east-southeast exposure. The Pégau terroirs are composed largely of a Miocene sandy marl, overlying a mass of limestone and large quartzite pebbles that cover the majority. The appellation is renowned for this glacial deposit, whose overall effect is to bring the vines to an early maturity by absorbing the heat during the day (and thus allowing the soil to retain its moisture) and then giving it out at night. The domaine is composed of many different plots of vineyards, with vines ranging from 20 to 92 years of age and yields of around 30 hectoliters per hectare.

The Pégau estate of Laurence Féraud and her father, Paul, produces one of Châteauneuf-du-Pape's most majestic, old-style, robust, super-concentrated, blockbuster wines. Not surprisingly, Paul Féraud was a high school classmate and chum of Henri Bonneau, and they remain dear friends to this day. I suppose that it is not just a coincidence that of all the wines of Châteauneuf-du-Pape, Pégau's Cuvée Réservée and Cuvée Laurence come closest to achieving the same glory as Henri Bonneau's Cuvée des Célestins.

Father and daughter could not have more different personalities. Paul, a diminutive, sinewy, no-nonsense, but deceptively funny man with a strong Provençal twang to his speech, looks as though he sprouted from one of the stone-covered Châteauneuf-du-Pape vineyards. He exudes the style of a man who works in the vineyards. His daughter, charming, articulate, and university-educated, is clearly in charge of the business side of Pégau, but she also gets down and dirty when cellar work is required. Although quite different, the two

complement each other, and on recent visits to Pégau it was Laurence rather than Paul who was climbing the ladder to extract juice from the large old wood *foudres* in the cellars next to the family's home in downtown Châteauneuf-du-Pape.

This morsellated estate, with holdings sprinkled throughout three sectors, Courthézon, La Solitude, and Bédarrides, possesses many old vines. The two finest parcels include one planted in 1902, in the northwestern sector, not far from La Gardine, and an old-vine parcel planted in 1905, in the heart of La Crau. Until 1987 (when Laurence became able to assist her father), this estate sold much of its production to *négociants.* This is winemaking with no compromises. These wines are made from physiologically ripe grapes, low yields, and are left to sit on their lees in the large *foudres* until Paul and Laurence decide it is time to bottle. Moreover, the wines suffer no bottle shock, because sulfur additions are low, and, more importantly, there is no fining or filtration for any Pégau red wine.

In 1998 they added another wine, the Cuvée da Capo, primarily old-vine Grenache, but all 13 authorized varietals are in this 600-case *cuvée* that originates from some of the estate's oldest parcels on La Crau. It has only been produced in 1998, 2000, and 2003, and is a massive wine of legendary potential.

I have long been a huge fan of this estate, and have put my money where my mouth has been, having purchased all of Pégau's vintages since 1979. Remarkably, a tasting I did for this book of all the Pégau wines I own did not reveal one wine that had passed its plateau of maturity. Accessible, if somewhat fiery and forceful when young, Pégau's Châteauneuf-du-Papes are among the most classic and long-lived of the appellation. The great vintages—1981, 1985, 1989, 1990, 1998, 2000, 2001, and 2003 (all potential legends)—can easily age well for two decades.

The Cuvée Laurence (about 650 cases produced in top vintages) is kept in cellars several miles away from those most visitors are shown. This wine is largely identical to the Cuvée Réservée, but it is kept two to three years longer in small oak casks (no new oak is ever used). I have tasted the available vintages blind against the Cuvée Réservée, and in most cases I have a slight preference for the more intense fruit and grapiness of the Cuvée Réservée, but the Cuvée Laurence is noticeably more complex and evolved because of its longer sojourn in wood. It is not meant to be a luxury *cuvée*, simply a wine that reflects the oldest traditions of Châteauneuf-du-Pape when the wine was often kept four or five years before being bottled.

CHATEAUNEUF-DU-PAPE CUVEE DA CAPO

2003 Châteauneuf-du-Pape Cuvée da Capo

RATING: 96–100 points

This wine was still fermenting after a year, which is similar to what both the 1998 and 2000 did. The potential of the wine is scary, it is that compelling and prodigious, but the Férauds need to be patient, as this wine needs to digest more of its sugar. A wine of enormous mass, concentration, and sweetness, with no hard edges, frightening levels of concentration, and almost the bottled essence of old-vine Grenache as well as Châteauneuf-du-Pape, this is the kind of wine that probably will rank right up there in terms of traditional Châteauneuf-du-Papes with Henri Bonneau's famed 1990 and 1990 Réserve des Célestins or, of course, this particular *cuvée*'s two predecessors, the 2000 and 1998 Capo. At this stage of its life—believe it or not—it exhibits even more potential than its two siblings, but of course, it still has to finish fermenting and be bottled, and of course they don't filter. I expect this wine is not going to hit the bottle until some time in 2006, given how slow it is evolving, but wow, is there awesome potential in the 2003 Cuvée da Capo! Anticipated maturity: 2010–2030+.

2000 Châteauneuf-du-Pape Cuvée da Capo

RATING: 100 points

The 2000 Châteauneuf-du-Pape Cuvée da Capo is a monument to old-vine Grenache as well as traditionally made Châteauneuf-du-Pape. Boasting a natural alcohol of 16%, the color is inky/ruby/purple to the rim. The extraordinary nose reveals aromas of kirsch, new saddle leather, animal fur, Provençal herbs, spice box, licorice, and a salty sea breeze character. On the palate, the wine is enormous, with an unctousness, thickness, and purity that must be tasted to be believed. Over 95% of this offering is old-vine Grenache, and the rest a field blend of ancient vines. Representing the essence of Châteauneuf-du-Pape, it possesses so much concentration that it is easy to pose the question "Where's the tannin?" Analytically, it has very high levels of tannin, but the tannin is barely noticeable given the wine's exaggerated wealth of richness and power. This is a modern-day legend in the making, and despite its precociousness and ease in smelling and consuming, it will not hit its prime for another decade. It should last for 25–30 years, and take its place among some of the greatest Châteauneuf-du-Papes ever made. Anticipated maturity: 2010–2030+.

1998 Châteauneuf-du-Pape Cuvée da Capo

RATING: 100 points

The debut release of 1998 Cuvée da Capo (made from incredibly low yields of 90% Grenache and 10% the other twelve permitted varietals) is profound. The color is a dense, thick-looking, ruby/garnet/purple. The aromas begin slowly, but then roar from the glass like an out-of-control locomotive, offering up a smorgasbord of candied black fruits, pepper, *garrigue*, earth, and truffles. Enormously thick and rich but, amazingly, not heavy, this blockbuster, full-bodied Châteauneuf-du-Pape is still youthful, but should age gracefully for three decades. The Cuvée da Capo is frightfully expensive by Châteauneuf-du-Pape standards, but if quality like this existed in Burgundy, consumers would be willing to pay $500 a bottle. Think it over! Anticipated maturity: now–2031.

CHATEAUNEUF DU PAPE CUVEE LAURENCE

2000 Châteauneuf-du-Pape Cuvée Laurence

RATING: 94 points

Given how well the 1998 Cuvée Laurence is performing out of bottle, I might be underestimating the 2000 Châteauneuf-du-Pape Cuvée Laurence. It exhibits better integration of wood than previous vintages, even though no new oak is used. Full-bodied, powerful, and backward, it requires further upbringing. Layered and rich, it will undoubtedly be very long-lived. Anticipated maturity: 2007–2020.

1998 Châteauneuf-du-Pape Cuvée Laurence

RATING: 96 points

The 1998 Châteauneuf-du-Pape Cuvée Laurence, the finest example of this offering I have yet tasted (even better than the 1989, 1990, and 1995), spent four years in small barrels prior to being bottled unfiltered. A spectacular effort, it is a monument to great Châteauneuf-du-Pape. A dense plum/purple color is followed by aromas of sweet black fruits intermixed with tobacco, cedar, pepper, and fruitcake. Powerful, rich, and concentrated, with a finish that lasts for nearly a minute, this wine is performing far better than when I tasted it a year ago. It is a legendary Châteauneuf-du-Pape in the making. Anticipated maturity: now–2025.

1990 Châteauneuf-du-Pape Cuvée Laurence

RATING: 95 points

Bottled at what I suspect is the whim of Paul Féraud, the 1989 and 1990 Châteauneuf-du-Pape Cuvée Laurence were tasted side by side with the Cuvée Réservée. Although the Cuvée

Laurence is no better than the Cuvée Réservée, it is more evolved, with more complexity from the extended cask aging. Ultimately, I think the Cuvée Réservée will surpass it, since the development of that wine will take place in the bottle, not in wood. Anticipated maturity: now–2020.

1989 Châteauneuf-du-Pape Cuvée Laurence

RATING: 95 points

The 1989 Cuvée Laurence is slightly sweeter, richer, and more opulent than its younger sibling. However, both wines are enormously constituted, thick, rich, classic, old-style Châteauneuf-du-Papes the likes of which are rarely seen today. Anticipated maturity: now–2018.

CHATEAUNEUF-DU-PAPE CUVEE RESERVEE

2003 Châteauneuf-du-Pape Cuvée Réservée

RATING: 95–97 points

In tasting through the different *cuvées* at Pégau, what was clear is that both Laurence and her father, Paul, have produced an extraordinary vintage, with some lots still fermenting because of unresolved residual sugar. The 2003 Cuvée Réservée could easily be called Capo in 2003 because of its incredible power and richness. It will undoubtedly exceed 16% natural alcohol in 2003, has enormous concentration and mass, hints of kirsch, plum, prune, spice box, and pepper in a massive, concentrated, very rich and intense style, but with no hard edges. This will be a provocative as well as fascinating wine to follow, as I am sure it will drink well young, because of the huge glycerin and generosity of the wine, but also have the capacity to age, much like the 1990, for 15–20 or more years.

2001 Châteauneuf-du-Pape Cuvée Réservée

RATING: 95 points

The 2001 Châteauneuf-du-Pape Cuvée Réservée is a prodigious effort. The dark plum/ruby/garnet color is followed by a spectacular smorgasbord of aromas, including roasted meats, lavender, ground pepper, and thick, sweet blackberry and brandy-macerated cherries. Full-bodied, dense, and chewy, it has high levels of tannin, a huge finish, and a monster upside. Although less voluptuous than the 2000, the 2001 looks to be potentially the longest-lived and finest Cuvée Réservée since the wonderful duo of 1989 and 1990, both of which are aging splendidly. Anticipated maturity: 2006–2020.

2000 Châteauneuf-du-Pape Cuvée Réservée

RATING: 95 points

The 2000 Châteauneuf-du-Pape Cuvée Réservée may be one of the few 2000s that is better than its 1998 counterpart. A deep ruby/purple color is accompanied by sweet aromas of crème de cassis, kirsch, cedar, licorice, and pepper. It smells like an open-air Provençal market. Sweet, fat, opulent, and voluptuous, with fabulous fruit concentration, sweet tannin, and a long, 45+–second finish, this powerful, deep, seamless 2000 is impeccably well balanced. A tour de force in traditional Châteauneuf-du-Pape, it is accessible now, but should age easily for 15–20 years.

1999 Châteauneuf-du-Pape Cuvée Réservée

RATING: 92 points

A powerful, concentrated 1999 Châteauneuf-du-Pape was produced at Château Pégau. The dense ruby/purple–colored 1999 Châteauneuf-du-Pape Cuvée Réservée boasts a powerful bouquet of pepper, *garrigue*, black fruits, and earth. Full-bodied and expansive, with sweet tannin giving it a more open-knit, accessible style than most young vintages of Pégau, this is a wine to drink while waiting for the 1998 and 1995 to become fully mature. Like all of this estate's red wines, it was bottled with neither fining nor filtration. Anticipated maturity: now–2014.

1998 Châteauneuf-du-Pape Cuvée Réservée

RATING: 94 points

The 1998 Cuvée Réservée is an old-style, full-bodied effort revealing notes of roasted meats, beef blood, *herbes de Provence*, kirsch, sandalwood, and spice. Rich, full-bodied, moderately tannic, super-pure and dense, this gorgeous offering is the finest Cuvée Réservée produced since 1990. Anticipated maturity: now–2020.

1995 Châteauneuf-du-Pape Cuvée Réservée

RATING: 94 points

The 1995 Cuvée Réservée exhibits an opaque black/purple color, and extraordinary rich, intense aromas of smoke, black raspberries, kirsch, and spice. Exceptionally full-bodied, with an unctuous texture, and a thick, rich, expansive mid-palate, this superbly concentrated wine appears to be a worthy rival to this estate's phenomenal 1989 and 1990. Interestingly, the average alcohol level achieved by Domaine du Pégau in 1995 was 14.5–15.5%. This is a blockbuster Châteauneuf-du-Pape. Anticipated maturity: now–2020.

1994 Châteauneuf-du-Pape Cuvée Réservée

RATING: 92 points

The superb 1994 is one of the top wines of the vintage. It reveals a deep ruby/purple color, followed by an expressive nose of black cherries, smoked meats, black olives, and Provençal herbs. Thick, rich, and full-bodied, as well as sweeter and softer than the more structured 1995, this is a huge wine for the vintage. Anticipated maturity: now–2015.

1990 Châteauneuf-du-Pape Cuvée Réservée

RATING: 96 points

The 1990 Cuvée Réservée is one of the appellation's super-stars. After bottling, the color is still an impenetrable, black/purple color. The huge nose of truffles, tar, superripe black fruits, licorice, tobacco, and spices is profound. In the mouth there is sweet, expansive fruit, a super-concentrated, powerful, tannic taste, lavish amounts of glycerin and body, as well as a finish that lasts well over a minute. With plenty of tannin, this wine is destined to have 20–25 years of evolution. And yes, this wine was bottled unfined and unfiltered, so expect considerable sediment to occur. Anticipated maturity: now–2020.

1989 Châteauneuf-du-Pape Cuvée Réservée

RATING: 92 points

Féraud's 1989 resembles something between a dry red table wine and vintage port. Its dark purple/black color, exceptional concentration, great extract, and huge body loaded with glycerin and tannin make it one of the most immense wines of this superlative vintage. Surprisingly forward (blame the superb ripeness and relatively low acidity of the 1989 vintage), this is a prodigious Châteauneuf-du-Pape. Anticipated maturity: now–2018.

1985 Châteauneuf-du-Pape Cuvée Réservée

RATING: 93 points

Most 1985 Châteauneuf-du-Papes matured quickly, and in most cases did not achieve the heights of richness and complexity predicted when they were young. Pegau's 1985 is an exception. The color is still an opaque ruby/purple with no lightening at the edge. The nose resembles a 3- to 5-year-old wine, rather than one that is nearly 20. Its huge fruit, muscular, thick, full-bodied, corpulent personality, and stunning length make for a rich, powerful glass of Châteauneuf-du-Pape. Anticipated maturity: now–2012.

1983 Châteauneuf-du-Pape Cuvée Réservée

RATING: 90 points

In complete contrast to the super-powerful, rich yet backward 1985, the 1983 appears to have reached full maturity. The color is a deep ruby with some amber/orange at the edge, and the flamboyant nose offers up oodles of sweet cedar, *herbes de Provence,* smoked meats, and jammy cherry fruit. Full-bodied, fleshy, and mouth-filling, this powerful yet soft, expansive, velvety-textured wine makes for a delicious glassful of Châteauneuf-du-Pape. Anticipated maturity: now.

1981 Châteauneuf-du-Pape Cuvée Réservée

RATING: 93 points

This has always been a magnificent example of the vintage. After having gone through nearly two cases, except for one corked bottle, I have found this to be consistently a thrilling wine. It has tasted fully mature since 1990, but the wine displays no loss of fruit, and continues to gain in terms of its aromatic development and complexity. The color is a deep, dark garnet with some amber at the edge. The huge, flashy, ostentatious nose of smoked meats, jammy berry fruit, Asian spices, and truffles is followed by an enormously constituted, big, fleshy, full-bodied wine that is crammed with glycerin, extract, and alcohol. This is a blockbuster, velvety-textured, decadent Châteauneuf-du-Pape that should continue to drink well for another 2–4 years.

CHATEAU RAYAS

WINES:

Rayas Châteauneuf-du-Pape

Fonsalette Côtes du Rhône Cuvée Syrah

Fonsalette Côtes du Rhône

OWNERS: Reynaud family

ADDRESS: 84230 Châteauneuf-du-Pape, France

TELEPHONE: 33 04 90 83 73 09

TELEFAX: 33 04 90 83 51 17

VISITING POLICY: Virtually no visits, but those dying to visit should at least write or telephone

VINEYARDS

SURFACE AREA:

Château Rayas: 37 acres (white—5 acres; Rayas—19.8 acres; Pignan—7.5 acres)

Château de Fonsalette: 27 acres (white—7.5 acres; red—19.8 acres)

GRAPE VARIETALS:

Château Rayas: Grenache, Clairette, other varietals

Château de Fonsalette: Grenache, Cinsault, Syrah, Marsanne, Clairette

AVERAGE AGE OF THE VINES:

Château Rayas (red)—30 years

Château de Fonsalette: 35 years

DENSITY OF PLANTATION:

Château Rayas: 3,000 vines per hectare

Château de Fonsalette: 3,000 vines per hectare

AVERAGE YIELDS:

Château Rayas: 15–25 hectoliters per hectare

Château de Fonsalette: 20–30 hectoliters per hectare

WINEMAKING AND UPBRINGING

For both Rayas and Fonsalette (kept in the same cellar on the property of Rayas), after fermentation, which is relatively short, the wines are moved into an assortment of ancient barrels, *demi-muids,* and moderate and larger *foudres.* A tasting process, always somewhat mysterious, results in the selection of which wines will end up being Rayas, Fonsalette, Fonsalette Syrah, and of course the other wines made from declassified Rayas, the Pignan and generic La Pialade. While the wines are not filtered, the time they spend in barrel and in these various sizes of neutral wood has been shortened from nearly two years by the father, Louis Reynaud, to 14–16 months by Jacques Reynaud. His nephew Emmanuel, who has run the estate since Jacques Reynaud's death in January 1997, continues that practice.

ANNUAL PRODUCTION

Château Rayas (red): 2,000 cases
Château de Fonsalette (red): 1,666 cases
Fonsalette Côtes du Rhône (red): 1,200 cases
Fonsalette Cuvée Syrah (red): 400 cases
AVERAGE PRICE (VARIABLE DEPENDING ON VINTAGE): $50–175

GREAT RECENT VINTAGES

2003, 2001, 2000, 1998, 1995, 1990, 1989, 1985, 1983, 1981, 1979, 1978

The late Jacques Reynaud

The reputation for this extraordinary estate was largely created by the eccentric but charmingly devilish Jacques Reynaud, who died of a massive heart attack in January 1997. His nephew, Emmanuel, and sister (who looks amazingly like her brother) now manage the estate. In my personal collection there are a few wines with which I would never part. Among the few "untouchables" are the finest vintages of Rayas. In some vintages, Rayas reaches a level of sumptuousness and extraordinary intensity, allied with an opulence in texture and flavor, that can even humble a great Bordeaux or Burgundy.

No one would suspect that inside the drab, unpainted building that houses Château Rayas (sitting unmarked at the end of a deteriorating dirt road in the appellation of Châteauneuf-du-Pape) are some of the world's most distinctive wines. The credit must be extended to the late Jacques Reynaud and his father, Louis, who passed away in 1978. Jacques Reynaud (who reminded me of a cross between Dr. Seuss's Grinch and Yoda from the *Star Wars* films) was the brilliant, unassuming genius behind these wines, which are made from frightfully low yields harvested incredibly late. Reynaud's sister, Françoise, who is cut from the same eccentric mold as her brother, lives on the estate and works together with Emmanuel Reynaud in producing the wines.

Château Rayas is the antithesis of modern-day winemaking. No stainless steel, no temperature controls, no new oak, and no oenologists are to be found in the Rayas cellar, which contains a hodgepodge of barrels, *demi-muids,* and *foudres.* The stories I could tell about Jacques Reynaud could fill a book, but behind his decidedly antifame, anti-20th-century façade was an extremely well-read gentleman with exceptional knowledge

and a love of many things, including fine food, as I discovered over several meals with him at the nearby bastion of artisanal Provençal cuisine, La Beaugravière.

Getting precise information on what goes on at Château Rayas has never been an easy task, and the tight-lipped attitude seems to be a family trait. Despite having visited and tasted at Rayas more than twenty times, I still have not figured out what magic takes place in these cellars. Given the extraordinary quality that emerges in the finest years, I have learned to live without the answers. After all, sometimes the mysteries of life are best kept secret. I got to know Jacques Reynaud reasonably well, and several stories give a glimpse of Reynaud's impish character. Early in my tasting experience with him, I became irritated after tasting through four different barrels without Reynaud saying one word about what was in each barrel. Finally, I asked what we were tasting. His response was, "You're the expert. You tell me." Another example of his sense of humor emerged over dinner at La Beaugravière while we were sharing a magnificent bottle of Chave Hermitage. I asked him whom he admired the most. His deadly serious yet comical response was, "You."

What I have learned over the last decade is that Château Rayas is a 56-acre estate, of which 37 acres are in vine. From that 37 acres, less than 3,000 cases of Châteauneuf-du-Pape are produced. When you consider that Château Pétrus produces an average of 4,500 cases from 28 acres, readers can understand just how small the yields are at Rayas. From this estate, the Reynauds produce two red wines, Rayas and Pignan. A controversial white Rayas is also made.

While Jacques Reynaud liked to play the role of a reclusive nomad, the fact that he never turned down a dinner invitation indicated that there was so much more to him than he liked to let on. Visitors to Rayas are advised to make an appointment, if possible, through the estate's importer. Once an appointment has been secured, there is no guarantee that visitors will be able to find the property. This is one of the few cellars (Henri Bonneau's is another) that is unmarked. The best advice I can provide is to follow the signs for Château Vaudieu, or take the road out of Châteauneuf-du-Pape in the direction Orange (D 68), passing Bosquet des Papes on the right and the ruined papal château on the left. Proceed another mile or so toward Orange and take a right at the unmarked road that sharply veers right in an easterly direction. About one mile down this road, Château Vaudieu can be spotted to the southeast, and on a very small, deteriorating sign will be the word "Rayas." The dark, drab cellars are nearly hidden behind the large trees. A mile or two to the west the plateau of Châteauneuf-du-Pape begins, and the famed *galets roulés* blanket the vineyards, but this part of Châteauneuf-du-Pape is noticeably different, with more sandy, red soils, and a marked absence of the large football and melon–shaped boulders. Rayas has a cool-climate vineyard in a warm appellation.

A tasting inside the low-slung, two-story, drab cellars is never going to produce a great deal of technical detail about just how these marvelous wines are made. In these cellars, the Reynauds make Rayas and the Fonsalette Côtes du Rhône and other miscellaneous *cuvées* that have been culled out for their all-purpose, rather innocuous La Pialade. The Reynauds are unlikely to provide much help, but the basic family response to any winemaking inquiry is essentially, "It's the vineyard and small yields, stupid." Yields here are considered commercial madness by peers, but to a person, I have never met anyone in Châteauneuf-du-Pape who did not regard Reynaud and his spiritual sidekick, Henri Bonneau, with extraordinary admiration and respect. In these cellars, tasting the component parts is never as satisfying as tasting the wine after it is bottled.

In the great vintages, it is the late harvest that gives Rayas the extraordinary essence of cherries and raspberries. There is no other wine I have ever tasted in the world, save perhaps for the old-vine Merlot and Cabernet Franc of Château Lafleur in Pomerol, that gives such a quintessentially raspberry/cherry/framboise liqueur intensity as does Château Rayas. As limited in

quantity as Rayas and its vinous siblings tend to be, it would be a shame to go through life without tasting at least one great vintage of this prodigious wine. For example, at a birthday party for a dear friend in 1996, a 1978 Rayas and a 1978 Domaine de la Romanée Conti La Tâche (one of the greatest red Burgundies I have tasted) were opened. Within 15 minutes, not a drop of Rayas remained in anyone's glass, but many glasses still contained plenty of La Tâche.

Although the Fonsalette wines are made at the cellars of Jacques Reynaud's Château Rayas, the vineyard is located near Lagarde-Paréol. This large 321-acre property, planted by Jacques's father, Louis, at the end of World War II, has only 27 acres under vine. The largest part of the property is a huge park that surrounds a dilapidated, unusual-looking edifice that might pass for a castle in a B-grade horror movie or the residence of the fictional Addams family.

Two extraordinary red wines emerge from this domaine. The remarkable Fonsalette, a 50% Grenache, 35% Cinsault, 15% Syrah blend, is better than the great majority of Châteauneuf-du-Papes. It is made in the exact same manner as Rayas, from yields that are amazingly low (about five barrels of wine per acre are produced from yields well under two tons of fruit per acre). There is also a legendary Cuvée Syrah that is made in microscopic quantities from what Jacques Reynaud does not blend in with Fonsalette. It is made from a Syrah vineyard planted with a northern orientation, which gives it a cooler microclimate than other vineyards in the south. The Syrah came from cuttings that Jacques's father, Louis, obtained from Gérard Chave in Hermitage. It is a remarkably dense, concentrated, opaque-colored wine that often needs 15–20 years to begin to evolve (the 1978 is just beginning to emerge from its infancy).

The red *cuvées* of Fonsalette Côtes du Rhône and Fonsalette Côtes du Rhône Cuvée Syrah can easily last for two decades, with the Syrah probably having 30–40 years of ageability. That this estate produces the singularly greatest, most monumental Côtes du Rhône is incontestable. It always confounds me that this wine is largely ignored by the trophy hunters in the wine commerce—so much the better, I suppose.

Reynaud has inspired and motivated a young generation of French winemakers to rediscover the methods of the past, and to recognize both the legitimacy and nobility of Grenache. Finally, Jacques Reynaud, part recluse, part philosopher, part gourmet, part superb winemaker, and part myth and legend, has left an indelible imprint on this author and, I suspect, on all those who have been touched by him or his extraordinary wines.

On January 14, 1997, one day before his 73rd birthday, Jacques Reynaud, while shopping for shoes in Avignon (probably his only materialistic addiction), collapsed and died from a heart attack. He was a *real* legend.

The jury still remains out on Emmanuel Reynaud, who, along with Jacques Reynaud's sister, has run the estate and made every vintage of Rayas since 1997. Certainly the greatness of Châteauneuf-du-Pape vintages in 1998, 2000, and 2001 didn't seem to translate into profound wines at Rayas, although what they produced is certainly very good, even outstanding. The 2003 looks to be the best yet under Emmanuel. However, the standards are very high, and some of the wines Emmanuel's uncle Jacques made were legendary stuff and almost impossible to replicate. Emmanuel Reynaud thinks he's moving in the right direction and seems to have changed very little in the cellars or in the general philosophy at Rayas. It's still a bit early to see if he can perform the same magic in the cellars, but certainly the 1998, 2000, and 2001, great years in Châteauneuf-du-Pape, produced wines that were not as profound as the quality that emerged elsewhere in Châteauneuf-du-Pape.

FONSALETTE COTES DU RHONE

2003 Fonsalette Côtes du Rhône
RATING: 90–92 points
The Cinsault, which represents 35% of the blend for this Côtes du Rhône, hit unprecedented levels of alcohol and richness in 2003. This wine doesn't have a lot of color but it is voluminous in the mouth, and that, combined with the very ripe Grenache, which represents the balance of this Côtes du Rhône, shows huge body, wonderful sweetness, medium ruby color, and a very seductive, sexy style that begs for consumption over the next 5–8 years.

1998 Fonsalette Côtes du Rhône
RATING: 90 points
The 1998 Fonsalette Côtes du Rhône is dark ruby/purple–tinged and tannic. The attack and mid-palate reveal rich, concentrated, peppery, earthy fruit. This full-bodied, dense, structured 1998 required cellaring, but is now ready to drink. Anticipated maturity: now–2020.

1996 Fonsalette Côtes du Rhône
RATING: 90 points
The 1996 Fonsalette Côtes du Rhône boasts a dense ruby/purple color, as well as a chocolaty, blackberry, super-concentrated palate impression, and considerable body. This wine is atypically massive for this vintage. Muscular and structured, with huge fruit and richness, it was made from fully ripened fruit and an extremely late harvest. While it has softened in the bottle, this offering is still dominated by its truffle and blackberry jam aspects. Anticipated maturity: now–2018.

1995 Fonsalette Côtes du Rhône
RATING: 90 points
The 1995 Château Fonsalette Côtes du Rhône is a 20-year wine that requires 4–5 years of cellaring. It exhibits a black/purple color, good acidity and tannin, a closed, dense, moderately tannic personality, exceptional richness, and a powerful, full-bodied finish. Yields of 30 hectoliters per hectare were slightly higher than the 15–20 achieved in 1996. This is a wine for those who cannot find or afford to purchase Rayas. Anticipated maturity: now–2017.

1994 Fonsalette Côtes du Rhône
RATING: 90 points
The 1994 Fonsalette Côtes du Rhône is a gorgeously rich wine with a deep ruby/purple color, a peppery, spicy, herb, and jammy black cherry nose, moderate tannin, full body, and super intensity and length. This wine has turned out to be an outstanding example of Côtes du Rhône that should drink well for another 6–7 years.

1990 Fonsalette Côtes du Rhône
RATING: 94 points
The 1990 red wine *cuvées* are prodigious. The 1990 Fonsalette Côtes du Rhône, made from yields that were well under 25 hectoliters per hectare, reached 14% alcohol, not surprising given the superripeness the southern Rhône enjoyed. The wine displays the essence of cherry and kirsch in its nose, followed by corpulent, sweet, expansive, rich flavors that linger and linger on the palate. It is a lavishly rich Côtes du Rhône, with an unctuous texture and enough alcohol and soft tannins to keep it going for at least another 2–3 years. Anticipated maturity: now–2007.

FONSALETTE COTES DU RHONE CUVEE SYRAH

2003 Fonsalette Côtes du Rhône Cuvée Syrah

RATING: 80–90? points

Part of the Syrah vineyards of Fonsalette suffered from the drought and heat, particularly those on the sandy soils. This wine does not have the saturated purple color of the great vintages, shows a bit more astringent tannin than the best examples, but there is plenty of weight, richness, and size to a wine that looks impressive but is still somewhat disjointed and needs time to sort its personality. I am not giving it the benefit of the doubt, but it does have much of the right stuff. It's just that the tannins need to soften for this to be completely harmonious. Anticipated maturity: 2008–2017.

2001 Fonsalette Côtes du Rhône Cuvée Syrah

RATING: 91+ points

A 100% Syrah offering, which was introduced by the late Jacques Reynaud in 1978, the 2001 Fonsalette Côtes du Rhône Cuvée Syrah is an inky/purple-colored effort displaying a provocative perfume of beef blood, composty/autumnal leaves, blackberries, and cassis. Firm and tannic as well as heady and full-bodied, it possesses the structure and grip of a Bordeaux Médoc, and boasts serious concentration. At present, it is quite austere, and in need of considerable aging. Anticipated maturity: 2010–2020.

2000 Fonsalette Côtes du Rhône Cuvée Syrah

RATING: 91 points

A monster effort, the deep purple–colored 2000 Fonsalette Côtes du Rhône Cuvée Syrah reveals characteristics of animal fur, licorice, blackberries, and mushroom/truffle notes. With superb concentration, huge body, and a monolithic, backward personality, it will be at its best between 2007 and 2018.

1999 Fonsalette Côtes du Rhône Cuvée Syrah

RATING: 91 points

The sensational, 250-case *cuvée* of black/purple-colored 1999 Fonsalette Côtes du Rhône Cuvée Syrah should be gobbled up by fans of this offering. This cool-climate vineyard planted on north-facing slopes consistently produces fabulous wines that age for 2–3 decades (the debut 1978 vintage is still an infant). The sweet, rich, full-bodied 1999 reveals ripe tannin along with notes of roasted meats, blackberries, truffles, and licorice. Cellar this monster for another 2–3 years, and enjoy the magic over the next 10–12 years. Anticipated maturity: 2007–2020.

1998 Fonsalette Côtes du Rhône Cuvée Syrah

RATING: 91 points

The 1998 Fonsalette Côtes du Rhône Cuvée Syrah exhibits a typical black/purple color as well as a knockout nose of animal fur, licorice, crème de cassis, truffles, and damp earth. This dense, huge, concentrated, formidably endowed wine is a superb expression of southern Rhône Syrah. It is for serious collectors only. Anticipated maturity: 2006–2020.

1996 Fonsalette Côtes du Rhône Cuvée Syrah

RATING: 90 points

The dense 1996 Fonsalette Côtes du Rhône Cuvée Syrah is, surprisingly, sweet and supple. It offers an intriguing nose of animal fur, blackberries, cassis, and earthy overtones. Medium to full-bodied, concentrated, chewy, and thick, this is a mouth-filling, palate-staining Syrah that should age well for another 10 or more years.

1995 Fonsalette Côtes du Rhône Cuvée Syrah

RATING: 94 points

The amazing 1995 Fonsalette Côtes du Rhône Cuvée Syrah should be cellared for 10–15 years. The wine is ferociously tannic, but wow, what extraordinary intensity of flavor it possesses. With its viscous texture, and peppery, smoky, sweet cassis, and truffle-scented nose and flavors, this wine offers a sensational mouthful of brutally savage and intense Syrah grown in the southern Rhône. I suspect this wine will evolve for 30–40+ years. Anticipated maturity: 2007–2037.

1994 Fonsalette Côtes du Rhône Cuvée Syrah

RATING: 94 points

The 1994 Fonsalette Côtes du Rhône Cuvée Syrah (only 4,000 bottles produced) achieved 14.5% alcohol naturally. This black-colored, staggeringly rich wine is not far behind the otherworldly 1995. It hits the palate with a crescendo of massive portions of cassis fruit, smoke, earth, and Asian spices. Extremely thick, unctuous, and moderately tannic, this is an enormously endowed, gargantuan Syrah that will require another 2–3 years of cellaring. It is another 30-year wine.

1991 Fonsalette Côtes du Rhône Cuvée Syrah

RATING: 92 points

The profound 1991 Fonsalette Côtes du Rhône Cuvée Syrah offers an amazing opaque black/purple color, followed by a huge nose of roasted herbs and cassis that roars from the glass. With a natural alcohol of more than 14% (from yields of 20–25 hectoliters per hectare), this massive, phenomenally extracted, gigantic wine needs another 2–4 years of cellaring. Anticipated maturity: now–2018.

1990 Fonsalette Côtes du Rhône Cuvée Syrah

RATING: 94 points

The 1990 Fonsalette Côtes du Rhône Cuvée Syrah is black in color, with an extraordinary perfume of hickory wood, chocolate, cassis, and other black fruits. In the mouth, there is staggering richness, astonishing opulence, plenty of alcohol, and gobs of tannin. The overall impression is one of massiveness and completeness. Anticipated maturity: now–2012.

RAYAS CHATEAUNEUF-DU-PAPE

2003 Rayas Châteauneuf-du-Pape

RATING: 92–95 points

This looks to be the best Rayas made under the relatively recent administration of Emmanuel Reynaud. Picked relatively late by the standards of the vintage (the harvest at Rayas occurred between September 5 and September 30), this wine shows a deep ruby color and a wonderful, sweet nose of framboise, kirsch, and some Asian spice. Very opulent, full-bodied, and lush, with that extraordinary intensity of flavor but remarkable lightness, this looks to be a terrific Rayas that could well turn out to be the best vintage for this eccentric estate since the profound 1995. It is certainly high in alcohol at just over 15%, but it is well concealed between a wealth of glycerin and fruit. Anticipated maturity: 2009–2020+.

2001 Rayas Châteauneuf-du-Pape

RATING: 93 points

The 2001 Rayas Châteauneuf-du-Pape is more structured and slightly deeper ruby-colored than the light-colored 2000. It also possesses more acidity as well as depth. This *terroir*-driven effort reveals aromas of raspberries and sweet kirsch as well as a medium-bodied, vigorously fresh, lively style. There is also good flavor authority. Give it 3–4 years of cellaring and consume it over the following 15.

2000 Rayas Châteauneuf-du-Pape

RATING: 90? points

The 2000 Rayas Châteauneuf-du-Pape, which Emmanuel Reynaud believes is better than 1998, came in at a whopping 15.2% alcohol. It is reminiscent of a hypothetical blend of the 1998 and 1999, with a medium to light ruby color, and a sumptuous bouquet of kirsch, spice box, and licorice. Full-bodied and fleshy, with low acidity, it is a sweet (from high glycerin and alcohol), seductive, intoxicating offering with no hard edges and a rich, fleshy mouth-feel. While it will be hard to resist, I feel the 1998 still has more structure. Anticipated maturity: now–2016.

1999 Rayas Châteauneuf-du-Pape

RATING: 92 points

The dark ruby–colored 1999 Rayas Châteauneuf-du-Pape admirably conceals its 15% alcohol. With serious structure and tannin, this medium to full–bodied, closed 1999 offers beautiful, sweet kirsch notes in the aromatics and on the attack, but it tightens in the finish. Anticipated maturity: now–2012.

1998 Rayas Châteauneuf-du-Pape

RATING: 94 points

Although the 1998 is not among the most compelling wines of the vintage, it continues to put on weight and performs better and better with each tasting. It appears to be the finest effort Emmanuel Reynaud has yet produced. Anticipated maturity: now–2017.

1995 Rayas Châteauneuf-du-Pape

RATING: 98 points

The 1995 is spectacular. When Emmanuel Reynaud said it was evolving quickly, in essence repudiating this vintage, I immediately drank two bottles of this glorious elixir. It does not reveal the overripeness of the 1990, bringing to mind a hypothetical blend of the great 1989 and 1978. Deeply colored and still young, with black currant/crème de cassis–like characteristics, huge body, yet great structure and delineation, this is a classic Rayas that is totally different from the 1990. It should continue to improve in the bottle and may merit an even higher score. While it can be drunk now, it will be even better with 3–4 years of cellaring. Anticipated maturity: 2007–2020.

1994 Rayas Châteauneuf-du-Pape

RATING: 90 points

A sleeper of the vintage, the 1994 offers up a fragrant perfume of kirsch, raspberries, leather, and tobacco in a medium to full–bodied, surprisingly authoritative style with outstanding depth, ripeness, and length. Compared to the cost of the 1990 and 1995, this is a steal. Anticipated maturity: now–2012.

1990 Rayas Châteauneuf-du-Pape

RATING: 100 points

As for the 1990, I have had the good fortune to drink nearly three cases, and it has been one of the triumphs of my cellar. A mere 1–2 years ago, I enjoyed a succession of perfect "100 point" bottles, but the last several bottles have merited 96–100 points, perhaps revealing the direction of this wine's evolution. Nevertheless, this is riveting stuff. A legendary Rayas made from extremely ripe Grenache, it exhibits notes of overripe kirsch, raspberries, cherries, game, licorice, and tobacco. This unctuously textured, thick, juicy Châteauneuf must tip the scale at 15.5% alcohol. It is truly a Rhône Valley monument. Owners, however, should consume it over the next 8–10 years.

1989 Rayas Châteauneuf-du-Pape

RATING: 99 points

A wine that continues to catch up to the 1990 (and probably has greater longevity) is the 1989. A dense-colored Rayas, but not as thick-looking as the 1990, this dark ruby–colored wine exhibits plenty of roasted herb notes intermixed with scents of tobacco, sweet crème de cassis, and kirsch. Full-bodied, highly extracted, powerful, and tannic (resembling 1995 more than 1990), it is shedding its cloak of tannin and beginning to approach full maturity. Anticipated maturity: now–2025.

1988 Rayas Châteauneuf-du-Pape

RATING: 92 points

A gorgeous effort, the 1988 has come on strong lately. While neither as flamboyant as the 1990 nor as extracted as the 1989, it is a gorgeously elegant example that would be interesting to insert in a top grand cru red Burgundy tasting. Flowery, sweet black cherries and raspberries, along with resiny, loamy soil aromas jump from the glass of this dark ruby–colored Châteauneuf. Full-bodied, rich, and just reaching its plateau of maturity, it will last for another 5–10 years.

1985 Rayas Châteauneuf-du-Pape

RATING: 93 points

The 1985 was great young, then went into a dormant state, but has bounced back with a vengeance. The medium ruby color is not particularly saturated, but the gorgeous bouquet offers up scents of balsam, pepper, black cherries, and leather. The wine is alcoholic, heady, and rich, but a sneaky tannic characteristic creeps up as the wine sits in the glass. The 1985 has continually played games, one bottle suggesting early maturity, and the next indicating far greater longevity. There is no color degradation, and it appears to be just now reaching its peak of maturity. I would opt for drinking it over the next 5–10 years.

1983 Rayas Châteauneuf-du-Pape

RATING: 94 points

This is a vintage that is nearing the end of its life, but which can still be spectacular where well stored. It is a classic Rayas vintage, with the 1983 potentially the wine of the vintage in Châteauneuf-du-Pape. The wine reveals considerable amber in its color, along with a huge, intoxicating aromatic display of red and black fruits, herbs, spices, earth, and licorice. It is a full-bodied, sweet, creamy-textured Châteauneuf-du-Pape that, while gorgeous to drink, should be drunk up.

1979 Rayas Châteauneuf-du-Pape

RATING: 90 points

The 1979 reveals a complex nose of dried herbs, leather, animal fur, black raspberries, cherries, and licorice. It is beginning to fade in the mouth, with the tannin and acidity poking through in the finish (always a sign of a wine turning the corner for the worse). It can still be spectacular, and there may well be some pristine bottles that remain perfect, but I have not seen one in many years.

1978 Rayas Châteauneuf-du-Pape

RATING: 94 points

A wine that once hit the magical three-digit score, it is now in decline. The 1978 started off life slowly, gathered steam, blossomed at age 8–10, and continued to add weight and richness until 1999–2000, when it began a slight decline. Although it is still a spectacular wine, it is no longer perfect.

WINES:

Côte Rôtie Côte Blonde

Côte Rôtie La Landonne

OWNER: René Rostaing

ADDRESS: 1 Petite Rue de Port, 69420 Ampuis, France

TELEPHONE: 33 04 74 56 12 00

TELEFAX: 33 04 74 56 13 32

VISITING POLICY: By appointment only

VINEYARDS

SURFACE AREA: 19.9 acres total (17.3 acres Côte Rôtie,
2.6 acres Condrieu)

GRAPE VARIETALS: Syrah, Viognier

AVERAGE AGE OF THE VINES: 40 years

DENSITY OF PLANTATION: 10,000 vines per hectare

AVERAGE YIELDS: 35 hectoliters per hectare

WINEMAKING AND UPBRINGING

René Rostaing takes a very enlightened approach to winemaking, always staying flexible depending on what the vintage provides. He can often be among the first or the last to harvest depending on the vintage character. There is always partial destemming according to his vineyards, but how much depends on the style of the vintage. In general, fermentation is kicked off early, the maceration lasting for three weeks, with regular *pigéages* as well as pumpovers. All the Côte Rôties are then moved into small Burgundy barrels as well as the larger 500-liter *demi-muids*. About 20% of the wood is new, with the balance between two and three years. After 15 months of aging, the wines are fined very lightly with egg whites and bottled without filtration.

ANNUAL PRODUCTION

Côte Rôtie La Landonne: 8,000 bottles

Côte Rôtie Côte Blonde: 6,000 bottles

AVERAGE PRICE (VARIABLE DEPENDING ON VINTAGE): $60–100

GREAT RECENT VINTAGES

2003, 2001, 1999, 1991, 1985, 1978, 1971

Fortune is smiling on René Rostaing, a fit young businessman who always wears a determined, serious expression. One taste of Rostaing's wine will no doubt convince anyone that he is a star of this appellation. A sort of French yuppie, Rostaing is also in the real

René Rostaing

estate business and manages apartment buildings in nearby Condrieu. He is an intelligent winemaker, having learned traditional techniques from his deceased father-in-law, Albert Dervieux, and balances that knowledge with some of the benefits of modern-day technology. Especially admirable is Rostaing's flexibility. On such issues as fining and filtration, he will await the results of laboratory analyses in order to make a decision if the wine is healthy enough to go into the bottle with no clarification. This open-minded attitude contrasts sharply with producers who fine and filter simply because "my father and grandfather did it."

Rostaing has become one of the most important producers of high-quality Côte Rôtie. When his father-in-law and his uncle, Marius Gentaz, retired, Rostaing inherited the responsibility for overseeing most of their vineyard holdings, thus significantly increasing his estate, as well as giving him some exceptional parcels of Côte Rôtie vineyards. His holdings include old-vine parcels in Fongent (Côte Brune), La Garde (Côte Blonde), and La Viaillère (85-year-old vines in Côte Brune). Moreover, in 1993, he acquired the right to manage the extraordinary ancient vines (over 70 years) of Marius Gentaz, also located in the Côte Brune, not far from Guigal's famed vineyard La Turque.

His small underground cellar, which is beautifully equipped and air-conditioned, is located by the river in Ampuis, just a block away from that of Emile Champet and the refurbished Château d'Ampuis of Marcel Guigal.

In Rostaing's meticulously clean cellars, there is an assortment of both new oak casks and, increasingly, the larger *demi-muids,* which, Rostaing is convinced, are the best size of oak vessels in which to age Côte Rôtie. His vinification, which takes place in state-of-the-art, stainless-steel, rotating, automatic *pigéage* fermenters, is typical of his intelligence and flexibility. Some *cuvées* will be 100% destemmed, depending on the vintage and the *terroir*; other *cuvées* will have a partial destemming. In the top years, Rostaing produces three *cuvées:* Cuvée Classique, Cuvée Côte Blonde, and La Landonne. When the vintage is suspect, Rostaing will often blend La Landonne into his Cuvée Classique. The top wines are the Côte Blonde and La Landonne. Rostaing often prefers to serve the Côte Blonde last in tastings in his cellar, largely because of its sumptuous texture as well as extraordinary richness and intensity. It is even more outstanding than his La Landonne, even though the latter wine comes from older vines than those owned by Marcel Guigal. In fact, his three parcels of La Landonne include a young-vine parcel and two parcels of 50- to 60-year-old vines, with 0.7 of an acre coming from Marius Gentaz's ancient 70-plus-year-old La Landonne vines!

COTE ROTIE COTE BLONDE

2003 Côte Rôtie Côte Blonde
RATING: 96–100 points
An explosive, legendary effort that may equal or even surpass the prodigious 1999 Côte Rôtie Côte Blonde, this wine (which has 3–4% Viognier co-fermented with it) already has an explosive nose consisting of marmalade, lychee, raspberry and blackberry jam, enormous body, a velvety texture, stunning concentration, virtually no acidity, but sweet tannin and massive extract and richness. I would give it 2–3 years of cellaring and drink it over the next 15–17 years.

2001 Côte Rôtie Côte Blonde
RATING: 94 points
A wine of great intensity and lushness with no hard edges is the dark ruby/purple–colored 2001 Côte Rôtie Côte Blonde. Sweet aromas of caramel, honeysuckle, black cherry liqueur, raspberries, currants, and subtle notes of toasty oak are followed by a plump, well-textured, opulent finish. I adore this *cuvée* of Côte Rôtie, and it's a shame more is not produced. Anticipated maturity: now–2014.

2000 Côte Rôtie Côte Blonde
RATING: 92 points
To no one's surprise, the most sexy and voluptuous of the 2000 *cuvées* is the 2000 Côte Rôtie Côte Blonde. It boasts honeysuckle-infused black cherry and currant fruit in a dense, rich, opulent, aromatic, velvety-textured, seamless format. With no hard edges, this 2000 will be hard to resist young; it is capable of lasting 10–12 years. Rostaing's Côte Blonde vineyard is sandwiched between La Mouline and Chatillonne.

1999 Côte Rôtie Côte Blonde
RATING: 100 points
What can I say about the 1999 Côte Rôtie Côte Blonde? This is a dry vintage port–like Côte Rôtie. It possesses extraordinary intensity, brilliant harmony, and a staggering bouquet of violets laced with other flowers (paperwhite narcissus comes to mind), blackberries, cassis, vanilla, and a touch of honey. The wine is unctuously textured yet remarkably well defined, with elegance married to intense concentration as well as an extremely long finish. It is one of the most profound and seductive Côte Rôties I have ever tasted. There are 500 cases of this nectar. Anticipated maturity: now–2018.

1998 Côte Rôtie Côte Blonde
RATING: 98 points
The exquisite, dense ruby/purple-colored 1998 offers up soaring aromas of peach and blackberry jam. The wine is velvety-textured and full, with layers of glycerin, extract, and concentrated fruit, superb richness, impressive purity, and a finish that lasts 40+ seconds. Anticipated maturity: now–2015.

1997 Côte Rôtie Côte Blonde
RATING: 91 points
The 1997 exhibits a dark ruby color, followed by a sexy apricot, blackberry, raspberry, bacon fat, and toasty nose, and luscious, medium to full–bodied, open-knit flavors that caress the palate with glycerin and fruit. The wine's low acidity, fleshy texture, and forward, evolved style are appealing. It should drink well for another 4–6 years.

1996 Côte Rôtie Côte Blonde
RATING: 90 points
The 1996 Côte Rôtie Côte Blonde is the epitome of elegance, finesse, and black raspberry fruit wrapped in smoky oak and pepper. Luscious, with an opulent texture, enough tangy acidity to provide delineation, and a fleshy, sweet finish, this well-structured wine is the most flashy of these offerings. Rostaing's

Côte Blonde always performs well regardless of its evolutionary stage. The 1996 should drink well for another 5–7 years.

1995 Côte Rôtie Côte Blonde

RATING: 95 points

The dense purple–colored 1995 Côte Rôtie Côte Blonde boasts an awesome, mind-boggling nose of violets, cassis, blueberries, and vanilla. Sumptuous and rich on the palate despite crisp acidity, this is a wine of exceptional intensity, a multilayered personality, and fabulous persistence and delineation. It is a tour de force for Côte Rôtie. Unfortunately, quantities are extremely limited as the yields of just over one ton of fruit per acre were well below normal. Anticipated maturity: 2007–2017.

1994 Côte Rôtie Côte Blonde

RATING: 94 points

The 1994s are excellent to outstanding, exhibiting plenty of opulence, power, and sweet fruit. The most hedonistic and voluptuously textured *cuvée* is the Côte Rôtie Côte Blonde. The 1994 exhibits a knockout sweet, expansive, penetratingly fragrant nose of flowers, rich, ripe cassis fruit, cedar, and black raspberries. The wine possesses an opulent texture, gorgeously unctuous, thick flavors, and a fabulous finish. It is a seductive Côte Rôtie for drinking over the next 2–4 years.

1991 Côte Rôtie Côte Blonde

RATING: 92 points

The 1991 Côte Blonde is a sweet, fat, voluptuously styled wine with soft tannin and none of the rusticity or animal character of La Viaillère. Sweet and expansive on the palate, it makes for a seductive, generous mouthful of wine. It should drink well for another 2–3 years.

1990 Côte Rôtie Côte Blonde

RATING: 93 points

The 1990 Côte Blonde exhibits that penetrating, smoky, roasted Côte Rôtie aroma, sweet black raspberry–scented, supple, medium to full–bodied flavors, and a chewy, fleshy, seductive finish. The tannins are covered by layers of fruit, and the acidity is low. Anticipated maturity: now–2009.

1988 Côte Rôtie Côte Blonde

RATING: 92 points

The 1988 Côte Blonde is a smooth, velvety-textured wine with fabulous reserves of fruit that gush from the glass. Extremely intense and ripe, with a raspberry, cassis-dominated bouquet touched judiciously by new oak, this profound, full-flavored wine is still tannic, so give it a few more years of cellaring. Anticipated maturity: now–2010.

1985 Côte Rôtie Côte Blonde

RATING: 91 points

A fully mature wine, Rostaing's Côte Blonde is much more velvety than the tannic La Landonne. Voluptuous on the palate, with an intense bouquet of roasted nuts and ripe, jammy black raspberry and cassis fruit, this wine offers a smorgasbord of exotic aromas and flavors. Anticipated maturity: now.

COTE ROTIE LA LANDONNE

2003 Côte Rôtie La Landonne

RATING: 94–96 points

Rostaing, who started the harvest of his Côte Rôtie vineyards on August 21 (which is unprecedented), produced only 40% of the normal crop. He refused to acidify and change the character of the vintage and also refused to destem everything, claiming that all of the stems were totally ripe. His decisions look brilliant. The 2003 Côte Rôtie La Landonne has virtually no acidity but has structure and definition largely because of the wine's concentration, extract, and tannin levels. The wine has a dense purple color to the rim and a glorious nose of scorched earth, licorice, graphite, blackberry, and creosote. Very full-bodied, rich, yet exceptionally pure and seamless, this wine still seems to require 3–4 years of cellaring and should drink well for 15–16 years.

2001 Côte Rôtie La Landonne

RATING: 93 points

The 2001 Côte Rôtie La Landonne reveals a roasted espresso character along with licorice, pepper, scorched earth, and dense blackberry and cassis fruit. Firm, tannic, and masculine as well as aromatic (a characteristic of this cool vintage), it requires another 1–2 years of cellaring, after which it should last for 7–8 years.

2000 Côte Rôtie La Landonne

RATING: 91 points

The 2000 Côte Rôtie La Landonne's saturated deep ruby/purple color is followed by a peppery bouquet revealing notes of scorched earth, blackberries, cassis, Asian spice, and toast. Full-bodied, dense, and rich, it is an impressive, authoritative example of the vintage. Anticipated maturity: now–2014.

1999 Côte Rôtie La Landonne

RATING: 98 points

The profound 1999 Côte Rôtie La Landonne boasts a saturated black purple color as well as scents of graphite, truffles, smoke, bacon, blackberry, and earth. This full-bodied, muscular, powerful effort displays surprisingly sweet tannin for a wine from this *terroir,* along with awesome concentration, and a finish that lasts for 40+ seconds. Give it another 1–2 years of cellaring and enjoy it over the next 25 years.

1998 Côte Rôtie La Landonne

RATING: 93 points

This spectacular offering boasts a deep purple color in addition to a dense nose that the French would call a *confiture* of black fruits, particularly plums, blackberries, and black currants. Superb aromatics jump from the glass of this young, unevolved 1998. On the palate, it is deep and dense, with a multilayered texture and terrific purity and concentration. It possesses a sweet, concentrated mid-palate, well-integrated tannin, and a long finish. This wine is thrilling to taste at present. It will drink well young, but will last for 15–20 years.

1995 Côte Rôtie La Landonne

RATING: 92 points

The 1995 Côte Rôtie La Landonne is a backward, tart, opaque purple–colored wine that is just beginning to reveal its character. Tannic and rich, with a chocolaty, smoky, black currant/cassis–scented nose, this powerful, impenetrable wine is just attaining full maturity. Anticipated maturity: now–2014.

1994 Côte Rôtie La Landonne

RATING: 90 points

The 1994s are excellent to outstanding, exhibiting plenty of opulence, power, and sweet fruit. The impressive 1994 Côte Rôtie La Landonne combines power and elegance in a densely colored, tannic, medium to full–bodied, cassis, pepper, grilled meat–scented and flavored wine. It should keep for another 7+ years.

1991 Côte Rôtie La Landonne

RATING: 94 points

Perhaps the best of the 1991s is the 1991 La Landonne. As you might anticipate, there is considerable rivalry between Rostaing and his neighbor, Marcel Guigal. Rostaing is quick to assert that his La Landonne vines are considerably older than those of Guigal. This black-colored wine offers up an exquisite perfume of licorice, violets, blackberries, and toast, staggering concentration, smooth tannin, and low acidity. It is a gorgeous, exceptionally opulent, multidimensional wine with layers of flavor. It should drink well for another 4–7 years.

1990 Côte Rôtie La Landonne

RATING: 91 points

Rostaing's 1990 La Landonne exhibits an earthy, animal, smoky character, superb richness of fruit, gobs of glycerin and extraction, soft tannins, and low acidity. Despite its considerable size, this is a wine that should be drunk in its first 10–12 years of life. Anticipated maturity: now–2006.

1988 Côte Rôtie La Landonne

RATING: 90 points

The 1988 La Landonne has a fabulously compelling bouquet of black raspberry and vanilla scents. The wine's rich, full-bodied, impeccably balanced flavors marry power with finesse. There are still some tannins to be resolved. Anticipated maturity: now–2012.

WINES:

Châteauneuf-du-Pape Le Secret des Sabon

Châteauneuf-du-Pape La Cuvée Prestige

CLASSIFICATION: EARL Domaine Roger Sabon

OWNERS: Jean-Jacques, Denis, and Gilbert Sabon

ADDRESS: Avenue Impériale, B.P. 57, 84232 Châteauneuf-du-Pape, France

TELEPHONE: 33 04 90 83 71 72

TELEFAX: 33 04 90 83 50 51

E-MAIL: roger.sabon@wanadoo.fr

CONTACT: Jean-Jacques Sabon

VISITING POLICY: Monday through Friday, 8 A.M.–noon, 2–6 P.M.; Saturday, 9 A.M.–noon and 2–6 P.M.

VINEYARDS

SURFACE AREA: 109 acres total (37 acres in Châteauneuf-du-Pape)

GRAPE VARIETALS:

La Cuvée Prestige (red)—Grenache, Syrah, Mourvèdre, Cinsault, Terret Counoise, Vaccarèse, and Clairette

Le Secret des Sabon (red)—An ancient field blend that is largely unidentifiable but believed to be Grenache, as well as the 12 other authorized varietals of the village, all well over 100 years of age.

AVERAGE AGE OF THE VINES: La Cuvée Prestige (red)—80 years; Le Secret des Sabon (red)—100+ years

DENSITY OF PLANTATION: La Cuvée Prestige (red)—3,500 vines per hectare; Le Secret des Sabon (red)—4,000 vines per hectare

AVERAGE YIELDS: 20–35 hectoliters per hectare

WINEMAKING AND UPBRINGING

The Cuvée Prestige, which comes from vines that are roughly 80 years of age, is made largely from destemmed grapes. Vinified in large tanks with indigenous yeasts, which the Sabons believe brings an expression of *terroir* to the wine, they do both pumpovers and *pigéage* but are very careful not to harshly crush the berries. The *cuvaison* lasts 20 days in top vintages, then the wine is moved to both *foudres* and smaller barrels. About 65% of the Cuvée Prestige spends 15 or so months in *foudres,* and the balance of 35% in small barrels of which a very tiny percentage, if any, is new. The very limited but prodigious Le Secret des Sabon is believed to be made from all 13 authorized varietals from an ancient parcel well over 100 years of age. The production is absurdly small, and no doubt this explains not only the extraordinary concentration but also the elegance and harmony of this compelling

wine. It is treated somewhat like the Cuvée Prestige, with the majority of this small *cuvée* aged in neutral wood *foudres* with a small amount in barrel, but that amount does see a slightly higher percentage of new oak than the Cuvée Prestige.

ANNUAL PRODUCTION

La Cuvée Prestige (red): 16,000 bottles

Le Secret des Sabon (red): 1,300 bottles

AVERAGE PRICE (VARIABLE DEPENDING ON VINTAGE): $40–200

GREAT RECENT VINTAGES

2003, 2001, 1998, 1995, 1990, 1988, 1981, 1978, 1972, 1967, 1961, 1959

Jean-Jacques Sabon (right) tastes with his family

The Sabon family (in this instance Jean-Jacques, Denis, and Gilbert) are some of the more intellectual and forward-thinking vignerons in Châteauneuf-du-Pape. This ancient family presided over the very beginning of the creation of Châteauneuf-du-Pape, when the great-grandfather of the current owners, Séraphin Sabon, along with the famous Baron Le Roy, held the first tastings and discussed how the appellation should operate. Perhaps it is because their family name has been associated with Châteauneuf-du-Pape since the early 17th century that the Sabons seem more concerned about the future than many vignerons. The Sabons own a moderately sized estate and produce a

solid white wine and four *cuvées* of red Châteauneuf-du-Pape. The vineyards are in such superbly situated sectors as Les Cabrières, La Crau, Courthézon, and Nalys. While the soils are slightly diverse, what they all have in common is the famed *galets roulés.*

Sabon is a traditional winemaker. He has moved toward raising his red wines in a tiny percentage of small oak casks (all old since he does not like the effect of new oak). Though pressured by his oenologist and European clients to do more fining and filtering, Sabon decided to make a qualitative rather than a business decision, and has refused to filter any of his wines. In fact, he is an outspoken critic of those oenologists who consistently advocate an intense filtration, not recognizing that it can harmfully remove much of the aromatics, body, and flavors of a wine. Sabon's wines are classic Châteauneuf-du-Papes, and, as one might imagine, they increase in intensity from the traditional *cuvée* of Les Olivets to the Cuvée Réserve, Cuvée Prestige, and very limited but colossal Le Secret des Sabon.

This estate has been making exceptionally high-quality wines for years, but recent vintages seem to have risen to a new level of quality. Moreover, Sabon's wines have not yet been discovered by the masses, so prices are surprisingly reasonable.

Roger Sabon produces a very delicious Côtes du Rhône and Lirac from vineyard holdings in those appellations.

CHATEAUNEUF-DU-PAPE CUVEE PRESTIGE

2003 Châteauneuf-du-Pape Cuvée Prestige
RATING: 91–94+ points
A primordial, full-bodied, earthy wine with notes of plum, saddle leather, roasted meat, and sweet kirsch and black fruits, this layered wine offers plenty of power along with striking finesse and precision. I'm sure the alcohol is well over 15%, and the high tannins combined with the high extract suggest a wine that needs 2–4 years of cellaring but should last for up to two decades. This is a very impressive Cuvée Prestige from the Sabons.

2001 Châteauneuf-du-Pape Cuvée Prestige
RATING: 94 points
Tipping the scales at 14.5–15% alcohol, the old-vine, full-bodied 2001 Châteauneuf-du-Pape Cuvée Prestige is a wine of impressive intensity and thickness. Aromas reminiscent of liqueur of roasted herbs intermixed with meaty, game-like smells, black cherries, ground pepper, beef blood, and *garrigue* are followed by a wine of noteworthy stature, complexity, and mouth-filling generosity. Serious tannin is largely obscured by the wealth of fruit and extract. Give it 2–3 years of cellaring, and drink it over the following 12–15 years.

2000 Châteauneuf-du-Pape Cuvée Prestige
RATING: 92 points
The Cuvée Prestige is full-bodied, sexy, concentrated, and loaded with the essence of Provence. The 2000 Châteauneuf-du-Pape Cuvée Prestige smells like liqueur of black pepper intermixed with lavender, game, and black fruits. It tastes so much like Provence that one almost expects some of their famous miniature figurines (*santons*) to jump out of the glass. Ripe, layered, and spicy, with soaring aromatics, this fleshy, chewy 2000 is undoubtedly hiding some serious tannin. Anticipated maturity: now–2016.

1999 Châteauneuf-du-Pape Cuvée Prestige
RATING: 90 points
The 1999 Châteauneuf-du-Pape Cuvée Prestige (14.5% alcohol) reveals a dark plum/garnet color as well as a gorgeously complex nose of licorice, pepper, black cherries, and cassis. As the wine sits in the glass additional nuances develop. It is a seductive, open-knit, layered, succulent, fleshy effort to enjoy now and over the next 10–12 years.

1998 Châteauneuf-du-Pape Cuvée Prestige
RATING: 94 points
The 1998 Cuvée Prestige is a fabulous Châteauneuf-du-Pape offering a classic bouquet of pepper, dried *herbes de Provence,*

balsam wood, black cherries, and blackberries displayed in a full-bodied, young, unevolved but fabulously concentrated style. Possessing moderately high tannin, huge fruit and glycerin, and great balance as well as purity, it should age effortlessly for 25 years.

1997 Châteauneuf-du-Pape Cuvée Prestige

RATING: 90 points

The 1997 Châteauneuf-du-Pape Cuvée Prestige is powerful, with elevated alcohol, and a full-bodied, weighty, concentrated personality. The sweet rich fruit includes plums, cherries, and cassis intermixed with aromas of dried herbs, black pepper, and Provençal *garrigue* scents. A decadently rich, superb 1997 offering, this pure, impressively rich, fruit-driven wine can be drunk now or cellared for another 5–6 years.

1995 Châteauneuf-du-Pape Cuvée Prestige

RATING: 93 points

The 1995 Cuvée Prestige boasts great sweetness, a pronounced black-fruit character, a high degree of ripeness, and admirable glycerin and alcohol. It is a dense, promising, formidably endowed Châteauneuf-du-Pape. Anticipated maturity: now–2012.

CHATEAUNEUF-DU-PAPE LE SECRET DES SABON

2003 Châteauneuf-du-Pape Le Secret des Sabon

RATING: 94–95+ points

Playing it close to the vest, still tightly knit, with some of the new-oak cask that part of this *cuvée* is aged in showing the telltale vanilla (this usually disappears at age two), this super-concentrated, inky/purple-colored wine shows notes of black currants, kirsch, Asian spice, licorice, and new oak. Very heady, with superb intensity, massive body, and a long finish that certainly conceals well over 15% alcohol, this is a gorgeously extracted, rich, full-throttle wine that should be at its best between 2009 and 2023.

2001 Châteauneuf-du-Pape Le Secret des Sabon

RATING: 100 points

A magical elixir, the 2001 Châteauneuf-du-Pape Le Secret des Sabon matches the otherworldly 1998 in its seamlessness, extraordinary richness, unctuous texture, and incredible perfume. Its inky ruby/purple color is accompanied by gorgeous aromas of roasted herbs, cassis, blackberries, graphite, wood smoke, and an assortment of red as well as black fruits. Amazingly full-bodied, with a viscous texture, beautifully integrated acidity, tannin, and alcohol, this massively proportioned yet gorgeously balanced, impeccably pure wine is one of the world's greatest expressions of ancient vines and natural/artisanal winemaking. Anticipated maturity: 2008–2025.

2000 Châteauneuf-du-Pape Le Secret des Sabon

RATING: 94 points

For readers fortunate enough to latch on to the super-expensive Châteauneuf-du-Pape Le Secret des Sabon, the 2000 may not be as profound as the 1998, but it is a terrific effort. A deep plum/purple color is accompanied by subtle notes of pepper, spice, truffles, earth, smoked meats, prunes, and a wealth of black currant and cherry fruit. Although full-bodied, rich, and concentrated, with majestic layers of flavor that unfold on the palate, the 2000 remains closed and tannic, so patience is suggested. Anticipated maturity: 2006–2020.

1999 Châteauneuf-du-Pape Le Secret des Sabon

RATING: 96 points

The 1999 Châteauneuf-du-Pape Le Secret des Sabon offers a blockbuster bouquet of roasted meats, truffles, smoked herbs, prunes, and black cherry jam. Akin to drinking dry vintage port, it tastes like a Châteauneuf-du-Pape on steroids. The alcohol level must be 15+%, but it is buried beneath the wealth of fruit and flesh. The 1999 appears more evolved and forward than the 1998 did at a similar age, so drinking it over the next 7–9 years is advised. It is a tour de force in winemaking.

1998 Châteauneuf-du-Pape Le Secret des Sabon

RATING: 100 points

The unreal, 100-case micro-*cuvée* produced from extraordinarily old vines called Le Secret des Sabon is a perfect Châteauneuf-du-Pape. It coats the palate with extraordinary levels of black cherry, kirsch, raspberry, and pepper-infused fruit. Unctuously textured, with a sumptuous, compelling, meaty richness revealing notes of barbecue spice and earth, it is extremely long with a finish that lasts 50+ seconds. This monumental as well as majestic Châteauneuf-du-Pape can be drunk now or cellared for 30–35 years.

DOMAINE SANTA DUC

WINE:

Gigondas Les Hautes Garrigues

OWNERS: Edmond and Yves Gras

ADDRESS: Les Hautes Garrigues, 84190 Gigondas, France

TELEPHONE: 33 04 90 65 84 49

TELEFAX: 33 04 90 65 81 63

E-MAIL: santaduc@wanadoo.fr

CONTACT: Yves Gras

VISITING POLICY: By appointment only

VINEYARDS

SURFACE AREA: 54.3 acres

GRAPE VARIETALS: Grenache, Mourvèdre, Syrah, Cinsault, Clairette

AVERAGE AGE OF THE VINES: 40 years (oldest planted in 1901)

DENSITY OF PLANTATION: Old vines—3,500 vines per hectare; young vines—5,000 vines per hectare

AVERAGE YIELDS: Hautes Garrigues—25 hectoliters per hectare; Gigondas—30 hectoliters per hectare

WINEMAKING AND UPBRINGING

Old vines and low yields are the defining factors for this splendid wine. There is no destemming, very long 40- to 60-day macerations, an upbringing on the lees, and 24 months' aging in both barrel and *foudre*.

ANNUAL PRODUCTION

Gigondas: 30,000 bottles

Hautes Garrigues: 15,000 bottles

AVERAGE PRICE (VARIABLE DEPENDING ON VINTAGE): $45–50

GREATEST RECENT VINTAGES

2001, 2000, 1999, 1998, 1995, 1990, 1989

The Domaine Santa Duc has emerged in just over a decade as the number one estate for quality in Gigondas. Much of the credit must go to Yves Gras, a tall, good-looking man who is probably in his early 40s, but looks even younger. He took over when his father, Edmond Gras, retired in 1985. Until then, virtually the entire production was sold to various *négociants*. Yves, fresh and enthusiastic, with the vigor of youth, decided the estate had to take a different direction and begin to estate bottle most of the production from its vineyards.

Santa Duc has become not only an important estate in Gigondas, but also a noteworthy producer of high-quality Côte du Rhône and Vaccarèse, made from the family's 17 acres of vineyards sprinkled in and around Vacqueyras, Séguret, and Roaix.

The Gras cellars are located in the plateau of Gigondas two miles from the village center. This estate has moved forward in a progressive manner, utilizing some small casks for aging their Gigondas. Yves Gras makes his Cuvée des Hautes Garrigues from a 50-year-old parcel of hillside vineyards (planted with 70% Grenache, 15% Syrah, 15% Mourvèdre) that tends to yield a shockingly low one-half ton of fruit per acre. The Hautes Garrigues has been produced only in 1989, 1990, 1993, 1995, 1996, 1998, 1999, 2000, 2001, and 2003. This wine, which sees more new oak than the regular *cuvée* (30% is aged in 100% new oak casks), also contains a healthy wallop of Mourvèdre (sometimes as much as 30%). All of the Gras vineyards are on either the plateau of Gigondas that faces the Côtes du Rhône village of Sablet to the north, or on the terraced limestone/clay hillsides of Les Hautes Garrigues. The low yields that are a hallmark of this estate's wines tend to produce Gigondas that reaches 13–14% alcohol for the classique, and in vintages like 1989 and 1990, 15% alcohol for the Cuvée des Hautes Garrigues. If that sounds intimidating, what is even more remarkable is that the alcohol is not noticeable given the wines' intensity of fruit and extract.

Today, over 90% of Santa Duc's wines are sold in the export market. It is not unusual for Yves to get requests for his exquisite Gigondas from such far-flung locations as Singapore, Australia, and South America.

Is this the finest estate in Gigondas? As the following notes demonstrate, Santa Duc combines the muscle, richness, and fire of a classic Gigondas with a degree of elegance and purity that many wines of this appellation lack.

Yves Gras

GIGONDAS LES HAUTES GARRIGUES

2003 Gigondas Les Hautes Garrigues

RATING: 90–93 points

Yves Gras produced an uncommonly tannic, full-bodied, backward-styled 2003 that he compares to his impressive 1989, which is just now drinking well. A blend of 80% Grenache, 15% Mourvèdre, and the rest equal parts Syrah and Cinsault has produced a blue/black-colored wine with notes of white flowers, blueberries, and scorched black fruits in a very tannic, dry, somewhat austere style, but with enormous body, density, and richness. It is a very backward wine that will reward patient connoisseurs. Anticipated maturity: 2010–2020.

2001 Gigondas Les Hautes Garrigues

RATING: 93 points

The luxury *cuvée,* the 2001 Gigondas Les Hautes Garrigues (20,000 bottles produced from a blend of 80% Grenache and the rest Mourvèdre and Syrah), boasts an inky/purple color along with deep, concentrated blackberry and blueberry fruit, crushed stone, white flower, and toasty oak characteristics. Chewy and rich, but not as ripe as the 2000 or 1998, this is a structured, elegant, seamless 2001 that should age effortlessly for 12–15 years. Anticipated maturity: 2007–2017.

2000 Gigondas Les Hautes Garrigues

RATING: 94 points

While more accessible than the 2001, the 2000 Gigondas Les Hautes Garrigues is explosive in its fruit-driven, powerful style. Inky/purple-colored, with a sumptuous perfume of liquid minerals, pepper, blackberries, acacia flowers, and hints of blueberries as well as cassis, this full-bodied classic has terrific palate penetration and mouth-staining levels of extract. There are no hard edges, but there is noticeable tannin in the finish. Anticipated maturity: now–2020.

1999 Gigondas Les Hautes Garrigues

RATING: 92 points

The stunning 1999 Gigondas Les Hautes Garrigues spent 23 months in *barriques,* of which 40% were new. Made from 80% Grenache and 20% Mourvèdre that achieved 15.5% natural alcohol, it boasts a saturated purple color as well as immense body, a layered texture, and pure cassis, kirsch, and blackberry flavors along with a subtle note of wood. The finish lasts for 30–35 seconds. There are 1,500 cases of this 1999, which appears to be the wine of the vintage. Anticipated maturity: now–2016.

1998 Gigondas Les Hautes Garrigues

RATING: 93 points

The 1998 Gigondas Les Hautes Garrigues achieved 15.64% alcohol, but the 1998 Mourvèdre battered all records as it came in at a whopping 15.8% natural alcohol. Of course, this wine would not merit its high score if it did not completely hide the lusty alcohol. One of the advantages of low yielding, concentrated Grenache is that it easily hides high alcohol. This full-bodied black beauty offers a terrific bouquet of licorice, blackberry, cassis liqueur, and a smoky, subtle dose of wood in the background. In the mouth, it is enormously endowed, very full-bodied and textured, exceptionally pure, with a creamy mid-palate, silky tannin, and a profound finish. Anticipated maturity: now–2018.

1996 Gigondas Les Hautes Garrigues

RATING: 90 points

The outstanding 1996 Gigondas Les Hautes Garrigues boasts a knockout nose of floral scents intermixed with blackberry fruit, pepper, and licorice. Subtle toast notes are present. The wine is medium to full–bodied, expansive, rich, and beautifully textured, with a supple finish. It is a remarkable wine given the vintage conditions. Drink it over the next 1–2 years. Probably the leading estate in Gigondas, Yves Gras's Santa Duc continues to turn out some of the most complete, concentrated, and potentially complex wines of the southern Rhône. In the two difficult vintages of 1996 and 1997, the wines are solidly made, with the 1996 Gigondas Les Hautes Garrigues stunning.

1995 Gigondas Les Hautes Garrigues

RATING: 95 points

The magnificent 1995 Gigondas Les Hautes Garrigues, a selection made only in the greatest years, is a powerhouse Gigondas with an alcohol percentage approaching the mid-teens. This opaque purple–colored wine offers a stunning nose of crushed minerals, black raspberries, blackberries, and vanilla. In spite of its huge extraction, marvelous concentration, and massive richness, this wine is brilliantly balanced by sweet tannin and tangy acidity. It possesses a viscosity and richness that make me think this may be among the half-dozen greatest bottles of Gigondas I have ever tasted. I own the 1989 and 1990 Les Hautes Garrigues, and the 1995 appears to be superior to those two classics! Made from a 50-year-old parcel of hillside vineyards planted with 70% Grenache, 15% Syrah, and 15% Mourvèdre, yields are as low as a half-ton of fruit per acre. Bottled without filtration, this remarkable wine represents the essence of Gigondas. How long will it last? This wine will age beautifully. Anticipated maturity: now–2017.

1993 Gigondas Les Hautes Garrigues

RATING: 92 points

The 1993 Gigondas Les Hautes Garrigues is the finest Gigondas I tasted from this vintage. The wine displays a black color and a superrich nose of raspberries, jammy cherries, and spice. Full-bodied, with splendid concentration, moderate tannin, and loads of glycerin, it should prove to be a large-scaled, impressively concentrated Gigondas for drinking during its first 15 years of life. Anticipated maturity: now–2011.

1990 Gigondas Les Hautes Garrigues

RATING: 92 points

The 1990's huge nose of cassis, vanilla, smoke, flowers, and minerals is followed by a deeply concentrated, full-bodied wine with soft tannins, considerable complexity, and a voluptuous, explosively long, rich finish. It can be drunk now, but the advantage of this style of wine is that it can also still be cellared. Anticipated maturity: now–2010.

1989 Gigondas Les Hautes Garrigues

RATING: 92 points

The 1989 Gigondas Les Hautes Garrigues displays more tannin than the regular *cuvée,* generous, smoky, vanilla, toasty, cassis-scented aromas, enticingly rich black/purple color, and huge flavors of coffee, chocolate, herbs, and superripe black fruits. In the mouth there is the same opulence, but the use of new barrels has resulted in a more muscular, structured, tannic wine. Very impressive! Anticipated maturity: now–2010.

WINES:

Châteauneuf-du-Pape Cuvée de Mon Aïeul

Châteauneuf-du-Pape Réserve des Deux Frères

Châteauneuf-du-Pape Tradition

OWNER: E.A.R.L. Domaine Pierre Usseglio et Fils

ADDRESS: Route d'Orange, 84230 Châteauneuf-du-Pape, France

TELEPHONE: 33 04 90 83 72 98

TELEFAX: 33 04 90 83 56 70

VISITING POLICY: Open Monday through Friday,
9:30 A.M.–noon and 2–6 P.M.

VINEYARDS

SURFACE AREA: 53.1 acres

GRAPE VARIETALS: Grenache, Syrah, Mourvèdre, Cinsault

AVERAGE AGE OF THE VINES: 65 years

DENSITY OF PLANTATION: 3,500 vines per hectare

AVERAGE YIELDS: 22–30 hectoliters per hectare

WINEMAKING AND UPBRINGING

This estate produced very good wines, but it was the ascension of the two sons of Pierre Usseglio, Thierry and Jean-Pierre, in the late 1990s that pushed the quality to world-class level with the acquisition of 20 acres of old-vine vineyards and the introduction of the two luxury *cuvées,* the Cuvée de Mon Aïeul in 1998 and the Réserve des Deux Frères in 2000.

These are very traditional wines made from extremely low yields in the vineyard. They begin with a triage both in the vineyard and in the cellars, followed by vinification in neutral vats and upbringing largely in small used barrels and cement *cuves* and larger wooden *foudres.* The Cuvée Tradition is aged completely in wood *foudres* for 15–18 months prior to being bottled, whereas half of the Cuvée de Mon Aïeul (which emerges from old vines in three sectors—La Crau, Guigasse, and Les Serres—averaging between 75 and 87 years old) is aged in neutral wood *foudres* and the other half in tank prior to being bottled unfined and unfiltered. The Réserve des Deux Frères, which was actually called the Cuvée de Cinquantenaire in 1999, is aged 60% in neutral wood *foudres* and 40% in one-, two-, and three-year-old small Burgundy barrels. The vineyard sources are the same as the Cuvée de Mon Aïeul, but the Deux Frères is a selection of the finest lots in the cellar, although in both cases the dominant percentage of the blend for Mon Aïeul and Deux Frères comes from the famed section of Châteauneuf-du-Pape called La Crau.

Jean-Pierre and Thierry Usseglio

ANNUAL PRODUCTION

Rouge Tradition: 60,000 bottles
Cuvée de Mon Aïeul: 8,900 bottles
Réserve des Deux Frères: 3,400 bottles
AVERAGE PRICE (VARIABLE DEPENDING ON VINTAGE): $30–150

GREAT RECENT VINTAGES

2003, 2001, 2000, 1999, 1998, 1995, 1990

There are a lot of Usseglios in Châteauneuf-du-Pape, but certainly at present the Usseglio family producing the highest quality is the Domaine Pierre Usseglio, run since 1998 by the two dynamic brothers, Thierry and Jean-Pierre. They have invested significantly in 20 acres of superb old-vine vineyards, giving Domaine Pierre Usseglio a total of 53.1 acres. Very old vines everywhere with extremely low yields result in wines of great concentration and intensity.

The Usseglio family came to Châteauneuf-du-Pape in the early 20th century from a family of Piedmontese winemakers. This estate, which had traditionally sold much of its wine to *négociants,* is now bottling the great majority itself. In many ways, this estate symbolizes the dramatic surge in quality that Châteauneuf-du-Pape has witnessed over the last decade, the result of the younger generation taking an existing vineyard, augmenting it through meticulous purchases of very fine plots of old vines, and introducing two new *cuvées* of truly spectacular wines.

CHATEAUNEUF-DU-PAPE

2003 Châteauneuf-du-Pape

RATING: 90–92 points
About 80% Grenache, 10% Syrah, and the rest Mourvèdre and Cinsault, this tannic, full-bodied, rather backward style from Usseglio has produced a wine of dense ruby/purple color, notes of pepper, salty sea breezes, Asian spice, along with black cherry, plum, and currant. Very tannic, full-bodied, and ripe, this is a wine to cellar for 2–3 years and drink over the following 15–16 years.

2001 Châteauneuf-du-Pape

RATING: 91 points
The brilliant 2001 Châteauneuf-du-Pape should not be overlooked (the 1998 and 2000 are drinking spectacularly well at present). A peppery, leathery, earthy effort with copious quantities of black cherries, this dense, full-bodied 2001 is surprisingly precocious by Usseglio's standards. Nevertheless, 1–2 years of cellaring is warranted given the size and structure of this big, chewy, 75% Grenache, 10% Mourvèdre, 10% Cinsault, and 5% Syrah blend. It was aged in neutral wood *foudres* for 15–18 months. Anticipated maturity: 2006–2014.

2000 Châteauneuf-du-Pape

RATING: 90 points
The 2000 Châteauneuf-du-Pape (a blend of 75% Grenache, 10% Mourvèdre, 10% Cinsault, and 5% Syrah) was aged in *foudre* for 15–18 months, and totally destemmed. It offers a deep ruby/purple color in addition to aromas of black currants, cherries, dried Provençal herbs, and licorice. Layered, sweet, accessible, and plump, this succulent effort was produced from the estate's younger vines (25–30 years). It should drink well for 10–15 years. Kudos to Thierry and Jean-Pierre Usseglio.

1999 Châteauneuf-du-Pape

RATING: 90 points
The classic, deep ruby/purple–colored 1999 Châteauneuf-du-Pape offers scents of *garrigue* (that Provençal mélange of herbs and earth), pepper, black cherries, and kirsch. With admirable structure, it is an authoritative expression of a Mediterranean-styled red with an unmistakable Provençal character. Rich, layered, and full-bodied, it will provide ideal drinking over the next 10–12 years.

1998 Châteauneuf-du-Pape

RATING: 90 points
The 1998 Châteauneuf-du-Pape exhibits a roasted herb, concentrated style with notes of scorched earth, licorice, cherry liqueur, and pepper. Full-bodied and intense, it is representative of a traditional Châteauneuf-du-Pape made primarily from Grenache. Anticipated maturity: now–2015.

1995 Châteauneuf-du-Pape

RATING: 90 points
At first, the outstanding 1995 Châteauneuf-du-Pape is tightly knit and difficult to penetrate, but airing brings forth marvelous richness and intensity. The dark ruby color is accompanied by copious amounts of sweet black cherry and raspberry fruit, along with pepper, iodine, and earth. It is full-bodied, powerful, and rich, with plenty of sweet fruit and glycerin on the attack, but then some of the wine's muscle and tannin kick in. This is a structured, intensely rich Châteauneuf-du-Pape that should drink well for another 5–7 years.

CHATEAUNEUF-DU-PAPE CUVEE DE MON AIEUL

2003 Châteauneuf-du-Pape Cuvée de Mon Aïeul
RATING: 96–98 points

This blend of 95% Grenache and the rest tiny portions of Cinsault and Syrah comes from three old-vine parcels owned by the Usseglios in Les Serres, Guigasse, and La Crau. It is one of the most prodigious wines of the vintage in 2003, a wine with all the right stuff. Inky ruby/purple in color, it has a classic nose of spring flowers intermixed with blueberry and blackberry liqueur as well as cassis and some sweet earth, almost truffle-like notes. Very full-bodied, opulently textured, and multilayered, this is a spectacular wine that should hit its peak in about 5–6 years and last for up to two decades. This is fabulous Châteauneuf-du-Pape.

2001 Châteauneuf-du-Pape Cuvée de Mon Aïeul
RATING: 97 points

The 2001 Châteauneuf-du-Pape Cuvée de Mon Aïeul (85% Grenache and equal parts Syrah, Mourvèdre, and Cinsault) tips the scales at a prodigious 15.8% alcohol. Half of the wine is aged in neutral wood *foudres* and the other half in tank prior to being bottled unfined and unfiltered. The sources for Mon Aïeul are three vineyard parcels with vines averaging between 75 and 87 years of age. The 2001 is much more structured and backward than the 2000, 1999, or 1998. The color is a dense purple, and the bouquet offers sweet but reserved aromas of blackberries, raspberries, crushed rocks, and kirsch. It possesses superb texture, enormous body, and tremendous purity as well as overall symmetry. The tannin is high, but it is largely concealed by the wealth of fruit and extract. Give it 3–4 years of cellaring, and drink it over the following 15–18 years. This fabulous 2001 will provide fascinating comparisons when tasted alongside the 2000, 1999, and 1998 over the next 10–15 years.

2000 Châteauneuf-du-Pape Cuvée de Mon Aïeul
RATING: 95 points

The profound 2000 Châteauneuf-du-Pape Cuvée de Mon Aïeul (85% Grenache and the rest equal parts Syrah, Mourvèdre, and Cinsault) tips the scales at 15% alcohol. From an old vineyard and cropped at 15 hectoliters per hectare, and aged only in *foudre,* it boasts a dense purple color in addition to an exquisite nose of violets, minerals, blueberries, and blackberries. Pure and concentrated, but atypically tannic, it requires considerable aging as it is one of the vintage's more backward, broodingly powerful efforts. Anticipated maturity: 2006–2020.

1999 Châteauneuf-du-Pape Cuvée de Mon Aïeul
RATING: 91 points

The 1999 Châteauneuf-du-Pape Cuvée de Mon Aïeul (10,000 bottles produced) has closed down since bottling. It is a dense purple–colored, concentrated effort made from incredibly low yields of 15–20 hectoliters per hectare from 80-year-old vines. A blend of 95% Grenache and 5% Cinsault, this tannic, backward, blockbuster *vin de garde* should open in another 1–2 years, and last for two decades. It is an extracted, dense, atypically powerful 1999.

1998 Châteauneuf-du-Pape Cuvée de Mon Aïeul
RATING: 98 points

I have been a great believer in this wine since I first tasted it, but never has it shown as well as it did at several tastings in New York City in the fall of 2001. The color is a dense blue/purple. The wine appeared closed after bottling, and is still tight, but oh, so promising and loaded. Crème de cassis intermixed with minerals and blueberries are reminiscent of a Napa Cabernet Sauvignon from the likes of Bryant Family Vineyards. In the mouth, earth, pepper, and Provençal notes tip the scales in favor of Châteauneuf-du-Pape. Awesomely concentrated, extraordinarily pure, with moderately high tannin, fabulous length, and a youthful personality, it will drink well for 2–3 decades. Anticipated maturity: now–2030.

CHATEAUNEUF-DU-PAPE RESERVE DES DEUX FRERES

2003 Châteauneuf-du-Pape Réserve des Deux Frères
RATING: 98–100 points

Selected by the two brothers from their Mon Aïeul *cuvées* as the best of the best, and then some press wine added, with 60% of this *cuvée* aged in old used barrels and *demi-muids* and the other 40% in cement tanks before blending, this spectacular wine is a candidate for one of the wines of the vintage. Actually, for the first time tasting it, the aromas smelled somewhat like the great Cuvée da Capo from Pégau. Dense purple to the rim with an extraordinary nose, almost like a great Amarone but with an additional freshness from lively blackberry and blueberry fruit, floral notes, and hints of pen ink, the wine is stunningly rich, very full-bodied, and much like its sibling with a natural alcohol that exceeds 16%. The wine is very layered, huge, yet remarkably well balanced and neither hot nor heavy. It is a tour de force in winemaking and a candidate for drinking between 2010 and 2025+.

2001 Châteauneuf-du-Pape Réserve des Deux Frères

RATING: 99 points

The 2001 Châteauneuf-du-Pape Réserve des Deux Frères elicits "wows." This 2001, which tips the scales at an awesome 16.2% natural alcohol, boasts an inky/purple color along with a sensationally pure bouquet of blackberries, graphite, acacia flowers, licorice, and sweet kirsch. Unctuously textured and full-bodied, with high tannin as well as a closed personality, this prodigious yet fabulous Châteauneuf-du-Pape is a potential legend in the making. It requires 3–5 years of cellaring, and should keep for two decades. The texture, purity, and magnificent concentration suggest tiny yields, old vines, and non-interventionalistic winemaking. By the way, this wine represents a selection of the finest lots in the cellar as the sources are the same as for the Cuvée de Mon Aïeul, although a large component of Deux Frères is from the Usseglio holdings in the sector of Châteauneuf-du-Pape called La Crau. Anticipated maturity: 2007–2022+.

2000 Châteauneuf-du-Pape Réserve des Deux Frères

RATING: 98 points

The 2000 Châteauneuf-du-Pape Réserve des Deux Frères, which has been one of the winners in several blind tastings, is a candidate for wine of the vintage. This blend of 95% Grenache and 5% Cinsault tips the scales at a whopping 15.8% alcohol. Its inky purple color is accompanied by succulent aromas of blackberry, cherry, and raspberry liqueur interwoven with licorice, mineral, and acacia flower characteristics. Fabulously concentrated and full-bodied, with a voluptuous texture, sweet tannin, and a flamboyant and accessible personality, this prodigious, majestic Châteauneuf-du-Pape needs to be tasted to be believed. Anticipated maturity: 2008–2030.

1999 Châteauneuf-du-Pape Cuvée de Cinquantenaire

RATING: 95 points

The debut release of the Reserve des Deux Frères was called Cinquantenaire in 1999 to celebrate the 50th anniversary of the domaine. The prodigious, saturated, opaque ruby/purple-colored 1999 Châteauneuf-du-Pape Cuvée de Cinquantenaire (200 cases) is a candidate for the wine of the vintage. A 100% Grenache *cuvée* aged in older *demi-muids*, it is exceptionally full-bodied with a fabulous perfume of blackberry liqueur, cassis, minerals, spice, and flowers. The texture is sumptuous and the wine accessible, although readers lucky enough to latch on to a few bottles can watch the magic unfold over the next two decades. Awesome stuff! Anticipated maturity: now–2020.

WINE: Châteauneuf-du-Pape

CLASSIFICATION: Châteauneuf-du-Pape

OWNER: Lucien Michel

ADDRESS: 9, avenue St.-Joseph, B.P. 66, 84232 Châteauneuf-du-Pape, France

TELEPHONE: 33 04 90 83 70 03

TELEFAX: 33 04 90 83 50 38

E-MAIL: vieux-donjon@wanadoo.fr

WEBSITE: www.vieux-donjon.com *(under construction)*

CONTACT: Marie José Michel

VISITING POLICY: By appointment only

VINEYARDS

SURFACE AREA: 32.1 acres total

GRAPE VARIETALS: *Red*—80% Grenache, 10% Syrah, 5% Mourvèdre, plus others

AVERAGE AGE OF THE VINES: *Red*: 10–90 years

DENSITY OF PLANTATION: Old vines—1.75 x 1.75 m; young vines—2.5 x 1 m

AVERAGE YIELDS: 30–32 hectoliters per hectare

WINEMAKING AND UPBRINGING

This is another traditional wine that is made more in the vineyard than cellar. Severe crop thinning is followed by triages of the harvest. Approximately 50–75% of the grapes are destemmed according to vintage character. The vinification takes place in cement tanks, the *cuvaison* lasts 18–21 days, and the wine spends 18–24 months in neutral wood *foudres* prior to bottling, with minimal clarification.

ANNUAL PRODUCTION

Châteauneuf-du-Pape (red): 50,000 bottles

AVERAGE PRICE (VARIABLE DEPENDING ON VINTAGE): $35–50

GREAT RECENT VINTAGES

2003, 2001, 1998, 1990, 1978

Lucien and Marie José Michel

This is one of the great unheralded estates of Châteauneuf-du-Pape. It is a relatively recent creation, founded in 1979 after the marriage of Lucien Michel to Marie José, members of two established wine families. Lucien's grandfather was both a barrel maker and transporter of wine in the first half of the 20th century (1914–1945), and also had a small vineyard. Marie José's grandfather had holdings also, and upon their marriage, a union of both people and vineyards became Vieux Donjon. The 32.1 acres include many old vines—25 acres of the estate possess vines over 80 years of age—all on the plateau near Mont Redon and Les Cabrières (the sector covered with the famed *galets roulés*). In 1990, the Michels planted one hectare with equal parts Clairette, Roussanne, and Grenache Blanc, from which they have begun to make a fruity, dry white Châteauneuf-du-Pape. However, the real glory from this estate is their majestic red wine.

The red wine is put through a traditional vinification, with some destemming, a relatively long maceration, and—perhaps the biggest secret of all—low yields from ancient vines. Moreover, the wine is one of the handful in Châteauneuf-du-Pape to be bottled with no fining or filtration. The modest, enthusiastic Michels farm their vineyard organically, harvest much later than most in Châteauneuf-du-Pape (except for Henri Bonneau and Jacques Reynaud), and let the wine make itself. The upbringing in large wood *foudres* (no new oak is employed) can last for two years.

Vieux Donjon wines are some of the great classics of the appellation, and are very long-lived. The estate has been remarkably consistent in lighter years. Moreover, prices have essentially remained stable for almost a decade!

My buying history with this estate goes back two decades, and I have enjoyed virtually every vintage I have purchased. At present, I'm working my way through the last of my 1985s and 1990s, and then I'll attack the 1995s and 1998s.

CHATEAUNEUF-DU-PAPE

2003 Châteauneuf-du-Pape

RATING: 95+ points

A very strong vintage for this traditionally made Châteauneuf-du-Pape, the 2003, a blend of 80% Grenache, 10% Syrah, and the rest Mourvèdre and Cinsault, has a deep ruby/plum/purple color and a big sweet nose of dried Provençal herbs, licorice, seaweed, and spice box. The wine is massively concentrated, relatively high in alcohol by the standards here (15+% on their component parts), and a long, concentrated, chewy finish with high tannin and equally high extract. If there is one Châteauneuf-du-Pape that smells like an open-air Provençal spice, flower, and food market, it is Vieux Donjon. It is a classic, concentrated essence of Provence, all in an alcoholic beverage. This wine will need 4–5 years of cellaring when released and drink well for 15–20 years.

2001 Châteauneuf-du-Pape

RATING: 93 points

For one of the appellation's classic, old-style offerings, the Michel family continues to produce an uncompromisingly long-lived, remarkably consistent Châteauneuf-du-Pape. The dark plum/purple-colored 2001 boasts a huge, Provençal-styled bouquet of ground pepper, lavender, roasted *herbes de Provence,* beef blood, and cranberry, as well as black cherry liqueur. This perfumed effort exhibits sweet, broad, full-bodied flavors, moderately high tannin, and admirable density and chewiness. There are also hints of underbrush, new saddle leather, incense, and black fruits. This striking 2001 needs 1–3 years of cellaring. It will drink well for 12–15 years.

2000 Châteauneuf-du-Pape

RATING: 91 points

The 2000 Châteauneuf-du-Pape represents an educational tour of the southern Rhône, in particular, Châteauneuf-du-Pape. It possesses all the appellation's classic components—underbrush, *garrigue,* licorice, pepper, lavender, sweet black cherries, and incense. Extremely perfumed and heady, this full-bodied, moderately tannic offering comes close to matching the mass and blockbuster power of the 1998. Firm tannin in the finish suggests a long aging curve. Given my experience with Vieux Donjon, most of the classic vintages hit their peak at 7–8 years, where they remain for 5–6 years.

Around age 15–16 they begin a slow decline. The 2000 should follow that path. Anticipated maturity: 2006–2016.

1999 Châteauneuf-du-Pape

RATING: 91 points

Le Vieux Donjon's 1999 Châteauneuf-du-Pape offers soaring aromas of barbecue spice, licorice, herbs, tar, black cherries, and blackberries. This powerful, rich, full-bodied effort is more up front and accessible than most vintages, but there is no compromise in the richness and mouth-filling characteristics consistently offered by this estate. Drink this sexy, compelling 1999 between now and 2020.

1998 Châteauneuf-du-Pape

RATING: 95 points

The 1998, a classic in the making, is, along with the 1990, one of the two finest Vieux Donjons I have tasted. The backward 1998 offers aromas of incense, roasted herbs, lavender, licorice, and kirsch in a full-bodied, sweet, expansive, structured style. It should last another 15–20 years.

1995 Châteauneuf-du-Pape

RATING: 90 points

The 1995 remains closed but promising. Its garnet/plum/purple color is followed by sweet aromas of roasted herbs, black cherries, incense, licorice, iodine, and earth. Medium to full–bodied, structured, and muscular, it is still youthful and exuberant, with plenty of tannin to shed. Anticipated maturity: 2006–2014.

1994 Châteauneuf-du-Pape

RATING: 91 points

The opaque dark ruby/purple–colored 1994 Châteauneuf-du-Pape exhibits a fabulous nose of sweet, jammy, black cherries, raspberries, smoke, and a vague hint of licorice and Provençal herbs. Full-bodied, with excellent concentration, power, and a sweet, expansive, chewy mid-palate, this is an outstanding example of Châteauneuf-du-Pape from what continues to be the most underrated great estate of the appellation. It should drink well for another 4–6 years.

1990 Châteauneuf-du-Pape
RATING: 95 points

The spectacular 1990 gets better every time I go back to it. Fully mature, yet seemingly capable of lasting another 8–10 years, it boasts a dark plum/garnet color in addition to a celestial bouquet of lavender and other Provençal herbs intermixed with licorice-infused cassis and black cherry liqueur. Powerful, full-bodied, unctuously textured, and loaded, there are no hard edges in this seamless, young classic. Don't miss it!

1989 Châteauneuf-du-Pape
RATING: 90 points

The 1989, like many of its peers in this vintage, has aged at a glacial pace. The color is still a dark plum/ruby, and the nose exhibits dusty sweet and sour cherry aromas intermixed with licorice, herbs, leather, and meat. While tight in the mouth, and medium to full–bodied, with high tannin, it possesses good balance. I suspect it is behaving like many 1978s did at a similar age. Anticipated maturity: 2007–2016.

1981 Châteauneuf-du-Pape
RATING: 90 points

The dark garnet–colored 1981 Châteauneuf possesses very deep, concentrated, seductively opulent and luxuriant flavors that fill the mouth. Smooth and velvety, but balanced, this wine has reached full maturity, but it displays no signs of losing its fruit. It is a high-class, distinctive wine from Vieux Donjon. Anticipated maturity: now–2009.

WINE: Châteauneuf-du-Pape

CLASSIFICATION: Châteauneuf-du-Pape AOC

OWNER: Brunier family

ADDRESS: 3 route de Châteauneuf-du-Pape, B.P. 5, 84370 Bedarrides, France

TELEPHONE: 33 04 90 33 00 31

TELEFAX: 33 04 90 33 18 47

E-MAIL: vignobles@brunier.fr

WEBSITE: www.vignoblesbrunier.fr

CONTACT: Daniel Brunier

VISITING POLICY: By appointment only

VINEYARDS

SURFACE AREA: 173 acres total

GRAPE VARIETALS: *Red*—65% Grenache, 15% Syrah, 15% Mourvèdre, 5% Cinsault and others

AVERAGE AGE OF THE VINES: 50 years

DENSITY OF PLANTATION: Traditional—3,300 vines per hectare

AVERAGE YIELDS: 30 hectoliters per hectare

WINEMAKING AND UPBRINGING

At Vieux Télégraphe the grapes are hand-picked, with double sorting in the vineyard and cellar. This is followed by gentle pressing and selective destemming, followed by 15–20 days of traditional fermentation in temperature-controlled stainless steel tanks. After malolactic fermentation, the wine is aged in concrete tanks for the first 9 months, and then transferred to *foudres* (50–70 hl capacity) at about 10 months, for a period of 8–12 months, depending on the vintage. Bottled without filtration at about 20 months, it is released to the market at two years.

ANNUAL PRODUCTION

Vieux Télégraphe (red): 200,000 bottles

AVERAGE PRICE: $40–55

GREAT RECENT VINTAGES

2003, 2001, 1998, 1995, 1989, 1978

Hippolyte Brunier established this domaine in 1898 on the highest terrace of the Châteauneuf-du-Pape appellation, called the Plateau de la Crau. The domaine takes its name from the optical telegraph, as its inventor, Claude Chaffe, chose this location for a relay tower in 1792. Today, the domaine extends over 173 acres and is run by Frédéric and Daniel Brunier, the fourth generation of the family.

Vieux Télégraphe is unquestionably one of Châteauneuf-du-Pape's most famous estates. No doubt the large production from the estate's large vineyard accounts for the effective distribution of this wine throughout the world's finest wine circles. Owned by the Brunier family since the early part of the 20th century, Vieux Télégraphe has one of the most privileged *terroirs* of Châteauneuf-du-Pape. Located in the eastern section of the appellation, in an area covered with large, football-sized *galets roulés,* the entire vineyard is in a sector known as La Crau. Along with the two famous estates on the plateau of Châteauneuf-du-Pape, Mont Redon and Les Cabrières, Vieux Télégraphe's vineyard has a distinct geographic advantage. Vieux Télégraphe's

Daniel and Frédéric Brunier

vineyards enjoy an extremely hot microclimate, enabling the Bruniers to harvest 7–10 days before many other estates in the appellation. Their early harvest is largely responsible for the property's success in years when other estates have had difficulties (i.e., 1993).

For most of the latter part of the 20th century, the fortunes of Vieux Télégraphe were guided by Henri Brunier, whom I first met in the late 1970s. Gregarious, open, always tanned, and with chiseled features (another *vigneron* with more than a vague similarity to the appellation's old, gnarled vines), Brunier retired in the late 1980s, turning over the operation of Vieux Télégraphe to his two capable sons, Daniel and Frédéric. Everything I have seen since these two enthusiastic

young men have taken over suggests that Vieux Télégraphe is raising the quality to an even higher level.

From the old vineyards (the average age of the vineyards is 50 years, with one-third an impressive 60 years of age), emerges a wine made from a traditional blend of 60–70% Grenache, 15–18% Syrah, 15–18% Mourvèdre, and a tiny amount of Cinsault. Since the two brothers have taken over there has been an effort made to decrease the percentage of Grenache and use slightly more Syrah and Mourvèdre. Yields are always conservative, with 30 hectoliters per hectare being the norm.

The winemaking style of Vieux Télégraphe did go through a metamorphosis of sorts when the sparkling new *cuverie* was constructed in 1979. In my 1987 book on the wines of the Rhône Valley, I lamented the fact that Vieux Télégraphe's winemaking style had moved away from their textbook, classic, ageworthy, thick, burly Châteauneuf-du-Papes best exemplified by the magnificent 1978 and excellent 1972, to a more modern, fruity style that was immensely appealing but lacked the longevity of the pre-1979 vintages. That style has gradually been refined, with most of the changes occurring in the 1990s. A second wine, Vieux Mas des Papes, (named after Daniel's residence) was introduced in 1994. This 100% Grenache Châteauneuf-du-Pape is made from younger vines. Another apparent change is that since the late 1980s, Vieux Télégraphe has been bottled unfiltered. The Bruniers had been doing several filtrations, a Kisselguhr filtration after malolactic, and a prebottling filtration. The latter has been eliminated for fear of losing too much extract and body.

From a vinification perspective, the wines are impeccably handled. The Bruniers are flexible regarding destemming, never removing the stems from their old-vine Grenache, but destemming the young-vine Grenache, as well as a hefty percentage of the Mourvèdre and Syrah. The wines never see any new oak, but they are vinified and raised in spotless stainless-steel tanks buried in a hill underneath the famed Autoroute de Soleil. After 8–10 months in tanks, the wines are moved to large wooden *foudres* until deemed ready for bottling.

Vieux Télégraphe can produce wines of surprising richness. However, nothing produced in the 1980s can match the extraordinary intensity and majestic richness and complexity of the 1978. In the 1990s, I thought the 1994, 1995, and 1998 were the finest wines made at this estate since the 1978. This success was furthered by the impressive 2000 and 2001. The style of Vieux Télégraphe is one that appeals to both neophytes and connoisseurs of Rhône Valley wines, and this renowned estate has achieved its worldwide popularity the hard way—it has earned it.

CHATEAUNEUF-DU-PAPE

2003 Châteauneuf-du-Pape
RATING: 90–94 points
Only the old vines were utilized in Vieux Télégraphe, and as a result, it is a relatively small production that is 40% less than normal. The result is a very tannic, almost austere, but formidably concentrated Vieux Télégraphe with a deep ruby/purple color and a sweet nose of raspberries, black cherries, nori (that seaweed wrap used in sushi preparation), pepper, and an almost crushed mineral note. Quite dense, full-bodied, and combining power and elegance with some austere, almost Bordeaux-like tannins in the finish, this is a *vin de garde* Châteauneuf-du-Pape to forget in the cellar for 4–6 years. It is all there, but patience will be required. Anticipated maturity: 2010–2022+.

2001 Châteauneuf-du-Pape
RATING: 93 points
The 2001 Châteauneuf-du-Pape is gorgeous, structured, and impressive. Full-bodied and backward, with great depth, purity, and heady aromatics, this 20,000-case blend of 60% Grenache, 15% Mourvèdre, 10% Syrah, and 15% miscellaneous amounts of the other permitted varietals will easily rival the 1998. A deep ruby/purple-tinged color is accompanied by a sweet perfume of salty sea breezes, seaweed, melted licorice, kirsch, crème de cassis, and iodine—a classic Vieux Télégraphe aromatic display. Powerful as well as firmly structured, this is a wine to lay away for 4–5 years. It should prove to be uncommonly long-lived, lasting a minimum of two decades. It gets my nod as the greatest Vieux Télégraphe since the 1998.

2000 Châteauneuf-du-Pape

RATING: 91 points

The elegant 2000 Vieux Télégraphe possesses 14.8% alcohol, along with a deep ruby/purple color, charming, rich fruitiness, and firm tannin in the finish. With loads of freshness, copious quantities of pepper, seaweed, and black fruit characteristics, and a distinctive minerality, this full-bodied, sweet 2000 requires another year or two of cellaring; it should age well for 15–16 years. Anticipated maturity: now–2018.

1998 Châteauneuf-du-Pape

RATING: 95 points

Just beginning to blossom, the 1998 is, for me, the finest Vieux Télégraphe made in twenty years (since the 1978). A spectacular effort, it boasts a deep ruby/purple color and huge concentration, but it was beginning to open in 2004. It is a very rich, full-bodied wine, yet it has considerable elegance. A beauty! Anticipated maturity: 2007–2020.

1995 Châteauneuf-du-Pape

RATING: 90 points

The deep ruby/purple-colored 1995 exhibits a sweet perfume of licorice, iodine, seaweed, black cherries, and plums. Dense, medium to full–bodied, well structured, and muscular, it will be at its peak between now and 2015.

1994 Châteauneuf-du-Pape

RATING: 93 points

A sleeper vintage for Vieux Télégraphe is 1994. Because this vineyard tends to mature quickly, the extraordinarily hot, dry summer allowed this estate to harvest in late August and early September, long before many other properties could, and before the rain began. The 1994 offers sweet floral, blue and black fruits intermixed with dried Provençal herbs, tree bark, and earth. Powerful, concentrated, and close to full maturity, it will last for another decade. Moreover, this wine sells for a song since the vintage does not have a reputation such as the 1995, 1998, 1999, 2000, and 2001.

1989 Châteauneuf-du-Pape La Crau

RATING: 90 points

While not one of the great Vieux Télégraphes, 1989 continues to perform well. It is dense, sweet, and ripe, with copious quantities of seaweed, iodine, smoke, black cherry, and plum-like fruit offered in a medium-bodied, slightly tannic style. Fully mature, it should last for another decade.

1983 Châteauneuf-du-Pape La Crau

RATING: 90 points

One of the top successes for this property during a period of very good rather than outstanding winemaking, the 1983 is spicy, peppery, and earthy, with a fragrant, in-your-face aromatic profile. This full-bodied, corpulent, muscular Vieux Télégraphe is one of the few wines made during the estate's high-tech period that displays some of the old, burly, thick character of pre-1979 vintages. Some amber/orange is creeping along the edge, but the wine reveals no loss of fruit. This fully mature wine should be drunk up.

1978 Châteauneuf-du-Pape La Crau

RATING: 94 points

One of the great classics of Châteauneuf-du-Pape is the 1978 made by Henri Brunier. This wine, which has given me immense pleasure, offers a sensational smorgasbord of aromas, including compost, pepper, black fruits, smoked meats, Vaucluse truffles, licorice, and incense. The aromatics easily merit a perfect 100-point score. In the mouth, this huge wine is massive, thick, and unctuous, with the concentration of a dry vintage port. An amazing effort, it remains the quintessential classic Vieux Télégraphe, that perhaps only the 1998 will come close to rivaling. The 1978 has been fully mature for over a decade, but the color remains a dark plum/purple with little signs of evolution. Drink it over the next decade. An amazing wine!

GERMANY

Germany remains the most confusing wine region in the world. Blame the complicated nomenclature that appears on the labels and the fact that the best wines are made in tiny quantities. To simplify things as much as possible: there are 11 major wine-producing zones in Germany, and within these zones there are subdistricts, the most general of which are called Bereich. By analogy these would be the equivalent to a generic appellation wine in France. Within the Bereich there are more specific parameters or boundaries called Grosslagen, to which the closest French equivalent would be a more specific appellation within the overall generic appellation, such as Appellation Morey St.-Denis within the more generalized Appellation Bourgogne Contrôlée. These are wines that are not from a specific vineyard but from a particular region or collection of sites for vineyards. There are well over 150 Grosslagen in Germany. The most specific zone in Germany is called Einzellage, which is a single site or vineyard. There are over 2,600 of them in Germany, and again by analogy, this is the closest German equivalent to what the French would call a château- or vineyard-designated premier cru or grand cru Burgundy.

The majority of the greatest producers in Germany are located in the following nine zones: the Middle Mosel, the Lower Mosel, the Saar, the Ruwer, the Rheingau, the Rheinhessen, the Rheinpfalz (which is often referred to as the Pfalz today), the Nahe, and the Franken. In the profiles that follow, not all of these areas are represented.

To add to the complicated German wine scene, the best German wines carry a designation such as Kabinett, Spätlese, Auslese, Beerenauslese, Trockenbeerenauslese, or Eiswein, which is essentially a level of ripeness or sweetness. Most wine consumers would not find a Kabinett to be particularly sweet, although these wines contain residual sugar. Because of the high natural acidity found in German wines, most Kabinetts generally taste fresh and fruity, but not sweet. However, most tasters would likely be able to determine some sweetness in the Spätlese and even more in an Auslese. Of course the Beerenauslese and Trockenbeerenauslese are clearly dessert wines, as are the Eisweins. Most of these wines average between 7 and 9% alcohol, although the alcohol can creep up to 12–14% depending on the grower, the viticultural region, and the vintage. One of the interesting things about the very finest German wines is that despite relatively low alcohol, they actually become drier as they age. Certainly a top producer's Spätlese or Auslese from a top vintage can last for 8–25 years, with the great sweet wines designated as Beerenauslese, Trockenbeerenauslese, or Eisweins lasting 30–50 and sometimes 100 or more years.

Another myth about German wines is that they don't work well with food. The fact is that none of them sees any new oak—they're aged in neutral, large oak *foudres* or stainless steel, which gives them much more flexibility with food than people suspect. Because the residual sugar is counterbalanced by equally high levels of fresh natural acidity, the wines never taste as sweet as their analysis indicates, and as they age they taste increasingly drier while gaining additional nuances and complexity in their aromatic and flavor profile.

The one downside, of course, is that the great producers who are profiled in the following pages do make extraordinary wines, but their top *cuvées* are, much like other small estates, extremely limited in production.

WINES:

Riesling Oberhäuser Brücke

Riesling Niederhäuser Hermannshöhle

Riesling Schlossböckelheimer Felsenberg

Riesling Schlossböckelheimer Kupfergrube

CLASSIFICATION: Nahe

OWNER: Helmut Dönnhoff

ADDRESS: Bahnhofstrasse 11, 55585 Oberhausen/Nahe, Germany

TELEPHONE: 49 67 55 263

TELEFAX: 49 67 55 1067

CONTACT: Winery address

VISITING POLICY: By appointment only

VINEYARDS

SURFACE AREA: 31.5 acres

GRAPE VARIETALS: 75% Riesling, 25% Weissburgunder and Granburgunder

AVERAGE AGE OF THE VINES: 30–45 years

DENSITY OF PLANTATION: 5,000–7,000 vines per hectare

AVERAGE YIELDS: 35–45 hectoliters per hectare

WINEMAKING AND UPBRINGING

The wines are handled very traditionally, fermented in large, neutral oak casks with indigenous yeasts and bottled in early spring following the vintage. Dönnhoff uses yeast cultures that he has created from his own wines, which allow for a very slow, controlled fermentation.

ANNUAL PRODUCTION

Total production—6,700 cases

AVERAGE PRICE (VARIABLE DEPENDING ON VINTAGE): $35–250

GREAT RECENT VINTAGES

2003, 2002, 2001

Readers looking for almost virginal purity of fruit and character should beat a path to the wines of Helmut Dönnhoff, who has become, over the last decade, a superstar from the tiny Nahe appellation. Yet he is certainly no newcomer, having made wine for over 30 years. Dönnhoff has extraordinary vineyards, most notably the Niederhäuser Hermannshöhle, an incredibly steep hillside with ideal exposure and an amazing combination of slate and volcanic soils. One of his other great sites is his monopole vineyard, the Oberhäuser Brücke, which often produces the biggest, most flamboyant, and powerful of the Dönnhoff wines, but they still exhibit plenty of nuances, transparency, and that extraordinary minerality that characterizes a great Riesling.

This estate has been in the Dönnhoff family since 1750, and I doubt any of the Dönnhoffs ever imagined the kind of international hysteria their wines would create at the turn of the 20th century. These are some of the most justifiably fashionable and hardest-to-find Rieslings in the wine world and worth all the effort that it takes to latch on to a few bottles.

RIESLING AUSLESE NIEDERHÄUSER HERMANNSHÖHLE

2003 Riesling Auslese Niederhäuser Hermannshöhle

RATING: 97 points

Tarragon, oregano, stones, and pears can be detected in the nuanced scents of the spectacular 2003 Riesling Auslese Niederhäuser Hermannshöhle. This offering blew me away with its juxtaposition of immense richness and elegant detail. Medium-bodied and satin-textured, it reveals an ample character awash in spices, herbs, poached pears, and superripe apples. Notes of red currants, slate, and candied minerals intermingled with linden blossoms can also be discerned in its complex flavor profile. This wine's lush, tremendous finish appears to last over a minute. Anticipated maturity: 2007–2035.

2002 Riesling Auslese Niederhäuser Hermannshöhle

RATING: 94 points

For the second year in a row, Helmut Dönnhoff has left me shaking my head in wonder. Tasting the greatest wines in the world, year in and year out, as a wine merchant and as a critic, did not prepare me for the awe-inspiring experience of tasting through Dönnhoff's 2001s and 2002s. They are magical, emotional, breathtaking. My words cannot do them justice. Dominated by botrytis and spices, the nose of the 2002 Riesling Auslese Niederhäuser Hermannshöhle leads to a broad, immensely rich core of enormous concentration. Medium-bodied, laced with spicy noble rot, it has tremendous depth, power, and length. It is rather fitting that both of the estate's 2002 Auslesen are only available in half-bottles, a sign that Dönnhoff himself realizes they are more than Auslesen, deserving to be treated (and served) as Beerenauslesen. Anticipated maturity: 2010–2030.

2001 Riesling Auslese Niederhäuser Hermannshöhle

RATING: 92 points

Buttery white fruits and stones can be found in the mouth of the smoked mineral–scented 2001 Riesling Auslese Niederhäuser Hermannshöhle. Medium-bodied and thick, this wine has a plush, velvety character whose effects linger on the palate for 30 seconds. It does not have the exceptional focus and delineation of Dönnhoff's greatest 2001s yet remains outstanding. Drink it between now and 2014.

RIESLING AUSLESE OBERHÄUSER BRÜCKE

2003 Riesling Auslese Oberhäuser Brücke

RATING: 95 points

The 2003 Riesling Auslese Oberhäuser Brücke exhibits a terrific nose of perfume, lilies, violets, and apples. Broad, supple, and round, this pure, medium-bodied wine has the personality and grace of a plump, joyful dancer. Its plush, sweet, white fruit–packed core is dusted with spices whose flavors are seamlessly extended into its prolonged finish. Anticipated maturity: 2007–2030.

2002 Riesling Auslese Oberhäuser Brücke

RATING: 97 points

The 2002 Riesling Auslese Oberhäuser Brücke screams Beerenauslese from its nose to its finish. Red fruits, smoky botrytis, and spices are found in its explosive aromatics. Syrupy, weighty, authoritative, and revealing remarkable richness, it is plush as well as impeccably balanced. Anticipated maturity: 2010–2030+.

2001 Riesling Auslese Oberhäuser Brücke

RATING: 94 points

Sweetened scallions can be discerned in the nose of the medium to full–bodied 2001 Riesling Auslese Oberhäuser Brücke. A wine of great harmony, depth, and power, it coats the palate with lingering poached pear and spice flavors. Lush, wonderfully elegant, and exceptionally long, it is a superb Auslese for drinking between 2010 and 2025.

RIESLING EISWEIN OBERHÄUSER BRÜCKE

2003 Riesling Eiswein Oberhäuser Brücke

RATING: 95 points

Deep aromas of honeyed botrytis can be found in its nuanced aromatics. Medium-bodied, unbelievably dense, concentrated, and long, this superb effort coats the palate with oily waves of black cherry jam, white chocolate, and molasses. Unlike most of the super-high-end, sweet 2003s I tasted from Germany, this one did not abandon grace and balance in favor of syrupy sweetness. That being said, while it will most certainly last for many decades, its burnt sugar flavors lead me to recommend drinking it over the next 15 years.

2002 Riesling Eiswein Oberhäuser Brücke

RATING: 100 points

The 2002 Riesling Eiswein Oberhäuser Brücke is another grand slam home run for Dönnhoff. It is so intense, so powerful, and so complex as to instill fear in the taster. Its apricot and peach cobbler aromas lead to a jellied core of cassis, raspberries, syrupy slate, and oodles of spices. It is simply amazing that a wine of this richness, ripeness, and depth can retain perfect definition, grip, and refinement. What is truly terrifying, however, is that Dönnhoff produced a three-star Eiswein from the same vineyard in 2002, one he presumably considers better than this sublime nectar. Bravo! Anticipated maturity: 2015–2040+.

2001 Riesling Eiswein Oberhäuser Brücke

RATING: 100 points

From a parcel that reached 100 Oeschle (the scale used in Germany for determining ripeness—in natural potential alcohol terms it is equivalent to 13%) before freezing, and therefore being concentrated, the 2001 Riesling Eiswein Oberhäuser Brücke is a wine of sumptuous ripeness and blazing acidity. Candied eggplants, sweetened herbal teas, minerals, and hints of banana can be found in its penetrating aromatics. It cuts a broad yet elegant and highly focused swath across the palate with exotic fruits and strawberries. An offering of magnificent purity, it is immensely concentrated, powerful, lush, refined, and vibrant. Its effects can still be discerned over a minute after having tasted it. This stupendous, complete gem will benefit from cellaring until 2012–2013 and will then last for 20 years or more. Bravo!

RIESLING SPÄTLESE NIEDERHÄUSER HERMANNSHÖHLE

2003 Riesling Spätlese Niederhäuser Hermannshöhle

RATING: 95 points

Loads of fresh herbs intermingled with a myriad of spices are found in the aromatic profile of the 2003 Riesling Spätlese Niederhäuser Hermannshöhle. A bold, sultry wine, it unleashes powerful waves of pears, candied apples, spices, melon balls, raspberries, and red currants that conquer the taster's palate. This offering's stupendous flavor profile, depth, and sensual nature led me to write "sexylicious!" in my notebook. Yet, what makes this Niederhäuser stand out most when compared to Dönnhoff's other 2003 Spätlesen is the extraordinary precision of its fruit. Anticipated maturity: 2006–2020.

2002 Riesling Spätlese Niederhäuser Hermannshöhle

RATING: 96 points

This Spätlese is extraordinary, hovering in that zone bordering perfection where wines touch the soul. Profound aromas of liquid slate and pepper emanate from the glass of the 2002 Riesling Spätlese Niederhäuser Hermannshöhle. Equally powerful, muscular, and masculine as the Oberhäuser Brücke, it has flavors of spices awash in pear syrup. A barely perceptible dip in intensity in the mid-palate is the reason this extraordinarily pure, concentrated, and persistent wine earned one fewer point than some of its peers. All Hail the King of Spätlese! Dönnhoff's lineup of Spätlesen is second to none. Anticipated maturity: 2009–2030.

2001 Riesling Spätlese Niederhäuser Hermannshöhle

RATING: 98 points

The medium to full–bodied 2001 Riesling Spätlese Niederhäuser Hermannshöhle is the greatest Spätlese I've ever tasted. Its liquid mineral and spice scents lead to a mind-boggling personality of otherworldly richness, depth, and concentration. This massive yet intensely pure wine bastes the taster's palate with oily layers of minerals, almonds, earth, and smoky slate whose flavors are seemingly unending (*unendlich*, as F. X. Pichler, Austria's superstar winemaker, says). This is a prodigious, benchmark-setting effort. Anticipated maturity: 2008–2020+.

RIESLING SPÄTLESE OBERHÄUSER BRÜCKE

2003 Riesling Spätlese Oberhäuser Brücke

RATING: 93 points

The 2003 Riesling Spätlese Oberhäuser Brücke is flint-scented, medium-bodied, and silky-textured. Well balanced, it explodes on the palate with loads of white fruits, notes of red berries, and spices. Suave, angle free, and exceptionally long in the finish, this effort is a candidate for drinking between now and 2020.

2002 Riesling Spätlese Oberhäuser Brücke

RATING: 97 points

The 2002 Riesling Spätlese Oberhäuser Brücke exhibits aromas and flavors of cherry-drenched quartz, raspberries, and minerals, as well as steel. Medium-bodied, muscular, powerful, and masculine, it is an oily-textured, broad-shouldered wine of spectacular depth and length. This concentrated, harmonious behemoth will be at its best between 2010 and 2030.

2001 Riesling Spätlese Oberhäuser Brücke

RATING: 94 points

Fresh citrus fruits, spring onions, and spices are found in the nose of the 2001 Riesling Spätlese Oberhäuser Brücke. A medium-bodied, complex, highly expressive wine, its satin-textured core reveals perfumed white fruits, green onions, minerals, and verbena in its rich yet crystalline character. Anticipated maturity: 2006–2018.

RIESLING SPÄTLESE SCHLOSSBÖCKELHEIMER FELSENBERG

2003 Riesling Spätlese Schlossböckelheimer Felsenberg

RATING: 92 points

The floral, white fruit–scented 2003 Riesling Spätlese Schlossböckelheimer Felsenberg is broad, ample, and light to medium–bodied. This pure, deep effort reveals loads of cotton candy–laced white fruit flavors. Its personality bursts forth on the palate with the same fervor as pop rocks candies, yet instead of fading away, this wine seamlessly retains its powerful hold on the taster from the attack to the finish. Anticipated maturity: now–2020.

2002 Riesling Spätlese Schlossböckelheimer Felsenberg

RATING: 95 points

The 2002 Riesling Spätlese Schlossböckelheimer Felsenberg explodes from the glass with sweet onion and black raspberry aromas. This decadent wine offers a goose-down duvet texture as well as wide, lush waves of juicy cassis fruit, sea salt, and flint. Powerful, edge free, pure, and magnificently long, this medium-bodied beauty is a candidate for drinking between 2008 and 2025.

RIESLING SPÄTLESE SCHLOSSBÖCKELHEIMER KUPFERGRUBE

2003 Riesling Spätlese Schlossböckelheimer Kupfergrube

RATING: 93 points

Intense scents of slate as well as minerals burst from the glass of the medium-bodied and seductively sexy 2003 Riesling Spätlese Schlossböckelheimer Kupfergrube. Broad, rich, and plush, it boasts plump, seamless layers of powerfully flavored poached pears, apples, and candied slate. This dense, fat, and prolonged wine should be drunk over the next 15 years.

2002 Riesling Spätlese Schlossböckelheimer Kupfergrube

RATING: 97 points

Medium-bodied and revealing scents reminiscent of sweet scallions, cassis, spices, and fresh herbs, the 2002 Riesling Spätlese Schlossböckelheimer Kupfergrube conquers the taster with ethereal waves of black currants, apples, minerals, baby powder, and pears. Satin-textured, as pure as crystal, and lasting over a minute on the palate, it is a masterpiece to drink with reverence between 2009 and 2030.

2001 Riesling Spätlese Schlossböckelheimer Kupfergrube

RATING: 95 points

Clay, smoke, and earth can be discerned in the aromatics of Dönnhoff's 2001 Riesling Spätlese Schlossböckelheimer Kupfergrube. This satin-textured, medium-bodied wine is stupendously pure and delineated as well as unbelievably concentrated, deep, and powerful. Typical of a wine from the Nahe, its flavors are dominated by minerals, earth, and smoky flint rather than primary fruit. Armed with a magnificently flavorful and lengthy finish, it is an exceptional Spätlese to drink between 2006 and 2020.

WINES:

Riesling Brauneberger

Riesling Brauneberger Juffer Sonnenuhr

CLASSIFICATION: Weingut Fritz Haag, Dusemonder Hof

OWNER: Wilhelm Haag

ADDRESS: Dusemonder Str. 44, D-54472 Brauneberg/Mosel, Germany

TELEPHONE: 49 6534 410

TELEFAX: 49 6534 1347

E-MAIL: weingut-fritz-haag@t-online.de

WEBSITE: www.weingut-fritz-haag.de

CONTACT: Wilhelm Haag

VISITING POLICY: By appointment only

VINEYARDS

SURFACE AREA: 19 acres

GRAPE VARIETALS: 100% Riesling

AVERAGE AGE OF THE VINES: 15 to 70 years (average—30 years)

DENSITY OF PLANTATION: 5,000 to 7,000 vines per acre

AVERAGE YIELDS: 60 hectoliters per hectare

WINEMAKING AND UPBRINGING

Depending on the quality of the fruit, a combination of both old wood and stainless steel is used for fermentation. Yields are moderate, and there is strict attention given to selection, both in hand sorts in the vineyards and at the winery. Vinifications are by indigenous yeast, and the wines are aged in the cold cellars until spring following the harvest and then bottled.

ANNUAL PRODUCTION

Fritz Haag Riesling: 10,000 bottles

Brauneberger Juffer Riesling Kabinett: 8,000 bottles

Brauneberger Juffer Sonnenuhr Riesling Kabinett: 15,000 bottles

Brauneberger Juffer Sonnenuhr Riesling Spätlese: 20,000 bottles

Brauneberger Juffer Sonnenuhr Riesling Auslese: 25,000 bottles

Brauneberger Juffer Sonnenuhr Riesling Beerenauslese: 800 bottles

Brauneberger Juffer Sonnenuhr Riesling Trockenbeerenauslese: 300 bottles

AVERAGE PRICE (VARIABLE DEPENDING ON VINTAGE): $25–150

GREAT RECENT VINTAGES

2001, 1999, 1997, 1994, 1993, 1990, 1985, 1983, 1979, 1976, 1975, 1969, 1966, 1953

The historic wine estate Fritz Haag "Dusemonder Hof" lies in the heart of the central Mosel River Valley. When first documented in 1605, the estate was located in a village then known as Dusemond. In 1925, the village was renamed Brauneberg in order to further promote the reputation of the world-renowned vineyards Brauneberger Juffer Sonnenuhr and Brauneberger Juffer—regarded as pearls of the Mosel region by no less a Frenchman than Napoleon. The vineyards are planted 100% with Riesling.

The excellent microclimate and deep slate soils of the Brauneberger Juffer slope give some of the most intense and highly structured Riesling wines of the Mosel region. Wilhelm Haag, the current proprietor, rigorously selects the clones most suited to the microclimate of his vineyards. With his cellar work Mr. Haag has few peers. His wines, produced very reductively, are pale to the eye and show pinpoint balance on the palate. With a fruit patina of honeysuckle, apples, and pears laced with citrus and underlying minerality that reflect the slate-based vineyards in Brauneberg, Fritz Haag wines take several years to fully develop. In fact, they are quite difficult to assess when young, but always have great potential for aging. His elegant, refined Rieslings are impressive examples of the finest the Mosel region has to offer.

BRAUNEBERGER JUFFER SONNENUHR RIESLING AUSLESE

2002 Brauneberger Juffer Sonnenuhr Riesling Auslese #12 (Gold Capsule)

RATING: 90 points

Revealing purity of fruit on the palate and good grip, the slate and limestone–scented 2002 Brauneberger Juffer Sonnenuhr Riesling Auslese #12 (Gold Capsule) is a lush, light to medium–bodied, satin-textured wine. It is generous, rich, and fruit-driven, and has a flavor profile dominated by spiced pears. Anticipated maturity: 2009–2024.

2001 Brauneberger Juffer Sonnenuhr Riesling Auslese

RATING: 97 points

Candied stones and liquid minerals are intermingled with honeysuckle blossoms in the aromatics of the 2001 Brauneberger Juffer Sonnenuhr Riesling Auslese. This stunner is elegant beyond words: powerful, crystalline, with a mind-boggling finish. Its light to medium–bodied, satin-textured personality is boldly flavored yet airy. Quartz, assorted minerals, verbena, and hints of candied limes are found in this complete offering's complex character. Anticipated maturity: 2007–2020+.

1992 Brauneberger Juffer Sonnenuhr Riesling Auslese #16 (Long Gold Capsule)

RATING: 93 points

Fritz Haag has turned in a bevy of lovely 1992s. Haag's 1992 Auslese #16 (Long Gold Capsule), from the same vineyard as the excellent Brauneberger Juffer Sonnenuhr Auslese #17 (Gold Capsule), is slightly richer, with a cherry, mineral, honeyed apple component, wonderful density, moderate sweetness, adequate acidity, and a penetrating, well-defined personality. It is a great Auslese, not withstanding its outrageous price, which reflects both Haag's reputation and the minuscule quantities available. Anticipated maturity: 2008–2025.

BRAUNEBERGER JUFFER SONNENUHR RIESLING KABINETT

2001 Brauneberger Juffer Sonnenuhr Riesling Kabinett

RATING: 92 points

The stunning, 2001 Brauneberger Juffer Sonnenuhr Riesling Kabinett has the depth and concentration generally associated with Ausleses. Creamy white flowers can be found in its lively aromas. Light to medium–bodied, lush, and softly-textured, this is a broad wine filled with tangy lime-soaked minerals. Rich, focused, and exquisitely balanced, this is a stupendous Kabinett! Drink it over the next five to six years.

BRAUNEBERGER JUFFER SONNENUHR RIESLING SPÄTLESE

2001 Brauneberger Juffer Sonnenuhr Riesling Spätlese

RATING: 94 points

The demure nose of the 2001 Brauneberger Juffer Sonnenuhr Riesling Spätlese offers delicate floral, mineral, and sweet citrus scents. On the palate, it bursts forth with candied lemons, awesome clarity of flavors, and a noble minerality. Light to medium–bodied and satin-textured, this is a penetrating wine with extraordinary detail and elegance. Its ethereal core of fruit lingers for over a minute in the focused, highly expressive finish. Anticipated maturity: 2005–2018.

WINES:

Rieslaner Mussbacher Eselshaut
Riesling Haardter Herrenletten
Scheurebe Haardter Mandelring
Muskateller Haardter Bürgergarten
Riesling Haardter Bürgergarten

CLASSIFICATION: Weingut Müller-Catoir

OWNER: Jakob Heinrich Catoir

ADDRESS: Mandelring 25, 67433 Neustadt-Haardt, Germany

TELEPHONE: 49 63 21 28 15

TELEFAX: 49 63 21 48 00 14

E-MAIL: weingut@mueller-catoir.de

WEBSITE: www.mueller-catoir.de

CONTACT: Call or write winery

VISITING POLICY: Monday through Friday 8 A.M.–noon and
1–5 P.M. (no parties)

VINEYARDS

SURFACE AREA: Vines cover 50 acres, of which 70% are flat
and 30% on slopes. Different types of soil include heavy
loam, clay, and loamy gravel.

GRAPE VARIETALS: Primarily Riesling, with some
Weißburgunder, Grauburgunder, Spätburgunder.
Rieslaner, Scheurebe, and Muskateller are grown as
rarities.

AVERAGE AGE OF THE VINES: 35 to 50 years or older

DENSITY OF PLANTATION: 5,000–6,000 vines per hectare

AVERAGE YIELDS: 54 hectoliters per hectare

WINEMAKING AND UPBRINGING

The wines of Müller-Catoir are surprisingly flavorful—full-bodied and very racy, rich in extract and with an impeccable fruit/acidity structure. All wines are made from grapes from the winery's own vineyards. The harvest is limited through restrictive vine pruning in the winter, supplemented by partial removal of grapes in the summer. Soil is given meticulous care and there is selective hand-picking, resulting in high extract figures, ripe acidity, and a definitive character for each variety, making even lesser vintages full-bodied and impressive. Since grapes are always harvested extremely late on this estate, the musts are cold when they arrive in the cellar and ferment very slowly. After racking to remove the yeasts, the wines are not touched again until they are bottled. During bottle storage, these wines usually precipitate tartrate crystals, a sign of a natural, unmanipulated wine.

ANNUAL PRODUCTION

Riesling: 80,000 bottles
Rieslaner: 19,000 bottles
Weißburgunder: 12,000 bottles
Grauburgunder: 3,000 bottles
Muskateller: 5,000 bottles,
Scheurebe: 8,000 bottles
Spätburgunder: 3,000 bottles
Total: 130,000 bottles

AVERAGE PRICE (VARIABLE DEPENDING ON VINTAGE): $25–75

GREAT RECENT VINTAGES

2002, 2001, 1992, 1990

The Weingut Müller-Catoir estate, now in the ninth generation, has been owned by the same family since 1744. For almost 100 years, the winery was run by women: the great-grandmother, grandmother, and mother of the present owner, Jakob Heinrich Catoir. His son, Philipp David Catoir, an architect by training, is the junior managing partner.

The winemaking at this famed Pfalz estate, in the sure hands of cellarmaster Hans-Günter Schwarz for 42 years, experienced a hiccup in 2002, the year Schwarz retired and owner Heinrich Catoir passed the reins to a young winemaker, Martin Franzen. The estate performed well in 2003, Franzen's first full year at the helm, but Franzen has gargantuan shoes to fill. His predecessor, Schwarz, had been a wizard with Rieslaner and Scheurebe, and while Franzen has a good résumé he has little experience with those two grapes.

Considering the extraordinary diversity of superior wines it produces, Müller-Catoir is the Pfalz's greatest estate. Who else has achieved such brilliance with not only Riesling, but with Muskateller, Scheurebe, and Rieslaner? Müller-Catoir is Germany's most fashionable winemaker, enjoying a position among connoisseurs much like that of such illustrious French winemakers as Jean-François Coche-Dury, Comte Lafon, Michel Niellon, and Olivier and Leonard Humbrecht. Müller-Catoir's aromatic wines are undoubtedly superripe and multidimensional, as well as exceptionally complex. Most important, they are delicious! Let's hope the change of winemakers in 2002 does not diminish the greatness of this estate's wines.

MUSKATELLER SPÄTLESE TROCKEN HAARDTER BÜRGERGARTEN

2003 Muskateller Spätlese Trocken Haardter Bürgergarten

RATING: 90 points

Earthy mineral scents are intermingled with delicate aromas of oranges in the nose of the 2003 Muskateller Spätlese Trocken Haardter Bürgergarten. A complex, concentrated wine, it reveals outstanding depth of fruit, a medium-bodied personality, and an exceptionally long finish. Its nuanced flavor profile, composed of minerals, notes of red berries, and demure traces of tangerine, will particularly appeal to those readers who find that most Muskatellers are too obvious and boisterous. Drink it over the next four to five years.

RIESLANER BEERENAUSLESE HAARDTER BÜRGERGARTEN

2003 Rieslaner Beerenauslese Haardter Bürgergarten

RATING: 92+ points

The 2003 Rieslaner Beerenauslese Haardter Bürgergarten is a wonderful late-harvest wine fashioned from Rieslaner, a cross of Riesling and Sylvaner. Sweet herbal teas, botrytis, and passion fruit are found in its boisterous aromatics. Light to medium–bodied and dense, its thick (almost unctuous) character offers caramelized bananas, mango purée, and papaya jam flavors. While numerous 2003 late-harvest Rieslings are cloying, this wine, made from a high acid varietal, retains enough freshness to provide balance and a lengthy, pure finish. Anticipated maturity: now–2030.

RIESLING EISWEIN HAARDTER HERRENLETTEN

1992 Riesling Eiswein Haardter Herrenletten

RATING: 99 points

Mere words cannot do justice to the 1992 Riesling Eiswein Haardter Herrenletten. One of the finest sweet wines I have poured across my palate, this superrich, hauntingly well-balanced, fresh wine is a winemaking tour de force. It should drink well for another 15–20 years.

RIESLING SPÄTLESE HAARDTER BÜRGERGARTEN

2001 Riesling Spätlese Haardter Bürgergarten A.P. #2134

RATING: 94 points

The A.P. #2134 bursts from the glass with white pepper, spice, and smoke aromas. On the palate, this broad, medium-bodied wine exhibits gorgeous layers of plump pears, red currants, apples, and raspberries. Its gorgeous fruit ("berries galore!" read my notes) are beautifully defined in this offering's rich, lush character. Anticipated maturity: 2006–2016.

Note: Consumers will need strong reading glasses to decipher Müller-Catoir's A.P. numbers (Amtliche Prufungsnummer, the licensing number that indicates a German wine has been subjected to the Qualitätswein testing), and there are a number of different 2001 Riesling Spätlese Haardter Bürgergartens.

RIESLING SPÄTLESE HAARDTER HERRENLETTEN

2003 Riesling Spätlese Haardter Herrenletten

RATING: 93 points

The 2003 Riesling Spätlese Haardter Herrenletten, an exciting, deep effort, bursts from the glass with flint, chalk, and sweet apples. Loads of pulp-laden pears vie for the taster's attention with candied apples and boisterous spices. Sultry yet focused, this lush effort is a candidate for drinking between 2006 and 2019.

RIESLING SPÄTLESE TROCKEN HAARDTER BÜRGERGARTEN

2003 Riesling Spätlese Trocken Haardter Bürgergarten "Im Aspen"

RATING: 90 points

Müller-Catoir is offering three 2003 Riesling Spätlese Trockens from the same vineyard yet from different parcels. Thankfully, the estate has elected to list the individual parcels on the labels. My favorite of the three (by a smidgen) is the 2003 Riesling Spätlese Trocken Haardter Bürgergarten "Im Aspen." It bursts from the glass with boisterous scents of white flowers and minerals. On the palate, this outstanding light to medium–bodied offering exhibits superb purity and detail. Complex flavors of white fruits are intermingled by a delicate assortment of minerals whose effects linger in its long finish. Anticipated maturity: now–2010.

2003 Riesling Spätlese Trocken Haardter Bürgergarten "Im Breumel"

RATING: 90 points

Pears, spices, and limestone can be detected in the aromatic profile of the 2003 Riesling Spätlese Trocken Haardter Bürgergarten "Im Breumel." Light to medium–bodied, it boasts a pear and apple–dominated personality with a noticeably intense underlying minerality. Well concentrated, this expressive effort reveals a lengthy finish redolent of notes of limestone. Drink it over the next six years.

2001 Riesling Spätlese Trocken Haardter Bürgergarten

RATING: 90 points

The 2001 Riesling Spätlese Trocken Haardter Bürgergarten offers a nose of lilies, acacia, pear, lime, and honeysuckle blossoms. Loads of lemon-infused stones, pears, and apples sit atop a powerful underlying smoky minerality in this wine's core. It would have merited a higher score if its personality had not dissipated before returning to fill out its long, focused finish. Anticipated maturity: now–2014.

SCHEUREBE SPÄTLESE HAARDTER MANDELRING

2003 Scheurebe Spätlese Haardter Mandelring

RATING: 93 points

An exotic wine, the 2003 Scheurebe Spätlese Haardter Mandelring offers a clamorous nose as well as flavor profile of passion fruits, pineapples, mangoes, and a myriad of spices. Big, rich, luxurious, and ample, it is concentrated and dense, and sports an apple-laced finish of impressive length. Anticipated maturity: now–2013.

2001 Scheurebe Spätlese Haardter Mandelring

RATING: 94 points

Produced from 35-year-old vines, the 2001 Scheurebe Spätlese Haardter Mandelring displays eucalyptus, freshly mowed grass, grapefruit, and pepper in its aromatics. Rich, layered, and exotic, this medium-bodied beauty is studded with fresh herbs, papaya, mangoes, pineapples, lemons, and red currants. This is a succulent, powerful, extroverted wine with a wild streak. Its medium-bodied, velvety-textured character reveals a sumptuous, exceptionally long finish. Drink it over the next 12 years.

WINE: Scharzhofberger Riesling

CLASSIFICATION: Saar

OWNER: Egon Müller

ADDRESS: Scharzhof, 5449 Wiltingen/Saar, Germany

TELEPHONE: 49 65 01 17 232

TELEFAX: 49 65 01 150263

E-MAIL: egon@scharzhof.de

WEBSITE: www.scharzhof.de

CONTACT: Egon Müller

VISITING POLICY: By appointment only

VINEYARDS

SURFACE AREA: 28 acres

GRAPE VARIETALS: Riesling

AVERAGE AGE OF THE VINES: 40–50 years

DENSITY OF PLANTATION: 5,000–10,000 vines per hectare

AVERAGE YIELDS: 45 hectoliters per hectare

WINEMAKING AND UPBRINGING

Late, selective harvest, no skin contact, racking of the must after 24 hours of sedimentation, fermentation with natural yeast in 1,000-liter old oak casks (Fuder) or stainless-steel vats. Fermentations often last into January. After the yeasts settle, the wine is racked and, typically in March, filtered with diatomaceous earth. There is no fining, but a sterile filtration is done at bottling, which takes place April–June.

ANNUAL PRODUCTION

Scharzhof Riesling: 24,000 bottles

Scharzhofberger Kabinett: 30,000 bottles

Scharzhofberger Spätlese: 15,000 bottles

Scharzhofberger Auslese: 5,000 bottles

Wiltinger Braune Kupp Kabinett: 8,000 bottles

Wiltinger Braune Kupp Spätlese: 4,000 bottles

Wiltinger Braune Kupp Auslese: 2,000 bottles

Beerenauslese, Trockenbeerenauslese, and Eiswein in small quantities, vintage permitting

AVERAGE PRICE (VARIABLE DEPENDING ON VINTAGE): $50–100

The Scharzhofberger is one of the finest vineyards in Germany. So great is its fame that it remains one of only a handful of German vineyards whose wines are sold without mention of the village name. The vineyard was likely planted by the Romans and belonged to the monastery St. Marien ad Martyres in Trier after its founding around 700.

After the French Revolution and the occupation of the west bank of the Rhine River by the revolutionary government, all church properties were seized and sold. Egon Müller's great-great-great-grandfather acquired the Scharzhof estate in 1797 from the "République Française." Ever since, it has remained in the family.

Egon Müller owns about 21 acres of prime vineyards in the Scharzhofberger and manages the small estate of Le Gallais in the Wiltinger Braune Kupp of 10 acres. About 7 acres of ungrafted Riesling vines in the Scharzhofberger date back to the last century. The old vineyards require traditional methods. Much work is done by hand. The vines are of low vigor and do not tolerate herbicides or weeds. As a result, the vineyards are plowed several times a year. Any fertilization is organic. Insecticides have not been used for 16 years. There is no treatment against botrytis.

The yields are very low with three tons per acre considered ideal. The juice is normally fermented by native yeasts in wooden 1,000-liter casks without need for temperature control. Due to cold weather at harvest (end of October/November) and the relatively small size of the casks, fermentation temperatures rarely exceed 60ºF and fermentation can last well into January.

Fermentation in the cold cellar at Scharzhof often stops before the wines are dry. Racking is done two to four weeks after fermentation. The wines are aged in casks for approximately six months, generally unfined, but filtered prior to bottling in May. The better casks in each category are bottled unblended. All of the Auslese as well as the Beerenauslese and Trockenbeerenauslese are bottled unblended.

SCHARZHOFBERGER RIESLING AUSLESE

2003 Scharzhofberger Riesling Auslese

RATING: 94 points

An extraordinary wine with a sweet nose of spring flowers intermixed with white peach, honeysuckle, and citrus. It has extraordinary minerality in the mouth, intense, huge flavors, and a notion of sweetness that is balanced perfectly by extraordinary acidity. This remarkable wine seems still to be an infant, but what an upside potential it has. Look for this wine to evolve for 20 more years.

SCHARZHOFBERGER RIESLING SPÄTLESE

2002 Scharzhofberger Riesling Spätlese

RATING: 92 points

This very concentrated Riesling tastes relatively dry although there is obvious residual sugar balanced perfectly by good underlying acidity. A very natural tasting wine with hints of peach, apricot, ripe apple, and some intriguing currant flavors, this medium-bodied Riesling has great penetration, almost liquid minerality, and a finish that goes on for a good 30+-seconds. A stunning wine with lemongrass notes that seem to develop with aging. It can be drunk now or cellared for another 10–15 years.

WEINGUT JOH. JOS. PRÜM

WINES:

Riesling Wehlener Sonnenuhr

Riesling Graacher Himmelreich

CLASSIFICATION: Weingut Joh. Jos. Prüm

OWNERS: Dr. Manfred Prüm and Wolfgang Prüm

ADDRESS: Uferallee 19, 54470 Bernkastel-Wehlen, Germany

TELEPHONE: 49 65 31 3091

TELEFAX: 49 65 31 6071

CONTACT: Dr. Manfred Prüm

VISITING POLICY: By appointment only

VINEYARDS

SURFACE AREA: 43 acres

GRAPE VARIETALS: 100% Riesling

AVERAGE AGE OF THE VINES: 50 years

DENSITY OF PLANTATION: About 7,500 vines per hectare

AVERAGE YIELDS: About 60 hectoliters per hectare (remarkably changing from year to year)

WINEMAKING AND UPBRINGING

From the gray Devonian slate slopes, grapes are hand-harvested and fermented in a combination of both stainless-steel and fiberglass tanks and then aged in the traditional 1,000-liter wood casks until bottling takes place in July following the harvest. The bottling at J. J. Prüm is a bit later than at many other Mosel estates.

ANNUAL PRODUCTION

Production varies for the four major sites of J. J. Prüm—Wehlener Sonnenuhr, Graacher Himmelreich, Zeltinger Sonnenuhr, and Bernkasteler Badstube—but the production in an abundant year from their 43 acres is approximately 10,000 cases.

AVERAGE PRICE (VARIABLE DEPENDING ON VINTAGE): $25–37

GREAT RECENT VINTAGES

2001, 1999, 1997, 1995, 1994, 1990, 1988, 1983, 1976, 1971, 1959, 1949

This is one of the most legendary German wine estates, and its reputation is well deserved. Not only are extraordinary wines made, but the wines have a well-established record of exceptional longevity. The estate, by German standards, is not terribly old—it was founded in 1911 by Johann Josef Prüm. Its reputation was largely built by his son Sebastian, who began working at age 18 and developed the distinctive style of the Prüm wines during the 1930s and 1940s. In 1969, Sebastian Prüm died, and his son, Manfred, became the estate's director and continues to run the winery today. He is assisted by his younger brother Wolfgang.

Manfred Prüm has said frequently that they have tried to modernize some parts of the winery, but they really don't want to change the fundamental style established by his father. Still, the Prüms tend to be notorious risk takers, often pushing the harvest as late as possible. Their wines are nevertheless always full of delicate fruit flavors while super-intensely flavored and always quite low in alcohol with very crisp acidity. There is a tendency in some vintages to use relatively noticeable quantities of SO_2, but in the long run this serves to protect the wines and gives them remarkable longevity. But it does mean consumers are best advised to defer gratification and cellar newly purchased vintages for three to five years. While their most famous and greatest wines come from the Wehlener Sonnenuhr and Graacher Himmelreich vineyards, in certain vintages they produce a superior quality Auslese that the estate designates "Gold Cap," which is easily recognized by a gold foil capsule. There is even a variation of this that is an even richer style of Auslese called "Long Gold Cap," and these have become liquid gold sought by collectors the world over.

RIESLING AUSLESE WEHLENER SONNENUHR

2003 Riesling Auslese Wehlener Sonnenuhr
RATING: 93 points

After some SO_2 blows off, this wine shows extraordinary notes of citrus oil, lemon blossom, white peach, and crisp minerals in a medium-bodied, sweet, but well-balanced style with great purity and texture. This wine should drink well for at least 15–20 years.

2001 Riesling Auslese Wehlener Sonnenuhr
RATING: 95 points

Extraordinary minerality intermixed with hints of pear, lime juice, white peach, and spring flower blossoms jumps from the glass of this very well-delineated, medium-bodied wine with tremendous intensity of flavor and a crisp, zesty finish with the acid completely counterbalancing the wine's sweetness. Look for it to drink well for 15 or more years.

RIESLING KABINETT WEHLENER SONNENUHR

2001 Riesling Kabinett Wehlener Sonnenuhr
RATING: 92 points

Deep, intense, smoky mineral aromas are intermingled with talcum powder and poached pears in the aromatic profile of the 2001 Riesling Kabinett Wehlener Sonnenuhr. Armed with the richness generally associated with a Spätlese (or higher!), this penetrating, ethereal wine coats the taster's palate with lush, silky waves of red currants, honeysuckles, pears, and raspberries. As is typical with wines from this estate,

this offering reveals some trapped CO_2, which adds to its lively, gorgeously precise, and refined personality. Drink it over the next six years.

RIESLING SPÄTLESE GRAACHER HIMMELREICH

2001 Riesling Spätlese Graacher Himmelreich
RATING: 94 points

A sensational Spätlese with gorgeous citrus oil notes intermixed with flowers, peach, honeysuckle, and vanilla cream, medium-bodied, with great purity, tremendous zestiness, and a finish over 30 seconds make this young, brilliant Spätlese a wine to drink now as well as over the next 15 or more years.

RIESLING SPÄTLESE WEHLENER SONNENUHR

2001 Riesling Spätlese Wehlener Sonnenuhr
RATING: 94 points

Aromas of candied limes, smoky slate, and white pepper are found in the explosive nose of the 2001 Riesling Spätlese Wehlener Sonnenuhr. A sultry, seductive wine, it luxuriously slathers the taster's palate with rich, yet focused, layers of juicy lemons, red cherries, currants, blueberries, limes, and pears. Notes of candied raspberries make an appearance in this exceptional offering's unbelievably long finish. Pure, elegant, powerful, deep, and densely packed, it should get even better with cellaring. Anticipated maturity: 2007–2020+.

WINES:

Riesling Graacher Himmelreich

Riesling Graacher Domprobst

CLASSIFICATION: Weingut Willi Schaefer

OWNERS: Willi Schaefer and Christoph W. Schaefer

ADDRESS: Hauptstrasse 130, D-54470 Graach (Mosel),
Germany

TELEPHONE: 49 65 31 8041

TELEFAX: 49 65 31 1414

CONTACT: Willi or Christoph Schaefer

VISITING POLICY: By appointment only

VINEYARDS

SURFACE AREA: 6.6 acres; exclusively steep slopes (up to a
70° angle), Devonian slate soil

GRAPE VARIETALS: 100% Riesling

AVERAGE AGE OF THE VINES: 50 years (70% ungrafted)

DENSITY OF PLANTATION: 8,000 vines per hectare

AVERAGE YIELDS: 58 hectoliters per hectare

WINEMAKING AND UPBRINGING

When I asked Willi Schaefer about his winemaking, he responded simply, "It's all about love and respect for nature and
terroir." He also went on to voice the common refrain among
the wine producers in this book that "less is more." After the
fruit is hand-harvested from his incredibly steep slopes, vinification takes place in 1,000-liter ancient wood *foudres.* After
six months' aging on the fine lees, the wine tends to be bottled
in May following the vintage. The goal is always to produce
individual wines that show the character of the *terroir* and the
vintage personality.

ANNUAL PRODUCTION

Graacher Himmelreich: 12,000 bottles various ripeness

Graacher Domprobst: 12,000 bottles various ripeness

Wehlener Sonnenuhr: 1,300 bottles various ripeness

AVERAGE PRICE (VARIABLE DEPENDING ON VINTAGE): $25–80

GREAT RECENT VINTAGES

2002, 2001, 1997, 1995, 1993, 1990, 1976, 1975, 1971, 1969,
1966, 1959, 1953, 1949, 1921

Willi Schaefer and his son Christoph

The winery has been in the Schaefer family only
since 1950. The current proprietors are Willi
Schaefer, a handsome, bearded, and bespectacled man
who seems to exude confidence, and since 2001, his son
Christoph Schaefer. The reason this winery remains
below the general public's radar could be simply that
the production is so tiny, a mere 2,200 or so cases from
a minuscule estate of 6.6 acres.

I've always thought of the Schaefer Rieslings as
wines for sybarites—glorious, pleasurable, but extraordinarily complex, savory, and just compelling. Willi
Schaefer seems to be one of those sybarites now, with his
son involved in the winemaking and a brand-new

Porsche to zip around the back roads of the Mosel. His greatest wines remain his Graacher Domprobst and his Graacher Himmelreich. His best-known vineyard is the Wehlener Sonnenuhr, but as good as it is, it simply never seems to have quite the majesty of his Graacher bottlings. These are wines of purity, integrity, and restraint, but understated power and intensity. Though skeptics may dismiss them as not ageworthy because of their glorious performance in their youth, older vintages I have tasted seem in no danger of falling off the table.

RIESLING AUSLESE GRAACHER DOMPROBST

2003 Riesling Auslese Graacher Domprobst A.P. #1404
RATING: 95 points

Concerning Schaefer's 2003 Riesling Auslese Graacher Domprobst A.P. #1404, my notes read: "Sophia Loren in a bottle!" Its raspberry, red currant, talcum powder, botrytis, and flower scents lead to an awesomely sexy and sensual personality. There isn't an angle to be found in this wine—it's a mouthful of voluptuous curves. Sweet, plush, and richly broad, its medium to full–bodied character offers apple compote and red fruit flavors that linger throughout its exemplary finish. Anticipated maturity: 2007–2030.

2003 Riesling Auslese Graacher Domprobst A.P. #1804
RATING: 95 points

The boisterous aromatics of the 2003 Riesling Auslese Graacher Domprobst A.P. #1804 explode from the glass with scents of lilies and red berries. Rich, dense, and medium to full–bodied, it slathers the palate with silky layers of raspberries, melons, salty spiced apples, and flowers. This thick, broad-shouldered offering remains surprisingly pure and detailed while wowing the taster with its luxurious breadth. Anticipated maturity: 2009–2030.

2002 Riesling Auslese Graacher Domprobst A.P. #1003
RATING: 97 points

Liquid minerals, spices, verbena, and linden can be found in the aromatic profile of the 2002 Riesling Auslese Graacher Domprobst A.P. #1003. Medium-bodied, elegant, and deep, this profound Auslese reveals harmonious layers of pears, slate, apples, fresh herbs, and spices. It is fruitier than the #1403, just as precise as well as equally long, complex, and graceful—it just has a touch less magic to it. Anticipated maturity: 2008–2038. Bravo!

2002 Riesling Auslese Graacher Domprobst A.P. #1403
RATING: 98 points

An unbelievable marriage of coiled power and refinement, the 2002 Riesling Auslese Graacher Domprobst A.P. #1403 is a slate and mineral–scented wine of massive breadth, concentration, purity, and harmony. It's all here: the detail, richness, elegance, muscle, depth, and stunning length. The lucky few who will encounter this jewel will be wowed by its intense minerality, shocking complexity, and graceful dance across the palate. Anticipated maturity: 2009–2038.

2001 Riesling Auslese Graacher Domprobst A.P. #1102
RATING: 98 points

Gunflint, smoky slate, sea salt, sweet limes, honeyed minerals, and poached pears are found in the boisterous nose of the 2001 Riesling Auslese Graacher Domprobst A.P. #1102. The combination of seamless harmony and unbridled power of this wine is mind numbing. Expansive, it slathers the palate with untold layers of poached pears, candied apples, red fruits, dried honey, and a distinctive note of cassis that permeates the taster's palate throughout its unbelievably long, compelling finish. Anticipated maturity: 2014–2030+.

2001 Riesling Auslese Graacher Domprobst A.P. #0902
RATING: 97 points

The epitome of refinement, the 2001 Riesling Auslese Graacher Domprobst A.P. #0902 reveals aromas of Johnson's baby powder, flowers, perfume, and underlying earthy notes. A wine of magnificent depth, it has a penetrating character of purity, breadth, and focus. Rich, yet impeccably balanced, its tangy flavor profile is composed of an assortment of minerals, citrus fruits, quartz, honeysuckle, and white flowers. Drink this ethereal, glorious wine between 2008 and 2025+.

RIESLING AUSLESE GRAACHER HIMMELREICH

2003 Riesling Auslese Graacher Himmelreich A.P. #1204
RATING: 93+ points

Produced from fruit harvested after the region's first late-October freeze, the 2003 Riesling Auslese Graacher Himmelreich A.P. #1204 displays a sweet, botrytis-laced nose and a personality that reveals a mini-Eiswein's focus and delineation. Powerful, deep, and with cutting precision, it releases sweet and sour flavors of minerals as well as hints of passion fruit. Anticipated maturity: 2009–2030.

2003 Riesling Auslese Graacher Himmelreich A.P. #1604

RATING: 92 points

Sweet earth and candied citrus fruits are found in the aromatic profile of the 2003 Riesling Auslese Graacher Himmelreich A.P. #1604. Medium-bodied, softly textured, and expressive, it coats the taster's palate with red berries, limes, and superripe yellow plums. Plump and giving, this wine's character sports impressive depth, precision, and length. Anticipated maturity: 2007–2027.

RIESLING BEERENAUSLESE GRAACHER DOMPROBST

2003 Riesling Beerenauslese Graacher Domprobst

RATING: 94 points

Delicate notes of botrytis are intermingled with candied apples as well as hints of caramel in the nose of the 2003 Riesling Beerenauslese Graacher Domprobst. An intense wine of massive concentration and density, it reveals jellied flavors of red fruits, slate, and gold raisins. Extremely well focused, it also displays a long, flavor-packed finish. Anticipated maturity: 2007–2035.

RIESLING KABINETT GRAACHER DOMPROBST

2003 Riesling Kabinett Graacher Domprobst A.P. #0504

RATING: 91 points

Another top-flight Kabinett, the 2003 Riesling Kabinett Graacher Domprobst A.P. #0504 detonates from the glass with boisterous aromas of lilies, pears, apples, and a myriad of spices. Less exotic than the Himmelreich, this light to medium–bodied wine wows with salt-laced slate, expressive minerals, delicate notes of kiwi, and hints of red berries. A highly focused offering, it also sports a tremendously long finish. Anticipated maturity: now–2013.

2002 Riesling Kabinett Graacher Domprobst A.P. #0703

RATING: 92 points

The broad, ample, medium-bodied 2002 Riesling Kabinett Graacher Domprobst A.P. #0703 sports a nose of spiced apples and smoky slate. It juxtaposes the fat, pulp-laden fruit found in the finest 2002s with superb

purity and liveliness. Apples, minerals, lemongrass, and currants can be discerned in its zesty character as well as in its huge length. Thank God nobody told Willi Schaefer that Kabinetts aren't supposed to be this great! Anticipated maturity: 2005–2020.

RIESLING KABINETT GRAACHER HIMMELREICH

2003 Riesling Kabinett Graacher Himmelreich

RATING: 90 points

A more complex and expressive wine, the 2003 Riesling Kabinett Graacher Himmelreich displays a profound nose of chalk, white flowers, spices, and limestone. Upon tasting this beauty I double-checked the bottle's label, as Kabinetts of this intensity, depth, and concentration are few and far between. Its personality bursts on the palate, expands, and releases flavors reminiscent of ripe green apples, raspberries, red currants, pears, limestone, and salty minerals that seamlessly extend into its impressively long finish. Anticipated maturity: now–2014.

2002 Riesling Kabinett Graacher Himmelreich

RATING: 90 points

The liquid mineral–scented 2002 Riesling Kabinett Graacher Himmelreich is a wide, lush, rich, yet superbly focused wine filled with kiwis, limes, and minerals. It has outstanding purity, depth, ripeness, and harmony, and an extremely long finish. Drink it over the next 15 years.

RIESLING SPÄTLESE GRAACHER DOMPROBST

2003 Riesling Spätlese Graacher Domprobst A.P. #0904
RATING: 94 points

Apples, limestone, and white flowers are found in the nose of the 2003 Riesling Spätlese Graacher Domprobst A.P. #0904. Armed with awesome breadth, this ample, medium-bodied wine bursts forth with crystalline freshness and verve. Loads of quartz, tea, and pear-laced minerals can be detected in its complex, pure, exceptionally long personality. Anticipated maturity: 2006–2022.

2003 Riesling Spätlese Graacher Domprobst A.P. #1004
RATING: 95 points

The 2003 Riesling Spätlese Graacher Domprobst A.P. #1004 reveals aromas reminiscent of talcum powder–dusted flowers immersed in perfume. A wine of immense sensuality, it seduces the taster with a rich, voluminous character that is packed with red berries and minerals. While medium to full–bodied and broad, this offering is also highly detailed, pure, and exceptionally long. Anticipated maturity: 2006–2025.

2003 Riesling Spätlese Graacher Domprobst A.P. #1504
RATING: 94 points

Flowers, baby powder, spices, linden tea, and ripe apples burst from the glass of the 2003 Riesling Spätlese Graacher Domprobst A.P. #1504. This sultry, medium-bodied wine is silky-textured, soft, and densely packed with angle-free waves of lilies as well as poached pears. This concentrated, generous, and prolonged wine should be drunk between 2006 and 2024.

2002 Riesling Spätlese Graacher Domprobst A.P. #0903
RATING: 93 points

The aromatic clarity of the 2002 Riesling Spätlese Graacher Domprobst A.P. #0903 is something to experience. Its red currant and floral scents penetrate the skull like a laser beam before blossoming into a magnificent bouquet of perfumes. Plush, yet detailed, its personality offers slate, pear, and tangy minerals in a rich, yet driven, style. Anticipated maturity: 2008–2028.

2002 Riesling Spätlese Graacher Domprobst A.P. #1203
RATING: 94 points

Smoke, gunflint, and minerals make up the aromatic profile of the 2002 Riesling Spätlese Graacher Domprobst A.P. #1203. The grapes that produced this beauty were the last Schaefer harvested in 2002 (on November 20). Soft, silky-textured, and light to medium–bodied, it is a supple wine of magnificent elegance and grace. Spiced pears, white pepper, and apples are found in its broad, nuanced personality. Anticipated maturity: 2008–2030.

RIESLING SPÄTLESE GRAACHER HIMMELREICH

2003 Riesling Spätlese Graacher Himmelreich
RATING: 91 points

Sweet herbal teas, flowers, and pears can be discerned in the nose of the 2003 Riesling Spätlese Graacher Himmelreich. Medium-bodied, silky-textured, and well balanced, this beauty reveals creamy flavors of spiced linden tea and chamomile that linger in its long finish. A plump yet fresh wine, it should be consumed over the next 12 years.

WINES:

Zeltinger Sonnenuhr

Wehlener Sonnenuhr

Graacher Domprobst

Zeltinger Himmelreich

CLASSIFICATION: Mosel-Saar-Ruwer

OWNER: Johannes Selbach

ADDRESS: Uferallee 23, D-54492 Zeltingen, Germany

TELEPHONE: 49 65 32 2081

TELEFAX: 49 65 32 4014

E-MAIL: info@selbach-oster.de

WEBSITE: www.selbach-oster.de

CONTACT: Johannes Selbach

VISITING POLICY: No tours; by appointment only

VINEYARDS

SURFACE AREA: 35 acres

GRAPE VARIETALS: 98% Riesling, 2% Pinot Blanc (new)

AVERAGE AGE OF THE VINES: 55 years (youngest are 20, oldest approximately 100 years)

DENSITY OF PLANTATION: Old vineyards—8,000 vines per hectare; young vineyards—5,500 vines per hectare

AVERAGE YIELDS: Old vineyards (Sonnenuhr, parts of Schlossberg): 45–50 hectoliters per hectare; young vineyards (Himmelreich, Domprobst, parts of Schlossberg): 78 hectoliters per hectare

WINEMAKING AND UPBRINGING

Johannes Selbach clearly desires to make elegant, crisp wines with exceptional aging potential, purity of fruit, and the telltale slate mineral character that is part of the typicity of his vineyards' *terroirs*. The grapes are hand-harvested, often in two or three passes in the vineyard. They are crushed gently and, using modern pneumatic presses as well as two old basket presses for their Eiswein, the clear wine must is racked off its deposit and aged in the traditional 1,000-liter oak *foudres*, with the balance in stainless-steel tanks as well as some fiberglass.

To a large extent, fermentations are the product of indigenous yeasts, although the winery will inoculate if certain wines don't ferment to a satisfactory level of dryness. All fermentations take place in small vats of 1,000–3,000 liters in a very cold environment. For those wines with residual sugar, this is achieved by interrupting fermentation. Selbach likes to age his wines on their fine lees for as long as possible, believing this adds texture and aromatic complexity. Bottling takes place in early spring.

ANNUAL PRODUCTION

Production varies significantly from vintage to vintage, with the bulk of the production in the Kabinett and Spätlese categories and very limited quantities of Auslese and higher category wines. In general, production runs from a high of 15,000 or so bottles for the estate Kabinetts to just over 1,000 bottles of the top Auslese *cuvées*. For the Beerenauslese and Trockenbeerenauslese *cuvées*, production ranges from 1,500 to 2,400 bottles.

AVERAGE PRICE (VARIABLE DEPENDING ON VINTAGE): $30–235

GREAT RECENT VINTAGES

2001, 1990, 1976, 1975, 1971, 1959, but I must add that Johannes Selbach loves 1997 for its delicacy and multifaceted aromas and also is very keen on 1995, 1994, and 1983.

The Selbach family began making wine in 1661, but in 1961 Selbach-Oster became a separate entity, adding Oster, the maiden name of Hans Selbach's mother, to distinguish it from the family's *négociant* business. Over the years the estate was slowly enlarged and now produces approximately 7,500 cases of wine from its impressive 35 acres of holdings. Johannes Selbach joined the family estate in 1988 and took over the business from his father, Hans, in 1993.

These are wines that grab the taster's attention with their extraordinary purity, transparency, and restraint, yet they are undeniably rich and intense. I suppose the nicest compliment a professional taster could offer is that these delicate, very nuanced wines simply hold your interest and keep drawing you back for further examination and pleasure. There is just always something more there, and that comes from great vineyard sites and non-interventionist winemaking. These are, of course, some of the greatest Rieslings produced in the world, and not surprisingly they came from the very finest vineyards: grand cru–quality vineyards in Zeltinger Sonnenuhr, from which emerge their biggest, fullest, and most intense wines; extraordinary sites in Graacher Domprobst, which produce wines that almost taste like liquid slate; and the Wehlener Sonnenuhr, with

its delicate herbal, floral, and ethereal character, a more feminine version of the Zeltinger. The Selbach family is planning to purchase, when available, additional parcels from the Zeltinger Sonnenuhr slope, which they believe has more top vineyard sites than even Wehlener. They also make some very impressive wines from Zeltinger Schlossberg and Bernkastler Badstube.

RIESLING AUSLESE BERNKASTLER BADSTUBE

2003 Riesling Auslese Bernkastler Badstube

RATING: 93 points

The Auslesen were the stars of the show at Selbach-Oster in 2003. Aromatically demure, yet expressive, expansive, and medium to full–bodied on the palate, the 2003 Riesling Auslese Bernkastler Badstube possesses an oily-textured and seductive as well as rich character. Bursting with thick layers of spiced red berries, it reveals additional flavors of sweet slate, apples, and honeyed minerals. Pure, deep, and lush, this wine also has a long, fruit-packed finish. Anticipated maturity: 2008–2020.

2002 Riesling Auslese Bernkastler Badstube

RATING: 94 points

I loved the 2002 Riesling Auslese Bernkastler Badstube. Its nose of red cherries, spices, and botrytis explodes from the glass and tastes like a cross between a Beerenauslese and an Eiswein. On the palate it is jammy, thick, medium-bodied, and crammed with cassis, assorted red fruits, ginger, and copious spices. Its Eiswein-like finish is exceptionally long and bright, and reveals traces of molasses intermingled with fresh herbs. Anticipated maturity: 2009–2035.

RIESLING AUSLESE ZELTINGER HIMMELREICH

2001 Riesling Auslese Zeltinger Himmelreich

RATING: 90 points

Austere aromas of minerals blended with sautéed onions and fresh scallions are found in the aromas of the 2001 Riesling Auslese Zeltinger Himmelreich. Pure, focused, and elegant, its deep character reveals caramelized minerals, spices, hints of tangy limes, and resin. Anticipated maturity: now–2018.

Opposite: Johannes Selbach

RIESLING AUSLESE ZELTINGER SCHLOSSBERG

2003 Riesling Auslese Zeltinger Schlossberg

RATING: 92 points

Though its nose is dominated by sulfur, a trait that will disappear within six months, the sultry Riesling Auslese Zeltinger Schlossberg is a sweet, soft, silky-textured wine filled with flavors reminiscent of apples, raspberries, red currants, and poached pears. A powerful underlying minerality comes to the fore in the mid-palate and is extended into this effort's impressively long finish. Anticipated maturity: 2008–2019.

2003 Riesling Auslese Zeltinger Schlossberg "Schmitt"

RATING: 92 points

Botrytis-laced pineapple and apples are found in the aromatic profile of the 2003 Riesling Auslese Zeltinger Sonnenuhr "Schmitt" (Schmitt is a parcel—or *lieu dit*—within the Zeltinger Sonnenuhr). Supple, soft, and plush, this wine also reveals outstanding freshness. Its fleshy character is riddled with botrytis that coats its guava and mineral flavors. Anticipated maturity: 2009–2025.

2002 Riesling Auslese Zeltinger Schlossberg

RATING: 91 points

The flint-scented 2002 Riesling Auslese Zeltinger Schlossberg is a generous, lush, broad wine filled with ripe white peaches, raspberries, and pears. Medium-bodied, satin-textured, and long, it's an outstanding Auslese to drink over the next 25 years.

2001 Riesling Auslese Zeltinger Schlossberg

RATING: 93 points

Resin, cinnamon, nutmeg, and cloves can be discerned in the nose of the 2001 Riesling Auslese Zeltinger Schlossberg. Candied red cherries, currants, and raspberries are interspersed with smoky slate, mint, and white chocolate in this muscular, highly expressive wine's personality. Broad, boisterous, and exotic, it explodes on the palate, demanding the taster's full attention. Medium-bodied and rich, this is not a delicate, lace-like wine, but one that bowls you over with richness, a flavorful core of fruit, and enormous length. Anticipated maturity: now–2020+.

RIESLING AUSLESE ZELTINGER SONNENUHR

2003 Riesling Auslese Zeltinger Sonnenuhr

RATING: 93 points

Boasting a nose of spicy apples, the 2003 Riesling Auslese Zeltinger Sonnenuhr is a large-scaled, medium to full–bodied, boldly assertive wine. Though immensely rich and thick, it has wonderful balance, freshness, and harmony. Loads of botrytis can be found among this effort's pineapple, passion fruit, poached pear, and raspberry flavors. Deep, concentrated, and pure, it also exhibits an exceptionally long finish. Anticipated maturity: 2008–2022.

2002 Riesling Auslese Zeltinger Sonnenuhr

RATING: 92 points

Botrytis-laced aromas are found in the nose of the medium-bodied 2002 Riesling Auslese Zeltinger Sonnenuhr. This highly concentrated, rich wine coats the taster's palate with oodles of pears, white peaches, minerals, orange blossoms, and red berries. It is complex, harmonious, and powerful. In addition, this beauty reveals a gorgeous, long, and expressive finish. Anticipated maturity: 2007–2030.

2001 Riesling Auslese Zeltinger Sonnenuhr

RATING: 95 points

A stunning wine, Selbach's 2001 Riesling Auslese Zeltinger Sonnenuhr is a study in power, concentration, and intensity. "It tastes just like the finest 1976s did when they were young," said Terry Theise, the estate's importer. Sweet aromas of onions long caramelized in butter, almonds, poached pears, candied apples, Margarita mix, and currants can be found in this beauty's glorious nose. Broad-shouldered, massive, and bulky, it dares the taster to penetrate its dense mass. Smoky notes of botrytis, melons, crisp pears, caramel-covered apples, and a vibrant punch of lemon are found in its thick yet well-balanced core. Not for the faint at heart, this wine combines the weight of a Beerenauslese with the zest of a Spätlese. Anticipated maturity: 2010–2030.

RIESLING BEERENAUSLESE ZELTINGER SONNENUHR

2003 Riesling Beerenauslese Zeltinger Sonnenuhr

RATING: 93 points

The 2003 Riesling Beerenauslese Zeltinger Sonnenuhr sports a nose of spiced and honeyed minerals as well as a sweet, immensely rich core of botrytis-laced fruit. Medium to full–bodied, its intense flavor profile is packed with pepper, smoke, apricots, honey, and slate, as well as notes of jammy red currants. Revealing exceptional harmony and a long finish brimming with fruit, this is a candidate for drinking between 2008 and 2035+.

RIESLING EISWEIN BERNKASTLER BADSTUBE

2002 Riesling Eiswein Bernkastler Badstube
RATING: 94 points
Superb aromatics of spiced/herbal lemons and slate are found in the nose of the 2002 Riesling Eiswein Bernkastler Badstube. A wine of awesome focus, purity, and clarity, it explodes on the palate, revealing precise kirsch and earth flavors. This crystalline offering is medium-bodied and supremely elegant. Anticipated maturity: 2010–2040.

2001 Riesling Eiswein Bernkastler Badstube
RATING: 99 points
Jammy cherries, currants, molasses, cinnamon, and white raisins can be found in the zesty, sharp aromas of the 2001 Riesling Eiswein Bernkastler Badstube. A wine of sumptuous depth, it is massively concentrated, possesses awesome levels of acidity, and has unreal purity of flavor. It soars onto the palate, permeating it with an assortment of red berries, wave after wave of candied limes, and syrupy layers of honeyed slate. This stupendous, mind-numbingly long, earth-shattering wine may outlive anyone old enough to purchase it upon release. Anticipated maturity: 2015–2050+. Wow!

RIESLING EISWEIN ZELTINGER HIMMELREICH

2003 Riesling Eiswein Zeltinger Himmelreich
RATING: 92 points
Spices, pears, and apples are interspersed with smoky minerals in the aromatics of the 2003 Riesling Eiswein Zeltinger Himmelreich. Baked red berries, yellow plums, and white fruits are found immersed in molasses in this big, brazen wine's character. Though undoubtedly capable of lasting for over 30 years, the presence of burnt sugar flavors at such a young age leads me to recommend drinking this effort between 2007 and 2018.

2002 Riesling Eiswein Zeltinger Himmelreich
RATING: 96 points
An awe-inspiring offering, Johannes Selbach's 2002 Riesling Eiswein Zeltinger Himmelreich displays aromas eerily reminiscent of a live lobster. Scents of the sea and a certain earth sweetness lead to a thick, rich, deep, and powerful core of red currants, tangy sugar-coated limes, and loads of spices. This wine has magnificent purity, sublime concentration, and massive length. It will most certainly earn an even higher score as it harmonizes with cellaring. Anticipated maturity: 2013–2050.

2001 Riesling Eiswein Zeltinger Himmelreich "Junior"
RATING: 93 points
The white pepper, candied lemon, eucalyptus, and lime-scented 2001 Riesling Eiswein Zeltinger Himmelreich "Junior" is the most reasonably priced Eiswein of outstanding quality I've encountered. Jellied red currants, raspberries, freshly cracked pepper, and lively limes are found in its plump, pure, zesty character. While it is concentrated and powerful it remains friendly and forward. Its acidity doesn't shock, as with many of its Eiswein brethren. Drink it between now and 2030+.

RIESLING KABINETT ZELTINGER SCHLOSSBERG

2001 Riesling Kabinett Zeltinger Schlossberg
RATING: 91 points
A fresh bouquet of flowers, sweet minerals, and hints of cinnamon can be detected in the aromatic profile of Selbach's 2001 Riesling Kabinett Zeltinger Schlossberg. This superb value is intense, crystalline, and layered, and exhibits awesome depth of fruit, particularly for a Kabinett. Light to medium-bodied, it coats the taster's palate with satiny waves of candied lemon-infused minerals and lilies. Drink this concentrated, broad, and deep wine between now and 2012.

RIESLING SPÄTLESE ZELTINGER SCHLOSSBERG

2001 Riesling Spätlese Zeltinger Schlossberg
RATING: 90 points
A medium-bodied and concentrated wine, the 2001 Riesling Spätlese Zeltinger Schlossberg reveals lime, mineral, and floral scents. On the palate it displays beautiful depth to its linear, pure, and focused character. Sweet minerals, spices, and lilies can be discerned in its vibrant character. Anticipated maturity: 2006–2016.

RIESLING SPÄTLESE ZELTINGER SONNENUHR

2003 Riesling Spätlese Zeltinger Sonnenuhr
RATING: 90 points
Though its aromatics were dominated by SO_2, the 2003 Riesling Spätlese Zeltinger Sonnenuhr's personality was terrifi-

cally expressive. Broad, ample, and forward, it conquers the palate with silky waves of superripe apples, raspberries, and chamomile. A harmonious, graceful effort, it reveals outstanding depth, concentration, and length. Anticipated maturity: 2006–2014.

2002 Riesling Spätlese Zeltinger Sonnenuhr

RATING: 91 points

Pretty, sweet minerals are found in the aromatics of the 2002 Riesling Spätlese Zeltinger Sonnenuhr. Armed with outstanding depth of fruit, this light to medium–bodied goose-down–textured wine has a flavor profile composed of cotton candy, spice, and pulp-laced pear. Its finish is exceptionally long, displaying additional waves of sweet white fruits. Anticipated maturity: now–2025.

2001 Riesling Spätlese Zeltinger Sonnenuhr

RATING: 93 points

Smoky, tangy minerals, sea salt, and verbena are found in the aromatic profile of the 2001 Riesling Spätlese Zeltinger Sonnenuhr. Exhibiting superb breadth, concentration, depth, and length, this lush, intense wine conquers the palate with loads of pears, apples, spices, and red currants. Revealing enormous elegance and purity, this Riesling impressively combines power with grace. Anticipated maturity: 2007–2018.

RIESLING TROCKENBEERENAUSLESE ZELTINGER SONNENUHR

2003 Riesling Trockenbeerenauslese Zeltinger Sonnenuhr

RATING: 93+ points

Copious wafts of powerfully smoky botrytis and minerals emanate from the glass of the 2003 Riesling Trockenbeerenauslese Zeltinger Sonnenuhr. As rich as it is expensive, this oily-textured (almost viscous) wine is plush, suave, and densely packed with apricots, white peach compote, and spiced superripe fruits. It is immense, mouth-coating, and lavish, and while time may civilize this boldly sweet jam of a wine, it comes across as perhaps too much of a good thing. Anticipated maturity: 2010–2040.

WINE: Riesling Kiedrich Gräfenberg

CLASSIFICATION: Weingut Robert Weil

OWNERS: Suntory, Wilhelm Weil

ADDRESS: Mühlberg 5, 65399 Kiedrich (Rheingau area), Germany

TELEPHONE: 49 6123 2308

TELEFAX: 49 6123 1546

E-MAIL: info@weingut-robert-weil.com

WEBSITE: www.weingut-robert-weil.com

CONTACT: Wilhelm Weil or Jochem Becker-Köhn

VISITING POLICY: Vinothek (hours of business): Monday through Friday, 8 A.M.–5:30 P.M., Saturday 10 A.M.–4 P.M., Sunday 11 A.M.–5 P.M., closed on holidays

VINEYARDS

SURFACE AREA: 160 acres

GRAPE VARIETALS: 98% Riesling, 2% Pinot Noir

AVERAGE AGE OF THE VINES: 25 years

DENSITY OF PLANTATION: 5,000–6,000 vines per hectare

AVERAGE YIELDS: 55 hectoliters per hectare (10-year average)

WINEMAKING AND UPBRINGING

Very strict viticultural practices are employed at Weil, including severe pruning and thinning of the bunches as well as removal of foliage to encourage air currents. All of Weil's vineyards are organically farmed with absolutely no herbicides. The grapes are whole-cluster pressed and vinified in stainless-steel tanks that are temperature-controlled. The tanks vary in size depending on the parcel. Weil believes that the fuller-bodied wines require some contact with wood and slower fermentations, but all the wines are bottled by late spring following the harvest in order to capture their primary fruit and freshness.

ANNUAL PRODUCTION

While Weil makes other wines, his most famous is clearly his extraordinary vineyard, which would be a grand cru in France, the Kiedrich Gräfenberg, and where the Weil winery first made wine in 1868. The vineyards are situated east of the village of Kiedrich on a southwestern-facing slope with a 60% gradient. Stony, fragmented soil of loess and sandy loams gives this wine a very distinctive *terroir* that is known for producing wines of great elegance, finesse, and longevity.

Kiedrich Gräfenberg Riesling Erstes Gewächs: 17,000 bottles

Kiedrich Gräfenberg Riesling Spätlese: 10,000 bottles

Kiedrich Gräfenberg Riesling Auslese: 9,000 bottles

Kiedrich Gräfenberg Riesling Beerenauslese: 2,000 bottles

Kiedrich Gräfenberg Riesling Eiswein: 2,200 bottles

Kiedrich Gräfenberg Riesling Trockenbeerenauslese: 600 bottles

AVERAGE PRICE (VARIABLE DEPENDING ON VINTAGE): $50–500

GREAT VINTAGES

2002, 2001, 1997, 1990, 1976, 1975, 1971, 1964, 1959, 1953, 1945, 1934, 1921, 1911, 1893

This estate earned its great renown with the Gräfenberg Riesling, which in the 19th century was sold to many of the emperors and kings of Europe, and in 1900 was one of the most expensive wines in Europe. However, its ancestry dates back even farther: wines from the extraordinary Kiedrich Gräfenberg vineyard (whose name means "hill of the Rhine counts") were first documented in 1258 and 1259.

The history of the Robert Weil estate is much more recent. It was founded in 1875 by Dr. Robert Weil, a professor of German at the Sorbonne who was forced to leave Paris because of the imminent outbreak of the Franco-Prussian War (1870–1871). His brother was a minister and choir director of the parish church in Kiedrich, which no doubt influenced Dr. Weil's decision to purchase vineyards in Kiedrich in 1868 and move there in 1875 to produce wine. Today's proprietor, Wilhelm Weil, represents the fourth generation of Weils to run this estate. In 2005, the Kiedrich Gräfenberg remains the single greatest wine of the Rheingau and seems to be only gaining greater stature with each new vintage.

RIESLING AUSLESE KIEDRICH GRÄFENBERG

2003 Riesling Auslese Kiedrich Gräfenberg (Gold Cap)

RATING: 94 points

Sporting a nose that combines aromatic characteristics typical of Beerenauslesen and Eisweins, the 2003 Riesling Auslese Kiedrich Gräfenberg (Gold Cap) reveals smoky botrytis-laced yellow fruits as well as hints of lemon-laced caramels. Armed with huge richness, this deep effort has superb purity, inten-

sity, and length. While it is somewhat heavy, like many 2003 high-end German late-harvest wines, it appears to have enough balancing acidity to provide lift. Anticipated maturity: 2008–2030. Note: A non–Gold Cap version of this wine exists and was tasted—it sells for $245 per half-bottle—but it was so raisiny, so heavy, as well as so dominated by caramel and molasses, that it was not reviewed.

2002 Riesling Auslese Kiedrich Gräfenberg
RATING: 95 points
The 2002 Riesling Auslese Kiedrich Gräfenberg bursts forth with highly expressive smoky botrytis aromas. On the palate, this broad, medium-bodied, satin-textured beauty is densely packed with mangoes, passion fruit, apricots, and a myriad of spices. Rich, immensely concentrated, and impeccably balanced, it also possesses an extensive finish. Anticipated maturity: 2015–2030.

2001 Riesling Auslese Kiedrich Gräfenberg
RATING: 94 points
Awesome aromas of red fruits, always a positive characteristic in wines from this varietal, can be found in the nose of the medium-bodied 2001 Riesling Auslese Kiedrich Gräfenberg. Jammy, baked cherries and apricots make up this stunner's character. Armed with the depth and concentration generally associated with Beerenausleses, it is a fat, plump, thickly-textured monster of a Riesling. Anticipated maturity: 2010–2025+.

2001 Riesling Auslese Kiedrich Gräfenberg (Gold Capsule)
RATING: 97 points
Big and dense, the 2001 Riesling Auslese Kiedrich Gräfenberg (Gold Capsule) sports a boisterous nose of honeyed minerals, botrytis, and spice. Surprisingly, given this wine's immense depth and thick personality, it retains great purity as well as exceptional balance. It is Bo Jackson in a bottle, capable of bowling over a 240-pound linebacker while tiptoeing along the sideline. Anticipated maturity: 2012–2030.

RIESLING BEERENAUSLESE KIEDRICH GRÄFENBERG

2001 Riesling Beerenauslese Kiedrich Gräfenberg
RATING: 93 points

Weil's botrytis and jellied apricot–scented 2002 Riesling Beerenauslese Kiedrich Gräfenberg is fat, hugely rich, dense, and concentrated. Soft, plump, and velvety-textured, this sweet, plush wine bastes the palate with honeyed yellow fruits. While unquestionably outstanding, it would have benefitted from having better focus. Anticipated maturity: 2018–2039.

RIESLING EISWEIN KIEDRICH GRÄFENBERG

2002 Riesling Eiswein Kiedrich Gräfenberg
RATING: 98 points

The jellied, big, exotic 2002 Riesling Eiswein Kiedrich Gräfenberg is a complete wine. It is massively rich yet not heavy, sweet but magnificently pure, and concentrated yet detailed. Medium-bodied, its lush tropical fruit and spice flavors are majestically delineated, complex, and intense. This is a spectacular Eiswein. Anticipated maturity: 2015–2040+.

2001 Riesling Eiswein Kiedrich Gräfenberg

RATING: 99 points

Spicy pears and apples can be found in the vibrant nose of the 2001 Riesling Eiswein Kiedrich Gräfenberg. This awe-inspiring wine conquers the palate with jellied apricots, cherries, white peaches, chamomile, and spices. Prodigiously rich, it is also impeccably balanced and reveals a seemingly never-ending finish. Sultry, thickly-textured, yet admirably focused, it has all the characteristics of perfection. Those fortunate enough to afford it should lay it away for many years if the intention is to taste it at full maturity. Anticipated maturity: 2020–2040.

RIESLING SPÄTLESE KIEDRICH GRÄFENBERG

2002 Riesling Spätlese Kiedrich Gräfenberg

RATING: 92 points

Smoky botrytis can be discerned in the timid nose of the 2002 Riesling Spätlese Kiedrich Gräfenberg. Awesomely rich, complex, and intense, this outstanding Spätlese will most certainly merit a more exalted review when its nose sorts itself out. It slathers the palate with honeyed minerals, botrytis, spices, and candied limes whose effects linger in its impressively long, lush finish. Anticipated maturity: 2008–2020.

2001 Riesling Spätlese Kiedrich Gräfenberg

RATING: 92 points

Aromatically demure, the 2001 Riesling Spätlese Kiedrich Gräfenberg has huge richness, breadth, and depth. Candied minerals, stones, and pears can be found in its concentrated core of fruit. Cellaring will be required for this wine's full potential to blossom. Anticipated maturity: 2008–2018.

RIESLING TROCKENBEERENAUSLESE KIEDRICH GRÄFENBERG

2002 Riesling Trockenbeerenauslese Kiedrich Gräfenberg

RATING: 99 points

Looking for something big, maybe in the $500 for a half-bottle range? Well, Weingut Robert Weil's got a wine for you! Honeyed minerals, spices, buckets of botrytis, red cherries, and apricots are found in the complex aromas of the 2002 Riesling Trockenbeerenauslese Kiedrich Gräfenberg. An unbelievably rich effort, its layered personality conquers the taster with lavish waves of honey-laced fruits. Hugely spicy, oily-textured, and nectar-like, it retains extraordinary balance while unleashing dense, luxurious red, yellow, and tropical fruits. Anticipated maturity: 2015–2045+. Bravo!

2001 Riesling Trockenbeerenauslese Kiedrich Gräfenberg

RATING: 95 points

The medium to full–bodied 2001 Riesling Trockenbeerenauslese Kiedrich Gräfenberg reveals aromas of botrytis-laced earth and mangoes. Bordering on being over-the-top, this syrup of a wine is as thick as 10W-40 motor oil. If time brings its dense core of caramelized/honeyed fruit focus and delineation, my score will appear nonsensically conservative. Anticipated maturity: 2015–2030+.

ITALY

No country's wine quality has enjoyed a more radical revolution than Italy's. In the two most famous areas of wine production, Piedmont and Tuscany, it is fashionable for journalists to argue whether the modern style or the traditional style produces the better wine. However, if the truth be known, both schools are capable of fashioning compelling wines. Certainly Tuscany has had its revolution in quality, as has Piedmont, and each year new producers come onto the scene who seem to be sensitive to their specific vineyard sites and uncompromising in their pursuit of excellence. Yet it is to the south of Tuscany that so many wondrous wines have emerged. Lamentably, most of those wineries are far too new and their vintages far too recent to be included in this book, but I do have to acknowledge the exceptional excitement and quality that are developing in Umbria, Lazio, Abruzzo, Campania, and the two islands of Sicily and Sardinia.

The diversity of soil types, microclimates, and varietals planted in Italy by ancient tribes that settled in the area long before the Phoenicians arrived is reflected in the extraordinary number of different types of wines produced in Italy today. Historically, while early Italian winemaking was influenced by Greek settlements, the Romans took viticulture far more seriously, developing systems of both vine training and pruning, and the fall of the Roman Empire did little to change Italian viticultural practices.

Although the international prestige and reputation of Italian wine has traditionally trailed other countries', particularly that of France, over the last twenty years it has enjoyed a renaissance. Its revival began in the late 1960s, plodded along during the 1970s, and exploded in the 1980s as many producers rediscovered the infinite number of microclimates and native varietals planted by their ancestors.

There have always been laws regarding the production of Italian wine, but they were largely ignored until 1963, when the Italian government passed its famous DOC (Denominazione di Origine Controllata) and DOCG (Denominazione di Origine Controllata e Garantita) classification systems. These were modeled in large part after the French appellation laws and dictated basic requirements for all wines that were entitled to these two tiers in the Italian hierarchy. In 1992, the law was modernized to a four-tiered hierarchy that included 300 DOCs and DOCGs, and recognized the thousands of varieties of wines made in Italy. The present system has four tiers, beginning at the bottom with *vini da tavola,* which is basically generic table wine. Next comes the *IGT,* or *Indicazione Geografica Tipica.* These wines, which are generally the equivalent of a French *vin de pays,* come from the same geographical region and must be vintage-dated. The two top levels are the aforementioned *DOC* and *DOCG.* The problem in Italy, however, is that many of the most creative, individualistic estates refuse to comply with the DOC and DOCG laws, believing they can make superior wine (which they often

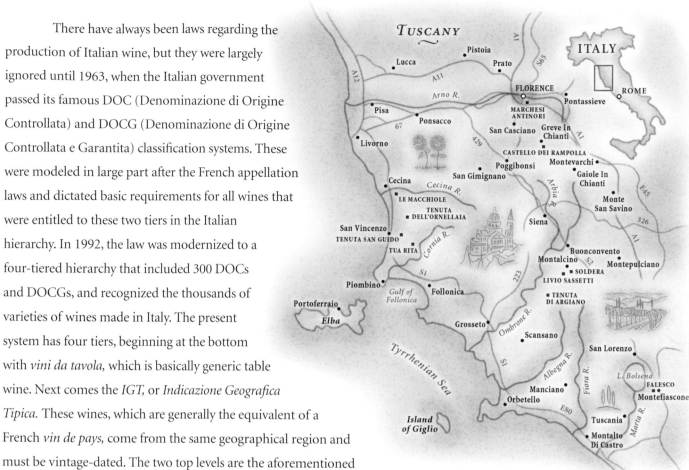

do), but thus are entitled to only an IGT or VDT designation. Consequently, the hierarchy designations are often meaningless.

Many of the estates profiled in this book are controversial. Add to that (1) the argument raging among wine consumers over the traditional Italian wine style versus the more progressive, modern style, and (2) whether the producer uses indigenous varietals or favors international varietals.

History and contemporary trends confirm that the greatness of Italy's wines still rests largely in Piedmont and Tuscany, which is why those two regions dominate the following chapter.

WINES:

Barolo Arborina

Barolo Brunate

OWNER: Elio Altare

ADDRESS: Localita Cascina Nuova, Frazione Annunziata, 51,
     12064 La Morra (CN), Italy

TELEPHONE: 39 0173 50835

TELEFAX: 39 0173 50835

E-MAIL: elioaltare@elioaltare.com

CONTACT: Silvia Altare

VISITING POLICY: By appointment only

VINEYARDS

SURFACE AREA: 25 acres

GRAPE VARIETALS: Nebbiolo d'Alba, Barbera d'Alba,
     Dolcetto d'Alba, Cabernet Sauvignon

AVERAGE AGE OF THE VINES: 30–35 years

DENSITY OF PLANTATION: 5,000 vines per hectare

AVERAGE YIELDS: Barolo: 4,500 kilograms per hectare;
     Dolcetto: 7,500 kilograms per hectare

WINEMAKING AND UPBRINGING

A surprisingly short vinification in rotary fermenters for 3–5 days and then a quick passage to French oak barrels (20% new and 80% two and three years old) for 24 months prior to bottling unfiltered. These wines exhibit the natural softness and suppleness that characterize vineyards in La Morra, and Altare emphasizes the local character with a very modern style of vinification. These are not the longest-lived wines of Barolo, but they are gorgeous to drink young and they actually age quite beautifully for 10–15 years. In addition to the Barolos, this is also a terrific source of proprietary reds called La Villa (60% Barbera and 40% Nebbiolo) and Larigi (100% Barbera).

ANNUAL PRODUCTION

Barolo Arborina: 5,500 bottles

Barolo Brunate: 1,600 bottles

AVERAGE PRICE (VARIABLE DEPENDING ON VINTAGE): $35–85

GREAT RECENT VINTAGES

2004, 2003, 2001, 2000, 1999, 1998, 1997, 1996

The dynamic Elio Altare has been considered one of the catalysts of change in Piedmont and a touchstone for young producers looking to produce high-quality, more modern-style wines. He himself has always recognized that while great wines made in the traditional style often need 10 years of cellaring before they are drinkable; at the same time, given the shortage of truly ideal wine cellars in the world, most consumers prefer something they can drink at a younger age. His commitment to quality was nowhere more in evidence than in the 1997 vintage, which produced some of the best wines of his lifetime; yet he refused to release them once he found that more than 25% of the wines had tainted corks. Unlike most producers, who would have put the wines on the market, he refused to sell even one bottle.

I first raved about Elio Altare's brilliant wines more than 20 years ago, and I remember some old-timers in the wine business raising their eyebrows about such praise for a producer who was then totally unknown in Piedmont. Now, most recognize that Altare has turned out as many sensational wines as anybody in Piedmont. In fact, he is making some of the most magnificent wines in Italy.

Elio Altare

BAROLO ARBORINA

2000 Barolo Arborina

RATING: 95 points

A gloriously fragrant bouquet of black fruits, flowers, rose water, and a hint of truffle and tar is followed by an opulently textured, very rich, supple wine that is already showing some amber at the edge of its dark plum/ruby color. Wonderfully sweet, expansive, and fleshy, with no hard edges, this is an atypically forward and precocious 2000 Barolo to drink now as well as over the next 10 years.

1999 Barolo Arborina

RATING: 92 points

A classic wine with hints of road tar, sweet currant and cherry fruit, dried Provençal herbs, and a hint of tobacco, this wine shows ripe tannins, medium body, and wonderful elegance and precision. It is already strutting its stuff, so don't hesitate to drink it now and over the next decade.

1998 Barolo Arborina

RATING: 91–93 points

The 1998 Barolo Arborina boasts a glorious perfume of overripe black cherries intertwined with Asian spices, new oak, and flowers. Layered, gorgeously concentrated, superbly balanced and seamless, with fabulous fruit, good underlying tannin, and a long, 40+-second finish, it can be drunk now and over the next 12 years.

1997 Barolo Arborina

RATING: 96 points (from an uncorked bottle)

The saturated dark ruby/purple–colored 1997 Barolo Arborina offers a stunning nose of smoky, sweet oak intertwined with jammy cassis, cherry liqueur, licorice, and white truffles. Full-bodied, with explosive fruit, terrific purity, and layers of glycerin and extract, this magnificent, mouth-filling, teeth-staining Barolo possesses extraordinary symmetry for its size, as well as low acidity and nearly overripe tannin. There is not a hard edge to be found. Anticipated maturity: now–2018.

1996 Barolo Arborina

RATING: 92 points

Altare's 1996 Barolo Arborina is reminiscent of a terrific grand cru from Burgundy's Côte d'Or. Intensely aromatic, with copious quantities of black cherry jam, earth, toast, and floral scents, this saturated dark ruby–colored offering reveals superb ripeness, substantial richness, a full-bodied, layered personality, adequate acidity, and sweet tannin in the finish. It is a stunning Barolo to drink now and over the next 10 years.

1995 Barolo Arborina

RATING: 91 points

Altare has turned in a stunning effort. The lush, voluptuously textured 1995 Barolo Arborina exhibits a saturated dark ruby/garnet color. Full-bodied, with great purity, the layered complexity that comes from low yields and ripe fruit, and a bouquet of Asian spices, tobacco, smoke, and black cherries, this is a sweet, rich, forward but hedonistically styled Barolo. Anticipated maturity: now–2008.

1994 Barolo Arborina

RATING: 90 points

This wine reveals Musigny-like complexity and finesse. When it was released, it exhibited a deep ruby color with amber at the edge, suggesting a fast evolutionary track. The fragrant bouquet offers exceptionally sweet aromas of toasty new oak, ripe black raspberry and cherry fruit, flowers, licorice, and spice. The wine is full-bodied and gorgeously rich, but it manages to avoid any notion of heaviness. Expansive and layered, with compelling richness and length, this is Barolo at its sexiest and most intellectually satisfying. However, it needs to be drunk soon.

1993 Barolo Arborina

RATING: 95 points

The 1993 Barolo Arborina is one of the vintage's most profound wines and not far from the spectacular 1990 and 1989 Arborinas. The wine boasts an opaque deep ruby color and a stunning concoction of aromas ranging from melted tar, toast, and smoked herbs to jammy black cherry fruit and roasted meats. Compelling in the mouth, with layers of opulence and sweet fruit presented in a medium to full–bodied, authoritatively rich, yet graceful style, this is an awesome, extremely rich, superbly balanced Barolo that should drink well from now until 2010.

1990 Barolo Arborina

RATING: 96 points

The highly saturated, opaque color of the 1990 Barolo Arborina suggests an exceptionally concentrated wine. The huge nose of new saddle leather, ripe plum/black cherry fruit, and smoky new oak is a turn-on. Full-bodied, with layers of chewy fruit and that elusive Nebbiolo flavor of tar, this seductive wine possesses a huge, expansive, chewy richness and a sweet finish due to the 1990 vintage's great ripeness. Drink it over the next 3–5 years.

1988 Barolo Arborina

RATING: 96 points

Altare's stunning 1988 Barolo Arborina is a brilliant example of Nebbiolo. The deep black/ruby color and huge nose of black fruits, tar, and spices are followed by a wine with explosive richness, layer upon layer of dense, chewy Nebbiolo fruit, and a blockbuster, moderately tannic, phenomenally long finish. Experience the magic until at least 2012.

BAROLO BRUNATE

2000 Barolo Brunate

RATING: 95 points

Typical of Altare's wines, this is absolutely seductive, with a gloriously fragrant nose of black cherries, tar, rose petal, herbs, and new oak. Seamless on the palate, with tremendous opulence and flesh, low acidity, and gorgeous layers of ripe black cherry, plum, fig, and blackberry fruit, this is an atypically forward wine even by Altare's standards. Drink it over the next 10–12 years.

1998 Barolo Brunate

RATING: 92–94 points

The dark ruby/plum–colored 1998 Barolo Brunate exhibits a smoky, mineral, jammy strawberry and black cherry–scented nose with notions of leather, toast, and spice box. The wine has fabulously well-integrated wood, tannin, and acidity in addition to a complex, layered mid-palate and finish. The outstanding balance, purity, and seamlessness are immensely admirable. Enjoy this 1998 Barolo over the next 9–12 years.

1997 Barolo Brunate

RATING: 93 points

The 1997 Barolo Brunate displays extraordinary fruit concentration, excellent purity, and the classic tar, cherry, and rose petal fragrance with subtle toasty new oak. It is muscular and tannic, with a finish lasting for more than 30 seconds. Anticipated maturity: now–2017.

1996 Barolo Brunate

RATING: 90 points

The 1996 Barolo Brunate is the proverbial "iron fist in a velvet glove." It possesses a dark ruby color, closed personality, powerful, muscular flavors of cherries, incense, smoke, and dried herbs, and a tannic finish. Enjoy it over the next 10–15 years.

1995 Barolo Brunate

RATING: 90 points

The outstanding 1995 Barolo Brunate is muscular and backward, though it possesses good density and superb ripeness, with lots of tannin and body. Consume it over the next 5–6 years.

WINES:

Guado al Tasso Bolgheri
Solaia
Tignanello
OWNER: Marchesi Antinori Srl
ADDRESS: Piazza Antinori 3, 50123 Florence (FI), Italy
TELEPHONE: 39 055 23595
TELEFAX: American importer Remy Amerique: (212) 399-9494
E-MAIL: antinori@antinori.it
WEBSITE: www.antinori.it
CONTACT: Public Relations
VISITING POLICY: By appointment only

VINEYARDS

SURFACE AREA: 4,183 acres
GRAPE VARIETALS: Sangiovese, Cabernet Sauvignon, Cabernet
    Franc, Syrah, Canaiolo, Merlot, and other complementary
    red varieties
AVERAGE AGE OF THE VINES: Ranges from 7 to 50 years old,
    with most about 20 years old
DENSITY OF PLANTATION: 1,500–2,500 vines per acre
AVERAGE YIELDS: 2,000–4,000 kilograms per acre

WINEMAKING AND UPBRINGING

Both the Tignanello and the Solaia come from the Tignanello
estate, located between the Greve and Pesa Valleys in the heart
of the Chianti Classico–making regions, 20 miles south of Florence. The Tignanello comes from southwest-facing parcels
that are planted with vines dating back to the 15th century.
The Tignanello tends to be 80% Sangiovese, 15% Cabernet
Sauvignon, and 5% Cabernet Franc. The Solaia vineyard is
contiguous and, like the Tignanello, is planted with Cabernet
Sauvignon and Sangiovese. The Solaia is a blend of 75%
Cabernet Sauvignon, 20% Sangiovese, and 5% Cabernet.

All three varietals are vinified separately and then macerated in 50-hectoliter wooden open-top fermenters, usually 15+
days for the Sangiovese and 20+ days for the Cabernet Franc
and Cabernet Sauvignon. After the wine completes its alcoholic
fermentation, it is transferred to 225-liter new French oak
casks. The wine is bottled after 14 months of barrel aging.

The Guado al Tasso from Bolgheri is a blend of 60%
Cabernet Sauvignon, 30% Merlot, and 10% Syrah from 150
acres of vines. As with its siblings, all the varietals are vinified
separately, macerated in stainless-steel tanks for 12–14 days,
moved to 100% new French oak for a minimum of 14
months of barrel aging, and then bottled.

ANNUAL PRODUCTION

Guado al Tasso: 10,000 cases
Solaia: 7,000 cases
Tignanello Vino da Tavola: 25,000–30,000 cases
AVERAGE PRICE (VARIABLE DEPENDING ON VINTAGE): $30–145

GREAT RECENT VINTAGES

2001, 2000, 1999, 1998, 1997, 1990, 1985, 1982

Palazzo Antinori is situated at the end of via de'
Tornabuoni in a small piazza of the same name,
overlooked by the Baroque Church of San Gaetano.
The palace is one of the most beautiful examples of
mid-15th-century Florentine architecture. Built between 1461 and 1466 by Giuliano da Maiano, the palace
was bought in 1506 by Niccolò di Tommaso Antinori
for "4,000 large florins." The Antinori family had already been in Florence since the beginning of the 13th
century. They had moved there from Calenzano, a small
village between Florence and Prato, where records date
their presence back to 1188. A family of merchants,
they joined the Silk Guild in 1285 and subsequently became members of the Banker's Guild. They also produced and sold wine, which gradually became their
primary business.

Francesco Redi (1626–1698), an eminent scientist
and man of letters, praised their wines in his short
poem on wine "Bacco in Toscana": "Là d'Antinoro in su
quelli colli alteri . . . un mosto sì puri che ne' vetri
zampilla, salta, spumeggia e brilla!" ("On those high
hills, from Antinori . . . a must so pure that in the glass
it jumped and sparkled!").

In 1898, a series of disparate estates was transformed into a modern, highly organized enterprise
founded by the two sons of the Marchese Niccolò, a direct descendant of the Marchese Niccolò who had acquired Palazzo Antinori in 1506 and had already done
so much to establish the reputation of Tuscan wines
around the world and to produce a high-quality product. Twenty-six generations later, the Antinori tradition
is still alive, guided by the charismatic and handsome
Piero Antinori.

Marchese Piero Antinori

The Antinori estates in Tuscany and Umbria have grown considerably over the last 50 years and have adopted many innovative techniques for growing grapes and making wine. For five centuries, through to the present day, Palazzo Antinori has been a symbol of the continuity of ancient winemaking tradition and family history, and the name Antinori is about as close to a guarantee of quality as one is likely to find. Just about everything Antinori does, in all price ranges, is good.

Of course, all this history would be irrelevant without the extraordinary commitment, energy, passion, and creativity of the current proprietor, Marchese Piero Antinori, one of the truly "good guys" in the wine business. A forward-looking innovator who has a healthy respect for tradition but is not trapped by it, Piero Antinori (along with Angelo Gaja in Piedmont) is one of the fathers of Italy's modern-day revolution in quality. In these pages, I have highlighted only the three wines I consider among the very greatest in the world, but Antinori is also a sensational source of terrific Chianti Classico Badia a Passignano, Chianti Classico Riserva Tenute Marchese Antinori, and Villa Antinori Chianti Classico Riserva, in addition to impressive wines from Piedmont (the Prunotto Barolos and Barberas, for example) and their newest baby, the very promising Tormaresca wines from Puglia.

GUADO AL TASSO BOLGHERI

2001 Guado al Tasso Bolgheri
RATING: 90 points
A rather reserved, restrained style for Guado al Tasso (a 60% Cabernet Sauvignon, 30% Merlot, 10% Syrah blend), this wine shows notes of black currant, tobacco leaf, crushed rocks, some spicy oak, and a hint of underbrush. It is medium to full–bodied with relatively austere tannins, considerable structure and muscle, but a rather austere finish. Drink it between 2008 and 2016.

2000 Guado al Tasso Bolgheri
RATING: 92 points
A very decadent, luxurious nose of spice box, roasted herbs, beef blood, blackberry, and coffee jumps from this rather unctuously textured, full-bodied wine with loads of flavor, relatively heady alcohol, and a meaty, almost sweet finish due to its high levels of glycerin. Drink it over the next decade.

1999 Guado al Tasso Bolgheri
RATING: 94 points
Spectacular, the 1999 Guado al Tasso possesses sweet tannin and accessibility. Its explosive aromatics consist of smoke, licorice, espresso, chocolate, vanilla, and celestial black currants. With its sensational concentration, flamboyant flavors, opulent texture, full body, and brilliant concentration as well as delineation, it comes across as intense, balanced, pure, and rich. Anticipated maturity: now–2016.

1998 Guado al Tasso Bolgheri
RATING: 92 points
Bolgheri is the source of some of Italy's greatest proprietary red wine blends of Cabernet Sauvignon and Merlot. No other region in the world (other than Pomerol and St.-Emilion) has produced such great Merlots. The 1998 Guado al Tasso was fashioned from extremely small yields of 30 hectoliters per hectare, spent 14 months in 100% new French oak, and was bottled with minimal clarification. Malolactic was also done in barrel, so the wood is nicely assimilated. The dense ruby/purple–colored 1998 offers a glorious perfume of coffee, chocolate, blackberries, cassis, and vanilla. Dense, rich, supple-textured, and fruity as well as elegant, it will drink well until 2012 or so.

SOLAIA

2001 Solaia

RATING: 91 points

A deep nose of crème de cassis intermixed with smoked herbs, licorice, espresso roast, and a hint of vanilla and chocolate is followed by a full-bodied wine with real opulence, depth, and a long, heady finish. Compared to the more reserved and restrained 2001 Guado al Tasso from the Antinori stable, this 2001 is rather exuberant, flamboyant, and very well delineated. Anticipated maturity: now–2020.

2000 Solaia

RATING: 90 points

A very full-bodied, rather earthy wine with hints of sweet cassis, crushed raspberries, smoky oak, and some licorice, this exuberant wine shows elevated but sweet tannin, a rather muscular mouth-feel, and loads of flavor and spice. Anticipated maturity: now–2015.

1999 Solaia

RATING: 94 points

The first two bottles of the 1999 Solaia I tasted were corked, but the third was brilliant. Its black/purple color is followed by a sumptuous bouquet of licorice, blackberries, mint, and cassis, all presented in a concentrated, medium to full–bodied, dense, yet elegant style. Although still young, it is undoubtedly the qualitative equivalent of a Bordeaux first or second growth. Anticipated maturity: now–2016.

1998 Solaia

RATING: 93 points

Solaia has been one of Italy's most brilliant wines since the early 1980s. Made in a Bordeaux-like style, it will age for two decades or more. The 1998, a blend of 75% Cabernet Sauvignon, 20% Sangiovese, and 5% Cabernet Franc (8,000 cases), was aged for 14 months in new and one-year-old French oak casks prior to being bottled without filtration. The yields were a low 30 hectoliters per hectare. The 1998 is a classically structured, dense, full-bodied, youthful, well-balanced wine designed for cellaring. Its opaque ruby/purple color is accompanied by a classic bouquet of black currants, vanilla, earth, tobacco, and a touch of mint. Moderately tannic, dense, and concentrated, this is a backward 1998. Anticipated maturity: now–2020.

1997 Solaia

RATING: 96 points

The unfiltered 1997 Solaia (75% Cabernet Sauvignon, 20% Sangiovese, and 5% Cabernet Franc, from a single 25-acre vineyard) is aged in 100% new French oak. There are 8,000 cases. This sensational, opaque blue/purple–colored wine exhibits a complex nose of cedar, spice box, cassis, and subtle oak. With yields of only 30 hectoliters per hectare, and malolactic fermentation in barrel (à la Tignanello), this wine reveals extraordinary concentration and a thick, viscous texture, yet no sense of heaviness or ponderousness. It is a thrilling Solaia to consume over the next 10–15 years. If a first-growth Pauillac were made in Tuscany, this would be it!

1990 Solaia

RATING: 94 points

The 1990 Solaia is slightly more concentrated than the 1990 Tignanello, with a saturated purple color and a classic international nose of cassis, lead pencil, vanilla, and smoke. It is gorgeously rich, with a fat, unctuous texture and a long, highly extracted finish. Well balanced and already delicious, it remains unevolved and is potentially a 12–20-year wine. In the context of recent Solaias, I would rate it a worthy competitor to the otherworldly 1985. It is certainly much more opulent, with sweeter, jammier, richer fruit than the 1988 (most recently rated 88 points). Anticipated maturity: now–2014.

1985 Solaia

RATING: 95 points

A huge nose of olives, toast, cedar, and cassis offers considerable enjoyment. In the mouth, this dark ruby/purple–colored, opulent wine is rich and medium to full–bodied, with a chewy texture, decent acidity, and well-integrated flavors of smoky new oak. The finish is supple and long, as the tannins have melted away quickly. Approachable and delicious, this offering should be consumed now.

TIGNANELLO

2001 Tignanello

RATING: 90 points

A rather supple-textured wine that is quite showy already. Normally a blend of 80% Sangiovese, 15% Cabernet Sauvignon, and 5% Cabernet Franc aged in French oak for 12 months and bottled with no filtration, this wine exhibits a deep ruby/purple–tinged color, hints of dried herbs intermixed with underbrush, loamy soil notes, black cherry, and currant. The wine is very elegant and quite stylish, with noticeable but silky tannin and a medium-bodied finish. Anticipated maturity: now–2012.

1999 Tignanello

RATING: 91 points

The deep ruby/purple–colored 1999 Tignanello exhibits rare elegance married to considerable flavor intensity as well as power. It offers up aromas of new saddle leather intertwined with black cherries, currants, creosote, vanilla, and spice box.

TIGNANELLO

2001

Vino prodotto con uve Sangiovese e, in piccola parte, Cabernet nell'antico podere sito nel cuore della Toscana, di proprietà dei Marchesi Antinori di Firenze, viticoltori dal 1385. Il terreno, in collina, è composto da roccia di "Galestro"e "Alberese" ha un' esposizione a solatìo ed un' altitudine che va dai 350 ai 400 metri sul livello del mare. Il vino è invecchiato esclusivamente in piccole botti di rovere pregiato e successivamente affinato in bottiglia.

TE DUCE PROFICIO

TOSCANA
INDICAZIONE GEOGRAFICA TIPICA

ANTINORI

Rich and medium-bodied, with adequate acidity as well as sweet but noticeable tannin, it is the third consecutive exceptional vintage from this reference winery for modern, aggressively styled Tuscan reds. Anticipated maturity: now–2012.

1998 Tignanello

RATING: 91 points

There are 30,000 cases of this well-known Tuscan proprietary red. The 1998 offers a classic bouquet of berry fruit, new saddle leather, underbrush, earth, and toast from its aging in new *barriques*. Medium to full–bodied, with good delineation and a firm, classic style, it should drink well for another 12–13 years.

1997 Tignanello

RATING: 93 points

The 1997 Tignanello possesses a dense, ruby/purple color, and an expansive nose of black currants, cherry compote, vanilla, and earth. Sweet, jammy, and opulently textured, this expansive, concentrated, low-acid wine is flashy and gorgeously proportioned. It should drink well for another 5–10 years, although who can ignore it now?

1990 Tignanello

RATING: 93 points

Antinori's 1990 Tignanello (a blend of primarily Sangiovese with some Cabernet Sauvignon) is the best example I have tasted of this wine since the marvelously opulent, rich 1985. Rich yet supple and expansive enough to be consumed with great pleasure, it offers a dark ruby/purple color, and a big, smoky, earthy nose of nearly overripe cherry and currant-like fruit. Full-bodied, with exceptional concentration and purity, this distinctive, spicy wine should drink well for another 5–10 years.

1988 Tignanello

RATING: 90 points

The color is deep ruby/purple, and the nose offers up penetrating aromas of sweet red and black fruits and toasty new oak. In the mouth, this medium to full–bodied wine offers wonderfully precise flavors, excellent richness, good acidity, soft tannins, and a spicy, long, rich finish. I would have to rank this vintage of Tignanello alongside the glorious 1985. Anticipated maturity: now.

1985 Tignanello

RATING: 92 points

This wine appears to have reached full maturity. The color is a healthy deep ruby/purple, and the nose offers up scents of roasted nuts, smoky oak, cassis, cedar, and leather. Medium to full–bodied, with lovely black fruit flavors wrapped gently in oak, this fleshy, supple, deliciously constituted wine is a treat to drink.

CASTELLO DEI RAMPOLLA

WINES:

Sammarco

Vigna d'Alceo

OWNERS: Luca and Maurizia di Napoli Rampolla

ADDRESS: Località Case Sparse 22, 50020 Panzano in Chianti
(FI), Italy

TELEPHONE: 39 055 852001

TELEFAX: 39 055 852533

E-MAIL: castellodeirampolla.cast@tin.it

CONTACT: Maurizia di Napoli Rampolla

VISITING POLICY: By appointment only

VINEYARDS

SURFACE AREA: 153 acres (104 acres in production)

GRAPE VARIETALS: Sangiovese, Cabernet Sauvignon, Merlot,
Petit Verdot, Chardonnay, Traminer, Sauvignon Blanc,
Malvasia

AVERAGE AGE OF THE VINES:

Oldest vines: 27 years old

Youngest vines: 2, 3, and 4 years old

Vigna d'Alceo: 10 years old

DENSITY OF PLANTATION:

10,000 vines per hectare (in 5 acres)

8,000 vines per hectare (in 25 acres)

5,500 vines per hectare (in 63 acres)

AVERAGE YIELDS:

Sangiovese: 50 quintals per hectare

Cabernet: 35 quintals per hectare

WINEMAKING AND UPBRINGING

The land is predominantly limestone with some clay and stones. The vineyards enjoy south, southeast, and southwest exposures, with altitudes ranging from 290 to 380 meters. Rampolla recently began biodynamic agriculture in order to reestablish a natural balance for the soil.

The winemaking is done in enameled vats. The grapes ferment at a temperature of 26–30°C, controlled by a veil of water running down the outside of the vats. Aging takes place in large oak ovals and small French *barriques*.

Castello dei Rampolla Chianti Classico is a blend of 95% Sangiovese and 5% Cabernet Sauvignon. It remains in steel vats for 3 months, in barrels of 3,000 liters for 12 months, and in bottle for 6 months before being put up for sale.

Sammarco is a blend of Cabernet Sauvignon and Sangiovese. The debut vintage was 1980. The vineyards where it is produced have a full southern exposure at 360 meters above sea level. The land is rocky and marly and has little clay or lime. The two varieties of grapes are vinified separately: about 15 days for the Cabernet Sauvignon and about 10 days for the Sangiovese. The Sangiovese is aged for 18–24 months in large barrels and the Cabernet Sauvignon in French Bordeaux *barriques*. For additional refinement, Sammarco is bottle-aged for another 6–8 months before being released.

Vigna d'Alceo, first produced in 1996, is a blend of 85% Cabernet Sauvignon and 15% Petit Verdot. After racking, it remains in new and second-passage French wood *barriques* of 225 liters for 10–12 months and is bottle aged nearly 8 months before being put up for sale.

ANNUAL PRODUCTION

Castello dei Rampolla Chianti Classico: 55,000–60,000
bottles

Sammarco red table wine: 28,000–32,000 bottles

Vigna d'Alceo red table wine: 15,000–18,000 bottles

Trebianco Vendemmia Tardiva (late harvest) white sweet
wine: 2,500–3,000 bottles

AVERAGE PRICE (VARIABLE DEPENDING ON VINTAGE): $45–245

GREAT RECENT VINTAGES

2001, 2000, 1999, 1990, 1985, 1982

The estate Santa Lucia in Faulle, where the Castello dei Rampolla wine is produced, is in the southern valley of Panzano, called "Conca d'Oro." It has been owned by the di Napoli Rampolla family since 1739. The first vinifications were done in 1970, the first bottling of wine done from the grape harvest of 1975. Today the business is run by Maurizia and Luca di Napoli Rampolla.

Castello dei Rampolla has long been one of my favorite Tuscan producers. I began purchasing its wines with the 1983 Sammarco. As I have said many times, Sammarco always reminds me of a top Graves, because of the tobacco/mineral component it often displays.

SAMMARCO

1999 Sammarco

RATING: 93 points

The 1999 Sammarco, a blend of 85% Cabernet Sauvignon and 15% Sangiovese, has been one of Tuscany's great classics for nearly two decades. The 1999 Sammarco is tight and closed, but wow, what potential! A dense ruby/purple color is followed by a sweet nose of high-class cigar tobacco intermixed with smoke, minerals, black currants, and vanilla. In the mouth, it is dense and medium to full–bodied, with superb richness, purity, and overall harmony. Cellaring is mandatory for this backward, still primary 1999. Anticipated maturity: 2010–2025. A classic!

1998 Sammarco

RATING: 90 points

What has always made this wine exceptional, especially in the top vintages, is its complexity and elegance. It is closer to a great Graves than any other wine I have ever tasted outside France. The 1998 Sammarco, a blend of 85% Cabernet Sauvignon and 15% Sangiovese, reveals structure and tannin. Additionally, it possesses formidable underlying concentration and depth, along with that multilayered mid-palate that always seems to separate exceptional wines from good ones. The 1998 Sammarco has a saturated ruby color and a complex bouquet of charcoal, roasted herbs, smoke, hot gravel, black currants, and cherries. Medium-bodied and deep, with high but sweet tannin, it has extraordinary purity as well as delineation. Anticipated maturity: now–2016.

1995 Sammarco

RATING: 92 points

The glorious, dark ruby/purple–colored 1995 Sammarco *vino da tavola* (primarily Cabernet Sauvignon with 30%–35% Sangiovese) is a rich, full-bodied, complex super-Tuscan reminiscent of a northern Graves from Pessac-Léognan. Notes of tobacco, tar, lead pencil, roasted herbs, and copious black cherries and cassis slowly emerge as the wine sits in the glass. It is full-bodied and elegant, with flavors of black cherries, cassis, and roasted minerals. Pure, rich, and structured but notably tannic in the finish, this wine should be at its finest between now and 2018.

1990 Sammarco

RATING: 93 points

The 1990 Sammarco may prove to be a worthy rival to the glorious 1985. The saturated ruby/purple/garnet color is followed by an intense yet youthful fragrance of ripe black fruits, vanilla, and minerals. Full-bodied, rich, and beautifully delineated and structured, it possesses considerable body, tannin, and extract. It should age well until 2012.

1985 Sammarco

RATING: 93 points

From time to time, this wine reminds me of a classic red Graves; at other times there is a Pauillac-like lead pencil and mineral fragrance to the nose. At my most recent tasting, this exceptionally elegant wine displayed a classic Pauillac aroma of cassis and lead pencil. A deep ruby color, the wine has softened and expanded, and the new oak and moderate tannins that were so noticeable after bottling have taken a backseat to the gorgeously rich cassis fruit and long, velvety textured finish. This 1985 Sammarco should be drunk up.

VIGNA D'ALCEO

2001 Vigna d'Alceo

RATING: 93+ points

Quite closed down but with superb potential, this deep ruby/purple–colored wine shows notes of blackberry, bay leaf, and smoky French oak. It is quite concentrated and very well delineated, with good acidity, tremendous depth, and a hint of licorice and blackberries continuing on the palate. This is a wine of extraordinary nobility, purity, and palate presence. Drink it over the following 15+ years.

2000 Vigna d'Alceo

RATING: 98 points

For whatever reason, the full-bodied 2000 Vigna d'Alceo was roaring the day I tasted it. A single-vineyard blend of 85% Cabernet Sauvignon and 15% Sangiovese, it tastes like the Sammarco on steroids. It boasts a deep purple color in addition to scents of espresso, sweet melted licorice, black currant jam, and toasty oak. It has great intensity, superb purity, and a finish that lingers for nearly a minute. This mythical wine will age effortlessly for two decades.

1999 Vigna d'Alceo

RATING: 99 points

The monumental 1999 Vigna d'Alceo is a 20,000-bottle *cuvée* of 85% Cabernet Sauvignon and 15% Sangiovese aged in oak. It boasts an exceptionally provocative nose of liquid minerals, graphite, plums, crème de cassis, and cherry liqueur. It is fabulously concentrated yet remarkably light on its feet, with medium to full body, sweet tannin, and layer upon layer of flavor nuances. There is plenty of glycerin in this rich but neither heavy nor overbearing effort. This is a thrilling tour de force! However, it requires cellaring. Anticipated maturity: now–2025. Bravo!

1998 Vigna d'Alceo

RATING: 92 points

The 1998 Vigna d'Alceo is a fine offering. An opaque purple-colored blend of Cabernet Sauvignon, Sangiovese, and small quantities of Syrah and Petit Verdot, it is a large-scaled wine with exceptional elegance and complexity as well as more power and richness than the 1998 Sammarco. A sweet entry on the palate is followed by abundant quantities of smoky, complex, black currant fruit intermixed with lead pencil and vanilla flavors. Medium bodied, beautifully knit, and suave, it possesses sweet tannin. Anticipated maturity: now–2017.

1996 Vigna d'Alceo

RATING: 92 points

This terrific wine bears more than a passing resemblance to a top-class Médoc. The opaque purple color is followed by gobs of toasty new oak and jammy cassis fruit intermixed with minerals, spice, and cedar. Medium bodied, with outstanding purity and concentration, exceptional harmony, and moderately high tannin, this is a promising, seriously endowed wine. It should keep for another 10–15 years.

WINES:

Barolo Bricco Rocche

Barolo Brunate

Barbaresco Bricco Asili

OWNERS: Bruno and Marcello Ceretto

ADDRESS: Località San Cassiano 34, 12051 Alba, Piedmont, Italy

TELEPHONE: 39 0173 282582

TELEFAX: 39 0173 282383

E-MAIL: ceretto@ceretto.com

WEBSITE: www.ceretto.com

CONTACT: Roberta Ceretto (External Relations)

VISITING POLICY: By appointment only, Monday through Friday; no large groups (maximum 20 people)

VINEYARDS

SURFACE AREA: 248 acres

GRAPE VARIETALS: Nebbiolo d'Alba, Barbera d'Alba, Dolcetto d'Alba, Arneis, Riesling, Cabernet, Merlot, Pinot Nero, Chardonnay, Moscato (I Vignaioli di Santo Stefano—Partnership)

AVERAGE AGE OF THE VINES: 35 years

DENSITY OF PLANTATION: 3,700–4,500 vines per hectare

AVERAGE YIELDS: 5–8 tons per hectare

WINEMAKING AND UPBRINGING

While the Ceretto family has always produced red wines fashioned from the area's traditional varietals, in the last few years they also have worked with international varietals, using these grapes to experiment with new technologies before applying them to the winemaking of the native grapes.

Ceretto's three greatest wines experience a relatively short (about 7–8 days) floating cap fermentation in steel vats. After that period, the cap is pushed below the surface for an additional 8–10 days of maceration. All of this is done under strict temperature control between 28 and 30°C. Once the wine goes through malolactic fermentation in tank, it is moved to French *barriques,* where it remains until bottling. These *barriques* are 300 liters in size, but in the case of the Barbaresco Bricco Asili, some smaller casks are also used.

The Bricco Rocche vineyard in the *comune* of Castiglione Falletto has a full southerly exposure, and the soil types are basically dominated by clay with alluvial silting and sand. The vines were planted in 1978. At the Bricco Rocche Brunate vineyard in the *comune* of La Morra, the exposure is 100% southeast. The soil is a combination of primarily clay with some sand and silt. These vines were planted in 1974.

Bricco Asili in the *comune* of Barbaresco is a vineyard with a south-southwest exposure planted in 1969 and composed of 48% clay, 33% silt, and 19% sand. I tend to agree with the Cerettos' position that these wines have an aging curve of up to 20 years after they have been released.

ANNUAL PRODUCTION

Barolo Bricco Rocche: 6,000 bottles
Barolo Brunate: 30,000 bottles
Barbaresco Bricco Asili: 6,000 bottles
AVERAGE PRICE (VARIABLE DEPENDING ON VINTAGE): $50–180

GREAT RECENT VINTAGES

2000, 1999, 1997, 1996, 1990, 1989, 1986, 1985, 1982, 1979, 1978, 1974, 1971

The Cerettos

The Ceretto wines are among the most elegant of Italy and seem to represent a blend of traditional wine-making and an enlightened, modern approach. They are wonderfully fragrant and stylish, and are accessible immediately when released. They are by no means the biggest, brawniest, or most ageworthy of Piedmont's Barolos and Barbarescos, but they are not lacking the potential for longevity. A new generation, Lisa and Alessandro (Marcello's daughter and son) and Roberta and Federico (Bruno's daughter and son) have now joined the firm; however, the two brothers, Bruno and the oenologist Marcello, are still the primary representatives of this great estate. Fiercely proud of what they have achieved—not only they themselves, but all of Piedmont—they are quick to criticize their French brethren for ignoring the greatness of the Piedmontese wines.

BARBARESCO BRICCO ASILI

1999 Barbaresco Bricco Asili
RATING: 94 points
A beautiful, sweet nose of raspberries, tobacco, saddle leather, and a hint of dried herbs is followed by a full-bodied wine with good structure, sweet tannin, and medium to full body. This wine has a certain firmness that is usually undetectable in this kind. It should age nicely for 10–15 years. It is a classically elegant, potentially very complex style of wine that is a wonderful blend of both traditional and progressive winemaking.

1996 Barbaresco Bricco Asili
RATING: 93 points
This wine exhibits a saturated ruby color with purple nuances. The seductive, dark ruby–colored 1996 Barbaresco Bricco Asili is rich, with lots of extract, tannin, and body. It offers a classic bouquet of road tar, cherry liqueur, tobacco, and dried herbs. Medium to full–bodied and surprisingly supple for the vintage, it exhibits firm tannin in the finish. Anticipated maturity: now–2014.

1990 Barbaresco Bricco Asili
RATING: 95 points
The most stunningly perfumed and richest of Ceretto's 1990 Barbarescos is the 1990 Bricco Asili. Deeper-colored than the 1990 Bricco Asili-Faset, with an intensely fragrant bouquet of roasted herbs, nuts, oak, and sweet, ripe fruit, this wine possesses great richness, full body, a succulent texture, and a finish that lasts for nearly a minute. Drink this gorgeously proportioned, decadently hedonistic Barbaresco between now and 2009. Bravo!

1989 Barbaresco Bricco Asili
RATING: 91 points
The exquisite 1989 Bricco Asili exhibits a smoky, roasted, vanilla element to its fruity character. Rich and full, with an intoxicating cigar box aroma, this concentrated, lush wine provides stunning drinking. Anticipated maturity: now–2009.

BAROLO BRICCO ROCCHE

2000 Barolo Bricco Rocche
RATING: 95 points
Surprisingly evolved but oh, so complex and delicious already! I have doubts about the ultimate aging potential of this vintage for many wines, but there is no question of their opulence. Very complex aromas and wonderfully fleshy, succulent flavors are the stuff that no one can resist. This wine is already showing considerable amber at the edge. It is very provocative,

with a fragrant nose of dried herbs, seaweed, sweet cherries, plums, and a hint of balsamic vinegar, followed by oodles of fruit with a layered, full-bodied mouth-feel and a complex, supple texture. The finish lasts nearly a minute. It is a brilliant wine for drinking now and over the next 10–12 years.

1999 Barolo Bricco Rocche

RATING: 92 points

A very elegant style of wine with a sweet nose of red fruits intermixed with a hint of new saddle leather, tar, and rose petals, this dark ruby-colored wine shows medium body, ripe but present tannins, good acidity, and a long, concentrated finish. Anticipated maturity: 2006–2016.

1998 Barolo Bricco Rocche

RATING: 92 points

Ceretto's finest Barolo of the vintage appears to be the 1998 Barolo Bricco Rocche. An incredibly complex perfume of creosote, minerals, smoke, soy, black cherries, and incense is accompanied by a full-bodied, sweet, layered, powerful wine with outstanding balance. Long as well as elegant, this beauty will be at its finest between now and 2017.

1997 Barolo Bricco Rocche

RATING: 96 points

The ostentatious, staggering 1997 Barolo Bricco Rocche possesses a dark garnet color with amber at the edge. The explosive bouquet of coffee liqueur, licorice, spice box, black cherries, kirsch, raspberries, and cedar is to die for. The wine reveals numerous dimensions and nuances as well as a boatload of glycerin. Full-bodied, massively concentrated, and exceptionally thick and juicy, with a sweetness due to its high glycerin and ripeness, this is Barolo on steroids. Anticipated maturity: now–2018.

1996 Barolo Bricco Rocche

RATING: 95 points

This wine exhibits a saturated ruby color with purple nuances. It is also rich, with lots of extract, tannin, and body. Ceretto's opaque ruby/purple–colored 1996 Barolo Bricco Rocche is sensational stuff. It combines explosive levels of fruit, glycerin, and extract with an uncanny sense of elegance and finesse. There are copious quantities of black cherry fruit, intermixed with raspberries, cedar, spicy oak, licorice, and tar. This terrific, complex, multidimensional Barolo should be at its finest between now and 2018.

1995 Barolo Bricco Rocche

RATING: 90 points

The 1995 Barolo Bricco Rocche is concentrated and massive. It offers a classic nose of melted tar, Asian spice, incense, and cedar, as well as gobs of black fruits, a whiff of high-quality tobacco, full body, and a layered, moderately tannic finish. Anticipated maturity: now–2015.

1990 Barolo Bricco Rocche

RATING: 94 points

The bouquet of the awesomely concentrated, compelling 1990 Barolo Bricco Rocche soars from the glass, offering aromas of melted road tar, sweet, jammy cherry fruit, tobacco, and fruitcake. Massive yet graceful flavors cascade over the palate, revealing considerable viscosity, glycerin, and extraction of flavor. The wine is deep, expansive, and chewy. The finish is something to behold. There is undoubtedly plenty of tannin lurking beneath the fruit, so this wine can be drunk now and over the next 5–10 years.

1989 Barolo Bricco Rocche

RATING: 93 points

The most tannic of Ceretto's 1989 single-vineyard offerings is the 1989 Barolo Bricco Rocche. A large-scaled, super-concentrated, muscular wine for Ceretto, it should last for another 10 or more years. Rich, with layers of fruit, it exhibits a promising bouquet, as well as superb ripeness and intensity. The finish goes on and on. This may turn out to be one of Ceretto's longest-lived Barolos.

BAROLO BRUNATE

2000 Barolo Brunate

RATING: 94 points

A very delicate nose of rose water intermixed with hints of road tar, sweet kirsch, loamy soil, and saddle leather is followed by a more firmly structured, medium-bodied wine that is elegant but that has a lot more structure and obvious tannin than many 2000 Barolos. The wine is a beauty that will drink well for 12–15 years. It's hard to know if it will be as long-lived as such vintages as 1989 and 1996, but time will tell.

1997 Barolo Brunate

RATING: 94 points

The 1997 Barolo Brunate displays an evolved, dark garnet color with an amber edge. However, in the mouth, it is dense, full-bodied, moderately tannic, structured, and backward with plenty of power, concentration, and youthfulness. This wine should age well for another 13–15+ years.

1996 Barolo Brunate

RATING: 93 points

This wine exhibits a saturated ruby color with purple nuances. Additionally, it is rich, with lots of extract, tannin, and body. The 1996 Barolo Brunate's dark ruby color is followed by aromas of Chinese black tea, pepper, earth, and cherries. Ripe, full-bodied, and structured, with excellent depth, a sweet mid-palate, and a firm finish, this wine requires moderate patience. Anticipated maturity: now–2016.

1990 Barolo Brunate

RATING: 94 points

Ceretto's 1990 offerings are all outstanding, combining fabulous extract levels with aromatic bouquets and opulent, voluptuously rich flavors, textures, and finishes. The 1990 Barolo Brunate is very aromatic and perfumed. Concentrated and full-bodied, with sweet tannin, ripe fruit, and a luscious, multidimensional personality, this wine should drink well for another 5–10 years.

1989 Barolo Brunate

RATING: 93 points

The 1989 Barolo Brunate is a dazzling effort. The huge bouquet of tobacco, herbs, sweet black cherry fruit, and roasted nuts is a knockout. Dense, concentrated, and full-bodied, with layers of flavor, this stunningly proportioned, large-scaled Barolo retains a sense of grace and elegance. Drink it over the next 5–10 years.

WINES:

Barolo Ciabot Mentin Ginestra

Barolo Mosconi Percristina

Barolo Pajana

OWNERS: Domenico and Giuliana Clerico

ADDRESS: Via Cucchi 67, Località Manzoni, 12065 Monforte d'Alba (CN), Italy

TELEPHONE: 39 0173 78171

TELEFAX: 39 0173 789800

E-MAIL: domenicoclerico@libero.it

WEBSITE: www.marcdegrazia.com

CONTACT: Mrs. Giuliana Clerico

VISITING POLICY: By appointment only

VINEYARDS

SURFACE AREA: 52 acres

GRAPE VARIETALS: Nebbiolo d'Alba, Barbera d'Alba, Dolcetto d'Alba

AVERAGE AGE OF THE VINES: 30–40 years

DENSITY OF PLANTATION: 4,200 vines per hectare

AVERAGE YIELDS: 5,500 kilograms per hectare

WINEMAKING AND UPBRINGING

Clerico aggressively thins crops when it appears there is an abundance of grapes. After harvesting ripe fruit and macerating on the skins in temperature-controlled steel rotary fermenters for 5–10 days, Clerico moves the wine to small French oak *barriques*. In most vintages 90% new and 10% used oak are employed. The wine stays in cask for 18–24 months before it is bottled unfiltered.

ANNUAL PRODUCTION

Barolo Ciabot Mentin Ginestra: 16,800 bottles

Barolo Mosconi Percristina: 5,500 bottles

Barolo Pajana: 6,500 bottles

AVERAGE PRICE (VARIABLE DEPENDING ON VINTAGE): $20–80

GREAT RECENT VINTAGES

2001, 2000, 1999, 1998, 1997, 1990

One of the singular winemakers in Piedmont, Domenico Clerico, with his big head of wavy hair, is a "wild and crazy guy" who could have just stepped out of a Steve Martin movie. He left a job as a salesman in 1977 to work full time for the family estate. Totally self-taught as both a vigneron and a winemaker, he was mentored by many of his friends, including Elio Altare and the young, dynamic wine broker Marc de Grazia, whom he first met in the early 1980s. He has some of the best vineyards in Barolo, all fascinating, top-quality sites from the village of Monforte d'Alba: Ginestra, which he purchased in 1983, Pajana in 1989, and his most recent purchase, Mosconi in 1995. His wines are clearly of the modern school, but they age nearly as well as some of the traditional *cuvées* made by the likes of Bruno Giacosa or Roberto (Giacomo) Conterno. They are also much easier to drink young. In most cases his top Barolos require 2–4 years of bottle age and drink well for up to 20 years.

Domenico Clerico

2000 Barolo Ciabot Mentin Ginestra

RATING: 92 points

This is an intriguing 2000 Barolo that shows some amber at the edge and wonderfully forward, evolved aromatics that smell almost as if they were a decade old. That's not a criticism. This is just a fleshpot of a Barolo with loads of concentrated herb and graphite-infused black cherry and currant fruit with plenty of toasty new oak. A very concentrated, velvety-textured wine, it is opulent, fleshy, and ideal for drinking over the next 10–12 years.

1999 Barolo Ciabot Mentin Ginestra

RATING: 91+ points

Quite ripe for a 1999, with notes of figs, black cherry liqueur, smoke, earth, and dried herbs, this is a full-bodied, rather heady wine that seems a bit richer and fleshier than the other Clerico 1999s. It may lack a touch of definition compared to those, but it is surprisingly opulent, and rich, and seems in this particular case to have more in common with the very showy 2000 vintage than the more austere, tannic, and classical 1999s. Anticipated maturity: 2007–2018.

1998 Barolo Ciabot Mentin Ginestra

RATING: 93 points

The super-extracted, blockbuster 1998 Barolo Ciabot Mentin Ginestra assaults the palate with a blast of broodingly tannic, super-concentrated black cherry and raspberry fruit infused with minerals, new oak, licorice, and truffles. With a huge mid-palate as well as an astonishingly long finish, it is not yet ready to drink. Anticipated maturity: 2006–2020.

1997 Barolo Ciabot Mentin Ginestra

RATING: 94 points

The 1997 Barolo Ciabot Mentin Ginestra is a fearsomely powerful, tannic, ultra-concentrated, explosively rich wine with a mid-palate in which one could get lost. A saturated ruby/purple color is accompanied by scents of lead pencil, cedar, black fruits, smoke, earth, and vanilla. Massive richness, monster extract, sweet tannin, and a blockbuster finish characterize this dazzling, 20–30-year wine. Anticipated maturity: now–2020.

1996 Barolo Ciabot Mentin Ginestra

RATING: 90 points

This is a spectacularly powerful, rich, concentrated wine. The 1996 Barolo Ciabot Mentin Ginestra possesses a deep, dark purple color and a nose of overripe plums, cherries, and cassis. Rich and full-bodied, with admirable glycerin, subtle oak, and licorice/floral nuances, it is a large-scaled yet beautifully balanced Barolo to drink between now and 2018.

1995 Barolo Ciabot Mentin Ginestra

RATING: 91 points

The 1995 Barolo Ciabot Mentin Ginestra offers a knockout nose of tobacco, mint, dried red fruits, balsam wood, and cherry liqueur. There are tons of glycerin, low acidity, medium to full body, and striking richness and lushness. It is about as sexy a 1995 Barolo as readers will find. Anticipated maturity: now–2012.

1994 Barolo Ciabot Mentin Ginestra

RATING: 91 points

The 1994 Barolo Ciabot Mentin Ginestra is a sumptuous, medium to full–bodied, multilayered, exceptionally complex Barolo; aromas of charcoal, smoke, tobacco, Asian spices, fruitcake, and framboise dominate. Deep, opulently textured, and full-bodied, it, like its sibling, the Pajana, is a tour de force in winemaking. Anticipated maturity: now–2007.

1993 Barolo Ciabot Mentin Ginestra

RATING: 90 points

One of the truly fun characters of Piedmont has once again turned in this superlative performance. The 1993 Barolo Ciabot Mentin Ginestra offers up truffle, earthy, spicy aromas accompanied by copious quantities of sweet black cherry fruit. As the wine hits the palate, it has the telltale sweetness and ripeness, as well as the beautifully knit, well-etched, medium to full–bodied character of the vintage. Neither the acidity, the tannin, nor the alcohol are obtrusive in this pure, expansive, tasty, and complex Barolo. Anticipated maturity: now–2009.

1990 Barolo Ciabot Mentin Ginestra

RATING: 94 points

The most tannic and closed of the three Clerico 1990 Barolos is the 1990 Barolo Ciabot Mentin Ginestra. Although the wine obviously has great depth and huge reserves of fruit, it is closed aromatically. Most of its richness and power are noticeable at the back of the mouth—always a good sign. It is a candidate for two decades of drinkability. Anticipated maturity: now–2014.

1989 Barolo Ciabot Mentin Ginestra

RATING: 95 points

The 1989 Barolo Ciabot Mentin Ginestra is compelling. It combines magnificent power and massiveness with exceptional elegance and finesse—a rare and difficult combination to achieve. The color is dense dark ruby/purple. Although reticent at first, with airing the nose offers huge aromas of smoked nuts, flowers, minerals, and black and red fruits. Spectacularly rich and deep, this staggeringly proportioned Barolo should be at its best between now and 2012.

1988 Barolo Ciabot Mentin Ginestra

RATING: 92 points

Clerico's 1988 Barolo Ciabot Mentin Ginestra is a super wine, with a dense, dark ruby color and a big, ripe nose of tar, spices, and earthy red fruit. In the mouth, the wine displays super-concentration, as well as a ripe, full-bodied, glycerin-dominated, tannic finish. The wine has terrific potential and extremely high tannins, but it is still backward and unevolved. Anticipated maturity: now–2007.

1985 Barolo Ciabot Mentin Ginestra

RATING: 90 points

The 1985 Barolo Ciabot Mentin Ginestra exhibits aromas and flavors of melted asphalt, dried herbs, underbrush, and sweet black and red fruits, all infused with smoke. Full-bodied, with sweet tannin, outstanding vigor and richness, and a concentrated finish, this is a fully mature, lively, intense wine. This Barolo is fully mature, yet reveals no signs of decline. Anticipated maturity: now–2013.

1982 Barolo Ciabot Mentin Ginestra

RATING: 92 points

The excellent 1982 Barolo Ciabot Mentin Ginestra is extraordinarily complex. A bouquet of dried herbs, smoked meats, tobacco, truffles, and earthy black fruits soars from the glass. Full-bodied, rustic, and animalistic, this is a thick, earthy, fully mature Barolo. Anticipated maturity: now–2011.

BAROLO MOSCONI PERCRISTINA

2000 Barolo Mosconi Percristina

RATING: 96 points

I'm not so sure the 2000 Barolo Mosconi Percristina (named after Clerico's daughter who, tragically, died at the age of seven) is going to make it past 10–12 years, but who cares? It is a spectacularly sumptuous, exotic, full-throttle, flamboyant Barolo with a dense plum/purple color already showing a hint of amber at the edge. A knockout nose of smoked herbs, sweet cherries, and blueberries with some toasty oak in the background leads to an opulently textured, almost viscous, very ripe wine that is almost over the top, an amazingly rich, concentrated wine that should drink well for at least a dozen years, assuming anyone can resist drinking it for that long. It is already remarkably complex and evolved, which is a characteristic of this vintage.

1998 Barolo Mosconi Percristina

RATING: 92 points

The 1998 Barolo Mosconi Percristina reveals aromas of sweet black fruit intermixed with new oak, blueberry, flowers, and an underlying minerality. Full-bodied, powerful, deep, and chewy, this youthful, backward 1998 is spectacular. Anticipated maturity: now–2018.

1997 Barolo Mosconi Percristina

RATING: 93 points

Clerico's 1997 Barolo Mosconi Percristina is tannic and backward. A dense ruby/purple color is followed by aromas of new saddle leather, licorice, black cherries, and the telltale rose petals. Closed aromatically, with huge flavors and copious glycerin, as well as abundant tannin, this full-bodied, loaded 1997 requires cellaring. Anticipated maturity: 2007–2030.

1996 Barolo Mosconi Percristina

RATING: 95 points

This is a spectacularly powerful, rich, concentrated wine. The profound 1996 Barolo Mosconi Percristina exhibits a black raspberry liqueur–like nose. As it sits in the glass, notes of cherries, cassis, toast, and smoke emerge. Massive, powerful, chewy, unctuously textured, and long, with subtle oak and immense fruit concentration, this spectacular Barolo should age effortlessly for another 10–15 years.

1995 Barolo Mosconi Percristina

RATING: 92 points

The amazing 1995 Barolo Mosconi Percristina is the richest, most complete of the 1995 offerings from Clerico. This debut vintage offers up kirsch, Chinese black tea, flowers, licorice, and subtle spicy new oak. Amazingly rich and full-bodied, with terrific purity, symmetry, and length, it will keep for another 7–10 years.

BAROLO PAJANA

2000 Barolo Pajana

RATING: 94 points

A very Pomerol-styled wine with notes of black cherry liqueur intermixed with black currant, smoke, and earth in a wonderfully sweet, ripe, forward style with low acidity and an almost shockingly seductive personality already. A beauty, this wine should drink well for at least a decade. This is an unusual vintage for Barolo and Barbaresco, but wow, the wines are gorgeous already.

1999 Barolo Pajana

RATING: 91+ points

In contrast to the showy 2000, the 1999 Pajana is more laid back and restrained, with medium to full body, notes of graphite, mineral, tobacco leaf, and black currant and cherry fruit as well as new oak. Medium-bodied, elegant and quite pure, this wine should be drunk over the next 12–15 years.

1998 Barolo Pajana

RATING: 92 points

The dense ruby/purple–colored 1998 Barolo Pajana reveals copious new oak along with lead pencil, black cherry, black-berry, licorice, and earth aromas. It is a structured, powerful, full-bodied, chewy wine. Anticipated maturity: now–2016.

1997 Barolo Pajana

RATING: 93 points

Clerico's saturated purple–colored 1997 Barolo Pajana offers a classic bouquet (reminiscent of a cross between Mouton and Lafite Rothschild) of cedarwood, cassis, licorice, lead pencil, and mineral scents. The wine possesses abundant quantities of black fruit, tar, truffle, and cigar box flavors. A huge, monstrous Barolo, it is not one of the most forward 1997s. Anticipated maturity: 2004–2018.

1996 Barolo Pajana

RATING: 94 points

This is a spectacularly powerful, rich, concentrated wine. The striking resemblance of the 1996 Barolo Pajana to a top-class Pomerol is unmistakable. This massive wine possesses fabulous purity of fruit and a sweet toast aroma that complements the wine's highly concentrated black cherry/chocolaty personality. Dense and layered, with considerable viscosity, low acidity, and moderate tannin in the impressive, long finish, it will be at its best between 2006 and 2020.

1995 Barolo Pajana

RATING: 90 points

Stylistically, the 1995 Barolo Pajana is somewhere between a grand cru Burgundy and a first-growth Bordeaux. It exhibits a saturated ruby/purple color, lush black raspberry and cherry fruit, and a touch of black currants. This medium to full–bodied, fruit-driven, low-acid wine should be at its best between now and 2012.

1994 Barolo Pajana

RATING: 91 points

The 1994 Barolo Pajana displays a Lafite Rothschild–like lead pencil note in its fragrant bouquet of black cherries, currants, minerals, and toast. This beautifully focused, well-delineated, dense, full-bodied wine possesses surprising depth and richness for a 1994, outstanding purity, and a multidimensional personality. It should be drunk now.

1993 Barolo Pajana

RATING: 94 points

Readers may remember my praise for the debut vintage of Clerico's Barolo Pajana in 1990. As I was dictating my tasting notes for the 1993, my first word was "kick-ass." I realize that doesn't say everything readers want or need to know about a wine, so consider the following description. It is an opaque dark color, with a chocolate, black raspberry, cherry, and truffle–scented nose; sweet, rich, concentrated fruit flavors; an expansive mid-palate; and impressive opulence and richness in the nicely textured, long finish. Although unevolved, the wine is accessible. Anticipated maturity: now–2010.

1990 Barolo Pajana

RATING: 96 points

The only evidence of the new oak is some spicy vanilla and smoke in the nose, which should give readers a good idea of this wine's splendid concentration of black and red fruits. Exceptionally long and sweet (because of the great ripeness and tiny yields), the wine's finish lasts for more than a minute. An intoxicating perfume of black fruits, spices, and smoke, with a touch of hickory and licorice, makes this a totally profound wine. Drink it over the next 10 years.

WINES:

Barolo Cascina Francia

Barolo Riserva Monfortino

OWNER: Roberto Conterno

ADDRESS: Località Ornati 2, 12065 Monforte d'Alba (CN),
  Italy

TELEPHONE: 39 0173 78221

TELEFAX: 39 0173 787190

WEBSITE: www.conterno.it

CONTACT: Mr. Roberto Conterno

VISITING POLICY: Small groups of 5–7 people only;
  reservation is required

VINEYARDS

SURFACE AREA: 34.6 acres

GRAPE VARIETALS: Nebbiolo d'Alba, Barbera d'Alba

AVERAGE AGE OF THE VINES: 28 years

DENSITY OF PLANTATION: 4,000 vines per hectare

AVERAGE YIELDS:

Barolo Cascina Francia: 35 hectoliters per hectare

Barolo Riserva Monfortino: 35 hectoliters per hectare

WINEMAKING AND UPBRINGING

All the grapes come from Cascina Francia, a small estate on a single plot located in the *comune* of Serralunga d'Alba. The vineyard is about 34.6 acres and faces south and southwest. This bastion of traditionalism utilizes the *cappello sommerso* (submerged cap) technique. The must is fermented in stainless-steel and open oak vats at temperatures from 28° to 30°C for about 3–4 weeks. No filtration or clarification is employed, nor are concentrators used. After the malolactic fermentation at natural temperatures, the wines are matured in large casks (*foudres*) of Slavonian oak—two years for the Barbera d'Alba, four years for the Barolo Cascina Francia, and a minimum of seven years for the Barolo Riserva Monfortino. After bottling, which is done once a year around mid-July as a rule, the wines are cellared for one to two years before release.

ANNUAL PRODUCTION

For some vintages the production is much lower than these averages.

Barolo Cascina Francia: 18,000 bottles

Barolo Riserva Monfortino: 7,000 bottles

AVERAGE PRICE (VARIABLE DEPENDING ON VINTAGE): $50–275

GREAT RECENT VINTAGES

Roberto Conterno is reluctant to identify his greatest vintages because, as he claims, "it doesn't do justice to the others." His philosophy (also held by his late father, Giovanni) is that he produces his Barolo Riserva Monfortino only when he considers the grapes exceptional. In fact, when the quality of the grapes is not satisfactory, no wine is produced. In 1991 and 1992, neither a Barolo Riserva Monfortino nor a Barolo Cascina Francia was produced. However, the favorites of the winery include 1996, 1995, 1990, 1989, 1988, 1987, 1985, 1982, 1978, 1974, 1971, 1970, 1968, 1964, 1961, 1958, and 1955. It's useful to know (and it's a most uncommon thing) that the Conternos had an unprecedented succession of great vintages from 1995 through 2002. All these vintages are considered of the same exceptional quality.

I have followed the wines of this bastion of traditionalism since the mid-1970s. It is the quintessential conservative, traditional winery that makes no concessions to modern-day tastes or the bottom line. Roberto Conterno makes his wines just as his father (Giovanni, who passed away in 2003) did. In fact, generations of Conternos have made Barolo in the same way: very low yields, ripe fruit, long maceration, and extensively prolonged aging in large oak ovals (or, as the French call them, *foudres*). The Conternos do not think twice about aging their famed Barolo Riserva Montfortino for more than a decade prior to its bottling and release. The Barolo Cascina Francia di Serralunga also spends up to four years in old large oak before being bottled, an unusually long period by modern standards. These are truly great wines that pay respect to their place of origin. The extraordinarily well-manicured vineyard is in the Serralunga sector of Barolo.

These wines sometimes shock modern-day palates since they can appear, at least early in life, to be rustic and sometimes possess what many technocrats consider relatively feeble color as well as elevated levels of volatile acidity. That said, they consistently develop into profoundly complex, multidimensional wines that stand the test of time. The style at this winery is unlikely to change under Roberto, and along with Bruno

Giacosa and a handful of other Piedmontese producers, these remain the most traditional, antiglobalist wines of the world. My advice is to forget these Barolos for 10 years after they are released. Then their magic is unleashed. They are monuments to the greatness of the Nebbiolo grape and to the glory of Piedmont.

BAROLO CASCINA FRANCIA

1999 Barolo Cascina Francia

RATING: 92 points

A classic Barolo, the 1999 Barolo Cascina Francia has a moderate ruby color with some amber at the edge. A huge, fragrant nose of tobacco leaf, spice box, licorice, sweet cherry, and autumnal, earthy, decaying vegetation jumps from the glass. It is very full-bodied with the sweet cherry, licorice, and underlying herbal notes still present. Very intense and massive with relatively high tannin, this wine needs another 5–6 years of cellaring and should keep for 20–25 years.

1995 Barolo Cascina Francia

RATING: 92 points

The 1995 Barolo Cascina Francia is a young, dense Barolo. It possesses the classic Nebbiolo traits of melted asphalt, cedarwood, sweet cherries, rose petals, and truffles. Full-bodied, deep, and chewy, with an intriguing earthy smokiness, this full-bodied, tannic, impressively concentrated and endowed Barolo can be drunk now, but it will last for another 10+ years. This impeccably made, traditional wine is not for everybody, but it will handsomely repay cellaring and represents a winemaking style that, hopefully, will never be extinguished by the new, more supple-textured, darker-colored, earlier bottled wines.

1994 Barolo Cascina Francia

RATING: 90 points

The 1994 Barolo Cascina Francia reveals amber in its ruby/garnet color. Scents of Chinese black tea, cedarwood, smoked duck, soy, licorice, and tobacco jump from the glass. This aromatic Barolo is forward with sweet, round, old-style flavors, dusty tannin, and wonderful glycerin and concentration. It should drink well for another 7–10 years.

1993 Barolo Cascina Francia

RATING: 91 points

The 1993 Barolo Cascina Francia exhibits a dark ruby color with purple nuances, in addition to aromas of roasted herbs, tobacco, tar, kirsch, and dried cherries as well as some volatile acidity. In the mouth, it is dense, medium to full–bodied, with good concentration and dusty tannin in the finish. It can be drunk now but promises to evolve for another 10–15 years.

Roberto Conterno

1990 Barolo Cascina Francia

RATING: 95 points

Just now approaching its adolescent stage, this spectacular Barolo exhibits a dark garnet color with amber edges. An extraordinary nose of spice box, new saddle leather, and sweet herb and licorice–infused black cherry/kirsch notes along with hints of fig and plum jump from the glass. An amazingly concentrated, full-throttle wine that still has some tannin to shed but is remarkably multidimensional and long, this wine is just hitting the beginning of its period of maturity and should continue to evolve for another 20–25 years.

1989 Barolo Cascina Francia

RATING: 94 points

This is a vintage that the Conternos always considered to be one of their all-time greatest, and while they could have made a Monfortino, the production was so tiny they decided to simply include it all in the Cascina Francia. The wine is a huge, broodingly backward, full-throttle Barolo that seems to have put on considerable weight over the last few years. I am not sure it equals the 1990, but it continues to impress and has the classic tar and rose petal–scented nose, huge body, a bit of amber at the edge of the color, and a massive finish. Anticipated maturity: 2006–2020+.

1988 Barolo Cascina Francia

RATING: 92 points

The 1988 Barolo Cascina Francia offers a rose and tar–scented nose, deep, full-bodied flavors with aggressive tannin, plenty of ripeness and glycerin, and a heady, spicy cherry, leather, and herb–flavored finish. Drink this huge, large-scaled, full-throttle Barolo over the next 10 years.

1985 Barolo Cascina Francia

RATING: 94 points

The fabulous 1985 Barolo Cascina Francia possesses the classic Nebbiolo nose of roses and tar, as well as masses of rich red and black fruits. Unctuous and intense, with spectacular fruit, it offers great fragrance and massive body to go along with its high extract and huge tannin. Anticipated maturity: now–2012.

1971 Barolo Cascina Francia

RATING: 96 points

One of the great Conterno vintages, the 1971 Cascina Francia is probably the best vintage of this wine I have ever tasted. Dark garnet–colored with an intense bouquet of tar, roasted herbs, damp earth, truffles, and black cherries, this wine has an amazing amount of concentration, good acidity, and sweet tannin. Very massive and full-bodied, with just a hint of balsamic/volatile acidity, this is a wine that can be drunk now or cellared for at least another 25 years. An amazing achievement.

BAROLO RISERVA MONFORTINO

1998 Barolo Riserva Monfortino

RATING: 93–96 points

Who can't admire a producer who won't even release his wine until 2006–2007? Tasted from a gigantic *foudre* (where the entire Monfortino *cuvée* is sitting), it is a ruby-colored wine with a forward, evolved style (typical of the 1998 vintage) and a sweet bouquet of rose water, tar, truffles, minerals, and cherry fruit. Full-bodied but beautifully balanced, it is delicious enough to drink now, although that would be considered heresy in these cellars. Interestingly, both Conternos considered 1998 to be a greater vintage for them for Monfortino than the 1997. Perhaps it is the more structured style of the 1998 that appeals to them. Anticipated maturity: 2009–2028.

1997 Barolo Riserva Monfortino

RATING: 94 points

The 1997 Barolo Monfortino appears to be an atypically forward wine for this estate. It is dense and sexy, with abundant glycerin, and lush, seamless, black cherry, kirsch, smoke, tar, and meatlike flavors presented in a full-bodied, concentrated style. Anticipated maturity: 2007–2022.

1996 Barolo Riserva Monfortino

RATING: 96 points

This wine is a very structured, potentially complex, backward Barolo with a huge nose of rose petals intermixed with sweet tar, licorice, cherry, and leathery notes. Very massive, full-bodied, and powerful, with incredibly high levels of tannin, some amber peeking through at the edge of the medium garnet color, and an amazing finish, this wine probably won't hit its peak until about 2015 and will last until 2025–2030.

1995 Barolo Riserva Monfortino

RATING: 94 points

This is one of the great Barolo Monfortinos of 1995. Significantly concentrated, it represents a tiny crop because of hail damage. The wine reveals the essence of licorice, kirsch, smoke, red currant, and cherries, as well as the telltale rose petal and licorice notes. It is ripe and full-bodied, with sweet fruit, copious glycerin, and a seamless finish that lasts for nearly 45 seconds. As the wine sat in the glass, it became even more floral and concentrated. There is abundant tannin, and the wine will undoubtedly taste more structured when it is released. Anticipated maturity: 2010–2040.

1993 Barolo Riserva Monfortino

RATING: 92 points

The light garnet/ruby–colored 1993 Barolo Monfortino is undoubtedly the wine of the vintage, which was a challenging one. Like all Conterno wines, it was bottled without fining and filtration, thus preserving its full *terroir* and varietal characteristics. It boasts a knockout aromatic profile of rose petals, tar, new saddle leather, sweet jammy black cherries, licorice, and raspberries, decent acidity, sweet tannin, copious alcohol, wonderful density, a fleshy texture, and beautiful harmony as well as elegance. It can be drunk now and over the next 12 years. Look for this effort to be one of the great sleeper wines of Piedmont, given the fact that most 1993 Barolos are austere and hard-edged.

1990 Barolo Riserva Monfortino

RATING: 96 points

This wine displays a medium ruby color with amber at the edge. The intensely fragrant bouquet offers aromas of smoky tobacco, jammy cherries, aged Parmesan cheese, licorice, dried herbs, and truffles. In the mouth, this old-style, monster Barolo boasts awesome extract, full body, mouth-searing levels of tannin, and a massive, 40+-second finish. It is hard not to be seduced by the wine's fabulous bouquet. Look for this Monfortino to age for another two decades! This profound 1990 wine appears to be an exhilarating effort in a succession of great Monfortinos. (The 1985, 1982, 1978, 1971, 1967, and 1964 remain Piedmontese classics.) This long-awaited yet surreal 1990 Barolo Monfortino Riserva spent 7 years in *foudre* before being bottled. (In the old days, it was often kept 10 or more years before bottling.)

1987 Barolo Riserva Monfortino

RATING: 93 points

While many producers have said that their 1987 Barolo vintage was average in quality, Conterno enjoyed great success. The 1987 Monfortino is unquestionably the best Barolo of the vintage. Its saturated dark color and huge nose of truffles, tar, and sweet tobacco tinged with black cherry fruit are followed by a wine with gobs of glycerin, amazing power and richness, and a monstrously long, tannic finish. A great wine from a so-so vintage, it should be at its best between now and 2020. Those of you who love wine loaded with lavish new oak, sweet, crunchy fruit, and squeaky-clean, simple flavors should be sure to taste this before you decide whether to buy it. Though a fabulous wine, it is not for everybody.

1985 Barolo Riserva Monfortino

RATING: 97 points

This superb Monfortino is actually one of the few relatively recent (if that is the appropriate expression) wines from the Conternos approaching some level of full maturity. An extraordinary nose of white truffles, smoked meats, dried herbs, spice box, saddle leather, and kirsch jumps from the glass of this dark garnet–colored wine. It is very full-bodied and, like most Monfortinos, supple-textured at present, with gorgeous texture, a very layered, multidimensional mouth-feel, and a sweet, very long, glycerin-imbued finish. Anticipated maturity: now–2025.

1971 Barolo Riserva Monfortino

RATING: 100 points

The perfect Monfortino! A wine that is still youthful but has now moved into the very beginning stages of its early mature period, this extraordinary Monfortino is the stuff of legends. The wine shows the classic nose of dried red and black fruits intermixed with loamy soil notes, smoked herbs, white truffles, rose petals, and meaty, leathery notes. The explosive aromatics are followed by a massively constituted, gigantically styled wine with sweet tannin, amazing symmetry and purity, and mouth-staining levels of extract. It has become much more supple and delicious and can be drunk after several hours of decantation with great pleasure. Anticipated maturity: now–2030+.

1970 Barolo Riserva Monfortino

RATING: 90 points

The monolithic 1970 Barolo Monfortino exhibits plenty of amber in its dark garnet color in addition to earthy, dried fruit, smoke, and tobacco scents. Angular in the mouth, it is big, rich, and well constituted. Anticipated maturity: now–2015.

1967 Barolo Riserva Monfortino

RATING: 95 points

Fully mature for the past decade, the 1967 Barolo Monfortino is one of Conterno's great successes. For some reason, this wine has long been ignored when top-notch Monfortinos are discussed by wine lovers/aficionados. The 1967 reveals a mature ruby/garnet color with considerable amber. The smoky, earthy bouquet offers up copious quantities of sweet tea and dried fruit aromas. There is a sweet, succulent, rich, fleshy mouth-feel with just enough acidity and tannin to provide delineation. Owners should not push their luck by holding this wine longer, as it needs to be consumed.

WINES:

Valpolicella Superiore

Amarone della Valpolicella

OWNER: Dal Forno Romano

ADDRESS: Località Lodoletta, 1, 37030 Cellore d'Illasi, Verona, Italy

TELEPHONE: 39 045 7834923

TELEFAX: 39 045 6528364

E-MAIL: info@dalforno.net

WEBSITE: www.dalforno.net (under construction)

CONTACT: Dal Forno Romano

VISITING POLICY: From Monday to Wednesday by appointment only

VINEYARDS

SURFACE AREA: Property of the winery: 30.8 acres; rented property: 30.8 acres

GRAPE VARIETALS: Corvina, Rondinella, Croatina, Oseletta

AVERAGE AGE OF THE VINES: 18 years

DENSITY OF PLANTATION: Old vineyards: 2,000–3,000 vines per hectare; new vineyards: 11,000–13,000 vines per hectare

AVERAGE YIELDS: 55–60 quintals per hectare

WINEMAKING AND UPBRINGING

The proprietor states explicitly, "The objective is to achieve the highest level of quality so that I can transfer to the final consumer not only the pleasure of drinking, but emotion." After temperature-controlled fermentation, which lasts about two weeks, the wine is decanted in another tank for the clarification and finally put in *barriques,* in which it stays for 36 months, both Amarone and Valpolicella. After maturing, the wine is bottled in February or March, and it remains in bottles for two years for Valpolicella, while the Amarone rests there for three years before being released.

ANNUAL PRODUCTION

Amarone DOC: 9,000 bottles

Valpolicella DOC Superiore: 19,000 bottles

AVERAGE PRICE (VARIABLE DEPENDING ON VINTAGE): $100–400

GREAT RECENT VINTAGES

2001, 2000, 1998, 1997, 1995, 1990, 1985

The Dal Forno estate, the standard for uncompromising Valpolicella and Amarone, is in Val d'Illasi, a valley, to the east of Verona. The estate is located about halfway up the valley where the slopes just begin to rise toward the mountains. The farm has always been a hospitable place to produce wine and olive oil, largely because of its altitude (290 meters above sea level).

Dal Forno has been in the same family for at least four generations and has been producing wine for at least three of them. Luigi Dal Forno played an essential role by reuniting the whole property after it had been split up among various family members. Though he reserved some of the land for the sowing of livestock crops, which at the time were the farm's only source of income, he envisaged the farm primarily as a vineyard.

Luigi's son Romano managed the winery during a period that witnessed significant changes in the valley. After the Second World War, many of the local inhabitants abandoned agriculture as incomes fell and the grueling farmwork lost its appeal. The increasing globalization of the market and the need for state-of-the-art mechanization presented significant financial problems, and as a result Luigi Dal Forno was never able to make wine a full-time enterprise.

Romano Dal Forno began producing wine in 1983, after weighing his options and decid-

ing to continue the family tradition. In 1990 he built the winery and the house that is now both his home and the center of the farm. The buildings are meant to evoke the style of the area's 19th-century villas, because the style is well suited to the environment and reflects his philosophy of winemaking: "Solidity, longevity, complexity, but above all, a love for natural materials and respect for history and traditions."

The Dal Forno family is unquestionably the leading Veneto producer of Valpolicella and Amarone. It is remarkable what Romano Dal Forno has accomplished in such a short period. By European winemaking standards, he has a brief résumé. The wines, which go from strength to strength, have established new benchmarks for Valpolicella and Amarone, redefining this category in both price and quality. Regrettably, they are both hard to find and priced in the upper stratosphere. However, anyone who has tasted a Dal Forno offering realizes that this is the reference point for prodigious Valpolicella and Amarone. They possess off-the-chart levels of complexity, richness, and aging potential, and reveal a style totally unlike that of anything else produced in the region.

AMARONE DELLA VALPOLICELLA

1998 Amarone della Valpolicella Vigneto di Monte Lodoletta

RATING: 96 points

An extraordinarily powerful, potent wine with an almost black color, a huge nose of graphite, licorice, white chocolate, espresso roast, and huge amounts of fruit, this full-bodied, almost over-the-top wine pulls it back in and shows some remarkable delineation, balance, and, yes, surprising elegance for something so huge. This is a wine that will last at least 20–25 years. It is quite prodigious. Anticipated maturity: 2008–2025.

1997 Amarone della Valpolicella

RATING: 99 points

The outrageous 1997 Amarone (17.5% alcohol) was aged 28 months in 100% new French oak. Its inky/purple color is followed by sumptuous aromas of blueberry liqueur intermixed with truffle, graphite, camphor, and vanilla scents. This remarkable offering is immensely full-bodied and super-concentrated, with great purity, symmetry, and length. It is the stuff of legends! How long will it last? Who knows? Certainly this wine is capable of evolving for 15–20 years.

1996 Amarone della Valpolicella

RATING: 99 points

Dal Forno's virtually perfect 1996 is undoubtedly the finest Amarone I have ever tasted. Its inky black/purple color is accompanied by extraordinarily pure, graphite-infused, blackberry, plum, mineral, licorice, and espresso flavors. Despite its monumental intensity and richness, this wine is not heavy, somehow managing to conceal its 17.5% alcohol! As compelling an Italian wine as I have ever tasted, it should prove to be unbelievably long-lived. Anticipated maturity: now–2030.

1995 Amarone della Valpolicella

RATING: 98 points

The opaque purple 1995 Amarone is nearly perfect. It is reminiscent of super-concentrated blackberry liqueur infused with incense, smoke, and minerals. Full-bodied, dense, and chewy, this huge offering possesses remarkable purity and liveliness for its size and intensity. Amarone is an acquired taste, given its size as well as its earthy, tarry characteristics. Certainly this wine reaches new levels of extract and richness, yet is dry, well balanced, and, because of its extravagant richness, able to hide the whopping 16.5% alcohol it possesses. This is the product of a true genius. It should drink well for a minimum of two decades.

1994 Amarone della Valpolicella

RATING: 97 points

The spectacular 1994 Amarone exhibits amazing freshness for a wine of such mass, size, and concentration. It oozes across the palate but never comes close to being heavy. There are amazing quantities of truffles, smoke, black fruits, and licorice present in this exquisite wine. Anticipated maturity: now–2020.

1990 Amarone della Valpolicella

RATING: 95 points

I do not drink much Amarone (although I methodically taste it every year), as I find most of it to be too pruny, somewhat oxidized, and not fresh enough, even allowing for the particular style of these wines. Yet even I get excited by such spectacular Amarones. The profound 1990 Amarone della Valpolicella is a magnificent example of Amarone. Dry and massively proportioned, with a dark plum color, this wine offers up copious quantities of chocolate, smoke, tar, and sweet, pruny fruit, with intriguing nuances. Full-bodied, powerful, and rich, with no hard edges, this is a heady, sensationally endowed wine that should drink well between now and 2012! An amazing wine.

1989 Amarone della Valpolicella

RATING: 96 points

Dal Forno Romano's 1989 Amarone is one of the greatest I have ever tasted. The color is a dark, saturated, murky garnet/ruby/charcoal. Incredibly sweet, rich aromas of prunes, chocolate, and overripe black fruits, intermixed with a touch of truffles, cedar, licorice, and spice soar from a glass of this extraordinary wine. Thick and unctuous but dry, this is a spectacularly endowed, multidimensional Amarone that can be drunk now and over the next 18 years. Sadly, only 50 cases were exported to the United States, most of which, I suspect, have been allocated to some of our country's finest Italian restaurants. It should be savored with cheese at the end of a meal.

VALPOLICELLA SUPERIORE

1998 Valpolicella Superiore

RATING: 93 points

The amazing 1998 Valpolicella boasts a saturated ruby/purple color in addition to a beautiful perfume of creosote, plums, prunes, blackberries, and currants with a hint of mineral in the background. It offers astonishing concentration, immense body, fine balance, purity, a stunning flavor profile, and a 50–60-second finish. Anticipated maturity: now–2013.

1997 Valpolicella Superiore

RATING: 93 points

The 1997 Valpolicella's opaque purple color is accompanied by a thick, glycerin-imbued texture with immense concentration, fabulous purity, and copious quantities of smoky, earth-infused blackberry and cherry fruit. This awesome effort must be tasted to be believed. Anticipated maturity: now–2012.

1996 Valpolicella Superiore

RATING: 94 points

This 1996 Valpolicella is amazing. Readers will have to redefine their definition of Valpolicella to understand this blockbuster. The color is a dense purple. The bouquet offers glorious levels of blackberry and cherry fruit intertwined with vanilla, minerals, lead pencil shavings, and spice. The wine is full-bodied and voluptuously textured, with sweet tannin and a seamless finish. It is an enormous yet incredibly symmetrical Valpolicella. It will last for another 12–15 years. Anticipated maturity: now–2018.

1995 Valpolicella Superiore

RATING: 91 points

This 1995 Valpolicella is an amazing effort, with an opaque dark ruby color, as well as an explosive nose of smoke, earth, jammy berry and blackberry fruit, great richness and purity, full body, and abundant glycerin and intensity. Remarkably, there is little evidence of new oak, even though the wine spent 36 months in barrel before being bottled without filtration. It tips the scales at a whopping 14.5% alcohol, high for Valpolicella. Anticipated maturity: now–2015.

1992 Valpolicella Superiore

RATING: 90 points

This 1992 Valpolicella boasts a huge, smoky, sweet, gamey, jammy nose. The wine is fabulously textured, rich, full-bodied, and loaded with extract. Elements of tar and sweet, chocolaty, cedar-like berry fruit cascade over the palate with an unctuous texture and an amazing finish. Readers weaned on the ocean of industrial swill that parades under the name of Valpolicella will have their senses shocked by this wine's complexity and intensity. Anticipated maturity: now–2007.

1988 Valpolicella Superiore

RATING: 91 points

This wine is unquestionably the greatest Valpolicella I have ever tasted. One does not expect a Valpolicella to be this complex, rich, and potentially ageworthy. The nose offers up huge aromas of ripe plums, spices, and sweet cedary scents. Unctuously textured, with lavish quantities of fruit, this medium to full-bodied, velvety-textured wine is undeniably seductive, as well as thoroughly delicious. Although the price seems high for a Valpolicella, this is a great red wine! Anticipated maturity: now–2009.

WINES:

Montiano

Marciliano

OWNERS: Riccardo and Renzo Cotarella

ADDRESS: Località Artigiana Le Guardie, 01027
Montefiascone (VT), Italy

TELEPHONE: 39 0761 825669; 830401; 1825803

TELEFAX: 39 0761 834012

E-MAIL: info@falesco.net

WEBSITE: www.falesco.it

CONTACT: Riccardo Cotarella

VISITING POLICY: Open Monday to Friday, 8 A.M.–1 P.M. and
2–5 P.M. Visitors should contact the winery to arrange
a visit.

VINEYARDS

SURFACE AREA: 750 acres

GRAPE VARIETALS:

Lazio (250 acres): Merlot, Roscetto, Trebbiano, Malvasia,
Aleatico

Umbria (500 acres): Sangiovese, Merlot, Cabernet
Sauvignon, Cabernet Franc

AVERAGE AGE OF THE VINES: 5–25 years

DENSITY OF PLANTATION: Montiano: 2,500 vines per acre;
Marciliano: 3,000 vines per acre

AVERAGE YIELDS: 1.6–2 tons per acre (reds)

WINEMAKING AND UPBRINGING

The vineyards are impeccably maintained under the watchful eye of the Cotarella brothers. Their density of planting continues to increase, with current plantings ranging from 5,000 to 8,000 vines per hectare. They also employ radical viticulture, including shoot positioning and crop thinning by as much as 10–50%, depending on the varietal and the season's growing conditions. Low yields and ripeness are fundamental at Falesco. They are attempting to produce wines rich in structure but also full of character, softness, and elegance. Long maceration at controlled temperatures and techniques such as *délestage* to extract soft tannins are utilized. Both the Montiano and Marciliano are stored in small French casks on their lees and bottled with no fining or filtration at the end of 12–15 months.

ANNUAL PRODUCTION

Montiano: 80,000 bottles

Marciliano: 10,000 bottles

AVERAGE PRICE (VARIABLE DEPENDING ON VINTAGE): $10–50

GREAT RECENT VINTAGES

2001, 2000, 1999, 1995

No one has done more to elevate the quality of wines from Umbria and Lazio than Riccardo and Renzo Cotarella, who established the Falesco winery in 1979. They recognized the historical importance of this viticultural area and the need to participate in the revolution in quality that had taken place in Piedmont and Tuscany. In the past, the wines of Umbria and Lazio were the wines of the Roman aristocracy and the popes, yet by the 1900s they had completely sunk into oblivion. The Cotarellas built a state-of-the-art winery, and their first harvest was

Riccardo and Renzo Cotarella

in 1991. Going against conventional wisdom, they planted the best clones of Merlot available, and in 1993, their famed Montiano was born, a wine of extraordinary richness, concentration, structure, and elegance. Their huge success allowed them to purchase the large Marciliano estate, a hillside vineyard south of Orvieto that has brought another extraordinary baby into the portfolio of Falesco wines: the Marciliano, 100% Cabernet Sauvignon, a wine of remarkable richness and complexity.

While Renzo Cotarella is the chief winemaker for Piero Antinori, it is Riccardo Cotarella who has been the catalyst behind Falesco. Consistently combating the declining quality of commercial modern-day winemak-

ing, Cotarella's battle plan includes (1) fighting for lower yields, (2) harvesting physiologically mature fruit by hand, (3) aging in small *barriques,* and (4) bottling the wines with minimal clarification, frequently with no fining or filtration.

These wines are among the most exciting modern-styled reds of Italy. Riccardo Cotarella remains one of the young geniuses who has revolutionized winemaking in Italy and is the spiritual brother of Michel Rolland in France.

MARCILIANO

2001 Marciliano
RATING: 95 points
An extraordinary blend of 70% Cabernet Sauvignon and 30% Cabernet Franc, the 2001 Marciliano has an inky ruby/purple color and a gorgeous nose of lead pencil shavings followed by a blackberry and currant nose with a hint of mint and smoke. Very expansively flavored, full-bodied, and moderately tannic, yet very layered and rich, this is a superb wine that is made from what are still very young vines. Anticipated maturity: now–2020.

1999 Marciliano
RATING: 94 points
The 1999 is the first vintage of Riccardo Cotarella's newest baby, the Marciliano. Aged 16 months in 100% new French oak and bottled unfined and unfiltered, this 70% Cabernet Sauvignon, 30% Cabernet Franc blend already displays a fab-

ulous, complex fragrance of lavender, mint, crème de cassis, licorice, spice box, and toasty oak. Dense, with great fruit and richness on the attack, extraordinary elegance and precision, and a long, layered finish, it is not as hedonistic as the Montiano, but it is potentially more complex, with greater subtlety and more nuances. Like the Montiano, the Marciliano is a wine of first-growth quality and deserves serious attention. Anticipated maturity: now–2018.

MONTIANO

2001 Montiano
RATING: 95 points
A luxurious, almost decadently rich wine, the deep ruby/purple–colored 2001 Montiano (100% Merlot, like every vintage to date) has an extraordinary nose of espresso roast and sweet kirsch intermixed with some licorice and mocha. The wine is very full-bodied, opulently textured, and just terrific. This has become the great Merlot of southern Italy and is on a par with the finest Merlots made in the world. Anticipated maturity: now–2016.

2000 Montiano
RATING: 94 points
Though Falesco's 2000 Montiano, a 100% *barrique*-aged Merlot, may not equal the quality of the 1999 or 1997, it comes close. The 2000 boasts an opaque purple color in addition to a sumptuous perfume of graphite, blackberries, currants, licorice, and subtle toast notes. With its great depth, full body, sweet tannin, and a long, layered, elegant finish, it should drink well between now and 2020. Bravo!

1999 Montiano

RATING: 95 points

The profound, dense ruby/purple–colored 1999 Montiano (2,500 cases of 100% Merlot aged in 100% new French oak and bottled unfined and unfiltered) offers a smorgasbord of aromas, including melted chocolate, espresso, blackberries, cherries, currants, and smoke. Full-bodied, with terrific purity, a multilayered texture, and surprising freshness for a wine of such depth, it can be drunk young or cellared. For technicians who care about such things, it has a whopping 37 grams per liter of dry extract. Anticipated maturity: now–2020.

1998 Montiano

RATING: 94 points

The terrific opaque purple–colored 1998 Montiano exhibits a spectacular bouquet of black cherry liqueur, licorice, and toasty vanilla. The wine explodes on the palate, offering copious quantities of glycerin, cassis, black cherries, and blackberries. As it sits in the glass, aromas and flavors of melted chocolate and toasty oak emerge. The finish lasts for 40+ seconds. Anticipated maturity: now–2016.

1997 Montiano

RATING: 95 points

The 1997 Montiano (100% Merlot, bottled unfined and unfiltered after spending 12 months in new French oak) is fabulous. It displays multiple layers that build in the mouth, exploding at the back of the palate. From its opaque purple color, the huge sweet notes of chocolate, smoke, black fruits, and toast satiate the olfactory senses yet please the mind's intellectual yearnings. Pure and powerful, yet brilliantly knit together with no hard edges and no sense of high alcohol or heaviness, this sensational wine is one of the finest Merlots made in Italy. Production was 1,000 cases. Anticipated maturity: now–2014.

1996 Montiano

RATING: 93 points

The 1996 Montiano was bottled unfined and unfiltered after aging in French oak casks. Sadly, only 500 cases were produced. It boasts an opaque purple color, followed by a knockout nose of blackberry liqueur intermingled with smoke, toast, and chocolate. Full-bodied and thick with a voluptuous texture, layered richness, superb purity, and a finish that lasts more than 30 seconds, this is a profoundly concentrated, complex Merlot to drink now. Anticipated maturity: now–2012.

1995 Montiano

RATING: 95 points

The 1995 Montiano (1,000 cases produced) is stunning. Made from 100% Merlot from vineyards planted on the hillsides of Lazio (at a relatively high altitude of 980 feet), this unfined/unfiltered, profoundly rich red wine is a knockout. The color is a saturated purple, and the nose offers up glorious aromas of smoked meats, cassis, chocolate, and vanilla. Spectacular richness, combined with beautifully integrated acidity, tannin, and wood, make for an opulently textured, multilayered, stunningly proportioned wine of exceptional purity and richness. With marvelous intensity but no sense of heaviness, this fabulous wine provides a strong case for the potential that exists in southern Italy. Anticipated maturity: now–2010.

1994 Montiano

RATING: 93 points

Two wines of which Cotarella is especially proud are the 1993 and 1994 Montiano (1,200 cases each), made from a tiny 10-acre Umbrian vineyard that produces about 2,000 bottles per acre (that is a small yield!). The impressive 1994 Montiano is even richer than the 1993. The opaque purple color is followed by sexy, smoky, toasty new oak aromas, a ripe, concentrated, black fruit character (black currants and cherries), formidable flavor intensity and extract, medium to full body, great purity, and a layered yet structured, rich finish. This is a compelling wine! Anticipated maturity: now–2010.

1993 Montiano

RATING: 90 points

1993 was the debut vintage of this 80% Merlot, 20% Cabernet Sauvignon blend that was aged in 100% new French oak and bottled with no clarification. It exhibits a saturated deep purple color, an intense, smoky, spicy, vanilla and cassis–scented nose, rich, elegant, authoritatively powerful flavors, good backbone and structure, and a long finish. Although young and unevolved, it is a very promising wine of first-growth quality. Anticipated maturity: now–2008.

WINES:

Barbaresco

Sorì San Lorenzo

Sorì Tildin

Costa Russi

Sperss

Conteisa

OWNER: Angelo Gaja

ADDRESS: Via Torino 36, 12050 Barbaresco (CN), Italy

TELEPHONE: 39 0173 635158

TELEFAX: 39 0173 635256

E-MAIL: gajad@tin.it

CONTACT: Stefano Bariani or Marco Rabellino

VISITING POLICY: Wine professionals only, by appointment

VINEYARDS

SURFACE AREA: 250 acres

GRAPE VARIETALS: Nebbiolo d'Alba, Barbera d'Alba, Chardonnay, Sauvignon Blanc, Cabernet Sauvignon

AVERAGE AGE OF THE VINES: 20 years

DENSITY OF PLANTATION: 1,120–2,200 vines per acre

AVERAGE YIELDS: 1.8 tons per acre

WINEMAKING AND UPBRINGING

Angelo Gaja is hardly a modernist in terms of his winemaking, as he doesn't do short fermentations nor does he use concentrators or rotofermenters. He does use a lot of new barrels, but his vinifications are classic, with an initial relatively warm fermentation at 30°C, then plenty of pumpovers, and then a drop of the temperatures in the fermenters down to 22°C for around 7–10 days, at which time pumping-over also stops. The wine is then left to sit in a postfermentation maceration period for another week, making the total skin-must contact time around three weeks.

The wine is aged in *barriques* for 12 months, followed by an additional 12 months of aging in large oak casks. The wines are then bottle-aged for one to two years before being released.

ANNUAL PRODUCTION

Barbaresco: 60,000 bottles

Sorì San Lorenzo: 12,000 bottles

Sorì Tildin: 12,000 bottles

Costa Russi: 12,000 bottles

Sperss: 32,000 bottles

Conteisa: 18,000 bottles

AVERAGE PRICE (VARIABLE DEPENDING ON VINTAGE): $50–350

GREAT RECENT VINTAGES

2001, 2000, 1998, 1997, 1996, 1990, 1989, 1985, 1982, 1978, 1971

The French writer Honoré de Balzac said something that is very much apropos of Angelo Gaja: "The genius resembles everyone, and no one resembles him." There are aspects of Angelo Gaja that often remind me of modern art: his impeccably rigid lines, his staccato speech, his hell-bent, frenetic pace. He represents the fifth generation of Gajas to run the family firm, located in the village of Barbaresco. He has long been an advocate of improved wine quality in Italy, and many even consider the quality revolution that started in Italy three decades ago to be largely a result of Gaja's quest for worldwide respectability and recognition of the brilliance of his wines. For many years he has been one of the most admired winemakers and successful businessmen in Italy, and he merits all the accolades. In short, he got to the top the hardest way of all—he earned it!

One of the first to recognize that production levels in the vineyards had to be cut in order to improve quality, Gaja began cutting yields in the early 1960s, going against time-honored traditions and the general philos-

Angelo Gaja

ophy that more is better. He was among the first to employ radical viticultural and vinification techniques that are now considered commonplace in the wine world. Long before it became accepted doctrine, he began buying wood from Central European forests, aging his wood three years before having the barrels constructed to his specifications, and aging the wines not in large oak ovals, or what the French call *foudres,* but in smaller *barriques*. He also began, in 1971, to isolate his finest parcels of Nebbiolo in the Barbaresco zone and began his single-vineyard offerings, known as Sorì San Lorenzo and Sorì Tildin, later adding Costa Russi. Gaja was also the first to plant non-Piedmontese varietals in Italy, first planting Cabernet Sauvignon in 1978 and calling it "Darmagi," which in the local dialect means "What a pity," which is exactly what his father said to him when he told him what his intentions were.

Gaja was probably the first wine producer in Italy to believe that his finest wines could not only sit on the table with the greatest produced in France but could actually eclipse them. Because of that, he raised his prices to reflect the quality of what he produced, recognizing that for his top wines (Sorì Tildin and Sorì San Lorenzo) in the early 1970s, he had only 4,000 to 5,000 bottles to sell. The exceptional quality of his wines and the fact that he earned Piedmont a spot on the world's most prestigious dining tables and cellars inspired a new generation of winemakers, not only in Piedmont but throughout Italy. His influence is unprecedented, and with his fanatical commitment to quality, he continues to be a reference point for many young growers who have just begun to estate-bottle their wines.

Gaja is a revolutionary, never content with the status quo. In the late 1990s, he decided to drop the appellations of Barbaresco and Barolo from the label of his finest wines, simply naming them after the vineyard sites. This gave him the option of adding a bit of Barbera to his famed crus of Sorì San Lorenzo, Sorì Tildin, Costa Russi, and his two crus in Barolo, Sperss and Conteisa. The blending was a nod to the history of old Piedmont and allowed him, as he said, to actually make better wines, but it was a controversial move that was widely criticized.

There are cynics who claim that Gaja is simply a brilliant marketer, a huckster in designer Italian clothes, but they fail to recognize the greatness of his wines and the fact that despite all the invitations by other multinational companies to bring Gaja in as a limited partner in some joint venture in California, South Africa, South America, or elsewhere, he has always said no. He recognizes that his greatest achievements must remain in Italy, at his beloved estates in Piedmont and of course his newer vineyards in Montalcino and Bolgheri. Why is it my impression that, at age 65, Angelo Gaja is just getting started?

Readers should note that these wines are not entitled to an appellation other than Langhe, which is the general regional appellation. For example, the Sorì San Lorenzo, Sorì Tildin, and Costa Russi are essentially Barbaresco wines, which means they are 95–96% Nebbiolo with 4–5% Barbera added. The Sperss and the Conteisa are 94–96% Barolo (Nebbiolo) with about 4–6% Barbera as well.

BARBARESCO

2000 Barbaresco
RATING: 90 points
Quite ripe, with relatively high extraction, sweet earth intermixed with tobacco, red cherry, and a hint of dried herb and anise, this is a full-bodied wine that is quite good but seems to lack a bit of complexity for a Gaja Barbaresco. Drink it during its first 10–15 years of life.

1999 Barbaresco
RATING: 90 points
A very elegant wine with more noticeable acidity than its counterpart in 2000, Gaja's 1999 Barbaresco has a big, sweet nose of minerals, tobacco, flowers, and smoky oak, as well as a sweet mid-palate, but crisp acids give a certain austerity to the tannins in the finish. Anticipated maturity: 2007–2017.

1998 Barbaresco
RATING: 91 points
The 1998 Barbaresco is a beautiful effort displaying fleshy, oaky, deep black cherry, raspberry, tar, and truffle scents with subtle new oak in the background. Dense, voluptuously textured, and full-bodied, with gorgeous overall symmetry and beautifully integrated tannin, acidity, alcohol, and wood, it will drink well for another 12 years or more.

1997 Barbaresco
RATING: 94 points
Gaja's 1997 Barbaresco is undoubtedly the finest he has yet made. An exquisite effort, it boasts a dense ruby/purple color in addition to an extraordinary nose of black cherry liqueur, smoke, licorice, mineral, and floral aromas. The wine is full-

bodied, opulent, and loaded with fruit. It should age effortlessly for another 20 years.

1996 Barbaresco

RATING: 91 points

The 1996 Barbaresco exhibits a dense ruby color as well as a forward nose of cherry liqueur, earth, truffle, mineral, and spicy scents. Rich, full-bodied, and seductive, with its moderate tannin largely concealed by the wine's wealth of fruit and extract, this gorgeously pure offering gets my nod as the finest Barbaresco produced by Gaja since 1990. Anticipated maturity: now–2016.

1995 Barbaresco

RATING: 90 points

1995 tended to be a good rather than great vintage in Piedmont, but Gaja's sensational 1995s are among the stars of the vintage. This wine possesses extremely saturated dark ruby/purple colors, almost atypical for Nebbiolo. The 1995 Barbaresco offers a superb nose of licorice, cherry fruit, strawberries, flowers, and toasty scents. Ripe, dense, and lush, with an alluring, sexy personality, it is one of the more forward, generic Barbarescos Gaja has produced. Anticipated maturity: now–2011.

1990 Barbaresco

RATING: 93 points

I do not think Angelo Gaja has made a better *cuvée* of his classic Barbaresco (there's nothing "regular" about either the price or the quality!) than the 1990. From its deep, saturated, dark ruby color to its big, spicy, roasted nose of red and black fruits, nuts, and cedar, this huge, massive, super-concentrated wine exhibits layers of flavors. Although tannin is present, it is sweet, giving the wine a precocious, approachable style. It is a blockbuster Barbaresco for drinking over the next 5–10 years.

1989 Barbaresco

RATING: 91 points

Gaja's 1989 Barbaresco offers sweet, rich, tobacco, black cherry, and spicy fruit touched gently by new oak. It is made in a full-bodied, powerful style, with admirable depth. Approachable now, this wine should continue to improve. Anticipated maturity: now–2014.

CONTEISA

2000 Conteisa

RATING: 92 points

Notes of mint, licorice, red currant, cherry, and earth are present in this dark ruby/plum–colored wine. As the wine sits in the glass, some hints of fig, tobacco leaf, and grilled meats and herbs are also present. It has a slightly cooler climate character

than the Sperss but is medium to full–bodied with firm tannin and a long finish. Anticipated maturity: 2007–2020+.

1999 Conteisa

RATING: 91 points

Some mint, anise, and dried herbs intermixed with plum, fig, and red currants are present in this very tannic, backward, structured wine that finishes with a rather elevated level of austere tannins. The concentration and depth are there, but the wine is nearly impenetrable and broodingly backward. Anticipated maturity: 2010–2025.

1998 Conteisa

RATING: 92 points

From the Barolo appellation, the 1998 Conteisa displays a distinctive bouquet of black cherry jam mixed with vitamins, smoke, iron, minerals, and spicy oak. In the mouth, earth, truffle, lead pencil, and espresso-infused cherry flavors make an appearance. Deep, rich, and full-bodied, with moderate tannin and power, this impressive offering should age well for two decades.

1997 Conteisa

RATING: 98 points

The 1997 Conteisa offers classic aromas of licorice, melted tar, black cherries, wet stones, and tobacco. It is a full-bodied, unctuously textured wine of remarkable density and thickness. The tannin is high but sweet. This brawny offering cuts an immense swath across the palate, but there are no hard edges and all the component parts are pure and well integrated. There are 15,000 bottles of this spectacular wine. Anticipated maturity: now–2030.

1996 Conteisa

RATING: 93–95 points

The opaque purple–colored 1996 Barolo Conteisa reveals a sweet, ripe nose with an element of *sur-maturité* given its over-ripe cassis, melted road tar, licorice, and spice–scented bouquet. It exhibits a voluptuous texture, layers of concentrated fruit, and full body. Its tannin is largely concealed by the wine's glycerin, alcohol, and extract. Anticipated maturity: now–2020.

COSTA RUSSI

2000 Costa Russi

RATING: 91 points

I always detect something Zinfandel-like when I taste this wine, and the 2000 seems to show plenty of expressive notes intermixed with white chocolate, raspberry, briary fruit with a hint of smoked herbs. Dry tannins and medium to full–

bodied, relatively plump and fleshy notes make this a wine to drink over the next 12–15 years.

1999 Costa Russi

RATING: 92 points

A very vibrant, fragrant nose of Valrhona chocolate intermixed with sweet cherry and smoky berry notes, dried herbs, and crushed rocks jumps from the glass of this medium to full–bodied, firmly tannic, slightly crisp and acidic style of Nebbiolo. The wine is well delineated and very spicy, but a bit austere and backward. Anticipated maturity: 2008–2020.

1998 Costa Russi

RATING: 92 points

The dark ruby/purple–colored, supple-textured 1998 Costa Russi possesses sweet, jammy raspberry and cherry fruit, medium to full body, gorgeous glycerin, low acidity, and a lightly tannic finish. Although large-sized, it has good finesse as well as beautifully pure fruit. Anticipated maturity: now–2020.

1997 Costa Russi

RATING: 96 points

The opaque ruby/purple colored 1997 Costa Russi (10,000 bottles produced) displays a striking bouquet of blackberry and cherry fruit intermixed with espresso and wood scents. Typically the most internationally styled Gaja offering, the 1997 comes across as a Nebbiolo on steroids. Full-bodied, gorgeously pure and symmetrical, it should be at its best between now and 2025.

1996 Costa Russi

RATING: 93 points

The 1996 Costa Russi reminds me of how a great Zinfandel or a great red Burgundy would taste if made by Angelo Gaja. A seductive nose of black raspberries, violets, licorice, and toast is followed by a rich wine with pure black fruit flavors intertwined with sweet, smoky oak. Full-bodied, with ripe tannin, this internationally styled, stunningly proportioned, big, compelling 1996 will be at its peak between now and 2023.

1995 Costa Russi

RATING: 90 points

The 1995 Barbaresco Costa Russi is a full-bodied, fruit-driven, powerful wine. It possesses copious quantities of black raspberry and cherry fruit, as well as toasty new oak. There is even an element of *sur-maturité* in this large-scaled, expansively flavored effort. I would not be surprised to see it age well for another 15–20 years. Anticipated maturity: now–2020+.

1990 Costa Russi

RATING: 94 points

I always find the Costa Russi to be the most New World–like of Gaja's Barbarescos, often resembling a hypothetical blend of a great California Zinfandel and a stunning French, small new oak–aged Châteauneuf du Pape. The 1990 Costa Russi displays the telltale Nebbiolo character in its thick, rich, jammy, black cherry–scented nose, complemented by wonderfully fragrant aromas of grilled vegetables and sweet vanilla from new oak. Deep and full-bodied, with chewy, unctuous, concentrated flavors, this is another awesome Barbaresco. It will last for another 10–15 years.

1989 Costa Russi

RATING: 90 points

Gaja's three 1989 single-vineyard Barbarescos include the Costa Russi, the most monolithic and New World–like wine of the trio. The deep ruby/purple color is followed by scents of new oak. There is less of a Nebbiolo character than I would like to see. One has to admire the wine's terrific concentration and overall sense of balance, but I found it interesting that in several tastings, lovers of Nebbiolo (including me) thought it to be the least impressive of these Barbarescos. Those who tend to like a more international style preferred it. Nevertheless, it is a superb wine for drinking between now and 2009.

1988 Costa Russi

RATING: 90 points

The full-bodied 1988 Costa Russi reveals a purple tinge to its color, as well as a straightforward, rich nose of black fruits and new oak. It is more monolithic than the other single-vineyard Barbarescos. All of Gaja's 1988 Barbarescos are backward, reserved wines. Even after sitting four days with the corks pulled, they exhibited no signs of oxidation. While they should be uncommonly long-lived, I did not see quite the flesh and richness possessed by such vintages as 1985 and 1982. Anticipated maturity: now–2012.

SORI SAN LORENZO

2000 Sorì San Lorenzo

RATING: 94 points

Notes of roasted nuts and balsamic vinegar interwoven with allspice, cedar, tobacco, clove, black cherries, and currants jump from the glass of this very seriously endowed, more structured, and gritty 2000. Medium to full–bodied, ripe, but quite tannic, this is a big wine that is showing a dense ruby color and plenty of sweetness but a bit more backward style than the Sorì Tildin. Anticipated maturity: 2009–2023.

1999 Sorì San Lorenzo

RATING: 93+ points

Notes of licorice, violets, plums, clove, spice box, and roasted herbs are present in this full-bodied wine that is quite powerfully structured, well built, muscular, and dense, with relatively high acidity and very noticeable tannin. Anticipated maturity: now–2022.

1998 Sorì San Lorenzo

RATING: 96 points

The multifaceted 1998 Sorì San Lorenzo offers up notes of lead pencil, smoke, tobacco, tar, rose petals, black fruits, and espresso. Already incredibly expressive, soft, sexy, and voluptuous, jammy fruits infused with toasty oak cascade over the palate. This easily understood, seamless, pure, classic 1998 should drink well for another 20 years.

1997 Sorì San Lorenzo

RATING: 98 points

Profound, the 1997 Sorì San Lorenzo is an elegant, nuanced, and complex Gaja offering. It exhibits a striking perfume of lead pencil, roasted nuts, black fruits, spice box, leather, cedar, and Chinese black tea. Forward yet enormously constituted and rich, with an ethereal elegance underpinning its personality, the Sorì Lorenzo displays a classic combination of power and finesse. Sadly, there are only 10,000 bottles. As this wine sat in the glass, notes of Japanese soy sauce made an appearance. Anticipated maturity: now–2030.

1996 Sorì San Lorenzo

RATING: 96 points

The dense opaque purple 1996 Sorì San Lorenzo possesses complex aromatics, consisting of classic Nebbiolo scents of rose petals, dried herbs, spice box, cedar, and abundant jammy black cherry and berry fruit. It is impressively powerful and muscular, with moderate tannin, a sweet, unctuous texture, and a 40+-second finish. Although the aromatics are stunning, this 1996 remains youthful and backward. Anticipated maturity: now–2025.

1995 Sorì San Lorenzo

RATING: 91 points

The 1995 Barbaresco Sorì San Lorenzo possesses extremely saturated dark ruby/purple colors, almost atypical for Nebbiolo. It offers telltale cigar tobacco, spice box, and cedar with black currant and cherry fruit in the background. The new oak plays a subtle role. Structured and noticeably tannic, this is a dense wine with surprising levels of glycerin, a saturated plum color, and intriguing flavors of black fruits, soy, and cedar. Anticipated maturity: now–2016.

1990 Sorì San Lorenzo

RATING: 95 points

Of Gaja's three single-vineyard Barbarescos, the most compelling is the Sorì San Lorenzo. The 1990 is a massive wine with a staggering yet unevolved nose of herbs, hickory, smoked meats, cedar, and red and black fruits. Spectacularly concentrated, with layers of flavor, this dense, blockbuster wine should be drunk through the first two or more decades of the 21st century.

1989 Sorì San Lorenzo

RATING: 96 points

The 1989 Sorì San Lorenzo is a monument to the Nebbiolo grape, as well as to Barbaresco. It is one of the most concentrated wines I have tasted from this vineyard. There is sweetness and unctuousness to the fruit that I did not detect in either the great 1985 or the 1982. Still tannic, backward, and unevolved, this huge, rich, spice, tobacco, and black cherry–scented wine is massive on the palate. It should be at its best between now and 2015. It is a remarkable winemaking effort!

1988 Sorì San Lorenzo

Of the three single-vineyard Barbarescos, the most aromatic and complex is the 1988 Sorì San Lorenzo. This intense wine offers up a bouquet of spices, vanilla, herbs, cedar, and red and black fruits. Though it is perfumed, the tannins once again dominate. There is freshness, full body, and plenty of length. Anticipated maturity: now–2014.

SORI TILDIN

2000 Sorì Tildin
RATING: 95 points

A very opulent, succulent style that shows the rather precocious character of this vintage, this deep ruby–colored wine has nearly overripe aromas of black raspberries, dates, plums, and currants, with a hint of truffle, smoke, and earth. A very fleshy, full-bodied wine with decent acidity, tremendous intensity of flavor, and a long finish with well-integrated tannins, it is uncommonly precocious and showy for a young Gaja Sorì Tildin. Anticipated maturity: now–2020.

1999 Sorì Tildin
RATING: 96 points

An extraordinary nose of roasted meats, smoked duck, soy, black currant, cherry, and truffle seems to have everything going for it in the extraordinarily perfumed aromatics of this wine. Very full-bodied, dense, concentrated flavors coat the palate with considerable extract and tannin. This is a beauty that shows tremendous intensity, definition, and length, and is certainly one of the candidates for the best Piedmontese wine of the vintage. Anticipated maturity: 2008–2025.

1998 Sorì Tildin
RATING: 95 points

Chocolate, coffee, smoke, licorice, and tobacco characteristics are found in the complex, deep purple–colored 1998 Sorì Tildin. Surprisingly seductive for such a young wine, it exhibits abundant aromatic fireworks, fabulous fruit concentration, a layered opulence, more intensity, glycerin, and depth than the Costa Russi, and a spectacularly long finish. Anticipated maturity: now–2025.

1997 Sorì Tildin
RATING: 99 points

The awesome 1997 Sorì Tildin (10,000 bottles produced) is a candidate for perfection. The saturated purple color is followed by a dense, full-bodied wine possessing extraordinary vibrancy for such a heavyweight, muscular Nebbiolo. It offers a supersweet entry, a boatload of glycerin, and notes of earth, licorice, cedar, blackberry and cherry liqueur, and a touch of blueberries. Extremely full, and gorgeously pure, with a seamless texture, this spectacular 1997 will enjoy three decades of cellaring.

1996 Sorì Tildin
RATING: 96 points

It is hard to argue with those who claim that the finest of Gaja's single-vineyard offerings is always the Sorì Tildin. The 1996 Sorì Tildin reveals a pigmented/saturated ruby/purple color in addition to a tight nose, with aromas of blackberries, cherry liqueur, smoke, licorice, incense, and spice box. Enormous on the palate, with multiple layers of fruit, soft tannin, huge body, and a knockout finish, it is backward and brawny. Anticipated maturity: now–2030.

1995 Sorì Tildin
RATING: 91 points

1995 tended to be a good rather than great vintage in Piedmont, but Gaja's sensational 1995s are among the stars of the vintage. This wine possesses extremely saturated dark ruby/purple colors, almost atypical for Nebbiolo. The 1995 Barbaresco Sorì Tilden reveals a liqueurlike viscosity to its richness. It offers spicy black raspberry fruit in addition to melted asphalt, smoke, truffle, and toast. This complex, expansive Barbaresco is deeply colored for the vintage, with superb richness, full body, and beautifully integrated acidity, tannin, and alcohol. Anticipated maturity: now–2020+.

1990 Sorì Tildin
RATING: 97 points

The most massive of Gaja's Barbarescos is the huge, thick, smoky 1990 Sorì Tildin. This enormously rich, profound wine is full-bodied and magnificently concentrated with admirable underlying acidity, and plenty of tannin. The finish lasts for more than a minute. Drink it over the next 25 years.

1989 Sorì Tildin
RATING: 96 points

The 1989 Sorì Tildin is a monument to the Nebbiolo grape, as well as to Barbaresco. Not surprisingly, it is the most backward, tannic, muscular, and masculine of the Gaja Barbarescos. With tons of tannin and a broad, rich, fleshy, expansive personality, it is the least flattering. It should last until 2020.

1988 Sorì Tildin
RATING: 94 points

My favorite of Gaja's 1988 Barbarescos is the Sorì Tildin. This compelling wine exhibits sweet scents of tobacco, black fruits, coffee, and herbs. There is more body, richness, and weight than in the other Barbarescos, as well as a rich, long, tannic finish. The wine will last for another two decades.

SPERSS

2000 Sperss
RATING: 95 points

A brilliant wine that shows this gorgeous vineyard's potential in Serralunga, the classic nose of road tar intermixed with rose water, sweet, smoky oak, black currants, and raspberries as well as truffle and licorice is present in a beautiful, aromatic display. It is quite full-bodied and broad, with high tannin but also equally high extract and richness, decent acidity, and a fleshy, full-bodied finish. Anticipated maturity: now–2035.

1999 Sperss

RATING: 93 points

Tar, sweet new saddle leather, white flowers, underbrush, black cherries, and a hint of white chocolate are present in this very powerful young Barolo that is expansive, rich, and full-bodied, with enormous potential. Anticipated maturity: 2010–2030.

1998 Sperss

RATING: 94 points

The 1998 Sperss reveals a perfume of black fruits, truffles, earth, and spice box. Dense and massive yet seamless, this beautifully integrated wine possesses low acidity as well as a terrific finish. Although evolved and delicious for such a youthful Barolo, it will age well for another 20 years.

1997 Sperss

RATING: 99 points

A virtually perfect effort is the 1997 Sperss (30,000 bottles), which represents the essence of truffles, earth, and black cherries in its striking aromatics and multidimensional, opulent, full-bodied palate. The acidity seems low because of the huge glycerin levels and prodigious concentration of fruit, but I suspect it is normal in the scheme of oenological measurement. Anticipated maturity: 2009–2035.

1996 Sperss

RATING: 96 points

The spectacular 1996 Sperss boasts an opaque ruby/purple color in addition to enormously ripe black cherries, tar, flowers, and white truffles. Extremely full-bodied, with compelling intensity and purity, this is a large-scaled, massive Barolo with plenty of tannin, and 2–3 decades of ageability. Anticipated maturity: now–2030.

1990 Sperss

RATING: 95 points

Gaja's 1990 Sperss is even richer, fuller, and deeper than the spectacular 1989 and outstanding 1988. The 1990 exhibits Gaja's signature in its extraordinary purity of flavor and layered richness, full body, and moderately tannic finish. It offers a huge, classic Barolo nose of roses, black fruits, smoke, and a whiff of tar. Dense and large-scaled, as well as stylish and graceful, this immensely impressive wine is supple enough to be drunk, but it is also capable of lasting another 15–20 years.

1989 Sperss

RATING: 93 points

The 1989 Sperss gives the impression of being more evolved, softer, and fatter than the single-vineyard Barbarescos. Although there appears to be more depth of fruit and the nose is more expressive, sweeter, and flamboyant, a thorough examination of the wine reveals considerable tannin. Nevertheless, the rich, ripe, broad, expansive fruit; full-bodied, chewy texture; and soft acids make for a decadently rich, complex, compelling bottle of Barolo. Drink it between now and 2012.

1988 Sperss

RATING: 92 points

The 1988 Sperss exhibits a deep color, tremendous extraction of fruit, and soft acids and tannins. It is a backward, unevolved, potentially exceptional wine. Tightly packed, full-bodied, and muscular, its wonderful tar, rose, and black cherry–scented nose is just beginning to emerge. Drink it between now and 2010.

GALARDI (TERRA DI LAVORO)

WINE: Terra di Lavoro

OWNER: Galardi SRL (Dora Catello, Francesco Catello, Maria Luisa Murena)

ADDRESS: S. P. Sessa-Mignano, Località Vallemarina, 81030 S. Carlo di Sessa Aurunca (CE), Italy

TELEPHONE: 39 0823 925003

TELEFAX: 39 0823 925003

E-MAIL: galardi@napoli.com

CONTACT: Arturo Celentano

VISITING POLICY: By appointment only

VINEYARDS

SURFACE AREA: 27 acres

GRAPE VARIETALS: 80% Aglianico, 20% Piedirosso

AVERAGE AGE OF THE VINES: 12 years

DENSITY OF PLANTATION: 4,500 vines per hectare

AVERAGE YIELDS: 50–60 quintals per hectare

WINEMAKING AND UPBRINGING

Since 1991, Riccardo Cotarella has been Galardi's winemaker. This is another treasure of a small vineyard where radical viticulture is practiced and almost excessive attention is paid to every detail of viticulture, vinification, and bottling. The primary fermentation takes place for up to two weeks in temperature-controlled steel tanks, followed by a malolactic fermentation in tanks for about two months. At that point the wine is moved into French oak barrels, of which about 80% are new, for 10–12 months. Bottled unfiltered, the wine is aged another 10 months prior to being released.

ANNUAL PRODUCTION

Terra di Lavoro IGT Roccamonfina: 10,000 bottles

AVERAGE PRICE (VARIABLE DEPENDING ON VINTAGE): $35–100

GREAT RECENT VINTAGES

2001, 2000, 1999, 1995, 1994

This remarkable operation in southern Italy owes its nobility to indigenous grapes, Aglianico and Piedirosso, planted on hillsides just outside Naples. In essence, Galardi renewed an ancient tradition of working with local varietals. A syndicate of owners had the foresight to bring in the brilliant Umbrian oenologist and winemaker Riccardo Cotarella, and then this wine just exploded onto the international scene, confirming the enormous potential Aglianico and Piedirosso have in this gorgeous windswept area dotted with vineyards, and chestnut and olive trees.

2001 Terra di Lavoro

RATING: 99 points

Inky blue/purple in color, with an extraordinary nose of creosote, blackberry liqueur, singed leather, and scorched earth, this full-bodied wine has fabulously sweet tannin and a magnificent mid-palate and finish, with layers of fruit. There is almost something wild about the flavor profile, but it is sophisticated, mouth-filling, and just a prodigious wine. When it is exposed to air, notes of truffles, seaweed, and additional blackberry and cassis fruit jump from the glass. This is an ethereal wine that can be drunk now or cellared for up to 20 years.

2000 Terra di Lavoro

RATING: 98 points

The 2000 Terra di Lavoro is the finest effort yet produced by Galardi. Aged 12 months in 100% new French oak and bottled unfined and unfiltered, it boasts an opaque purple color as well as a gorgeous bouquet of scorched earth, balsamic vinegar, blackberries, blueberries, tobacco, and sweet new saddle leather. It is full-bodied, with huge amounts of spice, a voluptuous texture, and a silky, 50-second finish. Despite the 100% oak aging, the wood note is only a minor nuance in the aromas and flavors. This prodigious Italian red will be at its finest between now and 2015.

1999 Terra di Lavoro

RATING: 96 points

Sadly, there are only 200+ cases of this offering from Galardi's vineyard. Some past vintages have been too rustic (no doubt due to the indigenous grapes used in the blend), but in 1999, the blend of 80% Aglianico and 20% Piedirosso resulted in a wine with sweet tannin as well as an extraordinary earthy, graphite character that undoubtedly is due to the vineyard's decomposed volcanic soils. The color is an opaque black/purple. The bouquet offers up scents of concentrated black cherries as well as blackberries intermixed with leather, licorice, lead pencil shavings, and new oak. An unfined, unfiltered effort aged for 12 months in new French oak, this spectacular 1999 is the most harmonious and complete Terra di Lavoro to date. This is compelling juice! Anticipated maturity: now–2018.

1998 Terra di Lavoro

RATING: 96 points

A 200+-case blend of 80% Aglianico and 20% Piedirosso, aged for 12 months in new French oak and bottled with neither fining nor filtering, this profoundly complex, black/purple-colored effort boasts wild blackberry/blueberry and mineral scents intertwined with smoke, tobacco, and licorice aromas. The flavors mirror the bouquet. Displaying a wealth of fruit, glycerin, concentration, and body, it is a massive, huge effort with sweet tannin, low acidity, and a spectacular 45+-second finish. This amazing offering is more civilized and less funky than some previous vintages, which have been stunning but clearly individualistic and rustic. Look for the 1998 to drink well for another 11+ years.

1997 Terra di Lavoro

RATING: 95 points

Wouldn't you know, there are only 50 cases of this beauty for the United States—one case per state. Let's hope it serves as a beacon for other Campania producers. Made from 80% Aglianico and 20% Piedirosso, the 1997 Terra di Lavoro was bottled unfined and unfiltered after 12 months in 100% new oak. Not surprisingly, it displays all the earmarks of a Riccardo Cotarella–crafted wine. A monster, with extraordinary intensity and richness, its black/purple color, and knockout aromas of tar, jammy black raspberries, licorice, truffles, and smoke are intoxicating. It is fabulously concentrated, with terrific glycerin, multiple layers of flavor, and a blockbuster, pure finish that lasts for more than 40 seconds. For the lucky few who are able to find a bottle, it will be absolutely amazing! Anticipated maturity: now–2020.

TERRA DI LAVORO

1999

RED WINE ROCCAMONFINA
Indicazione Geografica Tipica

Produced and bottled by Galardi s.r.l.
Sessa Aurunca - Caserta - Italia

IMPORTED BY WINEBOW, INC.,
NEW YORK, NY

750 ml. ℮   PRODUCT OF ITALY   ALC.13% BY VOL.

WINES:

Barbaresco Gallina

Barbaresco Santo Stefano

Barbaresco Asili

Barbaresco Rabajà

Barolo Falletto

Barolo Le Rocche del Falletto

Barolo Rionda di Serralunga (no longer produced)

OWNER: Famiglia Giacosa

ADDRESS: Via XX Settembre 52, 12057 Neive (CN), Italy

TELEPHONE: 39 0173 67027

TELEFAX: 39 0173 677477

E-MAIL: brunogiacosa@brunogiacosa.it

WEBSITE: www.brunogiacosa.it

CONTACT: Bruna Giacosa

VISITING POLICY: Monday to Friday, 8 A.M.–noon and
2–6 P.M., with notice

VINEYARDS

SURFACE AREA: 44.7 acres

GRAPE VARIETALS: Nebbiolo d'Alba, Barbera d'Alba, Dolcetto
d'Alba

AVERAGE AGE OF THE VINES: 15 years

DENSITY OF PLANTATION: 4,500–5,000 vines per hectare

AVERAGE YIELDS: 48 hectoliters per hectare

WINEMAKING AND UPBRINGING

Bruno Giacosa states, "Traditionalist philosophy for us means making wines that strongly convey the varietal properties of a native vine and its *terroir*. We always produce single-variety wines. Techniques have improved, and we take advantage of soft pressing and crushing, rational pumping-over systems, as well as optimized cold and hot technology." Certain traditional rules remain frozen in time in these hallowed cellars—prolonged maceration on the skins, followed by aging of the red wines in large oak casks. Giacosa believes that technology and tradition do not need to be at odds with each other. The red wines ferment in steel and are kept in wood for 3–4 months (Dolcetto), 6–12 months (Barbera d'Alba and Nebbiolo d'Alba), 18–30 months (Barbaresco), or 24–36 months (Barolo). They are then bottled without being filtered.

ANNUAL PRODUCTION

Barbaresco Gallina: 8,000–10,000 bottles

Barbaresco Santo Stefano: 10,000–14,000 bottles

Barbaresco Asili: 10,000–14,000 bottles

Barbaresco Rabajà: 6,000–8,000 bottles

Barolo Falletto: 15,000–20,000 bottles

Barolo Le Rocche del Falletto: 10,000–15,000 bottles

AVERAGE PRICE (VARIABLE DEPENDING ON VINTAGE): $75–170

GREAT RECENT VINTAGES

2001, 2000, 1998, 1997, 1996, 1990, 1989, 1985, 1982, 1978, 1971, 1967, 1964, 1961

There are some mysteries surrounding wine that cannot be explained even though I, as much as anyone, would prefer a logical explanation. Bruno Giacosa's consistent brilliance might well be considered illogical given the fact that until recently most of his wines were made from grapes purchased from other people's vineyards. I have been buying and drinking Bruno Giacosa's wines for close to 30 years, and they can often be relatively closed and uninspiring immediately after bottling, yet after 10 years of cellaring, their magic is irrefutable. I have seen this happen in Giacosa's greatest vintages, 1964, 1971, 1978, 1982, 1985, and 1988, as well as what was for him the extraordinary decade of the 1990s—1990, 1996, 1997, 1998, 1999—and of course the vintage that marked the new millennium, 2000.

Bruno Giacosa

Bruno Giacosa, a tall, handsome man with a stoic mien that recalls both Gary Cooper and Jimmy Stewart, has worked in the vineyards of Piedmont since 1944, when his father pulled him out of his school because Allied forces were bombing the area. In his mid-70s, he walks as straight as an arrow, and his wily smile is a treat, because he rarely lets any emotion show even as broad grins ripple across the faces of those tasting his wines. Historically, his family purchased grapes from the best vineyards, and for much of his career he followed suit. However, he has now acquired nearly 45 acres of vines, 32 in Barolo and the rest in Barbaresco. He is known by virtually all of his colleagues and peers in Piedmont as "The Professor of Nebbiolo" or "The Great Man" or "The Maestro." Working with his outstanding oenologist, Dante Scaglione, Bruno Giacosa is an unabashed traditionalist, but his wine has never been deprived of improvement and experimentation. All of his finest wines are fermented in stainless-steel tanks and raised in large oak barrels. No small *barriques* are to be found in the Giacosa cellars, which are always so clean that one could actually eat off the floor. He has experimented with crop thinning, which would have been unheard of 30 years ago. His 2000 wines seem slightly more evolved and sweeter than vintages in the past, but as he told me over dinner in November 2004, this had more to do with the vintage than with any decision to change his style.

Perhaps the greatest compliment I could confer on Bruno Giacosa is that there are no wines in the world I buy without tasting first, except for those of one producer—the Professor of Nebbiolo.

BARBARESCO ASILI

1998 Barbaresco Asili

RATING: 93 points

Giacosa's 1998 Barbaresco Asili exhibits a dark ruby color along with a big, sweet nose of dried herbs, cedar, tobacco, tar, and red fruits. Opulent on the attack, with moderately high tannin as well as good underlying acidity, this is a fragrant effort for Giacosa. Anticipated maturity: 2006–2020.

1997 Barbaresco Asili

RATING: 94 points

The 1997 Barbaresco Asili has developed stunningly since it was first tasted, a typical characteristic of Giacosa's wines.

Surprisingly precocious and evolved for a wine from this estate, it possesses a dark ruby color with an amber edge and abundant quantities of tobacco, cherry liqueur, incense, spice box, and licorice in its flamboyant nose. It is like candy: fleshy, full-bodied, unctuous, and silky. This seamless classic should drink well young and last for another 10–12 years.

1995 Barbaresco Asili

RATING: 90 points

Bruno Giacosa now owns a parcel of the renowned Asili vineyard in Barbaresco, from which he has fashioned a gorgeously elegant 1995 Barbaresco Asili. The color is a deceptively light ruby with some amber at the edge. The nose offers aromas redolent of kirsch, dried Provençal herbs, new saddle leather, and smoke. In the mouth, Asian spice and soy make an appearance in the rich, jammy cherry flavors that also offer an intriguing tomato-like characteristic. This lush, open-knit, full-bodied Barbaresco will drink well between now and 2014.

1990 Barbaresco Asili

RATING: 96 points

Giacosa produced a microscopic quantity of Barbaresco from a small parcel of the Asili vineyard, only 2,000 bottles. Is it the Musigny of Barbaresco? The 1990 Barbaresco Asili is a quintessentially elegant, ripe, fragrant wine with wonderfully sweet, harmonious cherry fruit intertwined with hints of cedar, truffles, and roasted nuts. Full-bodied, with layers of opulent fruit supported admirably by fine acidity and tannin, it should drink well until 2010 or beyond.

BARBARESCO ASILI (RED LABEL RISERVA)

2000 Barbaresco Asili (Red Label Riserva)

RATING: 98 points

Perhaps the most opulent and evolved vintage I have tasted from Bruno Giacosa, and no doubt a reflection of the year, this is still a spectacular wine, already showing a dark ruby color and a gorgeously penetratingly fragrant nose of kirsch, rose petal, licorice, and tobacco leaf. Very full-bodied and quite concentrated, with good underlying acidity, sweet tannin, expansive texture, and an extraordinary finish, this will be a wine that will evolve for 20 years but will be one of those rare Bruno Giacosa wines where an investment of 8–10 years will not be necessary. Anticipated maturity: now–2022+.

1996 Barbaresco Asili (Red Label Riserva)

RATING: 98 points

The utterly perfect, dense ruby/purple–colored 1996 Barbaresco Asili (Red Label Riserva) is a heroic offering brilliantly displaying both power and elegance. The bouquet develops incrementally, offering up aromas of black raspberries, cherries, cigar box, licorice, and leather. The wine impresses with its nuances as well as its extraordinarily rich, dense mid-palate, and a finish that lasts nearly a minute. There is huge tannin, but equally massive concentration, extract, and overall harmony. Anticipated maturity: 2006–2025.

BARBARESCO GALLINA

1990 Barbaresco Gallina

RATING: 90 points

The 1990 Barbaresco Gallina is a lusciously rich, deeply concentrated, full-bodied, spicy wine. It should last through 2007–2010.

1978 Barbaresco Gallina

RATING: 94 points

Of all Giacosa's wines from the 1978 vintage, the Barbaresco Gallina is the most developed. The color reveals some amber at the edge, but the nose offers intense aromas of mushrooms, cedar, leather, tobacco, and sweet, jammy red and black fruits. Full-bodied, velvety, and expansive, with a long finish, this fully mature wine has been delicious for over a decade. It should easily keep through 2007–2008.

2001 Barbaresco Rabajà

RATING: 96 points

With a wine that seems to transcend its vintage, Bruno Giacosa may have fashioned his finest Rabajà to date. An extraordinary, full-bodied, opulent Barbaresco with a potentially sublime perfume of high-quality cigar smoke, sweet cherries, forest floor, flowers (particularly roses), and licorice, it possesses crisp acids that buttress the wine's impressive richness and multilayered texture. A great achievement, it is another tour de force from the remarkable Bruno Giacosa. Anticipated maturity: 2008–2023.

2000 Barbaresco Rabajà

RATING: 94 points

A big, earthy, spicy nose of clove, cinnamon, ripe cherries, and hints of fig and plum jumps from the glass of this dark plum/ruby-colored wine. A relatively meaty, chewy wine with considerable body, loads of tannin, and a heady finish, this wine is a bit more muscular in structure and more backward than Gaja's brilliant 2000 Barbaresco Asili but is impressive in its own right. It will require a bit more patience. Anticipated maturity: 2008–2023.

1998 Barbaresco Rabajà

RATING: 95 points

The 1998 Rabajà is a terrific Barbaresco. Complex notes of soy, earth, candied cherry fruit, and cigar box emerge from this concentrated yet intellectually challenging effort. Full-bodied, with a soft attack as well as a tannic finish, it will be drinkable between 2007 and 2020.

1997 Barbaresco Rabajà

RATING: 96 points

Giacosa's 1997 Barbaresco Rabajà boasts a fabulous nose of caramel, soy, herbs, black cherries, plums, and kirsch. Dense and full-bodied, with a spectacular, silky texture, gobs of glycerin, and a layered, multidimensional palate, it is immensely satisfying from both hedonistic and intellectual perspectives. Anticipated maturity: now–2020.

1996 Barbaresco Rabajà

RATING: 96 points

The 1996 Barbaresco Rabajà (Giacosa's debut vintage from this noted vineyard) displays an intriguing nose of soy, dried Provençal herbs, new saddle leather, and red/black fruits. Tannic and full-bodied, with an enormous impact on the palate, it is extremely concentrated, yet the fruit, alcohol, tannin, and acidity are all marvelously well integrated. Anticipated maturity: 2006–2025.

2000 Barbaresco Santo Stefano

RATING: 92 points

A very open-knit style, somewhat atypical for Bruno Giacosa, this wine already shows some slight amber at the edge and a vivid, very expressive nose of sweet cherries, fennel, rose petals, and a hint of tar. Quite expansive, chewy, and opulent, with surprising forwardness and softness, this broadly textured, very succulent, sexy Barbaresco can be drunk now as well as over the next 12–15 years.

1998 Barbaresco Santo Stefano

RATING: 92 points

The renowned Barbaresco Santo Stefano is the most forward offering of 1998, with its medium ruby color already displaying amber at the edge. Aromas of new saddle leather, fennel, smoke, tobacco, kirsch, and licorice soar from the glass of this ripe, opulent, medium to full–bodied Barbaresco. Drink it over the next 10–12 years.

1997 Barbaresco Santo Stefano

RATING: 93 points

The classic 1997 Barbaresco Santo Stefano is evolved and flamboyant. A medium ruby/garnet color with an amber edge is followed by a sweet perfume of black cherries, tobacco, leather, spice box, licorice, and tar. Full-bodied, with a creamy texture, superb concentration, and an exquisite finish, it can be drunk now or cellared for another 12+ years.

1996 Barbaresco Santo Stefano

RATING: 96 points

The 1996 Barbaresco Santo Stefano (red label) is spectacular. The color is a dark ruby/garnet. The bouquet is just beginning to open, revealing scents of dried Provençal herbs, cherry liqueur, tobacco, spice box, and white truffles. In the mouth, the wine is stunningly concentrated and extremely full-bodied, with high tannin, and fabulously pure, sweet, cherry cough syrup, licorice, smoke, and dried herb flavors. The finish lasts for more than 45 seconds, although this 1996 is still young and tight. It should enjoy a glorious evolution. Anticipated maturity: 2006–2030.

1995 Barbaresco Santo Stefano

RATING: 91 points

One of the ironies when tasting Giacosa's wines is that he does not own any vines in the Santo Stefano vineyard, yet he consistently produces the finest wine from this hillside parcel. The 1995 Barbaresco Santo Stefano reveals an intensely fragrant nose of coffee, soy, tobacco, dried herbs, and cherry cough syrup. Full-bodied, with moderate tannin in the finish, this is an expressive, rich, expansively flavored Barbaresco that can be drunk now as well as over the next 7–10 years.

1989 Barbaresco Santo Stefano

RATING: 90 points

The 1989 Barbaresco Santo Stefano (which Giacosa compares to the 1982) is a firm, closed, densely concentrated wine that gives only hints of its potential. With airing, it offers up a sweet, gamey, cherry and tobacco–scented perfume. However, its richness is most noticeable at the back of the palate. Its full-bodied personality exhibits considerable tannin. Seven hundred cases of this wine were made. Interestingly, Giacosa did not make a Red Label Riserva of the 1989 Barbaresco Santo Stefano. Anticipated maturity: now–2015.

1988 Barbaresco Santo Stefano

RATING: 94 points

The 1988 Barbaresco Santo Stefano is a deep ruby–colored, fragrant wine with intense aromas of cedar, cherry jam, tobacco, and herbs. Full-bodied and expansive, with layers of sweet fruit, this wine offers immediate appeal, but it promises to evolve gracefully through 2010–2015. The rich, thick fruit nearly obscures the tannin. It is a monument to the heights Nebbiolo can achieve!

BARBARESCO SANTO STEFANO (RED LABEL RISERVA)

1990 Barbaresco Santo Stefano (Red Label Riserva)

RATING: 97 points

The blockbuster 1990 Barbaresco Santo Stefano (Red Label Riserva) exhibits a profound nose of sweet fruit, smoked meats, spice, and fruitcake-like scents. It is exceptionally deep, concentrated, and full-bodied, with wonderful richness as well as a layered, concentrated texture. If Giacosa is correct, this wine is a modern-day clone of the 1971. Anticipated maturity: now–2020.

1985 Barbaresco Santo Stefano (Red Label Riserva)

RATING: 96 points

The 1985 Barbaresco Santo Stefano (Red Label Riserva)'s medium ruby/garnet color displays considerable amber at the edge. Its intoxicating perfume of Chinese black tea, smoke, tobacco, cherries, and exotic spices jumps from the glass. The wine is full-bodied, gorgeously nuanced, and multidimensional, with considerable glycerin and layers of flavor. It unfolds fabulously in the mouth, exhibiting remarkable intensity and complexity. The 1985 has just reached full maturity, where it should remain for another decade.

1982 Barbaresco Santo Stefano (Red Label Riserva)

RATING: 94 points

The 1982 Barbaresco Santo Stefano (Red Label Riserva) possesses animal, dried herb, truffle, and earthy notes in its aromatics. Big, bold, tannic, and rich, the fully mature 1982 probably should be drunk between now and 2010–2015.

1978 Barbaresco Santo Stefano (Red Label Riserva)

RATING: 96 points

Still one of the most extraordinary wines produced from this vineyard by Bruno Giacosa, this wine has a darker color than the 1982, 1985, or 1988. It has an extraordinary nose of melted road tar, truffle, animal fur, and sweet saddle leather intermixed with kirsch, dried herbs, balsam, and black cherry fruit. Huge body, sweet tannin, mouth-coating levels of extract, and an amazing finish all characterize one of the modern-day legends of Barbaresco. Fully drinkable if decanted several hours in advance, this wine will continue to age for 10–15 more years.

1971 Barbaresco Santo Stefano (Red Label Riserva)

RATING: 100 points

Bottles now can be variable, but for several decades this was the single greatest wine I ever tasted from Italy. I thought it was in decline; then in 2003 I had another bottle that was pure perfection. An extraordinary, expressive nose of truffles, dried herbs, saddle leather, cedar, black and red fruits, earth, and spice jumps from the glass. Dense, opulent, and full-bodied, yet incredibly well balanced with no hard edges, it is one of those tours de force in winemaking that will never be forgotten by anyone who ever tasted it. Anyone who has access to a bottle should plan to drink it, as pushing its life is probably dangerous.

BAROLO FALLETTO

2000 Barolo Falletto

RATING: 95 points

A very sweet nose of white flowers intermixed with tobacco leaf, road tar, and a telltale rose water characteristic intermixed with hints of dates and black cherry fruit is followed by a very youthful, sweet, expansive, full-bodied wine with very ripe tannin, quite massive concentration, and a more forward style than Bruno Giacosa usually achieves. It is hard to know if this wine will firm up or not, as I tasted it when it had just been bottled, but my instincts suggest this wine should hit its peak in 2009–2011 and last for at least two decades. A somewhat atypically opulent style for a young Bruno Giacosa Barolo.

1999 Barolo Falletto

RATING: 95 points

A very full-bodied, ripe Barolo with notes of allspice, sweet cherries, new saddle leather, tobacco, and underbrush, this powerful, intense wine has an expansive mouth-feel, high tannin, good acidity, and a very backward finish. Give it until 2009–2010 to bottle-age. Anticipated maturity: 2008–2028+.

1998 Barolo Falletto

RATING: 95 points

The fabulous 1998 Barolo Falletto reveals intensity and volume. A dark plum color is accompanied by a classic Nebbiolo perfume of rose water, melted tar, truffles, and cherry jam. As the wine sits in the glass, aromas of spice box and cigar smoke also emerge. Full-bodied, dense, and powerfully tannic yet extremely harmonious, it will be at its finest between 2008 and 2030.

1997 Barolo Falletto

RATING: 93 points

Bruno Giacosa told me his maceration of this wine lasted 60 days. He is openly critical of the 1997 vintage, saying it was a difficult year—too hot and dry, with raisined grapes, low acidity, and excessive sugars and alcohol. That said, his 1997s appear to be beauties. The 1997 Barolo Falletto is typically full-bodied, with a knockout nose of kirsch, cherry liqueur, fruitcake, and cigar box smells. Expansive, lush, rich, and muscular, with the vintage's open-knit, forward character, it will mature quickly and last for 15–20 years. Anticipated maturity: now–2019.

1996 Barolo Falletto

RATING: 96 points

The saturated ruby/purple–colored 1996 Barolo Falletto exhibits an extraordinary nose of smoke, earth, white truffles, black fruits, licorice, and floral scents. Extremely massive, with layers of concentration, high tannin, a muscular personality, and a 40+-second finish, this classic young Barolo will require patience. Why can't I turn my body clock back 20 years? Anticipated maturity: 2012–2035.

1995 Barolo Falletto

RATING: 90 points

I enjoyed the outstanding 1995 Barolo Falletto. It possesses a medium dark ruby color with some lightening at the edge. The intense nose of cedar, spice box, soy, tar, rose petals, and black fruits is followed by a wine with a sweet attack, full body, and dense, layered, concentrated, spicy flavors. As this muscular, tannic wine sat in the glass, allspice and dried herbs became increasingly apparent. Consume it over the next 12 years.

1993 Barolo Falletto

RATING: 90 points

The 1993 Barolo Falletto was the first wine made from Giacosa's estate-grown vines. The wine exhibits a deep garnet color with some amber at the edge. A provocative, complex, compelling nose of dried fruits, cedar, spice, and roasted meat and herbs is followed by a deep, rich, outstandingly concentrated wine with bold, robust, deep flavors that exhibit abundant glycerin, as well as notes of white chocolate, figs, fruitcake, and sweet red and black fruits. This smoky, rich, nuance-filled, luscious, full-bodied Barolo should drink well through 2008–2010.

BAROLO FALLETTO (RED LABEL RISERVA)

2000 Barolo Falletto (Red Label Riserva)

RATING: 99 points

This 2000 Barolo Falletto (Red Label Riserva) is extraordinary and continues Bruno Giacosa's run of remarkable success. Giacosa crop-thinned one of the few times in his life to cut the yields down, and the deep ruby–colored wine he produced shows extraordinarily complex, relatively evolved notes of white truffles, dried red and black fruits, tobacco, smoke, underbrush, and wonderful sweet earthiness. Extraordinarily full-bodied, with massive concentration, huge precision and purity, and an opulent, long finish with very ripe, sweet tannin, this is a candidate for the best wine I have tasted from this vintage in Piedmont. Anticipated maturity: 2010–2030.

1996 Barolo Falletto (Red Label Riserva)

RATING: 98 points

The 1996 Barolo Falletto (Red Label Riserva) possesses extraordinary presence and stature. Dark garnet/ruby–colored, it offers a tight but promising nose of road tar, scorched earth, truffles, blackberries, cherries, and espresso. This muscular, massive wine gave me chills. It is an exquisite, virtually perfect Barolo that requires another 6–7 years of cellaring and should last for 30–40 years. I remember wishing I was 20 years younger when I tasted it prior to bottling; I still feel the same way. Awesome! Anticipated maturity: 2012–2040.

1990 Barolo Falletto (Red Label Riserva)

RATING: 95 points

Giacosa's 1990 Barolos are full-bodied, backward, and concentrated, as well as admirably rich and intense. The 1990 Barolo Falletto (Red Label Riserva) is huge, massively proportioned, thick, and muscular. Readers who adore Bruno Giacosa's faithful adherence to traditionally styled Barolo will be thrilled by this wine. Anticipated maturity: 2007–2025.

1989 Barolo Falletto (Red Label Riserva)

RATING: 94 points

Giacosa's 1989s are superb. The 1989 Barolo Falletto (Red Label Riserva) is the most backward, with a ferocious tannin level balanced by rich, concentrated, thick, chewy flavors. Full-bodied, but massive and nearly impenetrable, this wine of great dignity should be drunk over the next 30 years!

BAROLO RIONDA

1993 Barolo Rionda

RATING: 91 points

The 1993 Barolo from the famed Collina Rionda vineyard is an outstanding example of a traditionally made Barolo that never saw a day in new oak. Although it is *barrique*-aged, the emphasis is on Nebbiolo's varietal character. The wine reveals an amber edge to its garnet color. The nose offers up celestial aromas of ginger, cinnamon, spice, and sweet black cherry fruit. Full-bodied, exotic, and dense, with considerable opulence yet a firm underpinning of tannin, this old-style, impeccably made, mouth-coating Barolo will drink well through 2013–2015.

BAROLO RIONDA (RED LABEL RISERVA)

1989 Barolo Rionda (Red Label Riserva)

RATING: 100 points

This wine has gone from strength to strength over recent years and is now just beginning to enter its period of adolescence. Wonderfully dense plum/garnet–colored to the rim, with an extraordinary nose of tobacco, tar, red and black fruits, cedar, truffles, and smoke, this magnificently rich wine has layers of unctuously textured, full-bodied flavors that coat the palate, shows no hard edges, and has a good 90-second finish. This is an immortal wine that will continue to stand the test of time for at least another two decades.

1978 Barolo Rionda (Red Label Riserva)

RATING: 98+ points

Another monumental effort from this vineyard by Bruno Giacosa, this is perhaps the biggest, richest, most concentrated Barolo I have ever tasted, and it is still in its youth in 2005. With an amazing dark plum/garnet color to the rim, a huge nose of crushed stones, white truffle, underbrush, black plum, fig, cedar, tar, and God knows what else, this amazingly complex wine has massive concentration, thick proportion, full-bodied flavors, yet no sense of heaviness. Everything is impeccable, but this is still a very backward, broodingly concentrated, almost impenetrable wine with great nobility and the potential to evolve for at least another 20 years. A modern-day legend. Anticipated maturity: now–2030.

BAROLO LE ROCCHE DEL FALLETTO

1999 Barolo Le Rocche del Falletto

RATING: 95 points

Playing it close to the vest, with the classic nose of earth, truffle, dried fruits, roasted nuts, and underbrush, this elegant, medium to full–bodied wine seemed almost impenetrable the two times I tasted it. High levels of tannin are there, with a hint of mint and tar. This is a somewhat closed but very promising wine that will benefit from aging until 2010–2013 and will drink well for 20–30 years.

1998 Barolo Le Rocche del Falletto

RATING: 96+ points

The limited *cuvée* made from four blocks of the Falletto vineyard called Le Rocche, the 1998 Barolo Le Rocche del Falletto borders on perfection. This massive, full-bodied wine is spectacular. A dark plum color reveals lightening at the edge. Stunning aromatics offer up scents of crushed stones intermixed with cherry jam and sweet tobacco. There are loads of glycerin, moderately high tannin, and an amazingly long finish of nearly 50 seconds. As staggering as it is now, I am sure it will close down and require cellaring until 2009–2010. Anticipated maturity: 2008–2035.

1997 Barolo Le Rocche del Falletto

RATING: 96 points

Bruno Giacosa's 1997 Barolo Le Rocche del Falletto emerges from four blocks of his Falletto vineyard with a southeastern exposure. This amazing, deep plum/garnet–colored offering possesses huge body as well as a sweet, sexy, fleshy mid-palate and finish. Classic aromas of rose petals, melted tar, and cherry liqueur not only soar aromatically but saturate the palate and coat the taster's teeth. Profoundly complex and multilayered, with an exquisite texture and overall harmony, for a Giacosa Barolo it is uncommonly precocious, making me think it will provide profound drinking and last for three decades. Anticipated maturity: 2007–2030.

WINES:

Messorio

Scrio

Macchiole

Paleo Rosso

OWNER: Cinzia Merli Campolmi

ADDRESS: Via Bolgherese 189/A, 57020 Bolgheri (LI), Italy

TELEPHONE: 39 0565 766092

TELEFAX: 39 0565 763240

E-MAIL: lemacchiole@etruscan.li.it

WEBSITE: www.lemacchiole.it

CONTACT: Cinzia Merli Campolmi

VISITING POLICY: By appointment only

VINEYARDS

SURFACE AREA: 44.7 acres

GRAPE VARIETALS: Merlot, Cabernet Franc, Syrah, Sangiovese, Sauvignon Blanc, Chardonnay, Cabernet Sauvignon

AVERAGE AGE OF THE VINES: 4–18 years

DENSITY OF PLANTATION: 5,000–10,000 vines per hectare

AVERAGE YIELDS: Approximately a pound of fruit per vine

WINEMAKING AND UPBRINGING

These wines are the result of very low yields and ripe fruit, harvested by hand. Completely separate vinification in temperature-controlled stainless-steel vats is followed by malolactic fermentation in barrel and 15–18 months of aging in wood prior to being bottled with no filtration. Since there are a number of small-lot *cuvées* made at Le Macchiole, wood *barriques* of different sizes are utilized. Small *barriques* of 100% new oak are employed for the Messorio, the 100% Merlot *cuvée*. French *barriques* of 225 liters are also used for the Scrio, the 100% Syrah *cuvée*, but these are all once-used wood. The blend of Macchiole Sangiovese, Cabernet Franc, and Merlot is also aged only in 225-liter casks that have been used one time. Last, the flagship wine, the Paleo, which is 100% Cabernet Franc, is aged in 50% new oak casks and 50% 1-year-old casks. The wines are not marketed until 4 years after the harvest.

ANNUAL PRODUCTION

Messorio (100% Merlot): 5,000 bottles
Scrio (100% Syrah): 4,000 bottles

Paleo Rosso (70% Cabernet Sauvignon, 30% Cabernet
    Franc): 30,000 bottles
Macchiole (80% Sangiovese, 10% Cabernet Franc, 10%
    Merlot): 35,000 bottles
AVERAGE PRICE (VARIABLE DEPENDING ON VINTAGE): $40–200

GREAT RECENT VINTAGES

If owner Eugenio Campolmi were still alive, he wouldn't hesitate to recommend the 1998 because of its explosive concentration and power. Other important vintages he would recommend include the 1995 and 1997, which combine both power and elegance.

The name of the farm, Le Macchiole, means "the place where it was in the beginning." In 1975, Ottorino Campolmi and his son Umberto decided to sell the wine they were producing for their own table. In 1981, Umberto's son Eugenio took over management of the farm and changed it completely. First, he relocated the vineyards to the foot of Bolgheri's hills, where the soil was more suitable for growing grapes. Stubborn and radical in his choices, he devoted himself entirely to the vines and their care, converting this work to the main activity of the farm. With Luca D'Attoma joining him as wine consultant in 1991, Eugenio achieved his laudable qualitative targets in just a few years. Unfortunately, Eugenio died in the summer of 2002, well before his time—he was only 40. But the farm's mission had already been established: to capture the pureness of 100% Merlot, to meet the challenge issued by Syrah, and to transition the flagship wine, Paleo, from a blend of Cabernet Sauvignon and Cabernet Franc to 100% Cabernet Franc. Today the farm is being run by Eugenio's widow, Cinzia.

MACCHIOLE

2000 Macchiole

RATING: 90 points
The 2000 Macchiole is a blend of 80% Sangiovese, 10% Cabernet Sauvignon, and 10% Merlot aged 14–16 months in French oak prior to being bottled unfiltered. A dense ruby/purple color is accompanied by complex aromas of melted chocolate, espresso, leather, black cherries, currants, and licorice. There is considerable volume, all the Tuscan typicity one would want, superb ripeness, and a layered, concentrated finish. Anticipated maturity: now–2012.

1999 Macchiole

RATING: 90 points
The 1999 Macchiole is a blend of 95% Sangiovese and 5% Cabernet Sauvignon aged in French *barriques* before being bottled without fining or filtration. Its complex bouquet offers scents of cedar, new saddle leather, dried herbs, espresso beans, chocolate, and black fruits (plums and currants). Supple, complete, concentrated, and lush, it already drinks well. Anticipated maturity: now–2011.

1998 Macchiole

RATING: 91 points
There are approximately 2,000 cases of the 1998 Macchiole, a wine aged in barrel prior to being bottled with neither fining nor filtering. Aromas of blackberry/cassis fruit intertwined with smoke and licorice jump from the glass of this fragrant wine. Intense and opulently styled, with low acidity, medium to full body, and nicely integrated toasty oak, this blend of 95% Sangiovese and 5% Cabernet Sauvignon offers compelling drinking. Anticipated maturity: now–2010.

MESSORIO

2000 Messorio

RATING: 94 points

One of the great Merlots of western Europe and certainly among the top two or three Merlots made in Italy, the 2000 Messorio, from a relatively challenging vintage, has a dense plum/purple color and a big, sweet nose of chocolate, mint, espresso roast, blackberry, and cherry fruit. Quite full-bodied, concentrated, and expansively textured, with sweet tannin and a seamless integration of acidity, alcohol, and wood, this beauty should drink well for 10–15 years.

1999 Messorio

RATING: 98 points

The awesome, saturated purple–colored 1999 Messorio is a 100% Merlot aged 18 months in French oak prior to being bottled without filtration. The alcohol content is a lofty 14.6% and the dry extract number is about the highest technically that I have ever seen. The first vintage of this *cuvée* was 1995, so it is still an infant in terms of how well it develops in the bottle. However, the 1999 is packed and stacked. Aromas of cola, coffee, blackberries, and intense black cherry jam interspersed with mocha, licorice, and toast characteristics are followed by a massive wine with great precision, purity, concentration, and length. I don't want to get too carried away, since only 4,000 bottles were produced, but this is a riveting example of what can be achieved on the Tuscan coastline. Anticipated maturity: 2009–2019.

1998 Messorio

RATING: 96 points

There are only microscopic quantities available of this wine, so I will keep my tasting notes somewhat streamlined, even though it merits a near-perfect score. The 1998 Messorio (100% Merlot) rivals some of the finest Merlots being produced anywhere in the world. Mind-blowing in its richness and intensity, it can compete with the finest wines being made on the Pomerol plateau. Representing the essence of Merlot in its concentrated jammy blackberry and cherry notes, it is a well-defined, beautifully poised effort revealing both power and elegance. Full-bodied, dense, and super-concentrated, with an incredibly long 50-second finish, it is a tour de force in winemaking that must be tasted to be believed. Anticipated maturity: now–2016. This is a prodigious wine. It is a shame that the quantity is so limited.

1997 Messorio

RATING: 98 points

This is a brilliant effort, rivaling the finest made not only in Italy but also in France and the United States. Unfortunately, the quantity is very limited. Approximately 40–50 cases will be available, but production is expected to increase slightly in future vintages. The awesome 1997 Merlot Messorio is truly prodigious. Black/purple-colored, it boasts an astonishingly rich nose of black raspberries, smoky new oak, dried herbs, and cedar. Chocolate, new saddle leather, and exhilarating levels of black fruits give this wine a luxurious, voluptuous texture. The finish lasts for nearly a minute! A winemaking tour de force that is already accessible given its expansive, open-knit texture. Anticipated maturity: now–2015.

1995 Messorio

RATING: 95 points

The 1995 Merlot Messorio smells like a sensational vintage of the ostentatious Pomerol, Le Pin. Knockout aromas of new oak intermixed with jammy black cherry fruit, coconut, allspice, and licorice tumble out of the glass with little restraint. The wine is dense, with spectacular concentration and purity, a plush texture, and thrilling levels of glycerin, extract, and richness. Everything is velvety-textured in this flashy wine, which can be drunk now. Anticipated maturity: now–2012.

PALEO ROSSO

2000 Paleo Rosso

RATING: 90 points

A nose of smoke, black currant, dried herbs, tobacco leaf, and road tar are present in this medium-bodied, very flavorful, somewhat evolved 2000. The wine shows lots of complexity, though not quite the depth and richness of some of the previous vintages, but it is certainly an undeniable success for the vintage. Drink it over the next decade.

1999 Paleo Rosso

RATING: 92 points

A stunning wine of great depth, intensity, and blue/purple color saturation, with an extraordinary nose of graphite, crushed rocks, road tar, black fruits, and dried Provençal herbs, this supple-textured, full-bodied wine has stunning concentration, a sweet, expansive mid-palate, and a long finish with no hard edges. It is a big wine but brilliantly balanced. Drink it over the next decade.

1998 Paleo Rosso

RATING: 92 points

The 1998 Paleo is a *barrique*-aged blend of 85% Cabernet Sauvignon and 15% Cabernet Franc. Displaying a Cheval Blanc–like complexity, it offers a profound aromatic smorgasbord of spice box, cedar, licorice, menthol, and juicy black currants and blackberries. It is medium to full–bodied, with superb palate presence, great precision as well as purity, and well-integrated acidity, tannin, and alcohol (13.5%) in its long, seamless finish. Anticipated maturity: now–2014.

1997 Paleo Rosso

RATING: 92 points

The 1997 Paleo Rosso, an unfined, unfiltered, *barrique*-aged blend of 80% Cabernet Sauvignon, 10% Sangiovese, and 10% Cabernet Franc, is promising. Its opaque ruby/purple color is followed by a sweet nose of licorice, smoke, graphite, blackberries, and cassis. Full-bodied, with a roasted meat character to its flavors, extraordinary purity and concentration, and beautifully integrated acidity as well as tannin, this blockbuster is a candidate for drinking now. Anticipated maturity: now–2015.

1996 Paleo Rosso

RATING: 91 points

The 1996 Paleo Rosso (85% Sangiovese and 15% Cabernet Sauvignon) reveals chocolate, espresso, and mocha aromas, as well as new oak. Full-bodied and dense, with moderate tannin, outstanding concentration, and abundant quantities of sweet, jammy, black cherry fruit, the wine's low acidity and thick, juicy style suggest drinking. Anticipated maturity: now–2008.

1995 Paleo Rosso

RATING: 90 points

The dark plum/purple–colored 1995 Paleo (85% Sangiovese and 15% Cabernet Sauvignon) offers a striking nose of melted road tar, cedar, leather, strawberry jam, and kirsch. In addition to the splendid aromatics, the wine possesses a chewy texture, medium to full body, a silky palate, ripe tannin, adequate acidity, and a long finish. Anticipated maturity: now–2009.

SCRIO

2000 Scrio

RATING: 90 points

Big notes of eucalyptus, mint, chocolate, licorice, and tar jump from the glass of this full-bodied, concentrated, very supple-textured and evolved Syrah. This wine should drink well young yet age nicely for up to a decade. Anticipated maturity: now–2014.

1999 Scrio

RATING: 93 points

The 1999 Scrio (100% Syrah aged 18 months in French *demi-muids*) exhibits classic Syrah characteristics of camphor/creosote intertwined with blackberry liqueur, licorice, and vanilla. With phenomenally high extract as well as tannin, massive body, and a long, pure, concentrated finish, this unfiltered beauty's dry extract numbers are nearly off the charts. Patience is required for this formidable 1999. It should be at its best between 2007 and 2018. It is Italy's most compelling example of Syrah!

1998 Scrio

RATING: 95 points

Le Macchiole's Scrio is the most profound Syrah being made in Italy. Unfined, unfiltered, and produced from incredibly tiny yields, the black/purple-colored 1998 offers scents of licorice, melted tar, truffles, and blackberry liqueur. Full-bodied and opulent, with high tannin but compelling sweetness and a multilayered palate, it should age for two decades. It could easily compete with some of the Rhône Valley's great Hermitages. Anticipated maturity: now–2021.

WINE: Montevetrano

OWNER: Silvia Imparato

ADDRESS: Via Montevetrano 3, 84099 San Cipriano Picentino (SA), Italy

TELEPHONE: 39 089 882285

TELEFAX: 39 089 882010

E-MAIL: montevetrano@tin.it

WEBSITE: www.montevetrano.com

CONTACT: Silvia Imparato

VISITING POLICY: By appointment with Silvia Imparato

VINEYARDS

SURFACE AREA: 11.1 acres, but plans are to expand to 25 acres

GRAPE VARIETALS: 60% Cabernet Sauvignon. 30% Merlot, 10% Aglianico

AVERAGE AGE OF THE VINES: 10 years

DENSITY OF PLANTATION: 4,000 vines per hectare

AVERAGE YIELDS: Very low

WINEMAKING AND UPBRINGING

Overseen by her famed oenologist, Riccardo Cotarella, Silvia Imparato's wines are made from completely destemmed fruit, given up to a three-week classic fermentation and maceration, and then moved into totally new French oak. At the end of 12 months or so they are bottled without filtration.

ANNUAL PRODUCTION

Montevetrano: about 30,000 bottles

AVERAGE PRICE (VARIABLE DEPENDING ON VINTAGE): $50–80

GREAT RECENT VINTAGES

Ms. Imparato's own thoughts are revealing: "I'm not really able to say. All are my sons. I'm very severe with them, but they have changed my life. I have always defended the 1997, which seemed soft. I think it has 'nuances,' very deep and special. The strongest at the moment is 1993, but always 1995 and 1997. 1999 had a different acidity but now is 'formidable.' 2001 has a big personality. 1992 is the most elegant."

Silvia Imparato and Riccardo Cotarella continue to fashion one of southern Italy's most distinctive wines. Since its debut, this wine has been a testament to the conservative viticulture of the proprietor as well as the extraordinary winemaking skills of Cotarella. Sadly, this small vineyard of 11.1 acres produces only 500 cases of a blend of 60% Cabernet Sauvignon, 30% Merlot, and 10% Aglianico Tourasi. The wines are bottled unfined and unfiltered after spending 12 months in 100% new French oak, and amazingly, the new oak is completely absorbed by the fruit. I love these wines' individualistic style. Each year, regardless of vintage conditions, Montevetrano offers up compelling amounts of blueberry, blackberry, and black raspberry fruit presented in a distinctive, medium to full–bodied, fruit-driven, complex personality. It also exhibits a touch of minerals and marvelous purity and symmetry, as well as the potential for 10–20 years of evolution. Stylistically, it resembles an Italian version of the Colgin or Bryant Family Vineyard Cabernet Sauvignon and is generally staggering in its complexity and richness.

MONTEVETRANO

2001 Montevetrano

RATING: 95 points

An extraordinary achievement, this dense, almost black/ruby-colored wine has a tremendous nose of melted licorice, graphite, blackberry, and currant notes intermixed with some crushed minerals. Full-bodied, rich, and expansive with tremendous purity, this is a brilliant wine to drink over the next 10–15 years.

2000 Montevetrano

RATING: 94 points

A singular aromatic profile of blueberries, spice box, white flowers, and assorted fruits is followed by an opulent wine with extraordinary purity, medium to full body, and beautifully integrated tannin, acidity, and wood. It is a wine of uncharacteristic seamlessness as well as compelling intensity and length. In 2003, I opened a bottle of the 1993, which was still aging at a glacial pace and remained a young but promising wine of great power, elegance, and harmony. The only downside is that there is just not enough of it. Anticipated maturity: now–2015.

1999 Montevetrano

RATING: 94 points

A 19,000-bottle blend of 60% Cabernet Sauvignon, 30% Merlot, and 10% Aglianico produced from extremely small yields, this unfined/unfiltered, elegant yet singular wine boasts a deep ruby/purple color as well as a sweet nose of blueberry pie, cassis, minerals, and violets. Dense, medium to full–bodied, and harmonious, with a fabulous underlying liquid minerality, it is a distinctive, pure wine to drink now and over the next 12 years.

1998 Montevetrano

RATING: 92 points

The 1998 is an outstanding success, with elegance allied to power and intensity. Montevetrano's hallmark blackberry and black raspberry component is present as well as beautiful purity/symmetry and a long, medium to full–bodied, highly concentrated finish. Sadly, production was a mere 2,000 bottles from only 4 acres (subsequently expanded to 11.1). Like most of the wines made under the supervision of Riccardo Cotarella, it is aged in new French oak and bottled with neither fining nor filtration. The 1998 should drink well for another 6–11 years.

1997 Montevetrano

RATING: 96 points

This wine is staggering in its complexity and richness. Silvia Imparato is a shining star. Amazingly, the new oak is completely absorbed by the fruit. Stylistically, it can be described as an Italian version of the Colgin or Bryant Family Vineyard Cabernet Sauvignon. Its mild blackberry/vivid blueberry, fabulously fragrant, floral-scented nose jumps from the glass. Opaque purple–colored, with a layered, naturally textured feel, this full-bodied, spectacularly concentrated, multidimensional wine must be tasted to be believed. A prodigious effort, it may be the finest Montevetrano yet made—which is saying something, given how spectacular other vintages have been. Anticipated maturity: now–2020.

Montevetrano.®
imbottigliato dall'Azienda agricola
Montevetrano
di Silvia Imparato

2000

1996 Montevetrano

RATING: 94 points

This wine possesses a minimum of two decades of aging potential. It boasts an opaque purple color and dense, thick aromas of black raspberry ice cream intermingled with roasted herbs and grilled meats. In the mouth, the wine is rich and full-bodied, with an unctuous texture, loads of blackberry fruit, sweet tannin, and a layered, thick, low-acid finish. Anticipated maturity: now–2012.

1995 Montevetrano

RATING: 92 points

The 1995, like so many vintages of this wine, combines the elegance, richness, and intensity of a great Château Margaux with the lushness and succulence of a top Pomerol such as La Conseillante. Gorgeous levels of sweet blueberry and cassis fruit jump from the glass of this dense purple wine. The aromatics and fruit are sweet, ripe, and pure. On the palate, there is superb concentration, layers of flavor, medium to full body, impeccable balance, and that rare combination of finesse and strength. The wine is supple enough to be drunk at present, but rich and well balanced. This is a beautifully full, elegant wine that has to be tasted to be believed. Anticipated maturity: now–2010.

1994 Montevetrano

RATING: 93 points

The 1994 Montevetrano is a fabulously concentrated, opaque purple wine with a tight but promising nose of vanilla, chocolate, cassis, and wild blueberries. Full-bodied, rich, and layered, with highly extracted, sweet flavors, this graceful yet powerfully rich and flavored wine admirably combines elegance with force. It should last for another 6–7 years. Like its glorious predecessors, the 1994 was aged in 100% new French Allier oak and bottled without any fining or filtering.

WINES:

Barolo Cannubi Boschis

Barolo Le Vigne

OWNER: Luciano Sandrone

ADDRESS: Via Pugnane 4, 12060 Barolo (CN), Italy

TELEPHONE: 39 0173 560023

TELEFAX: 39 0173 560907

E-MAIL: info@sandroneluciano.com

WEBSITE: www.sandroneluciano.com

CONTACT: Mrs. Barbara Sandrone

VISITING POLICY: By appointment only

VINEYARDS

SURFACE AREA: 54.3 acres

GRAPE VARIETALS: Nebbiolo d'Alba, Nebbiolo da Barolo, Barbera d'Alba, Dolcetto d'Alba

AVERAGE AGE OF THE VINES: 35 years

DENSITY OF PLANTATION: 5,000 vines per hectare

AVERAGE YIELDS: 6,500 kilograms per hectare

WINEMAKING AND UPBRINGING

Very low yields and very ripe fruit are characteristics of Luciano Sandrone's wines. His vinification is relatively classical and lasts for 10–14 days, with part of the malolactic fermentation occurring in French oak casks. However, over the last decade, Sandrone has begun to prefer the larger 200-liter *tonneaux* over the 55-liter French *barriques,* so now a combination of both exists in his modern winery near the village of Barolo.

ANNUAL PRODUCTION

Barolo Cannubi Boschis: 14,000 bottles

Barolo Le Vigne: 16,000 bottles

AVERAGE PRICE (VARIABLE DEPENDING ON VINTAGE): $25–115

GREAT RECENT VINTAGES

2001, 2000, 1999, 1998, 1997, 1996, 1990, 1989, 1985, 1982

Extraordinary producers of Barolo, Luciano Sandrone and his wife worked at Marchesi di Barolo before acquiring a tiny plot of land outside their native village of Barolo in 1977. Theirs quickly became a cult wine, first with their 1982 and 1985 vintages. Then they made a wine that merited one of the first perfect scores I ever gave a Barolo, the 1990. There is attention to detail in the vineyard and in the winery at every level, and the results are wines that are hybrid creations, paying respect to both progressives and traditionalists. Of course, Sandrone knows his vineyards: His Cannubi Boschis, a magnificent site with a southeastern exposition, is extraordinary, and his Le Vigne, another top Barolo vineyard, is a site that is not nearly as well known but capable of making exceptional wine. These are extraordinary expressions of Nebbiolo that combine both power and elegance.

BAROLO CANNUBI BOSCHIS

2000 Barolo Cannubi Boschis

RATING: 97 points

A very forward style by Sandrone's standards, with some creeping amber at the edges, this wine shows an extraordinarily fragrant nose of black fruits intermixed with melted licorice, truffle, tar, and rose petals. Very opulent and full-bodied, with great delineation, tremendous purity, and intense concentration, this is a beauty and one of the few 2000s that actually needs bottle aging, even though it is atypically forward for a Sandrone. Its low acidity and fast-track evolutionary course should make this wine gorgeously delicious between 2008 and 2018.

1999 Barolo Cannubi Boschis

RATING: 90 points

A medium-bodied style for Sandrone with notes of cedarwood, dried herbs, sweet kirsch, and a hint of rose water and truffle, this medium-bodied wine has a certain austerity, moderately high tannin, and long finish. Anticipated maturity: 2008–2018.

1998 Barolo Cannubi Boschis

RATING: 94–96 points

The deep ruby/purple–colored 1998 Barolo Cannubi Boschis boasts a spectacular bouquet of mineral-infused black cherry liqueur, new saddle leather, and toast. This powerful, ripe wine offers full-bodied flavors, silky tannin, low acidity, gorgeous levels of glycerin, and a creamy mouthful of complex, layered, superbly pure Nebbiolo fruit. Anticipated maturity: 2006–2020.

1997 Barolo Cannubi Boschis

RATING: 96 points

The prodigious 1997 Barolo Cannubi Boschis possesses a dark saturated garnet color. The sweet nose of black fruits, minerals, scorched earth, smoke, dried herbs, and wet stones is stunning. Amazingly concentrated, with tremendous unctuousness yet superb delineation, this large-scaled and elegant Barolo possesses fabulous extract as well as a multidimensional mid-palate and finish. It is an amazing effort! Anticipated maturity: now–2020.

1996 Barolo Cannubi Boschis

RATING: 94–96 points

The spectacular 1996 Barolo Cannubi Boschis offers aromas of cassis, cherry liqueur, and flowers. It is dense, superb, and full-bodied, with fabulous intensity as well as layers of extract. Muscular, concentrated, broad, and powerful, it demands cellaring. Anticipated maturity: 2006–2020.

1994 Barolo Cannubi Boschis

RATING: 90 points

Sandrone's 1994 is a feminine-styled, elegant Barolo with a medium ruby color and an attractive, smoky, black cherry and raspberry–scented nose. Mineral and new oak notes are also apparent in the wine's fragrance. In the mouth, it is expansive and long, with considerable finesse and elegance. Not a blockbuster in the style of the 1990, it is an elegantly wrought wine with outstanding purity and harmony. Drink up.

1993 Barolo Cannubi Boschis

RATING: 92 points

The dark ruby–colored 1993 Barolo Cannubi Boschis is reserved, but it reveals a sweet, elegant nose of roasted meats and nuts intermixed with scents of underbrush and black fruits. As the wine sits in the glass, notes of melted tar and rose petals emerge. More firmly structured than many 1993s, it is full-bodied, with considerable character, outstanding concentration, and an expansive inner core of sweet fruit. Anticipated maturity: now–2012.

1990 Barolo Cannubi Boschis

RATING: 100 points

Sandrone appears to have topped what he achieved in 1982, 1985, 1988, and 1989 with a nearly perfect 1990 Barolo from the Cannubi Boschis vineyard. There are only 1,600 cases of this blockbuster Barolo for the world, but should you have the requisite contacts to be able to latch on to a few bottles, don't hesitate! It is an amazingly rich, superbly balanced, profound Barolo that is crammed with flavor. It exhibits a hauntingly intense bouquet of roses, black cherries, new leather, and a touch of tar. Great richness and extraordinary precision are its hallmarks. This massive wine is a riveting tasting and drinking experience. Do not be misled by the wine's immediate drinkability. Many of the 1989 and 1990 Barolos are so sweet and precocious that there is a temptation to forget how much tannin is buried beneath the decadent levels of fruit. The 1990 Cannubi Boschis should be peaking about now and should last for at least 20 years or more. An awesome effort!

1989 Barolo Cannubi Boschis

RATING: 97 points

The 1989 Barolo Cannubi Boschis is another treasure to be added to Sandrone's impressive résumé. Backward for a 1989, it exhibits a dense purple color, a blossoming nose of smoky new oak, black fruits, and tar; rich, full-bodied, multilayered flavors; and awesome dimension and persistence in the mouth. Anticipated maturity: now–2010.

1988 Barolo Cannubi Boschis

RATING: 93 points

Sandrone's 1988 Cannubi Boschis promises to rival his 1985, but will it be as stunning as his 1982? Traditionally styled, the 1988 is unbelievably intense, with a super nose of damp earth and black fruits. There is sensational chewy, ripe, opulent fruit, softer tannins than many producers appear to have obtained, and a massively long, heady finish. Anticipated maturity: now–2010.

1982 Barolo Cannubi Boschis

RATING: 95 points

This offering is a terrific example of just what heights the Nebbiolo grape can achieve. The huge, smoky, leathery, black cherry and truffle–scented nose is followed by a majestic wine with an expansive, broad-shouldered, rich palate, decent acidity, and a stunningly long, flashy finish. Sandrone has produced a spectacular Barolo. Anticipated maturity: now–2009.

BAROLO LE VIGNE

2000 Barolo Le Vigne

RATING: 93 points

A very decadent, almost luxurious nose of freshly crushed sweet red and black fruits, with a hint of dates/figs along with some tobacco leaf and truffle, jumps from the glass of this dark garnet-colored wine that is already showing a bit of lightening and amber at the edge. Quite low in acidity and very fleshy, opulent, and full-bodied, this comes across almost like an 8- to 10-year-old Barolo, but it shows great fruit, texture, and just a very seductive mouth-feel. Drink it over the next 10–16 years.

1999 Barolo Le Vigne

RATING: 91+ points

This dark ruby–colored wine offers up notes of allspice, herbs, tar, truffle, and sweet strawberry and cherry fruit. As the wine sits in the glass, a bit of raspberry also seems to emerge. Medium-bodied and elegant, with wonderful purity and good delineation, this is not a blockbuster but a very classic Barolo that should be at its best between 2007 and 2015.

1998 Barolo Le Vigne

RATING: 95 points

The multidimensional 1998 Barolo Le Vigne possesses huge layers of black cherry fruit infused with rose petals, tar, balsam wood, mineral, and subtle new oak notes. Full-bodied, awesomely concentrated, and extraordinarily pure, this exquisite, youthful Barolo will be at its prime between now and 2020.

1997 Barolo Le Vigne

RATING: 94 points

The dark ruby–colored 1997 Barolo Le Vigne reveals amber at the edge. It offers stunning aromatics consisting of flowers, black fruits, lead pencil, spice box, and minerals. As is typical of Sandrone's offerings, there is extraordinary purity as well as intensity to the blackberry and cherry fruit flavors. As the wine sits in the glass, mineral and tar notes become more apparent. This is a stunning, gorgeously pure, Château Margaux–like Barolo to consume between now and 2018.

1996 Barolo Le Vigne

RATING: 90–92 points

The dark ruby/purple–colored 1996 Barolo Le Vigne is an elegant, large-scaled Barolo with everything in balance. There is sweet tannin and a measured yet powerful, rich style with copious amounts of black fruits intermixed with minerals, spice, and dried herbs. Anticipated maturity: now–2018.

1995 Barolo Le Vigne

RATING: 90 points

The classic 1995 Barolo Le Vigne offers telltale aromas of tar, rose petals, and cherry liqueur. It provides medium to full body, a silky, open, accessible style, sweet, expansive flavors, a gorgeous texture, and a classic finish with no hard edges. This beautifully made Barolo can be drunk now. Anticipated maturity: now–2013.

1993 Barolo Le Vigne

RATING: 92 points

More precocious and exotic than the Barolo Cannubi Boschis, Sandrone's 1993 Barolo Le Vigne is a blend of five separate parcels. It boasts a dark ruby color, a Pomerol-like sweet, chocolaty, coffee, and jammy black cherry–scented nose, medium to full body, a lush, soft texture, and a heady, rich finish. Anticipated maturity: now–2012.

1990 Barolo Le Vigne

RATING: 95 points

In 1990, Sandrone produced 100 cases of this single-vineyard Barolo. Although more developed and less tannic and muscular than the 1990 Cannubi Boschis, it is a spectacularly ripe, rich, unctuously textured wine that is gorgeous to smell and taste. Anticipated maturity: now–2014.

1985 Barolo Le Vigne

RATING: 94 points

The 1985 Barolo demonstrates why Sandrone is so renowned. Still youthful when I last tasted it in 2002, it boasts a dark plum/purple color as well as sweet aromas of black fruits, minerals, asphalt, and underbrush. Full-bodied, with sweet tannin, no hard edges, gorgeous purity, and multiple dimensions, this is a spectacular, still vigorous and youthful Barolo. Anticipated maturity: now–2015.

1982 Barolo Le Vigne

RATING: 95 points

While the 1982 Barolo is rustic, it is loaded with admirable characteristics. The dark garnet color reveals some amber at the edge. The celestial perfume offers a gamut of spices infused with abundant jammy red and black fruits, tobacco, soy, licorice, tar, and smoke. Extremely full-bodied, powerful, and concentrated, with abundant tannin in the finish, this is a massive, mature Barolo. Anticipated maturity: now–2014.

LIVIO SASSETTI (PERTIMALI)

WINES:

Brunello di Montalcino

Brunello di Montalcino Riserva

OWNER: Livio Sassetti & Figli

ADDRESS: Azienda Agricola Pertimali, Podere Pertimali, 329,
53024 Montalcino (SI), Italy

TELEPHONE: 39 0577 848721

TELEFAX: 39 0577 848721

E-MAIL: lsasset@tin.it / info@sassettiliviopertimali.it

WEBSITE: www.sassettiliviopertimali.com

CONTACT: Lorenzo Sassetti

VISITING POLICY: By appointment only

VINEYARDS

SURFACE AREA: 40.8 acres

GRAPE VARIETALS: Sangiovese Grosso, Cabernet Sauvignon,
Moscadello, Trebbiano Toscano

AVERAGE AGE OF THE VINES: 20 years

DENSITY OF PLANTATION: 4,000 vines per hectare

AVERAGE YIELDS: 60 quintals per hectare

WINEMAKING AND UPBRINGING

Fermentation takes place in stainless-steel tanks for up to 2 weeks, and then, in the case of the Brunello di Montalcino, the wine is aged an additional 8 months in stainless steel before it is moved into large Slavonian oak *foudres* for 3 years. After bottling with no filtration, the wine is rested another 16 months in bottle prior to being released. One unusual thing Pertimali does is bottle half its Brunello di Montalcino in the summer after 3 years in wood and the other half 5 months later.

ANNUAL PRODUCTION

Brunello di Montalcino: 40,000–50,000 bottles

AVERAGE PRICE (VARIABLE DEPENDING ON VINTAGE): $25–65

GREAT RECENT VINTAGES

1999, 1997, 1995, 1990, 1988, 1985, 1975, 1970, 1964, 1961

This producer can be found in the northern village of Montalcino in an area called Montosoli. From an old family that always produced wines, olive oil, and cereals, Livio Sassetti began to devote himself entirely to the production of wine in the 1960s. Today his sons, Lorenzo and Luciano, continue the work of previous generations.

BRUNELLO DI MONTALCINO

1998 Brunello di Montalcino

RATING: 91 points

Typical of the vintage, the 1998 Brunello di Montalcino is forward, with a gorgeous perfume of roasted herbs, saddle leather, asphalt, truffles, spice box, and sweet cherry as well as currant fruit. This wine is round, generous, and complex but extremely accessible and evolved. Anticipated maturity: now–2010.

1997 Brunello di Montalcino

RATING: 96 points

Readers should note that with the 1997 Brunello di Montalcino, the label changed to emphasize the proprietor's name, Livio Sassetti, rather than the estate name, Pertimali. Always a top-notch Brunello, the 1997 is staggering in its aromatic fireworks and concentrated, long, intense flavors. Sumptuous aromas of dried Provençal herbs, roasted meats, soy, spice box, asphalt, truffles, and black fruits linger in the air. Flavors of new saddle leather are added to jammy black fruit characteristics. Opulently textured, full-bodied, and gorgeously pure, this wine creates an olfactory overload. Its low acidity, high glycerin, and huge fruit reserves suggest drinking it now and over the next 10–15 years. *Mamma mia!*

1995 Brunello di Montalcino

RATING: 91 points

Sassetti's 1995 Brunello di Montalcino is one of the finest tasted from the vintage. The dark garnet/ruby color is followed by complex characteristics of cedarwood, dried tobacco, licorice, Asian spices, and black cherry/currant fruit. Generous and full-bodied, with sweet fruit, light to moderate tannin, and a long finish, this Brunello can be drunk now. Anticipated maturity: now–2012.

1991 Brunello di Montalcino

RATING: 90 points

In late 1996, I participated in a blind tasting of Rosso and Brunello di Montalcino in which all twelve tasters preferred most of the Rosso di Montalcino to the Brunellos. What is the lesson to be gleaned? Brunello di Montalcino are more serious wines, but Rosso di Montalcino provide delicious, up-front, richly fruity drinking with no patience required. A great Brunello needs 7–10 years in the cellar, whereas a Rosso is meant to be drunk during its first 5–7 years of life. The 1991 Brunello di Montalcino is no 1990, but it is still an outstanding wine. It exhibits a deep ruby/garnet color; a fragrant licorice, smoke, roasted meat, and herb–scented nose; sweet black cherry, tobacco, cedar, and animal–like flavors; dense concentration; and a long, surprisingly soft, velvety-textured finish. I was surprised by how forward and delicious as well as complex this 1991 Brunello already was in 1997. Anticipated maturity: now–2010.

1990 Brunello di Montalcino

RATING: 94 points

The 1990 Brunello di Montalcino is full-bodied and expansive, offering a dark ruby color, a spice, cedar, tobacco, and fruitcake–scented nose, and a sensational attack. Even more noteworthy is the length, which unfolds and expands impressively. Loads of tannin and alcohol infuse this Brunello with a potential of 15–20 or more years of longevity. This is a stunning Brunello di Montalcino that can be drunk now or cellared. Anticipated maturity: now–2016.

1988 Brunello di Montalcino

RATING: 95 points

The awesome, inspirational 1988 Brunello di Montalcino is super-extracted, with an opaque deep ruby/purple color and a highly promising nose of roasted nuts, black fruits, herbs,

and Asian spices. The wine is massively rich yet impeccably well balanced, with fabulous purity and a multidimensional feel. If you can find any, it is a must purchase. Anticipated maturity: now–2010.

1985 Brunello di Montalcino

RATING: 92 points

The 1985 Brunello di Montalcino is a worthy successor to Pertimali's superb 1982 and 1983 Brunellos. With a deep, opaque color and a huge nose of grilled meats, saddle leather, and roasted black fruits, this opulent, sensationally rich wine exhibits brilliant delineation in its intense, full-bodied flavors. Surprisingly soft for a Brunello, it can be drunk now. Anticipated maturity: now–2008.

BRUNELLO DI MONTALCINO RISERVA

1997 Brunello di Montalcino Riserva

RATING: 92 points

The 1997 Brunello di Montalcino Riserva boasts an opaque ruby/purple color in addition to deep, full-bodied flavors, and more tannin as well as a more angular finish than the regular cuvée. Hence the lower rating. Although it does not possess the exuberance, fruit intensity, staggering aromatic fireworks, and concentration of the regular bottling, it is still a great meaty, leathery Brunello that should age well for another 10–13+ years. I'd be happy to drink it on any occasion.

1995 Brunello di Montalcino Riserva

RATING: 90 points

The 1995 Brunello di Montalcino Riserva is a safe bet, a full-bodied, sweet offering with a gorgeous bouquet of mushrooms, black fruits, earth, incense, and leather. Tobacco flavors intermingle with cherries, plums, and earth. Elegant, sweet, pure, and complex as well as accessible, it should drink well before 2010.

1993 Brunello di Montalcino Riserva

RATING: 91 points

The 1993 Brunello di Montalcino Riserva boasts a dazzling nose of cedar, cigar smoke, tea, soy, and kirsch. Rich, spicy, and peppery, with significant quantities of fruit and glycerin, this moderately tannic, full-bodied effort will be at its best between now and 2012.

1990 Brunello di Montalcino Riserva

RATING: 94 points

The 1990 Brunello di Montalcino Riserva is a wine of immense proportions and extraordinary complexity. I cannot say it is better than the regular cuvée since they both possess the same exuberance, personality, and depth of fruit. Anticipated maturity: now–2016.

1988 Brunello di Montalcino Riserva

RATING: 94 points

The 1988 Brunello di Montalcino Riserva is a wine of immense proportions and extraordinary complexity. I cannot say it is better than the regular cuvée since, in large measure, it possesses the same exuberance, personality, and depth of fruit. Yet it has an additional dimension of complexity and perfume. Dark ruby–colored, with a spicy, cedary, tobacco and fruitcake–scented nose, this full-bodied, expansive wine offers a sensational attack. Even more noteworthy is the wine's length, which unfolds and expands impressively. Loads of tannin and alcohol infuse this wine with a joyous potential of 15–20 or more years of longevity. It is a stunning Brunello di Montalcino Riserva that can be drunk now or cellared. As prodigious a wine as it is, it will be extremely hard to find given the microscopic quantities produced. Anticipated maturity: now.

Barolo Bric del Fiasc

Barolo Cannubi

Barolo Rocche dell'Annunziata

OWNER: Enrico Scavino

ADDRESS: Borgata Garbelletto, Via Alba-Barolo 59, 12060
    Castiglione Falletto (CN), Italy

TELEPHONE: 39 0173 62850

TELEFAX: 39 0173 62850

E-MAIL: info@aziendapaoloscavino.it

WEBSITE: www.aziendapaoloscavino.it/home.htm

CONTACT: Miss Enrica Scavino

VISITING POLICY: By appointment only

VINEYARDS

SURFACE AREA: 50 acres

GRAPE VARIETALS: Nebbiolo d'Alba, Barbera d'Alba,
    Dolcetto d'Alba, Sauvignon Blanc, Chardonnay,
    Cabernet Sauvignon

AVERAGE AGE OF THE VINES: 35 years

DENSITY OF PLANTATION: 4,500–5,000 vines per hectare

AVERAGE YIELDS: 6,000 kilograms of grapes per hectare

WINEMAKING AND UPBRINGING

Enrico Scavino is another of the modernist producers who use rotary fermenters. The wines are briefly macerated for 7–10 days and then moved to virtually all new French oak for aging for 12 months prior to bottling without filtration. Yields are always low, since in most vintages Scavino does a green harvest.

ANNUAL PRODUCTION

Barolo Bric del Fiasc: 8,800 bottles

Barolo Cannubi: 2,700 bottles

Barolo Rocche: 2,500 bottles

AVERAGE PRICE (VARIABLE DEPENDING ON VINTAGE): $35–120

GREAT RECENT VINTAGES

2001, 2000, 1999, 1998, 1997, 1996, 1990

From his modern cellars in Castiglione Falletto, Enrico Scavino and his two beautiful daughters, Enrica and Elisa, fashion wines that are clearly of the modern school and seem to possess very good aging potential as well. These are very savory, complex wines that exhibit the multidimensional perfume and flavors of Barolo,

show surprisingly judicious use of new oak, and pack quite a bit of power and potency without losing their elegance or typicity. This estate was founded in 1921, but its success has occurred over the last 10–15 years, in large measure because of the extraordinary efforts of Enrico Scavino and his daughters. The estate is located in Castiglione Falletto, as is their famous Bric del Fiasc vineyard, but they also have vineyards in La Morra. While the Scavino family deserves an enormous amount of credit for their efforts, the influence of the revolutionary wine broker Marc de Grazia can't be discounted, as it was he who discovered this estate and helped encourage its qualitative progress.

BAROLO BRIC DEL FIASC

2000 Barolo Bric del Fiasc

RATING: 94 points

Already showing some amber at the edge, this very forward, complex, flamboyant Barolo has a dark garnet color. A huge nose of new saddle leather, truffle, allspice, clove, and very ripe black cherry and currant fruit intermixed with some tobacco and licorice make for an amazing aromatic concoction. In the mouth it is pure velvet, full-bodied, viscous, and lush, with very low acidity and ripe tannin. I can't resist drinking it now, so why defer anyone else's gratification? Anticipated maturity: now–2015.

1998 Barolo Bric del Fiasc

RATING: 92 points

The 1998 Barolo Bric del Fiasc is a dramatic, provocative effort. It possesses awesome levels of concentration, considerable power, immense body, and a fabulously pure, concentrated style. With impressive quantities of black fruits, licorice, minerals, asphalt, earth, and truffles, this Barolo is notable for its purity, high extract levels, and seamlessness. Anticipated maturity: now–2016.

1997 Barolo Bric del Fiasc

RATING: 95 points

The 1997 Barolo Bric del Fiasc reveals the essence of cherry jam in its massive constitution. It is a powerful, full-bodied effort displaying pronounced black cherry liqueur–like aromas and flavors, huge extract and glycerin, and 14.5–15% alcohol. It is remarkably pure, delineated, and balanced for a wine of great massiveness. Anticipated maturity: now–2020.

1996 Barolo Bric del Fiasc

RATING: 91–94 points

The 1996 Barolo Bric del Fiasc displays a saturated plum color, a smoky, black cherry–scented nose, explosive, fleshy flavors with plenty of glycerin, an evolved and seductive character, extraordinary intensity, and impeccable balance. Exotic Asian spice and fruitcake aromas add to its complexity. Anticipated maturity: now–2018.

1995 Barolo Bric del Fiasc

RATING: 91 points

The 1995 Barolo Bric del Fiasc is backward, with scents of smoke, tar, soy, jammy black cherry and blackberry fruit, and toast. Full-bodied, concentrated, expansive, soft, and seductive, with 13.5% alcohol and moderate tannin in the finish, it should be drunk between now and 2011.

1994 Barolo Bric del Fiasc

RATING: 91 points

Scavino followed his splendid 1993s with strong efforts in the more difficult vintage of 1994. The 1994 Barolo Bric del Fiasc reveals a Château Margaux–like nose of violets, black currants, asphalt, and toasty new oak. In the mouth, it is deep, rich, and full-bodied, with the vintage's telltale silky texture, low acidity, and up-front, evolved personality. This deep, concentrated, layered, yet voluptuously textured Barolo is delicious. Anticipated maturity: now.

1993 Barolo Bric del Fiasc

RATING: 95 points

While the 1993s may not possess the power, intensity, and extract of the great 1990s, qualitatively they are equals. The awesome 1993 Barolo Bric del Fiasc (one-third new oak casks) is a candidate for the Barolo of the vintage. Made from 45-year-old vines, this full-bodied, blockbuster Barolo is amazingly rich, superbly balanced, and oh, so profound. The fragrant, penetrating bouquet of black cherries, new saddle leather, tar, and rose petals, intermixed with subtle spicy toast, is followed by an exceptionally rich, medium to full–bodied wine with terrific delineation and focus, as well as gorgeously integrated acidity, tannin, and alcohol. Anticipated maturity: now–2012.

1990 Barolo Bric del Fiasc

RATING: 96 points

Scavino's 1990s are immense, statuesque wines of exceptional richness and complexity. The 1990 Barolo Bric del Fiasc boasts the most saturated color. The bouquet suggests a flattering, up-front style of wine in its complex nose of Asian spices, smoky new oak, black cherries, and herbs. This wine possesses great density along with considerable structure and plenty of tannin. The formidable finish offers copious quantities of jammy fruit, glycerin, and heady alcohol. Drink this blockbuster Barolo between now and 2010.

1989 Barolo Bric del Fiasc

RATING: 92+ points

In the mid-1990s, I had the opportunity to taste a minivertical of Scavino's Barolo Bric del Fiasc, from the 1990, 1989, 1988, 1985, and 1982 vintages. All of these wines were made in the old style, without aging in small oak casks. The 1989 was spectacular, although more tannic, without the wealth of glycerin, extract, and massive fruit of the 1990. The 1989 should age effortlessly for 15–20+ years. How fortunate readers owning both the 1989 and 1990 vintages will be to have an opportunity to compare them as they evolve!

BAROLO CANNUBI

2000 Barolo Cannubi

RATING: 93 points

Dark plum/garnet with some amber at the edge, this wine offers notes of melted licorice, rose water, dried herbs, sweet berry, and a licorice-infused currant nose. It is plush, with medium to full–bodied flavors, low acidity, very ripe tannin, and considerable glycerin and alcohol. Drink this beauty over the next decade.

1998 Barolo Cannubi

RATING: 92 points

The full-bodied, seamless 1998 Barolo Cannubi offers the essence of black cherry jam/liqueur along with earth, mineral, new saddle leather, coffee, licorice, tobacco, and new wood. It saturates the mouth without any sense of heaviness. Drink this full-throttle, elegant, pure, classic Barolo between now and 2015.

1997 Barolo Cannubi

RATING: 95 points

The surreal 1997 Barolo Cannubi boasts a saturated ruby/purple color and an exquisite bouquet of black fruits, lead pencil, minerals, smoke, and licorice. Full-bodied and opulent, with obvious tannin, this structured, muscular, viscous, formidably concentrated effort will be at its best between now and 2020.

1996 Barolo Cannubi

RATING: 90–93 points

The dark plum/ruby–colored 1996 Barolo Cannubi reveals cherries galore intermixed with smoke, tobacco, and new saddle leather scents. This full-bodied, supple-textured, glorious Barolo possesses exceptional extract and can be drunk now or cellared for another 10–12 years.

1995 Barolo Cannubi

RATING: 91 points

The 1995 Barolo Cannubi is very sexy. The dark ruby color is accompanied by a sumptuous nose of tobacco smoke, coffee, black fruits, and toast. The wine is dense, velvety-textured, full-bodied, and silky, with no hard edges. This is a voluptuous wine to enjoy now. Anticipated maturity: now–2009.

1994 Barolo Cannubi

RATING: 90 points

The 1994 Barolo Cannubi boasts a deep ruby/garnet color, as well as a fragrant bouquet of smoked herbs, sweet berry/cherry fruit, licorice, and spice box notes. Rich, concentrated, and layered, this medium to full–bodied, pure, lush, silky smooth Barolo should be drunk now.

1993 Barolo Cannubi

RATING: 92 points

The 1993 Barolo Cannubi (50% new oak casks) is the most backward wine of the trio of 1993s from Scavino. The dark ruby/purple color is followed by a nose that reluctantly gives up aromas of smoke, earth, and black cherries. The wine makes a beautiful impression with its display of richness and well-integrated tannin and acidity. The finish lasts for nearly a minute. This is a youthful as well as one of the least evolved 1993 Barolos I tasted. It will drink well for another 8–12 years.

1990 Barolo Cannubi

RATING: 95 points

Scavino's 1990s are immense, statuesque wines of exceptional richness and complexity. The 1990 Barolo Cannubi is a stunningly elegant wine with great depth and richness. It offers a fascinating display of grace allied to considerable power and richness. The fruit's sweetness (from low yields and ripe grapes) is marvelous to behold. This flashy, complex wine is mature. Anticipated maturity: now–2011.

1989 Barolo Cannubi

RATING: 96 points

Scavino's three 1989 Barolos are spectacular. The 1989 Barolo Cannubi is a legend in the making. Its spectacular nose of sweet black fruits, licorice, grilled meats, and smoky new oak is followed by a wine with immense richness, stunning opulence, a multidimensional personality, and a spectacularly long, well-delineated finish. Anticipated maturity: now–2012.

BAROLO ROCCHE DELL'ANNUNZIATA

1998 Barolo Rocche dell'Annunziata

RATING: 94 points

The 1998 Barolo Rocche dell'Annunziata is an undeniable showstopper. An exquisite combination of black fruits, coffee, smoke, new oak, licorice, and incense is found in this medium to full–bodied, ripe, elegant, pure Barolo. Explosive aromatics are followed by equally riveting flavors as well as a 50-second finish. The tannin is sweet and beautifully integrated. Anticipated maturity: now–2018.

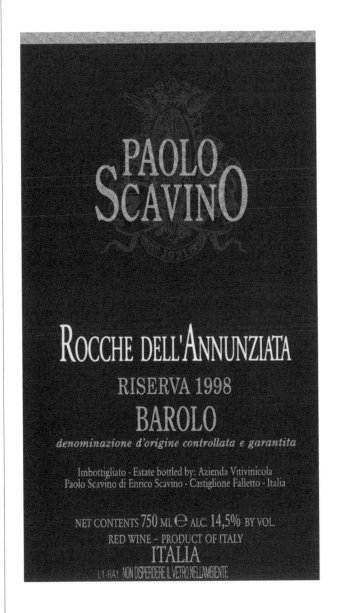

1996 Barolo Rocche dell'Annunziata

RATING: 95 points

Scavino produced one of the great wines of this classic year, the 1996 Barolo Rocche dell'Annunziata. The color is a healthy dark ruby. The nose offers scents of smoky charcoal, licorice, toast, black cherries, incense, tobacco, and leather. It is full-bodied and massive, with superb balance, nicely integrated acidity and tannin, and a finish that goes on for nearly a minute. A profound Barolo to drink now and over the next 10–15 years.

1995 Barolo Rocche dell'Annunziata

RATING: 92 points

The intensely fragrant (wood smoke, allspice, black fruits, and tobacco) 1995 Barolo Rocche dell'Annunziata boasts a dark ruby color, as well as terrific extract, full body, and copious quantities of glycerin. While it possesses a velvety, evolved personality, there are lots of stuffing and richness but few nuances. Anticipated maturity: now–2014.

1993 Barolo Rocche dell'Annunziata Riserva

RATING: 94 points

The 1993 Barolo Rocche dell'Annunziata Riserva is one of the great Barolos of the vintage. The wine is deep, dark garnet/ruby–colored, with a stunningly sweet nose of lead pencil, black currants, cherries, smoke, roasted meats, toast, and vanilla. Made from 56-year-old vines, it is broad, rich, and packed with fruit and extract. Full-bodied and broodingly deep and intense, this compelling Barolo manages to marry power and richness to a sense of elegance, harmony, and finesse. Anticipated maturity: now–2013.

SOLDERA (CASE BASSE)

WINES:

Brunello di Montalcino

Intistieti

OWNER: Gianfranco Soldera

ADDRESS: Località Case Basse, 53024 Montalcino (SI), Italy

TELEPHONE: 39 335 7727311

TELEFAX: 39 0577 846135

E-MAIL: gianfranco.soldera@casebasse.it

WEBSITE: www.soldera.it

CONTACT: Gianfranco Soldera

VISITING POLICY: By appointment only

VINEYARDS

SURFACE AREA: 17.3 acres in production and 5 acres recently
    planted

GRAPE VARIETALS: Sangiovese Grosso

AVERAGE AGE OF THE VINES: 25 years

DENSITY OF PLANTATION: 3,300–4,400 vines per hectare

AVERAGE YIELDS: Very conservative; actual yields per vine or
    acre were not divulged

WINEMAKING AND UPBRINGING

Made from very small yields, the wines are aged in large
Slavonian oak *foudres* for 4–5+ years before being bottled
without any fining or filtration. No added yeasts or technical
manipulation are utilized as the intention is to produce the
purest and most natural product of the Case Basse vineyard.

ANNUAL PRODUCTION

Brunello di Montalcino: 8,000–16,000 bottles

AVERAGE PRICE (VARIABLE DEPENDING ON VINTAGE): $120–370

GREAT RECENT VINTAGES

1999, 1985, 1979

Everyone I know who has met proprietor Gianfranco
Soldera has the same impression—that the man is an
uncompromising perfectionist who makes great wines
but seems not to want to sell them to anybody on planet
Earth unless they meet his "qualifications," a list of prerequisites Soldera keeps to himself. From his 17.3-acre
Case Basse vineyard (planted in 1973), Soldera produces
three wines: a *vino da tavola* called Intistieti and two
Brunellos, with the Riserva being made only in top years.

Soldera's vineyards have a southwest exposure and
sit at an altitude of 320 meters.

BRUNELLO DI MONTALCINO

1999 Brunello di Montalcino

RATING: 95+ points

This is a dark plum/garnet–colored wine with an explosive
bouquet of licorice, cedarwood, spice box, new saddle leather,
an open charcoal fire, and with that, associated notes of dried
herbs and sweet plum, cherry, and currant fruit; like most vintages of Soldera's wines, the extraordinary aromatics are followed by a very powerful, full-bodied, concentrated wine with
exceptional harmony among its elements. With beautiful purity, compelling complexity, and a long, heady finish, it is still
quite young but promises to evolve beautifully for 15–20 years.

1997 Brunello di Montalcino

RATING: 94 points

Dark ruby/garnet–colored with an exceptional nose of soy, ripe red fruits infused with smoke, herbs, and almost leathery roasted meat smells, this wine has relatively high tannin, a very concentrated attack and mid-palate, and a finish of just over a minute. Some hints of balsamic vinegar intermixed with sweet cherry, plum, and fig notes are also present as the wine aerates. Anticipated maturity: now–2017.

1993 Brunello di Montalcino

RATING: 90 points

The dark plum/garnet–colored 1993 Brunello di Montalcino offers a knockout nose of fruitcake, Asian spices, incense, flowers, red and black fruits, earth, and minerals. It is one of the most complex bouquets I have ever smelled in a wine. In the mouth, it is sweet, ripe, and round, with exceptional purity and ripeness but, surprisingly, not the weight one would associate with such a provocative and persistent fragrance. Medium-bodied, with a gorgeously layered, supple texture, it should drink well between now and 2010.

Gianfranco Soldera

1990 Brunello di Montalcino

RATING: 98 points

The 1990 Brunello di Montalcino from Case Basse is a modern-day classic, as well as one of the greatest Brunellos I have ever tasted. It exhibits a deep ruby color and a magnificent, rich, complex nose of roasted herbs, sweet, jammy red and black fruits, cedar, spice, and oak. The wine is extremely powerful and full-bodied, with layers of highly concentrated, ripe fruit. Despite its massive size, it retains a gracefulness and elegance. The velvety texture and layers of fruit conceal the wine's high tannin. It is approachable but should age effortlessly. Anticipated maturity: now–2015.

1988 Brunello di Montalcino

RATING: 93 points

This large-scaled, intensely fragrant Brunello offers a lavishly exotic and decadent bouquet of grilled meats, hickory smoke, and jammy peaches as well as red and black fruits, coffee, and spices. Full-bodied, with authoritatively rich, supple flavors oozing with glycerin and extract, this meaty, multidimensional, velvety-textured wine can be drunk now. Anticipated maturity: now–2011.

BRUNELLO DI MONTALCINO RISERVA CASE BASSE

1999 Brunello di Montalcino Riserva Case Basse
RATING: 96 points

Perhaps the greatest Brunello that Soldera has produced in over a decade, this extraordinary 1999 boasts a dark plum/garnet color as well as an intoxicating, flamboyant bouquet of melted licorice, dried herbs, pepper, incense, cherries, and smoke. As always, Soldera's full-bodied Brunello di Montalcino lives dangerously, with some noticeable volatile acidity. However, the extraordinary aromatics, backed up by a multilayered texture and sumptuous mid-palate and finish, are the stuff of legends. Readers looking for technically clean, correct, soulless wines will find this offering at the extreme end of the wine spectrum, yet totally compelling. It is capable of evolving for 20–25 years. Anticipated maturity: now–2030.

1995 Brunello di Montalcino Riserva Case Basse
RATING: 96 points

The medium garnet/ruby–colored 1995 Brunello di Montalcino Riserva Case Basse's exotic nose of truffle juice, roasted meats, minerals, smoke, red and black fruits, licorice, Chinese black tea, and incense reveals different nuances every ten seconds or so. It displays an Ausone-like austerity backed by powerful concentration and a steely delineation that's oh, so precise. At 14% alcohol, it is not a shy wine. It is a remarkable effort that must be tasted to be believed. Anticipated maturity: now–2020.

1994 Brunello di Montalcino Riserva Case Basse
RATING: 90 points

One of the most exotic, complex, and individualistic Brunellos produced, Soldera's 1994 Riserva Case Basse offers intense aromatic fireworks. A dark ruby/garnet color is followed by a stunning nose of spice box, cedar, soy, cinnamon, red and black fruits, earth, and truffle scents. Few wines achieve the aromatic intensity and complexity of Soldera's Brunello di Montalcinos. In the mouth, the 1994 is medium to full–bodied, with sweet ripeness, a firm tannic underpinning, and a pure, concentrated finish. Drink it over the next 10–13 years.

1993 Brunello di Montalcino Riserva Case Basse
RATING: 95 points

The 1993 Brunello di Montalcino Riserva Case Basse is sensational. A spectacular bouquet of tobacco, ginger, soy, roasted meat, black cherry, plum, and toast scents is followed by layer upon layer of fruit, sweet tannin, superripeness, and gorgeous complexity and symmetry. This is an exceptionally complex, full-flavored Brunello di Montalcino that can be drunk now or cellared for another 5–10 years. This idiosyncratic but brilliant effort is not for everybody (few will be able to afford it), but it is a wine of great originality and complexity.

1991 Brunello di Montalcino Riserva Case Basse
RATING: 94 points

Readers may remember my enthusiastic notes on the two *cuvées* of 1990 Brunello. In 1991, only a Riserva was made. It is a magnificent Brunello that gets my nod as the wine of the vintage. The wine is a dark ruby color with some amber at the edge. An extraordinary nose offers up provocative aromas of grilled meats, sweet black cherries, Asian spices, balsamic vinegar, and smoke. The wine exhibits superb richness, incredibly sweet, pure fruit, full body, and layers of depth. The finish easily lasts for 35–40 seconds. This is a terrific, remarkable, compellingly complex, already delicious Brunello that promises to age well. Anticipated maturity: now–2010.

BRUNELLO DI MONTALCINO RISERVA INTISTIETI

1995 Brunello di Montalcino Riserva Intistieti
RATING: 98 points

The 1995 Brunello di Montalcino Riserva Intistieti possesses prodigious aromatics, flavor nuances, and complexity. It reveals Asian spice notes in addition to an exotic, funky incense smell to the extraordinary ripe, surreal perfume. There is also a dry, layered, intriguing texture and a finish that lasts for nearly a minute.

This wine seems to change every ten seconds or so, offering provocative aromas and flavors. In short, I have never tasted anything quite like it. Kudos to the fanatical proprietor! I suspect the window of maturity will be now–2020+.

TENUTA DELL'ORNELLAIA

WINES:

Ornellaia

Masseto

OWNER: Constellation Brands

ADDRESS: Via Bolgherese 191, 57020 Bolgheri (LI), Italy

TELEPHONE: 39 0565 718242

TELEFAX: 39 0565 718230

E-MAIL: info@ornellaia.it

WEBSITE: www.ornellaia.com

CONTACT: Public Relations

VISITING POLICY: By appointment only

VINEYARDS

SURFACE AREA: 160.5 acres of vineyards, 207.5 in the estate

GRAPE VARIETALS: Cabernet Sauvignon, Merlot, Cabernet Franc

AVERAGE AGE OF THE VINES: 20–25 years

DENSITY OF PLANTATION: 5,000–7,000 vines per hectare

AVERAGE YIELDS: 35–45 hectoliters per hectare

WINEMAKING AND UPBRINGING

This estate has two major vineyard locations: the original vineyard, called Ornellaia, where the winery is located, and Bellaria, just to the east of the small town of Bolgheri. The vineyards are planted on very diverse but primarily marine, alluvial, and volcanic soils.

After hand-harvesting and complete destemming, the wine is fermented partially in wood but also in stainless-steel tanks, with the temperature never exceeding 30°C. The vineyard parcels are vinified separately. Postfermentation maceration is long, averaging up to 30 days or more, before the wines are transferred into French oak barrels (70% new and 30% used). The malolactic fermentation occurs in barrels.

The wine stays in wood for 18 months in the winery's temperature-controlled cellars, and after 12 months, the master blend is made by famed winemaking consultant Michel Rolland. The wine is gently fined prior to bottling but never filtered.

The Masseto, of which there are usually only around 2,000 to 2,400 cases, is close to 100% Merlot, whereas the Ornellaia tends to be dominated by Cabernet Sauvignon with small percentages of Cabernet Franc and more recently a bit of Petit Verdot.

ANNUAL PRODUCTION

Ornellaia: 8,000–12,500 cases

Masseto: 2,000–2,400 cases

AVERAGE PRICE (VARIABLE DEPENDING ON VINTAGE): $75–200

GREAT RECENT VINTAGES

2001, 1999, 1998, 1997

It is remarkable how far this wine has come since Lodovico Antinori founded the estate in 1981. Antinori, whose dream was to create truly exceptional wine, was inspired by Marchese Nicolò Incisa della Rochetta, the proprietor of Sassicaia. Ornellaia became a completely U.S.-owned company in 2001, when the Robert Mondavi Corporation of California, which owned a minority interest, purchased 100% of the estate.* The winemaking continued in the hands of two Frenchmen, Thomas Duroux and consulting oenologist Michel Rolland, until recently, when Duroux left Ornellaia to go back to work in Bordeaux at Château Palmer.

The Ornellaia winery, which looks more as though it belongs in Napa Valley than in Tuscany, has a modern pentagonal shape constructed of steel, concrete, and wood. Both stainless-steel vats and open-top oak fermenters are employed, along with a bevy of smaller French *barriques*.

MASSETO

2001 Masseto
RATING: 96 points

An extraordinary wine made with a gorgeous nose of white chocolate, espresso roast, blackberry and cherries, and some grilled herbs and smoke, it is opulent and full-bodied, with a voluptuous texture, tremendous purity, and a very heady, full-bodied finish. This is sumptuous stuff to drink over the next 10–12 years.

1999 Masseto
RATING: 94 points

The dense ruby/purple–colored 1999 Masseto offers a fabulous bouquet of sweet oak, black raspberries, blackberries, currants, new wood, and licorice. Firmly structured and medium to full–bodied yet remarkably elegant, this impressive beauty needs cellaring and should age for 15+ years. Anticipated maturity: 2007–2019.

*Subsequently, Constellation Brands purchased Robert Mondavi, and therefore acquired Ornellaia. Whether they will sell this asset remains open to conjecture.

1995 Masseto

RATING: 91 points

A superb single-vineyard Merlot from a high-quality Tuscan producer, the 1995 Masseto *vino da tavola* exhibits a saturated dark ruby/purple color in addition to a sweet nose of jammy black cherries, chocolate, and smoky new oak. The vintage's high tannin level is present, but it is complemented by admirable concentration, glycerin, and spice. Anticipated maturity: now–2016.

1994 Masseto

RATING: 91 points

The rich 1994 Masseto offers lavish quantities of spicy new oak. In addition to the obvious toast notes, the Masseto is less evolved than the 1995 Ornellaia. This full-bodied, spicy, rich wine cuts a broad swath across the palate. Anticipated maturity: now–2012.

1993 Masseto

RATING: 91 points

The 1993 Masseto reveals a deep, saturated ruby/purple color, plenty of sweet, toasty oak; gobs of gorgeously pure, sweet fruit; full body; and plenty of suppleness. In a blind tasting, it would be easy to mistake for a top-notch right bank Bordeaux. The 1993 can be drunk now. Anticipated maturity: now–2010.

ORNELLAIA

2001 Ornellaia

RATING: 92 points

Notes of black olive, chocolate, espresso, and oodles of black currant and cedary blackberry fruit tumble from the glass of this dark ruby/purple–colored wine that shows good structure, wonderful sweetness, a hint of licorice, and a very full-bodied finish. It is already approachable but promises to evolve for 10–15 years.

1998 Ornellaia

RATING: 93 points

Made in a relatively structured style for the normally succulent Ornellaia, the densely saturated ruby/purple–colored 1998 offers aromas of toast, spice, smoke, black fruits, and graphite. Full-bodied, concentrated, and exceptionally pure and long, it will be at its finest between 2005 and 2018. Very impressive.

1997 Ornellaia

RATING: 94 points

Probably the finest (and most sumptuous) Ornellaia yet produced, the 1997 has it all. A dense purple color offers smoky espresso and jammy black cherry aromas wrapped in new oak.

Full-bodied, opulent, thick, and juicy, this low-acid, seamless classic can be drunk now and over the next 10+ years.

1995 Ornellaia

RATING: 92 points

The 1995 Ornellaia is unquestionably another stunning wine in what has been a strong succession of top wines since 1988. The color is a saturated, thick-looking ruby/purple. The nose offers aromas of roasted coffee, jammy black cherry liqueur, and cassis intermixed with spice. On the palate, the wine is rich and full-bodied, with well-integrated wood, tannin, and acidity. Pure, youthful, and accessible, this is an impressively endowed wine. Anticipated maturity: now–2011.

1990 Ornellaia

RATING: 92 points

Another super effort from this producer, the 1990 Ornellaia is a worthy successor to the super 1988. Fat, supple, and loaded with black cherry and currant fruit and a dash of vanilla from new oak barrels, this full-bodied, velvety-textured, opulent wine should be drunk between now and 2008.

1988 Ornellaia

RATING: 93 points

This brilliant wine is one of the best new-breed Tuscan reds I have tasted. The color is a sensational black/purple, and the nose offers gorgeously intense aromas of black plums, cassis, licorice, and spicy new oak. In the mouth, there is extraordinary opulence and richness, enough acidity to provide grip, and plenty of tannin lurking behind the cascade of fruit. The explosive finish goes on and on. Approachable, even delicious now, this splendid wine promises to last through the first decade of the 21st century. Anticipated maturity: now–2012.

WINE: Solengo

OWNER: Countess Noemi Marone Cinzano

ADDRESS: Argiano S.R.L., Sant'Angelo in Colle, 53020
Montalcino (SI), Italy

TELEPHONE: 39 0577 844037

TELEFAX: 39 0577 844210

E-MAIL: argiano@argiano.net

WEBSITE: www.argiano.net

CONTACT: Dr. Pepe Schib Graciani

VISITING POLICY: By appointment only

VINEYARDS

SURFACE AREA: 118.6 acres

GRAPE VARIETALS: Sangiovese, Cabernet Sauvignon, Merlot,
Syrah

AVERAGE AGE OF THE VINES: 12 years

DENSITY OF PLANTATION: 5,000–7,000 vines per hectare

AVERAGE YIELDS: 0.8–1.0 kilograms per vine

WINEMAKING AND UPBRINGING

The vinification is done with traditional methods using
temperature-controlled stainless-steel vats. The soaking of the
grapes is prolonged for 15 days. During fermentation, the
temperature is rigorously controlled at 28–30°C. After the
malolactic fermentation and several decanting operations to
eliminate heavy lees, the wine is transferred to the cellars,
where it rests in both French *barriques* and traditional large
oak casks. The wines are transferred to stainless-steel vats and
are decanted before bottling takes place. There is no filtration.
The whole annual production for each type of wine produced
is bottled at the same time so as to ensure uniformity from
the first bottle to the last.

ANNUAL PRODUCTION

Solengo: 40,000 bottles

AVERAGE PRICE (VARIABLE DEPENDING ON VINTAGE): $25–75

GREAT RECENT VINTAGES

2001, 2000, 1999, 1998, 1997

Nestled on top of a hill 300 meters above sea level in the valley of the River Orcia, located a few kilometers south of Montalcino in the Tuscan province of Siena, Argiano is believed to be an ancient site. Local historians believe that the name Argiano may refer to an *Ara Jani,* or temple to the Roman god Janus, or perhaps the living place of a people called the Argia.

The Villa di Argiano, headquarters of the Tenuta di Argiano winery, was built between 1581 and 1596 by Baldassare Peruzzi. This Renaissance building, with its characteristic horseshoe shape, has survived time and inclemencies, and its ownership has changed many times over the centuries as it passed from one noble family to another. Documents confirming the existence of vineyards around the Villa di Argiano as early as the 16th century have been found. The property was acquired by the Gaetani family at the end of the 19th century, and since 1992, the management has been under the Countess Noemi Marone Cinzano with advice from oenologist Dr. Giacomo Tachis.

The estate lies on a hilltop plateau and stretches over 247 acres. Currently it is composed of 118 acres of vineyards, 25 acres of olive groves, and several parcels of arable and grazing land. The vineyard soil is composed mainly of marly limestone with some clay areas. The vineyard sites are particularly favorable because they face south, with a perfect midday exposition, and the altitude gives good ventilation. All the grapes are hand-picked and brought into the vinification cellar in small cases to avoid crushing in transport.

A new fermentation cellar was finished in the year 2000; it is furnished with the latest technology to conduct the most sophisticated analysis of the musts and wines. Connected by subterranean pipes to this cellar, the original aging cellar underneath the villa still holds the barrels and *barriques.* The conditions in the original cellar are mostly constant but fluctuate slightly with the seasons, thereby allowing the wines in the wood casks to develop according to natural cycles.

In 1995, Giacomo Tachis was able to produce the first super-Tuscan at Argiano. Recognizing the potential of the specific microclimate, influenced mostly by winds churning up from the coastal region of the Maremma, he had vineyards planted with Cabernet Sauvignon, Merlot, and Syrah. Each grape variety is vinified separately and then comprises 33% of the final blend. The wine is aged for 16 months in new French oak casks, resulting in a smooth Bordeaux-styled wine with Tuscan flair.

SOLENGO

2000 Solengo
RATING: 95 points
There is no doubting the phenomenal quality of the 2000 Solengo, a blend of equal parts Cabernet Sauvignon, Merlot, and Syrah with a tiny dollop of Petit Verdot. Its opaque ruby/purple color is followed by a stunning perfume of crème de cassis, blackberries, espresso, licorice, and new saddle leather. Full-bodied, sensationally concentrated, pure, and well textured, with a 45-second finish, this unformed, youthful black beauty possesses extraordinary upside potential. Anticipated maturity: 2008–2022.

1999 Solengo
RATING: 94 points
A fine offering, the 1999 Solengo is a blend of equal parts Cabernet Sauvignon, Merlot, Sangiovese, and Syrah. This opaque purple–colored offering exhibits gorgeously ripe blackberry and cassis fruit mixed with scents of leather, charcoal, earth, and wood. Dense, opulent, and full-bodied, with sweet tannin in the finish, it is still youthful and unevolved but promises to drink splendidly between now and 2015.

1998 Solengo
RATING: 91 points
The 1998 Solengo is a terrific offering. An intriguing blend aged in 100% new French oak for 16 months prior to bottling, it boasts an opaque ruby/purple color, as well as a classic black currant and blackberry–scented bouquet infused with high-quality, toasty oak, and elements of roasted espresso. Intense, medium to full–bodied, chewy, and rich, with a multi-layered mid-palate and sweet tannin, this mouth-filling, dry red can be drunk now. Anticipated maturity: now–2014.

1997 Solengo
RATING: 94 points
The profound 1997 Solengo *vino da tavola* (a blend of Sangiovese and Cabernet Sauvignon with a tiny dose of Syrah) is spectacular. Opaque purple–colored, it displays a fabulously sweet nose of crème de cassis, new saddle leather, toasty new oak, licorice, and flowers. This wine boasts amazing richness, a huge, full-bodied impact on the palate (yet no sense of heaviness), low acidity, gorgeous ripeness, and a finish that lasts for 35+ seconds. I predict a brilliant future for this compelling proprietary red wine. Anticipated maturity: now–2016.

1996 Solengo

RATING: 94 points

Argiano's 1996 Solengo, a blend of Cabernet Sauvignon, Sangiovese, Merlot, and Syrah (500 cases produced), is a blockbuster effort. The wine boasts a saturated ruby/purple color, as well as an excellent nose of jammy blackberries, cassis, toast, and spice. Full-bodied, with superb depth, a layered texture, low acidity, and a blockbuster finish, this is an impressively endowed, smoky, rich, exotic, accessible, dry red that should age nicely. Anticipated maturity: now–2012.

1995 Solengo

RATING: 92 points

The wine boasts a dense, saturated ruby/purple color, as well as a stunning nose of black currants, chocolate, smoke, and an elusive floral scent. Long, dense, and extravagantly rich, with full body and exceptional purity, this low-acid yet fleshy, powerful, silky-textured wine impressively conceals some serious tannin. The wine is exceptionally rich and layered in the mouth but unevolved. Still, it possesses enormous potential. Anticipated maturity: now–2015.

WINE: Sassicaia

OWNER: Marchese Nicolò Incisa della Rochetta

ADDRESS: Località Le Capanne 27, 57020 Bolgheri (LI), Italy

TELEPHONE: 39 0565 762003

TELEFAX: 39 0565 762017

E-MAIL: info@sassicaia.com

WEBSITE: www.sassicaia.com

CONTACT: Marchese Nicolò Incisa della Rochetta; Dottore Sebastiano Rosa

VISITING POLICY: By appointment through their distributors

VINEYARDS

SURFACE AREA: 173 acres, all included in the Bolgheri Sassicaia DOC zone

GRAPE VARIETALS: 85% Cabernet Sauvignon, 15% Cabernet Franc

AVERAGE AGE OF THE VINES: 25–30 years old

DENSITY OF PLANTATION: 4,000–5,000 vines per hectare

AVERAGE YIELDS: 1 kilogram per vine

WINEMAKING AND UPBRINGING

Vinification takes place in temperature-controlled stainless-steel vats of 35–110 hectoliters. Maceration lasts around 14 days. The wine is aged in 33% new 225-liter French oak barrels for 24 months.

Marchese Nicolò Incisa della Rochetta

ANNUAL PRODUCTION

Sassicaia: 180,000 bottles

AVERAGE PRICE (VARIABLE DEPENDING ON VINTAGE): $75–165

GREAT RECENT VINTAGES

2000, 1998, 1997, 1995, 1993, 1990, 1988, 1985, 1982, 1978, 1975

This Cabernet Sauvignon–based offering is one of Italy's most famous wines. The late Mario Incisa della Rocchetta, whose son Nicolò runs Sassicaia, refused to work under Italy's wine laws, which he found too rigid and reactionary. Therefore he decided to break out and simply make the best wine he could and call it a *vino da tavola* (a table wine). He was convinced that at his huge estate, the Tenuta San Guido in the Tuscan town of Bolgheri, he could plant and produce extraordinary Cabernet Sauvignon. The first wine, Sassicaia, now includes about 25% Cabernet Franc. The production has increased significantly since it was first produced, and there is also a second wine called Guidalberto, which accounts for 10,000 out of the estate's total of around 25,000 cases.

According to Nicolò, his father had dreamed as a student in Pisa during the 1920s of producing a "noble" wine based on the Bordeaux model. Cabernet Sauvignon provided the kind of bouquet that he considered majestic, and he believed the gravelly soils on what would become the Tenuta San Guido would prove ideal. Sassicaia, which in the Tuscan dialect means "stony ground," was produced between 1948 and the mid-1960s but during that time was consumed only at the estate. As the wine evolved, Mario came to realize there was more potential than even he had imagined.

All of the original wines came from a vineyard planted in an area called Castiglioncello. In 1965, Mario planted two new vineyards with Cabernet Sauvignon and Cabernet Franc, and these became the basis of the new Sassicaia vineyard, situated approximately 800 feet lower than the original vineyard at Castiglioncello. The debut vintage of 1968 was well received, and the rest, as they say, is history. There has been little change under Nicolò except for the conversion from old wood fer-

mentation vats to temperature-controlled stainless-steel tanks.

The great commercial success of and international acclaim for Sassicaia made it an influential lightning rod for the qualitative revolution that has taken place throughout Italy, particularly in Tuscany, and a catalyst for the extraordinary vineyard developments that have taken place along the Tuscan coastline, particularly in the Bolgheri area. It was among the first wines to earn international acceptance, and the fact that it was a Cabernet Sauvignon and competing with Bordeaux only added to its stature, nobility, and mystique.

The question that needs to be asked today: "Is Sassicaia as great as it was in vintages such as 1985 (the finest I've ever tasted), 1988, or 1990?" Certainly production is higher, but even if the vintages of the 1990s never hit the heights of the three great vintages in the 1980s, it is still one of the world's great wines and an extraordinarily elegant expression of Cabernet Sauvignon and Cabernet Franc grown in Italy.

SASSICAIA

1999 Sassicaia

RATING: 91+ points

A very elegant style of wine with notes of dried herbs, cedar, tobacco smoke, and sweet red and black currants, the 1999 is medium-bodied and delicately flavored, with nicely integrated wood, some spicy tannin, and a long finish. This deep ruby/purple–tinged wine is the quintessentially elegant style of Cabernet Sauvignon grown on the Tuscan coastline. Anticipated maturity: 2006–2016.

1998 Sassicaia

RATING: 90 points

The 1998 Sassicaia exhibits a dense ruby color with purple highlights and a classic nose of cedar, spice box, licorice, and black currants. Medium-bodied, powerful, extracted, and rich, as well as elegant and well balanced, it should evolve for another 12–17 years.

1995 Sassicaia

RATING: 92 points

This exceptional 1995 has another 12–14 years of aging potential ahead of it. The wine boasts a nearly opaque ruby/purple color, as well as a knockout nose of lead pencil, toast, minerals, licorice, and black currants. As the wine sat in the glass, violet/floral notes began to emerge. In the mouth, it is tightly knit and tannic but superbly concentrated as well as remarkably pure. It possesses that sweet, rich mid-palate that often distinguishes great wines from merely good ones. The finish lasts for over 30 seconds. The 1995 appears to be a Sassicaia to rival the estate's other top vintages. Anticipated maturity: now–2020.

1990 Sassicaia

RATING: 94 points

The 1990 Sassicaia appears to be the finest wine made at this estate since the nearly perfect 1985. It boasts a saturated purple, almost bluish, color and a sensational yet unevolved and youthful aromatic profile of sweet, nearly overripe black currants, cedar, tobacco, and toasty new oak. Full-bodied, with staggering concentration and extract levels, this tannic, super-pure, well-defined Cabernet possesses low enough acidity and sweet enough tannin to make it accessible. It will last through 2010.

1988 Sassicaia

RATING: 90 points

This firmly structured, medium-weight, restrained example of Sassicaia exhibits an impressive deep, dark ruby color and a perfumed, superripe nose of black fruits and toasty vanilla from aging in new oak casks. In the mouth there is excellent concentration, crisp acidity, and plenty of tannin, glycerin, and alcohol in the admirable finish. Though it is neither as multi-dimensional nor as concentrated as the otherworldly 1985, nor as opulent as the 1982, it is nevertheless another brilliant example of what heights Cabernet Sauvignon can achieve in the soils of Tuscany. Anticipated maturity: now–2012.

1985 Sassicaia

RATING: 100 points

I had this wine in a blind tasting in 1997; I have had it frequently, and have never failed to give it a perfect rating. (At the same time, I have often misidentified it in blind tastings as the 1986 Mouton Rothschild.) In this tasting, the wine was phenomenal. The color remained an opaque purple. The bouquet was beginning to develop secondary aromas of cedar and truffles to go along with its intense cassis, black raspberry, blackberry, tarry, toasty personality. Exceptionally dense, concentrated, and full-bodied, this wine possesses layers of concentrated fruit that are beautifully balanced by the wine's sweet tannin and well-integrated acidity. The finish lasts for nearly a minute. A monumental Cabernet Sauvignon, it is one of the greatest wines made in the 20th century. Tasting after tasting continues to confirm this wine's surreal level of quality. Despite being 11 years old at the tasting in 1997, it was still youthful. My best guess for when it will reach full maturity is between now and 2025. What a wine!

WINES:
Redigaffi
Giusto di Notri
OWNERS: Rita Tua and Virgilio Bisti
ADDRESS: Località Notri 81, 57028 Suvereto (LI), Italy
TELEPHONE: 39 0565 829237
TELEFAX: 39 0565 827891
E-MAIL: info@tuarita.it
WEBSITE: www.tuarita.it
CONTACT: Stefano Frascolla
VISITING POLICY: Only a few people, by appointment only

VINEYARDS

SURFACE AREA: 54 acres
GRAPE VARIETALS: Merlot, Cabernet Sauvignon, Cabernet
   Franc, Sangiovese
AVERAGE AGE OF THE VINES: 12 years
DENSITY OF PLANTATION: 8,000 vines per hectare
AVERAGE YIELDS: 42 quintals per hectare

WINEMAKING AND UPBRINGING

Ripe fruit, low yields, aging in barrel for 16–18 months, and
bottling without filtration is the *modus operandi* of Tua Rita.

ANNUAL PRODUCTION

Redigaffi: 3,200 bottles (1994–2001); 5,800 bottles in 2001
Giusto di Notri: 15,000 bottles (1991–2001); 23,000 bottles
   in 2001
AVERAGE PRICE (VARIABLE DEPENDING ON VINTAGE): $25–180

GREAT RECENT VINTAGES

1999 for the concentration, 2000 for the elegance, or so say
the proprietors; I would include 2001, 1998, 1997, and 1996

In the coastal Tuscan region known as Bolgheri, this
estate, acquired in 1985, has been graced by some of
Italy's finest winemaking consultants, including Riccardo Cotarella, Luca d'Attoma, and Stefano Chioccioli.
The wine has quickly become a legend. Under the guidance of its proprietors, Rita Tua and Virgilio Bisti, the
small vineyard was planted just outside the medieval
village of Suvereto in 1988, 1997, and 1998. It soon
gained international fame for its 100% Merlot wine
called Redigaffi and the blend of Merlot and Cabernet
Sauvignon called Giusto di Notri. Both are aged in
small French barrels.

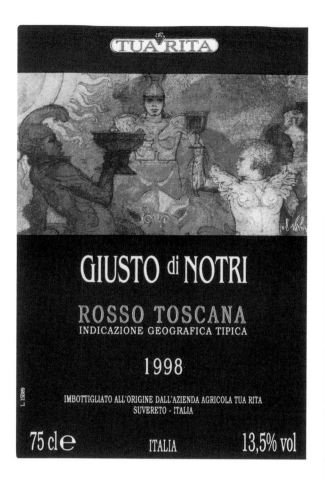

GIUSTO DI NOTRI

2001 Giusto di Notri

RATING: 95 points

A very potent, complex wine offering up notes of grilled meats, dried Provençal herbs, lead pencil shavings, crushed rocks, crème de cassis, and blackberries, this black/purple-colored wine is full-bodied, and has a seamless integration of acidity, tannin, and wood, and a blockbuster finish with no hard edges. Anticipated maturity: now–2020.

2000 Giusto di Notri

RATING: 95 points

The opaque purple–colored 2000 Giusto di Notri is impressive. A blend of 65% Cabernet Sauvignon, 30% Merlot, and 5% Cabernet Franc, it's aged 20 months in 100% new French oak before being bottled without filtration. The wine requires decanting to strut its stuff, but it is phenomenally rich with notes of blackberries, creosote, truffles, vanilla, and licorice presented in a full-bodied, powerful, concentrated style with remarkable precision and harmony for a wine of such massive intensity and richness. The finish lasts for 40–45 seconds. Anticipated maturity: 2007–2020.

1999 Giusto di Notri

RATING: 96 points

The brawny, serious, opaque purple–colored 1999 Giusto di Notri is a *barrique*-aged, unfined, unfiltered blend of 65% Cabernet Sauvignon and 35% Merlot. Its opaque purple color is accompanied by awesome aromas of weedy tobacco, espresso, smoke, chocolate, black currants, and blackberries. Dense, full-bodied, thick, viscous, rich, and pure, it should last for another 12+ years. Sadly, production was a measly 800 cases.

1998 Giusto di Notri

RATING: 93 points

The spectacular 1998 Giusto di Notri is a 60% Cabernet Sauvignon, 40% Merlot blend aged in French oak, of which 50% was new, and bottled unfined and unfiltered. A dense, murky ruby/purple color is followed by aromas of melted Valrhona chocolate, blackberries, smoke, and toast. Rich and full-bodied, with superb concentration, a seamless texture, low acidity, and a 40+-second finish, this huge, full-bodied wine should drink well between now and 2012.

1997 Giusto di Notri

RATING: 90 points

The outstanding 1997 Giusto di Notri (a 60% Cabernet Sauvignon and 40% Merlot blend aged in French oak and bottled with neither fining nor filtration) exhibits a dark ruby/purple color and excellent aromatics consisting of toasty new oak, lead pencil, black currants, chocolate, and smoke. Layered and rich but backward and unevolved, with copious tannin in the finish, this wine should improve with further cellaring. The low acidity and sweet fruit give it immediate accessibility, but the wine has not yet developed its secondary aromatics. Anticipated maturity: now–2012.

1996 Giusto di Notri

RATING: 90 points

The production of the 1996 Giusto di Notri *vino da tavola* (a blend of 60% Cabernet Sauvignon and 40% Merlot) was a meager 450 cases. An outstanding wine, it boasts a black ruby/purple color, as well as an intense nose of licorice, black currants, and a whiff of Provençal olives. Full-bodied, thick, and layered, with moderately high tannin, a slight austerity in the finish, and a concentrated, complete, and powerful feel, this pure, harmonious wine should be at its finest between now and 2012.

1994 Giusto di Notri

RATING: 93 points

The 1994 Giusto di Notri *vino da tavola* exhibits a saturated opaque purple color (it looked like a barrel sample of a profound vintage of Mouton Rothschild), as well as a knockout nose of black currants, sweet toasty oak, chocolate, smoke, and licorice. The wine is beautifully balanced, with superb purity, extraordinary concentration and length, medium to full body, and silky, sweet layers of flavor. It is both exceptionally intense and well balanced. Already accessible, it will continue to evolve gracefully. Anticipated maturity: now–2016.

REDIGAFFI

2001 Redigaffi

RATING: 97 points

This is an extraordinary wine with tremendous intensity of espresso roast intermixed with melted chocolate, black cherry liqueur, figs, and a hint of plum. Deep purple, almost black to the rim, with a big, smoky, earthy richness and tremendous viscosity and opulence, this is an amazing example of Merlot from the Tuscan coastline. Anticipated maturity: now–2018.

2000 Redigaffi

RATING: 100 points

The prodigious, unfined/unfiltered, inky/purple-colored 2000 Redigaffi (a 400-case 100% Merlot *cuvée*) is a wine of extraordinary distinction and intensity. It boasts a fabulous perfume of melted licorice mixed with high-quality espresso roast, black cherry and currant liqueur, white flowers, and toast. Boasting great intensity, glorious ripeness, formidable purity, and a finish that lasts nearly a minute, this is the stuff of dreams! Its dry extract number is about as high as one will find in a dry red wine. Additionally, its 15% alcohol is incredibly well concealed beneath the wealth of glycerin and fruit. A brilliant achievement! Kudos to winemaker Stefano Chioccioli and proprietors Rita Tua and Virgilio Bisti. Anticipated maturity: 2007–2018.

1999 Redigaffi

RATING: 99 points

The 1999 Redigaffi has an astonishing 36 grams per liter of dry extract, which exceeds most top Pomerols in a great vintage! Unfined and unfiltered, this 250-case *cuvée* of 100% Merlot is as close to perfection as a wine can get. The color is a deep saturated blue/purple. The powerful, pure nose offers smoke, licorice, black cherry, and blackberries. It boasts awesome concentration, a fabulously dense, viscous mid-section, and a finish that lasts for nearly a minute. This is riveting juice. Anticipated maturity: now–2015.

1998 Redigaffi

RATING: 96 points

The 1998 Redigaffi (2,000+ bottles produced) is profound. I do not normally quote dry extract numbers, because taste is more important than the numbers. However, I could not help but notice one of the highest measured dry extract numbers I have ever seen in a wine with the 1998 Redigaffi—39 grams per liter! Made from 100% Merlot, aged in 100% new Allier and Tronçais French barrels, it is bottled without fining or filtration. An opaque purple–colored, powerful, enormously endowed effort, it offers gorgeous black currant, plum, and blackberry fruit characteristics infused with spice box, chocolate, and vanilla. This harmonious wine oozes with extract and glycerin. Extraordinarily pure and impressive, with copious tannin nearly hidden beneath the wine's superb richness, this beauty should be at its apogee between now and 2020.

1997 Redigaffi

RATING: 94 points

This wine is a classic example of Merlot's potential in this coastal section of Tuscany. The spectacular, black/purple-colored 1997 Redigaffi boasts huge, chocolaty, blackberry, smoky nose and flavors, a full-bodied personality oozing with extract and ripe, juicy fruit, sensational length (45+ seconds), and brilliant purity and symmetry. Anticipated maturity: now–2012.

1996 Redigaffi

RATING: 94 points

The 1996 Redigaffi *vino da tavola* is a 100% Merlot made from yields of approximately 2 tons of fruit per acre. The first word in my tasting notes is "Wow!" An explosive nose of cherry liqueur, smoke, coffee, vanilla, and jammy black fruits is followed by a superbly delineated, rich, layered, multifaceted wine with full body, exceptional purity and concentration, a voluptuous texture, and a powerful, blockbuster finish. The high level of extract and richness conceals lofty tannin and alcohol. Anticipated maturity: now–2012.

1994 Redigaffi

RATING: 93 points

The 100% Merlot 1994 Redigaffi is awesome. I suspect the likes of Christian Moueix and Michel Rolland from Pomerol would be thrilled to taste this wine, as it possesses the quintessential Merlot characteristics: chocolate, mocha, jammy black cherries, and toast, as well as subtle herbs. This wine is extraordinarily rich, full-bodied, opulent, and, as my enthusiastic notes read, "great stuff." With full body, low acidity, luscious layers of chewy, jammy fruit, and a finish that lasts for more than 30 seconds, this is a terrific Merlot. It should drink well for another 5–8+ years.

ROBERTO VOERZIO

WINES:

Barolo La Serra

Barolo Brunate

Barolo Cerequio

Barolo Vecchie Viti dei Capalot e delle Brunate Riserva

OWNER: Roberto Voerzio

ADDRESS: Località Cerreto 7, 12064 La Morra (CN), Italy

TELEPHONE: 39 173 509196

TELEFAX: 39 173 509196

E-MAIL: voerzioroberto@libero.it

CONTACT: Roberto Voerzio's staff

VISITING POLICY: Phone before visiting

VINEYARDS

SURFACE AREA: 21.65 acres

GRAPE VARIETALS: Dolcetto d'Alba, Nebbiolo d'Alba, Barbera d'Alba, Cabernet Sauvignon

AVERAGE AGE OF THE VINES: La Serra: 18 years; Brunate: 15–40 years; Cerequio: 12–26 years; Capalot: 50 years

DENSITY OF PLANTATION: 4,000–6,000 vines per hectare

AVERAGE YIELDS: 4 tons per hectare

WINEMAKING AND UPBRINGING

An absolutely manic, uncompromising perfectionist runs this estate, and he is obsessed with getting full ripeness out of the grapes. Once harvested by hand, the grapes are fermented in 3- to 3.5-ton stainless-steel tanks for up to two weeks at temperatures of 30–35°C. They also complete malolactic fermentation in tank, and then, usually toward the end of November, the wine is transferred to 60-gallon small oak barrels for another 20–28 months of barrel aging. At the end of that period, the wine is again transferred back into stainless-steel tanks for several months and then finally bottled unfiltered and released after an additional 12 months of bottle aging. The sulfur dioxide levels are among the lowest in Piedmont.

ANNUAL PRODUCTION

Barbera d'Alba D.O.C. Vigneto Pozzo dell'Annunziata Riserva: 1,500 magnums

Barolo D.O.C.G. Brunate: 3,500 bottles

Barolo D.O.C.G. Cerequio: 4,000 bottles

Barolo D.O.C.G. Vecchie Viti dei Capalot e delle Brunate Riserva: 1,200 magnums

Barolo D.O.C.G. Rocche dell'Annunziata/Torroglione: 5,000 bottles

Barolo D.O.C.G. Sarmassa di Barolo: 650 magnums

Dolcetto d'Alba D.O.C. Priavino: 18,000 bottles

Langhe Rosso D.O.C. Vignaserra: 8,000 bottles

AVERAGE PRICE (VARIABLE DEPENDING ON VINTAGE): $75–500

GREAT RECENT VINTAGES

2001, 2000, 1999, 1998, 1997, 1996, 1990, 1989, 1988

Though Roberto Voerzio's estate is just under 22 acres, he has quickly emerged as one of Piedmont's superstars. In terms of quality, he is on fire, producing one of the region's most profound Barberas as well as some of the most majestic, complex Barolos. He believes in organic growing and is a fanatical crop thinner. He often thins his vineyard by as much as 50% prior to harvest, leaving only 4–5 bunches of grapes per vine (compare this to 30–50 bunches per vine in many Napa vineyards). Voerzio is a modernist, fermenting his wines with indigenous yeasts and putting them into a combination of Taransaud and Vicard French new oak.

Over the last decade, Voerzio has produced some of Italy's most stunningly complete, complex wines. In fact, an argument can be made that no one makes better Barbera than the Vigneto Pozzo dell'Annunziata. In addition to a tiny parcel of Sarmassa di Barolo he purchased in 1998, Voerzio owns three vineyards from which emerge the Cerequio (350–400 cases), the Serra (400 cases), and the Brunate (300 cases) cuvées. The single-vineyard Capalot Riserva is made from a plot of the oldest vines in the Brunate vineyard. This wine, bottled only in magnums (approximately 1,000) is produced only in the top vintages. In 2000, Voerzio added an additional cru, the famed Pozzo dell'Annunziata, to his portfolio. Consequently, beginning in 2000, there have been six crus, compared to four in 1997 and former vintages.

BAROLO BRUNATE

2000 Barolo Brunate

RATING: 94 points

With a stunning aromatic display of rose petals intermixed with truffle oil, sweet cherry, currant, tobacco, and date, this full-bodied wine shows no hard edges, very sweet integrated tannin, low acidity, and an opulent, full-bodied finish. It can be drunk now or cellared for up to 12–15 years.

1998 Barolo Brunate

RATING: 92 points

Dense, masculine, and muscular, the 1998 Barolo Brunate displays abundant quantities of blackberry and cherry liqueur aromas intertwined with vanilla, licorice, tobacco, and rose petals. The new oak is brilliantly absorbed by this medium to full–bodied, sweet, expansively flavored Barolo. Anticipated maturity: now–2016.

1997 Barolo Brunate

RATING: 92 points

A big wine, the dense, opaque ruby/purple–colored, tannic 1997 Barolo Brunate exhibits copious aromas of cassis, black cherry, kirsch, licorice, smoke, truffles, and new oak. Notes of coffee and chocolate emerge as the wine sits in the glass. It possesses amazing density, a lot of muscle, and a roasted character to its fruity personality. This backstrapping, full-bodied Barolo requires cellaring. Anticipated maturity: 2007–2025.

1996 Barolo Brunate

RATING: 95 points

The fabulous, black/purple-colored 1996 Barolo Brunate is gigantic. Monstrous in size, with huge alcohol, high tannin, and spectacular extract, this layered, chewy wine is sensationally promising. Although stubbornly backward, it possesses wonderful ripeness, but it is so huge it needs another year or two to evolve. Anticipated maturity: 2006–2030.

1988 Barolo Brunate

RATING: 91 points

All three 1988 Barolos from Roberto Voerzio were outstanding. It is hard to pick a favorite since they are young and un-evolved. The 1988 Barolo Brunate is the biggest, most masculine, and most full-bodied of the trio. It is also the most concentrated and tannic. If all the tannins melt away, it will have the highest potential for longevity. Anticipated maturity: now–2007.

BAROLO VECCHIE VITI DEI CAPALOT E DELLE BRUNATE RISERVA

2000 Barolo Vecchie Viti dei Capalot e delle Brunate Riserva

RATING: 98 points

A magnificent wine. Although far more evolved and forward than I would have suspected, nonetheless this is a compelling effort. Dense plum/purple to the rim with just a bit of lightening at the edge, this is a massive wine with oodles of glycerin-imbued black cherry fruit tinged with notes of new saddle leather, spice box, tobacco, and allspice. It is a huge, massive, full-bodied wine that needs bottle age. Anticipated maturity: 2009–2025.

1998 Barolo Vecchie Viti dei Capalot e delle Brunate Riserva

RATING: 95 points

From Voerzio's oldest vines (50 years), 1,200 magnums were produced of the 1998 Barolo Vecchie Viti dei Capalot e delle Brunate Riserva. This effort ratchets up the intensity level, offering volume, power, density, and flavor extraction. It is an incredible achievement. Its dense ruby/purple color is accompanied by a big, thick nose of black cherries, cherry syrup, espresso, toast, and roasted meats. This massive, huge, tannic 1998 requires cellaring. Anticipated maturity: 2009–2030.

1997 Barolo Vecchie Viti dei Capalot e delle Brunate Riserva

RATING: 98 points

The formidable 1997 Barolo Vecchie Viti dei Capalot e delle Brunate Riserva is a candidate for Barolo of the vintage. A massive wine, it exhibits aromas and flavors of vitamins, coffee, chocolate, black cherry liqueur, licorice, and toast, plus a terrific palate entry with oodles of glycerin as well as extract, multiple flavor layers, and sweet tannin in the 60-second finish. There is plenty of tannin lurking beneath the surface, so ideally, it needs to be aged. This is a tour de force in winemaking! Anticipated maturity: 2010–2030.

1996 Barolo Vecchie Viti dei Capalot e delle Brunate Riserva

RATING: 93+ points

The profound 1996 Barolo Vecchie Viti dei Capalot e delle Brunate Riserva boasts a dense ruby/purple color and a pure nose of black cherries, raspberries, and blackberries. Layered and multidimensional, with a sweet mid-palate and a blockbuster finish, this is an immense, full-throttle Barolo that should age effortlessly for another 10–20 years. Impressive!

1995 Barolo Vecchie Viti dei Capalot e delle Brunate Riserva

RATING: 91 points

The 1995 Barolo Vecchie Viti dei Capalot e delle Brunate Riserva is a thick, chewy offering with a stunning display of aromatics: cigar smoke, Chinese black tea, new oak, cherry liqueur, and dried Provençal herbs. Extremely full-bodied and rich, and surprisingly huge for a 1995, this Barolo possesses amazing extract as well as a finish that lasts for nearly a minute. Extremely rich and powerful but accessible, it can be drunk now. Anticipated maturity: now–2014.

BAROLO CEREQUIO

1999 Barolo Cerequio

RATING: 93 points

Rose petal notes intermixed with hints of truffle, saddle leather, herbs, sweet cherries, plums, and fig are followed by a medium to full–bodied wine with excellent texture, impressive concentration, and some spicy oak and loamy earthy scents. This very beautiful 1999 can be drunk now or cellared for 12–15 years.

1998 Barolo Cerequio

RATING: 90 points

The dark ruby/purple–colored 1998 Barolo Cerequio is structured and backward. It emerges from a south-facing vineyard from which Angelo Gaja produces his Conteisa. This tannic, structured, rigidly styled Barolo is loaded with black cherry fruit, rose petal, and tar notes. Anticipated maturity: 2006–2020.

1997 Barolo Cerequio

RATING: 92 points

The paradoxical 1997 Barolo Cerequio possesses exquisite purity as well as an open-knit bouquet but restrained, tannic, forceful, backward flavors. Dense and rich, with the vintage's thickness well displayed, it will be at its best between now and 2020.

1996 Barolo Cerequio

RATING: 91 points

The opaque ruby/purple–colored 1996 Barolo Cerequio possesses extremely high tannin and extract, but it is very backward, closed, and firm. Full-bodied, powerful, and rich, but broodingly backward and stubborn, it possesses all the correct component parts, but patience will be required by purchasers. Anticipated maturity: 2010–2025.

1988 Barolo Cerequio

RATING: 91 points

The 1988 Barolo Cerequio is rich and tight, with a beautiful inner core of sweet fruit, as well as a fragrant tar-scented Nebbiolo nose. Anticipated maturity: now–2015

BAROLO LA SERRA

1999 Barolo La Serra

RATING: 93 points

With a deep ruby/purple hue, this wine shows plenty of berry, crushed rock, and almost minty notes intermixed with a hint of espresso and licorice. The wine is medium-bodied, very elegant, and quite rich, sweet, and intense. Anticipated maturity: 2008–2020.

1998 Barolo La Serra

RATING: 91 points

The 1998 Barolo La Serra is a finesse-styled offering, exhibiting a deep ruby color in addition to a sexy nose of sweet black cherries, fennel, vanilla, and spice. Its velvety texture, full

body, and overall harmony suggest it will drink well young as well as over the next 8–12 years.

1997 Barolo La Serra
RATING: 92 points
The 1997 Barolo La Serra is a sexy, dense ruby/purple–colored effort offering notes of currants, black cherries, and licorice, a huge, chewy texture, plenty of glycerin, and a creamy, supple, velvety finish. Although impossible to resist, it will develop even more nuances. Anticipated maturity: now–2020.

1996 Barolo La Serra
RATING: 93 points
The superb 1996 Barolo La Serra's opaque ruby/purple color is followed by aromas of black fruits (blackberry, cherry, and a hint of raspberry); superb purity; highly extracted, powerful, monster-sized flavors; mouth-searing levels of tannin; and an impressively endowed, 40+-second finish. This backward, pure, intensely concentrated Barolo will require patience. Anticipated maturity: 2008–2025.

Portuguese table wines are increasingly available throughout the world, but they remain a work in progress. While the potential for exciting Portuguese table wines is unquestionable, for most people, Portugal means Port, particularly great Vintage Ports. In short, these are primarily red wines augmented by brandy, which stops the fermentation and produces a wine both sweet and high in alcohol.

During the 18th and 19th centuries, the Port trade was primarily controlled by British wine merchants who purchased casks of Port, shipped them to England, and bottled the wine at their leisure. Virtually all of the finest Port vineyards are in the Douro Valley, the epicenter of Port production. These vineyards were destroyed by a fungus in the mid-19th century, and were hit again by the phylloxera epidemic 20 years later. However, the 20th century saw a rebound in Port, and today many consumers consider it the world's most civilized and complex after-dinner alcoholic beverage.

There are many top Port houses, but the three greatest are included in the following chapter.

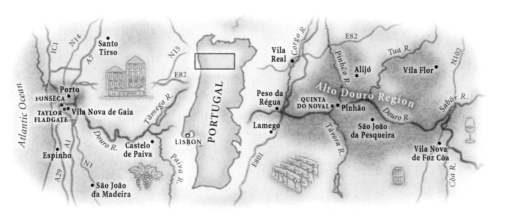

WINE: Vintage Port

CLASSIFICATION: Port Wine—Portugal

OWNER: Fonseca-Guimaraens Vinhos SA (Alistair Robertson, Chairman)

ADDRESS: P.O. Box 1313, E.C. Santa Marinha, 4401–501 Vila Nova de Gaia, Portugal

TELEPHONE: 351 223 742 800

TELEFAX: 351 223 742 899

E-MAIL: marketing@fonseca.pt

WEBSITE: www.fonseca.pt

CONTACT: Ms. Ana Margarida Morgado

VISITING POLICY: Quinta do Panascal open Monday–Friday, 10 A.M.–6 P.M.; open weekends from June to October. Closed on all national holidays between November and February. Tastings and audio tour available.

VINEYARDS

SURFACE AREA: Quinta do Panascal: 108.7 acres under vine; Quinta do Cruzeiro: 32 acres under vine; Quinta de Santo António: 14.8 acres under vine

GRAPE VARIETALS: Quinta do Panascal—16% Touriga Nacional, 29% Touriga Francesa, 32% Tinta Roriz, 2% Tinto Cão, 8% Tinta Barroca, 8% Tinta Amarela, 5% other varietals

Quinta do Cruzeiro—1% Touriga Nacional, 31% Touriga Francesa, 19% Tinta Roriz, 32% Tinta Barroca, 4% Tinta Amarela, 13% other varietals

Quinta de Santo António—12% Touriga Nacional, 33% Touriga Francesa, 18% Tinta Roriz, 2% Tinto Cão, 17% Tinta Barroca, 7% Tinta Amarela, 11% other varietals

AVERAGE AGE OF THE VINES: 30 years

DENSITY OF PLANTATION: 3,500 vines per hectare

AVERAGE YIELDS: 30–35 hectoliters per hectare

WINEMAKING AND UPBRINGING

For Vintage Port, the grapes are crushed in *lagares* (stone troughs in which the grapes are trodden—by feet—and fermented) over a 3-day period. Fermentation is arrested once approximately half the natural grape sugar has been turned into alcohol by adding 77% alc./vol. neutral grape spirit. The ratio of must to grape spirit is four to one. The Port is stored in large old oak vats until the following spring, when the wines are transported to Vila

Nova de Gaia to be matured. Vintage Port remains in large oak vats of 25,000–100,000 liters for 2 years before being bottled and then sold. Late Bottled Vintage Port remains in large oak vats for 4–6 years before being bottled and sold. It is sold ready to drink. The firm's 10, 20, 30, and 40–year-old Tawny Ports are matured in 630-liter "pipes" (old casks) before being bottled. Each age designation is an average age of the Tawny Port. These Ports are normally racked once a year.

ANNUAL PRODUCTION

Fonseca Vintage Port: 8,000–14,000 cases

AVERAGE PRICE (VARIABLE DEPENDING ON VINTAGE): $60-100

GREAT RECENT VINTAGES

2000, 1997, 1994, 1992, 1985, 1983, 1977, 1970, 1963

In 1822, M. P. Guimaraens bought the existing Port shippers of Fonseca, Monteiro & Co., and 25 years later Fonseca declared their first vintage. Over the next century, the company built a flourishing market and purchased additional vineyards, including Quinta do Cruzeiro (1973), Quinta do Panascal (1978), and Quinta de Santo António (1979).

This is always the most flamboyant, exuberant, and exotic of the Vintage Ports, with a character that is completely different from that of its peers. Whether it is the Asian spice or balsamic component, or just its tremendous, exotic perfume, Fonseca is unique. It also tends to reach full maturity at a slightly more rapid pace than other Vintage Ports, yet it has the extraordinary ability to hold its fruit and continue to drink well for 30–40 years.

FONSECA VINTAGE PORT

2000 Fonseca Vintage Port

RATING: 95 points

Dense ruby/purple–colored, with an exotic, exuberant perfume of black fruits, flowers, incense, and licorice, this unctuously textured, full-bodied port is one of the most concentrated of the vintage. Sweet, expansive, and succulent, this large-scaled but remarkably well-balanced effort is surprisingly

forward and accessible (by Fonseca's standards). Anticipated maturity: 2006–2025.

1997 Fonseca Vintage Port
RATING: 93 points

Somewhat of a lightweight for Fonseca but undeniably charming, this dark ruby/purple–colored wine offers a floral, exotic, flamboyant bouquet and a sweet, fleshy style, but not a great deal of weight or massiveness. Heady alcohol, sweet tannin, and a velvety texture make for a gorgeous finish. While I would have preferred to see more weight, structure, and intensity, this is an outstanding, albeit lighter than normal Fonseca. Anticipated maturity: now–2020.

1994 Fonseca Vintage Port
RATING: 97 points

One of the most spectacular 1994s, this opaque purple–colored wine is an exotic, flamboyant, ostentatious Port. Extremely fragrant and pungent, with a flashy display of jammy cassis, pepper, licorice, and truffles, this Port is an attention grabber. Awesomely rich and full-bodied, with superb length and overall balance, it possesses a huge mid-palate, layers of flavor, an unctuous texture, and a blockbuster finish. Everything is in place, with the brandy and tannin well integrated, even concealed, by the masses of fruit and glycerin. Anticipated maturity: now–2035.

1992 Fonseca Vintage Port

RATING: 97 points

Fonseca's 1992 is a majestic young Port that rivals this house's great efforts (1985, 1977, 1970, 1963). This colossal Vintage Port reveals a nearly opaque black/purple color, and an explosive nose of jammy black fruits, licorice, chocolate, and spices. Extremely full-bodied and unctuously textured, this multilayered, enormously endowed Port reveals a finish that lasts for over a minute. It is a magnificent Port that will age well for 30–40 years.

1985 Fonseca Vintage Port

RATING: 90 points

The 1985 looks to be one of the top successes of the vintage, yet I believe both the superb 1983 and the otherworldly 1977 are far superior. Dense ruby/purple with the Oriental spice box aroma, the 1985 is an expansive, sweet, broadly flavored wine with outstanding depth, concentration, and balance. It finishes with a solid lashing of alcohol and tannin. Anticipated maturity: now–2025.

1983 Fonseca Vintage Port

RATING: 92 points

The 1983 is magnificently scented (licorice, incense, balsam), full-bodied, creamy, and rather forward, but shows great length and character. While fully mature, it should last through 2015–2020.

1977 Fonseca Vintage Port

RATING: 93+ points

The 1977, which has developed nicely in the bottle, represents the finest Fonseca produced between 1970 and 1992. However, I am not convinced it has the extraordinary concentration of the best Fonseca vintages. It seems less impressive in 2004 than it was when it was first tasted. There is some amber at the edge of its color, but the perfume reveals the telltale Fonseca aromas of jammy fruit intermixed with crushed nuts, incense, and balsamic hints as well as plums. Medium to full–bodied and drier than most vintages, with muscular tannin in the finish, it appears to be at the end of its adolescence and is just beginning to blossom, so perhaps I am underestimating it. Anticipated maturity: now–2030.

1970 Fonseca Vintage Port

RATING: 97 points

An extraordinary Vintage Port, the powerful, exotic, multidimensional 1970 boasts a dark plum color with light amber at the rim. An intoxicatingly fragrant perfume of incense, licorice, caramel, black and red fruits, and notions of saddle leather soars from the glass of this unctuously textured, full-bodied, velvety offering. This magnificent Port is finally hitting full maturity, where it should rest for another 20+ years.

1963 Fonseca Vintage Port

RATING: 96 points

Cut from a mold similar to the 1977 but seemingly better (largely because it is fully mature), the ruggedly constructed, concentrated 1963 is more firmly structured and masculine than most Fonsecas. A fragrant bouquet of tar, licorice, red and black fruits, scorched earth, coffee, and leather is followed by a big, muscular, firm, still-tannic wine loaded with glycerin. It shows no signs of decline. Anticipated maturity: now–2035.

WINES:

Vintage Port

Vintage Port Nacional

CLASSIFICATION: Port Wine—Portugal

OWNER: AXA Millésimes

ADDRESS: Av. Diogo Leite, 256, 4400-III Vila Nova de Gaia,
Portugal

TELEPHONE: 351 223 770 270

TELEFAX: 351 223 750 365

WEBSITE: www.quintadonoval.com

CONTACT: Christian Seely, Managing Director, and Antonio
Agrellos, Technical Director

VISITING POLICY: By appointment only

VINEYARDS

SURFACE AREA: 247 acres

GRAPE VARIETALS: Touriga Nacional, Tinto Cão, Touriga
Francesa, Tinta Roriz, Tinta Barroca, Sousao, Tinta
Amarela

AVERAGE AGE OF THE VINES: 30 years

DENSITY OF PLANTATION: Variable

AVERAGE YIELDS: 30 hectoliters per hectare

WINEMAKING AND UPBRINGING

Quinta do Noval is unusual among the great traditional Port
houses in that it emphasizes the importance of the vineyard.
It is significant that the company is named after its vineyard,
that it is entirely based in the Douro Valley, and that its principal Vintage Ports, Quinta do Noval Nacional and Quinta do
Noval, are both single-vineyard wines. The aim is to produce
classic Vintage Ports that are harmonious and elegant expressions of Quinta do Noval's *terroir*. Strict selection in the vineyard, low yields, and strict selection again in the tasting room
result in a small production. Techniques are a blend of the
traditional and the modern. All Quinta do Noval production
is trodden in *lagares* as it always has been, but standards of
winemaking and hygiene are extremely rigorous. Noval is also
unique in that it has a five-acre parcel of ungrafted grapes,
from which it produces Nacional, a unique Vintage Port of
outstanding quality and longevity.

ANNUAL PRODUCTION

Quinta do Noval Vintage Port: 10,000–20,000 bottles

Quinta do Noval Vintage Port Nacional: 2,000 bottles

AVERAGE PRICE (VARIABLE DEPENDING ON VINTAGE): $75-450

GREAT RECENT VINTAGES

2000, 1997, 1994, 1967, 1966, 1963, 1962 (Nacional only),
1960, 1955, 1934, 1931

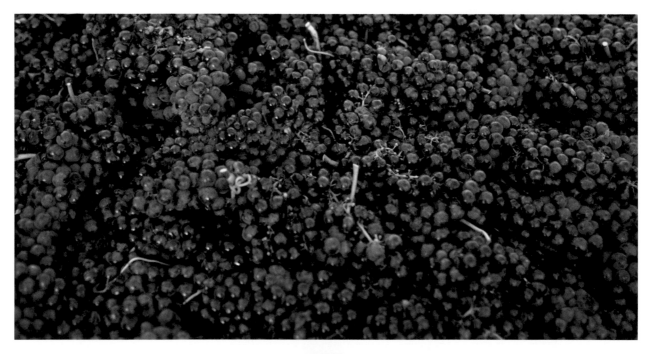

The name of Quinta do Noval first appeared in land registries in 1715. In the 19th century, the estate passed by marriage to the Viscount Vilar D'Allen, who was renowned for hosting wild parties at Noval for which he imported dancing girls from the Folies Bergère.

By the 1880s, the Douro Valley had been ravaged by phylloxera, and, like many estates, Quinta do Noval was put on the market. In 1894, it was bought by the distinguished Port shipper António José da Silva. Da Silva replanted the vineyards and renovated buildings on the estate. His work was continued by his son-in-law, Luiz Vasconcelos Porto, who was responsible for an extensive modernization program, transforming the old narrow terraces into the wide whitewashed ones seen today, allowing better use of space and more exposure to the sun. He also built Noval's reputation in the United Kingdom, focusing his attention on Oxford, Cambridge, and private clubs.

Noval made its name with the declaration of 1931—arguably the most sensational Port of the 20th century (and certainly the most expensive). Due to the world recession and vast shipments of the 1927s still on the market, only three shippers declared 1931.

Quinta do Noval has always been an innovator. The first stenciled bottles were introduced by Noval in the 1920s; Noval pioneered the concept of indicating age (10, 20, and over 40 years) on the Old Tawnies label,

and in 1958, it was the first house to introduce a Late Bottled Vintage, the 1954 Quinta do Noval LBV.

In 1963, Porto's grandsons, Fernando and Luiz Van Zeller, took over the company. Another extensive program of modernization was implemented, including new vinification equipment, new plantings, and the practice of bottling the vast majority of wines in Vila Nova de Gaia (in 1963 only 15% of Noval Ports were bottled there; 15 years later the figure was 85%).

In the autumn of 1981, a catastrophic fire swept through Noval's lodge, bottling plant, and offices in Vila Nova de Gaia, destroying 350,000 liters of stock, 20,000 bottles of the 1978 vintage, and more than two centuries' worth of records. The following year a new generation of the family entered the company: Cristiano and Teresa Van Zeller (great-grandchildren of Luiz Vasconcelos Porto), then aged 23 and 22, respectively.

In 1982, building began on a vast lodge at Quinta do Noval. In 1986, the Portuguese government changed the shipping laws, allowing Port houses to export directly from the Douro Valley. Noval was the first major house to be able to take advantage of the new legislation and announced in 1989 that it would be moving most of its stock there.

In May 1993, the Van Zeller family sold the company to AXA Millésimes, one of the world's largest insurance groups. The AXA group already owned a string of leading Bordeaux châteaux, such as Pichon-Longueville Comtesse de Lalande and Cantenac Brown, and an estate in Hungary's Tokay region named Disznöko. The Quinta do Noval deal included the 358-acre estate, together with stocks and production facilities.

In October 1993, Englishman Christian Seely was appointed managing director of Quinta do Noval. In 1994, Noval began a major program of technical improvements, including replanting and renovation of the vineyards, a new vinification center, improvements to the Douro lodge, and the construction of a new warehouse and bottling plant in the Douro. The results of Seely's administration and enormous investments have propelled Quinta do Noval into the top rank of Port houses.

QUINTA DO NOVAL VINTAGE PORT

2000 Quinta do Noval Vintage Port

RATING: 92 points

The saturated blue/purple/black–colored 2000 Vintage Port reveals a distinctive bouquet of graphite, crème de cassis, licorice, and spice. Sweet tannin, full body, and outstanding concentration provide an impressive entry on the palate. Notions of chocolate make an appearance in the long finish of this sweet, lush, precocious effort. Anticipated maturity: 2008–2030.

1997 Quinta do Noval Vintage Port

RATING: 100 points

The 1997 Vintage Port is the greatest Quinta do Noval I have ever tasted. The wine of the vintage, this black/purple-colored Port boasts fabulous aromatics (espresso, blackberries, licorice, tar, and flowers), followed by massive concentration, full body, and outstanding levels of depth and richness. Gorgeously sweet, stunningly concentrated, and full-bodied, this profound Vintage Port should be legendary. Quinta do Noval's production normally approaches 4,000 cases, but in 1997, only 1,200 cases were produced, so availability is extremely limited. Anticipated maturity: now–2035.

1994 Quinta do Noval Vintage Port

RATING: 95 points

The 1994 Vintage Port may be the finest regular Vintage Port I have tasted from this house in decades. Sadly, the production was absurdly small (approximately 800 cases), as the owners, France's AXA, wanted to make a statement about quality immediately after their acquisition. It is opaque ruby/purple-colored, with fabulous purity and richness, full body, moderate sweetness, layers of jammy fruit, and well-integrated alcohol. There is some tannin in the finish, but this is a large-scaled, authoritatively flavored as well as elegant Port. Anticipated maturity: now–2035.

QUINTA DO NOVAL VINTAGE PORT NACIONAL

1997 Quinta do Noval Vintage Port Nacional

RATING: 98+ points

This black/purple-colored effort reveals tight, reserved notes of graphite, blackberries, minerals, and espresso. Full-bodied, unctuously textured as well as hugely concentrated and dense, it remains 10–15 years away from drinkability. It should rival, and ultimately eclipse, the 1997 Vintage Port. Moreover, it will last 20–30 years longer. Anticipated maturity: 2018–2050+.

1994 Quinta do Noval Vintage Port Nacional

RATING: 96 points

This dense purple–hued Port reveals sweet aromas of blackberries, blueberries, nuts, scorched earth, and graphite. Full-bodied, powerful, and backward, it possesses massive concentration, huge tannin, and a long, spectacular finish. Anticipated maturity: 2015–2045.

1970 Quinta do Noval Vintage Port Nacional

RATING: 96 points

Exhibiting a dark plum-purple color with a bit of lightening at the edge as well as a huge, smoky nose offering up sweet fig, blackberry, currant, chocolate, plum, and fruitcake scents, this full-bodied Port has just passed adolescence. As the wine sits in the glass, a licorice note also emerges. Beautifully pure and concentrated, with plenty of tannin, it should remain at its peak until 2040.

1963 Quinta do Noval Vintage Port Nacional

RATING: 98 points

The dark plum/garnet–colored 1963 reveals a touch of amber at the rim. An enormous Port of great power, tannin, muscle, and concentration, it offers super notes of ripe dates/figs, blackberries, coffee, and chocolate. Still amazingly youthful for a 40+-year wine, it is a Vintage Port tour de force with immortal potential. Anticipated maturity: 2008–2050.

WINE: Vintage Port

CLASSIFICATION: Port Wine—Portugal

OWNER: Taylor, Fladgate & Yeatman Vinhos SA (known only in North America as "Taylor Fladgate," not "Taylor's"); Alistair Robertson, Chairman

ADDRESS: P.O. Box 1311, E. C. Santa Marinha, 4401–501 Vila Nova de Gaia, Portugal

TELEPHONE: 351 223 742 800

TELEFAX: 351 223 742 899

E-MAIL: marketing@taylor.pt

WEBSITE: www.taylor.pt

CONTACT: Ms. Ana Margarida Morgado

VISITING POLICY: Visitor's lodge in Vila Nova de Gaia open Monday–Friday, 10 A.M.–6 P.M. Closed weekends except in August.

VINEYARDS

SURFACE AREA: Quinta de Vargellas—187.7 acres under vine

Quinta de Terra Feita–148.2 acres under vine

Quinta de Junco–101.3 acres under vine

GRAPE VARIETALS:

Quinta de Vargellas—25% Touriga Nacional, 25% Touriga Francesa, 22% Tinta Roriz, 6% Tinto Cão, 7% Tinta Barroca, 5% Tinta Amarela, 10% other varietals

Quinta de Terra Feita—13% Touriga Nacional, 27% Touriga Francesa, 22% Tinta Roriz, 4% Tinto Cão, 13% Tinta Barroca, 7% Tinta Amarela, 15% other varietals

Quinta de Junco—20% Touriga Nacional, 15% Touriga Francesa, 20% Tinta Roriz, 10% Tinto Cão, 20% Tinta Barroca, 15% Tinta Amarela

AVERAGE AGE OF THE VINES: 40 years

DENSITY OF PLANTATION: 3,500 vines per hectare

AVERAGE YIELDS: 30–35 hectoliters per hectare

WINEMAKING AND UPBRINGING

For Vintage Port, the grapes are crushed by foot in stone *lagares* over a three-day period. Fermentation is arrested once approximately half the natural grape sugar has been turned into alcohol by adding 77% alc./vol. neutral grape spirit. The ratio of must to grape spirit is four to one. The Port is stored in large old oak vats until the following spring, when the wines are transported to Vila Nova de Gaia to be matured. The Vintage Port remains in large oak vats of 25,000–100,000 liters for two years before being bottled and then sold. The 10-, 20-, 30-, and 40-year-old Tawny Ports are matured in 630 liter "pipes" (old casks) before being bottled. Each age designation is an average age of the Tawny Port. These Ports are normally racked once a year.

ANNUAL PRODUCTION

Vintage Port: vintage sensitive, but on average, 20,000 cases

AVERAGE PRICE (VARIABLE DEPENDING ON VINTAGE): $60–100

GREAT RECENT VINTAGES

2000, 1997, 1994, 1992, 1983, 1977, 1970, 1963, 1955

Aside from the limited-production Quinta do Noval Nacional, Taylor Fladgate is the most expensive Vintage Port. The reasons for this are obvious. First of all, it is extremely long-lived, and second, it is a wine of extraordinary richness and complexity. For me, it is the Château Latour of Vintage Ports. It needs 10–15 years after its declaration to approach its adolescence, and should last 30–40 years. It is not the flashiest Vintage Port, nor does it possess the flamboyance, exuberance, or exoticism of Fonseca, but it is as good as gold in the bank.

The company is no youngster, having been founded in 1692. It was the first Port house to purchase real estate in the famed Douro Valley. In 1844 the company took the name Taylor, Fladgate & Yeatman. Over recent years, it has been building quite an empire, acquiring the famed Port house of Fonseca, then Croft and the well-known Delaforce firm. None of this has changed the intrinsic high quality of the Taylor Vintage Ports.

TAYLOR FLADGATE

2000 Taylor Fladgate

RATING: 98 points

Among the most saturated blue/purple/black–colored examples of the vintage, Taylor's 2000 tastes like a young vintage of Château Latour on steroids. Aromas of graphite, blackberry liqueur, crème de cassis, and smoke jump from the glass. Spectacularly concentrated and enormously endowed, with sweetness allied to ripe tannin, decent acidity, and layer upon layer of fruit and extract, this is the leading candidate for the Port of the vintage. Anticipated maturity: 2010–2040.

1997 Taylor Fladgate

RATING: 96 points

Saturated black/purple–colored, with stunning aromatics of blueberries, blackberries, licorice, and iron, this spectacular Vintage Port is one of the stars of the vintage. Extremely full-bodied, with silky tannin, spectacular concentration and purity, multiple flavor levels, and an evolved, forward personality, this is an exquisite yet precocious 1997 Vintage Port. Anticipated maturity: now–2030.

1994 Taylor Fladgate

RATING: 97 points

Among young Vintage Ports, Taylor is always the most backward. However, it has the potential to be the most majestic. This classically made, opaque purple–colored wine is crammed with blueberries and cassis. It reveals high tannin and a reserved style, but it has an enormous constitution with massive body, a formidable mid-palate, and exceptional length. It is a young, rich, powerful Taylor that, compared to the more flashy, forward style of the 1992, has more in common with such vintages as 1977 and 1970. Anticipated maturity: 2008–2045.

1992 Taylor Fladgate

RATING: 100 points

Taylor's 1992 Vintage Port is unquestionably the greatest young Port I have ever tasted. It represents the essence of what Vintage Port can achieve. The color is an opaque black/purple, and the nose offers up fabulously intense aromas of minerals, cassis, blackberries, licorice, and spices, as well as extraordinary purity and penetration. Yet this is still an unformed and infantile wine. If Château Latour made a late-harvest Cabernet Sauvignon, I suspect it might smell like this. In the mouth, the wine is out of this world, displaying layer upon layer of concentrated black fruits backed by well-integrated tannin and structure. This is a massive, magnificently rich, full-bodied Port, far more flattering in its youth than were such Taylors as the 1983, 1977, or 1970. It possesses awesome fruit, marvelous intensity, and lavish opulence, all brilliantly well delineated by the wine's formidable structure. This monumental 30- to 50-year Port is a must purchase for aficionados! Also noteworthy is the fact that the 1992 Taylor commemorates the 300th anniversary of this firm, and Taylor created a special bottle for this vintage. Anticipated maturity: now–2035.

1983 Taylor Fladgate

RATING: 94 points

Taylor's Ports are remarkably backward yet still impressive when young. Of all the Vintage Ports, those of Taylor need the longest time to mature and even when fully mature seem to have an inner strength and firmness that keep them going for decades. The 1983 Vintage Port is wonderfully aromatic and supple (a characteristic of this charming vintage), yet powerful, long, and deep on the palate. Anticipated maturity: now–2015.

1977 Taylor Fladgate

RATING: 96 points

This stubborn, slow-to-evolve Vintage Port possesses a dark plum/garnet color with a hint of amber at the edge. Full-bodied and dense, this mammoth effort exhibits huge tannin, power, structure, and concentration, but appears reluctant to reach its adolescence. Still young after surpassing a quarter of a century in age, this large-scaled Port is revealing more complexity aromatically, but remains tight in the mouth. Anticipated maturity: 2010–2030.

1970 Taylor Fladgate

RATING: 96 points

A gorgeous Port that is just emerging from adolescence, the dark garnet–hued 1970 reveals a touch of amber at the edge. An extraordinary nose of melted licorice, road tar, plums, fruitcake, and sweet currants is followed by a wine of great richness, huge body, a wonderful sweet, expansive mid-palate, and a blockbuster finish. It will provide sumptuous drinking over the next two decades.

1963 Taylor Fladgate

RATING: 95 points

Fully mature, the 1963 Taylor offers an exceptional aromatic display of smoked figs and earth intermixed with jammy red and black fruits, tar, saddle leather, and roasted herbs. Full-bodied but sweet, with well-integrated tannin and acidity, it will drink beautifully between now and 2025.

1955 Taylor Fladgate

RATING: 96 points

A spectacular Vintage Port, the 1955, which still possesses a certain firmness because of its structure, retains a dark plum color with moderate amber at the edge. Aromas of crushed rocks, plums, sweet currants, and walnuts are followed by a deep, muscular, powerful, structured, well-delineated wine. While fully mature, this beautiful Vintage Port exhibits no signs of decline. It has already thrown enormous sediment in the bottle. Drink it over the next 20 years.

SPAIN

The wine history of Spain began later than that of its neighbors, France and Italy. As in many regions of Western Europe, it was the Romans who first brought serious viticulture to this beautiful country. Viticulture continued under the domination of the Moors, who occupied much of Spain until their defeat in the 13th century.

The modern age for Spanish wine began in Rioja in the late 19th century. The 20th century saw little change until the 1960s, when a few estates began to receive international attention. Until recently, Spanish wine production was largely controlled by huge cooperatives for which quantity was far more important than quality. Spanish wine importers claim that the new constitution adopted in the late 1970s, which gave regional authorities great power and autonomy, gave credibility to more regional wines than ever before. Whether this is true or not remains to be seen, but 25 years ago there were very few interesting wines outside of Rioja. Today, Spain is a lightning rod for creativity and innovation, from the crisp, fragrant, dry white wines of Rias Baixas in the northwest to the red wines from such up-and-coming regions as Toro, Navarra, Ribera del Duero, Priorato, and Jumilla.

No other country, with the possible exception of Italy, is more of a hotbed for experimentation and passionate new wine operations. The dramatic revolution that began in Spain 20–25 years ago with a gradual movement away from the cooperative mentality has had a profound impact on the quality of wines today. Producers are increasingly rediscovering abandoned viticultural areas as well

as adopting a refreshing open-mindedness about what it takes to compete on the world's stage. The best-known historical vineyards of Rioja remain very important, but they have been upstaged by many other areas. If Rioja remains the best-known Spanish wine appellation, it is by no means the most exciting. New wineries in Priorato, Ribera del Duero, Toro, and such unheralded newcomers as Yecla, Jumilla, and Alicante are eliciting increasing oohs and aahs from the world's wine consumers. Many of the highest-quality offerings from wineries today are less than a decade old, as evidenced by several of the entries that follow. Of course, the popular ploy of many wine journalists in arguing the relative merits of modern-styled and traditionally made wines plays out in Spain as it does in every other viticultural area of the world, but in Spain perhaps it is somewhat different in that the Spanish are rediscovering and reinventing ancient vineyards and modernizing ancient practices. The fact is that Spain has become an extraordinarily fascinating country of remarkably diverse wine styles, with some offering a déjà vu of long-forgotten aromas, textures, and tastes, and enough newfangled wines to please progressives as well.

WINES:

Grandes Añadas

Pagos Viejos

Viña El Pisón

OWNER: Juan Carlos López de Lacalle

ADDRESS: Bodegas Artadi-Cosecheros-Alaveses SA, Ctra. de Logroño, s/n, 01300 Laguardia (Alava), Spain

TELEPHONE: 34 945 60 01 19

TELEFAX: 34 945 60 08 50

E-MAIL: info@artadi.com

WEBSITE: www.artadi.com

CONTACT: Ana Isabel Rodriguez

VISITING POLICY: Through importers and distributors only

VINEYARDS

SURFACE AREA: 173 acres

GRAPE VARIETALS: Tempranillo

AVERAGE AGE OF THE VINES: 15–90 years, with the main proportion between 25 and 40 years

DENSITY OF PLANTATION: 3,500 vines per hectare

AVERAGE YIELDS: 35 hectoliters per hectare

WINEMAKING AND UPBRINGING

The grapes are picked by hand and sorted on a selection table composed of five segments. The grapes are destemmed by hand on the first four segments, then released onto the fifth and last segment, which vibrates, allowing the grapes to be identified and separated. The grapes then go into wooden 110- to 170-hectoliter vats for about 4 days until they begin to ferment (with natural yeasts). Once the wine finishes the alcoholic fermentation, it is moved to barrels for malolactic fermentation and aging.

Except for Viña El Pisón, a 50-year-old single vineyard (actually a *clos*, as it's surrounded by a stone wall), the range is organized by the age of the vines. Artadi's philosophy is to separate the different qualities according to the age of the vineyards and their quality potential. Grandes Añadas is produced only in the best vintages, and then it is fashioned from the oldest (70+ years old) vineyards. Pagos Viejos is made from vineyards averaging 50+ years old.

All the wines experience malolactic fermentation in barrel. The top wines (Pagos Viejos, Grandes Añadas, and Viña El Pisón) remain in new French oak for about 14–18 months, depending on the wine and the vintage.

ANNUAL PRODUCTION

Artadi Pagos Viejos: 40,000–50,000 bottles

Artadi Grandes Añadas: 8,000–11,000 bottles

Artadi Viña El Pisón: 7,000–9,000 bottles

AVERAGE PRICE (VARIABLE DEPENDING ON VINTAGE): $35–120

GREAT RECENT VINTAGES

2001, 1998, 1996, 1995, 1994

In the medieval Spanish town of Laguardia, one could argue that the future of Rioja is being battled out in the cellars of Artadi, located on the road to Logrono.

One of Spain's most creative and brilliant visionaries, Juan Carlos López de Lacalle guided Artadi, which began as a cooperative in 1985, into a private enterprise by 1992. A short two years later, Lacalle was producing some of Spain's (and the world's) greatest wines. Under his guidance, Artadi has altered the Rioja landscape, introducing high-quality concepts such as low yields, malolactic fermentation in wood, and the use of French

Juan Carlos López de Lacalle

oak. Lacalle, a tall, intense, passionate man in his mid-40s, is a revolutionary. Bottling his wines early, he abandoned the traditional concept of Rioja, in which wines spent 8–20 years in huge oak tanks prior to bottling that reclassified them as Crianza, Reserva, and Gran Reserva, and instead stressed the age of the vines. He also began producing a single-vineyard *cuvée* of old-vine Tempranillo called Viña El Pisón. Artadi's offerings are among the most exciting wines being produced anywhere in the world.

ARTADI GRANDES AÑADAS

2001 Artadi Grandes Añadas

RATING: 98 points

The prodigious, inky/purple-colored 2001 Grandes Añadas marries elegance with tremendous power and flavor intensity. It represents Spain's version of Comte de Vogue's Musigny—in a top vintage. Aromas of spice box, violets, raspberries, blackberries, plums, cherries, and an undeniable minerality are found in this structured, ripe, phenomenally intense red. The finish exceeds one minute, yet it gives the impression that it is not even close to being mature. While it offers plenty of enjoyment now, it will be at its finest between 2007 and 2027.

1998 Artadi Grandes Añadas

RATING: 96 points

The 1998 Grandes Añadas (100% Tempranillo from 70- to 100-year-old vines) is tannic and highly extracted, with lots of body. It is a broodingly backward, formidable wine with amazing concentration, purity, and overall balance. Long and concentrated, with a 40- to 50-second finish, it is a classic yet singular expression of Rioja the likes of which can be found nowhere else in that viticultural area. Anticipated maturity: now–2031.

1994 Artadi Grandes Añadas Reserva Especial

RATING: 96 points

The 1994 Grandes Añadas Reserva Especial (made from a single Tempranillo vineyard planted 80–100 years ago) was aged for 40 months in 100% new French oak casks. Approximately 100 six-bottle cases were imported to the United States. This intellectually and hedonistically satisfying wine is one of the most compelling and prodigious Riojas I have ever tasted. It possesses amazing richness, and a fabulous smoky, black fruit–scented nose that soars from the glass. Full-bodied, with extraordinary richness, layers of fruit, beautifully integrated acidity, tannin, and wood, and a whoppingly long 45+-second finish, this wine must be tasted to be believed. It is also one of the most expensive Riojas I have ever tasted, but this wine has a 20-year upside potential. It is a tour de force in winemaking. Kudos to Artadi! Anticipated maturity: now–2020.

ARTADI PAGOS VIEJOS

2001 Artadi Pagos Viejos

RATING: 97 points

Aged 18 months in 100% new French oak from 75-year-old Tempranillo vines, the 2001 Pagos Viejos is one of Spain's greatest wines. A singular red of extraordinary stature and intensity, it exhibits an inky/ruby/purple color as well as a luxu-

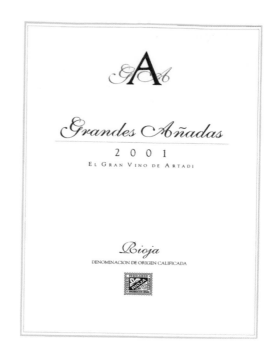

rious bouquet of lead pencil shavings, black and blue fruits, espresso roast, and floral notes. This full-bodied, dense 2001 possesses layers of flavor, a sweet integration of tannin and wood, and a finish that lasts for nearly a minute. Drink this riveting Rioja between now and 2015.

2000 Artadi Pagos Viejos

RATING: 94 points

The dense, rich 2000 Pagos Viejos possesses a saturated ruby/purple color; a layered, expansive texture; and additional oak, extract, and glycerin characteristics in the finish. Anticipated maturity: now–2018.

1999 Artadi Pagos Viejos

RATING: 90 points

The impeccable 1999 Pagos Viejos (100% Tempranillo from 60+-year-old vines, and aged in French oak) exhibits a dense ruby/purple color along with a sweet, Volnay-like bouquet of raspberries, cherries, minerals, and a hint of spicy wood. Medium-bodied, long, concentrated, and well balanced, it will be drinkable until 2010.

1998 Artadi Pagos Viejos

RATING: 96 points

The superb 1998 Pagos Viejos is one of the greatest Riojas I have ever tasted. A dense ruby/purple color is accompanied by a sweet nose of violets, black fruits, minerals, toasty new oak, and smoke. The wine is full-bodied, with gorgeous purity, amazing symmetry for its exceptional size, and an incredibly well-delineated finish. In short, it is great stuff! Anticipated maturity: now–2025.

1996 Artadi Pagos Viejos

RATING: 93 points

The dark ruby/purple–colored 1996 Pagos Viejos (400 six-packs available for the United States) is a fabulous Rioja. It boasts a complex bouquet of lead pencil, red as well as black currants, spice box, cedar, and tobacco. Made from low yields, the wine displays a gorgeous mid-palate, great depth and purity, and a finish that lingers for nearly 40 seconds. Drink this spectacular effort between now and 2025.

ARTADI PAGOS VIEJOS RESERVA

1995 Artadi Pagos Viejos Reserva

RATING: 96 points

This wine is spectacular, but there are only 350 cases. The wine is 100% Tempranillo grown at high altitudes, raised in French oak, and bottled without filtration. It has an extraordinary elegance and purity, as well as remarkable intensity and symmetry. The 1995 Pagos Viejos Reserva (from 50-year-old vines) displays an opaque purple color in addition to a superb, pure nose of blackberry and cherry liqueur intertwined with toast, smoke, mineral, and anise aromas. Concentrated and rich, this offering represents the essence of the Tempranillo grape. This medium to full–bodied, harmonious wine can be drunk between now and 2020.

1994 Artadi Pagos Viejos Reserva

RATING: 92 points

The 1994 Pagos Viejos Reserva is made from 100% Tempranillo (50-year-old vines) grown in a vineyard planted at 2000 feet. The wine is given a lengthy fermentation/maceration, and aged for 32 months in 100% new French oak casks. What I find so exceptional about this wine is that the oak is a very subtle component, which should give readers an idea of how rich and concentrated the wine's fruit is. The color is a saturated dark ruby/purple. The sweet nose of lead pencil, cassis, blackberries, minerals, and vanilla is followed by a full-bodied wine with opulent richness, a terrific texture, and sexy, open-knit, candied fruit flavors that gush across the palate with no hard edges. The finish exceeds 30 seconds. This is an immensely impressive, complex, compelling Rioja from a terrific vintage. Anticipated maturity: now–2014.

ARTADI VIÑA EL PISÓN

2001 Artadi Viña El Pisón

RATING: 98+ points

El Pisón is a 100% Tempranillo *cuvée* produced from a single vineyard planted in 1945. The soil is pure limestone, yields are a lowly 18–22 hectoliters per hectare, and the wine is aged for 18–24 months in French oak. The potentially perfect 2001 El Pisón has more of everything. While it possesses an extraordinary flavor intensity, it remains light on its feet. Anticipated maturity: 2007–2020.

2000 Artadi Viña El Pisón

RATING: 96 points

The rich, profound 2000 El Pisón boasts a dense ruby/purple color as well as full body, tremendous precision, and layers of sweet strawberry, cherry, raspberry, and black currant fruit intermixed with mineral, subtle wood, and floral notes. Anticipated maturity: now–2018.

1998 Artadi Viña El Pisón

RATING: 95 points

The 1998 El Pisón is made from a Tempranillo vineyard planted in 1945, and aged 18–24 months in new French oak from yields of only 22 hectoliters per hectare. It offers a deep ruby/purple color and a glorious nose of raspberry jam intermixed with cherries and smoky new oak. As the wine sits in the glass, more complex, floral aromas with a graphite-like character emerge. A sexy, elegant, medium to full–bodied, beautifully made wine transcends the Rioja appellation with a singular style and character. Anticipated maturity: now–2016.

1996 Artadi Viña El Pisón

RATING: 94 points

The spectacular limited-production 1996 Viña El Pisón was fashioned from a vineyard planted in 1931 on pure limestone. This wine is outrageously rich, complex, and profound. A dense ruby/purple color is followed by aromas of sweet black fruits, vanilla, flowers, and minerals. There are layers of fruit, great flavor extraction, unbelievable finesse, complexity, and elegance. The finish lasts for nearly a minute. Full-bodied and super-concentrated, this compelling Rioja will be at its peak between now and 2025. Sadly, only 300 six-packs were exported to the United States, but it is well worth seeking out.

1994 Artadi Viña El Pisón

RATING: 93 points

Made from a Tempranillo vineyard planted in 1945 on pure limestone soil, and aged 24 months in 100% French oak casks, this dazzling wine offers a saturated opaque ruby/purple color. The nose exhibits blackberry, cigar box, mineral, and toast notes. Well delineated, full-bodied, and well textured, this wine displays explosive richness and intensity at the back of the palate—always an encouraging sign of longevity. Outstanding purity and layers of fruit are buttressed by good acidity and sweet tannin. Anticipated maturity: now–2018.

WINE: Clos Erasmus

CLASSIFICATION: DOQ Priorat

OWNER: Daphne Glorian

ADDRESS: C/ La Font, 1, 43737 Gratallops (Tarragona), Spain

TELEPHONE: 34 977 83 94 26

TELEFAX: 34 977 83 94 26

E-MAIL: closerasmus@terra.es

CONTACT: Daphne Glorian

VISITING POLICY: By appointment only

VINEYARDS

SURFACE AREA: 17.3 acres in production; 6.2 acres planted in 2004

GRAPE VARIETALS: 70% Grenache, 20% Cabernet Sauvignon, 10% Syrah

AVERAGE AGE OF THE VINES: 8–50+ years

DENSITY OF PLANTATION: 2,000–6,500 vines per hectare

AVERAGE YIELDS: 18 hectoliters per hectare

WINEMAKING AND UPBRINGING

Organically grown from the beginning (1989), the vineyards have been worked biodynamically since 2004. Immediately after picking, the grapes are cooled at 2°C. Only whole, slightly crushed berries are utilized, as are indigenous yeast fermentations. Each parcel is vinified separately, hence the small size of the vats (15–20 hectoliters) and the practice of vinifying directly in barrel. Clos Erasmus is fermented in wooden vats or

Daphne Glorian

in 225-liter barrels. Clos Erasmus dislikes *remontage* (pumping over) and prefers to work the grapes with *pigéage* (pumping down), which they believe is a more gentle method of extraction. The macerations usually last 28–35 days. The wines go through malolactic fermentation in barrel. Clos Erasmus is aged in 100% new French barrels for 18 months and remains at the winery for 3–4 months before being shipped.

ANNUAL PRODUCTION

Clos Erasmus: 5,000 bottles

AVERAGE PRICE (VARIABLE DEPENDING ON VINTAGE): $51–75

GREAT RECENT VINTAGES

2001, 1998, 1995, 1994

Daphne Glorian, who is married to the well-known American boutique importer Eric Solomon, was born and raised in Switzerland. In the early 1990s, on a visit to Priorato with her friends René Barbier and Alvaro Palacios, she was talked into buying a piece of property and joining their efforts to revive this desolate, long-ignored viticultural area. As she said, in one day she became the owner of a tiny parcel of vines as well as the de facto winemaker. She decided to name the vineyard and the wine after the philosopher Erasmus von Rotterdam, author of the essay "In Praise of Folly," which seemed appropriate given the frivolity, perhaps even madness, of the venture. However, Daphne Glorian quickly joined the group of passionate young Spanish producers who were serious about taking this isolated region to new heights.

Priorato, situated at altitudes of 100–700 meters, possesses extraordinary soils of volcanic origin, primarily quartzite, slate, and schist. In the higher elevations, schist dominates. Priorato is one of those special places with an abundance of mountain scenery, wildflowers, and herbs. There is also a winemaking history: Carthusian monks established a monastery in Priorato in 1162, and the old, ruined monastic cellars reveal that wine was produced there over eight centuries ago. However, the area was not recognized as a legal Spanish viticultural region until 1975.

CLOS ERASMUS

2001 Clos Erasmus

RATING: 98 points

A wine of great intensity, this 415-case blend of 78% Grenache, 17% Cabernet Sauvignon, and 5% Syrah aged in 100% new French oak casks reveals an inky/purple color as well as a tight but promising bouquet of acacia flowers, raspberries, blackberries, and hints of blueberries, smoke, and the essence of minerality. With extraordinary richness, good underlying acidity, firm tannin, and a multilayered mouth-feel, this spectacularly concentrated 2001 is only hinting at its ultimate potential. Patience will be rewarded as this is a tour de force in winemaking, marrying the elegance and complexity of Priorato with the extraordinary concentration and intensity that comes from low yields and ripe fruit. Anticipated maturity: 2008–2020+.

2000 Clos Erasmus

RATING: 96 points

The blockbuster 2000 Clos Erasmus exhibits a saturated ruby/purple color as well as a gorgeous nose of jammy black fruits intermixed with a liquid minerality, and hints of vanilla as well as spice. With super purity, tremendous richness, and a full-bodied, long (45-second) finish, it will drink beautifully between 2006 and 2020.

1999 Clos Erasmus

RATING: 93 points

The 1999 Clos Erasmus, a blend of 65% Grenache, 20% Cabernet Sauvignon, and 15% Syrah aged in 100% new French oak, was fashioned from yields of only one ton of fruit per acre. Its dark ruby/purple color is followed by an elegant perfume of pure, sweet black raspberries, currants, creosote, and minerals. It reveals complex flavors, tremendous purity, and a long finish with no hard edges. Anticipated maturity: now–2018.

1998 Clos Erasmus

RATING: 99 points

The spectacular 1998 flirts with perfection. Its saturated opaque blue/purple color is not dissimilar to ink. Dazzling aromas of ripe, pure blackberries, violets, blueberries, wet stones, and smoky, toasty oak soar from the glass. Powerful, with an unctuous texture and super-extracted, rich, concentrated flavors, this blockbuster effort boasts extravagant quantities of fruit, glycerin, extract, tannin, and personality. The wine displays a firm, structured edge, but a viscous texture from super concentration gives it immediate accessibility. It is a winemaking tour de force. Anticipated maturity: 2007–2030.

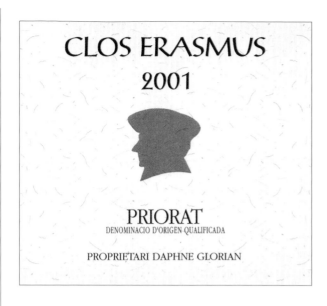

1997 Clos Erasmus

RATING: 93 points

The 1997 exhibits a dense ruby/purple color as well as scents of minerals, toasty new oak, blueberry, black raspberry, and currant fruit, and a full-bodied, impressively endowed, highly extracted personality. Gorgeously pure, with adequate underlying acidity and a well-delineated, structured, muscular, and concentrated finish, this unevolved 1997 is accessible because of its wealth of fruit and suppleness. Anticipated maturity: now–2020.

1996 Clos Erasmus

RATING: 90 points

Production of the 1996 Clos Erasmus was only 300 cases, from yields of a mere 18 hectoliters per hectare. This is a dark ruby/purple–colored wine with a spicy, oak-driven nose intermixed with black cherry and raspberry fruit notes. Spicy and dominated by wood at present, it is full-bodied, rich, and promising. Anticipated maturity: now–2015.

1995 Clos Erasmus

RATING: 96 points

The 1995 Clos Erasmus's levels of extract and richness are nearly off the chart. Only 280 cases were produced of this wine, which tips the scales at 14.6% alcohol. The wine had been open for 24 hours before I tasted it, yet it revealed no signs of oxidation or fruit deterioration! This is not a wine for the shy. It is a huge, massive, powerhouse example with a dense, Port-like purple color, and aromas of macerated black fruits intermixed with minerals and French oak. Huge in the mouth, with extraordinary purity, this wine is almost too much of a good thing—but I loved it! Anticipated maturity: now–2020.

1994 Clos Erasmus

RATING: 99 points

This wine, made from a blend of very old-vine Grenache and younger-vine Syrah and Cabernet Sauvignon grown on terraced vineyards, is among the most exciting wines I have tasted. Unfortunately, only 300 cases were produced, all of which were exported to the United States. It was aged in 100% new French oak casks and bottled without fining or filtration. 1994 is considered to be one of Spain's all-time great vintages, so it is not surprising that this wine possesses even more potential than the exceptional 1993 and 1992. Try to imagine a hypothetical blend of Pétrus, L'Evangile, Rayas Châteauneuf-du-Pape, and Napa's 1993 Colgin Cabernet Sauvignon. The color is an opaque black/purple. The nose offers up spectacularly rich, pure aromas of blackberries, black raspberries, minerals, and subtle vanilla from new oak barrels. Extremely rich and dense, with unbelievable levels of concentration and extract, this amazing wine can be drunk between now and 2021.

1993 Clos Erasmus

RATING: 94 points

The 1993 is spectacular. The opaque ruby/purple color is followed by a stunningly fragrant nose of black fruits, melted road tar, toasty new oak, and truffle/licorice scents. Extremely full-bodied, with layers of flavor, this immense but well-balanced wine is a winemaking tour de force. Anticipated maturity: now.

1992 Clos Erasmus

RATING: 93 points

The brilliant 1992 was macerated for more than five weeks (talk about extended *cuvaisons*). This prodigious wine exhibits a dense color and superrich, jammy black cherry and cassis fruit intertwined with toasty new oak (100% new oak casks are used). The wine is full-bodied, with layers of flavor, a sweet mid-palate, and a long, rich, well-defined finish. Anticipated maturity: now–2015.

WINE: L'Ermita

CLASSIFICATION: Priorat

OWNER: Alvaro Palacios

ADDRESS: C/ Afores, s/n 43737, Gratallops (Tarragona), Spain

TELEPHONE: 34 977 83 91 95

TELEFAX: 34 977 83 91 97

E-MAIL: alvaropalacios@ctv.es

CONTACT: Blanca Bathevell

VISITING POLICY: By appointment only

VINEYARDS

SURFACE AREA: L'Ermita: 5.93 acres; Finca Dofi: 22.24 acres

GRAPE VARIETALS: L'Ermita: 80% Grenache, 20% Cabernet Sauvignon

Finca Dofi: 55% Grenache, 30% Cabernet Sauvignon, 10% Syrah, 5% Merlot

AVERAGE AGE OF THE VINES: L'Ermita: 28–75 years old; Finca Dofi: 9–19 years old

DENSITY OF PLANTATION: L'Ermita: 2,230 vines per acre; Finca Dofi: 1,540 vines per acre

AVERAGE YIELDS: L'Ermita: 10 hectoliters per hectare; Finca Dofi: 15–20 hectoliters per hectare

WINEMAKING AND UPBRINGING

Alvaro Palacios, the architect behind L'Ermita, states succinctly, "The winemaking philosophy is to express the character of the *terroir* with the greatest transparency and purity." A unique training system for the head-pruned vines allows the steep, terraced vineyard to be worked by mules. The fruit is destemmed by hand. Maceration lasts 25 days, and fermentation is in oak vats with punching down. Since 1999, malolactic fermentation has occurred in barrel. An egg white fining is done, but there is no filtration. The wine spends 16–18 months in new French *barriques*.

ANNUAL PRODUCTION

L'Ermita: 3,000 bottles

Finca Dofi: 22,500 bottles

AVERAGE PRICE (VARIABLE DEPENDING ON VINTAGE): $200

GREAT RECENT VINTAGES

2003, 2001, 1999, 1998, 1995, 1994

In his early 40s, Alvaro Palacios seems to have done it all. While in his 20s, Palacios, who comes from a famous Rioja winemaking family (owners of the Bodegas Palacios Remondo), apprenticed with Christian Moueix at Château Pétrus and Château Trotanoy. He then followed Catalonian René Barbier to Priorato, where he was so impressed with the ancient soils and potential for high quality that he decided to establish his vineyard in this viticultural backwater, located 85 miles southwest of Barcelona. As Palacios has said, the belief was that there could be no commercial winemaking in Priorato because "the yields are too low, the terrain is impossible, and most of it requires cultivation by hand," and there was little chance of making a profit. The naysayers were proven wrong.

Alvaro Palacios

L'Ermita's first vintage was 1993 and it immediately became one of the superstars of modern Spanish winemaking. This *cuvée*, made primarily from 80–90% old-vine Grenache, with the balance Cabernet Sauvignon and old-vine Carignan, won an extraordinary reaction both in Spain and internationally. Alvaro Palacios's state-of-the-art winery, situated on a hilltop overlooking the village of Gratallops, attests to his dominating influence and his ongoing efforts to revolutionize the Spanish wine industry.

Like some of his peers, Palacios has been expanding his sphere of influence. In an even more challenging and long-forgotten viticultural region, Bierzo, he has begun to produce interesting wines. But make no mistake about it, he belongs in this book for what he has accomplished in Priorato with old-vine Grenache. Alvaro Palacios, with his boyish good looks, large smile, and dark eyes, is one of Spain's great visionaries, and there is no telling what other Spanish viticultural backwater he will next revive.

L'ERMITA

2001 L'Ermita
RATING: 96 points
The 2001 L'Ermita was produced from 60-year-old, head-pruned Grenache vines (85%) and old-vine Carignan and younger-vine Cabernet Sauvignon (15%). Yields were a meager 15 hectoliters per hectare in 2001. This 500-case *cuvée*, aged in 100% new French oak, represents the essence of Priorato as well as this particular vineyard source. The black/purple-colored 2001 boasts an extraordinary aromatic profile of charcoal, blackberries, raspberries, kirsch, melted licorice, and espresso. Full-bodied and unctuously textured, with sweet tannin and abundant quantities of fruit as well as glycerin, this is a remarkably well-balanced wine of great intensity and formidable aging potential. Anticipated maturity: 2007–2020.

1998 L' Ermita
RATING: 97 points
The blockbuster, opaque purple–colored 1998 L'Ermita (the finest since the 1995 and 1994) exhibits a full-bodied personality, with copious quantities of sweet oak, a boatload of glyc-

erin, and superb blackberry, cassis, and cherry fruit that explodes on the mid-palate and in the finish. The elevated quantities of new oak should become better integrated as the wine ages. This is an exceptionally impressive/expressive wine. Anticipated maturity: now–2021.

1996 L' Ermita

RATING: 92 points

The 1996 L'Ermita's color is a saturated purple. The expressive nose boasts aromas of toast, roasted coffee; chocolate-covered, jammy cherry candy; minerals; and new oak. Full-bodied, dense, and thick, with an unctuous texture, lower acidity, and higher alcohol than the 1995 and 1994, this is a meaty, chewy, masculine wine with a flamboyant personality in addition to a monster finish. It is super-intense, but exceptionally well balanced, especially in view of its proportions. Anticipated maturity: now–2020.

1995 L' Ermita

RATING: 94 points

A clone of the 1994, the 1995 L'Ermita does not reveal quite the power and density of its older sibling, but that is a tough call. The color is an opaque purple, and the wine displays more toast, grilled *jus de viande,* blackberry, and floral notes in its aromatics, which seem slightly more evolved than the 1994's. In the mouth, the 1995 is deep, powerful, and rich, with low acidity, better sweetness and integration of tannin (when compared to the massive 1994), layers of extract and flavor, and a 40-second finish. It is a remarkable wine with formidable style, intensity, and flavor. Anticipated maturity: now–2020.

1994 L' Ermita

RATING: 97 points

Quantities of the 1994 are absurdly small. The color is a saturated inky/purple, and the soaring nose provides thrilling levels of sweet blackberry and cherry liqueur–like fruit. In spite of being full-bodied, massive, and huge, it manages not to taste heavy despite its gargantuan proportions of fruit, glycerin, tannin, and extract. This chewy, glycerin-imbued, phenomenally intense wine possesses all the component parts necessary to become a modern-day legend. Anticipated maturity: now–2020.

WINES:

Pesquera Gran Reserva

Pesquera Janus Gran Reserva

OWNER: Alejandro Fernández and family

ADDRESS: Calle Real 2, 47315, Pesquera de Duero
(Valladolid), Spain

TELEPHONE: 34 983 87 00 37

TELEFAX: 34 983 87 00 88

E-MAIL: lfernandez@pesqueraafernandez.com

WEBSITE: www.grupopesquera.com

CONTACT: Luciá Fernández

VISITING POLICY: By appointment only

VINEYARDS

SURFACE AREA: 494 acres

GRAPE VARIETALS: 100% Tempranillo

AVERAGE AGE OF THE VINES: Approximately 15 years

DENSITY OF PLANTATION: 2,000–2,200 vines per hectare

AVERAGE YIELDS: 40–45 hectoliters per hectare

WINEMAKING AND UPBRINGING

The Fernández philosophy has always focused upon assiduous care of the vineyards, followed by precise timing of the largely individual-bunch harvest and careful, natural winemaking. Spontaneous fermentation with natural yeasts is followed by sufficient but not excessive macerations. Originally, Fernández fermented his wines in concrete troughs called *lagares* (better known for fermenting Vintage Port), but he quickly decided to build stainless-steel fermentation tanks, which were first used in 1982.

Alejandro Fernández

The young wine goes straight to new oak for malolactic fermentation, which also takes place spontaneously. Clarification is achieved entirely through racking. No filtration or cold stabilization is used. Predominantly American oak (from various origins) is used, although various French and Spanish types are employed each year for special lots. Bottling takes place after 18 months for Crianza, 24 for the Reserva, and 30 for the Gran Reserva. Further bottle aging prior to release includes 6 months for Crianza, 12 for the Reserva, and 30 for the Gran Reserva.

ANNUAL PRODUCTION

Tinto Pesquera Crianza: 500,000 bottles

Pesquera Reserva: 90,000 bottles

Pesquera Gran Reserva: 30,000 bottles

Pesquera Janus Gran Reserva: 10,000 bottles (only five
vintages produced)

Pesquera Millennium: 10,000 bottles (only one vintage
produced, 1996)

AVERAGE PRICE (VARIABLE DEPENDING ON VINTAGE): $85

GREAT RECENT VINTAGES

2001, 2000, 1999, 1996, 1995, 1994, 1992, 1991, 1986, 1982

In terms of success, only Vega Sicilia in the Ribera del Duero can match proprietor Alejandro Fernández's Pesquera. Producing wines of considerable richness and character at relatively realistic prices, Fernández is a modern-day success story. Born in 1932, he quit school at age 14 to work in the fields. His résumé includes work as a carpenter, blacksmith, and inventor of farm machinery (to improve the cultivation of beets and nongrape crops). However, he and his wife, Esperanza, along with their four daughters, dreamed of producing a world-class wine, and in 1972 his farm-tool company loaned him money to establish a winery. One of his chief assistants (and mentors), oenologist Teofio Reyes, had a defining influence on Fernández's wine style, emphasizing riper fruit and more limited aging in wood. At a time when Spanish viticulture was in the doldrums and vineyards were being uprooted and replaced with fields of beets, Fernández began to plant vineyards, and released his first wine in 1975. Unlike most Spanish wines, which were aged at the bodega and released only when fully mature, Pesquera, like a great Bordeaux, was designed to be aged in bottle. An inky ruby/purple-colored wine with huge fruit, loads of oak, tremendous ripeness and intensity, as well as plenty of structure and tannin, Pesquera quickly became regarded as the modern-day standard for what Spanish wines could achieve.

Fernández, whose face resembles one of his gnarled old Tempranillo vines, is allowing his daughters to take a more active role in the winery while he continues to build his empire. In 1989, his financial success with Pesquera allowed him to build a new bodega called Condado de Haza, which produces over 60,000 cases of wine each year. More recently, he purchased a nearly 2,000-acre estate in Toro and expanded into Spain's western province of Zamora. Against all odds Fernández has become a legend in winemaking circles, and is widely credited by many of his peers for bringing worldwide attention to Ribera del Duero. His huge success with Pesquera forced the Spanish government to grant official authorization to Ribera del Duero in 1982 as an official viticultural region. All this is remarkable for a man without any formal oenological education or training.

PESQUERA GRAN RESERVA

1995 Pesquera Gran Reserva

RATING: 91 points

The 1995 Gran Reserva possesses a deep ruby/garnet/plum color as well as a sweet nose of earth, licorice, black fruits, underbrush, and spicy new oak. In the mouth, it is medium to full-bodied, with refreshing acidity and outstanding depth, ripeness, and complexity. It should drink well for 10–15 years.

1994 Pesquera Gran Reserva

RATING: 92 points

Dense plum/ruby/purple–colored, with a sweet perfume of earth, herbs, jammy black fruits, and oak in the background, the opulently textured, round, fleshy 1994 Gran Reserva possesses full body, moderate tannin, and an accessible yet structured personality. Anticipated maturity: now–2016.

PESQUERA JANUS GRAN RESERVA

1995 Pesquera Janus Gran Reserva

RATING: 94 points

The full-bodied 1995 Janus Gran Reserva (a *cuvée* only produced previously in 1994, 1991, 1986, and 1982) is remarkably young and vibrant despite the fact that it was aged for

three years in oak casks. Sadly, there are only 1,000+ cases of this wine. It exhibits a deep ruby/purple color along with a bouquet of barbecue spices, creamy oak, melted licorice, and copious quantities of black currant and cherry fruit. This opulent, viscous, full-bodied, lusty 1995 reveals substantial tannin that is largely concealed by the wealth of fruit and extract. The heady finish lasts over 40 seconds. This big, solid Ribera del Duero should age effortlessly until 2019.

1994 Pesquera Janus Gran Reserva

RATING: 97 points

The 1994 Janus Gran Reserva may be the greatest Pesquera ever made. This wine is awesome in its richness, intensity, and potential complexity. It is a gentle giant, with no hard edges and profound levels of rich, concentrated black fruits nicely meshed with smoky, spicy new oak. Given its sweetness, opulence, and lush personality, it can be drunk through 2012.

WINE: Pingus

OWNER: Peter Sisseck

ADDRESS: Calle matador s/n, 47300 Quintanilla de Onesimo (Valladolid), Spain

TELEPHONE: 34 639 83 38 54

TELEFAX: 34 983 48 40 20

E-MAIL: pingus@telefonica.net

CONTACT: Peter Sisseck

VISITING POLICY: Professionals only

VINEYARDS

SURFACE AREA: Pingus: 11.1 acres; Flor de Pingus: 37 acres

GRAPE VARIETALS: Tinto Fino (a clone of Tempranillo)

AVERAGE AGE OF THE VINES: Pingus: 75 years; Flor de Pingus: 15 years

DENSITY OF PLANTATION: 3,000–4,000 vines per hectare for the old vineyards; 4,000–6,000 vines per hectare for the newer plantations

AVERAGE YIELDS: Pingus: 8–12 hectoliters per hectare; Flor de Pingus: 15–20 hectoliters per hectare

WINEMAKING AND UPBRINGING

A destalking is done by hand, which results in a selection of only perfect, unbroken berries. Small (20-hectoliter) open-top wooden fermenters are utilized. Because of the small volume, the fermentation temperature never goes higher than 28°C. Pingus undergoes a long, cold soak (up to two weeks), and there is a natural yeast fermentation. *Pigéage* (punching down) is done 2 or 3 times daily. There are short postfermentation rackings, long lees contact, and no micro-oxidation. The wine spends 20–23 months in barrel. No fining or filtration is done.

ANNUAL PRODUCTION

Pingus: 3,700–6,800 bottles

Flor de Pingus: 40,000 bottles

AVERAGE PRICE (VARIABLE DEPENDING ON VINTAGE): $230

GREAT RECENT VINTAGES

2003, 2001, 2000, 1999, 1996, 1995

In 1995, Peter Sisseck, an exuberant young Dane by birth who appears to spend most of his time traveling between Spain and France, created Pingus from an 11.1-acre plot of extremely old-vine Tinto Fino. The name "Pingus" is a double entendre: Danish slang for "Peter" as well as the name of a well-known European cartoon. However, there is nothing funny about this estate, especially (cynics will point out) the extraordinary price, which the wine market has been more than willing to accept given the wine's brilliant quality.

The vineyard, planted on gravelly soil in La Horra, is situated in the center of Ribera del Duero. Sisseck's objective was to employ a noninterventionist winemaking policy to create a world-class, completely natural wine that allowed the *terroir* and varietal character to come through. In 2000, Pingus moved to biodynamic farming, a logical decision since the vineyard was already organically farmed.

This is Spain's quintessential garage wine, made in an actual garage just off the highway to Valladolid.

PINGUS

2001 Pingus

RATING: 95 points

The opaque ruby/purple-colored, firmly structured 2001 Pingus is more closed and backward than the extravagantly rich, flamboyant 2000. It offers great fruit on the attack along with huge body, and notes of grilled meats intermixed with Provençal herbs, pepper, spice box, cigar smoke, and copious quantities of barbecue smoke–infused blackberry and cassis flavors. The finish lasts for nearly a minute. Anticipated maturity: 2010–2028.

2000 Pingus

RATING: 96 points

A freak, the 2000 Pingus is an exaggerated, extravagantly rich effort boasting an inky/purple color along with a sumptuous perfume of beef blood, lavender, Provençal herbs, ground pepper, melted licorice, and oodles of blackberry and crème de cassis–like fruit. Full-bodied, powerful, rich, and smoky, with great intensity and an unctuously textured, full-throttle finish, it should drink well for 15–20 years. Anticipated maturity: 2007–2025.

1999 Pingus

RATING: 98 points

The spectacular, nearly perfect 1999 Pingus boasts an opaque ruby/purple color, sensational extract, gorgeous concentration, and spectacularly intense blackberry and cherry aromas and flavors infused with incense, coffee, chocolate, and toasty new oak. Enormous levels of extract and richness are accompanied by a full-bodied, glycerin-imbued, thick, viscous finish. The tannin is nearly hidden by the wine's wealth of fruit and concentration. Anticipated maturity: now–2025.

1998 Pingus

RATING: 90 points

The 1998 Pingus exhibits chocolate, espresso, and leather characteristics as well as an expansive mid-palate, a dense, opaque ruby/purple color, medium to full body, moderate tannin, and gorgeous purity/sweetness. Although outstanding, it is not one of Sisseck's most prodigious efforts. Anticipated maturity: now–2020.

1996 Pingus

RATING: 96 points

The 1996 Pingus is an astonishing wine that continues to put on weight and add more nuances to its multidimensional personality. The explosive aromatics consist of smoke, jammy blackberry and currant fruit, incense, licorice, cedar, and toast. Massive in the mouth, with a sumptuous texture, immense body, high levels of glycerin, and a multilayered mid-palate, this spectacular wine is evolved and accessible. Anticipated maturity: now–2018.

1995 Pingus

RATING: 98 points

The 1995 Pingus exhibits an opaque purple color, and an extraordinary sweet nose of black fruits, truffles, and nicely integrated, subtle toast. The wine is massive, huge, and full-bodied, with layers of concentrated, pure fruit; loads of glycerin; and beautifully sweet tannin. Although one would think it would taste Bordeaux-like, it has its own individual style that falls somewhere between St.-Emilion's Valandraud, Pesquera's Janus, and Vega Sicilia's Unico! The 1995 will age effortlessly for 25–30+ years. This is a brilliant winemaking effort! Anticipated maturity: now–2027.

BODEGAS VEGA SICILIA

WINES:

Unico Reserva

Unico Reserva Especial

OWNERS: Alvarez family

ADDRESS: Carretera Nacional, 122, Km. 323, 47359, Valbuena
de Duero (Valladolid), Spain

TELEPHONE: 34 983 68 01 47

TELEFAX: 34 983 68 02 63

E-MAIL: vegasicilia@vega-sicilia.com

WEBSITE: www.vega-sicilia.com

CONTACT: Rafael Alonso Santos (34 916 31 09 13)

VISITING POLICY: Professionals only, by appointment

VINEYARDS

SURFACE AREA: 296 acres

GRAPE VARIETALS: Tempranillo, Cabernet Sauvignon, Merlot,
Malbec—no precise formula exists, but most top
vintages include approximately 70% Tinto Fino, 20%
Cabernet Sauvignon, and the rest Merlot and Malbec

AVERAGE AGE OF THE VINES: 30 years

DENSITY OF PLANTATION: 2,200 vines per hectare

AVERAGE YIELDS: 7–21 hectoliters per hectare

WINEMAKING AND UPBRINGING

Since its founding in 1864, Vega Sicilia has followed traditional vinification practices with the goal of producing wine
with the least manipulation possible in the vineyard and winery. Vinification, which takes place in oak, stainless steel, and
epoxy-lined concrete vats, is followed by malolactic fermentation, also in epoxy-lined concrete vats. The winery employs
both American and French wood barrels of various sizes
(7,000–20,000 liters). While there is considerable flexibility in
the Unico's upbringing, it is generally aged in small oak barrels (both new and used) for 2–4 years, and is then moved to
large oak vats for the final blending and settling. Unico is only
made in the greatest years, and some vintages reportedly
spent nearly 16 years in wood (e.g., the colossal 1970).

ANNUAL PRODUCTION

Vega Sicilia Unico Reserva: 40,000–100,000 bottles

Vega Sicilia Unico Reserva Especial (a blend of 3 vintages):
13,000–15,000 bottles

AVERAGE PRICE (VARIABLE DEPENDING ON VINTAGE): $220

GREAT RECENT VINTAGES

1999, 1996, 1994, 1991, 1990, 1989, 1987, 1986, 1985, 1983,
1982, 1981, 1976, 1975, 1974, 1970, 1968, 1966, 1964, 1962

Vega Sicilia, the beverage of Spanish kings, is one of
the world's most iconical wines. It emerges from
an isolated, windswept *terroir* located 25 miles east of
the town of Valladolid. For more than a century, it has
been the most renowned as well as the most expensive
wine produced in Spain. The vineyard was planted by a
Señor Lecanda in 1864 with some cuttings brought to
the area from Bordeaux. The early vintages were undistinguished, and much of the production in the late
1800s was sold off and bottled as Rioja. By the 20th
century, things were looking up, but the wine was still
referred to as Bodegas de Lecanda, and later as Antonio
Herrero. It did not take on its present name, Bodegas
Vega Sicilia, until the early 1900s.

Some vintages in the 1920s won huge acclaim at
international wine festivals. The person responsible for
many great vintages in the '40s, '50s, and '60s, Don
Jesus Anadon, continued to work at the estate after it
was sold in 1964 to a Czech/Venezuelan family by the

name of Neumann. Anadon had the foresight to bring in the brilliant young oenologist Mariano Garcia, who continued to fine-tune Vega Sicilia, building on its reputation as Spain's greatest wine. After working at the winery for 30 years, Garcia was let go in 1998, largely because (according to Vega Sicilia's CEO, Pablo Alvarez) his other winemaking projects were interfering with his responsibilities at Vega Sicilia.

Inspired winemaking and inspiring quality continue under the energetic visionary Alvarez, who manages Vega Sicilia for his family. Additionally, the bodega's owners have expanded with an exciting new project in Toro, an up-and-coming viticultural region that remains under the radar for most wine consumers.

VEGA SICILIA UNICO RESERVA

1994 Vega Sicilia Unico Reserva
RATING: 98+ points
This bodega has produced many profound wines, but the 1994 may be the greatest vintage released since their legendary 1970 and 1968. A truly prodigious effort, it boasts an opaque ruby/purple color as well as a gorgeously sweet, expansive bouquet of sweet cherries interwoven with black currant, truffle, licorice, and scorched-earth aromas. Full-bodied, potent, powerful, and well-delineated, with crisp acidity, sweet but noticeable tannin, a multidimensional, expansive, layered palate-feel, and a pure yet refreshing finish, it should be a wine for the history books. Anticipated maturity: now–2035.

1991 Vega Sicilia Unico Reserva
RATING: 95 points
Vega Sicilia's flagship offering, the 1991 Unico Reserva is a gorgeous, deep ruby/purple–colored, remarkably youthful effort offering sweet vanilla notes intertwined with black currants, cherry liqueur, flowers, spice box, and tobacco leaves. Full-bodied and intense, with sweet tannin, outstanding density as well as purity, and a layered mouth-feel, this unevolved 1991 is a wine of great elegance as opposed to power. Anticipated maturity: 2007–2029.

1990 Vega Sicilia Unico Reserva
RATING: 94 points
For an Unico Reserva, the 1990 exhibits a relatively unevolved style. A deep opaque plum/garnet color is accompanied by noticeable sweet toasty oak in the nose along with copious quantities of black cherry and cassis fruit. It is extremely youthful, vigorous, and full-bodied, with notes of overripeness, low

acidity, moderately high tannin, and a full-bodied, layered, concentrated personality. Anticipated maturity: now–2026.

1989 Vega Sicilia Unico Reserva

RATING: 94 points

The sensational 1989 Unico Reserva boasts a dark ruby/ purple color as well as a sweet, fragrant bouquet of plums, black currants, vanilla, caramel, and chocolate. It possesses tremendous density, an opulent, textured, full-bodied palate, great purity, and moderate tannin in the 60+-second finish. Anticipated maturity: 2006–2033.

1987 Vega Sicilia Unico Reserva

RATING: 92 points

The 1987 Unico Reserva's opaque ruby/purple color is accompanied by a glorious perfume of sweet cherries, flowers, licorice, and toasty oak. Full-bodied, with tremendous brightness and texture as well as an elegant, long, head-turning finish, it is undoubtedly super juice. Anticipated maturity: now–2022.

1986 Vega Sicilia Unico Reserva

RATING: 92 points

The opaque plum/garnet–colored 1986 Unico Reserva is a harmonious offering, with good glycerin, full body, copious tannin, and a backward yet promising style. This wine is less accessible than the 1985, 1983, or the 1981, and may merit an even higher score. It is one of the few Vega Sicilia wines that will require cellaring at its release. Anticipated maturity: now–2025.

1985 Vega Sicilia Unico Reserva

RATING: 93 points

The 1985 Unico Reserva reveals considerable complexity and low acid, and plump, round, rich flavors of cherries, figs, and plums. There is no amber to be found in the wine's deep ruby/purple color. The nose offers tobacco, smoke, tar, and gobs of sweet black cherry fruit aromas. Full-bodied, with a layered, nuanced character, high glycerin (hence the sweetness in the flavors), and a lush, round, generously endowed finish, this is a substantial as well as elegant, savory style of Unico Reserva. Anticipated maturity: now–2013.

1983 Vega Sicilia Unico Reserva

RATING: 95 points

The huge, opaque 1983 Unico Reserva is fat and grapy, with massive flavor concentration; an expansive, sweet, jammy, black currant fruitiness; spicy oak; and a long, robust, spicy finish. There is no doubting the wine's awesome levels of extract. Anticipated maturity: now–2020.

1982 Vega Sicilia Unico Reserva

RATING: 95 points

The 1982 Unico Reserva is fatter and richer than the 1985, displaying a dark plum/garnet color and a complex set of aromatics consisting of sweet tobacco, roasted herbs, tar, jammy kirsch, and caramel. Full-bodied, with a viscous texture; forward, fat, ripe flavors; low acidity; and a knockout finish with copious amounts of glycerin, this is a succulent, hedonistic, luxuriously rich Unico. Anticipated maturity: now–2025.

1981 Vega Sicilia Unico Reserva

RATING: 95 points

The 1981 Unico Reserva is more restrained than the 1982 or 1985, with a personality similar to a classic Médoc (i.e., Lafite Rothschild). Lead pencil, tar, smoke, black currant, and weedy tobacco notes are followed by a medium-bodied wine with beautiful fruit, a supple texture, and a long finish. While not as flamboyant or expansive as either the 1982 or 1985, it is a classy, complex offering with an intriguing lead pencil/smoky note in its aromatics, flavor, and finish. Anticipated maturity: now–2015.

1976 Vega Sicilia Unico Reserva

RATING: 93 points

The full-bodied, large-scaled 1976 Unico Reserva offers a smoky, roasted nose indicative of a hot, dry growing season. There are copious quantities of jammy black cherries and sweet, toasty, vanilla oak in the wine's multifaceted, intriguing bouquet. Sweet, lush, opulent fruit cascades across the palate, exhibiting low acidity, generous amounts of glycerin and alcohol, and layers of richness. Anticipated maturity: now–2015.

1975 Vega Sicilia Unico Reserva

RATING: 96 points

1975 has always been one of Vega Sicilia's great vintages, and it has the potential to be one of this historic winery's finest offerings. The wine's beautiful, saturated, dense ruby/purple color is followed by a tight but rich nose of black and red fruits, spices, and toasty oak. Deep, with huge body and massive flavor extraction, this wine combines awesome power and richness with considerable structure and delineation. It appears to be a legendary Vega Sicilia. Anticipated maturity: now–2025.

1970 Vega Sicilia Unico Reserva

RATING: 96 points (magnum)

This wine boasts an elegant, complex bouquet of cedarwood, blackberries, cherry liqueur, and vanilla. Opulently textured, with fabulous unctuousness, vivaciousness, and vigor, superb ripeness, a full-bodied, super-concentrated attack as well as lush mid-palate and finish, this seamless classic was brilliant from the 750-ml format, and is equally compelling from magnum. Anticipated maturity: now–2035.

1968 Vega Sicilia Unico Reserva

RATING: 98 points

An awesome wine! The nose offers up copious aromas of sweet, jammy black plums, black cherries, and cassis, as well as gorgeous smoky, vanilla, floral, and licorice scents that tease the olfactory senses with the promise of considerable thrills. Extremely full-bodied, massively rich, and unctuous, with layers of jammy fruit, adequate acidity, and moderate tannin, this huge wine's well-focused structural component keeps everything in balance. There is a freshness, youthfulness, and extraordinary degree of promise in this amazingly young, fabulously concentrated Unico Reserva. It should take its place in wine history beside the greatest clarets of the decade of the 1960s. Anticipated maturity: now–2025.

1966 Vega Sicilia Unico Reserva

RATING: 95 points

The 1966 Unico Reserva exhibits a huge, fragrant, penetrating bouquet of sweet, jammy black cherry fruit, cedar, smoke, and earth. The saturated, dark ruby color reveals a hint of amber at the edge. Full-bodied, succulent, and velvety, this gorgeously proportioned, decadently styled Vega Sicilia is fully mature, yet its balance, freshness, and thrilling level of flavor extraction suggest it should easily last through 2015.

1964 Vega Sicilia Unico Reserva

RATING: 94 points

This wine's graceful, spicy, cedary, black currant–scented nose is reminiscent of a classic St.-Julien or Pauillac. Any evidence of new oak has been well concealed by the wine's evolution. Medium to full–bodied, with an opulent texture, an attractive, sweet inner core of ripe fruit, and a soft, lightly tannic finish, this fully mature, beautifully made Vega Sicilia admirably balances power and finesse. Anticipated maturity: now–2010.

1962 Vega Sicilia Unico Reserva

RATING: 95 points

The deep, saturated, dark-ruby 1962 has been a consistently gorgeous wine. A huge, fragrant bouquet combining jammy red and black fruits, herbs, vanilla, smoke, and cedar is followed by a full-bodied wine with sweet, generous flavors, light tannin, and a finish that lasts for 30–40 seconds. This knockout Unico is fully mature, yet remains fresh, vibrant, and lively. Anticipated maturity: now–2015.

CALIFORNIA

Virtually every type of wine available elsewhere in the world is made in California. There is no question that the region's fine wines continue to be dominated by the vanilla and chocolate flavors of the wine world, Chardonnay and Cabernet Sauvignon. However, as some of the California wineries included in this book on the world's greatest estates prove, there has been considerable progress with the fickle Pinot Noir as well as with wines made from Syrah, Grenache, and Mourvèdre, the so-called Rhône Rangers. Certainly the top four or five dozen wineries produce wines that are as fine and multidimensional as those found anywhere in the world, but California's is still a young industry, and most wineries, even those that are 10–20 years old, are still trying to find the right vineyards, the right blends, and the right identity.

Certainly the time-honored philosophy of California winemaking—which consisted of an obsession with the vineyard as a manufacturing plant, a predilection for industrial winemaking in the cellars, and a preoccupation with monolithic, simplistic, squeaky clean wines—has evolved. Winemakers are now taking risks and realizing that 80–90% of the quality was in the vineyard, not the advice of some high-tech, college-educated oenologist with several master's degrees who often doesn't even drink wine for pleasure. The tradition of eviscerating wines, of stripping them by trying too hard to sculpt their aromas, flavor, soul, and personality, remains a problem for many wineries, but not for any of those that are discussed in the pages that follow. The old industrial, food-processor mentality has been

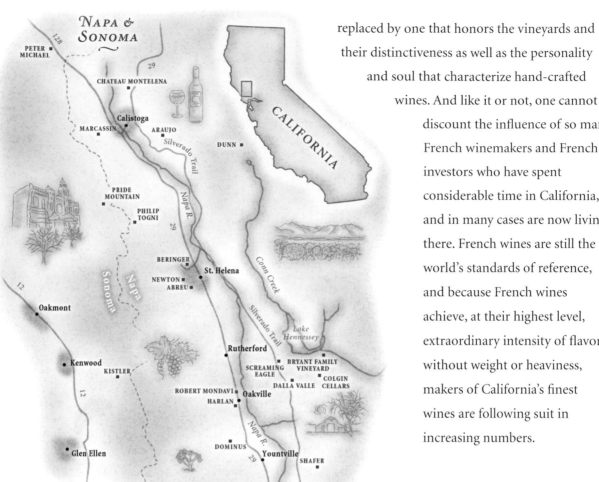

replaced by one that honors the vineyards and their distinctiveness as well as the personality and soul that characterize hand-crafted wines. And like it or not, one cannot discount the influence of so many French winemakers and French investors who have spent considerable time in California, and in many cases are now living there. French wines are still the world's standards of reference, and because French wines achieve, at their highest level, extraordinary intensity of flavor without weight or heaviness, makers of California's finest wines are following suit in increasing numbers.

ABREU VINEYARD

WINES:

Cabernet Sauvignon Madrona Ranch

Cabernet Sauvignon Thorevilos

OWNER: David Abreu

ADDRESS: P.O. Box 89, Rutherford, CA 94573

TELEPHONE: (707) 963-7487

TELEFAX: (707) 963-5104

E-MAIL: info@abreuvineyard.com

WEBSITE: www.abreuvineyard.com

CONTACT: Brad Grimes

VISITING POLICY: No tours or tastings are available

VINEYARDS

SURFACE AREA:

Madrona Ranch—25 acres

Thorevilos—20 acres

GRAPE VARIETALS: Cabernet Sauvignon, Cabernet Franc,
Merlot, Petit Verdot

AVERAGE AGE OF THE VINES.

Madrona Ranch—25 years

Thorevilos—15 years

DENSITY OF PLANTATION: Most of the newer plantings are
3 feet between the vines and 6 feet between the rows.
Some of the older vines at Madrona Ranch and
Thorevilos are planted 4–6 feet between the vines and
8 feet between the rows. The tendency is toward denser
and denser plantings.

AVERAGE YIELDS: Older vines—2.2 tons per acre; younger
vines—less than 2 tons per acre

WINEMAKING AND UPBRINGING

David Abreu, like most of the producers in this book, believes
that quality begins in the vineyard where the fruit is obtained.
Harvesting is done in the early morning to take advantage of
cool temperatures. The grapes are put into small lugs that hold
only 30 pounds of fruit. A sorting is performed prior to the
destemming, and a second sorting is done afterward to remove
any damaged fruit or vegetal material. Primarily whole berries
are used during the fermentation, which generally begins after
a 3–5 day prefermentation cold maceration. After a relatively
long maceration of 3–4 weeks, the wine goes through malolactic fermentation in 100% new French oak casks. It is aged
2 years in barrel, followed by another 2 years in bottle before
being released.

ANNUAL PRODUCTION

Madrona Ranch: 6,000 bottles

Thorevilos: 2,400 bottles

AVERAGE PRICE (VARIABLE DEPENDING ON VINTAGE): $150–175

GREAT RECENT VINTAGES

2003, 2002, 2001, 2000, 1997, 1995

David Abreu, a tireless viticulturist, consults for some
of California's finest producers, who recognize his
perfectionist attitude in planting and maintaining vineyards. His own Madrona Ranch vineyard, located at the
base of Spring Mountain, west of St. Helena, was planted
in 1980 with Cabernet Sauvignon and Cabernet Franc.
Merlot vines were added in 1986, and a small amount of
Petit Verdot was planted in 2000. In 1990, the Thorevilos
vineyard was planted with Cabernet Sauvignon, Cabernet Franc, Merlot, and Petit Verdot. The debut vintage
was 2000, and thus was born what is potentially one of
the most extraordinary wines in California.

Two other Abreu vineyards, both planted with Bordeaux varietals, are just coming into production. Cap-
pella, situated south of Madrona Ranch, was planted in
2000, and a vineyard on the top of Howell Mountain
was planted in 2001.

David Abreu

David Abreu is best known as a viticulturist, but the quality of his own wines speaks to the extraordinary work he does in the vineyard, keeping yields as small as any of his peers, and massaging the wines through the winemaking and upbringing in cask with virtually no intervention. There is no acidification or clarification, resulting in wines that represent the natural bottled essence of their vineyard sites. Moreover, as the following tasting notes suggest, they have extraordinary aging potential.

ABREU CABERNET SAUVIGNON MADRONA RANCH

2003 Abreu Cabernet Sauvignon Madrona Ranch
RATING: 93–95 points
The 2003 Cabernet Sauvignon Madrona Ranch does not possess the power and structure of the 2001, or the sweetness, density, and flamboyance of the 2002, but it possesses abundant concentration, elegance, and finesse. It is a racy, feminine expression of Cabernet Sauvignon. A deep purple color precedes a stunning nose of melted licorice, camphor, acacia flowers, new saddle leather, and copious black fruits. I would not be surprised to see this medium to full–bodied, rich, well-balanced, and accessible 2003 hit full maturity before its two older siblings. Anticipated maturity: 2007–2020.

2002 Abreu Cabernet Sauvignon Madrona Ranch
RATING: 94–96 points
The day I tasted it, the 2002 Cabernet Sauvignon Madrona Ranch was about ready to be bottled. Cut from the same mold as the 2001, it is an intense effort of first-growth Bordeaux proportions. An extraordinarily complex nose of Asian spices, soy, smoky barbecue scents, blackberries, crème de cassis, violets, licorice, and incense is followed by a wine of great purity as well as intensity, with a multidimensional mid-palate and a fabulously voluptuous finish with high but sweet tannin. In the more challenging vintage of 2002, Abreu has turned in another brilliant performance. Anticipated maturity: 2008–2028.

2001 Abreu Cabernet Sauvignon Madrona Ranch
RATING: 97+ points
The 2001 Cabernet Sauvignon Madrona Ranch is still an infant, but wow, what upside potential it possesses! A provocative inky purple color is accompanied by a sumptuous perfume of flowers, wood smoke, licorice, tobacco, blackberries, and cassis. Full-bodied, with perfect harmony, extraordinary concentration, and a 60+-second finish, it should be at its peak between 2011 and 2030+.

2000 Abreu Cabernet Sauvignon Madrona Ranch
RATING: 92 points
A candidate for wine of the vintage, the gorgeous 2000 Cabernet Sauvignon Madrona Ranch (93% Cabernet Sauvignon and the rest Cabernet Franc and Petit Verdot) boasts an inky purple color as well as a sumptuous perfume of violets, blackberries, blueberries, and coffee offered in a medium to full–bodied, supple-textured, accessible style. Anticipated maturity: now–2018.

1999 Abreu Cabernet Sauvignon Madrona Ranch
RATING: 93 points
The 1999 Cabernet Sauvignon Madrona Ranch (90% Cabernet Sauvignon, 5% Cabernet Franc, and 5% Merlot) exhibits a saturated purple color in addition to a gorgeous bouquet of espresso beans intermixed with licorice, incense, blueberries, and blackberries. There is more tannin in the unusually austere finish, but the wine is remarkably complex and should be exceptionally long-lived. There are 500 cases of this beauty, which should be at its finest between 2006 and 2025.

1998 Abreu Cabernet Sauvignon Madrona Ranch
RATING: 93 points
Abreu was ruthless with his phenomenally successful 1998 Cabernet Sauvignon Madrona Ranch (one of the half-dozen or so superstars of the vintage). He said the year was so cold that over one-half of his crop had to be cut off to accentuate maturity in the remainder of the grapes. A blend of 90% Cabernet Sauvignon and equal parts Cabernet Franc and Merlot, the 1998 boasts an opaque blue/purple color, as well as an explosive nose of black olives, licorice, new saddle leather, cassis, and blueberries. Soft, plush, and opulently textured, it will evolve effortlessly through 2020.

1997 Abreu Cabernet Sauvignon Madrona Ranch
RATING: 100 points
The 1997 boasts an opaque black/purple color as well as a gorgeous bouquet of roasted meats, scorched earth, blackberry, crème de cassis, minerals, and toast. The soaring aromatics are matched by a phenomenally intense, seamless palate, with full-bodied opulence, exquisite purity and symmetry, and a multidimensional finish that lasts for nearly a minute. This wine will last through 2031. It is a tour de force in winemaking.

1996 Abreu Cabernet Sauvignon Madrona Ranch
RATING: 98 points
The 1996 Cabernet Sauvignon Madrona Ranch reveals a blueberry/blackberry, crème de cassis character with smoky oak, new saddle leather, licorice, dried herbs, and mineral scents. Expansive, with terrific intensity, purity, and overall

symmetry, it has noticeable tannin in the finish. Anticipated maturity: now–2030.

1995 Abreu Cabernet Sauvignon Madrona Ranch
RATING: 95 points
The 1995 Cabernet Sauvignon Madrona Ranch is a strikingly superb Cabernet Sauvignon. It includes 5% Cabernet Franc and 5% Merlot in the blend, but I would never have guessed that. Aged in 100% new Taransaud oak barrels (as are all Abreu's wines), this wine boasts an opaque purple color in addition to a fabulous bouquet of blueberries, blackberries, cassis, licorice, minerals, and smoky, toasty oak. The wine's aromatics soar from the glass, and in the mouth the bouquet's promise is fulfilled. A thick, juicy, black-fruit character comes across in cascades of glycerin and extract. All of this has been buttressed by sweet tannin and good acidity. A voluptuously textured, blockbuster, yet remarkably harmonious wine, it is one of the finest efforts of the vintage. Anticipated maturity: now–2025.

1994 Abreu Cabernet Sauvignon Madrona Ranch
RATING: 94 points
The impressively rich, dense, purple-colored 1994 Cabernet Sauvignon Madrona Ranch exhibits a blueberry/blackberry/cassis-scented nose, with a touch of violets and subtle new oak. In the mouth, the wine has disguised its tannic clout with extraordinary extraction of fruit, medium to full body, and a silky yet powerful personality. Anticipated maturity: now–2022.

1993 Abreu Cabernet Sauvignon Madrona Ranch
RATING: 94 points
The 1993 Cabernet Sauvignon, another great wine from an often "maligned" vintage, boasts a fabulous dark purple color, as well as sweet, jammy, toasty black fruits, fruitcake, cedar, and black truffle–like smells. Packed with extract and glycerin, this is an expansive, chewy, pure Cabernet that will easily last until 2025. This is great stuff!

ABREU CABERNET SAUVIGNON THOREVILOS

2003 Abreu Cabernet Sauvignon Thorevilos
RATING: 95–97 points
The 2003 Cabernet Sauvignon Thorevilos is unquestionably one of the most compelling wines of the vintage. It possesses a dense purple color in addition to abundant quantities of blackberry, cedar, coffee, and blueberry characteristics, a silky texture, medium to full body, and a voluptuous finish. It should be accessible early on and provide delicious drinking for two decades or more.

2002 Abreu Cabernet Sauvignon Thorevilos
RATING: 98–100 points
The 2002 Cabernet Sauvignon Thorevilos is singing the same song as the 2001 . . . just more loudly. Slightly more precocious and fruit-forward, it exhibits an inky blue/purple color in addition to an explosive, exotic bouquet of blackberries, blueberries, vanilla, incense, licorice, and smoke. It is full-bodied and extraordinarily rich with mouth-staining levels of extract as well as a seamless integration of acidity, tannin, wood, and alcohol. Riveting! Anticipated maturity: 2009–2030.

2001 Abreu Cabernet Sauvignon Thorevilos
RATING: 99 points
The amazing, virtually perfect 2001 Cabernet Sauvignon Thorevilos (85% Cabernet Sauvignon, 10% Cabernet Franc, and 5% Petit Verdot) boasts an opaque purple color along with a tantalizing perfume of blueberry liqueur intermixed with scents of espresso roast, chocolate, and black truffles. Voluminous in the mouth, revealing flavors of cedar, chocolate, cassis, blueberry, and flowers along with a striking minerality, this full-bodied, opulently textured 2001 is as good as any red wine can possibly be. Anticipated maturity: 2008–2030.

2000 Abreu Cabernet Sauvignon Thorevilos
RATING: 92 points
The first release from the 20-acre Thorevilos Vineyard (co-owned by David Abreu and Ric Forman) is the 2000 Cabernet Sauvignon Thorevilos, a blend of 88% Cabernet Sauvignon, 10% Cabernet Franc, and 2% Petit Verdot. It is a dense, sweet, black currant–flavored effort with hints of scorched earth, cedar, and flowers in the background. Fruit-driven (mostly blue and black fruits), with a Pomerol-like succulence/lushness, it should drink well between now and 2018.

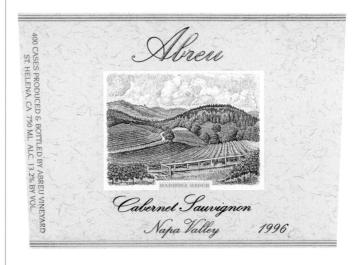

WINES:

Grenache

Syrah Lorraine Vineyard

Syrah Reva Vineyard

Syrah Seymour's Vineyard

OWNERS: John and Lorraine Alban

ADDRESS: 8575 Orcutt Road, Arroyo Grande, CA 93420

TELEPHONE: (805) 546-0305

TELEFAX: (805) 546-9879

E-MAIL: john@albanvineyards.com

WEBSITE: www.albanvineyards.com

CONTACT: John Alban

VISITING POLICY: Sorry, no visitors

VINEYARDS

SURFACE AREA: 60 acres currently planted. Room for 60 more.

GRAPE VARIETALS: Viognier, Roussanne, Grenache, Syrah

AVERAGE AGE OF THE VINES: 14 years

DENSITY OF PLANTATION: 1,000–2,400 vines per acre

AVERAGE YIELDS: Viognier—2 tons per acre; Syrah—2.5 tons per acre; Grenache—1 ton per acre; Roussanne—1.5 tons per acre

WINEMAKING AND UPBRINGING

John Alban has said, "Alban Vineyards focuses on the belief that the true measure of a wine's greatness is the pleasure it evokes. While we do not embrace the idea that there are noble varieties, we are forever pursuing the potential nobility of any given wine; it is not a matter of birthright, but a question of what is realized by each bottling . . . By planting what [in 1990] were unknown or disregarded grape varieties in a relatively unknown appellation, we could free ourselves of any preconceptions and focus on our own goals. There were no benchmarks for California Roussanne or Grenache Noir—they were not previously produced. Likewise, Edna Valley Syrah and Viognier were nonexistent. Using a blank canvas, we have sought to make your racing pulse our *terroir*, your gleaming eyes our typicity, and your lust for more our tradition."

With this objective, Alban handles each wine differently, but all of Alban's grapes are grown under high stress, which naturally results in low yields, which are fermented in small lots using indigenous yeasts. The small lots allow each tiny parcel to be kept separate, giving the winemaker the greatest flexibility for blending and the ability to isolate premier vineyard sites. All wines that complete primary and secondary fermentations are bottled unfined and unfiltered.

Syrah and Grenache are fermented open top in one to three barrel-sized lots. They are pumped over daily once fermentation starts and until the berries are soft enough for anyone under 150 pounds to punch down by hand. Then a mix of punching and pumping is employed until the wine is appropriately structured with skin tannins and the extraction of flavors appears complete. The wines are drained to a mix of new and once-filled barrels—95% or more French, regardless of sugar content, and complete primary and secondary in oak. The wines are bottled unfined and unfiltered flowing by gravity to bottle after 18–23 months in barrel.

Grenache is generally allowed to heat up faster and cool down faster than the Syrah. The Grenache is usually pressed earlier. As John Alban explains, "Syrah is much more even-keeled and can be given a longer lead; Grenache would merely use the extra rope to tie us up."

ANNUAL PRODUCTION

Syrah Reva: 8,400 bottles

Syrah Lorraine: 3,000 bottles

Syrah Seymour's: 1,000 bottles

Grenache: 3,000 bottles

AVERAGE PRICE (VARIABLE DEPENDING ON VINTAGE): $25–85

GREAT RECENT VINTAGES

Grenache and Syrah—2002, 2001, 1997, 1996

John Alban settled into a beautiful hillside location overlooking the Edna Valley in 1989, and began planting his vineyard the following year. From a family of doctors, Alban broke with tradition by becoming a viticulturist/oenologist. His impressive apprenticeship résumé includes working in Beaujolais and the northern Rhône. His 60 acre vineyard (which could be expanded to 120 acres) is planted with Rhône varietals save for a tiny block of Chardonnay. He produces only 5,000 cases each year, as he sells fruit to some of the best Rhône varietal producers (Manfred Krankl of Sine Qua Non is his most prominent client). All of Alban's wines are aged in small barrels, larger *demi-muids,* and *foudres* or tanks, blended together, and bottled with neither fining nor filtration. This estate is a reference point for what Rhône varietals can achieve in California. In short, John Alban not only talks the talk but walks the

walk. Low yields, ripe fruit, meticulous handling, and a policy of nonintervention result in stunning wines that go from strength to strength.

One of the most articulate winemakers and viticulturists in California, Alban always wondered why Europe grew and fermented over 500 different grape varieties, but California was using only about a half-dozen. He remembers a friend giving him his first glass of Condrieu in celebration of his 24th birthday, and he has come to believe that was "one of the most significant gulps" of wine in his life. Knowing nothing about wine at the time, the following day he started researching everything he could about the tiny appellation of Condrieu, and Alban ultimately became one of the pioneers of California's Rhône Valley grape variety movement.

He completed his master's degree in oenology at the University of California, Davis, but was still obsessed with the Rhône and started taking apprentice jobs designed to get him closer and closer to this fabled region. He realized that there was virtually no Grenache, Roussanne, or Viognier, three of the most noble varietals of the Rhône Valley, in California, and

what was there, if anything at all, was probably just poor commercial clones designed for blending. Using cuttings that he brought back from France, he began to propagate vines, working extensively in a greenhouse, and of course, all of this led to the planting of a vineyard in an area that was totally unheralded and unknown for its potential for Rhône varietals. John Alban believes that the progressive, passionate wine buyers and sommeliers who championed the early vintages of Alban Vineyards kept him in business. These were his missionaries, who nurtured what was then an infantile/fledgling California Rhône wine movement, and took the California wine trade out of the age of black and white (Cabernet Sauvignon and Chardonnay) into the age of what he calls "color and deliciousness."

In my experience, John Alban has always been one of California's finest viticulturists. His winemaking was sometimes a bit rustic in the early days, but now each vintage and each cellar visit indicates a sure hand in the cellar. There is no question that the fruit from his vineyards is as fabulous as can be produced in California, and now the winemaking is on an equal par.

GRENACHE

2003 Grenache

RATING: 89–92 points

The 2003 Grenache exhibits a dark ruby/purple color as well as sweet aromas of melted licorice, kirsch, black cherries, and berries. It is putting on weight, but the tannin remains edgy and gritty. They will need to soften for it to merit its projected score. Anticipated maturity: 2006–2014.

2002 Grenache

RATING: 95 points

As for the 2002 reds, this is a great vintage for Lorraine and John Alban. For starters, the 2002 Grenache (15% Syrah is included in the blend), which I tasted several days after bottling, is absolutely remarkable. The problem is, there is virtually no production, as the crop size was minuscule (0.6 tons of fruit per acre). This wine, which is destemmed, fermented with indigenous yeasts in open-topped fermenters, and is both punched down and pumped over, may be the finest Grenache the Albans have yet produced. Classic aromas of raspberries, kirsch, and hints of blackberries, anise, and loamy soil soar from the glass of this dense purple–colored Grenache (one of the blackest I have ever seen). Tipping the scales at 15.3% alcohol, this monumental Grenache is a tribute to just how great this varietal can be in Edna Valley. It should drink well for 10–12 years or more.

2001 Grenache

RATING: 92 points

The 2001 Grenache (blended 80% Grenache and 20% Syrah) exhibits an opaque blue/purple color in addition to peppery, kirsch, raspberry, and blackberry aromas and flavors. With a viscous texture, medium to full body, and a gorgeous up-front style, it begs to be drunk over the next decade.

2000 Grenache

RATING: 93 points

Its dense ruby/purple color is followed by a glorious perfume of raspberry and kirsch, blackberries, licorice, and pepper. Full-bodied, viscous, and opulent, it is an uncompromisingly rich, intense, authentic example of Grenache that should evolve for 10–15 years. A revelation!

1999 Grenache

RATING: 90 points

The 1999 Grenache exhibits sweet kirsch and raspberry fruit. It is sexy, opulent, and hedonistic. My tasting notes said, "a Pinot Noir on steroids." Drink it over the next 4–6 years for its blast of fruit and glycerin.

1997 Grenache

RATING: 90 points

I adore the 1997 Grenache. It boasts a dense, dark ruby/purple color as well as textbook Grenache aromas of black raspberry liqueur, cherries, and spice. Full-bodied, concentrated, and mouth-filling, this expansive, chewy, gorgeously rich Grenache can be drunk now as well as over the next 6 years. Impressive!

SYRAH LORRAINE VINEYARD

2003 Syrah Lorraine Vineyard

RATING: 94–97 points

The 2003 Syrah Lorraine Vineyard, named after John Alban's raven-haired wife, comes from stony soils with abundant amounts of fragmented rock and less clay. This is always the most voluptuous and opulent, and initially the most seductive of Alban's Syrahs. The saturated black/purple–hued 2003 boasts great intensity, fabulous concentration, and a long, chewy, blockbuster finish. It is very unevolved compared to the Reva. Anticipated maturity: 2008–2020.

2002 Syrah Lorraine Vineyard

RATING: 96 points

A flamboyant wine with a sensational nose of blackberry liqueur, melted licorice, acacia flowers, crushed stones, and a hint of blueberries, it is seamlessly assembled with fabulous concentration, an expansive, full-bodied palate, and an amazingly long finish that lasts well over a minute. Consume it during its first 10–12 years of life.

2001 Syrah Lorraine Vineyard

RATING: 94 points

The 2001 Syrah Lorraine Vineyard exhibits a saturated purple color to the rim along with explosive aromas of acacia flowers and blackberries, full body, and admirable acidity. Impressively endowed, thick, and multilayered, with considerable flavor dimension as well as character, it will drink beautifully for a decade or more.

2000 Syrah Lorraine Vineyard

RATING: 93 points

The inky/black/purple 2000 Syrah Lorraine Vineyard is saturated with color. It boasts a knockout nose of melted licorice, blackberry liqueur, and acacia flowers. Full-bodied, huge, tannic, but ripe, this is a stunningly rich wine that should hit its peak in 2–3 years, and last for 15+.

1999 Syrah Lorraine Vineyard

RATING: 90 points

With a saturated color as well as high extraction, the 1999 Syrah Lorraine offers a combination of structure, elegance, power, and concentration with beautifully integrated wood, tannin, and acidity. This backward effort should age well for another 10–12 years.

1998 Syrah Lorraine Vineyard

RATING: 93 points

A dynamite effort, the saturated opaque, murky, purple-colored 1998 Syrah Lorraine offers up aromas of bacon fat, mocha, licorice, and crème de cassis. This full-bodied, unctuously textured, stunningly rich, exuberant, robust, super-endowed Syrah is a total turn-on. Still youthful, it promises to evolve gracefully for another 8–10 years.

1997 Syrah Lorraine Vineyard

RATING: 91 points

The black/ruby/purple-colored 1997 Syrah Lorraine offers blackberry, tar, and licorice notes in its moderately powerful aromatics. Thick, rich, full-bodied, and concentrated, with excellent purity, this offering exhibits power, richness, symmetry, and the potential to improve for another 6–8 years.

1995 Syrah Lorraine Vineyard

RATING: 90 points

This superb wine displays a saturated dark ruby/purple color, and knockout aromatics consisting of hickory smoke, bacon, and cassis fruit. Opulent on the palate, this full-bodied, concentrated, lush, chewy Syrah has low enough acidity and sweet enough fruit to be drunk now, but it promises to develop nicely for another 4–9 years.

SYRAH REVA VINEYARD

2003 Syrah Reva Vineyard

RATING: 93–95 points

The 2003 Syrah Reva Vineyard emerges from one of Alban's cooler Syrah sites with considerable clay in the subsoil. Its dense purple color is accompanied by a gorgeous perfume of blackberries, cassis, and licorice. Full-bodied and opulent, it appears to be a terrific success. Anticipated maturity: 2007–2018.

2002 Syrah Reva Vineyard

RATING: 95+ points

The 2002 Syrah Reva Vineyard performs spectacularly well. Its opaque purple color is accompanied by a classic bouquet of crème de cassis, blackberries, and touches of new oak, tar, and sweet leather. It is a spectacular, dense, opulent, full-bod-

ied effort with good minerality as well as structure. It should drink well for 10–15 years.

2001 Syrah Reva Vineyard

RATING: 93+ points

The saturated blue/purple–hued 2001 Syrah Reva Vineyard reveals a huge nose of melted licorice, crushed rocks, crème de cassis, blackberries, pepper, and spice. This voluptuous, rich, intense Syrah possesses a 40 plus+-second finish. A beauty, it should hit its prime in 1–2 years, and last for 10–15.

2000 Syrah Reva Vineyard

RATING: 94 points

The saturated blue/purple–colored 2000 Syrah Reva Vineyard exhibits a slightly reduced nose, but with aeration of 60–90 minutes, glorious notes of blackberries, asphalt, singed leather, and wood emerge. Medium to full–bodied and moderately tannic, this young, unevolved, but promising 2000 will be at its finest between now and 2015.

1999 Syrah Reva Vineyard

RATING: 90 points

The opaque purple–colored 1999 Syrah Reva Vineyard reveals notes of bacon fat, cassis, spicy oak, and a Hermitage-like character. It comes from the coolest section of the vineyard, and perhaps that's why it seems the most French. There are 700 cases of this *cuvée*, which should age well for another 8–10 years.

1998 Syrah Reva Vineyard

RATING: 90 points

The 1998 Syrah Reva Vineyard reveals a dense ruby/purple color as well as a classic nose of bacon fat, smoke, blackberries, and licorice. Full-bodied and rich, with a vanilla note added to the black fruit and smoke characteristics, this lush, full-throttle Syrah is accessible, but should age nicely for another 8 years.

1997 Syrah Reva Vineyard

RATING: 92 points

The 1997 Syrah Reva Vineyard displays a saturated purple color along with an element of *sur-maturité* (overripeness), the telltale blackberry/cassis fruit, and notes of licorice. Full-bodied, superrich, and impeccably pure, this is an exceptional example of Syrah from Edna Valley. Drink it over the next 6–11 years.

SYRAH SEYMOUR'S VINEYARD

2003 Syrah Seymour's Vineyard

RATING: 95–100 points

A prodigious example of this varietal is the 2003 Syrah Seymour's Vineyard, named after John Alban's father. The most evolved of these *cuvées*, it exhibits classic acacia flower, blackberry liqueur, cassis, road tar, and licorice characteristics. A seamless integration of acidity, tannin, and wood is the stuff of legends. This will be an amazing wine upon release. Anticipated maturity: 2009–2020.

2002 Syrah Seymour's Vineyard

RATING: 95–97 points

The inky/purple-colored 2002 Syrah Seymour's Vineyard offers up a huge bouquet of scorched earth, crème de cassis, melted tar, camphor, and the entire black fruit spectrum. Superb, full-bodied flavors are expansive, rich, profoundly concentrated, and velvety textured. Two to three years of patience is warranted for this glorious Syrah. It should easily last 12–15 years.

2001 Syrah Seymour's Vineyard

RATING: 95+ points

The so-called pick of the best barrels (a difficult job at this winery), the 2001 Syrah Seymour's Vineyard possesses additional concentration, aromatics, and length. A blue/purple color is followed by meaty flavors that coat the palate with blackberries, mocha, cocoa, earth, and crème de cassis. A tour de force in winemaking, it is a spectacular, rich, broad yet remarkably well-balanced wine to drink over the next 10–15 years. Awesome stuff!

2000 Syrah Seymour's Vineyard

RATING: 96 points

The luxury *cuvée* of 2000 Syrah Seymour's Vineyard is a Syrah on steroids. A bottle left open for two weeks revealed no signs of oxidation. Amazing! The inky/blue/purple color is followed by a wine reminiscent of dry Vintage Port. Notes of scorched earth, blackberry liqueur, and asphalt are presented in an unctuous, thick, chewy style with marvelous extract and multiple dimensions. This is a tour de force in winemaking, and certainly any Rhône Ranger aficionado should be beating a path to Alban Vineyards to get a bottle or two of this elixir. Anticipated maturity: now–2017.

1999 Syrah Seymour's Vineyard

RATING: 91 points

There are 150 cases of the 1999 Syrah Seymour's Vineyard. It reveals an opaque purple color along with a classic Syrah nose of blackberry and cassis intermixed with toasty oak, bacon fat, and vanilla. Full-bodied, layered, rich, dense, and smoky, this impressively constituted wine will be at its finest between now and 2014.

1998 Syrah Seymour's Vineyard

RATING: 90 points

The 1998 Syrah Seymour's Vineyard is still relatively firm and closed. Its opaque ruby/purple color is followed by a dense, chewy, tannic, more backward wine revealing more new oak. Loaded with concentrated blackberry and cassis flavors with hints of smoke and underbrush, it should last for another 10–16 years.

ARAUJO ESTATE WINES

WINES:

Cabernet Sauvignon Eisele Vineyard

Syrah Eisele Vineyard

OWNERS: Bart and Daphne Araujo

ADDRESS: Eisele Vineyard, 2155 Pickett Road, Calistoga, CA 94515

TELEPHONE: (707) 942-6061

TELEFAX: (707) 942-6471

E-MAIL: bart@araujoestate.com; daphne@araujoestate.com

WEBSITE: www.araujoestatewines.com

CONTACT: Bart Araujo

VISITING POLICY: Not open to the public

VINEYARDS

SURFACE AREA: 40 acres

GRAPE VARIETALS: Cabernet Sauvignon, Cabernet Franc, Petit Verdot, Merlot, Syrah, Sauvignon Blanc, Viognier

AVERAGE AGE OF THE VINES: 12 years

DENSITY OF PLANTATION: 1,100–1,800 vines per acre

AVERAGE YIELDS: 2.5–3 tons per acre

WINEMAKING AND UPBRINGING

Individual vineyard blocks are harvested and fermented separately to retain the nuances of each vineyard location. All fruit is hand-picked by the estate's own vineyard workers. Currently, 15 lots are kept separate for Cabernet Sauvignon, and 5 lots for Syrah. Grapes are sorted twice on sorting tables before and after destemming. The individual berries are then delivered to fermentation tanks without the use of pumping.

Following the primary fermentation with the native yeasts, the wines are transferred to French oak barrels for malolactic fermentation. They use 100% new barrels for Cabernet Sauvignon, 50% new for Syrah. The Cabernet Sauvignon is aged for 22 months prior to bottling, the Syrah for 15 months.

ANNUAL PRODUCTION

Cabernet Sauvignon Eisele: 24,000 bottles

Syrah: 4,000 bottles

AVERAGE PRICE (VARIABLE DEPENDING ON VINTAGE): $50–125

GREAT RECENT VINTAGES

Cabernet Sauvignon—2003, 2002, 2001, 1999, 1996, 1995, 1994, 1993, 1992, 1991

Syrah—2002, 1999, 1998

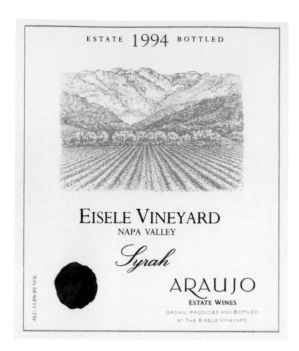

Since 1971, some of California's most ageworthy and intensely flavored Cabernet Sauvignons have been made from grapes grown at the Eisele Vineyard, located on benchland near the northern end of the Napa Valley, just east of Calistoga. Protected by the Palisades Mountains to the north and cooled by westerly breezes from the Chalk Hill Gap, this 40-acre vineyard is planted on warm cobbly soils that yield a small crop of exceptionally concentrated fruit. The wines produced in this remarkable place have a rare combination of forthright character with precisely defined flavors and fine textures, deep concentration without any sense of heaviness, and the capacity to develop profound complexity with age.

The Eisele Vineyard was originally planted in the 1880s with Zinfandel and Riesling, and has been under vine since. The first Cabernet was planted in 1964.

Milt and Barbara Eisele purchased the 137-acre property in 1969, including 35 acres of vineyard. Initially they sold their crop to the local co-op, but suspecting that their fruit was of exceptional quality, they were advised by the late wine gurus Barney Rhodes and Harry Waugh to explore a vineyard-designation for their wine. The Eiseles approached Paul Draper, winemaker at Ridge Vineyards, who produced the first Eisele Vineyard Cabernet Sauvignon in 1971. This landmark wine, one of the first vineyard-designated Cabernets in

California, is gracious and beautiful after more than three decades in the bottle, and is considered by many to be one of the finest wines ever produced in the Napa Valley. The 1972 and 1973 vintages went to the Robert Mondavi Winery to be included in their Reserve Cabernet. The second vineyard-designated Eisele Cabernet, which has equally impressive longevity, was produced by Conn Creek Winery in 1974 to great acclaim.

In 1975, wine visionary Joseph Phelps began producing what would become a long line of legendary Cabernets from the Eisele Vineyard. Throughout Joseph Phelps's tenure there, the wines reflected the incomparable character and quality of the Eisele Vineyard. The 1991 vintage yielded two significant Eisele Vineyard Cabernets—the final Phelps bottling from the property and the first Araujo Estate Cabernet Sauvignon.

The Araujos acquired the property in 1990. From that point, the vineyards have been dedicated exclusively to estate-bottled wines.

In 1993, Tony Soter, Araujo's initial consulting oenologist, hired Françoise Peschon as his assistant winemaker. Raised in California with roots in Luxembourg, Françoise received her oenology degree from UC Davis. After postgraduate work at the University of Bordeaux and an apprenticeship at Château Haut-Brion, she returned to California to join Napa Valley's Stag's Leap Wine Cellars, where she worked for seven years before joining Araujo. She became winemaker in 1996, while Tony and his associate, Mia Klein, continued as consultants until Tony's retirement in 1998. The consistent character of Araujo Estate wines derives largely from Françoise's cumulative experience with the vineyard and the wines, and her dedication to producing wines that express the character of the vineyard.

Michel Rolland, the esteemed French consulting oenologist, has been a part of the Araujo team since 2000.

At Araujo Estate, the goal is to produce world-class wine that clearly expresses the estate's distinct *terroir*. They believe that farming organically and biodynamically is the most effective and sustainable method of growing fruit unique to the site, and that improving the health of the soil inevitably improves the flavor of the wines.

To produce the estate's flagship wine, three quarters of the 40-acre Eisele Vineyard is dedicated to Cabernet Sauvignon and its companion varieties, Cabernet Franc, Petit Verdot, and Merlot. The resulting wine is an intense expression of the Eisele Vineyard *terroir*, showing the characteristic flavors of cassis, blackberry, black cherry, cedar, chocolate, and slate, with a lingering mineral finish. Cabernets from the Eisele Vineyard are known for their concentration without heaviness, silky texture, and ability to age for decades.

At the request of Joseph Phelps, Syrah was first planted on the property by Milt Eisele in 1978, but the intention of making an Eisele Vineyard–designated Syrah was abandoned due to lack of demand for Syrah in the marketplace. In 1986, the Syrah vines were budded over to Cabernet, although about 100 plants remained unchanged. The Araujos discovered these few remaining vines, and after making wine from them in 1991 and 1993, made a serious commitment to this an-

cient and noble grape, and increased the plantings in the vineyard. Viognier is co-fermented with some of the Syrah lots, making up 5% of the wine. Araujo Syrah is a profound, mysteriously compelling wine that reveals yet another aspect of the Eisele Vineyard's unique *terroir*.

This reference-point winery is always one of my favorite stops in Northern California. I have been an admirer of the Eisele Vineyard Cabernet Sauvignons since I first tasted the 1974 Conn Creek Eisele. I've been inspired by the proprietors Daphne and Bart Araujo, who have taken this superb *terroir* and built it into a world-class winery and vineyard operation, producing not only spectacular Cabernet Sauvignon, but also fabulous Syrah.

CABERNET SAUVIGNON EISELE VINEYARD

2003 Cabernet Sauvignon Eisele Vineyard

RATING: 96–98 points

The 2003 Cabernet Sauvignon Eisele Vineyard (1,600 cases made from 95% Cabernet Sauvignon and 5% Petit Verdot, but winemaker Françoise Peschon was quick to say they might tweak the blend as it evolves) is higher in alcohol than the 2002 or 2001, but it is another wine of great intensity and stature. Elegant notes of flowers, minerals, black fruits, and smoke are followed by a wine with beautiful fruit, medium to full body, tremendous intensity, and a finish that lasts nearly a full minute. A more streamlined style of Cabernet than the more voluptuous 2002 or the more muscular 2001, this beautifully made Cabernet should be accessible when released in a year. It will evolve for 15–20 years.

2002 Cabernet Sauvignon Eisele Vineyard

RATING: 98–100 points

A potential candidate for perfection is the exquisite 2002 Cabernet Sauvignon Eisele Vineyard. A 1,650-case blend of 92% Cabernet Sauvignon, 5% Cabernet Franc, and 3% Petit Verdot made from extremely low yields, it boasts superb intensity, flavor, elegance, and nobility in addition to a marvelously complex nose of minerals, licorice, cedar, crème de cassis, vanilla, and spice. Exceptionally rich, nuanced, and precise, it is a magnificent expression of Cabernet Sauvignon that offers the elegance of a Bordeaux with the power and potency of Napa Valley Cabernet. A tour de force, this wine can be drunk now or cellared for up to two decades.

2001 Cabernet Sauvignon Eisele Vineyard

RATING: 97 points

The 2001 Cabernet Sauvignon Eisele Vineyard was produced from a large crop, a total of 1,700 cases from a blend of 75% Cabernet Sauvignon and 25% Cabernet Franc. Its saturated purple color leads to a restrained but impressive nose of cassis, toast, earth, and a hint of cedar. Full-bodied and multilayered, with impeccable balance and a noteworthy juxtaposition of power and elegance, it is starting to close down ever so slightly and seems more masculine when compared to the 2002 and 2003. Anticipated maturity: 2008–2025.

2000 Cabernet Sauvignon Eisele Vineyard

RATING: 91 points

The 2000 Cabernet Sauvignon Eisele Vineyard is a 1,700-case blend of 84% Cabernet Sauvignon, 9% Cabernet Franc, and the rest Petit Verdot and Merlot. This vintage produced lighter wines, resulting in a Bordeaux-like example of this *cuvée*. This textured, perfumed Cabernet offers up aromas of black cur-

rants, earth, and lilacs (reminiscent of Château Margaux). It possesses a deep ruby/purple color as well as medium body, a good texture, a slight austerity, but brilliant purity and balance. A lighter-weight effort by Araujo's standards, it is extremely well balanced and approachable. Drink it over the next 10–12 years.

1999 Cabernet Sauvignon Eisele Vineyard

RATING: 95 points

The 1999 Cabernet Sauvignon Eisele Vineyard (a 1,750-case blend of 85% Cabernet Sauvignon, 7% Cabernet Franc, 5% Petit Verdot, and 3% Merlot) boasts explosive aromas of incense, crème de cassis, minerals, and flowers. It is medium to full–bodied, with great harmony and a sweet attack as well as finish. This is a classic example of power and richness allied to considerable elegance. Those in the foreign press who accuse California of being incapable of producing elegant wines have obviously never tasted this Cabernet. Anticipated maturity: now–2020.

1998 Cabernet Sauvignon Eisele Vineyard

RATING: 92 points

The 1998 Cabernet Sauvignon Eisele Vineyard was bottled earlier than usual as this vintage is not as massive or concentrated as its predecessors. It is supple and elegant, with a complex, evolved bouquet of smoke, black currants, spice box, and cedar. In the mouth, the wine is forward with sweet tannin, gorgeously rich, concentrated fruit, and impressively integrated acidity and tannin. Drink this alluring charmer now and over the next 12–15 years.

1997 Cabernet Sauvignon Eisele Vineyard

RATING: 92 points

The 1997 Cabernet Sauvignon Eisele Vineyard is a beauty. The healthy ruby/purple color is followed by classic, unevolved but promising aromas of minerals, cedar, smoke, and black currants. The wine is medium to full–bodied, with admirable purity, a sweet, lush mid-palate, and ripe tannin in the finish. The top-notch 1997 is a restrained classic. Anticipated maturity: now–2020.

1996 Cabernet Sauvignon Eisele Vineyard

RATING: 94 points

The saturated purple–colored 1996 Cabernet Sauvignon Eisele Vineyard offers an attractive nose of black fruits intermixed with toast, minerals, subtle tar, and wood smoke. Full-bodied, with impressive purity and a multilayered mid-palate and finish, it is an expressive, pure, powerful, and large-boned wine. Anticipated maturity: now–2014.

1995 Cabernet Sauvignon Eisele Vineyard

RATING: 98 points

The saturated purple/black color is followed by aromas of sweet vanilla intermixed with riveting scents of black currants, minerals, exotic spices, coffee, and toast. There is nothing garish about this subtle yet powerful giant of a wine. A Napa Valley classic, it is full-bodied and extremely rich, yet retains its sense of balance and symmetry. This fabulous Cabernet Sauvignon should age effortlessly for 30 or more years. Anticipated maturity: now–2030.

1994 Cabernet Sauvignon Eisele Vineyard

RATING: 95 points

The 1994 Cabernet Sauvignon Eisele Vineyard exhibits an impressively saturated dark purple color. Although slightly less powerful than the 1993 and marginally less concentrated than the 1995, the 1994 is still a profoundly rich, silky-textured wine with an uncanny balance between its smooth tannin and layers of cassis and blackberry/mineral–tinged fruit. This wine is particularly impressive if it is first decanted for 45 or so minutes. It will age well for 15–20 years.

1993 Cabernet Sauvignon Eisele Vineyard

RATING: 96 points

The color is an opaque purple, and the nose offers up smoky, chocolaty, black currant, licorice, and mineral scents. On the palate, the wine reveals fabulous density, concentration, and sweetness of fruit as well as tannin, and a 30–40-second finish. Although there is a high percentage of new oak, this wine has completely soaked it up, a testament to its extract and concentration of fruit. While the wine displays a certain precociousness, unusual for a 1993, there is plenty of tannin lurking in the finish, but it is well concealed by the wine's exceptional richness. This beauty is destined to age effortlessly for 20–25 years.

1992 Cabernet Sauvignon Eisele Vineyard

RATING: 96 points

The 1992 Cabernet Sauvignon Eisele Vineyard is another fabulous wine from this superb vineyard. It displays a sweet, pure nose of black currants, minerals, and spices. Full-bodied, tannic, and powerful, as well as undeveloped, it exhibits the potential for another 10–15 years of aging. It is a splendidly rich Cabernet Sauvignon, with outstanding balance and purity. Anticipated maturity: now–2020.

1991 Cabernet Sauvignon Eisele Vineyard

RATING: 95 points

This magnificent California Cabernet offers that exciting blend of power and elegance. The opaque purple color is followed by copious quantities of sweet, mineral, licorice, floral-laden, black currant fruit, full body, exceptional purity, good underlying well-integrated acidity and tannin, and a whoppingly long finish. Typical of many top California wines, it combines magnificent richness and ripeness with a sense of gracefulness and complexity. Look for the 1991 Araujo Estate Cabernet Sauvignon Eisele Vineyard to age effortlessly for another 10–15 years.

SYRAH EISELE VINEYARD

2003 Syrah Eisele Vineyard

RATING: 93–95 points

Sadly, the production of Syrah is limited—250 to 300 cases in most vintages. The winery tends to co-ferment 4–5% Viognier with it, which has a significant impact on uplifting the wine's aromatics. It spends time in equal parts new French oak and used barrels. The 2003 Syrah possesses sweet tannin, formidable intensity, yet not the length, power, and overall depth of the 2002. There is 5% Viognier co-fermented with it. It should drink well for 7–8 years.

2002 Syrah Eisele Vineyard

RATING: 95 points

The black/purple-colored 2002 Syrah exhibits tremendous ripeness along with scents of blackberries, charcoal, and white flowers. Made in a full-bodied, opulent style, I would opt for drinking it during its first 7–10 years of life.

2001 Syrah Eisele Vineyard

RATING: 94 points

The compelling 2001 Syrah (200 cases) includes 4% Viognier in the blend, adding a touch of spunk and exuberance to the already impressive aromatics (blackberry liqueur, flowers, truffles, and a hint of bacon). Full-bodied, with great intensity and purity, this may be the finest Syrah the Araujo team has yet fashioned. Anticipated maturity: now–2016.

2000 Syrah Eisele Vineyard

RATING: 92 points

A high-class, limited *cuvée*, the 2000 Syrah (470 cases) boasts a dense ruby/purple color in addition to deep, chewy, blackberry fruit intermixed with hints of white pepper, acacia flowers, and loamy, earthy notes. Dense and supple, with sweet tannin, it will provide delicious drinking over the next 5–6 years.

1999 Syrah Eisele Vineyard

RATING: 92 points

The 1999 Syrah Eisele Vineyard (a blend of 94% Syrah and 6% Viognier) boasts an opaque ruby/purple color along with gorgeous, complex aromatics of melted asphalt, graphite, blackberry liqueur, coffee, and a hint of pepper. This full-bodied Syrah reveals surprising freshness, finesse, and elegance despite its size. The wine is long, rich, and French in style. It is best drunk over the next 5–10 years.

1997 Syrah Eisele Vineyard

RATING: 90 points

The 1997 is a sexy, surprisingly evolved, extremely fragrant wine that typifies the vintage with its expansive aromatics and seductive personality. The wine's saturated dark purple color is followed by a textbook smoky, bacon fat, toasty, tropical fruit, blackberry, honeysuckle, pepper, and spice–scented nose. Evolved, juicy, rich, and concentrated, but surprisingly refined for a wine of such intensity, this beautifully made Syrah should age nicely for another 5–6 years.

1996 Syrah Eisele Vineyard

RATING: 92 points

The 1996 Syrah Eisele Vineyard is a full-bodied, brawny wine revealing the telltale peppery, blackberry, and cassis scents that seem so easy to obtain with this varietal in California. It is rich and pure, with sweet tannin and plenty of power harnessed in a symmetrical, large-scaled effort that is not without considerable elegance for its mass and volume. This wine can be drunk now, but should last for 5–10 or more years.

1995 Syrah Eisele Vineyard

RATING: 97 points

The spectacular 1995 Syrah Eisele Vineyard is one of the greatest New World Syrahs I have ever tasted. Approximately 300 cases were made, and it is even better out of bottle than it was in barrel. The color is an opaque purple. The bouquet offers explosive notes of wood fire, licorice, jammy blackberries, and cassis, in addition to the unmistakable scent of black truffles/licorice. Full-bodied and rich, with sensational flavor extraction, remarkable harmony, and a 35+-second finish, this is profoundly great Syrah. While it is approachable, it will not reach full maturity for another 5–7 years.

WINE: Cabernet Sauvignon Private Reserve

OWNER: Beringer Blass Wine Estates

ADDRESS: 2000 Main Street, St. Helena, CA 94574 (physical address); P.O. Box 111, St. Helena, CA 94574 (mailing address)

TELEPHONE: (707) 963-7115

TELEFAX: (707) 963-1735

E-MAIL: Beringer.Vineyards@beringerblass.com

WEBSITE: www.beringer.com

CONTACT: Allison Simpson, Public Relations

VISITING POLICY: Tours and tastings available every day except Thanksgiving Day and Christmas. Summer hours (June–Oct.) 10 A.M.–6 P.M., winter hours (Nov.–May) 10 A.M.–5 P.M. Tour information: (707) 963-4812.

VINEYARDS

SURFACE AREA: Beringer Vineyards owns or has long-term leases of 2,134 planted acres in Napa Valley and 600 in Knights Valley. Their Private Reserve Cabernet is one of their most limited production wines (usually 10,000–15,000 cases).

GRAPE VARIETALS: In Napa Valley and Knights Valley: 840 acres of Chardonnay, 442 acres of Merlot, 322 acres of Cabernet Sauvignon, 94 acres of Sauvignon Blanc, 82 acres of Syrah, and 73 acres of Pinot Noir, as well as assorted miscellaneous plantings of other varietals including Viognier, Johannisberg Riesling, Malbec, Petit Verdot, Cabernet Franc, etc.

AVERAGE AGE OF THE VINES: Varies widely between varietal/vineyard.

DENSITY OF PLANTATION: Varies. Majority is 8' x 6', 8' x 5', 6' x 7', and 6' x 6'.

AVERAGE YIELDS: Varies between varietal/vineyard. Cabernet Sauvignon is 2–4 tons per acre.

WINEMAKING AND UPBRINGING

In general, winemaster Ed Sbragia and winemaker Laurie Hook strive to extract as much of what the vineyard is trying to express as possible from the grapes, and showcase it in a balanced wine. Sbragia says, "If a vineyard has the potential to give me ripe, concentrated fruit, I would be wasting an opportunity if I picked the grapes before they had reached true maturity." Stylistically, Beringer's wines have a high intensity and complexity of aromas and flavors while maintaining good balance.

The first and most important key to quality is viticulture, keeping an eye on the vines as the season progresses, managing the canopies to maximize the amount of exposure each cluster receives, dropping crop where needed to balance the vines, etc., and making that all-important decision about the right time to harvest. Vineyard manager Bob Steinhauer has led his Beringer viticulture team for over two decades, working in partnership with the winemakers to provide the best fruit possible. Steinhauer says, "It's gotten so I can read Ed's mind just from the look on his face." Ed and Laurie spend several hours each morning during harvest walking the vineyards and tasting grapes to monitor their development and get a sense of how the vines are doing. They base their harvesting decisions on how the grapes taste, the sensation the skins leave on the inside of their palates, what the seeds look like, and how strong the vines look.

For Cabernet Sauvignon Private Reserve, Ed prefers French Nevers oak barrels and traditionally ages them between 18 and 24 months, depending on where the grapes are grown (mountain vineyards versus valley floor) and the vintage conditions. After bottling, the wines are usually aged for another 18 months to two years.

ANNUAL PRODUCTION

Private Reserve Napa Valley Cabernet Sauvignon: 10,000 cases

AVERAGE PRICE (VARIABLE DEPENDING ON VINTAGE): $75–100

GREAT RECENT VINTAGES

2002, 2001, 1999, 1997, 1994, 1992, 1991, 1987, 1986, 1985, 1978

The 215-acre property Jacob Beringer purchased on September 3, 1875, for $14,500 is still the heart of the Beringer Vineyards' Napa Valley estate. The purchase included a two-story farmhouse (the current Hudson House) and a 28-acre vineyard that was already planted with White Riesling, Chappelt, and Cabernet Sauvignon (St. Helena Home Vineyard, now 48 acres). The following year Jacob and Frederick Beringer established Beringer Brothers Winery. 1876 was their first harvest, yielding approximately 18,000 cases.

Then in 1919, along came Prohibition. Beringer continued to farm 200 acres of vineyard and produce about 15,000 cases of "altar" wines until 1933, when Prohibition was repealed. At the time the estate was growing Sauvignon Vert, Johannisberg Riesling, Cabernet Sauvignon, Petite Syrah, Alicante, Golden Chasselas, Semillon, Gutedel, Green Hungarian, and Burger.

In 1976, Beringer celebrated its centennial with two special bottlings: 1974 Chardonnay and 1973 Cabernet Sauvignon from St. Helena Home Vineyard. Ed Sbragia was hired as assistant winemaker. Then in 1980, the first releases of Private Reserve wines (1978 Private Reserve Chardonnay and 1977 Private Reserve Cabernet, Lemmon Ranch, now know as Chabot) won gold medals at the Orange County Fair.

Beringer's wines benefit from the consistency that comes from the longevity of its staff. In 2001, when the winery celebrated its 125th anniversary, it honored 125 employees who had worked there for over 15 years (the longest was 47 years!), and at least 80% of them worked in the winemaking and vineyard departments. Ed Sbragia believes that employee retention translates into experience with "compounded interest."

I cannot recall a disappointing vintage of Beringer's Private Reserve. That they are able to produce 10,000–15,000 cases and maintain outstanding quality is even more enviable. Statisticians should note that the Private Reserve is always at least 97% Cabernet Sauvignon, and aged for 22–24 months in 100% new French oak. One of the commonalities I find in the wines is a smoky, chocolaty, licorice character that works well with their lavish quantities of fruit and glycerin. One of the safest choices a consumer can make, the Private Reserve has been a consistently fine and accurate representation of Cabernet's varietal characteristics.

It is especially admirable when a winery of the size, stature, and importance of Beringer continues to push the quality of its offerings to greater and greater heights. Though this property could easily rest on its already sterling reputation, no one at this historic winery appears satisfied with maintaining the status quo. Beringer has been on an amazing hot streak.

CABERNET SAUVIGNON PRIVATE RESERVE

2002 Cabernet Sauvignon Private Reserve

RATING: 91–93 points

The 2002 Cabernet Sauvignon Private Reserve was grapy, unevolved, and primary when I tasted it. Nevertheless, it reveals loads of fruit as well as a big, heady, high glycerin style. I'm sure further barrel aging will bring forth some complexity. Anticipated maturity: 2010–2022.

2001 Cabernet Sauvignon Private Reserve

RATING: 96 points

All of Beringer's 2001 Cabernet Sauvignon *cuvées* blended together result in the finest Cabernet Sauvignon yet made by Ed Sbragia, the 2001 Cabernet Sauvignon Private Reserve (11,000 cases of truly divine Cabernet nectar). For statisticians, 44% came from the Steinhauer Vineyard, 1% from Bancroft Ranch, 17% from Rancho del Oso, 3% from Chabot, 13% from St. Helena Home Ranch, and the balance from Marston Vineyard. The 2001 is an extraordinary effort. Large-scale yet elegant, it boasts classic notes of crème de cassis, chocolate, and smoky oak. With extraordinary voluptuousness, great concentration, tremendous intensity, and a finish that lasts nearly 60 seconds, this saturated purple–colored, full-bodied Cabernet Sauvignon is one of the greatest wines ever made at Beringer. It is a tribute to the brilliant Ed Sbragia. Anticipated maturity: 2007–2023.

1999 Cabernet Sauvignon Private Reserve

RATING: 90 points

The dark ruby/purple–colored 1999 Cabernet Sauvignon Private Reserve exhibits a sweet, Bordeaux-influenced bouquet of tobacco, cedarwood, spice box, and black currants. It is moderately tannic, medium-bodied, and firm in the finish. Patience will be required. The cooler growing climate is clearly evident when tasting this wine. Anticipated maturity: now–2014.

1997 Cabernet Sauvignon Private Reserve

RATING: 94 points

The opaque plum/purple color is followed by a superb nose of smoked herbs, melted licorice, and black currant jam. Full-bodied, with a silky texture and an opulent personality, this sexy, full-throttle Cabernet Sauvignon will be delicious young, yet last for 18–20 years. Anticipated maturity: now–2020.

1996 Cabernet Sauvignon Private Reserve

RATING: 91 points

The 1996 Cabernet Sauvignon Private Reserve reveals more concentration as well as higher tannin than the 1995. I know it is a trade-off, but I suspect this vintage will not be as sexy in its youthfulness as the 1995. The black ruby/purple–colored 1996 offers more licorice, in addition to the obvious levels of toast, jammy black currant fruit, and spice notes. Structured, full-bodied, and powerful, this Private Reserve can be consumed between now and 2019.

1995 Cabernet Sauvignon Private Reserve

RATING: 93 points

The 1995 Cabernet Sauvignon Private Reserve is a full-bodied, explosively rich, deep purple–colored wine bursting with ripe fruit. It displays smoky oak, gobs of cassis, a touch of cigar box and cedar, and a layered, multidimensional feel. This voluptuous, seductive offering is already drinking well, yet should age effortlessly for 10–15 years.

1994 Cabernet Sauvignon Private Reserve

RATING: 94 points

Beringer's Private Reserve has always been one of my favorite California Cabernets, particularly since the late 1970s. They can be drunk young, but age exceptionally well, giving every indication of holding their fruit and evolving nicely for two decades. The terrific 1994 Cabernet Sauvignon Private Reserve offers an opaque purple color, a gorgeous nose of toasty oak, and a silky, concentrated texture with unobtrusive acidity or tannin. The wine possesses layered richness, remarkable balance, sweet, pure fruit, and a finish that lasts for nearly 30 seconds. These wines are aged in 100% new oak, and tend to possesses at least 97% Cabernet Sauvignon, with the balance Cabernet Franc. Amazingly, the oak is not a pronounced component in the final wine, a testament to excellent wine-making and the concentration these wines possess. Like so many top 1994s from Napa and Sonoma, this wine will age well for another 10–12 or more years.

1993 Cabernet Sauvignon Private Reserve

RATING: 92 points

The wine's opaque purple color is followed by a promising sweet, smoky, chocolaty, licorice, and black currant–scented nose, and deep, powerful, full-bodied flavors. Normally these Private Reserves possess a precociousness and silky, up-front richness. Aromatically, the 1993 Private Reserve is rewarding, but after the initial attack of sweet fruit, the wine's tannin takes precedence. It is an outstanding wine, but more of a long-term prospect. Compared with the flattering precociousness of the 1994, 1992, 1991, and 1990, the 1993 will offer less immediate appeal. Anticipated maturity: now–2015.

1992 Cabernet Sauvignon Private Reserve

RATING: 96 points

The opaque-colored 1992 exhibits a huge, chocolaty, smoky nose crammed with gobs of black fruits. This soft, voluptuously textured, full-bodied wine boasts remarkable concentration and purity. It is a round, flattering, luscious style of Cabernet Sauvignon that should keep for another 7+ years. Anticipated maturity: now–2010.

1991 Cabernet Sauvignon Private Reserve

RATING: 96 points

Beringer's 1991 Cabernet Sauvignon Private Reserve possesses excellent concentration, a smashing bouquet of smoky, unctuously textured black and red fruits, sweet, generous, decadently rich flavors, low acidity, and a voluptuously long, juicy finish. This fabulous Cabernet should drink well for another 7 or more years. Anticipated maturity: now–2010+.

1990 Cabernet Sauvignon Private Reserve

RATING: 93 points

The generously endowed, dark purple–colored 1990 Cabernet Sauvignon Private Reserve is a rich, opulent, full-bodied wine loaded with layers of flavor, copious amounts of juicy fruit, sweet tannin, and moderate amounts of lavish oak. Less muscular and concentrated than the 1991, it is a superb expression of a Napa Valley Cabernet Sauvignon. It should drink well for another 3–6 years. Anticipated maturity: now–2009.

1987 Cabernet Sauvignon Private Reserve

RATING: 93 points

Beringer continues to do everything right. Its staff of talented professionals may rank as the best in the business. Since 1984, its Private Reserve Cabernets have been among the top dozen Cabernets produced in California and are not likely to stumble over the next several years. The 1987 Reserve is a worthy competitor to the terrific 1986. The 1987's dark ruby/garnet color is followed by a super bouquet. There are huge aromas of chocolate, spicy new oak, herbs, cassis, and tobacco in this beautifully scented wine. In the mouth, it is full-bodied, voluptuous, spicy, and crammed with fruit, glycerin, and enough tannin to support another 5–6 years of cellaring. Like the 1986, the tannins are soft, and, fortunately, the acids are not shrill enough to prevent immediate drinkability. This is a skillfully made, complex Cabernet Sauvignon that will not linger long on retailers' shelves. Anticipated maturity: now–2009.

1986 Cabernet Sauvignon Private Reserve
RATING: 90 points

The fully mature, open-knit 1986 Cabernet Sauvignon Private Reserve is totally delicious. The color is dark garnet with some amber at the edge. The big, sweet, licorice, earthy, jammy, black fruit–scented nose is followed by a full-bodied, sweet, expansive, chewy wine with no hard edges. The acidity and tannin are both well integrated in this plump, sumptuous Cabernet Sauvignon. Anticipated maturity: now.

1985 Cabernet Sauvignon Private Reserve
RATING: 90 points

Beringer's 1985 Private Reserve is a superb, fully mature (atypical for the vintage), medium to full–bodied Cabernet Sauvignon with an enticing, chocolaty, herb, black currant–scented nose, rich, plump, expansive, sweet, jammy flavors, attractive spice, and a soft, lush finish. It has matured quickly for a 1985, but there is no rush to consume it as it reveals no signs of fatigue. It should hold at its current plateau for another 3–5 years.

1978 Cabernet Sauvignon Private Reserve
RATING: 93 points

A spectacular wine that is still remarkably vibrant, this dark plum/garnet-colored wine has a saturated color to the rim. A big, smoky, earthy nose intermixed with oak, and blackberry, cassis, chocolate, and coffee notes jump from the glass. On the palate, the wine is full-bodied, opulent, and very rich. A terrific wine that is just moving beyond its adolescence, this is a tour de force in great winemaking and a tribute to just how long the best California Cabernets can last. Anticipated maturity: now–2015.

WINE: Bryant Family Cabernet Sauvignon

OWNERS: Barbara and Donald Bryant, Jr.

ADDRESS: Winery: 1567 Sage Canyon Road, St. Helena, CA 94574

Executive Offices (mailing list inquiries): 701 Market Street, Suite 1200, St. Louis, MO 63101

TELEPHONE: Winery: (707) 963-0480; Executive Offices: (314) 231-8066

TELEFAX: Winery: (707) 963-0482; Executive Offices: (314) 231-4859

E-MAIL: Winery: bryantwinery@covad.net; Executive Offices: donald.bryant@bryantgroupinc.com and bill.wirth@ bryantgroupinc.com

CONTACT: Winery: Philippe Melka, Winemaker; Michel Rolland, Consulting Oenologist; Anna Monticelli, Cellar Master; Daniel Wojtkowiak, Facilities Engineer; Executive Offices: Bill Wirth, Chief Administrative Officer

VISITING POLICY: Not open to public

VINEYARDS

SURFACE AREA: 15 acres under vine

GRAPE VARIETALS: Cabernet Sauvignon, estate wines only

AVERAGE AGE OF THE VINES: 5 years

DENSITY OF PLANTATION: 2,000 vines per acre

AVERAGE YIELDS: 1.5 tons per acre

WINEMAKING AND UPBRINGING

The Bryant Family winery was built with the objective of producing the greatest-quality wine possible. The winery has three floors and is a gravity-flow system.

At harvest, the grapes are carefully selected. The sunny and shady sides of the vine and different parts of each parcel are picked separately. Grapes are brought into the winery in small picking baskets filled only halfway. They are then sorted, destemmed, and sorted again before gravity pulls them down into the tank.

All grapes are fermented in open-top stainless-steel vats that were custom-made to fit each vineyard block. The wine is then aged for about 18 months in 100% new French oak barrels. Shiners (unlabeled wine) are bottled and laid down for a year before being labeled.

ANNUAL PRODUCTION

Bryant Family Vineyard Cabernet Sauvignon

During planting: average of 900–1,000 cases

Upon completion: approximately 2000+ cases

AVERAGE PRICE (VARIABLE DEPENDING ON THE VINTAGE): $150–200

GREAT RECENT VINTAGES

2002, 2000, 1999, 1997, 1996, 1995, 1994, 1993, 1992

The Bryants chose a steep hillside vineyard, blessed with large and small rocks and ample sunshine.

This vineyard's beautiful topography no doubt accounts for its exceptional wine. The winds blow over the mountains from the west, are drawn down and across the cool waters of Lake Hennessey, then travel directly up a natural chute to the Bryant vineyard. This breezeway makes the vineyard unique and enhances the quality of fruit as the winds cool the grapes on hot summer days.

With ideal morning and afternoon sun ratios (60% morning sun and 40% afternoon sun) and the rocky vineyard drainage, the vines tend to develop deep root systems in search of moisture.

The vineyard has been reconfigured so that cooling breezes reach grapes on both sides of the vines. Thanks to such close spacing of the vines, in addition to very small yields per plant, a Cabernet of majestic proportions has been fashioned, first by winemaker Helen Turley (1992–2001) and more recently by Philippe Melka and Michel Rolland.

Though 1992 was the debut vintage, the wine from this hillside vineyard near Napa's Pritchard Hill has already reached mythical stature. This is a wine of world-class quality, and is certainly as complete and potentially complex as any first-growth Bordeaux. To date, it has been characterized by extraordinary richness, complexity, and harmony, as well as the potential to evolve and improve for 20 or more years.

CABERNET SAUVIGNON

2003 Cabernet Sauvignon

RATING: 96–98 points

After the upheaval and turbulent departure of former winemakers Helen Turley and John Wetlaufer, along with a major lawsuit between them and Don Bryant, things have settled down nicely, and this vineyard is again asserting itself as one of Napa's finest *terroirs*. While the viticulture for 2002 was not controlled by Philippe Melka and his team at Bryant, he did make the wine and had full control of the 2003. The 2003 (400 cases, half the production of the 2002) is the result of seven different harvests, as Melka and his team clearly wanted to show that they could turn out wine as great as any Bryant made to date under the ancien régime. Fermented in small open-top fermenters designed specifically for Bryant, this wine is exceptional. It boasts a black/purple color to the rim as well as an extraordinary nose of blueberry and blackberry liqueur intermixed with hints of barbecue spice, hickory wood, acacia flowers, and espresso roast. The wine, 100% Cabernet Sauvignon, has superb intensity, tremendous complexity, and at the same time, amazing elegance and finesse for its size and power (about 15% alcohol). The acidity is remarkably good and the pH (3.75) normal by a ripe Bordeaux vintage standard. Bryant's 2003 is a candidate for wine of the vintage. Anticipated maturity: 2008–2022+.

2002 Cabernet Sauvignon

RATING: 96 points

The 2002 was bottled (800 cases) in June 2004. It exhibits a classic Bryant profile of blueberries, blackberries, chocolate, and smoky notes (100% new Taransaud barrels are utilized), a full-bodied, powerful palate, great texture, tremendous purity, and a long, heady finish with high tannin, but it is well integrated and sweet. Anticipated maturity: 2006–2020.

2000 Cabernet Sauvignon

RATING: 95 points

The 2000 Cabernet Sauvignon is an amazing tour de force. Quality like this was rare, if not impossible, to obtain in 2000.

From bottle, the wine is performing even better than it did from cask. The color is an opaque black/ruby/purple, and the amazing aromatic concoction includes notes of melted licorice, minerals, smoky toast, and blackberry as well as cassis. Full-bodied, thick, and juicy, it is a voluptuous effort to drink now and over the next 15–16 years. It is a brilliant achievement, surpassed by none, and equaled only by a few other Northern California 2000s.

1999 Cabernet Sauvignon

RATING: 95 points

Readers wanting more structure and a Bordeaux-like tannin profile should check out the 1999 Cabernet Sauvignon. The tannin possesses a structure and astringency reminiscent of a young Bordeaux. The nose offers up scents of melted licorice, smoky barbecue, truffles, earth, blackberries, currants, coffee, graphite, and blueberries. It is more obviously muscular and less seductive than the 2000 or 2001, because the tannin is more aggressive. The finish is exceptionally long. The antithesis of the 2000, the 1999 will require patience. Anticipated maturity: 2007–2025. P.S. As this wine sat in the glass, its aroma brought to mind another wine—the 1983 Palmer.

1998 Cabernet Sauvignon

RATING: 93 points

The 1998 Cabernet Sauvignon is a fine wine. While it does not reveal much weight, it is a dense plum/purple–colored, big, thick, concentrated effort. Evolved aromas of smoke, cedar, tapenade, blackberries, crème de cassis, and creosote are followed by a lush, full-bodied, voluptuously textured 1998 exhibiting superb intensity as well as low acid, and sweet, pure flavors. This is a dazzling example of extremely ripe Cabernet Sauvignon made under less than ideal conditions. It will drink well over the next two decades.

1997 Cabernet Sauvignon

RATING: 100 points

I have consumed several bottles of the Bryant Family 1997 Cabernet Sauvignon. One of the most awesome young reds I have ever tasted, it possesses a black/purple color, a seamless texture, and freakishly high levels of intensity (cassis, blackberries, and blueberries infused with espresso, chocolate, and licorice) that are flawlessly presented in a full-bodied, massive yet elegant wine. Nothing is out of balance in this explosively rich, thick, highly extracted Cabernet. A compelling, historic Cabernet Sauvignon, it will drink well for 30–35 years. It is not too much to suggest that in the future, Bryant's Pritchard Hill Cabernet Sauvignon might well be one of the wines that redefines greatness in Cabernet Sauvignon.

1996 Cabernet Sauvignon

RATING: 99 points

The opaque purple–colored 1996 Cabernet Sauvignon offers a spectacular, exotic bouquet of Peking duck skins, blackberry, cassis, roasted herbs, and burning charcoal. It is phenomenally intense, with record levels of dry extract and glycerin. This hedonistic blockbuster is crammed with jammy fruits nicely buttressed and framed by adequate acidity and tannin. Drink this marvelous Cabernet Sauvignon now or cellar it for two decades. This is mind-boggling stuff!

1995 Cabernet Sauvignon

RATING: 97 points

The full-bodied, opaque purple–colored 1995 Cabernet Sauvignon possesses a sweet fragrance of jammy cassis and wild blueberries, intertwined with floral and mineral scents. The effect of the 100% new Taransaud oak barrels is minimal given the fact that only a background note of toast is noticeable. On the palate, the wine is extraordinarily dense and rich, but neither heavy nor flabby. With its remarkable purity, delineation, and layers of rich, concentrated fruit, this appears to be one of the superstars of the 1995 vintage. Although it will drink reasonably well young because of its sweet tannin and low acidity, this beauty will last for another 20–25 years. Is this a candidate for perfection? Anticipated maturity: now–2027.

1994 Cabernet Sauvignon

RATING: 93 points

The 1994 Cabernet Sauvignon boasts a provocative nose of cassis, cream, blueberries, violets, rhubarb, minerals, and spice. It smells like a hypothetical blend of L'Evangile, Clinet, and Mouton Rothschild. The opaque purple/black color is followed by a full-bodied wine stacked and packed with fruit, glycerin, and extract. No component part is out of place in this formidably endowed, remarkably well-balanced wine. The purity, richness, sweetness, and depth of fruit suggest that the wine's potential is limitless. Anticipated maturity: now–2015.

1993 Cabernet Sauvignon

RATING: 94 points

The extraordinary 1993 Cabernet Sauvignon possesses an opaque black/purple color and a huge bouquet of black raspberries, cassis, vanilla, licorice, and spices. The wine is superrich, with sweet tannin, an expansive mouth-feel, and an awesome finish. It will last for another decade.

1992 Cabernet Sauvignon

RATING: 91 points

The 1992 Cabernet Sauvignon (1,000 cases) offers an impressive black/purple color, rusty tannin, immense concentration, full body, and enormous richness in the finish. Anticipated maturity: now–2008.

WINES:

Cabernet Sauvignon Herb Lamb Vineyard

Cabernet Sauvignon Tychson Hill Vineyard

Cariad Proprietary Red Wine

OWNER: Colgin Partners LLC (Ann Colgin, President)

ADDRESS: P.O. Box 254, St. Helena, CA 94574

TELEPHONE: (707) 963-0999

TELEFAX: (707) 963-0996

E-MAIL: info@colgincellars.com

WEBSITE: www.colgincellars.com

CONTACT: Ann Colgin

VISITING POLICY: Not open to the public

VINEYARDS

SURFACE AREA:

IX Estate (referred to as "No. 9")—20 acres

Tychson Hill Vineyard—2.5 acres

They also purchase a selection of grapes from the Herb
    Lamb Vineyard and David Abreu's Madrona Ranch
    and Thorvilos Vineyards.

GRAPE VARIETALS: Cabernet Sauvignon, Merlot, Cabernet
    Franc, Petit Verdot, Syrah

AVERAGE AGE OF THE VINES:

IX Estate—4 years

Tychson Hill—7 years

Madrona Ranch—15 years

Herb Lamb—16 years (selective replanting occurring now)

DENSITY OF PLANTATION: At IX Estate and Tychson Hill, 3' x 6'
    spacing (approx. 2,400 vines per acre)

AVERAGE YIELDS: 2 tons per acre

WINEMAKING AND UPBRINGING

The Colgin winemaking philosophy is to try to bring the best
possible grapes from exceptional hillside vineyards into the
winery and then let them "speak for themselves." In order to
reach the vineyards' full potential, they emphasize small
yields, balanced water and nutrition, and finally physiologically ripe grapes that they determine primarily by taste but
also laboratory testing.

During harvest considerable care is taken to ensure that
the grapes arrive in the best possible condition. This includes
picking them early in the morning into small 35-pound boxes
and carefully transporting the fruit from the vineyards in a re-
frigerated truck to maintain a stable temperature and unbroken skins. Once at the winery, the grapes are gently sorted
twice, first in their "whole cluster" state and then after destemming in their "whole berry" state. After the double sorting, the
grapes are gravity fed into state-of-the-art stainless-steel tanks.
This also allows for a long, initial cold soak and fermentation.
Both cultivated yeast and natural indigenous yeast fermentations are utilized. Pumping-over is done twice a day, and fermentation usually lasts 2–3 weeks. Following is an extended
maceration for another 30–40 days on average.

Malolactic fermentation, which usually takes up to two
months, is done in barrel in a specially designed warm cellar to
encourage additional complexity. Wines may be racked after
the malolactics have been completed but not always. Some
light sulfuring is done to protect the young wines. Wines are
generally kept in barrel for 18–24 months and a carefully selected mix of barrels is used, with a predominance of 100%
new Taransaud oak barrels. The aging cellar is kept at a cool 55
degrees. The wines are bottled without fining or filtration and
then aged for another 10–12 months before being shipped.

ANNUAL PRODUCTION

Tychson Hill Vineyards: Approx. 300 cases (12 bottles per
    case)

Herb Lamb Vineyard: Approx. 350 cases

Cariad: Approx. 500 cases

IX Estate: They will produce two Napa Valley Red wines from the estate, approx. 750 cases each

IX Estate (Syrah): Approx. 500 cases

AVERAGE PRICE (VARIABLE DEPENDING ON VINTAGE): $165–175

GREAT RECENT VINTAGES

2002, 2001, 1999, 1997, 1996, 1995, 1994, 1993

Colgin Cellars quickly burst on the scene in the early 1990s when their winemaker, Helen Turley, was fashioning some spectacular Cabernet Sauvignons from the Herb Lamb Vineyard in Napa. The first vintages were strikingly provocative and enormously complex wines. However, proprietress Ann Colgin, who is a stylish woman of considerable charm, along with her fine wine–obsessed husband, Joe Wender, weren't content to simply purchase fruit from top vineyards. They have one of the most magnificent vineyards and estates I have ever seen, situated high up in the hills overlooking Lake Hennessey, and ultimately there will be approximately 750 cases of Bordeaux Proprietary Blend and 500 cases of Syrah from these estate wines when they come into full production. There's no reason to think that those wines won't qualify for a future edition of this book. However, at present, Colgin and Wender's three great wines are their Cabernet Sauvignon from the Tychson Hill Vineyard, their Cabernet Sauvignon from the Herb Lamb Vineyard, and their Proprietary Bordeaux blend (primarily Cabernet Sauvignon) from the Madrona Ranch in St. Helena called Cariad.

The departure of Helen Turley was not nearly as disruptive as expected, because Ann Colgin quickly decided to bring in a full-time winemaker, Mark Aubert, who had done great work at the Peter Michael winery. Along with vineyard manager David Abreu and Bordeaux winemaking consultant Dr. Alain Raynaud, they have quite an impressive team of talent overseeing the vineyards and the winemaking. Colgin Cellars is undeniably one of the most meticulously, passionately run wineries in the world, and with the new wines coming from their IX Estate (the aforementioned 120-acre parcel overlooking Lake Hennessey, planted at elevations of 950–1,400 feet), this estate's fame can only grow.

CABERNET SAUVIGNON HERB LAMB VINEYARD

2003 Cabernet Sauvignon Herb Lamb Vineyard

RATING: 91–94 points

The elegant 2003 Cabernet Sauvignon Herb Lamb Vineyard (225 cases) offers up notes of tobacco, lavender, spice box, black currants, and licorice in a medium to full–bodied, persistent, rich, well-focused style. It possesses gorgeous complexity, plenty of flavor, and moderate tannin, but not the weight, depth, or seamlessness of the 2002 and 2001. Anticipated maturity: 2007–2018.

2002 Cabernet Sauvignon Herb Lamb Vineyard

RATING: 96 points

The 2002 Cabernet Sauvignon Herb Lamb Vineyard (220 cases) exhibits a dense purple color in addition to a big, rich bouquet of grilled meats, dried herbs, ground pepper, espresso, blackberries, cassis, and blueberries. This seriously endowed yet elegant Cabernet is full-bodied, dense, and rich with sweet tannin as well as a surprising accessibility—a characteristic of this exciting vintage. Anticipated maturity: now–2020.

2001 Cabernet Sauvignon Herb Lamb Vineyard

RATING: 95+ points

There are 360 cases of the 2001 Cabernet Sauvignon Herb Lamb Vineyard. Slightly less exotic chocolaty, blackberry, blueberry, herbal tea, and floral notes are apparent in this densely saturated purple-colored 2001. Thick, juicy, succulent, black, crème de cassis and licorice–infused flavors proliferate. Sweet tannin, a beautiful texture, and superb purity as well as delineation suggest this stunning Cabernet may be the best Herb Lamb since the 1997. Anticipated maturity: now–2018.

2000 Cabernet Sauvignon Herb Lamb Vineyard

RATING: 91 points

The 2000 Cabernet Sauvignon Herb Lamb Vineyard reveals a singular, exotic bouquet of flowers (geraniums?) and a minty undertone intermixed with copious quantities of blueberries, cassis, and tar. Dense, rich, and full-bodied, it is a strong effort that should drink well for 10–12 years.

1999 Cabernet Sauvignon Herb Lamb Vineyard

RATING: 95 points

The 1999 Cabernet Sauvignon Herb Lamb Vineyard is performing significantly better out of bottle than it did from cask. Its opaque purple color is followed by a gorgeous perfume of graphite, crème de cassis, and licorice, and full-bodied, layered, concentrated flavors with superb balance and density. Surprisingly sweet tannin as well as an explosive finish have developed. Anticipated maturity: now–2020+.

1998 Cabernet Sauvignon Herb Lamb Vineyard

RATING: 90 points

From a tough vintage, the 1998 Cabernet Sauvignon Herb Lamb Vineyard possesses a dense plum/purple color as well as a sweet perfume of minerals, blackberries, and cassis, medium to full body, an excellent texture, ripe tannin, and an evolved personality. An undeniable success for the vintage, it should be consumed over the next 9–12 years.

1997 Cabernet Sauvignon Herb Lamb Vineyard

RATING: 99 points

Saturated black/purple–colored with a knockout nose of blackberries, blueberries, lavender, licorice, and toast, this is a profound, full-bodied Cabernet Sauvignon. It displays a seamless, velvety texture, layers of concentrated fruit, and a 45+-second finish. Am I being too conservative in not giving it a three-digit score? Anticipated maturity: now–2025.

1996 Cabernet Sauvignon Herb Lamb Vineyard

RATING: 97 points

The saturated black/purple–colored 1996 Cabernet Sauvignon Herb Lamb Vineyard displays this winery's hallmark—a provocative nose of blueberry jam, orchid flowers, and smoky new oak intertwined with cassis. Additional aromas of licorice and exotic Asian spices emerge as the wine sits in the glass. Extremely full-bodied and rich, with more noticeable tannin than the 1997, this large-scaled yet extraordinarily rich wine is like drinking cassis/blueberry liqueur. Its sweet tannin and remarkable 40+-second finish are amazing. Anticipated maturity: now–2022.

1995 Cabernet Sauvignon Herb Lamb Vineyard

RATING: 98 points

The 1995 possesses the telltale opaque black/purple color, phenomenal aromatics consisting of blackberries, raspberries, blueberries, cassis, subtle new oak, and a notion of floral scents (is it acacia or lilac?). In the mouth, the wine is full-bodied, remarkably supple, and opulent, with a purity and presence of fruit. Anticipated maturity: now–2020.

1994 Cabernet Sauvignon Herb Lamb Vineyard

RATING: 96 points

The 1994 Cabernet Sauvignon is a totally dry wine, but the sweetness and taste of this wine's fruit is akin to a savory blend of a chocolate-covered, herb-tinged, blueberry/cassis-filled candy bar and vanilla ice cream melting in the mouth. This full-bodied wine is silky, seductive, opulent, voluptuously textured, and extraordinarily fragrant, expansive, and rich. In spite of this, the wine remains graceful and well balanced, without any sense of heaviness, or obtrusive tannin or acidity. Anticipated maturity: now–2020+

1993 Cabernet Sauvignon Herb Lamb Vineyard

RATING: 95 points

The color is an opaque ruby/purple. The nose offers up cassis, blueberry, black raspberry, herbs, and toasty scents, followed by gorgeously rich, sweet (from extract, not sugar) flavors, full body, gobs of glycerin, and wonderfully ripe tannin in the intense finish that must last for 40+ seconds. It is an exceptional Cabernet Sauvignon that will age for another 12+ years. A tour de force in winemaking.

1992 Cabernet Sauvignon Herb Lamb Vineyard

RATING: 96 points

The wine boasts dark purple color, followed by a sweet nose of blueberries and blackberries intertwined with smoky, toasty oak and underbrush. The enormously opulent texture, viscous richness, and huge quantities of sweet, pure fruit were deftly balanced by just enough acidity and ripe tannin. This full-bodied wine is soft enough to be drunk now, but it promises to evolve for at least another 5–10 years.

CABERNET SAUVIGNON TYCHSON HILL VINEYARD

2003 Cabernet Sauvignon Tychson Hill Vineyard

RATING: 93–95 points

The 2003 Cabernet Sauvignon Tychson Hill Vineyard (250 cases) reveals the purity and nobility of pure cedar-infused crème de cassis fruit, medium to full body, striking concentration and clarity, and a long, heady, rich finish with moderate but sweet tannin. Anticipated maturity: 2007–2020.

2002 Cabernet Sauvignon Tychson Hill Vineyard

RATING: 100 points

The amazing 2002 Cabernet Sauvignon Tychson Hill Vineyard (100% Cabernet Sauvignon) offers up a fabulously fragrant perfume of chocolate, barbecue smoke, crème de cassis, crushed rocks, and spring flowers. A wine of enormous concentration, multiple dimensions, layers of flavor, and a sensational one-minute-plus finish, its purity, harmony, and symmetry are prodigious. It should be at its peak between 2009 and 2028.

2001 Cabernet Sauvignon Tychson Hill Vineyard

RATING: 96+ points

The 2001 Cabernet Sauvignon Tychson Hill Vineyard boasts an inky/purple color, thrilling concentration, and gorgeously pure aromas of blackberry, crème de cassis, toast, white chocolate, and vanilla ice cream. Incredibly long, pure, and dense, but tightly wound, this is a wine of enormous constitution and wonderfully sweet integrated tannin, yet I got the sense that it

was only revealing part of its personality. It needs 7–8 years of bottle age, and should last for 30 years. A brilliant effort!

2000 Cabernet Sauvignon Tychson Hill Vineyard

RATING: 92 points

The 2000 Cabernet Sauvignon Tychson Hill Vineyard is a classic as well as pure expression of Cabernet Sauvignon's crème de cassis, tobacco, cedary character. Expressive, rich, medium to full–bodied flavors, terrific ripeness, and surprising tannin and persistence are found in this pure 2000. Drink it over the next 12–15 years.

CARIAD PROPRIETARY RED WINE

2003 Cariad Proprietary Red Wine

RATING: 95–99+ points

A potential wine of the vintage is the 2003 Cariad, a 500-case blend of 65% Cabernet Sauvignon, 25% Merlot, and the balance equal parts Cabernet Franc and Petit Verdot. A color reminiscent of squid ink is accompanied by fabulous aromas of melted licorice, camphor, blackberries, cassis, spice box, earth, new saddle leather, and graphite. Full-bodied, with fabulous concentration, a multilayered, skyscraper-like mouth-feel, and sweet tannin in the texturally sensual finish, this beauty should be drinkable when released, and last for two decades or more. The 2003 may turn out to be as good or better than the 2002—and that's saying something! Anticipated maturity: 2009–2022.

2002 Cariad Proprietary Red Wine

RATING: 97 points

A proprietary blend of 58% Cabernet Sauvignon, 28% Merlot, and the balance equal parts Cabernet Franc and Petit Verdot, the 2002 Cariad (520 cases) is fashioned from the Madrona Ranch and Thorevilos vineyards. A California hybrid version of a big, rich St.-Emilion/Graves blend, it reveals a Bordeaux-like structure along with loads of tannin and a certain tightness. Extraordinarily elegant, exotic notes of orange rind, ground pepper, incense, and Indian spices are intermixed with chocolate and blackberry currant characteristics in a seamless, full-bodied style that coats the palate without any sense of heaviness. As it sits in the glass, meaty, bay leaf, smoked Peking duck, and new saddle leather characteristics also emerge. This singular red can be drunk early in life, or aged for two decades or more.

2001 Cariad Proprietary Red Wine

RATING: 98 points

Virtually perfect, the 2001 Cariad is a blend of 55% Cabernet Sauvignon, 31% Merlot, 7% Cabernet Franc, and 7% Petit Verdot. This seamless offering possesses a saturated ruby/purple color as well as a smorgasbord of aromas, including Valrhona chocolate, cigar tobacco, blackberries, black currants, licorice, incense, and espresso. Sweet on the entry, with a voluptuous mid-palate, and a spectacular finish with the tannin hardly noticeable, this is a proprietary red of extraordinary quality and singularity. As it sat in the glass, additional nuances continued to develop, and the wine seemed to swell and become even richer with each sip. I'm not sure it doesn't deserve a three-digit score. Anticipated maturity: now–2028.

2000 Cariad Proprietary Red Wine

RATING: 94 points

My favorite 2000 from Colgin is the proprietary red, the 2000 Cariad, a blend of 55% Cabernet Sauvignon, 35% Merlot, 5% Cabernet Franc, and 5% Petit Verdot. This is Colgin's California version of St.-Emilion. The dense ruby/purple–colored 2000 Cariad offers up a flamboyant nose of creosote, tobacco leaf, roasted coffee, chocolate, smoke, and earthy black currant as well as blackberry fruit. With great complexity, a firm, structured, tannic underpinning, medium to full body, and dazzling purity, this terrific 2000 is unquestionably one of the wines of the vintage. Anticipated maturity: now–2016.

1999 Cariad Proprietary Red Wine

RATING: 91 points

The 1999 Cariad is a Bordeaux-like blend of 55% Cabernet Sauvignon, 35% Merlot, 5% Cabernet Franc, and 5% Petit Verdot that could easily pass for a high-class Médoc. It offers a complex nose of cedar, spice box, minerals, currants, and loamy soil, with well-integrated sweet oak, a layered texture, wonderful elegance, sweet fruit, and terrific length. It is hard to believe this wine was aged in 100% new Taransaud barrels, as their influence is subtle. The vintage's austerity is evident in the wine's finish, so another 1–2 years of cellaring is suggested. Anticipated maturity: 2006–2018.

WINES:

Maya Proprietary Red Wine
Cabernet Sauvignon Estate
OWNER: Naoko Dalla Valle
ADDRESS: P.O. Box 329, Oakville, CA 94562
TELEPHONE: (707) 944-2676
TELEFAX: (707) 944-8411
E-MAIL: Info@DallaValleVineyards.com
WEBSITE: www.DallaValleVineyards.com
VISITING POLICY: Not open to the public

VINEYARDS

SURFACE AREA: 21 acres

GRAPE VARIETALS: Cabernet Sauvignon, Cabernet Franc

AVERAGE AGE OF THE VINES: 14 years

DENSITY OF PLANTATION: 6' x 10'; 4' x 8'

AVERAGE YIELDS: 1.5 tons per acre

WINEMAKING AND UPBRINGING

The wines at Dalla Valle emerge from the red soils overlooking Napa's Oakville corridor. Fermentation takes place in jacketed stainless-steel tanks. The frequency and duration of the pumpovers are monitored closely, along with fermentation temperatures, to optimize the extraction of color, texture, and flavor. Texture is further optimized by means of extended maceration times on the skin before pressing. Maceration times vary from 21–36 days, with 2–3 days as a prefermentation soak, 7–14 days fermentation time, and 4–21 days postfermentation maceration. After pressing, wines are aged as separate lots in 60–80% new French Château barrels, where they undergo malolactic fermentation and receive racking every 3–4 months. Blending happens right around the following harvest, either right before or soon after. Bottling occurs after approximately 22 months of barrel aging.

ANNUAL PRODUCTION

Cabernet Sauvignon: 2,000 cases
Maya (red table wine): 400 cases
AVERAGE PRICE (VARIABLE DEPENDING ON VINTAGE): $60–140

GREAT RECENT VINTAGES

2001, 2000, 1999, 1998, 1997, 1995, 1994, 1992, 1991

Dalla Valle Vineyards is a small, family-owned winery founded in 1986, located along the eastern hillside of Oakville, Napa Valley. When Gustav and Naoko Dalla Valle came to Napa Valley with aspirations of developing a restaurant and spa, they discovered a small site in the western hills of Napa that included a home and five acres of vineyards with a stunning panoramic view, and over time their plan changed.

Gustav Dalla Valle emigrated to the U.S. and founded Scubapro, a manufacturer of sport diving apparatuses and equipment. Back in Italy, however, his family has been involved in the wine business for over 175 years. Founding the winery in Oakville proved inevitable. Shortly after their arrival in Napa Valley in 1984, they planted approximately 16 acres of Cabernet Sauvignon and Cabernet Franc vineyards, and constructed a beautiful Tuscan-style winery in time for the first harvest and crush in 1986.

In 1988, the first grapes from Maya's vineyards (a small specific site where some of the best grapes were grown), named after Gustav and Naoko's daughter, came to maturity and were bottled separately.

Gustav Dalla Valle passed away in December 1995, but he was able to witness and enjoy the growing enthusiasm and demand for his wine during his lifetime. A commitment to maintain and improve the highest quality of Dalla Valle wines continues. An extensive replanting program began in the late 1990s, and the winemaking equipment is continually monitored and upgraded. Naoko Dalla Valle continues to manage the winery with the help of winemaker Mia Klein and the vineyard foreman, Fausto Cisneros.

In a little more than a decade, Dalla Valle has propelled itself into the top echelon of California Cabernet Sauvignon and proprietary red wines. The microscopic production of Dalla Valle's proprietary red wine, Maya, usually contains between 45 and 55% Cabernet Franc. I am not overstating the case by saying that the finest Cabernet Franc I have tasted in the New World is from Dalla Valle's vineyard.

I don't think I need to underscore the fact that these offerings are extremely difficult to find, but isn't that the way it always is with such extraordinary wines?

CABERNET SAUVIGNON ESTATE

2003 Cabernet Sauvignon

RATING: 88–91 points

The 2003 Cabernet Sauvignon (85% Cabernet Sauvignon and 15% Cabernet Franc) exhibits an elegant, sweet nose of bay leaves, tobacco smoke, loamy earth, licorice, and cassis fruit. Medium-bodied and elegant, with attractive sweet tannin as well as a plush finish, it should drink well young and evolve for 10–14 years.

2002 Cabernet Sauvignon

RATING: 92 points

A strong effort, the 2002 Cabernet Sauvignon displays a dense purple color along with scents of crème de cassis, asphalt, and minerals, medium to full body, beautiful purity, and a long, heady finish filled with spice box, earth, herb, and cedar characteristics. It is also very forward. Enjoy it over the next 15 years.

2001 Cabernet Sauvignon Estate

RATING: 92 points

The deep ruby/purple–colored 2001 Cabernet Sauvignon offers up aromas of minerals, licorice, acacia flowers, blackberries, and cassis. Tannic, medium-bodied, and tightly knit, with a long finish, the wine will require considerable cellaring. Anticipated maturity: 2009–2016.

2000 Cabernet Sauvignon Estate

RATING: 90 points

The dark ruby/purple-colored, medium-bodied, stylish 2000 Cabernet Sauvignon offers sweet, loamy, earthy notes along with pure cassis, licorice, and spice box. It is best consumed over the next decade.

1999 Cabernet Sauvignon Estate

RATING: 94 points

The opaque purple-colored 1999 Cabernet Sauvignon boasts exceptionally sweet fruit as well as a telltale perfume of melted licorice, black currant liqueur, and hints of blueberries and flowers. This wine is long, ripe, and full-bodied, with the vintage's more noticeable, astringent tannin. It will be at its apogee between 2006 and 2021.

1998 Cabernet Sauvignon Estate

RATING: 93 points

The spectacular, full-bodied 1998 Cabernet Sauvignon possesses great character, richness, and black currant fruit intermixed with licorice, tobacco, and smoke. While not as opulent as some vintages, it is exceptionally concentrated, long, and reminiscent of a ripe Bordeaux from a top vintage. Anticipated maturity: now–2018. Dalla Valle's 1998s are candidates for wines of the vintage.

1997 Cabernet Sauvignon Estate

RATING: 93 points

The 1997 Cabernet Sauvignon boasts an opaque purple color as well as a gorgeous nose of mineral-infused black currants and spicy oak. Full-bodied, structured, muscular, and multidimensional, it is approachable, but best cellared for another 1–2 years, and drunk over the following 10–15 years.

1996 Cabernet Sauvignon Estate

RATING: 93 points

The 1996 Cabernet Sauvignon is a powerful, concentrated, dense ruby/purple–colored wine. Full-bodied and muscular, it exhibits copious quantities of black currant fruit intermixed with blackberries, minerals, cedar, and Chinese black tea–like notes. The tannin is sweet in a vintage where this component

can be slightly coarse. It can be drunk now or aged for 20 or more years.

1995 Cabernet Sauvignon Estate
RATING: 94 points

The 1995 Cabernet Sauvignon exhibits an opaque blue/black/purple color, followed by sweet cassis aromas intermingled with scents of earth, spice, smoke, and grilled meats. This dense, powerful, muscular, concentrated wine provides an enormous mouth-feel. The tannin may be sweeter in the 1995 than in the 1994—imagine that. It will easily age for another 8–10 years or longer.

1994 Cabernet Sauvignon Estate
RATING: 94 points

The 1994 Cabernet Sauvignon possesses a full-bodied, multi-layered personality, with plenty of tannin, but sufficient earthy, black currant/plum–like fruit to balance out the wine's structure. With an opaque purple color, a high tannin level, and gorgeous layers of fruit and intensity, it will last for 10–15 years.

1993 Cabernet Sauvignon Estate
RATING: 93 points

The 1993 Cabernet Sauvignon is crammed with so much sweet black currant fruit that it does not take a genius to figure out what this wine is all about. It offers an opaque garnet/purple color, a moderately intense, cassis, smoky, herb, and earthy nose, fabulous concentration, good muscle, and a boatload of sweet tannin. It will easily last for 20 years.

Largely because of phylloxera damage to the vineyard and the consequent replanting, the production in 1993 was 40% less than that in 1992. The quantities of wine in 1994 were equally small.

1992 Cabernet Sauvignon Estate
RATING: 95 points

Dalla Valle's 1992 Cabernet Sauvignon Estate is a worthy successor to the blockbuster 1990 and 1991. Huge, sweet aromas of black fruits, spices, and oak are followed by a wine with great fruit extraction, full body, layers of richness, and that multidimensional, layered feel that this producer routinely obtains. The flattering personality of the 1992 has resulted in a more unctuous and voluptuous wine than even the 1991 or 1990. Moreover, it has another 5–7 years of aging potential.

1991 Cabernet Sauvignon Estate
RATING: 94 points

The 1991 Cabernet Sauvignon is an opaque, deeply saturated, purple-colored wine with a super-sweet, pure nose of black cherries, cassis, minerals, and vanilla. The wine possesses exceptional richness, full body, ripe tannin, and a blockbuster finish. It promises to evolve for another decade.

1990 Cabernet Sauvignon Estate
RATING: 93 points

The 1990 Cabernet Sauvignon Estate reveals an astonishingly deep color, as well as a huge aroma of smoky cassis, chocolate, and licorice. In the mouth, it is a powerful wine, with great stuffing, wonderful structure, enough acid and tannin to frame the wine's immense size, and a formidable finish. I was told the yields were a minuscule 2 tons per acre. It has the potential to easily last for 20 years. Anticipated maturity: now–2013.

MAYA PROPRIETARY RED WINE

2002 Maya Proprietary Red Wine
RATING: 93 points

The Maya is always a blend of 55% Cabernet Sauvignon and 45% Cabernet Franc, and in 2002 there were only 300 cases produced, since this vineyard is being replanted. Its dense ruby/purple color is followed by rich, sumptuous aromas of blueberries, raspberries, crushed rocks, dried herbs, a touch of smoke, and a long finish. Although not a blockbuster like some previous vintages, it remains a mid-weight, backward effort that requires 5–7 years of bottle age. It should last for 20 years.

2001 Maya Proprietary Red Wine
RATING: 92 points

The deep ruby/purple–colored 2001 Maya displays a reticent but promising perfume of Provençal herbs intermixed with new saddle leather, spice box, cedar, and black currants. Boasting beautiful intensity as well as purity, medium body, high tannin, and an austere, Bordeaux-like finish, it needs 4–5 years of cellaring, and should keep for 20–25 years.

2000 Maya Proprietary Red Wine
RATING: 91 points

The 2000 Maya is a medium-weight, elegant effort displaying spice box, incense, loamy soil, dried herb, crème de cassis, and smoky oak characteristics. Medium-bodied, lovely, and forward, it will drink well for 8–12 years.

1999 Maya Proprietary Red Wine
RATING: 97 points

The virtually perfect 1999 Maya is a wine of stupendous unctuousness, richness, fruit, and elegance. It is remarkable that the Cabernet Franc grown in these red volcanic soils can produce wines of such intensity as well as elegance. Notes of cassis, blueberries, blackberries, espresso, smoke, earth, and vanilla are offered in a full-bodied, profoundly concentrated and layered style. For whatever reason, the 1999 Maya revealed more forwardness than the Cabernet Sauvignon cuvée. Anticipated maturity: now–2024.

1998 Maya Proprietary Red Wine

RATING: 96 points

Another candidate for wine of the vintage, along with Dalla Valle's 1998 Cabernet Sauvignon, the 1998 Maya is an amazing effort, possessing multiple layers of fruit, sweet tannin, and no herbaceousness, astringency, or thinness. This is an amazing tour de force in winemaking for the vintage. It is loaded, with impeccable balance. Anticipated maturity: now–2020.

1997 Maya Proprietary Red Wine

RATING: 99 points

Close to perfection, the saturated blue/black–colored 1997 Maya exhibits complex aromatics of crème de cassis, smoke, spice box, iron, and espresso. The wine has a viscous texture, huge, concentrated, ripe fruit, remarkable body, and a seamless, multilayered finish. The tannin, acidity, and alcohol are all beautifully integrated. This is profound stuff! Anticipated maturity: now–2030.

1996 Maya Proprietary Red Wine

RATING: 96 points

The 1996 Maya is a blend of Cabernet Sauvignon and Cabernet Franc. Vivid, intense aromas of new saddle leather, plums, black currants, underbrush, and licorice are followed by a full-bodied, sensationally concentrated wine with sweet tannin, a deep, exceptionally pure and concentrated mid-palate, and an opulently textured finish. It is surprisingly open-knit and delicious, but there is more tannin lurking beneath the surface. Anticipated maturity: now–2025.

1995 Maya Proprietary Red Wine

RATING: 96 points

The terrific 1995 Maya is cut from the same mold as all the great Mayas of this decade. Its tannin may be even riper than in the 1994, but the wine is still an unevolved, massive, and unformed giant, although it is obvious that this will be another legendary effort. Anticipated maturity: 2007–2023.

1994 Maya Proprietary Red Wine

RATING: 99 points

The 1994 Maya is prodigious. The color is saturated opaque purple. The wine offers up restrained but gorgeously sweet earth, oak, mineral, and black fruit aromas. Full-bodied, with substantial quantities of glycerin and extract, this wine's large-scaled tannin seems to be well-submerged beneath the wine's fabulous layers of fruit. Although more accessible than I would have thought prior to bottling, it is a candidate for another 15–25 years of evolution.

1993 Maya Proprietary Red Wine

RATING: 98 points

The 1993 Maya is awesome. The opaque purple color accompanies a bouquet of stony, jammy cassis, roasted herbs, and smoky, meaty scents that are just beginning to unfold and soar from the glass. The wine possesses unbelievable concentration, powerful tannin, and a finish that lasts for 45+ seconds. It is an extraordinarily well-endowed and well-balanced wine that will age effortlessly through the first 25 years of this century.

1992 Maya Proprietary Red Wine

RATING: 98+ points

The 1992 Maya is a prodigious wine. This dark purple–colored wine has already developed an intense black currant, herb, cedar, and spicy bouquet that explodes upward from the glass. With layers of sweet, rich fruit lavishly presented in a full-bodied style, this large-scaled yet provocatively complex, multidimensional wine should last for another 5–15 years. A winemaking tour de force!

1991 Maya Proprietary Red Wine

RATING: 99 points

The 1991 Maya (made from equal proportions of Cabernet Franc and Cabernet Sauvignon) is black/purple-colored and offers up a compelling bouquet of flowers, minerals, black fruits, vanilla, and spices. There is huge extraction of fruit, full body, outstanding purity and balance, moderate tannin, and a tremendous layered feel on the palate. All of this intensity and richness is brilliantly pulled off without any sense of heaviness. It is a candidate for 25 years of aging as well as a strong candidate for a three-digit score in a few years. This is a winemaking tour de force!

1990 Maya Proprietary Red Wine

RATING: 96 points

The 1990 Maya (with almost equal proportions of Cabernet Franc and Cabernet Sauvignon) is a monster in the making. Its super-saturated, opaque black/ruby color is followed by a tight but promising nose of earth, cassis, smoke, and gobs of sweet fruit. In the mouth it is even richer, as well as more tannic than the regular Cabernet. The finish is long, sweet, and compelling. Anticipated maturity: now–2012.

WINE: Dominus

OWNER: Christian Moueix

ADDRESS: 2570 Napanook Road, Yountville, CA 94599

TELEPHONE: (707) 944-8954

TELEFAX: (707) 944-0547

E-MAIL: dominus@napanet.net

WEBSITE: www.dominusestate.com

CONTACT: Julia Levitan (Director, Finance and Administration)

VISITING POLICY: Due to a very restrictive use permit, they are not allowed to receive visitors.

VINEYARDS

SURFACE AREA: 120 acres

GRAPE VARIETALS: 80% Cabernet Sauvignon, 10% Cabernet Franc, 5% Merlot, 5% Petit Verdot

AVERAGE AGE OF THE VINES: 15–25 years

DENSITY OF PLANTATION: Old vines 10' x 7' = 622 vines per acre; Young vines 9' x 5' = 968 vines/acre

AVERAGE YIELDS: 3 tons of grapes per acre

WINEMAKING AND UPBRINGING

As one might expect from proprietor Christian Moueix, who is one of the few people in the world to make great wines in two countries, the United States and France, Dominus is a very French operation with a winemaking philosophy that is decidedly Bordeaux: impeccable attention to the vineyards, classic Bordeaux fermentation of three weeks, 18 months in barrels (50% new oak and 50% one-year), egg-white fining, and no filtration characterize a wine that, from its very beginning, has been a model of extraordinary elegance, distinctively French in personality. Christian Moueix was assisted in the early vintages by well-known winemakers Chris Phelps, David Ramey, and Daniel Baron, but later completely changed troops to an all-French cast, utilizing the services of his famous oenologist in Bordeaux, Jean-Claude Berrouet, and full-time French winemaker Boris Champy, who is assisted by Jean-Marie Maurèze.

ANNUAL PRODUCTION

Dominus: 85,000 bottles (first vintage 1983—the 1993 vintage was declassified)

Napanook: 50,000 bottles (first vintage 1996)

AVERAGE PRICE (VARIABLE DEPENDING ON VINTAGE): $30–120

GREAT RECENT VINTAGES

2002, 2001, 1997, 1994, 1991, 1990, 1987, 1985, 1984

The Dominus vineyard, which is called Napanook, is believed to be one of the first vineyards planted in Napa Valley, and is thus considered a historical landmark. Purchased in 1946 by the legendary John Daniel, it was the basis for some of the greatest wines made during the glorious Inglenook era. Daniel's daughters, Marcie Smith and Robin Lail, partnered with Christian Moueix to form Dominus in 1982, but Moueix purchased their shares in January 1995 and is now the sole owner. The winery itself, designed by the well-known Swiss architects Herzog and de Meuron, has a fascinating design that observers tend to either love or hate. (Put me in the former category.) The building is made from rocks encased in a sort of chicken wire, and actually looks like an extension of the vineyards' *terroir*. However, it is completely functional and very much in keeping with the landscape.

Dominus has changed in style but has maintained an unmistakably French personality. The first vintages, 1983 through 1989, have always exhibited a bit more tannin and toughness, although several of those vintages have matured beautifully and proven that Christian

Christian Moueix

Moueix's initial instincts were on target. Starting in 1990, the tannins became noticeably softer and the wine much more accessible in its youth. That style has remained throughout the 1990s and early part of the 21st century. When Dominus is great, it can be profoundly so, and that certainly is a characteristic of the 1991. The 1991 and 1994 were followed closely by the 1990, 1997, and 2001. This is a wine that tastes like a great Bordeaux, but obviously it is made from ripe Napa fruit. In tastings against other California Cabernet Sauvignons, it always stands out as a very distinctive French-styled wine, completely different from its peers.

As the letterhead of Christian Moueix says so astutely, this is a Napa *terroir*, but with a Bordeaux spirit.

DOMINUS PROPRIETARY RED WINE

2003 Dominus

RATING: 92–95 points

The 2003 Dominus (a 4,800-case blend of 88% Cabernet Sauvignon, 7% Cabernet Franc, and 5% Petit Verdot) is a firm, tannic wine offering aromas and flavors of dried herbs, smoke, saddle leather, coffee, sweet kirsch, and black currants. While the estate feels it is softer and more elegant than the 2002, it is, nevertheless, muscular and powerful with plenty going on. It should be at its best between 2010 and 2025+.

2002 Dominus

RATING: 96 points

The 2002 Dominus gets my nod as the greatest example of this *cuvée* since the 1991 and 1994. There are 4,500 cases of this 85% Cabernet Sauvignon, 8% Cabernet Franc, 4% Petit Verdot, and 3% Merlot blend fashioned from minuscule yields ranging from 1.8 to 2.8 tons of fruit per acre. Christian Moueix told me that while the phenolic material was higher analytically in 2002, so were the acids, which surprised everyone. The deep, saturated purple–colored 2002 boasts an extraordinary perfume of roasted coffee intermixed with black currants, cherries, cocoa, cedar, cigar smoke, and new saddle leather. A classic, full-bodied palate possesses great structure, tremendous depth, loads of tannin, and a multilayered, concentrated yet elegant finish. It is difficult to predict when this beauty will plateau in terms of maturity. My best guess is it needs 3–5 years of bottle age, and should last for 25 years.

2001 Dominus

RATING: 95 points

The impeccably made 2001 Dominus boasts a dense plum/purple color in addition to a fragrant, promising perfume of cocoa, cedar, coffee, roasted herbs, and copious quantities of black fruits. There are 7,000 cases of this 81% Cabernet Sauvignon, 10% Cabernet Franc, 4% Merlot, and 5% Petit Verdot blend. Rich and medium to full–bodied, with sweet but noticeable tannin, a layered mid-palate, and a long finish with obvious tannin, it will require 3–4 years of cellaring. It should last for two decades.

1997 Dominus

RATING: 94 points

The 1997 Dominus, a blend of 86.5% Cabernet Sauvignon, 9% Cabernet Franc, and 4.5% Merlot, is showing fabulously well. With 14.1% alcohol and a pH that would make many New World oenologists shudder (about 3.95), this wine is a fleshy, silky-textured, opulent wine with a gorgeous nose of roasted herbs, coffee, jammy black cherry, and plum-like fruit. Asian spice, licorice, and blackberry and cherry notes with tobacco spice all add to this complex, very involved, yet gorgeously symmetrical Dominus. This medium to full–bodied, very concentrated wine is gorgeous to drink now, but should age easily for 10–12 years.

1996 Dominus

RATING: 92 points

The 1996 Dominus, a blend of 82% Cabernet Sauvignon, 10% Cabernet Franc, 4% Merlot, and 4% Petit Verdot, tips the scales at 14.2% alcohol. Although this offering lacks the power, intensity, and compelling characteristics of the 1991 and 1994, it is not far off the pace of those two monumental wines. A super nose of roasted coffee, chocolate, dried herbs, black fruits, and kirsch is both intense and persuasive. The wine displays terrific richness, medium to full body, low acidity, a succulent, opulent texture, and superb purity. This beautifully made 1996 is one of the few wines that has successfully tamed the vintage's elevated tannin level. It should evolve nicely for two decades. Impressive!

1995 Dominus

RATING: 93 points

Christian Moueix and his talented winemaking team continue to rewrite the definition of a Napa Valley reference-point wine. The 1995 Dominus (6,000 cases produced from a blend of 80% Cabernet Sauvignon, 10% Cabernet Franc, 6% Petit Verdot, and 4% Merlot) is a ripe, plummy, supple, expansively flavored wine with copious quantities of black currant fruit. Full-bodied and low in acidity, it possesses exceptional concentration and purity. Qualitatively, it is built along the lines of the 1992 and 1990. While it is not as powerful or intense as the 1996 or 1994, the 1995 is a large-scaled, rich, concentrated wine that should provide splendid drinking for two decades.

1994 Dominus

RATING: 99 points

I have had a difficult time keeping the corks in my bottles of 1994 Dominus. Eight thousand cases were produced from a blend of 70% Cabernet Sauvignon, 14% Cabernet Franc, 12% Merlot, and 4% Petit Verdot. In this vintage, 174 days passed between bud break and the harvest, a remarkable period of time for any wine region in the world. The 1994 is a strikingly thick, compellingly rich wine with the texture of a great Pomerol, despite being made primarily from Cabernet Sauvignon. The wine exhibits a dense purple color and an incredibly fragrant nose of jammy black fruits, spice, smoke, and loamy, truffle-like scents. In the mouth, it is full-bodied, with thrilling levels of extract and richness, but no sense of heaviness or harshness. This seamless Dominus possesses no hard edges, as its acidity, tannin, and alcohol are beautifully meshed with copious quantities of ripe fruit. This wine offers early drinking, yet has the potential to last for another 25+ years.

1992 Dominus

RATING: 95 points

The 1992 Dominus is similar in style to the 1990. It exhibits an open-knit, opulent, rich, easygoing character with gorgeous levels of earthy, cassis fruit intertwined with scents of herbs, coffee, and chocolate/mocha ice cream. Rich and full-bodied, with thick, viscous flavors and low acidity, this is a forward, exceptionally concentrated, easy to understand Dominus that should drink well for another 10–12 years.

1991 Dominus

RATING: 98 points

The 1991 is the finest Dominus to date, although the 1994 may eventually rival it. The wine is incredibly expansive, rich, complex, fragrant, concentrated, and compelling in all respects. The opaque ruby/purple color is followed by huge quantities of sweet jammy fruit nicely touched by tar, licorice, and earthy scents reminiscent of the aroma of fresh black truffles. The wine is extremely concentrated, opulently textured, and voluptuous, with huge reserves of juicy fruit. It is a marvelous Pomerol-like wine of exceptional purity and harmony. It should last for another 10–15 years.

1990 Dominus

RATING: 95 points

In a blind tasting in 1997, I mistakenly thought the 1990 was a Médoc, with its cedary, spicy, tobacco, black currant–scented nose, sweet, full-bodied flavors, high tannin, and low acidity. In retrospect, I suppose I was somewhat surprised by just how great the 1990 performed in comparison with the profound 1991. It is a superb Dominus that was just beginning to close down in 1997. Rich and powerful, it is capable of lasting for another 10+ years.

1989 Dominus

RATING: 92 points

The 1989 is undoubtedly the Cabernet Sauvignon of the vintage. The color is a dark ruby/purple and the nose offers up

CALIFORNIA

sweet, fragrant scents of black fruits, cedar, herbs, and spicy wood. In the mouth, there is extraordinary concentration, medium to full body, and an authoritatively rich, lingering finish. I assume others will have as much difficulty as I did explaining why the wine tastes more like a Pomerol than a Napa Cabernet. Interestingly, Moueix stated that the key to his success in 1989 was to wait 6–7 days after the rains had stopped before harvesting so the vines could shed their excess moisture. Anticipated maturity: now–2009.

1987 Dominus

RATING: 96 points

It is one of the great wines of the vintage in a year when a handful of California producers made profound Cabernets (i.e., Robert Mondavi Reserve, Dunn Howell Mountain, and Chateau Montelena). The wine displays a rich ruby color and an intensely spicy, fragrant nose of toasty vanilla oak, cassis, and cedar. In the mouth, this medium to full–bodied wine displays considerable tannins, fine integrated acidity, and an opulent, rich, spicy finish. Anticipated maturity: now–2015.

1986 Dominus

RATING: 92 points

The color remains a deep, dark ruby, with purple hues. Dense, concentrated, and pure, with copious quantities of cassis fruit intermingled with earth, spice, and minerals, this large-scaled, concentrated wine appears to have aged at a glacial pace since I first tasted it. Accessible because of its well-integrated, low acidity, this wine should continue to evolve and drink well for another 5–6 years.

1985 Dominus

RATING: 94 points

The 1985 Dominus stands out for its smoky, ripe cassis, earthy nose, sweet, full-bodied, concentrated flavors, and opulently long, chewy finish. It was one of the most forward, precocious examples of this wine I have tasted. This bottling exhibited the plush, velvety texture that proprietor Christian Moueix achieves in top Pomerol vintages. The 1985 Dominus should continue to drink well for another 4–10 years.

1984 Dominus

RATING: 94 points

I have been fooled by this wine in blind tastings, mistaking it for a top Pomerol, although there is an insignificant percentage of Merlot in the blend. The complex bouquet of ripe, curranty fruit, coffee, and sweet black cherries has become increasingly complex and intense. Full-bodied, opulent, and soft, this fleshy wine appears to have reached an attractive plateau of maturity; it should easily last for another 3–6+ years.

1983 Dominus

RATING: 90 points

Only 2,100 cases were produced of the debut vintage of Dominus. While very backward, full-bodied, and tannic, with an austere Bordeaux personality, the wine continues to exhibit considerable promise. The nose offers damp woodsy aromas intermingled with rich, jammy cassis, cedar, licorice, and even some Oriental spice notes. This highly extracted, rich wine should prove to be extremely long-lived. It gives every sign of shedding its tannins and having the requisite extraction of fruit and concentration for future harmony. It is unquestionably among the finest 1983 California Cabernet Sauvignon–based wines. Anticipated maturity: now–2010.

DUNN VINEYARDS

WINE:

Cabernet Sauvignon Howell Mountain
OWNER: Dunn Vineyards, LLC (Dunn family)
ADDRESS: P.O. Box 886, Angwin, CA 94508
TELEPHONE: (707) 965-3642
TELEFAX: (707) 965-3805
WEBSITE: In development
CONTACT: Randy Dunn
VISITING POLICY: They are closed to the public—no tours
    or visits.

VINEYARDS

SURFACE AREA: 34 acres
GRAPE VARIETALS: Cabernet Sauvignon
AVERAGE AGE OF THE VINES: 10 years
DENSITY OF PLANTATION: 1,000 vines per acre
AVERAGE YIELDS: 3.3 tons per acre

WINEMAKING AND UPBRINGING

From the start at Dunn Vineyards, it was obvious that Dunn had grapes capable of producing very long-lived, complex wines, a trait that is not found in all fruit. Randy Dunn's winemaking has not changed significantly in the last 24 years. He continues to hand-pick the fruit at a sugar level that will produce wines in the 13.5–13.8% alcohol range. Mature fruit flavors are essential to quality Cabernet. Dunn does not believe grape maturity levels that produce wines over 14% are necessary.

The grapes are destemmed, then crushed into stainless-steel fermenters, where the temperature is controlled. The tanks are pumped over at least three times each day. When no residual sugar is left of the grape must, the free run juice is drawn off and the remainder is pressed.

The wines are aged 30 months in 50% new French oak 60-gallon barrels in very cool and damp tunnels. Malolactic fermentation is initiated in the stainless steel and generally is completed in the barrels by December the first year. The wines are not blended until shortly before bottling. The wines are filtered but never fined.

The main changes at Dunn's winery, tucked away in the woods on top of Howell Mountain, have involved upgrading equipment. Dunn has also implemented some viticultural changes—farming practices to provide better fruit, such as more crop thinning and shoot removal to provide more light exposure, etc. The objective is massive, age-worthy Cabernets. This style has been established and well-received, and Dunn avoids the trends of winemaking that are considered avant garde.

ANNUAL PRODUCTION

Cabernet Sauvignon Howell Mountain—The first vintage was 1979 (660 cases). Expansion has been modest: 1980—825 cases; 1981—940 cases; 1982—1250 cases, and by 1986 it leveled off at just over 2,000 cases.
There are also 2,000 cases of a very good Napa Cabernet Sauvignon.
AVERAGE PRICE (VARIABLE DEPENDING ON VINTAGE): $40–55

GREAT RECENT VINTAGES

2002, 2001, 1997, 1996, 1995, 1994, 1992, 1991, 1990, 1987, 1985, 1984, 1982

Randy Dunn began as a home winemaker. In 1971 his professor at UC Davis called him up one Friday night and asked if he wanted to learn how to make wine. The professor was involved in research on a new grape pesticide. Dunn picked the grapes and weighed them, and the untreated grapes were his to vinify. So this experiment became his first experience in oenology. That was in 1971. He then enrolled in all of the oenology courses at UC Davis. In 1975 Dunn was hired as "crush help" at Caymus and stayed until 1985.

Dunn Vineyards was started on essentially no budget, because they had no money. As Dunn says, "Even twenty years ago it was very easy to get so hugely in debt that a small winery would never be profitable." But Dunn kept his winery small, and after the release of his 1979, a huge cult demand of his wines followed.

The Howell Mountain subappellation is distinct from other areas of Napa Valley. Because of the 2,000-foot elevation, bud break in the spring is later than on the valley floor. The valley also frequently has a fog layer and 55 to 57 degree temperatures until 10:00 A.M. At Dunn, however, the days are about 10–15 degrees cooler. The warmer nights enable the vines to catch up with those in the valley, so the harvest time is not that different.

The brick-red volcanic soils tend to be shallow and well drained. This, along with being above the fog, gives Dunn an extreme advantage if there is any rain during harvest. The sun is on the vines by 6:30 A.M. Add a bit of breeze and the soils and berries dry out, so rot is usually not a problem. This is in contrast with the valley's heavier soils and cold fog that prevent the berries from drying. The thinking that temperature extremes (high days/low nights) are necessary for making wines of intense color does not seem to apply to Howell Mountain, as Dunn's Cabernets are among the blackest of Napa.

Dunn's basic philosophy is to keep it simple . . . and small. As he says, "If you make one or two wines in limited amounts, you can really streamline the operation. Small production enables you to have time to do everything—pruning, tractor driving, repairs, marketing, paperwork, and winemaking. This choice of what to do in a day is lost forever when production levels increase."

If Godzilla drank California Cabernet Sauvignon, this would be his choice. Anyone who has regularly tasted Randy Dunn's Cabernet Sauvignons realizes that they all possess the following characteristics: (1) remarkable color and richness, (2) massive personalities with huge tannic structures, (3) gorgeous purity, and (4) unreal aging potential. Not long ago I tasted all of Dunn's top wines back through the 1982. Remarkably, they had hardly budged in development, yet they were still exceptionally rich in their pure crème de cassis, black raspberry, and blackberry fruit notes.

Having closely followed Dunn's Cabernet Sauvignons since the debut 1979 vintage, I find it remarkable how consistent these wines have been. Dunn, who believes in filtering but not fining, tends to use the former technique as a way of bringing a measure of refinement to the brute strength and power his wines possess. It is too early to say, but if there is any weakness to Dunn's Cabernets it would be the surprising lack of bottle bouquet. Dunn vehemently believes that filtration has nothing to do with this, and that it is only a matter of time before his Cabernets exhibit more aromatic evolution.

Despite his success, Dunn has kept his operation modest in size. Approximately 4,000–5,000 cases are produced, and this is generally evenly split between the Napa and Howell Mountain bottlings. The two *cuvées* are similar in personality and quality, with the Napa sometimes revealing less astringent tannin. However, blind tastings reveal both wines to have similar aromatic and flavor profiles, but with age, it is the Howell Mountain Cabernet that proves its world-class pedigree.

Perhaps the question potential buyers need to ask themselves is, just how much patience are they willing to invest in Dunn's Cabernets? It is no crime to drink them young, since they are well balanced, and the fruit

Randy Dunn

is ripe, concentrated, and sweet. However, my experience has shown that these wines do not begin to develop secondary aromas for at least a dozen years. These are classic, very long-lived, mountain Cabernet Sauvignons meant to survive four to five decades of cellaring.

CABERNET SAUVIGNON HOWELL MOUNTAIN

2003 Cabernet Sauvignon Howell Mountain
RATING: 92–94+ points
The powerful 2003 Cabernet Sauvignon Howell Mountain may turn out to be richer and fuller than either the 2001 or 2002, an atypical scenario. Its dense blue/purple color is followed by a big, rich nose of cassis, blueberries, minerals, and flowers. Rich, full-bodied, and powerfully tannic, it is classic Dunn stuff. Anticipated maturity: 2012–2030.

2002 Cabernet Sauvignon Howell Mountain
RATING: 91–93+ points
The 2002 Cabernet Sauvignon Howell Mountain exhibits an inky blue/purple color along with a sweet perfume of pure blackberries, meat, new saddle leather, and flowers. From an unusually ripe harvest, this sweet, rich, fleshy offering displays more accessibility than many Howell Mountain vintages. Randy Dunn said it was important to drop crop, and he eliminated 40% of the fruit from the vines in both 2002 and 2001. The long, concentrated 2002 may not be the biggest Howell Mountain *cuvée,* but it will provide lovely drinking between 2009 and 2024.

2001 Cabernet Sauvignon Howell Mountain
RATING: 93+ points
The saturated purple–hued 2001 Cabernet Sauvignon Howell Mountain reveals a bouquet of acacia flowers, blueberries, blackberries, and raspberries. It is a full-bodied, intense, tannic, muscular, powerful effort that should be cellared for 5–10 years and drunk over the following 20–25.

1997 Cabernet Sauvignon Howell Mountain
RATING: 95 points
The enormous 1997 Cabernet Sauvignon Howell Mountain is a super-powerful, fabulously concentrated, 50-year wine. Aromas and flavors of blackberry/cassis jam, minerals, and subtle oak are found in this extravagantly rich, gargantuan Cabernet Sauvignon that should age effortlessly for half a century. Anticipated maturity: 2015–2050.

1996 Cabernet Sauvignon Howell Mountain
RATING: 96 points
The 1996 Cabernet Sauvignon Howell Mountain possesses a black/blue/purple color and a texture of unctuousness and thickness. Greatness is suggested by a wonderfully sweet midsection, gorgeous purity, and this humongous wine's overall symmetry. It also possesses sumptuous layers of concentration, remarkably sweet tannin, low acidity, and a 40+-second finish. Anticipated maturity: 2009–2040.

1995 Cabernet Sauvignon Howell Mountain
RATING: 96 points
The 1995 Cabernet Sauvignon Howell Mountain is similar in all respects to the Napa Valley, but somewhat heavier in the mouth, with an aggressive tannic bite and more length. It possesses mineral-tinged blackberry and cassis fruit, massive body, and extraordinary purity and length. It should not be touched for another 7–10 years. It will undoubtedly live through the first half of this century. 1995 appears to be a fabulous vintage. I doubt there will be much difference in quality between the 1995s and Randy Dunn's spectacular 1994s.

1994 Cabernet Sauvignon Howell Mountain
RATING: 96 points
Look out for the behemoth 1994 Cabernet Sauvignon Howell Mountain. This black/purple-colored wine adds a few more nuances (minerals, licorice, and floral scents) to the lavish display of crème de cassis. Full-bodied, with a blockbuster level of extract and density, this is an outstanding Cabernet Sauvignon for readers with patience, good genes for longevity, or the foresight to purchase it for their children. Anticipated maturity: 2006–2030.

1993 Cabernet Sauvignon Howell Mountain
RATING: 95 points
The 1993 Cabernet Sauvignon Howell Mountain reveals an opaque black color, huge tannin, terrific purity and density, a broad, heavyweight mouth-feel, and gobs of ripe tannin. It is a massive Cabernet Sauvignon that may require additional cellaring. This is another producer who turned out outstanding 1993s, a vintage that received some unjustifiably tough press. Anticipated maturity: now–2016.

1992 Cabernet Sauvignon Howell Mountain
RATING: 96 points
What makes Dunn's 1992 Cabernet Sauvignons so incredible is that one of the vintage's hallmarks is the voluptuous, opulent, and succulent nature of the fruit. In Dunn's offerings, that translates into wines that are huge, massive, and rich, but with a sweeter, more expansive, chewy middle palate. The 1992 Howell Mountain Cabernet is a 20–30-year wine.

WINE: Harlan Estate Proprietary Red

OWNER: H. William Harlan

ADDRESS: P.O. Box 352, Oakville, CA 94562

TELEPHONE: (707) 944-1441

TELEFAX: (707) 944-1444

E-MAIL: info@harlanestate.com

WEBSITE: www.harlanestate.com

CONTACT: Don Weaver (Director)

VISITING POLICY: No tours or tastings

VINEYARDS

SURFACE AREA: 36 acres

GRAPE VARIETALS: 70% Cabernet Sauvignon, 20% Merlot, 8% Cabernet Franc, 2% Petite Verdot

AVERAGE AGE OF THE VINES:

17 years—50%

6–11 years—33%

4 years—17%

DENSITY OF PLANTATION: 50% at 700 vines per acre; 50% at 2,200 vines per acre

AVERAGE YIELDS: 2 tons per acre

WINEMAKING AND UPBRINGING

The philosophy at Harlan Estate is certainly to keep the wines as natural as can be. There is a very gentle policy in regard to the grapes and fermentation. The use of small picking trays, severe cluster triage, destemming without crushing, and then a triage for the destemmed berries (very rare in the wine world) and no pumping of berries must result in the most gentle extraction methods possible. The wine is lightly punched down and pumped-over, then fermented in open-top small fermenters that are designed to provide as much harmony as possible with the tannins' more consistent temperatures. This is followed by malolactic fermentation in small, 100% new French oak barrels, where the wine rests a part of its time on the lees as well, for 23–36 months. It is usually bottled with neither fining nor filtration.

ANNUAL PRODUCTION

Harlan Estate (Napa Valley red wine): 19,000 bottles (current average); 28,000 bottles at vineyard maturity

The Maiden (Napa Valley red wine): 10,000 bottles (current average); 14,000 bottles at vineyard maturity

First commercial vintage: 1990, released January 1996

Most recent vintage: 2001, released May 2005

The labels of Harlan Estate and The Maiden each feature an allegorical vignette, intaglio engraved in the banknote tradition. This painstaking, time-honored method reinforces product authenticity and evokes a timeless elegance.

AVERAGE PRICE OF THE HARLAN ESTATE PROPRIETARY RED: $100–175

GREAT RECENT VINTAGES

2002, 2001, 1998, 1997, 1996, 1995, 1994, 1993, 1992, 1991

Set in the western hills of Oakville, rising above the fabled Napa Valley benchlands, the Harlan estate possesses over 240 acres of natural splendor—oak-studded knolls and valleys, roughly 15% of which are under vine.

Harlan Estate was founded in 1984 with the intent to build and establish one of the finest wine-growing estates in America. Bill Harlan, who is a very successful real estate developer and the proprietor of Napa Valley's exquisite Meadowood Resort, cuts a dashing figure. With his white hair and closely trimmed beard, he has the look of a noble Spanish conquistador. He also has a single-minded purposefulness that, in large part, explains the extraordinary quality and success Harlan Estate has enjoyed in such a short period of time. Bill Harlan has said authoritatively that his "mission is to consistently produce a wine of the highest quality and great longevity . . . in essence, to create a first growth of California."

The first vineyard development of the estate began in 1984 with just six acres. Planting has continued slowly and intermittently over the past 19 years. Today, the planting is complete, with 36 acres under vine, planted to the classic varietals: Cabernet Sauvignon, Merlot, Cabernet Franc, and Petit Verdot. The impressive mountainside vineyards are situated on the western side of Napa Valley, overlooking Martha's Vineyard.

Variously sited on the "tenderloin" of the well-drained slopes, the vineyards are uniquely beautiful—vertically trained vines in spartan soils over fractured rock, with some on terraces cut to contour, others flowing

with the lay of the land. The farming and cultural practices are uncompromising, emphasizing low vine vigor and low yields, employing enormous patience and care.

Since this wine debuted in 1990, Harlan Estate has produced one of California's most impressive Cabernet Sauvignons. No compromises are made when producing this dazzling wine. Bill Harlan, assisted by his winemaker, Bob Levy, and consulting oenologist, France's Michel Rolland, have turned out a wine of exquisite richness and complexity. The wine offers the intensity one expects from a top California Cabernet-based wine, yet it incorporates a sense of grace, complexity, and elegance that clearly places it in the top echelon of California wines. In 1996, I inserted the 1991 Harlan Estate as a ringer in a blind tasting of the top 1990 and 1989 Bordeaux. It scored impressively well against the likes of 1990 Latour, 1990 Margaux, and 1990 Pétrus. I have since repeated this tasting with the 1992, 1994, and 1995 Harlan, with similar ecstatic results for the Harlan. The wine, which

can be imagined as a blend of a great California Cabernet and equal parts La Mission Haut-Brion, Cheval Blanc, and Mouton Rothschild, is a must purchase for those with the requisite discretionary income and ability to track down a few bottles of this knockout wine.

The wine from Harlan Estate possesses all the elements of greatness—individuality, power combined with elegance, extraordinary complexity, remarkable aging potential, and compelling richness without ponderousness. The vintages produced to date give signs of improving in the bottle for 20–30+ years. In 1995, their second wine, The Maiden, was produced, the result of an even more severe selection process at this hillside vineyard.

While perfect wines are few and far between, history has taught me that wineries with such lofty aspirations as Harlan Estate will continue to push the envelope of quality. The objective at Harlan is simple—low yields, ripe fruit, no razzle dazzle in fermentation, a natural upbringing, and bottling without clarification.

HARLAN ESTATE PROPRIETARY RED

2002 Harlan Estate

RATING: 96–100 points

The huge heat wave during the third week of September 2002 gave the grapes an extra plushness, which is reflected in the brilliant 2002 Harlan Estate. The most flattering and precocious Harlan Estate I have tasted to date, it boasts an inky purple color along with an extraordinary nose of cappuccino, chocolate, crème de cassis, smoke, licorice, and graphite. Incredibly full-bodied and unctuously textured with low acidity, high but ripe tannin, and a blockbuster, flamboyant finish, this is the most decadent and extravagantly fruity Harlan I have tasted to date. I would not be surprised to see it firm up considerably once it is in bottle. Anticipated maturity: 2006–2020+.

2001 Harlan Estate

RATING: 100 points

Tasted on four separate occasions, this offering, which spent 28 months in oak before being bottled unfined and unfiltered, is an extraordinary effort that comes across as a hypothetical blend of Mouton Rothschild, La Mission Haut-Brion, and Montrose. A synthesis in style between the more elegant, delineated, structured 1994 and the Port-like, over-the-top, viscous 1997, this extraordinary 2001 was the wine of my trip, even though I had already had it from bottle several months earlier. An inky purple color is accompanied by a stupendous bouquet of lead pencil shavings interwoven with coffee, new saddle leather, melted licorice, cedarwood, black currant liqueur, and violets. Explosive richness, a marvelous, full-bodied texture, and fabulous purity, concentration, complexity, and nobleness are the stuff of legends. Anticipated maturity: 2009–2028+.

2000 Harlan Estate

RATING: 91 points

A Graves-like perfume of roasted coffee, scorched earth, black currants, cedar, and a hint of menthol emerge from this dense, dark ruby/purple–colored 2000. Lighter than normal, but medium to full–bodied and elegant, with soft tannin as well as a silky, precocious personality and texture, it can be drunk now and over the next 12 years.

1999 Harlan Estate

RATING: 92 points

The 1999 Harlan Estate reveals moderately intense aromatics of sweet vanilla, menthol, espresso, chocolate, and cassis. The wine is medium to full–bodied, suave, and elegant. It is more restrained and not as intense as previous vintages, reflecting 1999's cool growing season. Nevertheless, this is still an outstanding wine. The finish is long, elegant, and Bordeaux-like.

It is not as prodigious as the Harlans produced between 1991 and 1998. I would rank it behind all those wines. Anticipated maturity: now–2016.

1998 Harlan Estate
RATING: 95 points

This 1998, which is a candidate for the wine of the vintage, was produced from yields of 0.9 tons per acre. A spectacular achievement, it boasts an opaque plum/purple color as well as a sumptuous nose of espresso, mineral, blueberry, blackberry, tobacco, licorice, Asian spice, and roasted meat. In the mouth, it is seamless, full-bodied, with an unctuous texture, gorgeously sweet tannin, and layer upon layer of concentration. This is a tour de force in winemaking. It is hard to believe that a wine such as this has emerged from 1998. Anticipated maturity: now–2030.

1997 Harlan Estate
RATING: 100 points

A blend of 80% Cabernet Sauvignon, with the rest Merlot and Cabernet Franc, this enormously endowed, profoundly rich wine must be tasted to be believed. Opaque purple-colored, it boasts spectacular, soaring aromatics of vanilla, minerals, coffee, blackberries, licorice, and cassis. In the mouth, layer after layer unfold powerfully yet gently. Acidity, tannin, and alcohol are well balanced by the wine's unreal richness and singular personality. The finish exceeds one minute. Anticipated maturity: now–2030.

1996 Harlan Estate
RATING: 98 points

The opaque purple–colored 1996 Harlan Estate reveals extraordinary intensity, a spicy, black currant, tobacco, cedar, and fruitcake–scented bouquet, full body, a texture oozing with glycerin and concentrated fruit, and moderate tannin in the blockbuster finish. It is one of the most concentrated and complete red wines one could hope to taste. Anticipated maturity: now–2030.

1995 Harlan Estate
RATING: 99 points

The 1995 Proprietary Red Wine is almost as perfect as the 1994. It has gotten even better in the bottle, and remains one of the most remarkable young Cabernet Sauvignons I have tasted. This opaque purple–colored Cabernet offers up a nose of smoke, coffee beans, black and blue fruits, minerals, and roasted herbs. It is extremely full-bodied, with spectacular purity, exquisite equilibrium, and a seamless personality with everything in total harmony. The finish lasts for more than 40 seconds. Anticipated maturity: now–2027.

1994 Harlan Estate
RATING: 100 points

What can I say about the 1994? I tasted the wine for three consecutive years, and each time it satisfied all of my requirements for perfection. The opaque purple color is followed by spectacular aromatics that soar from the glass, offering up celestial levels of black currants, minerals, smoked herbs, cedarwood, coffee, and toast. In the mouth, this seamless legend reveals full body, and exquisite layers of phenomenally pure and rich fruit, followed by a 40+-second finish. It should easily last for 30+ years. Every possible jagged edge—acidity, alcohol, tannin, and wood—is brilliantly intertwined in what seems like a diaphanous format. What is so extraordinary about this large-scaled wine, with its dazzling display of aromatics and prodigious flavors and depth, is that it offers no hint of heaviness or coarseness. Harlan's 1994 comes close to immortality in the glass.

1993 Harlan Estate
RATING: 95 points

The 1993 should be as prodigious as the 1992. It is an opaque purple–colored wine with spectacular ripeness, purity, and potential. Dense, full-bodied, with a chocolaty, toasty, mineral, and black currant–scented nose, this wine has a rich, full-bodied, chewy texture nicely buttressed by ripe tannin. In addition, the wine reveals more noticeable tannin in the finish, particularly when it is compared to the 1992 or 1994. Anticipated maturity: now–2021.

1992 Harlan Estate
RATING: 96 points

Harlan's 1992 offers a dense purple color and a splendid sweet nose of minerals, black currants, toast, and spice. Opulent and rich, with full body, and well-integrated sweet tannin, this expansive yet graceful wine possesses layers of flavor that caress the palate. The wine is accessible, yet still youthful and unformed. It should drink well for 12+ more years.

1991 Harlan Estate
RATING: 98 points

This is a profoundly great wine. It came across in a blind tasting as one of the most remarkable wines there, with most tasters mistaking it for a first-growth Médoc. The wine revealed an opaque purple color, a fabulously complex, sweet nose of minerals, fruitcake, cedar, toasty new oak, and pure black currant fruit. Although huge in the mouth, the wine is remarkably well balanced, with its high tannin level well concealed by copious quantities of sweet ripe fruit, as well as huge amounts of glycerin and extract. I have consistently rated the 1991 Harlan Estate in the mid- to upper-90s, but in this blind tasting with so many high-quality wines, it was a big-time winner. Approachable now, this wine should last for 2–3 decades.

WINES:

Chardonnay Kistler Vineyard

Chardonnay McCrea Vineyard

Chardonnay Vine Hill Vineyard

Chardonnay Durell Vineyard

Chardonnay Cuvée Cathleen

Pinot Noir Cuvée Catherine

Pinot Noir Cuvée Elizabeth

OWNERS: Stephen Kistler and the Kistler family

ADDRESS: 4707 Vine Hill Road, Sebastopol, CA 95472

TELEPHONE: (707) 823-5603

TELEFAX: (707) 823-6709

E-MAIL: mfbixler@kistlerwine.com

WEBSITE: www.kistlerwine.com

CONTACT: Mark Bixler

VISITING POLICY: Not open to the public

VINEYARDS

SURFACE AREA: 210 acres

GRAPE VARIETALS: Chardonnay, Pinot Noir, Syrah

AVERAGE AGE OF THE VINES: Ranging from oldest of 36 years to most recent plantings in 2002

DENSITY OF PLANTATION: Spacing varies; meter x 7' / 4' x 7' / 4' x 8' / 5' x 7' / 5' x 8' / 5' x 10' / 6' x 10'

AVERAGE YIELDS: Lowest yield: $1/2$–2 tons; highest: 2–3 tons

WINEMAKING AND UPBRINGING

From the beginning, white Burgundy has been Kistler Vineyards' point of reference. Winemaker Steve Kistler and his assistant, Mark Bixler, are dedicated to using single-vineyard sources to develop the classic flavors and aromas of Chardonnay. For their Chardonnay, Kistler has always used whole-cluster pressing and 100% barrel fermentation in various percentages of new French oak (ranging from a low of 50% to a maximum of 75%). They prefer using a mixture of both indigenous and cultured yeast, and full malolactic fermentation occurs in oak rather than tank. All of the Chardonnays remain 12 months on their lees in barrel, then are racked into a settling tank and bottled 6 months later unfined and unfiltered. For their Pinot Noir, the fruit is destemmed but never crushed. They believe in a 5+-day cold maceration prior to kicking off fermentation. The Pinot Noirs are fermented in 2–4-ton open-top fermenters and only indigenous yeasts are used. After a 3–4-week *cuvaison*, malolactic fermentation occurs naturally in barrel. About 85% new French oak is used, and the wine spends 14–16 months in wood without any racking until it is assembled in a bottling tank and bottled unfined and unfiltered.

ANNUAL PRODUCTION

Chardonnay:

Kistler Vineyard: 900–2,700 cases (since 1986)

McCrea Vineyard: 1,800–3,600 cases (since 1988)

Vine Hill Vineyard: 1,800–2,700 cases (since 1988)

Durell Vineyard: 900–1800 cases (1986)

Cuvée Cathleen: 0–500 cases (1992)

Pinot Noir:

Cuvée Catherine: 250–500 cases (1991)

Cuvée Elizabeth: 250–500 cases (1999)

AVERAGE PRICE (VARIABLE DEPENDING ON VINTAGE): $60–150

GREAT RECENT VINTAGES:

Chardonnay—2003, 2002, 2001, 2000, 1999, 1997, 1994, 1992, 1990, 1988, 1987, 1979

Pinot Noir—2003, 2002, 2001, 2000, 1999, 1996, 1994, 1992, 1991

In 1978 Steve Kistler and his family founded this small winery in the Mayacamas Mountains, and the first vintage, the 1979, totaled 3,500 cases of Chardonnay. In 1992, the state-of-the-art winery was built on the Russian River, right off Vine Hill Road. The current production averages around 20,000 cases, 15,000 of which are Chardonnay and 5,000 Pinot Noir.

Since the beginning, Kistler Vineyards has been operated by its two principals, owner/winemaker Steve Kistler and his assistant, Mark Bixler. Kistler received his bachelor of arts from Stanford University, later studied at the University of California at Davis and Fresno State, and worked as an assistant winemaker at Ridge for two years before founding Kistler. Mark Bixler earned his degree at M.I.T. and then studied at the University of California at Berkeley before becoming a professor of chemistry at Fresno State, and then moving on to Fetzer Vineyards for two years.

Kistler Vineyards is at the pinnacle of California quality. Particularly admirable is the fact that they got there the hard way—they earned it.

After each visit to Kistler I am moved to write one accolade after another because of the extraordinary efforts and quality of the wines produced by Steve and Mark. I begin to sound like a broken record, but this winery is turning out prodigious wines. Everyone knows about Kistler's remarkable Chardonnays, but I believe their Pinot Noirs will ultimately prove even more historic. All are aged in 100% new oak, made in small lots (250–500 cases), and bottled with neither fin-ing nor filtration. They are trying to keep the levels of SO_2 to minimal dosages so the wines can be as expressive as possible. These Pinot Noirs can easily hold their own in blind tastings with the finest red Burgundies.

Steve Kistler and Mark Bixler feel that the key to making top-quality Chardonnay and Pinot Noir is patience. Some years the flavors come early, and in other years they arrive much later. The Chardonnays could easily pass as grand cru white Burgundies, as they possess incredible liquid minerality, great structure, and phenomenal purity. At the same time, these wines reflect their individual vineyard sites. All are put through full, slow malolactics, then racked off into the settling tanks, and bottled without filtration. Nothing is ever done in a hurry. Over the last decade, I have been assessing the Chardonnays' aging potential. It appears they hit their peak in 3–5 years, where they remain for 8–9 years before beginning to decline. While that is not lengthy by the standards of many white Burgundies, it is extremely long-lived for California Chardonnay. The wines will last longer, but longevity should be measured by the ability of a wine not just to survive, but to improve.

CHARDONNAY CUVEE CATHLEEN

2003 Chardonnay Cuvée Cathleen

RATING: 99 points

Named after one of Kistler's daughters, the 2003 Chardonnay Cuvée Cathleen, a selection of the very best barrels from the Kistler Vineyard, is undeniably sexy, full-throttle stuff. About 500 cases of this were made in 2003, and the wine comes across as a combination of the best that California can do with the complexity, minerality, and definition of a French white Burgundy. Very rich tropical fruits intermixed with some citrus oil, crushed rocks, and a steely backbone provide a canvas where a large-scale yet incredibly elegant, complex wine has been produced. This is a beauty, very long, impressive, and noble. It should drink well for 7–8 years.

2002 Chardonnay Cuvée Cathleen

RATING: 96 points

The 2002 Chardonnay Cuvée Cathleen appears more subdued than the Vine Hill and Kistler. I doubt that is actually the case, but that is the way it tasted. Nevertheless, you can serve me this wine any time, any day—it's that good. Powerful and rich, with a striking minerality, it comes across like a Coche-Dury Corton-Charlemagne that's been racheted up a few levels. Powerful as well as extremely well-delineated, but still playing it close to the vest, it is a spectacular Chardonnay that should hit its peak in two years, and last for a decade.

2001 Chardonnay Cuvée Cathleen

RATING: 96 points

From a selection of the best barrels, the light gold–colored 2001 Chardonnay Cuvée Cathleen (6,396 bottles) offers aromas of brioche, buttered pear, honeyed citrus oil, and hazelnuts. Opulent, full-bodied, and thick, with superb density and richness, this sublime effort represents the essence of its varietal. Impossible to resist now, it will age for 7–9 years, easily.

2000 Chardonnay Cuvée Cathleen

RATING: 95 points

There are 500 cases of the Chardonnay deemed by Steve Kistler and Mark Bixler as representing the finest barrels, the 2000 Chardonnay Cuvée Cathleen. It exhibits a gravelly liquid minerality intermixed with profound flavors of orange marmalade infused with hazelnut oil, candied citrus, white peaches, and lemon blossom. It possesses superb purity, remarkable palate presence, and great structure as well as definition. This amazing tour de force in Chardonnay (as it has been in every vintage in which it has been produced) should drink well for a decade.

1999 Chardonnay Cuvée Cathleen

RATING: 97 points

The 1999 Chardonnay Cuvée Cathleen is phenomenal. It is rich, mineral-dominated, and full, with an unctuous flavor profile, great purity, and stunning layers that unfold on the palate, and does not taste heavy or over the top. That's the brilliance of Steve Kistler and Mark Bixler. This profound Chardonnay rivals the greatest Burgundy grand crus. If you don't believe me, put it in a blind tasting, as I have done many times. Drink it over the next 6–7 years.

1998 Chardonnay Cuvée Cathleen

RATING: 95 points

Along with the 1998 Chardonnay Vine Hill Road Vineyard, this Chardonnay represents an evolution in style. It possesses all the power and concentration of Steve Kistler's most successful wines, but it also has a certain restraint allied with extraordinary complexity and elegance that a few years ago would have been found only in the finest Burgundy grand crus.

The 1998 Chardonnay Cuvée Cathleen is a spectacularly beautiful, well-delineated effort with everything hitting the olfactory senses and palate in measured doses. However, the overall impression is one of stunning concentration, perfect harmony, fabulous density and richness, and that layered, intense mid-palate and length that only great wines possess. It should evolve in an intriguing manner for up to a decade. Anticipated maturity: now–2010.

1997 Chardonnay Cuvée Cathleen

RATING: 94 points

It is difficult to find the adjectives and superlatives to describe the 1997 Chardonnay Cuvée Cathleen. This offering is produced from a selection of barrels that Steve Kistler and Mark Bixler believe to be the richest and most complete. Negligibly better than the other brilliant *cuvées*, it possesses exceptional richness, length, and intensity. Layers of fruit, smoky, buttery popcorn, tropical fruit, and mineral scents soar from the glass, and are exceptionally intense and well balanced. This terrific, full-bodied effort should age for another 3–5 years. Anticipated maturity: now–2008.

CHARDONNAY DURELL VINEYARD

2003 Chardonnay Durell Vineyard

RATING: 93 points

Liqueur of minerals in addition to lemon oil and egg custard might well be a worthy description for the 2003 Chardonnay Durell Vineyard. Light gold with a greenish hue, this wine is a bit more evolved in color than the McCrea Vineyard, but generous, full-bodied, and rich, with uplifting, vibrant acidity, giving freshness and zest to all the component parts. This is another candidate for 4–5 years of aging, although I suspect it is going to last longer.

2002 Chardonnay Durell Vineyard
RATING: 92 points

The light straw/greenish–colored 2002 Chardonnay Durell Vineyard offers up aromas of lemon oil and vanilla custard in a clean, crisp, tart manner. The wine opens in the glass to reveal lemons, orange rind, pineapple, and plenty of rocks and minerals. Fresh, zesty, and exceptionally well delineated, it is a candidate for 5–8+ years of ageability.

2001 Chardonnay Durell Vineyard
RATING: 94 points

The sensational 2001 Chardonnay Durell Vineyard's light gold color displays a greenish hue, and the bouquet is more reticent, offering up notes of minerals and citrus oil. With excellent acidity, abundant minerality, and a long, concentrated finish, this tight but promising 2001 tastes like a grand cru Chablis mixed with a grand cru Côte d'Or white Burgundy. It should drink well for 5–7 years.

2000 Chardonnay Durell Vineyard
RATING: 95 points

The blockbuster 2000 Chardonnay Durell Vineyard (produced from an old Wente Chardonnay clone) is an intensely steely offering with extraordinary texture, ripeness, and weight, with a liquid minerality, phenomenal precision, and a sensational finish that lasts nearly 40 seconds—remarkable for a dry white. It possesses a floral note intermixed with the minerality and citrus fruit aspect so prevalent in this vintage's finest wines. Enjoy it over the next decade.

1999 Chardonnay Durell Vineyard
RATING: 96 points

The astonishing 1999 Chardonnay Durell Vineyard tastes like a grand cru Chevalier-Montrachet or premier cru Meursault-Perrières, given its liquid minerality and extraordinary nose of honeysuckle/tropical fruits. It is full-bodied, with exceptional delineation for a wine of such size. This extraordinary Chardonnay marries unbridled power and richness with uncanny elegance and precision. This is a Chardonnay of great stature as well as majesty. It should drink well for another 6–7 years.

1998 Chardonnay Durell Vineyard
RATING: 92 points

The 1998 Chardonnay Durell Vineyard is tight and backward. Always the last to be harvested (because of the extremely cool microclimate), the 1998 possesses considerable force and intensity, with a mineral, citrusy, lemon blossom, orange peel

component to its full-bodied richness. It reveals good acidity and power, all of which is harnessed and beautifully balanced. Look for this wine to drink well for another 2–4 years.

1997 Chardonnay Durell Vineyard
RATING: 91 points

Readers looking for a Chardonnay that possesses the tropical fruit spectrum, without completely abandoning the complex mineral character, will be pleased with the 1997 Chardonnay Durell Vineyard. The poor vigor of these rocky soils, combined with such clones as Hyde, has resulted in a wine with zesty acidity, medium to full body, outstanding ripeness and purity, and loads of orange blossom/lemony fruit in addition to hints of peach and pineapple. This wine should have an unusually long life of 8–10 years. Anticipated maturity: now–2008.

CHARDONNAY KISTLER VINEYARD

2003 Chardonnay Kistler Vineyard
RATING: 95 points

The 2003 Chardonnay Kistler Vineyard has a Corton-Charlemagne-like personality. Notes of acacia flower, stone fruits, liqueur of rocks, some orange blossom notes intermixed with apple skin, and hints of hazelnut and lemon butter are all present in this full-bodied, stony, mineral-dominated wine that is undeniably impressive. Again, it is backward, but there is an inner core of concentration that just goes on and on. Drink it over the next 7–8 years.

2002 Chardonnay Kistler Vineyard
RATING: 95 points

Spectacular ripeness along with a liquid minerality give this large-scaled, bigger-than-life Chardonnay tremendous balance/equilibrium. This compelling, full-bodied, dense wine offers smoky hazelnut characteristics intermixed with oranges, lemons, tropical fruits, and hints of Grand Marnier as well as caramel. There is a lot going on in this full-bodied, concentrated yet impeccably well-balanced offering. It should drink well for a decade.

2001 Chardonnay Kistler Vineyard
RATING: 95 points

The 2001 Chardonnay Kistler Vineyard is a tightly knit offering. Light gold–colored with considerable glycerin and power, it exhibits a liquid minerality, and a big, rich, textured style with huge concentration. Most of the wine's character is at the back of the palate. This offering reminds me of a Bâtard-Montrachet from the likes of Louis Latour. With extraordinary length, richness, precision, and purity, this sensational Chardonnay will drink well for 6–8 years.

2000 Chardonnay Kistler Vineyard

RATING: 90 points

The tightly knit 2000 Chardonnay Kistler Vineyard is reminiscent of a grand cru Puligny-Montrachet. Lemony honeyed grapefruit, orange rind, and buttered citrus aromas are accompanied by subtle notions of liquid stones, roasted almonds, and a long, medium to full–bodied finish with refreshing levels of acidity. As with all of the Kistler Chardonnays, it is elegant, restrained, nuanced, yet intensely flavorful. Anticipated maturity: now.

1999 Chardonnay Kistler Vineyard

RATING: 93 points

The 1999 Chardonnay Kistler Vineyard boasts a phenomenal perfume of sweet white corn mixed with wet rocks, candied citrus, smoke, and tropical fruit. It is full-bodied, with remarkable length and intensity. This brilliant offering should last another 4–5 years.

1998 Chardonnay Kistler Vineyard

RATING: 94 points

The rich and wonderful 1998 Chardonnay Kistler Vineyard, made from a vineyard planted with the Mount Eden clone, is extremely full-bodied, with striking purity, and powerful, concentrated, honeyed flavors with nuances of butter, smoke, roasted nuts, and minerals. The creamy texture is buttressed by good acidity. Toast, gravel, and slate-like richness intermixed with fruit make this a compelling, intensely flavored Chardonnay. It should drink well for 2–4 more years, perhaps longer.

1997 Chardonnay Kistler Vineyard

RATING: 92 points

The 1997 Chardonnay Kistler Vineyard (made from the Mount Eden clone, which is alleged to be a suitcase clone from Burgundy's Corton-Charlemagne vineyard) is a multidimensional wine with a rich, full-bodied, creamy texture, superb buttery, honeyed fruit, subtle toast, gorgeously rich fruit, white flowers, buttered popcorn, and liquid gravel–like notes. Combining power with finesse, it should drink well for another 1–2 years.

CHARDONNAY MCCREA VINEYARD

2003 Chardonnay McCrea Vineyard

RATING: 95 points

The 2003 Chardonnay McCrea Vineyard has a more Chablis-like character because of its striking mineral notes in addition to lemon zest, orange rind, and a hint of tropical fruit. It is medium to full–bodied, dense, rich, layered, backward, and restrained, but powerful on the palate. It should drink well for 5–7 years.

2002 Chardonnay McCrea Vineyard

RATING: 93 points

The full-bodied 2002 Chardonnay McCrea Vineyard exhibits a distinctive composty/earthy component along with notes of liquid minerals, grapefruit, buttered citrus, and a steely, green-tinged flavor profile reminiscent of a full-bodied French Chablis on steroids. This impressive yet austere, intense Chardonnay should age nicely for 7–8 years.

2001 Chardonnay McCrea Vineyard

RATING: 90 points

The light gold–colored 2001 Chardonnay McCrea Vineyard offers a perfumed nose of buttered popcorn and honeysuckle along with medium to full body and a pure, nicely textured, long finish. It should drink well for 4–5 years.

2000 Chardonnay McCrea Vineyard

RATING: 90 points

The 2000 Chardonnay McCrea Vineyard is a crisp, lemony, zesty effort with hints of lemon butter, grapefruit, and assorted citrus characteristics. The wine possesses high acid, subtle wood notes, and a 1996 Burgundy-like style. It will age for another 4–5 years. For readers seeking opulence, flesh, and luxurious fruit, this wine will always play it close to the vest, although its striking minerality is impressive. There are 2,700 cases.

1999 Chardonnay McCrea Vineyard

RATING: 93 points

The 1999 Chardonnay McCrea Vineyard (2,000 cases) exhibits an intense liquid minerality, notes of white currants, a full-bodied personality with citrus oils and white flowers, and a remarkably well-delineated finish. Concentrated and extremely Burgundian, it should last for a decade. Anticipated maturity: now–2010.

1998 Chardonnay McCrea Vineyard

RATING: 91 points

The 1998 Chardonnay McCrea Vineyard (made from an old, low-producing Wente clone) exhibits a striking minerality in its lemony, buttery, citrusy style. Full-bodied and complex, it is reminiscent of a grand cru Chassagne-Montrachet. The wine, which becomes more complex in the glass, is powerful, rich, concentrated, and well balanced. It should drink well for another 2–4 years.

1997 Chardonnay McCrea Vineyard

RATING: 92 points

The 1997 Chardonnay McCrea Vineyard, made from an old Wente clone, personifies this varietal's lemony, buttery, citrusy, mineral style. It offers medium to full body, splendid concentration, considerable richness and texture on the mid-palate, and gorgeous elegance, purity, and overall balance. Tangy acidity gives the wine admirable freshness. Anticipated maturity: now.

CHARDONNAY VINE HILL VINEYARD

2003 Chardonnay Vine Hill Vineyard
RATING: 97 points

From the vineyard surrounding the winery, the 2003 Chardonnay Vine Hill looks to be one of the candidates for the Chardonnay of the vintage. Truly profound stuff, with a stunning nose of tangerines, orange marmalade, and lemon custard, this layered, full-bodied wine has superb purity, striking minerality, and builds incrementally in the mouth, finishing with rather high-toned flavors that are buttressed by good, crisp acidity. It is a prodigious Chardonnay and comes across like a California version of Chevalier-Montrachet. This wine is young and unevolved, and I suspect it will hit its prime in 1–3 years and last for up to a decade.

2002 Chardonnay Vine Hill Vineyard
RATING: 95 points

A spectacular offering, the 2002 Chardonnay Vine Hill Vineyard (adjacent to the Kistler winery) tastes like a California version of a great Bâtard-Montrachet. This dense, rich, layered, multidimensional Chardonnay builds incrementally in the mouth to reveal leesy notes intermixed with liquid minerals, lemon rind, citrus oils, and orange marmalade. Like its siblings, it reveals subtle oak notes along with great purity, tremendous palate presence, full body, and a majestic style. However, patience will be required. Anticipated maturity: now–2012.

2001 Chardonnay Vine Hill Vineyard
RATING: 95 points

A brilliant effort, the 2001 Chardonnay Vine Hill Vineyard is tightly knit, but full-bodied and powerful, with an oily texture buttressed by considerable acidity. Citrus oil, buttered tropical fruit, mineral, and roasted nut characteristics are present in this gorgeous offering. Full-bodied, pure yet well structured, this terrific effort will drink well for 5–8 years.

2000 Chardonnay Vine Hill Vineyard
RATING: 91 points

The 2000 Chardonnay Vine Hill Vineyard is long and textured. Along with its liquid minerality, it possesses orange marmalade/tangerine, citrus oil, white fruit, and subtle wood notes. The wine is medium to full–bodied and admirably perfumed. This is a stunning Chardonnay to enjoy over the next 6–7 years.

1999 Chardonnay Vine Hill Vineyard
RATING: 95 points

An awesome effort is the 1999 Chardonnay Vine Hill Vineyard. It exhibits telltale minerality as well as a gorgeous nose of white fruits, citrus oils, nuts, minerals, smoke, and butter. With fabulous intensity, purity, and an expansive, multilayered mid-palate, this powerful, impeccably balanced, restrained Chardonnay unfolds on the palate. This wine will have a long and compelling evolution. Anticipated maturity: now–2007.

1998 Chardonnay Vine Hill Vineyard
RATING: 95 points

The 1998 Chardonnay Vine Hill Vineyard is profound. It is a spectacular Chardonnay. Amazingly, a meager 23 tons of fruit emerged from this 15-acre vineyard, and this wine represents the essence of Chardonnay from Vine Hill. Its extraordinary precision, intense mouth-feel, and glorious display of pure fruit come across in a full-bodied, perfectly balanced fashion, making for a riveting drinking experience. It may last for more than a decade, and evolve much like a great grand cru white Burgundy. Anticipated maturity: now–2010+.

1997 Chardonnay Vine Hill Vineyard
RATING: 92 points

The 1997 Chardonnay Vine Hill Vineyard (from both Hyde and Dijon Burgundy clones) is a more restrained wine with noticeably higher acidity. It reveals suggestions of cold steel, wet stones, and that liquid minerality found in certain Chardonnays. Medium to full–bodied, with excellent depth. Anticipated maturity: now.

PINOT NOIR CUVEE CATHERINE

2003 Pinot Noir Cuvée Catherine
RATING: 94–96 points

The 2003 Pinot Noir Cuvée Catherine has a ruby/purple color, a big, ripe, framboise and currant fruit nose with some floral notes, forest floor, and a touch of new oak. The wine has great purity, medium to full body, and a long finish with good acidity. Anticipated maturity: 2007–2016.

2002 Pinot Noir Cuvée Catherine
RATING: 95 points

The 2002 Pinot Noir Cuvée Catherine, which comes from the Kistler Vineyard, is a 500-case cuvée that shows wonderful notes of flowers intermixed with black raspberries, cherries, and forest floor. It is medium-bodied, impressive, and long and authoritative. It should drink well for 10–12 years.

2000 Pinot Noir Cuvée Catherine

RATING: 96 points

The profound 2000 Pinot Noir Cuvée Catherine is a wine of extraordinary ripeness and richness, with intense violet aromas mixed with scents of blackberry and cherry liqueur. This exceptional Pinot Noir should drink well for another 9–11 years.

1999 Pinot Noir Cuvée Catherine

RATING: 95 points

The 1999 Pinot Noir Cuvée Catherine, a selection of the best barrels from the Kistler Vineyard, displays a bouquet of roasted meats, earth, truffle, blackberry, raspberry, and smoky cherry fruit. Full body, an unctuous texture, and terrific acidity define this large-scaled effort. A monumental Pinot Noir that has to be tasted to be believed, it should hit its prime within the next year and last for 12–15 years, if not longer.

1998 Pinot Noir Cuvée Catherine

RATING: 95 points

The dense ruby/purple–colored 1998 Pinot Noir Cuvée Catherine displays a spectacular floral, black raspberry, and cherry-scented nose. Compelling fruit purity offers jammy cherry, strawberry, and smoky aromas with hints of violets (or is it lilacs?). Full body, fine underlying acidity, and sweet tannin make for a sumptuous wine. Anticipated maturity: now–2012.

1997 Pinot Noir Cuvée Catherine

RATING: 95 points

The wine's 14% alcohol is totally obscured by its sensational concentration, extract, and overall equilibrium. A dense ruby/purple–colored, full-bodied Pinot Noir, it offers up aromas of blackberries, raspberries, and cherry liqueur intermixed with licorice, smoke, and meat. Chewy yet not heavy, this wine does reveal some tannin, but it is largely hidden by the wine's fruit, glycerin, and extract. Anticipated maturity: now.

PINOT NOIR CUVEE ELIZABETH

2003 Pinot Noir Cuvée Elizabeth

RATING: 92–95 points

While I don't like to choose between daughters, Kistler's other daughter gets her name on the 2003 Pinot Noir Cuvée Elizabeth. I preferred Kistler's 2003 Pinot Noir Cuvée Catherine to the 2003 Cuvée Elizabeth, which reveals raspberry, pomegranate, cherry, and plum notes, crisp, tart acidity, some flowery characteristics, a lovely, medium-bodied mid-palate, and a good finish with vibrant acidity. It is like picking between champion racehorses, as these are all impressive Pinot Noirs, but made in a far more feminine and delicate style than the Kistler Pinot Noirs of the past. Anticipated maturity: 2007–2019.

2002 Pinot Noir Cuvée Elizabeth

RATING: 95 points

This wine is spectacular, and it gets a slight nod over the 2002 Cuvée Catherine because it just seems to have a few more layers of flavor crammed into its medium to full–bodied personality. Wonderfully floral, raspberry, and kirsch notes emerge from this wine, which also shows a touch of toast, some rocky crushed-stone notes, beautiful texture, and vibrant acidity. I wouldn't be surprised to see this wine age effortlessly for 10–15 years. It is certainly a terrific Pinot Noir which, as I said last year, comes across as California's Musigny.

2000 Pinot Noir Cuvée Elizabeth

RATING: 99 points

The 2000 Pinot Noir Cuvée Elizabeth is profound. An opaque purple color is followed by gorgeous aromas of white flowers, minerals, black raspberries, cherries, and toast. It is slightly tight (from high tannin), and boasts layers of flavor, astonishing purity as well as fruit intensity, and a finish that lasts for nearly a minute. Anticipated maturity: now–2015.

1999 Pinot Noir Cuvée Elizabeth

RATING: 96 points

There are 150 cases of the dense purple–colored 1999 Pinot Noir Cuvée Elizabeth. Blueberry and boysenberry liqueur infused with minerals and violets make for dazzling olfactory fireworks. On the palate, the wine is sumptuous yet remarkably fresh and lively. The wine has incredible concentration, purity, and overall equilibrium. Anticipated maturity: now–2012.

WINES:

Chardonnay Marcassin Vineyard
Pinot Noir Marcassin Vineyard
Pinot Noir Blue Slide Ridge
Chardonnay Three Sisters Vineyard
OWNERS: Helen Turley and John Wetlaufer
ADDRESS: P.O. Box 332, Calistoga, CA 94515
TELEPHONE: (707) 258-3608 (voice mail for Marcassin)
TELEFAX: (707) 942-5633
VISITING POLICY: No reception of the general public

VINEYARDS

SURFACE AREA: 8.5–18.5 acres
Blue Slide and Three Sisters vineyards are on the same ridge on the Sonoma coast, developed and farmed by the Martinellis to Marcassin specifications and shared 50/50 with the Martinelli Winery.
GRAPE VARIETALS: Chardonnay and Pinot Noir
AVERAGE AGE OF THE VINES: Old vines 8.5–12 years
DENSITY OF PLANTATION: Various, but very dense spacing
AVERAGE YIELDS: 2–3 tons per acre, depending on vine age

WINEMAKING AND UPBRINGING

The Chardonnay is whole-cluster pressed very cold and fermented with native/indigenous yeasts. Helen Turley ferments the wines dry prior to malolactic fermentation, and then performs an *élevage* on the lees, with lee-stirring (*bâtonnage*) for 6–8 months. The Chardonnay is only racked once, and that is to a holding tank for bottling after 12 months in barrel. All the wines are bottled without filtration after having spent those 12 months in 100% new François Frères barrels. The Pinot Noir is destemmed, the berries uncrushed, and the wine is fermented in 2.5- to 3-ton stainless-steel fermenters. These temperature-controlled fermentation tanks are quite squat, and for part of the fermentation the Pinot is given a cold soak of 3–4 days. Natural yeasts kick off the fermentation, and there is gentle aerating and pumping-over. The wine is pressed very gently and moved by gravity to barrel where it is racked only once prior to bottling, after 12 months in 100% new François Frères barrels. Like the Chardonnay, it is bottled unfiltered.

ANNUAL PRODUCTION

Chardonnay Marcassin Vineyard: 400 cases
Pinot Noir Marcassin Vineyard: 600 cases
Pinot Noir Blue Slide: 400 cases
Chardonnay Three Sisters: 400 cases
AVERAGE PRICE (VARIABLE DEPENDING ON VINTAGE): $75

GREAT RECENT VINTAGES

2002, 2001, 2000, 1998, 1996

Winemaker/proprietor Helen Turley, a tall, statuesque blond of almost Viking proportions, and her husband, John Wetlaufer, believe the soils, elevation, and microclimate of a top vineyard site are essential. Their Marcassin Vineyard is planted on a ridge just east of the Pacific Ocean, with an exceptional exposition and slope. Their viticulture, which is radical by all means, is focused on harvesting fully mature and uniformly ripe fruit, something they seem able to achieve through meticulous viticultural techniques in every vintage. The soils of the Marcassin vineyard are 18–24 inches of gravelly loam over highly fractured rock of marine volcanic origin, known as greenstone or basalt. They have exceptional drainage, which in many ways sets the vineyard apart from others on the Sonoma coast that are a not pure rock, but with clays.

Fortunately for wine consumers and for the stature of California wines, there has been increasing attention paid to the philosophy of Helen Turley and John Wetlaufer. Ms. Turley is a strong-minded, immensely talented woman who began her career at Robert Mondavi, and has become a leading consultant for some of the finest wineries in California. She also deserves credit for her positive influence on a younger generation of winemakers that is increasingly dedicated to capturing the full character of the vineyard and the grape varietal. Hers is the antithesis of the industrial, food-processor mentality eschewed by technicians at the University of California at Davis that has dominated California winemaking. With Ms. Turley and her husband, as well as the growing number of similarly minded peers, rests the hope for what I see as a splendid golden age for California wine.

Bottled without fining or filtration, Marcassin's Chardonnays are extraordinary examples of this varietal. I utilize nearly all of my allocation each year in blind tastings with Burgundy experts, placing the Marcassin wines in vinous confrontations with France's greatest Montrachets, Chevalier-Montrachets, Bâtard-Montrachets, and Corton-Charlemagnes. Most of the time the Marcassin wines run away with top honors from other tasters who are admitted Burgundy wine fanatics. There are no secrets to Marcassin's success. Low yields, a noninterventionist winemaking philosophy that eschews any type of processing in favor of wild yeasts, and no acidification, fining, or filtration combine in a magical manner to produce intense wines of razor-sharp clarity and complexity.

Helen Turley and John Wetlaufer continue to rank at the top of a short list of producers making the world's most prodigious, complex wines. Their wines are available through the winery's mailing list, although some preferred Napa Valley restaurants, particularly the French Laundry, and some in New York (such as Daniel and Le Bernardin), seem to receive noteworthy allocations. For wine-lovers interested in California Chardonnay that is more complete, complex, and compelling than all but a handful of the greatest white Burgundies, Marcassin is a cherished name.

Marcassin's unfiltered Chardonnays are among the world's most concentrated and provocative wines, with a degree of complexity and balance that must be tasted to be believed.

CHARDONNAY MARCASSIN VINEYARD

2002 Chardonnay Marcassin Vineyard

RATING: 96+ points

As usual, the 2002 Chardonnay Marcassin Vineyard is the most noble, complex effort of Marcassin's Chardonnays, but it has unquestionably gone into a shell. This dense, chewy 2002 behaves more like a grand cru white Burgundy than a typical California Chardonnay. Powerful, concentrated, and profound, it requires 1–2 years of bottle age, and should last for a decade or more.

2001 Chardonnay Marcassin Vineyard

RATING: 96 points

From one of the New World's true grand cru vineyards, and always a candidate for Chardonnay of the vintage since its debut release in 1996, the 2001 Chardonnay Marcassin Vineyard boasts a liqueur of rocks in its big, leesy, honeysuckle-scented nose, along with buttery, caramelized citrus; a hint of tropical fruit; huge, ripe notes of nectarines; smoke; and minerals. This beautiful Chardonnay should hit its prime in 2–3 years, and last for a decade.

John Wetlaufer and Helen Turley

2000 Chardonnay Marcassin Vineyard

RATING: 98 points

The exquisite 2000 Chardonnay Marcassin Vineyard is a broad, gorgeously perfumed, light green/gold–colored effort revealing tremendous power as well as notes of hazelnuts intermixed with white peaches, citrus oils, and other exotic fruits. It has great depth, tremendous delineation, a firm underpinning of acidity, and a 50-second finish. Anticipated maturity: 2014.

1999 Chardonnay Marcassin Vineyard

RATING: 97+ points

The 1999 Chardonnay Marcassin Vineyard recalls the 1985 Niellon Bâtard-Montrachet or Chevalier. It offers up extraordinary, concentrated honeyed pineapple fruit intermixed with candied orange and lemon peel, liquid stones, and a steely finish. It is layered, with superb purity. This work of art should drink well for 10–12 years.

1998 Chardonnay Marcassin Vineyard

RATING: 99 points

The 1998 Chardonnay Marcassin Vineyard is a phenomenal effort! Its 14.9% alcohol is hidden beneath a cascade of aromas and flavors suggesting a liqueur made from crushed seashells, candied citrus, honeysuckle, and lemon butter. It is rich and full-bodied, with an unctuous texture, good acidity that provides a significant framework for the wine's intensity and concentration, and an extraordinary finish. This is a virtually perfect Chardonnay—again! Drink it over the next decade.

1997 Chardonnay Marcassin Vineyard

RATING: 96 points

Although tight, the 1997 Chardonnay Marcassin Vineyard offers up gorgeous notes of liquefied oranges, hazelnuts, and citrus oils, with high levels of acidity, a backward, full-bodied palate impression, and a finish that lasts over 40 seconds. It should age effortlessly for a decade.

1996 Chardonnay Marcassin Vineyard

RATING: 99 points

The 1996 Chardonnay Marcassin Vineyard boasts record setting levels of complexity, richness, individuality—and let's not forget joy. It is an extraordinary wine that somehow manages to juxtapose complexity, elegance, and finesse with unbridled power, richness, and layers of flavor. The 1996 Chardonnay Marcassin Vineyard should drink well for at least another 6–7 years. Bravo!

CHARDONNAY THREE SISTERS VINEYARD

2002 Chardonnay Three Sisters Vineyard

RATING: 96 points

Smoky hazelnuts intermixed with notions of caramel and buttered citrus are present in the 2002 Chardonnay Three Sisters Vineyard. While full-bodied, layered, dense, and flamboyant, it is closed when compared to my tasting notes from 2003. Anticipated maturity: 2006–2013.

2001 Chardonnay Three Sisters Vineyard

RATING: 95 points

The 2001 Chardonnay Three Sisters Vineyard is crisp, with minerality, definition, and subtle richness. Orange blossom, marzipan, citrus oil, crushed stones, and a touch of smoky scents emerge from this full-bodied wine. It offers beautiful honeyed richness, great definition, and a long finish. I even noticed a hint of papaya. Drink it over the next 7–10 years.

2000 Chardonnay Three Sisters Vineyard

RATING: 92 points

The 2000 Chardonnay Three Sisters Vineyard reveals a gorgeous minerality along with rich lemon oil, full body, and impeccably high quality. Anticipated maturity: now–2009.

1999 Chardonnay Three Sisters Vineyard

RATING: 97 points

The 1999 Chardonnay Three Sisters Vineyard possesses aromas of honeyed lemon, smoky hazelnuts, minerals, pineapples, and a hint of passion fruit. The oak is beautifully integrated, and the wine is exceptionally long in the mouth. This is a grand cru lookalike. Enjoy it over the next 4–6 years.

1998 Chardonnay Three Sisters Vineyard

RATING: 92 points

The 1998 Chardonnay Three Sisters Vineyard reveals copious amounts of mineral, lemon, and honeyed citrus characteristics, along with good underlying acidity and a custardy com-

plexity. There are hints of pineapple and smoky oak in the finish. Anticipated maturity: now–2012.

PINOT NOIR BLUE SLIDE RIDGE

2002 Pinot Noir Blue Slide Ridge

RATING: 90+? points

The 2002 Pinot Noir Blue Slide Ridge, which was virtually perfect a year ago, appears to be going through an unusual stage. I detected some noticeable volatile acidity along with jammy plum, animal, and composty characteristics, broad, provocative flavors, full body, loads of density, and DRC-like floral/forest floor notes. For all its positive attributes, there appear to be some burgeoning features that could prove to be flaws down the road. An awkward wine, it's hard to figure out where it's going—hence the question mark. Anticipated maturity: 2007–2013.

2001 Pinot Noir Blue Slide Ridge

RATING: 92 points

Fragrant aromas of damp earth, fresh mushrooms, gravel, anise, plums, and cherries emerge from the 2001 Pinot Noir Blue Slide Ridge, which reveals this vineyard's distinctive perfume and singular quality. An atypical note of herbaceousness is also present. Drink this gamy, rich, complex 2001 over the next 7–10 years.

2000 Pinot Noir Blue Slide Ridge

RATING: 96 points

The 2000 Pinot Noir Blue Slide Ridge, my candidate for a DRC Richebourg on steroids vote, possesses the extraordinary aromatics that this vineyard routinely produces. The blueberry, blackberry, forest floor, mushroom, and gamy notes are all offered in a provocative smorgasbord of aromas. There is tremendous fruit intensity, medium to full body, outstanding acid levels, and a long, textured, spectacular finish. It is a compelling Pinot Noir to drink over the next 7–8 years.

1999 Pinot Noir Blue Slide Ridge

RATING: 98 points

The 1999 Pinot Noir Blue Slide Ridge is composed of pure black fruits mixed with floral overtones. It is dense, opulent, and nearly viscous with extraordinary purity and concentration. It comes across as a New World version of perhaps Domaine de la Romanée-Conti's La Tache or Richebourg, or a Claude Dugat or Dugat-Py grand cru. It is an awesome effort that falls just short of perfection. Anticipated maturity: now–2010.

1998 Pinot Noir Blue Slide Ridge

RATING: 98 points

The 1998 Pinot Noir Blue Slide Ridge exhibits a grand cru Burgundy-like perfume of plum liqueur intermixed with soy, underbrush, and roasted meats in a more foresty, autumnal style than the 1999, 2000, and 2001. There is sweet black cherry fruit as well as a pronounced earthy, animal-like character to this wine. It is compelling Pinot Noir. Anticipated maturity: now–2010.

1997 Pinot Noir Blue Slide Ridge

RATING: 96 points

The spectacularly complex, opulently textured, lavishly rich 1997 Pinot Noir Blue Slide Ridge displays a saturated plum/purple color in addition to gorgeous aromas of blueberries, black cherries, lavender, and smoky oak. Intense and full-bodied, with fabulous concentration, a voluptuous texture, and a long finish, this is a stunning effort. Anticipated maturity: now–2008.

PINOT NOIR MARCASSIN VINEYARD

2002 Pinot Noir Marcassin Vineyard

RATING: 96 points

The brilliant 2002 Pinot Noir Marcassin Vineyard boasts copious quantities of blue, red, and black fruit in addition to a youthful, concentrated, full-bodied style with impressive minerality, and a liqueur of wet rocks intermingled with beautiful fruit, floral, and forest floor notes. With excellent acidity, it should prove to be uncommonly long-lived by California Pinot Noir standards. It should last for 10–15 years.

2001 Pinot Noir Marcassin Vineyard

RATING: 93 points

The plum/ruby-colored, earthy, meaty, smoky 2001 Pinot Noir Marcassin Vineyard possesses Morey-St.-Denis–like characteristics of plums, mushrooms, forest floor, and flowers. Rich, medium to full–bodied, moderately tannic, and structured, it should be enjoyed between 2007 and 2015.

2000 Pinot Noir Marcassin Vineyard

RATING: 97 points

The magnificent 2000 Pinot Noir Marcassin Vineyard continues to develop even more complexity. Truly great stuff, this medium to full–bodied 2000 exhibits scents of rose petals intertwined with charcuterie, spring flowers, blue and black fruits, and hints of raspberries, cola, and mint oil. This profound, extremely nuanced, powerful, exuberant Pinot Noir boasts terrific definition and personality. Anticipated maturity: now–2014.

1999 Pinot Noir Marcassin Vineyard

RATING: 95 points

The 1999 Pinot Noir Marcassin Vineyard is less flamboyant than the ostentatious Blue Slide *cuvée*. It exhibits more animal, plum, raspberry, and earthy characteristics (meaty porcinis come to mind) in its broodingly backward, mineral-dominated personality. Additionally, there is great structure and purity, as well as layers of fruit and intensity. Anticipated maturity: 2004–2014.

1998 Pinot Noir Marcassin Vineyard

RATING: 98 points

The 1998 Pinot Noir Marcassin Vineyard is similar to a hypothetical blend of a grand cru Musigny and a grand cru such as Clos de la Roche. This is an extraordinary accomplishment. This firmly structured, precise offering exhibits notes of figs, plum liqueur, black cherries, wet stones, smoked duck, and gorgeous red and black fruits. It is a very Burgundian, gamy, earthy effort with incredibly sweet fruit that hides the 14.9% alcohol. This Pinot Noir will drink well young, and last for at least a decade.

1997 Pinot Noir Marcassin Vineyard

RATING: 95 points

The 1997 Pinot Noir Marcassin Vineyard is a closed, backward offering. Its dark ruby/purple color is followed by aromas of compost, earth, plums, figs, black cherries, and raspberries. It behaves like a grand cru from Morey-St.-Denis, possessing bracing acidity, a dense, concentrated finish, and superb purity. It will last for 10–12 years.

1996 Pinot Noir Marcassin Vineyard

RATING: 95 points

To get a snapshot of what the outstanding 1996 Pinot Noir Marcassin Vineyard is really about is to recognize that it is reminiscent of the finest grand crus I have tasted from such sites as Clos de la Roche and Clos St.-Denis. It shares an extraordinary minerality with fabulously concentrated plum, black cherry, blueberry/blackberry characteristics. It is full-bodied, dense, concentrated and alcoholic. Anticipated maturity: now–2012.

WINES:

Les Pavots Proprietary Red

Chardonnay Belle Côte

Chardonnay Mon Plaisir

Chardonnay La Carrière

Chardonnay Cuvée Indigène

Chardonnay Point Rouge

OWNER: Sir Peter Michael

ADDRESS: 12400 Ida Clayton Road, Calistoga, CA 94515

TELEPHONE: (707) 942-4459

TELEFAX: (707) 942-8314

E-MAIL: info@petermichaelwinery.com

WEBSITE: www.petermichaelwinery.com

CONTACT: Bill Vyenielo (General Manager)

VISITING POLICY: By appointment only

VINEYARDS

SURFACE AREA: 112 acres of vines

GRAPE VARIETALS: Chardonnay, Sauvignon Blanc, Pinot Noir, Cabernet/Merlot/Cabernet Franc/Petit Verdot

AVERAGE AGE OF THE VINES: Chardonnay planted 1991–1994; Cabernet/Merlot/Cabernet Franc/Petit Verdot planted 1989

DENSITY OF PLANTATION: Vine spacing ranges from 3' x 6' to 5' x 8'

AVERAGE YIELDS: 2.5 tons of grapes per acre

WINEMAKING AND UPBRINGING

The essence of the handcrafted, naturally fermented wines of Peter Michael is the result of several key efforts. First and foremost is extremely gentle handling of the fruit. All vineyards at Peter Michael are hand-picked in very small capacity logs to avoid compaction and to prevent the grapes from bursting open. At the winery, a second major effort is made to meticulously sort through the fruit. Every major winery today has a triage table, and at Peter Michael it is a complicated, finely calibrated one that is designed to deliver the fruit by gravity to the press for the white wines and into the destemmer for the red wines, with virtually no damage or blemishes to the individual grape berries. The red grapes even go through a second triage after destemming in order to eliminate, berry by berry, small stems and any vegetal materials that can add bitter tannins to the finished wines.

All the Chardonnay grapes are whole-cluster pressed, which ferments to yield the gentlest and finest pure grape juice. The winemakers use Burgundian techniques for both the whites and reds. The whites are aged on their lees and given *bâ-tonnage* (lee-stirring) after malolactic fermentation in barrel. The lees are stirred at least once a week for 6–9 months, which adds roundness and complexity. Most of the Chardonnays spend a total of 10–14 months *sur-lies*. The barrels are then racked in to a cold storage tank and bottled without any filtration. The Cabernet-based Les Pavots is also fermented naturally with indigenous yeasts, and more recently has enjoyed very long, extended macerations ranging from 21 days to a record of 56 days for the 2001 vintage. A selection of only his finest barrels goes into the top wine, Les Pavots. Peter Michael is meticulous about the use of French oak barrels. Each barrel regime is tailored to the specific *terroir* and *cuvée*, and can range from as little as 12% new oak to as much as 80%.

ANNUAL PRODUCTION

Les Pavots Proprietary Red: 30,000 bottles

Chardonnay Belle Côte: 24,000 bottles

Chardonnay Mon Plaisir: 22,000 bottles

Chardonnay La Carrière: 21,000 bottles

Chardonnay Cuvée Indigène: 6,000 bottles

Chardonnay Point Rouge: 2,000 bottles

AVERAGE PRICE (VARIABLE DEPENDING ON VINTAGE): $60–120

GREAT RECENT VINTAGES:

Chardonnay: 2003, 2002, 2001, 1997, 1996, 1983

Les Pavots: 2002, 2001, 1997, 1994, 1992, 1991

Since its first vintage in 1987, the mission of the Peter Michael Winery has been to produce only a limited quantity of unique world-class quality wines from properly sited and meticulously maintained mountain vineyards. The winemaking philosophy can be defined as neoclassical—marrying the best of the New and Old World winemaking knowledge and traditions. It is irrefutable that the New World's technology and unhindered freedom to experiment in the winery and the vineyards have fostered incredible advances in wine quality in just the last 15 years. The Peter Michael Winery's Old World classical practices (hand sorting of grapes, fermenting with indigenous yeast, and not filtering their wines), modeled after the best French producers, embrace a minimal interventionist approach that guarantees that their wines are the most natural and authentic expressions of the vineyard.

The Peter Michael Winery has seen some of California's finest winemaking talents pass through its doors, including Helen Turley, Mark Aubert, Vanessa Wong, and the Burgundian Luc Morlet, who is currently serving as winemaker.

In the late 1980s, Peter Michael Winery was pioneering in the use of natural yeast present on the grapes to carry out fermentation. The resulting wine displayed a heightened aromatic complexity and an amazing texture, roundness, and length. Back then they added the designation "Cuvée Indigène" to honor this natural "indigenous" technique, a practice now employed in the making of every Peter Michael wine.

Dedication to this approach has made Peter Michael one of the most exciting wineries in not only Sonoma County, but the world. Englishman Sir Peter Michael had the foresight to hire the brilliant Helen Turley to oversee the winemaking (Ms. Turley has now left this estate in order to pursue her own venture), and the current vineyard/winemaking team shares Ms. Turley's winemaking philosophy. The present as well as upcoming releases are irrefutably brilliant wines. Rare is the winery that can make exceptional Sauvignon, multiple *cuvées* of profoundly rich Chardonnays, and a Bordeaux-styled, classy, complex red wine.

All of Peter Michael's top wines, including the Chardonnays, are bottled without filtration because of

its deleterious effect on the aging process of Chardonnay. Case in point: Peter Michael produced two *cuvées* of 1988 Chardonnay Mon Plaisir, one filtered (the one most likely to have been purchased commercially) and one unfiltered (called the Red Dot Cuvée because Helen Turley had put a red dot on the label). Both wines were exactly the same except for the handling they received at bottling. When I tasted the wines during a visit in 1994, the filtered wine was stale, with an absence of any fruit in the bouquet, and short, compact flavors. The unfiltered "Red Dot" Mon Plaisir was honeyed, vibrant, and rich, having lost none of its freshness or fruit.

The blend for Peter Michael's Les Pavots proprietary red wine varies year to year, but the composition usually includes at least 70% Cabernet Sauvignon, 5–15% Merlot, and 5–15% Cabernet Franc. They use 60% new French oak casks. The result is a wine that comes as close as any other California Cabernet Sauvignon–based wine to resembling a structured, rich, complex St.-Julien/Pauillac. The wine is more broad-shouldered and deep than most Bordeaux. Readers should be forewarned that Les Pavots is not made in an up-front, fruity style that begs for immediate consumption. They are rich, full-bodied, complex, restrained wines built for the long haul. That being said, Peter Michael's Les Pavots has enjoyed an unprecedented string of highly successful vintages.

Readers should make it a point to visit this winery situated in the beautiful Knights Valley, not far from the Napa/Sonoma county line. The quality is extraordinary, and the commitment and talent of the winery staff laudatory.

CHARDONNAY BELLE COTE

2003 Chardonnay Belle Côte
RATING: 95 points

The biggest production of any of Peter Michael's 2003 *cuvées* is the 2003 Belle Côte (2,900 cases; 15% alcohol). Exotic lychee, pineapple, and marmalade notes (which suggest tremendous ripeness) along with a refined, sophisticated structure result in a sensational glass of full-bodied Chardonnay that is well delineated for its size and power. This is pretty sensational stuff and has good availability. Anticipated maturity: now–2013.

2002 Chardonnay Belle Côte
RATING: 95 points

A big offering is the 2002 Chardonnay Belle Côte. Filled with pure tropical fruit characteristics, it is a full-bodied, exotic Chardonnay offering up tremendous notes of smoky hazelnuts as well as lychee nuts presented in a ripe, gorgeously balanced style with a decidedly California personality, but with more definition than most California Chardonnays of this size and intensity. It is made primarily from the old Wente clone of Chardonnay planted on clay-dominated soils. It is best drunk during its first 3–4 years of life.

2001 Chardonnay Belle Côte
RATING: 94 points

The 2001 Chardonnay Belle Côte exhibits exotic tropical fruit notes, a layered, opulent texture, medium to full body, less minerality than La Carrière, beautiful layers of fruit, and a stunning finish. This brilliant effort should drink well for another 4–6 years.

1999 Chardonnay Belle Côte
RATING: 90 points

The fourth vintage for this estate's Belle Côte Chardonnay, the 1999 was produced from three clones of Chardonnay (the Old Wente, Rued, and See). It reveals gorgeous aromas and flavors of tropical fruits, lemon zest, pears, and minerals. This authoritatively rich, complex, elegant Chardonnay is medium-bodied, well delineated, and beautifully concentrated, with exotic floral and spice notes in addition to well-integrated oak. It should drink well for another 1–2 years.

CHARDONNAY LA CARRIERE

2003 Chardonnay La Carrière
RATING: 97 points

The 2003 La Carrière tastes like a grand cru from Corton-Charlemagne, with yeasty, earthy, mineral notes that are present in liqueur-like levels. Some heady, honeyed citrus and orange blossom characteristics add to the complexity of this gorgeous, full-bodied effort with zesty acidity. It emerges from the volcanic ash (tufa) soils of this site. Look for this wine to drink well for 5–7 years.

2002 Chardonnay La Carrière
RATING: 95 points

A French-styled offering, it is made from a vineyard planted in soils filled with white volcanic ash, and is aged completely in Louis Latour barrels. It possesses an exquisite liquid minerality as well as gorgeous aromas of citrus oils intermixed with such exotic tropical fruits as guava and passion fruit. Full-

bodied, with dazzling palate penetration, fine balance, and an extraordinary, layered, multidimensional feel, this is one of the single greatest Chardonnays I have recently tasted. It is a brilliant blend of French finesse with California power that should drink well for 5–7 years, possibly longer.

2001 Chardonnay La Carrière

RATING: 94 points

The knockout 2001 Chardonnay La Carrière offers honeyed citrus, liquid mineral, floral, and exotic tropical fruit characteristics as well as admirable definition, texture, body, and richness. Although I suspect the acids are high, the wine is more concentrated than the 2000, with more depth as well as fruit. This brilliant effort should age nicely for another 4–7 years.

1999 Chardonnay La Carrière

RATING: 91 points

The 1999 La Carrière reveals roasted hazelnut/stony characteristics along with abundant spice, buttered pears, and guava-like fruit. Produced from extremely low yields of 1.7 tons of fruit per acre, it possesses a creamy texture, exotic fruit on the mid-palate, and a ripe, rich finish with fine underlying acidity. It is a brilliant Chardonnay that should last another 1–2 years.

CHARDONNAY CUVEE INDIGENE

2003 Chardonnay Cuvée Indigène

RATING: 97 points

The 2003 Cuvée Indigène (500 cases) has a big, smoky, roasted nut–scented nose intermixed with honeysuckle, buttered citrus, and crème brûlée characteristics, and a long, rich, mineral-laden finish with good acidity and definition. Some white peach notes are also present in this beauty, which should age nicely for 7–8 years.

2002 Chardonnay Cuvée Indigène

RATING: 95+ points

The 2002 Chardonnay Cuvée Indigène comes from a parcel of Chardonnay vines made famous by Helen Turley, the Upper Barn/Gauer Ranch, renamed the Alexander Valley Mountain Estate when it was acquired by Jess Jackson. This 2002 exhibits wonderfully buttered orange, brioche, and ripe citrus notes, terrific minerality, and a full-bodied, layered, concentrated, intense style. It is brilliantly balanced by zesty acidity that provides a refreshing as well as vigorous personality. Anticipated maturity: now–2014.

2001 Chardonnay Cuvée Indigène

RATING: 95 points

The blockbuster 2001 Chardonnay Cuvée Indigène possesses an oily, unctuous texture in addition to smoky, leesy, peach, honeysuckle, and lemon zest aromatics, and dense, deep, full-bodied flavors with great texture, richness, and purity. It is a superb Chardonnay to enjoy over the next 8–9 years.

1999 Chardonnay Cuvée Indigène

RATING: 93 points

The 1999 exhibits distinctive aromas of smoky tropical fruit intermixed with peaches, apricots, and pears. Long, full-bodied, and layered, with terrific texture, gorgeous purity, and loads of fruit, this effort can stand up against the finest Burgundy grand crus. The Cuvée Indigène possesses leesy, smoky notes in its rich, concentrated style. It is a young, pure, super-concentrated Chardonnay to enjoy over the next year (although it may last nearly a decade). Anticipated maturity: now–2006.

1998 Chardonnay Cuvée Indigène

RATING: 96 points

This Chardonnay is terrific on the palate, displaying explosive lemon/butter/honey flavors mixed with tropical fruit, mineral, and smoky, leesy components. Orange/tangerine notes also make an appearance. Anticipated maturity: now.

CHARDONNAY MON PLAISIR

2003 Chardonnay Mon Plaisir

RATING: 94 points

The 2003 Chardonnay Mon Plaisir offers wonderful lemon butter and tropical fruit notes with hints of brioche and hazelnut. It is a broad, flavorful, concentrated, lush, heady Chardonnay to drink over the next 4–5 years.

2002 Chardonnay Mon Plaisir

RATING: 94 points

The 2002 Chardonnay Mon Plaisir is a full-bodied, beautifully textured, opulent effort revealing notes of honeyed pineapple, orange marmalade, and oily flavors backed up by zesty acidity. This big, rich, exuberant Chardonnay is already purring on all cylinders. Drink it over the next 3–5 years.

2001 Chardonnay Mon Plaisir

RATING: 93 points

The 2001 Chardonnay Mon Plaisir boasts wonderfully sweet notes of orange marmalade, apple skins, buttered citrus, vanilla, and subtle wood. It is full-bodied, rich, and pure, with terrific acidity providing freshness as well as delineation. It will drink well for another 4–6 years.

1999 Chardonnay Mon Plaisir

RATING: 91 points

One of the most flamboyant Peter Michael Chardonnays is their *cuvée* Mon Plaisir. Produced from the Old Wente clone grown in the Alexander Mountain Estate Vineyard owned by Jess Jackson, and aged totally in French oak (50% new), the 1999 Chardonnay Mon Plaisir reveals abundant tropical fruit characteristics in its ostentatious bouquet. Aromas of oranges, ripe honeyed apples, and buttered citrus jump from the glass of this hedonistically styled Chardonnay. The integration of wood provides subtle notes of vanilla and toast, which add to the wine's complex personality. Medium to full–bodied, pure, long, and concentrated, with enough acidity to provide freshness and focus, it will drink well for another year or two.

CHARDONNAY POINT ROUGE

2003 Chardonnay Point Rouge

RATING: 98 points

The *tête de cuvée*, or selection of the finest barrels each year, receives the Point Rouge designation, named after the first bottling of Point Rouge done by Helen Turley in the late 1980s. This offering intentionally pushes the envelope of Chardonnay. It is a wine of fabulous purity, intensity, and ripeness with broad, expansive flavors, and a perfume of extraordinarily floral, honeysuckle notes intermixed with marmalade, lemon oil, and such exotic tropical fruits as mango and papaya. The wood is kept well in check because of good acidity, as it is for all these wines. Recent Chardonnay vintages, particularly those made under the administration of Luc Morlet, have possessed light straw colors with a greenish hue, similar to the color of a top-notch French white Burgundy. Morlet claims this comes from chlorophyll and considers it a good sign for the stability and aging of the wines. The 2001s, 2002s, and 2003s all share this color characteristic. Anticipated maturity: now–2014.

2002 Chardonnay Point Rouge

RATING: 98 points

One of California's two or three most extraordinary Chardonnays, the 2002 Chardonnay Point Rouge boasts great intensity, huge body, and massive fruit as well as impeccable balance and purity. It offers up honeysuckle, orange marmalade, and sweet, oily citrus notes along with pinpoint precision, good acidity, tremendous purity, and a massive finish that lasts 35–40 seconds. Like all of these Chardonnays, it is a remarkable effort. Anticipated maturity: now–2014.

2001 Chardonnay Point Rouge

RATING: 96 points

A light green/gold color is followed by aromas of roasted hazelnuts intermixed with honeysuckle, orange skin, and sweet citrus. This expansive, powerful, packed wine boasts loads of flavor, zesty underlying acidity as well as definition, and fabulous purity and length. This profound Chardonnay can compete with the finest grand cru white Burgundies— and then some! It should drink well for a decade or more.

1999 Chardonnay Point Rouge

RATING: 94 points

The 1999 Chardonnay Point Rouge is steely, as well as closed and unevolved, but there is no doubting its immense potential. It boasts honeyed citrus, orange, tangerine, liquid mineral, and smoky hazelnut aromas. The liquid minerality evident in the Point Rouge is a prominent characteristic of the better wines from such grand cru Burgundy vineyards as Le Montrachet, Chevalier-Montrachet, and Meursault-Perrières. The finish lasts for more than 40 seconds. This wine is backward and should have a slow evolution. Anticipated maturity: now–2010. Exquisite!

1998 Chardonnay Point Rouge

RATING: 95 points

The light gold–colored 1998 Chardonnay Point Rouge displays an emerging nose of honeyed tropical fruits and citrus. It possesses exquisite concentration, admirable singularity, full body, and terrific purity and delineation. Anticipated maturity: now.

1997 Chardonnay Point Rouge

RATING: 98 points

The 1997 Chardonnay Point Rouge exhibits a terrific texture and a sensational buttery, leesy nose with subtle toasty oak. Passion fruit, oranges, and honeyed lemons compete with minerals in this exceptionally rich, concentrated Chardonnay. A spectacular, full-throttle effort with impeccable balance, it should drink well for another 1–2+ years.

LES PAVOTS PROPRIETARY RED

2003 Les Pavots Proprietary Red

RATING: 92–94 points

More downsized and not as concentrated and expressive as the 2001 and 2002 is the 2003 Les Pavots, a blend of 61% Cabernet Sauvignon, 22% Cabernet Franc, 13% Merlot, and 4% Petit Verdot. There are 2,975 cases of this offering. A floral nose of violets—or is it acacia?—intermixed with espresso roast, chocolate, smoke, and black currants is followed by a medium to full–bodied, dense, concentrated, long, rich red. At this stage of development, it is not revealing the depth, length, or potential of either the 2002 or 2001. Nevertheless, it is an impressive wine to drink between 2008 and 2020.

2002 Les Pavots Proprietary Red

RATING: 98 points

Les Pavots, one of California's great dry red wines, seems to go from strength to strength. The 2002 is the finest Les Pavots to date. A monumental effort, it is a blend of 71% Cabernet Sauvignon, 12% Merlot, 10% Cabernet Franc, and 7% Petit Verdot. And there is even more good news—there are 2,800 cases of this exceptional wine. Dense purple–colored with an extraordinary nose of melted licorice, white chocolate, crème de cassis, licorice, and incense, the wine hits the palate with a silky opulence and marvelous, full-bodied power, but it is light on its feet, with great delineation, vibrancy, and freshness. Superb purity and a finish that goes on for 50+ seconds is the stuff of modern-day California leg-

ends. This beauty is already beginning to age well yet should last easily for 18–22 years.

2001 Les Pavots Proprietary Red

RATING: 95 points

The 2001 Les Pavots merits a score several points higher than it did last year, no doubt because it has recovered from bottling and continues to gain in the bottle. This 1,853-case blend of 72% Cabernet Sauvignon, 16% Merlot, 10% Cabernet Franc, and 2% Petit Verdot exhibits a floral, blueberry, blackberry, and licorice-scented nose with smoky black currants in the background. A wine of great richness with a distinctive Graves-like, scorched-earth component to the flavors, this full-bodied, elegant, pure, well-delineated 2001 will benefit from another 1–3 years of cellaring, and should age nicely for two decades.

1999 Les Pavots Proprietary Red

RATING: 90 points

The dense purple–colored 1999 Les Pavots exhibits sweet aromas of cassis, tapenade, cherries, licorice, and subtle wood. It is medium-bodied, with a cool-climate textural profile, noticeable tannin, and a Bordeaux-like finish. It will be drinkable between now and 2015. There are only 2,342 cases.

1997 Les Pavots Proprietary Red

RATING: 96 points

The 1997 blend consists of 79% Cabernet Sauvignon, 12% Merlot, and 9% Cabernet Franc. A blue/black/purple color is followed by an extraordinary bouquet of toast, blackberries, crème de cassis, licorice, and cedar. Full-bodied, with silky tannin, low acidity, and layers of concentrated, pure black fruits judiciously wrapped in subtle toasty oak, this wine can be drunk early, but promises to hit its peak in 2–4 years, and last for two or more decades.

1996 Les Pavots Proprietary Red

RATING: 96 points

The powerhouse, opaque purple/blue–colored 1996 Les Pavots is a blend of 74% Cabernet Sauvignon, 20% Merlot, and 6% Cabernet Franc. The nose offers up blackberry, licorice, cassis, and toast aromas. The superb extract, well-defined personality, and smoky, licorice, Asian spice, and blackberry flavors provide a thrilling tasting experience. It was bottled with neither fining nor filtration. There are approximately 2,800 cases of this fabulous effort. Anticipated maturity: now–2025.

1995 Les Pavots Proprietary Red

RATING: 91 points

The black/ruby/purple-colored 1995 Les Pavots (a 73% Cabernet Sauvignon, 14% Merlot, and 13% Cabernet Franc blend), which achieved 13.9% alcohol naturally, reveals a sweet, tobacco, lavender, and cassis–scented nose, medium-bodied, tannic, elegant flavors, outstanding purity, ripeness, and length, yet a measured, restrained style. Less forthcoming than either the 1996 or 1994, this rich, nicely proportioned proprietary red is California's answer to a graceful Médoc. Anticipated maturity: now–2020.

1994 Les Pavots Proprietary Red

RATING: 94 points

This deep, saturated purple–colored wine has taken on a gorgeous nose of cassis intermixed with violets, licorice, and attractive spicy oak. Sweet, rich, and surprisingly showy for a Les Pavots, this medium to full–bodied wine possesses a luscious, multilayered texture, outstanding depth, and attractively integrated tannin and acidity. Anticipated maturity: now–2026.

1993 Les Pavots Proprietary Red

RATING: 92 points

The 1993 Les Pavots, another impressive wine from a vintage that has plenty of skeptics in the West Coast press, reveals a dense, ruby/purple color, and a complex nose of smoke, spice, toast, and black fruits. Medium to full–bodied, with an inner core of sweet, rich fruit, outstanding purity, and a powerful yet elegant personality, this layered, multidimensional wine should drink well young, but keep for 10–15+ years. Anticipated maturity: now–2016.

1992 Les Pavots Proprietary Red

RATING: 91 points

The 1992 Les Pavots, reminiscent of a top-class St.-Julien/Pauillac, is the first vintage that has begun to exhibit some complex cedar, lead pencil, and cassis aromas. Medium to full–bodied, with impressive richness, this layered, intense, yet balanced wine reveals more immediate charm and secondary aromas than its three younger siblings. It is a wine that will last for at least 10+ years. Anticipated maturity: now–2016.

1991 Les Pavots Proprietary Red

RATING: 91 points

The 1991 Les Pavots is Bordeaux-like, with a fragrant pure, black currant–scented nose, rich, medium to full–bodied flavors, and a fine underpinning of acidity and moderate tannin. Its long finish admirably combines power and intensity with finesse. It is capable of lasting for another decade. Anticipated maturity: now–2014.

WINES:

Cabernet Sauvignon Reserve

Cabernet Sauvignon To Kalon Reserve

OWNER: Constellation Brands

ADDRESS: 7801 St. Helena Highway, Oakville, CA 94562

TELEPHONE: (707) 259-9463 or 1–888-RMONDAVI

TELEFAX: (707) 968-2174

E-MAIL: info@robertmondaviwinery.com

WEBSITE: www.robertmondaviwinery.com

VISITING POLICY: Robert Mondavi Winery is a leader in wine education and visitor programs. The winery is open to visitors daily from 9 A.M. to 5 P.M., and closed on Easter, Thanksgiving, Christmas, and New Year's Day. A vineyard and winery tour is available at various times throughout the day and reservations are recommended. A broad range of other tours, tastings, and courses are offered to those seeking wine education from novice to professional level.

VINEYARDS

SURFACE AREA:

Total acreage—1,540 acres

To Kalon Vineyard, Oakville District—513 planted acres

Wappo Hill Vineyard, Stags Leap District—261 planted acres

Huichica Hills Vineyard, Carneros District—405 planted acres

GRAPE VARIETALS: Cabernet Sauvignon, Fumé Blanc, Sauvignon Blanc, Pinot Noir, Chardonnay, Merlot, Zinfandel, Sauvignon Blanc Botrytis, Moscato d'Oro; other varieties grown in small amounts (Cabernet Franc, Malbec, Petit Verdot, Semillon)

AVERAGE AGE OF THE VINES: Variable (10–25 years)

Older blocks: 30–50 years

High-density, post-phylloxera blocks: 10+ years

DENSITY OF PLANTATION: They have customized the spacing to the soil, microclimate, and variety. Spacing varies from high density in newer, post-phylloxera blocks to wider spacing in older blocks.

AVERAGE YIELDS: 3–4 tons per acre

WINEMAKING AND UPBRINGING

Specific techniques vary for each varietal and are adjusted to get the maximum character for each variety and vineyard. In general, the Mondavis use gentle, natural processes whenever possible with widespread use of natural yeast ferments, native malolactic where appropriate, 100% French oak aging, and bottling without filtration.

Tim Mondavi states, "For our Cabernet Sauvignon Reserve program, in order to capture the elegance of our intense fruit, we incorporate gravity flow, vigorous hand-sorting of only the finest clusters, oak fermentation tanks, long, extended skin contact to extract more character and flavor, underground first year barrel *chai*, 100% French oak, and barrel to barrel racking to create natural clarity and enable bottling without filtration wherever possible."

ANNUAL PRODUCTION

Cabernet Sauvignon Reserve Napa Valley: 120,000–150,000 bottles

Cabernet Sauvignon To Kalon Reserve: 6,000 bottles

AVERAGE PRICE (VARIABLE DEPENDING ON VINTAGE): $150

GREAT RECENT VINTAGES

2002, 2001, 2000, 1999, 1994, 1992, 1991, 1990, 1987, 1984, 1978, 1974, 1973, 1971

This venerable Napa winery, which, justifiably, has enormous influence on the quality and direction of California winemaking, continues to perform admirably, pushing quality at both the vineyard and winery to greater heights. Readers who mistakenly believe size is not synonymous with quality must be surprised by the bevy of extraordinary wines turned out by the Mondavis. This winery's break with California's tradition of producing often tart, eviscerated wines that are the result of excessive amounts of added acidity and too much fining and filtering began in 1987 with their Reserve reds. The Mondavis are now bottling virtually all their top white wines without filtration as well—a tribute to this family's commitment and dedication to excellence.

My annual visit to the Mondavi winery is always a learning experience. The extraordinary amount of experimentation that goes on, both in the vineyard and the winery is, in my opinion, unprecedented and unequaled. It is refreshing to see a winery that is already recognized worldwide for its commitment to excellence and quality continue to push the envelope.

The Robert Mondavi family, which has now been making wine for four generations, started the flagship Robert Mondavi Winery in 1966 with an obvious passion for producing something special. This is a family that traveled to the great wine regions of the world, learned to respect the concept of *terroir*, and believed that great wines could be produced in the Napa Valley. In fact, it could be strongly argued that Robert Mondavi, along with his two sons Tim and Michael, were the first to fully understand and create great European-styled wines in Napa that could stand against the very best wines of France and Italy.

The winery has always been a leader in its wine-growing and winemaking innovations. In the late 1960s, the winery introduced cold fermentation, stainless-steel tanks, and the use of small French oak barrels, which were largely unheard of in the California wine industry. More recent innovations, such as gentle winemaking techniques that increase wine quality, high-density vineyard plantings to reduce yield per vine and increase flavor concentration, and natural viticultural practices to protect not only the environment but also the people in the vineyards, have been catalysts in creating fundamental changes in the wine industry's approach to winemaking and growing.

The Mondavis have also been some of the strongest proponents of wine tourism, believing as they do that wine is part of civilized culture and is best appreciated in celebration of both food and the arts. The Robert Mondavi Winery was one of the first wineries to open its doors to visitors and offer meaningful tours and tastings. They went on to add culinary programs, music concerts, art exhibits, and other cultural events, including a Great Chefs program started in 1976, all of which were largely the first of their kind in America. Every summer the winery sponsors a music festival and large fund-raiser to raise money for the Napa Valley Symphony.

Much of the recent press about the Mondavi operation has focused on its empire building, which is not always eagerly accepted, and critics have also decried some changes in management and the fact that the company went public. But the fact is, the Robert Mondavi Winery remains a beacon of innovation bonded to classic traditional techniques, and continues to produce some of the world's greatest wines that reflect honorably on Robert Mondavi and his family's lifelong commitment to quality. Their legacy, regardless of the corporate politics that now seem to dominate the headlines, is ensured, and has its place in the history of great wine in both California and in the world.

The sale of this winery and all of its assets to the gigantic Constellation Brands in 2004 certainly had a far-reaching effect on the public's perception of the winery, but hopefully they will keep the Mondavi family in charge of the most important vineyards in Oakville.

Robert, Michael, and Tim Mondavi

While many other top-quality wines are made at Mondavi, this is a great Cabernet Sauvignon house, and their two greatest wines are the Robert Mondavi Reserve Cabernet Sauvignon and, more recently, the To Kalon Reserve.

CABERNET SAUVIGNON RESERVE

2002 Cabernet Sauvignon Reserve

RATING: 92 points

The stylish, elegant 2002 Cabernet Sauvignon Reserve (8,300 cases of 83% Cabernet Sauvignon, 7% Merlot, and the balance Cabernet Franc, Petit Verdot, and Malbec) offers a beautiful marriage of power and elegance. Cedar wood, crème de cassis, spice box, and dried herb aromas soar from the glass of this medium-bodied, beautifully balanced, elegant Reserve, which is somewhat reminiscent of Mondavi's 1978. It's all about harmony, balance, and finesse in 2002. Drink it over the next 15+ years.

2001 Cabernet Sauvignon Reserve

RATING: 94+ points

The finest Private Reserve since the 1991, 1990, and 1987, the 2001 Cabernet Sauvignon Reserve is extraordinary. There are 8,000 cases of this blend of 88% Cabernet Sauvignon, 10% Cabernet Franc, and small dollops of Merlot as well as Petit Verdot. A perfume of smoke, camphor, crème de cassis, cedar, and fruitcake is accompanied by a gentle giant of a wine. Powerful and impeccably balanced, with outstanding concentration, well-integrated wood, acidity, and tannin, and a long, nearly 60-second finish, this saturated ruby/purple–hued effort is a prodigious example of Cabernet Sauvignon. Anticipated maturity: now–2020+.

2000 Cabernet Sauvignon Reserve

RATING: 91 points

One of the finest efforts from this difficult vintage, this wine is a blend of 80% Cabernet Sauvignon, 14% Cabernet Franc, and the rest Merlot and Malbec. It exhibits a deep purple color as well as an elegant, sweet perfume of black currants intertwined with licorice, loamy soil, and hints of mint as well as new oak. It is ripe, long, and structured, with medium to full body, outstanding purity and concentration, and a persistent finish. This elegant Cabernet will be at its finest between 2006 and 2020.

1997 Cabernet Sauvignon Reserve

RATING: 92 points

The 1997 Cabernet Sauvignon Reserve seemed be going through a relatively closed stage when tasted in 2000. As it sat in the glass, it took on an almost Ducru-Beaucaillou or Léoville-Las-Cases St.-Julien–like character, with notes of minerals, cedarwood, black currants, tobacco, and spice. This is a rich, dark ruby/purple–colored wine with very complex aromatics, medium to full body, tight structure, and plenty of tannin in the finish. There are 20,000 cases. Anticipated maturity: now–2025.

1996 Cabernet Sauvignon Reserve

RATING: 92 points

The 1996 Cabernet Sauvignon Reserve may be no better than the Oakville, but it is made in a slightly different style. The color is opaque purple, and the wine reveals more vanilla, a touch of mint, and plenty of black currant fruit in its moderately intense aromatics. Some of the vintage's dry tannin (from this year's stressed vineyard conditions) is present in the wine's finish. A more stylish, restrained, less exuberant example than the 1996 Oakville, it is an outstanding offering that should be consumed between now and 2025.

1996 Cabernet Sauvignon 30th Anniversary Reserve

RATING: 95 points

There is a majesty, richness, and breadth to the 1996 Cabernet Sauvignon 30th Anniversary Reserve. This special bottling (about 1,000 cases) is a fabulous wine. From its opaque purple color and stunning aromatics of blackberries, cassis, toast, licorice, and Asian spices to its full-bodied, concentrated, superbly extracted style, this wine possesses virtually everything. Layers of fruit, glycerin, extract, and sweet tannin are presented in a flamboyant format. The tannin level is high, but so is the wine's richness and length. It is a sensational effort. Anticipated maturity: now–2030.

1995 Cabernet Sauvignon Reserve

RATING: 93 points

The 1995 has great promise and raw materials, with superb fruit and richness, medium body, and subtle lead pencil notes to go along with black currant, mineral, and toast scents and flavors. Based on this tasting, I would lower my overall rating, but it is still an exceptional California Cabernet Sauvignon made in a compellingly elegant, graceful style. Anticipated maturity: now–2018.

1994 Cabernet Sauvignon Reserve

RATING: 98 points

The deep opaque purple color and tightly wound nose and flavors still reveal enough profound aromas and flavors to mark this as one of Mondavi's most sensational efforts. The nose possesses a Margaux/Mouton-like cassis, lead pencil, floral aroma, backed up by copious quantities of black currant fruit. As for mouth-feel, my notes said, "great stuff." The wine is full-bodied, layered, multidimensional, and astonishingly well balanced, with an inner depth and core of exceptional richness and intensity. All of this has been accomplished without any notion of obtrusive weight, tannin, or alcohol. The finish lasts for 35+ seconds. Because of its luxurious quantity of fruit, this wine will be accessible young, thus much of it will be drunk long before it ever reaches full maturity. However, for those who possess the discipline to wait another 3–8 years, this wine should prove to be a formidable California Cabernet with a rare complexity, elegance, and richness. It should be at its best between now and 2025.

1993 Cabernet Sauvignon Reserve

RATING: 93 points

The 1993 Cabernet Sauvignon Reserve outperformed the 1992 at the winery, revealing a concentrated, splendidly saturated dark purple color, and wonderfully sweet, intense aromas of chocolate, smoke, vanilla beans, and rich black currant fruit. The wine tastes more extracted than the 1992, with a sweeter, more expansive, glycerin-imbued mid-section and

finish. Although it carries as much tannin as the 1992, the tannin is riper as well as better integrated. The 1993 is a 15- to 20-year wine. Anticipated maturity: now–2025.

1991 Cabernet Sauvignon Reserve

RATING: 97 points

The fabulous 1991 Reserve is the quintessential Napa Cabernet that represents a synthesis in style between the elegance of a first-growth Bordeaux and the ripe, intense, generous fruit of Napa Valley. It is just hitting its peak of maturity, where it should remain for 10–20 years.

1990 Cabernet Sauvignon Reserve

RATING: 96 points

This wine is just beginning to drink spectacularly well. The rustic, big, thick 1990 is Californian in its orientation. It is loaded with flavor, but the tannin is coarser when compared to the seamlessness of the 1991s. Anticipated maturity: now–2014.

1987 Cabernet Sauvignon Reserve

RATING: 97 points

This extraordinary wine is backward and unevolved, but even neophytes will recognize its potential greatness. The opaque, saturated, dark purple color reveals no sign of age. The huge, smoky, oaky, black currant, herb, and vanilla–scented nose only hints at what will be achieved with further evolution. Sweet, decadently rich, dense, highly extracted flavors are wrapped around a full-bodied, chewy, super-concentrated, moderately tannic wine that, ideally, needs 7–8 more years of cellaring. It is a 25- to 30-year California Cabernet Sauvignon that is just beginning to become civilized. A potential legend in the making! Anticipated maturity: now–2024.

1978 Cabernet Sauvignon Reserve

RATING: 90 points

The 1978 Cabernet Sauvignon Reserve has consistently been a 90-point wine. It remains a beautiful Cabernet, displaying cedar, tobacco, and black currant fruit. Medium to full–bodied and fully mature, with sweet ripeness on the attack, excellent purity, and a long, supple finish, this wine should keep for another 2–4 years.

1974 Cabernet Sauvignon Reserve

RATING: 93 points

A consistent star of the vintage, this fully mature wine exhibits no sign of losing its fruit. The color is saturated dark plum/garnet with slight amber at the edge. The bouquet has always been ostentatious, with pungent aromas of cassis, pepper, herbs, licorice, cedar, and Asian spices. Full-bodied and superbly balanced, with that layered, expansive richness found in top, highly extracted wines, the acidity is low but sound, and the tannin has nearly melted away. This stunning, opulent, complex California Cabernet Sauvignon should continue to drink well for several more years.

1971 Cabernet Sauvignon Reserve
RATING: 90 points

The 1971 Cabernet Sauvignon Reserve (the first vintage to carry a Reserve designation) includes a significant percentage of Cabernet Franc. This has always been one of the more compelling Reserve wines. It reached its peak in the late 1970s, and continued to drink well for many years. At a tasting in October 1997, I rated the wine 90 points, but I must say it had a 96-point bouquet. It seemed to be drying out ever so slightly in the mouth. The wine still possesses an astonishing fragrance, reminiscent of a hypothetical cross between a top vintage of Cheval Blanc and a classic cassis-dominated California Cabernet. In the mouth, it never was a blockbuster, but a medium-bodied, graceful wine that relied more on its harmony than power to attract attention. The fruit is just beginning to dry out, and the tannin and acidity are becoming more noticeable. This wine, which drank beautifully for 25 years, is still hanging on to life.

CABERNET SAUVIGNON TO KALON RESERVE

2001 Cabernet Sauvignon To Kalon Reserve
RATING: 95+ points

There are 1,000 cases of the 2001 Cabernet Sauvignon To Kalon Reserve. Fashioned from 31-year-old vines, it is a powerful, firmly structured offering revealing notes of charcoal, creamy black currants, loamy soil, and tobacco leaf. Although its pH of 3.78 is relatively high, seemingly suggesting a more forward style, it is broodingly backward and less accessible than the Reserve Cabernet Sauvignon. It's a classic Oakville Cabernet Sauvignon that may not be quite as generous or complex as the Reserve or perhaps the M-Bar, but it is almost too backward to fully evaluate at present. Give it 5–6 years of cellaring, and drink it over the following 20–25 years.

2000 Cabernet Sauvignon To Kalon Reserve
RATING: 91+ points

The 2000 Cabernet Sauvignon To Kalon Reserve is rich with graphite and cassis flavors. There are 1,000 cases of this intensely concentrated blend of 97% Cabernet Sauvignon and 3% Cabernet Franc. It is made from Mondavi's home vineyard in Oakville, and boasts a saturated ruby/purple color in addition to a sweet nose of crème de cassis, vanilla, licorice, tobacco, and smoke. The wine is sweet in the mouth, with medium to full body, and excellent precision as well as purity. It represents a synthesis between the Margaux-like, perfumed

style of the Stags' Leap District Cabernet, and the more powerful, structured, Pauillac-like Oakville *cuvée*. Anticipated maturity: 2008–2025+.

1999 Cabernet Sauvignon To Kalon Reserve
RATING: 90 points

The 1999 Cabernet Sauvignon To Kalon Vineyard is 100% Cabernet Sauvignon. This wine boasts an excellent texture, although the finish is austere. Sweet black currant and blackberry fruit are wrapped with subtle oak and a weedy, tobacco herbaceousness. It is deep, dense, full-bodied, and impressively textured as well as concentrated. However, the high tannin profile suggests it should be cellared for another 1–2 years; it will last 20–25 years.

1997 Cabernet Sauvignon To Kalon Reserve
RATING: 94 points

The 1997 Cabernet Sauvignon To Kalon Reserve, made from 100% Cabernet Sauvignon, is a brilliant wine that has a dark ruby/purple color, a gorgeously broad, complex nose of cedar, black fruits, new saddle leather, and mineral. In the mouth, it is full-bodied, showing slightly higher tannin and austerity than it did previously, but there is no doubt that this wine has depth, multiple layers of flavor, an expansive texture, and a long, reassuring, concentrated finish. It should age for at least 30+ years. Anticipated maturity: now–2030.

WINE: Cabernet Sauvignon Estate

OWNERS: James L. Barrett, Managing General Partner; Laura G. Barrett, Limited Partner; James P. "Bo" Barrett, Limited Partner

ADDRESS: 1429 Tubbs Lane, Calistoga, CA 94515

TELEPHONE: (707) 942-5105

TELEFAX: (707) 942-4221

E-MAIL: customer-service@montelena.com

WEBSITE: www.montelena.com

CONTACT: Tom Inlay

VISITING POLICY: The winery is open daily (except major holidays) from 9:30 A.M. to 4 P.M.

VINEYARDS

SURFACE AREA: 200 acres farmed and another 52 acres under long-term contract

GRAPE VARIETALS: Cabernet Sauvignon, Chardonnay, Zinfandel, Cabernet Franc, Merlot

AVERAGE AGE OF THE VINES: 20 years

DENSITY OF PLANTATION: Varies from 8' x 12' to 5' x 10'

AVERAGE YIELDS: 2–2.5 tons per acre

WINEMAKING AND UPBRINGING

All of the Cabernet Sauvignon is fermented in temperature-controlled stainless-steel tanks. This is to provide a warm (70–80 degrees), slow fermentation rather than a hot, fast fermentation. Manual pumpovers twice a day. When enough color and tannin have been extracted from the skins, between 8–40 days, the wine is drained from the skins and pumped into another oak or stainless-steel tank to further clean it up before going into barrels. The malolactic fermentation occurs in large oak casks, 1,200–3,000 gallons. The selection and assemblage occurs in January following the vintage. French oak, primarily from Nevers, is utilized to age the Cabernet. Montelena tends to utilize between 20 and 25% new oak for the Estate Cabernet, with older barrels (up to 7 years old) for the rest. The purpose of the Cabernet barrel-aging program is to soften the wine and add nuances of spice rather than to make the wine taste oaky. The Estate Cabernet ages for up to 22 months in oak, then is bottled and aged for another 18 months in bottle before release.

ANNUAL PRODUCTION

Montelena Cabernet Sauvignon Estate: 108,000 bottles

AVERAGE PRICE (VARIABLE DEPENDING ON VINTAGE): $85–125

GREAT RECENT VINTAGES

Best overall balance—1997, 1994, 1990, 1986, 1978
Biggest wines—2002, 2001, 1999, 1996, 1987, 1984
Most Bordeaux-like—1991, 1985, 1979
Best in challenging years—2000, 1998, 1989, 1983

The Barrett family is only the second family to operate this estate since it was founded in 1882 by Senator Alfred Tubbs. By the 1890s, Montelena had established itself as one of the northern Napa Valley's premier producers. After Prohibition, Tubbs's grandson, Chapin F. Tubbs, only operated the winery until the beginning of World War II, although the Tubbs heirs continued to farm the vineyards. Montelena was one of Napa's ghost wineries until 1972, when Jim Barrett formed a partnership to rebuild the château. Recognizing the potential of the vineyard, Barrett's team began an ambitious replanting, replacing the Prohibition-era varieties with Cabernet Sauvignon. The main blocks of the estate vineyard were planted in 1972 and 1974. Since the partnership determined that quality, not quantity, was the priority, the new vines were planted on St. George rootstock, which only gives about half the yield of the then-popular AXR rootstock. That decision proved to be very wise, because those plantings are still in production and were unaffected by the phylloxera epidemic that swept through the valley in the 1980s and 1990s. As a result, Château Montelena has one of the oldest mature-vine Cabernet plantings in the

Bo and Jim Barrett

Napa Valley. The vines don't produce much tonnage and the resulting fruit concentration is one of the signatures of the Montelena Estate's wines.

Seven years passed between the time the Cabernet vines were planted and the sale of the first bottle of wine. So in order to avoid financial suicide, the Barretts' team, with their winemaker Mike Grgich, made Cabernet Sauvignon, Chardonnay, Riesling, and Zinfandel, mostly from purchased fruit, to keep them alive while waiting for the estate vineyards to produce.

Bo Barrett, a tall, charismatic, remarkably down-to-earth guy, has been the winemaker since 1982, but has worked on every single vintage since 1973. His father, Jim Barrett, serves as the estate's no-nonsense fearless leader and philosopher-taskmaster. From the beginning the Barretts have maintained the same lands, same vines (mostly), same small size, same dedication of a small professional team, and same unwavering commitment to the place and quality.

Modern-day society seems to always be in search of new stars, but this winery has been a Cabernet Sauvignon superhero for nearly 30 years! Chateau Montelena's Estate Cabernet Sauvignon remains one of California's most remarkable Cabernets. I have been following it since the early 1970s, and even the most difficult vintages are still drinking beautifully. The home vineyard is so consistent that even in difficult vintages such as 1989 and 1998, this wine is far better than its competition.

Buying Montelena's Estate Cabernet Sauvignons is equivalent to buying blue-chip stock. They get better and better with age, and as the vertical tastings I have attended so persuasively attest, they are still relatively young wines at 20 years of age!

CABERNET SAUVIGNON ESTATE

2003 Cabernet Sauvignon Estate

RATING: 92–95 points

The 2003 Cabernet Sauvignon Estate looks to be another great success at Montelena. No shy wine with 14.3% alcohol, it exhibits a dense purple color along with a big, sweet perfume of crème de cassis intermixed with smoke, earth, and forest floor scents. Noble purity, an opulent attack and mid-palate, and a long, tannic, rich, full-bodied finish suggest it should be consumed between 2010 and 2020+.

2002 Cabernet Sauvignon Estate

RATING: 95+ points

The 2002 Cabernet Sauvignon Estate, one of the most powerful Cabernets the Barretts have made, is reminiscent of the profound 1987. A blend of 99% Cabernet Sauvignon and 1% Cabernet Franc, it tips the scales at 14.3% alcohol. The wine has a sensational nose of sweet crème de cassis intermixed with notes of beef blood, licorice, and underbrush. Full-bodied and more flamboyant than the more structured, muscular 2001, the 2002 is fleshier with more glycerin and higher alcohol. This chewy effort should be ready for prime-time drinking a few years ahead of the more rigid 2001. Anticipated maturity: 2008–2025.

2001 Cabernet Sauvignon Estate

RATING: 95+ points

The 2001 Cabernet Sauvignon Estate is one of Bo Barrett's finest efforts. While tightly knit, 24 hours of aeration reveals its upside potential. Dense ruby/purple with a nose of crushed rocks intermixed with crème de cassis and a hint of licorice, this full-bodied, pure, deep offering will be at its peak between 2010 and 2025. It is a blend of 96% Cabernet Sauvignon and 4% Cabernet Franc that came in at 14.1% alcohol.

2000 Cabernet Sauvignon Estate

RATING: 90 points

The thrilling Cabernet Sauvignon Estate is one of the longest-lived wines produced in California, typically lasting for 15–30+ years. The dense purple–colored 2000 Cabernet Sauvignon Estate (97% Cabernet Sauvignon and 3% Cabernet Franc) reveals a sweet perfume of black currants, an expansive, full-bodied palate, and surprising elegance as well as accessibility, excellent purity, and a long, layered finish. It is a successful 2000 Cabernet to drink now and over the next 12–15 years.

1999 Cabernet Sauvignon Estate

RATING: 95 points

The 1999 Cabernet Sauvignon Estate is considered by Bo Barrett to be a "great" year. The wine boasts a saturated inky/purple color as well as extraordinary density of fruit and cassis, and huge tannin, body, and extract. It is a substantial, palate-staining, long, muscular Cabernet that should only be purchased by connoisseurs with cold cellars as well as patience. Anticipated maturity: 2006–2030.

1998 Cabernet Sauvignon Estate

RATING: 93 points

The 1998 Cabernet Sauvignon Estate (13,000 cases) will disprove all the naysayers about how bad the vintage was in the North Coast. It possesses an opaque ruby/purple color, a gorgeous perfume of loamy soil, new saddle leather, chocolate, and black cherry and black currant fruit, full body, and ripe tannin in the finish. As it sits in the glass, notes of cedar and spice box also emerge. Although it was more evolved than most four-year-old Montelena Cabernets when last tasted, there is no doubting that it will still provide considerable pleasure at age 15 or 16. Kudos to the Barretts for producing this impressive 1998 Cabernet Sauvignon, one of the vintage's few stars.

1997 Cabernet Sauvignon Estate

RATING: 98 points

Opaque purple–colored with a dense, chewy, full-bodied personality, it displays abundant cassis, mineral, and earth notes. This brilliantly made, super-concentrated, pure blockbuster possesses sweet tannin as well as a terrific finish. Having added additional weight, this sumptuous, multilayered, profoundly concentrated Cabernet contains 14% alcohol. It is a candidate for 25–30 years of longevity. Anticipated maturity: now–2030.

1996 Cabernet Sauvignon Estate

RATING: 93 points

A behemoth Cabernet Sauvignon is the stern, tannic, concentrated 1996 Cabernet Sauvignon Estate (13.5% alcohol). Full-bodied, but closed, with gorgeously pure black fruits, powerful, loamy, earthy scents along with fruit and extract, this wine also needs another 2–3 years of cellaring, and should easily last through the first 2–3 decades of the new century.

1995 Cabernet Sauvignon Estate

RATING: 94 points

This is another winery where the 1995 Cabernet Sauvignon may be as strong as the 1994. The color is an opaque purple. The wine is full-bodied and powerful, with classic notes of cassis intermixed with loamy soil scents, underbrush, and spice. There is massive body and elevated but sweet tannin that is well integrated with the wine's other components, a blockbuster mid-palate, and a finish that lasts for 30+ seconds. Anticipated maturity: now–2025.

1994 Cabernet Sauvignon Estate

RATING: 95 points

The 1994 Cabernet Sauvignon Estate has begun to open and display its enormous potential. The saturated black/purple color is followed by aromas of gorgeously pure blackberry and cassis scents. Toasty oak notes are barely discernible given the wine's bombastic display of black fruits, huge, chewy glycerin level, and sensational finish. Anticipated maturity: now–2013.

1993 Cabernet Sauvignon Estate

RATING: 91 points

The 1993 Cabernet Sauvignon Estate possesses the most aggressive tannin of the 1993–1996 Estate Cabernets. It is a

weighty, hefty, powerful wine, with a dense purple color, ripe, sweet black fruit flavors, considerable muscle and depth, and a spicy, full-bodied, tannic finish. This wine has all the necessary components to age effortlessly for 20+ years. Anticipated maturity: now–2017.

1992 Cabernet Sauvignon Estate

RATING: 95 points

The 1992 Cabernet Sauvignon Estate is slightly richer than the 1993. There is an extra line on its label honoring Chateau Montelena's 20th Cabernet Sauvignon vintage (1972–1992). The wine's opaque ruby/purple color is followed by a sweet, jammy nose of black fruit and minerals, huge body, a sweet inner core of ripe fruit, and a long, low-acid, opulent finish. Rich and full, this Cabernet is destined for 20+ years of gorgeous drinking. Anticipated maturity: now–2015.

1991 Cabernet Sauvignon Estate

RATING: 95 points

Montelena's incredible 1991 Cabernet Sauvignon Estate is an exceptional wine, rivaling even the winery's profound 1987. The color is a dense, opaque purple. The nose offers up Château Montelena's telltale signature—abundant, pure aromas of cassis, minerals, and spicy oak. Full-bodied, spectacularly rich, and highly extracted, with moderate to high tannin, this is a youthful, exuberant, stunning example of blockbuster Napa Cabernet Sauvignon. Its inner core of cassis fruit is something to savor. Don't miss it! Anticipated maturity: now–2020.

1990 Cabernet Sauvignon Estate

RATING: 93 points

The 1990 Cabernet Sauvignon Estate is a backward, but splendidly concentrated, broad, expansively flavored, full-bodied Cabernet with a high level of tannin. Its stunning display of highly extracted, black currant fruit judiciously wrapped in toasty oak is impressive. It is a 20–30 year wine. Anticipated maturity: now–2024.

1989 Cabernet Sauvignon Estate

RATING: 91 points

I firmly believe that the 1989 Cabernet Sauvignon Estate is one of the top three or four Cabernets made in that maligned vintage. Extremely full-bodied and tannic, the wine possesses a smoky, chocolaty component in the cassis-dominated bouquet. Consumers should keep an eye out for this wine at their favorite retailers. Anticipated maturity: now–2014.

1987 Cabernet Sauvignon Estate

RATING: 98 points

Château Montelena has made so many sensational Cabernets that it seems almost impossible to believe that their 1987

Cabernet Sauvignon Estate could be even more profound than any of the exceptional wines made previously at this property. The black/purple color, the extraordinary bouquet of rich cassis, violets, and licorice, the massive extraction of flavors, sensational depth, superripeness, and a length that must last over a minute, suggest to me that this is easily the most concentrated and potentially longest-lived Cabernet Sauvignon that Château Montelena has ever made. The extract level is incredible, yet the balance is there. Anticipated maturity: now–2025.

1986 Cabernet Sauvignon Estate

RATING: 96 points

This great wine exhibits a black/purple color, a fabulous, sweet, pure, cassis-scented nose, massive body and richness, and total harmony among its components—fruit, wood, alcohol, acidity, and tannin. Still exceptionally youthful and vigorous, with no signs of age in either its color or taste, this 1986 is an extraordinary effort that appears to be a legitimate candidate for the wine of the vintage. Anticipated maturity: now–2016.

1985 Cabernet Sauvignon Estate

RATING: 92 points

Consistently a low- to mid-90-point Cabernet Sauvignon, Château Montelena's 1985 remained frightfully backward at nearly 10 years of age. The 1991, 1987, and 1985 have the potential to be three of the longest-lived Montelena Cabernets this fine winery has ever produced. In a tasting in 1995, the 1985 was unevolved and youthful, with an opaque ruby/purple color, and a closed but promising nose of cassis fruit, earth, minerals, and oak. Full-bodied, marvelously concentrated and pure, this highly extracted, muscular, blockbuster effort is finally ready to drink. It is a candidate for 10 more years of longevity. Anticipated maturity: now–2015.

1984 Cabernet Sauvignon Estate

RATING: 92 points

Château Montelena's wines possess gorgeous potential when young, and are even better when revisited later. The 1984 Cabernet Sauvignon exhibits the forward, jammy, cassis and other black fruit character of the vintage, marvelously rich, full-bodied, concentrated flavors, high extract, gobs of glycerin, and moderate tannin in the finish. Its virtues—purity, richness, and opulence—along with a firm underpinning of tannin should serve it well for another five years. Anticipated maturity: now–2010.

1982 Cabernet Sauvignon Estate

RATING: 90 points

Very elegant, fully mature, with notes of sandalwood, earth, black currants, and a hint of cherries with a slight note of ashtray, this wine is dark plum/garnet with some amber at the edge. Medium to full–bodied, expansive, but rather elegant and just beginning to show some drying, astringent tannin in the finish, this wine is best consumed over the next 2–3 years.

1980 Cabernet Sauvignon Estate

RATING: 90 points

Extremely deep in color and youthful, with pure aromas of cassis and new oak, this full-bodied, expansively flavored, supple wine has shed much of its tannin and has now reached its plateau of maturity. The wonderful texture and long flavors are a complete turn-on. Anticipated maturity: now.

1978 Cabernet Sauvignon Estate

RATING: 95 points

One of the all-time great Montelena Cabernet Sauvignons, and at age 27 still going strong, this dark plum/garnet–colored wine is still saturated to the rim. A huge, sweet nose of licorice, tobacco, black currant, cedar, other assorted juicy black fruits, and earth jumps from the glass. Quite opulent, voluptuous, powerful, with great integration of tannin and acidity, this is a full-throttle, multidimensional Cabernet Sauvignon that proves just how remarkably the best Cabernets of Napa and of Montelena can age. Just past its adolescence, this wine still has at least another 10–12 years of life left in it.

1977 Cabernet Sauvignon Estate

RATING: 91 points

Still a very vibrant, full-bodied wine showing some amber at the edge, this full-throttle Cabernet displays notes of new saddle leather, blackberry, cassis, plum in the nose, substantial body on the palate, some earthy tannins beginning to poke their head through in the finish, but loads of intensity and richness. It is fully mature and probably best drunk over the next 3–4 years.

WINES:

Epic Merlot
Chardonnay Unfiltered
Cabernet Sauvignon Unfiltered
OWNERS: Peter and Su Hua Newton and Clicquot, Inc.
ADDRESS: 2555 Madrona Avenue, St. Helena, CA 94574
TELEPHONE: (707) 963-9000
TELEFAX: (707) 963-5408
E-MAIL: marketing@newtonvineyard.com
WEBSITE: www.newtonvineyard.com
CONTACT: Dr. Su Hua Newton
VISITING POLICY: By appointment only

VINEYARDS

One of the most gorgeous mountain estates in California, the Newton Vineyards (comprising a total of 120 acres) are sprinkled over a massive area of knolls and steep hills encompassing a 565-acre ranch. Newton also has a smaller vineyard of 20 acres in Carneros. The average age of the vines is approximately 25 years, but in order to increase density of vineyards, there has been significant interplanting, and those vines average between 10–12 years.

GRAPE VARIETALS: Merlot, Cabernet Franc, Cabernet Sauvignon, Petit Verdot, Chardonnay, Viognier

WINEMAKING AND UPBRINGING

Su Hua Newton was born in China, and often quotes the following Chinese proverb: "Nurture nature, it will smile upon you. Control nature, it will bite you hard." From the gorgeous

Su Hua Newton

flower gardens at the entrance to the impeccable viticulture on the hillsides, producing the best possible grapes is the operative rule at Newton. Harvest begins at dawn and the picking is finished by 11 A.M. so that the fruit comes into the winery very cool. Their profound unfiltered Chardonnay is naturally made, as the juice gets very little settling time and is put directly into the barrels to ferment on the natural yeasts. The cool underground cellars encourage a slow fermentation, and this is one producer of high-quality Burgundy that actually avoids doing much *bâtonnage* for fear of eliminating any of the *terroir* character and fragile fruit from the wine. In most years, the complete fermentation cycle for Chardonnay takes about eight months, after which the wine is blended and left in barrel for another 7–10 months, depending on its level of concentration.

Su Hua Newton was one of the first to make unfiltered Chardonnay in California, and she claimed it wasn't an easy decision, because her colleagues thought she was crazy and many of her distributors as well as assistant winemakers threatened to boycott the product. But she stayed the course, largely because of her admiration for the great white Burgundies made by Jean-François Coche-Dury and Dominique Lafon, unfiltered classics year in and year out.

With respect to the red wines, they treat every lot as if it were a child. Every winemaking decision—whether to ferment in stainless-steel or open wood fermenters, how much pumping-over will be done, whether to do malolactic in tank or barrel—depends on the individual lot. In short, each vintage requires a different equation, and there is never any overriding formula for producing their world-class Epic Merlot (not made in every vintage) and their unfiltered Cabernet Sauvignon. The wines are generally blended after fermentation and put into various French oak casks, where they are racked every 3 months until bottling without fining or filtration after 22 months in barrel. The success of Newton's very Bordelais style of upbringing is no doubt a tribute to classic advice from their French wine consultant, the famous Michel Rolland.

ANNUAL PRODUCTION

Chardonnay Unfiltered: 48,000 bottles
Epic Merlot: only in exceptional vintages, at the most 12,000 bottles
Cabernet Unfiltered: 30,000 bottles
AVERAGE PRICE (VARIABLE DEPENDING ON VINTAGE): $35–65

GREAT RECENT VINTAGES

2002, 2001, 1997, 1994, 1992, 1990

The inspiration for Newton came from a much better-known and older winery, Sterling, which Su Hua Newton and her husband, Peter Newton, owned. Their favorite wines at the time always came from their Diamond Mountain vineyards, and after they sold Sterling, they began to search the mountains of western Napa for slopes that were suitable for higher-elevation planting. They ended up on Spring Mountain, and while there are many beautiful estates on Spring Mountain, Newton's is one of remarkable viticulture and pure beauty. The cool nights and winds from the north and northwest give these high vineyards a much cooler microclimate than those on the valley floor. Su Hua Newton often quotes the late Vincent Leflaive from Puligny-Montrachet and the great winemaker and administrator of Haut-Brion, Jean Delmas; both, she says, said, "Love your land, and nurture your vines; nature will do the rest."

It is obvious that Su Hua Newton, who now seems to have total control over the day-to-day operations of Newton, was a quick learner. She's the first to say she could have made a great Cabernet Sauvignon in 1983, but was convinced by assistant winemakers to add tartaric acid, thus ruining the wine. All of these wines from their beautiful mountain vineyards are among the most natural wine made in the world. The three classics, of course, are the Chardonnay Unfiltered, which I have been buying and drinking since the 1992 vintage (it is a wine that has striking longevity for a California Chardonnay, usually 6–10 years), the Epic Merlot (which is only made in the greatest of the greatest vintages), and Cabernet Sauvignon Unfiltered. These last two wines probably have much more in common with a great French Bordeaux than most other Napa wines. They are elegant, restrained, but authoritatively rich wines, with tremendous purity and intensity. They each have at least two decades of longevity.

CABERNET SAUVIGNON UNFILTERED

2003 Cabernet Sauvignon Unfiltered

RATING: 92–94 points

The most impressive *cuvée* of 2003 from Newton is the Cabernet Sauvignon Unfiltered. Deep ruby/purple to the rim, with a terrific nose of dark chocolate, crème de cassis, underbrush, and plums, the wine is deep and medium to full–bodied, with outstanding richness and a layered, fleshy mouth-feel. Anticipated maturity: 2008–2020+. Release date: Spring 2007.

2002 Cabernet Sauvignon Unfiltered

RATING: 91+ points

Patience is definitely required for the dense ruby/purple–colored 2002 Cabernet Sauvignon Unfiltered. Tightly knit and structured with a reticent but promising nose of dusty black currants, cedar, and licorice, the wine reveals plum, anise, and underbrush notes in the mouth, good acidity, firm tannin, but loads of concentration as well as impressive complexity. Anticipated maturity: 2007–2018.

2001 Cabernet Sauvignon Unfiltered

RATING: 90 points

The 2001 Cabernet Sauvignon Unfiltered is made in a typically *vin de garde* (for long aging) European style. Medium to full–bodied, with a classic combination of tobacco leaf, cedarwood, black currants, and earth, this dense purple–colored Cabernet is firmly structured and loaded with concentration. However, it is years away from being fully accessible. Anticipated maturity: 2008–2020.

2000 Cabernet Sauvignon Unfiltered

RATING: 90–91 points

The 2000 Cabernet Sauvignon Unfiltered (which includes small quantities of Cabernet Franc and Petit Verdot) is a potentially outstanding offering. The wine reveals backward, dense, smoky, black currant fruit intertwined with earth, spice box, cedar, and saddle leather. It is tannic and chewy, requiring 5–6 years of bottle age. Anticipated maturity: 2008–2020.

1999 Cabernet Sauvignon Unfiltered

RATING: 91 points

The brilliant 1999 Cabernet Sauvignon Unfiltered possesses pure notes of melted licorice, crème de cassis, smoky oak, and a touch of foresty elements. This full-bodied, powerful 1999 is reminiscent of a New World version of a famed Pauillac such as Pontet-Canet or Mouton Rothschild. A stunning effort! Anticipated maturity: now–2025.

1996 Cabernet Sauvignon Unfiltered

RATING: 93 points

The 1996 Cabernet Sauvignon Unfiltered exhibits an opaque purple color, as well as a robust, nearly massive constitution, a boatload of tannin, and considerable power, depth, and muscle. Atypically rugged and brawny for a Newton Cabernet Sauvignon, it should age effortlessly for 2–3 decades. Prospective purchasers should be aware that this vintage may require another year or two of cellaring for some of the tannin to melt away. Newton's Cabernets have a broader, more textured mouth-feel than do the Merlots.

1995 Cabernet Sauvignon Unfiltered

RATING: 92 points

Tannic, but classically constructed, the 1995 Cabernet Sauvignon Unfiltered offers rich cassis fruit intermixed with loamy soil scents, toast, and floral notes. Long in the mouth, with an expansive texture, impeccable symmetry, and fine overall balance, this wine finishes with a tannic clout, as well as outstanding ripeness and presence in the mouth. It should be long-lived, but will be ready to drink at an early age. Anticipated maturity: now–2020.

1993 Cabernet Sauvignon Unfiltered

RATING: 92 points

In contrast to the 1992, the 1993 Cabernet Sauvignon (once again unfined and unfiltered) is more precocious and flattering with seemingly lower acidity, a more velvety texture, wonderful richness, and an opulent, forward, cassis fruitiness that is easy to understand. Highly extracted, rich, and full, with no hard edges, unlike the more structured and tannic 1992, the 1993 will age effortlessly for another 12–17 years.

1992 Cabernet Sauvignon Unfiltered

RATING: 92 points

The 1992 Cabernet Sauvignon is a powerful, cassis-scented and-flavored wine with an opaque ruby/purple color, and youthful, expansive aromas and flavors. It cuts a deep swath on the palate. This wine is ready to drink now and will last for 10–15 years.

1991 Cabernet Sauvignon Unfiltered

RATING: 94 points

The extraordinary, blockbuster 1991 Cabernet Sauvignon offers a spectacular nose of black currants, truffles, vanilla, mineral, floral, and menthol scents. Massive, with huge extraction, beautiful balance, and a finish that lasts for over a minute, this majestic Cabernet should prove a worthy rival to Newton's 1990. It will keep for another 5–7 years.

1990 Cabernet Sauvignon Unfiltered

RATING: 95 points

The 1990 Cabernet Sauvignon is the first Newton Cabernet to have an extended maceration of 25–35 days and to include an important percentage of Cabernet Franc in the final blend. With a huge nose of chocolate, cedar, and cassis, this rich, full-bodied, spectacular wine offers unbelievably concentrated flavors, firm, sweet tannins, and enough acidity to give it grip and delineation. It is unfiltered. Anticipated maturity: now–2012.

CHARDONNAY UNFILTERED

2003 Chardonnay Unfiltered

RATING: 97 points

Although less impressive than the 2002, the well-made 2003 Chardonnay Unfiltered offers beautiful leesy, nectarine, and brioche notes along with hints of custard and orange rind. Medium to full-bodied, ripe, dense, and expansive and rich, this beauty should drink well for 5–6 years.

2002 Chardonnay Unfiltered

RATING: 96 points

I was blown away by the 2002 Chardonnay Unfiltered, one of California's finest Chardonnays, made from a 30-year-old vineyard planted with old Wente clones. This *cuvée* ages well, as a gorgeous bottle of 1992 I tasted recently demonstrated. Nevertheless, I prefer drinking them within their first 6–7 years. A huge floral and white peach nose with some oily citrus and tropical fruit (primarily pineapple) jumps from the glass of this powerful, broad, but beautifully layered wine that is harmonious and pure. As the wine sits in the glass, some of that famous *goût de petrol* emerges, which is a characteristic I often find in Montrachets and Meursault-Perrières. The wine has good acidity and should prove to be one of the top Chardonnays of the vintage.

2001 Chardonnay Unfiltered

RATING: 94 points

The compelling 2001 Chardonnay Unfiltered possesses a re strained but powerful bouquet of citrus oils intermixed with lemon blossoms and buttery popcorn presented in a full-bodied, layered, textured style with gorgeous richness. It is a powerful, intense Chardonnay that is performing far better out of bottle than it did from the barrel. It will drink well for 6–7 years.

1999 Chardonnay Unfiltered

RATING: 91 points

Newton's 1999 Chardonnay Unfiltered exhibits plenty of texture as well as handsome honeyed citrus, orange, smoky hazelnut, and tropical fruit characteristics. It is very elegant, offering a striking texture, great minerality, medium to full body, and flavors that unfold gracefully in the mouth. This serious, Burgundian-styled effort will last 5–6 years, an uncommonly long life for a California Chardonnay.

EPIC MERLOT

2002 Epic Merlot

RATING: 92–94 points

The 2002 Epic Merlot reveals a dramatic nose that suggests plum/cherry jam intermixed with spice box, incense, and a hint of licorice. Superb richness, full body, and ripe Merlot flavors with good underlying acidity, structure, and firm tannins give this wine an elegant yet authoritative mouth-feel. This beauty is set to have two decades of longevity. Anticipated maturity: 2007–2024.

2001 Epic Merlot

RATING: 93+ points

In great vintages, Su Hua Newton makes a selection of the finest barrels called Epic, a Merlot-dominated wine. The unfiltered 2001 Epic could be mistaken for a Pomerol/St.-Emilion. Composty aromas of earth, licorice, black cherry liqueur, mocha, and cocoa along with a hint of white chocolate jump from the glass of this saturated ruby/purple–colored 2001. Attractive, medium to full–bodied, with good acidity and firm tannin, this still-youthful Merlot needs 2–4 years of cellaring; it should keep for two decades.

2000 Epic Merlot

RATING: 90 points

The 2000 Epic Merlot exhibits complex characteristics of chocolate, cocoa, and sweet cherry and black currant fruit. It is Bordeaux-like, with moderately high tannin, medium body, and a structured, muscular demeanor. Anticipated maturity: now–2016.

1999 Epic Merlot

RATING: 91 points

The 1999 Epic Merlot offers a broodingly backward, intense, concentrated mouthful of wine with high tannin and structure in addition to impressive layers of both richness and extract. The wine is thick, with notes of black fruits, espresso, and chocolate submerged into its earthy personality, with a dry, austere finish. Patience is required. Anticipated maturity: 2006–2020.

WINES:

Cabernet Sauvignon

Merlot Vintner's Select

Cabernet Sauvignon Reserve

Cabernet Franc

Reserve Claret

OWNER: Pride family

ADDRESS: 4026 Spring Mountain Road, St. Helena, CA 94574

TELEPHONE: (707) 963-4949

TELEFAX: (707) 963-4848

E-MAIL: contactus@pridewines.com

WEBSITE: www.pridewines.com

CONTACT: Wendy Brooks

VISITING POLICY: Tours and tastings welcomed by appointment

VINEYARDS

SURFACE AREA: 220 total acres; 82 vine acres

GRAPE VARIETALS: Cabernet Sauvignon, Merlot, Cabernet Franc, Petit Verdot, Syrah, Sangiovese, Viognier, Chardonnay

AVERAGE AGE OF THE VINES: 16–30 years through new

DENSITY OF PLANTATION: Various ranging on the contour and slope of the hillsides

AVERAGE YIELDS: 3.5 tons per acre

WINEMAKING AND UPBRINGING

The Pride Mountain Vineyards property cloaks the summit of the Mayacamas ridge, which undulates down either side of the county line. Soil types and depths vary greatly along this ridge, and the resulting geologic mosaic causes vineyards to ripen fruit in small zones. Every year these ripening lots are identified, harvested, and vinified separately in order to capture their individual viticultural expression. Each resulting *cuvée* is subsequently elevated in French oak cooperage selected for its complementary personality aimed at producing the most complete wine from each aging lot. Final blends are assembled toward the end of the barrel-aging cycle, which is usually 18–24 months in total. One of the interesting practices at Pride Mountain is they actually age the wine in old oak prior to moving it into new oak for a period of time, after which the actual final blending is accomplished right before bottling. This is somewhat different from most other wineries. A minimum of processing and no fining or filtration are used in the production of the wines.

ANNUAL PRODUCTION

Cabernet Sauvignon: 6,200 cases

Cabernet Sauvignon Reserve: 1,300 cases

Reserve Claret: 400 cases

Merlot Vintner's Select: 300 cases

Cabernet Franc: 1,200 cases

AVERAGE PRICE (VARIABLE DEPENDING ON VINTAGE): $40–130

GREAT RECENT VINTAGES

2003, 2002, 2001, 1999, 1997

This mountaintop vineyard area has 7 separate soil types and 25–40% of the surface is covered by stones. In some of the vineyards there is virtually no topsoil, but great drainage and sun exposure from all directions. At 2,000+-feet elevation, Pride Mountain Vineyards is above the fog line, and is believed to be the first vineyard planted on Spring Mountain, in 1869, with the first winery constructed (called Summit Winery) in 1890.

Winemaker Robert Foley, who is certainly one of the great talents in Northern California, has worked at Pride Mountain since its inception, and has had carte blanche from owner Jim Pride, who passed away in 2004. While the history of the Pride Mountain Vineyards under the Pride-Foley regime is relatively short, the quality of their achievement is prodigious.

The late Jim Pride

CABERNET FRANC

2002 Cabernet Franc

RATING: 93 points

I loved the penetrating aromatics and floral, blueberry, and menthol notes of the deep ruby/purple–colored 2002 Cabernet Franc. The blend is actually 75% Cabernet Franc and 25% Merlot. The flamboyant fragrance jumps from the glass of this sweetheart of a wine. There is tremendous concentration and intensity of flavor, yet the wine is light on its feet, with a surreal, ethereal flavor profile. Cabernet Franc can do some special things in California, and it is good to see this wine perform so well. Already drinkable, it should last for 10–15 years.

2001 Cabernet Franc

RATING: 95 points

Hard to find is the brilliant 2001 Cabernet Franc, a blend of 75% Cabernet Franc and 25% Merlot. Cabernet Franc's floral and blueberry characteristics are found in this intense, medium-bodied 2001, along with extraordinary elegance and palate presence. A hedonistic as well as intellectual turn-on, it should age nicely for 10–15 years, but who can resist it now?

1999 Cabernet Franc

RATING: 94 points

The terrific, extremely textured 1999 Cabernet Franc boasts a floral and black fruit–scented nose with an underlying mineral/earthiness. The wine is medium to full–bodied with an ethereal sense of lightness. The finish goes on and on. There is plenty of sweet tannin to go along with the copious fruit and extract. Pride Mountain does an amazing job with Cabernet Franc. They somehow achieve superb flavor and aromatic intensity without the weight one would expect from a wine so rich and full. Anticipated maturity: now–2018.

1998 Cabernet Franc

RATING: 94 points

The fabulous 1998 Cabernet Franc is a noteworthy achievement in this difficult vintage. Its deep purple color is accompanied by a gorgeous bouquet of cedar, spice box, black fruits, smoke, and earth. In the mouth, there is a smorgasbord of sweet black fruits with a hint of dried Provençal herbs. Opulent and full-bodied, with marvelous concentration yet an eerie sense of weightlessness, this rich, complex 1998 can be drunk now as well as over the next decade. Bravo!

1997 Cabernet Franc

RATING: 93 points

The extraordinary 1997 Cabernet Franc boasts an opaque purple color as well as a fabulously sweet nose of black currants, cranberry liqueur, new oak, and roasted notes. Chewy, full–bodied, and exceptionally huge, this offering should become even more complex with another 1–2 years of cellaring. It should keep for nearly two decades. Anticipated maturity: now–2020.

1996 Cabernet Franc

RATING: 91 points

This wine (a blend of 75% Cabernet Franc and 25% Cabernet Sauvignon) has filled out considerably, exhibiting a dense ruby/purple color, followed by a knockout nose of black cherries, herbs, and spice. In the mouth, the wine is rich, with more layers of flavor than I originally noted when I tasted it at the winery. This superb, medium to full–bodied example is the quintessential Cabernet Franc, offering elegance along with plenty of power and richness. It should drink well for another 5–10 years.

1995 Cabernet Franc

RATING: 92 points

For a Cabernet Franc, the wine possesses an uncommonly dense black/purple color, and a sweet nose of licorice, underbrush, red as well as black currants, and toast. Amazingly extracted, yet somehow retaining its elegance, this wine offers the essence of black fruits in its long, rich, medium to full–bodied flavors. There is enough acidity and some tannin, but the wine's extraordinary purity and equilibrium are hallmarks of this smashing effort. Anticipated maturity: now–2016.

CABERNET SAUVIGNON

2002 Cabernet Sauvignon

RATING: 92 points

The 2002 Cabernet Sauvignon (5,000 cases made from 100% Cabernet Sauvignon) is a supple, flamboyant, and more accessible version of the 2001 Cabernet Sauvignon. Deep ruby/purple–colored, with a classic nose of tobacco leaf, black currant, licorice, and smoke, the wine is medium to full–bodied, has a supple texture, an attractive textural mouth-feel, and a plush, heady finish. Drink it over the next 8–10 years.

2001 Cabernet Sauvignon

RATING: 95+ points

The 2001 Cabernet Sauvignon is structured and closed. Its inky/purple color is followed by scents of pure crème de cassis intertwined with licorice, smoke, and cigar tobacco. Sweet tannin forms a backdrop for a wine of admirable texture, intensity, and purity. A tremendous experience to smell and taste, it should be at its peak between 2006 and 2020.

1998 Cabernet Sauvignon

RATING: 90 points

The outstanding 1998 Cabernet Sauvignon boasts a dark ruby/purple color as well as surprising opulence for a wine from this vintage, admirable elegance, abundant black currant fruit, a dense, chewy mid-palate, a fleshy texture, low acidity, and a tannic finish. It is a classic Cabernet Sauvignon with medium weight, as well as outstanding ripeness, richness, and balance. Drink it over the next 10 years.

1997 Cabernet Sauvignon

RATING: 91–93 points

The opaque black/purple–colored 1997 Cabernet Sauvignon offers sensational notes of black currants, minerals, smoke, licorice, and new oak. Full-bodied, with fabulous extract and power, the acidity, tannin, and potentially harsh components are well meshed with the wine's personality. This is a large, ripe, impeccably balanced Cabernet Sauvignon that achieved 14.1% alcohol naturally. Anticipated maturity: now–2020.

1994 Cabernet Sauvignon

RATING: 90 points

The massive, opaque purple–colored 1994 Cabernet Sauvignon is formidably endowed, with gobs of smoky black currant fruit intelligently wrapped with toasty oak from aging in new barrels. Full-bodied, rich, powerful, muscular, and tannic, this is an impressive, immense Cabernet Sauvignon that is impeccably well balanced for its huge size. Anticipated maturity: now–2015.

CABERNET SAUVIGNON RESERVE

2002 Cabernet Sauvignon Reserve

RATING: 98 points

The 2002 Cabernet Sauvignon Reserve (100% Cabernet Sauvignon) has an inky ruby/purple color and a gorgeously sweet nose of crème de cassis and cherries intermixed with some vanilla and spice. The wine is opulent and full-bodied, with an unctuous texture and blockbuster finish with no hard edges. It seems to be on a faster evolutionary track than the 2001, but who's complaining? This is still a 15–18-year wine.

2001 Cabernet Sauvignon Reserve

RATING: 99 points

A potentially perfect wine is the 2001 Cabernet Sauvignon Reserve, which is now in bottle after having spent 30 or so months in a combination of old and new oak. The 2001 Cabernet Sauvignon Reserve (a 1,300-case blend of 100% Cabernet Sauvignon aged 27 months in oak) offers gorgeously fresh, lively, but super-concentrated fruit. Inky

blue/purple to the rim, with a spectacular nose of crème de cassis, licorice, camphor, and a hint of vanilla, this wine is sensationally rich, has remarkable intensity, a multidimensional palate, and fabulous concentration and depth. It needs another 1–3 years of bottle-aging, and should easily and effortlessly evolve for 20 or more years.

1999 Cabernet Sauvignon Reserve

RATING: 94 points

The 1999 Cabernet Sauvignon Reserve is closed, revealing remarkably concentrated crème de cassis fruit intermixed with licorice, mineral, and toasty oak aromas and flavors, along with high tannin in the finish. It tastes like an oversized Bordeaux given its tannin profile, but the huge wealth of fruit, glycerin, and extract are exceptional. Patience will be essential. Anticipated maturity: 2006–2025.

1998 Cabernet Sauvignon Reserve

RATING: 95 points

The opaque purple–colored 1998 Cabernet Sauvignon Reserve is extraordinarily full-bodied and powerful, with unbelievable finesse and harmony for a wine of such great extract and richness. Pure crème de cassis intermixed with licorice, minerals, smoke, and incense is accompanied by sweet tannin, well-integrated acidity, wood, and alcohol, and a stupendous finish lasting nearly 45 seconds. The wine is approachable, but should age easily for two decades. The limited-production Reserve *cuvée* (450 cases) is an expression of California winemaking at its most compelling.

1997 Cabernet Sauvignon Reserve

RATING: 97 points

The 1997 Cabernet Sauvignon Reserve pushes richness to unreal levels. Despite its intense, full-bodied, ultra-concentrated style, it possesses a sense of balance and definition. The color is a saturated inky purple. The aromatics consist of lead pencil shavings, minerals, blackberries, cassis, and flowers. Extremely full-bodied, with amazing purity, mouth-coating richness, sweet tannin, and low acidity, it offers profound drinking even though it has not yet begun to develop secondary nuances. Anticipated maturity: now–2025.

1996 Cabernet Sauvignon Reserve

RATING: 99 points

The virtually perfect 1996 Cabernet Sauvignon Reserve is 100% Cabernet Sauvignon. Opaque purple–colored, with a profound bouquet of minerals, flowers, black fruits, and spice, this awesomely concentrated, multilayered wine represents the essence of Cabernet Sauvignon. Amazingly, it is neither ponderous nor heavy-handed, with the oak, acidity, and tannin woven into the wine's formidable, concentrated personality. The finish lasts for nearly a minute. Sadly, it is extremely limited in availability, but what a compelling wine it is! Anticipated maturity: 2008–2025. This is a spectacular wine that must be tasted to be believed.

1995 Cabernet Sauvignon Reserve

RATING: 91 points

The promising opaque purple–colored 1995 Cabernet Sauvignon Reserve offers exceptionally sweet, rich cassis in the nose, and pure, well-delineated, full-bodied flavors that marry power with elegance. This wine is also structured and tannic, and in need of 1–2 more years of cellaring. Anticipated maturity: now–2025.

1994 Cabernet Sauvignon Reserve

RATING: 95 points

The wine's opaque purple color and huge, massive richness do not come across as heavy, despite the wine's extraordinary intensity and thickness. There is enough acidity for freshness, and plenty of sweet, well-integrated tannin. This large-scaled, magnificently endowed Cabernet Sauvignon should keep for another 10+ years.

RESERVE CLARET

2002 Reserve Claret

RATING: 98 points

The opaque purple–colored 2002 Reserve Claret reveals more aromatic development and complexity than the 2002 Cabernet Sauvignon Reserve. It boasts chocolate, blackberry, blueberry, currant, and licorice notes, a voluptuous texture, and a luscious personality. Already delicious, it will be impossible to resist young, and will last for 12–15 years.

2001 Reserve Claret

RATING: 99 points

Along with the 2001 Cabernet Sauvignon Reserve, another potentially perfect wine is the 2001 Reserve Claret, a 450-case blend of two-thirds Merlot and one-third Cabernet Sauvignon. It is a spectacular wine, offering up a dense purple color and a nose of lead pencil shavings, blackberries, crème de cassis, chocolate, and espresso roast. The wine is full-bodied, opulent, and layered, with tremendous purity and persistence on the palate. It is a stunning example of mountain viticulture that can be drunk now, although it is still an adolescent in its evolutionary development and will age for 15–20 years.

1999 Reserve Claret

RATING: 96 points

It boasts an opaque purple color in addition to a sumptuous, sweet bouquet of espresso, blackberries, cassis, maple syrup, and vanilla. It is long, layered, multidimensional, sweet, and thick on the palate, possessing an unctuousness and concentration that must be tasted to be believed. Nevertheless, it is well balanced and incredibly pure as well as long. Anticipated maturity: now–2020.

1998 Reserve Claret

RATING: 93 points

The opaque purple–colored 1998 Reserve Claret (a blend of 60% Merlot, 35% Cabernet Sauvignon, and 5% Petit Verdot) reveals red and black fruit scents intermixed with vanilla, underbrush, and mocha/coffee. It is long and opulently textured, with low acidity, fabulous fruit, a succulent, expansive mid-palate, and a blockbuster, long finish. This is compelling stuff! Drink it over the next 12–15 years.

1997 Reserve Claret

RATING: 95 points

The 1997 Reserve Claret offers an opaque purple color in addition to a sumptuous bouquet of sweet blackberries, crème de cassis, and minerals, superb richness, exceptional concentration, and huge body. However, it manages to avoid being overbearing or unmanageable. Purity and delineation are also present in this multidimensional, prodigious wine. Although an infant in terms of development, it is accessible because of the ripe tannin and spectacularly concentrated fruit. Anticipated maturity: now–2025.

1996 Reserve Claret

RATING: 95 points

The 1996 Reserve Claret is a blend of 63% Merlot, 32% Cabernet Sauvignon, and 5% Petit Verdot. It is a gorgeously balanced, super-concentrated yet hauntingly symmetrical wine with copious quantities of black fruits, spicy new oak, minerals, licorice, and roasted herbs. Full-bodied, with a cherry liqueur–like richness to its fruit, this wine has loads of glycerin, fabulous extract, and no hard edges. The velvety finish lasts for 40+ seconds. This is a spectacular wine that must be tasted to be believed. Anticipated maturity: now–2020.

1995 Reserve Claret

RATING: 90 points

The promising 1995 Reserve Claret, made from equal portions of Cabernet Sauvignon and Merlot with a microscopic portion of Petit Verdot included, reveals a saturated ruby/purple color, a dense, black cherry, cassis, and mineral–scented nose, deep, full-bodied, powerful flavors, outstanding richness, and a layered, long aftertaste. Anticipated maturity: now–2020.

MERLOT VINTNER'S SELECT

2002 Merlot Vintner's Select

RATING: 93 points

Ratcheting up the level of concentration, complexity, and persistence in the mouth is the 2002 Merlot Vintner's Select (400 cases). An opulent, heady wine that reveals gorgeously melted toffee notes intermixed with blackberry and cherry liqueur, a hint of smoke, underbrush, and fabulous power and richness, this is extraordinarily pure, dense wine that is about as good as Merlot can be in California. Drink it over the next decade.

2001 Merlot Vintner's Select Mountaintop Vineyard

RATING: 97 points

The amazing 2001 Merlot Vintner's Select Mountaintop Vineyard is a candidate for the finest Merlot-based wine I have ever tasted from Northern California. As I tasted this wine with Bob Foley, I couldn't help asking myself, "How in the hell does he get Merlot to be this great?!" This knockout effort's notes of mocha, chocolate, and black cherry liqueur form into an amazingly concentrated, rich yet elegant wine with no hard edges. This seamless classic is worth twisting a few arms to get a bottle or two. It's that spectacular . . . and I'm not a fan of New World Merlot! Drink it over the next 12–15 years.

1999 Merlot Vintner's Select Mountaintop Vineyard

RATING: 94 points

The 1999 Merlot Vintner's Select Mountaintop Vineyard, a new offering, is a selection of Jim Pride and Robert Foley's favorite Merlot lots. Approximately 20% Cabernet Sauvignon has been added to the blend. This is a "balls to the walls" sort of wine—opaque purple–colored, with notes of melted fudge intermixed with dense black cherry, tightly wound, but oh so concentrated flavors. The depth, sweetness of fruit, and richness of the tannin are incredible given the fact that this wine emerged from such a cool year. This is one of the finest California Merlots I have tasted. It will drink well for 12–15 years.

WINES:

Monte Bello Vineyard (primarily Cabernet Sauvignon)

Geyserville (primarily Zinfandel)

Lytton Springs (primarily Zinfandel)

OWNER: Ridge Vineyards, Inc.; Shareholder, Akihiko Otsuka; Chief Executive Officer, Paul Draper

ADDRESS: 17100 Monte Bello Road, P.O. Box 1810, Cupertino, CA 95015

TELEPHONE: (408) 867-3233

TELEFAX: (408) 868-1350

E-MAIL: wine@ridgewine.com

WEBSITE: www.ridgewine.com

CONTACT: Michael Perry

VISITING POLICY: Monte Bello Tasting Room, open Saturday and Sunday from 11 A.M. to 4 P.M., weekdays for sales, please call; Lytton Springs Tasting Room, 650 Lytton Springs Road, Healdsburg, CA 95448, open every day from 11 A.M. to 4 P.M.

VINEYARDS

SURFACE AREA: 653.3 acres total

GRAPE VARIETALS: Cabernet Sauvignon, Merlot, Petit Verdot, Cabernet Franc, Chardonnay, Zinfandel, Petite Syrah, Carignane, Matarro (Mourvèdre), Syrah, Grenache, Viognier, Alicante Bouschet

AVERAGE AGE OF THE VINES: Oldest planted 1880; youngest planted 2003

Monte Bello Vineyard (Bordeaux varietals)—35 years old

Lytton Springs Vineyards (Zinfandel and traditional blending varietals)—33 years old

Geyserville Vineyards (Zinfandel and traditional blending varietals)—47 years old

DENSITY OF PLANTATION: Ranges from 310–1,350 vines per acre

AVERAGE YIELDS: Ranges from 1.6–2.8 tons per acre

WINEMAKING AND UPBRINGING

All of the Bordeaux varietals at Ridge enjoy natural malolactic fermentations carried out in barrel, and the wine remains on its gross lees for at least three months. One of the interesting twists is that, unlike most of the top Cabernet Sauvignon producers of the world, Ridge has always used American white oak. They constantly conduct experiments with the finest French oak and have done so for nearly 20 years, but consistently prefer what the fruit from their Monte Bello vineyard does in the dried white American oak. Moreover, 100% new oak is used for the Monte Bello Cabernet Sauvignon, although very little is used in

producing their two great proprietary reds based on Zinfandel: Lytton Springs and Geyserville.

ANNUAL PRODUCTION

Monte Bello: 46,400 bottles

Lytton Springs: 139,000 bottles

Geyserville: 121,500 bottles

AVERAGE PRICE (VARIABLE DEPENDING ON VINTAGE): $25–125

GREAT RECENT VINTAGES

Monte Bello (Bordeaux varietals)—2002, 2001, 1999, 1997, 1996, 1995, 1992, 1991, 1988, 1985, 1981, 1977, 1974, 1971, 1970, 1968, 1964, 1962

Lytton Springs (Zinfandel and traditional blending varietals)—2001, 1999, 1995, 1990, 1987, 1974, 1973

Geyserville (Zinfandel and traditional blending varietals)— 2002, 2001, 1999, 1997, 1993, 1987, 1977, 1973, 1970

Nestled high in the Santa Cruz Mountains, with a precipitous view of the San Andreas Fault, Ridge Vineyards has long been one of the classic reference points for high-quality California wines. While the winery now has a Japanese owner, longtime winemaker Paul Draper continues to have complete control of vineyard management and winemaking.

For the last 40 years, one of Ridge's fundamental goals has been to identify vineyard sites capable of producing the finest wines without blending in other vineyards, and without using mechanical and chemical

Paul Draper

processing. Paul Draper's position, supported by the new owner, is that the finest wines of the world should "represent something more real, more authentic than an industrial process and a winemaker's blend."

The history at Ridge is impressive. The ridge itself is limestone, 12 miles long, and dates back 100 million years. The original winery was built in 1886, but it wasn't until 1949 that Cabernet Sauvignon vines were planted on limestone subsoils in a region that they believe is as cool as Bordeaux. Full-scale commercial operation at Ridge began in 1962. The famed Monte Bello Ridge vineyard, where the best vines are planted, is 20 miles south of San Francisco. The records show that Osea Perrone, a doctor from northern Italy, built the Monte Bello Winery in 1886. He carved terraces into the surrounding steep slopes, planted the first grapes at a 2,700-foot altitude, and bottled the first vintage of Monte Bello in 1892. The winery stopped producing during Prohibition and was subsequently abandoned.

The current Ridge Vineyards was founded when three friends, all working at Stanford Research Institute, as well as their wives, set out in the late 1950s to find a piece of land in the hills where they could bring their kids on weekends and camp out. Dave and Fran Bennion, Hew and Sue Crane, and Charlie and Blanche Rosen purchased this vineyard from a retired theologian, William Short, in 1959. The winery was reopened in 1962, and Ridge's famous label, which has remained largely unchanged since its inception, was designed by the late Jim Robertson. It was later, at a fortuitous meeting at a friend's house, that Dave and Fran Bennion met Paul Draper. Although not an oenologist (his major at Stanford was philosophy), Draper did know about wine and he joined Ridge as the winemaker in 1969. The rest, as they say, is history.

In 1986 Ridge was purchased by the Japanese-born fine-wine collector Akihiko Otsuka, who had the foresight to leave Paul Draper, also one of the company's principal shareholders, responsible for the operation. While the Geyserville Vineyard is under a long-term lease from its owners, the Trentadues, the Monte Bello Vineyard is owned by the winery, as is the Lytton Springs Vineyards, which was purchased in two separate transactions. More recently, Donn Reisen, who had worked at Ridge for some time, became the president, but Paul Draper has continued as winemaker and chief executive officer. The only major change has been the construction of the Lytton Springs Winery, which has allowed that wine to be made on-site, so the fruit no longer has to be shipped down to the Monte Bello site.

CABERNET SAUVIGNON MONTE BELLO

2002 Monte Bello Proprietary Red
RATING: 94+ points
The 2002 Monte Bello Proprietary Red is a blend of Cabernet Sauvignon, Merlot, and Petit Verdot, with more of the Cabernet component than the 2001 possesses. Aromas of white chocolate, charred oak, black currants, tar, cedar, and earth are followed by a full-bodied, tannic red that is not as fleshy or fat in the mid-palate as its older sibling. This structured, ageworthy 2002 should be consumed between 2011 and 2030.

2001 Monte Bello Proprietary Red
RATING: 96 points
A candidate for one of the longest-lived Cabernet Sauvignon–based wines in California is Ridge's Monte Bello. The 2001 Monte Bello Proprietary Red is this historic vineyard's 40th anniversary *cuvée*. It boasts a saturated purple color in addition to a luxurious perfume of smoky oak, plums, cedarwood, espresso, black cherries, and cassis. As the wine sits in the glass, a hint of tar also emerges. This full-bodied, broad, expansively flavored offering exhibits high tannin along with a huge finish. In blind tastings, I consistently mistake these *cuvées* for French Bordeaux, and also underestimate their age since they last for 30+ years. Over 90% of this offering is aged in new American oak, yet it never displays that sappy American oak character, thanks to the superb cooperage of the barrels. This top-notch 2001 Monte Bello should be at its best between 2012 and 2035.

2000 Monte Bello Proprietary Red
RATING: 90 points
The 2000 Monte Bello Proprietary Red (75% Cabernet Sauvignon, 23% Merlot, and 2% Cabernet Franc) is a surprisingly forward example of a Ridge Monte Bello. Its dense ruby/purple color is accompanied by sweet toasty oak along with crème de cassis, licorice, and resin-like aromas. Medium to full–bodied, nicely textured, and elegant with soft tannin as well as a forward style (surprising in view of winemaker Paul Draper's typical style), it could firm up considerably in the bottle and last for 12–13 years. Anticipated maturity: now–2016.

1997 Cabernet Sauvignon Monte Bello
RATING: 91+ points
The 1997 Cabernet Sauvignon Monte Bello exhibits an opaque purple color, as well as an elegant, black currant, mineral, and smoky oak–scented nose. The wine is medium to

full–bodied, tannic, and in need of another 5 years of cellaring. Not a blockbuster, this offering is more elegant and finesse-styled than usual. As with previous Monte Bellos, it will take a long time to come around, yet it will keep for 2–3 decades. Anticipated maturity: 2008–2028.

1996 Cabernet Sauvignon Monte Bello

RATING: 95 points

The 1996 Cabernet Sauvignon Monte Bello (80% Cabernet Sauvignon, 11% Merlot, and 9% Petit Verdot that reached 13.4% alcohol) represents a severe selection of only 40% of the vineyard's crop. A blockbuster, powerful, concentrated Monte Bello, it possesses an opaque purple color, plenty of spicy oak in the nose, and a deep, layered, concentrated style. There is plenty of tannin, but it is sweeter than that found in the 1997, and the wine is more concentrated and extracted. There is a touch of oak in the flavors, which are otherwise dominated by minerals and jammy black fruits. This is a terrific Monte Bello that will have another 25+ years of life.

1995 Cabernet Sauvignon Monte Bello

RATING: 91 points

The 1995 Monte Bello is actually a Proprietary Red Wine, as the blend is 69% Cabernet Sauvignon, 18% Merlot, 10% Petit Verdot, and 3% Cabernet Franc. It was made from an extremely severe selection of only 25% of the harvest. Paul Draper feels it is the biggest, brawniest, and most muscular Monte Bello of the 1990s, and in need of 5–10 more years of cellaring. This saturated ruby/purple–colored effort is still backward, with a closed nose of minerals, oak, and subtle black fruits. In the mouth, it is large-scaled, tannic, rich, and long, but nearly abrasive because of the wine's high tannin level. This youthful, muscular, monster Monte Bello will require significant cellaring. Anticipated maturity: 2010–2035.

1994 Cabernet Sauvignon Monte Bello

RATING: 91+ points

The 1994 Cabernet Sauvignon Monte Bello was one of the most backward Cabernets in a tasting in March 1996. It almost defies inspection given its austere, extremely tannic, hard style. The opaque purple color is accompanied by a wine that smells and tastes ripe, rich, and brilliantly made, but it will require a minimum of another 3–5 years of cellaring to shed enough tannin to become civilized. Although it should be a winner, it may not be as sure a bet as such vintages as 1995, 1992, and 1991. When young, this wine rarely reveals its full potential. Having said that, the 1995, 1994, and 1993 vintages of the Monte Bello Cabernet Sauvignon are immensely impressive, with perhaps the 1994 the least expansive—for now.

1993 Cabernet Sauvignon Monte Bello

RATING: 93 points

The 1993 Ridge Monte Bello is a tightly wrapped, densely colored, pure, rich, full-bodied Cabernet with moderately intense aromas of vanilla, black raspberries, currants, and minerals. This rich wine cuts a deep path on the palate, with high tannin, adequate acidity, and a long, muscular, formidably endowed finish. Anticipated maturity: now–2015.

1992 Cabernet Sauvignon Monte Bello

RATING: 97 points

This 1992 looks to be one of the greatest examples of Monte Bello Cabernet Sauvignon that Ridge has produced. Only 40% of the crop made it into the final blend, which consists of 75% Cabernet Sauvignon, 11% Merlot, 10% Petit Verdot, and 4% Cabernet Franc. The wine offers a black/purple color, a profound nose of minerals, cassis, licorice, and spices, spectacular richness, and a great mid-palate that boasts layers of fruit. Admirable purity, fine underlying acidity, and considerable sweet, ripe tannin make this another compelling effort. Assuming good cellar conditions, the 1992 Monte Bello should have another 20–25 years of longevity. Anticipated maturity: now-2028.

1991 Cabernet Sauvignon Monte Bello

RATING: 92 points

The top-notch 1991 Cabernet Sauvignon Monte Bello exhibits the classic austerity found in Bordeaux, with a reserved but highly complex bouquet of licorice, cassis, and lead pencil. It is a rich, almost measured wine in its restraint, but there is considerable intensity, and the wine offers outstanding extraction of flavor, full body, and gobs of tannin. Given the glacial pace at which most Monte Bellos evolve, this wine is not likely to be fully mature for another 2–5 years. Anticipated maturity: 2008–2030.

1990 Cabernet Sauvignon Monte Bello

RATING: 93 points

The 1990 Monte Bello remains backward, tannic, and rich, and is just beginning to approach adolescence. Its cassis, mineral, and oak-scented nose offered considerable promise. With medium to full body, crisp acidity, and a long, tight, closed finish, it requires considerable patience. Anticipated maturity: 2007–2017.

1987 Cabernet Sauvignon Monte Bello

RATING: 90 points

The 1987 Monte Bello is one of those profound mountain Cabernets that should last for 20–25 years. There is not much of it available, as quantities produced from the Monte Bello Vineyard in 1987 were tiny. Dark black/ruby, with a rich, ripe yet reticent bouquet of minerals, black currants, and toasted oak, this wine is exceptionally concentrated, full-bodied, and extremely firm and closed. With airing, some blossoming flavors of licorice, black currants, and vanilla emerge. The finish is long, but forbiddingly tannic. This is a large-scaled yet impeccably balanced wine for drinking during the first two decades of this century. Anticipated maturity: now–2020.

1985 Cabernet Sauvignon Monte Bello
RATING: 94 points

The beautiful ruby/purple color exhibits no signs of age. The sweet nose of cassis fruit, lead pencil, flowers, and minerals is followed by a full-bodied, opulent wine with a boatload of tannin. This huge, massive, yet well-delineated and focused wine should prove to be uncommonly long-lived. Drink it between now–2030.

1984 Cabernet Sauvignon Monte Bello
RATING: 95 points

The saturated purple color of this blockbuster Cabernet Sauvignon displays no amber or signs of evolution at the edge. The nose reluctantly offers up pure aromas of black fruits, minerals, and licorice. Extremely full-bodied, with layers of rich, glycerin-dominated, sweet, jammy fruit buttressed by zesty acidity and abundant tannin, this large-scaled, surprisingly well-proportioned and balanced Cabernet Sauvignon is a candidate for 10–15+ years of longevity. So what's new? Anticipated maturity: now–2024.

GEYSERVILLE PROPRIETARY RED

2002 Geyserville Proprietary Red
RATING: 92 points

Another reference-point effort from Ridge, the 2002 Geyserville Proprietary Red (84% Zinfandel, 12% Carignan, and 4% Petite Syrah) boasts a rich, sumptuous bouquet of blackberries, kirsch, damp earth, and licorice. Full-bodied and powerful, with good acidity as well as surprising elegance, this ruby/purple-colored, heady 2002 can be drunk over the next 7–8 years.

2001 Geyserville Proprietary Red
RATING: 91 points

The 2001 Geyserville Proprietary Red, a blend of 74% Zinfandel, 18% Carignan, and 8% Petite Syrah, is a beautiful effort. Its deep ruby/purple color is followed by a tight but promising nose of raspberry and briery fruit intermingled with notions of oak, pepper, and resin. This dense, full-bodied, textured, voluptuous offering is both exuberant and dramatic on the palate. Although the aromatics have not caught up with the flavors, this appears to be an exceptional example of this renowned *cuvée*. Its 14.4% alcohol is well disguised beneath some serious concentration. It will drink well for 5–6 years.

1999 Geyserville Proprietary Red
RATING: 91 points

The exceptional 1999 Geyserville Proprietary Red (a blend of 68% Zinfandel, 16% Carignan, and 16% Petite Syrah with 14.8% alcohol) offers aromas of black currants, kirsch, minerals, smoky oak, earth, and spice. It possesses superb concentration, excellent definition, tremendous purity, and mouth-staining extract without heaviness. A long finish further enhances this sensational, Zinfandel-dominated offering. Consume it over the next 4–5 years.

1998 Geyserville Proprietary Red
RATING: 90 points

A classic effort, the 1998 Geyserville (74% Zinfandel, 15% Petite Syrah, 10% Carignan, and 1% Matero) possesses Bordeaux-like complexity and elegance. The alcohol is listed as 14.1%. The wine was reticent on the day I tasted it, but as it sat in the glass, sweet aromas of minerals, smoky wood, red/black currants, and dried herbs emerged. This classy, elegant, restrained, yet authoritatively rich Zinfandel should be consumed over the next 1–2 years.

1997 Geyserville Proprietary Red
RATING: 91 points

The 1997 Geyserville Proprietary Red (74% Zinfandel, 15% Carignan, 10% Petite Syrah, and 1% Mourvèdre, with 14.9% alcohol) offers explosive aromas of jammy berry fruit and flavors redolent with notes of plums, cherries, raspberries, and smoky wood. Open-knit and expansive, with low acidity, this evolved, forward, hedonistic wine will drink well for another 1–2 years.

LYTTON SPRINGS PROPRIETARY RED

2002 Lytton Springs Proprietary Red
RATING: 93 points

One of the most famous names in Zinfandel-land is Lytton Springs, and Ridge's 2002 Lytton Springs (75% Zinfandel, 20% Petite Syrah, and 5% Carignan) boasts a deep ruby/purple hue along with a big, sweet nose of brier, blueberry and blackberry fruit, full body, good acidity, and notions of pepper, loamy earth, and licorice. While this beauty will undoubtedly last a decade, it should be at its finest over the next 5–6 years.

2001 Lytton Springs Proprietary Red

RATING: 92 points

The superb 2001 Lytton Springs Proprietary Red is a blend of 76% Zinfandel, 17% Petite Syrah, and 7% Carignan (14.7% alcohol). I was knocked out by its multiple dimensions and combination of jammy, briery raspberry and currant fruit intermingled with licorice, spice, and pepper. Its dense purple color is accompanied by a rich, full-bodied palate presentation and a long, seamless finish. Enjoy this outrageously delicious Zinfandel over the next 5–6 years.

1999 Lytton Springs Proprietary Red

RATING: 90 points

An exceptional offering from Ridge's portfolio is the 1999 Lytton Springs Proprietary Red. This superb blend of 70% Zinfandel, 17% Petite Syrah, 10% Carignan, and 3% Mataro boasts a deep ruby/purple color in addition to a big, sweet bouquet of jammy berries, and a hint of raspberries as well as strawberries. Elegant and full-bodied, with layers of flavor, superb purity, a subtle dosage of American oak, and a full, long finish, it should drink well for another 3–5 years.

1998 Lytton Springs Proprietary Red

RATING: 90 points

A Ridge classic, the deep ruby/purple–colored 1998 Lytton Springs (14.3% alcohol; 77% Zinfandel, 16% Petite Syrah, 4% Matero, 2% Carignan, and 1% Alicante) boasts a sweet nose of briery fruit intermixed with red and black currants, minerals, pepper, and smoke. Medium to full–bodied, with dried Provençal herb characteristics that emerge with airing, this fleshy, beautifully pure, and stunningly proportioned Zinfandel can be drunk now as well as over the next 1–2 years.

1997 Lytton Springs Proprietary Red

RATING: 92 points

Made from a blend of 80% Zinfandel, 15% Petite Syrah, 2% Carignan, 2% Mataro, and 1% Grenache, the 1997 Lytton Springs Proprietary Red (14.9% alcohol) exhibits a saturated purple color in addition to sumptuous aromas of truffles, licorice, loamy soil, blackberry liqueur, and cherries. There are layers of concentration, sweet glycerin in the mid-palate, and a blockbuster, concentrated, opulently textured finish. It should drink well for 1–2 more years.

WINE:

Cabernet Sauvignon

OWNER: Jean Phillips

ADDRESS: P.O. Box 134, Oakville, CA 94562

TELEPHONE: (707) 944-0749

TELEFAX: (707) 944-9271

VISITING POLICY: Not open to the public

VINEYARDS

SURFACE AREA: Approximately 57 acres

GRAPE VARIETALS: Cabernet Sauvignon, Cabernet Franc,
    Merlot

AVERAGE AGE OF THE VINES: Approximately 15 years

DENSITY OF PLANTATION: Varies from 5' x 5' spacing to 6' x 11'

AVERAGE YIELDS: From 2 to 4 tons per acre

WINEMAKING AND UPBRINGING

I keep asking Jean Phillips what she does in order to achieve such purity of fruit. Essentially, her comments are "less is more," and she wants to show "the fingerprints of our vineyard." The winemaking approach has been to harvest healthy, ripe Cabernet Sauvignon fruit and blend it with small amounts of Cabernet Franc and Merlot. There are no secrets —yields are modest, grapes are harvested at 24 Brix (which is normal), the wine is aged in Seguin-Moreau French barrels (about 65% new) for 18 months and bottled with little or no filtration. Considerable punching down is done at Screaming Eagle, and the small, half-ton fermenters may hold the secret to the extraordinary fruit quality Phillips achieves. On the other hand, it may simply be the *terroir* combined with the owner's obsession with brilliant wines. And let's not forget the consulting oenologist, Napa Valley's Heidi Barrett.

ANNUAL PRODUCTION

Cabernet Sauvignon: 500–850 cases

AVERAGE PRICE (VARIABLE DEPENDING ON VINTAGE): $125–$300

GREAT RECENT VINTAGES:

2002, 2001, 1999, 1997, 1995, 1994, 1992

This impressive operation is run by real estate broker Jean Phillips. Ms. Phillips owns 57 acres well situated on the Napa Valley floor, from which she culls the finest fruit for the 500–800+ cases she produces in a micro-sized stone winery perched on a stony hillside overlooking the valley. Since she first started selling in 1992, in many ways Screaming Eagle has become the poster child for limited production, high-quality, super-expensive California wines. Only the winery price for mailing list customers is realistic. In the secondary market (the auction market) the wine has shot up in price to $700–1,000 a bottle.

Screaming Eagle is an extraordinary expression of Cabernet Sauvignon grown in Napa's tenderloin section, the Oakville Corridor. While accessible upon release, even the debut vintages are still relatively young wines that are developing slowly but assuredly. Jean Phillips has taken all of this fame in stride. It often appears that she would prefer to be riding one of her Ducati motorcycles. Having visited her annually to taste since Screaming Eagle was first produced, I've always found her extraordinary energy and down-to-earth personality refreshing. She met Heidi Barrett (the wife of Château Montelena's Bo Barrett, and one of Napa Valley's most respected consultants) through her friend Robert Mondavi, and Barrett has been the one and only winemaker at Screaming Eagle.

Phillips began acquiring her property in 1986 in a piecemeal fashion. The vineyard is planted in rocky soils on a mostly west-facing slope, east of the Napa River, and enjoys superb drainage. Even in the hottest vintages, the fruit never appears to get a cooked or baked character. Only a tiny percentage of the 57 acres is used in the wine's production, and, at the suggestion of the late André Tchelistcheff, the primary varietal is Clone 7. What makes Screaming Eagle wines so stunning is the black currant/cassis fruit, which may be the most extravagantly rich expression of cassis one can find short of drinking cassis itself. There is an unbelievable purity to these wines, as well as phenomenal concentration and richness, yet in no sense are they heavy, ponderous, or out of balance. Getting on the winery's mailing list is the only way to latch on to a bottle, unless you get lucky and find a bottle at one of Napa Valley's wine shops or restaurants.

Opposite: Jean Phillips

Jean Phillips has summed it up as beautifully as anyone who has enjoyed such extraordinary success. "I followed my heart, and have always felt I was doing something I genuinely loved. If I was successful at it, great. If I wasn't, at least I was enjoying my life. This is a philosophy I have followed forever."

CABERNET SAUVIGNON

2003 Cabernet Sauvignon

RATING: 95–97 points

The 2003 is a superb effort from this winery, but production is down significantly, with only 600 cases produced. A dense purple color is followed by a sweet nose of charcoal-infused crème de cassis intermixed with licorice, graphite, and a subtle hint of vanilla. Full-bodied, dense, and powerful, with more tannin and structure than the 2002 exhibited at a similar age, the 2003 looks set for a long life of 20–25 years. Anticipated maturity: 2009–2025. (Release date: 2006.)

2002 Cabernet Sauvignon

RATING: 99 points

The 2002 is reminiscent of the 1992, exhibiting a precociousness out of the gate, but capable of lasting 20–25 years. Deep purple–colored to the rim, with a gorgeously pure nose of crème de cassis and hints of sweet cherry, licorice, and smoke, this wine is beautifully voluptuous, full-bodied, yet incredibly elegant, with a finish that goes on for close to a minute. It is more showy than either the 2001 or the 2003. Anticipated maturity: 2008–2025.

2001 Cabernet Sauvignon

RATING: 98 points

The 2001 (of which only 450 cases were produced) is a blend of 88% Cabernet Sauvignon, 10% Merlot, and 2% Cabernet Franc. Dense purple with a classic nose of black currant liqueur intermixed with licorice, a touch of earth, smoke, and discreet toast, this wine is a powerful, tannic, dense, young offering revealing Screaming Eagle's classic trademarks of fragrance, purity, nobility, and an extraordinary intensity of black currant fruit in a full-bodied, seamless style. Anticipated maturity: 2010–2025+.

1999 Cabernet Sauvignon

RATING: 97 points

The bottled 1999 (a blend of 88% Cabernet Sauvignon, 10% Merlot, and 2% Cabernet Franc) is as profound as I predicted in early 2001. It boasts an opaque purple color along with a gorgeously pure nose of crème de cassis, charcoal, and floral characteristics. The wine is opulent, dense, and rich, with exceptional purity, a viscous texture, and impressive underlying tannin that frames its large but elegant personality. Not surprisingly, this is a candidate for the wine of the vintage. Anticipated maturity: now–2020.

1998 Cabernet Sauvignon

RATING: 94 points

The 1998 Cabernet Sauvignon, which was bottled in late June 2000, has turned out even better than I originally thought. It boasts a saturated ruby/purple color in addition to an expressive bouquet of cassis, minerals, and smoke. This multitextured, round wine exhibits sweet, well-integrated tannin, a great midpalate and finish, as well as spectacular purity and palate presence. Consume it now and over the next 10–15 years.

1997 Cabernet Sauvignon

RATING: 100 points

It doesn't get any better than Screaming Eagle's 1997 Cabernet Sauvignon, a perfect wine. Representing the essence of cassis intermixed with blackberries, minerals, licorice, and toast, this full-bodied, multidimensional classic is fabulous, with extraordinary purity, symmetry, and a finish that lasts for nearly a minute. It has the overall equilibrium to evolve for nearly two decades. Anticipated maturity: now–2020.

1996 Cabernet Sauvignon

RATING: 98 points

The 1996 Cabernet Sauvignon reveals lots of structure, an opaque purple color, and the hallmark blackberry and cassis–like notes. It is silky-textured, fabulously concentrated, and gorgeously balanced; every component part—acidity, alcohol, tannin, and extract—is flawlessly presented. Anticipated maturity: now–2020.

1995 Cabernet Sauvignon

RATING: 99 points

The 1995 Cabernet Sauvignon is as close to a perfect wine as I could hope to taste. This opaque purple–colored wine exhibits a sensational purity of black currant fruit, intermixed with a notion of raspberries, violets, and well-disguised sweet vanilla. Full-bodied, with remarkable intensity, exquisite symmetry, and a mid-palate and finish to die for, this is a compelling, astonishingly seductive Cabernet Sauvignon that can be drunk now, or cellared for another 12–18 years. I may have done this wine a disservice by not giving it the big 3-digit score.

1994 Cabernet Sauvignon

RATING: 94 points

The opaque purple–colored 1994's forward, gorgeously scented nose offers up a smorgasbord of black fruits, along with a subtle dose of toasty oak and minerals. Full-bodied, with a seamless, lush texture, this is a profoundly generous wine with everything going for it. The finish lasts for 35 seconds. As gorgeous as it is, this wine can be drunk young or cellared for another 12–17 years.

1993 Cabernet Sauvignon

RATING: 97 points

The 1993 Cabernet Sauvignon is a remarkable wine, not dissimilar from the 1992. It reveals an opaque purple color, as well as a rich, jammy, pure nose of black currant/cassis fruit intertwined with scents of minerals and high-quality, spicy oak. The wine offers a cascade of lavishly rich, opulently textured, super-extracted fruit that is beautifully buttressed by the oak and sweet tannin. Remarkably long, pure, and rich, this is a compelling Cabernet Sauvignon with no hard edges. Perfectly balanced, marvelously concentrated, and exciting, look for this wine to drink well for another 15 years.

1992 Cabernet Sauvignon

RATING: 99 points

The 1992 Screaming Eagle Cabernet Sauvignon is exceptionally impressive. The wine's opaque purple color is followed by a sensational nose of jammy black currant and subtle toasty oak. As stunning as the aromatics are, the wine reveals even greater richness and intensity on the palate, offering up layers of stunningly proportioned, ripe, intense fruit; full body; great purity; and an inner core of sweet, creamy, highly extracted black currant/cassis fruit. The tannin is nearly concealed behind the massive extract and richness. All the component parts are brilliantly focused and in balance. The finish is awesome! This is a spectacular debut release that should age effortlessly until at least 2015.

WINE:

Cabernet Sauvignon Hillside Select

OWNER: Doug Shafer, President; John Shafer, Chairman

ADDRESS: 6154 Silverado Trail, Napa, CA 94558

TELEPHONE: (707) 944-2877

TELEFAX: (707) 944-9454

E-MAIL: info@shafervineyards.com

WEBSITE: www.shafervineyards.com

CONTACT: Doug Shafer

VISITING POLICY: By appointment only

VINEYARDS

SURFACE AREA: 200 acres

GRAPE VARIETALS: Cabernet Sauvignon, Chardonnay,
Sangiovese, Merlot, Syrah; also, small quantities for
blending, Cabernet Franc and Petite Syrah

AVERAGE AGE OF THE VINES: 10 years

DENSITY OF PLANTATION: 1100 per acre

AVERAGE YIELDS: 3.5 tons per acre

WINEMAKING AND UPBRINGING

The Shafers claim to simply "let the fruit dictate the style," but
that's a lot more difficult than it sounds, because letting the
fruit dominate the winemaking process requires a detailed
knowledge of every block of vines in their vineyards. They
make no excuses for the fact that their vineyards produce
"big, bold, no-holds-barred flavors" and that "we take advantage of the climate to go after truly ripe fruit that delivers
massive flavors with lots of color, concentration, and extract."

At Shafer, the winemaking team of John and Doug Shafer,
along with the brilliant Elias Fernandez, has been in place for
20 years. Only at Château Montelena and a handful of other estates has the same lineup done the same thing for so long. The
Shafers were also quick learners, recognizing early on that the
standard winemaking recipe prescribed by the University of
California at Davis and other wine experts (which calls for 18
months in oak) wasn't working from their greatest vineyard,
the Hillside Selections, for their Cabernet Sauvignon. So, in the
1980s, "The cookbook went out the window," and the Hillside
Select ended up getting 24 months in barrel, later increased to a
full 34 months.

ANNUAL PRODUCTION

Cabernet Sauvignon Hillside Select: 28,800 bottles
(2,400 cases)

AVERAGE PRICE (VARIABLE DEPENDING ON VINTAGE): $100–$150

GREAT RECENT VINTAGES

2003, 2002, 2001, 1999, 1997, 1996, 1995, 1994, 1992, 1991,
1985, 1978

The Cabernet Sauvignon Hillside Select, one of the most prodigious Cabernet Sauvignons in the world, is indeed a wine of its place of origin. The Shafers claim that in the great years of Napa it is by far the easiest wine to make, but in the drought-stricken years, the poor soils, which have no moisture-retentive qualities, can effectively defoliate the vineyard. The fruit for the Cabernet Sauvignon Hillside Select is tiny, usually no bigger than the size of blueberries, but there are different clones planted. Today, only 2,400 cases of Cabernet Sauvignon Hillside Select are produced, all of it gobbled up by the extremely faithful band of Shafer enthusiasts.

The winery, which has been making wine since 1978, was the creation of John Shafer, who, several years shy of his 50th birthday, visited California wine country ready to start a second career after a very successful life in the corporate world. After visiting several sites, he developed a fondness for a neglected 30-acre vineyard site planted with an assortment of white and red varietals with a run-down house on the property. Undeterred by the fact that several well-known growers in Napa had already turned the site down, it had what John Shafer was looking for—hillsides of thin, volcanic soils that offered quick drainage. It was also located at the southern end of the valley, in what is now known as the Stags Leap district, which offers a balanced combination of midday heat and cool, late-day breezes off the San Francisco Bay. He purchased this 209-acre property and quickly moved there, leaving the corporate life of Chicago and becoming a grape grower. At first, the fruit was sold to the St. Helena cooperative, where it was then trucked to Gallo Brothers' huge industrial plant in Modesto and blended into hearty Burgundy. However, the fruit quality was so good that local vintners began to pay even higher premiums for it. After a homemade wine off the estate in 1977, John Shafer decided to take the plunge, and the first vintage, the 1978 Shafer Vineyards Cabernet Sauvignon, was made. His son Doug graduated from UC Davis having studied oenology and viticulture, and in 1983 was ready to become the full-time winemaker at Shafer. He was joined one year later by Elias Fernandez, and this team has remained in place ever since. Both Doug Shafer and Elias Fernandez are quick to admit that their first four or five vintages were made the way they had been taught, and their product was very stable, sound, and totally free from any potential spoilage, but

Doug and John Shafer, and Elias Fernandez

was uninteresting and tasted generic. "By 1986, we threw out the textbooks, because we wanted to listen to the wine. We wanted to make the kind of wine that was dictated by the place where it was grown. We wanted big, lush, bold, hedonistic wines, not something safe and sound." Some of those early vintages turned out to be brilliant, but there's no question that since the early 1990s, the quality at Shafer has improved further and resulted in some of the world's greatest wines. Their Cabernet Sauvignon Hillside Select, in particular, is one of the most compelling Cabernets in the world. As the Shafers say somewhat reflectively, "In 2004, we celebrated 25 years of winemaking, but even with that kind of experience under our belts, it's impossible to sit back on our laurels. It all comes down to this—every year you get one shot, and just like Charlie Brown used to say, you get to be the hero or the goat. At every point in the grape-growing and winemaking process, there are about 100 things that can go haywire. While we have learned a great deal about how to make a bottle of wine, being the 'goat' is always only a few missteps away."

CABERNET SAUVIGNON HILLSIDE SELECT

2003 Cabernet Sauvignon Hillside Select

RATING: 94–98 points

A lighter vintage than both 2001 and 2002, the 2003 Cabernet Sauvignon Hillside Select exhibits a surreal elegance, restraint, and beauty that comes across as a hybrid blend of a great Médoc and a Stags Leap Cabernet Sauvignon. Notes of flowers intermixed with black currants, blueberries, and minerals are present in this medium to full–bodied, pure, concentrated effort. It has a strikingly seamless personality despite being so young and still in barrel. The wine reveals style, nobility, and character, and should be approachable when released in several years. This looks like another candidate for two decades of aging potential.

2002 Cabernet Sauvignon Hillside Select

RATING: 98–100 points

Equally impressive but more muscular and flamboyant than the structured and restrained 2001 is the 2002 Cabernet Sauvignon Hillside Select. It boasts an explosive nose of crème de cassis intermixed with smoke, licorice, camphor, and vanilla. This full-bodied, extravagantly rich, opulent, dense, chewy 2002 possesses low acidity, tremendous concentration, and a fabulous finish. More sumptuous, lush, and voluptuous than the 2001, it will be showy young, but should age for 20–25 or more years.

2001 Cabernet Sauvignon Hillside Select

RATING: 99 points

The 2001 Cabernet Sauvignon Hillside Select is a potentially perfect wine in the making. A skyscraper that builds in the mouth with multiple dimensions, amazing layers of flavor, great delicacy, and tremendous purity, this inky purple–colored Cabernet offers extraordinarily pure crème de cassis notes intermixed with crushed rocks, flowers, sweet oak, an amazingly powerful yet impeccably balanced mid-palate, and a sweet, 70-second finish. This prodigious Cabernet Sauvignon is about as good as Cabernet can be.

2000 Cabernet Sauvignon Hillside Select

RATING: 93 points

The 2000 Cabernet Sauvignon Hillside Select was performing even better this year than it was last year. While not as weighty and ageworthy as some of the more hallowed vintages, it is a seriously endowed wine. Deep ruby/purple to the rim, with a gorgeous nose of crème de cassis, licorice, graphite, spice, and cedar, it is more forward than most vintages, but full-bodied, concentrated, and beautifully seductive. Drink it over the next 15 or so years.

1999 Cabernet Sauvignon Hillside Select

RATING: 97 points

The 1999 Cabernet Sauvignon Hillside Select is one of the finest wines of the vintage. The 14.9% alcohol is barely noticeable given the amazing concentration and intensity. A saturated opaque purple color is followed by scents of vanilla, blackberry liqueur, crushed minerals, and a hint of white flowers. There is stunning intensity, tremendous purity, full body, and a remarkable, seamless finish (amazing given the elevated, austere tannin). Give the 1999 another 2–3 years of cellaring, and enjoy it over the following two decades or longer. A brilliant effort!

1998 Cabernet Sauvignon Hillside Select

RATING: 94 points

The 1998 Cabernet Sauvignon Hillside Select is a candidate for wine of the vintage. It continues to gain weight, and is better each time I retaste it. Its opaque purple color is accompanied by gorgeous aromas of graphite, vanilla, black currant liqueur, and minerals. This rich, full-bodied Cabernet offers sweet tannin, a layered texture, and a finish that lasts for 45–50 seconds. It is a splendid accomplishment in a difficult vintage. Anticipated maturity: now–2017.

1997 Cabernet Sauvignon Hillside Select

RATING: 99 points

Is the prodigious 1997 Cabernet Sauvignon Hillside Select a perfect wine? This effort is about as spectacular as Cabernet Sauvignon can be. The soaring bouquet of sweet, lavishly rich black currants, plums, cherries, toast, minerals, and smoke cascades from the glass. Opaque purple–colored, extraordinarily intense, and full-bodied, yet amazingly well-balanced, this flawless Cabernet Sauvignon will be at its peak between now and 2030. One of the greatest young Cabernet Sauvignons I have ever tasted, it represents the quintessential Napa Cabernet, combining both elegance and power.

1996 Cabernet Sauvignon Hillside Select

RATING: 98 points

The 1996 Cabernet Sauvignon Hillside Select is one of the vintage's superstars. Its opaque purple color is accompanied by super aromatics, immense body, great fruit extraction, superb purity, and overall symmetry, as well as a 40+-second finish. Revealing exceptional intensity (but no heaviness) as well as perfectly integrated acidity, tannin, and alcohol, this fabulous Cabernet will drink wonderfully for three decades. Anticipated maturity: now–2030.

1995 Cabernet Sauvignon Hillside Select

RATING: 99 points

The 1995 Cabernet Sauvignon Hillside Select possesses lots of fatness in the mid-palate. There is plenty of tannin in this full-bodied, rich effort. It is remarkable how the finest California Cabernets combine extraordinary power and richness with balance and elegance. A stupendous wine, it is worth a special effort to obtain. Anticipated maturity: now–2030.

1994 Cabernet Sauvignon Hillside Select

RATING: 99 points

The 1994 Cabernet Sauvignon Hillside Select is a prodigious Cabernet. I had it at a tasting in Japan, and the Japanese were as enthusiastic about it as my rating suggested they should be. They were crestfallen when informed they probably would not be able to buy multiple cases of the wine! The 1994 combines the vintage's spectacularly ripe, luscious fruit with a rarely seen degree of elegance and finesse. The wine is extremely rich, as well as gorgeously poised and graceful. The saturated ruby/purple color is accompanied by Médoc-like, lead pencil aromas intermixed with cassis, cedar, minerals, and spice. I wrote the word "great" four different times in my most recent tasting note, which mirrored every other tasting note I have for this wine. It is full-bodied and seamless, with a silky texture, voluptuous richness, and fabulous purity. The finish lasts for over 40 seconds. Anticipated maturity: now–2025.

1993 Cabernet Sauvignon Hillside Select

RATING: 94 points

The 1993 Cabernet Sauvignon Hillside Select is an outstanding wine that is close in quality to the 1992 and 1991. The 1993 boasts an opaque purple color, as well as a sweet, smoky nose of licorice, black currants, minerals, and vanilla. Huge, rich, and full-bodied, with fabulous concentration and extract, but harder tannin than the 1992 or 1994, this is a large-scaled, well-balanced, powerful Cabernet Sauvignon to drink between now and 2020.

1992 Cabernet Sauvignon Hillside Select

RATING: 95 points

I extolled the virtues of the 1992 Cabernet Sauvignon Hillside Select prior to its release, and now that it is in the marketplace, it is as fabulous as I had hoped. It possesses an opaque dark purple color, and a profoundly complex nose of minerals, ripe cassis fruit, cedar, chocolate, and subtle herbs. Full-bodied yet silky, with layers of concentrated, highly extracted fruit, this wine is exceptionally well balanced, beautifully pure, and already delicious. It is still an infant in terms of development, but I would not fault anybody for wanting to drink it. Anticipated maturity: now–2012.

1991 Cabernet Sauvignon Hillside Select

RATING: 94 points

This knockout Cabernet Sauvignon boasts a youthful purple color; a sweet black currant, vanilla, and earth-scented nose; great ripeness and sweetness of fruit; high flavor extraction; well-integrated acidity and tannin; and a layered, multidimensional, complete feel in the mouth with no hard edges or toughness. There is splendid balance and concentration. The 3.63 pH gives the wine a juicy, succulent, up-front feel, and a chewy, expansive, layered texture. This wine has the potential of 30+ years of aging. A terrific 1991! Anticipated maturity: now–2020.

1990 Cabernet Sauvignon Hillside Select

RATING: 92 points

The first vintage of Hillside Select that was not sterile-filtered at bottling, the 1990 reveals far greater aromatic intensity and complexity. Sweet scents of red and black fruits, spicy oak, roasted herbs, toast, and vanilla jump from the glass. The wine possesses full body, great fruit extraction, plenty of glycerin, and chewy, gorgeously proportioned, supple, rich flavors unaccompanied by the hard, tannic structure and heaviness usually associated with wines of this level of extraction. Anticipated maturity: now–2020.

WINES:

Wines change names with every vintage, but there are four categories: a Syrah-dominated blend, a Grenache-dominated blend, a Roussanne-dominated white wine blend, and the Mr. K sweet wines.

OWNERS: Elaine and Manfred Krankl

ADDRESS: Office, 918 El Toro Road, Ojai, CA 93023; Winery, 1750 N. Ventura Ave., #5, Ventura, CA 93001

TELEPHONE: (805) 640-0997

TELEFAX: (805) 640-1230

E-MAIL: mkrankl@netzero.net

CONTACT: Elaine or Manfred Krankl

VISITING POLICY: Not licensed for tastings and tours. Call for "special" visits.

VINEYARDS

SURFACE AREA: 22.9 acres of contract vineyards of which all or most will be eliminated as the estate holding comes into full production. There are 30 acres of Estate Vineyard.

GRAPE VARIETALS: Syrah, Grenache, Pinot Noir, Roussanne, Chardonnay, and Viognier; also Gewurztraminer for Ice Wine and Sémillon for dessert wine (Vin de Paille)

AVERAGE AGE OF THE VINES: 12 years on Vineyard Contracts; 3 years (new) for Estate Vineyard

DENSITY OF PLANTATION: Between 871 and 1,675 vines per acre on Vineyard Contracts; 2,420 vines per acre on Estate Vineyard

AVERAGE YIELDS: 2.0 tons per acre on white varietals; 1.7 tons per acre on red varietals

WINEMAKING AND UPBRINGING

Manfred Krankl states, "It is our objective to make perfectly ripe, full-bodied, full-flavored wines that are still lively and agile, and retain grace and individuality and express the uniqueness of each vintage.

"It is our philosophy to treat the wine/must/grapes exceedingly gently. Thus no pumping-over, extremely careful handling from vineyard to bottle, long and careful sorting of the fruit to eliminate any and all unwanted parts, such as leaves, stems, jacks, underripe or rotten berries. No fining or filtration, unless absolutely necessary. Some 40–60% new French oak barrels are used on white wines (numerous forests and coopers) and 60–100% new oak is used on red wines (numerous forests and coopers). Whites are typically in barrel between 13–15 months (some Roussanne *cuvées* longer) and Pinot Noir between 9–13 months. Syrah and Grenache about 18–24 months. TBA and Vin de Paille 3+ years." In 2001, Krankl began to experiment with 38–40 months in oak for specific *cuvées* of Syrah.

ANNUAL PRODUCTION

White Cuvée: 6,000 bottles

Syrah: 8,500 bottles

Grenache: 3,200 bottles

Ice Wine: 900 half-bottles

TBA: 1,450 half-bottles

Vin de Paille: 1,350 half-bottles

AVERAGE PRICE (VARIABLE DEPENDING ON VINTAGE): $60–95

GREAT RECENT VINTAGES

Syrah—2003, 2002, 2000, 1997

Grenache—2002, 2000

White Wines—2003, 2002, 2001, 2000, 1999, 1995

Ice Wine—2002, 2000, 1999

TBA—2002, 2000, 1999

Vin de Paille—2002, 2001, 2000, 1999, 1998

After experimenting at other wineries, Elaine and Manfred Krankl started their own brand and winery, Sine Qua Non, with the 1994 vintage. Small amounts of Syrah were produced from fruit of the Bien Nacido Vineyard Block ZA. The Krankls are proud to let their senses be their guide during the winemaking process, not numbers or technical instruments in a lab. They believe that great wine is first made in the vineyard, but also in the winery via an uncompromising, exceptionally gentle approach to every step in the upbringing of the wines.

One of the world's most creative wineries, Sine Qua Non is turning out world-class wines of extraordinary complexity and individuality. The Krankl husband-and-wife team remains wholly dedicated to the pursuit of perfection. I suspect no detail goes unnoticed in their warehouse/winery, which is located adjacent to several appalling junkyards in the commercial hindquarters of Ventura. The Rhône varietals from Sine Qua Non consistently score above 90 points, and Austrian-born Manfred Krankl has also joined with the famed Austrian wine producer, Alois Kracher, to produce limited quantities of Ice Wines and Vin de Paille, all of which appear under the name "Mr. K." They are truly magnificent efforts that must be tasted to be believed.

Sine Qua Non's Rhône Ranger offerings are the products of a craftsman who works endlessly in the vineyards to ensure the ripest, healthiest fruit from incredibly small yields. Krankl then massages the fruit through the fermentation and upbringing process, the objective being to bottle it naturally so tasters get the uncompromised essence of each vintage and varietal blend. Despite relatively expensive prices (which are realistic considering what is in the bottle) and labels by Manfred Krankl that are works of art, no one seems to be able to latch on to many bottles of this stuff, and demand is insatiable. The good news is that the Krankls have purchased a large tract of land north of Santa Barbara (22 acres planted in the Santa Rita Hills) as well as a ranch in Ventura County where the 6-acre vineyard has been planted. So a few more cases should become available in the future to help placate the hordes of wine lovers who can't get enough of these remarkable elixirs.

Oh, how I wish there were more small producers such as Elaine and Manfred Krankl.

Manfred and Elaine Krankl

DESSERT WINES

2002 Mr. K. The Iceman Eiswein (Gewurztraminer)
RATING: 96 points

The 2002 Mr. K The Iceman (made from Gewurztraminer from the Babcock Vineyard) tastes like a wonderfully rich yet crisp Beerenauslese with a sweet, honeyed personality, tremendous richness, great delineation, and an amazing finish. These wines look like motor oil, but they possess superb underlying acidity, freshness, and purity. The residual sugar is 272 grams per liter, and the finished alcohol is 12%, all with 7.6 grams per liter of acidity! Anticipated maturity: now–2020.

2002 Suey TBA (100% Botrytised Roussanne)
RATING: 100 points

The 2000 Suey TBA, made from 100% botrytis-infected Roussanne from the Alban Vineyard, was harvested berry by berry, spent 38.5 months in new oak, and at harvest, had residual sugar of nearly 59.7%—an unheard-of number. At bottling, there were 241 grams of sugar per liter and the finished alcohol was 12.5%. This looks to be the stuff of legends. Unfortunately, only 597 half bottles were produced. Will it age as gracefully as a 1921 Yquem or 1949 Climens? Who knows, but anyone who loves prodigious, individualistic wine and the nectars produced from meticulous, even obsessive harvesting and vinification concerns should make every effort to latch on to a bottle of this unbelievable elixir. It's as good as it gets. Anticipated maturity: now–2030+.

2001 Mr. K. The Nobleman (Chardonnay)
RATING: 97 points

The rich, sweet, and unctuous 2001 Mr. K The Nobleman (Chardonnay), a Trockenbeerenauslese lookalike, possesses nervy, vibrant acidity that is hard to imagine in a wine of this mass and richness. The residual sugar is 255 grams per liter, with an amazing 11.1 grams per liter of acidity, and 11.7% finished alcohol.

2001 Mr. K The Strawman (Botrytised Sémillon)
RATING: 97 points

The 2001 Mr. K The Strawman is a 100% Sémillon made in the style of a *vin de paille*. There is an astonishing 371 grams per liter of residual sugar, with 8.63 grams per liter of total acidity, and a finished alcohol of 10%. It is a wine of extraordinary richness, honeyed complexity, and a finish that lasts over 60 seconds. The sweet wines of Sine Qua Non almost defy description. Anyone who has access to them is indeed very lucky. How they will age remains to be seen, as no one has achieved anything like this in California, but they should certainly evolve for 20+ years.

RED WINES

2002 Just for the Love of It (Syrah)
RATING: 100 points

A dead ringer (at least aromatically) for Guigal's single vineyard Côte-Rôtie La Mouline, the 2002 Just for the Love of It is the greatest California Syrah I have yet tasted. A 1,000-case blend of 96% Syrah, 2% Grenache, and 2% Viognier, it is nearly equal parts Alban, Bien Nacido, and Stolpman fruit with a small amount from both Shadow Canyon and White Hawk. It boasts a provocative perfume of crème de cassis, toast, blackberries, licorice, barbecue spice, and exotic floral scents. Extremely full-bodied, with fabulous intensity, great purity, awesome length, and a finish that lasts over a minute, this classic is a must-purchase. Already accessible, it will drink well for 10–15 years.

2002 SQN (Grenache/Syrah)
RATING: 96+ points

The finest Grenache-based wine I have tasted from California is Manfred Krankl's 2000 Incognito, but his 2002 SQN (80% Grenache and 20% Syrah) is nearly as good. The bulk of the grapes come from the Alban Vineyard along with significant quantities from Stolpman and Shadow Canyon vineyards. The wine spent 19 months in wood prior to being bottled with neither fining nor filtration. There are only a measly 110 cases of this nectar. Its dense purple color is accompanied by a spectacular bouquet of licorice, kirsch, black currants, earth, and notions of smoky toast in the background. A stunning wine of great intensity, multiple flavor dimensions, and a long finish, it will hit its prime in 2–3 years, and should age well for a decade or more.

2001 Midnight Oil (Syrah)
RATING: 96 points

The impeccable 2001 Midnight Oil (95.5% Syrah, 3% Grenache, and 1.5% Viognier) is a product of four vineyards: Alban, Stolpman, Bien Nacido, and White Hawk. The good news is that there are 950 cases of this compelling effort. With a "midnight" black color and the viscosity of 10W-40 oil, its aromas of violet/acacia flowers, melted licorice, camphor, blackberries, crème de cassis, and subtle toasty new oak are accompanied by a wine boasting terrific texture, good underlying acidity, ripe tannin, and a 60+-second finish. This stunning effort competes with the 2000, and what looks to be Krankl's greatest Syrah-based wine to date, the 2002. Anticipated maturity: now–2020.

2001 On Your Toes (Syrah)

RATING: 99 points

An experiment for Krankl, the 2001 On Your Toes Syrah was given a much longer time in barrel in an effort to emulate Marcel Guigal's incredibly long barrel-aging routine for his top single-vineyard Côte-Rôties (42 months in 100% new oak casks). Made from 70% Alban and 30% Stolpman fruit, the 2001 looks very promising, and may end up being as compelling as the Just for the Love of It. It reveals a deep purple hue to the edge along with a gorgeous nose of bacon fat, camphor, vanilla, licorice, crème de cassis, and blackberries. There is fascinating intensity as well as tremendous balance and symmetry, and a harmonious, opulent, long finish with a prominent floral component. Beautifully made, it is ideal for drinking over the next 10–12 years.

2001 Ventriloquist (Grenache / Syrah)

RATING: 92 points

The 2001 Ventriloquist is a blend of 82% Grenache and 18% Syrah. 60% of the fruit came from the Alban Vineyard, 32% from the Stolpman Vineyard, and 8% from the Shadow Canyon Vineyard. There are approximately 400 cases of this nectar. While it may not hit the surreal prodigiousness of the 2000 Incognito, it is a spectacular effort from a cooler growing season. It boasts a saturated purple color as well as beautiful aromatics of red and black fruits, with hints of licorice, earth, and spice in the background. There is great purity, more austere tannin in the finish than most Krankl wines, gorgeous depth and texture, and a finish that lasts 45+ seconds. Anticipated maturity: now–2015.

2000 In Flagrante (Syrah)

RATING: 96 points

The 2000 In Flagrante (a 725-case blend of 86% Syrah, 10% Grenache, and 4% Viognier) is a world-class, provocative effort. It reveals many of the same aromatic and flavor components found in the 2001 Midnight Oil and 2002 Just for the Love of It. A black color is followed by a seamless effort loaded with blackberry, honey, and flower aromas, and an extraordinarily long, concentrated finish. As with all great wines, tasting notes/descriptors just can't do it justice. Among the recent SQN Syrahs, it is a strikingly elegant and powerful wine that has a decidedly French flair to it. Anticipated maturity: now–2015.

2000 Incognito (Grenache / Syrah)

RATING: 98 points

The 2000 Incognito (a blend of 95% Grenache and 5% Syrah) is the finest Grenache-based effort the Krankls have yet produced. A black/ruby/purple color is followed by a lavishly exotic nose of superrich as well as superripe black cherries, black currants, blackberries, licorice, pepper, and other heavenly delights. It is a wine of extraordinary opulence, texture, and purity with a finish that lasts 65+ seconds. Undeniably the greatest Grenache I have tasted from California, it is a reference point for what can be achieved by someone pushing the envelope of quality—viticultural, winemaking, and cellar work. Kudos to the Krankls. It should drink well for 10–15 years, but who can resist it that long?

1999 Icarus (Grenache / Syrah / Viognier)

RATING: 91 points

The 1999 Icarus (a blend of 80% Grenache, 18% Syrah, and 2% Viognier, three-fourths from the Alban Vineyard and one-fourth from the Stolpman) was closed on the two occasions I tasted it. Its deep ruby color is accompanied by sweet black cherry and kirsch–like aromas with an underlying peppery earthiness. Full-bodied and moderately tannic, it is an austere and tightly knit offering. It should be decanted 45 minutes prior to consumption as these wines beg for aeration. Anticipated maturity: now–2015.

1999 The Marauder (Syrah)

RATING: 95 points

The outrageously rich 1999 The Marauder (100% Syrah from the Alban, Stolpman, and Bien Nacido vineyards) is tightly structured, but crammed with blackberry and cassis fruit infused with subtle notes of camphor and licorice. Full and rich, it is a candidate for 14–18 years of graceful evolution.

1998 Syrah E-Raised

RATING: 95 points

The 1998 Syrah E-Raised is great stuff. The blended Syrah comes from different vineyard sources, primarily the Alban Vineyard in San Luis Obispo, and Bien Nacido and Stolpman vineyards in Santa Barbara. It is black-colored, jammy, and super-intense, with awesome concentration, terrific, chewy, explosive flavors of blackberries, cherries, and cassis interfused with creosote, pepper, and vanilla. All the *cuvées* are gorgeously pure, thick, and rich. As they sit in the glass, notes of roasted coffee, licorice, smoke, and barbecue spices emerge, giving them another dimension of complexity. Anticipated maturity: now–2015.

1997 Syrah Imposter McCoy

RATING: 96 points

The funky artwork on the bottle reveals Manfred Krankl's whimsical side, but as the label says, "The truth is in the inside." By early 2000, I had already wolfed down two bottles of the 1997 Imposter McCoy (529 cases) with equally voracious friends. A thick, juicy, massive Syrah, it gushes copious quantities of licorice-infused blackberry fruit offering smoke, coffee, and meaty notes. The wine is mouth-filling, teeth-staining, and loaded. Its high alcohol (15.3%), glycerin level, and low acidity make it easy to drink, but I suspect it will age easily for 5–15+ years. Anticipated maturity: now–2020.

1996 Against the Wall (Syrah)

RATING: 94 points

Sine Qua Non has produced some spectacular Syrahs, buying fruit from the best sources in Santa Barbara—the Alban, Stolpman, and Bien Nacido vineyards. The color is opaque black/purple, and the nose offers a combination of cassis/ blackberry jamminess intermixed with tar, pepper, and spice. Thick, massively full, yet wonderfully rich and expansive, with admirable purity and mouth-staining levels of glycerin and extract, this full-bodied, silky-smooth Syrah is deceptively easy to drink, but I suspect it will age effortlessly for another 5–10 more years. Anticipated maturity: now–2012.

1995 The Other Hand (Syrah)

RATING: 92 points

The 1995 The Other Hand is made from 100% Syrah grown in the Alban, Bien Nacido, and Stolpman vineyards, situated respectively in Edna Valley, Santa Maria, and Los Olivos. Aged 18 months in oak, of which 70% is new, this blockbuster, opaque purple–colored wine offers glorious notes of black fruits (primarily blackberry and cassis), subtle smoke, toast, and licorice, and a whiff of plant material and spice. Full-bodied, yet gorgeously layered and nearly seamless in its flamboyant display of fruit, glycerin, and extract, this large-scaled Syrah is drinkable now. It is another example of why I think wineries in this region should be ripping out their Pinot Noir vines and replanting with Syrah! Look for this super Syrah to age effortlessly for another 9 or more years. Anticipated maturity: now–2012.

1995 Red Handed (Grenache/Syrah/Mourvèdre)

RATING: 95 points

The limited-production 1995 Red Handed is a blend of 43% Grenache, 40% Syrah, and 17% Mourvèdre aged 18 months in oak, of which 50% was new. This wine wants to be a Southern California Châteauneuf-du-Pape, and comes close to duplicating the character of a hedonistic southern Rhône. Sadly, only 80 six-bottle cases were produced. The color is an impressively saturated red/black/purple. The wine offers up aromas of cigar box, fruitcake, cedar, pepper, Provençal herbs, and glorious levels of kirsch and other black fruits. The influence of oak frames the wine rather than adding much to the aromas or flavors. Extremely full-bodied, rich, chewy, and loaded with per-

sonality (another wine that reflects its makers), with a multidimensional palate, and beautifully integrated alcohol, acidity, and tannin, this wine has a singular personality and stupendous quality. Anticipated maturity: now–2014.

WHITE WINES

2003 Proprietary White Sublime Isolation (Chardonnay/Roussanne/Viognier)

RATING: 95 points

The spectacular 2003 Proprietary White Sublime Isolation is a blend of 44% Chardonnay, 37% Roussanne, and 19% Viognier, all from the Alban Vineyard. A nose of citrus blossoms intermixed with honeysuckle, butter, sealing wax, and tropical fruit is accompanied by a stunningly textured, opulent, dry, full-bodied white that caresses the palate without tasting over the top or too heavy. I suspect this is Manfred Krankl's version of a French southern Rhône, but it has its own distinctive style, and should be flexible with an assortment of cuisines given its individuality and intense character allied to tremendous vibrancy and delineation. This is a tour de force in winemaking, but believe it or not, it was not the finest dry white I tasted in this cellar. I suspect it will drink well for 5–7 years, perhaps even longer.

2002 Proprietary White Whisperin' E (Roussanne/Viognier/Chardonnay)

RATING: 95 points

The 2002 Proprietary White called Whisperin' E is a concoction of 50% Roussanne, 31% Viognier, and 19% Chardonnay, most from the Alban Vineyard with a tiny dollop of Stolpman fruit. There are 524 cases of this light gold–colored 2002. A superb perfume of smoky hazelnuts intermixed with exotic lychee, honeysuckle, peach, and beeswax notes is followed by a full-bodied wine with a multilayered texture that pulls back in the finish to reveal surprising uplift, acidity, and lightness— an amazing feat given a wine of this power, dimension, and intensity. It should drink well for another 5–7 years.

2001 Proprietary White Albino (Chardonnay/Roussanne/Viognier)

RATING: 95 points

The 2001 Albino (46% Chardonnay, 40% Roussanne, and 14% Viognier) emerged primarily from John Alban's vineyard in Arroyo Grande as well as the Stolpman Vineyard. Possessing fabulous intensity (it actually should be decanted 30–45 minutes prior to serving), it is a full-bodied white offering aromas of lychee nuts, citrus oils, honeysuckle, and rose petals. Fabulously rich and well delineated in spite of its large size (15.1% natural alcohol), it is surprisingly light on its feet, and finishes with considerable zestiness. Anticipated maturity: now–2012.

2001 Rien Ne Va Plus (Roussanne)

RATING: 98 points

One of the most amazing dry whites I have ever tasted is the 2001 Rien Ne Va Plus. Fashioned from 100% Roussanne, and aged on its lees for an extremely long period, my initial image when I tasted it was of the great Barsac, the 2001 Climens. However, the Sine Qua Non wine is bone-dry with no sweetness evident. It gains in both stature and aromatic dimension as it sits in the glass. At first, I did not like it as well as the Whisperin' E or the 2003 Proprietary White, but after 30–45 minutes in a decanter, the Rien Ne Va Plus was a symphony of exotic aromas and flavors. Dense, rich, and full-bodied, with impeccable balance, superb honeyed richness, and wonderfully integrated wood, it is undeniably the greatest New World expression of Roussanne made to date. For another dramatic characteristic, its golden color seemed to lighten as it sat in the glass and sucked up oxygen. This is an amazing achievement! Sadly, production is less than 100 cases. Anticipated maturity: now–2018.

2000 Proprietary White The Hussy (Roussanne)

RATING: 93 points

The 100% Roussanne that emerged from both the Stolpman and Alban vineyards is the 2000 Hussy. Its light gold color is accompanied by fabulously decadent levels of fruit, luxurious glycerin, and a dry, full-bodied, amazingly well delineated finish. This is a sumptuous white that is among the most creative produced in California. Anticipated maturity: now–2011.

the hussy

PHILIP TOGNI VINEYARD

WINE: Cabernet Sauvignon

OWNERS: Lisa Togni, Birgitta Togni, Philip Togni

ADDRESS: P.O. Box 81, St. Helena, CA 94574 (Physical address: 3780 Spring Mountain Road, St. Helena, CA 94574)

TELEPHONE: (707) 963-3731

TELEFAX: (707) 963-9186

WEBSITE: www.philiptognivineyard.com

CONTACT: Philip Togni

VISITING POLICY: Very small numbers of individuals by appointment. Except for mailing list customers, they are often unable to accept requests.

VINEYARDS

SURFACE AREA: 10.5 acres

GRAPE VARIETALS: Cabernet Sauvignon (82%), Merlot (15%), Cabernet Franc (2%), Petit Verdot (1%)—all for a single wine; also, half-acre of Black Hamburgh

AVERAGE AGE OF THE VINES: 12 years

DENSITY OF PLANTATION: 519–871 per acre

AVERAGE YIELDS: 3.5 tons per acre—50 hectoliters per hectare

WINEMAKING AND UPBRINGING

The philosophy of winemaking at Philip Togni is that of classic Bordeaux, adapted to the conditions of Spring Mountain. The grapes are picked very ripe, but not so ripe that they don't have sufficient acidity. Fermentations are hot, reaching 85°F, and then there is a total maceration/*cuvaison* of nearly four weeks. Togni still uses an old Willmes bladder press, and then moves his wine to 225-litre Nevers barrels (always coopered by Nadalie and Taransaud). The wines stay 19 to 20 months, are racked every three months in the Bordeaux fashion, and see about 40% new oak. The wines used to be egg-white fined until the 1990s, when Philip Togni started wondering whether it really accomplished anything, and since then the wines have been neither fined nor filtered. Malolactic fermentation occurs spontaneously in the barrel, and afterward, the contents are tasted and the best barrels are selected for the famous Philip Togni Cabernet Sauvignon.

These are some of the longest-lived Cabernet Sauvignons of California. If you taste Togni's most prodigious efforts when he worked at Chappellet and Cuvaison, none of those great vintages (for example the 1969 Chappellet) are anywhere near over-the-hill. Under his own label, the wines, when well stored, are still vibrant and, for the most part, relatively young. Even wines from the early vintages of the mid-1980s haven't yet passed their adolescence.

ANNUAL PRODUCTION

Cabernet Sauvignon: 20,000 bottles

AVERAGE PRICE (VARIABLE DEPENDING ON VINTAGE): $50–80

GREAT RECENT VINTAGES

2003, 2001, 1997, 1996, 1995, 1994, 1992, 1991, 1990, 1987, 1986, 1985, 1984

Philip Togni bears a striking resemblance to the late actor George C. Scott and is probably both tough and contrary enough to have played the title role in the movie *Patton*. All of Togni's wines are, as Togni likes to say, "made as Bordeaux was . . . a long, long time ago."

This artisanal producer tucked away on the steep hillsides of Spring Mountain continues to fashion some of the most concentrated, inky black–colored Cabernet Sauvignons in California. The more I taste the Cabernets of Philip Togni, the more I admire what he has achieved. One of the legendary Philip Togni wines is the 1969 Chappellet Cabernet Sauvignon, which remains one of the most memorable California Cabernets I have ever had. The Cabernet Sauvignons Togni has produced at his small boutique winery since the early 1980s are every bit as profound, if not better than, the 1969. In most wines, there's always a battle between the fruit and the tannin, with the tannin often winning out, but Togni's wines are the exception. At a vertical tasting, his Cabernet Sauvignons from his first vintages in the early 1980s remain extraordinary; these are remarkably young wines that still possess fabulous fruit concentration. Older vintages

Philip and Lisa Togni

still taste superb, with the 1991 and the 1990 meriting mid-90-point scores. The 1985 Cabernet Sauvignon is marginally lighter, but this massive example of the vintage is extremely well endowed, and perhaps underrated vis-à-vis the other Cabernet Sauvignons.

Togni's Cabernet Sauvignon, generally made from a Bordeaux-like blend of 82% Cabernet Sauvignon, 15% Merlot, and 3% Cabernet Franc, and aged 22 months in small French oak casks (of which 25–40% are new), is one of the richest, most complex Cabernets made in California. Every time I have the opportunity to go back and taste an older vintage I am impressed with the complex aromatics the wine develops. How reassuring it is to see these Cabernets become even more impressive with bottle age. The first Philip Togni Cabernet Sauvignon vintage was 1983, a wine that remains not only young, but one of the top wines from what was an unimpressive vintage for most other Napa wineries. Togni has been a longtime believer in not acidifying, and his wines are never fined or filtered at bottling.

Togni, a legendary California winemaker, must be the least self-promoting member of his profession—but then with wines such as these, why not let them do the talking for you? Since nearly 70% of Togni's wines are sold directly to wine consumers, those wanting an opportunity to buy this wine must get their name on the winery's mailing list.

It seems that Philip Togni was destined to make great Cabernet Sauvignon. But who would have thought it would be on Spring Mountain in Napa Valley? He had the privilege of studying under Emile Peynaud at the University of Bordeaux in 1955 and from 1956 to 1957, and received from that university a Diplôme National d'Oenologie. He jokes that it was in Bordeaux that he made the most of his studies, learning all his prejudices and idiosyncracies. His résumé is impressive, with his having worked in France, Algeria, Chile and, of course, California before launching his own label with his wife, Birgitta, in 1983. Their charming daughter Lisa has been trained in the European fashion of working harvests and vineyards in both France and Australia, and is clearly in line to take over if Philip Togni ever decides that those steep hills he briskly climbs like a mountain goat become too steep.

CABERNET SAUVIGNON

2003 Cabernet Sauvignon

RATING: 92–94+ points

Philip Togni, who makes classic, long-lived, uncompromising wines from low yields, indigenous yeast fermentations, malolactic fermentation in barrel, and no trickery or tomfoolery, has fashioned a brilliant 2003 Cabernet Sauvignon. There are 2,100 cases of this dense purple–colored effort. Its beautiful bouquet of black currants, blackberries, dried herbs, white chocolate, and smoke is followed by a rich, full-bodied, moderately tannic wine with well-integrated acidity, tannin, and wood. This 2003 may not require as much patience as some Togni Cabernets (usually 5–10 years), but it should be at its finest between 2010–2023.

2001 Cabernet Sauvignon

RATING: 96 points

The 2001 Cabernet Sauvignon is the finest Cabernet Togni has produced since the mid-1990s. In bottle, it is even better than it was from barrel. Even better, there are 2,100 cases, a humongous quantity by this property's measly production standards. The color is an inky/black, and the nose offers up spectacular aromas of melted licorice intermixed with crème de cassis, acacia flowers, roasted meats, tapenade, and subtle toast. Opulent and voluptuous, with huge body brilliantly balanced by sweet tannin and adequate acidity, this Cabernet possesses impeccable equilibrium, admirable purity, and a 50-second finish. It is one of Togni's great Cabernet Sauvignons, of which there have been many over the last quarter of a century. While masochists might enjoy it young, I would opt for cellaring it 4–5 years, and drink it over the following two decades. It is a brilliant achievement!

2000 Cabernet Sauvignon

RATING: 91 points

The 2000 Cabernet Sauvignon is performing well. There are 1,600 cases of this medium-bodied, Bordeaux-like effort. Notes of cedar, spice box, black currants, subtle oak, and a hint of saddle leather emerge from a pretty, rich, concentrated Cabernet. It is an exceptionally successful effort for the vintage. Anticipated maturity: now–2018.

1999 Cabernet Sauvignon

RATING: 91 points

Its dense purple color is followed by a big, spicy nose of black currant liqueur, licorice, and foresty/fernlike scents. It is sweet, medium to full–bodied, and deep, as well as structured, with a Bordeaux-like tannic profile in the finish. It will require patience. Anticipated maturity: 2007–2026+.

1998 Cabernet Sauvignon

RATING: 90 points

The 1998 Cabernet Sauvignon exhibits a dense ruby/purple color. Made from fruit that was harvested between October 30 and November 4 (50% of the crop was cut off to guarantee only ripe fruit), it reveals aromas of tapenade, licorice, black currants, smoked herbs, and earth. The wine offers abundant black fruits, with outstanding richness and complexity. It can be drunk early but will easily age for another 12 or more years. Anticipated maturity: now–2015+.

1997 Cabernet Sauvignon

RATING: 95 points

The glorious 1997 Cabernet Sauvignon (a blend of 82% Cabernet Sauvignon, 15% Merlot, and 3% Cabernet Franc) is the most opulently textured Togni offering since his 1992. It possesses a saturated purple color in addition to a thrilling but still reticent nose of blackberries, cassis, minerals, dried herbs, and smoky oak. Full-bodied, pure, thick, and creamy-textured, this wine's superb concentration conceals its lofty but sweet tannin. Togni's wines possess exceptional aging potential, but it will be hard to keep your hands off this one. Anticipated maturity: now–2025+.

1996 Cabernet Sauvignon

RATING: 96 points

The opaque purple-colored 1996 Cabernet Sauvignon is a blockbuster monster crammed with phenomenal potential. It offers up a sensational nose of licorice, chocolate, cassis, Provençal herbs, and toast. The wine is succulent and full-bodied, as well as extraordinarily powerful and backward. It should be drinkable within another year or two, and age beautifully for three decades.

1995 Cabernet Sauvignon

RATING: 95 points

Cabernet Sauvignon is king at Togni, and they are wines of extraordinary concentration, flavor dimension, and aging potential. The 1995 Cabernet Sauvignon, a vintage that produced a number of top-notch wines (as well as some with rough tannin and muted personalities), is one of the year's bright shining successes. The wine displays an opaque purple color, as well as a lavishly intense nose of blackberry/blueberry/cassis fruit intermingled with chocolate and olive nuances. Dense and fruit-driven, with awesome levels of glycerin and extract, this formidably endowed, moderately tannic wine should be at its best with another 1–2 years of cellaring. Once again, Philip Togni has produced a wine with 25 or more years of aging potential.

1994 Cabernet Sauvignon

RATING: 97 points

As is the practice at this winery, they hold back 50 or so cases of their finest vintages for release after a decade. The current release of their library selection is the 1994 Cabernet Sauvignon, a magnificent effort that, for me, is one of Togni's six or seven finest wines. Its deep plum/purple color reveals only a touch of lightening at the edge. A glorious perfume offers up aromas of plums, figs, crème de cassis, smoke, hickory spice, and high-quality cigar tobacco. In a blind tasting, this California Cabernet could easily be mistaken for a great Pauillac given its structure, density, richness, and perfume. This 1994 is just beginning to move into its adolescence. Even though it has 20–25 years of life remaining, it is approachable. It is a monumental Cabernet Sauvignon from one of the valley's legendary producers.

1993 Cabernet Sauvignon

RATING: 94 points

This wine delivers a complex Cabernet that is just approaching mid-adolescence. Its tastes are similar to a hybrid blend of a Pauillac and St.-Julien. Cedarwood, spice box, black currants, and tobacco leaf aromas soar from the glass of this aromatically exciting 1993. A dark plum/purple/garnet color reveals a touch of lightening at the edge. The wine is rich and medium to full-bodied, with impressive purity as well as intensity. Already beautiful to drink, it should evolve for another 10–15 years.

1992 Cabernet Sauvignon

RATING: 97 points

Since bottling, the 1992 Cabernet Sauvignon continues to display the remarkable richness and opulence it possessed from cask. The wine offers a saturated dark purple color, a jammy, plum, black cherry, herb, and spice–scented nose, expansive, chewy, full-bodied flavors, superb depth, moderate tannin, low acidity, and a blockbuster finish. It should drink well for at least another decade. Anticipated maturity: now–2014+.

1991 Cabernet Sauvignon

RATING: 96+ points

The wine possesses a very fragrant bouquet of plums, wood smoke, cassis, and dried herbs. The 1991 deep purple–colored Cabernet Sauvignon reveals wonderfully sweet black cherry, spicy fruit, and cassis flavors, full body, an unctuous texture, and lavish quantities of fruit obscuring the wine's moderate tannin. It has finally reached its plateau of maturity, where it should remain for another decade or more.

1990 Cabernet Sauvignon

RATING: 96 points

Togni's ability to harvest ripe, sweet fruit is evident in the 1990 Cabernet Sauvignon, a wine with awesome intensity. According to Togni, 1990 produced his smallest crop, which may account for the wine's extraordinary concentration and intensity. It exhibits ripe fruit buttressed by sweet toasty oak, and jammy black cherry and black currant flavors. Anticipated maturity: now–2018.

1985 Cabernet Sauvignon

RATING: 93 points

A strong showing for Togni's Cabernet Sauvignon, the youthful, unevolved 1985 is undoubtedly one of the top wines of the vintage. The opaque plum/purple color is followed by a huge, fragrant nose of cedar, smoke, and jammy blackberry and currant fruit. With superb concentration, admirable underlying acidity, and moderate tannin, this intense, mouth-filling, youthful, forceful wine is capable of evolving for another 10–12 years. Anticipated maturity: now–2015.

WASHINGTON

Though it is an increasingly important player in the fine-wine marketplace, Washington state still seems to be in search of an identity. In every famous wine region, quality can be irregular, but Washington produces only a handful of extraordinary wines. The most compelling ones consistently emerge from the Quilceda Creek winery. The fact that wines of such intensity, complexity, and prodigious quality can be produced is a measure of what this state can achieve, but unfortunately, for reasons that escape me, the state in general still produces too many average and poor wines. Nevertheless, consumers should pay attention to this state, where the upside potential appears to have no limit.

Viticulturally speaking, virtually all of Washington state's finest wines come from the Columbia Valley appellation, which includes the sub-regions of Yakima and Walla Walla. The appellation is a primarily desert area in southeastern Washington, running to and slightly across the Oregon border. Seattle may have considerable rainfall and a jungle-like coastal climate thanks to the precipitation that emerges from the Pacific Ocean, but the moisture gets trapped on the western slopes of the Olympic Mountains. In the Walla Walla and Yakima valleys, no vines could grow without irrigation. The landscape is barren except for the well-irrigated farms and vineyards. Climatically, the area enjoys significant sun and heat in the summer, but the drop in temperature in the evening is dramatic, even more so in the Columbia Valley than in most areas of California. This explains the fresh levels of acidity that naturally complement the region's finest wines, which are made from Bordeaux

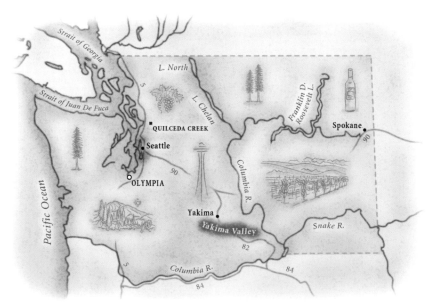

varietals and are extremely rich as well as concentrated.

There are other serious Washington state wineries, but none approaches the extraordinary world-class quality of Quilceda Creek. My hope for the future is that many others will emulate this impeccably run winery, which is turning out compelling wines of irrefutable richness and complexity.

WINES:

Cabernet Sauvignon

Cabernet Sauvignon Champoux Vineyard

Cabernet Sauvignon Reserve

OWNER: Quilceda Creek

ADDRESS: 11306 52nd Street SE, Snohomish, WA 98290

TELEPHONE: (360) 568-2389

TELEFAX: (360) 568-1609

E-MAIL: alex@quilcedacreek.com

WEBSITE: www.quilcedacreek.com

CONTACT: Alex Golitzin

VISITING POLICY: Not open to the public

VINEYARDS

SURFACE AREA: 32 acres

GRAPE VARIETALS: Cabernet Sauvignon, Merlot, Cabernet Franc

AVERAGE AGE OF THE VINES: Cabernet Sauvignon—18 years;
    Merlot—7 years; Cabernet Franc—8 years

DENSITY OF PLANTATION:

Champoux Vineyards—726 vines per acre and 968 vines per
    acre

Golitzin Estate Vineyards—2,074 vines per acre (first case
    was in 2004)

AVERAGE YIELDS: 2.5–3.0 tons per acre

WINEMAKING AND UPBRINGING

Quilceda Creek concentrates its physical and mental resources
into one varietal—Cabernet Sauvignon. A small amount of
Merlot is also produced, but is limited because of Merlot's sensitivity to the very low winter temperature that occurs in eastern Washington every five or six years. Quilceda Creek also
produces a declassified red wine from grapes deemed not good
enough for the Cabernet Sauvignon or Merlot.

The Cabernet Sauvignon is usually blended with less
than 5% of either Merlot or Cabernet Franc to boost aromatics without sacrificing the varietal identity of Cabernet Sauvignon. The objective is to produce a wine that is delicious
upon release but has the potential to age 20 or more years.

Grapes are picked only when the fruit tastes totally ripe.
The grapes are destemmed and extremely lightly crushed, and
fall by gravity into the fermenters. Fermentation is carried out
using specific commercial yeast cultures. The extraction is
done by punching the caps. Fermentation is continued until
dryness (no residual sugar remains), at which point the wine
is pumped into new French oak barrels. There it is racked,
and malolactic fermentation is done in the barrels.

All wines are barrel-aged for approximately 22 months
before bottling. The wines are not fined or filtered. Wines are
bottle-aged about 9 months prior to release.

ANNUAL PRODUCTION

Cabernet Sauvignon: 38,000 bottles

AVERAGE PRICE (VARIABLE DEPENDING ON VINTAGE): $50–75

GREAT RECENT VINTAGES

2002, 2001, 1999, 1998, 1994, 1989, 1983

Alex Golitzin, the force behind the creation and
emergence of Quilceda Creek, was born in France
at the beginning of World War II and lived in Paris for
the duration of the war. In 1946 his family immigrated to
California and settled in San Francisco, close to the Napa
Valley. His uncle, the well-known André Tchelistcheff,
was at the time the winemaker at Beaulieu Vineyards.

In 1974, with Tchelistcheff's help, Golitzin made his
first barrel of Cabernet Sauvignon. Following three more
vintages and three more barrels, the winery was bonded in

Alexander, Jeanette, and Paul Golitzin

1978 and produced the first Quilceda Creek Cabernet in 1979. Four years later this wine received a Gold Medal and a Grand Prize at the Enological Society Festival in Seattle, the only Cabernet to achieve the honor to this day.

Today, Golitzin's son Paul is the lead winemaker for Quilceda Creek. Having begun his career with the remarkable 1988 Cabernet Sauvignon Reserve, Paul has been instrumental in driving the improvements of quality at Quilceda Creek. While influenced by two great winemakers—his father, Alex Golitzin, and grand-uncle André Tchelistcheff, Paul's style is all his own. He fashions big wines elegantly balanced with fruit, layers of oak, and rounded tannins. They are enjoyable upon release, but can be cellared for 20+ years. As Paul says, "It is all about pleasure."

Of all the producers profiled in this book, Quilceda Creek may be the only one that still remains below the radar of even the most knowledgeable wine enthusiasts. These are prodigious, world-class wines.

CABERNET SAUVIGNON

2002 Cabernet Sauvignon

RATING: 98 points

The dark ruby–colored 2002 Cabernet Sauvignon (3,400 cases) contains 2% Merlot and 1% Cabernet Franc. It displays blackberry, tar, violet, herb, and cassis aromas that lead to a velvety-textured, penetrating character. Effortlessly sporting that mind-boggling juxtaposition of power and elegance, it slathers the palate with red cherries, blackberries, raspberries, cassis, and spices. Enormously rich yet fresh, this broad, expansive wine is plush, packed with sweet tannin, and has an immensely long finish. Anticipated maturity: 2007–2019.

2001 Cabernet Sauvignon

RATING: 97 points

The saturated black–colored 2001 Cabernet Sauvignon continues this winery's brilliant string of successes. Its intense aromas reveal a huge depth of blackberry and cassis fruit. Concentrated, backward, and deep, it is a medium to full–bodied wine with exceptional balance, purity, focus, and length. Powerful yet refined, it coats the palate with cassis and jammy blackberries

whose flavors linger for almost a minute. Anticipated maturity: 2008–2020+.

2000 Cabernet Sauvignon

RATING: 94 points

The dark ruby–colored 2000 Cabernet Sauvignon has a nose of blackberry-flavored Yoplait yogurt laced with roasted oak and hints of licorice. A full-bodied wine of power and structure, it is crammed with black currants, blackberries, and spices. Its dense fruit is matched blow for blow by a muscular, firm structure. Anticipated maturity: 2008–2020.

1999 Cabernet Sauvignon

RATING: 98 points

The sumptuous 1999 Cabernet Sauvignon is a dark ruby–colored wine with mouthwatering aromas of highly expressive blackberries awash in toasted oak and roasted spices. Medium to full–bodied, thick, concentrated, and exquisitely balanced, this mouth-coating tour de force is densely packed with jammy black fruits and cassis. It combines elegance with power in a manner reminiscent of Châteaux Margaux's prodigious 1990. This velvety-textured wine is complete, with magnificent depth of fruit, a profound personality, and the requisite structure for long-term cellaring. Anticipated maturity: 2006–2020.

1998 Cabernet Sauvignon

RATING: 96 points

Blackberry jam, juniper berries, and spices can be found in the rich aromatics of the stunning, dark-colored 1998 Cabernet Sauvignon. A wine of awesome breadth, width, concentration, and power, this full-bodied beauty is crammed with lush layers of blackberries, plums, and cassis. This offering's prodigious fruit envelops its copious silky tannin. Additionally, it displays an extraordinarily long finish. Drink it between now and 2016.

1997 Cabernet Sauvignon

RATING: 94 points

The 1997 Cabernet Sauvignon was fashioned from 89% Cabernet Sauvignon, 9% Merlot, and 2% Cabernet Franc. It offers a boisterous rosemary and black fruit–scented nose. Big, broad, and chewy, this medium to full–bodied wine is packed with black fruits, spices, and hints of tar. Masculine and concentrated, it can be drunk until 2020.

1996 Cabernet Sauvignon

RATING: 95 points

Produced from a blend of 85% Cabernet Sauvignon, 9% Merlot, and 6% Cabernet Franc, the saturated, dark ruby–colored 1996 Cabernet Sauvignon exhibits sweet cherries, herbal spice, and candied blackberries in its elegant, sexy aromatics. This delightful, medium-bodied, and harmonious wine offers blueberry, cassis, and spice flavors. It is seamless and refined, and possesses a harmony, equilibrium, and delineated finish rarely seen in the New World. Anticipated maturity: now–2018.

1995 Cabernet Sauvignon

RATING: 92 points

The dark ruby–colored 1995 contains 12% Merlot, a high figure for this Cabernet Sauvignon–dominated wine. It reveals an expressive, ripe, and violet-laced nose as well as wonderful layers of blackberry, red currant, cassis, and floral flavors. This medium to full–bodied, elegant, and refined wine is intensely concentrated and flavorful, but certainly not on the level of the blockbuster 1994. In its youth this silky-textured wine is quintessential Golitzin, polished, precise, focused, and gracefully exhibiting highly defined sweet fruit. Anticipated maturity: now–2010+.

1994 Cabernet Sauvignon

RATING: 94 points

The 1994 Cabernet Sauvignon offers deep and compelling aromas of red and black fruits, lead pencil, and traces of oak spices. This full-bodied, concentrated, and chewy wine is thick, dense, and gorgeously defined for such a massive wine. Its combination of power and elegance brought to mind the 1986 Margaux, one of the finest wines ever produced by that illustrious estate. When I first tasted this wine at the estate in Snohomish, Golitzin was worried that it was too big and powerful. I found myself in the all-too-rare position of defending a wine's qualities to the person who had made it! At a subsequent tasting, the wine had lost some of its youthful exuberance and Golitzin was delighted to see that it was gaining focus and elegance. This is a truly magnificent wine, and it will age remarkably well. Drink it between now and 2015+.

1991 Cabernet Sauvignon

RATING: 90 points

This winery's hallmark is great purity allied with considerable body and structure, without sacrificing any of the superb cassis fruit, all of which is gently kissed by high-quality oak. It is a shame Quilceda Creek's wines are rarely seen outside of Washington, but who can blame that state's chauvinistic wine enthusiasts for keeping these heroic wines to themselves? Anticipated maturity: now–2015.

1990 Cabernet Sauvignon

RATING: 90 points

The 1990 is a deep, rich, full-bodied wine with a saturated color and copious amounts of sweet cassis fruit intelligently married with toasty new oak. Ripe, concentrated, graceful, and harmonious, with well-integrated acidity, tannin, and alcohol, it should drink well between now and 2008.

CABERNET SAUVIGNON CHAMPOUX VINEYARD

1997 Cabernet Sauvignon Champoux Vineyard

RATING: 91 points

The medium to dark ruby–colored 1997 Cabernet Sauvignon Champoux Vineyard displays creamy, sweet, Connecticut white corn, and black cherry aromas. Medium to full–bodied and satin-textured, it is an intense, blackberry and dark cherry–flavored wine. This expressive, flavorful offering has outstanding follow-through from its attack to its long, seamless, and focused finish. Anticipated maturity: now–2008.

CABERNET SAUVIGNON RESERVE

1990 Cabernet Sauvignon Reserve

RATING: 96 points

Quilceda Creek's Reserves are outrageously rich, complex wines. Less evolved than the 1988 or 1989, the 1990 Reserve Cabernet exhibits a huge, chocolaty, cassis, herb, and mineral–scented nose, and rich, full-bodied flavors judiciously touched by sweet, toasty new oak. With exceptionally well-integrated acid, elevated but sweet and ripe tannin, and a finish that lasts for almost a minute, this is another stunning example of what heights Cabernet Sauvignon can reach in Washington state. Anticipated maturity: now–2010.

1989 Cabernet Sauvignon Reserve

RATING: 96 points

The 1989 Cabernet Sauvignon Reserve is an outrageously rich, complex wine. Lamentably, only 200 cases are available. It is an awesome bottle of wine, with a huge nose of cedar, cassis, minerals, and vanilla. It reveals spectacular purity, great extraction of flavor, full body, and layers of fruit that come across as phenomenally well delineated and well balanced. This is a winemaking tour de force! Anticipated maturity: now–2013.

1988 Cabernet Sauvignon Reserve

RATING: 94 points

The 1988 Cabernet Reserve offers a huge nose of spicy, cedary cassis fruit, and dense, superrich, concentrated flavors with gorgeous texture, huge body, and an impeccable sense of balance. A superb Cabernet Sauvignon from start to finish, it should drink well between now and 2013.

FUTURE STARS

SOME PROSPECTS TO THINK ABOUT

ALSACE

Domaine Bott-Geyl
1 rue du Petit Château
68980 Beblenheim
Telephone: 33 3 89 47 90 04
Fax: 33 3 89 47 97 33

Domaine Albert Boxler
78 rue Trois Epis
68230 Niedermorschwihr
Telephone: 33 3 89 27 11 32
Fax: 33 3 89 27 70 14

Domaine Albert Mann
13 rue du Château
68920 Wettolsheim
Telephone: 33 3 89 80 62 00
Fax: 33 3 89 80 34 23

AUSTRALIA

Amon-Ra (produced by Glaetzer Wines)
Glaetzer Wines Head Office:
34 Barossa Valley Way
Tanunda SA, 5352
Telephone: 61 8 8563 0288
Fax: 61 8 8563 0218
www.glaetzer.com

Kaesler
P.O. Box 852
Nuriootpa SA 5355
Telephone: 61 8 8562 4488
Fax: 61 8 8562 4499
www.kaesler.com.au

Kilikanoon
P.O. Box 205
Auburn SA 5451
Telephone: 61 8 8843 4377
Fax: same number
www.kilikanoon.com.au

Leeuwin Estate
P.O. Box 724
Fremantle WA 6959
Telephone: 61 8 9430 4099
Fax: 61 8 9430 5687
www.leeuwinestate.com.au

Mitolo
P.O. Box 520
Virginia SA 5120
Telephone: 61 8 8282 9012
Fax: 61 8 8282 9062
www.mitolowines.com.au

Rockford
P.O. Box 142
Tanunda SA 5352
Telephone: 61 8 8563 2720
Fax: 61 8 8563 3787
www.rockfordwines.com.au

Rusden
P.O. Box 257
Tanunda SA 5352
Telephone: 61 8 8563 2976
Fax: 61 8 8563 0885
www.rusdenwines.com.au

Two Hands
P.O. Box 94
Walkerville SA 5081
Telephone: 61 8 8367 0555
Fax: 61 8 8367 0655
www.twohandswines.com

Yalumba
P.O. Box 10
Angaston SA 5353
Telephone: 61 8 8561 3200
Fax: 61 8 8561 3465
www.yalumba.com

AUSTRIA

Schloss Gobelsburg
Schlosstrasse 16
A-3550 Langenlois
Telephone: 43 2734 2422
www.gobelsburg.at

Weingut Alzinger
3601 Unterloiben 11
Telephone: 43 2732 77900
www.alzinger.at

Weingut Hiedler
Am Rosenhügel 13
A-3550 Langenlois
Telephone: 43 2734 2468
Fax: 43 2734 24685
www.hiedler.at

Weingut Hirsch
Hauptstrasse 76
3493 Kammern/Langenlois
Telephone: 43 2735 2460
Fax: 43 2735 36089
www.weingut-hirsch.at

BORDEAUX

Bellevue Mondotte
33330 Saint-Laurent-des-Combes
Mailing address:
c/o Château Pavie
33330 Saint-Emilion
Telephone: 33 5 57 55 43 43
Fax: 33 5 57 24 63 99
www.chateaupavie.com

Branaire Ducru
33250 Saint-Julien
Telephone: 33 5 56 59 25 86
Fax: 33 5 56 59 16 26
www.branaire.com

Château Canon La Gaffelière
SCEV Comtes de Neipperg
BP 34
F-33330 Saint-Emilion
Telephone: 33 5 57 24 71 33
Fax: 33 5 57 24 67 95
www.neipperg.com

Clos l'Eglise
33500 Pomerol
Mailing address:
c/o Haut-Bergey
BP 49
33850 Léognan
Telephone: 33 5 56 64 05 22
Fax: 33 5 56 64 06 98

Clos St.-Martin
33330 Saint-Emilion
Telephone: 33 5 57 24 71 09
Fax: 33 5 57 24 69 72

Ducru Beaucaillou
33250 Saint-Julien-Beychevelle
Telephone: 33 5 56 73 16 73
Fax: 33 5 56 59 27 37
www.chateau-ducru-beaucaillou.com

Haut-Bailly
33850 Léognan
Telephone: 33 5 56 64 75 11
Fax: 33 5 56 64 53 60
www.chateau-haut-bailly.com

Magrez Fombrauge
Saint-Christophe des Bardes
33330 Saint-Emilion
Telephone: 33 5 57 24 77 12
Fax: 33 5 57 24 66 95
www.fombrauge.com

Marojallia
Route de Bordeaux
33460 Margaux
Mailing Address:
287 avenue de la Libération
33110 Le Bouscat
Telephone: 33 5 56 49 69 50
Fax: 33 5 56 42 62 88

Pape-Clément
216 avenue du Dr Nancel Penard
33600 Pessac
Mailing address:
BP 164 33600 Pessac
Telephone: 33 5 57 26 38 38
Fax: 33 5 57 26 38 39
www.pape-clement.com

Château Pavie Decesse
33330 Saint-Emilion
Mailing address:
c/o Château Pavie
33330 Saint-Emilion
Telephone: 33 5 57 55 43 43
Fax: 33 5 57 24 63 99
www.chateaupavie.com

Le Pin
33500 Pomerol
Mailing address:
Hof te Cattebeke
Bossenaar 14
9680 Etikhove
Belgium
Telephone (France): 33 5 57 51 33 99
Fax (France): 33 5 57 31 09 66
Telephone (Belgium): 32 55 31 17 59
Fax (Belgium): 32 55 31 09 66

Pontet-Canet
125 Château Pontet-Canet
33250 Pauillac
Telephone: 33 5 56 59 04 04
Fax: 33 5 56 59 26 63
www.pontet-canet.com

Sociando Mallet
33180 Saint-Seurin-de-Cadourne
Telephone: 33 5 56 73 38 80
Fax: 33 5 56 73 38 88

Vieux Château Certan
33500 Pomerol
Telephone: 33 5 57 51 17 33
Fax: 33 5 57 25 35 08
www.vieux-chateau-certan.com

BURGUNDY

Domaine Arnaud Ente
12 rue Mazeray
21190 Meursault
Telephone: 33 3 80 21 66 12
Fax: same number

Domaine Robert Arnoux
3 Route Nationale 74
21700 Vosne-Romanée
Telephone: 33 3 80 61 08 41
Fax: 33 3 80 61 36 02

Domaine du Clos de Tart
7 Route des Grands Crus
21220 Morey-Saint-Denis
Telephone: 33 3 80 34 30 91
Fax: 33 3 80 51 86 70

Domaine Vincent Dancer
23 Route Santenay
21190 Chassagne-Montrachet
Telephone: 33 3 80 21 94 48
Fax: 33 3 80 21 39 48

Domaine Dujac
7 rue de la Bussière
21220 Morey-Saint-Denis
Telephone: 33 3 80 34 01 00
Fax: 33 3 80 34 01 09
www.dujac.com

Domaine des Epeneaux / Comte Armand
Place de l'Eglise
21630 Pommard
Telephone: 33 3 80 24 70 50
Fax: 33 3 80 22 72 37

Domaine Vincent Girardin
Chemin Champs Lin
21190 Meursault
Telephone: 33 3 80 20 81 00
Fax: 33 3 80 20 81 10
www.vincentgirardin.com

Domaine Henri Gouges
7 rue du Moulin
21704 Nuits-Saint-Georges
Telephone: 33 3 80 61 04 40
Fax: 33 3 80 61 32 84
www.gouges.com

Domaine Robert Groffier
3 Route Grands Crus
21220 Morey-Saint-Denis
Telephone: 33 3 80 34 31 53
Fax: 33 3 80 34 15 48

Domaine Michel Lafarge
Rue La Combe
21190 Volnay
Telephone: 33 3 80 21 61 61
Fax: 33 3 80 21 67 83

Domaine Lecheneaut
14 rue des Seuillets
21700 Nuits-Saint-Georges
Telephone: 33 3 80 61 05 96
Fax: 33 3 80 61 28 31

Maison Frédéric Magnien
26 Route Nationale
21220 Morey-Saint-Denis
Telephone: 33 3 80 58 54 20
Fax: 33 3 80 51 84 34

Domaine Michel Magnien
4 rue Ribordot
21220 Morey-Saint-Denis
Telephone: 33 3 80 51 82 98
Fax: 33 3 80 58 51 76

Domaine Méo-Camuzet
11 rue des Grands Crus
21700 Vosne-Romanée
Telephone: 33 3 80 61 11 05
Fax: same number
www.meo-camuzet.com

Domaine Denis Mortet
22 rue de l'Eglise
21220 Gevrey-Chambertin
Telephone: 33 3 80 34 10 05
Fax: 33 3 80 34 16 26

Domaine H. Perrot-Minot
54 Route des Grands Crus
21220 Morey-Saint-Denis
Telephone: 33 3 80 34 32 51
Fax: 33 3 80 34 13 57
www.perrot-minot.com

CALIFORNIA

David Arthur
1521 Sage Canyon Road
St. Helena, CA 94574
Telephone: (707) 963-5190
Fax: (707) 963-3711
www.davidarthur.com

L'Aventure
2815 Live Oak Road
Paso Robles, CA 93446
Telephone: (805) 227-1588
Fax: (805) 227-6988
www.aventurewine.com

Bond
Harlan Estates
P.O. Box 352
Oakville, CA 94562
Telephone: (707) 944-1441
Fax: (707) 944-1444
www.harlanestate.com

Brewer-Clifton
1704 Industrial Way
Lompoc, CA 93436
Telephone: (805) 735-9184
Fax: (805) 735-9185
www.brewerclifton.com

Carlisle
P.O. Box 556
Santa Rosa, CA 95402
Telephone: (707) 566-7700
Fax: (707) 566-7200
www.carlislewinery.com

Diamond Creek
1500 Diamond Mountain Road
Calistoga, CA 94515
Telephone: (707) 942-6926
Fax: (707) 942-6936
www.diamondcreekvineyards.com

DuMOL
11 El Sereno
Orinda, CA 94563
Telephone: (925) 254-8922
Fax: (925) 254-8942
www.dumol.com

Hartford Court
8075 Martinelli Road
Forestville, CA 95436
Telephone: (800) 588-0234 or (707) 887-1756
Fax: (707) 887-7158
www.hartfordwines.com

Paul Hobbs
3355 Gravenstein Highway North
Sebastopol, CA 95472
Telephone: (707) 824-9879
Fax: (707) 824-5843
www.paulhobbswinery.com

Hourglass
Ricky Sander Wine Company
1104 Adams Street, Suite 103
St. Helena, CA 94574
Telephone: (707) 968-9332
Fax: (707) 968-9337
www.rswco.com

Hundred Acre Vineyard
P.O. Box 380
Rutherford, CA 94573
Telephone: (707) 967-9398
Fax: (707) 968-9658

Kongsgaard
P.O. Box 349
Oakville, CA 94562
Telephone: (707) 963-5918
Fax: (707) 963-5919
www.kongsgaardwine.com

Kunin Wines
458 Terrace Road
Santa Barbara, CA 93109
Telephone: (805) 689-3545
Fax: (805) 564-4172
www.kuninwines.com

Linne Calodo
3845 Oakdale Road
Paso Robles, CA 93446
Telephone: (805) 227-0797
Fax: (805) 227-4868
www.linnecalodo.com

Ojai Vineyard
P.O. Box 952
Oak View, CA 93022
Telephone: (805) 649-1674
Fax: (805) 649-4651
www.ojaivineyard.com

Pax Wine Cellars
3352-D Coffey Lane
Santa Rosa, CA 95403
Telephone: (707) 591-0782
Fax: (707) 591-0784
www.paxwines.com

Rochioli Vineyard and Winery
6192 Westside Road
Healdsburg, CA 95448
Telephone: (707) 433-2305
Fax: (707) 433-2358

Saxum
2810 Willow Creek Road
Paso Robles, CA 93446
Telephone: (805) 610-0363
Fax: (805) 238-2268
www.saxumvineyards.com

Seavey
1310 Conn Valley Road
St. Helena, CA 94574
Telephone: (707) 963-8339
Fax: (707) 963-0232
www.seaveyvineyard.com

Sloan Estate
P.O. Box 507
Rutherford, CA 94573
Telephone: (707) 967-8627
Fax: (707) 967-8918
www.sloanestate.com

Spottswoode
1902 Madrona Avenue
St. Helena, CA 94574
Telephone: (707) 963-0134
Fax: (707) 963-2886
www.spottswoode.com

Switchback Ridge
4292 Silverado Trail
Calistoga, CA 94515
Mailing address: 1104 Adams Street, Suite 103
St. Helena, CA 94574
Telephone: (707) 967-8987
Fax: (707) 569-9255
www.switchbackridge.com

Tablas Creek
9339 Adelaida Road
Paso Robles, CA 93446
Telephone: (805) 237-1231
Fax: (805) 237-1314
www.tablascreek.com

Talley Vineyards
3031 Lopez Drive
Arroyo Grande, CA 93420
Telephone: (805) 489-0446
Fax: (805) 489-0996
www.talleyvineyards.com

Turley Wine Cellars
3358 St. Helena Highway
St. Helena, CA 94574
Telephone: (707) 963-0940
Fax: (707) 963-8683
www.turleywinecellars.com

Verité
4611 Thomas Road
Healdsburg, CA 95448
Telephone: (707) 433-9000
Fax: (707) 431-1261

CHILE

Almaviva
Avda. Santa Rosa 08219
Casilla 274
Puente Alto
Telephone: 56 2 852 9300
Fax: 56 2 852 5405
www.almavivawinery.com

Casa Lapostolle
Av. Vitacura 5250, Of. 901
Vitacura
Santiago
Telephone: 56 2 426 99 60
Fax: 56 2 426 99 66

GERMANY

Weingut Emrich-Schönleber
Naheweinstrasse 10a
55569 Monzingen/Nahe
Telephone: 49 67 51 27 33
Fax: 49 67 51 48 64
www.schoenleber.de

Weingut Josef Leitz
Theodor-Heuss-Strass 5
D-65385 Rüdesheim-am-rhein
Telephone: 49 67 224 8711
Fax: 49 67 224 7658
www.leitz-wein.de

Weingut Schäfer-Fröhlich
Schulstrasse 6
D-55595 Bockenau
Telephone: 49 67 58 65 21
Fax: 49 67 58 87 94
www.weingut-schaefer-froehlich.de

Weingut St. Urbans-Hof
St. Urbans-Hof
Oekonomierat Nic. Weis
D-54340 Leiwen/Mosel
Telephone: 49 65 0793 770
Fax: 49 65 0793 7730
www.weingut-st-urbans-hof.de

ITALY

Allegrini
Corte Giara
37022 Fumane di Valpolicella
Telephone: 39 45 683 2011
Fax: 39 45 770 1774
www.allegrini.it

Tommaso Bussola
Via Molino Turri, 30
37024 Negrar (VR), Loc.S.Peretto
Telephone: 39 45 750 1740
Fax: 39 45 210 9940
www.bussolavini.com

Poderi Aldo Conterno
Localita Bussia, 48
12065 Monforte d'Alba (CN)
Telephone: 39 173 78150
Fax: 39 173 787240
www.il-vino.com/poderialdoconterno

Fattoria di Felsina
S. S. 484 Chiantigiana, 101
53019 Castelnuovo Berardenga (SI)
Telephone: 39 577 355 117

Fontodi
50020 Panzano in Chianti (FI)
Telephone: 39 55 852 005
Fax: 39 55 852 537
www.fontodi.com

Giuseppe Mascarello
Strada del Grosso, 1
12060 Castiglione Falletto (CN)
Winery and cellars: via Borgonuovo, 108
12060 Monchiero (CN)
Telephone: 39 173 79 21 26
Fax: 39 173 79 21 24
www.mascarello1881.com

Luigi Pira
Via XX Settembre 9
12050 Serralunga d'Alba (CN)
Telephone: 39 173 613 106

Podere Rocche dei Manzoni
loc. Manzoni Soprani 3
12065 Monforte d'Alba (CN)
Telephone: 39 173 78421
Fax: 39 173 787161
www.barolobig.com

Quintarelli
Via Cerè, 1
37024 Negrar
Telephone: 39 45 750 0016
Fax: 39 45 601 2301

La Spinetta di Giuseppe Rivetti
Via Annunziata, 17
14054 Castagnole Lanze
Telephone: 39 141 877 396
Fax: 39 141 877 566
www.la-spinetta.com

Vietti
Piazza Vittorio Veneto, 5
12060 Castiglione Falletto (CN)
Telephone: 39 173 62825
Fax: 39 173 62941
www.vietti.com

LANGUEDOC-ROUSSILLON

Domaine La Grange des Pères
34150 Aniane
Telephone: 33 4 67 57 70 55
Fax: 33 4 67 57 32 04

Château de la Negly
11560 Fleury-d'Aude
Telephone: 33 4 68 32 36 28
Fax: 33 4 68 32 10 69
e-mail: lanegly@wanadoo.fr

RHONE VALLEY

Domaine de Cristia
Fauburg-Saint-Georges, 33
84350 Courthézon
Telephone: 33 4 90 70 89 15

Yves Cuilleron
Verlieu
42410 Chavanay
Telephone: 33 4 74 87 02 37
Fax: 33 4 74 87 05 62

Domaine Grand Veneur
Vignobles Alain Jaume et Fils
Route de Châteauneuf-du-Pape, 84100 Orange
Telephone: 33 4 90 34 68 70
Fax: 33 4 90 34 43 71
www.domaine-grand-veneur.com

Domaine des Remizières
Quartier les Remizières, 26600 Mercurol
Telephone: 33 4 75 07 44 28
Fax: 33 4 75 07 45 87

Château Saint Cosme
Louis Barroul
84190 Gigondas
Telephone: 33 4 90 65 80 80

Cuvée du Vatican
SCEA Diffonty Félicien et Fils
Route de Courthézon, 10
84231 Châteauneuf-du-Pape
Telephone: 33 4 90 83 70 51
Fax: 33 4 90 83 50 36
e-mail: cuvee-du-vatican@mnet.fr

SPAIN

J. C. Conde
Pizarro s/n
09400 Aranda de Duero (Burgos)
Telephone: 34 669 403 169
Fax: 34 947 511 861
www.bodegasconde.com

Bodegas Muga
Barrio de la Estación s/n
26200 Haro (La Rioja)
Telephone: 34 941 311 825
Fax: 34 941 312 867
www.bodegasmuga.com

Bodega Uvaguilera
Crta. de la Aguilera Km. 5,400
09400 Aranda de Duero (Burgos)
Telephone: 34 947 54 54 19
Fax: 34 947 54 69 04
www.uvaguilera.com

Hermanos Sastre
San Pedro, s/n
09311 La Horra (Burgos)
Fax: 34 947 542 108
www.vinasastre.com

Numanthia
Real s/n
49882 Valdefinjas (Zamora)
Telephone: 34 980 560 012
Fax: 34 941 33 43 71
e-mail: vega-de-toro@fer.es

Rotllan Torra
Balandra no. 8 (Torroja del Priorat)
43737 Tarragona
Telephone: 977 839 285
Fax: 933 050 112
www.rotllantorra.com

WASHINGTON

Andrew Will Winery
12526 S.W. Bank Road
Vashon Island, WA 98070
Telephone: (206) 463-9227
Fax: (206) 463-3524
www.andrewwill.com

DeLille Winery
P.O. Box 2233
Woodinville, WA 98072
Telephone: (425) 489-0544
Fax: (425) 402-9295
www.delillecellars.com

Januik Winery
19730 144th Ave. NE
Woodinville, WA 98072
Telephone: (425) 481-5502
www.januikwinery.com

ACETIC: Wines, no matter how well made, contain quantities of acetic acid. If the amount is excessive, the wine will have a vinegary smell.

ACIDITY: The acidity level in a wine is critical to its enjoyability and livelihood. The natural acids that appear in wine are citric, tartaric, malic, and lactic. Wines from hot years tend to be lower in acidity, whereas wines from cool, rainy years tend to be high in acidity. Acidity in a wine preserves the wine's freshness and keeps the wine lively, but an excess of acidity results in wine that is tart and sour.

AFTERTASTE: As the term suggests, this is the taste left in the mouth after one swallows. This word is a synonym for length or finish. The longer the aftertaste lingers in the mouth (assuming it is a pleasant taste), the finer the quality of the wine.

AGGRESSIVE: Aggressive is usually applied to wines that are high either in acidity or harsh tannins, or both.

ANGULAR: Angular wines are wines that lack roundness, generosity, and depth. Wine from poor vintages or wines that are too acidic are often described as being angular.

AROMA: Aroma is commonly used to mean the smell of a young, relatively unevolved wine before it has had sufficient time to develop nuances, which are then called its bouquet.

ASTRINGENT: Wines that are astringent are not necessarily bad or good wines. Astringent wines are harsh and coarse to taste, either because they are too young and tannic and just need time to develop or because they are not well made. The level of tannin in a wine contributes to its degree of astringence.

AUSTERE: Wines that are austere are generally not terribly pleasant wines to drink. An austere wine is a hard, rather dry wine that lacks richness and generosity. However, young, promising Bordeaux can often express itself as austere, and with aging such a wine will reveal considerably more generosity than its youthful austerity suggested.

BACKWARD: Essentially a wine that is firm, closed, or needs more time in the bottle to attain maturity and become more interesting.

BALANCE: One of the most desired traits in a wine is good balance, where the concentration of fruit, level of tannin, and acidity are in total harmony. Well-balanced wines are symmetrical and tend to age gracefully.

BARNYARD: An unclean, farmyard, fecal aroma that is imparted to a wine because of unclean barrels or generally unsanitary winemaking facilities.

BERRYLIKE: As this descriptive term implies, wines, particularly Bordeaux wines that are young and not overly oaked, have an intense berry fruit character that can suggest blackberries, raspberries, black cherries, mulberries, or even strawberries and cranberries.

BIG: A big wine is a large-framed, full-bodied wine with an intense and concentrated feel on the palate. Bordeaux wines in general are not big wines in the same sense that Rhône wines are, but the top vintages of Bordeaux produce very rich, concentrated, deep wines.

BIODYNAMIC VITICULTURE: Based on the theories of the late Rudolf Steiner, biodynamic farming is organic viticulture taken to the extreme. The biodynamic viticulturist sees the greater philosophical and symbiotic relationships among soils, vines, humans, and the cosmos, and most pure biodynamic farmers consider all unnatural treatments in the vineyard totally forbidden. The only component used by biodynamic viticulturists against rot or mildew is sulfur. This is the quintessential homeopathic/holistic philosophy of operating a vineyard, and it is practiced by some of the great wine producers profiled in this book, including Domaine Leflaive in Puligny-Montrachet, Domaine Leroy in Vosne-Romanée, Chapoutier in Hermitage, and Huet in Vouvray.

BLACK CURRANT: A pronounced smell of the black currant fruit is commonly associated with red Bordeaux wines. It can vary in intensity from faint to very deep and rich.

BODY: Body is the weight and fullness of a wine that can be sensed as it crosses the palate. Full-bodied wines tend to have a lot of alcohol, concentration, and glycerine.

Botrytis cinerea: The fungus that attacks the grape skins under specific climatic conditions (usually interchanging periods of moisture and sunny weather). It causes the grape to become super-concentrated because it causes a natural dehydration. *Botrytis cinerea* is essential for the great sweet white wines of Barsac and Sauternes.

BOUQUET: As a wine's aroma becomes more developed from bottle-aging, it is transformed into a bouquet, which is hopefully more than just the smell of the grape.

BRAWNY: A hefty, muscular, full-bodied wine with plenty of weight and flavor, although not always the most elegant or refined sort of wine.

BREADTH AND CHARACTER: Breadth refers to a wine's expansive and relatively broad flavor profile, although it can also suggest a textural thickness. Character is a generic term that refers to a wine that has a singular style, a very specific expression; it is used as a positive descriptor.

BRIERY: I usually think of California Zinfandel rather than Bordeaux when the term briery comes into play. Briery suggests that the wine is aggressive and rather spicy.

BRILLIANT: Brilliant describes the color of the wine. A brilliant wine is one that is clear, with no haze or cloudiness.

BROWNING: As red wines age, their color changes from ruby/purple, to dark ruby, to medium ruby, to ruby with an amber edge, to ruby with a brown edge. When a wine is browning it is usually fully mature and is not likely to get better.

CARBONIC MACERATION: A vinification method used to make soft, fruity wines. Whole clusters of grapes are put in the vat, and then the tank is filled with carbonic gas. This system is used to emphasize the fruit in the final wine as opposed to structure and tannin.

CEDAR: Bordeaux reds often have a bouquet that suggests either faintly or overtly the smell of cedarwood. It is a complex aspect of the bouquet.

CHEWY: If a wine has a rather dense, viscous texture from a high glycerine content, it is often referred to as being chewy. High-extract wines from great vintages can often be chewy.

CLOSED: The term closed denotes that the wine is not showing its potential, which remains locked in because the wine is too young. Young Bordeaux often close up about 12–18 months after bottling and, depending on the vintage and storage conditions, may remain in such a state for several years to more than a decade.

COMPLEX: One of the most subjective descriptive terms used. A complex wine is one that the taster never gets bored with and finds interesting to drink. Complex wines tend to have a variety of subtle scents and flavors that hold one's interest.

CONCENTRATED: Fine wines, whether they are light, medium, or full-bodied, should have concentrated flavors. Concentrated denotes that the wine has a depth and richness of fruit that gives it appeal and interest. Deep is a synonym of concentrated.

CONCENTRATOR: A relatively recent (over the last 30 years) development, a concentrator is generally one of two types of devices. The most commonly encountered concentrator uses reverse osmosis. A second method, called entrophy, removes water from the grape must via a vacuum system. Both types of concentrators must be used gently and subtly to avoid concentrating the wrong things. Concentrators are increasingly being employed by wineries in troublesome vintages. They do not take the place of conservative viticulture practices and low yields in the vineyards. Moreover it is important to remember that if a winery concentrates wine with flaws—high unripe tannins, for example—the defects are merely magnified and exaggerated by the use of concentrators.

CORKED: A corked wine is a flawed wine that has taken on the smell of cork as a result of an unclean or faulty cork. It is perceptible in a bouquet that shows no fruit, only the smell of a musty cork or damp cardboard. Technically, a corked wine is contaminated with TCA (2,4,6 trichloroanisole).

DECADENT: If you are an ice cream and chocolate lover, you know the feeling of eating a huge sundae lavished with hot fudge, real whipped cream, and rich vanilla ice cream. If you are a wine enthusiast, a wine loaded with opulent, even unctuous, layers of fruit, with a huge bouquet, and a plump, luxurious texture can be said to be decadent.

DEEP: Essentially the same as concentrated, the word deep expresses the fact that the wine is rich, full of extract, and mouth-filling.

DELICATE: As this word implies, delicate wines are light, subtle, understated wines that are prized for their shyness rather than an extroverted robust character. White wines are usually more delicate than red wines.

DELINEATED: An adjective used to describe wine with impeccable focus and definition.

DENSITY OF PLANTATION: A tricky concept, density of plantation essentially refers to the number of vines planted per acre or hectare. As evidenced by this book, density can vary considerably, but a general observation is that vine density in European vineyards is two to five times higher than most vineyard plantations in the New World. Viticultural evidence suggests that the greater the vine density, the more the vine pushes its root system deeper in search of nutrients, thus producing smaller berries and fewer bundles of higher quality.

DIFFUSE: Wines that smell and taste unstructured and unfocused are said to be diffuse. Often when red wines are served at too warm a temperature they become diffuse.

DUMB: A dumb wine is also a closed wine, but the term dumb is used in a more pejorative sense. Closed wines may only need time to reveal their richness and intensity. Dumb wines may never become any better.

EARTHY: This term may be used in both a negative and a positive sense; however, I prefer to use earthy to denote a positive aroma of fresh, rich, clean soil. Earthy is a more intense smell than woodsy or truffle scents.

ELEGANT: Although more white wines than red are described as being elegant, the lighter-styled, graceful, well-balanced Bordeaux wines can be elegant.

EVOLVED: An adjective used to suggest a wine relatively mature and/or developing at a quicker rate than anticipated.

EXUBERANT: Like extroverted, somewhat hyper people, wines too can be gushing with fruit, and seem nervous and intensely vigorous.

FAT: When Bordeaux has a very hot year, the grapes attain a state of super-maturity, and the wines are often quite rich and concentrated with low to average acidity. Often such wines are said to be fat, which is a prized commodity. If they become too fat, that is a flaw and they are called flabby.

FERMENTATION: Wine is made simply. After the grapes are harvested, they are often destemmed and then moved to an open or closed vat that can be made from cement, wood, stainless steel, or fiberglass. After pressing, the wine is then fermented, meaning the sugar is converted into alcohol. Immediately after the alcoholic fermentation, many red wines remain in vat, where they go through a malolactic fermentation, which softens their sharp malic acids into softer, more pleasing lactic acids. Or, many old, traditional producers (especially in Burgundy) move the wine into barrels for the malolactic fermentation. While red wines tend to be fermented at relatively high temperatures, white wines are fermented at low temperatures. There are enormous variations with regard to fermentation methods. In fact, entire books have been written on this subject. In short, the critical decision for red wine producers is whether to destem the grapes or leave a portion or even 100% of the stems before pressing. The highest-quality white wine producers tend to do whole cluster pressings, and allow the juice very little skin contact during fermentation. With red wines, the skin contact can be prolonged for a month or more.

FINING: This is a traditional technique of clarifying wine by introducing various agents. The most common fining agents are egg whites and, more recently, bentonite (powdered clay) or gelatin. These agents precipitate to the bottom of the tank or barrel, carrying suspended particles with them. More artistic/artisanal wineries only resort to fining if the wine requires it, preferring to let the wine fall brilliant naturally without using any procedure that may strip the wine of aromas, flavor concentration, or texture.

FLABBY: A wine that is too fat or obese is a flabby wine. Flabby wines lack structure and are heavy to taste.

FLESHY: Fleshy is a synonym for chewy, meaty, or beefy. It denotes that the wine has considerable body, alcohol, and extract, and usually a high glycerin content.

FLORAL: Many wines possess a floral or flowery aspect to their bouquets or aromas. This can take the smell of roses (Gewurztraminer and Roussanne), acacia flowers (Marsanne), and honeysuckle (Chenin Blanc and Chardonnay).

FOCUSED: Both a fine wine's bouquet and flavor should be focused. Focused simply means that the scents, aromas, and flavors are precise and clearly delineated. If they are not, the wine is like an out-of-focus picture: diffuse, hazy, and problematic.

FORTIFIED: A fortified wine is one whose alcohol content has been increased by the addition of brandy or neutral spirits.

FORWARD: A wine is said to be forward when its charm and character are fully revealed. While it may not be fully mature yet, a forward wine is generally quite enjoyable and drinkable. Forward is the opposite of backward.

FOUDRE: A *foudre* is usually a large, oversized wooden vessel that can be 10 to 100 times larger than a typical wine barrel (*barrique* in French), which generally holds 225 liters (59 gallons). There are many different size barrels, ranging from *demi-muids* (500–600 liters) to *foudres,* which in Italian are called *botti.* The Australians call their large barrels hogsheads, which hold 300 liters or more. Another commonly employed descriptor is *puncheon;* a *puncheon* usually holds 450–500 liters.

FRESH: Freshness in both young and old wines is a welcome and pleasing component. A wine is said to be fresh when it is lively and cleanly made. The opposite of fresh is stale.

FRUITY: A very good wine should have enough concentration of fruit so that it can be said to be fruity. Common sense dictates that a wine, and especially great ones, should taste not only of the place (*terroir*) they came from, but also the fruit from which they were made.

FULL-BODIED: Wines rich in extract, alcohol, and glycerin are full-bodied wines.

GARRIGUE: In the southern Rhône Valley and Provence, the landscape of small slopes and plateaus is often referred to as the *garrigues.* This Provençal word applies to these windswept hilltops/slopes inhabited by scrub brush and Provençal herb outcroppings. The smell of the *garrigues* is often attributed to southern Rhône Valley wines and means more than simply the smell of *herbes de Provence.* It includes an earthy/herbal concoction of varying degrees of intensity.

GLYCERIN: This is a by-product of the wine's fermentation that is found in all wines. It becomes noticeably higher as the alcohol percentage increases, as well as in late-harvest wines. Glycerin provides a smooth textural impression and encourages fullness in a wine's body.

GREEN: Green wines are those made from underripe grapes; they lack richness and generosity and have a vegetal character. Green wines were often made in Bordeaux in poor vintages such as 1972 and 1977.

HARD: Wines with abrasive, astringent tannins or high acidity are said to be hard. Young vintages of Bordeaux can be hard, but they should never be harsh.

HARSH: If a wine is too hard, it is said to be harsh. Harshness in a wine, young or old, is a flaw.

HECTARE: A metric measurement of land. One hectare equals 2.47 acres.

HECTOLITERS PER HECTARE: The manner in which most European wineries provide production figures for their vineyards. The American equivalent is tons of fruit per acre. A rough conversion is that each 15 hectoliters per hectare equals approximately one ton of fruit per acre. This figure represents a general guideline. More important is the actual production in terms of kilos (or pounds) of fruit per vine. However, this figure is almost impossible to procure from producers.

HEDONISTIC: Certain styles of wine are meant to be inspected, and their appreciation requires introspection and intellectual effort. Others are designed to provide sheer delight, joy, and euphoria. Hedonistic wines can be criticized as "obvious" because they provide so much ecstasy, but in essence, they are totally gratifying wines meant to fascinate and enthrall—pleasure at its best.

HERBACEOUS: Many wines have a distinctive herbal smell that is generally described as herbaceous. Specific herbal smells can be of thyme, lavender, rosemary, oregano, fennel, or basil.

HERBES DE PROVENCE: Provence is known for the wild herbs that grow prolifically throughout the region. These include lavender, thyme, sage, rosemary, and oregano. It is not just an olfactory fancy to smell many of these herbs in Rhône Valley wines, particularly those made in the south.

HOLLOW: A synonym for shallow; hollow wines are diluted and lack depth and concentration.

HONEYED: A common personality trait of sweet Barsacs and Sauternes, a honeyed wine is one with the smell and taste of bees' honey.

HOT: Not meaning the wine is too warm to drink, hot denotes that the wine is too high in alcohol and therefore leaves a burning sensation in the back of the throat when swallowed. Wines with alcohol levels in excess of 14.5% are often hot.

INOX VATS: This is the French term for stainless-steel vats that are used for both fermentation and storage of wine.

INTENSITY: Intensity is one of the most desirable traits of a high-quality wine. Wines of great intensity must also have balance. They should never be heavy or cloying. Intensely concentrated great wines are alive, vibrant, aromatic, layered, and texturally compelling. Their intensity adds to their character, rather than detracting from it.

JAMMY: When Bordeaux wines have a great intensity of fruit from excellent ripeness they can be "jammy," which denotes a very concentrated, flavorful wine with superb extract. In great vintages such as 1961 and 1982, some of the wines are so concentrated that they are said to be jammy.

KISSELGUHR FILTRATION SYSTEM: This is a filtration system using diatomaceous earth as the filtering material, rather than cellulose, or in the past, before it was banned, asbestos.

LEAFY: A leafy character in a wine is similar to a herbaceous character, but it refers to the smell of leaves rather than herbs. A wine that is too leafy is a vegetal or green wine.

LEAN: Lean wines are slim, rather streamlined wines that lack generosity and fatness but can still be enjoyable and pleasant.

LEES: Lees are the sediment that is naturally suspended in wine during and after fermentation. Most of this sediment will ultimately precipitate out during fermentation or aging in barrel if the wine has not been excessively clarified. Lees consist primarily of dying yeast cells and proteins. Modern-day winemakers, copying the long-established Burgundian practice for Chardonnay, often employ an aging in cask on the lees, as they believe—assuming the lees are healthy—that this promotes additional texture as well as aromatic complexity, resulting in an improved wine with a more natural character. The expression "aged on its lees" means exactly what it says.

LIVELY: A synonym for fresh or exuberant, a lively wine is usually a young wine with good acidity and a thirst-quenching personality.

LONG: A very desirable trait, length relates to a wine's finish, meaning that after you swallow the wine, you sense its presence for a long time. (Thirty seconds to several minutes is great length.)

LUSH: Lush wines are velvety, soft, richly fruity wines that are both concentrated and fat. A lush wine can never be an astringent or hard wine.

MASSIVE: In great vintages with a high degree of ripeness and superb concentration, some wines can turn out to be so big, full-bodied, and rich that they are called massive. Great wines, such as the 1961 Latour and Pétrus and the 1982 Pétrus, are textbook examples of massive wines.

MEATY: A chewy, fleshy wine is also said to be meaty.

MICROBULLAGE: This is a technique developed in the southwestern France area of Madiran to soften tannins by adding small dosages of controlled oxygen into barrels or vats filled with red wine. In English, it is referred to as micro-oxygenation. Like any technique, it needs to be used and monitored carefully. Critics claim it promotes standardization of wine, but its defenders—and there are some brilliant ones, including such great Bordeaux wine consultants as Michel Rolland and Stéphane Dérenoncourt—believe that when employed judiciously, it is far less deleterious to the wine than frequent racking of barrels (the removal of wine from one barrel to another), which they claim is far more violent and dangerous to the wine's overall health. Like most technical applications, a balanced approach is best, and the polemics over its use seem to miss the point.

MONOCÉPAGE: A wine made totally of one specific varietal.

MONOPOLE: A term used for a vineyard owned exclusively by one proprietor. The word monopole appears on the label of a wine made from such a vineyard.

MORSELLATED: Many vineyards are fragmented, with multiple growers owning a portion of the same vineyard. Such a vineyard is often referred to as a morsellated vineyard.

MOUTH-FILLING: Big, rich, concentrated wines that are filled with fruit extract and high in alcohol and glycerine are wines that tend to texturally fill the mouth. A mouth-filling wine is also a chewy, fleshy, fat wine.

NOSE: The general smell and aroma of a wine as sensed through one's nose and olfactory senses is often called the wine's nose.

OAKY: Most top Bordeaux wines are aged from 12 to 30 months in small oak barrels. At the very best properties, a percentage of the oak barrels are new, and these barrels impart a toasty, vanilla flavor and smell to the wine. If the wine is not rich and concentrated, the barrels can overwhelm the wine, making it taste overly oaky. However, when the wine is rich and concentrated and the winemaker has made a judicious use of new oak barrels, the results are a wonderful marriage of fruit and oak.

OFF: If a wine is not showing its true character, or is flawed or spoiled in some way, it is said to be off.

ORGANIC FARMING: This is a system of viticulture that eschews industrial, synthesized compounds, or any inorganic additions to the soil designed to increase the vines' productivity or inhibit pests. There is considerable debate about what actually constitutes pure organic farming, but an avoidance of pesticides, fungicides, and fertilizers is the generally accepted description.

OVERRIPE: An undesirable characteristic; grapes left too long on the vine become too ripe, lose their acidity, and produce wines that are heavy and imbalanced. This happens more frequently in hot viticultural areas.

OXIDIZED: If a wine has been excessively exposed to air during either its making or its aging, the wine loses freshness and takes on a stale, old smell and taste. Such a wine is said to be oxidized.

PEPPERY: A peppery quality to a wine is usually noticeable in many Rhône wines, which have an aroma of black pepper and a pungent flavor. It occasionally appears in some Bordeaux wines.

PERFUMED: This term usually is more applicable to fragrant, aromatic white wines than to red Bordeaux wines. However, some of the dry white wines and sweet white wines can have a strong perfumed smell.

pH: This is a chemical measurement (hydrogen ions in solution) used by wineries to measure the ripeness of the grapes and the total acidity level in the finished wine. Most red wines are significantly higher in pH (lower in acidity) than whites. It is difficult to suggest acceptable pH levels in wines, but finished, bottled white wines tend to have a pH of 3.0 to 3.5, and reds generally fall between 3.5 and 4.0. There is a correlation between higher pH levels and greater ripeness and warmer climate wines, although even cool-climate varieties from hot vintages can have pHs approaching 4.0, which is considered high.

PIGÉAGE: A winemaking technique of punching down the cap of grape skins that forms during the beginning of the wine's fermentation. This is done several times a day, occasionally more frequently, to extract color, flavor, and tannin from the fermenting juice.

PLUMMY: Rich, concentrated wines often have the smell and taste of ripe plums. When they do, the term plummy is applicable.

PONDEROUS: Ponderous is often used as a synonym for massive, but in my usage a massive wine is simply a big, rich, very concentrated wine with balance, whereas a ponderous wine is one that has become heavy and tiring to drink.

PRECOCIOUS: Wines that mature quickly—as well as those wines that may last and evolve gracefully over a long period of time, but taste as if they are aging quickly because of their tastiness and soft, early charms—are said to be precocious.

PRUNY: Wines produced from overripe grapes take on the character of prunes. Pruny wines are flawed wines.

RAISINY: Late-harvest wines that are meant to be drunk at the end of a meal are often slightly raisiny, which in some Ports and sherries is desirable. However, in dry Bordeaux wines a raisiny quality is a major flaw.

RESIDUAL SUGAR: Most table wines are technically dry, although they may have a slight degree of residual sugar, which is the amount of sugar remaining in the wine. Experts have tended to adopt the following formula: If a wine has less than 0.5% residual sugar, it is considered very dry. Wines with 0.6–1.4% residual sugar are considered slightly off dry, although most consumers would find them to be dry. When residual sugar is over 1.5%, a sweet character can be discerned by even the most neophyte taster. Sweet dessert wines possess residual sugar levels in excess of 5%.

REVERSE OSMOSIS: This is a technique used to concentrate wine or to remove unpleasant characteristics (volatile acidity) by pushing the wine through a fine membrane to remove water. Like any technique, it is a question of application, as it can be abused or used subtly. Many top estates use a reverse osmosis concentrator machine only in rain-plagued vintages, and then only for the most diluted fruit. The problem with any type of concentration machine is that it concentrates everything. For example, if there is a flaw such as sharp green tannin, it tends to be concentrated/exaggerated as well.

RICH: Wines high in extract, flavor, and intensity of fruit are described as being rich.

RIPE: A wine is ripe when its grapes have reached the optimum level of maturity. Less than fully mature grapes produce wines that are underripe, and overly mature grapes produce wines that are overripe.

ROUND: A very desirable character of wines, roundness occurs in fully mature red wines that have lost their youthful, astringent tannins, and in young reds that are low in tannin and acidity and are meant to be consumed young.

SAVORY: A general descriptive term that denotes that the wine is round, flavorful, and interesting to drink.

SHALLOW: A weak, feeble, watery, or diluted wine lacking concentration is said to be shallow.

SHARP: An undesirable trait; sharp wines are bitter and unpleasant with hard, pointed edges.

SILKY: A synonym for velvety or lush; silky wines are soft, sometimes fat, but never hard or angular.

SMOKY: Some wines, either because of the soil or because of the barrels used to age the wine, have a distinctive smoky character. Some *terroirs* result in smoky characteristics in wine (the Graves in Bordeaux and Pouilly Fume in the Loire Valley). The use of some types of new oak casks can also promote aromas of smoke.

SOFT: A soft wine is one that is round and fruity and low in acidity, with an absence of aggressive, hard tannins.

SPICY: Wines often smell quite spicy, with aromas of pepper, cinnamon, and other well-known spices. These pungent aromas are usually lumped together and called spicy. Scents and flavors of Oriental spices refer to wines with aromas and/or flavors of soy sauce, ginger, hoisin sauce, and sesame oil.

STALE: Dull, heavy wines that are oxidized or lack balancing acidity for freshness are called stale.

STALKY: A synonym for vegetal, but used more frequently to denote that the wine has probably had too much contact with the stems and the result is a green, vegetal, or stalky character to the wine.

SUPPLE: A supple wine is one that is soft, lush, velvety, and very attractively round and tasty. It is a highly desirable characteristic, as it suggests that the wine is harmonious.

TANNIC: The tannins of a wine, which are extracted from the grape skins and stems, are, along with a wine's acidity and alcohol, its lifeline. Tannins give a wine firmness and some roughness when young, but gradually fall away and dissipate. A tannic wine is one that is young and not yet ready to drink.

TART: Sharp, acidic, lean, unripe wines are called tart. In general, a red Bordeaux that is tart is not pleasurable.

TCA: The technical terminology for a wine flawed or contaminated by a musty cork. TCA is 2,4,6 trichloroanisole. Experts have estimated that 3–7% of all wines are tainted by TCA contamination. It has also ruined some wineries' entire vintages, as they have experienced TCA contamination from the use of chlorine cleaning products.

THICK: Rich, ripe, concentrated wines that are low in acidity are often said to be thick.

THIN: A synonym for shallow; a thin wine is watery, lacking in body, and just diluted—all undesirable characteristics.

TIGHTLY KNIT: Young wines with good acidity levels and good tannin levels and are well made are called tightly knit, meaning they have yet to open up and develop.

TOASTY: A smell of grilled toast can often be found in wines because the barrels the wines are aged in are charred or toasted on the inside.

TOBACCO: Many red Graves wines have the scent of fresh burning tobacco. It is a distinctive and wonderful smell in wine.

TRONCAIS OAK: A type of oak from the forest of Troncais in central France.

UNCTUOUS: Rich, lush, intense wines with layers of concentrated, soft, velvety fruit are said to be unctuous. In particular, the sweet wines of Barsac and Sauternes are unctuous.

UNFILTERED: A wine that has been bottled without exposure to any type of centrifugation, cold stabilization, or filtration through membrane or cellulose pad filters is said to be an unfiltered wine. These are usually artisanal efforts made by producers pushing for the highest quality and refusing to compromise the wine. An argument can be made that a very light, coarse filtration does not harm the wine's aromas, texture, or flavors. Like most winemaking techniques, it is a question of balance. There are flawed wines that should have been filtered, but by and large, wines that are bottled unfiltered tend to reflect a greater sensitivity by the winemaker to preserve the vintage, the vineyard, and the wine's integrity.

UNFINED: An unfined wine has not received any type of fining agent in order to protect its full vineyard and vintage character as well as its flavor profile.

VEGETAL: An undesirable characteristic; wines that smell and taste vegetal are usually made from unripe grapes. In some wines a subtle vegetable garden smell is pleasant and adds complexity, but if it is the predominant characteristic, it is a major flaw.

VELVETY: A textural description and synonym for lush or silky, a velvety wine is a rich, soft, smooth wine to taste. It is a very desirable characteristic.

VIEILLES VIGNES: This is the classic French expression for "old vines." Since it is not controlled by law, it can be used loosely by unscrupulous producers.

VISCOUS: Viscous wines tend to be relatively concentrated, fat, almost thick wines with a great density of fruit extract, plenty of glycerine, and high alcohol content. If they have balancing acidity, they can be tremendously flavorful and exciting wines. If they lack acidity, they are often flabby and heavy.

VOLATILE: A volatile wine is one that smells of vinegar as a result of an excessive amount of acetic bacteria being present. It is a seriously flawed wine.

WOODY: When a wine is overly oaky it is often said to be woody. Oakiness in a wine's bouquet and taste is good up to a point. Once past that point the wine is woody and its fruity qualities are masked by excessive oak aging. However, one has to be careful. Many young wines often reveal markedly oaky aromas after bottling and in the first year or so of their life. Yet wines with the requisite concentration absorb this oak and it will completely disappear in 4–10 years or more of bottling. Of course the crucial issue is whether the wine has sufficient fruit and concentration to absorb its oak.

YIELDS: This refers to how the production from a vineyard is encapsulated. In Europe it is stated as hectoliters per hectare, and in the New World, it is tons per acre. A more meaningful number would be pounds or kilos per vine, but virtually no winery provides that information.

ACKNOWLEDGMENTS

Books such as this are huge collaborative efforts, and if they succeed, the author often receives all the credit, and those behind the scenes who have done so much to make the book a success rest in obscurity. With the following passages, I hope to change at least part of that perception.

To the tiny staff at *The Wine Advocate* who were heavily involved in gathering information and putting it into some sort of sensible arrangement, I owe a great deal of thanks. They include my longtime assistant and the true brain of *The Wine Advocate*, Joan Passman. God knows where I would be in my career without her manning the gates and taking care of all the day-to-day problems. Annette Piatek, a hardworking, conscientious freelancer who has worked for me for a number of years, was extremely meticulous in gathering information, sorting through it, and assembling it into a workable format. She was also responsible for pulling the bulk of the tasting notes from the database on eRobert-Parker.com, editing the notes, and inserting them into the proper chapters. My longtime colleague Pierre-Antoine Rovani was generous in providing many of the tasting notes on the wines in the Alsace, Austria, Burgundy, Germany, and Washington chapters.

At the professional publishing level, my editor, Amanda Murray, deserves an enormous amount of credit for successfully making sense of my verbose commentary, cleaning it up, and assisting me in making certain ideas clearer. In short, her efforts have made the book dramatically better, and I deeply appreciate all her efforts. I would also like to thank the rest of the S&S production team, including Annie Orr, Aja Shevelew, Linda Dingler, Joel Avirom, Meghan Day Healey, and Peter McCulloch.

Every author requires plenty of psychological support, and I suspect I receive more than most. The love of my life, my beautiful wife, Patricia, always provides wisdom and counsel, and is an encouraging voice when things seem gloomiest. I must not forget my wonderful dogs: the late, beloved George, an English bulldog, was at my side during most of time I spent working on this book. He passed away soon after he won the top animal award at the 2004 Cannes Film Festival for his performance in the movie *Mondovino*. His basset hound sidekick, Hoover, is still by my side, as is the newest baby, Buddy the bulldog, named in honor of my deceased father.

I also want to acknowledge two longtime friends: literary agent, bon vivant, and very wise man Robert Lescher, and my older spiritual brother, Dr. Park B. Smith.

My thanks to the 156 wine producers who made this very special list. They represent the heart and soul of what makes wine so compelling and important, and it is their work in the vineyard and in the cellars that has sustained me in this career that has now endured for over a quarter of a century.

Finally, to the following friends, supporters, and advisors, a heartfelt "million thanks": Jim Arseneault, Anthony Barton, Ruth and the late Bruce Bassin, Hervé Berlaud, Bill Blatch, Thomas B. Böhrer, Barry Bondroff, Daniel Boulud, Rowena and Mark Braunstein, Christopher Cannan, Dick Carretta, Jean-Michel Cazes, Corinne Cesano, Jean-Marie Chadronnier, M. and Mme. Jean-Louis Charmolue, Charles Chevallier, Bob Cline, Jeffrey Davies, Hubert de Boüard, Jean and Annie Delmas, Jean-Hubert Delon and the late Michel Delon, Jean-Luc Le Dû, Dr. Albert H. Dudley III, Barbara Edelman, Fédéric Engérer, Michael Etzel, Paul Evans, Terry Faughey, the legendary Fitzcarraldo—my emotional soulmate, Joël Fleischman, Doug Flower, Mme. Capbern Gasqueton, Laurence and Bernard Godec, Dan Green, Josué Harari, Alexandra Harding, Dr. David Hutcheon, Barbara G. and Steve R.R. Jacoby, Joanne and Joe James, Jean-Paul Jauffret, Daniel Johnnes, Nathaniel, Archie and Denis Johnston, Ed Jonna, Elaine and Manfred Krankl, Bernard Magrez, Patrick Maroteaux, Pat and Victor Hugo Morgenroth, Christian, Jean-François and the late Jean-Pierre Moueix, Jerry Murphy, Bernard Nicolas, Jill Norman, Les Oenarchs (Bordeaux), Les Oenarchs (Baltimore), François Pinault, Frank Polk, Paul Pontallier, Bruno Prats, Jean-Guillaume Prats, Judy Pruce, Dr. Alain Raynaud, Martha Reddington, Dominique Renard, Michel Richard, Alan Richman, Dany and Michel Rolland, Yves Rovani, Robert Roy, Carlo Russo, Ed Sands, Erik Samazeuilh, Bob Schindler, Ernie Singer, Betsy Sobolewski, Elliott Staren, Daniel Tastet-Lawton, Lettie Teague, Alain Vauthier, Steven Verlin, Peter Vezan, Robert Vifian, Sonia Vogel, Jeanyee Wong, and Gérard Yvernault.

pages iv–v: CEPHAS/R & K Muschenetz; page v: CEPHAS/Diana Mewes; page vii: CEPHAS/Mick Rock; page viii: CEPHAS/Nigel Blythe; page xii: CEPHAS/Mike Herringshaw; page 2: CEPHAS/Ian Shaw; page 7: CEPHAS/Mick Rock; page 9: CEPHAS/Ian Shaw; page 11: CEPHAS/Mick Rock; page 12: CEPHAS/Ian Shaw; page 15: CEPHAS/Nigel Blythe; page 17: CEPHAS/StockFood; page 20: Image courtesy the Global Photo Library; page 24: Image courtesy the Global Photo Library; page 29: ©Bindy Welsh, Indigo Images; page 34: Image courtesy the Global Photo Library; page 60: CEPHAS/Herbert Lehmann; page 66: photo by Herbert Lehmann; page 69: photo by Weingut Weinlaubenhof Kracher; page 80: Image courtesy the Global Photo Library; page 107: ©Serge Bois-Prevost; page 108: ©Serge Bois-Prevost; page 111: CEPHAS/Ian Shaw; page 116: Image courtesy the Global Photo Library; page 123: CEPHAS/Mick Rock; page 133: Image courtesy the Global Photo Library; page 137: CEPHAS/Mick Rock; page 141: Image courtesy the Global Photo Library; pages 142–143: Image courtesy the Global Photo Library; page 149: CEPHAS/Mick Rock; page 150: Image courtesy the Global Photo Library; page 154: Image courtesy the Global Photo Library; page 160: CEPHAS/Mick Rock; page 161: Image courtesy the Global Photo Library; page 165: Image courtesy the Global Photo Library; page 169: CEPHAS/Mick Rock; page 189: CEPHAS/Ian Shaw; page 195: Image courtesy the Global Photo Library; page 198: Photo Burdin; page 200: Photo Burdin; page 202: CEPHAS/Stephen Wolfenden; page 207: Régis Duvignau; page 209: Régis Duvignau; page 215: M. Le Collen; page 231: CEPHAS/Herbert Lehmann; pages 250–251: CEPHAS/Mick Rock; page 252: CEPHAS/Mick Rock; page 256: CEPHAS/Mick Rock; page 267: CEPHAS/Herbert Lehmann; page 272: CEPHAS/Mick Rock; page 273: CEPHAS/Mick Rock; page 279: CEPHAS/Mick Rock;

page 282: Image courtesy the Global Photo Library; page 286 top center: Photo Marie-Pierre Morel; page 289: CEPHAS/Mick Rock; page 296: ©Veuve Clicquot Ponsardin; page 304: CEPHAS/Mick Rock; page 308: CEPHAS/Mick Rock; page 311: CEPHAS/Mick Rock; page 322: CEPHAS/Mick Rock; page 328: Image courtesy the Global Photo Library; page 336: CEPHAS/Geraldine Norman; page 337: CEPHAS/Mick Rock; page 349: CEPHAS/Mick Rock; page 352: Image courtesy the Global Photo Library; page 361: photo James Andanson, Sipa Press; page 371: Image courtesy the Global Photo Library; page 383: Emmanuel Perrin; page 387: CEPHAS/Mick Rock; page 393: Patrick Taurignan; page 398: CEPHAS/Mick Rock; page 399: CEPHAS/Geraldine Norman; page 422: Vignobles Brunier; page 423: Vignobles Brunier; page 426: CEPHAS/Mick Rock; page 431: CEPHAS/Clay McLachlan; page 448: by Robin Head; pages 452–453: by Robin Head; page 458: Image courtesy the Global Photo Library; pages 480–481: Image courtesy the Global Photo Library; page 499: Arturo Celentano; page 521: Image courtesy the Global Photo Library; page 525: Angelo Tonolini; page 526: Angelo Tonolini; page 529: CEPHAS/Mick Rock; page 549: Image courtesy the Global Photo Library; page 550: Image courtesy the Global Photo Library; page 565: The Rare Wine Co.; pages 566–567: Alvaro Palacios; page 570: CEPHAS/Diana Mewes; page 571: CEPHAS/Mick Rock; page 576: Steven Rothfeld©2005; page 579: ©Michael Landis; page 597: Jen L. Molander Photography; page 599: Jen L. Molander Photography; page 619: Steven Rothfeld©2005; pages 620–621: Steven Rothfeld ©2005; page 631: Photography by Kent Hanson; page 632: Photography by Matt Phillips; page 634: Photography by Matt Phillips; page 644: Al Francis 2001

All other photos courtesy of individual vineyards